Basic
Marketing
Research

Basic Marketing Research

Gilbert A. Churchill, Jr.
University of Wisconsin

The Dryden Press
Chicago   New York   San Francisco   Philadelphia
Montreal   Toronto   London   Sydney   Tokyo

Acquisitions Editor: Rob Zwettler
Developmental Editor: Judy Sarwark
Project Editor: Cate Rzasa
Design Director: Alan Wendt
Production Supervisor: Diane Tenzi
Permissions Editor: Doris Milligan
Director of Editing, Design, and Production: Jane Perkins
Text and Cover Designer: Image House, Inc., Stuart Paterson
Copy Editor and Indexer: Margaret Jarpey
Compositor: The Clarinda Company
Text Type: 10/12 ITC Garamond Light

Library of Congress Cataloging-in-Publication Data
Churchill, Gilbert A.
   Basic marketing research.

   Bibliography: p.
   Includes index.
   1. Marketing research. I. Title.
   HF5415.2.C49   1988   658.8'3   87-5288
   ISBN 0-03-007278-6

Printed in the United States of America
789-032-98765432
Copyright © 1988 by The Dryden Press, a division of Holt, Rinehart and Winston, Inc.

Address orders:
111 Fifth Avenue
New York, NY 10003

Address editorial correspondence:
One Salt Creek Lane
Hinsdale, IL 60521

The Dryden Press
Holt, Rinehart and Winston
Saunders College Publishing

Cover Source: Photo by Michel Tcherevkoff

To our grandchildren, Kayla Marie and
Johnathan Winston

The Dryden Press Series in Marketing

Balsley and Birsner
Selling: Marketing Personified

Barry
Marketing: An Integrated Approach

Blackwell, Engel, and Talarzyk
Contemporary Cases in Consumer Behavior, *Revised Edition*

Blackwell, Johnston, and Talarzyk
Cases in Marketing Management and Strategy

Block and Roering
Essentials of Consumer Behavior, *Second Edition*

Boone and Kurtz
Contemporary Marketing, *Fifth Edition*

Churchill
Basic Marketing Research

Churchill
Marketing Research: Methodological Foundations, *Fourth Edition*

Czinkota and Ronkainen
International Marketing

Dunn and Barban
Advertising: Its Role in Modern Marketing, *Sixth Edition*

Engel, Blackwell, and Miniard
Consumer Behavior, *Fifth Edition*

Futrell
Sales Management, *Second Edition*

Hutt and Speh
Industrial Marketing Management: A Strategic View of Business Markets, *Second Edition*

Kurtz and Boone
Marketing, *Third Edition*

Park and Zaltman
Marketing Management

Patti and Frazer
Advertising: A Decision-Making Approach

Rachman
Marketing Today, *Second Edition*

Rogers and Grassi
Retailing: New Perspectives

Rosenbloom
Marketing Channels: A Management View, *Third Edition*

Schellinck and Maddox
Marketing Research: A Computer-Assisted Approach

Schnaars
MICROSIM
A marketing simulation available for IBM PC® and Apple®

Sellars
Role Playing the Principles of Selling

Shimp and DeLozier
Promotion Management and Marketing Communications

Talarzyk
Cases and Exercises in Marketing

Terpstra
International Marketing, *Fourth Edition*

Zikmund
Exploring Marketing Research, *Second Edition*

Preface

Basic Marketing Research is designed for the introductory, undergraduate course in marketing research and can be used either in one- or two-quarter sequences or in semester courses.

The topic of marketing research is a complex one. It involves a number of questions that need to be answered and a number of decisions that need to be made with respect to the choice of techniques used to solve a research problem. Without some overriding framework, which this book attempts to provide, it is easy for students to "fail to see the forest for the trees," that is, to become so overwhelmed by the bits and pieces that they fail to see the interrelationships of the parts to the whole. Yet, an understanding of these interrelationships is essential both to the aspiring manager and the aspiring researcher, for in a very real sense, marketing research is one big trade-off.

Decisions made with respect to one stage in the research process have consequences for other stages. Managers need an appreciation of the subtle and pervasive interactions among the parts of the research process so that they can have the appropriate degree of confidence in a particular research result. Researchers also need to appreciate the interactions among the parts. The parts serve as the "pegs" on which to hang the knowledge accumulated about research methods. Researchers need to resist the temptation of becoming enamored of the parts to the detriment of the whole.

This book attempts to serve both the aspiring manager and the aspiring researcher by breaking the research process down into some basic stages that must be completed when answering a research question. The specific stages are

1. Formulate problem.
2. Determine research design.
3. Determine data-collection method.
4. Design data-collection forms.
5. Design sample and collect data.
6. Analyze and interpret data.
7. Prepare research report.

The organization of the book parallels these stages in the research process. Thus, the book is organized into seven corresponding parts. Each part (or stage) is then broken into smaller parts, so that a given stage is typically discussed in multiple chapters. This modular treatment allows students to see the forest for the trees. It also allows instructors some latitude with respect to the order in which they cover topics.

◆ Organization

Part One consists of three chapters. Chapter 1 provides an overview of the subject of marketing research and describes the kinds of problems for which it is used, who is doing research, and how the research function is organized. Chapter 1 also provides a perspective on career opportunities available in marketing research. Chapter 2 then overviews the research process and discusses the issue of ethics in the conduct of marketing research. Chapter 3 discusses the problem-formulation stage of the research process and explains the issues that must be addressed in translating a marketing decision problem into one or more questions that research can productively address. It also covers the preparation of a research proposal.

Part Two concerns the choice of research design and consists of two chapters. Chapter 4 overviews the role of various research designs and discusses one of the basic types, the exploratory design. Chapter 5 then discusses the two other basic types, descriptive and causal designs.

Part Three discusses the general issue of the choice of data-collection method and contains four chapters. Chapter 6 focuses on secondary data as an information resource and includes a discussion of commercial marketing information services, and the appendix to Chapter 6 discusses the many sources of published secondary data. Chapter 7 describes the issues involved when choosing between the two primary means by which marketing information can be collected—through observing or questioning subjects. Chapter 8 then describes the main alternatives and the advantages and disadvantages of each when subjects are to be questioned. Chapter 9 does the same for observational techniques.

Part Four addresses the actual design of the data-collection forms that will be used in a study. Chapter 10 discusses a sequential procedure that can be used to design a questionnaire or observation form. Chapter 11 then discusses some basic measurement issues that researchers and managers need to be aware of so that they will neither mislead others nor be misled themselves when interpreting the findings. Chapter 12 describes some of the most popular techniques marketers currently use to measure customers' attitudes, perceptions, and preferences.

Part Five, which consists of four chapters, examines sample design and deals with the actual collection of data needed to answer questions. Chapter 13 overviews the main types of samples that can be used to determine the population elements from which data should be collected. It also describes the main types of nonprobability samples and simple random sampling, the most basic probability sampling technique. Chapter 14 discusses the use of stratified sampling and cluster sampling, which are more sophisticated probability sampling techniques. Chapter 15 treats the question of how many population elements need to be sampled for research questions to be answered with precision and confidence in the results. Chapter 16 discusses data collection and the many errors that can occur in completing this task from a perspective that allows managers to better assess the quality of information they receive from research.

Once the data have been collected, emphasis in the research process logically turns to analysis, which is a search for meaning in the collected information. The search for meaning involves many questions and several steps, and the three chapters in Part Six attempt to overview these steps and questions. Chapter 17 reviews the preliminary analysis steps of editing, coding, and tabulating the data. Chapter 18 discusses the procedures that are appropriate for examining whether the differences between groups are statistically significant. Chapter 19 describes the statistical procedures that can be used to examine the degree of relationship between variables.

Part Seven discusses the last, yet critically important, part of the research process: the research report. Because it often becomes the standard by which any research effort is judged, the research report must contribute positively to that evaluation. Chapter 20 discusses the criteria a research report should satisfy and a form it can follow so that it does contribute positively to the research effort. Chapter 21 provides a similar perspective for oral reports. Chapter 21 also discusses some graphic techniques that can be used to communicate the important findings more forcefully. Chapter 22 then goes on to discuss the relationship between a decision support system approach to the gathering of marketing intelligence and the project emphasis stressed in this book. It also covers some of the more important issues that must be addressed in designing a decision support system.

Organizing the material in this book around the stages in the research process produces several significant benefits. First, it allows the subject of marketing research to be broken into very digestible bites. Second, it demonstrates and continually reinforces how the individual bits and pieces of research technique fit into a larger whole. Students can see readily, for example, the relationship between statistics and marketing research, or where they might pursue additional study to become research specialists. Third, the organization permits the instructor some flexibility with respect to the order in which the parts of the process may be covered.

◆ Special Features

In addition to its pedagogically sound organization, *Basic Marketing Research* has several special features that deserve mention. First, the book is relatively complete with respect to its coverage of the most important techniques available for gathering marketing intelligence. The general approach employed when discussing topics is not only to provide students with the pros and cons of the various methods by which a research problem can be addressed, but also to develop an appreciation of why these advantages and disadvantages occur. The hope is that through this appreciation students will be able to creatively apply and critically evaluate the procedures of marketing research. Other important features include the following:

1. A set of learning objectives highlights the most important topics discussed in the chapter. The chapter summary then recaps the learning objectives point by point.

2. A "Case in Marketing Research" opens each chapter. These scenarios are adapted from actual situations and should prove to be very interesting to students. Furthermore, periodic references to the introductory case ("Back to the Case") illustrate how the scenario can be brought into sharper focus using the methods described in the chapter.

3. A running glossary appears throughout the text. Key terms in each chapter are boldfaced, and their definitions appear in the margin where the terms are discussed. Each key term is also indexed.

4. The "Research Windows" provide a view of what is happening in the world of marketing research. "Research Windows" describe some influential marketing research pioneers, what is going on at specific companies, and offer some specific "how to" tips. Like the "Case in Marketing Research" features, they serve to breathe life into the subject and strongly engage the students' interest.

5. Discussion questions, problems, and/or projects are found at the end of each chapter. This feature allows students the opportunity to apply the chapter topics to focused situations, thereby honing their analytical skills and developing firsthand knowledge of the strengths and weaknesses of various research techniques.

6. A worked-out research project is discussed throughout the book. This project is found at the end of each part and concerns retailers' attitudes toward advertising

in various media. The project represents an actual situation faced by a group of radio stations in one community. It begins with a description of the radio stations' concerns and objectives. Each of the sections then describes how the research was designed and carried out, demonstrating the interrelationships of the stages in the research process and providing students with a real, hands-on perspective as to how research is actually conducted.

7. Several cases occur at the end of each part and deal with a stage in the research process. The twenty-seven cases assist students in developing their own evaluation and analytical skills. They are also useful in demonstrating the universal application of marketing research techniques. The methods of marketing research can be used not only by manufacturers and distributors of products, as is commonly assumed, but also by the private and public sectors to address other issues.

   The cases include such diverse entities or issues as the Big Brothers program, computerized bibliographic data services, rent control, generic drugs, banking services, legal services, and university extension programs. All cases represent actual situations, although some of them have been disguised to protect the proprietary nature of the information.

8. Raw data are provided for four of the cases to allow students to perform their own analyses to answer questions. The data are listed in the *Instructor's Manual* (IM) for the convenience of those who can enter the data into their computer systems. The data are also available on computer disk to adopters. The disk allows those who have statistical packages available to use them for analysis. Others may find it more convenient to upload the data from the disk onto the school's mainframe computer and have students use the larger systems for analyses. To obtain a copy of the disk, which is available for the IBM microcomputer, adopters must send the insert card in the *IM* to the nearest Dryden regional sales office.

◆ Ancillaries

A complete, carefully developed ancillary package accompanies *Basic Marketing Research*.

Instructor's Manual/Transparency Masters   Developed with the assistance of Jacqueline C. Hitchon of the University of Wisconsin–Madison, the *Instructor's Manual* contains alternative course outlines, instruction suggestions for each chapter, answers to discussion questions, solutions to cases, and over 50 transparency masters with notes.

Test Bank   The *Test Bank*, which is included in the *Instructor's Manual*, contains more than 1,500 questions, including true-false and multiple-choice questions.

Computerized Test Bank   A computerized version of the text bank is available for the IBM PC® and IBM-compatible computers. The questions on the disks are identical to those that appear in the printed version of the *Test Bank*. This system also gives instructors the option of entering the program and adding or deleting questions.

Case Data Disk   A disk containing research data necessary to solve certain text cases is available upon request for the IBM PC®.

Marketing Research: A Computer-Assisted Approach   Written by D. A. Schellinck and R. N. Maddox of Dalhousie University, this stand-alone package consists of innovative utility programs, tutorial simulations, spreadsheet models, and easy-to-use statistical information that will enable instructors to use personal computers in the teaching of marketing research. The package includes an instructor's manual with two disks, which can be copied by the instructor and distributed to students. The text is available for sale to students.

◆ Acknowledgments

While writing a book is never the work of a single person, one always runs the risk of omitting some important contributions when attempting to acknowledge the help of others. Nonetheless, the attempt must be made because this book has benefited immensely from the many helpful comments I have received along the way from interested colleagues. I especially wish to acknowledge the following people who reviewed the manuscript. While much of the credit for the strengths of the book is theirs, the blame for any weaknesses is strictly mine. Thank you one and all for your most perceptive and helpful comments.

David Andrus
Kansas State University

Donald Bradley
University of Central Arkansas

David Gourley
Arizona State University

D. S. Halfhill
California State University, Fresno

Vince Howe
University of Kentucky

Glen Jarboe
University of Texas, Arlington

Leonard Jensen
Southern Illinois University, Carbondale

Roland Jones
Mississippi State University

Subhash Lonial
University of Louisville

Douglas MacLachan
University of Washington

Thomas Noordewier
Ohio State University

David Urban
Georgia State University

Joe Welch
North Texas State University

Linda Tischler worked closely with me on *Basic Marketing Research*. Her editorial assistance was invaluable in fine-tuning the manuscript and developing the pedagogy.

My colleagues at the University of Wisconsin have my thanks for the intellectual stimulation and psychological support they have always provided.

I also wish to thank Janet Christopher who did most of the typing on the manuscript. She was efficient in her efforts and patient with mine. I also wish to thank students Joseph Kuester, Jayashree Mahajan, and David Szymanski for their help with many of the tasks involved in completing a book such as this. I would like to thank the editorial and production staff of The Dryden Press for their professional efforts on my behalf. I am also grateful to the Literary Executor of the late Sir Ronald A. Fisher, F.R.S., to Dr. Frank Yates, F.R.S., and to Longman Group Ltd., for permission to reprint Table III from their book *Statistical Tables for Biological, Agricultural and Medical Research* (6th Edition, 1974).

Finally, I once again owe a special debt of thanks to my wife, Helen, and our children. Their unyielding support and generous love not only made this book possible but worthwhile doing in the first place.

Gilbert A. Churchill, Jr.

Madison, Wisconsin
September 1987

About the Author

Gilbert A. Churchill, Jr., DBA (Indiana University), is the Donald C. Slichter Professor in Business Research at the University of Wisconsin—Madison. He joined the Wisconsin faculty in 1966 and has taught there ever since, except for one year spent as a visiting professor at Bedriftsokonomisk Institutt in Oslo, Norway. Professor Churchill was named Distinguished Marketing Educator by the American Marketing Association in 1986, only the second individual so honored. The award recognizes and honors a living marketing educator for distinguished service and outstanding contributions to the field of marketing education.

Professor Churchill is a past recipient of the William O'Dell Award for the outstanding article appearing in the *Journal of Marketing Research* during the year. He has also been a finalist for the award three other times. He was named Marketer of the Year by the South Central Wisconsin Chapter of the American Marketing Association in 1981. He is a member of the American Marketing Association and has served as vice-president of publications and on its board of directors as well as on the Association's Advisory Committee to the Bureau of the Census. In addition, he has served as consultant to a number of companies, including Oscar Mayer, Western Publishing Company, and Parker Pen.

Professor Churchill's articles have appeared in such publications as the *Journal of Marketing Research,* the *Journal of Marketing,* the *Journal of Consumer Research,* the *Journal of Retailing,* the *Journal of Business Research, Decision Sciences, Technometrics, Organizational Behavior and Human Performance,* among others. He is author or co-author of several other books including *Marketing Research: Methodological Foundations,* Fourth Edition (Hinsdale: Ill.: Dryden, 1987); *Sales Force Management: Planning, Implementation, and Control,* Second Edition (Homewood, Ill.: Irwin, 1985); and *Salesforce Performance* (Lexington, Mass.: Lexington Books, 1984). He is a former editor of the *Journal of Marketing Research* and has served on the editorial boards of *Journal of Marketing Research, Journal of Marketing, Journal of Business Research,* and the *Journal of Health Care Marketing.* Professor Churchill currently teaches undergraduate and graduate courses in marketing research and sales management.

Contents

Part One   **Introduction to Marketing Research and Problem Definition**   1

Chapter 1   Role of Marketing Research   2

Learning Objectives   2   *Case in Marketing Research*   3   Role of Marketing Research in Marketing Management   4   Who Does Marketing Research?   9   *Back to the Case*   12   Organization of Marketing Research   13   *Back to the Case*   14   *Research Window 1.1: Marketing Research—On the Job at Quaker Oats*   16   Job Opportunities in Marketing Research   17   *Back to the Case*   18   Summary   21

Chapter 2   Process of Marketing Research   24

Learning Objectives   24   *Case in Marketing Research*   25   Sequence of Steps in Marketing Research   28   *Back to the Case*   29   Ethical Issues in Marketing Research   33   *Back to the Case*   36   *Research Window 2.1: Ethical Dilemmas — What Would You Do?*   38   Summary   39

Chapter 3   Problem Formulation   42

Learning Objectives   42   *Case in Marketing Research*   43   Problem Formulation   44   *Back to the Case*   48   Translating Decision Problem into Research Problem   50   Decision Trees   52   *Back to the Case*   52   The Research Proposal   54   *Back to the Case*   54   When Is Marketing Research Justified?   58   Choosing and Using a Research Supplier   60   *Research Window 3.1: How Clients and Marketing Research Firms Should Not Work Together*   62   Summary   62

Part One   Research Project   64

Cases to Part One   66

Part Two   **Research Design**   71

Chapter 4   Types of Research Designs and Exploratory Research   72

Learning Objectives   72   *Case in Marketing Research*   73   Research Design as a Plan of Action   74   Types of Research Design   75   *Research Window 4.1: Market Facts: A Firm Built on Determination, Hard Work — and a Little Bit o'Luck*   76   Exploratory Research   79   *Back to the Case*   80   *Research Window 4.2: Stouffer Does Its Homework and Comes Up with a Winner*   85   *Back to the Case*   86   Summary   87

Chapter 5   Descriptive and Causal Research Designs   90

Learning Objectives 90   *Case in Marketing Research* 91   Descriptive Research Designs 92   *Back to the Case* 103   Causal Research Designs 104   **Research Window 5.1: Rice Paddies or Pagodas? Test Marketing Helps the National Geographic Society Decide** 112   *Back to the Case* 115   Summary 117

Part Two   Research Project   123

Cases to Part Two   125

Part Three   **Data-Collection Methods**   141

Chapter 6   Secondary Data   142

Learning Objectives 142   *Case in Marketing Research* 143   Advantages of Secondary Data 144   Disadvantages of Secondary Data 147   Types of Secondary Data: Internal and External 149   *Back to the Case* 152   Standardized Marketing Information Services 155   *Back to the Case* 162   **Research Window 6.1: A Marketing Research Pioneer — A. C. Nielsen** 167   Summary 168   **Appendix 6A: Published External Secondary Data** 172

Chapter 7   Collecting Primary Data   182

Learning Objectives 182   *Case in Marketing Research* 183   Types of Primary Data 184   *Back to the Case* 185   *Back to the Case* 189   **Research Window 7.1: Calvin Klein Designs the World's Best-Known Underwear Ads** 190   Obtaining Primary Data 195   Summary 197

Chapter 8   Collecting Information by Questionnaire   200

Learning Objectives 200   *Case in Marketing Research* 201   Communication Methods 202   *Back to the Case* 209   Methods of Administering Questionnaires 216   **Research Window 8.1: Apple Juice or Antifreeze? Researchers Help Consumers Sort Out the Difference** 217   *Back to the Case* 230   Summary 231

Chapter 9   Collecting Information by Observation   236

Learning Objectives 236   *Case in Marketing Research* 237   Methods of Observation 238   *Back to the Case* 243   *Back to the Case* 247   **Research Window 9.1: The Eyes Have It** 249   Summary 251

Part Three   Research Project   254

Cases to Part Three   256

Part Four   **Data-Collection Forms**   265

Chapter 10   Designing the Questionnaire or Observation Form   266

Learning Objectives 266   *Case in Marketing Research* 267   Questionnaire Design 268   *Back to the Case* 277   **Research Window 10.1: A Rogue's Gallery of Problem Words** 286   *Back to the Case* 292   Observational Forms 299   Summary 302

Chapter 11   Measurement Basics   308

Learning Objectives 308   *Case in Marketing Research* 309   Scales of
Measurement 310   Scaling of Psychological Attributes 313   Introduction to
Psychological Measurement 314   Variations in Measured Scores 317   *Back to the
Case* 318   Classification and Assessment of Error 319   *Research Window 11.1:
Marketing Researchers Face the Real Pepsi Challenge: Interpreting Taste
Tests* 320   *Back to the Case* 323   Developing Measures 328
Summary 330

Chapter 12   Measuring Attitudes, Perceptions, and Preferences 334

Learning Objectives 334   *Case in Marketing Research* 335   Attitude-Scaling
Procedures 338   Other Ratings Scales 344   *Back to the Case* 348
Determining Which Scale to Use 350   Multidimensional Scaling 350
Back to the Case 351   *Research Window 12.1: Product Positioning in the
Automotive Industry* 352   Conjoint Measurement 358   Summary 361

Part Four   Research Project   367

Cases to Part Four   374

Part Five   **Sampling and Data Collection**   389

Chapter 13   Types of Samples and Simple Random Sampling   390

Learning Objectives 390   *Case in Marketing Research* 391   Required Steps in
Sampling 393   Types of Sampling Plans 394   Nonprobability Samples 396
Back to the Case 398   *Research Window 13.1: The Ad Is Slick, Clever,
Expensive — But Is Anybody Reading It?* 400   Probability Samples 403
Back to the Case 403   Simple Random Sampling 404   Summary 416

Chapter 14   Stratified and Cluster Sampling   420

Learning Objectives 420   *Case in Marketing Research* 421   Stratified
Sample 422   *Back to the Case* 429   Stratified versus Quota Sample 430
Cluster Sample 431   *Back to the Case* 432   *Research Window 14.1:
Designing a Sample — Or, Who Are Those Nielsen Viewers Anyway?* 438
Summary Comments on Probability Sampling 440   Summary 441

Chapter 15   Sample Size   446

Learning Objectives 446   *Case in Marketing Research* 447   Basic
Considerations in Determining Sample Size 448   *Back to the Case* 449   Sample
Size Determination When Estimating Means 450   *Research Window 15.1: Seeking
Consensus for the Census* 450   Sample Size Determination When Estimating
Proportions 458   Population Size and Sample Size 460   Other Probability
Sampling Plans 463   Sample Size Determination Using Anticipated Cross
Classifications 464   *Back to the Case* 465   Determining Sample Size Using
Historic Evidence 467   Summary 468

Chapter 16   Collecting the Data: Field Procedures and Nonsampling Errors 474

Learning Objectives 474   *Case in Marketing Research* 475   Impact and
Importance of Nonsampling Errors 476   Types of Nonsampling Errors 478
Research Window 16.1: A Day in the Life of a Telephone Interviewer 484
Back to the Case 490   *Back to the Case* 500   Total Error Is Key 501
Summary 504

Part Five   Research Project   507

Cases to Part Five   510

Part Six

Data Analysis   529

Chapter 17   Data Analysis: Preliminary Steps   530

Learning Objectives 530   *Case in Marketing Research* 531   Editing 532
Coding 534   Tabulation 537   **Research Window 17.1: Are the Rich Really
Getting Richer?** 548   *Back to the Case* 558   *Back to the Case* 562
Summary 565   **Appendix 17A: Hypothesis Testing** 570

Chapter 18   Data Analysis: Examining Differences   582

Learning Objectives 582   *Case in Marketing Research* 583   Goodness of
Fit 584   *Back to the Case* 586   Kolmogorov-Smirnov Test 588
Hypotheses about One Mean 590   Hypotheses about Two Means 594
Back to the Case 598   **Research Window 18.1: Caveat Emptor . . . or,
Beware the Butchers!** 602   Hypotheses about Two Proportions 603
Summary 604   **Appendix 18A: Analysis of Variance** 608

Chapter 19   Data Analysis: Investigating Associations   614

Learning Objectives 614   *Case in Marketing Research* 615   Simple Regression
and Correlation Analysis 616   **Research Window 19.1: The Importance of Theory
in Marketing Research** 617   *Back to the Case* 622   Multiple-Regression
Analysis 630   **Research Window 19.2: Walkup's Laws of Statistics** 630   *Back
to the Case* 638   Summary Comments on Data Analysis 642   **Research
Window 19.3: Life on the Mississippi — 742 Years from Now** 642   Summary 643
Appendix 19A: Nonparametric Measures of Association 646

Part Six   Research Project   655

Cases to Part Six   659

Part Seven

Research Reports and Marketing Intelligence   677

Chapter 20   The Written Research Report   678

Learning Objectives 678   *Case in Marketing Research* 679   Research Report
Criteria 680   *Back to the Case* 681   Writing Criteria 682   **Research
Window 20.1: How to Write Your Way Out of a Job** 684   Forms of Report 687
Back to the Case 694   Summary 695

Chapter 21   The Oral Research Report   698

Learning Objectives 698   *Case in Marketing Research* 699   Preparing the
Oral Report 700   Delivering the Oral Report 700   *Back to the Case* 701
Research Window 21.1: How to Use a Microphone Well 702   Graphic
Presentation of the Results 703   **Research Window 21.2: Computer Graphics
Take the Worry out of Charts and Graphs** 705   *Back to the Case* 707
Summary 713   **Research Window 21.3: Putting Slide Graphics to Use** 713

Chapter 22   The Research Project and the Firm's Marketing Intelligence System   716

Learning Objectives 716   *Case in Marketing Research* 717   The Research Process Revisited 718   ***Research Window 22.1: The Research Results May Be Enlightening—But Will They Be Used?*** 720   The Research Project and the Marketing Intelligence System 722   *Back to the Case* 723   ***Research Window 22.2: A Glossary of Computer Terms for the Slightly Bewildered*** 727   *Back to the Case* 731   Summary 734

Part Seven   Research Project   736

Appendix   739

Index   747

Part One   Introduction to Marketing Research and Problem Definition

1. Formulate Problem

Part One gives an overview of marketing research. Chapter 1 looks at the kinds of problems for which marketing research is used, who is doing the research, and how it is organized. Chapter 2 provides an overview of the research process, and Chapter 3 contains a detailed discussion of the problem formulation stage in the research process.

Chapter 1

Role of Marketing Research

Learning Objectives

Upon completing this chapter, you should be able to

1. Define marketing research.
2. Cite the two factors that are most responsible for how the research function is organized in any given firm.
3. List some of the skills important for careers in marketing research.

Case in Marketing Research

An icy sleet was falling on North Quad, but inside Rossman Hall lights were bright and there was a flurry of activity. The newest recruiting schedule had just been posted, and the university's seniors were jostling each other to sign up for interviews.

Leaving their marketing research class, Rob Daniels and his friend, Marcia Glazer, joined the melee. Marcia skillfully negotiated her way to a position near the bulletin board. As she finished signing her name opposite three interview times, she turned to Rob, who lingered near the edge of the crowd.

"Rob, hurry up or you'll miss out. Do you want me to put your name down for a slot with Allied? How about Smith & Zuckerman? B. G. Swensen?"

Rob wavered. "I don't know, Marcia. . ."

"Oh, come on. Sign up. Just talking with them doesn't commit you to a lifetime of employment and a gold watch, and maybe it'll help you decide what you want to do after graduation."

Rob paused again.

"Rob . . . it's either this or the family drapery business."

"Okay, okay. Put me down. I guess it won't hurt to talk."

Walking across the wintry campus, Rob confided the thoughts that had been bothering him since last semester.

"You know, Marcia, I never thought I'd be so undecided so close to graduation. I know I want a career in marketing, but there are so many different options that I can't figure out how to decide."

"Well, Rob, you're really burning up the track in this marketing research course. Why not pursue that area?"

"But how? Even narrowing the field to marketing research still leaves so many choices. Do I work in-house doing marketing research with a manufacturer like Procter & Gamble, or even a service firm like Merrill Lynch? Or should I begin with a big marketing research supplier like A. C. Nielsen or Burke? Or would it be best to start in the research department of an ad

agency where I could work on a variety of clients' accounts? How do I decide?"

"Well, that's why you should talk to these people when they're on campus. Let them tell you what each position offers," Marcia suggested.

"You're right, as usual. If my research courses have taught me anything, it's to get the facts before making a decision. I guess the first place I should use my research skills is in finding myself a job."

Discussion Issues

1. If you were Rob, what information might help you decide between various marketing research careers?

2. If you were a recruiter, what information would you want about Rob before deciding whether to hire him?

3. Besides a background in research methods, what skills do you think are important for a marketing researcher?

As our opening scenario suggests, the field of marketing research presents a wide variety of exciting career options. Those options are likely to increase as more enterprises discover the benefits of marketing research.

Many people think that marketing research is simply a scientific way of discovering consumer likes and dislikes. Television advertisers tend to reinforce this misconception by broadcasting the results of various cola taste tests or heralding the latest winner in the continuing saga of the "battle of the burgers." But the consumer survey is only one type of marketing survey, and the marketing survey is only one kind of marketing research.

For most companies it is not only more economical but more practical to check data that already exist before embarking upon an expensive and time-consuming original study. Before switching from Coke to Pepsi in all its outlets in 1983, researchers at Burger King, for example, spent two years studying existing data from the soft drink industry.[1]

Many companies use commercially supplied research data. The Toy Manufacturers of America, an industry trade group, discovered from National Panel Diary data that distribution patterns for toys are changing as people buy more often from toy supermarkets (like Toys "Я" Us) than from department and discount stores.[2] Some organizations base their research on data they generate internally. At Eastman Kodak, technical researchers looked at 10,000 pictures by amateur photographers to determine what kinds of mistakes the average user made. Based on their analysis of the pictures, researchers designed a camera that helped eliminate almost one-half of the out-of-focus and underexposed shots.[3] Organizations often use data generated externally by means other than surveys. American Airlines researchers studied garbage from various flights before deciding to quit serving butter on short-range flights.[4] (The amount of discarded butter showed that few people were eating it.)

Marketing research can be used to assess marketing opportunities for a new product or an improved version of an old product. It can be used to evaluate the effectiveness of various elements of the marketing mix as well, such as an advertising campaign or a new package design—or even the relative success or failure of the total marketing effort. Numerous specific uses of marketing research could be listed, since its basic purpose is to help marketing managers make better decisions in any of their areas of responsibility.

◆ Role of Marketing Research in Marketing Management

Anyone planning a career in marketing management should understand what marketing research can do. Managers at all levels and in all areas of business must make decisions. Accurate, effective decision making is often dependent on the quality of information provided. Marketing research plays an essential role in providing accurate and useful information.

You may recall from your introductory course in marketing the emphasis that many organizations place on the marketing concept. In today's hotly competitive

---

[1]John Koten, "Fast-Food Firms' New Items Undergo Exhaustive Testing," *The Wall Street Journal,* 64 (January 5, 1984), p. 21.

[2]"Toy Departments Are Fading Away," *Wisconsin State Journal,* (December 16, 1984), p. 12.

[3]John Koten, "You Aren't Paranoid If You Feel Someone Eyes You Constantly," *The Wall Street Journal,* 65 (March 29, 1985), pp. 1 and 21. See also "Credit Success of Kodak Disc Camera to Research," *Marketing News,* 17 (January 21, 1983), pp. 8 and 9.

[4]"Business Bulletin," *The Wall Street Journal,* 63 (August 11, 1983), p. 1.

marketplace, that marketing concept has been gaining in importance. In a management context the marketing concept states that the principal task of the marketing function is to serve the interests of the customer rather than the interests of the business. Many organizations have failed to embrace this notion though—sometimes with dire consequences. American auto manufacturers, for example, believed for decades that marketing was less important than engineering, finance, and manufacturing. But as sales figures fell in the face of high fuel prices, Japanese competition, and quality-conscious consumers, the industry had to reassess its beliefs. As one auto executive noted ruefully, "If there's a growing respect for the market, it's because we've learned that disrespecting it cost us an arm and a leg."[5]

Once an organization decides to focus its attention on marketing, it often discovers that satisfying customers means juggling a number of factors to achieve a balance that will enable its product to compete successfully in the marketplace. Marketing managers generally focus their efforts on the four Ps—price, product, place, and promotion.[6]

The marketing manager's essential task is to combine these variables, known as the *marketing mix,* into an effective marketing program in which all the elements complement each other. This task would be much simpler if all the elements that could affect customer satisfaction were under the manager's control and if consumer reaction to any contemplated change could be predicted. Usually, however, a number of factors affecting the success of the marketing effort are beyond the marketing manager's control, and the behavior of individual consumers is largely unpredictable. In addition, the objectives and internal resources of the firm may not coincide with the marketing manager's proposed strategy. The competitive, technological, economic, cultural, social, political, or legal environments may not be conducive to the marketing department's goals.

Figure 1.1 summarizes the task of marketing management. Customers are at the center of the figure because they are the focus of the firm's activities. Their satisfaction is achieved through simultaneous adjustments in the elements of the marketing mix, but the results of these adjustments are uncertain because the marketing task takes place within an uncontrollable environment. Consequently, as director of the firm's marketing activities, the marketing manager has an urgent need for information—and marketing research is traditionally responsible for providing it. Marketing research is the firm's formal communication link with the environment. It is the means by which the firm generates, transmits, and interprets feedback information from the environment relating to the success of the firm's marketing plans.

The definition of **marketing research** emphasizes its information-linkage role.

> Marketing research is the function which links the consumer and the customer to the organization through information—information used to identify and define marketing problems; generate, refine, and evaluate marketing actions; monitor marketing performance; and improve our understanding of marketing as a process.[7]

Note that this definition indicates that marketing research provides information feedback to the organization for use in at least four areas: (1) the generation of ideas for marketing action, including the definition of marketing problems, (2) the evaluation

• Marketing research

The function that links the consumer and the customer to the organization through information—information used to identify and define marketing problems; generate, refine, and evaluate marketing actions; monitor marketing performance; and improve our understanding of marketing as a process.

---

[5]"Chrysler Tries to Sharpen Its Brand Identity," *Business Week,* (November 21, 1983), p. 104.

[6]E. Jerome McCarthy and William D. Perreault, Jr., *Basic Marketing: A Managerial Approach,* 9th ed. (Homewood, Ill.: Richard D. Irwin, 1987), pp. 37–40.

[7]Peter Bennett, ed., *Glossary of Marketing Terms* (Chicago: American Marketing Association, forthcoming).

Figure 1.1

Task of Marketing Management

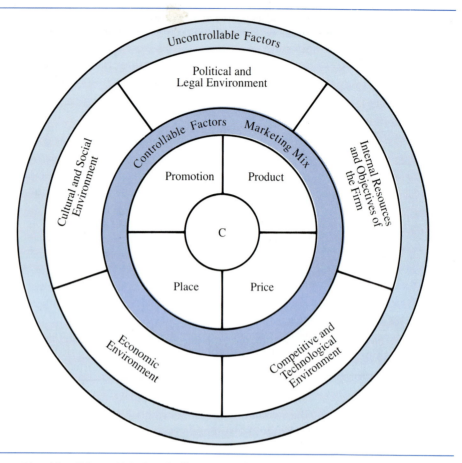

Source: Adapted from E. Jerome McCarthy and William D. Perreault, Jr., *Basic Marketing: A Managerial Approach,* 9th ed. (Homewood, Ill.: Richard D. Irwin, 1987), p. 47. Used with permission.

of marketing ideas, (3) the comparison of performance versus objectives, and (4) the development of general understanding of marketing phenomena and processes.[8] Further, marketing research is involved with all phases of the information-management process, including (1) the specification of what information is needed, (2) the collection and analysis of the information, and (3) the interpretation of that information with respect to the objectives that motivated the study in the first place.

The definition of marketing research implies a role in each of the sectors of Figure 1.1. A periodic survey (Table 1.1) conducted by the American Marketing Association details more specifically how many organizations use marketing research.[9] Al-

[8]Lawrence D. Gibson, "Some Strategic Aspects of Marketing Research Management," paper presented at American Marketing Association Research Conference, October 13, 1985.

[9]Dik Warren Twedt, *1983 Survey of Marketing Research* (Chicago: American Marketing Association, 1983). This survey is the seventh in a series begun in 1947. This latest survey was sent to 2,153 marketing research executives, and the tabulation in Table 1.1 is based on the returns from the 650 usable questionnaires.

Table 1.1   Research Activities of Respondent Companies

	Percent of Companies Engaged in Research Activity	Percent in Which Activity Is Done by Marketing Research Department	Percent in Which Activity Is Done by Another Department	Percent in Which Activity Is Done by Outside Firm
Advertising Research				
A. Motivation research	47	30	2	15
B. Copy research	61	30	6	25
C. Media research	68	22	14	32
D. Studies of ad effectiveness	76	42	5	29
Business Economics and Corporate Research				
A. Short-range forecasting (up to one year)	89	51	36	2
B. Long-range forecasting (over one year)	87	49	34	4
C. Studies of business trends	91	68	20	3
D. Pricing studies	83	34	47	2
E. Plant and warehouse location studies	68	29	35	4
F. Acquisition studies	73	33	38	2
G. Export and international studies	49	22	25	2
H. MIS (Management Information System)	80	25	53	2
I. Operations research	65	14	50	1
J. Internal company employees	76	25	45	6
Corporate Responsibility Research				
A. Consumers' "right to know" studies	18	7	9	2
B. Ecological impact studies	23	2	17	4
C. Studies of legal constraints on advertising and promotion	46	10	31	5
D. Social values and policies studies	39	19	13	7
Product Research				
A. New product acceptance and potential	76	59	11	6
B. Competitive product studies	87	71	10	6
C. Testing of existing products	80	55	19	6
D. Packaging research: design or physical characteristics	65	44	12	9
Sales and Market Research				
A. Measurement of market potentials	97	88	4	5
B. Market share analysis	97	85	6	6
C. Determination of market characteristics	97	88	3	6
D. Sales analyses	92	67	23	2
E. Establishment of sales quotas, territories	78	23	54	1
F. Distribution channel studies	71	32	38	1
G. Test markets, store audits	59	43	7	9
H. Consumer panel operations	63	46	2	15
I. Sales compensation studies	60	13	43	4
J. Promotional studies of premiums, coupons, sampling, deals, etc.	58	38	14	6

Source: Dik Warren Twedt, *1983 Survey of Marketing Research* (Chicago: American Marketing Association, 1983), p. 41. Reprinted with permission.

Table 1.2   Kinds of Questions Marketing Research Can Help Answer

I. *Planning*

A. What kinds of people buy our product? Where do they live? How much do they earn? How many of them are there?

B. Is the market for our product increasing or decreasing? Are there promising markets that we have not yet reached?

C. Are there markets for our products in other countries?

II. *Problem Solving*

A. Product
   1. Which, of various product designs, is likely to be the most successful?
   2. What kind of packaging should we use for our product?

B. Price
   1. What price should we charge for our new product?
   2. As production costs decline, should we lower our prices or try to develop a higher quality product?

C. Place
   1. Where, and by whom, should our product be sold?
   2. What kinds of incentives should we offer to induce dealers to push our product?

D. Promotion
   1. How effective is our advertising? Are the right people seeing it? How does it compare with the competition's advertising?
   2. What kinds of sales promotional devices—coupons, contests, rebates, and so forth—should we employ?
   3. What combination of media—newspapers, radio, television, magazines—should we use?

III. *Control*

A. What is our market share overall? In each geographic area? By each customer type?
B. Are customers satisfied with our product? How is our record for service? Are there many returns?
C. How does the public perceive our company? What is our reputation with dealers?

though the table is organized somewhat differently from the figure, the relationship between the two is readily apparent. Much research, for example, is done to measure consumer wants and needs. Other research assesses the impact of previous adjustments in the marketing mix or gauges the potential impact of new changes. Some research deals directly with the environment, such as studies of legal constraints on advertising and promotion[10] and studies of social values, business policy, and business trends.

---

[10]Marketing research is also increasingly being employed in legal suits and to assist in the formulation of new regulations. See Michael T. Brandt and Ivan L. Preston, "The Federal Trade Commission's Use of Evidence to Determine Deception," *Journal of Marketing,* 41 (January 1977), pp. 54–62; Robert F. Dyer and Terence A. Shimp, "Enhancing the Role of Marketing Research in Public Policy Decision Making," *Journal of Marketing,* 41 (January 1977), pp. 63–67; and John Koten, "More Firms File Challenges to Rivals' Comparative Ads," *The Wall Street Journal,* 64 (January 12, 1984), p. 21.

Another way of looking at the function of marketing research is to consider how management uses it. Some marketing research is used for planning, some for problem solving, and some for control. When used for planning, it deals largely with determining which marketing opportunities are viable and which are not promising for the firm. Also, when viable opportunities are uncovered, marketing research provides estimates of their size and scope, so that marketing management can better assess the resources needed to develop them. Problem-solving marketing research focuses on the short- or long-term decisions that the firm must make with respect to the elements of the marketing mix. Control-oriented marketing research helps management to isolate trouble spots and to keep abreast of current operations. The kinds of questions marketing research can address with regard to planning, problem solving, and control decisions are listed in Table 1.2. The relationship between each of these questions and a marketing manager's area of responsibility is easy to see.

◆ Who Does Marketing Research?

Marketing research, as a sizable business activity, owes its existence to this country's shift from a production-oriented to a consumption-oriented economy at the end of World War II. However, some marketing research was conducted before the war, and the origins of formal marketing research predate the war by a good number of years.

> More by accident than foresight, N. W. Ayer & Son applied marketing research to marketing and advertising problems. In 1879, in attempting to fit a proposed advertising schedule to the needs of the Nichols-Shepard Company, manufacturers of agricultural machinery, the agency wired state officials and publishers throughout the country requesting information on expected grain production. As a result, the agency was able to construct a crude but formal market survey by states and counties. This attempt to construct a market survey is probably the first real instance of marketing research in the United States.[11]

There were even formal marketing research departments and marketing research firms before World War II.[12] However, marketing research really began to grow when firms found they could no longer sell all they could produce, but rather had to gauge market needs and produce accordingly. Marketing research was called upon to estimate these needs. As consumer discretion became more important, many firms shifted their orientation to accommodate the new business climate. Marketing began to assume a more dominant role and production a less important one. The marketing concept emerged, and along with it a reorganization of the marketing

---

[11]From Lawrence C. Lockley, "History and Development of Marketing Research," pp. 1–4, in Robert Ferber, ed., *Handbook of Marketing Research*. Copyright © 1974 by McGraw-Hill, 1974. Used with permission of McGraw-Hill Book Company.

[12]The Curtis Publishing Company is generally conceded to have formed the first formal marketing research department with the appointment of Charles Parlin as manager of the Commercial Research Division of the Advertising Department in 1911, while the A. C. Nielsen Company, the largest marketing research firm in the world, began operation in 1934. For a detailed treatment of the development of marketing research, see Robert Bartels, *The Development of Marketing Thought* (Homewood, Ill.: Richard D. Irwin, 1962), pp. 106–124, or Jack J. Honomichl, *Marketing Research People: Their Behind-the-Scenes Stories* (Chicago: Crain Books, 1984), especially Part II on pages 95–184, which deals with the evolution and status of the marketing research industry.

Figure 1.2

Organization for Marketing Research

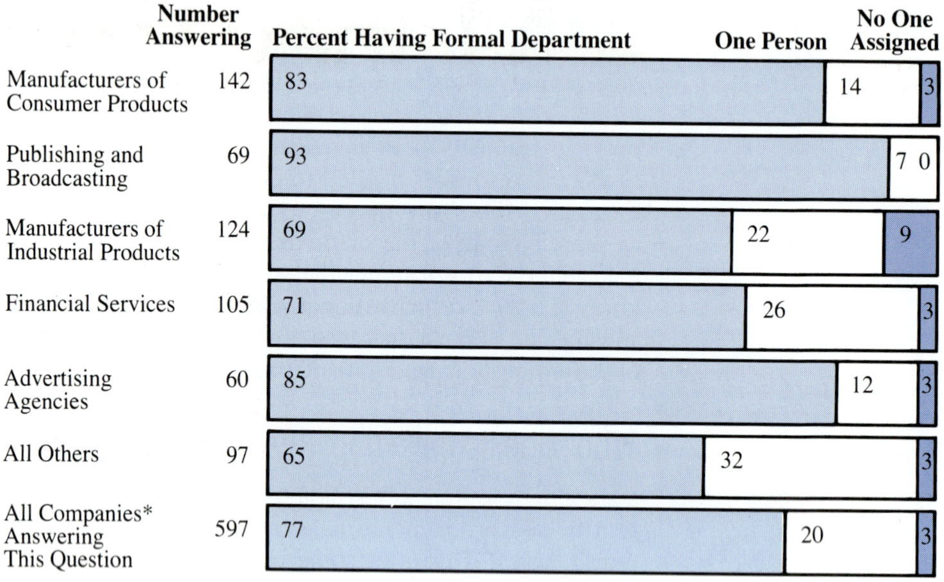

	Number Answering	Percent Having Formal Department	One Person	No One Assigned
Manufacturers of Consumer Products	142	83	14	3
Publishing and Broadcasting	69	93	7	0
Manufacturers of Industrial Products	124	69	22	9
Financial Services	105	71	26	3
Advertising Agencies	60	85	12	3
All Others	97	65	32	3
All Companies* Answering This Question	597	77	20	3

*Excludes marketing research and consulting firms.

Source: Dik Warren Twedt, *1983 Survey of Marketing Research* (Chicago, American Marketing Association 1983), p. 11. Reprinted with permission.

effort. Many marketing research departments were born in these reorganizations. The growth of these departments was stimulated by a number of factors, including past successes, increased management sophistication, and the data revolution created by the computer. The success of firms with marketing research departments caused still other firms to establish departments.

While the growth in the number of new marketing research departments has slowed recently, the firm that does not have a formal department, or at least a person assigned specifically to the marketing research activity, is now the exception rather than the rule (see Figure 1.2).[13] Marketing research departments are still most prevalent among industrial and consumer manufacturing companies, but they also exist in other types of companies. Publishers and broadcasters, for example, do a good deal of research. They attempt to measure the size of the market reached by their message and construct a demographic profile of this audience. These data are then used to sell advertising space or time (Figure 1.3). Also, financial institutions such as banks and brokerage houses do research involving forecasting, measurement of market potentials, determination of market characteristics, market-share analyses, sales analyses, location analyses, and product-mix studies.[14] Although these institutions use marketing research less than manufacturers, almost three-fourths of those responding to a recent survey had formal departments.

[13]Twedt, *1983 Survey,* p. 23. A plot of the number of departments on the Y-axis and time on the X-axis using semilogarithmic graph paper indicates the number of marketing research departments increased at a relatively constant rate between 1918 and 1978, but the growth rate now may be leveling off.

[14]*Ibid.,* p. 43.

Figure 1.3

Use of Marketing Research Data by a Magazine Publisher

Money Boomers are better boomers.

© 1985 Time Inc.

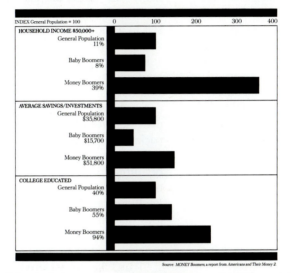

Source: *MONEY Boomers, a report from Americans and Their Money 2.*

Are things really booming for the baby boomers? Not really. Because as these charts show, most of America's 25 to 39's barely keep up with the entire U.S. population.

But there is an elite segment of baby boomers who are quite different. And clearly superior.

MONEY magazine's Executive Editor, Landon Jones (author of the definitive book on the baby boom generation, *Great Expectations*), has called them the Super Class. Others have labeled this elusive audience Yuppies, or Super Boomers. By any name, they are the rich topping that has given marketing allure to the plain vanilla of the baby boom.

And it is the members of this segment who are most likely to subscribe to MONEY. Here's how MONEY magazine's boomer-age subscribers stack up against their ordinary contemporaries and the U.S. as a whole.

First, consider a real yardstick of affluence—$50,000+ households. Only 11 per cent of the U.S. population earns that much. And just 8 per cent of baby boomers.

But for MONEY boomers, the figure is a startling 39 per cent.

Next, examine savings and investments. Where the general population controls $35,800, the typical baby boomer has just $15,700. But the MONEY boomers are working with a hefty $51,800.

As you might expect, these disparities in earnings/investments reflect differing levels of education. For though 55 per cent of all boomers are college educated, a whopping 94 per cent of MONEY boomers are.

In sum, MONEY attracts a financially mature segment of the baby boomers. To learn more about these extraordinary consumers, please request a copy of *MONEY Boomers*, a report from *Americans and Their Money 2.* Just call: (212) 841-4925, or ask your MONEY representative.

MONEY boomers. For advertisers, these readers are themselves—the rewards of MONEY.

Money®
America's Financial Advisor

Source: © 1986, *Money* Magazine, Time Inc.

Of the advertising agencies that responded to the survey, all but one of those with billings of more than $25 million had formal marketing research departments, and 69 percent of the medium-sized agencies (those with billings between $5 and $25 million) had formal research departments. Much of the research conducted by these agencies deals directly with creating the advertisement itself. That may involve testing alternative approaches to copy and art or investigating the effectiveness of various celebrity spokespersons. However, many agencies also do marketing research for their clients to determine the marketing potential of a proposed new product or the client firm's market share.

Back to the Case

The weather had turned unseasonably hot for March. Rob Daniels felt uncomfortably warm in his best wool suit as he opened the glass door to the reception room of the ad agency of Brett, Case, and Bowman. A dazzling young woman looked up from a flashing switchboard to greet him. Assuming his most winning smile, Rob silently thanked Marcia for encouraging him to check out this job before he met with recruiters on campus.

"Rob Daniels?" the receptionist asked. "Ms. Reiss is expecting you. Second door on the left."

Rob headed slowly in the direction she indicated, pausing to admire the agency's stylish front office furnishings as he headed down a long corridor. It wouldn't be hard to get accustomed to working in such posh surroundings, he thought.

Connie Reiss rose to meet him as he entered the room.

"Hi Rob, sit down. I'm sorry this is going to have to be brief. We just had an emergency on the "Robot-toasties" cereal account, and I have to be in a meeting in fifteen minutes. I've seen your resume, but tell me, what made you respond to our ad?"

"I liked the idea of getting a lot of experience on different accounts that an agency job would provide. I also liked your size—large enough for diversity, small enough so that I wouldn't get lost in the shuffle—and the kind of creative work your shop does," Rob responded.

"Well, if you like diversity, this is the place. If anything, you may often feel that there are too many balls in the air. On any given day you might find yourself in a shopping mall in the suburbs asking kids their favorite color lollipop, running video equipment for a group discussion of laundry detergents, or calling a list of a hundred executives' secretaries to see what package express service they prefer and why. At other times you'll be mired in reams of data and be expected to come up with an intelligent analysis by a ridiculous deadline. Sound like fun?"

Rob laughed. "It sounds like exam time at State."

"True," Reiss answered, turning serious, "but it's always exam time here, and the stakes are much higher. If you blow an exam at school, only you are the loser. If we muff a research project, millions of the client's dollars could be lost—and ultimately that could mean the loss of the account, and of our jobs. We have fun here, but I can't afford to hire someone who isn't dead serious about the quality and integrity of his work."

Rob was silent, not knowing if he should attempt to defend his integrity or just keep quiet.

After consulting her watch, Connie Reiss perched on the edge of her desk and smiled. "Look, I have five more minutes. Tell me what you know about psychology."

Rob brightened. He had a strong interest in psychology, and had taken as many elective

psych courses as his business schedule would allow. After explaining what he had done at school, he ventured, "Why do you ask?"

"We have found a familiarity with basic psychology an invaluable background for research. We'd like to hire someone who can pick up on nonverbal cues in group discussions with consumers, who can effectively pursue a line of questioning to get to the root of motivation issues, and who is sensitive to respondents' anxieties, frustrations, and concerns about products. Those kinds of observations can often be of much more use to us than a mountain of data spelling out consumer likes and dislikes. Such information could form the basis for copy for an ad, an idea for a promotional campaign, or a suggestion for a product improvement. Many people use the information we generate in many ways. The greater depth we can give to that information, the more helpful it will be in decision making.

"I'm sorry, Rob," she said hurriedly, "but I've got to run. The cereal account people are waiting. We'll be in touch."

In his first interview, Rob is introduced to the multifaceted, bustling world of an advertising agency. In such a setting he could expect to use both his technical research skills and the knowledge he has gleaned from his social science courses.

The enterprises included in the "All Others" category shown in Figure 1.2 include public utilities, transportation companies, and trade associations, among others. Public utilities and transportation companies often provide their customers with useful marketing information, particularly statistics dealing with area growth and potential. Trade associations often collect and disseminate operating data gathered from members.

The entire spectrum of marketing research activity also includes specialized marketing research and consulting firms, government agencies, and universities. While most specialized marketing research firms are small, a few are sizable enterprises.[15] Some of these firms provide syndicated research; they collect certain information on a regular basis, which they then sell to interested clients. The syndicated services would include such operations as the A. C. Nielsen store audit and the National Purchase Diary consumer panel. Such services are distinguished by the fact that their research is not custom designed, except in the limited sense that the firm will perform special analyses for a client from the data it regularly collects. Other research firms, though, specialize in custom-designed research. Some of these provide only a field service; they collect data and return the data-collection instruments directly to the research sponsor. Some are limited-service firms that not only collect the data, but also analyze them for the client. And some are full-service research suppliers that help the client in the design of the research, as well as in collecting and analyzing data.

Government agencies provide much marketing information in the form of published statistics. Indeed, the federal government is the largest producer of marketing facts through its various censuses and other publications.[16]

Much university-sponsored research of interest to marketers is produced by the marketing faculty or by the bureaus of business research found in many schools of business. Faculty research is often reported in marketing journals, while research bureaus often publish monographs on various topics of interest.

◆ Organization of Marketing Research

The organizational form of marketing research depends largely on the size and organizational structure of the individual company. In small firms, where one person often handles all the organization's research needs, there are few organizational questions other than determining to whom the research director shall report. Most often, this will be the sales or marketing manager, although some marketing research managers report directly to the president or the executive vice-president. Larger research units can take a variety of organizational forms, although three types are common:

1. Organization by area of application, such as by product line, by brand, by market segment, or by geographic area;

2. Organization by marketing function performed, such as field sales analysis, advertising research, or product planning;

3. Organization by research technique or approach, such as sales analysis, mathematical and/or statistical analysis, field interviewing, or questionnaire design.

Many firms with very large marketing research departments combine two or more of these organizational structures.

---

[15]For a list of the 40 largest, see Jack J. Honomichl, "Top Research Companies' Revenues Rise 13.7%," *Advertising Age,* 56 (May 23, 1985), p. 16.

[16]Some government publications containing useful marketing information are reviewed in the appendix to Chapter 6.

Whether the firm is centralized or decentralized also affects the organization of the marketing research function.[17] With decentralized companies—those in which authority and decision making are spread among a fairly large number of people—each division or operating unit might have its own marketing research department, or a single department in central headquarters might serve all operating divisions, or research departments might exist at both levels. The primary advantages of a corporate-level location are greater coordination and control of corporate research activity, economy, increased capability from an information system perspective, and greater usefulness to corporate management in planning. The primary advantage of a division or group-level location is that it allows research personnel to acquire valuable knowledge about divisional markets, products, practices, and problems. While shifting between the corporate and divisional structures occurs quite frequently, the recent trend is toward a mixed arrangement, in an attempt to secure the advantages of each.

In sum, the organization of the marketing research function will depend on the relative importance of that function within the firm and on the scale and complexity

---

[17]For a discussion of management of the research function, see Lee Adler and Charles S. Mayer, eds., *Readings in Managing the Marketing Research Function* (Chicago: American Marketing Association, 1980).

Back to the Case

Rob Daniels sat anxiously twisting his resume outside the office where the recruiter from Allied Foods was holding interviews. The door opened, and Rob jumped to his feet as a tall, pleasant-looking young man called his name.

"Rob Daniels? Hi, I'm Mel Jacobs. Come on in."

After glancing over Rob's resume, Jacobs leaned back in his chair and studied Rob for a moment. Rob anxiously wondered if he had really managed to get the spot out of his tie.

"Well, Rob, it looks as though you've been doing fairly well in a rigorous degree program here at State. Let me first tell you a little about the job at Allied, and then if you have any questions we can address them.

"As you may know, Allied Foods is a highly decentralized company. Our various divisions have a great deal of control over their own operations—as long as they continue to show a profit.

"We're currently looking for people to work in the marketing research departments of a few of our subsidiaries, such as "Country Farms" yogurt and "Happy Pup" dog food. Much of the nitty gritty of our research—the actual questionnaire design, the collection and coding of the data, etc.—is farmed out to a research supplier. In-house, our focus is on the general approach taken and in determining what marketing implications such research may have for our products. If the data show, for example, that vegetable-flavored yogurt is likely to

be the wave of the future, that information could influence product planning, budgeting, sales forecasting—a variety of issues."

"What kind of growth potential is there in this job?" Rob asked.

"If you do well at the junior level, you can expect to move up to a senior analyst, and then a research supervisor's position. Eventually, if you are good, you could be made a research manager for a specific brand, perhaps with another of our subsidiaries. In that position, you would work with management to determine what marketing problems need to be addressed and how to go about investigating them. You would also supervise a staff of junior researchers and of the research activities to be undertaken. Moreover, the organizational form is subject to sudden changes from time to time, some arising from changes within the firm. As the firm's size and market position change, the emphasis and organization of the marketing research function must also change, so that it is continually tailored to suit the firm's information needs. Research Window 1.1 describes the emphasis on and organization of the research function at Quaker Oats.

The data indicate that large firms are likely to spend a larger proportion of the marketing budget on research than are small firms. Among firms with sales of $25 million and over, approximately 3½ percent of the average marketing budget is spent on research, while among smaller firms, only about 1½ percent of the average marketing budget is spent on research.[18] As Figure 1.4. indicates, a few firms spend a very large proportion of their total marketing budget on research.

One important change that has been occurring in marketing research in recent years is the transition from a specific-problem perspective to a total marketing intelligence perspective. This perspective is usually called a marketing information system (MIS) or decision support system (DSS). The emphasis in those systems is on diagnosing the information needs of each of the marketing decision makers so that

---

[18]A. Parasuraman, "Research's Place in the Marketing Budget," *Business Horizons,* 26 (March–April 1983), pp. 25–29.

---

coordinate with the research supplier.

"Following that, you could move into a slot at corporate headquarters. In such a position, you would focus less on research as it pertains to a particular brand or product and more on issues that would affect the corporation's long-term planning. In our case, for example, that may mean determining what kind of influence the increasing numbers of working mothers will have on the food industry. Are there growth opportunities in gourmet frozen dinners, in restaurants offering take-out menus, or in foods that are designed specifically for microwave oven preparation? By the way, have you had much experience with computers?"

"Yes," Rob answered, "I've taken a few programming courses and one on management information systems."

"Good," Jacobs noted. "This job wouldn't require much, if any, actual programming, but you should know how to use various software programs to manipulate the data. I assume you've had some courses in management?"

Rob nodded.

"Then you recognize how critical the information this department generates is to the organization's management— especially in marketing. As you can see, we're looking for a rare combination of assets: someone who can, on the one hand, feel comfortable wading through in-house and industry sales figures,

estimates of market share, and questionnaire responses. To move up, however, that same person should show an ability to take a broader perspective and to see what those numbers mean in a larger context.

"Do you think you're the person for the job?"

In this interview, Rob learned how an organization's structure could influence a marketing research job. He also was reminded of the function marketing research serves as a tool for management decision making. As he discovered, jobs with user companies may provide less of an opportunity to get involved with the actual mechanics of research but more of a chance to determine the ramifications of that research for the company.

Research Window 1.1

Marketing Research—On the Job at Quaker Oats

Most students beginning a course in marketing research have only a fuzzy idea of what a researcher actually does on the job or how that position fits with the rest of an organization. Obviously, the details of the position differ from one firm to another, but let us examine the place of the researcher in one giant consumer organization that has a healthy respect for what marketing research can offer—the Quaker Oats Company. This company willingly admits that its officers rarely make critical decisions without input from the marketing research department. Its philosophy regarding marketing research follows:

Marketing research exists at Quaker for one reason: to recommend data-based courses of action which will improve corporate profits. More specifically, the stated mission of the Marketing Information Department is to contribute to Quaker's long-term grocery products' sales and profits through the collection and analysis of marketing information. This data—whether it is from survey research or the analysis of business problems—is used by the researcher to form points of view about likely consumer behavior to alternative marketing actions being considered by the company.

The importance of the marketing research function is recognized throughout the organization and primarily in the marketing area. In fact, according to the vice-president of marketing, "Quaker's Marketing Research Department is significantly involved in and makes substantial contributions toward identifying and addressing major marketing issues faced by Brand Management."

Quaker is one of the few companies to have its marketing research department led by a vice-president—another clear indication of the importance of the function to the company. Reporting to the vice-president are seven functional units designed to provide facilities for tracking existing markets, investigating new areas, and developing and executing consumer research. These reporting functions include three divisional research units, as well as marketing information systems, sales research, business development, and a project administration function.

The typical entry-level position within the Marketing Information Department is that of a research analyst. The research analyst receives on-the-job training from the research supervisor or manager while learning the business of his or her assigned brand. Once the analyst has demonstrated a knowledge of the business and the ability to operate independently, the usual progression of positions in terms of responsibility and compensation is as follows: senior research analyst, research supervisor, research manager, group research manager, and director.

A position in marketing research at Quaker requires a high level of research and analytical ability and experience with survey research and statistical analysis (usually obtained through graduate level studies or equivalent work experience). Good human relations and communications skills are also critical in dealing with professionals in other departments, as well as in ensuring that one's recommendations are included in marketing plans. Finally, a research analyst must be the type of person who will develop a sense of personal responsibility for the sales progress of assigned brands, even though the final responsibility for a brand's success rests with product management.

Source: "Marketing Research, a Career for You. . ." The Quaker Oats Company, Chicago, IL.

Figure 1.4

Share of Marketing Budgets Allocated to Research

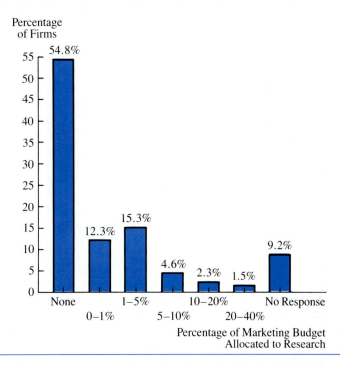

Source: Developed from data in A. Parasuraman, "Researcher's Place in the Marketing Budget," *Business Horizons,* 26 (March–April 1983), pp. 25–29.

they have the kinds of information they need, when they need it, to make the kinds of decisions they must make. We will discuss marketing intelligence systems in more detail in the final chapter of this book.

◆ Job Opportunities in Marketing Research

It is hard to generalize about the kinds of tasks a marketing researcher might perform. As previously suggested, the tasks will depend upon the type, size, and organizational structure of the firm with which the individual is employed. They will also depend upon whether the person works for a research supplier or for a consumer of research information.

The responsibilities of a marketing researcher could range from the simple tabulation of questionnaire responses to the management of a large research department. Table 1.3, for example, lists some common job titles and the functions typically performed by occupants of these positions. Figure 1.5 illustrates what they are likely to be paid and how that compares with salaries of those in similar positions in 1978.[19]

---

[19]For further discussion of the opportunities in marketing research, see Linden A. Davis, Jr., "What's Ahead in Marketing Research," *Journal of Advertising Research,* 21 (June 1981), pp. 49–51. For a discussion of threats to the future of marketing research, see Stephen W. McDaniel, Perry Verille, and Charles S. Madden, "The Threats to Marketing Research: An Empirical Reappraisal," *Journal of Marketing Research,* 22 (February 1985), pp. 74–80.

Back to the Case

After the interview with Allied Foods, Rob felt more confident about his upcoming meeting with B. G. Swensen, the big research firm. He was happy he had been able to work his computer experience into the conversation, and he felt that he had answered most of the interviewer's questions effectively. Feeling relaxed and comfortable, Rob settled back in his chair as the Swensen recruiter finished a phone conversation.

Jack Callahan, B. G. Swensen's delegate to academe, slammed down the phone and turned to Rob.

"How well do you write?" he asked abruptly.

Rob faltered. "Write? What do you mean?" he stammered.

"Write. You know . . . reports, memos, proposals. What have you done?" Callahan demanded.

"Well, I took comp and got a B+. I was on the newspaper staff in my sophomore year, but had to drop it when I started to work part-time. We're working on a research project in my marketing research course, and we have to write up our results. I should be done in two weeks," Rob volunteered hesitantly.

"Listen," Callahan said brusquely, "the person we hire must meet several requirements. First, he or she must have a solid academic background in marketing research. Your transcript shows that you have that. But we also need somebody who knows his

way around a paragraph. Somebody who can take complex data and turn it into a report that doesn't sound like the flight program for a satellite launch.

"Swensen is one of this country's largest research firms. We have some of the most sophisticated computer equipment short of the Pentagon. We can analyze data until the cows come home. But our clients range from whiz kids in electronics firms to small banks. We need to be able to make our research intelligible and meaningful to people who never heard of multivariate hypothesis testing and who think a random sample is something you buy at an off-price clothing outlet. What have you done that would prepare you for a job like that?"

Rob paused for a moment. Then an idea occurred to him.

"This may sound a little off-the-wall, sir, but for the past two years I've been earning money as a tutor in the university's "Computers for Poets" class. I've been helping liberal arts majors learn programming techniques and decipher users' manuals for various software programs. The professor who teaches the class says I'm the best tutor she's ever had since I can communicate in both languages: computerese and the King's English.

Callahan seemed interested.

"Sounds promising," he acknowledged. "In this job you'll start off tabulating and coding re-

sponses to questionnaires. From there you may begin working on questionnaire design, sampling, etc. We tend to move people around a lot so that they'll learn all the ins and outs of research. However, as I said earlier, just crunching numbers won't get you far. We're big, and we're busy. Your supervisors won't have time to spend hours picking your brain to determine what you've uncovered. They will want brief, accurate, well-written reports that they, in turn, can incorporate into their own reports to clients or upper management.

"If you're serious about research, you couldn't find a better place to learn the ropes," he concluded.

In his final interview, Rob discovered that research suppliers are good places to learn the mechanics of research. However, even in such technically and analytically oriented places, there is a need for strong communication skills.

Each of the marketing research jobs for which Rob interviewed presents unique opportunities and challenges. Each could serve as the first step in a career path or as a starting point for other careers in marketing. While some of the skills Rob would need are common across jobs, the different jobs place different emphases on the balance of skills required.

Table 1.3   Marketing Research Job Titles and Responsibilities

1. **Research Director:** This is the senior position in research. The director is responsible for the entire research program of the company. Accepts assignments from superiors or from clients or may, on own initiative, develop and propose research undertakings to company executives. Employs personnel and exercises general supervision of research department. Presents research findings to clients or to company executives.

2. **Assistant Director of Research:** This position usually represents a defined "second in command," a senior staff member having responsibilities above those of other staff members.

3. **Statistician/Data-Processing Specialist:** Duties are usually those of an expert consultant on theory and application of statistical techniques to specific research problems. Usually responsible for experimental design and data processing.

4. **Senior Analyst:** Usually found in larger research departments. Participates with superior in initial planning of research projects and directs execution of projects assigned. Operates with minimum supervision. Prepares, or works with analysts in preparing, questionnaires. Selects research techniques, makes analyses, and writes final report. Budgetary control over projects and primary responsibility for meeting time schedules rest with the senior analyst.

5. **Analyst:** The analyst usually handles the bulk of the work required for execution of research projects. Often works under senior analyst's supervision.

The analyst assists in questionnaire preparation, pretests them, and makes preliminary analyses of results. Most of the library research or work with company data is handled by the analyst.

6. **Junior Analyst:** Working under rather close supervision, junior analysts handle routine assignments. Editing and coding of questionnaires, statistical calculations above the clerical level, simpler forms of library research are among the duties. A large portion of the junior analyst's time is spent on tasks assigned by superiors.

7. **Librarians:** The librarian builds and maintains a library of reference sources adequate to the needs of the research department.

8. **Clerical Supervisor:** In larger departments, the central handling and processing of statistical data are the responsibility of one or more clerical supervisors. Duties include work scheduling and responsibility for accuracy.

9. **Field Work Director:** Usually only larger departments have a field work director who hires, trains, and supervises field interviewers.

10. **Full-time Interviewer:** The interviewer conducts personal interviews and works under direct supervision of the field work director. Few companies employ full-time interviewers.

11. **Tabulating and Clerical Help:** The routine, day-to-day work of the department is performed by these individuals.

Source: Dik Warren Twedt, *1983 Survey of Marketing Research* (Chicago: American Marketing Association, 1983), p. 4. of the Appendix. Reprinted with permission.

As these job descriptions reveal, there are opportunities in marketing research for people with a variety of skills. There is room for technical specialists, such as statisticians, as well as for research generalists whose skills are relevant to managing the people and resources needed for a research project rather than the mathematical detail any study may involve. The skills required to perform each job satisfactorily will, of course, vary.

In consumer-goods companies, the typical entry-level position is research analyst, usually for a specific brand. While learning the characteristics and details of the industry, the analyst will receive on-the-job training from a research manager. The usual career path for an analyst is to advance to senior analyst, then research supervisor, and on to research manager for a specific brand. At that time the researcher's responsibilities often broaden to include a group of brands.

Among research suppliers, the typical entry-level position is research trainee, a position in which the person will be exposed to the types of studies in which the supplier specializes and to the procedures required for completing them. Quite

Figure 1.5

Mean Compensation for Research Positions

Position	Number Positions	(chart)	Compared with 1978 Mean ($000)	Percent Change
Directors	512	$51.0	$35.8	+42
Assistant Directors	301	$44.7	$31.1	+44
Senior Analysts	430	$34.0	$24.2	+40
Statisticians	96	$30.7	$22.6	+36
Analysts	484	$25.1	$18.2	+38
Field Work Directors	28	$23.5	$15.8	+49
Librarians	55	$20.8	$13.9	+50
Junior Analysts	204	$18.8	$13.9	+35
Clerical Supervisors	163	$16.8	$14.0	+20
Full-Time Interviewers	22	$13.1	$10.0	+31
Tabulating & Clerical Help	237	$14.0	$10.0	+40
Total Number of Positions	**2,532**	$0 $10,000 $20,000 $30,000 $40,000 $50,000 $60,000		

Source: Dik Warren Twedt, *1983 Survey of Marketing Research* (Chicago: American Marketing Association, 1983), p. 57. Reprinted with permission.

often, trainees will spend some time actually conducting interviews, coding completed data-collection forms, or possibly even assisting with the analysis. The goal is to expose trainees to the processes the firm follows so that when they become account representatives, they will be familiar enough with the firm's capabilities to respond intelligently to clients' needs for research information.

The requirements to enter marketing research include analytical, communication, and human relations skills.[20] Marketing researchers also should have some basic statistical skills, or at least the capacity to develop such skills. They must be comfortable with numbers and with the techniques and technologies of marketing research. The best marketing researchers tend to initiate action rather than simply respond to the explicit requests for information given them.

Successful marketing researchers realize that marketing research is conducted to help make better marketing decisions. Thus, they are comfortable in the role of a staff person who makes recommendations to others rather than having responsibility for the decisions themselves.

---

[20]For discussion of the characteristics of successful researchers and typical career paths, see John R. Blair, "Marketing Research Offers Highly Visible Action-Oriented Career with Growth Potential," Emanuel H. Demby, "The Marketing Researcher: A Professional Statistician, Social Scientist—Not Just Another Business Practitioner," and Lawrence D. Gibson, "Confused New Marketing Researchers Soon Feel Confidence, Then Challenge," *Student Edition Marketing News,* 2 (March 1984), pp. 1, 3, and 7. For some suggestions for preparing for a career in marketing research, see Michael Boudreaux, "Prepare for Your Future in Marketing, Your Interviews, and Something 'Extra'," *Student Edition Marketing News,* 2 (March 1984), p. 3.

◆ Summary

Learning Objective 1: Define marketing research.

Marketing research is the function that links the consumer and the customer to the organization through information. The information is used to identify and define marketing problems; generate, refine, and evaluate marketing actions; monitor marketing performance; and improve general understanding of marketing as a process.

Learning Objective 2: Cite the two factors that are most responsible for how the research function is organized in any given firm.

The two factors that are most significant in determining this organization are the firm's size and the degree of centralization or decentralization of its operations.

Learning Objective 3: List some of the skills important for careers in marketing research.

Most positions in marketing research require analytical, communication, and human relations skills. In addition, marketing researchers must be comfortable working with numbers and statistical techniques, and they must be familiar with a great variety of marketing research methods.

Discussion Questions, Problems, and Projects

1. Indicate whether marketing research is relevant to each of the following organizations and if so, how each might use it.
   (a) Pepsico, Inc.
   (b) Your university
   (c) The Chase Manhattan Bank
   (d) The American Cancer Society
   (e) A small dry-cleaner

2. What do the following two research situations have in common?

   Situation I: The Bugs-Away Company marketed a successful insect repellent. The product was effective and a leader in the market. It was available in blue aerosol cans with red caps. The instructions were clearly specified on the container in addition to a warning to keep the product away from children. Most of the company's range of products were also produced by competitors in similar containers. The CEO was worried because of declining sales and shrinking profit margins. Another issue that perturbed him was that companies such as his were being severely criticized by government and consumer groups for their use of aerosol cans. The CEO contacted the company's advertising agency and requested it to do the necessary research to find out what was happening.

   Situation II: In early 1986 the directors of Adams University were considering the expansion of the business school due to increasing enrollments over the past ten years. Their plans included constructing a new wing, hiring five new faculty members, and increasing the number of scholarships from 100 to 120. The funding for this ambitious project was to be provided by some private sources, internally generated funds, and the state and federal government. A prior research study (completed in 1978), using the Box-Jenkins forecasting methodology, indicated that student enrollment would peak in 1985. Another study conducted in November 1980 indicated universities could expect gradual declining enrollments during the late 1980s. The directors were concerned about the results of the later study and the talk it stimulated about budget cuts by the government. A decision to conduct a third and final study was made to determine likely student enrollment.

3. What do the following two research situations have in common?

   Situation I: The sales manager of Al-Can, an aluminum can manufacturing company, was delighted with the increase in sales over the past few months. He was wondering whether the new cans, which would be on the market in two months, should be priced higher than the traditional products. He confidently commented to the vice-president of marketing, "Nobody in the market is selling aluminum cans with screw-on tops. We can get a small portion of the market and yet make substantial profits." The product manager disagreed with this strategy. In fact, she was opposed to marketing these new cans. The cans might present problems in preserving the contents. She thought to herself, "Aluminum cans are recycled, so nobody is going to keep them as containers." There was little she could do formally because these cans were the president's own idea. She strongly recommended to the vice-president that the cans should be priced in line with the other products. The vice-president thought a marketing research study would resolve this issue.

Situation II: A large toy manufacturer was in the process of developing a tool kit for children in the five-to-ten-year age group. The tool kit included a small saw, screwdriver, hammer, chisel, and drill. This tool kit was different fom the competitors' as it included an instruction manual with "101 things to do." The product manager was concerned about the safety of the kit and recommended the inclusion of a separate booklet for parents. The sales manager recommended that the tool kit be made available in a small case, as this would increase its marketability. The advertising manager recommended a special promotional campaign be launched in order to distinguish it from the competitors' products. The vice-president thought that all the recommendations were worthwhile but that the costs would increase drastically. He consulted the market research manager, who further recommended that a study be conducted.

4. List the key attributes that an individual occupying the following positions must possess. Why are these attributes essential?
   (a) Senior analyst
   (b) Full-time interviewer
   (c) Research director

Suggested Additional Readings

For examples of marketing research techniques, see

Robert P. Viehas, *Complete Handbook of Profitable Marketing Research Techniques* (Englewood Cliffs, N. J.: Prentice-Hall, Inc., 1982).

For discussion of the trends in marketing research, some threats to it, and its role in corporate decision making, see

Stephen W. McDaniel, Perry Verille, and Charles S. Madden, "The Threats to Marketing Research: An Empirical Appraisal," *Journal of Marketing Research,* 22 (February 1985), pp. 74–80.

A. Parasuraman, "Research's Place in the Marketing Budget," *Business Horizons,* 26 (March–April 1983), pp. 25–29.

Dik Warren Twedt, ed., *1983 Survey of Marketing Research* (Chicago: American Marketing Association, 1983).

For a historical perspective on the evolution of the marketing research industry, see

Jack J. Honomichl, *Marketing Research People: Their Behind-the-Scenes Stories* (Chicago: Crain Books, 1984).

For discussion of what is happening at the largest marketing research suppliers, see

Jack J. Honomichl, "Worldwide Revenues for top 44 up 11.5%," *Advertising Age* (May 19, 1986), pp. S1–S64.

For discussion of the careers available in marketing research, see

John R. Blair, "Marketing Research Offers Highly Visible, Action-Oriented Career with Growth Potential," *Student Edition Marketing News,* 2 (March 1984), pp. 1 and 3.

Lawrence Gibson, "Confused New Marketing Researchers Soon Feel Confidence, Then Challenge," *Student Edition Marketing News,* 2 (March 1984), pp. 1 and 3.

Neil Holbert, *Careers in Marketing* (Chicago: American Marketing Association, 1976), pp. 18–23.

Chapter 2

Process of Marketing Research

Learning Objectives

Upon completing this chapter, you should be able to

1. Explain the difference between a program strategy and a project strategy to research.
2. Outline the steps in the research process and show how the steps are interrelated.
3. Cite the most critical error in marketing research.
4. List five research practices that are nearly always considered to be unethical by consumers.
5. Specify the most difficult ethical problems facing marketing researchers.

Case in Marketing Research

The faces around the conference table at Burger Delight were grim. Fourth-quarter sales had just been reported, and they were anything but encouraging. The fast food chain's competitors were clearly pulling further ahead in the great American hamburger race, while Burger Delight continued to limp along with sagging sales and declining profits. Something had to be done, and soon. The company's president, Martin Turnbull, turned from the downward-sloping graph on the flip chart and faced his assembled managers. "All right, troops," he said. "Where do we go from here?"

Hands shot in the air. Everyone, it seemed, had a suggestion about what should be done.

"Okay, Huxley," the president said, turning to the vice-president of production, "what do you think we should do?"

"Well, sir," Huxley began, "I think our problem is service. People who eat at our restaurants want fast food. With our antiquated equipment, they often have to wait ten minutes for a burger when we get busy. I think if we invested in state-of-the-art broiling units, we could be the fastest burger on the block and beat the competition."

"Hmmm," Turnbull muttered, "you might have a point."

"Smithfield?" The president turned to the eager new advertising manager.

"I think our advertising is dated," she said. "Happy jingles are fine for the good times, but in this competitive market I think we need a more aggressive approach. Something hard-hitting that tells the customer why our burger is better than the competition's."

"But is it?" The voice from the back of the room belonged to Jamison, who headed quality control. "We may have the best beef on the market, but it's not charbroiled like Burger King's, it's an ounce smaller than McDonald's, and the buns don't even have sesame seeds. If we don't upgrade our operation, I don't see why anybody would buy our burger over theirs."

"Price, Jamison, price," said Kaplan, the national sales manager. "We have to make certain compromises in order to keep our prices lower than anybody else's. Price is our main competitive advantage."

Everyone had spoken now but Abbott, the vice-president of marketing.

Burger Delight's president turned to her. "Well, Allison, we've had a lot of opinions here. What do you think?"

"With all due respect, sir," Abbott ventured, "I'd rather not offer a solution without exploring the problem a bit more first. It seems to me that all of the criticisms and suggestions offered here have merit, but we still don't know where the real problem lies. I'd like to commission a marketing research study before we begin throwing money into a solution that may not be addressing the real reason for our sales decline."

The room was silent. All heads turned to the president.

When he spoke, his voice was soft but firm. "I think you're right, Allison. Call Smith & Cahners. They are a good research firm. But don't take too long. I can't stall the stockholders much longer. We need results. And fast."

Discussion Issues

1. If you were president of Burger Delight, what would you see as the company's major decision problem?

2. What specific research questions might you ask?

• **Program strategy**

A company's philosophy of how marketing research fits into its marketing plan.

• **Project strategy**

The design of the individual studies that are to be conducted.

Chapter 1 highlighted the many kinds of problems that marketing research can be used to solve. It emphasized that marketing research is the firm's communication link with the environment and can help the marketing manager in planning, problem solving, and control. Every company has its own way of using marketing research. Some use it on a continuous basis to track sales or to monitor the firm's market share. Others resort to it only when a problem arises or an important decision—such as the launching of a new product—needs to be made. A company's overall philosophy of how marketing research fits into its marketing plan determines its **program strategy** for marketing research.[1] A program strategy specifies the types of studies that are to be conducted and for what purposes. It might even specify how often these studies are to take place.

How the individual studies are designed is the basis of a firm's **project strategy.** A look at how marketing research is handled at Procter & Gamble, one of the nation's leading consumer manufacturers, should help to clarify the difference between a program strategy and a project strategy.

It is Procter & Gamble's policy that at least once a year marketing research will be conducted on each of its brands. These studies always include such information as people's likes and dislikes about P & G products, the products' names, packaging, and hundreds of other details. This mountain of information is then funneled monthly to every major segment of the company, including the executive suite, where it is sifted and resifted for implications for P & G's marketing, advertising, manufacturing, and research and development operations. This ongoing process may be thought of as P & G's program strategy for marketing research.

The project strategies P & G employs may vary widely, however. In addition to the usual types of marketing research—such as extensive questionnaires about existing products and test marketing in supermarkets—P & G takes some further steps. For example, P & G's researchers might follow housewives around while they do the laundry, noting how they sort the clothes, how many loads they do, and what temperature settings they use on their washing machines. This kind of research has led to some breakthroughs. Cheer, for example, was formulated in response to researchers' observations that housewives needed one detergent that could handle all fabrics and all water temperatures.[2]

The details of this research, as well as the specific design of consumer questionnaires, or the format in which a new product is sampled to customers in supermarkets, all reflect the company's project strategy.

Program strategies typically answer such questions as "Should we do marketing

---

[1]Walter B. Wentz, *Marketing Research: Management and Methods* (New York: Harper and Row Publishers, 1972), pp. 19–24.

[2]John A. Prestbo, "At P & G Success Is Largely Due to Heeding Consumer," *The Wall Street Journal,* 60 (April 29, 1980), pp. 1 and 35.

research?" and "How often?" and "What kind?" Project strategies address the issue of "Now that we've decided to go ahead with marketing research, how should we proceed? Should we use in-store surveys, self-administered printed questionnaires, or one of the new electronic interviewing devices? Should we question more people or fewer? More often or less often?" In sum, project strategy deals with how a study should be conducted, whereas program strategy addresses the question of what type of studies the firm should conduct.

Table 2.1 outlines the kinds of studies that constitute the Gillette Company's program strategy for marketing research. As you can see, each type of study is planned to meet a certain objective. The design of each individual study defines the firm's project strategy—for example, the use of personal interviews in the national consumer studies, mail questionnaires in the brand-tracking studies, and telephone interviews when measuring brand awareness. The goal of all this research is to help Gillette maintain its 60 percent share of the blade and razor market.

All research problems require their own special emphases and approaches. Since every marketing research problem is unique in some ways, the research procedure is usually custom tailored. Nonetheless, there is a sequence of steps called the **research process** (see Figure 2.1) that can be followed when designing the research project. This chapter overviews that process, and the remaining chapters discuss the stages in the process in more detail.

◆ **Research process**

Sequence of steps in the design and implementation of a research study, including problem formulation, determination of research design, determination of data-collection method, design of data-collection forms, design of the sample and collection of the data, analysis and interpretation of the data, and preparation of the research report.

Table 2.1   Major Thrusts of Marketing Research at Gillette Company

1. Annual National Consumer Studies

The objectives of these annual studies are to determine what brand of razor and blade was used for the respondents' last shave, to collect demographic data, and to examine consumer attitudes toward the various blade and razor manufacturers. These studies rely on personal interviews with national panels of male and female respondents, who are selected using probability sampling methods.

2. National Brand Tracking Studies

The purpose of these studies is to track the use of razors and blades so as to monitor brand loyalty and brand switching tendencies over time. These studies are also conducted annually and use panels of male and female shavers. However, the information for them is collected via mail questionnaires.

3. Annual Brand Awareness Studies

These studies are aimed at determining the "share of mind" Gillette products have. This information is collected by annual telephone surveys that employ unaided as well as aided recall of brand names and advertising campaigns.

4. Consumer Use Tests

The key objectives of the use-testing studies are to ensure that "Gillette remains state of the art in the competitive arena, that our products are up to our desired performance standards, and that no claims in our advertising, packaging, or display materials are made without substantiation." At least two consumer use tests are conducted each month by Gillette. In these tests, consumers are asked to use a single variation of a product for an extended period of time, at the end of which their evaluation of the product is secured.

5. Continuous Retail Audits

The purpose of the retail audits is to provide top management with monthly market share data, along with information regarding distribution, out-of-stock, and inventory levels of the various Gillette products. This information is purchased from the commercial information services providing syndicated retail audit data. The information is supplemented by special retail audits which Gillette conducts itself that look at product displays and the extent to which Gillette blades and razors are featured in retailer advertisements.

Source: Adapted from "Mature Products Remain as the Mainstays in the Gillette Company," *Marketing News,* 17 (June 10, 1983), p. 17. Published by the American Marketing Association. Adapted with permission.

Figure 2.1

**Stages in the
Research Process**

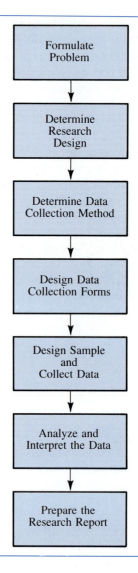

◆ Sequence of Steps in Marketing Research

Formulate Problem

One of the more valuable roles marketing research can perform is helping to define the problem to be solved. Only when the problem is precisely defined can research be designed to provide pertinent information. Part of the process of problem definition includes specifying the *objectives* of the specific research project or projects that might be undertaken. Each project should have one or more objectives, and the next step in the process should not be taken until these can be explicitly stated.

Determine Research Design

The sources of information for a study and the research design go hand in hand. They both depend on how much is known about the problem. If relatively little is known about the phenomenon to be investigated, *exploratory research* will be warranted. Typically, **exploratory research** is used when the problem to be solved is

◆ **Exploratory research**

Research design in which the major emphasis is on gaining ideas and insights; it is particularly helpful in breaking broad, vague problem statements into smaller, more precise subproblem statements.

⊸ Descriptive research

Research design in which
the major emphasis is on
determining the frequency
with which something
occurs or the extent to
which two variables covary.

• Causal research

Research design in which
the major emphasis is on
determining a cause and
effect relationship.

• Secondary data

Statistics not gathered for
the immediate study at
hand but for some other
purpose.

broad or vague. Burger Delight's sales decline presents this type of problem. Exploratory research may involve reviewing published data, interviewing knowledgeable people, or investigating trade literature that discusses similar cases. In any event, one of the most important characteristics of exploratory research is its flexibility. Since researchers know little about the problem at this point, they must be ready to follow their intuition about possible areas and tactics of investigation.

If instead of being broad or vague, a problem is precisely and unambiguously formulated, *descriptive* or *causal* research is needed rather than exploratory research. In these research designs, data collection is not flexible but rigidly specified, both with respect to the data-collection forms and the sample design. The **descriptive design** emphasizes determining the frequency with which something occurs or the extent to which two variables covary. The **causal design** uses experiments to identify cause and effect relationships between variables.

Determine Data-Collection Method

Often the information that a firm needs to solve its problem already exists in the form of **secondary data,** or data that have already been collected for some purpose other than the question at hand. Such data may exist in the firm's own internal

Back to the Case

Back at her office, Allison began sifting through her predecessor's files. Shortly after she had taken the job eight months ago, a colleague had offhandedly mentioned to Allison that she was but the most recent in a long line of marketing vice-presidents that had passed through this office in the company's fifteen-year history. It wasn't until now, however, that Allison had had a chance to examine the old files closely and see for herself just how many people had preceded her. She was shocked.

One result of the rapid turnover was that there had been no consistent examination of the firm's marketing strategy. Ad campaigns had come and gone,

seemingly determined by whim. Nine years ago, when the company was expanding rapidly, one vice-president had managed to push through a study of possible locations for new restaurants. The results of the study had led to the firm's decision to build in urban and middle-income neighborhoods. Since then, precious little had been done to update the study.

Allison grimly replaced the files. She had every intention of staying with Burger Delight for years to come. However, under her management, she vowed, the marketing function would be handled very differently. First she'd launch this study with Smith & Cahners, and then once

the company's direction was established, she would lobby for a program of ongoing research.

As Allison discovered, Burger Delight had no program strategy for research. The location study that Allison's predecessor commissioned represented a project focus, with its emphasis on questionnaires, an analysis of sales data, and an examination of demographic trends.

Smaller firms often do not have formal program strategies for marketing research. Larger firms, which routinely budget set sums each year for research, are more likely to have concrete plans as to how that money should be spent.

information system as feedback on warranty cards, call reports from the sales force, or orders from wholesalers. If the firm itself does not have the necessary information, it may be readily available from a good business library in the form of government statistics or trade association reports. Finally, if neither of those sources prove fruitful, the data may have already been collected by a commercial research supplier. While the firm must pay for such information, the fee is usually less than the cost of an original study. In any case, for reasons of both cost and time, researchers should always look first at existing sources of data before launching a research project.

• Primary data

Information collected specifically for the purpose of the investigation at hand.

If the information needed is not readily available, or if it is available only in a form unsuitable for the problem at hand, then the research must depend on **primary data,** which are collected specifically for the study. The research questions here are several, including: Should the data be collected by observation or questionnaire? How should these observations be made — personally or electronically? How should the questions be administered — in person, over the telephone, or through the mail?

Design Data-Collection Forms

Once the researcher has settled on the method to be used for the study, he or she must decide on the type of observation form or questionnaire that would best suit the needs of the project. Suppose a questionnaire is being used. Should it be structured as a fixed set of alternative answers, or should the responses be open ended to allow respondents to reply in their own words? Should the purpose be made clear to the respondent, or should the study objectives be disguised? Should some kind of rating scale be used? What type?

Design Sample and Collect Data

After determining how the needed information will be collected, the researchers must decide what group will be observed or questioned. Depending on the study, this group might be housewives, preschoolers, sports car drivers, Pennsylvanians, or tennis players. The particular subset of the population chosen for study is known as a *sample*.

• Sampling frame

List of sampling units from which a sample will be drawn; the list could consist of geographic areas, institutions, individuals, or other units.

In designing the sample, the researcher must specify (1) the **sampling frame,** which is the list of population elements from which the sample will be drawn, (2) the sample selection process, and (3) the size of the sample. While people often assume the frame is implicit in the research problem and thus take it for granted, that assumption can be erroneous.

> Take the case of the manufacturer of dog food . . . who went out and did an intensive market study. He tested the demand for dog food; he tested the package size, the design, the whole advertising program. Then he launched the product with a big campaign, got the proper distribution channels, put it on the market and had tremendous sales. But two months later, the bottom dropped out — no follow-up sales. So he called in an expert, who took the dog food out to the local pound, put it in front of the dogs — and they would not touch it. For all the big marketing study, no one had tried the product on the dogs.[3]

---

[3]Joseph R. Hochstim, "Practical Uses of Sampling Surveys in the Field of Labor Relations," *Proceedings of the Conference on Business Application of Statistical Sampling Methods* (Monticello, Ill.: The Bureau of Business Management, University of Illinois, 1950), pp. 181–182.

Today's easy-to-load, easy-to-use cameras reflect years of effective marketing research.

Source: Reprinted courtesy of Eastman Kodak Company.

As this old but classic example illustrates, the dog population was not part of the sampling frame, probably because it is people who buy dog food and not the dogs themselves. Nevertheless, the careless specification of population elements had dire consequences. While the consequences may be less dire in other cases, it is important to realize that when we sample from, say, a phone book or a mailing list, we are not sampling from the population as a whole, but are only sampling from people whose names appear in the phone book or on the mailing list. Answers to a questionnaire on frequency of air travel would clearly be quite different if the sample were selected from the Greenwich, Connecticut, phone book than if it were selected from the book covering rural West Virginia.

The sample selection process requires that the form of the sample be specified. Will it be a **probability sample,** in which each member of the population has a known chance of being selected? Or will it be a **nonprobability sample,** in which the researchers subjectively decide which particular group will be part of the study?

Sample size addresses the issue of how many institutions or subjects it is necessary to use in the project in order to get reliable answers without exceeding the time and money budgeted for it.

Once the dimensions of the sample design are specified, data collection can begin. Data collection requires a field force of some type, although field methods are largely dictated by the data-collection method, the kinds of information to be obtained, and the sampling requirements. The use of personnel to collect data raises a host of questions with respect to selection, training, and control of the field staff. For example, what kind of background should interviewers have in order to glean the most information from respondents? What specific training is necessary to en-

• Probability sample

Sample in which each population element has a known, nonzero chance of being included in the sample.

• Nonprobability sample

Sample that relies on personal judgment somewhere in the element selection process and therefore prohibits estimating the probability that any population element will be included in the sample.

sure that interviewers administer the questionnaires accurately? How often, and in what way, should the accuracy of the answers on the questionnaires be checked by validation studies? These questions should be anticipated in designing the research.

Analyze and Interpret the Data

Researchers may amass a mountain of data, but it is useless unless the findings are analyzed and the results interpreted in light of the problem at hand. Data analysis generally involves several steps. First, the data-collection forms must be scanned to be sure that they are complete, consistent, and that the instructions were followed. This process is called **editing.** After being edited, the forms must be **coded,** which involves assigning numbers to each of the answers so that they may be analyzed by a computer. The final step in analyzing the data is **tabulation.** This refers to the orderly arrangement of data in a table or other summary format achieved by counting the frequency of responses to each question. At this point the data may also be cross-classified by other categories. Suppose researchers asked women if they like a certain new cosmetic. Their responses may be cross-classified by age group, income level, and so forth.

The coding, editing, and tabulation functions are common to most research studies. Any statistical tests applied to the data are generally unique to the particular sampling procedures and data-collection instruments used in the research. These tests should be anticipated before data collection is begun, if possible, to assure that the data and analyses will be appropriate for the problem as specified.

- **Editing**
  Inspection and correction, if necessary, of each questionnaire or observation form.

- **Coding**
  Technical procedure by which data are categorized; it involves specifying the alternative categories or classes into which the responses are to be placed and assigning code numbers to the classes.

- **Tabulation**
  Procedure by which the number of cases that fall into each of a number of categories are counted.

Prepare the Research Report

The research report is the document submitted to management that summarizes the research results and conclusions. It is all that many executives will see of the research effort, and it becomes the standard by which that research is judged. Thus, it is imperative that the research report be clear and accurate, since no matter how well all previous steps have been completed, the project will be no more successful than the research report. One empirical study that investigated the factors determining the extent to which research results are used by firms found that the research report was one of the five most important determinants.[4]

Additional Comments on Marketing Research Steps

The steps in the research process serve to structure the remainder of this book. The following chapter, for example, deals with the first step, or Stage 1, problem formulation, while each of the remaining stages warrants a special section in the book.

These stages in the research process can also be used to direct additional study in research method. The aspiring research student needs more sophistication in at least some of the stages than this book could possibly provide. Each chapter will include some suggestions of where in-depth study might be most useful.

Although these stages have been presented as if one would proceed through them in a lockstep fashion when designing a research project (Figure 2.1), nothing could be further from the truth. Rather, Figure 2.1 could be drawn with a number of feedback loops suggesting a possible need to rethink, redraft, or revise the various

---

[4]Rohit Deshpande and Gerald Zaltman, "A Comparison of Factors Affecting Researcher and Manager Perceptions of Market Research Use," *Journal of Marketing Research,* 21 (February 1984), pp. 32–38.

elements in the process as the study proceeds. The process would begin with problem formulation, and then could take any direction. The problem may not be specified explicitly enough to allow the development of the research design, in which case the researcher would need to return to Stage 1 to define the research objectives more clearly. Alternatively, the process may proceed smoothly to the design of the data-collection forms, the pretest of which may require a revision of the research objectives or the research design. Still further, the sample necessary to answer the problem as specified may be prohibitively costly, again requiring a revision of the earlier steps. Once the data are collected, no revision of the procedure is possible. It is possible, though, to revise the earlier steps on the basis of the *anticipated* analysis, and it is critical that the methods used to analyze the data be determined before the data are collected.

Although it is hard for beginning researchers to understand, the steps in the research process are highly interrelated. A decision made at one stage will affect decisions at each of the other stages, and a revision of the procedure at any stage often requires modifications of procedures at each of the other stages. Unfortunately, it seems that this lesson is only understood by those who have experienced the frustrations and satisfactions of being involved in an actual research project.

The important error to avoid when designing a research project is the *total error* likely to be associated with the project. All the steps are necessary and vital, and it is dangerous to emphasize one to the exclusion of one or more others. Many beginning students of research, for example, argue for large sample sizes. What they fail to realize is that sample size is a decision with respect to one subset of one stage in the process. Further, and more important, an increase in the sample size to reduce sampling error can often lead to an increase in the total error of the research effort, since other errors increase more than proportionately with sample size. For example, a study may require researchers to call people from a list of randomly selected phone numbers. Even if the numbers themselves represent an excellent cross section of the population, a funny thing may happen on the way to the study's results. Researchers working a nine-to-five day will doubtlessly have trouble connecting with families in which both spouses work or with households made up of single working people. If this potential error is not accounted for, the study may overly represent the homebound—the elderly, families with a baby or an invalid, or the unemployed.[5] The larger the sample size, of course, the larger would be the weight of this group's opinions. The magnitude of the error caused by a large sample would then have a significant effect on the total error associated with the project.

Total error, rather than errors incurred in any single stage, is the important error in research work, except insofar as those individual errors increase total error. Quite often, *part error,* or *stage error,* will be increased so that total error may be decreased. Table 2.2 lists some of the typical questions that must be addressed so that total error can be minimized.

◆ Ethical Issues in Marketing Research

Ethical issues, by their very nature, always seem to be sensitive and complex. And as a future marketer, you face the prospect of being forced at some point in your career to make decisions that require ethical judgments. As a consumer you may have already been a subject in a marketing research project. Perhaps you have participated in the Pepsi Challenge on campus or at a local shopping mall. Or you might

---

[5]Bernice Kanner, "What Makes an Ad Work?" *New York,* 16 (May 23, 1983), p. 16.

Table 2.2   Questions Typically Addressed at the Various Stages of the Research Process

Stage in the Process	Typical Questions
Formulate problem	What is the purpose of the study — to solve a problem? Identify an opportunity? Is additional background information necessary? What information is needed to make the decision? How will the information be utilized? Should research be conducted?
Determine research design	How much is already known? Can a hypothesis be formulated? What types of questions need to be answered? What type of study will best address the research questions?
Determine data-collection method	Can existing data be used to advantage? What is to be measured? How? What is the source of the data? Can objective answers be obtained by asking people? How should people be questioned? Should the questionnaires be administered in person, over the phone, or through the mail? Should electronic or mechanical means be used to make the observations?
Design data-collection forms	Should structured or unstructured items be used to collect the data? Should the purpose of the study be made known to the respondents? Should rating scales be used in the questionnaires? What specific behaviors should the observers record?
Design sample and collect data	Who is the target population? Is a list of population elements available? Is a sample necessary? Is a probability sample desirable? How large should the sample be? How should the sample be selected? Who will gather the data? How long will the data gathering take? How much supervision is needed? What operational procedures will be followed? What methods will be used to ensure the quality of the data collected?
Analyze and interpret the data	Who will handle the editing of the data? How will the data be coded? Who will supervise the coding? Will computer or hand tabulation be utilized? What tabulations are called for? What analysis techniques will be used?
Prepare the research report	Who will read the report? What is their technical level of sophistication? What is their involvement with the project? Are managerial recommendations called for? What will be the format of the written report? Is an oral report necessary? How should the oral report be structured?

Source: Adapted from William G. Zikmund, *Exploring Marketing Research,* 2nd ed., p. 56. Copyright © 1986, 1982 by Holt, Rinehart and Winston, Inc. Reprinted by permission of Holt, Rinehart and Winston, Inc.

have agreed to answer questions in a telephone survey or responded to a mail questionnaire. Usually such research is totally aboveboard. However, in the late 1960s and early 1970s consumer groups began investigating some research practices that were less straightforward, and in some cases downright fraudulent. Among the various research practices considered deceptive by consumer groups, the following five were most often cited:[6]

- Falsified sponsor identification (fictitious name, "official" name)
- Faked promise of anonymity (invisible ink, special codes)
- Lying about length of questionnaire, time required to complete interview, possible follow-up survey, and so forth
- Promise of undelivered compensation (premiums, summaries of results)
- Selling under the guise of marketing research

Ethical issues involving researchers and respondents have received more media attention than those arising within a company or between research agencies and their clients. However, all of these types of ethical conflict may confront the researcher at one time or another.

A recent study found that three job situations were most often cited when researchers were asked to name "the most *difficult* ethical or moral problem for you."[7] They were as follows:

1. The most difficult ethical problem facing all types of marketing researchers was that of maintaining the integrity of their research efforts. Sometimes people higher in the firm pressure the researcher to modify his or her research so that it confirms their preexisting opinions. Or others in the company make decisions that the researcher is asked to accept even though they compromise the integrity of the project.

   Specific problems researchers cite include (1) deliberately withholding information, (2) falsifying figures, (3) altering research results, (4) misusing statistics, (5) ignoring pertinent data, (6) compromising the design of a research project, and (7) misinterpreting the results of a research project with the objective of supporting a predetermined personal or corporate point of view. Many other ethical problems are involved in marketing research, but the issue of maintaining fundamental research integrity dominates.

2. The primary ethical conflicts for in-house researchers are two: balancing the interests of self against the interests of other parties and balancing the interests of the company against the interests of other parties.

   For example, one in-house researcher reported, "[I] refused to alter research results, and as a result I was eventually fired for failure to think strategically." A sporting goods marketing researcher said he was often asked to supply ballpark estimates of certain figures for managers to use in their reports to a corporate parent. While he was careful to warn of the imprecise nature of these numbers, he found managers putting "these gross estimates, guesses, and sometimes completely fake figures into their reports with two-decimal accuracy," rather than admit that they did not have the time or money to do a thorough study.

---

[6]See Kenneth C. Schneider and Cynthia K. Holm, "Deceptive Practices in Marketing Research: The Consumer's Viewpoint," *California Management Review,* (Spring 1982), pp. 89–96.

[7]This section draws heavily from a study by Shelby D. Hunt, Lawrence B. Chonko, and James B. Wilcox, "Ethical Problems of Marketing Researchers," which appeared in *Journal of Marketing Research,* 21 (August 1984), pp. 309–324.

3. All of the primary ethical conflicts of *agency* researchers involve balancing the interests of their outside clients against the interests of various other parties, including company, self, society, competitors, and other clients. For example, one agency researcher reported a conflict between his own interest in conducting an honest project, and the client's insistence on using a methodology that would guarantee the results he wanted. Another agency vice-president said the most difficult moral problem he encountered was when the agency made a mistake in a study that resulted in unreliable findings. Do you tell the client about the mistake or try to bury the mistake?

Most marketing researchers responding to the preceding study believed that such unethical behavior is rare and that it can be effectively stopped by top management. As the authors of the study note, "When top management lets it be known that unethical behavior will not be tolerated, marketing researchers experience fewer ethical problems."[8]

---

[8]Hunt, *Journal of Marketing Research,* p. 319.

Back to the Case

Allison Abbott sat at her desk, poring over sketches of ideas for promotional items submitted by the company's advertising agency. She had just rejected a plastic and rubber-band slingshot as too dangerous when Stan Jamison appeared at her door.

"Hi, Stan. Come on in. How would your kids react to a re-usable snap-top cup that looks like a caterpillar with straws for antennae?"

"My son would probably love it—especially if he could blow in one antenna and squirt Coke at his sister out of the other," Jamison replied.

"Actually, Allison, these promo items are what I wanted to talk to you about. I had a great idea that would save the company a bundle of money and get you in very tight with Turnbull very quickly."

"What's that, Stan?" Allison asked. She had always felt a little suspicious of Jamison, and she now sensed her guard going up.

"That marketing research study you suggested at this morning's meeting is going to cost this company a fortune when we can least afford it. You're a smart girl. You know something about marketing research. Why don't you just print up a bunch of questionnaires and send them out to the managers of each franchise. Then advertise these bug cups like crazy on kiddie TV. Say they're free. The kids will drag their parents into the restaurant. Then, before we hand over the cups, we will ask the parents to answer our questionnaire. We'll get a great response and boost sales in the process!"

Allison was silent for a moment. Then she said quietly, "I don't think that sounds very ethical, Stan."

"Ethics, shmethics! The point is, the kids get the loot you were going to give them anyway, we get the data . . . and it won't cost us an arm and a leg. My unit has a dozen ways we could use that money to better advantage. If you were a team player, Allison, you'd see it my way."

In recent years marketing researchers have increasingly had to address the ethical considerations they must face in doing business. Allison finds that these issues are not limited to the researcher-respondent relationship. They often involve differences between co-workers as well.

Figure 2.2   Code of Marketing Research Ethics for the American Marketing Association

A. *For Research Users, Practitioners and Interviewers*

1. No individual or organization will undertake any activity which is directly or indirectly represented to be marketing research, but which has as its real purpose the attempted sale of merchandise or services to some or all of the respondents interviewed in the course of the research.

2. If a respondent has been led to believe, directly or indirectly, that he is participating in a marketing research survey and that his anonymity will be protected, his name shall not be made known to anyone outside the research organization or research department, or used for other than research purposes.

B. *For Research Practitioners*

1. There will be no intentional or deliberate misrepresentation of research methods or results. An adequate description of methods employed will be made available upon request to the sponsor of the research. Evidence that field work has been completed according to specifications will, upon request, be made available to buyers of research.

2. The identity of the survey sponsor and/or the ultimate client for whom a survey is being done will be held in confidence at all times, unless this identity is to be revealed as part of the research design. Research information shall be held in confidence by the research organization or department and not used for personal gain or made available to any outside party unless the client specifically authorizes such release.

3. A research organization shall not undertake marketing studies for competitive clients when such studies would jeopardize the confidential nature of client-agency relationships.

C. *For Users of Marketing Research*

1. A user of research shall not knowingly disseminate conclusions from a given research project or service that are inconsistent with or not warranted by the data.

2. To the extent that there is involved in a research project a unique design involving techniques, approaches or concepts not commonly available to research practitioners, the prospective user of research shall not solicit such a design from one practitioner and deliver it to another for execution without the approval of the design originator.

D. *For Field Interviewers*

1. Research assignments and materials received, as well as information obtained from respondents, shall be held in confidence by the interviewer and revealed to no one except the research organization conducting the marketing study.

2. No information gained through a marketing research activity shall be used directly or indirectly for the personal gain or advantage of the interviewer.

3. Interviews shall be conducted in strict accordance with specifications and instructions received.

4. An interviewer shall not carry out two or more interviewing assignments simultaneously unless authorized by all contractors or employers concerned.

Members of the American Marketing Association will be expected to conduct themselves in accordance with the provisions of this Code in all of their marketing research activities.

Source: American Marketing Association.

In an attempt to provide some guidelines both for researchers and for top management, the American Marketing Association has published a "Code of Marketing Research Ethics" (Figure 2.2). While it does not cover all the issues that researchers may face, it does provide some guidelines for acceptable practices in conducting marketing research.

It is critical that all marketers adhere to these standards. Not only one's personal integrity, but the integrity of the entire profession is at stake even though the course to take is not always clear—as Research Window 2.1 illustrates.

Research Window 2.1
Ethical Dilemmas—What Would You Do?

Even with a code of ethics, the choices facing researchers are not always easily decided. Following are some scenarios in which marketing researchers face ethical dilemmas. Read them and decide what you would do if faced with the same situation.

1. A leading manufacturer of breakfast cereals was interested in learning how consumers decide to buy a particular brand of cereal. To gather this information, the company instructed researchers to go to supermarkets in several cities. They were to assume a position out of the shoppers' way and observe the shoppers' behavior in the cereal aisles.

   Is it ethical to systematically observe another person's behavior without his or her knowledge? What if the behavior had been more private in nature? What if the behavior had been recorded on videotape?

2. A leading pharmaceutical supply company, which derived its major source of revenue from physician-prescribed drugs, found itself losing market share to a new competitor. The company's management decided to commission a study to find out how doctors decide which drugs to prescribe. The company's marketing research director instructed interviewers to call doctors and identify themselves as employees of a fictitious marketing research firm instead of the pharmaceutical company for which they actually worked. The marketing research director felt that revealing the company's actual name would bias the doctors' responses.

   Was the director's decision to withhold the sponsor's true name and purpose ethical? Do the physicians have a right to know who is conducting the research? What kind of results might have been obtained if the physicians knew the true sponsor of the study?

3. A local business group asked a marketing research consultant to give a talk at its monthly meeting about some of the research methods currently being used in the field. To make the presentation more meaningful, the consultant discussed the details of some recent studies her firm had undertaken. The details she revealed were such that most of the audience could identify the clients for whom the research had been conducted.

   What might be the consequences for the client of such a presentation? Should the consultant have obtained the client's consent before revealing the nature of the studies? What are the rights of the clients?

4. A beer company wanted to know whether consumers could really tell the difference in taste between beers, or whether their preferences were more psychological than actual. As part of a study to investigate this question, subjects were asked to taste three unmarked

Is it ethical to observe shoppers as a part of a marketing research study?

Source: Courtesy of Information Resources, Inc.

cans of beer, and to describe the taste of each. Although subjects had been led to believe that the three cans contained different brands, at the end of the session researchers revealed that the three cans were, in fact, the same beer. A fair number of the participants had thought the beers tasted quite different.

Some analysts argue that such an experiment may induce stress in some participants since it could cause them to doubt their competence as shoppers. Do you think that is a valid issue? Should the researchers have offered some sort of psychic support upon completion of the experiment in order to counteract any possible negative effects?

◆ Summary

Learning Objective 1: Explain the difference between a program strategy and a project strategy to research.

A company's overall philosophy of how marketing research fits into its marketing plan determines its *program strategy* for marketing research. A program strategy specifies the types of studies that are to be conducted, and for what purposes. It might even specify how often these studies are to take place. The design of the individual studies themselves constitutes the firm's *project strategy*.

Learning Objective 2: Outline the steps in the research process, and show how the steps are interrelated.

The steps in the research process are: (1) formulate the problem, (2) determine research design, (3) determine the data-collection method, (4) design the data-collection forms, (5) design the sample and collect the data, (6) analyze and interpret the data, and (7) prepare the research report. These steps are highly interrelated in that a decision made at one stage will affect decisions in every other stage, and a revision of the procedure in any stage often requires modification of procedures in every other stage.

Learning Objective 3: Cite the most critical error in marketing research.

Total error is the most critical error in research work, rather than the size of the error that occurs in any single stage.

Learning Objective 4: List five research practices that are nearly always considered to be unethical by consumers.

The following five research practices are most often cited by consumers as being deceptive: falsified sponsor identification; faked promise of anonymity; lying about length of questionnaire, the time required to complete interview, or the probability of a follow-up survey; promise of undelivered compensation; and selling under the guise of marketing research.

Learning Objective 5: Specify the most difficult ethical problems facing marketing researchers.

The most difficult ethical problems cited by respondents in a recent study were: maintaining the integrity of their research efforts; balancing the interests of self and/or the company against the interests of other parties; and, for agency researchers, balancing the interests of outside clients against the interest of other parties, including company, self, society, competitors, and other clients.

Discussion Questions, Problems, and Projects

1. Using the steps of the research process to structure your thinking, evaluate the following marketing research effort.

   The FlyRight Airline company was interested in altering the interior layout of its aircrafts to suit the tastes and needs of an increasing segment of its market—businesspeople. Management was planning to reduce the number of seats and install small tables to enable businesspeople to work during long flights. Prior to the renovation, management decided to do some research to ensure that these changes would suit the needs of the passengers. To keep expenses to a minimum the following strategy was employed.

   The questionnaires were completed by passengers during a flight. Due to the ease of administration and collection, the questionnaires were distributed only on the short flights (those less than one hour). The study was conducted during the second and third week of December, as that was when flights were full. To increase the response rate, each steward and stewardess on the flight was responsible for a certain number of questionnaires. The management thought this was a good time to acquire as much information as possible; hence, the questionnaire included issues apart from the new seating arrangement. As a result, the questionnaire took twenty minutes to complete.

2. Schedule an interview with the marketing research director of a firm near your home or where you go to school. In the interview, try to develop as exhaustive a list as you can regarding the general types of studies the firm conducts and for what purposes. Pick two of the studies and secure as much detail as you can on their specifics, such as the type and size of the sample, the data-collection instruments used, what is done with the data after it is collected, and so on. Report on what you found, organizing that report into the firm's program and project strategies for research.

Suggested Additional Readings

For a general discussion of the ethical issues facing marketers, including marketing research, see

Gene R. Laczniak and Patrick E. Murphy, eds., *Marketing Ethics: Guidelines for Managers* (Lexington, Mass.: Lexington Books, 1985).

Chapter 3

Problem Formulation

Learning Objectives

Upon completing this chapter, you should be able to

1. Explain what is meant by a decision situation.
2. List the factors that make up a decision maker's environment.
3. Describe the various elements a researcher must understand in order to address the real decision problem.
4. Distinguish between a decision problem and a research problem.
5. Explain why a decision tree can be useful in problem solving.
6. Outline the various elements of the research proposal.

Case in Marketing Research

In Chapter 2 we met Allison Abbott, vice-president of marketing at Burger Delight, a fast food chain with plummeting sales. Burger Delight's president, Martin Turnbull, had authorized a marketing research study to determine the reasons behind the company's decline. One of Abbott's co-workers suggested to her a way of doing the research that would save money but would depend on a degree of customer deception.

Closing the door softly behind her, Allison Abbott left President Turnbull's office. As she headed down the corridor, she felt an enormous sense of relief and a new confidence. Turnbull had been unequivocal in his support of the study—and unequivocal in his insistence that the study be totally ethical.

Back at her office, Allison found Jay Nichols, the researcher from Smith & Cahners assigned to the Burger Delight account, huddled over a stack of printouts of sales from the chain's restaurants across the country.

"Jay, you look as though you haven't moved an inch since I left you here an hour ago," Allison said. "I hope you've been able to make more sense out of that data than I've been able to. I've been poring over it for days, and have only become more confused in the process."

"Sales have been declining for five consecutive quarters and were, at best, merely stable for months before that. But what is responsible? Our competition? Our product? Our target market? Our advertising? It could be any one of those things or all of them! How can we sort this out?"

"Well, Allison, there are a lot of possible variables in this problem, but I think we can begin to tackle it by starting with those facts we know for sure.

"We know, for example, that Burger Delight's beef is probably the best quality on the market. In addition, Baxter from accounting told me that the company has ironclad contracts with suppliers for at least the next five years, so that pretty much eliminates turning Burger Delight into a quiche and fern bar or a chicken outlet.

"We also know that your prices are lower than those of competitors for a standard burger but that lower pricing structure is dependent on selling smaller portions and making customers pay for extras like tomatoes. Low prices have traditionally attracted large families who want an inexpensive way to feed lots of hungry but reasonably undiscriminating kids."

"You know, Jay," said Allison, "our sales reports indicate that we are doing best in lower-income neighborhoods. We're holding steady in middle-class locations and positively dying in the affluent suburbs. I think I sense a trend, but the exact reason is still unclear."

Jay and Allison have begun to formulate the problem facing Burger Delight by analyzing existing information. But the direction the research should take is still not well defined. Jay Nichols needs to know more about his client and its business environment before suggesting a research strategy.

Discussion Issues

1. If you were Allison Abbott, what existing information do you think it would be valuable to give to a marketing researcher?

2. What issues might a marketing researcher address?

◆ Problem Formulation

An old adage says, "A problem well-defined is half-solved." This is especially true in marketing research, for it is only when the problem has been clearly defined and the objectives of the research precisely stated that research can be designed properly. "Properly" here means not only that the research will generate the kinds of answers needed, but that it will do so efficiently.

Problem formulation requires good communication between decision maker and marketing researcher. The decision maker needs to understand what research can and cannot accomplish. The researcher needs to understand the nature of the decision managers face and what they hope to learn from research—in other words, the project objectives.

> Nothing in marketing research requires more creativity and insight than the definition of the research problem and the establishment of project objectives. In many ways the marketing researcher is like a doctor. A patient who is not feeling well describes his symptoms to the doctor. The patient may or may not be able to diagnose his own case. A broken arm can easily be identified. In most instances, however, the patient has several complaints (symptoms) resulting from underlying disorders (causal factors). The source of the disorder may not be as easy to pinpoint. The creative challenge for the doctor is in diagnosis. Once an accurate diagnosis has been made, the doctor can ascertain whether the fundamental problem is curable and take appropriate measures. . . .
>
> The marketing researcher, like the doctor, is responsible for an accurate diagnosis. Again like the doctor, the marketing researcher normally cannot fulfill his responsibility without some help from the client. It is with respect to this issue that one of the most frequent and crucial errors made in marketing research often occurs. When the research director allows the project to be based on a client's request for specific information he not only allows the client to diagnose the cause of the problem but to specify a prescription for the cure as well. The doctor's responsibility is to cure the patient; the marketing researcher's responsibility is to solve the client's problem. In each case the cure may or may not have any relationship to the information presented by the patient.[1]

A proper understanding of the basic structure of the problems involved in reaching a decision can help a researcher reach a diagnosis. The simplest of decision situations can be characterized by the following conditions. See Figure 3.1.

1. Person or organization X has a problem. That problem is the result of something that is taking place in X's environment (E).
2. There are at least two courses of action, A_1 and A_2, that X can follow.
3. If X chooses to follow A_2, for example, there are at least two possible outcomes of that choice $(O_1$ and $O_2)$. Of these outcomes, one is preferred to the other, so the decision process must have an objective.

---

[1] Robert W. Joselyn, *Designing the Marketing Research Project* (New York: Petrocelli/Charter, 1977), pp. 25–26.

Figure 3.1

A Sample Decision Situation

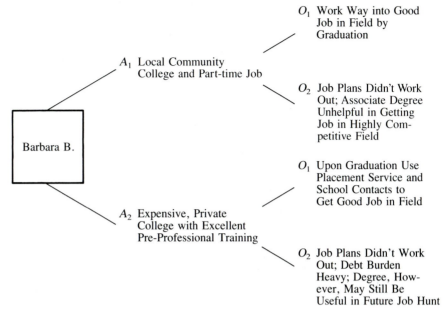

O_1 Work Way into Good Job in Field by Graduation

A_1 Local Community College and Part-time Job

O_2 Job Plans Didn't Work Out; Associate Degree Unhelpful in Getting Job in Highly Competitive Field

Barbara B.

O_1 Upon Graduation Use Placement Service and School Contacts to Get Good Job in Field

A_2 Expensive, Private College with Excellent Pre-Professional Training

O_2 Job Plans Didn't Work Out; Debt Burden Heavy; Degree, However, May Still Be Useful in Future Job Hunt

Barbara B., a high-school student interested in a broadcasting career, must decide whether to go to

College A_1—an inexpensive community college nearby; she can live at home and work part-time as a secretary in a local radio station in hopes of getting experience that would lead to a good job in her field, *or*

College A_2—an expensive, but excellent private college far from home, with a well-known communications department and a good track record in job placement and in percentage of students accepted to graduate school.

What might be the advantages—and disadvantages—of each choice?

4. There is a chance, but not an equal chance, that each course of action will lead to the desired outcome. If the chances were equal, the choice would not matter.[2]

To sum up, a person faces a decision situation if he or she has a problem, knows several good, but not equally good, ways of solving it, and must pick between the various choices available. Research can assist in clarifying any of these characteristics of the decision situation. Let us briefly consider how.

The Decision Maker and the Environment

It is important that the researcher understand the personality of the decision maker and the environment in which that person operates. That environment will include the state of the economy in general and also the economic situation of the particular industry involved and the particular company in that industry. In the mid-1980s, for example, the environment for manufacturers of fast-selling products like videocassette recorders was quite different from that for the ailing steel industry, despite the fact that they were both part of the same national economy.

Even within the same company, decision makers' environments may differ. At the same time that Coleco Industries was deciding to dump its entire computer operation (after sales of its Adam home computers and ColecoVision video games fizzled), it was also struggling to fill the huge demand for its highly successful Cabbage Patch

[2]See Russell L. Ackoff, *The Art of Problem Solving* (New York: John Wiley & Sons, Inc., 1978).

Kids.[3] Decision makers in these two divisions of the company faced very different challenges from their environments.

Surprisingly, sometimes the decision maker's original position will not change regardless of what is found by the researcher. Research merely represents "conscience money" in these cases. The results are readily accepted when they are consistent with the decision the individual "wants to make," or with the person's perceptions of the environment or the consequences of alternative actions. Otherwise, the results are questioned, at best, or discarded as being inaccurate, at worst. The reason, of course, is that the individual's view of the decision problem is so strongly held that research will do little to change it. When this is the case, research will be a waste of the firm's resources. The first task of the researcher, therefore, is to discover whether the decision maker is truly willing to consider the results of the research.

An example of pointless research was found by the Advertising Research Foundation in surveying financial service companies such as banks, brokers, and insurers. Although such companies spend almost as much as other consumer goods industries on television ads, they spend relatively little on research to test the effectiveness of their ads ($28,300 median for banks, $45,800 for diversified financial companies, and only $22,500 for insurance companies compared with upwards of $500,000 for other consumer goods industries). And among the 60 percent of this group who bother to test at all, 58 percent admit that the results of such research do not play an important part in their marketing decision making.[4]

Often the task of determining whether the management decision might change with research information is complicated by the fact that the researcher's contact is not the final decision maker but a liaison. Yet, this determination should be made before the researcher begins work on the decision problem. Next, as previously mentioned, the researcher also needs to understand the environment of the enterprise in which the decision maker operates. What are the constraints on that person's actions? What are the resources at the decision maker's disposal? What is the time frame in which the manager is operating? It does little good to design a study, however accurate, that costs $20,000 and takes six months to complete when the decision maker needs the results within one month and has only $2,000 for the research. Obviously, some compromises must be made, and it is the researcher's responsibility to anticipate them by carefully examining the decision environment.

The corporate culture, of course, is an important factor in the environment and should be carefully studied by the researcher.[5] In some firms the process by which decisions are made is dominant, while in other firms the personality of management is more important. At General Mills, for example, the emphasis is on research that evaluates alternatives, and the culture at General Mills tries to force all information requests into action alternatives. Thus, instead of asking the question, "What proportion of potato chips is eaten at meals?" General Mills would ask, "How can I advertise my potato chips for meal consumption?" or "Will a 'meal commercial' sell more chips than my present commercial?" (both action questions). To design effective research for General Mills, therefore, a researcher would need to be aware of this aspect of the general corporate culture.

---

[3]"Adam Hits the Briar Patch," *Newsweek,* 107 (January 14, 1985), p. 61.

[4]Bill Abrams, "Financial Service Advertisers Seen Neglecting Ad Research," *The Wall Street Journal,* 63 (August 8, 1983), p. 23.

[5]Joel Levine, the vice-president of marketing research at The Pillsbury Company in Minneapolis, suggests that awareness of the corporate culture is one of the most important factors that distinguishes researchers who affect strategic marketing decisions from those who do not. See "Six Factors Mark Researchers Who Sway Strategic Decisions," *Marketing News,* 17 (February 4, 1983), p. 1. See also Bernie Whalen, "Researchers Stymied by 'Adversary Culture' in Firms," *Marketing News,* 16 (September 17, 1982), pp. 1 and 7.

Figure 3.2

The Best Laid Models of Mice and Men. . .

The late Bob Keith, then president of the Pillsbury Company, was once persuaded by Pillsbury's operations researchers to review one of his major marketing decisions using a formal decision model. He agreed to the outcomes, their values, and their probabilities, and chose the decision rule he felt most appropriate. The computer then calculated the expectations, compared them, and reported the alternative that should be chosen according to that rule. Mr. Keith disagreed, noting that another alternative was obviously the only correct choice — indeed, it was the choice that *had* been made not long before. "How can that be?" the researchers asked. "You accepted all the values and probabilities and chose the decision rule yourself. The rest is just arithmetic." "That's fine," Keith replied, "but you forgot to ask me about a few other things that were more important."

Source: Adapted from Charles Raymond, *The Art of Using Science in Marketing* (New York: Harper & Row, 1974), p. 17.

Alternative Courses of Action

Research can be properly designed only when the alternative courses of action being considered are known. The more obvious ones are typically given to the researcher by the decision maker, and the researcher's main task is to determine whether the list provided indeed exhausts the alternatives. Quite often the researcher will not be informed of some of the options being considered. The researcher should check to see that all implicit options have been made explicit, since it is important that the research be relevant to all alternatives.

Let us consider an example of the types of alternative courses of action that a company may consider. The Campbell Soup Company has a strong commitment to keeping pace with consumer and technological trends. As part of its ongoing research, the company's product managers team up with in-house and outside researchers to probe for openings in the market. In addition to Campbell's traditional family market, the research teams have investigated the eating habits and flavor preferences of career women, Hispanics, consumers over age 55, and owners of microwave ovens — each of these groups suggesting an alternative course of action. And now that the company's "Soup is Good Food" campaign is well established, the team has begun work on positioning soup as a convenient snack food. Some of the other alternatives the company is considering are to create other value-added food items, advertise heavily to attract consumers to try Campbell's products, and be a low-cost producer.[6]

Researchers at times must adopt the role of detective in order to uncover the hidden agendas and alternatives lurking beneath the surface in any decision situation. If a critical piece of information remains undiscovered, even the most sophisticated research techniques cannot solve the problem. Attempting to impress the company president, researchers at Pillsbury discovered this fact belatedly — to their embarrassment (Figure 3.2).

Objectives of the Decision Maker

As a part of understanding the decision maker, the researcher should be aware that individuals differ in their attitudes toward risk and that these differences influence their choices. Some people are willing to assume a good deal of risk for the chance of even a small gain.[7] Others are unwilling to assume any risk, even when the potential gain is great. And some individuals walk a middle ground.

---

[6]"Soup Maker Bets Future on Monitoring Technological Consumption Changes," *Marketing News,* 18 (October 12, 1984), p. 44.

[7]The types of decision makers are more formally defined in decision theory literature. See, for example, the classic work by Howard Raiffa, *Decision Analysis: Introductory Lectures on Choices under Uncertainty* (Reading, Mass.: Addison-Wesley, 1968), pp. 51–101. See also James O. Berger, *Statistical Decision Theory* (New York: Springer-Verlag, 1980).

A person's attitude toward risk changes with the situation. When feeling secure in his or her position in the company, a person may take greater risks than at another time when feeling less secure.

Take the case of Jimmy Spradley, young president of Standard Candy of Nashville, manufacturers of Goo Goo Clusters—a gooey confection dear to the hearts of Southerners. When Spradley took over Standard Candy, it was close to bankruptcy. The new president immediately turned his focus to marketing, offering brokers trips as incentives for improved sales performance and enticing retailers to stock the brand by offering appealing discounts. By the summer of 1983 sales were strong,

Back to the Case

Jay was back in Allison's office after having investigated some literature on demographic trends with a view to their effect on the restaurant industry.

"Allison," he said, "I think I've turned up some information that may give us a clue as to what is going on. The Baby Boomers who used to be your primary market are getting older. They still want to eat out, but they are not so interested in food that is just quick and cheap anymore. Industry analysts all claim that quality is the key to attracting them."

"What does that mean for Burger Delight?" Allison asked.

"Well, as I see it, we could investigate a number of options," Jay said. "As you had suggested earlier, Burger Delight could continue to focus on its primary existing market—families with young children—by designing an appealing advertising campaign, perhaps with accompanying sales promotion items —glasses, hats, games, coupons, or such—and hold the line on prices. This is a pretty conservative strategy, and it should increase sales without the company having to make any serious changes.

"A second alternative that we talked about in our last meeting is to increase the size of the patty and bump up prices a bit. With this strategy you risk alienating your price-conscious customers, but if it works, you might attract a new market segment, one less concerned about price than quality.

"A third, more drastic alternative, would be to reposition the chain entirely—to invent an 'all-new Burger Delight'—that features large, high-quality burgers at premium prices. This approach would fit in with demographic trends, but you could say good-bye to your current market. You would probably have to sacrifice your locations in less affluent areas in the hopes of cultivating an upscale clientele in the suburbs and in your better in-town locations.

"These aren't the only options, Allison, but they represent three approaches with varying degrees of risk—and possible reward. What do you think?"

"Well, to be frank, I like your last idea. However, it does represent the greatest risk and a major upheaval in the way we do business. While I could give you the go-ahead to test a new advertising approach, or even to explore various pricing strategies, it would be pointless for me to put you to work on a study of such a major revision when I don't have the power to act on it should the results be positive. Before we go any further, let me consult with the president and get back to you."

Jay has presented Allison with an alternative that Burger Delight had never considered—revamping its entire operation. While it may have a great deal of potential in light of existing market trends, it's also a very risky proposal. A venture of that magnitude would require a substantial commitment of time and company resources. To pursue marketing research in that area without the assurance that top management would buy the plan if research results were encouraging would be a waste of time and money. Hence, Allison must seek a consensus from the top before authorizing Jay to begin.

and the company's debts were being paid off. It was then that Spradley took a big risk.

Impatient to boost sales even further, he doubled his discounts for certain customers. Sales soared, but profits plummeted, and the company began to lose money. Spradley quickly stopped the practice, admitting ruefully, "I've learned there's more to my company's health than fast growth."

Spradley could afford to take risks. After all, his father owned 50 percent of the company's stock, sales were on the upswing, and his decision could easily be reversed if initial results were bad. A year earlier, with the wolves at the door, Spradley's tactics were less risky. He knew that at that point one serious slip meant financial disaster for the company.[8]

It is the researcher's task to discover what attitude toward risk the decision maker has. Often some hint of the decision maker's posture can be gained from intensive probing, using "what-if" hypothetical outcomes of the research.

Closely allied to the need to determine the decision maker's attitude toward risk is the need to determine the decision maker's specific objectives. It is unfortunate, but true, that these are rarely explicitly stated.

> Despite a popular misconception to the contrary, objectives are seldom given to the researcher. The decision maker seldom formulates his objectives accurately. He is likely to state his objectives in the form of platitudes which have no operational significance. Consequently, objectives usually have to be extracted by the researcher. In so doing, the researcher may well be performing his most useful service to the decision maker.[9]

The researcher must transform the platitudes into specific operational objectives that the research can be designed to serve.

> One effective technique for uncovering these objectives consists of confronting the decision maker with each of the possible solutions to a problem and asking him whether he would follow that course of action. Where he says "no," further probing will usually reveal objectives which are not served by the course of action.[10]

Once the objectives for the research are finally decided upon, they should be committed to writing. In the course of this effort, additional clarity in thinking and in communication between the decision maker and researcher is often achieved. They should then agree formally on their written expression (by each initialing each statement of purpose, by initialing the entire document, or by some other means). This tends to prevent later misunderstandings.

Consequences of Alternative Courses of Action

A great deal of marketing research is intended to determine the consequences of various courses of action. Much of the research highlighted in Tables 1.1 and 1.2, for example, deals with the impact of manipulating one of the Ps in the marketing mix. This is not surprising since, as we have seen, the marketing manager's task basically involves manipulating the elements of the mix to achieve customer satisfaction. What is a more natural marketing research activity than seeking answers to such questions as, What will be the change in sales occasioned by a change in the prod-

---

[8]John F. Persinos, "Sugar Baby," *Inc.,* 6 (May 1984), pp. 85–92.

[9]Russell L. Ackoff, *Scientific Method* (New York: John Wiley, 1962), p. 71.

[10]*Ibid.,* p. 71.

uct's package? If we change the sales compensation plan, what will be the effect on the sales representatives' performance and on their attitudes toward the job and company? Which ad is likely to generate the most favorable customer response?

Researchers are primarily responsible for designing research that accurately assesses the outcomes of past or contemplated marketing actions. In this capacity, they must gauge the actions against all the outcomes management deems relevant. Management, for example, may want to know the impact of the proposed change on sales as well as on consumer attitudes. If the research addresses only consumer attitudes, management will most assuredly ask for the relationship between attitudes and sales. Embarrassing questions of this nature can only be avoided if researchers painstakingly probe for all relevant outcomes before designing the research.

◆ Translating Decision Problem into Research Problem

A detailed understanding of the decision maker's personality, environment, objectives, and preconceived ideas of possible alternative courses of action should enable researchers to translate the **decision problem** into a **research problem.** A research problem is essentially a restatement of the decision problem in research terms. Consider, for example, the new product introduction for which sales are below target. The decision problem faced by the marketing manager is deciding what to do about the shortfall. Should the target be revised? Should the product be withdrawn? Should one of the other elements in the marketing mix, such as advertising, be altered? Suppose the manager suspects that the advertising campaign supporting the new product introduction has been ineffective. This suspicion could serve as the basis for a research problem. For example, as the demand for denim jeans faded in the mid-1980s, Wrangler made the decision to expand its market beyond Western wear into a broad range of garments. To promote the line, Wrangler launched an advertising campaign with the theme, "Live it to the Limit," featuring people in exciting situations wearing Wrangler shirts, pants, and swimwear. However, subsequent consumer research showed that shoppers continued to perceive Wrangler as a maker of jeans, and not other, non-denim apparel. Wrangler's decision to stay with an expanded clothing line remained firm, but it was clear that the advertising had failed to convey that message. Consequently, Wrangler revised its advertising again to feature mini-adventure movies in which the heroes and heroines wore fashionable Wrangler non-denim outfits.[11]

Some illustrations of the distinctions between decision problems and research problems can be found in Table 3.1. Though the two problems are obviously related, they are not the same. The decision problem involves what needs to be done. The research problem involves determining what information should be provided in order to make the decision on what needs to be done—and how that information can best be secured.

In making this determination, the researcher must make certain that the real decision problem, not just its symptoms, is being addressed. The plight of the *Chicago Daily News,* which folded during the 1970s, is interesting in this regard. The *Chicago Daily News* was historically one of the most intellectual and best written of the Chicago daily papers. By the time it ceased publishing, it had won more Pulitzer Prizes than any other newspaper in the country except *The New York Times.*

◆ **Decision problem**

The problem facing the decision maker for which the research is intended to provide answers.

◆ **Research problem**

A restatement of the decision problem in research terms.

---

[11]Pat Sloan, "Wrangler Campaign Soft-Pedals Denim," *Advertising Age,* 55 (November 1, 1984), p. 3, and Bernice Kanner, "Raiders of the Lost Market," *New York,* 17 (November 26, 1984), pp. 18–24.

Table 3.1   Examples of the Relationship between Decision Problems and Research Problems

Decision Problems	Research Problems
Develop package for a new product	Evaluate effectiveness of alternative package designs
Increase market penetration through the opening of new stores	Evaluate prospective locations
Increase store traffic	Measure current image of the store
Increase amount of repeat purchasing behavior	Assess current amount of repeat purchasing behavior
Develop more equitable sales territories	Assess current and proposed territories with respect to their potential and workload
Allocate advertising budget geographically	Determine current level of market penetration in the respective areas
Introduce new product	Design a test market through which the likely acceptance of the new product can be assessed

---

Marketing research seems to have contributed to its demise. "Yes, it was market research that ultimately killed the *Chicago Daily News*. But, oddly enough, it wasn't bad research that did it. The research was right on target."[12] Apparently, the decision problem was incorrectly defined as being how to stimulate circulation, rather than how to appeal better to the basic market segment that the newspaper already served. As a result, the newspaper shifted its emphasis, which led to its demise.

How does one avoid the trap of researching the wrong decision problem? The main way is to delay research until the decision problem is properly defined.

There is an old saying that applies here, "If you do not know where you want to go, any road will get you there." It is the same in decision making. If the decision maker does not know what he or she wants to achieve, any alternative will be satisfactory and research will be of little use. Too often the researcher's initial step is to write a proposal describing the methods that will be used to conduct the research. Instead, the researcher should take the time to examine the situation carefully so as to acquire the necessary appreciation for (1) the decision maker and the environment, (2) the alternative courses of action, (3) the objectives of the decision maker, and (4) the consequences of alternative actions.

One useful mechanism for making sure that the real decision problem will be addressed by the research is to execute a **research request step** before preparing the research proposal.[13] This step requires that the decision maker and researcher have a meeting in which the decision maker describes the problem and the information that is needed. The researcher then drafts a statement describing his or her

◆ Research request step

The initial step that sets the research process in motion; this statement, which is prepared by the researcher after meeting with the decision maker, summarizes the problem and the information that is needed to address it.

---

[12]Joe Cappo, "The Failure to Properly Interpret Market Research Ruins Many Firms," *Marketing News,* 13 (January 11, 1980), pp. 1 and 18.

[13]Paul W. Conner, " 'Research Request Step' Can Enhance Use of Results," *Marketing News,* 19 (January 4, 1985), p. 41. See also Paul D. Boughton, "Marketing Research and Small Business: Pitfalls and Potential," *Journal of Small Business Management,* 21 (July 1983), pp. 36–42, for a list of questions small business managers (any decision maker, actually) can ask so as to make sure they are getting the most from their research.

understanding of the problem. The statement should include, but is not limited to, the following items:

1. Action: The actions that are contemplated on the basis of the research.

2. Origin: The events that led to a need for the decision to act. While the events may not directly affect the research that is conducted, they help the researcher understand more deeply the nature of the research problem.

3. Information: The questions that the decision maker needs to have answered in order to take one of the contemplated courses of action.

4. Use: The way each piece of information will be used to help make the action decision. Supplying logical reasons for each piece of the research ensures that the questions make sense in the light of the action to be taken.

5. Targets and their subgroups: The groups from whom the information must be gathered. Specifying these groups helps the researcher design an appropriate sample for the research project.

6. Logistics: Approximate estimates of the time and money that are available to conduct the research. Both of these factors will affect the techniques finally chosen.

This written statement should be submitted to the decision maker for his or her approval. The approval should be formalized by having the decision maker initial and date the entire document or each section. Following a procedure like this helps ensure that the *purpose* of the research is agreed upon before the research is designed.

◆ **Decision tree**

Decision flow diagram in which the problem is structured in chronological order, typically with small squares indicating decision forks and small circles chance forks.

◆ Decision Trees

One way of deciding between alternative courses of action is to diagram the problem by means of a **decision tree.** The root of the decision tree is the problem at hand. It then branches off to show various ways of approaching the problem. The

Back to the Case

It was 4:30 in the afternoon when Allison finally managed to squeeze in a call to Jay.

"Jay," she said wearily, "it's been a long day, but I think we're a little closer to reaching a decision here. The president and I have been meeting all day to discuss the various alternatives before us. He, too, likes the idea

of a total repositioning of the chain, but we can't do it overnight. We just don't have the capital resources for such an expensive venture, nor can we afford to embark on such a 'winner-take-all' strategy. We must decide instead between expanding the advertising campaign and trying the new, bigger burger.

We're meeting again tomorrow at 10 A.M. to finalize our decision. Do you have any further suggestions?"

"Allison, let me map out a little sketch of the problem before you two get together. I'll drop it at the office before your meeting. It might help you to clarify your decision."

Figure 3.3

**Sample Decision Tree
of Burger Delight's
Alternatives**

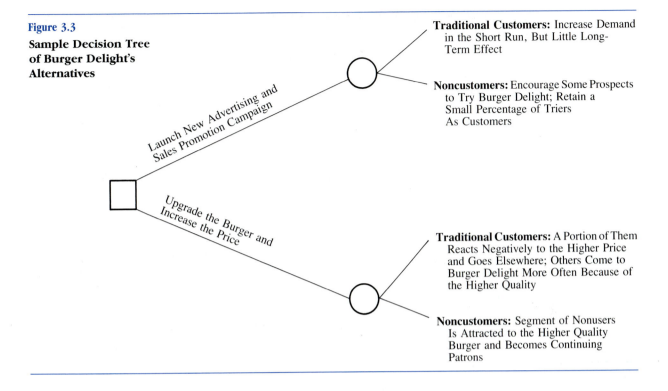

Traditional Customers: Increase Demand
in the Short Run, But Little Long-
Term Effect

Noncustomers: Encourage Some Prospects
to Try Burger Delight; Retain a
Small Percentage of Triers
As Customers

Traditional Customers: A Portion of Them
Reacts Negatively to the Higher Price
and Goes Elsewhere; Others Come to
Burger Delight More Often Because of
the Higher Quality

Noncustomers: Segment of Nonusers
Is Attracted to the Higher Quality
Burger and Becomes Continuing
Patrons

Launch New Advertising and Sales Promotion Campaign

Upgrade the Burger and Increase the Price

tree's branches are connected by either *decision forks* or *chance forks*. A decision
fork is usually depicted as a small square and a chance fork as a small circle. Most
important in using a decision tree is to lay out the problem completely before attempting to solve it by "pruning," or crossing off the undesirable branches.

Figure 3.3 is a decision tree showing the possible consequences of the two
courses of action Burger Delight is considering. Reading from left to right, Burger
Delight's initial decision is whether to launch a new advertising and sales promotion
campaign or to upgrade the burger with a corresponding increase in price. The
choice will depend on the expected value of the two options. If, for example, the
decision maker chooses the new advertising campaign, there is a chance that demand will increase and sales will improve for the duration of the campaign.
However, once the campaign is over, sales may return to their previous levels.

If, on the other hand, the company opts to upgrade its product with a corresponding price increase, demand may increase in certain locations but fall in others. An
improved product may, however, assist in stemming a long-term sales decline.

In each case there are some encouraging possibilities and some serious risks.
What happens ultimately depends on many factors beyond the decision maker's control. But it is not necessary to formally solve the problem diagrammed in the decision tree to benefit from the device. It helps conceptualize the problem and communicate its basic structure to others. In diagramming a problem, one reveals the
interrelationship of the decisions that need be made. This illuminates the role of
research in the decision and encourages communication between decision maker
and researcher. A decision tree can cast a formerly murky decision problem into
bold relief and make various options clearer.

◆ The Research Proposal

Once the purpose and scope of the research are agreed upon, researchers can turn their attention to the *techniques* that will be used to conduct the research. The decision maker should be informed of these techniques before the research begins. Typically, this is done via a formal research proposal, which also affords the researcher another opportunity to make sure that the research being contemplated will provide the information needed to answer the decision maker's problem.

Some **research proposals** are very long and detailed, running twenty pages or more. Others are as short as a single page. Regardless of their length, however, most proposals contain the following elements.[14]

◆ **Research proposal**

A written statement that describes the marketing problem, the purpose of the study, and a detailed outline of the research methodology.

1. *Tentative project title.*

2. *Statement of the marketing problem.* This is a brief statement that outlines or describes the general problem under consideration. Its brevity gives the reader a general sense of the reason for the project before reading the proposal in detail.

   This section of the proposal sums up preliminary discussions that have taken place between the decision maker and the writer. From it the decision maker can determine whether the researcher comprehends the problem and the decision maker's information needs accurately. It is a good way for both parties to make sure they understand each other before committing further time and money to the project.

3. *Purpose and limits of the project.* In this section the writer states the purpose(s) and scope of the project. *Purpose* refers to the project's goals or objectives. Often a *justification* for the project—a statement of why it is important to pursue research on this topic—is included here. *Scope* refers to the actual limitations of the research effort: in other words, what is *not* going to be investigated. In this

---

[14]This section draws heavily from J. Paul Peter and James H. Donnelly, Jr., *A Preface to Marketing Management,* 3rd ed. (Plano, Tex.: Business Publications, Inc., 1985), pp. 48–49.

Back to the Case

Jay's decision tree seemed to be the key to resolving the fuzzy thinking at Burger Delight. After considering the various alternatives, Allison and the president decided it wasn't enough simply to look for short-term solutions to the problem of continuing sales decline. Instead, they would seek to use one of the company's strengths—its high-quality beef—to begin a gradual reposi-

tioning of the chain into a more upscale eating place. Hence, they would ask Jay to design a marketing research study that would help them to introduce a new product—a deluxe burger.

When informed of the decision, Jay suggested a three-part study. One aspect would be to design a test-market through which the proposed new product might be tested. Another phase

of the study would be to test various names for the new product, and still another would address the various advertising approaches that might be used.

If the initial tests went well, marketing research could be used to determine the best locations for future restaurant sites. Table 3.2 shows what a research proposal for Burger Delight might look like.

Table 3.2   Sample Burger Delight Marketing Research Proposal

1. Tentative Project Title
Deluxe Burger Market Reaction

2. Statement of the Marketing Problem
Sales at Burger Delight have been decreasing. The company seeks to reverse this decline. It appears that changing environmental factors may have contributed to this problem. Baby Boomers, who as children and young adults were the chain's primary market, are getting older. While they still eat out, there is some indication that they are no longer interested in food that is just quick and cheap but now seek higher quality as well. There is a belief that the introduction of a higher quality burger would produce a positive reaction and help to stem the sales decline.

3. Definition and Limitations of the Project
The purpose of the study will be to assess consumer reaction to the new burger and to investigate its effect on sales. The study will not investigate other possible ways of stemming the sales decline such as relocating existing outlets or conducting special promotions to increase sales. The study will also not attempt to determine what is optimal with respect to other elements of the marketing mix, such as best level of ad expenditures, what distribution might be useful, special promotions for the product, or even the best price. Rather, some preliminary research will be conducted to determine what competitors charge for similar burgers. The burgers will be priced competitively, and some additional advertising will be conducted when the product is introduced to bring the product to the attention of those who do not normally patronize Burger Delight

4. Outline of Project
- Investigation of trade publications, annual reports, and secondary data sources to assess general industry trends and what is happening to Burger Delight's competition.
- Check of competitors' products and prices to determine appropriate price to charge.
- Selection of some markets and outlets in which the new burger will be introduced.
- Design of questionnaires to measure awareness and attitudes of Burger Delight's patrons towards the new burger.
- Measurement of attitudes and sales in the designated outlets prior to introducing the new burger.
- Introduction of the burger accompanied by advertising to promote its availability.
- Measurement of attitudes and sales in the designated outlets after introducing the new burger.
- Assessment of attitude and sales differences between the post- and pre-introduction periods.

5. Data Sources and Research Methodology
Secondary sources of data such as the *Census of Business* and *Annual Surveys of Business,* as well as annual reports for the last five years for McDonald's, Burger King, and Wendy's will be investigated. A search will be conducted of the *Reader's Guide to Business Literature and Periodicals* for any articles dealing with trends in the fast food industry and changing eating habits of the population.

The burger will be introduced into all the outlets in four of the smaller markets. Four other markets will be chosen in which the demographics match the test markets as closely as possible. Sales will be monitored for each outlet for four weeks prior to when the burgers are introduced.

For two weeks before the burgers are introduced, a random sample of customers frequenting each outlet will be personally interviewed for their attitudes toward Burger Delight. Interviews will be conducted throughout each day.

For four weeks after the introduction, randomly selected respondents in each outlet will be personally interviewed for their attitudes toward Burger Delight.

6. Estimate of Time and Personnel Requirements
- Preliminary investigation: two weeks
- Development of questionnaire: one week
- Pretest of the questionnaire: one week
- Selection of test markets: one week
- Determination of interview locations and times: two weeks
- Collection of sales and attitude data: six weeks
- Analysis and preparation of the research report: three weeks

7. Cost Estimates

Field staff for personal interviews, includes travel expenses	$20,000
Computer charges	500
Overhead charges	6,000
	$26,500

section the writer spells out the various hypotheses to be investigated or the questions to be answered. At this point the writer may also want to address what effect time and money constraints may have on the project or what the potential limitations are of the applicability of the project's findings. Far from being a hedge, documenting these issues early in the project may help in avoiding misunderstandings and disagreements when the project is completed.

4. *Outline.* This is a tentative framework for the entire project. It should be flexible enough to allow for unforeseen difficulties. Statistical tables or graphs reflecting proposed hypotheses that the writer intends to incorporate should be shown in outline form.

5. *Data sources and research methodology.* The types of data to be sought (primary or secondary) are briefly identified here, and a brief explanation is given as to how the necessary information will be gathered (e.g., surveys, experiments, library sources). *Sources* for data may be government publications, company records, actual people, and so forth.

   If measurements, such as consumer attitudes, will be involved, the techniques to be used should be stated. Since this proposal is designed to be read by management, not fellow researchers, the language used in describing these techniques should be as nontechnical as possible. The nature of the problem will probably indicate the types of techniques to be employed.

   The population or sample to be studied and its size should be described. The writer should mention whether the group will be divided into segments (i.e., rather than studying 1,000 teenagers, a study may focus only on those who own cars). The writer should also justify why that kind of sampling strategy is necessary.

   The kinds of data-collection forms the researcher plans to use should be discussed and included in the plan if possible. Depending on the nature of the study, these may be questionnaires, psychological tests, or observation forms. The proposal should indicate the reliability and validity of the measure to be used.

6. *Estimate of time and personnel requirements.* The number of people required to complete the study should be listed, along with an indication of their level of responsibility and rate of pay. The various phases of the study, and the amount of time required for each, should also be made clear. An example follows:

   1. Preliminary investigation: two months

   2. Final test of questionnaire: one month

   3. Sample selection: one month

   4. Mail questionnaire, field follow-up, etc.: four months, etc.

   As mentioned earlier, if the project is to be completed under serious time constraints, the researcher may wish to indicate what effect this circumstance may have on the study's results.

7. *Cost estimates.* The cost of the personnel required should be combined with expenses for travel, materials, supplies, computer charges, printing and mailing costs, and overhead charges, if applicable, to arrive at a total cost for the project. As mentioned with regard to time, if the project is to be completed under serious financial constraints, the effect of this should be made clear at this point. It is better to face these potential problems early in the project rather than to run out of money or miss a deadline once a project has begun. The researcher, not the client, is usually the one to bear the responsibility for such shortcomings.

Table 3.3   A Sample Proposal from General Mills for Protein Plus

1. **Problem and Background.** Protein Plus has performed below objectives in test-market. New product and copy alternatives are being readied for testing. Three alternative formulations—Hi Graham (A), Nut (B), and Cinnamon (C)—that retain the basic identity of current Protein Plus but have been judged to be sufficiently different and of sufficient potential for separate marketing have been developed for testing against the current product (D).

2. **Decision Involved.** Which product formulations should be carried into the concept fulfillment test?

3. **Method and Design.** An in-home product test in which one product is tested at a time. Each of the four test-products will be tested by a separate panel of 150 households. Each household will have purchased adult ready-to-eat cereal within the past month and will be interested in the test-product, as evidenced by their selection of Protein Plus as one or more of the next ten cereal packages they say they would like to buy. They will be exposed to Protein Plus in a booklet that will also contain an ad for several competitive products such as Product 19, Special K, Nature Valley, and Grape Nuts. A Protein Plus ad will be constructed for each of the four test-products, differing primarily in the kind of taste appeal provided. Exposure to these various executions will be rotated so that each of the four test-panels is matched on ready-to-eat cereal usage.

The study will be conducted in eight markets. Product will be packaged in the current Protein Plus package flagged with the particular taste appeal for that product.

The criterion measure will be the homemakers' weighted share after their exposure to the product, adjusted to reflect the breadth of interest in the various Protein Plus taste appeals that have been promoted.

Rather than trust a random sampling procedure to represent the population at large, a quota will be established to ensure that the sample of people initially contacted for each panel will conform as closely as possible to the division of housewives under 45 (56 percent) and over 45 (44 percent) in the U.S. population.

4. **Criteria for Interpretation.** Each formulation generating a higher weighted homemaker share than standard will be considered for subsequent testing. If more than one formulation beats standard, each will be placed in concept fulfillment test unless one is better than the other(s) at odds of 2:1 or more.

5. **Estimated Project Expense:** within ±500: $22,000

6. Individual who must finally approve recommended action: _____

7. Report to be delivered by _____ if authorized by _____ and test materials shipped by _____.

Source: Used with permission of General Mills.

Once the decision maker has read and approved the proposal, he or she should formalize acceptance of it by signing and dating the document. Table 3.3 contains a portion of an actual research plan, with some authorization and budget information removed, that was prepared by the research department at General Mills.[15] Note the clearly stated criteria that will be used to interpret the results and the carefully crafted action standards specifying what will be done depending upon what the research results indicate. The effort expended by the marketing research department in translating information requests into specific, action-oriented statements like this helps account for the wide acceptance of and enthusiastic support for the research function at General Mills.

---

[15]For a sample copy of the complete project proposal and expenditure approval form used at General Mills, see Lawrence D. Gibson, "Use of Marketing Research Contractors," in Robert Ferber, ed., *Handbook of Marketing Research* (New York: McGraw-Hill, Inc., 1974), p. 1–135.

◆ When Is Marketing Research Justified?

While the benefits of marketing research are many, it is not without its drawbacks. There is no denying that the process is often time-consuming and expensive, and if it is done incorrectly (as in the case of the *Chicago Daily News*), it can hurt more than help a company. There are also cases where even the best marketing research either cannot provide the answers a company seeks or poses disadvantages that outweigh its possible advantages (Table 3.4).

For example, ABC lavishly launched an experimental entertainment recording service called Telefirst in Chicago in January 1984. The service was designed to provide first-run movies, uncut concerts, children's programs, and so forth to homes equipped with videocassette recorders and special decoders. By June 11, 1984, ABC had decided to cancel it for many reasons, including discount-pricing trends in the videocassette rental industry, technical problems, and competition from the local subscription-television service. Could marketing research have predicted—and prevented—such a disaster? Yes and no.

ABC had conducted some consumer surveys prior to introduction but had failed to test the high price of Telefirst versus its convenience. ABC assumed people would rather pay for movies delivered to their homes than travel to and from stores to rent cassettes. That assumption proved false and was a major cause of Telefirst's failure.

But an ABC spokesman maintained that more thorough marketing research could not have prevented the death of Telefirst. According to him, "You can ask consumers about new technologies, but they really have to experience them before they can render a meaningful response. Also, ABC had to actually experiment with the system before it could decide whether it would work out."[16]

In other cases, the benefits of marketing research must be weighed against the risks of tipping off a competitor, who can then rush into the market with a similar product at perhaps a better price or an added product advantage. Airwick Industries was especially proud of its new product, Carpet Fresh, a rug and room deodorant. It did very well in test-markets and was launched nationally. Unfortunately for Airwick, an initially skeptical competitor, Sterling Drug, had been carefully monitoring the product's test-market performance and saw signs of its potential success. Sterling began a crash project to duplicate Carpet Fresh and within six months was on the market with a competing product, Love My Carpet.[17]

Some companies will forgo test-marketing if there is little financial risk associated with a new product introduction. Or the expense and effort of marketing research may outweigh the influence its findings will have on company decisions. Such was the case in our earlier example of financial service advertisers.

Despite these reservations, few companies are willing to risk such endeavors as launching a new product or developing a major advertising campaign without doing preliminary marketing research. A. C. Nielsen data indicate that roughly three out of four test-marketed products succeed, whereas four out of five products not fully tested fail.[18] Telecom Research, a company that does advertising testing, estimates that half of the $65 billion spent by U.S. companies on advertising in 1982 was

---

[16]Bernie Whalen, "Why ABC's Telefirst Didn't Last," *Advertising Age,* 55 (November 9, 1984), p. 32.

[17]Bill Abrams, "Some Tales of 'Copycat' Products Are Best Left Untold, Sterling Drug Learns," *The Wall Street Journal,* 60 (May 11, 1980), p. 18.

[18]Lee Adler, "Test Marketing—It's the Pitfalls," *Sales and Marketing Management,* 128 (March 15, 1982), pp. 74–77.

Table 3.4   Ten Situations When Marketing Research May Not Help

When you honestly know what you need to know without research.

When the information already exists.

When time is an enemy.

When conducting research would tip your hand to a competitor.

When a test doesn't represent future conditions.

When the cost of research would exceed its value.

When the budget is insufficient to do an adequate job.

When research findings would not affect the product's introduction.

When the problem is unclear and the objectives are vague.

When the research is not feasible technically.

Source: Lee Adler, "Secrets of when, and when not, to embark on a marketing research project," *Sales and Marketing Management,* 124 (March 17, 1980), p. 108 and 124 (May 19, 1980), p. 77.

Table 3.5   Six Common Situations Where Marketing Research Can Help

When you lack information needed to make a marketing decision.

When you are weighing alternatives and are not sure which one to choose.

When there is conflict within the organization over some policy, objective, or strategy.

When you detect symptoms of a problem, such as declining market share or weakening distribution.

When a marketing program is going well, and you want to know *why,* so that you can further exploit whatever it is that you're doing right.

When you undertake something different: a new product, revised price, new distribution channel, new package, market segment.

Source: Lee Adler, "Secrets of when, and when not, to embark on a marketing research project," *Sales and Marketing Management,* 123 (September 17, 1979), p. 108.

wasted. As the company's president notes, "Marketers don't want it to be their money, so they turn to research to find out how people see their sell."[19]

With such enormous money, time, and effort at stake, marketing research, despite its limitations, often seems the best way for a company to hedge its bets in a volatile marketplace (Table 3.5).

Besides, when it is good, marketing research can be very, very good. Based on marketing research, G. D. Searle developed a highly effective positioning strategy for Equal, its now popular sugar replacement; Kenner developed a "Kissing Barbie Doll" based on little girls' observed play habits; Sunset Books picked the title for a highly successful cookbook based on focus-group interviews; and designers at Berni Corporation changed the background color on Barrelhead Sugar-Free Root Beer cans after researchers found that people swore the drink tasted more like old-fashioned root beer in a frosty mug when it was served from beige cans instead of blue.[20]

[19]Kanner, *New York,* p. 16.

[20]"To Test or Not to Test Seldom the Question," *Advertising Age,* 55 (February 20, 1984), p. M-10; Daisy Maryles, "Market Research Sets Style, Content of Sunset Cookbook," *Publisher's Weekly,* (October 8, 1982), p. 41; and Ronald Alsop, "Color More Important in Catching Consumer's Eyes," *The Wall Street Journal,* 64 (November 29, 1984), p. 37.

One Possible, But Not Recommended, Method for Choosing a Research Supplier

"All right, Miss Burton, start the music and take away another chair."

Source: Drawing by Peter Steiner. Reprinted by permission.

Human nature, it seems, is nothing if not quirky and unpredictable. Often marketing research can reduce the risk inherent in that fact.

◆ Choosing and Using a Research Supplier

Most sizable business organizations today have formal marketing research departments. However, except for the very largest consumer products companies, these departments tend to be small—sometimes consisting of one person. In such cases, the firm's researcher may spend less time conducting actual research than supervising projects undertaken by research suppliers hired by the firm. Marketing managers in many large companies also use outside suppliers.

There are many advantages to using research suppliers. If the research work load tends to vary over the course of the year, the firm may find it less expensive to hire suppliers to conduct specific projects when needed than to staff an entire in-house department that may sit idle between projects. Also, the skills required for various projects may differ. By hiring outside suppliers, the firm can match the project to the vendor with the greatest expertise in the particular area under investigation. In addition, hiring outside suppliers allows the sponsoring company to remain anonymous, and it avoids problems that might arise with regard to internal politics.

Although it has become increasingly common to buy marketing research, many managers are uncertain as to how one goes about selecting a research supplier. Perhaps the first step is to decide when research is really necessary. Although there is no simple formula for assessing this need, most managers turn to research when they are unsure about their own judgment and other information sources seem inadequate. If the research is to be successful, however, the manager must be willing to be guided by it.[21]

---

[21]David W. Flegal, "How to Make Better Use of Dollars and Sense in Buying Market Research," *Management Review*, 72 (January 1983), pp. 49–51.

Once a manager has determined the most critical area for research, he or she is ready to seek the right supplier for the job. The selection process is not easy, for there are thousands of qualified marketing research companies in the United States. Some are full-service "generalist" companies; others are specialists in qualitative research, advertising-copy testing, concept testing, and so on, and still others are services that only conduct interviews, process data, or work with statistics.

It is important that the manager carefully evaluate the company's research needs as well as the capabilities of suppliers. Some issues require small-scale qualitative studies while others require large-scale quantitative research projects. It is essential that the vendor selected understand the firm's information needs and have the expertise required to conduct the research.

Experts suggest that managers should seek proposals from at least three companies.[22] They also urge that the research user talk with the persons at the supplier company who will be processing and analyzing the data, writing the report, supervising the interviewers, and making presentations to management.

Marketing research is still an art, not a science. It benefits from heavy involvement of senior research professionals, who provide insights that come only from years of training and experience. The most important asset of a research firm is the qualifications of the research professional(s) who will be involved in the design, day-to-day supervision, and interpretation of the research.[23]

The research user's responsibility is to communicate effectively with the prospective vendor and provide the necessary background and objectives for the study. Research users should also ask about the supplier's quality control standards. Most research firms are pleased when clients show concern about the quality of their work and will gladly explain their quality control steps in the areas of field work, coding, and data processing.

After reading the proposals and meeting key personnel, the manager should perform a comparative analysis. He or she should use the proposals to evaluate each vendor's understanding of the problem, how each will address it, and the cost and timing estimates of each.

The research should cost no more than the information is worth to the manager. There is a simple equation that can help the manager make this determination.[24] It uses the amount that could be lost or gained as a result of being better informed for the decision as a guide to determine how much to spend on research. As an example, if the advertising campaign is budgeted at $250,000, and the copy question being explored through research is judged to have the potential to increase advertising effectiveness by at least 10 percent, then the amount invested in the research should be no more than 10 percent of $250,000, or $25,000.

Of course, common sense must be applied in using this formula, for as the amount of risk or gain increases, this sort of logic will spin off unreasonable amounts for research. A $5 million investment in advertising probably would not justify a $500,000 investment in research.

When evaluating suppliers that seem equally competent, a manager must rely on his or her intuitive assessment regarding the soundness of the research design proposed, the supplier's responsiveness to the manager's specific questions, and the vendor's understanding of the subtler aspects of the marketing problem.

---

[22]Martin Katz, "Selecting the Right Research Firm: Step-by-Step Guidelines," *Marketing News,* 18 (January 6, 1984), pp. 1 and 27.

[23]David W. Flegal, "How to Buy Marketing Research," *Management Review,* 72 (February 1983), pp. 63–66.

[24]Flegal, "Dollars and Sense," *Management Review,* p. 51.

Research Window 3.1
How Clients and Marketing Research Firms Should Not Work Together

Both clients and marketing research firms may contribute to faulty designs, missed schedules, cost overruns, and inappropriate analyses. Client rules for creating such problems are as follows:

1. Keep the real purpose and objectives of the research hidden from the research firm.

2. Try to reduce the cost estimate by glossing over anticipated problems.

3. Change the questionnaire frequently. Include at least one change after interviewing has begun.

4. Delay the start of data collection. Cancel and restart the project, but insist upon receiving the report by the original deadline.

5. Delay approving analytical and tabulation plans as long as possible, then change the plan verbally without written confirmation.

6. Demand all possible cross tabulations, whether or not they are relevant to the purpose of the study.

7. Fail to pay for the research within a reasonable time.

Rules that a research firm can follow to reduce the likelihood of being burdened with client work in the future are as follows:

1. Modify the objectives of the research to fit the methodology that you find convenient.

2. Low-ball the cost estimate; then use minor changes in the project to raise the budget after being awarded the job.

3. Agree with the client on changes to be made; then after the project has been completed, tell the client it was just too late to make the changes.

4. Tell the client that all is on-schedule when it is not.

5. Bill the client before submitting the final report. Make it more than the original estimate, but do not bother to explain why until asked.

6. Send the report late, then avoid the client's phone calls.

In the most successful client/research firm relationships, both sides treat each other as professionals, are open with one another, and work together in designing the project to meet objectives and in handling the problems that inevitably arise.

Source: Michael Hardin, "How Clients and Marketing Research Firms Should Not Work Together," *Marketing Today*, Volume 23; No. 1, 1985.

In this section we have provided some guidelines for a successful partnership between research suppliers and users. As we all know, however, reality often seems to follow Murphy's Law rather than a textbook model. Research Window 3.1 suggests how to tailor a research partnership for a perfect fit with failure.

◆ Summary

Learning Objective 1: Explain what is meant by a decision situation.

A person faces a decision situation if he or she has a problem, knows several good, but not equally good, ways of solving it, and must pick between the various choices available.

Learning Objective 2: List the factors that make up a decision maker's environment.

A decision maker's environment includes not only the state of the economy in general, but the economic situation of the particular industry involved and the specific company in that industry. Researchers also need to be aware that the corporate culture can affect decision making and consequently the research that supports that decision making.

Learning Objective 3: Describe the various elements a researcher must understand in order to address the real decision problem.

In order for the research to address the real decision problem and not some symptom of it, the researcher working on the problem must develop an understanding of the personality of the decision maker and his or her environment; the alternative courses of action being considered; the objectives of the decision maker, including his or her attitude toward risk; and the potential consequences of the alternative courses of action.

Learning Objective 4: Distinguish between a decision problem and a research problem.

Decision problems involve what needs to be done. Research provides the necessary information to make an informed choice, so the research problem essentially involves determining what information to provide and how that information can best be secured.

Learning Objective 5: Explain why a decision tree can be useful in problem solving.

The decision tree is a useful device for conceptualizing a problem and communicating its basic structure to others. Diagramming a problem forces a focus on the interrelationship of the decisions that need to be made. A decision tree can cast the problem into bold relief and make various options clearer.

Learning Objective 6: Outline the various elements of the research proposal.

Most research proposals contain the following elements: tentative project title, statement of the marketing problem, definition and limitations of the project, outline, data sources and research methodology, estimate of time and personnel requirements, and cost estimates.

Discussion Questions, Problems, and Projects

1. Given the following decision problems, identify the corresponding research problems: (a) pricing strategy to follow for a new product, (b) whether to increase the level of advertising expenditures on print, (c) whether to expand current warehouse facilities, (d) whether to change the sales force compensation package.

2. Given the following research problems, identify corresponding decision problems for which they might provide useful information: (a) design a test market to assess the impact on sales volume of a particular discount program, (b) evaluate stock level at different warehouses, (c) evaluate sales and market share of grocery stores in a particular location, (d) develop sales forecasts for a particular product line.

3. Schedule an interview with the marketing manager of a firm near your home or your school. In the interview, attempt to isolate a problem with which the manager is wrestling and for which research information would be helpful. Explore each of the parts of a "research request step" with the manager. After the interview, prepare a short report that summarizes your discussion with respect to actions being considered, origin of the problem, information that would be useful to solve it, how each bit of information might be used in its solution, and the targets and subgroups for the study. Submit your report to the manager and secure an evaluation from him or her as to whether your report effectively captures the situation confronting the firm.

Suggested Additional Readings

For useful discussions of how to go about problem solving, see

Russell L. Ackoff, *The Art of Problem Solving* (New York: John Wiley & Sons, Inc., 1978).

Robert D. Behn and James W. Vaupel, *Quick Analysis for Busy Decision Makers* (New York: Basic Books, Inc., 1982).

For more detailed treatment of the content of the various parts of a research proposal and some sample proposals, see

Kenneth W. Houp and Thomas E. Pearsall, *Reporting Technical Information,* 4th ed. (Encino, California: Collier Macmillan Publishers, 1980), especially pages 342–365.

Part One   Research Project

In the following description of an actual research project, note the kind of background information the researchers received when they first met their client, a group of radio station managers. Subsequent sections will show how the researchers tackled the project and will analyze what they did well—or could have done better or differently.

In a small midwestern city, radio station owners and operators banded together to form a group called the Centerville Area Radio Association (CARA) to promote radio advertising. Station managers in the group were interested in finding out what their customers—specifically the local businesses who advertised on their stations—liked and disliked about radio advertising. They decided to commission a marketing research study to investigate the situation.

Members of CARA hoped the study would uncover ways that they could compete more effectively with the other major media, television and newspapers. They also hoped that the research could show them how they might better satisfy customers and thus increase their advertising sales volume.

When the study began, radio held a 13.5 percent share of the market in the Centerville area. CARA data showed that radio's sales volume had been growing at an annual rate of 9 to 10 percent for the past several years, and group members expected that this level of growth would continue for the foreseeable future.

CARA members thought that radio offered some advantages over newspapers and television. The group was especially proud of its sales philosophy, which embodied the marketing concept at its best. "The client comes first," was the watchword with CARA. CARA members thought that this philosophy combined with their "consultant-sell" sales approach, made customers perceive radio sales representatives as more concerned, more cooperative, and better trained than other media reps. Hence, it was CARA's opinion that radio sales reps had a better image in the business than sales reps from other media. These opinions, while widely held by CARA members, had never been tested for accuracy.

The groups that interested CARA the most were local business people who were already their customers or those whom they would like to have as customers. Businesses that were not yet advertisers were included in the study if they showed an interest in using one of the three major media in the future.

Finally, CARA wanted to know (1) if the amount of money a given business spent every year on advertising had any effect on its attitudes towards media and sales representatives and (2) what characteristics business people sought in these representatives.

The researchers formulated a number of hypotheses or conjectures from the information presented them by CARA managers. For example, it was hypothesized that there would be differences in business peoples' attitudes toward television, radio, and newspaper, and that differences would also be found in attitudes toward sales representatives of each of the media. The various characteristics of the advertising media, as well as the attributes of the sales people for each medium, were hypothesized to vary in importance to business people. It was also hypothesized that the attitudes of business people who were not managers or owners, and who were not involved in buying advertising, would differ from those of the population of interest.

After further probing, researchers were able to translate these hypotheses into problems that could be addressed by research. Specifically, they restated the problem in the form of two objectives:

1. Identify business decision makers' attitudes toward the advertising media of newspaper, radio, and television.

2. Identify business decision makers' attitudes toward the advertising sales representatives of newspaper, radio, and television.

They pointed out to CARA members that the information acquired from investigating these two areas could subsequently be used to make informed choices about what strategy to pursue in competing with other media.

It is, of course, too early to know what the actual results of the study might be. However, we can speculate on how varying results might affect management decisions. What might management want to do if the study showed that business people had a negative opinion of radio advertising? What might they do if they found that advertisers liked their sales approach? Using the steps in the research process as a guide, how would you suggest the research proceed?

Cases to Part One

Case 1.1 Big Brothers of Fairfax County

Big Brothers of America is a social service program designed to meet the needs of boys ages six to eighteen from single-parent homes. Most of the boys served by the program live with their mothers and rarely see or hear from their fathers. The purpose of the program is to give these boys the chance to establish a friendship with an interested adult male. Big Brothers of America was founded on the belief that an association with a responsible adult can help program participants become more responsible citizens and better adjusted young men.

The program was started in Cincinnati in 1903. Two years later, the organization was granted its first charter in New York State through the efforts of Mrs. Cornelius Vanderbilt. By the end of World War II, there were 30 Big Brothers agencies. Today there are 300 agencies across the United States, and 120,000 boys currently are matched with Big Brothers.

The Fairfax County chapter of Big Brothers of America was founded in Fairfax in 1966. In 1971 United Way of Fairfax County accepted the program as part of its umbrella organization and now provides about 85 percent of its funding. The remaining 15 percent is raised by the local Big Brothers agency.

Information about the Big Brothers program in Fairfax County reaches the public primarily through newspapers (feature stories and classified advertisements), radio, public service announcements, posters (on buses and in windows of local establishments), and word-of-mouth advertising. The need for volunteers is a key message emanating from these sources. The agency phone number is always included so that people wanting to know more about the program can call for information. Those calling in are given basic information over the telephone and are invited to attend one of the monthly orientation sessions organized by the Big Brothers program staff. At these meetings, men get the chance to talk to other volunteers and to find out what will be expected of them should they decide to join the program. At the end of the session, prospective volunteers are asked to complete two forms. One is an application form and the other is a questionnaire in which the person is asked to describe the type of boy he would prefer to be matched with, as well as his own interests.

The files on potential Little Brothers are then reviewed in an attempt to match boys with the volunteers. A match is made only if both partners agree. The agency stays in close contact with the pair and monitors their progress. The three counselors for the Big Brothers program serve as resources for the volunteer.

The majority of the inquiry calls received by the Fairfax County agency are from women who are interested in becoming Big Sisters or from people desiring information on the Couples Program. Both programs are similar to the Big Brothers program and are administered by it. In fact, of fifty-five calls concerning a recent orientation meeting, only five were from males. Only three of the five callers actually attended the meeting, a typical response.

Although informational campaigns and personal appeals have had some impact on the public, the results have fallen short of expectations. There are currently 250 boys waiting to be matched with Big Brothers, and the shortage grows weekly.

Big Brothers of Fairfax County believes a lack of awareness and accurate knowledge could be the cause of the shortage of volunteers. Are there men who would volunteer if only they were made aware of the program and its needs? Or is the difficulty a negative program image? Do people think of Little Brothers as problem children, boys who have been in trouble with the law or who have severe behavioral problems? Or could there be a misconception of the type of man who would make a good Big Brother? Do people have stereotypes with respect to the volunteers—for example, that the typical volunteer is a young, single, professional male?

Questions

1. What is (are) the marketing decision problem(s)?
2. What is (are) the marketing research problem(s)?

3. What types of information would be useful to answer these questions?
4. How would you go about securing this information?

Case 1.2   Supervisory Training at the Management Institute

University of Wisconsin-Extension is the outreach campus of the University of Wisconsin System. Its mission is to extend high-quality education to people who are not necessarily college students in the normal sense. The Management Institute (MI) is one of the departments within UW-Extension. It conducts programs aimed at providing education and training in at least a dozen areas of business and not-for-profit management.

The supervisory training area within the MI designs and conducts continuing education training programs for first-level supervisors. The training programs are designed to improve a trainee's managerial, communication, decision-making, and human relations skills. They consequently cover a broad range of topics.

A continuing decline in enrollments in the various programs during the past several years had become a problem of increasing concern to the three supervisory program directors. They were at a loss to explain why, although informal discussions among the supervisors raised a number of questions to which they did not know the answers. Have people's reasons for attending supervisory training programs

changed? What are their reasons for attending them? Was the decline caused by economic factors? Was it because of increased competition among continuing education providers? Was it due to the content or structure of MI's programs themselves? Was it due to the way the programs were structured or promoted? Were the programs targeted at the right level of supervisor?

Typically, the major promotion for any program involved mailing brochures that described the content and structure of the course. The mailing list for the brochures consisted of all past attendees of any supervisory training program conducted by the MI.

Questions

1. What is the decision problem?
2. What is (are) the research problem(s)?
3. How would you recommend the MI go about addressing the research problem(s)? That is, what data would you collect, and how might that data be used to answer the research question(s) posed?

Case 1.3   Bonita Baking Company (A)[1]

Frank Fortunada, Jr., is the sales manager of Bonita Baking Company. Bonita is a moderate-sized regional bakery in southern California, specializing in breads and bread products for markets, restaurants, and institutional accounts. Established in 1910 by Frank's grandfather, Vito Fortunada, Bonita bakes and sells a

number of well-known brands of bread under licensing agreements. Among these brands are Holsum,

[1]Source: From: *Cases in Marketing Research* by William G. Zikmund, William J. Lundstrom, and Donald Sciglimpaglia, pp. 3–4. Copyright © 1982 by CBS Publishing. Reprinted by permission of Holt, Rinehart and Winston, Inc.

Butter-top, and Hillbilly bread and rolls. Since his grandfather's retirement many years ago, Bonita has been run by Frank's father. To this day, everyone refers to them as Frank and Frank Junior (except in the latter's presence).

Frank Fortunada, Jr., has been involved in the bread business all of his life. As a boy he cleaned up at the bakery and later drove a route truck while attending high school. After serving four years in the U.S. Navy (as a baker), Frank, Jr., continued to work as a routeman while attending college on a part-time basis. A year after graduating with a degree in marketing from the local state college, Frank's father appointed him retail sales manager, in charge of sixty-five driver salespeople. Within two years, he was put in charge of both retail and commercial accounts. As such, Fortunada was the ranking marketing person at Bonita Baking, with his father in charge of operations of the bakery.

The Marketing Problem

About ten years ago, Bonita Baking introduced a line of specialty bread under the brand name of Bonita Health Bread. Specialty bread is made from special or mixed grain flour and is heavier than regular bread. National brands that have gained popularity include Roman Meal, Millbrook, and Pepperidge Farm. Not only has specialty breads been a rapidly growing segment of the bread market, but it is a higher gross margin product. Industry trade publications identified the specialty bread consumer as coming from a higher-income household and as being more highly educated than the typical bread consumer.

Fortunada knew that Bonita's specialty breads were high quality and that they should be selling well, but sales figures indicated otherwise. The Bonita Health line was apparently losing market share rapidly to the national brands and to another regional brand, Orowheat, which was the market leader. All, including Bonita Health, were actively promoted with con-

sumer advertising, coupons, and price deals. Also bothersome was the fact that many supermarket chains were also selling their own private brands of specialty bread. Fortunada's salespeople could offer no real insight as to why Bonita Health was doing poorly.

Fortunada decided to do something that had never been attempted at Bonita—to undertake some marketing research. He knew he would have trouble selling the idea to his father, but he also knew that he needed more information. Taking out a pad of paper, Fortunada began making notes as to what he would like to know about Bonita Health's position. Except for his own sales records and the trade publication reports, he decided that he knew very little.

Fortunada knew almost nothing about the size or growth rates of the specialty bread market in his area. He had no idea who bought his brand or those of his competitors, or how much consumers bought and how often. Except for his own experience, he really didn't even know who in the household requested specialty bread or who selected the brand. Another point that troubled him was not knowing the relative awareness of Bonita Health and its image among consumers. Lastly, since he hadn't been on a bread route in some time, Fortunada thought that he had better get to know retailers' attitudes toward the brands and the associated marketing practices.

Questions

1. How would you define the problem at Bonita Baking Company?

2. What are some of the major objectives of any research to be conducted with consumers?

3. What are some major objectives of any research to be conducted with retailers?

4. Why do you think that research has not been done previously at Bonita? Why will Fortunada have difficulty convincing his father of the need for research now?

Part Two   Research Design

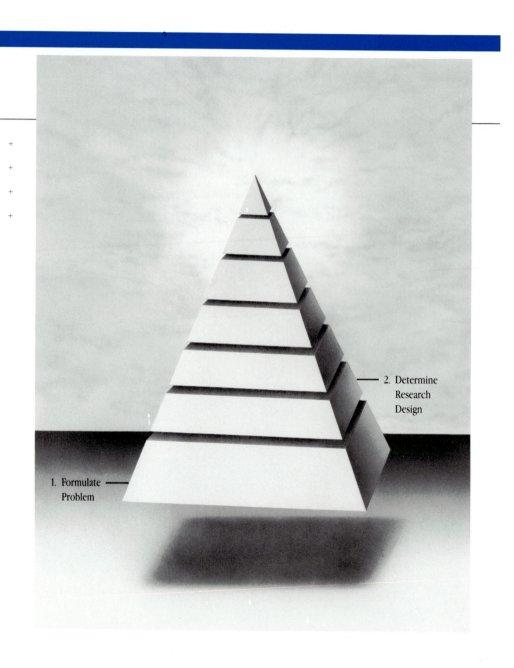

1. Formulate Problem

2. Determine Research Design

Part Two deals with the general issue of designing research so that it addresses the appropriate questions efficiently. Chapter 4 provides an overview of various research designs and discusses the exploratory design at some length. Chapter 5 then discusses descriptive and causal designs, two other primary types of research design.

Chapter 4

Types of Research Designs and Exploratory Research

+ + + +

+ + + +

+ + + +

+ + + +

Learning Objectives

Upon completing this chapter, you should be able to

1. Explain what is meant by a research design.
2. List the three basic types of research design.
3. Describe the major emphasis of each type of research design.
4. Cite the crucial principle of research.
5. Describe the basic uses of exploratory research.
6. Specify the key characteristic of exploratory research.
7. Discuss the various types of exploratory research and identify the characteristics of each.

Case in Marketing Research

Does the world need another variety of potato chip? Executives at Tasti-Snax thought so. After all, it was their job to discover new ways to excite the taste buds of America. But they were hard-pressed to think of a unique variation on an old idea. Supermarket shelves were already bursting with chips with ridges, chips in cans, taco chips and nacho chips, barbecue chips and corn chips, sour cream-and-onion chips and already-been-dipped chips. What could possibly be left?

Russell Atkins, head of the firm's marketing department, had already spent weeks polling his own advertising, sales, and promotion people for ideas, with few promising results. Now he was convinced that the problem really needed a more scientific approach. It was clearly time to put the company's researchers on the case.

He called Dave Reiss, the firm's bright new head of marketing research, and invited him to lunch at a popular pub across the street from the company's headquarters.

Both men laughed as a waitress arrived bearing plates on which a mound of potato chips threatened to bury the accompanying club sandwiches.

"Dave, what's wrong with these chips?" Atkins asked Reiss.

"Well, for one thing, they're stale," Reiss responded. "For another, they're too salty and lack potato flavor. Worst of all, they're our competitor's chips, not ours. We could probably both retire comfortably if we had the proceeds from this account alone."

"Look, Dave, if those jokers over at Consolidated Foods can sell this many mediocre chips, think what we could do with a really fine, first-quality chip. This brings me to the point of this lunch. We need a new product. As you know, we already dominate the corn chip market, so I want you and your team to look into the potato chip category for something novel . . . something that will satisfy consumers' needs for variety. Something that you'd be proud to serve at your next barbecue."

"Actually, we've heard rumors about top management's interest

in something like this and already have been thinking about this very problem in the marketing research department and have come up with some interesting ideas. Let me call a meeting of the troops and see what we can find out," Reiss said.

Reiss crumpled his napkin and began to push his chair away from the table.

"Dave, before you go too far, I want you to know that the executive committee has recently set certain standards for new products," Atkins said. "First, I'm going to have trouble selling an idea upstairs unless it's worth at least $75 million in sales per year. I want a product with broad national appeal, so don't give me some yuppie bacon-and-goat cheese concoction.

"Finally, whatever you and your people come up with had better be unique. I don't want to spend a fortune in new product development, only to have our competitors come out six months later with a knock-off product at a cheaper price."

"That's a tall order, Mr. Atkins, but I'm sure we can come up with something. Let me do some preliminary studies and get back to you with some ideas in a week or two," Reiss said.

Discussion Issues:

1. If you were Dave Reiss, what would be the first thing you would do in launching a marketing research study for a new potato chip?

2. What kinds of information might Reiss need to begin his study?

3. What important questions did Reiss neglect to ask Russell Atkins?

Source: This fictitious case was based on Frito-Lay's development strategy for its very successful O'Grady potato chips. In its first year on the market, O'Grady's had sales of $200 million. For more information about Frito-Lay's actual research program, see the keynote speech by Norman Heller, President and Chief Executive Officer, PepsiCo Wines & Spirits International, at the Association of National Advertisers' New Product Marketing Workshop reprinted in *Marketing News* 18 (December 21, 1984), p. 4; "Spotting Competitive Edges Begets New Product Success"; and Tom Bayer, "Frito-Lay in All-Out Snack Search," *Advertising Age,* 56 (November 4, 1985), p. 77.

The preceding chapters present some of the kinds of problems marketing research can help to solve. As you may have noticed, there was a great variation as to the nature of the questions researchers sought to investigate. Some questions were very specific: "Should we continue serving butter on short-run airline flights?" Others were much more general: "What factors account for our recent sales decline?"

In this chapter we will discuss the basic concepts central to research design. We will also outline the most common types of designs and show how they relate to each other. Exploratory research will be discussed in detail in this chapter, while descriptive and causal research will be explored more completely in the next chapter. The discussion should help to illuminate the first steps researchers take when they begin to tackle a marketing problem.

◆ Research Design as a Plan of Action

◆ Research design

Framework or plan for a study that guides the collection and analysis of the data.

A **research design** is simply the framework or plan for a study used as a guide in collecting and analyzing data. It is the blueprint that is followed in completing a study. It resembles the architect's blueprint for a house. While it is possible to build a house without a detailed blueprint, the final product will more than likely be somewhat different from what was originally envisioned by the buyer. A certain room is too small; the traffic pattern is poor; some things really wanted are omitted, other less important things are included, and so on. It is also possible to conduct research without a detailed blueprint. The research findings are also likely to differ widely from what was desired by the consumer or user of the research. "These results are interesting, but they do not solve the basic problem" is a common lament. Further, just as the house built without a blueprint is likely to cost more because of midstream alterations in construction, research conducted without a research design is likely to cost more than research properly executed using a research design.

Thus, a research design ensures that the study (1) will be relevant to the problem, and (2) will use economical procedures. It would help the student learning research methods if there were a single procedure to follow in developing the framework or if there were a single framework to be learned. Unfortunately, this is not the case.[1]

> There is never a single, standard, correct method of carrying out research. Do not wait to start your research until you find out *the* proper approach, because there are many ways to tackle a problem—some good, some bad, but probably several good ways. There is no single perfect design. A research method for a given problem is not like

_____

[1]Julian L. Simon, *Basic Research Methods in Social Science: The Art of Empirical Investigation* (New York: Random House, 1969), p. 4.

the solution to a problem in algebra. It is more like a recipe for beef stroganoff; there is no one best recipe.

Rather, there are many research design frameworks, just as there are many unique house designs. Fortunately though, just as house designs can be broken into basic types (for example, ranch, split-level, two-story), research designs can be classified into some basic types. One very useful classification is in terms of the fundamental objective of the research: exploratory, descriptive, or causal.[2]

◆ Types of Research Design

◆ **Exploratory research**

Research design in which the major emphasis is on gaining ideas and insights; it is particularly helpful in breaking broad, vague problem statements into smaller, more precise subproblem statements.

The major emphasis in **exploratory research** is on the discovery of *ideas* and *insights*.[3] The soft drink manufacturer faced with decreased sales might conduct an exploratory study to generate possible explanations. **Descriptive research** is typically concerned with determining the *frequency* with which something occurs or the relationship between two variables. It is typically guided by an initial hypothesis. Suppose the soft drink manufacturer thought that sales of his diet cola were slipping because the number of teenaged girls who constituted his primary market had declined over the past five years. He might decide to commission a study to see if trends in soft drink consumption were related to characteristics such as age or sex. This would be a descriptive study.

◆ **Descriptive research**

Research design in which the major emphasis is on determining the frequency with which something occurs or the extent to which two variables covary.

A **causal research** design is concerned with determining cause-and-effect relationships. Causal studies typically take the form of experiments, since experiments are best suited to determine cause and effect. For instance, our soft drink manufacturer may be interested in determining which of several different advertising appeals is most effective. One way for such a company to proceed would be to use different ads in different geographic areas and investigate which ad generated the highest sales. In effect, the company would perform an experiment, and if it was designed properly, the company would be in a position to conclude that one specific appeal caused the higher rate of sales.

◆ **Causal research**

Research design in which the major emphasis is on determining a cause-and-effect relationship.

Although it is useful to divide research designs into these neat categories—exploratory, descriptive, and causal research—as a way of helping to explain the research process, three warnings are in order. First, the distinctions among the three are not absolute. Any given study may serve several purposes. Nevertheless, certain types of research designs are better suited for some purposes than others. The crucial principle of research is that *the design of the investigation should stem from the problem*. Each of these types is appropriate to specific kinds of problems.

Second, in the remainder of this chapter and in the next two chapters, we shall discuss each of the design types in more detail. The emphasis will be on their *basic characteristics* and *generally fruitful approaches*. Whether or not the designs are useful in a given problem setting depends on how imaginatively they are applied. Architects can be taught basic design principles; whether they then design attractive, well-built houses depends on how they apply these principles. So it is with research. The general characteristics of each design can be taught. Whether they are productive in a given situation depends on how skillfully they are applied. There is no single best way to proceed, just as there is no single best floor plan for, say, a ranch-type house. It all depends on the specific problem to be solved. Research analysts, then, need an understanding of the basic designs so that they can modify them to suit specific purposes.

---

[2]Claire Selltiz, Lawrence S. Wrightsman, and Stuart W. Cook, *Research Methods in Social Relations,* 3rd ed. (New York: Holt, Rinehart and Winston, 1976), pp. 90–91.

[3]The basic purposes are those suggested by Selltiz, Wrightsman, and Cook, *Research Methods.*

Figure 4.1

Relationship among Research Designs

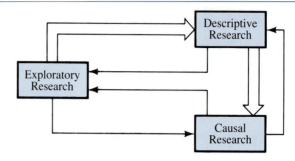

William F. O'Dell, founder of the multimillion-dollar research firm, Market Facts, built his reputation and his company on his ability to determine what, if any, research was needed and the most creative way to obtain it. A profile of this imaginative pioneer appears in Research Window 4.1.

Finally, it should be noted that the three basic research designs can be viewed as stages in a continuous process. Figure 4.1 shows the interrelationships. Exploratory

Research Window 4.1

Market Facts: A Firm Built on Determination, Hard Work—and a Little Bit o' Luck

But for a chance meeting on a train, Market Facts, the country's eighth largest research company, might never have gotten off the ground. In 1946 thirty-seven-year-old William F. O'Dell, Market Facts's founder, had assets of one typewriter, three prospective employees, and the idea for a business. In post-war Chicago, office space was virtually unavailable, but O'Dell was lucky enough to find a 400-square-foot sublet in the downtown business area, a few windows up from where streetcars screeched around a corner.

The day he stopped to pick up the keys, he learned that the deal for the sublet was off because the man from whom he had rented the office was embroiled in a personal feud with the building's owner and didn't have the authority to rent the space. Dejected, O'Dell boarded the train for home, thinking his money and that of his investors was gone.

As luck would have it, the man sitting next to O'Dell on the train was an attorney for the building's owner. Upon hearing O'Dell's story, he had a partner call the owner and fix the deal. Market Facts was on its way.

By going without pay for months at a time, working late nights, and meeting deadlines in spite of power outages that knocked out electric-

ity, O'Dell and his fledgling firm began to make a name for themselves. But the concepts that today form the basis for marketing research were new ideas then, and clients were skeptical as to whether they were worthy of trust—not to mention worth paying for.

For example, O'Dell's biggest problem with his largest account, the Ford Motor Company, was convincing executives that a sample survey could reflect the views of a larger population on such things as auto body styling, pricing, and new products.

"A former chairman at Ford found it almost impossible to grasp the concept of a sample survey, which made it extremely difficult to sell the idea that you could infer [things] from a small sample," O'Dell said.

Market Facts also developed the reputation of a firm that was willing to challenge a client's assumptions about the need for research, the optimum size of a project, and the potential benefits to be derived from it. This devil's advocate style contrasted sharply with the nice-guy midwestern image of other growing Chicago advertising agencies.

"It wasn't a situation where other companies were doing bad research," O'Dell said. "It was studies are often seen as the initial step. When researchers begin an investigation, it stands to reason that they lack a great deal of knowledge about the problem. Consider: "Brand X's share of the disposable diaper market is slipping; why?" This statement is too broad to serve as a guide for research. To narrow and refine it would logically be accomplished with exploratory research, in which the emphasis would be on finding possible explanations for the sales decrease. These tentative explanations, or **hypotheses,** would then serve as specific guides for descriptive or causal studies. Suppose the tentative explanation that emerged was that "Brand X is an economy-priced diaper, originally designed to compete with low-cost store-brand diapers. Families with children have more money today than when the brand was first introduced and are willing to pay more for higher quality baby products. It stands to reason that our market share would decrease." The hypothesis that families with small children have more real income to spend, and that a larger proportion of that money is going toward baby products, could be examined in a descriptive study of trends in the baby products industry.

Suppose the descriptive study did support the hypothesis. The company might then wish to determine whether mothers were, in fact, willing to pay more for higher quality diapers and, if so, what features (such as better fit or greater absor-

• Hypothesis

A statement that specifies how two or more measurable variables are related.

William F. O'Dell
Market Facts Founder

not so much bad as unnecessary, simply because people felt they needed data when they really didn't, or that it was too large a study for what was needed."

Market Facts's growth is a direct result of helping clients optimize allocation of their research dollars, O'Dell said. This is typified by its early creation of consumer mail panels, which provide accurate data at a cost one-third or less than that of personal interviews. Today, Market Facts's Consumer Mail Panel is among the nation's largest with 250,000 households.

Pressed to identify the most important factor in building a successful research business, O'Dell said, "Creativity is the one most important ingredient in decision making, bar none. My advice to people getting into the industry today is to view market research from a management view. In other words, look at the need for the information and how it is to be used. Let technology be the last thing you worry about.

"Understanding people is as important as the decision making process itself."

Source: Richard Edel, "O'Dell's Luck, Good Sense Lead to Market Facts," *Advertising Age,* 57, (May 19, 1986), p. S-64.

Originally a product of successful exploratory research, Pampers suffered a temporary decline in sales when a competitor acted on up-to-date research that showed a new willingness by consumers to purchase a more expensive, improved disposable diaper. Further research by Procter & Gamble led to today's high-selling "new" Pampers and Luvs.

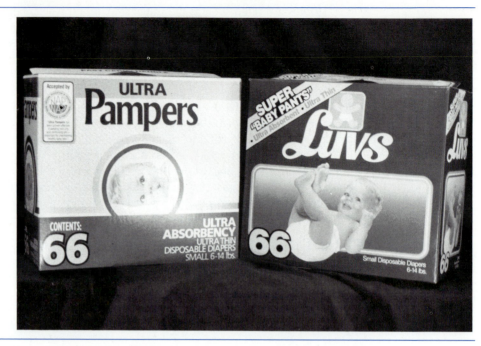

bency) were most important to them. This might be accomplished through a test-marketing study, a causal design.

Each stage in the process thus represents the investigation of a more detailed statement of the problem. Although we have suggested that the sequence would be from exploratory to descriptive to causal research, alternative sequences might occur. The "families with small children have more money to spend on baby products" hypothesis might be so generally accepted that the sequence would be from exploratory directly to causal. That sequence was more typical of what actually happened in the hard-fought battle between Procter & Gamble and Kimberly-Clark for shares of the lucrative diaper market.

Procter & Gamble, which had an enormous hit with Pampers, grew uncharacteristically complacent about the brand in the two decades following its introduction. By the early 1980s, Pampers had become P & G's single largest business, at $1 billion per year. But Kimberly-Clark spotted an opening in the market that P & G had neglected. In response to its perception that mothers were willing to pay more for a diaper with greater absorbency and less leakage, Kimberly-Clark developed Huggies, a premium-priced diaper.

The introduction of Huggies had a drastic effect on Pampers' market share. Realizing it was rapidly being beaten at its own game, in 1985 P & G poured $725 million into revamping production facilities and advertising a new generation of higher quality, more expensive Pampers. Since the success of competing Huggies had already proved that mothers were willing to pay extra for better diapers, P & G did not have to waste time or money testing that concept. Instead they could concentrate on causal research to refine design and fine-tune price and advertising approaches in their test market in Wichita, Kansas.[4]

The potential for conducting research in the reverse direction also exists. If a hypothesis is disproved by causal research (e.g., the product bombs in taste tests), the analyst may then decide that another descriptive study, or even another exploratory study, is needed. Also, not every research problem will begin with an exploratory study. It depends on how specific researchers can be in formulating the problem before them. A general, vague statement leads naturally to exploratory work, while a specific cause-effect hypothesis lends itself to experimental work.

◆ Exploratory Research

As previously stated, the general objective in exploratory research is to gain insights and ideas. The exploratory study is particularly helpful in breaking broad, vague problem statements into smaller, more precise subproblem statements, ideally in the form of specific hypotheses. In effect, a hypothesis is a statement that specifies how two or more measurable variables are related.[5]

In the early stages of research, we usually lack sufficient understanding of the problem to formulate a specific hypothesis. Further, there are often several tentative explanations for a given marketing phenomenon. For example: sales are off because our price is too high; our dealers or sales representatives are not doing the job they should; our advertising is weak, and so on. Exploratory research can be used to establish priorities in studying these competing explanations. Top priority would usually be given to whichever hypothesis appeared most promising in the exploratory study. Priorities may also be established according to the feasibility of researching the hypotheses. Exploratory studies should help to eliminate ideas that are not practical.

An exploratory study is also used to increase the analyst's familiarity with a problem. This is particularly true when the analyst is new to the problem arena, for example, a marketing research consultant going to work for a company for the first time.

The exploratory study may also be used to clarify concepts. For instance, if management is considering a change in service policy intended to increase dealer satisfaction, an exploratory study could be used to (1) clarify what is meant by dealer satisfaction and (2) develop a method by which dealer satisfaction could be measured.

The Reagan administration found itself facing the kind of broad, ill-defined problem that exploratory studies are designed to address when it set out to make the tax code more fair. The first issue to be resolved was what fairness in the tax code really meant. Several studies had supported the notion that a majority of Americans felt the system then in place was unfair; 82 percent responding to an Internal Revenue Service–sponsored survey felt this way, and two-thirds responding to a Louis Harris poll said they were "fed up" with the current system because of its unfairness. As Kent Smith, who headed a study of taxpayer compliance for the American Bar Association, commented, though, "the polls don't explain precisely why people think the current system is unfair. We've been frustrated by the way the fairness questions

[4]Nancy Giges and Laurie Freeman, "Wounded Lion? Trail of Mistakes Mars P & G Record," *Advertising Age,* 56 (July 29, 1985), pp. 1 and 50.

[5]See Fred N. Kerlinger, *Foundations of Behavioral Research,* 3rd ed. (New York: Holt, Rinehart and Winston, 1986), pp. 17–20, for a discussion of the criteria of good hypotheses and of the value of hypotheses in guiding research.

have been asked. . . . Is it tax enforcement that bothers people? Tax rates? The way laws are written? Tax avoidance by other people? Or is it because they believe their taxes are poorly spent by government?"[6] Exploratory research would play a particularly important role in clarifying a concept like this.

In sum, an exploratory study is used for any or all of the following purposes.[7]

- Formulating a problem for more precise investigation
- Developing hypotheses
- Establishing priorities for further research
- Gathering information about the practical problems of carrying out research on particular issues

---

[6]Alan Murray, "To Revamp Tax Code, Reagan Will Tap Belief That System Is Unfair," *The Wall Street Journal,* 65 (April 15, 1985), p. 21.

[7]Selltiz, Wrightsman, and Cook, *Research Methods,* p. 91.

Back to the Case

Three weeks after their initial luncheon meeting, Atkins and Reiss met again to go over the results of the marketing research department's preliminary survey for a new potato chip for Tasti-Snax.

Dave Reiss, the company's head researcher, arranged a number of files across the conference table and reached for an outline that he had carefully clipped to the top file.

"We've been very busy on new chip research, Mr. Atkins," he said. "We've uncovered what we think are some great new product ideas."

"Where did these come from, Dave?" Atkins asked.

"We've been talking with scientists, home economists, and consumers, as well as some people in your own department. We've collected and studied a number of cookbooks. We've also gathered samples of all our

competitors' snack products, and have been sampling them for new ideas and for needs that aren't being satisfied, and we're studying industry data detailing their sales patterns," Reiss said.

"So what have you discovered through all this snacking and studying?" Atkins asked.

"So far we've come up with four different product ideas," Reiss answered. He reached for the first file.

"We first considered a better version of Pringles, the potato chip in a can, but rejected it since the original Pringles was never much of a success.

"Then we came up with the idea for a thick, processed chip that would be similar to our corn chips, but made from potatoes. That is still a possibility.

"We also have toyed with the idea of a super-crispy chip, and a bite-sized lattice chip."

"Well, I'll be curious to see how these ideas translate into products," Atkins said. "Where do you go from here?"

"Next we're going to develop some prototypes of the ideas we think are worth pursuing and try them out on consumers in product-evaluation groups," Reiss said. "We'll keep you posted on developments."

Typically, a great deal of background research precedes the expensive development of a prototype, or sample version, of a new product. In this case, the examination of competitors' products and their respective market shares, brainstorming sessions with people familiar with the product category, and product-evaluation groups in which consumers react to the proposed product concept, all could be classified as exploratory research.

- Increasing the analyst's familiarity with the problem
- Clarifying concepts

In general, exploratory research is appropriate for any problem about which little is known. It becomes the foundation for a good study.

Because so much is typically unknown at the beginning of an inquiry, exploratory studies are generally very flexible with regard to the methods used for gaining insight and developing hypotheses. "Formal design is conspicuous by its absence in exploratory studies."[8] Exploratory studies rarely use detailed questionnaires or involve probability sampling plans. Rather, investigators frequently change the research procedure as the vaguely defined initial problem is transformed into one with more precise meaning. Investigators often follow where their noses lead them in an exploratory study. Ingenuity, judgment, and good luck inevitably play a part in leading to the one or two key hypotheses that, it is hoped, will account for the phenomenon. While exploratory research may be conducted in a variety of ways, experience has shown that literature surveys, experience surveys, and the analysis of selected cases are particularly productive.[9]

Literature Search

• Literature search

Search of statistics, trade journal articles, other articles, magazines, newspapers, and books for data or insight into the problem at hand.

One of the quickest and cheapest ways to discover hypotheses is in the work of others, through a **literature search.** The search may involve conceptual literature, trade literature, or, quite often, published statistics. The literature that is searched depends naturally on the problem being addressed. For example, a firm with a dissatisfied field sales force would probably begin its study with a search of literature on concepts and ideas related to satisfaction in such personnel. The search might include research studies in psychology, sociology, and personnel management, in addition to marketing journals. The focus would be on the factors determining employee satisfaction and dissatisfaction. The analyst would keep a keen eye for those factors also found in the company's environment. The question of how to measure an employee's satisfaction would also be researched at the same time.

Suppose the problem was one that typically triggers much marketing research: "Sales are off; why?" Exploratory insights into this problem could easily and cheaply be gained by analyzing published data and trade literature. Such an analysis would quickly indicate whether the problem was an industry problem or a firm problem. For example, it was readily apparent to P & G that the decline in Pampers' market share was a company problem, since the disposable diaper industry as a whole showed no signs of weakening.

Very different research is in order if the firm's sales are down, but (1) the company's market share is up, since industry sales are down further, (2) the company's market share has remained stable, or (3) the company's market share has declined. The last situation would trigger an investigation of the firm's marketing-mix variables, while the first condition would prompt an analysis to determine why industry sales are off. The great danger in omitting exploratory research is obvious from the preceding example; without the analysis of secondary data as a guide, there is a great danger of researching the wrong "why."

---

[8]Harper W. Boyd, Ralph Westfall, and Stanley F. Stasch, *Marketing Research: Text and Cases,* 6th ed. (Homewood, Ill.: Richard D. Irwin, 1985), p. 40.

[9]Selltiz, Wrightsman, and Cook, *Research Methods:* Chapter 4 has a particularly informative discussion of the types of research that are productive at the exploratory stages of an investigation. Our treatment follows theirs closely.

A company's own internal data should be included in the literature examined in exploratory research, as Mosinee Paper Company found to its pleasant surprise. The company was contemplating dropping one of its products because of its dismal sales performance. Before doing so, though, the company tallied sales of the product per salesperson and found that only a single salesperson was selling that specific grade of industrial paper. Upon further investigation, Mosinee discovered how the buyers "were using the paper—an application that had been known only to the one salesman and his customers. This information enabled management to educate its other salesmen as to the potential market for the paper and sales rose substantially."[10]

It is important to remember that in a literature search, as in any exploratory research, the major emphasis is on the discovery of ideas and tentative explanations of the phenomenon and not on demonstrating which explanation is *the* explanation. The demonstration is better left to descriptive and causal research. Thus, the analyst must be alert to the hypotheses that can be derived from available material, both published material and the company's internal records.

Experience Survey

• Experience survey

Interviews with people knowledgeable about the general subject being investigated.

Sometimes called the *key informant survey,* the **experience survey** attempts to tap the knowledge and experience of those familiar with the general subject being investigated. In studies concerned with the marketing of a product, anyone who has any association with the marketing effort is a potential source of information. This would include the top executives of the company, the sales manager, product manager, and sales representatives. It would also include wholesalers and retailers who handle the product, as well as consumers who use the product. It might even include individuals who are not part of the chain of distribution but who might, nevertheless, possess some insight into the phenomenon. For example, a children's book publisher gained valuable insights into the reason for a sales decline by talking with librarians and schoolteachers. These discussions indicated that an increased use of library facilities, both public and school, coincided with the product's drop in sales. The increase in library usage was, in turn, traced to an increase in federal funds, which had enabled libraries to buy more books for their children's collections.

Usually, a great many people know something about the general subject of any given problem. However, not all of them should be contacted.

> Research economy dictates that the respondents in an experience survey be carefully selected. The aim of the experience survey is to obtain insight into the relationships between variables rather than to get an accurate picture of current practices or a simple consensus as to best practices. One is looking for provocative ideas and useful insights, not for the statistics of the profession. Thus the respondents must be chosen because of the likelihood that they will offer the contributions sought. In other words, a *selected* sample of people working in the area is called for.[11]

Never, therefore, should a probability sample, in which respondents are chosen by some random process, be used in an experience survey. It is a waste of time to interview those who have little competence or little relevant experience in the subject under investigation. It is also a waste of time to interview those who cannot

[10] Jon G. Udell and Gene R. Laczniak, *Marketing in an Age of Change* (New York: John Wiley, 1981), p. 154.

[11] Selltiz, Wrightsman, and Cook, *Research Methods,* p. 94.

Exploratory research may include in-house interviews with company executives as well as key people who can provide experiential information relevant to the issue.

Source: Courtesy of *Ambassador* published by Hiram Walker-Gooderham & Worts Limited.

articulate their experience and knowledge. It is important, though, to include people with differing points of view. The children's book publisher we mentioned earlier interviewed company executives, key people in the product group, sales representatives, managers of retail outlets in which the books were sold, teachers, and librarians in the process of investigating the book's sales decline.

The interviews were all unstructured and informal. The emphasis in each interview among those immediately concerned with the distribution of the product was "How do you explain the sales decrease? In your opinion, what is needed to reverse the downward slide?"[12] Most of the time in each interview was then devoted to exploring in detail the various rationales and proposed solutions. A number of sometimes conflicting hypotheses emerged. This provided the researchers with an opportunity to "bounce" some of the hypotheses off groups with differing vantage points and, in the process, get a feel for which of the hypotheses would be most fruitful to research. The interviews with librarians and teachers approached the problem from a different angle. Here the emphasis was on discovering changes in children's reading habits.

The respondents were given a great deal of freedom in choosing the factors to be discussed. This is consistent with the notion that the emphasis in exploratory research is on developing tentative explanations and not on demonstrating the viability of a given explanation.

This emphasis, as well as the conduct of the experience survey, is reflected in the experience of an industrial goods manufacturer who used this technique to gain insight into a declining sales situation.

---

[12]Selltiz, Wrightsman, and Cook suggest it is often useful in an exploratory study to orient questions towards "what works." That is, they recommend that questions be of the following form: "If (a given effect) is desired, what influences or what methods will, in your experience, be most likely to produce it?" p. 95.

After several years of declining revenues followed ten years of revenue and profit growth, the firm's board of directors questioned the advisability of continuing with one line of business. A review of internal sales records revealed that their market for the service line was limited to approximately thirty large packaged goods manufacturers. No significant external secondary data sources were located. Executives of the firm were then asked to identify the three most knowledgeable persons in the country with respect to the service line characteristics, its market, and the capabilities of competitive suppliers. All three persons nominated were executives of present or past customers of the firm. Appointments for personal interviews were made with each nominee by telephone, using the firm's president as a reference.

Each of the three personal interviews were conducted at the informant's place of business, and lasted from 1½ to 3½ hours. . . . The sessions ranged over a wide variety of topics. Informants were asked to assess the past, current, and probable future developments of the service line, the market, and the comparative strengths and weaknesses of the major suppliers of the service line, including the research sponsor.

The findings . . . revealed that there had been no decline in market activity during the past two years. There had been, however, a concerted effort by a number of packaged goods manufacturers to divert business to two new service suppliers during the period. This was done to assure additional sources of supply and capacity in order to handle a significant expansion of demand that was expected to occur within two years. As a result, established suppliers were allocated less business during the period but could expect a resumption of their previous growth in the near future. The manufacturers were reluctant to divulge these plans to the established suppliers for fear they would add excess capacity and act to limit the competitiveness of the new suppliers.[13]

The insight from these three interviews was used to focus further personal interviews investigating its general truth, and the notion of continued growth was indeed supported.

One very common type of experience survey is a focus group session among users or potential users of a product in which typically 8 to 12 people are prompted to engage in group discussion about some issue. Stouffer's, for example, used focus groups among panels of consumers to find out what dieters did not like about diet meals when researching its Lean Cuisine line. Stouffer's experience in developing the product is detailed in Research Window 4.2. We will discuss focus groups at greater length in Chapter 8.

Analysis of Selected Cases

◆ Analysis of selected cases

Intensive study of selected examples of the phenomenon of interest.

Sometimes referred to as the analysis of *insight-stimulating examples,* the **analysis of selected cases** involves the intensive study of selected cases of the phenomenon under investigation. Researchers may examine existing records, observe the phenomenon as it occurs, conduct unstructured interviews, or use any one of a variety of other approaches to analyze what is really happening in a given situation. The focus may be on entities (individual people or institutions) or groups of entities (sales representatives or distributors in various regions).

---

[13]William E. Cox, Jr., *Industrial Marketing Research* (New York: John Wiley, 1979), pp. 25–26. For further discussion about the general conduct and uses of experience surveys, see Michael J. Houston, "The Key Informant Technique: Marketing Applications," in Thomas V. Greer, ed., *Conceptual and Methodological Foundations of Marketing* (Chicago: American Marketing Association, 1974), pp. 305–308; John Siedler, "On Using Informants: A Key Technique for Collecting Qualitative Data and Controlling Measurement Error in Organization Analysis," *American Sociological Review,* 39 (December 1974), pp. 816–831; Lynn W. Phillips, "Assessing Measurement Error in Key Informant Reports: A Methodological Note on Organizational Analysis in Marketing," *Journal of Marketing Research,* 18 (November 1981), pp. 395–415; and George John and Torger Reve, "The Reliability and Validity of Key Informant Data from Dyadic Relationships in Marketing Channels," *Journal of Marketing Research,* 19 (November 1982), pp. 517–524.

The method is characterized by several features.[14] First, the attitude of the investigator is the key. The most productive attitude is one of alert receptivity, of seeking explanations rather than testing explanations. The investigator is likely to make fre-

---

[14]These features are detailed further in Selltiz, Wrightsman, and Cook, *Research Methods*, pp. 98–99. See also Thomas V. Bonoma, "Case Research in Marketing: Opportunities, Problems, and a Process," *Journal of Marketing Research*, 22 (May 1985), pp. 199–208.

Research Window 4.2
Stouffer Does Its Homework and Comes Up with a Winner

It took Stouffer nearly thirteen years of research and development to launch its frozen food line, Lean Cuisine, but the product's phenomenal success has shown that the time and money invested were well worth it.

In the early 1970s, as American consumers' interest in health and diet grew, so did Stouffer's interest in serving this potentially lucrative market segment. The company launched a seven-year study of medical and consumer literature on the topic, followed by an intensive review of the entire diet food market.

Stouffer examined not only the psychology of those who used such products, "but also of those who didn't, but for one reason or other should consider using these types of products," said Milton C. Miles, a vice-president at Nestlé Enterprises, Stouffer's parent company.

Consumer media were studied to determine what people were buying, reading, and doing about their diet. Stouffer scrutinized such trends as jogging. Researchers talked with doctors for their views on dietary needs for the overweight and those with heart conditions.

Researchers at Stouffer conducted consumer panels and focus groups to find out what dieters didn't like about diet meals. These very informal, loosely structured group discussions uncovered four common objections: the food didn't look good, it didn't taste good, it wasn't filling, and it was boring in variety and appearance.

This kind of information helped Stouffer researchers decide the kinds of qualities their product should possess. They considered such issues as what the product should look like and taste like and how big the portions should be.

Stouffer's consumer affairs manager said the company decided to develop meals with ample

Source: Courtesy of Stouffer Foods Corporation.

portions but with fewer than 300 calories. This figure was based on the American Dietetic Association's recommendation that women consume 1,200 calories a day (1,600 for men), with 400 to 500 calories allotted for the main meal. Lean Cuisine therefore allows the consumer to add a salad or other food item to the meal.

Once the package design was tested, the product was test marketed in several large markets, including Cleveland and Omaha. Lean Cuisine was an immediate hit in the test markets. In its first year in national distribution, it rang up sales of $125 million. An industry observer said he believes Lean Cuisine is "heading for the $500 million mark in total annual sales." Stouffer recently had to face the enviable chore of building a new plant to meet the demand for existing and planned products.

Source: Based on Anna Sobczynski, "Reading the Consumer's Mind," *Advertising Age*, 55 (May 1984), p. M-16; and Kevin Higgins, "Meticulous Planning Pays Dividends at Stouffer's," *Marketing News*, 17 (October 1983), pp. 1 and 20.

quent changes in direction as new information emerges. He or she may have to search for new cases or secure more data from previously contacted cases. Second, the success of the method depends heavily on how well the investigator can integrate the diverse bits of information he or she has amassed into a unified interpretation. Finally, the method is characterized by its intensity. The analyst attempts to obtain sufficient information to characterize and explain both the unique features of the case being studied and the features it has in common with other cases.

> In one study to improve the productivity of the sales force of a particular company, the investigator studied intensively two or three of the best sales representatives and two or three of the worst. Data was collected on the background and experience of each representative and then several days were spent making sales calls with them. As a result, a hypothesis was developed. It was that checking the stock of retailers and suggesting items on which they were low were the most important differences between the successful and the poor sales representatives.[15]

---

[15]Boyd, Westfall, and Stasch, *Marketing Research,* p. 51.

Back to the Case

It had been a frenzied few months at Tasti-Snax. The marketing research department had had encouraging results from consumer tests of both the thick, processed potato chip and the very crunchy one, and both were in the process of being developed further. Neither, however, met the company's business objective of being a new potato chip.

The lattice chip had initially been rejected by consumers as being too light and thin. It had subsequently been reformulated as a thicker, heavier, crunchier chip. Tests by consumers at home showed that Tasti-Snax had hit on a potential winner.

Further tests were conducted that simulated market conditions and gave researchers an idea of what the potential sales volume of the brand might be and how well the actual product fit the concept of a hearty, crunchy potato chip.

Reiss was fairly bursting with enthusiasm over the product's success in early tests. Atkins brought him back to earth with a jolt.

"Dave, remember what I said way back at our lunch about the executive committee's standards for new products? I'm encouraged by your success so far, but I'm not convinced that this product, as it stands, will pass our $75 million corporate hurdle," Atkins said. "I suggest you develop additional flavors to enable the product to do the volume required to meet our internal standards. I'd also like further data on whether consumers will buy this product repeatedly."

"We've already planned a diary panel to test just that concept," Reiss said. "We're also testing various advertising approaches, and developing a system by which we can monitor distribution and out-of-stock levels. I'm confident that this chip will be one of our most successful new products."

Once a product has been developed, various other types of research are used to further refine the product and to measure potential consumer acceptance. In this case, the diary panel would be considered descriptive research, while the market simulation test and the advertising tests would be classified as causal research, all of which are described in the next chapter.

In this example, the key insight that good sales representatives had in common, and in which they differed from poor sales representatives, led them to check retailer inventory.

Some situations that are particularly productive of hypotheses are as follows:

1. *Cases reflecting changes and, in particular, abrupt changes.* For example, the way a market adjusts to the entrance of a new competitor can reveal a great deal about the structure of an industry.

2. *Cases reflecting extremes of behavior.* The case of the best and worst sales representatives just cited is an example. Similarly, to determine the factors responsible for the differences in sales performance among a company's territories, one could learn more by comparing the best and worst territories than by looking at all territories.

3. *Cases reflecting the order in which events occurred over time.* For example, in the case of the differing sales performance by territory, it may be that in one territory a branch office replaced a manufacturer's agent, while in another it replaced an industrial distributor.

Which cases will be most valuable depends, of course, on the problem in question. It is generally true, though, that cases that display sharp contrasts or have striking features are most useful. This is because minute differences are usually difficult to discern. Thus, instead of trying to determine what distinguishes the average case from the slightly above-average case, it is better to contrast the best and worst and thereby magnify whatever differences may exist.

◆ Summary

Learning Objective 1: Explain what is meant by a research design.

A research design is the framework or plan for a study that guides the collection and analysis of data.

Learning Objective 2: List the three basic types of research design.

One basic way of classifying designs is in terms of the fundamental objective of the research: exploratory, descriptive, or causal.

Learning Objective 3: Describe the major emphasis of each type of research design.

The major emphasis in *exploratory research* is on the discovery of ideas and insights. *Descriptive research* is typically concerned with determining the frequency with which something occurs or the relationship between variables. A *causal research* design is concerned with determining cause-and-effect relationships. Causal studies typically take the form of experiments.

Learning Objective 4: Cite the crucial principle of research.

The crucial principle of research is that *the design of the investigation should stem from the problem.*

Learning Objective 5: Describe the basic uses of exploratory research.

Exploratory research is basically "general picture" research. It is quite useful in becoming familiar with a phenomenon, in clarifying concepts, in developing but not testing "if-then" statements, and in establishing priorities for further research.

Learning Objective 6: Specify the key characteristic of exploratory research.

Exploratory studies are characterized by their flexibility.

Learning Objective 7: Discuss the various types of exploratory research and identify the characteristics of each.

Among the various types of exploratory research are literature searches, experience surveys, and analyses of selected cases. Literature searches may involve conceptual literature, trade literature, or, quite often, published statistics. Experience surveys, sometimes known as *key informant surveys,* attempt to tap the knowledge and experience of those familiar with the general subject being investigated. The analysis of selected cases is sometimes referred to as the analysis of *insight-stimulating examples.* By either label, the approach involves the *intensive study of selected cases* of the phenomenon under investigation.

Discussion Questions, Problems, and Projects

1. The Communicon Company was a large supplier of residential telephones and related services in the southeast United States. The Department of Research and Development recently designed a prototype with a memory function that could store the number of calls and the contents of the calls for a period of forty-eight hours. A similar model, introduced by Communicon's competitor three months earlier, was marginally successful. However, both the models suffered from a technical flaw. It was found that a call lasting for over twenty minutes would result in a loss of the dial tone for ninety seconds. This was mainly attributable to the activation of the memory function. Notwithstanding the flaw, management was excited about the efforts of the research and development department. They decided to do a field survey to gauge consumer reaction to the memory capability. A random sample of 1,000 respondents was to be chosen from three major metropolitan centers in the Southeast. The questionnaires were designed to find out respondents' attitudes and opinions toward this new instrument.

   In this situation, is the research design appropriate? If yes, why? If no, why not?

2. A medium-sized manufacturer of high-speed copiers and duplicators was introducing a new desktop model. The vice-president of communications had to decide between two advertising programs for this product. He preferred advertising program Gamma and was sure it would generate more sales than its counterpart, advertising program Beta. The next day he was to meet with the senior vice-president of marketing to plan an appropriate research design for a study that would aid in the final decision as to which advertising program to implement.

   What research design would you recommend? Justify your choice.

3. A local mail-order firm was concerned with improving its service. In particular, management wanted to assess if customers were dissatisfied with current service and the nature of this dissatisfaction.

   What research design would you recommend? Justify your choice.

4. The Write-It Company was a manufacturer of writing instruments such as fountain pens, ballpoint pens, soft-top pens, and mechanical pencils. Typically, these products were retailed through small and large chains, drugstores, and grocery stores. The company had recently diversified into the manufacture of disposable cigarette lighters. The distribution of this product was to be restricted to drugstores and grocery stores. The reason was that management believed that its target market of low- and middle-income classes would use these outlets. Your expertise is required in order to decide on an appropriate research design to determine if this would indeed be the case.

   What research design would you recommend? Justify your choice.

5. Feather-Tote Luggage is a producer of cloth-covered luggage, one of the primary advantages of which is its light weight. The company distributes its luggage through major department stores, mail-order houses, clothing retailers, and other retail outlets such as stationery stores, leather goods stores, and so on. The company advertises rather heavily, but it also supplements this promotional effort with a large field staff of sales representatives,

numbering around 400. The numbers vary because one of the historical problems confronting Feather-Tote Luggage has been the large number of sales representatives' resignations. It is not unusual for 10 to 20 percent of the sales force to turn over every year. Since the cost of training a new person is estimated at $5,000 to $10,000, not including the lost sales that might result because of a personnel switch, Mr. Harvey, the sales manager, is rightly concerned. He has been concerned for some time and, therefore, has been conducting exit interviews with each departing sales representative. On the basis of these interviews, he has formulated the opinion that the major reason for this high turnover is general sales representatives' dissatisfaction with company policies, promotional opportunities, and pay. But top management has not been sympathetic to Mr. Harvey's pleas regarding the changes needed in these areas of corporate policy. Rather, it has tended to counter Mr. Harvey's pleas with arguments that too much of what he is suggesting is based on his gut reactions and little hard data. Top management desires more systematic evidence that job satisfaction, in general, and these dimensions of job satisfaction, in particular, are the real reasons for the high turnover before they would be willing to change things. Mr. Harvey has called on the Marketing Research Department in Feather-Tote Luggage to assist him in solving his problem.

(a) As a member of this department, identify the general hypothesis that would guide your research efforts.

(b) What type of research design would you recommend to Mr. Harvey? Justify your answer.

Suggested Additional Readings

For an excellent discussion of the three types of research designs, their basic purposes, and generally fruitful approaches, see

Claire Selltiz, Lawrence S. Wrightsman, and Stuart W. Cook, *Research Methods in Social Relations,* 3rd ed. (New York: Holt, Rinehart and Winston, 1976).

Fred N. Kerlinger, *Foundations of Behavioral Research,* 3rd ed. (New York: Holt, Rinehart and Winston, 1986).

For some illustrations of their use in the industrial marketing context see

William E. Cox, Jr., *Industrial Marketing Research* (New York: John Wiley, 1979).

Chapter 5

Descriptive and Causal Research Designs

$$+ \quad + \quad + \quad +$$
$$+ \quad + \quad + \quad +$$
$$+ \quad + \quad + \quad +$$
$$+ \quad + \quad + \quad +$$

Learning Objectives

Upon completing this chapter, you should be able to

1. Cite three major purposes of descriptive research.
2. List the six specifications of a descriptive study.
3. Explain what a dummy table is.
4. Discuss the difference between cross-sectional and longitudinal designs.
5. Explain what is meant by a *panel* in marketing research and explain the difference between a traditional panel and an omnibus panel.
6. Explain what is meant by a turnover table, or brand-switching matrix.
7. Distinguish between field studies and sample surveys.
8. Distinguish between the scientific notion of causality and the commonsense notion.
9. Define *concomitant variation.*
10. List three ways of determining a causal relationship.
11. Clarify the difference between laboratory experiments and field experiments.
12. Explain which of the two types of experiments has greater internal validity and which has greater external validity.
13. List the three major problems in test marketing.
14. Discuss the advantages and disadvantages of simulated test marketing.
15. Distinguish between a controlled test market and a standard test market.

Case in Marketing Research

Don Harris was hooked on exotic peanuts. While working for an engineering firm in the Philippines, he discovered a nut coating popular among local residents that he thought would be a surefire hit back home in Tennessee. He spent the long evenings far from his family working on a business plan for launching his idea, and munching nuts. Harris was tired of the life of the itinerant engineer anyway, and he felt the little nest egg he had put aside from accepting overseas assignments would be just enough to start his new company. He could hardly wait to get home.

Once back in Tennessee, however, things did not go as smoothly as he had envisioned. For one thing, he found himself short of cash. His once tidy bank account was dwindling alarmingly in the face of the start-up costs of a new business. For another, his partner, Tony Sorrenti, a former college friend who was looking for more challenges than his accounting firm could provide, kept insisting that their product be test marketed before they attempted retail distribution.

Don was discouraged.

"Look, Tony," he said in one of their endless discussions of the business plan, "we're almost broke. We can't afford some pricey research right now.

"You know and I know the product is great. People will love it. Trust me. Let's spend the money on some catchy advertising instead. I think that would make a lot more sense."

"I don't know, Don," Tony said uneasily. "I think that may be the shortsighted approach. I still think we have too many unanswered questions to plunge ahead like this."

Discussion Issues

1. If you were Tony Sorrenti, what questions would you want marketing research to answer before you launched the product?

2. In what circumstances might a marketer be justified in *not* doing research?

3. How might a small business minimize some of the costs of marketing research?

Source: This fictitious case is based on the experience of John Werner, founder of "John Werner Select" nuts, as depicted in an article by Amy Saltzman, "Vision vs. Reality," *Venture* 37 (October 1985), pp. 40–45.

In the last chapter we learned that research designs typically fall into one of three categories: exploratory, descriptive, or causal research. We examined exploratory research and noted that one of its primary uses is to generate ideas and insights for additional, more targeted research. In this chapter we will see how descriptive and causal research might be used to test the validity of the hypotheses that exploratory studies evolve.

◆ Descriptive Research Designs

A great deal of marketing research can be considered descriptive research, which is used for the following purposes:

1. To describe the characteristics of certain groups. For example, based on information gathered from known users of our particular product, we might attempt to develop a profile of the "average user" with respect to income, sex, age, educational level, and so on.

2. To estimate the proportion of people in a specified population who behave in a certain way. We might be interested, say, in estimating the proportion of people within a specified radius of a proposed shopping complex who would shop at the center.

3. To make specific predictions. We might be interested in predicting the level of sales for each of the next five years so that we could plan for the hiring and training of new sales representatives.

Descriptive research encompasses an array of research objectives. However, a descriptive study is more than a fact-gathering expedition.

> Facts do not lead anywhere. Indeed, facts, as facts, are the commonest, cheapest, and most useless of all commodities. Anyone with a questionnaire can gather thousands of facts a day—and probably not find much real use for them. What makes facts practical and valuable is the glue of explanation and understanding, the framework of theory, the tie-rod of conjecture. Only when facts can be fleshed to a skeletal theory do they become meaningful in the solution of problems.[1]

The researcher should not fall prey to the temptation of beginning a descriptive research study with the vague thought that the data collected should be interesting. A good descriptive study presupposes much prior knowledge about the phenomenon being studied. It rests on one or more specific hypotheses. These conjectural statements guide the research in specific directions. In this respect, a descriptive study design is very different from an exploratory study design. Whereas an exploratory study is characterized by its flexibility, descriptive studies can be considered rigid. Descriptive studies require a *clear specification* of the *who, what, when, where, why,* and *how* of the research.

Suppose a chain of food convenience stores is planning to open a new outlet, and the company wants to determine how people usually come to patronize a new outlet. Consider some of the questions that would need to be answered before data collection for this descriptive study could begin. Who is to be considered a patron? Anyone who enters the store? What if they do not buy anything but just participate

---

[1]Robert Ferber, Donald F. Blankertz, and Sidney Hollander, Jr., *Marketing Research* (New York: The Ronald Press Co., copyright 1964), p. 153. See also, "Marketing Research Needs Validated Theories," *Marketing News,* 17 (January 21, 1983), p. 14. For an alternative view, see Raymond J. Lawrence, "To Hypothesize or Not to Hypothesize? The Correct 'Approach' to Survey Research," *Journal of the Market Research Society,* 24 (October 1982), pp. 335–343.

in the grand-opening prize giveaway? Perhaps a patron should be defined as anyone who purchases anything from the store.

Should patrons be defined on the basis of the family unit or should they be defined as individuals, even though the individuals come from the same family? What characteristics of these patrons should be measured? Are we interested in their age and sex, or perhaps in where they live and how they came to know about our store? When shall we measure them, while they are shopping or later? Should the study take place during the first weeks of operation of the store or should it be delayed until the situation has stabilized somewhat? Certainly if we are interested in word-of-mouth influence, we must wait at least until that influence has a chance to operate.

Where shall we measure the patrons? Should it be in the store, immediately outside the store, or should we attempt to contact them at home? Why do we want to measure them? Are we going to use these measurements to plan promotional strategy? In that case the emphasis might be on measuring how people become aware of the store. Or are we going to use them as a basis for locating other stores? In that case the emphasis might shift more to determining the trading area of the store.

How shall we measure them? Shall we use a questionnaire or shall we observe their purchasing behavior? If we use a questionnaire, what form will it take? Will it be highly structured? Will it be in the form of a scale? How will it be administered? By telephone? By mail? Perhaps by personal interview?

These questions are not the only ones that would be or should be asked. Certainly, some of the answers will be implicit in the hypothesis or hypotheses that guide the descriptive research. Others, though, will not be obvious. The researcher will only be able to specify them after some labored thought or even after a small pilot or exploratory study. In either case, the researcher is well advised to delay collecting that first item of information with which to test the hypotheses until clear judgments of the who, what, when, where, why, and how of descriptive research have been made.

The researcher should also delay data collection until it has been clearly determined how the data are to be analyzed. Ideally, a set of dummy tables should be prepared before beginning the collection process. A **dummy table** is used to catalog the data to be collected. It shows how the analysis will be structured and conducted. Complete in all respects save for filling in the actual numbers, it contains a title, headings, and specific categories for the variables making up the table. All that remains after collecting the data is to count the number of cases of each type. Table 5.1 shows what might be used by a women's specialty store preparing to investigate whether its customers are predominantly from one age group, and if so, how that group differs from the customers who frequent competitors' stores.

Note that the table lists the particular age segments the store's owner wishes to compare. It is crucial that the exact variables and categories to be investigated be specified before researchers begin to collect the data. The statistical tests that will be used to uncover the relationship between age and store preference in this case should also be specified before data collection begins. Inexperienced researchers often question the need for such hard, detailed decisions before collecting the data. They assume that delaying these decisions until after the data are collected will somehow make them easier. Just the opposite is true, as any experienced researcher will attest.

> Most difficult for the beginning researcher to anticipate will be the analytical problems he may face after the data are gathered. He tends to believe that a wide variety of facts will be enough to solve anything. Only after struggling with sloppy, stubborn, and intractable facts, with data not adequate for the testing of hypotheses and with data that

• Dummy table

A table that is used to catalog the collected data.

Table 5.1   Dummy Table

	Store Preference by Age		
Age	Prefer A	Prefer B	Prefer C
Less than 30			
30–39			
40 or more			

are interesting but incapable of supporting practical recommendations for action will he be fully aware that the big "mistakes" of research usually are made in the early stages. Each definition of a problem or problem variable will create different facts or findings, and a formulation once made serves to restrict the scope of analysis. No problem is definitely formulated until the researcher can specify how he will make his analysis and how the results will contribute to a practical solution.[2]

Once the data have been collected and analysis is begun, it is too late to lament "if only we had collected information on that variable" or "if only we had measured the Y variable using a finer scale." Correcting such mistakes at this time is next to impossible. Rather, the analyst must take such considerations into account when planning the study. And dummy tables make such planning easier.

Another way of ensuring that the information collected in a descriptive study will address the objectives of the research is to specify in advance the objective each question addresses, the reason the question is included in the study, and the particular analysis in which the question will be used.

For example, a meat packer is interested in investigating the potential market for a new hot dog.[3] Before allowing the study to begin, he may well ask his researchers to justify the questions they seek to have answered. One question researchers plan to ask respondents is, "How many packages of hot dogs does your family eat every month, and how many hot dogs are in a typical package?"

In keeping with the preliminary planning we have suggested, let us imagine a scenario between the meat packer (MP) and his head researcher (R).

MP: What objectives does this question address?

R: This question will give us the information we need to classify people who eat hot dogs into specific categories based on how many hot dogs they eat. This information can help us predict future patterns, and may be related to a group's interest in our new hot dog. If one of the study's objectives is to find the group most likely to buy our proposed new product, then this question may help us find that group and ultimately learn if its members share any characteristics, such as age, size of household, family income, etc.

MP: Are there any other reasons why this question is included in the study?

---

[2]Ferber, Blankertz, and Hollander, *Marketing Research,* p. 171.

[3]Benjamin D. Sackmary, "Data Analysis and Output Planning Improve Value of Marketing Research," *Marketing News,* 17 (January 21, 1983), p. 6.

Figure 5.1

Classification of Descriptive Studies

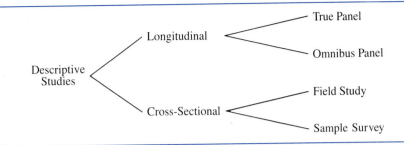

R: Yes, once we have developed a profile of our typical customer, we may be able to use that information to choose advertising media that will reach high-usage households at the least cost.

MP: How will the responses to this question be analyzed?

R: First, we will generate a frequency distribution. This will help us to sort respondents into three categories: light, moderate, and heavy users. Then we will try to relate usage types to such demographic variables as size of household, age of household shopper, total income, etc. We may also be able to determine how different prices would affect purchasing behavior.

This kind of exercise is called *output planning.* It is especially useful if it is done before the study in conjunction with the development of dummy tables, as suggested earlier. The dummy tables provide some additional clues on how to phrase the individual questions and code the responses.

Figure 5.1 is an overview of the various types of descriptive studies. The basic distinction is between **cross-sectional designs,** which are the most common and most familiar, and **longitudinal designs.** Typically, the cross-sectional design involves researching a sample of elements from the population of interest. If the population under investigation is hot dog eaters, the elements of the sample may include heavy users, moderate users, or people who eat hot dogs only on the Fourth of July. Most characteristics of the elements, or sample members, are measured only once. Researchers may ask sample members their age, sex, income, and education, for example.

Longitudinal studies, on the other hand, involve *panels,* which are fixed samples of elements. The elements may be stores, dealers, individuals, or other entities. The panel, or sample, remains relatively constant through time, although members may be added to replace dropouts or to keep it representative. The sample members in a panel are measured repeatedly, in contrast to the one-time measurement in a cross-sectional study. Both cross-sectional and longitudinal studies have weaknesses and advantages.

Longitudinal Analysis There are two types of panels. The older type (called a **true panel** in this text) relies on repeated measurements of the same variables. For example, the National Purchase Diary (NPD) maintains a consumer panel of 13,000 families.[4] Each family records its purchases of each of a number of products monthly. Similarly, the Nielsen Retail Store Audit involves a sample of 10,000 stores.[5]

• Cross-sectional study

Investigation involving a sample of elements selected from the population of interest at a single point in time.

• Longitudinal study

Investigation involving a fixed sample of elements that is measured repeatedly through time.

• Panel (true)

Fixed sample of respondents who are measured repeatedly over time with respect to the same variables.

---

[4]*We Make the Market Perfectly Clear* (New York: National Purchase Diary Panel, Inc., undated).

[5]*Management with the Nielsen Retail Index System* (Northbrook, Ill.: A. C. Nielsen Company, 1980).

Each store is checked monthly for its sales of each of a number of products. The operations of these panels will be examined more thoroughly when we discuss secondary sources of information in Chapter 6, but the important point to note now is that analysts measure each sample member with regard to the same characteristics each time. In the NPD panel, researchers would measure purchases; in the Nielsen Retail Store Audit, they would measure sales.

In recent years, a new type of panel, called the **omnibus panel,** has sprung up. The information collected from the members selected for this type of panel varies. At one time, it may be attitudes with respect to a new product. At another time, the panel members might be asked to evaluate alternative advertising copy. In each case, a sample might be selected from the larger group, which is in turn a sample of the population. The subsample might be drawn randomly. More than likely, though, participants with the desired characteristics will be chosen from a total panel. For example, the Parker Pen Company maintains a panel of 1,100 individuals, who were chosen because they expressed some interest in writing instruments and, of course, because of their willingness to participate. Parker Pen will often use selected members of this panel to evaluate new writing instruments. If the new instrument is a fountain pen, the company will often choose individuals who prefer fountain pens to test the products. Those chosen and the information sought will vary from project to project.

R. J. Reynolds, manufacturer of Camels, Vantage, and Winston cigarettes, chooses its panel members based on ability rather than interest. The company maintains a panel of 350 of its employees whose job it is to provide information for quality control and new brand development.[6] Only those employees who can successfully pass a screening test in which they smoke three cigarettes and can then identify which two were alike are allowed in the panel. As members of the panel, the employees are called upon to smoke, sniff, feel, and draw on unlit cigarettes and then provide their sensory evaluations. While the information that is collected is fairly standardized, the cigarettes being evaluated vary from test to test.

The distinction between the traditional panel and the omnibus panel is important. True longitudinal analysis, also called *time series analysis,* can be performed only on the first type of data, repeated measurements of the same entities over time. We shall see why when we discuss the method of analysis unique to panel data—the turnover table. The turnover table can be used only when individuals and variables are held constant through time. This is not to deny the value of the newer types of panels. Rather, we wish only to raise a cautionary flag because in other respects (for example, sample design, information collection, and so forth) both types of panels have about the same advantages and disadvantages when compared to cross-sectional studies. Consequently, we shall treat both types together when discussing these general advantages.

Probably the single most important advantage of true panel data is the way it lends itself to analysis. Suppose we are presently subscribing to the type of service that generates consumer purchase data from a panel of 1,000 families. Suppose further that we manufacture a laundry detergent, which we will call Brand A, and our brand has two main competitors, Brands B and C. There are also a number of other smaller competitors, which we will classify together in the single category, Brand D.

We have recently changed the package design of our product, and we are now interested in determining what impact the new design has on sales. Let us consider

◆ Panel (omnibus)

Fixed sample of respondents who are measured repeatedly over time but on variables that change from measurement to measurement.

---

[6]Margaret Loeb, "Testers of Cigarettes Find On-Job Puffing Really Isn't a Drag," *The Wall Street Journal,* 64 (August 22, 1984), pp. 1 and 15.

Table 5.2   Number of Families in Panel Purchasing Each Brand

Brand Purchased	During First Time Period t_1	During Second Time Period t_2
A	200	250
B	300	270
C	350	330
D	150	150
Total	1,000	1,000

the performance of our brand at time period t_1 before the change, and time period t_2 after the package change.

We could perform several types of analyses on these data.[7] We could look at the proportion of those in the panel who bought our brand in period t_1. We could also calculate the proportion of those who bought our brand in period t_2. Suppose these calculations generated the data shown in Table 5.2, which indicates that the package change was successful. Brand A's market share increased from 20 percent to 25 percent. Further, Brand A seemed to make its gains at the expense of its two major competitors, whose market shares decreased.

But that is not the whole story or even a completely accurate picture of the market changes that occurred. Look at what happens when, in assessing the impact of the package change, we maintain the identity of the sample members. Since we have repeated measures of the same individuals, we can count the number of families who bought Brand A in both periods, those who bought B or C or one of the miscellaneous brands in both periods, and those who switched brands between the two periods. Suppose Table 5.3 resulted from these tabulations. This table, which is a **turnover table**, or a **brand-switching matrix**, contains the same basic information as Table 5.2. That is, we see that 20 percent of the families bought Brand A in period t_1, while 25 percent did so in period t_2. But Table 5.3 also shows that Brand A did not make its market share gains at the expense of Brands B and C as originally suggested, but rather captured some of the families who previously bought one of the miscellaneous brands; 75 families switched from Brand D in period t_1 to Brand A in period t_2. And, as a matter of fact, Brand A lost some of its previous users to Brand B during the period; 25 families switched from Brand A in period t_1 to Brand B in period t_2.

Table 5.3 also allows the calculation of brand loyalty. Consider Brand A, for example; 175 of the 200, or 87.5 percent, of those who bought Brand A in period t_1 remained "loyal to it" (bought it again) in period t_2. By dividing each cell entry by the row or previous period totals, one can assess these brand loyalties and can also throw the basic changes that occurred in the market into bolder relief. Table 5.4, produced by such calculations, suggests, for example, that among the three major

• **Brand-switching matrix**

Two-way table that indicates which brands a sample of people purchased in one period and which brands they purchased in a subsequent period, thus highlighting the switches occurring among and between brands as well as the number of persons that purchased the same brand in both periods.

---

[7]Hans Zeisel, *Say It With Figures,* 5th ed. (New York: Harper & Row, 1968), pp. 200–239, has a highly readable version of the analyses that can be performed with panel data. See also David Rogosa, "Comparisons of Some Procedures for Analyzing Longitudinal Panel Data," *Journal of Economics and Business,* 32 (Winter 1980), pp. 136–151, and Gregory B. Markus, *Analyzing Panel Data* (Beverly Hills, Calif.: Sage Publications, 1979).

Table 5.3   Number of Families in Panel Buying Each Brand in Each Period

		During Second Time Period t_2				
		Bought A	Bought B	Bought C	Bought D	Total
During First Time Period t_1	Bought A	175	25	0	0	200
	Bought B	0	225	50	25	300
	Bought C	0	0	280	70	350
	Bought D	75	20	0	55	150
	Total	250	270	330	150	1,000

Table 5.4   Brand Loyalty and Brand Switching Probabilities among Families in Panel

		During Second Time Period t_2				
		Bought A	Bought B	Bought C	Bought D	Total
During First Time Period t_1	Bought A	.875	.125	.000	.000	1.000
	Bought B	.000	.750	.167	.083	1.000
	Bought C	.000	.000	.800	.200	1.000
	Bought D	.500	.133	.000	.367	1.000

brands, Brand A exhibited the greatest buying loyalty and Brand B the least. This is important to know because it indicates whether families like the brand when they try it.[8]

Whether we can conclude that those who switched from one of the miscellaneous brands to Brand A were prompted to do so by the package change is open to question for reasons that we will discuss later in the chapter. The point is that turnover, or brand-switching, analysis can be performed only when there are repeated measures over time for the same variables for the same subjects. It is not appropriate for omnibus panel data, in which the variables being measured are constantly changing, nor is it appropriate for cross-sectional studies, even if successive cross-sectional samples are taken.

Thus, the unique advantage of longitudinal analysis is that since it reveals changes in individual members' behavior, researchers can determine the effect of a change in a particular marketing variable—a package design, for example—better than if

[8]Table 5.4 can also be viewed as a transition matrix, since it depicts the brand-buying changes occurring from period to period. Knowing the proportion switching allows early prediction of the ultimate success of some new product or some change in market strategy. See, for example, Seymour Sudman and Robert Ferber, *Consumer Panels* (Chicago: American Marketing Association, 1979), pp. 19–27, which also provides an excellent review of the literature on such facets of consumer panels as uses of, sampling and sampling biases, data-collection methods, conditioning, data processing and file maintenance, costs of operating, and choosing a consumer panel service.

they had conducted separate studies using samples made up of different individuals. Had two different groups been used to study a change in a particular variable, it would not be clear whether variations in the data were due to changes in the marketing variable or to differences between the two groups.

Although the major advantage of a panel is analytical, it also provides some advantages in the kind of information it yields. Panels are probably a researcher's best format for collecting classification information, such as respondents' incomes, ages, education levels, and occupations. And this information allows a more sophisticated analysis of a study's results.

Cross-sectional studies are limited in this respect, since respondents being contacted for the first and only time are rarely willing to give lengthy, time-consuming interviews. Panel members are usually compensated for their participation, so their interviews can be longer and more exacting, or there can be several interviews. Further, the sponsoring firm can afford to spend more time and effort securing accurate classification information, as this information can be used in a number of studies.

Panel data are also believed to be more accurate than cross-sectional data because panel data tend to be freer from the errors associated with reporting past behavior. Errors arise in reporting past behavior because humans tend to forget, partly because time has elapsed, but partly for other reasons. In particular, research has shown that events and experiences are forgotten more readily if they are inconsistent with attitudes or beliefs that are important to the person or that threaten the person's self-esteem. If, for example, subjects are asked how often they brush their teeth, they might overstate the number of times—either because they genuinely do not remember or because they fear the interviewer will think less of them for brushing too seldom. In a panel, on the other hand, behavior is recorded as it occurs, so less reliance is placed on a respondent's memory. When diaries are used to record purchases, the problems should be virtually eliminated because the respondent is instructed to record the purchases immediately upon returning home. When other behaviors, such as television viewing, are of interest, respondents are asked to record those behaviors as they occur, thus minimizing the possibility they will be forgotten or misremembered.

In one study, for example, 261 mothers were asked to record the kinds of products and services—cereals, toys, fast foods, and so on—their children requested. Each mother was asked to keep three daily diaries: a product-request diary, a product-purchase diary, and a television viewing log. The product-request diary is shown in Table 5.5.

Researchers chose the panel diary method for the study because they deemed it the most accurate. As mentioned earlier errors often occur because respondents say what they think the interviewers want to hear or what they feel will make them look good in the interviewers' eyes. The panel design helps reduce this interaction bias. First, respondents come to trust the interviewer to a greater degree because of repetitive contact. Second, more frequent contact creates rapport.

The main disadvantage of panels is that they are nonrepresentative. The agreement to participate involves a commitment on the part of the designated sample member, and many individuals refuse this commitment. They do not wish to be bothered with testing products, evaluating advertising copy, or filling out consumer diaries. Because these activities require a sizable time commitment, families in which both husband and wife work, for example, may be less well represented than those in which one partner works and the other is at home. Consumer panels that require households to keep a record of their purchases generally have cooperation

Table 5.5 Product Request Diary

Date: / Product Type	1 Products — Brand Name (if child asks for a specific brand)	2 Where were you when your child asked? (check as many as apply)				3 How did your child try to get you to buy it? (check as many as apply)								4 If you said yes to child's request, did you: (check one and skip to column 8)			5 If you didn't say yes to child's request, did you (check one)				6 If you didn't say yes, how did your child react? (check one)				
		At home	On the way to the store	At the store	Other	Just asked, didn't nag about it	Really pleaded with you over and over	Said he/she had seen product on TV	Said brother, sister, or friend has or likes it	Bargained (offered to do chores, pay for part, etc.)	Gave bunch of ways he or she would use product	Just put in shopping basket at store	Other	Didn't mind buying it—said yes right away	Didn't mind buying it, but discussed with child before saying yes	Said yes, but not to the brand the child wanted	Said no, and that was that	Said no and explained why	Said no, but agreed to buy something else instead	Said maybe sometime, but not now	Seemed to take it okay	Disappointed, but didn't say anything more	Argued a little, then let it drop	Argued a lot, kept nagging	Got really angry with you

Source: Leslie Isler, Edward Popper, and Scott Ward, *Children's Purchase Request and Parental Responses: Results from a Diary Study* (Cambridge, Mass.: Marketing Science Institute, 1979), pp. 26–27. Reprinted with permission.

rates of about 60 percent when members are contacted in person and lower participation rates if telephone or mail is used for the initial contact.[9]

The better ongoing panel operations select prospective participants very systematically. They attempt to generate and maintain panels that are representative of the total population of interest with respect to such characteristics as age, occupation, education, and so on. Quite often, to create a representative panel, they will use *quota samples,* in which the proportion of sample members possessing a certain characteristic is approximately the same as the proportion possessing that characteristic in the general population. As a very simplified example of this, consider an organization that wishes to study sports car owners. If the organization knows that of the people owning sports cars, 73 percent are men and 27 percent are women, then it will want its quota sample to reflect that percentage.

All the research organization can do, however, is designate the families or respondents that are to be included in the sample. Researchers cannot force individuals to

---

[9]See Sudman and Ferber, *Consumer Panels.* p. 31. For suggestions on recruiting and maintaining cooperation from panel members, see William H. Motes, "How to Solve Common Problems in Longitudinal Studies," *Marketing News,* 18 (January 6, 1984), p. 3.

Table 5.5   *continued*

7 — If child argued or got angry, how did you respond to the child's reaction? (check as many as apply)					8 — Main reason(s) child asked for this (check as many as apply)						9 — Has child asked for this product before?		10 — If you said yes to #9: When was the last time child asked for it? (check one)							11 — If you said yes to #9: How often does your child ask for this product? (check one)							12 — Has your child asked for this specific brand before? (check one)			13 — If you said yes to #12: How often does your child ask for this specific brand (check one)						
Ignored it	Repeated what you'd said before	Got angry with child	Made some compromise	Decided to buy what child asked for	Saw it in store	Saw TV commercial for it	Brother, sister, or friends have it	Saw other advertising for it (not TV)	Don't know	Other	Yes	No	Yesterday	Earlier this week	Last week	In last 2 weeks	In last month	Over a month ago	Don't know	3–4 times a week	1–2 times a week	Once every couple of weeks	About once a month	Once every few months	Once or twice a year	Don't know	Yes	No, child doesn't prefer any particular brands of this product	No	3–4 times a week	1–2 times a week	Once every couple of weeks	About once a month	Once every few months	Once or twice a year	Don't know

participate, nor can they require continued participation from those who initially agreed to cooperate. True, they often encourage participation by offering some premium or by paying panel members for their cooperation. Nevertheless, a significant percentage of the individuals the organization may have hoped to include often refuse to cooperate—or drop out quickly once the panel has begun. Some individuals are lost to the panel because they move away or die. Depending on the type of cooperation needed, the refusal and *mortality,* or drop-out, rate might run over 50 percent. And, of course, the question then arises as to whether the panel is still representative of the population. Further, the payment of a reward for cooperation raises the question of whether particular types of people are attracted to such panels. It seems, for example, that "panel cooperation appears to be best in households with more than two members, in households having wives in the younger age groups, and in households with more education."[10] Nonrepresentation may not be a problem in every study. Unfortunately, one never knows in advance whether it will occur and how it will affect the results.

---

[10]Sudman and Ferber, *Consumer Panels,* p. 32. Winer demonstrates the biasing effects of attrition on the parameters of models fit to panel data. See Russell S. Winer, "Attrition Bias in Econometric Models Estimated with Panel Data," *Journal of Marketing Research,* 20 (May 1983), pp. 177–186.

Cross-Sectional Analysis Despite the advantages of longitudinal analysis, in actual practice cross-sectional designs are the best known and most important descriptive designs. In cross-sectional analysis, a sample of elements from the population of interest is measured at a single point in time. It may be helpful to think of a cross-sectional study as a snapshot of the situation under investigation and a longitudinal study as a series of pictures that, when pieced together, form a movie of the situation and the changes that are occurring in it.

Just as there are two types of panels, there are two types of cross-sectional studies: **field studies** and **sample surveys.** Although the distinction is not a fine one, there are practical differences between field studies and sample surveys that call for somewhat different techniques and skills. The basic difference is between the greater scope of the survey and the greater depth of the field study. The survey attempts to be representative of some known universe, both in terms of the number of cases included and in the manner of their selection. The field study is less concerned with the generation of large representative samples, and more concerned with the in-depth study of a few typical situations. The emphasis in a survey is on generating summary statistics such as averages and percentages, and on determining the relationship between these summary statistics. The emphasis in a field study is on the interrelationship of a number of factors. The field study is particularly useful when a number of factors bear on a phenomenon and when it is difficult to understand the phenomenon without considering the interrelationships among the factors.

A toy manufacturer, for example, may want to learn about the kinds of toys that four- to six-year-old boys like best as a way to guide future product development. The company may choose to commission a field study in which researchers observe boys of that age playing in a room full of various kinds of toys in a natural environment, such as a nursery school. They may record the kind of toys the children are initially attracted to, the amount of time they spend with a given toy, the ways the children use the toys, and so on. Then they may correlate the children's toy preferences with information about the preferred toys' price and sales history. If the most popular toy is an expensive train set, but research shows the product's sales are relatively small because of its high price, researchers may suggest developing a similar product at a lower price.

Contrast this method with a sample survey approach in which the manufacturer deploys a group of researchers to a variety of toy stores on a Saturday afternoon to interview parents of four- to six-year-old boys about the toys their children have purchased.

The main advantages of field studies over sample surveys are their realism, the strength of their variables, and their ability to guide research.[11] They are realistic because they involve the investigation of phenomena in the natural setting of that phenomena. No attempt is made to manipulate a control variable. Because the variables are allowed to exert their influence in a natural setting, their effects are typically strong. Researchers engaged in field studies must be particularly alert, however, because other factors in the study's natural setting may also act to obscure the effect being studied. An attempt, for example, to clock precisely how long one small boy will play with a set of blocks is disrupted if an older bully repeatedly knocks down the younger one's towers.

Field studies are also particularly useful in providing direction in a study. The intensive study of a few cases often produces a great many additional hypotheses.

---

[11]See Fred N. Kerlinger, *Foundations of Behavioral Research,* 3rd ed. (New York: Holt, Rinehart and Winston, 1986), pp. 373–375, for a general discussion of the advantages and disadvantages of field studies.

• Field study

In-depth investigation of a few cases typical of the target population, emphasizing the interrelationship of a number of factors.

• Sample survey

Cross-sectional study in which the sample is selected to be representative of the target population and in which the emphasis is on the generation of summary statistics such as averages and percentages. Also called a field survey.

Consequently, the investigator must be continually on guard against being diverted from examining the basic hypotheses guiding the descriptive research. As this comment suggests, the field study is often used in exploratory research where the emphasis is on generating, rather than testing, hypotheses. When used for descriptive research, though, there should be a clear specification of the who, what, why, when, where, and how questions, and the investigator must hold steadfast in this regard.

Field studies also have weaknesses. They do not, for example, permit the control possible in field and laboratory experiments. A great many variables always affect the response the researcher seeks to measure, and it is hard to separate their effects. Part of the difficulty lies in the precision with which variables can be measured in a field study. A questionnaire of some sort must often be used.

As mentioned earlier, surveys attempt to be representative of some portion of the population. Therefore, a great deal of emphasis is placed on selecting sample members, and usually a probability sampling plan is used to allow for the calculation of sampling error. The relatively large number of cases usually resulting from a sample survey also allows for cross classification of the variables.

The objective of cross-classification analysis is to establish categories such that classification in one category implies classification in one or more other categories. The method of cross-classification analysis will be detailed later, in the discussion of tabulation. For the moment, simply note that it involves counting the *simultaneous occurrence* of the variables of interest. For example, suppose management feels that occupation is an important factor in determining the consumption of its product. Further, suppose the proposition to be examined is that white-collar workers are more apt to use the product than blue-collar workers. If this hypothesis were ex-

Back to the Case

Don Harris sat next to a bowl of his treasured nuts in a hotel bar in Midtown and listened to some brutal comments about his product.

"Hey, Mike, what's this?" one young, obviously regular patron asked the bartender, pointing to Don's peanuts. "Looks like some kind of dog food."

Harris hunched his shoulders a bit more and stared into the beer he had been nursing for the past hour.

Tony was right. This little marketing research study had already uncovered problems with the product's taste and texture, not to mention the way it looked.

Harris admitted he had been suspicious of the whole project. But he had let Tony talk him into it when Tony had found a small agency that was willing to take on the job for a price that even Don thought was fair. Best of all, the head of the agency had no qualms about letting Don himself get involved in the research process.

Now here he was, in a bar, trying to conduct a survey on how people liked his snack product. The process was illuminating but painful. Some people thought the nuts were some kind of cereal. Many disliked Don's favorite flavor, "Oriental."

As discouraging as some of the findings were, Don was relieved that he was finding them out before rather than after introducing the product.

A survey such as what Don Harris is doing is an example of descriptive research. The patrons of the bar form one element of a broader population—consumers of snack food—that this project is studying. Because this group's responses will be measured only once, not over a long period of time, it is a cross-sectional design.

amined in a cross-sectional study, measurements would be taken from a representative sample of the population with respect to their occupation and use of the product. In cross tabulation, researchers would count the number of cases that fell in each of the following classes:

- White-collar and use the product
- Blue-collar and use the product
- White-collar and do not use the product
- Blue-collar and do not use the product

That is, the emphasis would be on the relative frequency of occurrence of the joint phenomenon, white-collar occupation and user of the product. If the hypothesis is to be supported by the sample data, the proportion of white-collar workers using the product should exceed the proportion of blue-collar workers using the product.

Causal Research Designs

Often exploratory or descriptive research will turn up several cause-and-effect hypotheses that a marketing manager may want to examine. For example, if a price change is planned, a manager may want to test this hypothesis: "A 5 percent increase in the price of the product will have no significant effect on the amount of the product that customers will buy." If the marketing department is considering a change in packaging, planners may first want to test this hypothesis: "A redesign of the cereal package so that it is shorter and less likely to tip over will improve consumer attitudes toward the product."

When the research question can be framed this explicitly, the researcher is dealing with a situation ripe for causal analysis. Descriptive research is fine for testing hypotheses, but it is not as effective as causal designs for testing cause-and-effect relationships. To understand why, one must understand the notion of causality, the types of evidence that establish causality, and the effect of outside variables in a research setting.

Concept of Causality

The concept of causality is complex, and a detailed discussion of it would take us too far afield. However, a few essentials will allow us to properly determine the role of the experiment in establishing the validity of a hypothesis that X causes Y.

In nontechnical language, the statement that one thing (X) is the cause of another thing (Y) suggests that there is a single cause of an event. The scientific notion of causality differs from this commonsense notion in three respects. First, the scientific notion holds that X would only be one of a number of determining conditions rather than the single one. Second, it holds that X does not make the occurrence of Y certain, but just makes it more likely. Finally, the scientific notion holds that we can never prove that X really is a cause of Y, but rather we only *infer* from some observed data (perhaps acquired in a very controlled experimental setting) that such a relationship exists.[12]

The scientific notion recognizes the fallibility of the procedures used to obtain data, or evidence, and for that reason, a causal statement is never demonstrated

---

[12]See Claire Selltiz, Lawrence S. Wrightsman, and Stuart W. Cook, *Research Methods in Social Relations*, rev. ed. (New York: Holt, Rinehart and Winston, 1959), pp. 80–82, for a brief but lucid discussion of the differences between the common-sense and scientific notions of causality. See also David A. Kenny, *Correlation and Causality* (New York: John Wiley, 1979), especially Chapter 1.

conclusively. Three basic kinds of evidence can be used to support scientific inferences: concomitant variation, time order of occurrence of variables, and elimination of other possible causal factors.[13]

Evidence of Causality

One type of evidence for the scientific inference, *"X is a cause of Y,"* is *concomitant variation*—the extent to which a cause, X, and an effect, Y, occur together or vary together in the way predicted by the hypothesis.

Consider the example of a foreign car manufacturer who wanted to test the relationship between the quality of its dealers and the company's market share in an area. The manufacturer's hypothesis is, "The success of our marketing efforts is highly dealer-dependent. Where we have good dealers, we have good market penetration, and where we have poor dealers, we have unsatisfactory market penetration." Now if X is to be considered a cause of Y, we should expect to find the following: In those territories where our good dealers are located, we should have satisfactory market shares, while in those territories where our poor dealers are located, we should have unsatisfactory market shares. However, if we find that in a large number of territories with good dealers we also have unsatisfactory market shares, we must conclude that our hypothesis is faulty.

Perfect evidence of concomitant variation would be provided, of course, if all good dealers were located in territories with satisfactory market shares, and all poor dealers were located in territories with unsatisfactory market shares. The "pure" case will rarely be found in practice, as other causal factors will produce some deviation from a one-to-one relationship between X and Y. Some good dealers, for example, may be located in territories where "Buy American" sentiment is very strong and hence foreign car sales are very low. A poor dealer may have no nearby competition in a territory where foreign cars are popular and thus have an excellent market share despite a reputation for poor service.

Suppose that when we analyzed the relationship between X and Y, we found evidence of concomitant variation. What can we say? All we can say is that *the association makes the hypothesis more likely; it does not prove it.*[14] Similarly, the lack of an association between X and Y cannot be taken as conclusive evidence that there is no causal relationship between them—because we are always inferring, rather than proving, that a causal relationship exists.

We will explore the idea of concomitant variation more closely in a later chapter. For the moment, let us emphasize that concomitant variation is one type of evidence supporting the existence of a causal relationship between X and Y; but its absence does not necessarily negate a relationship between X and Y, nor does its presence guarantee one.

The *time order of occurrence of variables* is another type of evidence of a causal relationship between two variables. This evidence is based on the following simple concept:

One event cannot be considered the "cause" of another if it occurs *after* the other event. The occurrence of a causal factor may precede or may be simultaneous with the

---

[13]*Ibid.,* pp. 83–88.

[14]Chapter 17 will discuss the various conditions that can arise when looking at evidence of concomitant variation. For the moment, we simply wish to emphasize through example that association between X and Y does not mean there is causality between X and Y, and that the absence of such association does not mean there is no causality.

In order to conclude that the display was responsible for any observed increase in sales, the manager of the produce department would need to eliminate other possible reasons for the sales increase such as a change in overall store traffic and the weather.

Source: Courtesy of Sunkist Growers, Inc.

occurrence of an event; by definition, an effect cannot be produced by an event that occurs only after the effect has taken place. However, it is possible for each term in the relationship to be both a "cause" and an "effect" of the other term.[15]

Though conceptually simple, time-order evidence requires the close attention of the researchers. Sometimes it is difficult to establish the time sequence governing a phenomenon. For example, consider the relationship between a firm's annual advertising expenditures and its sales. Marketing managers often attribute a sales increase to an increase in spending on advertising. However, many companies follow a rule of thumb that uses past sales as a guide to allocating resources to advertising. For example, an amount equal to 10 percent of last year's sales may be earmarked for this year's advertising budget. This practice confuses the issue of which event is the cause and which is the effect. Does advertising lead to higher sales or do higher sales lead to an increased ad budget? An intimate understanding of the way the company establishes the ad budget should resolve the dilemma in this situation.

The *elimination of other possible causal factors* is very much like the Sherlock Holmes approach to analysis. Just as Sherlock Holmes holds that if you can eliminate all of the possible suspects but one, the remaining one is guilty, this type of evidence of causality focuses on the elimination of possible explanations other than the one being studied. This may mean physically holding other factors constant, or it may mean adjusting the results to remove the effects of factors that do vary.

Take the situation of the divisional manager of a chain of supermarkets investigating the effects of end-of-aisle displays on orange sales. Suppose that the manager found that per store sales of oranges increased during the past week, and that a number of stores were using end-of-aisle displays for oranges. To conclude that the end displays were indeed the factor responsible for the sales increase, the manager would need to eliminate such other possible variables as price, size of store, and

---

[15]Selltiz *et al., Research Methods,* p. 85.

orange type and quality. This might involve looking at orange sales for stores of approximately the same size, checking to see if prices were the same in stores having an increase in sales and stores with no increase, and checking to determine if the type and quality of oranges were consistent with the previous week's.

A controversy over the 1983 Nielsen television ratings provided an interesting example of eliminating other possible causal factors. During the ratings period under investigation, the Nielsen ratings were so high that many people questioned the numbers. Some felt the dramatic increase in the number of people watching broadcast television had been affected by Nielsen's recent change to a larger sample of households. The Nielsen numbers were especially suspect because a study commissioned by the National Association of Broadcasters during the same period had indicated that people were dissatisfied with the offerings on broadcast television and were spending less time watching it. Were the Nielsen data wrong?

Investigators suggested that there were several other possible explanations for the phenomenon. Among them were (1) an increase in the amount of special-event programming, (2) the weather, (3) economic conditions, (4) a change in the proportion of working women, and (5) a change in the number of pay cable homes. Through systematic investigation of each of these factors, it was discovered that broadcast television viewing was indeed up, and the most likely explanation was the especially foul weather the country experienced in 1983, particularly in the East Central, Pacific, and Northeast states.[16]

Experimentation as Causal Research

Because of the control it affords investigators, an **experiment** can provide more convincing evidence of causal relationships than an exploratory or descriptive design can. For this reason, experiments are often called causal research.

> An experiment is taken to mean a scientific investigation in which an investigator manipulates and controls one or more independent variables and observes the dependent variable or variables for variation concomitant to the manipulation of the independent variables. An *experimental design,* then, is one in which the investigator *manipulates* at least one independent variable.[17]

Because investigators are able to control at least some manipulations of the presumed causal factor, they can be more confident that the relationships discovered are so-called true relationships.

Two types of experiments can be distinguished—the laboratory experiment and the field experiment. Since each has its own advantages and disadvantages, research analysts need to be familiar with both. A **laboratory experiment** is one in which an investigator creates a situation with the desired conditions and then manipulates some variables while controlling others. The investigator is thus able to observe and measure the effect of the manipulation of the variables while the effect of other factors is minimized.

In one laboratory experiment designed to measure the effect of price on the demand for coffee and cola, for example, 135 homemakers in a small town in Illi-

* ### Experiment
Scientific investigation in which an investigator manipulates and controls one or more independent variables and observes the dependent variable for variation concomitant to the manipulation of the independent variables.

* ### Laboratory experiment
Research investigation in which investigators create a situation with exact conditions so as to control some, and manipulate other, variables.

---

[16]Kevin Burns, "TV Viewing Up—Maybe," *Media Message: An Ogilvy & Mather Commentary on Media Issues* (October 1983), pp. 1–7.

[17]Fred N. Kerlinger, *Foundations of Behavioral Research,* p. 293. See also Geoffrey Keppel, *Design and Analysis: A Researcher's Handbook,* 2nd ed. (Englewood Cliffs, N.J.: Prentice-Hall, 1982), especially Chapter 1 for a description of the essential ingredients in experiments.

One objective of both laboratory and field experiments is to discover which choices consumers make among products. Laboratory experiments take place in an artificial setting, created by the investigators. Field experiments take place in a natural setting, although one or more variables may be manipulated there, too.

Source: Courtesy of Marketing Intelligence Service Ltd.

nois were asked to take part in simulated shopping trips.[18] On each of the eight simulated trips, which were conducted in subjects' homes, the homemakers could choose their favorite brands from a full assortment of coffees and colas listed on index cards. The only change on each trip was the products' prices. Each homemaker was free to switch brands to obtain the best product for the money. In this respect, the trial purchase was not unlike an actual purchase. In other respects, however, this trial was unlike conditions in a real supermarket. In the laboratory experiment, the homemakers were free from the distractions of other variables such as packaging, position on the shelf, and in-store promotions.

♦ **Field experiment**

Research study in a realistic situation in which one or more independent variables are manipulated by the experimenter under as carefully controlled conditions as the situation will permit.

A **field experiment** is a research study in a realistic or natural situation, although it, too, involves the manipulation of one or more variables under as carefully controlled conditions as the situation will permit. The laboratory experiment is distinguished from the field experiment, then, primarily in terms of environment, although the distinction is one more of degree than of kind, as both involve some manipulation. The degree of control and precision afforded by each individual field or laboratory experiment varies.[19]

A similar investigation to test the effect of price on the demand for coffee and cola was also conducted in a field experiment. In this case, the experiment was conducted in two small towns in Illinois, ten miles apart. The manipulations here involved actual changes in price for the respective brands.

Four supermarkets were used in all, two from each town. Two units in one town were designated as control stores, where the price of each brand was maintained at its regular level throughout the experiment. In the experimental town, the prices were systematically varied in the two stores during the experiment. Prices were

---

[18]John R. Nevin, "Using Controlled Experiments to Estimate and Analyze Brand Demand," unpublished Ph.D. dissertation, University of Illinois, 1972. See also John R. Nevin, "Laboratory Experiments for Estimating Consumer Demand: A Validation Study," *Journal of Marketing Research,* 11 (August 1974), pp. 261–268. Another area in which laboratory and field experiments have been used to examine the same phenomenon is comparative advertising. See George E. Belch, "An Examination of Comparative and Noncomparative Television Commercials: The Effects of Claim Variation and Repetition on Cognitive Response and Message Acceptance," *Journal of Marketing Research,* 18 (August 1981), pp. 333–349; and William R. Swinyard, "The Interaction Between Comparative Advertising and Copy Claim Variation," *Journal of Marketing Research,* 18 (May 1981), pp. 175–186.

[19]Laboratory and field experiments typically play complementary roles in providing managerially useful marketing information. For a discussion of their respective roles, see Alan G. Sawyer, Parker M. Worthing, and Paul E. Sendak, "The Role of Laboratory Experiments to Test Marketing Strategies," *Journal of Marketing,* 43 (Summer 1979), pp. 60–67.

marked on the package of each brand so as to be clearly visible but not conspicuous. After each price change, a cooling-off period was introduced to offset any surplus accumulated by consumers. The impact of the price change was monitored by recording weekly sales for each brand. This allowed brand market shares for each price condition to be determined. No displays, special containers, or other devices were used to draw consumer attention to the fact that the relative prices of the brands had been altered. All other controllable factors were also held as constant as possible.

Note the distinction between the two studies. In the field experiment, no attempt was made to set up special conditions. The situation was accepted as found, and manipulation of the experimental variable—price—was imposed in this natural environment. The laboratory experiment, on the other hand, was contrived. Subjects were told to behave as if they were actively shopping for the product. The prices of the respective brands were varied for each of these simulated shopping trips.

The results of the two experiments were consistent for one product and inconsistent for the other. The laboratory experiment generated reasonably valid estimates of consumers' reactions to real-world (field experiment) price changes for brands of cola. However, the data for coffee was considered invalid since it tended to overstate the effects of the price changes.

Internal and External Validity of Experiments Certain advantages and disadvantages result from the difference in procedure in laboratory and field experiments. The laboratory experiment typically has the advantage of greater **internal validity** because of the greater control of the variables that it affords. To the extent that we are successful in eliminating the effects of other factors that may obscure or confound the relationships under study, either by physically holding these other factors constant or by allowing for them statistically, we may conclude that the observed effect was due to the manipulation of the experimental variable. That is, we may conclude the experiment is internally valid. Thus, internal validity refers to our ability to attribute the effect that was observed to the experimental variable and not other factors. In the pricing experiment, internal validity focused on the need to obtain data demonstrating that the variation in the criterion variable—brand demanded—was the result of exposure to the experimental variable—relative price of the brand—rather than other factors, such as advertising, display space, store traffic, and so on. These other factors were nonexistent in the simulated shopping trip.

Whereas the laboratory experiment has the advantage in internal validity, the field experiment has the advantage in **external validity,** which focuses on how well the results of the experiment can be generalized to other situations.[20] The artificiality of laboratory experiments limits the extent to which the results can be generalized to other populations and settings.[21] In the simulated shopping trip, no real purchase

• **Internal validity**

One criterion by which an experiment is evaluated; the criterion focuses on obtaining evidence demonstrating that the variation in the criterion variable was the result of exposure to the treatment or experimental variable.

• **External validity**

One criterion by which an experiment is evaluated; the extent, to what populations and settings, to which the observed experimental effect can be generalized.

---

[20]Cook and Campbell distinguish four types of validity: (1) statistical conclusion, (2) internal, (3) construct, and (4) external. Their definitions of internal and external validity parallel ours. Statistical conclusion validity addresses the extent and statistical significance of the covariation that exists in the data; construct validity examines the operations used in the experiment and attempts to assess whether they indeed capture the construct they were supposed to measure. We will have more to say on construct validity in the measurement chapters and statistical conclusion validity in the analysis chapters. Thomas D. Cook and Donald T. Campbell, *Quasi-Experimentation: Design and Analysis Issues for Field Settings* (Chicago: Rand McNally College Publishing Company, 1979), pp. 37–94.

[21]For a general discussion of how the usefulness of experimental results is affected by the researcher's treatment of unmanipulated background factors in the experiment, see John G. Lynch, Jr., "On the External Validity of Experiments in Consumer Research," *Journal of Consumer Research,* 9 (December 1982), pp. 225–244.

took place. Further, we might suppose that the experimenter's calling attention to the price may have caused people to be more price conscious than they would have been in a supermarket. They may have attempted to act more "rationally" than they normally would. Further, those who agreed to participate in the laboratory experiment may not be representative of the larger population of shoppers, either because the location of the study was not typical or because those who willingly participated in such a study may be different in some significant way from those who declined to participate. Such problems would seriously jeopardize the external validity of the findings.

The controls needed for internal validity often conflict with the controls needed for external validity. A control or procedure required to establish internal validity may lessen the value of the results for generalization. The conditions needed to establish external validity may cast doubt on a study's internal validity. Both internal and external validity are matters of degree rather than all-or-nothing propositions.

Role of Experimentation in Marketing Research Experiments in marketing were rare before 1960, but their growth since then has been steady. One of the most significant growth areas has been in market testing, or *test marketing*. Although some writers make a distinction between the terms, the essential feature of the **market test** is that "it is a controlled experiment, done in a limited but carefully selected part of the marketplace, whose aim is to predict the sales or profit consequences, either in absolute or relative terms, of one or more proposed marketing actions."[22] Very often the action in question is the marketing of a new product or an improved version of an old product.

Notwithstanding previous tests of the product concept, the product package, the advertising copy, and so on, the test market is still the final gauge of consumer acceptance of the product. A. C. Nielsen data, for example, indicate that roughly three out of four products that have been test marketed succeed, while four out of five that have not been test marketed fail.[23]

Test marketing is not restricted to testing the sales potential of new products, but has been used to examine the sales effectiveness of almost every element of the marketing mix: for example, to measure the sales effectiveness of a new display, the responsiveness of food sales to supermarket shelf space changes, the impact of a change in retail price on the product's market share, the price elasticity of demand for a product, the effect of different commercials upon sales of a product, the sales effects of two different campaign themes, and the differential effects of price and advertising on demand in addition to their use in determining the sales potential of new products.

Experimentation is not restricted to test marketing. Rather, it can be used whenever the manager has some specific mix alternatives to consider — for example, package design A versus B — and when the researcher can control the conditions sufficiently to allow an adequate test of the alternatives. Experiments are often used, therefore, when testing product or package concepts and advertising copy, although

• Market test
(test marketing)

Controlled experiment, done in a limited but carefully selected sector of the marketplace; its aim is to predict the sales or profit consequences, either in absolute or relative terms, of one or more proposed marketing actions.

---

[22]Alvin R. Achenbaum, "Market Testing: Using the Marketplace as a Laboratory," in Robert Ferber, ed., *Handbook of Marketing Research* (New York: McGraw-Hill, 1974), pp. 4-31 to 4-54. For recent assessments of what is happening in the test market arena, see, "Test Marketing," *Sales and Marketing Management*, 136 (March 1986), pp. 87–117. See also "To Test or Not to Test Seldom the Question," *Advertising Age,* 55 (February 20, 1984), pp. M10–M11.

[23]"Test Marketing: What's in Store," *Sales and Marketing Management,* 128 (March 15, 1982), pp. 57–85.

An important part of marketing research involves experimenting with television commercials and assessing consumers' reactions to the various executions.

Source: Courtesy of Information Resources, Inc.

they have also been used for such things as determining the optimal number of sales calls to be made upon industrial distributors.[24]

An interesting example of the use of experimentation to examine the appeal of a new product while simultaneously fine-tuning the other elements of the marketing mix can be found in the experience of the National Geographic Society in marketing *Journey into China,* a 518-page book with 400 full-color illustrations, which is reported in Research Window 5.1.

Future and Problems of Experimentation Although marketing experiments will probably be used more frequently in the future, particularly when the research problem is one of determining which is the best of an available set of limited marketing alternatives, experimentation is not without its problems. Test marketing, which has been described as a double-edged sword, is a useful vehicle for illustrating these problems. As Larry Gibson, former director of corporate marketing research for General Mills, states: "It costs a mint, tells the competition what you're doing, takes forever, and is not always accurate. . . . For the moment, it's the only game in town."[25] Although Gibson is referring specifically to test marketing, similar problems beset other types of experiments as well. Three of the more critical problems in experimentation in general, and test marketing in particular, are cost, time, and control.

Cost Always a major consideration in test marketing, the cost includes the normal research costs associated with designing the data-collection instruments and the sample, the wages paid to the field staff that collects the data, and a number of other indirect expenses as well. For instance, the test market should reflect the marketing strategy to be employed on the national scale if the results are to be useful. So the test also includes marketing costs for advertising, personal selling, displays, and so on.

---

[24]There are several references that provide useful overviews of the use in marketing of experiments in general and test markets in particular. In addition to the Banks reference previously cited, one should also see David M. Gardner and Russell W. Belk, *A Basic Bibliography on Experimental Design in Marketing* (Chicago: American Marketing Association, 1980).

[25]"To Test or Not to Test Seldom the Question," *Advertising Age,* 55 (February 20, 1984), pp. M10–M11.

Philip Morris test marketed Like, its "99% caffeine-free" cola, in eight cities. Its ad budget for those eight cities, which contain approximately 5 percent of the U.S. population, was $2.3 million. If that level of advertising were done nationally, it would amount to $45 million, which is more than either Pepsi or Coke spends annually. The market test also included coupons, free samples, and other promotions, the cost of which was approximately equal to the ad budget.[26]

With new product introductions, there are also the costs associated with producing the merchandise. To produce the product on a small scale is typically inefficient. Yet to gear up immediately for large-scale production can be tremendously wasteful if the product proves a failure. It usually costs about $3.1 million to take a new product from the research-and-development stage through test marketing in 2 percent of the United States.[27]

[26]"Seven-Up's No-Caffeine Cola," *The Wall Street Journal,* 62 (March 25, 1982), p. 27.

[27]Eleanor Johnson Tracy, "Testing Time for Test Marketing," *Fortune,* 110 (October 29, 1984), pp. 75–76.

Research Window 5.1

Rice Paddies or Pagodas? Test Marketing Helps the National Geographic Society Decide

The National Geographic Society had set aside $1.8 million to use in selling its book, *Journey into China.* The society hoped to sell 380,000 copies of the book, which came with a separate wall map of China, to its members and subscribers.

Rather than spend the entire amount on a mass mailing, the society decided to conduct a test mailing first in order to resolve two questions: the best price for the book and the most appealing cover design for the brochure.

One cover design displayed a photograph of a person carrying two baskets through a deep-green rice paddy, bannered with the caption, "Take a spectacular tour of today's China." The other cover was red with a small color photograph of a pagoda and a waterfall. Its caption read, "Take a family tour of China for only (book's price)."

The brochure was accompanied by a perforated order card and a two-toned (blue and black) photograph of the Forbidden City in Peking. A four-page sales letter on National Geographic Society letterhead used the blue and black ink for alternating paragraphs. A half-page letter from the publisher, folded inside a small map of China, completed the package.

The society was considering three possible prices for the book: $19.95, $22.95, and $24.95. In addition, for the first time it offered buyers the choice of a more expensive deluxe edition for an extra $10.

The version with the photograph of the rice paddy achieved the best response in the test, so it was chosen for the mass mailing. The most profitable price turned out to be $19.95.

The results were stunning. It was the second most successful direct-mail campaign for a single book in the society's history. The original mailing to society members produced sales of more than 410,000 copies (a 4.28 percent response), well above the goal of 380,000. Moreover, 30 percent requested the deluxe edition. Since only 420,000 copies were printed in the first run, two additional press runs of 50,000 were required that year to fill later orders resulting from an insert card sent out with bills and from the society's Christmas catalog.

Source: Courtland L. Bovée and William F. Arens, *Contemporary Advertising,* 2nd ed. (Homewood, IL: Richard D. Irwin, Inc., 1986), p. 468.

Time The time required for an adequate test market can also be substantial. It took Procter & Gamble nine years to go national with Pampers disposable diapers after they were first introduced in Peoria, Illinois.[28] One reason for extending the period of test marketing is that the empirical evidence indicates that their accuracy increases directly with time. According to A. C. Nielsen data, after two months the forecast accuracy is only 1 out of 7, meaning that when test market results were compared to national sales figures, the test market statistics predicted national sales accurately in only 13 percent of the cases. The odds steadily increased, though, to 5 out of 6 after ten months.[29] Consequently, a year is often recommended as a minimum before any kind of "go–no go" decision is made. The year allows researchers to account for possible seasonal variations and to study repeat purchasing behavior. Such lengthy experiments are costly, and they raise additional problems of control and competitive reaction. However, experiments conducted over short periods do not allow for the cumulative impact of marketing actions.[30] These disadvantages must be weighed against one another in each individual situation before deciding on the length of the test marketing period.

Control The problems associated with control manifest themselves in several ways. First, there are the control problems in the experiment itself. What specific test markets will be used? How will product distribution be organized in those markets? Can the firm elicit the necessary cooperation from wholesalers? From retailers? Can the test markets and control cities be matched sufficiently to rule out market characteristics as the primary reason for different sales results? Can the rest of the elements of the marketing strategy be controlled so as not to cause unwanted aberrations in the experimental setting? Too much control can often be as much of a problem as too little. Precisely because the product is being test marketed, it may receive more attention than it would ever receive on a national scale. In the test market, for example, store shelves may be better stocked, the sales force more diligent, and the advertising more prominent than would normally be the case.

One example of this phenomenon is Pringle's potato chips, which were very successful in the test market but bombed nationally. Their failure has often been attributed to a decline in quality that occurred when the product had to be produced in quantities large enough for national distribution.[31]

There are control problems associated with competitive reaction, too. While the firm might be able to coordinate its own marketing activities, and even those of intermediaries in the distribution channel so as not to contaminate the experiment, it can exert little control over its competitors. Competitors can, and do, sabotage

[28]Julie B. Solomon, "P & G Rolls Out New Items at Faster Pace, Turning Away from Long Marketing Testing," *The Wall Street Journal,* 64 (May 11, 1984), p. 25.

[29]"How to Improve Your Chances for Test-Market Success," *Marketing News,* 18 (January 6, 1984), pp. 12–13.

[30]Some work has been done on early prediction of a new product's success, but these efforts still must have a sufficient time frame to allow assessment of repeat purchasing tendencies. See Chakravarthi Narasimhan and Subrata K. Sen, "New Product Models for Test Market Data," *Journal of Marketing,* 47 (Winter 1983), pp. 11–24, for a review of a number of these models. For an empirical comparison of the predictive power of five of them, see Vijay Mahajan, Eitan Muller, and Subhash Sharma, "An Empirical Comparison of Awareness Forecasting Models of New Product Introduction," *Marketing Science,* 3 (Summer 1984), pp. 179–197.

[31]Damon Darden, "Faced With More Competition, P & G Sees New Products as Crucial to Earnings Growth," *The Wall Street Journal,* 63 (September 13, 1983), pp. 37 and 53. For discussion of the general problems of overcontrolling the marketing effort in test markets, see "How to Keep Well-Intentioned Research from Misleading New-Product Planners" and "How to Improve Your Chances for Test-Market Success," *Marketing News,* 18 (January 6, 1984), pp. 1 and 8, and pp. 12 and 13, respectively.

Table 5.6   Examples of Misfires in Test Marketing

1. **Example:** When Campbell Soup first test marketed Prego Spaghetti sauce, Campbell marketers say they noticed a flurry of new Ragu ads and cents-off deals that they feel were designed to induce shoppers to load up on Ragu and to skew Prego's test results. They also claim that Ragu copied Prego when it developed Ragu Homestyle spaghetti sauce, which was thick, red, flecked with oregano and basil, and which Ragu moved into national distribution before Prego.

2. **Example:** P & G claims that competitors stole its patented process for Duncan Hines chocolate chip cookies when they saw how successful the product was in test market.

3. **Example:** A health and beauty aids firm developed a deodorant containing baking soda. A competitor spotted the product in test market, rolled out its own version of the deodorant nationally before the first firm completed its testing, and later successfully sued the product originator for copyright infringement when it launched its deodorant nationally.

4. **Example:** When P & G introduced its Always brand sanitary napkin in test market in Minnesota, Kimberly-Clark Corporation and Johnson & Johnson countered with free products, lots of coupons, and big dealer discounts, which caused Always not to do as well as expected.

5. **Example:** A few years ago, Snell (Booz Allen's design and development division, which does product development work under contract) developed a nonliquid temporary hair coloring that consumers used by inserting a block of solid hair dye into a special comb. "It went to market and it was a bust," the company's Mr. Schoenholz recalls. On hot days when people perspired, any hair dye excessively applied ran down their necks and foreheads. "It just didn't occur to us to look at this under conditions where people perspire," he says.

Source: Example 1: Betty Morris, "New Campbell Entry Sets off a Big Spaghetti Sauce Battle," *The Wall Street Journal,* 62 (December 2, 1982), p. 31; Example 2: Eleanor Johnson Tracy, "Testing Time for Test Marketing," *Fortune* 110 (October 29, 1984), pp. 75–76; Example 3: Kevin Wiggins, "Simulated Test Marketing Winning Acceptance," *Marketing News,* 19 (March 1, 1985), pp. 15 and 19; Example 4: Damon Darden, "Faced with More Competition, P & G Sees New Products as Crucial to Earnings Growth," *The Wall Street Journal,* 63 (September 13, 1983), pp. 37 and 53; Example 5: Roger Recklefs, "Success Comes Hard in the Tricky Business of Creating Products," *The Wall Street Journal,* 58 (August 23, 1978), pp. 1 and 27.

marketing experiments by cutting the prices of their own products, gobbling up quantities of the test marketer's product—thereby creating a state of euphoria and false confidence on the part of the test marketer—and by other devious means. It has been called the most dangerous game in all of marketing because of the great opportunity it affords for misfires, as shown by the examples in Table 5.6.

One could argue that the misfire reflected in the fifth example in Table 5.6 represents one of the fundamental reasons why test markets are desirable. It seems better to find out about product performance problems like this in test market than after a product is introduced nationally. Consider, for example, the losses in company prestige that would have resulted if the following problems had not been discovered in test markets.[32]

1. Because packages would not stack, the scouring pads fell off the shelf.
2. A dog food discolored on the store shelves.
3. In cold weather, baby food separated into a clear liquid and a sludge.
4. In hot weather, cigarettes in a new package dried out.
5. A pet food gave the test animals diarrhea.
6. When a product change in a liquid detergent was combined with a price reduction, consumers thought the product had been diluted with water.

[32]Examples 1–8 are discussed in Jay E. Klompmaker, G. David Hughes, and Russell I. Haley, "Test Marketing in New Product Development," *Harvard Business Review,* 54 (May–June 1976), pp. 135–136, while Example 9 is taken from Lynn G. Reiling, "Consumer Misuse Mars Sampling for Sunlight Dishwashing Liquid," *Marketing News,* 16 (September 3, 1982), pp. 1 and 12.

Back to the Case

Tony Sorrenti, Don Harris, and a representative of the marketing research firm they had hired sat around a table in the makeshift office the fledgling firm had rented. Before them were the results of the studies the market researchers had conducted.

It had been an eye-opening nine months for the new company. Many of Harris's plans for his product had been shown to be inefficient and unworkable, and some were potentially disastrous.

A survey of retailers had helped Harris decide on the best and most cost-efficient means of packaging—stackable bags. This discovery had totally surprised Harris, who had always assumed that vacuum-packed cans were the natural choice.

Pricing—$3.25 for an 8-ounce bag of peanuts, and $4.25 for al-

monds—had been determined by observing consumers on a simulated shopping trip in which the prices of Harris's nuts had been systematically varied in relation to the prices of competitive nuts.

Perhaps the most significant finding, aside from the formulation of the product itself, was the discovery that without extensive advertising and a known brand name, it would be nearly impossible to sell the product in supermarkets. Given the company's precarious financial standing, it seemed wiser to begin selling through specialty food stores, cheese shops, and liquor stores.

"It's been tough trimming my dreams to fit reality," Harris admitted. "But it would have been tougher to see the whole plan go down to defeat."

Don Harris's experience in readying his product for the market shows the many ways marketing research can be used to fine-tune a concept. Harris's firm engaged in both descriptive and causal research studies to answer the new company's questions about the product. The many surveys the firm conducted regarding the product's appearance, taste, size, and flavor, and the design of the package were all examples of descriptive research. The price tests with consumers were an example of causal research. The decision to sell through specialty stores may have been arrived at by studying industry data on competitors' advertising expenditures and distribution arrangements—all exploratory research designs.

7. Because of insufficient glue, over half of the packages came apart during transit.

8. Excessive settling in a box of paper tissues caused the box to be one-third empty at purchase.

9. Sunlight dishwashing liquid was confused with Minute Maid lemon juice by at least 33 adults and 45 children who became ill after drinking it.

Examples 1 through 4 in Table 5.6, however, are of a different sort. By exposing the product to competitors through a test market, each of the firms lost much of its differential development advantage.

The simple point is that the marketing manager contemplating a market test must weigh the costs of such a test against its anticipated benefits. While it may serve as the final yardstick for consumer acceptance of the product, in some cases it may be less effective and more expensive than a carefully controlled laboratory or in-home test.[33]

[33]On the basis of in-depth interviews with thirty-one marketing executives, Klompmaker, Hughes, and Haley, "Test Marketing in New Product Development," offer some specific suggestions regarding when a firm should conduct a test market, what can be learned from such a test, and how information from test markets should be used. See also "How to Improve Your Chances for Test Market Success."

Table 5.7   Most Popular Standard Test Markets

Akron	Dayton	Louisville	Raleigh-Durham
Albany-Schenectady-Troy	Denver	Lubbock, TX	Reading, PA
Albuquerque	Des Moines	Macon, GA	Roanoke-Lynchburg
Ann Arbor	Detroit	Madison	Rochester, NY
Atlanta	Duluth	Manchester, NH	Rockford
Augusta, GA	El Paso	Memphis	Sacramento-Stockton
Austin	Erie, PA	Miami-Fort Lauderdale	Salt Lake City
Bakersfield	Eugene, OR	Milwaukee	St. Louis
Baltimore-Washington, DC	Evansville	Minneapolis-St. Paul	San Antonio
Bangor	Fargo, ND	Mobile	San Diego
Baton-Rouge	Flint	Modesto	San Francisco-Oakland
Beaumont-Port Arthur-Orange, TX	Fort Wayne	Montgomery	Savannah
Binghamton, NY	Fresno	Nashville	Seattle-Tacoma
Birmingham-Anniston	Grand Rapids-Kalamazoo-Battle Creek	New Orleans	Shreveport
Boise	Green Bay, WI	Newport News	South Bend-Elkhart
Boston	Greensboro-Winston-Salem-High Point	New York	Spokane
Buffalo		Oklahoma City	Springfield-Decatur-Champaign, IL
Cedar Rapids-Waterloo	Greenville-Spartanburg-Asheville	Omaha	Syracuse
Charleston, SC	Harrisburg	Orlando-Daytona Beach	Tallahassee
Charleston, WV	Houston	Pensacola	Tampa-St. Petersburg
Charlotte	Huntsville	Peoria	Toledo
Chattanooga	Indianapolis	Philadelphia	Topeka
Chicago	Jacksonville, FL	Phoenix	Tucson
Cincinnati	Kansas City	Pittsburgh	Tulsa
Cleveland	Knoxville	Portland, ME	West Palm Beach
Colorado Springs	Lansing	Portland, OR	Wichita-Hutchinson
Columbus, GA	Las Vegas	Providence	Youngstown
Columbus, OH	Lexington, KY	Quad Cities: Rock Island & Moline, IL, Davenport & Bettendorf, IA (Davenport-Rock Island-Moline metro market)	
Corpus Christi	Little Rock		
Dallas-Fort Worth	Los Angeles		

Source: "Test Marketers on Target," *Sales and Marketing Management*, 134 (March 11, 1985), pp. 110 and 112.

◆ **Standard test market**

A test market in which the company sells the product through its normal distribution channels.

Types of Test Markets Table 5.7 lists in alphabetical order the most commonly used **standard test markets,** markets in which companies sell the product through their normal distribution channels. The results are typically monitored by one of the standard distribution services discussed in the next chapter.

Controlled test market

The entire testing program is conducted by an outside service in a market in which it can guarantee distribution.

Simulated test market

Interviews are conducted to determine consumer ratings of products, then consumers are given the opportunity to purchase the product at a reduced price in a simulated store environment.

An increasingly popular variation of the standard test market is the **controlled test market,** sometimes called the *forced-distribution test market.* In the controlled market, the entire test program is conducted by an outside service. The service pays retailers for shelf space and can therefore guarantee distribution to those stores that represent a predetermined percentage of the marketer's total food store sales volume. A number of research firms operate controlled test markets, including Audits & Surveys' Burgoyne, Inc.; A. C. Nielsen; and Dancer, Fitzgerald, Sample.[34]

Another relatively recent variation in test marketing is the **simulated test market** (STM). STM studies are usually employed prior to a full-scale market test. Typically an STM study begins with consumer interviews, either in shopping malls or occasionally in their homes. During the interview, consumers are shown the new product and asked to rate its features. They are then shown commercials for it and for competitors' products. In a simulated store environment, they are then given the opportunity to buy the product at a reduced price or with cents-off coupons. Those who choose not to purchase the test product are typically given free samples.

After a predetermined use period, researchers conduct follow-up telephone interviews with the participants to assess their reactions to the product and their repeat-purchase intentions.

All the information is fed into a computer model, which has equations for the repeat purchase and market share likely to be achieved by the test model. The key to the simulation is the equations built into the computer model. Studies have indicated that in 80 percent of the cases, STM models can come within 10 percent of predicting actual sales.[35]

A prime advantage of STM studies is the protection from competitors they provide. They are also faster and cheaper than full-scale tests, and they are particularly good for spotting weak products. This allows firms to avoid the expense of full-scale testing of those products likely to fail anyway.

The Achilles heel of STM is that it does not provide any information about the firm's ability to secure retail support for the product, nor does it indicate what competitive reaction is likely to be. Thus, STM is better suited for evaluating product improvements or additional products in an established product line than for examining the likely success of radically different new products.

Summary

Learning Objective 1: Cite three major purposes of descriptive research.

Descriptive research is used when the purpose is (1) to describe the characteristics of certain groups, (2) to estimate the proportion of people in a specified population who behave in a certain way, and (3) to make specific predictions.

Learning Objective 2: List the six specifications of a descriptive study.

Descriptive studies require a clear specification of the answers to who, what, when, where, why, and how in the research.

---

[34]For a full list of the research firms operating controlled test markets and the cities that they use, see "Test Marketers on Target," *Sales and Marketing Management,* 134 (March 11, 1985), pp. 81–116.

[35]"Simulated Test Marketing Winning Acceptance," *Marketing News,* 19 (March 1, 1985), pp. 15 and 19. See also Henry P. Khost, "Pretesting to Avoid Product Postmortems," *Advertising Age,* 53 (February 22, 1982), pp. M10–M11; and "'Magic Town' Doesn't Exist for Test Marketers," *Marketing News,* 19 (March 1, 1985), pp. 5 and 18, for other discussions of the operation, advantages, and disadvantages of STMs.

Learning Objective 3: Explain what a dummy table is.

A dummy table is used to catalog the data collected. It serves as a statement of how the analysis will be structured and conducted. Complete in all respects save for filling in the actual numbers, it contains a title, headings, and specific categories for the variables making up the table.

Learning Objective 4: Discuss the difference between cross-sectional and longitudinal designs.

A cross-sectional design involves researching a sample of elements from the population of interest. Various characteristics of the elements are measured once. Longitudinal studies involve panels of people or other entities whose responses are measured repeatedly over a span of time.

Learning Objective 5: Explain what is meant by a *panel* in marketing research and explain the difference between a traditional panel and an omnibus panel.

A panel is a fixed sample of elements. In a traditional panel, a fixed sample of subjects is measured repeatedly with respect to the same type of information. In an omnibus panel, a sample of elements is still selected and maintained, but the information collected from the members varies with the project.

Learning Objective 6: Explain what is meant by a turnover table, or brand-switching matrix.

A turnover table, or brand-switching matrix, is a two-way table that indicates which brands a sample of people purchased in one period and which brands they purchased in a subsequent period, thus highlighting the switches occurring among brands, as well as the number of persons who purchased the same brand in both periods.

Learning Objective 7: Distinguish between field studies and sample surveys.

The basic difference between field studies and sample surveys is the greater depth of the field study and the greater scope of the sample survey. The survey attempts to be representative of some known universe, both in terms of the number of cases included and in the manner of their selection. The field study is less concerned with the generation of large representative samples and more concerned with the in-depth study of a few typical situations.

Learning Objective 8: Distinguish between the scientific notion of causality and the commonsense notion.

The commonsense notion of causality suggests that there is a single cause of an event. The scientific notion of causality holds that there may be a number of determining conditions that are probable causes for an event, but that said relationship can be only inferred, never proven conclusively.

Learning Objective 9: Define *concomitant variation.*

Concomitant variation is the extent to which a cause and an effect occur together or vary together in the way predicted by the hypothesis.

Learning Objective 10: List three ways of determining a causal relationship.

Three ways of determining a causal relationship are (1) concomitant variation, (2) time order of occurrence of variables, and (3) eliminating other possible sources of explanation.

Learning Objective 11: Clarify the difference between laboratory experiments and field experiments.

The laboratory experiment is distinguished from the field experiment primarily in terms of environment. The analyst creates a setting for a laboratory experiment, while a field experiment is conducted in a natural setting. The distinction is one more of degree than of kind, as both involve control and manipulation of one or more presumed causal factors.

Learning Objective 12: Explain which of the two types of experiments has greater internal validity and which has greater external validity.

The laboratory experiment typically has the advantage of greater internal validity because of the greater control of the variables that it affords. Field experiments are generally considered more externally valid, meaning that their results are better able to be generalized to other situations.

Learning Objective 13: List the three major problems in test marketing.

Three of the more critical problems in experimentation in general, and in test marketing in particular, are cost, time, and control.

Learning Objective 14: Discuss the advantages and disadvantages of simulated test marketing.

Simulated test marketing studies provide the following advantages: (1) they protect a marketer from competitors, (2) they are faster and cheaper than full-scale tests, and (3) they are particularly good for spotting weak products. However, they do have disadvantages in that they cannot provide any information about the firm's ability to secure retail support for a product, nor do they indicate what competitive reaction is likely to be.

Learning Objective 15: Distinguish between a controlled test market and a standard test market.

A standard test market is one in which companies sell the product through their normal distribution channels, and results are typically monitored by a standard distribution service. In a controlled test market, the entire program is conducted by an outside service. The service pays retailers for shelf space and therefore can guarantee distribution to those stores that represent a predetermined percentage of the marketer's total store sales volume.

Discussion Questions, Problems, and Projects

1. The management of a national book club was convinced that the company's market segment consisted of individuals in the 25–35 years age group, while its major competitor's market segment seemed more widely distributed with respect to age. It attributed this difference to the type of magazines in which the competitor advertised. Management decided to do a study to determine the socioeconomic characteristics of the company's market segment. Management formed a panel of 800 heads of households who had previously shown a strong interest in reading. Mail questionnaires would be sent to all the panel members. One month after receiving all the questionnaries, the company would again send similar questionnaires to all the panel members.

   In this situation, is the research design appropriate? If yes, why? If no, why not?

2. Mr. Pennymarch, as the advertising manager for *Chemistry Today* magazine, is charged with the responsibility for selling advertising space in the magazine. The magazine deals primarily with chemical processing technology and is distributed solely by subscription. Major advertisers in the magazine are the producers of chemical processing equipment since the magazine is primarily directed at engineers and other technical people concerned with the design of chemical processing units.

   Since the size and composition of the target audience for *Chemistry Today* are key concerns for prospective advertisers, Mr. Pennymarch is interested in collecting more detailed data on the readership. While he presently has total circulation figures, he feels that these understate the potential exposure of an advertisement in *Chemistry Today*. In particular, he feels that for every subscriber, there are several others in the firm to whom the magazine is routed for their perusal. He wishes to determine how large this secondary audience is and also wishes to develop more detailed data on readers, such as degree of technical training, level in the administrative hierarchy, and so forth.

   (a) Does Mr. Pennymarch have a specific hypothesis? If yes, state the hypothesis.
   (b) What type of research design would you recommend? Justify your answer.

3. The Allure Company, a large manufacturer of women's beauty aids, conducted a study in 1986 in order to assess how its brand of hair dye was faring in the market. Questionnaires were mailed to a panel of 1,260 families. Allure brand of hair dye had three major competitors: Brand A, Brand B, and Brand C. A similar study conducted in 1985 had indicated

the following market shares: Allure 31.75 percent (i.e., 400 families), Brand A 25 percent (315 families), Brand B 32.54 percent (410 families), and Brand C 10.71 percent (135 families). The present study indicated that its market share had not changed during the one-year period, although Brand B had increased its market share to 36.5 percent (460 families). However, this increase could be accounted for by a decrease in Brand A's and Brand C's market shares. (Brand A now had a market share of 22.23 percent, or 280 families; Brand C now had a market share of 9.52 percent, or 120 families). The management of Allure Company decided it had little to worry about.

The study of 1986 also revealed some additional facts. Over the one-year period 70 families from Brand A and 30 families from Brand C had switched to Allure. Five families from Brand B and 30 families from Brand C had switched to Brand A, while none of Allure users had switched to Brand A. These facts further reassured management. Finally, 45 families switched from Brand B to Brand C, but none of the families using Allure or Brand A had switched to Brand C. Brand C's loyalty was estimated to be .556.

(a) Do you think that management of Allure Company was accurate in analyzing the situation? Justify your answer.
(b) You are called upon to do some analysis. From the data given above construct the brand-switching matrix. (Hint: Begin by filling in the row and column totals.)
(c) Indicate what this matrix reveals for each of the brands over the one-year period.
(d) Complete the following table and compute the brand loyalties.

	At Time t_1				
	Bought Allure	**Bought A**	**Bought B**	**Bought C**	**Total**
At Time t_0: Bought Allure					
Bought A					
Bought B					
Bought C					

(e) What can be said about the degree of brand loyalty for each of the four products?

4. The Nutri Company was a medium-sized manufacturer of highly nutritional food products. The products were marketed as diet foods with high nutritional content. Recently, the company was considering marketing these products as snack foods but was concerned about its present customers' reaction to the change in the products' images. The company decided to assess customers' reaction by conducting a study using one of the established consumer panels.

What type of panel would you recommend in this situation? Why?

5. The American Diabetic Association wanted to determine the socioeconomic and demographic characteristics of the adult population that supported the association. The association decided to conduct a study using cross-sectional analysis.

In this situation would you recommend a field study or a sample survey? Why?

6. Super Savers is a chain of department stores located in large towns and metropolitan centers in the northeast United States. In order to improve its understanding of the market, management decided to develop a profile of the so-called average customer. You are requested to design the study.
(a) What kind of research design would you select? Justify your choice.
(b) List at least ten relevant variables.
(c) Specify at least four hypotheses. (Note: A hypothesis is a conjecture as to how two or more variables are related. You should indicate the direction of the suggested relationship and how each of the variables would be measured.)
(d) Construct dummy tables using four of the variables that were specified in part b.

7. Consider the following statement: "The increase in sales is due to the new sales personnel that we recruited from the vocational school over the last several years. Sales of the new

salespeople are up substantially while sales for longer-term salespeople have not increased."

Identify the causal factor X and the effect factor Y in the above statement.

8. The research department of the company in Question 7 investigated the change in sales for each of the company's salespeople. Using criteria supplied by management, the department categorized all territory sales changes as increased substantially, increased marginally, or no increase. Consider the following table, in which 260 sales personnel have been classified as old or new:

Salesperson Assigned	Territory Sales Change			
	Increased Substantially	Increased Marginally	No Increase	Total
New	75	30	5	110
Old	50	40	60	150

(a) Does this table provide evidence of concomitant variation? Justify your answer.
(b) What conclusions can be drawn about the relationship between X and Y on the basis of the preceding table?

9. Six months later, the research department in Question 8 investigated the situation once again. However, a new variable was considered in the analysis, namely, the type of territory to which the salesperson was assigned; more specifically, whether the salesperson was assigned to an essentially urban metropolitan or nonmetropolitan territory. The following table summarizes the research department's findings:

Salesperson Assigned	Metropolitan Territory			
		Territory Sales Change		
	Increased Substantially	Increased Marginally	No Increase	Total
New	70	20	—	90
Old	54	16	—	70

Salesperson Assigned	Nonmetropolitan Territory			
		Territory Sales Change		
	Increased Substantially	Increased Marginally	No Increase	Total
New	5	10	5	20
Old	20	40	20	80

(a) If the type of territory to which the salesperson was assigned is ignored, does this table provide evidence of concomitant variation between change in sales and whether the salespeople are new or old? Justify your answer.
(b) If type of territory is considered, does the table provide evidence of concomitant variation between sales changes and whether the salespeople are new or old? Justify your answer.

Suggested Additional Readings

For a review of the structure, purposes, and useful approaches on descriptive designs, see
Claire Selltiz, Lawrence S. Wrightsman, and Stuart W. Cook, *Research Methods in Social Relations,* 3rd ed. (New York: Holt, Rinehart, and Winston, 1976).

For a discussion of the criteria of good hypotheses and the value of hypotheses in guiding research, see
Fred N. Kerlinger, *Foundations of Behavioral Research,* 3rd ed. (New York: Holt, Rinehart, and Winston, 1986).

For a discussion of the operation of consumer panels, see

Seymour Sudman and Robert Ferber, *Consumer Panels* (Chicago: American Marketing Association, 1979).

While for a discussion of methods for analyzing panel data, see

Gregory B. Markus, *Analyzing Panel Data* (Beverly Hills, Calif.; Sage Publications, 1979).

For general discussions regarding the design of experiments, see

Thomas D. Cook and Donald T. Campbell, *Quasi-Experimentation: Design and Analysis Issues for Field Settings* (Chicago: Rand McNally College Publishing Company, 1979).

Geoffrey Keppel, *Design and Analysis: A Researcher's Handbook,* 2nd ed. (Englewood Cliffs, N.J.: Prentice-Hall, 1982).

For a bibliography of marketing experiments, see

David M. Gardner and Russell W. Belk, *A Basic Bibliography on Experimental Design on Marketing* (Chicago: American Marketing Association, 1980).

Part Two   Research Project

The second stage in the research process is to determine the research design. As we have seen in Chapters 4 and 5, the design may take one of three forms, depending on the objective of the research. In these chapters we discussed the three basic types of research: exploratory, descriptive, and causal.

You will recall that the major emphasis in exploratory research is on the discovery of ideas and insights. A descriptive study is typically concerned with determining the frequency with which something occurs or the relationship between two variables, and it is generally guided by an initial hypothesis. A causal research design is concerned with determining cause-and-effect relationships.

Researchers for the Centerville Area Radio Association (CARA) decided to begin their study by conducting some exploratory research. This research consisted primarily of two types: (1) a literature review; and (2) experience surveys.

They began the literature review by reading articles dealing with the positive and negative perceptions held by users of television, radio, and newspaper advertising. This secondary information was found in marketing research studies, general articles, and reference works dealing with the three major advertising media.

They found "The Radio Marketing Consultants Guide to Media" published by the Radio Advertising Bureau to be a particularly helpful source. This source provided extensive coverage of the advantages and problems associated with each of the three major media.

They supplemented what they had found in the literature review with an experience survey. They began by interviewing various people who had specialized knowledge and experience with these media and then used their input to develop a revised list of advantages and problems associated with each.

Next, they discussed each of the media attribute items on the list with a group of CARA advertising sales representatives in order to obtain their input. Although the sales reps' feedback and suggestions were valued highly and weighed heavily, researchers also recognized that the group's opinions were not free of bias. Consequently, the final list of attribute items included in the study were determined by the researchers alone.

The resulting criteria decided upon were then discussed with three local retail businesses. This was done in order to determine the relevancy of each of the items and to make any appropriate additions, corrections, or deletions. In these interviews, it was obvious that individuals were going to have strong opinions and biases about the effectiveness of one medium versus another. However, there was virtually total agreement that the criteria chosen would be sufficient and broad enough in scope to assess the three media and respective sales representatives accurately.

The information gleaned from the literature review and experience survey were then used to develop the various hypotheses that would guide further research. A complete list of these hypotheses was given at the end of Part One.

Among them were the hypotheses that there would be differences in business-peoples' attitudes toward television, radio, and newspaper, and that differences would also exist in attitudes towards sales representatives of each of the media.

As we pointed out in Chapter 2, the stages in the research process should not be viewed as discrete entities, but rather as elements in a continuous process. Information uncovered at one stage in the process is often used to refine decisions made earlier in the study. The information researchers for CARA discovered in the course of their exploratory research may well have been used to formulate the research problem more clearly.

In this case, once the hypotheses were formed, the decision was made to test them by examining the perceptions of a cross section of retailers.

Given the hypotheses, if you were one of the researchers for CARA,

- What kinds of information would you attempt to secure from retailers?
- How would you go about selecting retailers to contact?

Cases to Part Two

Case 2.1 Nostalgia, Inc.[1]

The Nostalgia Company was founded on March 23, 1950, in Corpus Christi, Texas, by Douglas J. Kennedy. The company, which employs 35 full-time workers, manufactures and sells one basic product, a datebook calendar. These calendars are distinguished by their large 5- by 8-inch size, one week of days to the page, and a picturesque scene on the facing page of each week. In addition, the calendar has a space for each day that provides considerable room for recording appointments and other important events. The calendar has consistently been one of the least expensive in its competitive market.

Industry Background

The calendar printing industry is by nature one of the most difficult to analyze. The industry comprises hundreds of companies both large and small, some dealing primarily with calendar printing but most doing it only as a sideline. For this reason there is very little published data on the calendar industry per se, except for a few trade statistics from the advertising specialty and printing industries.

The calendar business generates over $250 million in sales each year. It is divided into three main categories: custom-produced, stock, and calendars for retail sales to customers. The first two categories are sometimes combined under the heading of advertising specialty calendars. These calendars are made up on special order for firms that wish to use them as promotional items to customers. Most of the calendars produced for this part of the industry are done by printing firms; however, there are nonprinting firms that have set up in-house print shops.

In the calendar printing for retail sales side of the industry, of which Nostalgia is part, the leading manufacturer is Hallmark Cards, Inc., of Kansas City, Missouri. Hallmark offers a number of different styles of calendars ranging from the traditional wall type to posters, address books, diaries, desk models, and towels. In the retail part of the industry 50 percent of the sales occur in November and December, with these months representing 20 percent and 30 percent of the total annual sales, respectively. It is estimated that 90 percent of all customers for this part of the industry are women, and that most calendars are priced between $6.95 and $8.95.[2]

The major types of calendars are art or wall calendars, which come in 12, 6, or 4 sheets per calendar; year-at-a-glance calendars, which are a one-sheet calendar; pin-up calendars, which have twelve or six sheets; commercial calendars, which have one illustration with a calendar pad attached; desk calendars or calendar pads; diary calendars; and one-a-day calendars, which consist of a stack of sheets with one date per page. The Nostalgia calendar is considered a desk calendar.[3]

Company Background

Doug Kennedy began his business in 1950 after five moderately successful years as a commercial photographer. Mr. Kennedy believed that if he put his pictures together in a calendar, it would serve two major purposes. First, it would bring in additional revenues, which he needed to purchase more photography equipment. Second, it would increase the sales of the pictures printed in the calendar.

As it turned out, the calendar business became much more lucrative than he had imagined, and in

[1]The contributions of Larry Foy to the development of this case are gratefully acknowledged.

[2]Supplied through the courtesy of Specialty Advertising Association, Chicago, Illinois. See also Marcia Newlands Fero, "Calendars—The Essential Sideline," *Publishers Weekly* (April 22, 1983), p. 45.

[3]For a description of the calendars available from each of 125 publishers and the prices for each, see "Calendars 1985," *Publishers Weekly* (April 27, 1984), pp. 32–64.

Table 1   Nostalgia Calendar Sales Data

Calendar	No. Printed	Calendar Printing Cost	Unit Cost (cents)	Total Income	Gross Profit	Total Sold	Total Refunds
1975	226,982	221,288.28	195.36	415,615.74	194,327.46	226,026	17,280
1976	221,498	226,365.48	208.35	401,894.70	175,529.22	221,120	25,266
1977	261,682	286,356.00	219.72	453,781.98	167,425.98	259,902	33,732
1978	305,880	320,419.74	204.84	480,674.04	160,254.30	256,902	46,302
1979	285,800	314,126.70	221.46	503,784.06	189,657.36	278,140	NOT ALLOWED
1980	288,400	411,607.86	286.95	577,861.56	166,253.70	244,366	NOT ALLOWED
1981	254,530	358,936.50	286.92	554,561.52	195,625.02	242,470	NOT ALLOWED
1982	256,430	364,771.44	285.18	566,691.18	201,919.74	197,660	23,094
1983	209,202	316,435.86	302.61	534,322.08	217,886.22	190,246	43,032
1984	188,500	352,105.92	373.47	593,130.66	241,024.74	162,124	6,822

Table 2   Nostalgia Calendar Group Sales

Segments	Total Calendars Sold				
	1980	1981	1982	1983	1984
Individuals (over 12 copies)	14,396	13,106	11,868	10,244	7,206
Schools & libraries	39,426	42,208	24,954	27,508	8,846
Church groups	8,566	10,550	6,374	6,008	3,798
General organizations	34,980	33,078	23,938	14,282	15,130
Institutions	7,082	8,456	7,956	7,352	8,076
Professional	8,022	8,568	6,420	5,290	5,808
Manufacturing	2,180	3,020	2,968	1,808	1,890
Complimentary	1,810	2,276	3,874	3,164	3,428
Information desk	1,380	1,602	1,480	970	1,016
Staff	594	752	492	640	688
Retailers	55,744	55,092	47,776	57,076	49,782
Imprinters	57,334	48,990	45,990	45,410	38,500
Individuals (under 12 copies)	12,852	12,530	11,434	10,494	9,236

1958 he dropped the sale of individual photographs completely and concentrated all his efforts on the datebook calendar. Calendar sales data for the recent ten-year period of 1975–1984 are presented in Table 1.

Nostalgia sells its calendar to a number of seg-ments of the market, as indicated in Table 2. These segments are contacted through two primary chan-nels of distribution: direct orders from consumers, and direct orders from retailers and resellers. To reach these segments Nostalgia does a small amount of advertising. Retailers are mailed a flyer three times

Table 3 Nostalgia Price Increases and Discount Structures

			Discount Structures			
Price Increases		**Retail**		**Resale**		
Year	**Retail Price**	**Quantity**	**Discount**	**Quantity**	**Discount**
1979	$3.00				
1980	$3.00	48–96	35%	12–49	25%
1981	$3.75	97–144	40%	50–150	30%
1982	$3.75	145–288	45%	151–250	35%
1983	$4.50	289–432	45%	251–500	40%
1984	$6.00	433–616	47%	501–999	45%
1985	$7.50	617 +	50%	1,000 +	50%

a year, and all other segments are mailed a flyer once a year, in May. In addition, each calendar contains a blank for ordering more copies of the current year's calendar, and/or a copy of the following year's calendar. Table 3 traces the rate of retail price increases for the period of 1979–1984 and includes the discount schedules at retail and resale for the calendars.

As an added feature for retailers, Nostalgia allows all customers who order directly to return unsold calendars by February 15 of the calendar year. This is done in the hope that retailers will be induced to order larger amounts. The retailer pays the postage for returns. The cost to mail calendars through the U.S. Postal Service for this period was 72 cents each.

The Problem

As J. M. Evans, marketing manager for Nostalgia, reviewed the sales results from 1984, he was well aware

of the problem the company faced. Calendar sales had reached a peak of 278,140 in 1979 but had declined steadily every year thereafter (see Table 1). Evans had originally believed it to be a temporary decline due to general economic conditions, but with a sales drop of 28,000 calendars for 1984, this decline had placed the company in a very weak position.

Evans began to ponder the possible sources of the problem. He was due in Kennedy's office at the end of the week with a full report of the company's dilemma.

Questions

1. What kind of research is in order to solve Mr. Evans's problem? Why?
2. Describe the procedure you would follow in determining the reason for the sales decrease. Be specific.

Case 2.2 Bonita Baking Company (B)[1]

As sales manager at Bonita Baking Company, Frank Fortunada, Jr., has elected to undertake a research project concerned with Bonita Health Breads. Bonita Health is a line of specialty breads competing with

[1]Source: From: *Cases in Marketing Research* by William G. Zikmund, William J. Lundstrom, and Donald Sciglimpaglia, pp. 61–64. Copyright © 1982 by CBS College Publishing. Reprinted by permission of Holt, Rinehart and Winston, Inc.

national brands (such as Roman Meal and Pepperidge Farms) and regional brands (such as Orowheat—the market leader). Although the specialty bread segment was rapidly growing, the Bonita Health line has not been performing well. Most specialty brands (including Bonita) are actively promoted through television, radio and newspaper advertising, coupons, and special price promotions.

Fortunada decided to undertake a research study to help him determine the source of the problem underlying the Bonita Health line's poor sales results. He was interested in ascertaining Bonita's relative position and image in the specialty bread market. Fortunada also needed to know more about the consumer profile of specialty bread users and how to reach them most effectively.

Fortunada solicited and received three separate proposals for the research study.

Proposal One—Consumer Research Analysts

The proposal from Consumer Research Analysts (CRA) suggested doing a two-stage mail survey to better understand the behavior of the specialty bread market. CRA had a reputation for doing sophisticated research for a number of consumer product areas. The proposal itself had been prepared by an associate of the firm who had recently completed an M.B.A. degree with an emphasis in consumer behavior. Excerpts from the proposal are shown below.

Statement of the Problem

Studies examining the process of adoption of products support the fact that consumers follow a general procedure that involves a series of stages:

1. **Awareness.** Before a person can consider purchase, the first requirement is that he or she be aware of the product's existence.

2. **Interest.** Often the level of interest is dictated by the need the consumer feels he or she has for a product. At other times, the mere awareness of the product stimulates interest.

3. **Evaluation.** At this stage the consumer will determine whether or not the product should be considered for purchase.

4. **Trial.** In most cases the consumer will try the product—if possible—and form attitudes and further evaluations based on this trial.

5. **Reevaluation.** Attitudes toward the product are formed based on the trial.

6. **Adoption.** At this stage the consumer continues to use the product on a continuous basis or abandons it in search of another.

The problem to be studied here includes the determination of how many consumers (or potential consumers) currently are at each stage of the process, why they are there, and how they might be moved toward adoption of Bonita Health Breads.

Objectives

To determine the above, the following objectives will be sought:

1. Determination of levels of awareness of the product;

2. Determination of attributes considered important in purchasing Bonita Health (or competitive lines);

3. Determination of number of individuals trying Bonita Health and evaluation of the same;

4. Analysis of those attributes considered as important in evaluating Bonita Health Bread (or competitive lines).

In addition, demographic and media-viewing characteristics of the users and nonusers will be provided.

Method

Preliminary evaluation of existing data will constitute the initial phase of the research. This procedure will utilize any existing sources of information that may provide insight into the problem.

The second phase will involve a two-step mail survey of consumers. The initial sample will consist of approximately 4,000 households selected from a city directory. The first survey will be used to identify the market profile for specialty breads and for Bonita Health specifically. A second (follow-up) survey questionnaire will be sent to those households identified in the first survey as Bonita Health and other specialty brand consumers. Its purpose will be to assess the objectives noted above.

Results

The results of the research presented will include a report covering:

1. levels of awareness of Bonita Health, attitudes toward the same, and attributes considered salient in the determination of these attitudes;

2. positioning of Bonita Health relative to the competition and relative strengths and weaknesses; and

3. demographic and media-viewing characteristics of users and nonusers.

A copy of the computer output generated will be included.

Costs

The total cost of this project would be $8,000.

Proposal Two — Lancaster Associates

Another proposal was received from James Lancaster, a local management and marketing consultant. Lancaster's proposal was in the form of the following letter to Fortunada in which he suggested using focus groups to research the problem.

Dear Frank,
   Thank you for allowing me to propose my research approach for the Bonita Health study.
   I think that we need to really do an in-depth study of consumer awareness, attitudes, and behavior regarding specialty breads in general and Bonita Health specifically. In this way we can get an understanding of the reasons behind the consumer purchase or nonpurchase of your product. I strongly feel that the way to do this is by using a series of focus group studies.
   I propose to conduct four focus groups of roughly twelve specialty bread buyers each. The consumers would be recruited by phone to meet certain criteria. The panelist screening criteria include:
1. Total household income — $20,000 plus
2. Female head of household who is the principal shopper
3. Fourteen (14) plus years of education
4. Specialty bread users of the following breads:
   a. Bonita Health
   b. Orowheat
   c. Northridge
   d. Fresh Horizons
   e. Pepperidge Farms
   f. Millbrook
   g. Roman Meal
   h. Specialty store brands

   I will personally conduct the focus groups and provide a written summary report of the findings. The total cost, including recruiting and participant incentives, is $4,000.

Sincerely,
James Lancaster
Lancaster Associates

Proposal Three — Action Research

The third proposal came from Action Research. Dale Dash, the person that Fortunada spoke to on the phone, suggested that the most fruitful course of action would be to conduct what he termed an experience survey. He suggested that his firm would telephone roughly 20 bread department managers or store managers to determine their feelings about specialty breads and the Bonita line. In addition, Dash proposed that baking industry people in other parts of the country could be interviewed to get an understanding of what other regional marketers were doing to promote and market their brands of specialty breads. Dash thought that about ten baking industry marketing persons should be interviewed.
   Dash told Fortunada that the total cost of the project would be between $1,500 and $3,000, although he could not say for sure. He indicated that he would be glad to give Fortunada a written proposal if he wished.

Questions

1. What are the strengths and weaknesses of each suggested approach?
2. Which (if any) proposal should Fortunada accept?
3. Write a short proposal that indicates how you would research this problem. You may want to refer to Part A of the Bonita Baking Company case for more information about the problem.

Case 2.3 Rumstad Decorating Centers (A)

In 1929 Joseph Rumstad opened a small paint and wallpaper supply store in downtown Rockford, Illinois. For the next 45 years the store enjoyed consistent, though not spectacular, success. Sales and profits increased steadily but slowly as, in order to keep pace with the competition, the original line of prod-

ucts was expanded to include unpainted furniture, mirrors, picture framing material, and other products. In 1974, due to a declining neighborhood environment, Jack Rumstad, who had taken over management of the store from his father in 1970, decided to close the downtown store and to open a new outlet

Table 1   Profit and Loss Statement for Rumstad Decorating Centers

	East Side Store		West Side Store	
	1985	1984	1985	1984
Total Sales	$114,461	$91,034	$87,703	$108,497
Cash sale discounts	4,347	2,971	4,165	2,930
Net sales	110,114	88,063	83,538	105,567
Beginning inventory	53,369	49,768	1,936	0
Purchases	64,654	56,528	163,740	59,366
Total	118,023	106,206	165,676	59,366
Ending inventory	51,955	53,369	115,554	1,936
Cost of sales	66,068	52,837	50,122	57,430
Gross profit or loss	44,046	35,226	33,416	48,137
Direct Costs				
Salaries	24,068	19,836	24,549	26,583
Payroll taxes	2,025	1,814	1,764	2,060
Depreciation—furniture and fixtures	92	92	92	92
Freight	6	43	511	800
Store supplies	694	828	607	4,153
Accounting and legal expenses	439	433	439	433
Advertising	2,977	4,890	4,820	5,252
Advertising—yellow pages	1,007	618	1,387	956
Convention and seminar expenses	0	33	83	216
Insurance	226	139	1,271	1,643
Office expense and supplies	4,466	4,393	5,327	5,010
Personal property tax	139	139	140	140
Rent	7,000	7,000	4,900	4,900
Utilities	2,246	1,651	2,746	2,359
Total direct costs	45,385	41,909	48,636	54,597
Profit or loss	(1,339)	(6,683)	(15,220)	(6,460)

on the far west side of the city. The west side was chosen because it was experiencing a boom in new home construction. In 1983 a second store was opened on the east side of the city and the name of the business was changed to Rumstad Decorating Centers. The east side store was staffed with sales clerks but was basically managed by Jack Rumstad himself from the west side location. All ordering, billing, inventory control, and even the physical storage of excess inventory was concentrated at the west side store.

In 1984, the east side store was made an independent profit center. Jack Rumstad personally took over the management of the outlet and hired a full-time manager for the west side store. With the change in accounting procedures occasioned by this organizational change, it became possible to examine the profitability of each outlet separately.

Jack Rumstad conducted such an examination early in 1986, using the profit and loss figures in Table 1, and became very concerned with what he discovered. Both stores had suffered losses for 1985, and, while he had anticipated incurring a loss during the first couple of years of operation of the east side store, he was not at all prepared for a second successive loss at the west side outlet. He blamed the 1984 loss on the disruptions caused by the change in organizational structure. Further, from 1984 to 1985, the east side had a 25 percent increase in net sales, a 25 percent increase in gross profits, an 8 percent increase in total direct costs, and although the east side store still showed a net loss, it was 80 percent less than the previous year's loss. The west side store, on the other hand, had shown a 21 percent decrease in net sales, a 31 percent decrease in gross profit, an 11 percent decrease in direct costs, and a 136 percent increase in net loss. Mr. Rumstad is very concerned about the survival of the business and particularly concerned with what is happening to the west side store. He has called you in as a research consultant to help him pinpoint what is happening so that he might take corrective action.

West Side Store

The west side store is located in the heart of the census tract with the highest per capita income in the city. Most of the residents in the area are professional people or white-collar workers. The store is a freestanding unit located on a frontage road with the word "Rumstad" printed across the front. Since Jack Rumstad's transfer to the east side store, there has been a succession of managers at the west side store.

The first one lasted six months, the second and third four months, while the current manager, previously a sales clerk at the store for four years, has held the job for ten months. While the products carried and the prices charged are the same in both stores, there is some difference in advertising emphasis. The west side store does all of its advertising in the *Shopper's World,* a weekly paper devoted exclusively to advertising, which is distributed free to all households in the community. Delivery is by and large door-to-door, although it is quite typical for a group of newspapers to be placed at the entrance to apartment buildings and for residents to pick up a copy if they so choose.

East Side Store

The east side store is located in a predominantly blue-collar area. Most of the residents in the immediate vicinity work for one of the various machine tool manufacturers that comprise one of the basic industries in Rockford. The store is located in a small shopping center. It has a large window display area with a readily visible "Rumstad Decorating Center" sign above the store. The east side store advertises periodically in the *Rockford Morning Star* in addition to its yellow pages advertising.

Question

1. How would you proceed to answer Mr. Rumstad's problem?

Case 2.4   Gibbons College Library[1]

The library staff of Gibbons College in Iowa has been deeply committed to serving the needs of the college's undergraduate student body. The library offers its students an attractive atmosphere in which to conduct individual or group study and provides numerous workshops and seminars designed to improve student study, writing, and test-taking skills. Of special significance has been the administration's commitment to meeting the information needs of library

patrons. For example, during the past academic year the library received some 70,000 requests for information and reference referral, and it had more than 169,000 library items checked out to registered students.

Because of the diversity in student backgrounds, meeting patron information demands is a very difficult and challenging activity. The facilities and installations must be specific enough to serve individual student needs, yet targeted to reach as large an audience as possible. Careful staff consideration must be continually given, therefore, to the establishment of new library policies and procedures.

[1]The contributions of David M. Szymanski to the development of this case are gratefully acknowledged.

Recently, the library staff contemplated the installation of a computer data base of bibliographic references to replace the manual methods of searching indexes and abstracts for information on research topics. The need for a computer search facility at the library had become especially acute in the last several years because of the following reasons:

- Library users had become more sophisticated in their awareness of the potential resources available to them.
- Library users and staff had become increasingly cognizant of the use and application of computers in educational and library settings.
- Library staff had become aware of the ways in which reference questions and search strategy problems could be solved through on-line data bases.

By having computer search facilities available, students could—for a relatively small fee that was based on the amount of computer time used and the length of the computer printout—quickly access information and coordinate research activities.

Since well over 150 bibliographic data bases are on the market, the library staff decided to conduct a study that would provide information directly related to decisions on choosing a computer data base searching service. First, the staff wanted to learn more about who currently uses the library and to what extent, what are the characteristics of people using the library, and what differences exist between heavy and low-level users of library facilities. Second, the staff wanted to focus on preferred features of a data base searching service. For example, how large is the potential user population for the service, and what characteristics of the service will best meet the needs of an undergraduate student body?

Sampling Procedure

To obtain information necessary for making an informed judgment on the best data base to install, the library staff conducted a survey of library patrons. The population was defined as all undergraduate users of the college's library.

Because a list of known sampling units was not available, a nonprobability convenience sample was used for the study. The staff decided to draw the sample from individual users of the library during one particular day. A sample of 300 subjects was projected as being necessary (1) to be representative of the user population and (2) for cross-tabulation analysis. Because a convenience sample is dependent on volunteer returns, it was recommended that researchers secure an adequate response by sampling morning, afternoon, and evening library patrons. A questionnaire (see Figure 1) was therefore distributed to stu-

Figure 1   Gibbons College Library Survey

The College Library needs information from you in order to improve library service. We would appreciate it if you could answer the following questions and place the completed survey in the questionnaire return box (located at all exits) when you leave the library.

1. *What one thing do you like most about the College Library?*

2. *What one thing do you like least about the College Library?*

3. *Approximately how many times per week have you used the College Library this semester?*

_____ this is my first visit to the College Library

_____ less than once a week

_____ once a week

_____ 2–4 times a week

_____ 5 or more times a week

continued

Figure 1   *continued*

4. ***For what purpose do you most often use the College Library?***

_____ to study

_____ to do homework (nonresearch-work homework)

_____ to do research work

_____ other: please specify _____

5. ***Have you used the* Reader's Guide to Periodical Literature, The Magazine Index, Business Periodicals Index, *or any other index to find magazine and journal articles this semester?***

_____ yes   _____ no

If yes, how often during the current school year have you used such indexes?

_____ 1–2 times   _____ 3–4 times   _____ 5 or more times

6. ***A computer data base searching service finds references to magazine and journal articles as in a printed index but retrieves them from an on-line computer data base. Have you ever used such a service before?***

_____ yes   _____ no

If yes, how often have you used such a service before?

_____ 1–2 times   _____ 3–4 times   _____ 5 or more times

If yes, did you find these indexes:

_____ very easy to use   _____ difficult to use

_____ easy to use   _____ very difficult to use

7. ***If a computer data base service was available at the College Library, would you use it?***

_____ yes   _____ no   _____ don't know

If yes, how often would you anticipate having a need for such a service?

_____ 1–2 times a year   _____ 3–4 times a year

_____ 5 or more times a year

8. ***When using a computer data base service, the user must pay the library a fee based on the amount of computer time used and the length of the computer printout. How important would the cost of the service be in your decision to use a computer data base?***

_____ not at all important

_____ somewhat unimportant

_____ neither important nor unimportant

_____ somewhat important

_____ very important

9. ***One of the advantages of a computer data base is that it can provide many bibliographic references in a short period of time. How important is this factor in your decision to use a computer data base?***

_____ not at all important   _____ somewhat important

_____ somewhat unimportant   _____ very important

_____ neither important nor unimportant

continued

Figure 1 *continued*

---

10. *Of the many types of data bases available to library users, which would you find most useful (check all relevant categories)?*

    _____ psychological abstracts

    _____ business & economic abstracts

    _____ science abstracts

    _____ engineering abstracts

    _____ health-related indexes

    _____ general periodical indexes

    _____ Other: please specify _____

11. *What is your current class standing?*

    _____ freshman   _____ junior

    _____ sophomore   _____ senior

    _____ special student

    _____ other: please specify _____

12. *What is your declared or intended major area of study?*

    _____ agriculture and life sciences

    _____ allied health fields

    _____ business

    _____ education

    _____ engineering

    _____ family resources

    _____ letters & sciences

    _____ nursing

    _____ other: please specify _____

13. *What is your sex:*

    _____ male   _____ female

---

dents entering the building during three periods: 9 to 11 a.m., 2 to 4 p.m., and 7 to 9 p.m. A large sign was posted informing patrons about the survey, and a questionnaire return box was placed near the library exits to facilitate survey returns.

The number of questionnaires distributed and returned for each period is listed in Table 1. Question- naires lacking responses to major questions and questionnaires appearing to be carelessly done (for example, all "4's" being checked) were eliminated from the analysis. For the final tabulations, 100 arbitrarily chosen responses from each of the three surveyed time frames were used, making the total number of subjects included in the analysis 300.

Table 1 Questionnaires Distributed and Returned During Each of the Time Periods Surveyed

Time Period	Questionnaires Distributed	Questionnaires Returned	Response Rate
7–9 a.m.	855	317	.37
2–4 p.m.	600	217	.36
7–9 p.m.	790	237	.30
TOTAL	2,245	771	.34

Questions

1. Using the research objectives as guidelines, construct dummy tables that can be used to help analyze the results obtained from the questionnaire.

2. Critique the research design. Will the research study as presented here lead to an "ideal" marketing research study of users' needs for a computer data base? Why or why not?

Case 2.5 Chestnut Ridge Country Club[1]

The Chestnut Ridge Country Club has long maintained a distinguished reputation as one of the outstanding country clubs in the Elma, Tennessee, area. The club's golf facilities are said by some to be the finest in the state, and its dining and banquet facilities are highly regarded as well. This reputation is due in part to the commitment by the board of directors of Chestnut Ridge to offer the finest facilities of any club in the area. For example, several negative comments by club members regarding the dining facilities prompted the board to survey members to get their feelings and perceptions of the dining facilities and food offerings at the club. Based upon the survey findings, the board of directors established a quality control committee to oversee the dining room and a new club manager was hired.

Recently, the board became concerned with the number of people seeking membership to Chestnut Ridge. Although no records are kept on the number of membership applications received each year, the board sensed that this figure was declining. They also believed that membership applications at the three competing country clubs in the area—namely, Alden, Chalet, and Lancaster—were not experiencing similar declines. Because Chestnut Ridge had other facilities, such as tennis courts and a pool, that were comparable to the facilities at these other clubs, the board was perplexed as to why membership applications would be falling at Chestnut Ridge.

To gain insight into the matter, the board of directors hired an outside research firm to conduct a study of the country clubs in Elma, Tennessee. The goals of the research were (1) to outline areas where Chestnut Ridge fared poorly in relation to other clubs in the area, (2) to determine people's overall perception of Chestnut Ridge, and (3) to provide recommendations for ways to increase membership applications at the club.

Research Method

The researchers met with the board of directors and key personnel at Chestnut Ridge to gain a better understanding of the goals of the research and the types of services and facilities offered at a country club. A literature search of published research relating to country clubs uncovered no studies. Based solely upon their contact with individuals at Chestnut Ridge,

[1]The contributions of David M. Szymanski to the development of this case are gratefully acknowledged.

Table 1   Average Overall Ratings of Each Club by Club Membership of the Respondent

| | Club Membership | | | Composite Ratings Across |
Club Rated	Alden	Chalet	Lancaster	All Members
Alden	4.57	3.64	3.34	3.85
Chalet	2.87	3.63	2.67	3.07
Chestnut Ridge	4.40	4.44	4.20	4.35
Lancaster	3.60	3.91	4.36	3.95

Table 2   Average Ratings of the Respective Country Clubs Across Dimensions

| | | | Country Club | |
Dimension	Alden	Chalet	Chestnut Ridge	Lancaster
Club landscape	6.28	4.65	6.48	5.97
Clubhouse facilities	5.37	4.67	6.03	5.51
Locker room facilities	4.99	4.79	5.36	4.14
Club management	5.38	4.35	5.00	5.23
Dining room atmosphere	5.91	4.10	5.66	5.48
Food prices	5.42	4.78	4.46	4.79
Food quality	a	4.12	5.48	4.79
Golf course maintenance	6.17	5.01	6.43	5.89
Golf course challenge	5.14	5.01	a	4.77
Condition of tennis courts	b	5.10	4.52	5.08
Number of tennis courts	b	4.14	4.00	3.89
Swimming pool	b	b	4.66	5.35
Membership rates	4.49	3.97	5.00	4.91

[a]Question not asked.
[b]Not applicable.

therefore, the research team developed a survey. Because personal information regarding demographics and attitudes would be asked of those contacted, the researchers decided to use a mail questionnaire.

The researchers thought it would be useful to survey members from Alden, Chalet, and Lancaster country clubs in addition to those from Chestnut Ridge for two reasons. One, members of these other clubs would be knowledgeable regarding the levels and types of services and facilities desired from a country club, and, two, they had at one time represented potential members of Chestnut Ridge. Hence, their perceptions of Chestnut Ridge might reveal why they chose to belong to a different country club.

No public documents were available that contained a listing of each club's members. Consequently, the researchers decided to contact each of the clubs personally to try to obtain a mailing list. Identifying themselves as an independent research firm conducting a study on country clubs in the Elma area, the researchers first spoke to the chairman of the board at Alden Country Club. The researchers told the chairman they could not reveal the organization sponsoring the study but that the results of their

Table 3   Attitudes Toward Chestnut Ridge by Members of the Other Country Clubs

Dimension	Alden	Chalet	Lancaster
Club landscape	6.54	6.54	6.36
Clubhouse facilities	6.08	6.03	5.98
Locker room facilities	5.66	5.35	5.07
Club management	4.97	5.15	4.78
Dining room atmosphere	5.86	5.70	5.41
Food prices	4.26	4.48	4.63
Food quality	5.52	5.75	5.18
Golf course maintenance	6.47	6.59	6.22
Condition of tennis courts	4.55	4.46	4.55
Number of tennis courts	4.00	4.02	3.98
Swimming pool	5.08	4.69	4.26
Membership rates	5.09	5.64	4.24

study would not be made public. The chairman was not willing to provide the researchers with the mailing list. The chairman cited an obligation to respect the privacy of the club's members as the primary reason for turning down the research team's request.

The researchers then made the following proposal to the board chairman: in return for the mailing list, the researchers would provide the chairman a report on Alden members' perceptions of Alden Country Club. In addition, the mailing list would be destroyed as soon as the surveys were sent. The proposal seemed to please the chairman, for he agreed to give the researchers a listing of the members and their addresses in return for the report. The researchers told the chairman they must check with their sponsoring organization for approval of this arrangement.

The research team made similar proposals to the chairmen of the board of directors of both the Chalet and Lancaster country clubs. In return for a mailing list of the club's members, they promised each chairman a report outlining their members' perceptions of their clubs, contingent upon their securing approval from their sponsoring organization. Both agreed to supply the requested list of members.

The researchers subsequently met with the Chestnut Ridge board of directors. In their meeting, the researchers outlined the situation and asked for the board's approval to provide each of the clubs with a report in return for the mailing lists. The researchers emphasized that the report would contain no infor-

mation regarding Chestnut Ridge nor information by which each of the other clubs could compare itself to any of the other clubs in the area, in contrast to the information to be provided to the Chestnut Ridge board of directors. The report would only contain a small portion of the overall study's results. After carefully considering the research team's arguments, the board of directors agreed to the proposal.

Membership Surveys

A review of the lists subsequently provided by each club showed Alden had 114 members, Chalet had 98 members, and Lancaster had 132 members. The researchers believed that 69 to 70 responses from each membership group would be adequate. Anticipating a 70 to 75 percent response rate because of the unusually high involvement and familiarity of each group with the subject matter, the research team decided to mail 85 to 90 surveys to each group, and a simple random sample of members was chosen from each list. In all, 87 members from each country club were mailed a questionnaire (348 surveys in total). Sixty-three usable surveys were returned from each group (252 in total), for a response rate of 72 percent.

Summary results of the survey are presented in Tables 1 through 3. Table 1 gives people's overall ratings of the country clubs, while Table 2 shows people's ratings of the various clubs on an array of dimensions. Table 3 is a breakdown of attitudes toward Chestnut Ridge by the three different membership groups, Alden, Chalet, and Lancaster. The data are average ratings of respondents. Table 1 scores are based upon a five-point scale, where 1 is poor and 5 is excellent. Tables 2 and 3 are based upon seven-point scales where 1 is an extremely negative rating and 7 an extremely positive rating.

Questions

1. What kind of research design is being used? Is it a good choice?

2. Do you think it was ethical for the researchers not to disclose the identity of the sponsoring organization? Do you think it was ethical for the board of directors to release the names of their members in return for a report that analyzes their members' perceptions toward their own club?

3. Overall, how does Chestnut Ridge compare to the three country clubs: Alden, Chalet, and Lancaster?

4. In what areas might Chestnut Ridge consider improvements to attract additional members?

Part Three   Data-Collection Methods

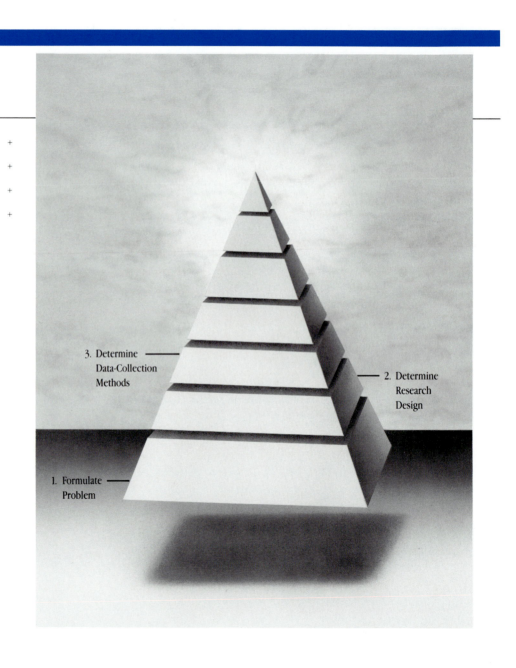

3. Determine
Data-Collection
Methods

2. Determine
Research
Design

1. Formulate
Problem

Part Three covers the third stage in the research process, determination of the methods used to collect data. Chapter 6 focuses on secondary data as an information resource. Chapter 7 compares the two methods marketing researchers have available for collecting marketing data—communication and observation. Chapter 8 then discusses the main alternatives if communication methods are used, and Chapter 9 explains the alternatives if observation methods are used.

Chapter 6   Secondary Data

Learning Objectives

Upon completing this chapter, you should be able to

1. Explain the difference between primary and secondary data.
2. Cite the two primary advantages offered by secondary data.
3. Specify two problems common to secondary data.
4. List the three criteria researchers should use in judging the accuracy of secondary data.
5. State the most fundamental rule in using secondary data.
6. Explain the difference between internal and external data.
7. List some of the key sources researchers should consider in conducting a search process.
8. Specify the primary drawback researchers face in using data from a standardized marketing information service.

Case in Marketing Research

It was still six months before next year's budget projections were due, but Mike Sebastian, vice-president of marketing at Diversified Foods, had already begun burning the midnight oil trying to come up with a figure that he could sell to top management. Previous years' advertising and promotional budgets had been well in excess of $50 million, most of which had traditionally been used to advertise the company's products in women's magazines, in the "food" pages of major newspapers, and on television programs with a high proportion of viewers who were homemakers.

In recent years Sebastian had begun using a substantial percentage of the budget for promotional devices: cents-off coupons, refunds with proof-of-purchase, free recipe books with proof-of-purchase, and cooperative advertising, whereby Diversified Foods would help pay for a store's large newspaper advertisement if it included a small ad for a Diversified Foods' product.

Sebastian liked the promotional strategy and thought that, in general, response had been very positive. But upper management was uneasy about the program since no attempt had yet been made to measure the promotions' effectiveness.

Sebastian knew that this year he would have to fight to maintain his department's current level of funding. The company had recently spent a fortune fighting off a particularly nasty takeover bid, and word had gone out that all budgets were going to be subjected to the closest scrutiny.

Sebastian decided to call in Bob Markson, the corporate marketing research manager, to help him build a case for the budget.

"Bob, I need your help," Sebastian said. "As you know, we've been running a variety of promotions to consumers and to the trade. Consumer promotions are designed to get our current users to buy even more, to get people who use competing brands to switch to ours, and to get nonusers of our products to try them. The point of our trade-oriented promotions, such as our cooperative advertising deals and special discounts, is to get retailers to give us better display space, to carry sizes or items they hadn't stocked previously, or to get stores who weren't our customers to start carrying our line.

"I think the promotions have been very effective, but I need concrete data to convince upper management. Can you help?" Sebastian asked.

"That's a tall order, Mike," Markson said, "but I'll put some of my best people on it and we'll see what we can do."

Discussion Issues

1. What kinds of data might Bob Markson consult to answer Sebastian's questions?

2. Would it be necessary to undertake primary research to find out what he needs to know?

3. Which do you think it might be easier to investigate — consumer responses or trade? Why?

Once the research problem is defined and clearly specified, the research effort logically turns to data collection. The natural temptation among beginning researchers is to advocate some sort of survey among appropriate respondent groups. This should be a last rather than a first resort. "A good operating rule is to consider a survey akin to surgery—to be used only after other possibilities have been exhausted."[1] First attempts at data collection should logically focus on **secondary data,** which are statistics not gathered for the immediate study at hand but previously gathered for some other purpose. Information originated by the researcher for the purpose of the investigation at hand is called **primary data.** The purpose therefore defines the distinction.

If General Electric Company conducted a survey on the demographic characteristics of refrigerator purchasers to determine who buys the various sizes of refrigerators, this would be primary data. If, instead, the company used its existing files and compiled the same data from warranty cards its customers had returned, or if it used already published industry statistics on refrigerator buyers, the information would be considered secondary data.

Beginning researchers are apt to underestimate the amount of secondary data available. Table 6.1, for example, lists some of the information on people and households that has already been collected by the U.S. Government Census and is readily available for use by researchers. It is important for researchers to know what is available in secondary sources, not just to avoid "reinventing the wheel," but because secondary data possess some significant advantages over primary data. Further, because of the recent "information explosion," such an oversight will have even greater consequences in the future.

◆ Advantages of Secondary Data

The most significant advantages of secondary data are the time and money they save the researcher. If the information being sought is available as secondary data, the researcher need simply go to the library, locate the appropriate source or sources, and extract and record the information desired. This should take no more than a few days and involve little cost. If instead the information were to be collected in a sample survey, the following steps would have to be taken: data-collection form designed and pretested; field interviewing staff selected and trained; sampling plan devised; data gathered and then checked for accuracy and omissions; data coded and tabulated. As a conservative estimate, this process would take two to three months and could cost several thousand dollars since it would include expenses and wages for a number of additional field and office personnel. For fledgling businesses, cost savings are especially critical. Not only is secondary data useful as a way of conducting a preliminary assessment of the marketplace, but as Walter Kearns, director of Arthur D. Little Enterprises, so delicately put it, " 'Entrepreneur' generally translates as 'poor.' "[2] If you're launching the next Apple Computer Corporation in your garage, secondary data may be the only data you can afford!

With secondary data, the expenses incurred in collecting the data have already been paid by the original compiler of the information. Even if there is a charge for using the data (unlike statistics compiled by government or trade associations, commercial data are not free), the cost is still substantially less than if the firm collected the information itself.

◆ **Secondary data**
Information not gathered for the immediate study at hand but for some other purpose.

◆ **Primary data**
Information collected specifically for the purpose of the investigation at hand.

---

[1]Robert Ferber and P. J. Verdoorn, *Research Methods in Economics and Business* (New York: Macmillan, 1962), p. 208.

[2]Joanne Kelleher, "Getting to Know Your Market," *Venture,* 35 (May 1983), pp. 70–74.

Table 6.1   Information Items Available from the 1980 Census of Population

Population	Housing
Items collected at every household ("complete-count items")	
Household relationship[a]	Number of units at address
Sex	Complete plumbing facilities[a]
Race	Number of rooms
Age	Tenure (whether the unit is owned or rented)
Marital status	Condominium identification[a]
Spanish/Hispanic origin or descent[a]	Value of home (for owner-occupied units and condominiums)
	Rent (for renter-occupied units)
	Vacant for rent, for sale, and so forth; and period of vacancy
Additional items collected at sample households[c]	
School enrollment	Type of unit
Educational attainment	Stories in building and presence of elevator
State or foreign country of birth	Year built
Citizenship and year of immigration	Year moved into this house[a]
Current language and English proficiency[b]	Acreage and crop sales
Ancestry[b]	Source of water
Place of residence 5 years ago	Sewage disposal
Activity 5 years ago	Heating equipment
Veteran status and period of service	Fuels used for house heating, water heating, and cooking
Presence of disability or handicap	Costs of utilities and fuels[a]
Children ever born	Complete kitchen facilities
Marital history	Number of bedrooms
Employment status last week	Number of bathrooms
Hours worked last week	Telephone
Place of work	Air-conditioning
Travel time to work[b]	Number of automobiles
Means of transportation to work[a]	Number of light trucks and vans[b]
Persons in carpool[b]	Homeowner shelter costs for mortgage, real-estate taxes, and hazard insurance[b]
Year last worked	
Industry	
Occupation	
Class of worker	
Work in 1979 and weeks looking for work in 1979[b]	
Amount of income by source[a] and total income in 1979	
Derived variables (illustrative examples)	
Families	Persons per room ("crowding")
Family type and size	Household size
Poverty status	Plumbing facilities
Population density	Institutions and other group quarters
Size of place	Gross rent
	Farm residence

[a]Changed relative to 1970.

[b]New items.

[c]For most areas of the country in 1980, one out of every six housing units or households received the sample form. Areas estimated to contain 2,500 or fewer persons in 1980 had a 3-out-of-every-6 sampling rate, which is required in order to obtain reliable statistics needed for participation in certain federal programs.

Source: Charles P. Kaplan and Thomas L. VanValey, *Census '80: Continuing the Factfinder Tradition* (Washington, D.C.: U.S. Bureau of the Census, 1980), p. 173.

Table 6.2   Use of Secondary Data by a Manufacturer of Pet Foods to Assess the Potential Demand for a Dog Food That Included Both Moist Chunks and Hard, Dry Chunks

The question was, "Is there currently a significant number of persons who mix moist or canned dog food with dry dog food?" At this early stage in the exploration of this product concept, the firm did not want to expend funds for primary research. While an actual survey of pet owners would have yielded the best answer, such a survey would have required the expenditure of several thousand dollars. In addition, further development of the idea would have required a delay of several weeks to obtain the survey results. An effort to develop an acceptable first answer to the question of demand using secondary sources was initiated.

The firm identified the following information:

1. From published literature on veterinary medicine, the firm identified the amount (in ounces) of food required to feed a dog each day by type of food (dry, semimoist, moist), age, size, and type of dog.

2. From an existing survey conducted annually by the firm's advertising agency, the firm obtained information on
   a. the percentage of U.S. households owning dogs;
   b. the number, sizes, and types of dogs owned by each household in the survey;
   c. the type(s) of dog food fed to the dogs; and
   d. the frequency of use of various types of dog food.

It was assumed that dog owners who reported feeding their dogs two or more different types of dog food each day were good prospects for a product that provided premixed moist and dry food. Combining the information in the survey with the information from the literature on veterinary medicine and doing some simple multiplication produced a demand figure for the product concept. The demand exceeded 20 percent of the total volume of dog food sales, a figure sufficiently large to justify proceeding with product development and testing.

Source: David W. Stewart, *Secondary Research: Information Sources and Methods* (Beverly Hills, Calif.: Sage Publications, 1984), p. 112. Reprinted by permission of Sage Publications, Inc.

Given the substantial amount of time and money at stake, we offer the advice: *Do not bypass secondary data.* Begin with secondary data, and only when the secondary data are exhausted or show diminishing returns, proceed to primary data. Sometimes the secondary data are sufficient, especially when all the analyst needs is a ballpark estimate, which is often the case. For example, a common question that confronts marketing research analysts is, what is the market potential for the product or service? Are there enough people or organizations interested in it to justify providing it?

Entrepreneur George Campos, for example, thought there might be enough of a market to start a darkroom rental business. To validate his instinct, he bought a copy of *The Wolfman Report,* a national survey of the photographic industry, for $75. He also consulted local market surveys published by various photography magazines. By the time he was ready to approach potential financial backers for his business, Campos had amassed a convincing body of research to support his idea. Campos now has two photography centers in operation, and a third in the works.[3]

Table 6.2 illustrates how secondary data were used to advantage by a manufacturer of pet foods to assess the potential demand for a dog food that included both moist chunks and hard, dry chunks. As the example indicates, when using secondary data it is often necessary to make some assumptions in order to use the data effectively (e.g., the number of owners who were good prospects). The key is to make reasonable assumptions and then to vary these assumptions to determine how sensitive a particular conclusion is to variations in them. In the dog food example, "altering the

---

[3]*Ibid.*

assumption regarding the number of owners who were good prospects for the new product to include as few as one-tenth of the original number did not alter the decision to proceed with the product. Under such circumstances, the value of additional information would be quite small."[4]

While it is rare that secondary data completely solve the particular problem under study, they usually will (1) help the investigator to better state the problem under investigation, (2) suggest improved methods or further data that should be collected, and/or (3) provide comparative data by which primary data can be more insightfully interpreted.

◆ Disadvantages of Secondary Data

Two problems that commonly arise with secondary data are (1) they do not completely fit the problem, and (2) they are not totally accurate.

Problems of Fit

Since secondary data are collected for other purposes, it is rare when they fit the problem as defined perfectly. In some cases, the fit will be so poor as to render them completely inappropriate. Usually the problem is unsuitable (1) units of measurement, (2) class definitions, or (3) publication currency.

The size of a retail store, for instance, can be expressed in terms of gross sales, profits, square feet, and number of employees. Consumer income can be expressed by individual, family, households, and spending unit. So it is with many variables, and a recurring source of frustration in using secondary data is that the source containing the basic information desired presents that information in units of measurement different from that needed.

Assuming the units are consistent, we find that the class boundaries presented are often different from those needed. If the problem demands income by individual in increments of $5,000 (0–$4,999, $5,000–$9,999, and so on), it does the researcher little good if the data source offers income by individual using boundaries $7,500 apart (0–$7,499, $7,500–$14,999, and so on).

Finally, secondary data are often out of date. The time from data collection to data publication may be long. Government census data, for example, take three years to get into print. Although census data have great value while current, this value diminishes rapidly with time. Most marketing decisions require current, rather than historical, information.

Problems of Accuracy

The accuracy of much secondary data is also questionable. As this book should indicate, there are a number of sources of error possible in the collection, analysis, and presentation of marketing information. When a researcher is collecting primary data, firsthand experience helps in judging the accuracy of the information being collected and even aspects that might be in error. But when using secondary data,

---

[4]David W. Stewart, *Secondary Research: Information Sources and Methods* (Beverly Hills, Calif.: Sage Publications, 1984), p. 113. See also *Measuring Markets: A Guide to the Use of Federal and State Statistical Data* (Washington, D.C., U.S. Department of Commerce, 1979) for discussion of the marketing-related information that is available from the federal and state governments and how that information can be used for such marketing tasks as market potential estimation, establishing sales quotas, allocating advertising budgets, locating retail outlets, and so on.

the researcher's task in assessing accuracy is more difficult.[5] It may help in this task to consider the primacy of the source, the purpose of publication, and the general quality of the data-collection methods and presentation.[6]

Primacy of Source Consider the source first. Secondary data can be secured from either a primary source or a secondary source. A **primary source** is the source that originated the data. A **secondary source** is a source that in turn secured the data from an original source. The *Statistical Abstract of the United States,* for example, which is published each year and contains a great deal of useful information for many research projects, is a secondary source of secondary data. All of its data are taken from other government and trade sources. The researcher who terminated a search for secondary data with the *Statistical Abstract* would violate the most fundamental rule in using secondary data—*always use the primary source of secondary data.*

There are two main reasons for this rule. First and foremost, the researcher will need to search for general evidence of quality (e.g., the methods of data collection and analysis). The primary source will typically be the only source that describes the process of collection and analysis, and thus it is the only source by which this judgment can be made. Second, a primary source is usually more accurate and complete than a secondary source. Secondary sources often fail "to reproduce significant footnotes, or textual comments, by which the primary source had qualified the data or the definition of units."[7] Errors in transcription can also occur in copying the data from a primary source. Once made, transcription errors seem to hold on tenaciously, as the following example illustrates.

In 1901 Napoleon Lajoie produced the highest batting average ever attained in the American League when he batted .422 on 229 hits in 543 times at bat. In setting the type for the record book after that season, a printer correctly reported Lajoie's .422 average, but incorrectly reported his hits, giving him 220 instead of 229. A short time later, someone pointed out that 220 hits in 543 at bats yields a batting average of .405, and so Lajoie's reported average was changed. The error persisted for some fifty years until an energetic fan checked all the old box scores and discovered the facts.[8]

Purpose of Publication A second criterion by which the accuracy of secondary data can be assessed is by the purpose of publication.

> Sources published to promote sales, to advance the interests of an industrial or commercial or other group, to present the cause of a political party, or to carry on any sort of propaganda, are suspect. Data published anonymously, or by an organization which is on the defensive, or under conditions which suggest a controversy, or in a form which reveals a strained attempt at "frankness," or to controvert inferences from other data, are generally suspect.[9]

• Primary source
Originating source of secondary data.

• Secondary source
Source of secondary data that did not originate the data but rather secured them from another source.

[5]Jacob has a particularly helpful discussion on the various errors that are present in published data and what remedies are available to the analyst for treating these errors. See Herbert Jacob, *Using Published Data: Errors and Remedies* (Beverly Hills, Calif.: Sage Publications, 1984).

[6]For an alternative list of criteria, see Stewart, *Secondary Research,* pp. 23–33.

[7]Erwin Esser Nemmers and John H. Myers, *Business Research: Text and Cases* (New York: McGraw-Hill, 1966), p. 38.

[8]*The Chicago Tribune,* September 19, 1960. If there had not been a cult of "baseball superfans whose passion is to dig up obscure facts about the erstwhile national pastime," the error might never have been discovered. See "You May Not Care But 'Nappie' Lajoie Batted .422 in 1901," *The Wall Street Journal,* 54 (September 13, 1974), p. 1.

[9]Nemmers and Myers, *Business Reseach,* p. 43.

This is not to say that such data cannot be used by the researcher, but only that they should be viewed most critically. A source that has no ax to grind but, rather, publishes secondary data as its primary function deserves confidence. If a source's business is to publish data, high quality must be maintained. Such a firm would gain no competitive advantage by publishing inaccurate data. Indeed, the success of any organization whose primary function is to supply data depends on its reputation for accuracy and its customers' satisfaction to ensure that it stays in business.

General Evidence of Quality The third criterion by which the accuracy of secondary data can be assessed is through the general evidences of quality. One way of determining this quality is to evaluate the ability of the supplying organization to collect the data. The Internal Revenue Service, for example, has greater leverage in securing income data than an independent marketing research firm. However, researchers also have to weigh whether this additional leverage may introduce bias. Would a respondent be more likely to hedge in estimating his income in completing his tax return or in responding to a consumer survey?

   In judging the quality of secondary data, a user also needs to understand how the data were collected. A primary source should provide a detailed description of the data-collection process, including definitions, data-collection forms, method of sampling, and so forth. If it does not, researcher beware! Such omissions are usually indicative of sloppy methods.

   When the details of data collection are provided, the user of secondary data should examine them thoroughly. Was the sampling plan sound? Was this type of data best collected through questionnaire or by observational methods? What about the quality of the field force? What kind of training was provided? What kinds of checks of the fieldwork were employed? What was the extent of nonresponse, due to refusals, not at home, and by item? Are these statistics reported? Is the information presented in a well-organized manner? Are the tables properly labeled, and are the data within them internally consistent? Are the conclusions supported by the data? As these questions suggest, the user of secondary data must be familiar with the research process and the potential sources of error. The remainder of this book should provide much of the needed insight for evaluating secondary data. For the moment, though, let us examine some of the main types of secondary data.

◆ Types of Secondary Data: Internal and External

The most common way of classifying data is by source, whether internal or external. **Internal data** are those found within the organization for whom the research is being done, while **external data** are those obtained from outside sources. The external sources can be further split into those that regularly publish statistics and make them available to the user at no charge (e.g., the United States government), and those commercial organizations that sell their services to various users (e.g., A. C. Nielsen Company). In the remainder of this chapter, we will review some of the more important sources of commercialized statistics, while Appendix 6A treats some of the main sources of published statistics. Together they represent some of the most commonly used sources of secondary data, the ones with which the researcher would typically begin a search.

   Internal data that were collected for some purpose other than the study at hand are *internal secondary data*. For example, the sales and cost data compiled in the normal accounting cycle represent promising internal secondary data for many research problems—such as evaluation of past marketing strategy or assessment of the firm's competitive position in the industry. Such data are less helpful in guiding

◆ **Internal data**

Data that originate within the organization for which the research is being done.

◆ **External data**

Data that originate outside the organization for which the research is being done.

Table 6.3 How to Get Started When Searching Published Sources of Secondary Data

Step 1: Identify what you wish to know and what you already know about your topic. This may include relevant facts, names of researchers or organizations associated with the topic, key papers and other publications with which you are already familiar, and any other information you may have.

Step 2: Develop a list of key terms and names. These terms and names will provide access to secondary sources. Unless you already have a very specific topic of interest, keep this initial list long and quite general.

Step 3: Now you are ready to use the library. Begin your search with several of the directories and guides listed in Appendix 6A. If you know of a particularly relevant paper or author, start with the *Social Science Citation Index* (or *Science Citation Index*) and try to identify papers by the same author, or papers citing the author or work. At this stage it is probably not worthwhile to attempt an exhaustive search. Only look at the previous two or three years of work in the area, using three or four general guides. Some directories and indices use a specialized list of key terms or descriptors. Such indices often have thesauri that identify these terms. A search of these directories requires that your list of terms and descriptors be consistent with the thesauri.

Step 4: Compile the literature you have found. Is it relevant to your needs? Perhaps you are overwhelmed by information. Perhaps you've found little that is relevant. Rework your list of key words and authors.

Step 5: Continue your search in the library. Expand your search to include a few more years and one or two more sources. Evaluate your findings.

Step 6: At this point you should have a clear idea of the nature of the information you are seeking and sufficient background to use more specialized resources.

Step 7: Consult the reference librarian. You may wish to consider a computer-assisted information search. The reference librarian can assist with such a search but will need your help in the form of a carefully constructed list of key words. Some librarians will prefer to produce their own lists of key words or descriptors, but it is a good idea to verify that such a list is reasonably complete. The librarian may be able to suggest specialized sources related to the topic. Remember, the reference librarian cannot be of much help until you can provide some rather specific information about what you want to know.

Step 8: If you have had little success or your topic is highly specialized, consult the *Directory of Directories, Directory Information Guide, Guide to American Directories, Statistics Sources, Statistical Reference Index, American Statistics Index, Encyclopedia of Geographic Information Sources,* or one of the other guides to information listed in Appendix 6A. These are really

Source: David W. Stewart, *Secondary Research: Information Sources and Methods* (Beverly Hills, Calif.: Sage Publications, 1984), pp. 20–22. Reprinted by permission of Sage Publications, Inc.

future-oriented decisions, such as evaluating a new product or a new advertising campaign, but even here they can serve as a foundation for planning other research.

Internal secondary data are the least costly (and most readily available) of any type of marketing research. If maintained in an appropriate form, internal sales data can be used to analyze the company's past sales performance by product, geographic location, customer, channel of distribution, and so on, while cost data help in determining how profitable these segments of the business are. This type of information typically forms the basis of a firm's marketing intelligence system. We shall not go into the details of this type of analysis here because it is a somewhat specialized topic and is extensively reported elsewhere.[10] Most studies should begin with internal secondary data.

Published external data are so plentiful that researchers are often unsure where to begin investigating them. Table 6.3 provides some general guidelines. Key sources

---

[10]See, for example, Charles H. Sevin, *Marketing Productivity Analysis* (New York: McGraw-Hill, 1965); or Sanford R. Simon, *Managing Marketing Profitability* (New York: American Management Association, Inc., 1969) for two of the best treatments of sales and profitability analysis.

Table 6.3 *continued*

directories of directories, which means that this level of search will be very general. You will first need to identify potentially useful primary directories, which will then lead you to other sources.

Step 9: If you are unhappy with what you have found or are otherwise having trouble, and the reference librarian has not been able to identify sources, use an authority. Identify some individual or organization that might know something about the topic. The various *Who's Who* publications, *Consultants and Consulting Organizations Directory, Encyclopedia of Associations, Industrial Research Laboratories in the United States,* or *Research Centers Directory* may help you identify sources. Don't forget faculty at universities, government officials, or business executives. Such individuals are often delighted to be of help.

Step 10: Once you have identified sources you wish to consult, you can determine whether they are readily available in your library. If they are not, ask for them through interlibrary loan. Interlibrary loan is a procedure whereby one library obtains materials from another. This is accomplished through a network of libraries that have agreed to provide access to their collections in return for the opportunity to obtain materials from other libraries in the network. Most libraries have an interlibrary loan form

on which relevant information about requested materials is written. Interlibrary loans are generally made for some specific period (usually one to two weeks). Very specialized, or rare, publications may take some time to locate, but most materials requested are obtained within a couple of weeks. If you would like to purchase a particular work, consult *Ulrich's International Periodicals Directory, Irregular Serials and Annuals: An International Directory,* or *Books in Print* to determine whether a work is in print and where it may be obtained. Local bookstores often have computerized or microform inventories of book wholesalers and can provide rapid access to books and monographic items.

Step 11: Even after an exhaustive search of a library's resources, it is possible that little information will be found. In such cases, it may be necessary to identify experts or other authorities who might provide the information you are seeking or suggest sources you have not yet identified or consulted. Identifying authorities is often a trial-and-error process. One might begin by calling a university department, government agency, or other organization that employs persons in the field of interest. Reference librarians often can suggest individuals who might be helpful. However, a large number of such calls may be necessary before an appropriate expert is identified.

are reference librarians, associations, on-line computer searches, and general guides to useful marketing information.

Reference Librarians

Reference librarians are specialists who have been trained to know the contents of many of the key information sources in a library, as well as how to search those sources most effectively. It is a rare problem indeed for which a reference librarian cannot uncover some relevant published information.

Associations

Most associations gather and often publish detailed information on such things as industry shipments and sales, growth patterns, environmental factors affecting the industry, operating characteristics, and the like. Trade associations are often able to secure information from members that other research organizations cannot because of the working relationships that exist between the association and the firms who belong to it. Two useful sources for locating associations serving a particular indus-

Back to the Case

Bob Markson called together his two top researchers, Pamela Tyler and Josh Epstein.

"Listen, you two," he said. "I have a big assignment here from Sebastian in marketing. It has to be done in a hurry, it has to be done well, and we have no money. Interested?"

Pamela sighed. "Someday, Bob, I'd like to come in here and hear you say, 'I have a leisurely little project here with lots of money, so go to it.' But since I'll probably be rocking on the veranda of the nursing home when that day comes, I guess I have little choice but to do an-

other one of these complicated, quick, and cheap projects. What have you got?"

"Pam, I want you to check out how well Sebastian's promotional schemes have been working with the trade," Markson said. "Start by seeing if you can find some information on company shipments to chains, wholesalers, and large independent stores. Then see if you can get hold of some warehouse withdrawal data. If we can correlate that information with the timing of Sebastian's promotions, we might begin to see a connection.

"Josh, I want you to look into the consumer end of things," Markson said. "Check out retail sales, and see if there is any purchase diary data available that we can use.

"I want both of you to get back to me in two weeks."

Markson is suggesting that his researchers use two kinds of secondary data: internal records on shipments and sales, and commercial data collected by organizations that sell their services to various users. What might be the advantages and disadvantages of each type of data?

try are the *Directory of Directories* and the *Encyclopedia of Associations* described in Appendix 6A.

On-Line Computer Searches

On-line computer searches have become increasingly useful for locating published information and data in the last ten years as computer-readable storage systems for data bases have come into their own.[11] Many public libraries, as well as college and university libraries, have invested in the equipment and personnel that are necessary to make data-base searching available to their patrons. One of the most useful aspects of the on-line computer search is that users themselves can search through the available information and retrieve precisely what they need. (See Table 6.4.)

Increasingly, businesses are expanding their own libraries through subscriptions to data bases and through hiring trained librarians, often called *information managers,* to conduct the search most efficiently. It has been estimated that the nation's 1,000 or so largest companies spend $20,000 to $25,000 a year for data-base services.

[11]Kenneth Duzy of Quadra Assoc., Inc., of Santa Monica, which publishes the *Directory of On-Line Data Bases,* estimates that at the end of 1983 there were 1,878 individual data bases. (*Boston Globe,* December 11, 1983, p. A54); W. Kiechel III, "Everything You Always Wanted to Know May Soon Be On-Line," *Fortune,* 101 (May 5, 1980), pp. 226–240. For discussion on how to go about using on-line data bases effectively, see Robert Donati, "Decision Analysis for Selecting Online Data Bases to Answer Business Questions," *Database,* 13 (December 1981), pp. 49–63; and H. Webster Johnson, Anthony J. Faria, and Ernest L. Maier, *How to Use the Business Library. With Sources of Business Information,* 5th ed. (Cincinnati: South-Western Publishing, 1984), pp. 29–57.

Table 6.4   How to Conduct a Data-Base Search

Step 1: Discuss information sought with specialist who will be doing the search to develop a "search strategy." The search strategy is a set of words that will be entered into the computer for the actual search.

Step 2: Once a search strategy is determined, the specialist uses a telephone to dial the number of the particular data base to be used. When the connection is made, the search specialist hooks up his or her terminal to the data-base computer via a modem.

Step 3: The data-base computer will then ask for identification to determine whether the search specialist is an authorized user of the system. The search specialist will reply by typing in a code. If it is accepted, the data-base computer will then ask for the name of the data base or file to be searched.

Step 4: If the file is available, the computer will ask the user to input a search strategy. When the search strategy has been entered, the computer will begin the search.

Step 5: The computer then informs the user of the number of matches made by the search. If the number of matches made is large, the user may wish to add further qualifiers of the terms used in the search to find the specific information he or she needs.

Step 6: If the results are satisfactory, the user must decide the level of detail he or she wants to see for each match made. Choices range from a simple bibliography, an annotated bibliography, a bibliography with abstracts, or even a copy of the references themselves.

Step 7: The user must also decide whether to have the information printed at the computer site and delivered later by mail or United Parcel Service, or printed immediately at the user's terminal. Having the results delivered by mail or UPS is generally cheaper, since charges for the service are generally based on the amount of time the computer is connected to the user's terminal time, and printers are considered slow devices in computer terms.

Source: Based on H. Webster Johnson, Anthony J. Faria, and Ernest L. Maier, *How to Use the Business Library: With Sources of Business Information,* 5th ed. (Cincinnati: South-Western Publishing Co., 1984), pp. 29–32.

In addition, many companies are creating their own data bases from information generated internally and from outside materials of particular interest.[12]

GTE's Sylvania Division has taken data-base use one step further: It has constructed a computer data base that continuously tracks the activities of fifty-one competitors. The system combines information from Securities and Exchange Commission filings and articles from industry publications with reports and analyses submitted by GTE's field staff. Each competitor record monitors seventeen strategic categories, such as pricing, production, distribution, marketing, and new technology. GTE's nationwide strategic business units (SBUs) and its marketing and sales staff members in the field feed information into the system through the company's headquarters in Connecticut.[13]

Most companies use on-line data bases to search for journal articles, reports, speeches, marketing data, economic trends, legislation, and any of a number of other types of information on a particular topic. Some especially useful guides to on-line data bases are described in Appendix 6A.

General Guides to Secondary Data

Other very useful sources for locating information on a particular topic are the general guides to secondary data described in Appendix 6A. Table 6.5, for example, lists what the *Encyclopedia of Business Information Sources* has to say about data

[12]Johnnie L. Roberts, "As Information Swells, Firms Open Libraries," *The Wall Street Journal,* 63 (September 28, 1983), pp. 25 and 29.

[13]Taken from "Intelligence Update," a newsletter published by Information Data Search, 1218 Massachusetts Ave., Cambridge, Mass. 02138.

Table 6.5   Sources of Data on the Chocolate Industry

Chocolate Industry

See also: CANDY INDUSTRY; COCOA INDUSTRY

Trade Associations and Professional Societies
American Cocoa Research Industry. 7900 Westpark Drive, Suite 514, McLean, Virginia 22101.

Chocolate Information Council. 777 Third Avenue, New York, New York 10017.

Chocolate Manufacturers Association of the U.S.A. 7900 Westpark Drive, Suite 514, McLean, Virginia 22101.

Periodicals
Choc-Talk. Chocolate Information Council, 777 Third Avenue, New York, New York, 10017. Quarterly. Free.

International Chocolate Review. Verlag Max Glättli, Post Office Box CH6934 Bioggio, Switzerland. Monthly. $12.00 per year.

Statistics Sources
Highlights of United States Export and Import Trade: FT990. U.S. Bureau of the Census. U.S. Government Printing Office, Washington, D.C. 20402. Monthly. $37.75 per year.

Price Sources
Estimated Retail Food Prices by Cities. U.S. Bureau of Labor Statistics, Washington, D.C. 20210. Monthly, with separate summary for annual average. Free.

Executive. Southam Business Publications Limited, 1450 Don Mills Road, Don Mills M38 2X7, Ontario, Canada. Monthly. Canadian subscribers $14.00 per year, others $16.00 per year.

Journal of Commerce. Twin Coast Newspapers, Incorporated, 99 Wall Street, New York, New York 10005. Daily except Saturday and Sunday. $80.00 per year.

Producer Prices and Price Indexes. U.S. Bureau of Labor Statistics. U.S. Government Printing Office, Washington, D.C. 20402. Monthly.

Wall Street Journal. Dow Jones and Company, Incorporated, 22 Cortlandt Street, New York, New York 10007. Daily. $49.00 per year.

General Works
The Book of Chocolate. Carol A. Rinzler. St. Martin's Press, Incorporated, 175 Fifth Avenue, New York, New York 10010. 1977. $8.95.

Chocolate, Cocoa and Confectionery: Science and Technology. Bernard W. Minifie, Avi Publishing Company, Incorporated, Post Office Box 831, Westport, Connecticut 06880. 1970. $25.00.

Cocoa and Chocolate Processing. H. Wieland. Noyes Data Corporation, Mill Road at Grand Avenue, Park Ridge, New Jersey 07656. 1972. $36.00

Sugar Confectionery and Chocolate Manufacture. R. Lees and B. Jackson. Chemical Publishing Company, Incorporated, 155 West 19th Street, New York, New York 10011. 1973. $22.50.

Online Data Bases
ABI/Inform. Data Courier, Inc., 620 South Fifth Street, Louisville, Kentucky 40202. General business literature, August 1971 to present. Inquire as to online cost and availability. Covers journal literature.

Foods Adlibra. K and M Publications, Inc., 2000 Frankfort Avenue, Louisville, Kentucky 40206. Food industry literature, 1974 to present, including food packaging. Inquire as to online cost and availability.

Management Contents. Management Contents, Inc., Box 1054, Skokie, Illinois 60076. General business journal literature, September 1974 to present. Inquire as to online cost and availability.

PTS F and S Indexes. (Predicasts Terminal System; Funk and Scott). Predicasts, Inc., 11001 Cedar Avenue, Cleveland, Ohio 44106. Indexes company, product, and industry news, 1972 to present. Inquire as to online cost and availability.

sources on the chocolate industry. Aspiring researchers are also well advised to acquaint themselves with the more important general sources of marketing information so that they know what statistics are available and where they can be found. Many of the most important of these are listed and briefly described in Appendix 6A.

◆ Standardized Marketing Information Services

The many standardized marketing information services that are available are another important source of secondary data for the marketing researcher. These services are available at some cost to the user and in this respect are a more expensive source of secondary data than published information. However, they are also typically much less expensive than primary data, because the costs incurred by the supplier in collecting, editing, coding, and tabulating the data are shared by the companies who pay to use the service. Because the information offered by the service must be suitable for use by a variety of companies, however, the type of data collected and the methods used to gather them must be uniform. It is that lack of precise fit that is the main disadvantage of this type of data as compared to primary data. Some of the main types and sources of standardized marketing information service data follow.

Industrial Market Services There are more information services available to the consumer goods manufacturer than to the industrial goods supplier. The consumer goods services are also much older than the industrial goods services. For instance, whereas the Nielsen Retail Index dates from 1934, the industry information services were born in the 1960s. This means that the industrial goods services are still evolving in terms of the type of information being collected and how it is made available to users.

One of the more important suppliers of industry market data is the Dun and Bradstreet "Market Identifiers" (DMI), which has a roster of over 4,300,000 establishments that is updated on a monthly basis so that the record on each company is accurate and current. Figure 6.1 is an example of a three- by five-inch-card record. These detailed records on a company-by-company basis allow a sales manager to construct sales prospect files, define sales territories and estimate their potential, and to identify potential new customers with particular characteristics. They allow advertising managers to select prospects by size and location; to analyze market prospects and select the media to reach them; to build, maintain, and structure current mailing lists; to generate sales leads and qualify them by size, location, and quality; and to locate new markets for testing. Finally, these records allow marketing researchers to assess market potential by territory, to measure market penetration in terms of numbers of prospects and numbers of customers, and to make comparative analyses of overall performance by districts or sales territories and between individual industries.

Distribution Services In an increasingly competitive marketplace, it is critical that the marketing manager have accurate information about the possible effects of any change in marketing decision variables. Sales volume (or market share) is a typical yardstick managers use to judge the effectiveness of various marketing strategies. Unfortunately, by itself it is an elusive yardstick. If shipments from the factory are used as a barometer of sales, then there is no way of judging whether those shipments are actually being converted to sales or whether they are sitting in a warehouse somewhere along the distribution pipeline. Yet the measurement of actual purchases by consumers raises a whole host of other questions about what samples were measured and how the data were gathered. The distribution services have come to grips with these problems, and they now collect consumer sales data on a continuing basis through store audits or via retail food store scanners. Others measure sales by monitoring warehouse withdrawals.

The basic concept of a store audit is very simple. The research firm sends field workers, called auditors, to a select group of retail stores at fixed intervals. On each

Figure 6.1

DMI Record

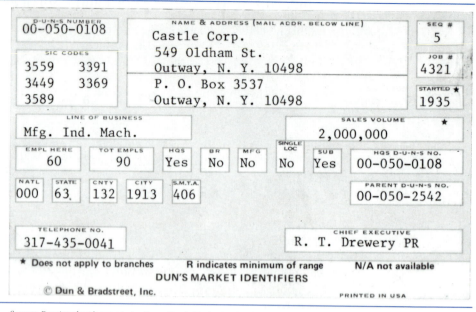

Source: Reprinted with permission from *Dun's Marketing Services* © Dun & Bradstreet, Inc.

visit the auditor takes a complete inventory of all products designated for the audit. The auditor also notes the merchandise moving into the store by checking wholesale invoices, warehouse withdrawal records, and direct shipments from manufacturers. Sales to consumers are then determined by the following calculation:

Beginning Inventory + Net Purchases (from wholesalers and manufacturers) − Ending Inventory = Sales

Some of the better known distribution information services follow.

Nielsen Retail Index Based on national samples of more than 7,500 supermarkets, 2,400 drugstores, 550 mass merchandisers, and 900 alcoholic beverage outlets, Nielsen Retail Index collects data every two months—not only the basic product turnover data described previously, but also information on retail prices, store displays, promotional activity, and local advertising using in-store observers or auditors.

The company takes these records and in turn generates the following information for each of the brands of each of the products audited:

- Sales to consumers
- Purchases by retailers
- Retail inventories
- Number of days' supply
- Out-of-stock stores
- Prices (wholesale and retail)
- Special factory packs
- Dealer support (displays, local advertising, coupon redemption)
- Total food store sales (all commodities)
- Major media advertising (from other sources)

Subscribers to the Nielsen service can get this data broken down by competitor, geographic area, or store type. Nielsen will also provide, on a fee basis, special

Figure 6.2

Sample Structure for Nielsen Retail Index

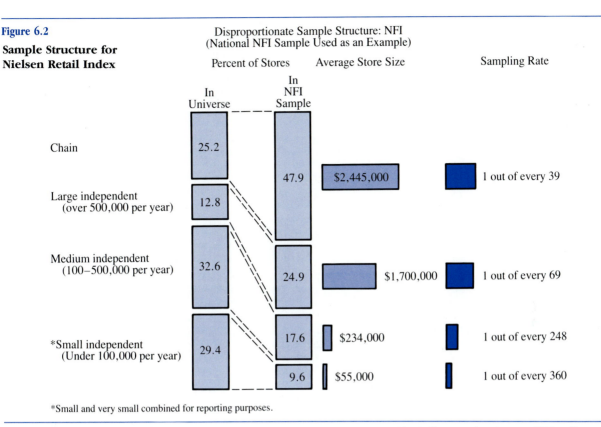

Disproportionate Sample Structure: NFI
(National NFI Sample Used as an Example)

	Percent of Stores		Average Store Size	Sampling Rate
	In Universe	In NFI Sample		
Chain	25.2	47.9	$2,445,000	1 out of every 39
Large independent (over 500,000 per year)	12.8			
Medium independent (100–500,000 per year)	32.6	24.9	$1,700,000	1 out of every 69
*Small independent (Under 100,000 per year)	29.4	17.6	$234,000	1 out of every 248
		9.6	$55,000	1 out of every 360

*Small and very small combined for reporting purposes.

Source: *Management with the Nielsen Retail Index System* (Northbook, Ill.: A. C. Nielsen Company, 1980), p. 11.

reports on such subjects as the effect of shelf facings on sales; the sales impact of different promotional strategies, premiums or prices; or the analysis of sales by client-specified geographic areas.

The stores included in all Nielsen index samples (regular, test, major market, and so on) are determined by using a "disproportionate, stratified" sampling technique. Larger stores, whose sales vary a great deal, are sampled most heavily. The proportion of smaller stores, whose sales typically will not vary much, are sampled less. For reasons that we will explain in the chapters on sampling, this type of sampling plan is more efficient than other sampling methods in terms of information accuracy versus cost. Figure 6.2 shows how the Nielsen sample is composed. The sample results are then adjusted using a complex weighting scheme to provide population estimates of the key statistics. The stores pinpointed for inclusion in the panel are contacted personally to secure their cooperation. Further, the stores are compensated for their cooperation on a per-audit basis. The auditors collecting the data are full-time people with college educations who have all undergone an in-house six-month training program.

Nielsen Scantrack Since the late 1970s Nielsen has been supplementing its Retail Index service with its Scantrack service, which emerged from the revolutionary installation of scanning equipment in retail food stores to read Universal Product Codes. These codes are eleven-digit numbers imprinted on each product sold in a supermarket. The first digit, called the *number system character,* indicates the type of product (grocery or drug). The next five digits identify the manufacturer, and the

Figure 6.3

Universal Product Codes

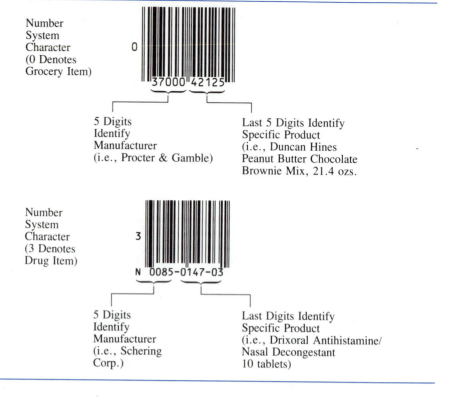

Number System Character (0 Denotes Grocery Item)

0

37000 42125

5 Digits Identify Manufacturer (i.e., Procter & Gamble)

Last 5 Digits Identify Specific Product (i.e., Duncan Hines Peanut Butter Chocolate Brownie Mix, 21.4 ozs.

Number System Character (3 Denotes Drug Item)

3

N 0085-0147-03

5 Digits Identify Manufacturer (i.e., Schering Corp.)

Last Digits Identify Specific Product (i.e., Drixoral Antihistamine/ Nasal Decongestant 10 tablets)

last five identify a particular product of the manufacturer, be it a different size, variety, or whatever (Figure 6.3).

There is a unique eleven-digit code for every product in the supermarket. As the product with its bar code is pulled across the scanner, the scanner identifies the number, looks up the price in the attached computer, and immediately prints the description and price of the item on the cash register receipt. The computer is simultaneously keeping track of each item's sales for the store's own inventory and sales records.[14]

The Scantrack service provides weekly sales data from a nationwide sample of scanner-equipped stores. The data allow clients to evaluate the effectiveness of short-term promotions, to evaluate pricing changes, to follow new product introductions, and to monitor unexpected events such as product recalls and shortages, among other things.

Audits and Surveys' National Total-Market Index Similar to the Nielsen Retail Index in some ways, the Audits and Surveys' National Total-Market Index differs from it in three respects: It is based on a product audit rather than a type-of-store audit; it uses part-time rather than full-time auditors; and the Audits and Surveys program is based on a calendar bimonthly schedule—January–February, and so on. Nielsen's schedule varies by type of outlet: drug is reported for December–January, food for

---

[14]For discussion of the trends in bar coding, see "Bar Codes are Black-and-White Strips and Soon They Will Be Read All Over," *The Wall Street Journal,* 65 (January 8, 1985), p. 37. For discussion of the trends in optical scanners, see Bob Gatty, "The Spreading Computer Revolution," *Nation's Business,* 71 (February 1983), pp. 72–73 and 76.

January–February. Audits and Surveys employs a permanent staff of six regional supervisors to administer its field quality control program.

The product audit emphasizes the total retail market for a product in all the outlets in which the product is sold. If the product under scrutiny is something like breath fresheners, auditors will canvass department stores, drugstores, grocery stores, general stores, variety stores, cigar stores, and other stores where breath fresheners might be sold. The product audit can provide the firm subscribing to the service the following types of information:[15]

1. *Retail sales.* How large is the total market? What is your brand's market share . . . and each of your competitors'? Is your position different by outlet type, by region, by size of city?

2. *Retailer inventory.* How much inventory is stocked by all retailers? How does your brand compare with competition in the struggle for store space? Does it vary by store type or geographically?

3. *Distribution and out-of-stock.* How many stores handle your brand? What volume of the product category's business do these stores represent? What is the prevalence of out-of-stock conditions on your brand? Your competition? What are the patterns by region, by outlet type?

The Audits and Surveys Index publishes bimonthly reports thirty days after the close of each audit period. Since its primary focus is on products, some of the items it measures are very different from those covered by the Nielsen Retail Index. The Audits and Surveys Index tracks activity in such product categories as automotive products, electrical products, food products, tobacco products, photographic products, health and beauty aids, household products, and writing instruments.

Selling Areas—Marketing, Inc. Another distribution service, Selling Areas—Marketing, Inc. (SAMI), issues reports based on warehouse withdrawals rather than retail store sales.[16] Only food operators participate, but since the SAMI sample includes warehouses of chains, wholesalers, rack jobbers, and frozen food warehousemen, the product movement figures include the volume retailed by chain supermarkets, "mom and pop" stores, independent supermarkets, and food discounters. SAMI reports the movement of all dry grocery and household supplies, frozen food, health and beauty aids, and certain warehoused refrigerated items. However, fresh meat, perishables, and store delivered items such as milk, bread, and soft drinks do not appear in the SAMI reports.

The basic SAMI reports are generated from food distribution records. SAMI reports are available for each of fifty-one major markets, which together account for over 86 percent of national food sales. A manufacturer may purchase any or all markets in a given category and any or all products. SAMI audits are conducted every four weeks, and reports are delivered to manufacturers purchasing the service three to four weeks following the end of the reporting period. Since the reports detail each brand's share and volume movement every month, they allow participating manufacturers to assess continuously the competitive conditions in each market. The manufacturer can therefore make appropriate changes in marketing strategy and can evelute the impact of these changes rather quickly.

---

[15]Taken from "The National Total-Market Audit Index," a division of Audits & Surveys, Inc., 1 Park Avenue, New York, N.Y.

[16]Taken from *The Facts of Sami, Saudi, and Market Segmentation* (Chicago: Selling Areas—Marketing, Inc., 1984).

Consumer Market Services A number of standardized marketing information services directly involve consumers and their behavior. Some are concerned with purchase or consumption behavior (the National Purchase Diary Panel and Behavior-Scan), some with viewing and reading habits (the Nielsen Television Index, the Starch Advertisement Readership Service, and the Simmons Media/Marketing Services), and others with a broad range of purposes (the National Family Opinion Panel and the Consumer Mail Panel).

National Purchase Diary Panel The largest diary panel in the United States is the National Purchase Diary Panel (NPD).[17] Over 13,000 families use a preprinted diary to record their monthly purchases in approximately fifty product categories. Figure 6.4 illustrates the sample diary for soup products. Note the diary asks for significant details regarding the brand and amount bought, the price paid, whether there were any deals involved (by type), the store where purchased, the flavor, and intended use.

The families comprising NPD are geographically dispersed, and the panel is demographically balanced so it can be used to project total U.S. purchasing. The total panel contains twenty-nine miniature panels, each representative of a local market. Panel members are recruited quarterly and are added to the active panel only after they have maintained a training diary and satisfactorily met NPD's standards for accuracy. Families are recruited so that the composition of the panel mirrors the population of the United States with respect to a variety of measures, including such things as family size, age of housewife, income, and census region. Panel members receive gifts for participating. Families are dropped from the panel at their request or if they fail to return three of their last five diaries.

The diaries are returned to NPD monthly, the purchase histories are gathered and recorded, and reports prepared. Using these reports the subscribing company is able to assess, among other things, the following:[18]

- Size of the market, proportion of families buying over time, and amount purchased per buyer
- Brand share over time
- Brand loyalty and brand-switching behavior
- Frequency of purchase and amount purchased per transaction
- Influence of price and special price deals as well as average price paid
- Characteristics of heavy buyers
- Impact of a new brand on the established brands
- Impact of a change in advertising or distribution strategy

Market Research Corporation of America Another service that maintains a consumer panel is the Market Research Corporation of America (MRCA). It details purchases in fifty categories of prepared foods, household products, and health and beauty aids. This information is fed into a data base that subscribers can access through their own computer terminals.

MRCA's DYANA (Dynamic Analysis System) allows subscribers to choose the basic data to be analyzed (such as product types or composition of household) and to specify the type of analysis that is to be undertaken (such as repeat buying behavior, brand shifting, or a demographic profile of buyers).

---

[17]See *We Make the Market Perfectly Clear* (New York: NPD Research, Inc., undated).

[18]See *Insights: Issues 1–13* (New York: NPD Research, Inc., undated) for discussion of these and other analyses using diary panel data.

Figure 6.4 Sample Page from National Purchase Diary

PAGE EIGHT

NOTE: Extra space page 1. Free Gift and Samples, on Back cover.

Dairy Tip: Enter all kinds of soups in this section that come in cans, boxes, pouches, or other containers including dry packaged ingredients for making homemade soup.

Date Of Month purchase was made	Write in **BRAND NAME** as shown on label — **SOUPS** Include Canned, Dry and Bouillon (Write in Brand and/or Company Name — Not Flavor)	HOW MANY of each kind did you buy? Write in number of packages, or other containers	TOTAL CASH PAID Don't include taxes $	¢	Check (✓) ONE — Did you redeem a coupon or was there a special price offer? No Special Price	Price Off on Label	Mail-in Cash Refund	Redeemed Coupon from Newspaper	Redeemed Coupon from Magazine	Redeemed Coupon received in Mail	Redeemed Coupon from prior purchase of same item	Redeemed Coupon from Other Purchase	Other Special Price	TOTAL CENTS OFF IF ANY WRITE IN	WHERE DID YOU PURCHASE? NAME OF STORE (or company if purchased from door-to-door or home delivery salesperson)	KIND OF STORE Check (✓) or Write In — GROCERY OR FOOD	Other — Describe	WEIGHT (size) shown on label — Write in weight (such as: ounces, pints, etc.) per item or can/or number of packets or cubes.	FLAVOR — Describe Flavor Write in Such as: Tomato, Chicken Noodle, Beef Broth, etc.	TYPE Check (✓) One — CANNED: Condensed	CANNED: Ready to Serve	DRY MIX: REGULAR — to be cooked	DRY MIX: INSTANT — No cooking needed	Dry Packaged Ingredients for Homemade Soup	CUBE	INTENDED USE Check (✓) One — Used as Soup	Used as Ingredient in another dish	MANUFACTURER CODE — On many cans or packages, you will find a 6 digit or 10 digit code number underneath a series of vertical lines or bars. Please fill in these code numbers below. If you can't find them, leave this question blank.

Perhaps MRCA's best-known service, however, is its Menu Census. In this panel, 2,000 households are asked what they typically eat and drink. Respondents report every food dish eaten at home plus the time of day it was served, any food eaten away from home, any ingredient added to a dish, recipes used, brand names of packaged products used, who prepared the meal, and who ate it, among other things.

This service allows marketers to determine how such factors as working women, nutritional concerns, an aging population, and various sorts of diets are changing the ways Americans eat.[19]

BehaviorScan A service provided by Chicago-based Information Resources, Inc., is BehaviorScan. Instead of relying on diary panels, it makes use of supermarket scanners to measure household consumption behavior. Scanner data have one obvious advantage over panel data in that they reflect purchasing behavior that is not subject to the interview, recording, or expert biases that may be present with diary panels. However, diary panels have the advantage of allowing the recorded purchase behav-

---

[19]See *DYANA* (1982) and *Menu Census* (1981) (Stamford, Conn.: Market Research Corporation of America).

Back to the Case

Two weeks later, Markson, Epstein, and Tyler sat around a conference table and discussed what they had found.

"Well, Pamela, what did you discover about the trade promotions?" Markson asked.

"I began by getting hold of the SAMI reports for the periods during which Mike's promotions ran. I then correlated the date at which he first began a special trade promotion with the warehouse withdrawal data that SAMI provides to see if there was any relationship. From what I can gather, Mike has quite a case for continuing the promotions. Warehouse withdrawals increased 11 percent over the previous year's activity during his first promotion, and subsequent promotions did even better. Al-

though the SAMI data doesn't tell us whether the product sold once it got to the retail store, I think we can infer that it did well, since retailers obviously took advantage of later promotional discounts to stock up. I think Mike may be on to something," Pamela said.

"How about you, Josh?" Markson said. "How did you fare?"

"I got some data from Nielsen's Retail Index that gives us a good indication of sales, but they do not tell us what we need to know about the effects of our promotions," Josh said.

"However, I think I got what we're looking for from National Panel Diary. NPD data show consecutive purchases by the same families and identify whether a

coupon was used, as well as how much a customer paid for an item. NPD is sending me the information we need about a long list of our products. If the results are good, this could be just what Sebastian needs to make his case."

Commercial sources of secondary data can often give marketers the information they need to make decisions at a fraction of the cost of amassing the same data through primary research. While researchers should always be careful when using such data to account for problems of fit and accuracy, secondary sources should always be investigated first before developing plans for gathering primary data.

ior to be linked to the demographic characteristics of those forming the panel. Information Resources, Inc., has tried to combine the advantages of both methods through its BehaviorScan system.

BehaviorScan started in two test markets—Marion, Indiana, and Pittsfield, Massachusetts—in 1979 and was intended to operate in twenty-four sampling areas by the end of 1985.[20] In each of these markets, Information Resources has recruited members of more than 2,500 households to serve as its panelists. Each household is given an identification card, which members present at grocery stores when they make a purchase.

Almost all the supermarkets in each area have scanners provided by Information Resources. Each household presents its identification card when checking out. The card is scanned along with the household's purchases allowing Information Resources to relate a family's purchases by brand, size, and price to the family's demographic characteristics and the household's known exposure to coupons, newspaper ads, free samples, and point-of-purchase displays.

Information Resources also has the capability to direct different advertising spots to different households through the "black boxes" that have been attached to the television sets in each test household in cooperation with the cable television systems serving the markets. This allows Information Resources the opportunity to monitor the buying reactions to different advertisements, or to the same advertisement in different types of households (e.g., whether the buying reactions to a particular ad are the same or different among past users and nonusers of the product). This targetable TV capability allows Information Resources to balance the panel of members for each ad test within each market according to the criteria the sponsor chooses (e.g., past purchasers of the product), thereby minimizing the problem of having comparable experimental and control groups.

Nielsen Television Index Probably the most well known commercial information service is the Nielsen Television Index. The most casual television watcher has probably heard of the Nielsen ratings and their impact on which TV shows are canceled by the networks and which are allowed to continue. The service provides estimates of the size and nature of the audience for individual television programs. The basic data are gathered through the use of Audimeter® instruments, which are electronic devices attached to the television sets in approximately 1,200 cooperating households. Each Audimeter is connected to a central computer that records when the set is on and to what channel it is tuned.

Through the data provided by these basic records, Nielsen develops estimates of the number and percentage of all television households viewing a given television show. The most popular report (the "Pocketpiece") is issued biweekly, forty-eight weeks a year, and is generally available to clients less than two weeks after a measurement period. For those requiring more frequent reports, Nielsen installs a special terminal in the client's office which permits receipt of national household ratings within twenty-four hours of a broadcast. Nielsen also breaks down these aggregate ratings by ten socioeconomic and demographic characteristics, including territory, education of head of house, county size, time zones, household income,

[20]See *BehaviorScan Market Profiles* (Chicago: Information Resources, undated), and *The Marketing Fact Book* (Chicago: Information Resources, undated). For discussion of the tremendous impact such "test market" systems are having on marketing research, see "New Tools Revolutionize New Product Testing," *Marketing and Media Decisions,* (November 1984), pp. 76–78 and 128–134; Richard Kreisman, "Buy the Numbers," *Inc.,* 7 (March 1985), pp. 104–112; and "Big Brother Gets a Job in Market Research," *Business Week,* (April 8, 1985), pp. 96–97.

age of woman of house, color television ownership, occupation of head of house, presence of nonadults, and household size.

Recently several firms, including Nielsen, have developed a way to refine their data on viewers even further. In participating households, each member of the family is assigned a viewing number, which he or she enters into a "people meter" upon turning on the television set, changing channels, or turning off the set. This information is transmitted immediately to the central computer for processing.[21] These breakdowns assist the network, of course, in selling advertising on particular programs, while they assist the advertiser in choosing to sponsor programs that reach households with the desired characteristics.[22]

Starch Advertisement Readership Service Consumer reading of advertisements in magazines and newspapers is measured by the Starch Readership Service. Some 75,000 advertisements in 1,000 issues of consumer and farm magazines, business publications, and newspapers are assessed each year using over 100,000 personal interviews.

The Starch surveys employ the *recognition method* to assess a particular ad's effectiveness. With the magazine open, the respondent is asked to indicate whether he or she had read each ad. Four degrees of reading are recorded:[23]

1. Non-reader: a person who did not remember having previously seen the advertisement in the issue being studied.

2. Noted: a person who remembered seeing the advertisement in that particular issue.

3. Associated: a person who saw or read some part of the advertisement that clearly indicated the brand or advertiser.

4. Read most: a person who read 50 percent or more of the written material in the advertisement.

During the course of the interview, data are also collected on the observation and reading of the component parts of each ad such as the headlines, subheadings, pictures, copy blocks, and so forth.

Interviewing begins a short time after the issue of the magazine is placed on sale. For weekly and biweekly consumer magazines, interviewing begins three to six days after the on-sale date and continues for one to two weeks. For monthly magazines, interviewing begins two weeks after the on-sale date and continues for three weeks.

The interviews are conducted by a trained staff of field interviewers, who have the responsibility of selecting those to be interviewed, since a quota sample is employed. Each interviewer must locate an assigned number of readers within a particular area who are eighteen years of age and over, with various occupations, family sizes, and marital and economic statuses. The quotas are determined so that different characteristics will be represented in the sample in proportion to their representation in the population. Readers are included in the sample when they conform to the specified demographic characteristics and they reply in the affirmative when

[21]For discussions of the operation of the people meter and experiments testing its effectiveness, see Elizabeth Berry, "Nielsen May Face U.K. Rival in Researching TV Audiences," *The Wall Street Journal,* 64 (February 2, 1984), p. 31; and Fred Gardner, "Test for the People Meter," *Marketing and Media Decisions,* 19 (April 1984), pp. 74–75 and 115.

[22]Greater detail regarding the Nielsen television rating can be found in *The Nielsen Ratings in Perspective* (Northbrook, Ill.: A. C. Nielsen Company, 1980).

[23]*Starch Readership Report: Scope, Method, and Use* (Mamaroneck, N.Y.: Starch INRA Hooper, undated).

asked if they had read the particular magazine issue in question. The size of the sample varies by publication. Most Starch studies, though, are based on 100 to 150 interviews per sex.

Since newspaper and magazine space cost data are also available, a "readers-per-dollar" variable can be calculated. The final summary report from Starch shows each ad's (one-half page or larger) overall readership percentages, readers per dollar, and rank when grouped by product category. The summary sheet is attached to the labeled copy of the issue in which each ad is marked to show the readership results for the ad as a whole and for each component part. The data allow the magazine and newspaper advertiser to compare (with respect to readership) its ads with those of competitors, its current ads with prior ads, and its current ads against product averages. This process can be effective in assessing changes in theme, copy, layout, use of color, and so on.

Simmons Media/Marketing Service A national sample of some 19,000 respondents is used by the Simmons Media/Marketing Service to compile data relating product usage to media exposure. Four different interviews are conducted with each respondent so that magazine, television, newspaper, and radio can all be covered by the Simmons Service. Information is reported for total adults and for males and females separately.[24]

Simmons researchers interview each respondent twice—first to measure the reading of magazines and newspapers and second to ask about radio-listening behavior. A self-administered questionnaire is used to gather product purchase and use information for over 800 product categories, which remain relatively fixed from year to year. Finally, television viewing behavior is determined by means of a personal viewing diary that each respondent is asked to keep for two weeks.

The Simmons sample does not attempt to be representative of the population as a whole. High-income households are sampled more than proportionately, while low-income households are sampled less than proportionately to their number. All households receive a premium for participating, and a minimum of six calls are made in an attempt to interview respondents who could not be reached earlier. A large number of demographic characteristics are gathered from each respondent included in the study.

Simmons determines magazine readership using the "through-the-book," or editorial interest, method for forty-three major magazines and by the "recent-reading" method of ninety-five smaller monthly magazines. In the "through-the-book" method respondents are screened to determine which magazines they might have read during the past six months. They are then shown actual issues of magazines stripped of confusing material (for identification purposes), such as advertising pages and recurring columns and features. Interviewers show respondents ten feature articles unique to the issue and ask them to indicate which they find especially interesting. At the end, interviewers ask a qualifying question: "Now that you have been through this magazine, could you tell me whether this is the first time you happened to look into this particular issue, or have you looked into it before?" In order to qualify as readers, respondents must confirm that they had seen that particular issue before coming to the interview. If the respondent expresses uncertainty, he or she is disqualified from the study.

[24]*The 1984 Study of Media and Markets* (New York: Simmons Market Research Bureau, Inc., 1984). See also *Dependable Data for Advertising and Marketing Decisions* (New York: Simmons Market Research Bureau, Inc., undated).

In the "recent-reading" method, respondents are asked to sort a deck of four-color cards featuring magazines' distinctive logos into two piles: magazines read, and magazines not read in the past six months.

This information about magazine and newspaper reading habits, television viewing, and radio-listening behavior is then cross-referenced with the information Simmons gathers on 800 different products, which includes

- Users of products, brands, or services
- Ownership of products
- Price paid for selected items
- Brand used most often
- Volume/frequency of use
- Store at which purchased

By analyzing these data and comparing them with demographic characteristics, a client can identify target groups and determine what combination of media should be used to reach them most efficiently and with what frequency.

NFO Research, Inc. As an independent research firm specializing in custom-designed consumer surveys using mail panels, NFO Research is not a source of secondary data in the true sense of the word, since the data collected are specifically designed to meet the client's needs. NFO maintains representative panels drawn from a sample of well over 250,000 U.S. families who have agreed to complete self-administered questionnaires on a variety of subjects. The topics may include specific product usage, reaction to the product or advertising supporting it, reaction to a product package, attitude toward or awareness of some issue, product, service or ad, and so on. The national panel is dissolved and rebuilt every two years so that it matches current family population characteristics with respect to income, population density, age of homemaker, and family size, for the continental United States and each of the nine geographic divisions in the census.

A current demographic profile is maintained for each family in the data bank. Included are such characteristics as size of family, education, age of family members, number of children and their sex, occupation of the principal wage earner, race, and so on. This information is used to generate highly refined population segments. If the user's needs require it, NFO can offer the client panels composed exclusively of mothers of infants, teenagers, elderly people, dog and cat owners, professional workers, mobile home residents, multiple car owners, or other specialized types. Each of these panels can be balanced to match specific quotas dictated by the client.[25]

Consumer Mail Panel A part of Market Facts, Inc., the Consumer Mail Panel (CMP) is a sample of households that have agreed to respond to mail questionnaires and product tests. Samples of persons for each product test or use are drawn from the 120,000 persons in the CMP pool. The pool is representative of the geographical divisions in the United States and Canada, and it is broken down, within these divisions, according to census data on total household income, population density and degree of urbanization, and age of panel member.

---

[25]More detailed information regarding the mail panel can be found in the company's publication *NFO* (Toledo, Ohio: NFO Research, Inc., undated).

Research Window 6.1

A Marketing Research Pioneer—A. C. Nielsen

The A. C. Nielsen Company is the world's largest and best-known marketing and advertising research company. But surprisingly little is known about Arthur C. Nielsen, Sr., the extraordinary man who invented the concept of "share of market," developed the first index services, and pioneered the field of broadcast audience measurement.

Today A. C. Nielsen Company has over 17,000 employees, subsidiaries in twenty-one foreign countries, and annual revenues in excess of $400,000,000, but in the company's first ten years, the going was rough.

Arthur C. Nielsen, Sr., started his business in 1923, four years after graduating from the University of Wisconsin with the highest scholastic average (95.8) ever recorded in the college of engineering, and after two years of duty as a naval officer in World War I. He was twenty-six years old when he took $45,000 raised from a group of friends and launched his company in a fledgling industry: marketing and advertising research.

"We were broke, and it was a terribly risky thing," Nielsen reminisced in a *New York Times* interview in 1967. "I had a mortgage on everything, and there wasn't another dime in the world that we could beg or borrow." Even so, in 1933—at the height of the Depression—he started a new service, the Nielsen Drug Index (NDI), which would become the mainspring for his company's growth in the future.

Developed for package goods manufacturers, the NDI was based on a novel idea for that time: draw a sample of drugstores and then visit them periodically to develop, through audits of purchase invoices and shelf stock, a measure of unit sales. This was a logical thing for Mr. Nielsen, however, since both his parents were accountants.

These store-movement data, when projected, provided a measure of category size and a record of sales velocity, which then could be related to marketing efforts. In the process, an exciting new concept was produced: share of market. This turned marketing into a horse race, and only Mr. Nielsen had the scorecard. More marketing decisions, expenditures, and careers have been influenced by that single statistic—share of market—than any other.

A companion service, the Nielsen Food Index, was started seven months after NDI, and since then, the adaptation of the index methodology to other store categories and the expansion of index services in foreign countries have been the main thrust of the Nielsen company. Today, ACN (A. C. Nielsen) Index services have over 1,500 corporate clients in twenty-three countries.

Mr. Nielsen was also one of the pioneers in broadcast audience measurements, starting in 1936 when radio set ownership grew to the level where there was commercial interest. His Nielsen Radio Index service brought the share-of-market concept to the communications industry The radio service was discontinued in 1964, but by then the Nielsen name had become a household word because of his television ratings service—and a curse word among entertainers who were cancelled because of low ratings.

In his prime, Mr. Nielsen worked sixty to seventy hours a week, some of that time out of the back of his eight-passenger blue Fleetwood Cadillac, which—complete with blue shag rug—was equipped as a moving office. The trunk of his car was equipped to carry the voluminous files he took on his long auto trips through countries he toured in the process of building his overseas empire.

In the midst of all this activity, he still found time to play championship tennis, and he was elected to the National Lawn Tennis Hall of Fame in 1971.

Arthur C. Nielsen, Sr., died in 1980 at the age of eighty-two. He was succeeded in the business by his son, Arthur, Jr.

Source: Jack J. Honomichl, *Marketing Research People* (Chicago: Crain Books, 1984), pp. 103–107.

According to CMP, their mail panel is ideally suited for experimental studies since the samples are matched. In particular, CMP is felt to be particularly valuable when

1. Large samples are required at low cost because the size of the subgroups is large or there are many subgroups to be analyzed.
2. Large numbers of households must be screened to find eligible respondents.
3. Continuing records are to be kept by respondents to report such data as products purchased, how products are used, television programs viewed, magazines read, and so on.

CMP has recorded a number of other characteristics with respect to each participating household that allow for cross-tabulation of the client's criterion variable against such things as place of residence (state, county, and standard metropolitan area), marital status, occupation and employment status, household size, age, sex, home ownership, type of dwelling, and ownership of pets, dishwashers, washing machines, dryers, other selected appliances, and automobiles.[26]

◆ Summary

Learning Objective 1: Explain the difference between primary and secondary data.

Secondary data are statistics not gathered for the immediate study at hand, but for some other purpose. Primary data are originated by the researcher for the purpose of the investigation at hand.

Learning Objective 2: Cite the two primary advantages offered by secondary data.

The most significant advantages offered by secondary data are the time and money they save the researcher.

Learning Objective 3: Specify two problems common to secondary data.

Two problems that commonly arise when secondary data are used are (1) they do not completely fit the problem, and (2) they are not completely accurate.

Learning Objective 4: List the three criteria researchers should use in judging the accuracy of secondary data.

The three criteria researchers should use in judging the accuracy of secondary data are (1) the source, (2) the purpose of publication, and (3) general evidence regarding the quality of the data.

Learning Objective 5: State the most fundamental rule in using secondary data.

The most fundamental rule in using secondary data is to *always use the primary source of secondary data*.

Learning Objective 6: Explain the difference between internal and external data.

Internal data are those found within the organization for which the research is being done, while external data are those obtained from outside sources.

Learning Objective 7: List some of the key sources researchers should consider in conducting a search process.

The key sources researchers should keep in mind in conducting a search process are reference librarians, associations, on-line computer searches, and general guides to useful marketing information.

---

[26]More detail regarding the Market Facts mail panel can be found in *Why Consumer Mail Panel is the Superior Option* (Chicago: Market Facts, Inc., undated) or *Market Facts, Inc.: Data Collection and Analysis for Reducing Business Decision Risks* (Chicago: Market Facts, Inc., undated).

Learning Objective 8: Specify the primary drawback researchers face in using data from a standardized marketing information service.

Because the information offered by the service must be suitable for use by a variety of companies, the type of data collected and the methods used to gather them must be uniform. It is that lack of precise fit that accounts for a service's main disadvantage over primary data.

Discussion Questions, Problems, and Projects

1. List some major secondary sources of information for the following situations.
   (a) The marketing research manager of a national soft drink manufacturer has to prepare a comprehensive report on the soft drink industry.
   (b) Mr. Baker has several ideas for instant cake mixes and is considering entering this industry. He needs to find the necessary background information to assess its potential.
   (c) The profit margins in the fur business are high! This is what Mr. Adams has heard. The fur industry has always intrigued him, so he decides to do some research to determine if the claim is true.
   (d) A recent graduate hears that condominiums are the homes of the eighties. He decides to collect some information on the condominium market.
   (e) Owning a grocery store has been Mrs. Smith's dream. She finally decides to make this into a reality. The first step she wishes to take is to collect information on the grocery business in her hometown.

2. Assume you are interested in opening a fast food Italian restaurant in Kansas City, Missouri. You are unsure of its acceptance by consumers and are considering doing a marketing research study to evaluate their attitudes and opinions. In your search for information you find the following studies:

   Study A was recently conducted by a research agency. In order to secure a copy of this study you would be required to pay the agency $225. The study evaluated consumers' attitudes toward fast food in general. The findings, based on a sample of 500 housewives for the cities of Springfield, Illinois; St. Louis and Kansas City, Missouri; and Topeka, Kansas, indicated that respondents did not view fast food favorably. The major reason for the unfavorable attitude was the low nutritional value of the food.

   Study B was completed by a group of students as a requirement for an M.B.A. marketing course. This study would not cost you anything as it is available in your university library. The study evaluated consumers' attitudes toward various ethnic fast foods. The respondents consisted of a convenience sample of 200 students from St. Louis. The findings indicated a favorable attitude toward two ethnic fast foods, Italian and Mexican. Based on these results, one of the students planned to open a pizza parlor in 1985 but instead accepted a job as sales representative in General Foods Corporation.
   (a) Critically evaluate the two sources of data.
   (b) Which do you consider better? Why?
   (c) Assume you decide that it will be profitable to become a franchisee in fast food. Identify five specific secondary sources of data and evaluate the data.

3. Interior Decor Products for many years had been a leading producer of paint and painting-related equipment such as brushes, rollers, turpentine, and so on. The company is now considering adding wallpaper to its line. At least initially, it does not intend to manufacture the wallpaper but rather to subcontract the manufacturing. Interior Decor will, however, assume the distribution and marketing functions.

   Before adding the wallpaper to its product line, the company secures some secondary data assessing the size of the wallpaper market. One mail survey made by a trade association showed that, on the average, families in the United States wallpapered two rooms in their homes each year. Among these families, 60 percent did the task themselves. Another survey, which had also been done by mail, but by one of the major home magazines, found that 70 percent of the subscribers answering the questionnaire had wallpapered one complete wall or more during the last twelve months. Among this 70 percent of the families, 80 percent had done the wallpapering themselves. Interior Decor thus has two sets of secondary data on the same problem, but the data are not consistent.

Discuss the data in terms of the criteria one would use to determine which set, if either, is correct. Assuming that you are forced to make the determination on the basis of the information in front of you, which would you choose?

4. Using the *1985 U.S. Statistical Abstract,* answer the following questions.
   (a) Which metropolitan area in the United States has the largest population?
   (b) What is the population of this metropolitan area?
   (c) What was the estimated median age of the U.S. population as of 1983?
   (d) Complete the following table:

Marital Status of U.S. Population	1983 (million)	Percent of Total
Single		
Married		
Widowed		
Divorced		

   (e) What percent of the households consist of five or more persons as of 1983?
   (f) List three major food commodities that have declined in terms of per capita consumption from 1960 to 1983.
   (g) Complete the following table on school enrollment for 1983. What do the percentages indicate?

	18–19 Years Old	20–24 Years Old	25–34 Years Old
Percent of males enrolled in school			
Percent of females enrolled in school			

   (h) Which of the following recreational products/services had the highest personal consumption expenditures in 1983?
   (1) Magazines and newspapers
   (2) Admissions to specified amusements
   (3) Radio and television receivers
   (4) Nondurable toys and sport supplies
   (i) Complete the following table:

Income Category	Percent of Families 1983
Under $5,000	
$5,000 to $9,999	
$10,000 to $14,999	
$15,000 to $19,999	
$20,000 to $24,999	
$25,000 to $34,999	
$35,000 to $49,999	
$50,000 and over	

(j) What was the Consumer Price Index for all items in 1983? What was the base year? What does this indicate?

(k) Complete the following table:

Industry Group	Ratio of Profits to Equity (1983) (percent)	Profits Per Dollar of Sales (1983) (percent)
Nondurable Good Industries		
Food and kindred products		
Tobacco manufacturers		
Textile mill products		
Paper and allied products		

(l) Based on the preceding table, which of the nondurable industries was the most profitable in 1983?

5. The *Statistical Abstract* is a secondary source of secondary data. As it is always better to use the primary source, identify the primary source for the following data that were referred to in the previous example.
   (a) The estimated median population of the U.S. population for 1983.
   (b) The per capita consumption of major food commodities.
   (c) Personal consumption expenditures for recreation.
   (d) The Consumer Price Indexes by major groups.
   (e) The manufacturing corporations' profits to stockholders equity, to sales, and to debt ratios.

6. John Smith is interested in becoming a wholesaler in household appliances. He has collected some general information but requires your help in finding answers to the following questions.
   (a) What is the SIC code for household appliance manufacturers?
   (b) How many retail establishments sell household appliances in the United States?
   (c) What are the total sales of all the retail establishments?

   Instead of attempting to handle all household appliances, John is considering specializing in household refrigerators and freezers.
   (d) What are the total number of establishments manufacturing household refrigerators and freezers?
   (e) How many wholesale establishments are there in the United States dealing in this category?

   John thinks that Dayton, Ohio, would be a profitable place to locate. He needs to know the following:
   (f) What is the total population of Dayton, Ohio?
   (g) What is the total civilian labor force in Dayton, Ohio?
   (h) How many persons are employed in Dayton, Ohio?
   (i) What are the total number of home furnishing and equipment stores that have a payroll in Dayton, Ohio?
   (Hint: In order to complete the above exercise, refer to the *Census of Manufacturers, Census of Retailers, Census of Wholesalers,* and *County and City Data Book.*)

7. Suppose you are interested in introducing a four-inch by two-inch FM/AM radio that could be carried in a person's pocket.
   (a) What data would be useful in making your decision?
   (b) Identify the specific secondary sources and the data they would provide that would assist you in making your decisions.
   (c) Develop a brief report on the data you find.

8. The Radiant Company is very much interested in determining how its position in the toothpaste market has changed since it changed the product package for its toothpaste, Freshen. The company is considering purchasing secondary data to conduct this analysis.

    Compare and contrast the information provided by the Market Research Corporation of America Consumer Panel with that provided by the A. C. Nielsen Company Retail Index in answering Radiant's problem.

Suggested Additional Readings

For general discussions of secondary data sources and how to go about finding secondary data, see

H. Webster Johnson, Anthony J. Faria, and Ernest L. Maier, *How to Use the Business Library: With Sources of Business Information,* 5th ed. (Cincinnati: South-Western Publishing, 1984).

For discussion of the marketing-related information that is available from the federal and state governments and how that information can be used for such marketing tasks as market potential estimation, establishing sales quotas, allocating advertising budgets, locating retail outlets, and so on, see

Measuring Markets: A Guide to the Use of Federal and State Statistical Data (Washington, D.C.: U.S. Department of Commerce, 1979).

Appendix 6A   Published External Secondary Data

There is so much published external secondary data that it is impossible to mention all of it in a single appendix. For this reason, only items of general interest are included.[1] The material is organized by the source of data.

Census Data

The Bureau of the Census of the U.S. Department of Commerce is the largest gatherer of statistical information in the country. The original census was the *Census of Population,* which was required by the Constitution to serve as a basis for apportioning representation in the House of Representatives. The first censuses were merely head counts. Not only has the *Census of Population* been expanded, but the whole census machinery has also been enlarged—at this point there are nine different censuses, all of which are of interest to the marketing researcher. Table 6.1, for example, listed some of the most useful data on population and housing that is available in the *Census of Population.* Table 6A.1 lists some of the most useful data that are collected in the various economic censuses described in this appendix.

    Census data are of generally high quality. Further, they are quite often available on the detailed level that the researcher needs. When not available in this form, the researcher can purchase either computer tapes or flexible diskettes from the Bureau of the Census for a nominal fee to create one's own tabulations. Alternatively, the researcher can contract with one of the private companies that market census-related products for information on a particular issue.[2] Not only does this allow one to obtain the information tailored to individual needs, but it is also one of the fastest ways to get census data. Further, many of the private providers update the census data at a detailed geographic level for the between-census years.

[1]For more detailed treatment, see H. Webster Johnson, Anthony J. Faria and Ernest L. Maier, *How to Use the Business Library: With Sources of Business Information,* 5th ed. (Cincinnati: South-Western Publishing, 1984); Eleanor G. May, *A Handbook for Business on the Use of Federal and State Statistical Data* (Washington, D.C.: Department of Commerce, 1979); and David W. Stewart, *Secondary Research: Information Sources and Methods* (Beverly Hills, Calif.: Sage Publications, 1984).

[2]Martha Farnsworth Riche, "Choosing 1980 Census Data Products," *American Demographics,* 3 (December 1981), pp. 12–16. See also Martha Farnsworth Riche, "Data Companies 1983," *American Demographics,* 5 (February 1983), pp. 28–39.

There are two major drawbacks to the use of census data: (1) censuses are not taken every year, and (2) the delay from time of collection to time of publication is quite substantial, often two years or more. This last weakness, however necessary because of the massive editing, coding, and tabulation tasks involved, renders the data obsolete for many research problems. The first difficulty requires that the researcher supplement the census data with current data. Unfortunately, current data are rarely available in the detail the researcher desires. This is particularly true with respect to detailed classifications by small geographic area, unless one takes advantage of the services of a private provider with update capability.

Census of Population The *Census of Population* is taken every ten years, in the years ending with a zero. The census reports the population by geographic region. It also provides detailed breakdowns on such characteristics as sex, marital status, age, education, race, national origin, family size, employment and unemployment, income, and other demographic characteristics. The *Current Population Reports,* which are published annually and make use of the latest information on migrations, birth and death rates, and so forth, update the information in the *Census of Population.*

Census of Housing Also published decennially for the years ending in zero, the *Census of Housing* was first taken in 1940 in conjunction with the *Census of Population.* It lists such things as type of structure, size, building condition, occupancy, water and sewage facilities, monthly rent, average value, and equipment including stoves, dishwashers, air conditioners, and so on. For large metropolitan areas, it provides detailed statistics by city block. The periods between publications of the *Census of Housing* are covered by the bureau's annual *American Housing Survey.*

Census of Retail Trade The *Census of Retail Trade,* which is taken every five years in the years ending in the numerals 2 or 7, contains detailed statistics on the retail trade. Retail stores are classified by type of business, and statistics are presented on such things as the number of stores, total sales, employment, and payroll. The statistics are broken down by small geographic areas such as counties, cities, and standard metropolitan statistical areas. Current data with respect to some of the information can be found in *Monthly Retail Trade.*

Census of Service Industries The *Census of Service Industries* is taken every five years in the years ending in the numerals 2 or 7. The service trade census provides data on receipts, employment, type of business (for example, hotel, laundry, and so on), and number of units by small geographic areas. Current data can be found in *Monthly Selected Services Receipts.*

Census of Wholesale Trade The *Census of Wholesale Trade,* which is taken every five years in the years ending in the numerals 2 or 7, contains detailed statistics on the wholesale trade. For instance, it classifies wholesalers into over 150 business groups and contains statistics on the functions they perform, sales volume, warehouse space, expenses, and so forth. It presents these statistics for counties, cities, and standard metropolitan statistical areas. Current data can be found in *Monthly Wholesale Trade.*

Census of Manufacturers The *Census of Manufacturers* has been taken somewhat irregularly in the past, but is now authorized for the years ending in the numerals 2 or 7. It categorizes manufacturing establishments by type using some 450 classes, and it contains detailed industry and geographic statistics for such items as the number of establishments, quantity of output, value added in manufacture, capital expenditures, employment, wages, inventories, sales by customer class, and fuel, water, and energy consumption. The *Annual Survey of Manufacturers* covers the years between publications of the census, while *Current Industrial Reports* contains the monthly and annual production figures for some commodities.

Census of Mineral Industries The *Census of Mineral Industries* is taken in the years ending in the numerals 2 or 7. The information here parallels that for the *Census of Manufacturers* but is for the mining industry. The census offers detailed geographic breakdowns

Table 6A.1   Information Available from Economic Censuses

Major Data Items	Retail Trade	Wholesale Trade	Service Industries	Construction Industries	Manufactures	Mineral Industries
Number of Establishments and Firms:						
All establishments	X			X		
Establishments with payroll	X	X	X	X	X	X
Establishments by legal form of organization	X	X	X	X	X	X
Firms	X	X	X		X	X
Single-unit and multi-unit firms	X	X	X		X	X
Concentration by major firms	X	X	X		X	
Employment:						
All employees	X	X	X	X	X	X
Production (construction) workers				X	X	X
Employment size of establishments	X	X	X	X	X	X
Employment size of firms	X	X	X			
Production (construction) worker hours				X	X	X
Payrolls:						
All employees, entire year	X	X	X	X	X	X
All employees, first quarter	X	X	X	X	X	
Production (construction) workers				X	X	X
Supplemental labor costs, legally required and voluntary	X	X	X	X	X	X
Sales Receipts, or Value of Shipments:						
All establishments	X			X	X	X
Establishments with payroll	X	X	X	X		
By product or line or type of construction	X	X	X	X	X	X
By class of customer	X	X				
By size of establishment	X	X	X	X	X	X
By size of firm	X	X	X			

Source: Adapted from *Guide to the 1982 Economic Censuses and Related Statistics* (Washington, D.C.: Bureau of the Census, U.S. Department of Commerce, 1984), p. 3.

Major Data Items	Retail Trade	Wholesale Trade	Service Industries	Construction Industries	Manufactures	Mineral Industries
Operating Expenses:						
Total	X	X	X			
Cost of materials, etc.	X	X		X	X	X
Specific materials consumed (quantity and cost)	X	X			X	X
Cost of fuels	X	X	X	X	X	X
Electric energy consumed (quantity and cost)	X	X	X		X	X
Contract work		X		X	X	X
Products bought and sold					X	X
Advertising	X	X	X			
Rental payments, total	X	X	X	X	X	X
Buildings and structures	X	X	X	X	X	X
Machinery and equipment	X	X	X	X	X	X
Communications services	X	X	X	X	X	X
Purchased repairs	X	X	X	X	X	
Capital Expenditures:						
Total	X	X	X	X	X	X
New, total	X	X	X	X	X	X
Buildings/equipment	X	X	X	X	X	X
Used, total	X	X	X	X	X	X
Buildings/equipment				X		X
Depreciable Assets, Gross Value Buildings/Equipment:						
End of 1981	X	X	X	X	X	X
End of 1982	X	X	X	X	X	X
Depreciation (total and detail for buildings/equipment)	X	X	X	X	X	X
Retirements (total and detail for buildings/equipment)	X	X	X	X	X	X
Inventories:						
End of 1981	X	X		X	X	X
End of 1982	X	X		X	X	X
Other:						
Value added	X	X		X	X	X
Specialization by type of construction/manufacturing				X	X	
Central administrative offices and auxiliaries	X	X	X	X	X	X
Water use					X	X

175

with respect to some fifty mineral industries on such things as the number of establishments, production, value of shipments, capital expenditures, cost of supplies, employment, payroll, power equipment, and water use. The *Minerals Yearbook,* published by the Bureau of Mines of the Department of the Interior, supplements the *Census of Mineral Industries* by providing annual data, although the two are not completely comparable in that they employ different classifications—an industrial classification for the Census Bureau data and a product classification for the Bureau of Mines data.

Census of Transportation The *Census of Transportation,* too, is taken in the years ending in the numerals 2 or 7. It covers three major areas: passenger travel, truck and bus inventory and use, and the transport of commodities by the various classes of carriers.

Census of Agriculture The *Census of Agriculture* was formerly taken in the years ending in the numerals 4 or 9. Since 1982, it is taken in years ending in 2 or 7. This census offers detailed breakdowns by state and county on the number of farms, farm types, acreage, land-use practices, employment, livestock produced and products raised, and value of products. It is supplemented by the annual publications *Agriculture Statistics* and *Commodity Yearbook.* In addition, the Department of Agriculture issues a number of bulletins, which often contain data not otherwise published.

Census of Government The *Census of Government* presents information on the general characteristics of state and local governments, including such things as employment, size of payroll, amount of indebtedness, and operating revenues and costs. The census is authorized in the years ending in the numerals 2 or 7.

Other Government Publications

The federal government also collects and publishes a great deal of statistical information in addition to the censuses. Some of this material is designed to supplement the various censuses and is gathered and published for this purpose (e.g., *Current Population Reports*), while other data are generated in the normal course of operations, such as collecting taxes, social security payments, claims for unemployment benefits, and so forth. Some publications also result from the desire to make the search for information more convenient. This section reviews some of the more important publications, chosen because they are of general interest in that they present a number of data series. Many of them also provide references to original sources, where more detailed data can be found. The sources are presented in alphabetical order.

Business Statistics Published every two years by the Department of Commerce, this publication provides an historical record of the data series appearing monthly in the *Survey of Current Business* (see the following).

County Business Patterns This annual publication of the Department of Commerce contains statistics on the number of businesses by type and their employment and payroll broken down by county. These data are often quite useful in industrial market potential studies.

County and City Data Book Published once every five years by the Bureau of the Census, this publication serves as a convenient source of statistics gathered in the various censuses and provides breakdowns on a city and county basis. Included are statistics on such things as population, education, employment, income, housing, banking, manufacturing output and capital expenditures, retail and wholesale sales, and mineral and agricultural output.

Economic Indicators This monthly publication by the Council of Economic Advisors contains charts and tables of general economic data such as gross national product, personal consumption expenditures, and other series important in measuring general economic activity. An annual supplement presenting historical and descriptive material on the sources, uses, and limitations of the data is also issued.

Economic Report of the President This publication results from the President's annual address to Congress regarding the general economic well-being of the country. The back portion of the report contains summary statistical tables using data collected elsewhere.

Federal Reserve Bulletin Published monthly by the Board of Governors of the Federal Reserve System, this publication is an important source of financial data including statistics on banking activity, interest rates, savings, the index of industrial production, an index of department store sales, prices, and international trade and finance.

Federal Statistical Directory This directory lists the names, office addresses, and telephone numbers of key people engaged in statistical programs and related activities, including agencies of the executive branch of the federal government. It is published by the Department of Commerce and is a useful source of who in Washington might be of some help in locating specific types of data.

Handbook of Cyclical Indicators Published monthly by the Department of Commerce, this publication contains at least seventy indicators of business activity designed to serve as a key to general economic conditions.

Historical Statistics of the United States from Colonial Times to 1970 This volume was prepared by the Bureau of the Census to supplement the *Statistical Abstract*. The *Statistical Abstract* is one of the more important general sources for the marketing researcher, since it contains data on a number of social, economic, and political aspects of life in the United States. One problem a user of *Statistical Abstract* data faces is incomparability of figures at various points in time because of the changes in definitions and classifications occasioned by a dynamic economy. *Historical Statistics* contains annual data on some 12,500 different series using consistent definitions and going back to the inception of the series.

Monthly Labor Review Published monthly by the Bureau of Labor Statistics, this publication contains statistics on employment and unemployment, labor turnover, earnings and hours worked, wholesale and retail prices, and work stoppages.

State and Metropolitan Area Data Book This book is a statistical abstract supplement put out by the Department of Commerce. It contains information on population, housing, government, manufacturing, retail and wholesale trade, and selected services by state and standard metropolitan statistical areas.

Statistical Abstract of the United States Published annually by the Bureau of the Census, this publication reproduces more than 1,500 tables originally published elsewhere that cover such areas as the economic, demographic, social, and political structure of the United States. The publication is intended to serve as a convenient statistical reference and as a guide to more detailed statistics. This latter function is fulfilled through reference to the original sources in the introductory comments to each section, the table footnotes, and a bibliography of sources. The *Statistical Abstract* is a source with which many researchers begin the search for external secondary data.

Statistics of Income Published annually by the Internal Revenue Service of the Treasury Department, this publication is prepared from federal income tax returns of corporations and individuals. There are different publications for each type of tax report—one for corporations, one for sole proprietorships and partnerships, and one for individuals. The *Corporate Income Tax Return* volume, for example, contains balance sheet and income statement statistics compiled from corporate tax returns and broken down by major industry, asset size, and so on.

Survey of Current Business Published monthly by the Bureau of Economic Analysis in the Department of Commerce, this publication provides a comprehensive statistical summary of the national income and product accounts of the United States. There are some 2,600 different statistical series reported, covering such topics as general business indicators, commodity prices, construction and real estate activity, personal consumption expenditures by major type, foreign transactions, income and employment by industry, transportation and communications activity, and so on. Most of the statistical series present data on the last four years.

U.S. Industrial Outlook Produced annually by the Department of Commerce, this publication covers the recent trends and outlook for over 350 manufacturing and service industries.

Privately Produced Publications and Marketing Guides

In addition to the censuses and other government publications, a number of private publications containing secondary data are of general interest to the marketing researcher. This section lists some of the more important ones in alphabetical order.

Almanac of Business and Industrial Financial Ratios Published annually by Prentice-Hall, this publication contains number of establishments, sales, and selected operating ratios for a number of industries (e.g., food stores). The figures are derived from tax return data supplied by the Internal Revenue Service and are reported for twelve categories, based on assets, within each industry. The data thus allow the comparison of a particular company's financial ratios with competitors of similar size.

CRB Commodity Yearbook Published annually by the Commodity Research Bureau, this publication contains data on prices, production, exports, stocks, and so on, for approximately 100 individual commodities.

Editor and Publisher Market Guide Published annually by *Editor and Publisher* magazine, this guide contains data on United States and Canadian cities, including location, population, number of households, principal industries, retail sales and outlets, and climate.

Fortune Directory Published annually by the editors of *Fortune* magazine, this directory provides information on sales, assets, profits, invested capital, and employees for the 500 largest United States industrial corporations.

Handbook of Basic Economic Statistics Published annually by the Economics Statistics Bureau, this handbook contains current and historical U.S. statistics on industry, commerce, labor, and agriculture.

Marketing Economics Guide Published annually by the Marketing Economics Institute, this publication provides detailed operating information on 1,500 retailing centers throughout the country on a regional, state, county, and city basis. It contains information on population, percent of households by income class, disposable income, total retail sales, and retail sales by store group.

Million Dollar Directory Published annually by Dun's Marketing Services this five-volume reference source lists the offices, products, sales, and number of employees by company.

Moody's Manuals Published annually, these manuals—*Banks and Finance, Industrials, Municipals and Governments, Public Utilities, Transportation*—contain balance sheet and income statements for individual companies and government units.

Poor's Register of Corporations, Directors and Executives Published annually by Standard and Poor, this register lists officers, products, sales, addresses, telephone numbers, and employees for some 45,000 U.S. and Canadian corporations.

Rand McNally Zip Code Atlas Published annually by Rand McNally Company, this atlas contains marketing data and maps for cities and towns in the United States. Included are such things as population, auto registrations, and retail trade.

Sales and Marketing Management Survey of Buying Power Published annually by *Sales and Marketing Management* magazine, this survey contains market data for states, a number of counties, cities, and standard metropolitan statistical areas. Included are statistics on population, retail sales, and household income and a combined index of buying power for each reported geographic area.

Thomas Register Published annually by Thomas Publishing Company, this seventeen-volume publication lists the specific providers of individual products and services and provides information on their address, branch offices, and subsidiaries.

United Nations Statistical Yearbook This annual United Nations publication contains statistics on a wide range of foreign and domestic activities including forestry, transportation, manufacturing, consumption, and education.

World Almanac and Book of Facts Issued annually by the Newspaper Enterprise Association, this publication serves as a well-indexed handbook on a wide variety of subjects. Included are industrial, financial, religious, social, and political statistics.

Guides to Secondary Data

The preceding sources are general. They contain information applicable to a wide number of research problems. Typically they provide a productive start in the search for secondary data. If this search results in a dead end, the required secondary data may still be available in industry trade publications. The amount of data available on an industry-by-industry basis is extensive indeed, and researchers are well advised not to finish their search without reviewing the appropriate industry sources. Often the source of industry statistics will be the industry trade association, while in other cases it may be trade journals serving the industry. Researchers new to an area may not be aware of these sources and thus may feel they face a hopeless task in ferreting them out. Fortunately, a number of published guides should be of assistance. This section lists some of the main guides. It includes guides to government statistics as well as privately produced statistics.

American Statistics Index (Washington, D.C.: Congressional Information Service). Published annually and updated monthly, the publication is intended to serve as a comprehensive index of statistical data available to the public from any agency of the federal government.

Brownstone, David M., and Gorton Carruth, *Where to Find Business Information* (New York: John Wiley, 1979). This publication lists over 5,000 books, periodicals, or data bases of current interest and contains subject, title, and publisher indexes.

Consultants and Consulting Organizations Directory, 7th ed. (Detroit: Gale Research, 1987). This directory lists firms and individuals who are active in consulting and briefly describes their services and fields of interest.

Daniells, Lorna M., *Business Information Sources,* rev. ed. (Berkeley, Calif.: University of California Press, 1986). A guide to the basic sources of business information organized by subject area.

Directory of Directories, biennial (Detroit: Gale Research, with supplements). This directory, which is arranged by subject matter, lists, among other things, commercial and manufacturing directories, directories of individual industries, trades, and professions, and rosters of professional and scientific societies.

Directory of Federal Statistics for Local Areas: A Guide to Sources (Washington, D.C.: U.S. Bureau of the Census, 1978). A guide to the sources of federal statistics for local areas on such topics as population, health, education, income, and finance.

Directory of Federal Statistics for States: A Guide to Sources (Washington, D.C.: U.S. Bureau of the Census, 1976). Similar to the guide for local sources, this guide outlines the sources of federal statistics for states on such topics as population, income, education, and so on.

Directory of Nonfederal Statistics for State and Local Areas: A Guide to Sources (Washington, D.C.: U.S. Bureau of the Census, 1970). Similar to the preceding census guides, this guide details the private, local, and state organizations collecting and publishing data on economic, political, and social subjects for state and local areas.

Encyclopedia of Associations (Detroit: Gale Research). Published annually, this encyclopedia lists the active trade, business, and professional associations and briefly describes each organization's activities and lists their publications.

Encyclopedia of Business Information Sources, 5th ed. (Detroit: Gale Research, 1983). A guide to the information available on various subjects, including basic statistical sources, associations, periodicals, directories, handbooks, and general literature.

Frank, Nathalie D., *Data Sources for Business and Market Analysis,* 3rd. ed. (Metuchen, N.J.: Scarecrow Press, 1983). An annotated guide to original statistical sources arranged by source of information rather than by topic.

Guide to American Directories (Coral Springs, Fla.: B. Klein Publications, biennial). This guide provides information on directories published in the United States, categorized under 300 technical, mercantile, industrial, scientific, and professional headings.

Guide to Foreign Trade Statistics (Washington, D.C.: U.S. Bureau of the Census, 1972). A guide to the published and unpublished sources of foreign trade statistics.

Guide to Industrial Statistics (Washington, D.C.: U.S. Bureau of the Census, 1977). A guide to the Census Bureau's programs relating to industry, including the type of statistics gathered and where these statistics are published.

Directory of American Research and Technology, 20th ed. (New York: Bowker, 1986). A guide to research and development capabilities of more than 6,000 industrial organizations in the United States. It contains an alphabetical listing of the organizations, address of facilities, sizes of staffs, and fields of research and development.

How to Find Information About Companies (Washington, D.C.: Washington Researchers, 1983). A useful guide to locating information about specific companies.

Nelson, Theodore A., *Measuring Markets: A Guide to the Use of Federal and State Statistical Data* (Washington, D.C.: Department of Commerce, 1979). This book serves as an excellent guide to both federal and state statistical data.

Social Sciences Citation Index (Philadelphia: Institute for Scientific Information). Published three times yearly, with annual cumulations, this publication indexes all articles in about 1,400 social science periodicals and selected articles in approximately 1,200 periodicals in other disciplines.

Statistics and Maps for National Market Analysis (Washington, D.C.: Small Business Administration, 1978). This small reference booklet (only eight pages) contains sources of interest to researchers needing statistics and maps for such market analysis projects as allocation of sales effort by area and appraisal of market opportunity by area.

Statistical Reference Index (Washington, D.C.: Congressional Information Service). Published annually, this publication is intended to serve as a selective guide to American Statistical publications from private organizations and state government sources.

Wasserman, Paul, *et al., Statistics Sources,* 10th ed. (Detroit: Gale Research, 1986). A guide to federal, state, and private sources of statistics on a wide variety of subjects.

Who's Who in Consulting (Detroit: Gale Research, 1982). This directory provides biographical information on consultants in a variety of fields including their subject area and geographical location.

Guides to Information Banks

As mentioned, the growth in computer-readable storage systems for data bases has been spectacular. Keeping up with the growth is difficult as new on-line search services are being created all the time. Fortunately, there are several good guides to the on-line data bases and search services that are available.

Directory of Online Databases (Santa Monica, Calif.: Cuadra Associates, Inc.). Published quarterly, this publication describes more than 275 bibliographic and nonbibliographic data bases.

Garven, Andrew P., and Hubert Bermont, *How to Win with Information or Lose Without It* (New York: Find/SVP, 1984). This publication, written in nontechnical language especially for executives, discusses data banks and information retrieval services.

Hoover, Ryan E., *et al., The Library and Information Manager's Guide to Online Services* (White Plains, N.Y.: Knowledge Industry Publications, 1980). See also *Online Search Strategies* by the same author, which contains practical tips on the effective use of bibliographic data bases and search systems.

Kruzas, Anthony T., and Linda Varekamp Sullivan, eds., *Encyclopedia of Information Systems and Services,* 6th ed. (Detroit: Gale Research, 1985). This encyclopedia lists and describes over 2,500 organizations involved in data storage and retrieval. Included are data base producers and publishers, on-line vendors, information centers, research centers, and banks.

Chapter 7

Collecting Primary Data

Learning Objectives

Upon completing this chapter, you should be able to

1. List the kinds of demographic and socioeconomic characteristics that interest marketers.
2. Relate the premise on which life-style analysis rests.
3. Specify the four main groups used to classify people in value and life-style (VALS) research.
4. Cite the three main approaches used to measure the effectiveness of magazine ads.
5. Give two reasons why researchers are interested in people's motives.
6. Describe the two basic means of obtaining primary data.
7. State the specific advantages of each method of data collection.

Case in Marketing Research

Karl Taft strolled through the parking lot of a large high school in suburban Dallas.

"Look at this," he said, beckoning to a row of Chevy C10 pickup trucks parked neatly at the edge of the lot. "I want to know what went wrong here, and I want to know soon."

Margaret Downing winced. She was the head marketing researcher hired recently by Taft, who had arrived in Dallas from North Dakota last month to run the city's largest Ford dealership. He did not have a reputation for being a patient man.

"Where I come from," Taft said, "when a youngster gets to choose his first vehicle, it's naturally a Ford F150 pickup. Now either something's going on here that I don't understand, or my predecessor was too distracted by the Cowboy Cheerleaders to keep his mind on the important business in life—selling trucks.

"By the end of next week I want some information on the pickup truck market. What's Chevy doing that we aren't? Why don't these cowboys recognize a good four-wheel-drive truck when they see one?" Taft asked petulantly.

"I'll get right on it, sir," said Downing.

Having been raised in Dallas, she had some opinions on the subject, but she was too astute a researcher to offer them to such a client without the hard data to back them up.

Discussion Issues

1. What kind of secondary information would you look for if you were Downing?

2. What are the probable limitations to the secondary data that Downing might find in researching this problem?

3. What kind of primary research might be necessary to answer Taft's questions?

Source: This fictitious case is based on Eugene Carlson, "Personality of Area's Drivers Offers Key to Auto's Success," *The Wall Street Journal,* 63 (December 13, 1983), p. 33.

In Chapter 6 we emphasized the advantages of using secondary data. Such research information is usually fast, inexpensive, and fairly easy to obtain. We also noted that researchers who give secondary data only a casual look are being reckless. However, as we have seen, such data also have certain shortcomings and rarely will provide a complete solution to a research problem. The units of measurement or classes used to report the data may be wrong; the data may be nearly obsolete by the time of their publication; the data may be incomplete; and so on. When these conditions occur, the researcher logically turns to primary data.

This chapter is the first of three dealing with primary data, and it serves as an introduction to the subject. In this chapter we will discuss the various types of primary data researchers collect from and about subjects, and will examine the two main means they employ to do it: communication and observation. In subsequent chapters we will explore each of these methods in more detail.

◆ Types of Primary Data

Demographic/Socioeconomic Characteristics

One type of primary data of great interest to marketers is the subject's demographic and socioeconomic characteristics, such as age, education, occupation, marital status, sex, income, or social class. Researchers often match these variables with the data they have collected to gain greater insight into the subject under investigation. They might be interested, for example, in determining whether people's attitudes toward ecology and pollution are related to their level of formal education. Alternatively, they may ask whether the use of a particular product is in any way related to a person's age, sex, education, income, and so on, and if so, in what way. These are questions of market segmentation. Demographic and socioeconomic characteristics are often used to delineate market segments (see "Back to the Case").

Until the early 1980s, American Express, for example, never made a serious effort to woo women or the young, according to one of the company's executives. The company's primary interest was in those it considered to be serious business travelers, who were largely men. But by 1982, the company determined that almost 40 percent of the American Express card's eligible universe had already been secured, and it cast about for ways to broaden the pool of potential users.

In focus groups, the marketing team discovered that although career women aged twenty-five to forty knew and enjoyed the company's "Do you know me?" campaign, they never imagined that the cards were for them. They identified the American Express card as an almost exclusively male product.

Researchers also discovered that men and women see success differently—for women, it is not synonymous with business achievement. Focus groups told researchers that women put less value than men on career advancement and possessions and more on having interesting lives.

Based on that research, the "interesting lives" campaign was launched, in which women are portrayed taking their husbands to dinner, cross-country skiing with an infant in a Snugli, or disembarking a plane toting a briefcase—and a teddy bear.

The campaign has been wildly successful. In 1980 only 16 percent of cardholders were women; by 1985 that number had soared to 29 percent.[1]

Demographic and socioeconomic characteristics are sometimes called states of being, in that they represent attributes of people. Some of these states of being such

---

[1]Bernice Kanner, "Think Plastic," *New York,* 18 (March 4, 1985), pp. 19–24.

as a respondent's age, sex, and level of formal education, can be readily verified. Some, such as social class, cannot be verified except very crudely, since they are relative and not absolute measures of a person's standing in society.[2] A person's income can also be a fairly difficult piece of information to verify. Although the amount a person earns in a given year is an absolute, not a relative, quantity, in our society money is such a sensitive topic that exact numbers may be hard to determine.

Psychological/Life-style Characteristics

• Personality

Normal patterns of behavior exhibited by an individual; the attributes, traits, and mannerisms that distinguish one individual from another.

Another type of primary data of interest to marketers is the subject's psychological and life-style characteristics in the form of personality traits, activities, interests, and values. **Personality** refers to the normal patterns of behavior exhibited by an individual—the attributes, traits, and mannerisms that distinguish one individual from another. We often characterize people by the personality traits—aggressiveness, dominance, friendliness, sociability—they display. Marketers are interested in per-

---

[2]See James H. Myers and William H. Reynolds, *Consumer Behavior in Marketing Management* (Boston: Houghton Mifflin, © 1967), pp. 206–216, for a useful discussion of social class, its role in marketing-related phenomena, and the various ways in which it is measured. See Charles M. Schaninger, "Social Class Versus Income Revisited: An Empirical Investigation," *Journal of Marketing Research,* 18 (May 1981), pp. 192–208, for a comparison of the ability of social class and income to predict consumption of a number of household products.

Back to the Case

For several days Margaret Downing has been poring over data from R. L. Polk & Company of Detroit relating to car sales in several states. What she found confirmed her earlier suspicions.

In sixteen states, the most popular car on the road wasn't a car. It was a pickup truck. In fact, if plotted on a map, a well-defined "truck belt" would emerge that would run from the upper Midwest, south through Texas and the Gulf states.

After checking vehicle registrations, Downing found that in the six upper-Midwest states, plus West Virginia and New Mexico, the single most popular vehicle on the road is a Ford F150, a

half-ton pickup. Given Mr. Taft's North Dakota roots this would account for his perception that the Ford pickup is the vehicle of choice among teenage drivers.

However, in seven Southern states, including Texas, Chevrolet's half-ton model, the C10, is the most popular vehicle model.

Downing knew she had the data to convince Taft that what he was seeing was not simply the result of an inept predecessor in the local Ford dealership. But what was the reason behind such a geographic preference in pickup trucks? That was going to be the harder question to answer.

As an experienced researcher, Margaret Downing wisely consulted secondary data before suggesting a more involved and expensive study. In the process, she uncovered information that would support Taft's perception that something was different about the pickup truck market in Texas than the one in North Dakota. Downing discovered a fact that the auto industry has known for a long time: there are vast regional differences in the kinds of cars people like. But the reasons for this phenomenon are much more complex than the simple fact of there being differences. Only primary research can uncover those.

sonality because it seems as if it would affect the way consumers and others in the marketing process behave. Many marketers maintain, for example, that personality can affect a consumer's choice of stores or products, or an individual's response to an advertisement or point-of-purchase display. Similarly, they believe that successful salespeople are more likely to be extroverted and understanding of other people's feelings than are unsuccessful salespeople. While the empirical evidence regarding the ability of personality to predict consumption behavior or salesperson success is weak, personality remains a variable dear to the hearts of marketing researchers.[3] Typically, it is measured by one of the standard personality inventories that have been developed by psychologists.

Life-style analysis rests on the premise that the firm can plan more effective strategies to reach its target market if it knows more about its customers in terms of how they live, what interests them, and what they like. The general thrust of such research, which is often called **psychographic analysis,** has been to develop a number of statements that reflect a person's *AIO*—activities (A), interests (I), and opinions (O)—and consumption behavior. The statements might include such things as "I like to watch football games on television," "I like stamp collecting," "I am very interested in national politics." Such a psychographic test would typically contain a great many such statements and be administered to a large sample of respondents.[4]

For example, the advertising agency of Needham, Harper, and Steers conducts an annual life-style study that asks 3,500 respondents to answer 700 questions.[5] Table 7.1 contains the list of characteristics that are usually assessed with AIO inventories. The analysis attempts to identify groups of consumers who are likely to behave similarly toward a product, and who have similar life-style profiles.

While the idea seems like a good one in the abstract, marketers discovered that in actual practice the technique has problems. One problem is that the categories of users, as identified by psychographics or AIO inventories, keeps changing from product to product. This means that each product required a new data collection and analysis exercise. Because the profiles across products are so unstable, it is also impossible to develop demographic descriptions of the various groups that would be useful in planning marketing strategies for new products or brands.

Value and life-style research (VALS) was developed to avoid these problems by creating a standard psychographic framework that could be used for a variety of

• Psychographic analysis

Technique that investigates how people live, what interests them and what they like; it is also called *life-style,* or *AIO, analysis* since it relies on a number of statements about a person's activities (the *A* in AIO), interests (the *I*), and opinions (the *O*).

---

[3]For a review of the evidence regarding the relationship of personality to consumer behavior, see Harold H. Kassarjian, "Personality and Consumer Behavior: A Review," *Journal of Marketing Research,* 8 (November 1971), pp. 409–418; or Richard C. Becherer and Lawrence M. Richard, "Self-Monitoring as a Moderator Variable in Consumer Behavior," *Journal of Consumer Research,* 5 (December 1978), pp. 159–162. For a review of the evidence regarding the relationship between personality characteristics and salesperson success, see Gilbert A. Churchill, Jr., Neil M. Ford, Steven W. Hartley, and Orville C. Walker, Jr., "The Determinants of Salesperson Performance: A Meta Analysis," *Journal of Marketing Research,* 22 (May 1985), pp. 103–118.

[4]One of the more popular lists is the 300-question inventory that appears in William D. Wells and Douglas Tigert, "Activities, Interests, and Opinions," *Journal of Advertising Research,* 11 (August 1971), pp. 27–35. For a general review of the origins, development, and thrust of life-style and psychographic research, see William D. Wells, ed., *Life Style and Psychographics* (Chicago: American Marketing Association, 1974). For evidence regarding the reliability and validity of psychographic inventories, see Alvin C. Burns and Mary Carolyn Harrison, "A Test of the Reliability of Psychographics," *Journal of Marketing Research,* 16 (February 1979), pp. 32–38; John L. Lastovicka, "On the Validation of Lifestyle Traits: A Review and Illustration," *Journal of Marketing Research,* 19 (February 1982), pp. 126–138; and Ian Fenwick, D. A. Schellinck, and K. W. Kendall, "Assessing the Reliability of Psychographic Analyses," *Marketing Science,* 2 (Winter 1983), pp. 57–74.

[5]Cara S. Frazer, "Staying Afloat in Oceans of Data," *Advertising Age,* 54 (October 31, 1983), pp. m42–m43.

Table 7.1   Life-Style Dimensions

Activities	Interests	Opinions
Work	Family	Themselves
Hobbies	Home	Social issues
Social events	Job	Politics
Vacation	Community	Business
Entertainment	Recreation	Economics
Club membership	Fashion	Education
Community	Food	Products
Shopping	Media	Future
Sports	Achievements	Culture

Source: Adapted from Joseph T. Plummer, "The Concept and Application of Life Style Segmentation," *Journal of Marketing,* 38 (January 1974), p. 34. Published by the American Marketing Association.

products. One particularly popular VALS classification scheme, for example, divides people into four main groups—need-driven, outer-directed, inner-directed, and combined outer-and-inner-directed—and nine subgroups.[6] Table 7.2 describes these groups and their size.

Attitudes/Opinions

Some authors distinguish between attitudes and opinions, while others use the terms interchangeably. Most typically **attitude** is used to refer to an individual's "preference, inclination, views or feelings toward some phenomenon," while **opinions** are "verbal expressions of attitudes." We shall not make the distinction between the terms in this text but will treat attitudes and opinions interchangeably as representing a person's ideas, convictions, or liking with respect to a specific object or idea.

Attitude is one of the more important notions in the marketing literature, since it is generally thought that attitudes are related to behavior.

> Obviously, when an individual likes a product he will be more inclined to buy it than when he does not like it; when he likes one brand more than another, he will tend to buy the preferred brand. Attitudes may be said to be the forerunners of behavior.[7]

Thus, marketers are often interested in people's attitudes toward the product itself, their overall attitudes with respect to specific brands, and their attitudes toward specific aspects or features possessed by several brands. Attitude is such a pervasive notion in behavioral science, and particularly in marketing, that Chapter 12 is devoted to various types of instruments used to measure it.

But, as many a marketer has discovered, it is risky to assume that people's attitudes toward products will remain consistent. General Mills discovered this fact to its dis-

◆ **Attitude**

An individual's preference, inclination, views or feelings toward some phenomenon.

◆ **Opinion**

Verbal expressions of attitudes.

---

[6]Arnold Mitchell, *The Nine American Lifestyles* (New York: MacMillan, 1983).

[7]Fred L. Schreier, *Modern Marketing Research: A Behavioral Science Approach* (Belmont, Calif.: Wadsworth, 1963), p. 273. For a general review of the relationship between attitude and behavior, see Susan T. Fiske and Shelley E. Taylor, *Social Cognition* (Reading, Mass.: Addison-Wesley, 1984), pp. 369–399.

Table 7.2   The Nine American Life-Styles

Need-Driven Groups

Survivor

Old, intensely poor; fearful; despairing; far
removed from the cultural mainstream;
misfits
Number: 7 million
Age: Most over 65
Sex: 73% female
Income: Most under $7,500
Education: Few have completed high school

Sustainer

Living on the edge of poverty; angry and
resentful; streetwise; involved in the
underground economy
Number: 12 million
Age: 67% under 35
Sex: 57% female
Income: Median, under $10,000
Education: More than half did not graduate from
high school

Outer-Directed Groups

Belonger

Aging; traditional and
conventional; contented;
intensely patriotic;
sentimental; deeply stable
Number: 64 million
Age: Median, 57
Sex: 58% female
Income: Median, $17,300
Education: Median, high school
graduate

Emulator

Youthful and ambitious;
macho; show-off; trying to
break into the system, to
make it big
Number: 17 million
Age: Median 28
Sex: 53% male
Income: Median, $18,000
Education: High school graduate
plus

Achiever

Middle-aged and prosperous;
able leaders; self-assured;
materialistic; builders of the
"American dream"
Number: 35 million
Age: Median 42
Sex: 58% male
Income: Median, over $40,000
Education: 25% college
graduates

Inner-Directed Groups

I-Am-Me

Transition state; exhibitionist
and narcissistic; young;
impulsive; dramatic;
experimental; active; inventive
Number: 5 million
Age: 94% under 25
Sex: 51% male
Income: Median, $8,800
Education: Some college

Experiential

Youthful; seek direct
experience; person-centered;
artistic; intensely oriented
toward inner growth
Number: 8 million
Age: Median, 28
Sex: 55% female
Income: Median, over $30,000
Education: 38% college
graduates or more

Societally Conscious

Mission-oriented; leaders of
single-issue groups; mature;
successful; some live lives of
voluntary simplicity
Number: 20 million
Age: Median, 37
Sex: 51% male
Income: Median, over $35,000
Education: 70% college
graduates, many have
attended graduate school

Combined Outer-and-Inner-Directed Group

Integrated

Psychologically mature; large
field of vision; tolerant and
understanding; sense of
fittingness
Number: 3.2 million

Source: Adapted with permission of Macmillan Publishing Company from *The Nine American Lifestyles: Who We Are and Where We Are Going* by Arnold Mitchell, and the Values and Lifestyles (VALS™) Program, SRI International, Menlo Park, CA. Copyright © 1983 by Arnold Mitchell.

Back to the Case

Margaret Downing sat outside Karl Taft's office at the Ford dealership waiting for Taft to close a deal on a Thunderbird. With her she had the results of the study she and her colleagues had recently completed investigating regional preferences in pickup trucks. The results were fascinating, but Downing was not eager to share them with the abrasive Taft.

Her company's surveys had shown that there were long-standing differences in the market that seemed to be the result of the regions' motorists' unique personalities. In the Midwest Farm Belt, the Ford pickup had earned a reputation for brawn, an image that sat well in an area where small trucks are often used for heavy-duty farm work. As one car salesman at a Chevrolet dealership in North Dakota

had told her, "We're right on the dividing line of cow country and farm country, and here it's a little more macho to have a four-wheel-drive truck than one built closer to the ground. It just looks tougher. Ford started stronger in four-wheel trucks, and it's taken time to overtake them."

In the South, tradition seems to be a major influence on a young person's preference in pickup trucks. Downing remembered one Chevy dealer telling her, "If your daddy bought a Chevrolet pickup and had good results, you probably will too."

Another dealer told her that status played a part in Southerners' preference for Chevy pickups, since Chevrolet was quicker to offer fancier options for trucks. That, he said, was a big selling point in an area

where gussied-up pickups are called "cowboy Cadillacs."

Downing knew Taft had a reputation as a crackerjack car salesman, but it was clear it was going to take more than simple salesmanship to change the area's attitudes and opinions when it came to the subject of pickup trucks.

Primary research on people's attitudes and opinions regarding pickup truck ownership uncovered some of the reasons for the differences between the two markets. This kind of information can then be used by marketing decision makers to design a strategy that might be able to influence truck buyers' purchase behavior. Obviously, however, overcoming a deep-seated regional preference for a brand is no easy feat!

may when sales of its Izod brand knit shirts, with their distinctive alligator emblem, dropped dramatically when the "preppy" look went out of vogue.[8]

Awareness/Knowledge

Awareness/knowledge as used in marketing research refers to what respondents do and do not know about some object or phenomenon. For instance, a problem of considerable importance is the effectiveness of magazine ads. One measure of effectiveness is the "awareness" generated by the ad, using one of the three approaches described in Table 7.3. All three approaches are aimed at assessing the respondent's awareness of and knowledge about the ad, although the three approaches can produce dramatically different results.

---

[8]Pamela G. Hollis, "Izod's Fall from Vogue a Drag on General Mills," *New York Times,* 133 (November 15, 1984), pp. D1 and D5.

Table 7.3   Approaches Used to Measure Awareness

Unaided recall: The consumer is given no cues at all, but is simply asked to recall what advertising he or she has seen recently. No prompting is used because, presumably, if prompting even in a general category were used (for example, cake mixes), the respondent would have a tendency to remember more advertisements in that product category.

Aided recall: The consumer is given some prompting. Typically this prompting might be in the form of questions about advertisements in a specific product category. Alternatively, the respondent might be given a list showing the names or trademarks of advertisers which appeared in the particular magazine issue, along with names or trademarks that did not appear, and is asked to check those to which he or she was exposed.

Recognition: The consumer is actually shown an advertisement and is asked whether or not he or she remembers seeing it.

Source: Adapted from James H. Myers and William H. Reynolds, *Consumer Behavior in Marketing Management* (New York: Houghton Mifflin, © 1967), pp. 65–67. Used by permission of the publisher.

Research Window 7.1
Calvin Klein Designs the World's Best-Known Underwear Ads

In an effort to increase reader awareness of his ads, Calvin Klein has pushed advertising to the limits of good taste.

Klein's first foray into controversial advertising was when a fifteen-year-old Brooke Shields scandalized television viewers in 1980 by announcing that "nothing" came between her and her Calvins. That ad created such a furor that many television stations refused to run it, and feminist groups denounced it as nothing more than pornography. In comparison with Klein's underwear advertising, those ads now seem the height of innocence.

In 1985 one of Klein's ads for underwear pictured two men and a woman (wearing Klein's briefest briefs) sleeping together on a towel-strewn bed. There was no caption, no explanation. The reader was left wondering what activities preceded their nap.

According to Klein, that ambiguity was intentional. "I'm not out to offend anyone, but the ads are meant to be ambiguous—to make people stop and think. I don't want women flipping through 600 pages of *Vogue* and not even noticing my ads."

Some advertising executives on Madison Avenue are critical of Klein's approach. Others doubt the selling power of the racier ads and dismiss his more offbeat creations as "ineffectual self-indulgence."

Klein doesn't worry. In their first five days at Bloomingdale's, 400 dozen pairs of Klein's basic briefs, bikini briefs, and athletic shirts for men were sold, at the same time that Bloomingdale's was promoting its own, virtually identical line at just over half the price.

If that weren't enough, there was other empirical evidence of reader awareness of Klein's advertising: at dozens of bus-stop shelters throughout New York, fans managed to break the glass and steal ads featuring a muscular young pole-vaulter reclining in the sun wearing nothing but a pair of briefs.

Source: Based on "A Kinky New Calvinism," *Newsweek,* 107 (March 11, 1985), p. 65; and Bernice Kanner, "The New Calvinism," *New York,* 17 (September 17, 1984), pp. 31–36.

A Starch readership report includes a copy of the ad that has been rated. In this advertisement, the labels show readership (i.e., recall and recognition) of the ad as a whole and the component parts (i.e., headline, illustrations, copy).

Source: Courtesy of Starch INRA Hooper, Inc.

Retention rates are much higher when knowledge is measured by recognition rather than by recall and by aided rather than unaided recall. This, of course, raises the question of which method is the most accurate. There are problems with each method.[9] The important thing to note is that when marketers speak of a person's awareness, they often mean the individual's knowledge of the advertisement. A person "very much aware" or possessing "high awareness" typically knows a great deal about the ad. (See Research Window 7.1.)

_____

[9]See Myers and Reynolds, *Consumer Behavior,* pp. 68–72, for a succinct discussion of the problems common to each.

Awareness and knowledge are also used interchangeably when marketers speak of product awareness. Marketing researchers are often interested in determining whether the respondent is aware of the following:[10]

- The product
- Its features
- Where it is available
- Its price
- Its manufacturer
- Where it is made
- How it is used, and for what purpose
- Its specific distinctive features

Although framed in terms of awareness, these questions, to a greater or lesser degree, aim at determining the individual's knowledge of the product. For our purposes, then, knowledge and awareness will be used interchangeably to refer to what a respondent does indeed know about an advertisement, product, retail store, and so on.

Intentions

♦ Intention

Anticipated or planned future behavior.

A person's **intentions** refer to the individual's anticipated or planned future behavior. Marketers are interested in people's intentions primarily with regard to purchasing behavior. One of the better known studies regarding purchase intentions is that conducted by the Survey Research Center at the University of Michigan. The center regularly conducts surveys for the Federal Reserve Board to determine the general financial condition of consumers and their outlook with respect to the state of the economy in the near future. The center asks consumers about their buying intentions for big ticket items such as appliances, automobiles, and homes during the next few months. The responses are then analyzed, and the proportion of the sample that indicates each of the following is reported:

- Definite intention to buy
- Probable intention to buy
- Undecided
- Definite intention not to buy

Intentions receive less attention in marketing than do other types of primary data, largely because there is often a great disparity between what people say they are going to do and what they actually do. This is particulary true with respect to purchase behavior. Researchers are most likely to use purchase intentions when investigating the likelihood of consumers buying items that require a large sum of money. For a family this might be an automobile, a new house, or even a vacation trip. For a business, a study of purchase intentions would usually focus on a new plant or equipment.

The general assumption researchers make is that the more an item costs, the more time a consumer will spend in planning the purchase. If that assumption is true,

---

[10]Schreier, *Modern Marketing Research,* pp. 269–273.

then there should be a significant correlation between anticipated and actual behavior. Unfortunately, the evidence of such a correlation is weak.[11]

Motivation

The concept of motivation seems to contain more semantic confusion than most terms in the behavioral sciences.

> Some writers insist that *motives* are different from *drives* and use the latter term primarily to characterize the basic physiological "tissue" needs (e.g., hunger, thirst, shelter, sex). Others distinguish between *needs* and *wants,* stating that needs are the basic motivating forces which translate themselves into more immediate wants which satisfy these needs (e.g., hunger needs give rise to wanting a good steak dinner).[12]

• Motive

Need, want, drive, wish, desire, or an impulse, or any inner state that energizes, activates, or moves and that directs or channels behavior toward goals.

For our purposes, a **motive** may refer to a need, a want, a drive, an urge, a wish, a desire, an impulse, or any inner state that directs or channels behavior toward goals.

A marketing researcher's interest in motives typically involves determining *why* people behave as they do. There are several reasons that explain this interest. In the first place, researchers believe that a person's motives tend to be more stable than an individual's behavior and therefore offer a better basis for predicting future behavior than does past behavior. For example, a young couple living in an apartment may say that they want to buy a house. Just because they did not buy a house last year, or the year before, does not mean that their motives have changed. Once they have saved enough for a down payment, or once a baby is on the way, they may be spurred to act on their motives, and past behavior will have no bearing on this action.

The second reason researchers are interested in motives is that by understanding what drives a person's behavior, it is easier to understand the behavior itself. A desire for status may motivate one car buyer to purchase a Mercedes-Benz, while a concern for safety may send another to the local Volvo showroom. If researchers understand the forces underlying consumer behavior, they are in a better position to influence future behavior, or at least to design products consistent with what they anticipate that behavior to be.

Behavior

• Behavior

What subjects have done or are doing.

Behavior concerns what subjects have done or are doing. In marketing this usually means purchase and use behavior. Now, behavior is a physical activity. It takes place under specific circumstances, at a particular time, and involves one or more actors or participants. A marketing researcher investigating behavior would be interested in a description of the activity and its various components. Table 7.4 is a checklist of the key elements involved in purchase behavior that researchers can use to design data-collection instruments.[13]

---

[11]Manohar U. Kalwani and Alvin J. Silk, "On the Reliability and Predictive Validity of Purchase Intention Measures," *Marketing Science,* 1 (Summer 1982), pp. 243–286; Murphy A. Sewall, "Relative Information Contributions of Consumer Purchase Intentions and Management Judgment as Explanations of Sales," *Journal of Marketing Research,* 18 (May 1981), pp. 249–253; and Gary M. Mullett and Marvin J. Karson, "Analysis of Purchase Intent Scales Weighted by Probability of Actual Purchase," *Journal of Marketing Research,* 22 (February 1985), pp. 93–96.

[12]Myers and Reynolds, *Consumer Behavior,* p. 80.

[13]The checklist is adapted from Schreier, *Modern Marketing Research,* p. 251. Schreier also has a productive discussion of the many kinds of questions that need to be answered to complete the checklist.

Table 7.4   Behavior Checklist

	Purchase Behavior	Use Behavior
What		
How much		
How		
Where		
When		
In what situation		
Who		

Source: Fred L. Schreier, *Modern Marketing Research: A Behavioral Science Approach* (Belmont, Calif.: Wadsworth Publishing Company, 1963), p. 251.

As a researcher fills in each category, he or she must make a decision about what information to include or omit. Consider the "where" category, for example. The "where of purchase" may be specified with respect to kind of store, the location of the store by broad geographic area or specific address, size of the store, or even the name of the store. So it is with each of the many categories. The study of behavior, then, involves the development of a description of the purchase or use activity, either past or current, with respect to some or all of the characteristics contained in Table 7.4.

To obtain primary data by observation, a mechanical device, such as a supermarket scanner, may serve as the "observer," or volunteers might be sought to deliver a pantry audit showing what brands are stocked in their homes.

Sources: Courtesy of Information Resources, Inc., and Courtesy of Starcraft Company.

◆ Obtaining Primary Data

The researcher attempting to collect primary data has a number of choices to make among the means that will be used. Figure 7.1 presents an overview of these choices. The primary decision is whether to employ communication or observation. **Communication** involves questioning respondents to secure the desired information, using a data-collection instrument called a questionnaire. The questions may be oral or in writing, and the responses may also be given in either form. **Observation** does not involve questioning. Rather, it means that the situation of interest is scrutinized and the relevant facts, actions, or behaviors recorded. The observer may be one or more persons or a mechanical device. For instance, supermarket scanners may be used to determine how many boxes of a particular brand of cereal are sold in a given region in a typical week. Alternatively, a researcher interested in the brands of canned vegetables a family buys might arrange a pantry audit in which the family's shelves are checked to see which brands they have on hand.

Choosing a primary method of data collection necessitates a number of additional decisions. For example, should we administer questionnaires by mail, over the telephone, or in person? Should the purpose of the study be disguised or remain undisguised? Should the answers be open-ended, or should the respondent be asked to choose from a limited set of alternatives? While Figure 7.1 implies that these decisions are independent, they are actually intimately related. A decision with respect to method of administration, say, has serious implications regarding the degree of structure that must be imposed on the questionnaire.

Each method of obtaining primary data has its own advantages and disadvantages. For the remainder of this chapter we will review these general pluses and minuses.

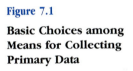

◆ Communication

Method of data collection involving questioning of respondents to secure the desired information using a data-collection instrument called a questionnaire.

◆ Observation

Method of data collection in which the situation of interest is watched and the relevant facts, actions, or behaviors recorded.

Figure 7.1

Basic Choices among Means for Collecting Primary Data

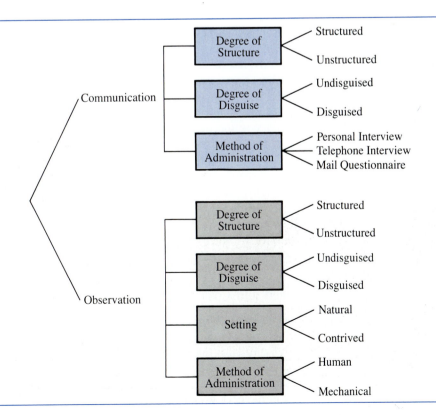

In the next chapter we will discuss the decisions that must be made when using the communication method, and in the chapter after that the decisions involved in the observational method.

In general, the communication method of data collection has the general advantages of versatility, speed, and cost, while observational data are typically more objective and accurate.

Versatility

Versatility is the ability of a technique to collect information on the many types of primary data of interest to marketers. A respondent's demographic/socioeconomic characteristics and life-style, the individual's attitudes and opinions, awareness and knowledge, intentions, the motivation underlying the individual's actions, and even the person's behavior may all be ascertained by the communication method. All we need to do is ask, although the replies will not necessarily be truthful.

Not so with observation. Observational techniques can provide us only with information about behavior and certain demographic/socioeconomic characteristics, but even here there are certain limitations. Our observations are limited to present behavior, for example. We cannot observe a person's past behavior. Nor can we observe the person's intentions as to future behavior. If we are interested in past behavior or intentions, we must ask.

Some demographic/socioeconomic characteristics can be readily observed. Sex is the most obvious example. Others can be observed but with less accuracy. A person's age and income, for example, might be inferred by closely examining the individual's mode of dress and purchasing behavior. Clearly, though, both of these observations may be in error, with income likely to be the farthest off. Still others, such as social class, cannot be observed with any degree of confidence about the accuracy of the recorded data.

The other basic types of primary data cannot be measured by observation at all. We simply cannot observe an attitude or opinion, a person's awareness or knowledge, or motivation. Certainly we can attempt to make some inferences about these variables on the basis of the individual's observed behavior. For instance, if a person is observed purchasing a box of new XYZ detergent, we might infer that the person had a favorable attitude toward XYZ. There is a real question, though, as to the accuracy of the inference. A great deal of controversy exists over whether attitudes precede behavior or behavior precedes attitude formation. If the latter explanation is correct, the person buying XYZ has no particular attitude toward it but just decided to try it. He or she may not have even been aware of XYZ previously. Or he or she may have been induced to try XYZ by a sizable cents-off coupon from the local newspaper or by an attractive promotional price offered by the supermarket. Then again, the person might be buying the box for a neighbor. Generalizing from behavior to states of mind is clearly risky, and researchers need to recognize this. Questioning clearly affords a broader base of primary data.

Speed and Cost

The speed and cost advantages of the communication method are closely intertwined. Assuming the data lend themselves to either means, communication is a faster means of data collection than observation, because it provides a greater degree of control over data-gathering activities. With the communication method, the researcher is not forced to wait for events to occur as she or he is with the observation method. In some cases, it is impossible to predict when the event will occur precisely enough to observe it. For still other behaviors, the time interval between events can be substantial. For instance, an observer seeking to determine the brand purchased most frequently in one of several appliance categories might have to wait a long time to make any observations at all. Much of the time the observer would be idle. Such idleness is expensive, as the worker will probably be compensated on an hourly rather than a per-contact basis. Events that last a long time can also cause difficulty. An observational approach to studying the relative influence of a husband and wife in the purchase of an automobile would be prohibitive in terms of both time and money.

Objectivity and Accuracy

Although the observational method has some serious limitations in terms of scope, time, and cost, it does have certain advantages with regard to objectivity and accuracy. Data that can be secured by either method will typically be more accurately secured by observation. This is because the observational method is independent of the respondent's unwillingness or inability to provide the information desired. For example, respondents are often reluctant to cooperate whenever their replies might place them in an unfavorable light. Sometimes respondents conveniently forget embarrassing events, while in other cases the events are not of sufficient importance for them to remember what happened. Since observation allows the recording of behavior as it occurs, it is not dependent on the respondent's memory or mood in reporting what occurred.

Observation typically produces more objective data than does communication. The interview represents a social interaction situation. Thus, the replies of the person being questioned are conditioned by the individual's perceptions of the interviewer. The same is true of interviewers' perceptions, but their training should afford a greater degree of control over their perceptions than would be true of the interviewee. Also, with the observation method, the subject's perceptions play less of a role than in the communication method. Sometimes people are not even aware that they are being observed. Thus, they are not tempted to tell the interviewer what they think the interviewer wants to hear or to give socially acceptable responses that are not truthful. The problems of objectivity are concentrated in the observer's methods, and this makes the task easier. The observer's selection, training, and control, and not the subject's perceptions of the field worker, become the crucial elements.

◆ Summary

Learning Objective 1: List the kinds of demographic and socioeconomic characteristics that interest marketers.

Marketers are interested in such socioeconomic and demographic characteristics as age, education, occupation, marital status, sex, income, and social class.

Learning Objective 2: Relate the premise on which life-style analysis rests.

Life-style analysis rests on the premise that the firm can plan more effective strategies to reach its target market if it knows more about its customers in terms of how they live, what interests them, and what they like.

Learning Objective 3: Specify the four main groups used to classify people in value and life-style (VALS) research.

One particularly popular VALS classification scheme divides people into four main groups: need-driven, outer-directed, inner-directed, and combined outer-and-inner-directed. So-called *survivors* (older, extremely poor people) and *sustainers* (streetwise people living on the edge of poverty) make up the need-driven group. *Belongers* (a stable group of highly conventional, patriotic middle-aged people), *emulators* (young, ambitious types on the make), and *achievers* (prosperous, middle-aged people who are builders of the "American Dream") make up the outer-directed groups. The inner-directed groups include the *"I-Am-Me"* group of impulsive, narcissistic young people; the artistic, inner-growth-oriented *experiential* group; and the mature, mission-oriented *societally conscious* group. Finally, the combined outer-and-inner-directed group is made up of persons described as *integrated*, who are psychologically mature, tolerant, and understanding.

Learning Objective 4: Cite the three main approaches used to measure the effectiveness of magazine ads.

The three main approaches used to measure awareness of magazine ads are (1) unaided recall in which the consumer is given no cues at all, (2) aided recall in which the consumer is given some prompting, and (3) recognition in which the consumer is actually shown an advertisement and asked whether or not he or she remembers seeing it.

Learning Objective 5: Give two reasons why researchers are interested in people's motives.

First, researchers believe that motives tend to be more stable than behavior and therefore offer a better basis for predicting future behavior than does past behavior. Secondly, researchers believe that by understanding what drives a person's behavior, it is easier to understand the behavior itself.

Learning Objective 6: Describe the two basic means of obtaining primary data.

The two basic means of obtaining primary data are communication and observation. Communication involves questioning respondents to secure the desired information, using a data-collection instrument called a questionnaire. Observation involves scrutinizing the situation of interest and recording the relevant facts, actions, or behaviors.

Learning Objective 7: State the specific advantages of each method of data collection.

In general, the communication method of data collection has the advantages of versatility, speed, and cost, while observational data are typically more objective and accurate.

Discussion Questions, Problems, and Projects

Should the communication or observational method be used in the situations captured in Questions 1 and 2? (Justify your choice.)

1. In 1985 the Metal Product Division of Miracle Ltd. devised a special metal container to store plastic garbage bags. Plastic bags posed household problems, as they gave off unpleasant odors, looked disorderly, and provided a breeding place for insects. The container overcame these problems as it had a bag-support apparatus that held the bag open for filling and sealed the bag when the lid was closed. In addition, there was enough storage area for at least four full bags. The product was priced at $53.81 and was sold through hardware stores. The company had done little advertising and relied on in-store promotion and displays. The divisional manager was wondering about the effectiveness of these displays. She has called on you to do the necessary research.

2. Friendship is a national manufacturer and distributor of greeting cards. The company recently began distributing a lower-priced line of cards that was made possible by using a lower-grade paper. Quality differences between the higher- and lower-priced cards did not seem to be noticeable to laypeople. The company followed a policy of printing its name and the price on the back of each card. The initial acceptance of the new line of cards convinced the vice-president of production, Sheila Howell, that the company should use this lower grade paper for all its cards and increase its profit margin from 12.3% to 14.9%. The sales manager was strongly opposed to this move and commented, "Sheila, consumers are concerned about the quality of greeting cards; a price difference of 5 cents on a card does not matter." The vice-president has called upon you to undertake the study.

3. Would you disguise the data-collection method you decided upon for Question 1? Why or why not?

4. Would you disguise the data-collection method you decided upon for Question 2? Why or why not?

5. Stop-Buy, Inc., recently opened a new convenience store in Galveston, Texas. The store is open every day from 7:00 A.M. to 11:00 P.M. Management is interested in determining the trading area from which this store draws its customers so that it can better plan the location of other units in the Galveston area.

   How would you determine this information by the questionnaire method? By the observation method? Which method would be preferred? Be sure to specify in your answer how you would define "trading area."

Suggested Additional Readings

There are a number of guides to the various personality inventories. Three of the better ones for marketers are

C. M. Bonjean, R. J. Hill, and S. D. McLemore, *Sociological Measurement: An Inventory of Scales and Indices* (San Francisco: Chandler, 1974);

Ki-Taiek Chun, Sidney Cobb, and J. R. P. French, *Measures for Psychological Assessment* (Ann Arbor, Mich.: Institute for Social Research, University of Michigan, 1975);

D. G. Lake, M. B. Miles, and R. B. Earle, Jr., *Measuring Human Behavior: Tools for the Assessment of Social Functioning* (New York: Teachers College Press, Columbia University, 1973).

For a general review of the origins, development, and thrust of life-style and psychographic research, see

William D. Wells, ed., *LifeStyle and Psychographics* (Chicago: American Marketing Association, 1974).

For a general discussion of the purpose and procedures followed in value and life-style research, see

Arnold Mitchell, *The Nine American Lifestyles* (New York: Macmillan, 1983).

Chapter 8

Collecting Information by Questionnaire

+ + + +

+ + + +

+ + + +

+ + + +

Learning Objectives

Upon completing this chapter, you should be able to

1. Explain the concept of *structure* as it relates to questionnaires.
2. Explain what is meant by *disguise* in a questionnaire.
3. Discuss why structured-undisguised questionnaires are the type most frequently used by marketing researchers.
4. Cite three drawbacks of fixed-alternative questions.
5. List the kinds of information usually generated by focus groups.
6. Identify the key person in a focus group.
7. Explain the reason why researchers use projective methods in conducting some studies.
8. List three common types of stimuli used in projective techniques.
9. Differentiate among the three methods of administering questionnaires.
10. Cite the points researchers generally consider when they compare the various methods of administering questionnaires.

Case in Marketing Research

Ten women, ages twenty-three to fifty-six, sat around a table in an all-white room on the fourteenth floor of a large office building in Manhattan on a blustery January day. They were part of a focus group exploring a lip problem that a major cosmetics company hoped to fix. Each woman held a hand mirror and peered closely at her lips as the group's moderator, Melissa Cavanaugh, explained what a rhytide was.

"Look closely," Cavanaugh said. "See those vertical lines above and below your lips? Those are called 'rhytides.' When your lips are dry and chapped, you may notice that they become more pronounced. Have any of you ever noticed them before?"

"I never paid much attention before," Carol Owen, one of the group members, said, "but now that you point them out, I can see that they are really there. Maybe they're why my lipstick keeps running."

"You're right, Carol," Anna Holmes chimed in. "In the winter when my lips get chapped, putting on lipstick only makes

them look worse. But then smearing my lips with Chapstick doesn't make me look very alluring either," she said ruefully.

The rest of the group laughed.

"Well, group members, the company I represent may have something that will help solve your problems," Cavanaugh said. "As a way of thanking you for your participation in this focus group, we will send you a sample as soon as it is approved for general release. You've been very helpful, and we certainly appreciate your taking the time to come in on such a nasty day. Jim Henley will show you the way out."

As the women filed into the corridor, Cavanaugh stopped by her boss's office further down the hall.

"Well, Jane, I think that group about wraps up our preliminary research. We've now held focus groups for 600 women and surveyed about 300 more on the rhytide problem by phone, and it seems we have enough evidence to begin thinking about launch-

ing the product," Cavanaugh said.

"That's true, Melissa, but it has also been clear from these group sessions that these women may not even know they have the problem until we tell them they do. We still have to figure out how to sell them on the idea that they have a problem for which we have the solution. Where do you propose we go from here?" Jane Hopkins asked.

Discussion Issues

1. If you were Melissa Cavanaugh, what other kinds of research would you propose before launching the product?

2. What kind of problems can you foresee in launching a product that solves a problem people don't know they have?

3. How might research help in resolving these issues?

4. Why was a focus group a good way of exploring these questions? Or was it?

Source: This fictitious case is based on Elizabeth Arden's program to launch its extremely successful lip repair product, "Lip Fix." For a more complete and factual discussion of the process, see Bernice Kanner, "Putting in the Fix," *New York,* 17 (April 16, 1984), pp. 17–20.

In Chapter 7 we discussed the types of primary data that interest marketing researchers. We also briefly examined the two methods, communication and observation, that researchers employ to gather such data. In this chapter we will investigate communication techniques more closely, paying particular attention to the many types of questionnaires researchers use and the means by which they are administered.

◆ Communication Methods

As we saw in Figure 7.1, if researchers choose to use the communication method of securing data, they must then decide on the kind of questionnaire that would best serve the problem at hand. They must determine the degree of **structure,** or standardization, to be imposed on the questionnaire and the degree of **disguise** that is appropriate to the problem they are investigating.[1]

In a highly structured questionnaire the questions to be asked and the responses permitted the subjects are completely predetermined. In a highly unstructured questionnaire the questions to be asked are only loosely predetermined, and the respondents are free to respond in their own words. A questionnaire in which the questions are fixed but the responses are open-ended would represent an intermediate degree of structure. A disguised questionnaire attempts to hide the purpose of the study, whereas an undisguised questionnaire makes the purpose of the research obvious by the questions posed.

Structured-Undisguised Questionnaires

Marketing researchers often use structured-undisguised questionnaires in which questions are presented with exactly the same wording and in exactly the same order to all respondents most frequently in collecting data. The reason for standardizing the wording is to ensure that all respondents are replying to the same question.[2] If one interviewer asks, "Do you drink orange juice?" and another asks, "Does your family use frozen orange juice?" the replies would not be comparable.

In the typical structured-undisguised questionnaire, the responses as well as the questions are standardized. **Fixed-alternative questions,** in which the responses are limited to the stated alternatives, are used. Consider the following question regarding the subject's attitude toward pollution and the need for more government legislation to control it.

Do you feel the United States needs more or less antipollution legislation?

☐ Needs more
☐ Needs less
☐ Neither more nor less
☐ No opinion

◆ **Structure**

Degree of standardization imposed on the data-collection instrument. A highly structured questionnaire, for example, is one in which the questions to be asked and the responses permitted subjects are completely predetermined, while a highly unstructured questionnaire is one in which the questions to be asked are only loosely predetermined, and respondents are free to respond in their own words and in any way they see fit.

◆ **Disguise**

Amount of knowledge concerning the purpose of a study communicated to the respondent by the data-collection method. An undisguised questionnaire, for example, is one in which the purpose of the research is obvious.

◆ **Fixed-alternative questions**

Questions in which the responses are limited to stated alternatives.

---

[1]The simultaneous treatment of structure and disguise was suggested by Donald T. Campbell, "The Indirect Assessment of Social Attitudes," *Psychological Bulletin,* 47 (January 1950), pp. 15–38. A similar treatment can be found in Harper W. Boyd, Jr., Ralph Westfall, and Stanley F. Stasch, *Marketing Research: Text and Cases,* 6th ed. (Homewood, Ill.: Richard D. Irwin, 1985), pp. 115–121.

[2]Claire Selltiz, Lawrence S. Wrightsman, and Stuart W. Cook, *Research Methods in Social Relations,* 3rd ed. (New York: Holt, Rinehart and Winston, 1976), p. 309. See also Ed Blair, Seymour Sudman, Norman M. Bradburn, and Carol Stocking, "How to Ask Questions about Drinking and Sex: Response Effects in Measuring Consumer Behavior," *Journal of Marketing Research,* 14 (August 1977), pp. 316–321; and Norman M. Bradburn and Seymour Sudman, *Improving Interview Method and Questionnaire Design: Response Effects to Threatening Questions in Survey Research* (San Francisco: Jossey Bass, 1979).

This question is a good example of a structured-undisguised question for two reasons. First, its purpose is clear: it seeks to discover the subject's attitudes toward antipollution legislation in a very straightforward manner. Second, it employs a highly structured format. Respondents are limited to only one of four stated replies.

Probably the greatest advantages of structured-undisguised questionnaires are that they are simple to administer and easy to tabulate and analyze.[3] Subjects should be reliable in that if they were asked the question again, they would answer in a similar fashion (assuming, of course, the absence of some attitude-changing event).

Such reliability is facilitated by the consistency of fixed-alternative questions. These questions help standardize responses by providing subjects with an identical frame of reference. In contrast, consider the question, "How much television do you watch?" If no alternatives were supplied, one respondent might say "every day," another might say "regularly," and still another might respond with the number of hours per day. Responses from such an open-ended question would be far more difficult to interpret than those from a fixed-alternative question limiting replies to the categories of "every day," "at least three times a week," "at least once a week," or "less than once a week."

Providing alternative responses also often helps to make the question clear. "What is your marital status?" is less clear in its intent than, "Are you married, single, widowed, or divorced?" The latter question provides the dimensions in which to frame the reply.

Although fixed-alternative questions tend to provide the most reliable responses, they may also elicit misleading answers. For example, fixed alternatives may force an answer to a question on which the respondent has no opinion. Even when a "no opinion" category is provided, interviewers often try to keep the number of "no opinions" to a minimum by pressing the respondent for a reply. The individual may agree, under pressure, to one of the other alternatives offered, but the alternative may not accurately capture the individual's true position on the issue. For example, the antipollution example presented earlier makes no allowance for those who feel that something probably should be done about pollution and that more legislation may possibly be one answer, but fundamentally favor other approaches.

Fixed-alternative responses may also produce inaccuracies when the response categories themselves introduce bias. This is particularly true when a reasonable response is omitted because of an oversight or insufficient prior research as to the response categories that are appropriate. The provision of an "other" category does not eliminate this bias either, since subjects are often reluctant to respond in the "other" category. In posing a fixed-alternative question, one should make sure the alternatives offered adequately cover the range of probable replies.

The fixed-alternative question is thus most productive when possible replies are "well known, limited in number, and clear-cut. Thus they are appropriate for securing factual information (age, education, home ownership, amount of rent, and so on) and for eliciting expressions of opinion about issues on which people hold clear opinions."[4] They are therefore not very appropriate for securing primary data on motivations but certainly could be used (at least sometimes) to collect data on attitudes, intentions, awareness, demographic/socioeconomic characteristics, and behavior.

---

[3]This general discussion of advantages and disadvantages of the structured-undisguised question follows that of Selltiz, Wrightsman, and Cook, *Research Methods,* pp. 309–321.

[4]Selltiz, Wrightsman, and Cook, *Research Methods,* p. 316.

Unstructured-Undisguised Questionnaires

In the unstructured-undisguised questionnaire, the purpose of the study is clear, but the responses to the question are open-ended. Consider the question, "How do you feel about pollution and the need for more antipollution legislation?" This initial question (which is often called a *stimulus* by researchers) is clear in its purpose. With it the interviewer attempts to get the subject to talk freely about his or her attitudes toward pollution. This is an **open-ended question,** because it leads to a very unstructured interview (called a **depth interview**). The respondent's initial reply, the interviewer's follow-up questions that seek elaboration, and the respondent's subsequent answers determine the direction of the interview. The interviewer may attempt to follow a rough outline. However, the order and the specific framing of the questions will vary from interview to interview, and the specific content will therefore vary.

The freedom permitted the interviewer in conducting these depth interviews reveals the major advantages and disadvantages of the method. By not limiting the respondent to a fixed set of replies, and by careful probing, an experienced interviewer should be able to derive a more accurate picture of the respondent's true position on some issue. This is particularly true with respect to sensitive issues in which there is social pressure to conform and to offer a "socially acceptable" response. Note, however, that we qualified our description of this method by specifying that "experienced interviewers" be used, and "careful probing" be done. The depth interview requires highly skilled interviewers. They are hard to find and expensive to hire. But they are essential to accurate results with this type of questionnaire, in which the lack of structure allows the interviewer to strongly influence the result. Keen judgment as to when to probe and how to word the probes is required of the interviewer, and good depth interviews often take a long time to complete. This makes it difficult to secure the cooperation of respondents. It also means that a study using depth interviews, as opposed to fixed-alternative questions, will not only take longer to complete, but will involve fewer respondents or will require a greater number of interviewers. And the more interviewers there are, the more likely it will be that responses will vary based on each interviewer's personal technique in administering the questionnaire.[5]

The depth interview also causes severe problems in analysis. The services of one or more skilled psychologists are typically required to interpret the responses—an expensive service. Further, the psychologist's own background and frame of reference will affect the interpretation. This subjectivity raises questions about both the reliability and validity of the results. It also causes difficulty in determining what the correct interpretation is and thus presents problems when tabulating the replies.[6]

Some of the problems with coding open-ended questions may be changing with new technology. Researchers today often feed respondents' answers into computers programmed to recognize a large vocabulary of words in their search for regularities in the replies. The computers are able to rank each word by the frequency of usage and then can print out sentences containing the key words. The detailed analysis of these sentences allows researchers to pick up on recurring themes.[7] While these

[5]Barbara Bailar, Leroy Bailey, and Joyce Stevens, "Measures of Interviewer Bias and Variance," *Journal of Marketing Research,* 14 (August 1977), pp. 337–343; and J. R. McKenzie, "An Investigation into Interviewing Effects in Market Research," *Journal of Marketing Research,* 14 (August 1977), pp. 330–331.

[6]Martin Collins and Graham Kalton, "Coding Verbatim Answers to Open Questions," *Journal of the Market Research Society,* 22 (October 1980), pp. 239–247.

[7]Jeffrey Zaslow, "A Maverick Pollster Promotes Verbosity That Others Disdain," *The Wall Street Journal,* 65 (February 13, 1985), pp. 1 and 23.

• Open-ended question

Question characterized by the condition that respondents are free to reply in their own words rather than being limited to choosing from among a set of alternatives.

• Depth interview

Unstructured personal interview in which the interviewer attempts to get subjects to talk freely and to express their true feelings.

systems automate the coding of unstructured interviews, they still leave interpretation to the individual analyst. Nevertheless, the systems can achieve in hours what a purely human review might take weeks to accomplish.

The depth interview is probably best suited to exploratory research, since it is productive with respect to just about all of the common purposes of exploratory research.

♦ **Focus-group interview**

Personal interview conducted among a small number of individuals simultaneously; the interview relies more on group discussion than on a series of directed questions to generate data.

Focus Group   A variation of the depth interview is the **focus-group interview,** in which a small number of individuals are brought together for interviewing, rather than being interviewed one at a time as in the depth interview. The dynamics of the encounter are quite different from the individual interview, in which the flow of information is one-way (from the respondent to the interviewer). The focus-group setting allows the comments of each person to be considered in group discussion.

The interaction among the group members is only loosely directed by the group interviewer, called the moderator. Focus groups are currently one of the most frequently used techniques in marketing research; they have proven productive for the following purposes:[8]

1. Generating hypotheses that can be further tested quantitatively.

2. Generating information helpful in structuring questionnaires.

3. Providing overall background information on a product category.

4. Securing impressions on new product concepts for which there is little information available.

5. Stimulating new ideas about older products.

6. Stimulating ideas for new creative concepts.

7. Interpreting previously obtained quantitative results.

Pillsbury, for example, held focus-group discussions around the United States in early 1976 to find out what consumers did not like about frozen pizza. "The response was overwhelming; about 60 percent hated the crust, which many said tasted like cardboard."[9] This initial insight, which was further verified by other research, led to the development of Pillsbury's very successful Totino's Crisp Crust Frozen Pizza.

Most focus groups consist of eight to twelve members. Smaller groups are too easily dominated by one or two members, while frustration and boredom can set in with larger groups as individuals have to wait their turn to respond or get involved. Researchers have found that by grouping people with similar backgrounds, experiences, and verbal skills, conflicts over issues not relevant to the study are minimized. Most firms conducting focus groups use screening interviews to determine the individuals that will compose a particular group. One type they try to avoid is the individual who has participated before in a focus group, since some of these people

---

[8]See Danny N. Bellenger, Kenneth L. Bernhardt, and Jac L. Goldstucker, *Qualitative Research in Marketing* (Chicago: American Marketing Association, 1976), pp. 7–28, for an elaboration of these uses with examples and for other insightful comments on the conduct of focus groups. Another useful general reference is James B. Higgenbotham and Keith K. Cox, eds., *Focus Group Interviews: A Reader* (Chicago: American Marketing Association, 1979).

[9]Lawrence Ingrassia, "A Matter of Taste: There's No Way to Tell If a New Food Product Will Please the Public," *The Wall Street Journal,* 60 (February 26, 1980), pp. 1 and 23. For similar experiences of Fisher-Price, Coke, and GE with focus groups, see, respectively, Ronald Alsop, "Fisher-Price Banks on Name, Design in Foray into Playwear," *The Wall Street Journal,* 64 (August 2, 1984), p. 23; "In Soft-Drink Wars, Brand Loyalty Can Last as Long as a Few Minutes," *The Wall Street Journal,* 65 (May 13, 1985), p. 21; and "Getting Consumers in Focus," *Dun's Business Month,* 119 (May 1982), pp. 78–80.

Table 8.1   Key Qualifications of Focus-Group Moderators

1. Kind but firm—In order to elicit necessary interaction, the moderator must combine a disciplined detachment with understanding empathy. To achieve this, he must simultaneously display a kindly, permissive attitude toward the participants, encouraging them to feel at ease in the group interview environment, while insisting that the discussion remain germane to the problem at hand. Only with experience can the moderator achieve an appropriate blending of these two apparently antithetical roles.

   It is also the moderator's responsibility to encourage the emergence of leadership from within the group, while at the same time avoiding tendencies of domination of the group by a single member. The kindly but firm moderator must be sensitive to bids for attention and must maintain his leadership without threatening or destroying the interactional process.

2. Permissiveness—While an atmosphere of permissiveness is desirable, the moderator must be at all times alert to indications that the group atmosphere of cordiality is disintegrating. Before permissiveness leads to chaos, the moderator must reestablish the group purpose and maintain its orientation to the subject.

   The moderator must be ready and willing to pursue clues to information that may at first appear tangential to the subject for it may open new areas of exploration. He must also be prepared to cope with expressions of unusual opinions and eruptions of personality clashes within the group. The manner in which these are

handled may well be the difference between a productive and an unproductive group session.

3. Involvement—Since a principal reason for the group interview is to expose feelings and to obtain reactions indicative of deeper feelings, the moderator must encourage and stimulate intensive personal involvement. If the moderator is unable to immerse himself completely in the topic being discussed, the group will sense his detachment, and the depth contribution of the interview will be lost.

4. Incomplete understanding—A most useful skill of the group moderator is his ability to convey lack of complete understanding of the information being presented. Although he may understand what the participant is trying to express, by carefully inserting noncommittal remarks, phrased in questioning tones, the respondent is encouraged to delve more deeply into the sources of his opinion. He is, by this process, able to reveal and elaborate on the kinds of information for which the group interview is designed. The goal is to encourage respondents to be more specific about generalized comments made by group members.

   The usefulness of this technique can be endangered if its application is inappropriate. If the "incomplete understanding" is a superficially assumed role, the group will soon detect this artificiality, and will feel that the moderator is playing some sort of cryptic game with the group. The group interview will then

Source: Donald A. Chase, "The Intensive Group Interview in Marketing," MRA Viewpoints 1973 as adopted by Danny N. Bellenger, Kenneth L. Bernhardt, and Jac L. Goldstucker, *Qualitative Research in Marketing* (Chicago: American Marketing Association, 1976). Reprinted with permission.

tend to behave as "experts." They continually try to make their presence felt, which can impair the functioning of the group.

As focus groups have become more popular it has become more difficult to recruit rookies for them.[10] Firms also try to avoid groups in which some of the participants are friends and relatives, since this tends to inhibit spontaneity in the discussion as the acquaintances begin talking to each other.

The typical focus-group session lasts from one and one-half to two hours. Groups can be arranged at a number of sites, including the client's home office, a neutral site, the office of the research agency, or even one of the respondents' homes. Each of these sites has its own advantages and disadvantages with respect to the ability to

[10]See, for example, The Unknown Researcher, "Shoddy Recruiting Practices Lead to Focus Group Biases," *Marketing News*, 12 (May 18, 1979), p. 2, for a comment on the seriousness of the problem; and Joel Henkin, "Time to Stop Talking about Problems and Do Something, Such as 'Cold' Recruiting," *Marketing News*, 13 (September 21, 1979), p. 4, for a reply.

Table 8.1   *continued*

deteriorate into a sterile collection of mutual suspicions. Incomplete understanding on the part of the moderator must be a genuine curiosity about the deeper sources of the participant's understanding.

5. Encouragement—Although the dynamics of the group situation facilitate the participation of all members in the interaction, there may be individuals who resist contributing. The skillful moderator should be aware of unresponsive members and try to break down their reserve and encourage their involvement.

   The unresponsive member offers a real challenge to the group moderator. There are numerous ways in which a resistant or bashful member can be encouraged to participate, such as by assigning him a task to perform, or by providing an opening for his remarks. If this is inappropriately attempted, it may only reinforce a reluctance to participate in a verbal fashion. The ability to interpret nonverbal clues may provide a means of discovering a tactic to broaden the scope of the group's active participation.

6. Flexibility—The moderator should be equipped prior to the session with a topic outline of the subject matter to be covered. By committing the topics to memory before the interview, the moderator may use the outline only as a reminder of content areas omitted or covered incompletely.

   If a topic outline is followed minutely, the progress of the interview will be uneven and artificial, jumping from topic to topic without careful transitions. This procedure communicates a lack of concern to the participants, for its mechanical nature makes the moderator appear to lack genuine interest in their responses.

   At the same time, the interview cannot be allowed to wander aimlessly. Under such conditions, control of the situation soon passes from the moderator to a self-appointed group leader.

   The group interview should be conducted the way one walks across a rope bridge. The handrails are gripped firmly and the objective is kept in mind constantly. If the bottom foot rope should break, the walk is continued hand over hand until the destination is reached. This requires an ability to improvise and alter predetermined plans amid the distractions of the group process.

7. Sensitivity—The moderator must be able to identify, as the group interview progresses, the informational level on which it is being conducted, and determine if it is appropriate for the subject under discussion. Sensitive areas will frequently produce superficial rather than depth responses. Depth is achieved when there is a substantial amount of emotional responses, as opposed to intellectual information. Indications of depth are provided when participants begin to indicate how they feel about the subject, rather than what they think about it.

recruit respondents, the costs of the session, the rapport that can be induced, and the ability to record the interviews for later transcription and analysis.[11]

   The moderator in the focus group has a key role. The moderator must not only lead the discussion so that all objectives of the study are met, but must do so in such a way that *interaction* among the group members is stimulated and promoted. A good moderator tries to avoid having the session dissolve into a series of individual interviews in which each participant takes a turn answering a predetermined set of questions. This is an extremely delicate role. It requires someone who is intimately familiar with the purpose and objectives of the research and at the same time possesses good interpersonal communication skills. Some of the key qualifications moderators must have are described in Table 8.1.

[11]Wells discusses the pros and cons of the various sites as well as a number of other operational questions that arise with the conduct of focus groups. See William D. Wells, "Group Interviewing," in Robert Ferber, ed., *Handbook of Marketing Research* (New York: McGraw-Hill, 1974), pp. 2-133 to 2-146. See also *Focus Groups: Issues and Approaches*, prepared by the Qualitative Research Counsel of the Advertising Research Foundation, 1985.

Table 8.2   Claimed Advantages of Focus-Group Interview over Individual Depth Interviews

---

Respondent Interaction Advantages

1. Synergism: The combined effort of the group will produce a wider range of information, insight, and ideas than will the cumulation of the responses of a number of individuals when these replies are secured privately.

2. Snowballing: A bandwagon effect often operates in a group interview situation in that a comment by one individual often triggers a chain of responses from the other participants.

3. Stimulation: Usually after a brief introductory period the respondents get "turned on" in that they want to express their ideas and expose their feelings as the general level of excitement over the topic increases in the group.

4. Security: In an interviewer—interviewee situation, respondents may not be willing to expose their views for fear of having to defend these views or fear of appearing "unconcerned" or "radical" or whatever the case may be. In the well-structured group, on the other hand, "the individual can usually find some comfort in the fact that his feelings are not greatly different from those of his peers, and that he can expose an idea without necessarily being forced to defend, follow through or elaborate on it. He's more likely to be candid because the focus is on the group rather than the individual; he soon realizes that the things he says are not necessarily being identified with him."

5. Spontaneity: Since no individual is required to answer any given question in a group interview, the individual's responses can be more spontaneous, less conventional, and should provide a more accurate picture of the person's position on some issue. In the group interview, people speak only when they have definite feelings about a subject and not because a question requires a response.

Sponsor Advantages

1. Serendipity: It is more often the case in a group rather than an individual interview that some idea will "drop out of the blue." The group also affords the opportunity to develop it to its full significance.

2. Specialization: The group interview allows the use of a more highly trained, but more expensive, interviewer, since a number of individuals are being "interviewed" simultaneously.

3. Scientific scrutiny: The group interview allows closer scrutiny. First, the session itself can be observed by several observers. This affords some check on the consistency of the interpretations. Second, the session itself may be tape-recorded or even video-taped. Later detailed examination of the recorded session allows additional insight and also can help clear up points of disagreement among analysts.

4. Structure: The group interview affords more control than the individual interview with regard to the topics that are covered and the depth with which they are treated, since the "interviewer" in the role of moderator has the opportunity to reopen topics that received too shallow a discussion when initially presented.

5. Speed: Since a number of individuals are being interviewed at the same time, the group interview permits the securing of a given number of interviews more quickly than do individual interviews.

Source: John M. Hess, "Group Interviewing," in R. L. King, ed., *New Science of Planning* (Chicago: American Marketing Association, 1968), p. 194. Reprinted with permission.

Some advantages that focus-group interviews have over individual depth interviews are listed in Table 8.2.[12] An interesting example of the benefits of a group interview was reported by one researcher who was investigating young men's perceptions of cigar smoking. In discussion many of the men in the group condemned the habit and ridiculed the macho-tycoon image cigar smokers try to project. However, when cigars were passed around the table, panelists all "lit up with a flourish,

---

[12]The list of advantages is taken from John M. Hess, "Group Interviewing," in *New Science of Planning,* ed. R. L. King (Chicago: American Marketing Association, 1968), pp. 193–196. See also Bobby J. Calder, "Focus Groups and the Nature of Qualitative Marketing Research," *Journal of Marketing Research,* 14 (August 1977), pp. 353–364, and *Focus Groups: Issues and Approaches* for a discussion of some philosophical and operational issues surrounding the use of focus groups.

sat back expansively, gestured with their cigars and, in general, appeared to be adopting the very image they had been mocking moments earlier."[13]

Focus-group interviews also lead to some problems that are not encountered with individual interviews. Although they are easy to set up, they are difficult to moderate and to interpret. It is easy to find evidence in one or more of the group discussions that supports almost any preconceived position. Because executives can observe the discussions through one-way mirrors or listen to the tape recordings of the sessions, focus groups seem more susceptible to executive and even researcher biases than do other data-collection techniques.[14]

---

[13]Bernice Kanner, "Out of the Ashes," *New York,* 17 (October 24, 1984), pp. 17–22.

[14]"Focus Groups Being Subverted by Clients," *Marketing News,* 18 (June 8, 1984), p. 7.

Back to the Case

Melissa Cavanaugh was having a bad day. Executives from the cosmetics company on whose account she was working were in town today observing her focus group from behind a one-way mirror. Naturally, of all the groups she had run on this particular study, the one she had today seemed to be particularly confrontational. She was having a hard time keeping the group members focused on the issue at hand, and an even more difficult time keeping one especially outspoken woman from totally dominating the group.

"Dorothy, if you had to describe what happens to your lipstick when your lips are dry, what would you say?" Cavanaugh asked one middle-aged woman who had contributed little to the group so far.

"Well, it always seemed to me that my lipstick would, like, bleed," Dorothy said.

"Bleed? Oh, that's a really clever way of putting it," Margo Hirsch chimed in. "That makes it

sound like Dracula or something," she snorted.

"Please, Mrs. Hirsch. Let the other group members say what they think. It's important that we can all feel free to say exactly what we feel," Cavanaugh said, trying hard to be patient.

So far Mrs. Hirsch had found something sarcastic to say about three other group members' comments. No wonder none of them wanted to speak, Cavanaugh thought.

"I think Dorothy's right," a young woman in a severely tailored suit said firmly. " 'Bleeding' is a good way of describing what happens to your lipstick in the winter. I think it's better than 'running' or 'feathering' or any of the other terms that have been suggested."

"Bless you, Justine," Cavanaugh thought to herself.

"Thank you, Justine," Cavanaugh said to the young woman. "I appreciate your comments. Does anyone else agree with Justine that 'bleeding' is a good way

of describing this problem? Could I see a show of hands?"

Nine hands went up. Mrs. Hirsch sat glaring with her arms folded over her chest.

Cavanaugh suppressed a smile. Maybe this group could be salvaged after all, she thought.

Melissa Cavanaugh is experiencing one of the problems common to focus-group interviews. One outspoken member can disrupt the whole group's functioning. It is the job of the moderator to keep the group focused on the problem at hand and to try to circumvent any problems that may crop up.

The point of this group was to explore how to describe the problem that the cosmetic company's product could solve. A focus group is a type of research that is particularly suited to such a problem, since it allows group members the freedom to generate ideas and discuss concepts in an open-ended and unstructured way.

A researcher has to keep in mind constantly that the discussion, and consequently the results, are greatly influenced by the moderator and the specific direction he or she provides. Moderators possessing all of the desired skills listed in Table 8.1 are extremely rare. Researchers also have to remember that since the groups are intentionally designed to be homogeneous, the results are not representative of the general population. Trying to project such results to a broader group is a hazardous research practice.

Further, the unstructured nature of the responses makes coding, tabulation, and analysis difficult. Focus groups should not be used, therefore, to estimate the proportion of people who feel a particular way. Like the individual depth interview, the focus-group interview is better suited to exploratory research than to descriptive or causal research. The method is better for generating ideas and insights than for systematically examining them.[15]

Unstructured-Disguised Questionnaires

Unstructured-disguised questionnaires lie at the heart of what has become known as motivation research.

> A person needs only limited experience in questionnaire type surveys to realize that many areas of inquiry are not amenable to exploration by direct questions. Many important motives and reasons for choice are of a kind that the consumer *will not* describe because a truthful description would be damaging to his ego. Others he *cannot* describe, either because he himself does not have the words to make his meaning clear or because his motive exists below the level of awareness. Very often such motives are of paramount importance in consumer behavior. If one tries to inquire into them with direct questions, especially categorical questions, one tends to get replies that are either useless or dangerously misleading.[16]

As evidence of the preceding observation, consider the following example. When consumers began complaining about the amount of salt in many prepared foods, a number of food companies flooded grocery store shelves with dozens of low-salt items. Sales of most of the items are either flat or declining. "All the market research showed that 60 percent of the people in this country were concerned about salt in their diet," said the marketing research director at Campbell Soup. "[But] in fact, only a fraction of those are willing to trade taste to get the salt out." Campbell's low-sodium soups never sold as well as the company had expected.[17]

Researchers have tried to overcome subjects' reluctance to discuss their feelings by developing techniques that are largely independent of the subjects' self-awareness and willingness to reveal themselves. The main thrust of these kinds of techniques, known as **projective methods,** has been to conceal the true subject of the study by using a disguised stimulus. Among the most common stimuli used are word association, sentence completion, and storytelling.

Though the stimulus is typically standardized, subjects are allowed to respond to it in a very unstructured form, which is why this method is known as an unstruc-

♦ Projective method

Term used to describe questionnaires containing ambiguous stimuli that force subjects to rely on their own emotions, needs, motivations, attitudes, and values in framing a response.

---

[15]For an empirical assessment of the relative ability of individual interviews versus focus groups of various sizes and composition to generate ideas, see Edward F. Fern, "The Use of Focus Groups for Idea Generation: The Effects of Group Size, Acquaintanceship, and Moderator on Response Quantity and Quality," *Journal of Marketing Research,* 19 (February 1982), pp. 1–13.

[16]F. P. Kilpatrick, "New Methods of Measuring Consumer Preferences and Motivation," *Journal of Farm Economics* (December 1957), p. 1314.

[17]Betsy Morris, "Study to Detect True Eating Habits Finds Junk-Food Fans in the Health Food Ranks," *The Wall Street Journal,* 64 (February 3, 1984), p. 19.

Sometimes direct questions produce misleading answers from consumers. For example, marketing research indicated more of an interest in low-salt or salt-free products than actually existed. Among the flood of items introduced to the market, only a few were successful, including Mrs. Dash.

Source: Courtesy of Alberto Culver; model: Kate O'Connor.

tured-disguised questionnaire. The basic assumption in projective methods is that the way an individual responds to a relatively unstructured stimulus provides clues as to how that person really perceives the subject under investigation and what his or her true reactions are to it.

> [T]he more unstructured and ambiguous a stimulus, the more a subject can and will project his emotions, needs, motivations, attitudes, and values. The *structure* of a stimulus . . . is the degree of choice available to the subject. A highly structured stimulus leaves very little choice: the subject has unambiguous choice among clear alternatives. . . . A stimulus of low structure has a wide range of alternative choices. It is ambiguous: the subject can "choose" his own interpretation.[18]

It is worth looking at each of these techniques more closely to see the kinds of information they can provide researchers.

---

[18]Fred N. Kerlinger, *Foundations of Behavioral Research,* 3rd ed. (New York: Holt, Rinehart and Winston, 1986), p. 471. For an overview of projective tests from the standpoint of psychology, see W. G. Klopfer and E. S. Taulkie, "Projective Tests," in M. R. Rosenzweig and L. W. Porter, eds., *Annual Review of Psychology* (1976), pp. 543–567.

• Word association

Questionnaire containing a
list of words to which
respondents are instructed
to reply with the first word
that comes to mind.

Word Association In the projective methods of **word association,** subjects respond to a list of words with the first word that comes to mind. The test words are
intermixed with neutral words to conceal the purpose of the study. In the study of
pollution, some of the key words might be

- *Water*   _____
- *Air*   _____
- *Lakes*   _____
- *Industry*   _____
- *Smokestack* _____
- *City*   _____

Responses to each of the key terms are recorded word-for-word and later analyzed
for their meaning. The responses are usually judged in three ways: by the frequency
with which any word is given as a response, by the average amount of time that
elapses before a response is given, and by the number of respondents who do not
respond at all to a test word after a reasonable period of time.

Any common responses that emerge are grouped to reveal patterns of interest,
underlying motivations, or stereotypes. It is often possible to categorize the associations as favorable-unfavorable, pleasant-unpleasant, modern–old-fashioned, and so
forth, depending upon the problem.

To determine the amount of time that elapses before a response is given to a test
word, a stopwatch may be used or the interviewer may count silently while waiting
for a reply. Respondents who hesitate (which is usually defined as taking longer
than three seconds to reply) are judged to be sufficiently emotionally involved in
the word so as to provide not their immediate reaction but rather what they consider to be an acceptable response. If they do not respond at all, their emotional
involvement is judged to be so high as to block a response. An individual's pattern
of responses, along with the details of the response to each question, are then used
to assess the person's attitudes or feelings on the subject.

• Sentence
  completion

Questionnaire containing a
number of sentences that
subjects are directed to
complete with the first
words that come to mind.

Sentence Completion The method of **sentence completion** requires that the
respondent complete a number of sentences similar to the following:

- *Many people behave as if our natural resources were* _____.
- *A person who does not use our lakes for recreation is* _____.
- *The number-one concern for our natural resources is* _____.
- *When I think of living in a city, I* _____.

Again, respondents are instructed to reply with the first thoughts that come to mind.
The responses are recorded word-for-word and are later analyzed.

In one study, Kassarjian and Cohen asked 179 smokers who believed cigarettes to be a
health hazard why they continued to smoke. The majority gave responses such as "Pleasure is more important than health," "Moderation is OK," "I like to smoke." One gets
the impression that smokers are not dissatisfied with their lot. However, in a portion
of the study involving sentence-completion tests, smokers responded to the question,
"People who never smoke are _____," with comments such as "better off," "hap-
pier," "smarter," "wiser," "more informed." To the question, "Teenagers who smoke
are _____," smokers responded with "foolish" "crazy," "uninformed," "stupid,"
"showing off," "immature," "wrong."

Clearly the impression one gets from the sentence completion test is that smokers
are anxious, uncomfortable, dissonant, and dissatisfied with their habit. This is quite
different from the results of a probed open-end question.[19]

[19]Harold H. Kassarjian, "Projective Methods," in Robert Ferber, ed., *Handbook of Marketing Research*
(New York: McGraw-Hill, 1974), p. 3–91.

One advantage of sentence completion over word association is that respondents can be provided with a more directed stimulus. There should be just enough direction to evoke some association with the concept of interest. The researcher needs to be careful not to convey the purpose of the study or provoke the "socially acceptable" response. Obviously, skill is needed to develop a good sentence-completion or word-association test.

· Storytelling

Questionnaire method of data collection relying on a picture stimulus such as a cartoon, photograph, or drawing, about which the subject is asked to tell a story.

· Thematic Apperception Test (TAT)

Copyrighted series of pictures about which the subject is asked to tell stories.

Storytelling Pictorial material such as cartoons, photographs, or drawings are often used in the **storytelling** approach, although other stimuli are also used. These pictorial devices are descendants of the psychologists' **Thematic Apperception Test (TAT).** The TAT consists of a copyrighted series of pictures about which the subject is asked to tell stories. Some of the pictures are of ordinary events and some of unusual events; in some of the pictures the persons or objects are clearly represented, and in others they are relatively obscure. The way a subject responds to these events helps researchers interpret that individual's personality. For example, the nature of the response might show a subject to be impulsive or controlled, creative or unimaginative, or so on.

When used in a marketing situation, the same pattern is followed. Respondents are shown a picture and asked to tell a story about the picture. However, the responses are used to assess attitudes toward the phenomenon under investigation, rather than to interpret the subject's personality. Continuing with the pollution example, the stimulus might be a picture of a city, and the respondent might be asked to describe what it would be like to live there. The analysis of the individual's response would then focus on the emphasis given to pollution in its various forms. If no mention were made of traffic congestion, dirty air, noise, and so on, the person would be classified as displaying little concern for pollution and its control.

One of the classic examples of the storytelling approach involves Nescafé instant coffee, one of the early instant food preparations.[20] When women who did not use instant coffee were asked directly, "What do you dislike about it?" most of them replied that they did not like the flavor. The investigators suspected that this might be a stereotyped answer, so they switched to a storytelling approach.

[20]Mason Haire, "Projective Techniques in Marketing Research," *Journal of Marketing,* 14 (April 1950), pp. 649–652.

Table 8.3   Reported Differences in Shopping List Study

Nescafé Shopper	Maxwell House Shopper
48% said lazy	4% said lazy
48% said failed to plan household purchases	12% said failed to plan household purchases
4% said thrifty	16% said thrifty
12% said spendthrift	0% said spendthrift
4% said good wife	16% said good wife

Source: Mason Haire, "Projective Techniques in Marketing Research," *Journal of Marketing,* 14 (April 1950), pp. 649–651. Published by the American Marketing Association.

A new sample of homemakers was split into two groups of fifty homemakers each. One group was then shown the following shopping list:

- pound and a half of hamburger
- 2 loaves Wonder Bread
- bunch of carrots
- 1 can Rumford's baking powder
- Nescafé instant coffee
- 2 cans Del Monte peaches
- 5 lb potatoes

The other half of the sample was shown the same list except that "1 lb. Maxwell House coffee (drip ground)" was substituted for the Nescafé instant coffee. Each homemaker was asked to read the shopping list and then describe the personality and character of the woman who made it out. Some of the reported differences were rather striking, as Table 8.3 indicates.

The evidence in Table 8.3 was interpreted as showing that the decision of whether or not to buy instant coffee was influenced as much by prevailing social ideas of what constituted good housekeeping in the late 1940s as it was by the flavor of instant coffee. Yet the direct approach failed to uncover this perhaps subconscious, but certainly important, attitude. Interestingly, when the same study was done again in 1968, researchers found no significant differences between subjects' descriptions of the Nescafé shopper versus the Maxwell House shopper. Both, actually, were seen in a more negative light than in the earlier study. In fact, by 1968 convenience foods had become so acceptable that the basically simple ingredients on both shopping lists led respondents to characterize the shoppers as having "no imagination." If anything, the Nescafé shopper was considered a bit more "with it" than the Maxwell House shopper, who was described as being "dull, phlegmatic," and having "no spirit of adventure."[21]

[21]Frederick E. Webster, Jr., and Frederick Von Peckmann, "A Replication of the Shopping List Study," *Journal of Marketing,* 34 (April 1970), pp. 61–63. For similar shopping list studies involving beer brands and cat food, see, respectively, A. G. Woodside, "A Shopping List Experiment of Beer Brand Images," *Journal of Applied Psychology,* 56 (December 1972), pp. 512–513; and L. N. Reid and L. Buchanan, "A Shopping List Experiment of the Impact of Advertising on Brand Images," *Journal of Advertising,* 8 (Spring 1979), pp. 26–28.

Each of the projective methods we have discussed differs somewhat in how structured its stimulus is. In the word-association and sentence-completion methods, researchers present each respondent with the same stimulus in the same sequence, and in this sense these methods are quite structured. However, both methods are typically categorized with storytelling as unstructured techniques, because, like the storytelling techniques, they allow very unstructured responses. Respondents are free to interpret and respond to the stimuli with their own words and in terms of their own perceptions.

Many of the same difficulties encountered with the unstructured-undisguised methods of data collection are also encountered with projective methods. Although having a standardized stimulus is a distinct advantage in interpreting the replies, the interpretation often reflects the researcher's frame of reference as much as it does the respondent's. Different researchers often reach different conclusions about the same response. This wreaks havoc with the editing, coding, and tabulating of replies and suggests that projective methods are also more suited for exploratory research than for descriptive or causal research.

Structured-Disguised Questionnaires

Structured-disguised questionnaires are the least used in marketing research. They were developed as a way of combining the advantages of disguise in uncovering subconscious motives and attitudes with the advantages of structure in coding and tabulating replies. Those who favor the structured-disguised approach usually base their support on the importance of a person's attitudes in his mental and psychological makeup.

One theory holds, for example, that an individual's knowledge, perception, and memory of a subject are conditioned by his attitudes toward it. Thus, in order to secure information about people's attitudes when a direct question would produce a biased answer, this theory suggests we simply ask them what they know, not what their opinion is. Presumably greater knowledge reflects the strength and direction of an attitude. Democratic voters, for example, could be expected to know more about Democratic candidates and the Democratic platform than would those intending to vote Republican. This argument is consistent with what we have learned about the process that psychologists call *selective perception*. That concept holds that individuals tend to selectively expose themselves, selectively perceive, and selectively retain ideas, arguments, events, and phenomena that are consistent with their previously held beliefs. Conversely, people tend to avoid, see differently, and forget situations and items that are inconsistent with their previously held beliefs.

This theory would suggest that one way of discovering a respondent's true attitudes toward pollution and the need for antipollution legislation, for example, would be to ask the person what he or she knows about the subject. Thus, the researcher might ask, "What is the status of the antipollution legislation listed below?" and then present some actual and some hypothetical bills for the respondent to check: "In committee," "Passed by the House but not the Senate," "Vetoed by the President," and so on. Respondents' attitudes toward the need for more legislation would then be assessed by the accuracy of their responses.

The main advantages of this approach emerge in analysis. Responses are easily coded and tabulated and an object measure of knowledge quickly derived. Whether this measure of knowledge can also be interpreted as a measure of the person's attitude, though, is another matter. Is high legislative awareness indicative of a favorable or an unfavorable attitude toward the need for more antipollution legislation? Or is it simply indicative of someone who keeps abreast of current events? In general, the evidence suggests that it is possible to obtain results with a structured-disguised approach that are at least comparable to those obtained with unstructured-disguised approaches.[22]

Methods of Administering Questionnaires

Questionnaires can also be classified by the method that will be used to administer them. The main methods are by personal interview, telephone interview, and mail questionnaire.

A **personal interview** implies a direct face-to-face conversation between the interviewer and the respondent, as compared to the **telephone interview**. In both cases, the interviewer asks the questions and records the respondent's answers either while the interview is in progress or immediately afterward. The **mail questionnaire** is sent to designated respondents with an accompanying cover letter. The respondents complete the questionnaire at their leisure and mail their replies back to the research organization.

A number of variations are possible on these so-called pure methods of administration. Questionnaires for a mail administration may simply be attached to products or printed in magazines and newspapers. Questionnaires in a personal interview may be self-administered, meaning the respondents complete the questionnaire themselves as opposed to having the interviewer ask the question and fill in the respondent's answer. This might be done in the interviewer's presence, in which case there would be an opportunity for the respondents to ask the interviewer to clarify any points that may be confusing. Or the respondents might complete the questionnaire in private for later pickup by a representative of the research organization, in which case the interaction would resemble a personal interview even less. Another possibility is for the interviewer to hand the designated respondent the questionnaire personally, but then have the respondent complete it in private and mail it directly to the research organization. In this case, the personal interview is indistinguishable from the mail-questionnaire method.

Each of these methods of administration possesses some advantages and disadvantages. When we discuss the various pros and cons of each method, we will use so-called pure cases as a frame of reference. By modifying the method of administration, researchers may also change some of the general advantages and disadvantages that normally characterize the method.

Other factors peculiar to a specific situation may also influence the strengths and weaknesses of each method. Nevertheless, a general discussion of advantages and disadvantages will help to clarify the various criteria that researchers must keep in mind when deciding on the method they will use to collect the data. Sampling control, information control, and administrative control are the points researchers generally consider when comparing the methods.

Sampling Control

Sampling control involves the researcher's ability to direct the inquiry to a designated respondent and to get the desired cooperation from that respondent.

The direction of the inquiry is guided by the **sampling frame,** that is, by the list of population elements from which the sample will be drawn. With the telephone method, for example, one or more phone books typically serve as the sampling

• Personal interview
Direct, face-to-face conversation between a representative of the research organization, the interviewer, and a respondent or interviewee.

• Telephone interview
Telephone conversation between a representative of the research organization, the interviewer, and a respondent or interviewee.

• Mail questionnaire
Questionnaire administered by mail to designated respondents under an accompanying cover letter and its return, by mail, by the subject to the research organization.

• Sampling control
Term applied to studies relying on questionnaires and concerning the researcher's dual abilities to direct the inquiry to a designated respondent and to secure the desired cooperation from that respondent.

• Sampling frame
List of sampling units from which a sample will be drawn; the list could consist of geographic areas, institutions, individuals, or other units.

[22]Ralph Westfall, Harper W. Boyd, Jr., and Donald T. Campbell, "The Use of Structured Techniques in Motivation Research," *Journal of Marketing,* 22 (October 1957), pp. 134–139.

frame. Respondents are selected by some random method from phone books serving the areas in which the study is to be done. Phone book sampling frames are inadequate because they do not include those without phones or those who have unlisted numbers. Though most of the U.S. population has phones—90 percent of all households in 1983—there are some notable variations in that percentage by demographic characteristics: 92 percent in the Midwest compared with 88 percent in the South, and 91 percent in urban areas compared with 88 percent in rural areas.[23]

---

[23]*Annual Housing Survey, 1983* (Washington: U.S. Bureau of the Census, 1984).

Research Window 8.1
Apple Juice or Antifreeze? Researchers Help Consumers Sort Out the Difference

How would consumers react to a frozen juice concentrate that remains liquid even when frozen? In interviews with the product's marketers, Sawyer Fruit & Vegetable Co-op Corporation of Bear Lake, Michigan, executives said they thought consumers would be delighted by how easy it would be to pour and prepare. But the company's advertising agency, The Berni Corporation, thought "AppleFresh" was a product ripe for consumer confusion.

In order to head off potential problems before they developed, marketing researchers at Berni staged focus groups to test consumer reaction. While group members liked the taste well enough, they incorrectly thought that the juice's liquidity was a result of adding artificial ingredients. "The only thing I know of that doesn't freeze solid is antifreeze—or alcohol," one consumer said. "Is that what this stuff is?"

Participants also said they might mistakenly believe AppleFresh had spoiled or defrosted when they got it home because of its liquidity. Some suggested confusion with single-strength, no-water-added juice might occur.

A telephone survey of supermarket buyers turned up the same concerns. Buyers said employees would have to be educated about product properties and benefits to head off consumer confusion.

Armed with the research, marketers at the Berni Corporation decided that instead of emphasizing product convenience first and foremost, as the client had originally preferred, a campaign for AppleFresh had to emphasize "100 percent natural and delicious" first, with easy preparation a secondary benefit. In addition, packaging had to be designed that would minimize confusion, as well as generate excitement, awareness, and trial.

To distinguish AppleFresh from traditional frozen concentrates, a distinctive plastic container that looked like a red apple with a green cap was designed. That design satisfied the focus groups' desire for a frozen juice package that was easy to open, reseal, and reuse. Because it was plastic, it wouldn't leak like paperboard containers.

Advertising and product copy for the juice emphasized "100% Natural/No Preservatives or Additives," with product convenience relegated to secondary status. Information about the "gentle freezing" method used to achieve liquidity was on the neck label. That copy was clear enough to dispel doubts about spoilage and avoid confusion with single-strength juices, yet it did not overshadow the "natural and delicious" positioning.

After several months of excellent success in test markets, marketers of AppleFresh began making plans for a national rollout. Fortunately, marketers responsible for launching the product realized that while a technological breakthrough may cause great excitement for the manufacturer, consumers may not greet the product with the same enthusiasm. Research is necessary to uncover possible negative product perceptions before the product is introduced, or the launch may go over like a lead balloon.

Source: Laurie. N. Yarnell, "Research, Packaging Stave off Negative Perceptions," *Marketing News,* 20 (May 9, 1986), p. 16.

Census data also indicate that there are more telephones in white households than in black, and more in high-income households than in low-income ones. The proportion of households with telephones increases each year, however, so the problem of bias due to the exclusion of nontelephone households should diminish in the future.

More serious is the underrepresentation of households where people have recently moved and whose numbers were assigned after the current directory was published, as well as the segment of the population that has requested an unlisted telephone number. The latter segment has been growing steadily and now represents approximately 20 percent of all residential phones.[24] The former segment accounts for another 40 percent of the total telephone households in some metropolitan areas.

According to one study, people with unlisted numbers tend to be younger, nonwhite, living in a large city, not college graduates, and employed by someone else in an unskilled or semi-skilled job.[25] These characteristics conflict with the stereotype that someone with an unlisted number is probably among the rich and famous!

An attempt at overcoming the sampling bias of unlisted numbers is **random-digit dialing,** in which a computer generates a list of random numbers, and often dials them automatically as well. The calls are typically handled through the central interviewing facility employing the Wide Area Telephone Service (WATS).[26] This procedure allows geographically wide distribution or coverage.

One problem with the random generation of phone numbers is that it can increase survey costs. While there are approximately 340 million possible phone numbers that can be called in the continental United States, there are only about 80 million working residential telephone numbers. Hence, when using random dialing, interviewers may only make a residential contact in about one out of four calls. This makes random-digit dialing very costly both in dollars and in time.[27]

An alternative scheme to random-digit dialing is **Plus-one sampling,** where a probability sample of phone numbers is selected from the telephone directory and a single, randomly determined digit is added to each selected number.[28]

One or more mailing lists typically serve as the sampling frame in mail questionnaires. The quality of these lists determines the sampling biases. If the list is a re-

◆ Random-digit dialing

Technique used in studies employing telephone interviews in which the numbers to be called are randomly generated.

◆ Plus-one sampling

Technique used in studies employing telephone interviews in which a single, randomly determined digit is added to numbers selected from the telephone directory.

[24]Clyde L. Rich, "Is Random Digit Dialing Really Necessary," *Journal of Marketing Research,* 14 (August 1977), pp. 300–305.

[25]Tyzoon T. Tyebjee, "Telephone Survey Methods: The State of the Art," *Journal of Marketing,* 43 (Summer 1979), pp. 68–78; A. B. Blankenship, "Listed Versus Unlisted Numbers in Telephone-Survey Samples," *Journal of Advertising Research,* 17 (February 1977), pp. 39–42; and Patricia E. Moberg, "Biases in Unlisted Phone Numbers," *Journal of Advertising Research,* 22 (August–September 1982), pp. 51–55.

[26]G. J. Glasser and G. D. Metzger, "Random-Digit Dialing as a Method of Telephone Sampling," *Journal of Marketing Research,* 9 (February 1972), pp. 59–64; *The Use of Random Digit Dialing in Telephone Surveys: An Annotated Bibliography* (Monticello, Ill.: Vance Bibliographies, 1979); and *Telephone Interviewing Bibliography,* (Washington, D.C.: U.S. Bureau of the Census, 1981).

[27]Albert G. Swint and Terry E. Powell, "CLUSFONE Computer-Generated Telephone Sampling Offers Efficiency and Minimal Bias," *Marketing Today,* 21 (Elrick and Lavidge, 1983). There is some evidence to suggest that certain sampling schemes can produce a higher proportion of working residential numbers without introducing any appreciable bias in the process. See, for example, Joseph Waksberg, "Sampling Methods for Random Digit Dialing," *Journal of the American Statistical Association,* 73 (March 1978), pp. 40–46; and Robert Groves and Robert L. Kahn, *Surveys by Telephone* (New York: Academic Press, 1979). More sophisticated sampling schemes have also been used with random-digit dialing to locate relatively rare segments of the population. See Johnny Blair and Ronald Czaja, "Locating a Special Population Using Random Digit Dialing," *Public Opinion Quarterly,* 46 (Winter 1982), pp. 585–590.

[28]T. Laird Landon, Jr., and Sharon K. Banks, "Relative Efficiency and Bias of Plus-One Telephone Sampling," *Journal of Marketing Research,* 14 (August 1977), pp. 294–299.

The use of central interviewing facilities and WATS line is currently the most popular method for administering questionnaires.

Source: Courtesy of Burgoyne Information Services, Cincinnati, Ohio.

sonably good one, the bias may be small. For example, some firms have established panels, which can be used to answer mail questionnaires and which are representative of the population in many important respects. Further, some mailing lists that may be ideally suited for certain types of studies can be purchased.

> Say you run a direct-mail business that specializes in selling monogrammed baby bibs. For a fee at any given time you can obtain a mailing list containing the names and addresses of up to one million pregnant women. And if it should suit your purposes, it's easy enough to get the list limited to women whose babies are expected in a certain month or who are expecting their first child.[29]

The fact remains, though, that the mailing list determines the sampling control in a mail study. If there is an accurate, applicable, and readily available list of population

---

[29]"Mailing List Brokers Sell More than Names to Their Many Clients," *The Wall Street Journal,* 54 (February 19, 1974), pp. 1 and 18. For other discussions of how firms go about developing mailing lists and their value, see Jeffrey H. Birnbaum, "Firms Try Shredders, Special Tasks to Protect Valuable Mailing Lists," *The Wall Street Journal,* 61 (April 27, 1981), p. 27; "Lists Make Targeting Easy," *Advertising Age,* 55 (July 9, 1984), p. 20; "Making a List, Selling It Twice," *The Wall Street Journal,* 65 (May 20, 1985), pp. 64–65.

elements, the mail questionnaire allows a wide and representative sample, since it costs no more to send a questionnaire across country than it does to send one across town. Even ignoring costs, it is sometimes the only way of contacting the relevant population, such as busy executives who will not sit still for an arranged personal or telephone interview but may respond to a mail questionnaire. It is estimated that the average consumer has his or her name on anywhere from twenty-five to forty separate mailing lists and receives eighty pieces of unsolicited mail per year. All those who think unsolicited mail is a bother, however, can send one letter to the Direct Mail Marketing Association, a trade group of more than 2,600 direct mail marketers, and that organization will remove the name from every member's list. The statistics indicate, however, that for every person requesting to have his or her name removed, two more request that their names be added.[30]

Sampling control for personal interviewing is a bit more difficult than for telephone interviewing or mail questionnaires, but is still possible. For some populations, such as doctors, architects, or business firms, trade associations or directories will furnish names from which a sample can be drawn. For consumer studies, however, there are few lists available, and those that are available are typically out-of-date. Instead of seeking names, researchers often choose their samples based on geographic areas and houses or apartments, termed *sampling units,* within that area. In this method, instead of inaccurate lists of people, interviewers use accurate, current lists of sampling units in the form of maps. We will discuss how such *area sampling,* as it is called, works in a later chapter.

While there is still the problem of ensuring that the field interviewer will contact the right household and person, the personal interview does provide some sampling control in directing the questionnaire to specific sample units.

It is one thing to figure out whom to contact in a study; it is quite another to get that person to agree to participate. For example, of the three methods of data collection we have discussed, the personal interview affords the most sample control with respect to obtaining cooperation from the designated respondent. With a personal interview, the respondent's identity is known, and thus there is little opportunity for anyone else to reply. People are also less likely to refuse a personal interview than they are a telephone interview or a mail questionnaire. There is sometimes a problem with not-at-homes, but this can often be handled by calling back at a different time.

Telephone methods also suffer from not-at-homes or no-answers. In one very large study involving more than 259,000 telephone calls, it was found, for example, that over 34 percent of the calls resulted in a no-answer.[31] Even more disturbing was that the probability of making contact with an eligible respondent on the first call was less than 1 in 10 (see Table 8.4). Of course, calling back by phone is much simpler and more economical than is trying to rearrange a personal interview. The relatively low expense of a telephone contact allows a number of follow-up calls to secure a needed response, while the high cost of field contact restricts the number of follow-ups that can be made in studies using personal interviews. However, making sure the intended respondent replies is somewhat more difficult with telephone

---

[30]Bruce Shawkey, "Mail Order Peddlers Pan Gold in Them Thar Lists," *Wisconsin State Journal* (July 31, 1983), pp. 1 and 4.

[31]Roger A. Kerin and Robert A. Peterson, "Scheduling Telephone Interviews," *Journal of Advertising Research,* 23 (April–May 1983), pp. 41–47.

Table 8.4   Results of First Dialing Attempts

Result	Number of Dialings	Probability of Occurrence
No answer	89,829	.347
Busy	5,299	.020
Out-of-service	52,632	.203
No eligible person	75,285	.291
Business	10,578	.041
At home	25,465	.098
Refusal	3,707	.014 (.146)[a]
Completion	21,758	.084 (.854)
Total	259,088	1.000

[a]Probability of occurrence given eligible individual is at home.

Source: Roger A. Kerin and Robert A. Peterson, "Scheduling Telephone Interviews." Reprinted from the *Journal of Advertising Research,* 23 (April/May 1983), p. 44. Copyright 1983 by the Advertising Research Foundation.

interviews than with personal interviews, as is the problem of determining which person in the household should be interviewed.[32]

Mail questionnaires afford the researcher little control in securing a response from the intended respondent. Although the researcher can offer the individual some incentive for cooperating,[33] a great many subjects may nevertheless refuse to respond. In many cases, only those most interested in the subject will respond. In other cases subjects will be incapable of responding because they are illiterate. For example, the International Reading Association estimates that some 20 million English-speaking, native-born American adults read or write so poorly that they have trouble holding jobs, and the author of *Illiterate America* suggests that 60 million adult Americans are illiterate.[34] Since many of these people have difficulty with everyday tasks such as reading job notices, making change, or getting a driver's license, it is no wonder that they might not respond to a mail questionnaire!

[32]Ronald Czaja, Johnny Blair, and Jutta P. Sebestik, "Respondent Selection in a Telephone Survey: A Comparison of Three Techniques," *Journal of Marketing Research,* 19 (August 1982), pp. 381–385; Diane O'Rourke and Johnny Blair, "Improving Random Respondent Selection in Telephone Interviews," *Journal of Marketing Research,* 20 (November 1983), pp. 428–432; and Terry L. Childers and Steven J. Skinner, "Theoretical and Empirical Issues in the Identification of Survey Respondents," *Journal of the Market Research Society,* 27 (January 1985), pp. 39–53.

[33]See Paul L. Erdos, *Professional Mail Surveys* (Malabar, Fla.: Robert E. Kreiger, 1983), for a discussion of the problem of sample control in mail surveys and what can be done to overcome respondent resistance. For general references on conducting telephone surveys, see A. B. Blankenship, *Professional Telephone Surveys* (New York: McGraw-Hill, 1977); or James H. Frey, *Survey Research by Telephone* (Beverly Hills, Calif.: Sage Publications, 1983).

[34]Daniel Machalaba, "Hidden Handicap: For Americans Unable to Read Well, Life Is a Series of Small Crises," *The Wall Street Journal,* 64 (January 17, 1984), pp. 1 and 12; and Chris Martell, "Illiteracy Hurts All, Author Says," *Wisconsin State Journal,* (April 3, 1985), pp. 1 and 2. The illiteracy problem is also severe in England. See *Journal of the Market Research Society,* 26 (April 1984), for a number of articles on the subject and its consequences for survey research.

Whatever the reason for nonresponse, it causes a bias of unknown size and direction. Lack of control also exists in respect to identifying who is responding to the mail questionnaire. The researcher cannot even ensure the preferred respondent from the household replies.

Information Control

◆ Information control

Term applied to studies using questionnaires and concerning the amount and accuracy of the information that can be obtained from respondents.

Information control, which involves the kinds of questions that can be asked and the amount and accuracy of the information that can be obtained from respondents, varies according to the method of data collection that is used. The personal interview, for example, can be conducted using almost any form of questionnaire, from structured-undisguised through unstructured-disguised. The personal nature of the interaction allows the interviewer to show the respondent pictures, examples of advertisements, lists of words, scales, and so on, as stimuli. In contrast, the telephone interview rules out most aids. The mail questionnaire, however, allows the use of some of them.

Figures 8.1 and 8.2 display an example of a questionnaire for a study on lighting fixtures. The study is designed in such a way that respondents must be allowed to see the lamps, but exposure to them is to be carefully controlled by the interviewer. Because the respondents must be able to view the merchandise, a personal interview is the only method that would be appropriate to this study.

Note the detailed instructions to the interviewer that are part of the research design. Note also the open-ended questions and the difficulty one will likely encounter in tabulating the responses. (The numbers in parentheses indicate the computer record columns that will be used for the coded answers.) Some of the open-ended questions require extensive probes. Mail questionnaires simply do not allow the use of questions requiring extensive probes for a complete response. Telephone interviews can incorporate them, but not nearly to the same extent. Note, finally, the automatic sequencing of questions; for example, if the answer to Question 4 is positive, ask Questions 5 and 6. If it is negative, ask Questions 7 and 8. While automatic sequencing is also possible with telephone interviews, mail questionnaires permit much less of it.

The computer-controlled cathode-ray terminal (CRT) has had a significant impact on how telephone interviews are conducted and the amount of information control they allow, both with respect to the questions asked and the analysis of replies. After dialing the selected number, the computer leads the interviewer through the survey questionnaire. The computer displays the exact wording of the question to be asked the respondent on the CRT. The interviewer records the responses on a keyboard for direct entry into the computer. Only when an acceptable answer is provided will the computer display the next question. If a respondent says she or he bought a brand that is not available in that particular area, for example, the computer is programmed to reject the answer and automatically go on to the next appropriate question. This saves considerable time and confusion in administering the questionnaire and allows the interview to flow more naturally. It also assures that there will be no variation in the sequence in which the questions are asked, as can happen with personal interviews or mail questionnaires.[35]

[35]The empirical evidence indicates that computer-assisted telephone interviewing indeed produces less interviewer variability and fewer skip problems than normal telephone interviews, although no time savings. See Robert A. Groves and Nancy Mathiowetz, "Computer Assisted Telephone Interviewing: Effects on Interviewers and Respondents," *Public Opinion Quarterly,* 48 (Spring 1984), pp. 356–359.

Figure 8.1

Interviewer Instructions for Portable Lighting Fixtures Study (Courtesy Ray-O-Vac Corporation)

Background

Your city will be responsible for the completion of 100 interviews, half with males between the ages of 20 and 64, the other half with females in the same age category. Quota sheets have been enclosed to ensure that about:

30% of the males are 20–29

25% of the males are 30–39

30% of the males are 40–54

15% of the males are 55–64

Female quota sheets have been enclosed so as to obtain the following approximate distribution:

30% of the females are 20–29

20% of the females are 30–39

35% of the females are 40–54

15% of the females are 55–64

Inventory

Please inventory for the following materials:

1 Rectangular lamp (#381 on back)

1 Round (brown) lamp (#492 on back)

Preprinted numbered ID stickers which will attach to front of display area directly above the respective lamps

One laminated concept statement which will attach to the wall under the rectangular #381 lamp

One laminated concept statement for use in Question 3

One laminated exhibit card for use in Question 4

One laminated price card for use in Question 11

Two laminated age/income cards fixed back to back

The Display

Both lamps will be attached to the wall approximately 5½' from the floor with the string switches hanging straight down. The number 381 will be attached to the wall right under the rectangular lamp; the number 492 will be under the round brown fixture.

A laminated concept statement will be attached to the wall right under the number identifier for model 381.

A white towel will be used to cover the brown fixture. This can most easily be accomplished by tacking the towel to the wall several inches above the brown fixture and placing a second tack far to the right so that when the towel is removed it can be hung off to the right side (see drawing enclosed).

When a consumer first enters the display area, only lamp #381 will be visible to him/her.

The Interview

Approach adult shoppers who appear to be at least 20 years old or older and read the introduction. This interview should not take much more than 5 to 8 minutes, which is specified in the introduction.

Question 1:   Terminate any adult consumer who has been in a research study within the last three months.

Question 2:   Terminate any consumer who is affiliated with a marketing research firm, advertising agency or lighting appliance manufacturer.

continued

Figure 8.1

continued

The Interview continued

Question 3:   Hand a laminated copy of the concept statement to the consumer, then read aloud with him/her. Once you have finished reading, hand the exhibit card for Question 4 and allow the respondent to evaluate the concept/lamp.

DO NOT ALLOW THE RESPONDENT TO TOUCH THE LAMPS. IF THE RESPONDENT WANTS TO TURN THEM ON OR MENTIONS LIGHTING CAPABILITY, SAY . . . This is only a model and the batteries are not installed.

DO NOT ATTEMPT TO PULL THE ON/OFF STRING ON ANY OF THESE LAMPS.

If the respondent likes the idea (Question 4 — one of the top 3 responses) you will ask Questions 5 and 6. If the respondent does not like the idea (Question 4 — the last 2 responses) you will ask Questions 7 and 8.

Question 5/6:   These are open-end questions which deal with the respondent's likes and dislikes. Probe and clarify fully, then skip to Question 9.

Question 7/8:   These open ends are almost identical to those references above but they ask the respondent for dislikes first, then likes. Once again, probe and clarify fully, then skip to Question 9.

Question 9:   Read the first paragraph of Question 9 slowly and pause so the respondent has time to think of the various places where he/she could use such a lamp. Then continue with the second paragraph. Put a number 1 next to the very first place the respondent mentions — and then ask why it would be used there? Then ask the third paragraph of Question 9 probing for additional places. Put a number 2 in the left hand blank provided for the second place mentioned and repeat the above probe. Continue placing 3's, 4's, 5's, 6's etc. next to the places where they would be used in the order mentioned until the respondent indicates no additional places of use.

Again, if the respondent would not use the light anywhere, merely circle the x at the bottom of the page and go on to Question 10.

Question 10:   Encourage the respondent to best guess — without batteries.

Question 11:   Be sure to use the exhibit card.

Question 12:   Remove the covering from Fixture 492 — allow inspection — obtain overall preference.

Question 13:   Self-explanatory. Read slowly.

Question 14:   This question reveals the difference in price — be absolutely sure to point to the different models as you are reading the prices. Allow the respondent ample time to make up his/her mind and then record final choice.

Question 15, 15A: Self-explanatory.

Question 16, 17:   Self-explanatory. Use the exhibit card.

At the completion of the interview circle the quota cell group on the top of page one and the city.

Your city is responsible for the completion of 100 interviews. Other cities are waiting for the use of the lights, so as soon as you have completed field work, ship the lights (well packed) and the exhibit cards:

Milwaukee — ship to Livingston, New Jersey
Houston — ship to Los Angeles, California

Ship via Federal Air Express — priority service and notify M. Maloney of the date and time of shipment.

Figure 8.2

Questionnaire Used in Portable Lighting Fixtures Study (Courtesy Ray-O-Vac Corporation)

(APPROACH SHOPPERS WHO APPEAR TO BE 20 YEARS OLD OR OVER AND SAY . . .)
Hi, I'm _____ from U.S. Testing Co. Many companies are asking consumers for their opinions in order to develop the kinds of products that you really want, and if you have about 5 minutes, I'd like to include your opinions in our market research study. **(IF REFUSED, TERMINATE)**

1. Have you participated in any consumer research studies in this center within the last three months? **(IF YES, TALLY AND TERMINATE)**   (07)

2. Do you, or any members of your family, or close friends, work for any marketing research firm, advertising agency, or lighting appliance manufacturer? **(IF YES, TALLY AND TERMINATE)**   (08)

3. Here is a brief description of this new type of area light.

"This is a battery operated light fixture . . . it operates on four regular flashlight batteries . . . designed to give you light in places where you don't have electricity available or in places where expensive wiring jobs can be avoided.

Both the non-globes and body are made of rugged high impact plastic which will not rust or corrode—ideal wherever you need wireless light; made by Ray-O-Vac, a United States manufacturer of quality lighting devices."

4. Which of the following phrases best describes your overall reaction to the product you have just read?

(09)—1 It's a great idea

     2 It's a pretty good idea   **—(ASK Q. 5 AND 6)**

     3 So-so

     4 It's not a very good idea

     5 It's a poor idea   **—(ASK Q. 7 AND 8)**

(IF RESPONSE WAS POSITIVE, ASK:)

5. What is it that you particularly like about this idea? **(Probe and Clarify)**

Likes
(10)
(11)
(12)
(13)
(14)

6. What, if anything, do you dislike about this idea? **(Probe and Clarify)**

(15)
(16)
(17)
(18)
(19)

continued

Figure 8.2
continued

(SKIP to Q. 9)

(IF RESPONSE WAS NEGATIVE, ASK:)

7. *What is it that you* dislike *about this idea?* **(Probe and Clarify)**

Dislikes

(20)
(21)
(22)
(23)
(24)
(25)
(26)
(27)
(28)
(29)

8. *Is there anything at all that you particularly* like *about this idea?* **(Probe and Clarify)**

9. *Now, take a minute or two to think about all the places where you might use a product of this type.* **(ALLOW TIME AND THEN CONTINUE BY SAYING . . .)**

Where would you use a product of this type and why? **(RECORD FIRST ITEM MENTIONED ON THE LINE PROVIDED IN THE LEFT HAND COLUMN. USE THE SPACE PROVIDED TO PROBE AND CLARIFY REASONS WHY, THEN CONTINUE BY SAYING . . .)**

What other areas would you use it in? **(RECORD SECOND MENTIONED, ETC., CONTINUE TO PROBE FOR OTHER AREAS UNTIL RESPONDENT INDICATES THERE ARE NO MORE)**

Left column	Right column
(30) _____ Tent	(40)
	(41)
(31) _____ Camper	(42)
	(43)
(32) _____ Boat	(44)
	(45)
(33) _____ Cottage/Cabin	(46)
	(47)
(34) _____ Home	(48)
	(49)
(35) _____ Garage	(50)
	(51)
(36) _____ Porch/Patio	(52)
	(53)
(37) _____ Car	(54)
	(55)
(38) _____ Other (SPECIFY)	(56)
	(57)
(39) _____ Other (SPECIFY)	(58)
	(59)

X _____ Would not use anywhere

10. *About how much would you expect a light like this to cost, without batteries?*

(URGE A GUESS IF NECESSARY)

$_____

(60-61-62)

Figure 8.2
continued

11. *Assuming this light sold for $_____ in your local discount store, how likely would you be to buy it? Would you say you would . . . (SHOW CARD)*

(63) — 1		I definitely would buy it
2		I probably would buy it
3		I might or might not buy it
4		I probably would not buy it
5		I definitely would not buy it

12. (UNCOVER 492 LIGHT AND SAY . . .)
Here is another light fixture that is basically the same as the first one, but its styling and design are somewhat different. Considering just the design of these two lights, which one do you prefer?

(64) — 1 381
2 492

13. *If you were going to buy a light fixture like either of these, would you be satisfied with the colors we've shown here, or would you prefer a wider variety of colors be available to coordinate with the decor in the places where you might use a light of this type?*

(65) — 1 Satisfied with these colors
2 Prefer a wider variety

14. *While model 381 and 492 are basically the same type of light, they do differ in styling and quality. Model 492 sells for $3.00 without batteries, compared to model 381 which sells for $5.00 without batteries. Please take one last look at them and then considering their overall appearance, features, and prices, please tell me which one you'd be most likely to buy.*

(66) — 1 381
2 492

15. *Just for classification purposes, do you live in a single family house or apartment?*

(67) — 1 Single family house
2 Apartment
Other _____ **(SPECIFY)**

15a. *Do you own or rent it?*

(68) — 1 Own
2 Rent

16. *Please look at this card* **(HAND CARD)** *and tell me which letter best represents your age group.*

(69) — 1 A 18–20	6 F 40–44
2 B 21–24	7 G 45–49
3 C 25–29	8 H 50–54
4 D 30–34	9 I 55–59
5 E 35–39	0 J 60–64
	X K 65 and over

17. *Which letter on the other side of that card best represents your total family income before taxes?*

(70) — 1 A Up to $5,000 a year
2 B $5,000–$7,499
3 C $7,500–$9,999
4 D $10,000–$12,499
5 E $12,500–$14,999
6 F $15,000–$19,999
7 G $20,000–$24,999
8 H $25,000 or more

Two other advantages are the personalization and customizing of questions offered by computer control. As the interview proceeds, the computer stores information on all previous responses (e.g., name of wife, cars owned, supermarket patronized) and can personalize the wording of future questions. For example, the computer could retrieve enough information to ask, "When your wife, Ann, shops at the Acme, does she usually use the Fiat or the Buick?" Such personalized questions could enhance rapport and thus provide for higher quality interviews.

Moreover, key information that the respondent has given early in the interview can be used to tailor the questionnaire to that individual. For example, a respondent may say that one of the main things she looks for when buying a car is styling. At that point the computer can then design questions to measure her opinion of various makes and models based on that particular attribute, rather than asking her about a long list of features such as gas mileage and trunk space that might be common concerns of all respondents.[36]

Another advantage to CRT interviews is that preliminary tabulations of the answers are available at a moment's notice, since the replies are already stored in memory. One does not have the typical two-to-three-week delay for coding and data entry that happens when questionnaires are completed by hand. Partly because of the advantages that are possible through CRT administration of questionnaires, telephone interviews are currently the most popular and have also experienced the greatest increase in popularity over the last few years among members of the Council of American Survey Research Organization (CASRO). (See Table 8.5.)

A CRT can also be used in personal interviews. Because of the need for an electronic hookup, however, these interviews must be conducted at central locations instead of door to door. Typically, this will mean shopping malls, in which case the previous comments on possible sampling control with personal interviews no longer apply.[37]

One of the primary obstacles to information control in mail questionnaires is that respondents may answer the questions out of order. This introduces a problem known as *sequence bias.* Since the respondent can see the whole questionnaire at once, he or she may be tempted to read ahead. Information contained in later questions may then bias the respondent's answers to other questions. This problem cannot arise in personal or telephone interviews.

The mail questionnaire, however, avoids the bias caused by interviewer-interviewee interaction. With a mail questionnaire, respondents are also able to work at their own pace. This may produce better-thought-out responses than would be obtained in personal or telephone interviews, where there is a certain urgency associated with giving a response. Of course, a thought-out response, is no guarantee of an informative reply if the question is vaguely worded. The mail survey offers no opportunity for clarification, so each question must succeed or fail on its own merits.

Each respondent brings his or her unique experiences and opinions to a study. An interviewer can minimize these differences by imposing a consistent frame of reference on the replies. This is impossible in a mail questionnaire. To take an extreme example, imagine a study that seeks to determine if people are more likely

[36]Tyebjee, "Telephone Survey Methods," p. 76.

[37]For a discussion of desirable sampling procedures to use with mall intercept interviewing, see Seymour Sudman, "Improving the Quality of Shopping Center Sampling," *Journal of Marketing Research,* 17 (November 1980), pp. 423–431. See also Alan J. Bush and Joseph F. Hair, Jr., "An Assessment of the Mall Intercept as a Data Collection Method," *Journal of Marketing Research,* 22 (May 1985), pp. 158–167, for an empirical assessment of response quality and the extent of the nonresponse problem in mall intercept interviewing.

Table 8.5 Popularity of Various Data-Collection Techniques among CASRO Members

Technique	1983	1982	1981
WATS/centralized telephone	41%	38%	38%
Central location/mall	19	17	16
Personal interview/door-to-door	13	19	20
Non-WATS telephone (local)	7	8	7
Mail/diary	7	7	6
Focus group	6	5	6
All other	7	6	7

Source: Jack J. Honomichl, "Survey Results Positive," *Advertising Age,* 55 (November 1, 1984), p. 23.

to go to a restaurant that has a separate nonsmoking section. In a personal or telephone interview, a researcher could keep respondents focused on the question at hand. If such an open-ended question were asked in a mail questionnaire, responses might range from the excessive to the inadequate based on the respondent's attitude toward smoking.

Answers to structured questions in a mail questionnaire may reflect merely the differences in the respondents' frame of reference rather than any real differences in opinion about the subject under investigation. An offsetting advantage, however, is that the anonymity sometimes associated with a mail questionnaire encourages people to be more frank on certain sensitive issues (such as sexual behavior).

As mentioned, both personal and telephone interviews can cause interviewer bias because of the respondent's perception of the interviewer or because of the individual interviewer's style of asking questions. Both of these biases can be more easily controlled in telephone surveys than in personal interviews. On the telephone there are fewer interviewer actions to which the respondent can react, and a supervisor can be present to ensure that the interviews are being conducted consistently. It is typically more difficult, though, to establish rapport over the phone than in person. The respondent in a telephone interview often demands more information about the purposes of the study, the credentials of the interviewer and research organization, and so on.[38]

With regard to length of questionnaire or amount of information to be collected, the general rule of thumb is that long questionnaires can be handled best by personal interview and least well by telephone interview. So much, however, depends on the subject of inquiry, the form of the questionnaire, and the approach used to secure cooperation that a rigid interpretation of this advice would be unwarranted and possibly hazardous.

Administrative Control

• **Administrative control**

Term applied to studies relying on questionnaires and referring to the speed, cost, and control of the replies afforded by the mode of administration.

Administrative control involves the time and cost of administering the questionnaire, as well as the control of the replies afforded by the administrative method chosen. The telephone survey is one of the quickest ways of obtaining information.

[38]Peter U. Miller and Charles F. Cannell, "A Study of Experimental Techniques for Telephone Interviewing," *Public Opinion Quarterly,* 46 (Summer 1982), pp. 250–269; Charles F. Cannell, Peter U. Miller, and Lois Oksenberg, "Research on Interviewing Techniques," in Samuel Leinhardt, ed., *Sociological Methodology 1981* (San Francisco: Jossey-Bass, 1981); and Pamela G. Guengel, Tracy R. Berchman, and Charles F. Cannell, *General Interviewing Techniques: A Self-Instructional Workbook for Telephone and Personal Interviewer Training* (Ann Arbor, Mich.: Survey Research Center, University of Michigan, 1983).

A number of calls can be made from a central exchange in a short period, perhaps as many as fifteen or twenty per hour per interviewer if the questionnaire is short. The personal interview affords no such time economies, since there is unproductive time between each interview in which the interviewer travels to the next respondent. If the researcher wishes to speed up the replies secured with personal interviews, the size of the field force must be increased. However, as the number of interviewers increases, so do problems of interviewer-related variations in responses. By properly selecting and training interviewers, researchers can minimize some of the differences in approach that lead to variations, but personal interviews still present more problems of control than telephone interviews.

Personal interviews also give researchers little control over possible interviewer cheating. Since the researcher can supervise telephone interviewers directly when they are making their calls, problems of variation in administration and cheating should be minimized.

While the mail questionnaire represents a standardized stimulus, and thus allows little variation in administration, it also affords little speed control. It often takes several weeks to secure the bulk of the replies, at which time a follow-up mailing is often begun. It, too, will involve a time lapse of several weeks for the questionnaires to reach the respondents, be completed, and find their way back. Depending on the number of follow-up mailings required, the total time needed to conduct a good

Back to the Case

For Melissa Cavanaugh, today's meeting with the top executives of the cosmetics company for whom she had been working represented the culmination of many long months of painstaking research. With her she had a carefully prepared report detailing all the studies she and her team had conducted, and the recommendations they were proposing.

It had been a fascinating project, and it had allowed her to conduct research in a variety of ways. Her focus groups had helped clarify the problem that the company's product was capable of solving. They had also

been influential in deciding the name of the secret ingredient in the product. A series of telephone interviews had determined that a product that would help treat dry lips would be of equal interest to young women and older women, blacks and whites, Midwesterners and those on either coast. Advertising awareness studies had shown that before-and-after pictures were essential in educating women as to product benefits.

Melissa was confident not only that the cosmetics company had a potentially big hit on its hands, but that she had done a good job in helping to make sure that

when it finally became available, the product would find its market.

Often a firm will use a combination of data-collection methods to investigate a problem. Each method has its advantages and disadvantages, and each can offer something that another method cannot provide. In this case, focus groups were most useful in the exploratory phase of the project; telephone interviews gave the study breadth; and personal interviews helped to clarify the advertising approach.

mail study can often be substantial.[39] With a mail study it also takes as long to get replies from a small sample as it does from a large sample. This is not so with personal and telephone interviews, where there is a direct relationship between the number of interviews and the time required to complete them.

In general, personal interviews tend to be the most expensive per completed contact, and the mail questionnaire tends to be the cheapest. However, many factors can change the cost picture dramatically.[40] For example, it costs relatively little, per contact, to mail a questionnaire; but if the response rate is very low, the cost per return may actually be quite high.

For the most part, the cost of the various methods hinges on the problem of assuring quality control. It is generally true that the larger the field staff is, the greater the problems of control. Mail surveys require the fewest staffers. Telephone, mall, and in-home personal interview methods require progressively larger field staffs. Hence, a personal interview in the home is typically the most expensive method of data collection.

Combining Administration Methods

Each method of data collection thus has its advantages and disadvantages, and none is superior in all situations. The research problem itself will often suggest one approach over the others, but the researcher should recognize that a combination of approaches is often the most productive. In one home product use test, for example, interviewers distributed the product, self-administered questionnaires, and return envelopes to the respondents, while telephone interviews were used for follow-up. The combination of methods produced telephone cooperation from 97 percent of the testing families, while 82 percent of the mail questionnaires were returned.[41]

◆ Summary

Learning Objective 1: Explain the concept of *structure* as it relates to questionnaires.

The degree of structure in a questionnaire is the degree of standardization imposed on it. In a highly structured questionnaire the questions to be asked and the responses permitted the subjects are completely predetermined. In a highly unstructured questionnaire, the questions to be asked are only loosely predetermined, and the respondents are free to respond in their own words. A questionnaire in which the questions are fixed but the responses are open-ended would represent an intermediate degree of structure.

---

[39]Because of the need to send follow-up mailings to reduce the typically high incidence of nonresponse that occurs to any single mailing, researchers sometimes attempt to predict the ultimate response rate to a mailing based on the early returns. See Stephen J. Huxley, "Predicting Response Speed in Mail Surveys," *Journal of Marketing Research,* 17 (February 1980), pp. 63–68; and Richard W. Hill, "Using S-Shaped Curves to Predict Response Rates," *Journal of Marketing Research,* 18 (May 1981), pp. 240–242, for discussion of how this can be done.

[40]The National Opinion Research Council, for one, has conducted a number of studies aimed at investigating the information quality-cost trade-offs associated with the various data-collection methods. The results of some of these studies are contained in Seymour Sudman, *Reducing the Cost of Surveys* (Chicago: Aldine, 1967). See also R. M. Groves and R. L. Kahn, *Surveys by Telephone: A National Comparison with Personal Interviews* (New York: Academic Press, 1979).

[41]Stanley L. Payne, "Combination of Survey Methods," *Journal of Marketing Research,* 1 (May 1964), p. 62.

Learning Objective 2: Explain what is meant by *disguise* in a questionnaire.

The amount of disguise in a questionnaire is the amount of knowledge hidden from the respondent as to the purpose of the study. An undisguised questionnaire makes the purpose of the research obvious by the questions posed, while a disguised questionnaire attempts to hide the purpose of the study.

Learning Objective 3: Discuss why structured-undisguised questionnaires are the type most frequently used by marketing researchers.

Structured-undisguised questionnaires are the most popular type of data collection because they are simple to administer and easy to tabulate and analyze. They are also relatively reliable, since they typically use fixed-alternative questions.

Learning Objective 4: Cite three drawbacks of fixed-alternative questions.

Fixed-alternative questions may force a subject to respond to a question on which he does not really have an opinion. They may also prove inaccurate if none of the response categories allows the accurate expression of the respondent's opinion. The response categories themselves may introduce bias if one of the probable responses is omitted because of an oversight or insufficient prior research.

Learning Objective 5: List the kinds of information usually generated by focus groups.

Focus groups have proven productive for generating hypotheses that can be further tested quantitatively, generating information helpful in structuring questionnaires, providing overall background information on a product category, securing impressions on new product concepts for which there is little information available, stimulating new ideas about older products, stimulating ideas for new creative concepts, and interpreting previously obtained quantitative results.

Learning Objective 6: Identify the key person in a focus group.

The moderator is key to successful functioning of a focus group. The moderator must not only lead the discussion so that all objectives of the study are met but must do so in such a way that interaction among group members is stimulated and promoted.

Learning Objective 7: Explain the reason why researchers use projective methods in conducting some studies.

Researchers use projective techniques as a way of overcoming subjects' reluctance to discuss their feelings. The main thrust of these techniques has been to conceal the true subject of the study by using a disguised stimulus. The basic assumption in projective methods is that the way an individual responds to a relatively unstructured stimulus provides clues as to how that person really perceives the subject under investigation and what his or her reactions are to it.

Learning Objective 8: List three common types of stimuli used in projective techniques.

Three common types of stimuli used are word association, sentence completion, and storytelling.

Learning Objective 9: Differentiate among the three methods of administering questionnaires.

Personal interviews imply a direct face-to-face conversation between the interviewer and the respondent, as opposed to the *telephone interview.* In both types, the interviewer asks the questions and records the respondents' answers, either while the interview is in progress or immediately afterward. *Mail questionnaires* are sent to designated respondents with an accompanying cover letter. The respondents complete the questionnaire at their leisure and mail their replies back to the research organization.

Learning Objective 10: Cite the points researchers generally consider when they compare the various methods of administering questionnaires.

Sampling control, information control, and administrative control are the points researchers generally consider when comparing the methods of personal interviewing, telephone interviewing, and mail questionnaires.

Discussion Questions, Problems, and Projects

1. Pick three of your friends and conduct a depth interview with each one of them to determine their feelings toward purchasing designer jeans.
   (a) What factors were mentioned in the first interview?
   (b) What factors were mentioned in the second interview?
   (c) What factors were mentioned in the third interview?
   (d) Based on the findings for Questions a, b, and c, what specific hypotheses would you suggest?
   (e) Briefly discuss the strengths and weaknesses of depth interviews.

2. Design and administer a word-association test to determine a student's feelings toward eating out.
   (a) List ten stimuli and the subject's responses and the amount of time that elapsed before the subject reacted to each stimulus.

STIMULUS	RESPONSE	TIME
1.		
2.		
3.		
4.		
5.		
6.		
7.		
8.		
9.		
10.		

   (b) On the basis of your mini-survey, what tentative conclusions can you infer regarding the person's feelings toward eating out?
   (c) Briefly discuss the strengths and weaknesses of this technique.

3. Design and administer a sentence-completion test to determine a student's feelings toward coffee consumption.
   (a) List at least eight sentences that are to be used in the sentence completion exercise.
   1.
   2.
   3.
   4.
   5.
   6.
   7.
   8.
   (b) On the basis of the respondent's reactions, how would you describe the person's attitudes toward drinking coffee?
   (c) How would a researcher analyze the responses?

4. Design and administer a storytelling test to determine a student's reasons for not living in the residence halls or dormitories.
   (a) Develop a stimulus (verbal or pictorial) for the story-completion exercise. (Hint: It might be easier to use a verbal stimulus.)
   (b) Based on this exercise, what are your findings as to the person's reasons for not living in residence halls.

5. Select eight to ten fellow students and conduct a focus-group interview with the following specific objectives: to find out respondent's attitudes toward video games in general and likes and dislikes of home-video games.
   (a) Report your findings with respect to both objectives.
   (b) Briefly discuss the usefulness of focus-group interviews.

6. You are requested to design an appropriate communication method to find out students' feelings and opinons about the various food services available on campus.
   (a) What degree of structure would be appropriate? Justify your choice.
   (b) What degree of disguise would be appropriate? Justify your choice.
   (c) What method of administration would be appropriate? Justify your choice.

Which survey method (mail, telephone, or personal) would you use for the situations listed in Questions 7 through 11? Justify your choice.

7. Administration of a questionnaire to determine the number of people who listened to the "100 Top Country Tunes in 1986," a program that aired on December 31, 1986.

8. Administration of a questionnaire to determine the number of households having a mentally ill individual in the household and a history of mental illness in the family.

9. Administration of a questionnaire by a national manufacturer of microwave ovens in order to test people's attitudes and opinions toward a new model.

10. Administration of a questionnaire by a local dry cleaner who wants to determine customers' satisfaction with a recent discount scheme.

11. Administration of a questionnaire by the management of a small hotel that wants to assess customers' opinions of their service.

Suggested Additional Readings

For a useful discussion of the advantages and disadvantages of structured, unstructured, disguised, and undisguised questions, see

Claire Selltiz, Lawrence S. Wrightsman, and Stuart W. Cook, *Research Methods in Social Relations,* 3rd ed. (New York: Holt, Rinehart and Winston, 1976).

For a useful discussion of how to go about organizing and conducting focus groups, see

Focus Groups: Issues and Approaches (New York: Qualitative Research Counsel of the Advertising Research Foundation, 1985).

For a general discussion of projective research methods, see

Fred N. Kerlinger, *Foundations of Behavioral Research,* 3rd ed. (New York: Holt, Rinehart and Winston, 1986).

For details as to how to go about conducting studies, especially using mail surveys or telephone interviews, see

Paul L. Erdos, *Professional Mail Surveys* (Malabar, Fla.: Robert E. Kreiger, 1983).

A. B. Blankenship, *Professional Telephone Surveys* (New York: McGraw-Hill, 1977).

Chapter 9

Collecting Information by Observation

Learning Objectives

Upon completing this chapter, you should be able to

1. List the different methods by which observational data can be gathered.
2. Cite the main reason researchers may choose to disguise the presence of an observer in a study.
3. Explain the advantages and disadvantages of conducting an observational experiment in a laboratory setting.
4. Discuss the principle that underlies the use of a psychogalvanometer.
5. Explain the function of a tachistoscope.
6. Explain how researchers use eye cameras.
7. Define *response latency* and explain what it measures.
8. Define *voice-pitch analysis* and explain what it measures.

Case in Marketing Research

Brian Carmichael sat clutching his briefcase on a leather sofa in the posh suburban headquarters of MacIntosh Foods, one of the giants of the food industry. As a new account executive at Target Marketing, Inc., he was about to pitch his first big account, and the prospect both excited and terrified him. Brian's goal was to sell the company's vice-president of marketing on the idea of using Target Marketing's new electronic test-marketing service. If he could land the account, Brian knew his future with Target would be off and running.

While he sat contemplating his rosy future, the door to the corner office opened, and a tall, silver-haired man emerged.

"Hello, Mr. Carmichael. I'm John Sargeant," the man said, jolting Brian out of his reverie. "Come in my office and tell me about your service. From what I've read, it sounds fascinating."

"Oh, it is, sir," Brian said, launching enthusiastically into his sales talk as the two entered Sargeant's office. "We've had great success so far in test marketing products for a wide range of clients."

"Tell me how it works," Sargeant said, leaning back in his chair.

"In a nutshell, it's like this," Brian said. "We have 3,000 households in Fairfax, Pennsylvania, as our sample. Each adult member of a participating household has a plastic card that he or she presents when checking out at a local supermarket. Computers we've installed at the markets record members' purchases, and feed them into our records. By showing the card, participants have a chance at a variety of prizes, including vacations in Mexico and Hawaii, small electrical appliances, and gift certificates at local restaurants and retail stores.

"The beauty of the system, however, is how it links with members' television-viewing habits," Brain continued. "Each of our households has a microprocessor inside its cable converter that tells us what the family watches and for how long. Fairfax is a terrific site for test marketing. It's located in a valley at the foot of a mountain, which makes television reception rot-

ten, so most residents get cable television.

"Our people sit in an electronic control room at the local cable-television franchise from 6:30 A.M. until midnight 'cutting' into commercials on the three local network affiliates. Say, for example, that you have bought time during 'General Hospital.' We could cut in on the commercial you are showing nationally and overlay a test ad if you wanted. Or you could buy local time to test a new ad. Local viewers can't tell which ads are standard and which are being tested.

"We can then correlate their exposure to your ads with their subsequent purchase behavior," Brian said earnestly.

"Sounds interesting, Mr. Carmichael," Sargeant said, "but as you no doubt know, we've been fairly successful for the past forty-five years with what you might call more 'traditional' methods of marketing research. This new approach of yours has a certain 'Big Brother' quality that makes me a bit uneasy. I'd like to see more data before I made any decisions."

Discussion Issues

1. If you were John Sargeant, what else would you want to know about Target Marketing's service?

2. How do you feel about the Orwellian aspects of this approach to test marketing? Under what conditions might this method be justified?

3. If you were a resident of Fairfax, would you be willing to participate in the study? Why, or why not?

Source: This is a fictitious case based on the actual service provided by Information Resources, Inc. The information in this vignette was provided by Michael Days, "Wired Consumers: Market Researchers Go High-Tech to Hone Ads, Weed Out Flops," *The Wall Street Journal*, 66 (January 23, 1986), p. 33.

In Chapter 8 we examined how researchers use communication techniques to collect data, specifically by questioning respondents. In this chapter we will look at another method by which researchers gather information—observation.

◆ Methods of Observation

Observation is a fact of everyday life. We are constantly observing other people and events as a means of securing information about the world around us. Admittedly, some people make more productive use of those observations than do others. One interesting story of a man who put his powers of observation to work is told about William Benton, one of the co-founders of the Benton and Bowles advertising agency. On a steamy day in 1929 Benton took a walk along a street in Chicago. Since it was hot, most of the windows in the apartments he passed were open, and he could hear the radios playing inside. As he strolled along, he repeatedly heard the voices of the actors in "Amos and Andy," one of the leading comedy programs at that time. Struck by this, Benton retraced his steps, this time counting the radios he could hear. He counted twenty-three of them in all and found that twenty-one were tuned to "Amos and Andy." Rushing back to his advertising firm, Benton suggested that they advertise one of their client's products, Pepsodent toothpaste, on "Amos and Andy." The sales of Pepsodent took off like a rocket, all because of Benton's first audience survey of radio listenership.[1]

Observation is also a tool of scientific inquiry. When used for that purpose, the observations are systematically planned and recorded so as to relate to the specific phenomenon of interest. While planned, they do not have to be sophisticated to be effective. They can be as basic as the method employed by the retailer who used a different color promotional flyer for each zip code to which he mailed. When customers came in the store with the flyers, he could then identify which trading areas the store was serving.

A more sophisticated scheme is used by many malls to determine their trading areas. People are hired to walk the parking lot of the mall and record every license number they find. A typical day yields 2,500 different numbers. The data are then fed into computers at R. L. Polk & Company of Detroit, specialists in auto industry statistics. Polk matches the license plates to zip code areas or census tracts and returns a color-coded map showing customer density from the various areas. At a cost of anywhere from $5,000 to $25,000, these studies are not only less expensive, but they are quicker and more reliable than store interviews or examinations of credit card records.[2]

[1]Edward Cornish, "Telecommunications: What's Coming," paper delivered at the American Marketing Association's 1981 Annual Conference held in San Francisco, California, June 14–17, 1981.

[2]See James G. Barnes, G. A. Pym, and A. C. Noonan, "Marketing Research: Some Basics for Small Business," *Journal of Small Business Management*, 20 (July 1982), pp. 62–66; Steve Raddock, "Follow That Car," *Marketing and Media Decisions*, 16 (January 1981), pp. 70–71, 103; and "I've Got Your Number," *The Wall Street Journal*, 61 (February 5, 1981), p. 21.

Figure 9.1

Basic Choices among Observational Means for Collecting Data

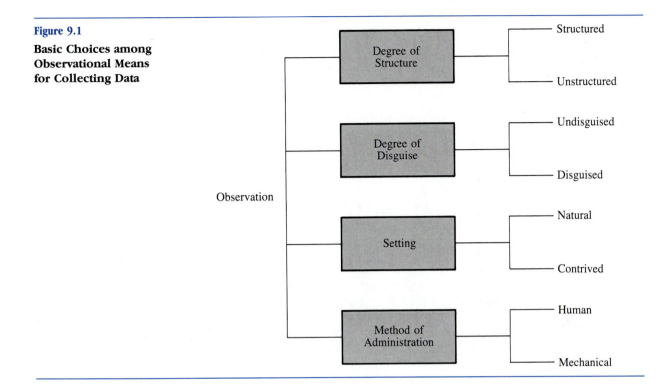

Like communication methods, observation methods may be structured or unstructured, disguised or undisguised. Further, as Figure 9.1 shows, the observations may be made in a contrived or a natural setting and may be secured by a human or mechanical observer.

Structured versus Unstructured Observation

• Structured observation

The problem has been defined precisely enough so that the behaviors that will be observed can be specified beforehand, as can the categories that will be used to record and analyze the situation.

• Unstructured observation

The problem has not been specifically defined, so a great deal of flexibility is allowed the observers in terms of what they note and record.

The distinction between a **structured** and **unstructured observation** is similar to that for communication methods. Structured observation applies when the problem has been defined precisely enough so that the behaviors that will be observed can be specified beforehand, as can the categories that will be used to record and analyze the situation. Unstructured observation is used for studies in which the problem has not been so specifically defined, so that a great deal of flexibility is allowed the observers in terms of what they note and record.

Consider a study designed to investigate the amount of search and deliberation that a consumer goes through in buying a detergent. On the one hand, the observers could be told to stand at one end of a supermarket aisle and record whatever behavior they think is appropriate with respect to each sample customer's deliberation and search. This might produce the following record: "Purchaser first paused in front of ABC brand. He picked up a box of ABC, glanced at the price, and set it back down again. He then checked the label and price for DEF brand. He set that back down again, and after a slight pause, picked up a smaller box of ABC than originally looked at, placed it in his cart, and moved down the aisle." Alternatively, observers might simply be told to record the first detergent examined, the total number of boxes picked up by any customer, and the time in seconds that the customer spent

What makes the consumer's hand go toward one product rather than another? Unstructured observation allows the investigator to determine what factors he or she thinks are significant to that choice. Structured observation requires that the investigator select among certain predetermined factors.

Source: Courtesy of Nielsen Marketing Research, a company of the Dun & Bradstreet Corporation.

in front of the detergent shelves by checking the appropriate boxes in the observation form. The last situation represents a good deal more structure than the first.

To use the more structured approach, researchers must decide precisely which behaviors are to be observed and which specific categories and units will be used to record the observations. In order to make such decisions, researchers must have specific hypotheses in mind. Thus, the structured approach is again more appropriate for descriptive and causal studies than for exploratory research. The unstructured approach would be useful in generating insights about the various aspects of the search and deliberation behavior in the preceding example. But it is less appropriate for testing hypotheses about it. Since so many different kinds of behaviors could be recorded, it would be difficult for researchers to code and quantify the data in a consistent manner.

One way to develop consistency in coding is to make sure that the coders are well-trained. A number of trained coders were used, for example, in an observational study examining the patterns of interactions between parents and children in choosing breakfast cereals. The observers in this study recorded word-for-word the verbal exchanges between parent and child when making the choice. The coders then tried to assess:

1. Which party initiated the selection episode.

2. How the other party responded.

3. The content and tone of the communication.

4. The occurrence of unpleasant consequences such as arguments or unhappiness.

The ultimate aim of the study was to determine if the child was unhappy with the resolution of the situation.[3]

The advantages and disadvantages of structure in observation are very similar to those in communication. Structuring the observation reduces the potential for bias and increases the reliability of observations. However, the reduction in bias may be accompanied by a loss of validity, since the number of seconds spent in deliberation or the number of boxes of detergent picked up and examined may not represent the complete story of deliberation and search. What about the effort spent simply looking at what is available but not picking them up, or the discussion between husband and wife as to which detergent to select? A well-trained, highly qualified observer might be able to interpret these kinds of behavior and relate them in a meaningful way to search and deliberation.

> The major problem of behavioral observation is the observer himself. . . . In behavioral observation the observer is both a crucial strength and a crucial weakness. Why? The observer must digest the information derived from observations and then make inferences about constructs. . . . The strength and the weakness of the procedure is the observer's powers of inference. If it were not for inference, a machine observer would be better than a human observer. The strength is that the observer can relate the observed behavior to the constructs or variables of a study: he brings behavior and construct together.[4]

Disguised versus Undisguised Observation

• Undisguised
observation

The subjects are aware that
they are being observed.

• Disguised
observation

The subjects are not aware
that they are being
observed.

In **undisguised observation,** the subjects know they are being observed; in **disguised observation,** they do not. In the search and deliberation study just described, observers could assume a position well out of the way of shopper's notice. Or the disguise could be accomplished by observers becoming part of the shopping scene. One firm, for example, uses observers disguised as shoppers to assess package designs by recording how long shoppers spend in the display area, whether they have difficulty finding the product, and whether the information on the package appears hard to read.[5] Other retailers are increasingly turning to on-site cameras not only to assess packaging designs, but also to determine what general improvements in counter space and floor displays are needed and to study traffic flows.[6] Still others are using paid observers disguised as shoppers to evaluate the attitude, courtesy, and promptness of service provided by their own employees.[7]

The reason the observer's presence is disguised, of course, is to control the tendency for people to behave differently when they know their actions are being watched. At least two disadvantages are entailed in disguised observation, though. First, it is often very difficult to disguise an observation completely, and second, one cannot obtain the other relevant information such as background data that can often be obtained by identifying oneself as a research worker. There is also an ethical question associated with disguised observation.

---

[3]Charles K. Atkin, "Observation of Parent-Child Interaction in Supermarket Decision Making," *Journal of Marketing,* 42 (October 1978), pp. 41–45.

[4]Fred N. Kerlinger, *Foundations of Behavioral Research,* 3rd ed. (New York: Holt, Rinehart and Winston, 1986), p. 487.

[5]David A. Schwartz, "Research Can Help Solve Packaging Functional and Design Problems," *Marketing News,* 9 (January 16, 1976), p. 8.

[6]"On-Site's Cameras Focus on the Retail Marketplace," *Marketing News,* 18 (November 9, 1984), p. 46.

[7]Larry Gulledge, "Evaluation Services Pay Off in Bigger Bottom Lines," *Marketing News,* 18 (October 12, 1984), p. 30.

An observer who counted the units on hand at the beginning and end of a time period and who adjusted the results for shipments received to determine how much of each brand was sold would be engaged in indirect observation.

Source: Courtesy of Burgoyne Information Services, Cincinnati, Ohio.

[T]he investigator who proposes to enter a situation without revealing his research purpose has an obligation to ask himself whether there is any possibility that his disguised activities will harm any of the people in the situation and if so, whether the potential results of his research are valuable enough to justify their acquisition under these circumstances.[8]

Disguised observations may be *direct* or *indirect*. A direct observation, for example, might be a person at the checkout counter counting the number of boxes of each brand of detergent being purchased. An indirect observation might involve counting the inventory on hand by brand at the end of each day and adjusting the results for shipments received to determine how much of each brand was sold. The key difference is that the behavior itself is observed in direct observation, whereas the *effects* or *results* of that behavior are observed in indirect observation.

There are many types of indirect observation.[9] One could, for example, determine the market share held by each brand of detergent by conducting pantry audits. In a

[8]Claire Selltiz, Lawrence S. Wrightsman, and Stuart W. Cook, *Research Methods in Social Relations,* 3rd ed. (New York: Holt, Rinehart and Winston, 1976), p. 218.

[9]For insight into some of the many ingenious ways that have been developed to make indirect measurements by observation, see Eugene J. Webb, *et al., Unobtrusive Measures: Nonreactive Research in the Social Sciences* (Chicago: Rand McNally, 1966); Lee Sechrest, *New Directions for Methodology of Behavior Science: Unobtrusive Measurement Today* (San Francisco: Jossey-Bass, 1979); and Thomas J. Bouchard, Jr., "Unobtrusive Measures: An Inventory of Uses," *Sociological Methods and Research* (February 1976), pp. 267–301.

pantry audit, researchers would visit respondents' homes and ask permission to examine the "pantry inventory." Their goal would be to determine what brands the family had on hand and the amount of each. While it is rare that researchers would go to the expense of a pantry audit for one product, they might use this method if they wanted to determine consumption of a number of products at once.

Over the years a number of innovative, indirect measures of behavior have been developed. For example, a car dealer in Chicago checked the position of the radio dial of each car brought in for service. The dealer then used this as a way of determining the appropriate share of the listening audience each station held, and used that information to decide where to advertise. As further examples, the number of different fingerprints on a page has been used to assess the readership of various ads in a magazine, and the age and condition of the cars in the parking lot have

Back to the Case

Brian Carmichael had done his homework and was ready to try again to convince John Sargeant to use Target Marketing's test-marketing services.

"Good to see you, Mr. Sargeant," Brian said confidently as he entered the executive's corner office with its spectacular view. "I think I have the information you wanted.

"I investigated the reliability of our service versus that of the purchase diaries that you said MacIntosh has traditionally used to track sales.

"Our researchers ran a test in which they asked people to write down what products they had bought in the previous three months. They then compared those answers to consumers' actual purchases. They found, for example, that only about a third of those who reported buying

Kellogg's Frosted Flakes had done so; only about one in ten of those claiming to have purchased Pledge furniture polish had bought the product.

"Diaries are only as reliable as the people who keep them, and human recall is somewhat less than perfect," Brian concluded.

"You have a point," Sargeant agreed, "but I'm still uncomfortable with the electronic snooping aspects of this research."

"I would agree, Mr. Sargeant, if participation in this project weren't totally voluntary. The people in the households we've signed up were told exactly what we intended to do. Besides qualifying for prizes, participants get free repair service if their cable reception ever goes bad. We work hard to keep participants happy. If anybody feels uncomfortable with the arrangement,

they are free to drop out at any time. We've had very few people choose that option," Brian said.

"Sounds intriguing," Sargeant admitted. "Can you tell me about the experiences of other companies using your service?"

"Yes, sir," Brian said happily. He sensed a softening in the older man's attitude. Maybe there was still a chance to reel in the account.

As Brian pointed out, human beings can be notoriously unreliable in reporting their own behavior. In some cases, observation techniques can overcome these inaccuracies in reporting. Some disguised observation techniques can be used without informing subjects; but do researchers have an ethical obligation to inform the participants anyway?

been used to gauge the affluence of the group patronizing a given business estab-lishment.[10]

Observation is often more useful than surveys in sorting fact from fiction with respect to desirable behaviors. For example, a group of electric utilities had been accustomed to using pollsters' reports of consumer interviews to project energy usage. Despite their attempt to forecast demand scientifically, they found their pro-jections continually fell short of reality. They asked a marketing research firm to investigate. The research firm put television cameras focused on the thermostat in 150 homes. The cameras revealed that what people said they did and what they actually did were vastly different. Many people claimed they set the thermostat at 68 degrees and left it there. It turned out that they fiddled with it all day. "Older rela-tives and kids—especially teenagers—tended to turn [it] up, and so did cleaning ladies. Even visitors did it. In a lot of homes, it was guerrilla warfare over the ther-mostat between the person who paid the bill and everyone else."[11]

Natural versus Contrived Setting for Observation

- Natural setting

Subjects are observed in the environment where the behavior normally takes place.

- Contrived setting

Subjects are observed in an environment that has been specially designed for recording their behavior.

Observations may be obtained either in **natural** or **contrived settings.** Sometimes the natural setting is altered to some degree for experimental purposes. In the search and deliberation study, for example, researchers may choose to keep the setting completely natural and study only the extent of the activities that normally go into the purchase of detergents. Alternatively, they may wish to introduce some point-of-purchase display materials and measure their effectiveness. One measure of effectiveness might be the amount of search and deliberation the materials stimulate for the particular brand being promoted.

If a contrived setting is desired, the researcher could bring a group of people into a very controlled environment such as a multi-product display in a laboratory and ask them to engage in some simulated shopping behavior. This controlled environ-ment might contain, for example, a detergent display that would enable researchers to study the degree of deliberation and search each participant goes through as he or she decides what to buy.

The advantage of the laboratory environment is that researchers are better able to control outside influences that might affect the interpretation of what happened. For example, shoppers in a natural setting might pause to chat with neighbors in the midst of deciding what detergent to buy. If researchers were measuring the time spent in deliberation, this interruption could raise havoc with the accuracy of the measurement. The disadvantage of the laboratory setting is that the contrived setting itself may cause differences in behavior and thus raise real questions about the external validity of the findings.

A contrived setting usually speeds the data-collection process, results in lower-cost research, and allows the use of more objective measurements. The researcher need not wait for events to occur, but rather instructs the participants to engage in the

---

[10]See Bouchard, "Unobtrusive Measures," for a relatively detailed list of studies using indirect measures of behavior.

[11]Frederick C. Klein, "Researcher Probes Consumers Using 'Anthropological Skills,'" *The Wall Street Journal,* 63 (July 7, 1983), p. 21.

kind of behavior he or she seeks to measure. This means that a great many observations can be made in a short period of time—perhaps an entire study can be completed in a few days or a week—with substantial cost savings. The laboratory also allows the greater use of electrical and/or mechanical equipment than does the natural setting and thereby frees the measurement from the observer's own selective processes.

Human versus Mechanical Observation

• **Human observation**

Individuals are trained to systematically observe a phenomenon and to record on the observational form the specific events that take place.

• **Mechanical observation**

A mechanical device observes a phenomenon and records the events that take place.

Much scientific observation is of the pencil-and-paper variety. One or more individuals are trained to observe a phenomenon systematically and to record on the observational form the specific events that took place—this is **human observation** as opposed to **mechanical observation.** DuPont, for example, relies on a human observer to deal with one of the most difficult problems it faces in its automotive paint division: color matching. It seems that no matter how much time and energy goes into the metal repair work after an accident, slight differences in color shading can occur, greatly upsetting the customer. There is no problem in matching colors for domestic cars, since new models are introduced each fall in an orderly fashion, and factory color information is available well before the vehicles reach the showrooms. However, new models of imported cars tend to reach dealer showrooms on a random basis throughout the year, and having paint shades available for their repair is a much greater problem.

DuPont handles this problem via Charlie Smith, color matcher par excellence. Smith operates out of a dockside laboratory in Jacksonville, Florida, the port of entry for thousands of imported cars each month. He not only has all the equipment necessary to mix the colors that will match the cars outside, but he also has a direct computer hookup to DuPont's Troy, Michigan, laboratory, where the formulas for 17,000 different colors are stored. "DuPont has formulas to match almost any color I see coming ashore," reports Smith. "As each new color arrives, I spray out the DuPont formula on a test panel and compare it to the new car. If the spray-out matches the color, I report this to our Troy lab to verify the formula already in the computer. If it doesn't match, I go back to my lab and make adjustments in the formula."

This process may take a few hours or a few days. Once satisfied with the match, Smith relays the new formula directly to the Troy computer, and the new information is distributed to body shops through DuPont's "refinish sales" network.[12]

Electrical and/or mechanical observation also has its place in marketing research. In Chapter 6 we saw, for example, that television ratings use data collected by an Audimeter®, an electronic device that is attached to a participant's television set, to indicate when the set is on and to which channel it is tuned. As we discussed, several firms are also introducing *people meters,* which attempt to measure not only the channels to which a set is tuned, but who in the household is watching. Each member of the family has his or her own viewing number. Whoever turns on the set, sits down to watch, or changes the channel, is supposed to enter his or her number into

---

[12]"Mixing and Matching," *Special Report News from DuPont of Interest to the College Community,* 76 (November–December 1982), p. 18.

When using a people meter to monitor TV viewing, each member of the family has a viewing number, which he or she enters into the meter before watching a program.

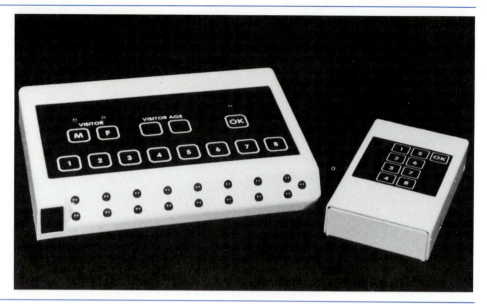

Source: Courtesy of Nielsen Media Research.

the people meter first. All of this information is transmitted immediately to the central computer for processing.[13]

Advertisers complain that the traditional household meters and the diaries that accompany them have become antiquated because there is much more to watch and record than ever before. Cable television, which covered 25 percent of the country in 1981, now reaches almost 47 percent; as of 1985, 83 percent of American homes carried at least nine channels. And videocassette recorders, which were in 3 percent of homes in 1981, are in 29 percent today.

With all these channel options, keeping the diaries is difficult, and so is evaluating the tallies. What is more, when it comes to filling out the diaries, "usually the lady of the house winds up doing it for everyone," said one network executive. Short snatches of programs—say, fifteen minutes of a movie—are underreported, as is late-night watching, when people doze and forget to fill in the blanks.

Unlike the diaries, which record what's viewed in fifteen-minute segments, the people meter gives minute-by-minute figures on the number and type of people watching. With it, advertisers can map the audience flow both during and between programs. And the relatively easy task of pressing a button instead of writing complicated entries in a diary "means that the same people can be kept on the panel for as long as is required, not rotated for only one week in three, as is necessary under the present national meter and diary system," said the vice-president of one company offering the people-meter service.[14]

The *optical scanner* (described in Chapter 6), which has automated the checkout process at many supermarkets, is another electronic device used in marketing re-

---

[13]For discussions of the operation of the people meter and experiments testing its effectiveness, see Elizabeth Berry, "Nielsen May Face U.K. Rival in Researching TV Audiences," *The Wall Street Journal,* 64 (February 2, 1984), p. 31; and Fred Gardner, "Acid Test for the People Meter," *Marketing and Media Decisions,* 19 (April 1984), pp. 74–75 and 115.

[14]Bernice Kanner, "Now, People Meters," *New York,* 19 (May 19, 1986), pp. 16–20.

search. Scanners allow retailers and manufacturers to receive prompt sales feedback on ads, point-of-purchase displays, special promotions, special prices, and so on.[15]

Some other electrical/mechanical devices used in marketing research—the psychogalvanometer, tachistoscope, and eye cameras—are commonly used in copy research. The **psychogalvanometer** is used to measure a person's emotional reaction to specific advertising copy. It operates on the same principle as the lie-detector apparatus used in criminal investigations. Psychogalvanometers record changes in the electrical resistance of the skin associated with the minute degree of sweating that accompanies emotional arousal. The subject is fitted with small electrodes on the palms or forearms to monitor this electrical resistance. As different advertising

• Psychogalvanometer

Device used to measure the emotion induced by exposure to a particular stimulus by recording changes in the electrical resistance of the skin associated with the minute degree of sweating that accompanies emotional arousal; in marketing research the stimulus is often specific advertising copy.

[15]For general discussions of the impact scanners are having on marketing research for frequently purchased items, see Edward Tauber, "Checkout Scanner Ultimately a Marketing Data Goldmine," *Marketing News,* 12 (May 18, 1979), pp. 1 and 13; Jack J. Honomichl. "Turning a Dream into a Reality," *Advertising Age,* 52 (February 9, 1981), pp. 54 and 59; "Checkout Scanners Soon Will Revolutionize Market Research, Packaged Goods Marketing," *Marketing News,* 14 (December 12, 1980), p. 5; Derek Bloom, "Point of Sale Scanners and Their Implications for Market Research," *Journal of the Market Research Society,* 22 (October 1980), pp. 221–238; "Supermarket Scanners Get Smarter," *Business Week* (August 17, 1981), pp. 88, 91–92; Carol Posten, "Scanning the Market for Changes in Tempo," *Advertising Age,* 53 (February 22, 1982), pp. M19–M20; and Fern Schumer, "The New Magicians of Market Research," *Fortune,* 108 (July 25, 1983), pp. 72–74.

Back to the Case

Brian knew he had piqued Sargeant's interest. Now all he had to do was close the deal. For a week prior to his last meeting with the MacIntosh Foods executive, he worked late gathering data to support his case. When the day for the meeting finally came, he was ready.

"I've got the information you requested, Mr. Sargeant," Brian said. "I have a testimonial here from the director of marketing and research at the country's best known soup company. He used our service to evaluate new products and to determine the marketing strategy that will sell them most effectively. He said he likes our service because it allows researchers to observe consumers' reactions without tipping them off about what is

being studied. He said they weren't able to do that with questionnaires and focus groups.

"A major drug company engaged our services after a national poisoning scare," Brian continued. "They wanted to know if consumers would buy their product if it were packaged differently.

"An added benefit of this service," Brian said, warming to his subject, "is that we can pinpoint audiences demographically. We have detailed information about each of our households," he said. "If you want to target families that own a cat, a dog, a microwave oven, or a personal computer, we can do it. If you want to run two different ads to two families with similar demographic profiles, and see which

produces better, we can do that too."

Sargeant smiled at the young man's eagerness. "All right," he said. "I think we'll give your service a try. I'll call a meeting next week to work out the details with our marketing people. We have a new line of cake mixes we'd like to test, and Target Marketing sounds like the firm to do it for us."

Optical scanners have the potential to truly revolutionize marketing research on package goods. When the precise measurements they provide are linked with advertising and demographic information, their usefulness for researchers can be enormous.

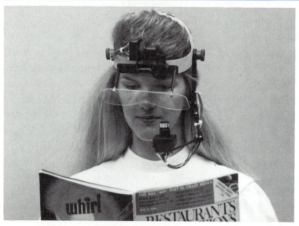 

The effectiveness of billboards and other advertising can be analyzed by tracking the path of people's eyes (by an eye camera) to see what part of the ad they notice first, how long they linger on each part of it, and whether or not they finish reading it. The ASL head-band mounted Eye View Monitor (*left*) makes accurate measurements and records over an almost unlimited field of view. One camera "looks" down at the reflection of the eye on the visor. Another camera "looks" up at the reflection from the other side of the visor to show the scene being viewed by the subject.

Sources: Courtesy of Applied Science Laboratories, a division of Applied Science Groups, Inc., Waltham, Massachusetts, and Sunkist Growers, Inc.

◆ Tachistoscope

Device that provides the researcher timing control over a visual stimulus; in marketing research, the visual stimulus is often a specific advertisement.

◆ Eye camera

Used by researchers to study a subject's eye movements while he or she is reading advertising copy.

copy is shown, the strength of the current that results is used to gauge the subject's attitude.[16]

The **tachistoscope** is a device that tells researchers how long it takes a subject to get the intended point of an ad. It does this by flashing the ad before the subject for an exposure interval that may range from less than a hundredth of a second to several seconds. After each exposure, the subject is asked to describe everything he or she saw and to explain what it meant. By systematically varying the exposure, the researcher is able to measure how quickly and accurately a particular stimulus—in this case, the ad—can be perceived and interpreted. Note, however, that since the subject is asked to respond verbally to what he or she saw, the tachistoscope is not a mechanical observer, but rather a mechanical means of presenting stimuli.

The **eye camera** is now used by researchers to study a subject's eye movements while he or she is reading advertising copy. The original eye cameras, which were introduced at the Chicago World's Fair in 1890, established the fact that people's eyes do not move smoothly along a line of type as they read and that people's reading habits differ widely.[17] Until recently eye cameras used a light that was positioned to bounce off the cornea of the subject's eye on to a moving film. The reflected light traced eye movements on the film. The researcher had to then project the film, frame-by-frame, while manually recording eye movements on a sheet of paper. Since the mid-1970s, computers have been developed that can automatically perform this analysis from videotape. There have also been significant advances in the cameras themselves. Some of the new videocameras weigh only a few ounces and are so small that they can be clipped to a respondent's eyeglasses. The visual

[16]A review of 118 studies on involuntary responses to advertising found that pupil dilation, skin moisture, and heart rate are the most commonly used. See Paul J. Watson and Robert J. Gatchel, "Autonomic Measures of Advertising," *Journal of Advertising Research,* 19 (June 1979), pp. 15–26.

[17]S. Watson Dunn and Arnold M. Barban, *Advertising: Its Role in Modern Marketing,* 5th ed. (Chicago: Dryden Press, 1982), pp. 281–282.

record produced as an individual reads an advertisement allows researchers to study the person's behavior in great detail. It can reveal the part of the ad the subject noticed first, how long his or her eyes lingered on a particular item, and whether the subject read all the copy or only part of it. The small videocameras that follow the path of the eye have also been used to analyze package designs, billboards, and displays in the aisles of supermarkets.[18]

Two other mechanical observers that promise to provide useful supplementary information in telephone interviews—response latency and voice-pitch analysis—

[18]For discussions of the operation and use of eye camera technology to study the effectiveness of ads, packages, and displays, see J. E. Russo, "Eye Fixation Can Save the World," in H. K. Hunt, ed., *Advances in Consumer Research* (Ann Arbor, Mich.: Association for Consumer Research, 1978), pp. 561–570; J. Treistman and J. P. Gregg, "Visual, Verbal, and Sales Response to Print Ads," *Journal of Advertising Research,* 19 (August 1979), pp. 41–47; "Determining How Ads Are Seen," *Dun's Business Month,* 119 (February 1982), pp. 85–86; "Recall Scores Are Giving Short Shrift to Outdoor Ads, Study Finds," *Marketing News,* 18 (November 23, 1984), p. 16; and "Study Disputes Earlier Findings," *Marketing News,* 19 (May 24, 1985), pp. 1 and 38.

Research Window 9.1
The Eyes Have It

As if advertisers didn't have enough to worry about, Perception Research Services, Inc., a firm that electronically measures consumers' reactions to ads, has found that readers notice the brand names in only six out of ten magazine ads.

The company discovered this information when it used beams of infrared light, computers, and cameras to track the movement of people's eyes as they glanced through magazines. "There's a lot of talk today about how people use remote-control devices to zap TV commercials," said Elliot Young, president of the Englewood Cliffs, N. J., firm. "But advertisers forget sometimes how easy it is for readers to turn the page of a magazine."

Perception Research plans to conduct eye-tracking studies with twenty magazines on a regular basis. Mr. Young believes visual cues are more reliable than consumers' memories in judging whether an ad really attracted their attention.

Some of Perception Research's conclusions clash with commonsense notions about advertising. For example, the company says food marketers may be thwarting themselves by running mouth-watering photographs of cakes and cookies. Often in such ads, the reader's eye lingers on the luscious illustration and overlooks the product name. The eye-tracking study also revealed that automobile ads catch readers' attention surprisingly well in women's magazines. And contrary to popular belief, Perception Research did not find that people were naturally more inclined to read ads on right-hand pages or in the front of magazines.

Some ad agency executives believe such research can help them decide which size ad to run in particular magazines and where to place headlines and copy for maximum impact. Yet, many also are suspicious of the artificial conditions in eye-tracking studies. Subjects don't leisurely browse through magazines as they would at home. Rather, they position their heads on chin rests and watch pictures of the magazine pages flash on a screen.

"I put this in the same dubious category as galvanic skin response measurement," said Morgan Neu, a vice-president at Starch INRA Hooper, Inc., another firm that does magazine readership research. "Just knowing someone's eye passed across an ad doesn't tell whether the message registered and had any meaning."

Source: Ronald Alsop, "Study of Magazine Ads Yields Some Eye-Opening Findings," *The Wall Street Journal,* 65 (December 5, 1985), p. 33.

◆ Response latency

The amount of time a respondent deliberates before answering a question.

owe their current popularity to mechanical/electronic recorders and the computer's ability to diagnose what is recorded. **Response latency** is the amount of time a respondent deliberates before answering a question. Since response time seems to be directly related to the respondent's uncertainty in the answer, it assists in assessing the individual's strength of preference when choosing among alternatives. It helps researchers judge how strongly an individual prefers one brand over another when asked to choose between alternatives. It also provides an unobtrusive way of measuring a subject's ambiguity in responding to a particular question.

The measure of response depends upon a voice-operated relay that triggers an electronic stopwatch. When an interviewer approaches the end of a question, he or she simply presses a pedal that sets the stopwatch to zero and alerts the electronic mechanism to listen for the offset (end of the question) of the interviewer's voice. The stopwatch is automatically triggered at the offset. The moment the respondent begins answering, the watch is stopped by the voice-operated relay system and a digital readout system indicates response latency to the interviewer, who can then record the deliberation time on the interview form.

There are several advantages in such a system. First, the method provides an accurate response latency measure without respondents being aware that this dimension of behavior is being recorded. Second, since the time is measured by an automatic device, the technique does not make the interviewer's task any more difficult, nor does it appreciably lengthen the interview.[19]

In an otherwise routine research study, and with little additional effort, DuPont, for example, used response latency to assess potential users' brand awareness and perception of quality of an industrial product compared to many competing brands.[20]

◆ Voice-pitch analysis

Type of analysis that examines changes in the relative frequency of the human voice that accompany emotional arousal.

Voice-pitch analysis relies on the same basic premise as the psychogalvanometer. Subjects experience a number of involuntary physiological reactions, such as changes in blood pressure, rate of perspiration, or heart rate when emotionally aroused by external or internal stimuli. Voice-pitch analysis examines changes in the relative vibration frequency of the human voice that accompanies emotional arousal. All individuals function at a certain physiological pace, called the *baseline*. The baseline in voice analysis is established by recording the respondent's speech while he or she is engaged in unemotional conversation. Deviations from the baseline level indicate that the respondent has reacted to the stimulus question. These deviations can be measured by special computer equipment adapted to hear abnormal frequencies in the voice caused by changes in the nervous system. Such changes may not be discernable to the human ear. The amount the individual was affected by the stimulus can be measured by comparing the person's abnormal frequency to his or her normal one. The greater the difference, the greater the emotional intensity of the subject's reaction is said to be.

Voice-pitch analysis has at least two advantages over other physiological reaction techniques. First, unlike the other techniques it measures not only the intensity but

---

[19]For general discussions of the use of response latency measures in marketing research, see James MacLachlan, John Czepiel, and Priscilla LaBarbera, "Implementation of Response Latency Measures," *Journal of Marketing Research*, 16 (November 1979), pp. 573–577; James MacLachlan and Priscilla LaBarbera, "Response Latency in Telephone Interviews," *Journal of Advertising Research*, 19 (June 1979), pp. 49–56; Tyzoon T. Tyebjee, "Response Latency: A New Measure for Scaling Brand Preference," *Journal of Marketing Research*, 16 (February 1979), pp. 96–101; and David A. Aaker, Richard P. Bagozzi, James M. Carman, and James M. MacLachlan, "On Using Response Latency to Measure Preference," *Journal of Marketing Research*, 17 (May 1980), pp. 237–244.

[20]Robert C. Grass, Wallace H. Wallace, and Samuel Zuckerkandel, "Response Latency in Industrial Advertising Research," *Journal of Advertising Research*, 20 (December 1980), pp. 63–65.

also the direction of the individual's feeling, since subjects are asked the nature of their opinions while the intensity of their emotions is being measured mechanically. Second, voice-pitch analysis allows a natural interaction between researcher and participant because subjects do not need to be connected to any equipment. This also tends to make it less time-consuming and expensive to use.[21]

At the other extreme, **brain-wave research,** which is still in its infancy and surrounded by a good deal of controversy, requires a rather elaborate hookup of the subject to equipment. The purpose of this technique is to assess the stimuli that subjects find arousing or interesting. To do this, subjects are fitted with electrodes that monitor the electrical impulses emitted by the brain as the subject is exposed to various stimuli. While researchers have been able to determine that the two hemispheres of the brain seem to respond differently to specific stimuli (the right hemisphere responding more to emotional stimuli), the full implications of this finding for the study of consumer behavior and for the practice of marketing research are not known.[22]

As we have mentioned, electrical/mechanical equipment frees the observation from the observer's selective processes. This is both its major strength and major weakness. Certainly recording when a TV set is turned on and to what channel it is tuned, for example, can be accomplished much more accurately by the Audimeter® than by any other means. The fact the set is tuned to a particular channel does not say anything, however, about whether anyone is watching, the number that might be watching, or their level of interest. A trained human observer's record might be more difficult to analyze, and it might be less objective, but the human powers of integration can produce a more valid assessment of what occurred.

Marketing researchers need to be aware of the electrical/mechanical equipment that is available so that they can make an informed choice as to the best technique for a particular study. Would a piece of equipment make a better observer than a human in a given instance, or vice versa? Or would a combination approach be more productive? These are difficult decisions that can greatly affect the quality of a study. A researcher who keeps abreast of the developments in the field is in the best position to make those decisions.

◆ Summary

Learning Objective 1: List the different methods by which observational data can be gathered.

Observational data may be gathered using structured or unstructured methods that are either disguised or undisguised. The observations may be made in a contrived or a natural setting and may be secured by a human or mechanical observer.

Learning Objective 2: Cite the main reason researchers may choose to disguise the presence of an observer in a study.

Most often an observer's presence is disguised in order to control the tendency of people to behave differently when they know their actions are being watched.

[21]For general discussions of the use of voice-pitch analysis in marketing research, see *ibid.,* or see Ronald G. Nelson and David Schwartz, "Voice Pitch Analysis," *Journal of Advertising Research,* 19 (October 1979), pp. 55–59; Glen A. Buckman, "Uses of Voice-Pitch Analysis," *Journal of Advertising Research,* 20 (April 1980), pp. 69–73; and Linda Edwards, "Hearing What Consumers Really Feel," *Across the Board,* 17 (April 1980), pp. 62–67.

[22]For general discussions of the status of brain-wave research, see F. Hansen, "Hemispherical Lateralization: Implications for Understanding Consumer Behavior," *Journal of Consumer Research,* 8 (June 1981), pp. 23–36; and A. Weinstein, "A Review of Brain Hemisphere Research," *Journal of Advertising Research,* 22 (June–July 1982), pp. 59–63.

Learning Objective 3: Explain the advantages and disadvantages of conducting an observational experiment in a laboratory setting.

The advantage of a laboratory environment is that researchers are better able to control outside influences that might affect the interpretation of what happened. The disadvantage of the laboratory setting is that the contrived setting itself may cause differences in behavior and thus threaten the external validity of the findings. A contrived setting, however, usually speeds the data-collection process, results in lower-cost research, and allows the use of more objective measurements.

Learning Objective 4: Discuss the principle that underlies the use of a psychogalvanometer.

The psychogalvanometer records changes in the electrical resistance of the skin associated with the minute degree of sweating that accompanies emotional arousal. When the subject is shown different advertising copy, the strength of the current that results is used to gauge his or her attitude toward the copy.

Learning Objective 5: Explain the function of a tachistoscope.

The tachistoscope is a device that tells researchers how long it takes a subject to get the intended point of an ad. It does this by flashing the ad before the subject for a short interval of time and then asking that subject to describe everything he or she saw and to explain what it meant.

Learning Objective 6: Explain how researchers use eye cameras.

Eye cameras are used by researchers to study a subject's eye movements while he or she is reading advertising copy. The visual record produced can allow researchers to determine the part of the ad the subject noticed first, how long his or her eyes lingered on a particular item, and whether the subject read all the copy or only part of it.

Learning Objective 7: Define *response latency* and explain what it measures.

Response latency is the amount of time a respondent deliberates before answering a question. Since response time seems to be directly related to the respondent's uncertainty in the answer, it assists in assessing the individual's strength of preference when choosing among alternatives.

Learning Objective 8: Define *voice-pitch analysis* and explain what it measures.

Voice-pitch analysis examines changes in the relative vibration frequency of the human voice that accompany emotional arousal. The amount an individual is affected by a stimulus question can be measured by comparing the person's abnormal frequency to his or her normal one. The greater the difference, the greater the emotional intensity of the subject's reaction is said to be.

Discussion Questions, Problems, and Projects

1. Next time you go shopping (grocery or otherwise) do the following disguised observation study with a fellow student. The objective is to assess the service provided to customers while checking out your groceries. One of you should complete the following structured observation table. The other should conduct an unstructured observation study by observing and recording all that seems relevant to the objective.

    (a) Store _____ Date _____

    Location _____ Time _____

Too few checkout counters	Yes	No
Long wait in line	Yes	No
Cashier: Quick and efficient	Yes	No
Cashier: Prices well recorded	Yes	No
Cashier: Friendly and pleasant	Yes	No
Purchases packed quickly	Yes	No
Purchases packed poorly	Yes	No

Bags were carried to car	Yes	No
Bags provided were flimsy	Yes	No
Bags provided were attractive	Yes	No
Other facts _____		

(b) Compare the two sets of results and discuss the strengths and weaknesses of structured versus unstructured observation.

2. Discuss the ethical ramification of a disguised observation versus an undisguised observation.

3. What is the biggest problem associated with the data collected by diary panels? What techniques can be used to avoid these problems?

4. Discuss the strengths and weaknesses of a natural setting versus a contrived setting.

5. What advantages does the people meter have over the more traditional diary panel?

6. Describe how each of the following instruments work and in what area of marketing they are most useful.
   (a) Psychogalvanometer
   (b) Tachistoscope
   (c) Eye camera

7. If you were the product manager of a leading brand of toothpaste, how would observational studies in a grocery store help you do your job?

Suggested Additional Readings

For general discussion of the strengths and weaknesses of observation as a data-collection method, see

Fred N. Kerlinger, *Foundations of Behavioral Research,* 3rd. ed. (New York: Holt, Rinehart and Winston, 1986).

For discussion and examples of unobtrusive measurement techniques, see

Thomas J. Bouchard, Jr., "Unobtrusive Measures: An Inventory of Uses," *Sociological Methods and Research* (February 1976), pp. 267–301.

Lee Sechrest, *New Directions for Methodology of Behavioral Science: Unobtrusive Measurement Today* (San Francisco: Jossey-Bass, 1979).

The third stage in the research process is to determine the data-collection method. As we have seen from the chapters in this section, two types of data may be useful in addressing the research problem: secondary data and primary data. While a beginning researcher's initial impulse may be to advocate a survey among respondent groups, the prudent and experienced researcher will always begin the study by investigating available secondary data first. Only if the answer the decision maker is seeking is unavailable in the secondary data should the researcher consider gathering primary data.

If a research study seems to be warranted, many other decisions must be made. In the data-collection stage, one of the primary decisions is whether to collect information by questionnaire or by observation.

Researchers for CARA sought to determine whether differences existed in the attitudes of local businesspeople toward the advertising media of television, radio, and newspaper, and toward the sales representatives of those media. They also wanted to test the hypothesis that differences in attitudes were associated with differences in annual advertising budgets.

As the researchers told their clients, when the purpose of a study is to determine the association between variables, the most common research design is descriptive. Descriptive designs presuppose a good deal of knowledge about the phenomenon to be studied, and they are guided by one or more hypotheses. Knowledge about the phenomenon under investigation was gleaned from the exploratory research phase of the study. The hypotheses mentioned here and discussed in earlier parts of this textbook guided the descriptive design.

Researchers used secondary data—existing data gathered for some purpose other than the study at hand—during the exploratory research phase to help in understanding the topic of advertising and its perceived strengths and weaknesses.

The information gained from the descriptive phase of the study, however, was based on primary data (data collected to solve the particular problem under investigation) and was secured with a structured-undisguised questionnaire. This type of data-collection instrument is characterized by standardized questions and responses, which simplify administration, make the purpose of the study clear, facilitate easy tabulation and analysis of the data, and provide reliable responses.

The researchers chose to administer the questionnaire by mail. This method was chosen partly to avoid the disadvantages posed by telephone and personal interviews and also because researchers wanted a tangible form that would allow a respondent to view all of the alternative responses. The mail questionnaire's format was designed with standardized questions and responses for reporting attitudes.

While the mail questionnaire format had many advantages, researchers were also aware of its possible drawbacks. For one, researchers often find it difficult to get individuals to respond to this type of questionnaire. In many studies researchers find that offering respondents an incentive of some sort may help to increase the response rate. Nonetheless, the problem of determining how those who do respond differ from those who do not remains.

Despite these problems, mail questionnaires are often the least expensive method of administration per completed contact. Researchers for CARA estimated that the cost per contact for personal interviews would be about $25; the cost per contact for mail questionnaires was $1.70. When the cost of an incentive for return was added in, the cost jumped to between $4.50 and $5.50. While substantially higher than the cost per contact, this cost was still much lower than the cost of a personal interview.

Besides lower cost and the opportunity for the respondent to mull over a list of possible alternative answers, what other advantages might the mail questionnaire have over personal or telephone interviews in this study?

Cases to Part Three

Case 3.1   Generic Drugs (A)

The state of Wisconsin passed a law in 1977 that permitted generic drugs to be substituted for brand name drugs when prescriptions were being filled. Consumers simply had to request the substitution, and the pharmacist was legally bound to make it. The legislation was designed to save customers money on their prescriptions. Thus, it proved disconcerting to the Department of Health and Social Services when, some eight years after its passage, few customers were taking advantage of the law by asking for the substitution.

The experience in Wisconsin was not unusual. By 1985 almost every state and every province in Canada had passed legislation enabling pharmacists to substitute interchangeable generic drugs for the brand prescribed. Yet the empirical evidence suggested that less than 15 percent of all the prescriptions written were filled with generic drugs.[1]

One speculation held that use of the law was low because awareness of the law was low. *American Druggist,* for example, conducted an informal survey among pharmacists regarding generic drug substitution. The pharmacists indicated that approximately 12 percent of chain drugstore customers and 9 percent of independently owned drugstore customers asked outright for substitutions on prescriptions.

Another speculation held that requests for drug substitutions were lower than expected because customers had unfavorable expectations of the quality of generic drugs and thought the price differential was less than it actually was.

Still a third speculation was that requests for generic drug substitutions were affected by a number of personal and situational factors: whether customers paid for their own medication or were part of a third-party pay plan, the number of prescriptions filled per year, and the amount spent per year on prescriptions. Given two consumers who were both favorably inclined toward generics, for example, it was expected that the customer who spent relatively more on prescriptions would be more likely to buy generic drugs than the one who spent less. Since the elderly spend a greater percentage of their incomes on prescription drugs than any other age group, they might be more likely to purchase generic drugs. There also might be some correlation between family size and generic drug purchase behavior, the expectation being that larger families had more expenses and, therefore, also had a greater need to search for bargains. Family income also might be related to use of the law, with lower income families likely to have a greater need to take advantage of the lower generic prices. Finally, it was believed that educational level might be influencing generic drug purchasing behavior. People with more formal education might be expected to be more aware of current social trends, especially consumer-oriented trends, and would therefore be more likely to purchase a generic drug.

Questions

1. Develop specific hypotheses as to why generic drug purchasing behavior has not been greater.

2. Should observation or communication methods of data collection be used in gathering the information that addresses these hypotheses? Why?

3. Design a data-collection instrument and methods for using it so as to secure information bearing on each of the hypotheses.

---

[1]M. Stratman and T. T. Tyebjee, "Strategic Responses to Changes in Public Policy: The Case of the Pharmaceutical Industry and Drug Substitution Laws," *Journal of Public Policy and Marketing,* 3 (1984), pp. 99–112.

Case 3.2   Suchomel Chemical Company

Suchomel Chemical Company was an old-line chemical company that was still managed and directed by its founder, Jeff Suchomel, and his wife, Carol. Jeff served as president and Carol as chief research chemist. The company, which was located in Savannah, Georgia, manufactured a number of products that were used by consumers in and around their homes. The products included waxes, polishes, tile grout, tile cement, spray cleaners for both windows and other surfaces, aerosol room sprays, and insecticides. The company distributed its products regionally. It had a particularly strong consumer following in the northern Florida and southern Georgia areas.

The company had not only managed to maintain but had increased its market share in several of its key lines in the past half-dozen years in spite of increased competition from the national brands. Suchomel Chemical had done this largely through product innovation, particularly innovation that emphasized modest product alterations rather than new technologies or dramatically new products. Jeff and Carol both believed that the company should stick to the things it knew best rather than trying to be all things to all people and in the process getting the company's resources spread too thin, particularly given its regional nature. One innovation the company was now considering was a new scent for its insect spray that was rubbed or sprayed on a person's body. The new scent had undergone extensive testing in both the laboratory and in the field. The tests indicated it repelled insects, particularly mosquitos, as well as, or even better than, the two leading national brands. One of the things that the company was particularly concerned about as it considered the introduction of the new brand was what to call it.

The Insecticide Market

The insecticide market had become a somewhat tricky one to figure out over the past several years. While there had been growth in the purchase of insecticides in general, much of this growth had occurred in the tank liquid market. The household spray market had decreased slightly over the same time span. Suchomel Chemical had not suffered from the general sales decline, though, but had managed to increase its sales of spray insecticides slightly over the past three years. The company was hoping that the new scent formulation might allow it to make even greater market share gains.

The company's past experience in the industry led it to believe that the name that was given to the new product would be a very important element in the product's success, because there seemed to be some very complex interactions between purchase and usage characteristics among repellent users. Most purchases are made by women for their families. Yet repeat purchase is dependent on the husband's supporting opinion that the product works well. Therefore, the name must appeal to both the buyer and the end user, but the two people are not typically together at the time of purchase. To complicate matters further, past research had indicated that a product with a name that appeals to both purchaser and end user will be rejected if the product's name and scent do not match. In sum, naming a product like this that is used on a person's body is a complex task.

Research Alternatives

The company followed its typical procedures in developing possible names for the new product. First, it asked those who had been involved in the product's development to suggest names. It also scheduled some informal brainstorming sessions among potential customers. Subjects in the brainstorming sessions were simply asked to throw out all the names they could possibly think of with respect to what a spray insecticide could or should be called. A panel of executives, mostly those from the product group but a few from corporate management as well, then went through the names and reduced the large list down to a more manageable subset based on their personal reactions to the names and subsequent discussion as to what the names connoted to them. The subset of names was then submitted to the corporate legal staff, who checked them for possible copyright infringement. Those that survived this check were then discussed again by the panel, and a list of twenty possibles was generated. Those in the product group were charged with the responsibility of developing a research design by which the final name could be chosen.

The people in the product group charged with the name test were considering two different alternatives for finding out which name was preferred. Both alternatives involved personal interviews at shopping malls. More specifically, the group was planning to conduct a set of interviews at one randomly determined mall in Atlanta, Savannah, Tallahassee, and Orlando. Each set of interviews would involve 100 respondents. The target respondents were married females, ages twenty-one to fifty-four, who purchased the product category during the past year. Likely respondents were to be approached at random and were to be asked if they used any insect spray at all over the past year and asked their age. Those that qualified would be asked to complete the insecticide-naming exercise using one of the two alternatives being considered.

Alternative 1 involved a sort of the twenty tentative names by the respondents. The sort would be conducted in the following way. First, respondents would be asked to sort the twenty names into two groups based on their appropriateness for an insect repellent. Group 1 was to consist of the ten best names and Group 2 the ten worst. Next, respondents would be asked to select the four best from Group 1 and the four worst from Group 2. Then they would be asked to pick the one best from the subset of the four best and the one worst from the subset of the four worst. Finally, all respondents would be asked why they picked the specific names they did as the best and the worst.

Alternative 2 also had several stages. All respondents would first be asked to rate each of the twenty names on a seven-point semantic differential scale with end anchors, "extremely inappropriate name for an insect repellent" and "extremely appropriate name for an insect repellent." After completing this rating task, they would be asked to spray the back of their hands or arm with the product and would then be asked to repeat the rating task using a similar scale, but this time one in which the polar descriptors referred to the appropriateness of the name with respect to the specific scent. Next they would be asked to indicate their interest in buying the product by again checking one of the seven positions on a scale that ranged from "definitely would not buy it" to "definitely would buy it." Finally, each respondent would be asked why she selected each of the names she did as being most appropriate for insect repellents in general and the specific scent in particular.

Questions

1. Evaluate each of the two methods being considered for collecting the data. Which would you recommend and why?

2. How would you use the data from each method to decide what the brand name should be?

3. Do you think personal interviews in shopping malls are a useful way to collect this data? If not, what would you recommend as an alternative?

Case 3.3   Suncoast National Bank[1]

Suncoast National Bank maintains its headquarters and twenty-three branch offices in the San Diego metropolitan area. As such, Suncoast National is one of the largest locally headquartered banks in the region. Most of the other major financial institutions located in the San Diego area (such as Bank of America and Security Pacific Bank) are headquartered in either Los Angeles or San Francisco.

The San Diego metropolitan area presently has a population of about 1.8 million persons. It is the second largest city in California and is the eighth largest metropolitan area in the United States. Figures from the U.S. Census show that the San Diego area grew roughly 35 percent in population between 1970 and 1979. Estimates indicate further growth of about 20 percent by 1985.

[1]Source: From: *Cases in Marketing Research* by William G. Zikmund, William Lundstrom, and Donald Sciglimpaglia, pp. 45–52. Copyright © 1982 by CBS College Publishing. Reprinted by permission of Holt, Rinehart and Winston, Inc.

Exhibit 1   Suncoast National Bank — Interdepartmental Communication

TO: Robert R. Redmund, Vice President, Marketing
FROM: Steven R. Bennett, Marketing Research Analyst
DATE: July 21, 1981
SUBJECT: NEWCOMER RESEARCH PROPOSAL

Purpose and Background. That we live in a highly mobile society is reflected by the fact that approximately one out of five U.S. citizens changes residence every year.

As people relocate, their life-styles are temporarily disrupted and certain "needs" become self-evident at their new locale. Among those needs are services provided by financial institutions.

The match between newcomers and financial institutions seems to be a natural one; however, many feel that the difficulty in reaching prospective newcomers outweighs the advantages of designing a newcomer program. Contrary to this belief, the newcomer is one of the best retail markets available to the bank. Rather than expend an entire marketing effort to redistribute the existing market, we should develop a program to tap this newcomer segment with the advantage being that we would have little or no competition from other institutions.

The newcomer program will have to be based upon information. In order for us to identify, locate, and capture this market segment, we must understand the key issues of the newcomer segment, their needs as newcomers to San Diego, and what it will take to attract them to our bank. We must understand how newcomers learn about banks (and savings and loans), who in a family will make the banking decision, at what point do they decide on a bank, and what their profile is.

Research must be undertaken to provide us with the necessary information to design and effectively market a newcomer program.

Methodology: A survey instrument will be designed to gather the above information via mail questionnaire of prospective San Diego residents and newcomers to San Diego. Address lists will be generated by the San Diego Chamber of Commerce and from San Diego Hospitality Hostess. The survey will be conducted among those persons most responsible in a household for the banking activities, and it will be designed to gather the necessary attitudinal and demographic information in order to maximize the success of a future newcomer program.

Focus Groups: To better understand the problems that newcomers experience, we need to conduct some focus group research. This research will result in our being better able to design a survey instrument which relates to the needs of this segment. I think that two or three group sessions should be sufficient.

Time Schedule:	Completed By:
■ Focus groups	August 21
■ Questionnaire design	September 7
■ Pre-test questionnaire	September 12
■ Survey	September 29
■ Data analysis	October 5

Newcomer Project

Steven Bennett, the marketing research analyst for Suncoast National, was impressed with these population growth figures. In recent years Suncoast had been losing market share to other banks, and its management was looking to the marketing area to help retain its place in the market. Bennett's direct superior, Bob Redmund, had asked him to give some thought to any research that could be conducted to help him formulate Suncoast National's marketing strategy.

Bennett was aware of programs used by banks in other cities that targeted new people moving into the area. In particular, he was familiar with one such newcomer program conducted by a bank in Atlanta that was so successful that it had earned the bank an award from the Bank Marketing Association. No doubt, Bennett thought, it probably also earned its originator a substantial raise in salary.

As he understood it, the Atlanta program worked this way: The bank accumulated the names of persons about to move to Atlanta from elsewhere and names of persons who had moved there within a very short time. The names were obtained through Atlanta employers, the Chamber of Commerce, realtors, and welcoming services such as Welcome Wagon and

Exhibit 2   Newcomers Study Focus Group Outline

General Purpose: (1) To determine problems and inconveniences experienced in moving to San Diego or shortly after arrival; (2) to understand how initial banks were selected, and (3) to determine problems associated with banking transactions.

Topics

1. Reasons for moving to San Diego

2. Problems in *planning* the move

3. Problems *during* the move

4. Problems *after* the move

5. How problems could have been corrected

6. Problems related to banking

7. How participants learned about various banks available in the city

8. How they selected initial bank

9. What banks could do to make move less inconvenient

10. What other groups or organizations could do to make the move easier

Hospitality Hostess. The bank offered each person a complete kit to help make his or her transition a little easier. Included in the kit were such things as maps, city guides, guides to services, bus schedules, and discount coupons. Each person contacted was sent an engraved invitation that entitled him or her to receive a newcomer kit at one of the bank's branch offices. Reportedly, the Atlanta bank had been successful in converting into new customers many of those who accepted the invitation.

Since San Diego is a high-growth and highly mobile community, Bennett thought that such a program should be investigated by Suncoast National. Accordingly, he wrote the memo seen in Exhibit 1 to Redmund.

Newcomer Focus Group Studies Bennett received approval to proceed with the project. He knew that, in addition to information that would be available from industry sources, he needed to know more about the feelings and experiences of newcomers.

This would assist him in designing a better survey questionnaire for the mail study. Bennett was especially interested in knowing about the problems that were encountered in moving, how newcomers selected a new bank, and what kinds of information newcomers thought would be useful to them. All of this would be thoroughly evaluated in the survey.

Bennett selected Professional Interviewing to conduct two focus groups to help find out more about problems experienced by newcomers. That firm, a local field interviewing company, was instructed to recruit 12 persons who had moved into San Diego within the last month for each of two group interview sessions. Bennett prepared the outline seen in Exhibit 2 for the interviews.

Paula Jackson, the owner of Professional Interviewing, was to be the group moderator. For the first group session, seven participants, six women and one man, attended. The transcript of that session is seen in Exhibit 3.

Exhibit 3   Newcomers Study Focus Group

Moderator I'm Paula from Professional Interviewing and I really appreciate your participation in this group session. As you can see, we are taping this session because after the end of this it would be impossible to remember what has transpired. First of all, we are here tonight to talk about your reasons for moving to San Diego. Let's start out by having each of you introduce yourself and state how you came about coming to San Diego . . . how you got here and where you're from.

Exhibit 3 *continued*

Mary My name is Mary—and we came to San Diego because my husband works here, and I came from New York.

Brenda Brenda Cole from Maine—was headed for Arizona but came to San Diego by chance. Came west because of the weather.

Marian Marian from Kansas City—came here because my husband took a job here.

Lisa Lisa, Pacific Northwest, read in a magazine that San Diego had the most perfect climate and wanted to get away from Redlands where it was all smog. Came alone by bus.

Anna I'm Anna, from Sacramento area, and I came to go to San Diego State, pre-med student.

Carolyn Carolyn, from Virginia. My husband took a job in San Diego.

Roger Roger from Los Angeles, came because of a transfer in the company and liked a smaller city.

Moderator Undoubtedly, some of you had situations that arose when you got ready to come here, inconveniences that happened to you. They may have been major things or minor things, but no matter what, they were still problems that came about when you got ready to move. I'd like to talk about the problems and inconveniences you had in getting ready to come to San Diego.

Brenda What do you mean by inconveniences?

Marian Like changes of addresses in banks or your subscriptions?

Moderator Things that disrupted your living the way you were living.

Marian Taking my daughter, who is a senior in high school, away and leaving all her friends. She despises it. That is an inconvenience. The move itself. The movers were late naturally. The furniture was broken. The claim is still not settled.

Moderator You mentioned banking, was that a problem?

Marian I've changed banks since I've been here. I don't like the banking hours here. In Kansas City, the banks were open just like department stores, day and night. So the banking was very easy. Here I started with Bank of America, but they were never open so I switched real quick.

Moderator What do you mean they were never open?

Marian They didn't open early, the one near me didn't open until 10:00 in the morning and is only open until 3:00 and we're used to 7:00 to 7:00 hours. I'm surprised by the banks. In such a big place, why not open longer and on Saturdays. I found a bank that is open Saturdays for my checking account. I've never seen such long lines in my whole life. With so many working in such a large population you would think they would accommodate more. You could wait an hour just to get a check cashed. I'm trying to get my account going, just to add a name. The drive-up is open, but they can't pass the card. I have to go inside and stand in the hour-long lines to do that, and I'm not willing to do that. I learned a long time ago that anything you open up, use the word *or* not *and*. Like Marty *or* Marian—not *and*. Then you don't have any trouble.

Moderator Brenda, how about you?

Brenda Trying to weed out what to bring or throw away. We brought only what we could take in the car. We have a few things in storage but not much. Like everyone, I feel the banks out here are the most horrendous situations I've ever seen. I've never found it so hard to get a check cashed. My husband, in his own bank, has to show his driver's license, and if you don't have a picture ID, you're out of luck. They are too untrusting, it's outrageous. I've been in many cities in many states and have never run into anything so outrageous in my entire life.

Moderator Then your difficulty in cashing a check is your main difficulty in banking?

Brenda Just everything . . . people's attitudes. Out here it's like everyone is for themselves, no one wants to help anyone else. Everybody is on their own. The last place I lived was a small town and the people were more willing to help you out. Most people I've run into out here are not willing to be helpful, especially the banks. I haven't been here long enough for firsthand evidence, but from what I've heard, even the residents have trouble. The lady I'm staying near has had to change banks three times in the last year.

Moderator Lisa, what problems have you encountered?

Lisa Well, not really very much. I take life as it comes, living day-to-day. I don't have any money in banks. I would never put money in a bank. Why? Because I don't like the way they do business. I don't like what they do with the money while it's in there. I don't like the interest they give you and I don't like the waiting in lines. I don't like anything about it. The banks aren't interested in us, they just want the money so they can use it.

Moderator Carolyn?

Carolyn The moving van gave us the most problems. Many of our things were damaged and many stolen. I don't know how to claim these items. We were delayed one day because the vans won't move less than five tons and we only had two. We paid for five. Also the banks . . . cashing out-of-state checks in your own bank. My husband applied for a Visa card here. Our credit is fantastic but we

Exhibit 3   *continued*

were denied the credit because they say they have no record of our credit rating. We could not transfer it out here, so fine, they won't use our money, we'll just keep sending it back to Virginia. The service charge out here is outrageous. I had a totally free checking account. No service charge, no minimum balance, everything was free. The checks were free. We figured it will cost about $40 a year to maintain a checking account.

Lisa So she has the right idea not to put money in the bank, put everything in cash. Also your records are not closed. The government can get your records. They can come in and construct a whole life-style by your transactions, so if you want the whole world to know about you, where you bank, where you buy, where you borrow, what church you donate or go to, then just use a bank!

Carolyn Another thing that surprised me is that when you buy a money order, even in the city, the banks won't cash it. That's wrong. This is just like cash. It was bought and paid for. Where can you cash them? You have to open an account and leave them there for so many days . . . in the city a couple of days, out of the city probably two weeks, and out of state up to eighteen to twenty days. A cashier's check is the same. Nobody trusts nobody. It took a friend about thirty days to cash a cashier's check. It was for $1,000 from Las Vegas so they couldn't cash it. The money is there so why can't they cash it? Travelers checks are not acceptable everywhere. Some stores and gas stations will not accept them.

Moderator Anna, tell us about your problems.

Anna You wouldn't believe it. Being a student, I have no credit cards, no credit. I have a driver's license and a military ID and it's impossible to cash a check without a credit card. Also, trying to find a place to live. I'm not twenty-one so they won't let you rent an apartment. They would not take my signature. I had to call my Dad and have him fly down, which is $50 one-way, and sign for me to get the apartment, and then fly back home. My parents send me money each month in a cashier's check, but I go through the problem all the time to cash it. I could get my parents to put me on their Visa card as a signer.

Roger Couldn't you go to a bank and get a check guarantee card?

Anna I've heard of it, but I don't have one. I have a military ID and a driver's license. I feel those two should be sufficient.

Moderator Did you experience any other problems as you were planning the move?

Anna Yes, getting into school. They sent my application to San Jose instead of San Diego State, so by the time I got it

back it was too late to register and I had to go contract register and it cost me $40 more per unit. At the time I was taking fifteen units, so I dropped all but ten units. I paid $400 instead of $100 and after moving down here and everything, I couldn't move back home.

Moderator Roger, how about you? When you were planning to move from Los Angeles?

Roger I had no problems moving down as I moved all my own stuff so if anything was broken, it was no one's fault but my own. As far as banking, you just go down and open an account and hope the bank has interest in other personal accounts in California. Most banks don't. I don't feel San Diego is any different than Los Angeles. In transferring down here, Bank of America would not give me a check guarantee card here, even though my account was with them in L.A., because they say I have not established my record with them. I closed my account with them. I switched. Of course, I had the same problem, but I'd rather give them the chance and build my record than a bank that didn't consider my past twelve-year record where I held two existing loans. I think it's like a franchise, you should get the same service here that you did in the other place if it's the same bank.

Moderator What bank do you bank with now?

Roger Security Pacific Bank.

Moderator Do you notice any difference?

Roger No. No difference. They all have the same policy. Their cause is not for you. You put a large sum of money into their savings account, you don't ask them their life history, they just take your money and put it in there. Just try to borrow money or try to get your own money out . . . it seems to be a different story. The interest they pay you is nothing. They're using that to invest at a much higher rate. You're donating to their cause when you have money in the bank, but yet they're a necessary evil, I wouldn't feel safe with that money at home. I think you need a bank. It's a must! They need some of the starch taken out of them. There are exceptions, some managers are nice but they're very few. Most are VIPs and we are the peons.

Lisa If we could figure some other way to handle our money that would put them down to size and then they wouldn't be VIPs anymore. They would be human beings and maybe they would treat us better.

Roger Credit unions are an alternative to banks if you have one; they are good.

Lisa Why do you feel credit unions are better than banks?

Roger I think they are more concerned with the people that are in that organization. They make loans to people in

Exhibit 3 *continued*

their organizations. They come first, not just someone who comes in off the street. If you're not a member, you don't get a loan. They deal more with people who are willing to invest some of their savings with them. They in turn give priority to that person. When you borrow money from a bank, they decide whether it's a good investment or not. What is a good investment to one person may not be to another. If he has a past record of paying back money, they should give him the same responsibility. The money is there to lend. And money should be there to lend when they hold "X" amount of money in savings accounts. When they have money to build new branches and furnish them quite lavishly, then I think they've got money. The bank manager shouldn't feel like the money is coming out of his own personal checking account. Their business is making loans. They don't make it on checking accounts. Even if checking accounts aren't free, that $2 or $3 a month isn't paying the salaries, it's the loans. As an example, we took out a loan for $125,000 for constructing apartments in L.A. through a savings and loan. We were putting $25,000 of our own money into the S & L when they OK'd the loan. We then sold the land prior to construction, never used one penny out of the account, but it cost us for that loan . . . $10,000 — it was never used. Not only the cost for the loan but there was the prepayment penalty on the construction loan. Now in personal loans, if I was to borrow that amount of money from someone here, they would not be allowed to do that.

Lisa What makes a bank an exception? I don't understand, but there is nothing you can do. It's in the fine print, they are above the law.

Moderator Let's talk about immediately after you all moved here . . . what situations you came up against and what inconveniences.

Marian Finding the shopping areas and schools. It's pretty hard to find out which schools are for which districts . . . and which ones are good. We have found that the schools here are a little behind in their teaching. Getting your children to feel as though they belong in the new school . . . everyone is in their little cliques and no one wants new people.

Carolyn I find the people here very unfriendly. It seems that it's each to themselves. The drivers here are wild. I need to get a new driver's license and, I think, California plates. I'm not sure.

Moderator Brenda, how about you?

Brenda Finding an apartment was hard. Knowing what area is good or not. Getting the apartment is hard. They need your life history even though you have the first month's rent and the deposit. They expect you to take a motel for awhile. They feel their apartments are worth gold and you are going to destroy them or something.

Carolyn They don't want to rent to people with children. I have only an infant but they don't want to rent to me. I think the best thing going on now are the people that are trying to stop these apartment owners from not renting to families.

Brenda Oh yea . . . and I'd bet that some of you had trouble finding out where to pay your utility deposits for gas and electricity and for the telephone. I had to go to four separate places. We had to wait two weeks for our phone to be installed.

Moderator If you had it to do over again, can you come up with any suggestions or other ways you may have handled the move to prevent some of these problems?

Brenda I don't think I would move here. The weather is great, but that's about it. I've lived in a lot of big and little cities, all over, and the people around here are the hardest to get to know of anyplace I've lived. There is a housing shortage here for renting and buying.

Roger There is no way to solve the problems of housing since it is a bureaucracy. If you could get the bureaucracy out of it, then private enterprises would take over and meet the demands of the people, but it can't be done.

Moderator Well, thanks very much for coming in to participate. You've been very helpful.

Questions

1. What kind of information should Bennett attempt to get from banking industry sources about newcomer programs?

2. Do you think it was wise to have a group with both men and women included and with participants of various ages?

3. Did the moderator do an adequate job of getting at the information needed by Bennett?

4. Analyze the focus group transcript very thoroughly. Make a list of problems generated and ideas for the proposed newcomer kit.

Part Four   Data-Collection Forms

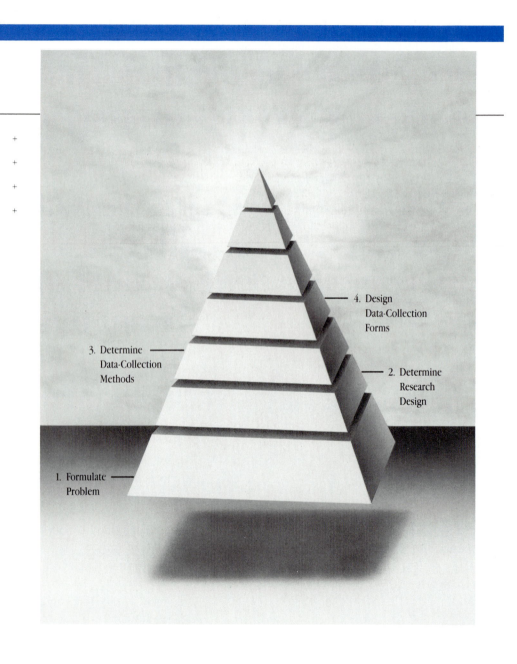

4. Design
Data-Collection
Forms

3. Determine
Data-Collection
Methods

2. Determine
Research
Design

1. Formulate
Problem

Once the data-collection method has been decided, the researcher needs to design the data-collection forms that will be used. Chapter 10 discusses the construction of questionnaires and observation forms. Chapter 11 provides some measurement basics that researchers need to be aware of so that they do not mislead others. Chapter 12 then discusses the measurement of attitudes, perceptions, and preferences.

Chapter 10

Designing the Questionnaire or Observation Form

Learning Objectives

Upon completing this chapter, you should be able to

1. Explain the role of research hypotheses in developing a questionnaire.

2. Define *telescoping error* and *recall loss* and explain how they affect a respondent's ability to answer questions accurately.

3. Cite some of the techniques researchers use to secure respondents' cooperation in answering sensitive questions.

4. Explain what is meant by an open-ended question.

5. Name two kinds of fixed-alternative questions and tell the difference between them.

6. List some of the primary rules researchers should keep in mind in trying to develop bias-free questions.

7. Explain what is meant by the funnel approach to question sequencing.

8. Explain what is meant by a branching question and discuss when it is used.

9. Explain the difference between basic information and classification information and tell which should be asked first in a questionnaire.

Case in Marketing Research

Karen Clark, a young staffer at Dunfey Communication Research, sat at her desk and stared out the window at the lush green landscape of early summer. The sun was shining, the flowers blooming, the birds singing, but Karen's mind was deep in the heart of a supermarket.

She had recently been assigned the job of developing a questionnaire to determine what improvements Wallach's, a small chain of supermarkets, should make to attract more customers. The family-owned stores had always been profitable until recently, when business had begun to decline. It was Karen's job to try to pinpoint what was causing the drop in sales.

After consulting a variety of secondary data, Karen and her colleagues had hypothesized that part of the stores' problem could be their limited hours. While competing stores had expanded their hours to allow for earlier opening, later closing, and limited hours on Sundays, Wallach's kept to the schedule that it had had for twenty years: 9 A.M. to 8 P.M., Monday through Saturday, and closed on Sunday.

Karen thought that the increase in the numbers of working women shown by recent demographic studies might be a clue to Wallach's problem.

Karen had already decided that the study would be in the form of a structured questionnaire administered personally by field staffers in the stores. She planned to have staffers posted at varying times in each of the stores to interview shoppers. Just as she was to begin drafting her first questions, Susan Malone, her supervisor, stopped in the office.

"Hi, Karen. How's the questionnaire for Wallach's going?" she asked.

Karen told Susan her preliminary plans for the study.

"Well, I think you're on the right track, but I already anticipate a few problems," Susan said. "If Wallach's former customers have indeed been driven away by their limited shopping hours, then interviewing current shoppers isn't going to answer our questions, is it?"

Karen blushed. "Gee, Susan, I never thought of that. You're right. I better rethink my sample before I start writing questions. I guess I got ahead of myself."

Discussion Issues

1. How might Karen find an appropriate sample on which to conduct her study?

2. How might that sample influence the design of her questionnaire?

3. What kinds of information might Karen want to collect in this study?

In the previous chapters we discussed the various types of questionnaires and observation forms researchers use and how they are administered, as well as the pros and cons of the specific types of questionnaire and observation methods. We also examined the various advantages and disadvantages of using communication and observational research techniques.

In this chapter we will build on that discussion by reviewing the procedures researchers can follow in developing a questionnaire or observational data-collection form.

◆ Questionnaire Design

Although much progress has been made, designing questionnaires is still an art and not a science. Much of the progress has been simply an awareness of what to avoid, namely, leading questions and ambiguous questions. Few guidelines exist, however, on how to develop questions that are not leading or ambiguous.

Figure 10.1 offers a method the beginning researcher might find helpful to develop questionnaires.[1] More experienced researchers would be expected to develop their own patterns, although the steps listed in Figure 10.1 would certainly be part of that pattern.

While the stages of development are presented in the figure in sequence, researchers will rarely be so fortunate as to develop a questionnaire in that step-by-step fashion. A more typical development will involve circling back to clarify some aspects of earlier steps after they have been found to be faulty later on in the questionnaire's design. The researcher may find, for example, that the way a question is worded tends to elicit unhelpful responses. Researchers should not be surprised, then, if they find themselves working back and forth among some of the stages. That is natural.

Researchers should also be warned not to take the stages too literally. They are presented as a guide or a checklist. With questionnaires, the proof of the pudding is very much in the eating. Does the questionnaire produce accurate data of the kind needed? Blind adherence to procedure is no substitute for creativity in approach, nor is it any substitute for a pretest (Step 9 of Figure 10.1) with which one can discover if the typical respondent indeed understands each question and is able and willing to supply the information sought.

Step 1: Specify What Information Will Be Sought

The first step in questionnaire design, deciding what information will be sought, is easy, provided that researchers have been meticulous and precise at earlier stages in the research process. Careless earlier work will make this decision difficult.

Both descriptive and causal research require that researchers have enough knowledge about the problem to frame some specific hypotheses to guide the research. The hypotheses also guide the questionnaire. They determine what information will be sought, and from whom, because they specify what relationships will be investigated. If researchers have already established dummy tables to structure the data analysis, their job of determining what information is to be collected is essentially complete. You may remember that a dummy table is a table that is used to catalog

---

[1] This procedure is adapted from one suggested by Arthur Kornhauser and Paul B. Sheatsley, "Questionnaire Construction and Interview Procedure," in Claire Selltiz, Lawrence S. Wrightsman, and Stuart W. Cook, *Research Methods in Social Relations,* 3rd ed. (New York: Holt, Rinehart and Winston, 1976), pp. 541–573.

Figure 10.1

Procedure for Developing a Questionnaire

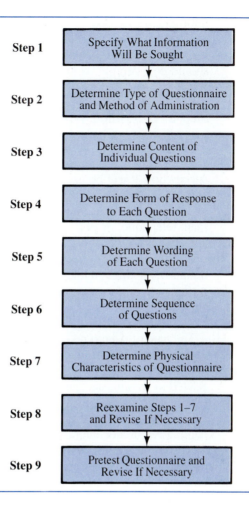

Step 1	Specify What Information Will Be Sought
Step 2	Determine Type of Questionnaire and Method of Administration
Step 3	Determine Content of Individual Questions
Step 4	Determine Form of Response to Each Question
Step 5	Determine Wording of Each Question
Step 6	Determine Sequence of Questions
Step 7	Determine Physical Characteristics of Questionnaire
Step 8	Reexamine Steps 1–7 and Revise If Necessary
Step 9	Pretest Questionnaire and Revise If Necessary

the data collected. It is identical to the one that will be used in the actual research, but in this early stage it has no numbers.

Researchers must collect information on the variables specified in the dummy tables in order to investigate these hypotheses. Further, researchers must collect this information from the right people and in the right units. Hence, it is clear that hypotheses are not only guides to what information will be sought, but also affect the type of question and form of response used to collect it.

Of course, the preparation of the questionnaire may itself suggest further hypotheses and other relationships that might be investigated at slight additional effort and cost. A most important warning is in order here. If the new hypothesis is indeed vital to understanding the phenomenon, by all means include it and use it to advantage when designing the questionnaire. On the other hand, and we are repeating ourselves, if it simply represents one of those potentially "interesting findings" but is not vital to the research effort, forget it. The inclusion of interesting but not vital items simply lengthens the questionnaire, causes problems in administration and analysis, and often increases nonresponse.

The exploratory research effort is, of course, aimed at the discovery of ideas and insights and not at their systematic investigation. The questionnaire for an exploratory study is therefore loosely structured, with only a rough idea of the kind of information that might be sought. This is particularly true at the earliest stages of exploratory research. It is also true, but to a lesser extent, at the later stages of exploratory research, when the emphasis is on determining the priorities that should be given to various hypotheses in guiding future research.

Step 2: Determine Type of Questionnaire and Method of Administration

After specifying the basic information that will be sought, the researcher needs to specify how it will be gathered. Decisions on the type of questionnaire and method of administering it constitute the second step. Such decisions center on the structure and disguise to be used in the questionnaire and whether it will be administered by mail, telephone, or personal interviews. We saw in the last chapter that these decisions are not independent of one another. If the researcher decides on a disguised-unstructured questionnaire in which subjects will be shown a picture and asked to tell a story about it, a telephone interview would be out of the question, and even a mail survey might pose serious problems.[2] Similarly, it is probably not a good idea to use a mail survey for an unstructured-undisguised questionnaire that asks open-ended questions.

The type of data to be collected will have an important effect, of course, on these questions. A researcher investigating the relationship between some behavior and a series of demographic characteristics (for example, how is dishwasher ownership related to income, age, family size, and so on?), might use either mail, telephone, or personal interviews to gather the data. The methods would not be equally attractive because of cost and other considerations, but they all could be used. On the other hand, a researcher interested in measuring attitudes could not use all of the methods. The method that would be most appropriate would be largely determined by decisions made earlier about structure and disguise. If researchers decided to use a lengthy attitude scale, for example, they would probably have to rule out telephone interviews. Such data could be gathered best either by mail or in personal interviews. Likewise, an open-ended questionnaire on attitudes might be unsuitable for mail administration. Thus, the researcher must specify precisely what primary data are needed, how these data might be collected, what degree of structure and disguise will be used, and then how the questionnaire will be administered.

Figure 10.2 offers an example. The primary data at issue are use of 6-volt batteries, and attitudes and purchase intentions toward a 6-volt battery recharger. The questions are all highly structured and totally undisguised. The questionnaire is to be administered by mail, using part of the NFO panel. Note the ease with which most of the responses could be coded and tabulated, except for the statements about likes and dislikes.

Step 3: Determine Content of Individual Questions

The researcher's previous decisions regarding information needed, the structure and disguise to be imposed on its collection, and the method for administering the questionnaire will largely control the decisions regarding individual question con-

---

[2]The two methods might possibly be used in combination through the locked-box approach.

Figure 10.2   Letter and Mail Questionnaire for 6-Volt Battery Study

National Family Opinion, Inc.

CONSUMER MARKET RESEARCH SINCE 1946

444 N. MICHIGAN AVENUE
CHICAGO, ILLINOIS 60611

TELEPHONE | AREA CODE 312
467-5222

Dear Homemaker:

Today's questionnaire is about 6-VOLT LANTERN BATTERIES. Please give this
questionnaire to the person in your family who is most responsible for
purchasing 6-VOLT LANTERN BATTERIES.

TO THE PERSON WHO IS MOST RESPONSIBLE FOR PURCHASING 6-VOLT LANTERN-TYPE
BATTERIES:

This questionnaire is about a new 6-Volt Lantern Battery with a recharger.
I would like for you to read the descriptions, look at the pictures and
then give me your opinions of the battery and recharger. Remember, it is
just as important for me to know what you DO NOT like about the ideas as it
is to know what you like about them.

After you have answered all my questions, please return this questionnaire
in the enclosed postage-paid envelope.

Thank you so much for your help!

                                        Sincerely,

                                        Carol Adams

TOLEDO (HOME OFFICE): P.O. BOX 315 43691   NEW YORK: 630 THIRD AVENUE 10017
WEST COAST: 43 QUAIL COURT, WALNUT CREEK, CALIF. 94596

Source: Courtesy Ray-O-Vac Corporation

continued

Figure 10.2

continued

1. *During the past 12 months, have you, or any member of your family (living at home) purchased a 6-VOLT LANTERN BATTERY?*

☐ Yes—Continue_____   ☐ NO—Stop here, return questionnaire!

2. a) *In Column "A", please write in the number of 6-Volt lantern batteries your family purchased during the past 12 months for each of the devices listed on the left.*
   b) *In Column "B" for each of the devices you bought 6-volt lantern batteries for, please write in the number of batteries that fit into that device at one time.*

	Number of 6-Volt Lantern Batteries purchased for this device in the past 12 months.	Number of 6-Volt Lantern Batteries that fit into this device at one time.
Toy.................	_____	_____
Lantern..............	_____	_____
Depth/Fish Finder	_____	_____
Lighting Device........	_____	_____
Garden Tool..........	_____	_____
Alarm/Security Device ..	_____	_____
Other (Specify): _____	_____	_____
_____	_____	_____

3. *Below are pictures of a new type of 6-Volt Lantern Battery and Recharger. This battery is the same size and works the same way as the 6-Volt lantern battery you usually purchase. However, this battery is rechargeable. When the battery wears down all you do is plug the charger into a regular household electrical outlet and put the battery upside down in the charger for an overnight recharge. This battery is made by a leading U.S. battery manufacturer and is guaranteed for three years or 150 charges (cycles), whichever comes first.*

THE PRODUCT   HOW TO RECHARGE BATTERY

4. *Which of the following phrases best describes your feelings about the type of battery described above?*

☐ It's a great idea

☐ It's a pretty good idea

☐ It's a "so-so" idea

☐ It's not a very good idea

☐ It's a poor idea

Figure 10.2

continued

5. *About how much would you expect this lantern-type battery and recharger combination to cost at your local discount store?*

$_____ for battery and recharger combination

6. *Is there anything that you particularly LIKE about this idea? Please be as specific as possible.*

_____

_____

_____

7. *Is there anything that you particularly DISKLIKE about this idea? Please be as specific as possible.*

_____

_____

_____

8. *Let us assume this battery and recharger combination would sell for about $20. Extra rechargeable batteries would cost about $10.*

Thinking only about the $20 battery and recharger combination, please indicate below how likely you would be to buy it at that price. Please check ONE box.

☐ I definitely would buy it_____

☐ I probably would buy it   ⟶**Continue with Question 9**

☐ I might or might not buy it_____

☐ I probably would not buy it_____

☐ I definitely would not buy it_____   ⟶**Stop here, return questionnaire**

9. a) *In Column "A" below, check the device(s) for which you would buy the combination lantern-type battery and recharger.*
   b) *In Column "B" below, check the devices for which you would purchase any additional rechargeable batteries mentioned above in Question 8.*
   c) *In Column "C" below, write in the number of additional rechargeable batteries you think you would purchase during the next year for each item you checked in column "B".*

	A Would buy combination lantern-type battery and recharger for this item(s).	B Would purchase *additional* rechargeable batteries for this item(s).	C For item(s) checked in "B", number of *additional* rechargeable batteries I would purchase in next year.
Toy..........................	☐	☐	____
Lantern.....................	☐	☐	____
Depth/Fish Finder	☐	☐	____
Non-Lantern Lighting Device.............	☐	☐	____

continued

Figure 10.2

continued

Garden Tool . . . .   ☐   ☐   ____

Alarm/Security
  Device . . . .   ☐   ☐   ____

Other(s) (Specify). . . . .   ☐   ☐   ____

_____   ☐   ☐   ____
_____   ☐   ☐   ____

10. *Suppose that the battery/recharger combination were available just as described in Question 3, except that the charger would charge two batteries at the same time (See Picture B). Also, this new battery charger combination would cost $22 instead of $20.*

A

Battery and single unit charger for $20

B

Battery and a charger that would charge 2 batteries at one time for $22

The Product   How To Recharge Battery   The Product   How To Recharge Battery

Now, looking at the two different combinations, please indicate which one you would prefer:

☐ Prefer battery and single unit charger for $20 (Illustration "A")

☐ Prefer battery and a charger that would charge 2 batteries at one time for $22 (Illustration "B")

tent, which is the third step. But the researcher can and should ask some additional questions.[3]

Is the Question Necessary? Suppose an issue is important. Then the researcher needs to ask whether the point has been adequately covered by other questions. If not, a new question is in order. The question should then be framed to secure an answer with the required detail, but not an answer with more detail than needed. Very often in marketing, for example, we employ the concept of *stage in the life cycle* to explore family consumption behavior. Stage in the life cycle is a variable

---

[3]These questions were suggested by Kornhauser and Sheatsley, "Questionnaire Construction." For a systematic treatment of questionnaire construction, see the classic work by Stanley L. Payne, *The Art of Asking Questions* (Princeton, N.J.: Princeton University Press, 1979). Three other good general sources are A. N. Oppenheim, *Questionnaire Design and Attitude Measurement* (New York: Basic Books, 1966); Douglas R. Berdie and John F. Anderson, *Questionnaires: Design and Use* (Metuchen, N.J.: Scarecrow Press, 1974); and Seymour Sudman and Norman M. Bradburn, *Asking Questions: A Practical Guide to Questionnaire Design* (San Francisco: Jossey-Bass, 1982). For specific suggestions on the construction of mail and telephone questionnaires, see Paul L. Erdos, *Professional Mail Surveys* (Malabar, Fla.: Robert E. Krieger, 1983); and A. B. Blankenship, *Professional Telephone Surveys* (New York: McGraw-Hill, 1977). For a general bibliography on questionnaire construction, see Wayne G. Daniel, *Questionnaire Design: A Selected Bibliography for the Survey Researcher* (Monticello, Ill.: Vance Bibliographics, 1979).

made up of several elements, including marital status, presence of children, and the ages of children. The presence of children is an important factor, because it most often indicates a dependency relationship. This is especially true if the youngest child is under six years old and thus represents one type of responsibility, or over six but under seventeen and thus another type of responsibility for the parents. In a study using stage in the life cycle as a variable, there is no need to ask the age of each child. Rather, all that is needed is one question aimed at securing the age of the youngest child if there are any children. Once again, the roles of the hypotheses and dummy tables are obvious when designing the questionnaire.

Are Several Questions Needed Instead of One? There will often be situations in which several questions are needed instead of one. Consider the question, "Why do you use Crest?" One respondent may reply, "To reduce cavities," while another may reply, "Because our dentist recommended it." Obviously two different frames of reference are being employed to answer this question. The first respondent is replying in terms of why he is using it now, while the second is replying in terms of how she started using it. It would be better to break this one question down into separate questions that reflect the possible frames of reference that could be used, for example:

How did you first happen to use Crest?
What is your primary reason for using it?

Do Respondents Have the Necessary Information? The researcher should carefully examine each issue to determine whether the typical respondent can be expected to have the information sought. Respondents will give answers. Whether the answers mean anything, though, is another matter. In one public opinion survey, the following question was asked:[4]

Which of the following statements most closely coincides with your opinion of the Metallic Metals Act?

- ☐ It would be a good move on the part of the United States.
- ☐ It would be a good thing, but it should be left to the individual states.
- ☐ It is all right for foreign countries, but it should not be required here.
- ☐ It is of no value at all.
- ☐ No opinion.

The proportion of respondents checking each alternative was, respectively, 21.4 percent, 58.6 percent, 15.7 percent, 4.3 percent, and 0.3 percent. The second alternative captures the prevailing sentiment, right? Wrong! There was no Metallic Metals Act, and the point of the example is that *most questions will get answers, but the real concern is whether the answers mean anything.*[5] In order for the answers to mean

---

[4]Sam Gill, "How Do You Stand on Sin?" *Tide,* 21 (March 14, 1947), p. 72

[5]There are a number of other examples in the literature that report findings of people having opinions about totally fictional issues like the Metallic Metals Act. See, for example, George F. Bishop, Robert W. Oldendick, Alfred J. Tuchfarber, and S. E. Bennett, "Pseudo-Opinions on Public Affairs," *Public Opinion Quarterly,* 44 (Summer 1980), pp. 198–209; Herbert Schuman and Stanley Presser, "Public Opinion and Public Ignorance: The Fine Line Between Attitudes and Nonattitudes," *American Journal of Sociology,* 85 (March 1980), pp. 1214–1225; and Del I. Hawkins and Kenneth A. Coney, "Uninformed Response Error in Survey Research," *Journal of Marketing Research,* 18 (August 1981), pp. 370–374. The phenomenon is not unique to opinions. It also applies when measuring brand awareness, where it has been observed that the more plausible sounding a brand name, the more likely consumers are to claim they are aware of it even though it does not exist. See "'Spurious Awareness' Alters Brand Tests," *The Wall Street Journal,* 64 (September 13, 1984), p. 29.

anything, the questions need to mean something to the respondent. This means that, first, the respondent needs to be informed with respect to the issue addressed by the question, and, second, the respondent must remember the information.

Consider the question, "How much does your family spend on groceries in a typical week?" Unless the respondent does the grocery shopping or the family operates with a fairly strict budget, he or she is unlikely to know. In a situation like this, it might be helpful to ask "filter questions" before this question to determine if the individual is indeed likely to have this information. An example filter question might be "Who does the grocery shopping in your family?" It is not unusual, for example, to use filter questions of the sort, "Do you have an opinion on . . .?," before asking about the specific issue in question in opinion surveys. The empirical evidence indicates that providing a filter like this will typically increase the proportion responding "no opinion" by 20 to 25 percentage points.[6]

Not only should the individual have the information sought, but he or she should remember it. Our ability to remember various events is influenced by the event itself and its importance, the length of time since the event, and the presence or absence of stimuli that assist in recalling it. Important events are more easily remembered than are unimportant events. While most people might be able to remember who shot President John F. Kennedy or the make of the first car they ever owned, many of them will be unable to recall the particular shows they watched last Wednesday evening. Returning to our toothpaste example, many people will be unable to recall the first brand they ever used, when they switched to their current brand, or why they switched. While the switching and use information might be very important to a *brand manager for toothpastes,* it is unimportant to most individuals, a condition we have to keep in mind continually when designing questionnaires. We need to put ourselves in the shoes of the respondent, not those of the product manager, when deciding whether the information is important enough for the individual to remember.

We also need to recognize that an individual's ability to remember an event is influenced by how long ago it happened. While we might recall the television programs we watched last evening, we might have much greater difficulty remembering those we watched last week on the same evening, and might find it all but impossible to recall our viewing pattern of a month ago. The moral of this is that if the event could be considered relatively unimportant to most individuals, we should ask about very recent occurrences of it. For more important events, there are two forces, operating in opposite directions, that affect a respondent's ability to provide accurate answers to questions referring to some specified time period. **Telescoping error** is one; it is the tendency to remember an event as having occurred more recently than it did. **Recall loss** is the other; it is the tendency to forget the relatively important event entirely. The degree to which the two sources of error affect the accuracy of the reported information depends on the length of the period in question. For long periods, the telescoping effect is smaller while the recall loss is greater. For short periods, the reverse is true: "Thus, for short reference periods, the telescoping error may outweigh the recall loss, while for long periods the reverse will apply; in between there will be a length of reference periods at which the two effects coun-

• Telescoping error

A type of error resulting from the fact that most people remember an event as having occurred more recently than it did.

• Recall loss

A type of error caused by a respondent forgetting that an event happened at all.

---

[6]Herbert Schuman and Stanley Presser, "The Assessment of 'No Opinions in Attitude Surveys,'" in Karl F. Schnessler, ed., *Sociological Methodology, 1979* (San Francisco: Jossey-Bass, 1979), pp. 241–275. See also George F. Bishop, Robert W. Oldendick, and Alfred J. Tuchfarber, "Effects on Filter Questions in Public Opinion Surveys," *Public Opinion Quarterly,* 47 (Winter 1983), pp. 528–546.

terbalance each other."[7] Unfortunately, there is no single reference period that can be used to frame questions for all events, because what is optimal depends on the importance of the event to those involved.

Will Respondents Give the Information? A situation sometimes arises in which respondents have the necessary information, but they will not give it. Their unwillingness may be a function of the amount of work involved in producing an answer, their ability to articulate an answer, or the sensitivity of the issue.

While a purchasing agent may be able to determine to the penny how much the company spent on cleaning compound last year, or the relative amount spent on each brand bought, the agent is unlikely to take the time to look up this data to reply to an unsolicited questionnaire. Questionnaire developers need to be constantly mindful of the amount of effort it might take respondents to give the information sought. When the effort is excessive, the respondent may either ignore it or

---

[7]Graham Kalton and Howard Schuman, "The Effect of the Question on Survey Responses: A Review," *Journal of the Royal Statistical Society, Series A,* 145 (Part 1, 1982), pp. 44–45.

Back to the Case

Karen had drastically revised her plans for the Wallach's questionnaire based on Susan Malone's comments. Instead of personal interviews by staffers in the Wallach stores, she had decided on a telephone survey in the stores' trading area. That way, she figured, she would be able to get information both from people who shopped at Wallach's and those who preferred the competition.

Recognizing that the people she wanted to speak with would often be at work during the day, she planned to have interviewers call in the evening as well as during the morning and afternoon.

Karen had decided that the questionnaire would combine both multiple-choice and open-ended questions and would also seek classification information about respondents.

To make sure that she was talking to the most informed person in the household, she had instructed interviewers to begin by asking to speak to the person who does the majority of the grocery shopping in the family. Once she got the family's primary shopper on the line, she was confident that the twenty-six questions she had planned would result in a complete picture of what was going on at Wallach's.

Showing her questionnaire draft to Susan, she was surprised to see her frown.

"Karen, these are good questions," Susan said, "but think of your sample. If many of the respondents are working women,

and you're planning to call them during the evening, when they're busy with dinner, children, and laundry, and probably exhausted after a hard day's work, I doubt that many will sit still long enough to answer this many questions. I suggest you cut this questionnaire in half. Promise them it will take only five minutes, and you may get some cooperation. Otherwise you risk a lot of irritated respondents."

Researchers must always keep their respondents' needs in mind. Researchers are dependent on respondents' goodwill and cooperation to conduct their studies. If the effort involved in participating in a survey is excessive, respondents may refuse to cooperate.

give only an approximate answer. It may be wiser to omit these types of questions since they tend to irritate respondents and lessen their cooperation in responding to the rest of the survey.

Otherwise, the researcher needs to use a good deal of creative energy designing a mechanism that allows respondents to articulate their views. While they might not be able to express their preferences in car styling, for example, they should be able to indicate the style they like best when shown pictures of different body styles. General Motors used this picture scheme to determine preferences for grill designs when it found that respondents could not articulate their likes and dislikes.[8]

When an issue is embarrassing or otherwise threatening to respondents, they are also apt to refuse to cooperate. Such issues should be avoided whenever possible. If that is impossible because the issue is very significant to the study, then the researcher needs to pay close attention to how the issue is addressed, particularly with respect to question location and question phrasing. Income, for example, is often a sensitive issue. Respondents' willingness to cooperate depends on how and when the researcher asks for income data. One particularly interesting study investigated the four different versions of the income question shown in Table 10.1 as part of a larger study in which researchers conducted 1,000 telephone interviews. The total sample was divided into four groups of 250 each. Each group was given one of the four versions of the income question. The study found that Versions 2 and 3 produced better cooperation and better income estimation. Versions 1 and 4, which each asked if the respondent's income was "more than" a certain amount, caused respondents to answer quickly, resulting in an overrepresentation in the lower-income categories. The general conclusion was that Versions 2 and 3 were less threatening to respondents. This study demonstrates that researchers should be careful to try to design question forms that take both the nature of the respondents' expectations and their sensitivity to what they perceive as threatening questions into account.[9]

In general, it is better to address sensitive issues later, rather than earlier, in the survey.[10] Most surveys will produce some initial mistrust in respondents. One has to overcome this skepticism and establish rapport. This is made easier when respondents have the opportunity to warm to the task by answering nonthreatening questions early in the interview, particularly questions that establish the legitimacy of the project.

When sensitive questions must be asked, it helps to consider ways to make them less threatening. Some helpful techniques in this regard follow:[11]

1. Hide the question in a group of other more innocuous questions.
2. State that the behavior or attitude is not unusual before asking the specific questions of the respondent, for example, "Recent studies show that one of every four households has trouble meeting their monthly financial obligations." This tech-

[8]Harper W. Boyd, Jr., Ralph Westfall, and Stanley F. Stasch, *Marketing Research: Text and Cases,* 6th ed. (Homewood, Ill.: Richard D. Irwin, 1985), p. 272.

[9]William B. Locander and John P. Burton, "The Effect of Question Form on Gathering Income Data by Telephone," *Journal of Marketing Research,* 13 (May 1976), p. 192.

[10]Question sequence will be discussed more fully later in the chapter.

[11]For more extensive treatments on how to handle sensitive questions, see Kent H. Marquis, *et al., Response Errors in Sensitive Topic Surveys: Estimates, Effects, and Correction Options* (Santa Monica, Calif.: Rand Corporation, 1981); and Thomas W. Mangione, Ralph Hingson, and Jane Barrett, "Collecting Sensitive Data: A Comparison of Three Survey Strategies," *Sociological Methods and Research,* 10 (February 1982), pp. 337–346.

Table 10.1   Four Versions of an Income Question

Form 1
What was the approximate annual income for all members of your family before taxes during 1974? Was it . . .
(REPEAT UNTIL "NO." THEN CIRCLE)

more than $5,000	no 1	more than $20,000	no 5
more than $7,500	no 2	more than $25,000	no 6
more than $10,000	no 3		yes 7
more than $15,000	no 4	Don't know/refused	 X

Form 2
What was the approximate annual income for all members of your family before taxes during 1974 . . . would it be $15,000 or more or would it be less than that?

	less than $15,000 .... **ASK:**
	IF LESS would it be ....
$15,000 or more .... **ASK:**	Over $10,000 4
IF MORE would it be	Under $10,000 .... **ASK:**
Under $20,000 or 5	IF UNDER would it be ....
Over $20,000 .... **ASK:**	Over $7,500 3
IF OVER would it be	Under $7,500 .... **ASK:**
Under $25,000 6	IF UNDER would it be ....
Over $25,000 7	Over $5,000 2
	Under $5,000 1

Form 3
What was the approximate annual income for all members of your family before taxes during 1974? Was it . . .
(REPEAT UNTIL "YES." THEN CIRCLE)

less than $5,000	yes 1	less than $20,000	yes 5
less than $7,500	yes 2	less than $25,000	yes 6
less than $10,000	yes 3		no 7
less than $15,000	yes 4	Don't know/refused	 X

Form 4
What was the approximate annual income for all members of your family before taxes during 1974? Was it . . .
(REPEAT UNTIL "YES." THEN CIRCLE)

more than $25,000	yes 7	more than $7,500	yes 3
more than $20,000	yes 6	more than $5,000	yes 2
more than $15,000	yes 5		no 1
more than $10,000	yes 4	Don't know/refused	 X

Source: William B. Locander and John P. Burton, "The Effect of Question Form and Gathering Income Data by Telephone," *Journal of Marketing Research,* 13 (May 1976), pp. 189–192. Published by the American Marketing Association.

nique, known as the use of counterbiasing statements, makes it easier for the respondent to admit the potentially embarrassing behavior.

3. Phrase the question in terms of others and how they might feel or act, for example, "Do you think most people cheat on their income tax? Why?" While respondents might readily reveal their attitudes toward cheating when preparing income tax forms when asked these questions, they might be very reluctant to do so if they were asked outright if they ever cheat on their taxes and why.

4. State the response in terms of a number of categories that the respondent may simply check. Instead of asking women for their age, for example, one could simply hand them a card with the age categories

   A: 20–29   D: 50–59
   B: 30–39   E: 60+
   C: 40–49

   and ask them to respond with the appropriate letter.

• Randomized-
response model

Interviewing technique in
which potentially
embarrassing and relatively
innocuous questions are
paired, and the question
the respondent answers is
randomly determined.

5. Use the **randomized-response model,** in which the respondent answers one of several paired questions at random.[12] For example, the respondent may draw colored balls from an urn, being instructed to answer Question A if the ball is blue and Question B if the ball is red. The interviewer is unaware of the question being answered by the respondent, because he or she never sees the color of the ball drawn. Under these conditions the respondent is less likely to refuse to answer or to answer untruthfully. A study to investigate the incidence of shoplifting might pair the sensitive question, "Have you ever shoplifted?" with the innocuous question, "Is your birthday in January?" The incidence of shoplifting can still be estimated by using an appropriate statistical model, since the percentage of respondents answering each question is controlled by the proportion of red and blue balls in the urn. Since the researcher cannot determine specifically which respondents have admitted to shoplifting by this technique, though, there is no opportunity to examine such questions as whether shoplifting behavior was associated with any particular demographic characteristics.

Step 4: Determine Form of Response to Each Question

If a fixed-alternative format is chosen, researchers must decide whether to use questions that are open-ended or that have multiple choices, two choices, or perhaps represent a scale.

• Open-ended
question

Question that respondents
are free to answer in their
own words rather than
being limited to choosing
from among a set of
alternatives.

Open-Ended Questions Respondents are free to reply to **open-ended questions** in their own words rather than being limited to choosing from a set of alternatives. The following are examples:

_____

[12]James E. Reinmuth and Michael D. Geurts, "The Collection of Sensitive Information Using a Two-Stage Randomized Response Model," *Journal of Marketing Research,* 12 (November 1975), pp. 402–407. For an elementary overview of the randomized-response model, see Cathy Campbell and Brian L. Joiner, "How to Get the Answer Without Being Sure You've Asked the Question," *American Statistician,* 26 (December 1973), pp. 229–231. For reviews of its use, see D. G. Horvitz, B. G. Greenberg, and J. R. Abernathy, "Randomized Response: A Data Gathering Device for Sensitive Questions," *International Statistical Review* (August 1976), pp. 181–195; and Paul E. Tracy and James Alan Fox, "The Validity of Randomized Response for Sensitive Measurements," *American Sociological Review,* 46 (April 1981), pp. 187–200. For discussion of randomization devices and methodologies for self-administered and telephone interview applications of the randomized response method, see Donald E. Stem, Jr., and R. Kirk Steinhorst, "Telephone Interview and Mail Questionnaire Applications of the Randomized Response Model," *Journal of the American Statistical Association,* 79 (September 1984), pp. 555–564.

How old are you? _____

Do you think laws requiring passengers in motor vehicles to wear seat belts are needed? _____

Who sponsors the Monday night football games? _____

Do you intend to purchase an automobile this year? _____

Why did you purchase a Zenith brand color television set? _____

Do you own a sewing machine? _____

These questions span the gamut of the types of primary data that could be collected from demographic characteristics, through attitudes and intentions, and behavior. The open-ended question is indeed a versatile device.

Open-ended questions are often used to begin a questionnaire. The general feeling is that it is best to proceed from the general to the specific in constructing questionnaires. So an opening question like, "When you think of television sets, which brands come to mind?" gives some insight into the respondent's frame of reference and could be most helpful in interpreting the individual's replies to later questions. The open-ended question is also often used to probe for additional information. The probes "Why do you feel that way? Please explain" are often used to seek elaboration of a respondent's reply.

In a fixed-alternative format, respondents choose their answer from a predetermined number of responses. Researchers generally use one of three types of fixed-alternative formats.

• **Multichotomous question**

Fixed-alternative question in which respondents are asked to choose the alternative that most closely corresponds to their position on the subject.

Multichotomous Questions Despite the daunting name, every college student is probably familiar with the **multichotomous question.** From grade school to graduate school, students answer questions in the same format on multiple-choice exams. In a multichotomous question, respondents are asked to choose the one alternative from several choices that most closely reflects their position on the subject. Table 10.2, for example, presents some of the open-ended questions in the preceding list as multichotomous questions. Respondents would be instructed to check the box or boxes that apply.

The examples in Table 10.2 illustrate some of the difficulties encountered in using multiple-choice questions. None of the alternatives in the seat belt question, for example, may correctly capture the respondent's true feeling on the issue. The individual's opinion may be more complex. He may feel that seat belts should be required on school buses but not in private vehicles. Or she may think that seat belts should be required but that tickets for noncompliance should be issued only in conjunction with another traffic violation. The multiple-choice question does not permit individuals to elaborate their true position but requires them to condense their complex attitude into a single statement. Of course, a well-designed series of multiple-choice questions could allow for such elaborations. Researchers must be careful, however, not to allow so many possible choices that the questionnaire becomes too long to be used effectively.

The seat belt question also illustrates a general problem in question design: should respondents be provided with a "don't know" or "no opinion" option? If a respondent truly does not know an answer, or has no opinion on an issue, he or she should obviously be allowed to state so. But should the option be *explicitly* provided to the respondent in the form of a "don't know" or "no opinion" category by asking a filter question like "Do you have an opinion on . . . "? The arguments about the desirability of a neutral point or "no opinion" category center on the need

Table 10.2   Examples of Multichotomous Questions

Age

How old are you?

☐ Less than 20
☐ 20–29
☐ 30–39
☐ 40–49
☐ 50–59
☐ 60 or over

Seat Belt Legislation

Do you think laws requiring passengers in motor vehicles to wear seat belts are needed?

☐ Definitely needed
☐ Probably needed
☐ Probably not needed
☐ Definitely not needed
☐ No opinion

Television Purchase

Why did you purchase a Zenith brand color TV?

☐ Price was lower than other alternatives
☐ Feel it represents the highest quality
☐ Availability of local service
☐ Availability of a service contract
☐ Picture is better
☐ Warranty was better
☐ Other

---

for data accuracy versus the desire to have as many respondents as possible answer the question at issue.

Those against including a "no opinion" answer argue that most respondents are unlikely to be truly neutral on an issue. Instead of providing them an easy way out, they say, it is much better to have them think about the issue so that they can frame their preference, however slight it may be. That tact is much better than allowing the researcher to infer the majority opinion from the responses of those taking a stand on the issue. The argument for including a neutral or "no opinion" category among the responses claims that forcing a respondent to make a choice when his or her preference is fuzzy or nonexistent simply introduces response error into the results. Further, it makes it harder for respondents to answer, and it may turn them off to the whole survey. The jury is still out with respect to which form better captures respondents' true position on an issue. There is no question, however, that the two alternatives can produce widely differing proportions regarding the number holding a neutral view, potentially in the range of 10 to 50 percent.[13]

For example, in one fairly large study using four-point versus five-point purchase-intention scales, which were the same except for the provision of the neutral category in the five-point scale, it was found that if one used only the extreme points (i.e., definitely will buy/definitely will not buy) for evaluating a new product or idea, *either* scale could be used. On the other hand, the researcher who wanted to use two categories as the percentage likely to buy the product (i.e., definitely will buy or probably will buy) would find a difference in the two scales, with the four-point scale providing more positive responses than the five-point scale.[14]

The television set purchase question illustrates a number of problems associated with multiple-choice questions. First, the list of reasons cited for purchasing a Zenith

---

[13]Kalton and Schuman, "The Effect of the Question on Survey Responses: A Review," pp. 51–52.

[14]Gregory J. Spagna, "Questionnaires: Which Approach Do You Use?" *Journal of Advertising Research,* 24 (February/March 1984), pp. 67–70.

color television may not exhaust the reasons that could have been used by the respondent. The person may have purchased a Zenith out of loyalty to a friend who owns the local Zenith distributorship or because she really supports the "buy locally" plea advanced by many small-town chambers of commerce. The "other" response category attempts to solve this problem. If a great many respondents check the "other" category, however, they could render the study useless. Thus, the burden is on the researcher to make the list of alternatives in a multiple-choice question exhaustive. This may entail a good deal of prior research into the phenomenon that is to serve as the subject of a multiple-choice question.

Unless the respondent is instructed to check all alternatives that apply, or is to rank the alternatives in order of importance, the multiple-choice question also demands that the alternatives be mutually exclusive. The income categories of $5,000–$10,000 and $10,000–$15,000 violate this principle. A respondent with an income of $10,000 would not know which alternative to check. A legitimate response with respect to the color television purchase question might include several of the alternatives listed. The respondent thought the picture, warranty, and price were all more attractive on the Zenith than they were on other makes. Thus, the instructions would necessarily have to be "Check the most important reason," "Check all those reasons that apply," or "Rank all the reasons that apply from most important to least important."

A third difficulty with the television purchase question is its great number of alternative responses. The list should be exhaustive. Yet the number of alternative statements an individual can process simultaneously appears to be limited. In one early study, the researchers presented each respondent with a card with six alternative statements. After each respondent had made his or her choice, the card was immediately replaced with another. On the second card, two of the six statements had been changed, and one statement from the original list was omitted. Yet only one-half of the respondents "could identify the changes and a mere handful located the omission."[15] The meaning of all this is that in designing multiple-choice questions the researcher should remain aware of human beings' limited data-processing capabilities. Perhaps a series of questions is more appropriate than one question. If there are a great many alternatives to a single question, then they should be shown to respondents using cards, and not simply read to them.

The fourth weakness of the television purchase question is that it is susceptible to an order bias. Respondents have a tendency to check either the first or last statement on a list with a somewhat heavier concentration of replies on the first.[16] The recommended procedure for combating this order bias is to prepare several forms of the questionnaire, or several cards, if cards are used to list the alternatives. The order in which the alternatives are listed is then altered from form to form. If each alternative appears once at the extremes of the list, once in the middle, and once somewhere in between, the researcher can feel reasonably comfortable that the possible effects of position bias have been neutralized.[17]

[15]Hadley Cantril and Edreta Fried, *Gauging Public Opinion* (Princeton, N.J.: Princeton University Press, 1944), chap. 1, as reported in Payne, *The Art of Asking Questions,* p. 93. For a discussion of people's limited information-processing abilities, see Jacob Jacoby, "Perspectives on Information Overload," *Journal of Consumer Research,* 10 (March 1984), pp. 432–435.

[16]Payne, *The Art of Asking Questions,* p. 84. This tendency to reply at the extremes is reversed when numbers are attached to the alternatives. Then respondents tend to choose an alternative near the middle of the list.

[17]Although it is commonly done, Niels J. Blunch, "Position Bias in Multiple-Choice Questions," *Journal of Marketing Research,* 21 (May 1984), pp. 216–220, argues to the contrary that position bias in multiple-choice questions cannot be eliminated by rotating the order of the alternatives.

Dichotomous Questions Also a fixed-alternative question, the **dichotomous question** is one in which there are only two alternatives listed, as in the following examples:

Do you think laws requiring passengers in motor vehicles to wear seat belts are needed?

☐   Yes
☐   No

Do you intend to purchase an automobile this year?

☐   Yes
☐   No

We have already seen how the first of these questions could also be handled as a multiple-choice question. The second could also be given a multichotomous structure. Instead of simply presenting the yes-no alternatives, the list could be framed as "definitely intend to buy," "probably will buy," "definitely intend not to buy," and "undecided." Dichotomous questions can often be framed as multichotomous questions, and vice versa. (The two possess similar advantages and disadvantages, which were reviewed earlier when discussing structured questions. They will not be repeated here.) The dichotomous question offers the ultimate in ease of coding and tabulation, and this probably accounts for its being the most commonly used type of question in communication studies.

One special problem with the dichotomous question is that the response can well depend on how the question is framed. This is true, of course, of all questions, but with the dichotomous question it represents a special problem. Consider two alternative questions:

Do you think that gasoline will be more expensive or less expensive next year than it is now?

☐   More expensive
☐   Less expensive

Do you think that gasoline will be less expensive or more expensive next year than it is now?

☐   Less expensive
☐   More expensive

Now the questions appear identical, and certainly we might want to expand each to include categories for "no opinion" and "about the same." The fact remains, though, that the two questions will elicit different responses.[18] The simple switching of the positions of "more expensive" or "less expensive" can affect the response an individual gives. Which then is the correct wording?

One generally accepted procedure for combating this order bias is to employ a split ballot. One phrasing is used on one-half of the questionnaires, and the alternative phrasing is employed on the other one-half of the questionnaires. The averaged percentages from the two forms should then cancel out any biases.

Scales Another type of fixed-alternative question is the question that employs a scale to capture the response. For instance, when inquiring about the various sewing machine features that home seamstresses use, the following question might be asked:

---

[18]Two of the best discussions of this are to be found in Payne, *The Art of Asking Questions,* and Howard Schuman and Stanley Presser, *Questions and Answers in Attitude Surveys* (Orlando: Academic Press, 1981), especially pp. 56–77.

How often do you use the zigzag stitch on your machine?

☐   Never
☐   Occasionally
☐   Sometimes
☐   Often

In this form, the question is a multichotomous question. However, the responses also represent a scale of use. The scale nature of the question would be more obvious perhaps if the following form were used to secure the replies:

Never	Occasionally	Sometimes	Often

The advantage of this scheme is that the descriptors or categories could be presented at the top of the page, and a number of possible features could be listed along the left margin, for example, decorative stitch, blind stitch, built-in button holer, and so on. The respondent would then be instructed to designate the frequency of use for each feature. The instruction would only need to be given once at the beginning, and thus a great deal of information could be secured from the respondent in a short period of time.

Step 5: Determine Wording of Each Question

Step 5 in the questionnaire development process involves the phrasing of each question. This is a critical task, in that poor phrasing of a question can cause respondents to refuse to answer it even though they agreed to cooperate in the study. Poor phrasing may also cause respondents to answer a question incorrectly, either on purpose or because of misunderstanding. The first condition, known as **item nonresponse,** can create a great many problems in analyzing the data. The second condition produces measurement error in that the recorded or obtained score does not equal the respondent's true score on the issue.[19]

Experienced researchers know that the phrasing of a question can directly affect the responses to it. One humorous anecdote in this regard involves two priests, a Dominican and a Jesuit, who are discussing whether it is a sin to smoke and pray at the same time. "After failing to reach a conclusion, each goes off to consult his respective superior. The next week they meet again. The Dominican says, 'Well, what did your superior say?' The Jesuit responds, 'He said it was all right.' 'That's funny,' the Dominican replies, 'my superior said it was a sin.' Jesuit: 'What did you ask him?' Reply: 'I asked him if it was all right to smoke while praying.' 'Oh,' says the Jesuit, 'I asked my superior if it was all right to pray while smoking.' "[20]

While researchers recognize that question wording can affect the answers obtained, there are, unfortunately, few basic principles researchers can rely upon to develop bias-free ways of framing a question. Instead, the literature is replete with rules of thumb. Although these rules of thumb are often easier to state than to practice, researchers need to be aware of them.

Use Simple Words   Because most researchers are more highly educated than the typical questionnaire respondent, they tend to use words familiar to them but not understood by many respondents. This is a difficult problem because it is not easy

♦ Item nonresponse

Source of nonsampling error that arises when a respondent agrees to an interview but refuses or is unable to answer specific questions.

---

[19]For a review of the literature on the quality of questionnaire data, including item omission, see Robert A. Peterson and Roger A. Kerin, "The Quality of Self-Report Data: Review and Synthesis," in Ben Enis and Kenneth Roering, eds., *Annual Review of Marketing 1981* (Chicago: American Marketing Association, 1981), pp. 5–20.

[20]Sudman and Bradburn, *Asking Questions*, p. 1.

Research Window 10.1

A Rogue's Gallery of Problem Words

"Use Simple Words!" "Use unambiguous words!" Students of questionnaire design are accustomed to hearing those rules cited loudly and often. But, unfortunately, some of the simplest words may still be ambiguous in meaning. Here's a short list of words that may cause trouble if you're not sensitive to their possibilities for misinterpretation.

You

"You" is extremely popular with question worders since it is implicated in every question they ask. In most cases "you" gives no trouble, since it is clear that it refers to the second person singular. However, and here is the problem, the word sometimes may have a collective meaning. Consider the question:

> How many television sets did you repair last month?

The question seems to be straightforward, until it was asked of a repairman in a large shop, who counters with, "Who do you mean, me or the whole shop?"

Sometimes "you" needs the emphasis of "you, yourself," and sometimes it just isn't the word to use, as in the above situation where the entire shop was meant.

All

"All" is one of those dead-giveaway words. From your own experience with true-false exams, you probably know that it is safe to count almost every all-inclusive statement as false. That is, you have learned in such tests that it is safe to follow the idea that all statements containing "all" are false, including this one. Some people have the same negative reaction to opinion questions that hinge upon all-inclusive or all-exclusive words.

They may be generally in agreement with a proposition, but nevertheless hesitate to accept the extreme idea of *all, always, each, every, never, nobody, only, none,* or *sure.*

Bad

In itself the word "bad" is not at all bad for question wording. It conveys the meaning desired and is satisfactory as an alternative in a "good or bad" two-way question. Experience seems to indicate, however, that people are generally less willing to criticize than they are to praise. Since it is difficult to get them to state their negative views, sometimes the critical side needs to be softened. For example, after asking, "What things are good about your job?" it might seem perfectly natural to ask, "What things are bad about it?" But if we want to lean over backwards to get as many criticisms as we can, we may be wise not to apply the "bad" stigma, but to ask, "What things are not so good about it?"

Dinner

"Dinner," the main meal of the day, comes at noon with some families and in some areas. Elsewhere it is the evening meal. The question should not assume that it is either the one or the other.

Government

"Government" is one of those words heavily loaded with emotional concepts. It is sometimes used as a definite word meaning the federal gov-

Source: Stanley L. Payne, *The Art of Asking Questions* (Princeton: Princeton University Press, 1979), pp. 158–176.

ernment, sometimes as an inclusive term for federal, state, and local government, sometimes as an abstract idea, and sometimes as the party in power as distinct from the opposition party. The trouble is that the respondent does not always know which "government" is meant. One person may have a different idea from another. It is best to specify if we want all respondents to answer with the same government in mind.

Like

"Like" is on the problem list only because it is sometimes used to introduce an example. The problem with bringing an example into a question is that the respondent's attention may be directed toward the particular example and away from the general issue which it is meant only to illustrate. The use of examples may sometimes be necessary, but the possible hazard should always be kept in mind. The choice of an example can affect the answers to the question—in fact, it may materially change the question, as in these two examples:

Do you think that leafy vegetables like spinach should be in the daily diet?

Do you think that leafy vegetables like lettuce should be in the daily diet?

Where

The frames of reference in answers to a "where" question may vary greatly. Consider the possible answers from this simple question:

Where did you read that?

Three of the many possible answers are

In the *New York Times*.
At home in front of the fire.
In an advertisement.

Despite the seemingly wide variety of these three answers, some respondents could probably have stated them all: "In an ad in the *New York Times* while I was at home sitting in front of the fire."

When designing a questionnaire, one must be aware of words like "dinner," that mean one thing to some people (the noon meal in this case) and something else to others (the evening meal).

Source: Grant Wood, American, 1891–1942; Dinner for Threshers, 1934; Oil on masonite, 20″ × 81″. Gift of Mr. and Mrs. John D. Rockefeller 3rd, 1979.7.105. Reproduced by permission of The Fine Arts Museums of San Francisco.

to dismiss what one knows and put oneself instead in the respondent's shoes when trying to determine appropriate vocabulary. A significant proportion of the population, for example, does not understand the word *Caucasian,* although most researchers do.[21] The researcher needs to be constantly aware that the average person in the United States has a high school, not a college, education and that many people have difficulty in coping with such routine tasks as making change, reading job notices, or completing a driver's license application blank. The best advice is to keep the words simple.

Avoid Ambiguous Words and Questions   Not only should the words and questions be simple, they should also be unambiguous. Consider again the multichotomous question:

How often do you use the zigzag stitch on your machine?

- ☐   Never
- ☐   Occasionally
- ☐   Sometimes
- ☐   Often

For all practical purposes, the replies to this question would be worthless. The words *occasionally, sometimes,* and *often* are ambiguous. For example, to one respondent, the word *often* might mean "every time I sew." To another it might mean, "yes, I use it when I have the specific need. This happens on about one of every four projects." Thus, while the question would get answers, it would generate little real understanding of the frequency of use of the zigzag stitch. A much better strategy would be to provide concrete alternatives for the respondent, such as the following:

- ☐   Never use
- ☐   Use on approximately one of ten projects
- ☐   Use on approximately one of three projects
- ☐   Use on almost every project

Another way to avoid ambiguity in asking about the frequency of behavior is to ask when the behavior last occurred. Our earlier question might be framed in the following way, for example:

When you last sewed, did you use the zigzag stitch?

- ☐   Yes
- ☐   No
- ☐   Can't recall

The proportion responding yes would then be used to infer the frequency with which the zigzag stitch was used, while the follow-up question among all those responding yes, "For what purpose?" would give insight as to how respondents are using it. Among the people responding, there will be some who normally use the zigzag stitch but did not use it the last time they sewed. There will be others who do not normally use that particular stitch but did use it the last time they sewed.

---

[21]Alan E. Bayer, "Construction of a Race Item for Survey Research," *Public Opinion Quarterly,* 36 (Winter 1972–1973), p. 596. Payne, *The Art of Asking Questions,* has a list of the recommended words, while John O'Brien, "How Do Market Researchers Ask Questions?" *Journal of the Market Research Society,* 26 (April 1984), pp. 93–107, reports on the relative frequency with which Payne's recommended words are used on a sample of British questionnaires.

These variations should cancel each other out if a large enough sample of respondents is used.

The total sample should provide a good indication of the proportion of times the zigzag stitch is used, and for what purposes. The researcher, in effect, relies on the sample to provide insight into how frequently the phenomenon occurs, rather than on a specific question that may contain ambiguous alternatives. In such cases it is important that the sample be large enough so that the proportions can be estimated with the appropriate degree of confidence.

Avoid Leading Questions A question framed so as to give the respondent a clue as to how he or she should answer is a **leading question.** Consider the question:

Do you feel that limiting taxes by law is an effective way to stop the government from picking your pocket every payday?

<table>
<tr><td>☐</td><td>Yes</td></tr>
<tr><td>☐</td><td>No</td></tr>
<tr><td>☐</td><td>Undecided</td></tr>
</table>

This was one of three questions in an unsolicited questionnaire that the author received as part of a study sponsored by the National Tax Limitation Committee. The committee intended to make the results of the poll available to Congress and to state legislators. Given the implied purpose, it is probably not surprising to see the leading words "picking your pocket" being used in this question, or the leading word "gouge" being used in another question. What is especially unfortunate is that it is unlikely the questions themselves accompanied the report to Congress. Rather, it is more likely that the report suggested that some high percentage, e.g., 90 percent of those surveyed, favored laws that limited taxes. Conclusion: Congress should pay attention to the wishes of the people and pass such laws.

One sees instances of this phenomenon every day in the newspaper. The public is treated to a discussion of the results of this or that study with respect to how the American people feel on issues but is not shown the questionnaire. One interesting report in this regard was published during New York City's financial crisis.

> Question: What percentage of the American public favors federal aid for New York City?
> Choose one of the following: a. 69; b. 55; c. 42; d. 15; e. all of the above.
> Answer: All of the above.
> One apparent key to the different responses was whether the aid was described as a "bailout," "federal funds," or "the federal government guaranteeing loans."[22]

The correct phrasing of this or almost any question could of course be argued. The important point for both researchers and managers to remember is that the phrasing finally chosen will affect the responses secured. If one truly wants an accurate picture of the situation, one needs to avoid leading the respondent as to how he or she should answer.

Avoid Implicit Alternatives An alternative that is not expressed in the options is an **implicit alternative.** In one study, researchers wanted to know the attitudes of nonworking housewives toward the the idea of having a job outside the home. They asked two random samples of housewives the following two questions:[23]

• Leading question

A question framed so as to give the respondent a clue as to how he or she should answer.

• Implicit alternative

An alternative answer to a question that is not expressed in the options.

[22]"Why the Polls Get Differing Results on Aid to New York," *Capital Times* (November 8, 1975), p. 2.

[23]E. Noelle-Neumann, "Wanted: Rules for Wording Structured Questionnaires," *Public Opinion Quarterly,* 34 (Summer 1970), p. 200.

- ***Would you like to have a job, if this were possible?***
- ***Would you prefer to have a job, or do you prefer to do just your housework?***

While the two questions appear very similar, they produced dramatically different responses. In the first version, 19 percent of the housewives said they would not like to have a job. In the second version, 68 percent said they would prefer not to have one, over three and one-half times as many. The difference in the two questions is that the second version makes explicit the alternative only implied in the first version. As a general rule, one should avoid implicit alternatives unless there is a special reason for including them. Thus, the second version is better than the first. Further, because the order in which the alternatives appear can affect the responses, one should rotate the order of the options in samples of questionnaires.

Avoid Implicit Assumptions   Questions are frequently framed so that there is an **implicit assumption** as to what will happen as a consequence. The question, "Are you in favor of placing price controls on crude oil?" will elicit different responses from individuals, depending on whether they think price controls will result in rationing, long lines at the pump, or lower prices. A better way of stating this question is to make explicit the possible consequence(s). For example, the question could be altered to ask, "Are you in favor of placing price controls on crude oil if it would produce gas rationing?"

Avoid Generalizations and Estimates   Questions should always be asked in specific rather than general terms. Consider the question: "How many salespeople did you see last year?" which might be asked of a purchasing agent. To answer the question, the agent would probably estimate how many salespeople call in a typical week and would multiply this estimate by 52. This burden should not be placed on the agent. Rather, a more accurate estimate would be obtained if the purchasing agent were asked, "How many representatives called last week?" and the researcher multiplied the answer provided by 52.

Avoid Double-Barreled Questions   A question that calls for two responses and thereby creates confusion for the respondent is a **double-barreled question.** The question, "What is your evaluation of the price and convenience offered by catalog showrooms?" is asking respondents to react to two separate attributes by which such showrooms could be described. The respondent might feel the prices are attractive, but the location is not, for example, and thereby is placed in a dilemma as to how to respond. The problem is particularly acute if the individual must choose an answer from a fixed set of alternatives. One can and should avoid double-barreled questions by splitting the initial question into two separate questions. A useful indicator that two questions might be needed is the use of the word *and* in the initial wording of the question.

• Implicit assumption

A problem that occurs when a question is not framed so as to explicitly state the consequences, and thus it elicits different responses from individuals who *assume* different consequences.

• Double-barreled question

A question that calls for two responses and thereby creates confusion for the respondent.

Step 6: Determine Question Sequence

Once the form of response and specific wording for each question have been decided, the researcher is ready to begin putting them together into a questionnaire. The researcher needs to recognize immediately that the order in which the questions are presented can be crucial to the success of the research effort. Again, there are no hard-and-fast principles but only rules of thumb to guide the researcher in this activity.

Use Simple and Interesting Opening Questions The first questions asked the respondent are crucial. If respondents cannot answer them easily or if they find them uninteresting or threatening in any way, they may refuse to complete the remainder of the questionnaire. Thus, it is essential that the first few questions be simple, interesting, and in no way threatening to respondents. Questions that ask respondents for their opinion on some issue are often good openers, as most people like to feel their opinion is important. Sometimes it is helpful to use such an opener even when responses to it will not be analyzed, since opinion questions are often effective in relaxing respondents and securing their cooperation.

• Funnel approach

An approach to question sequencing that gets its name from its shape, starting with broad questions and progressively narrowing down the scope.

Use Funnel Approach One approach to question sequencing is the **funnel approach,** which gets its name from its shape, starting with broad questions and progressively narrowing down the scope. If respondents are to be asked, "What improvements are needed in the company's service policy?" and also, "How do you like the quality of service?" the first question needs to be asked before the second. Otherwise, quality of service will be emphasized disproportionately in the responses simply because it is fresh in the respondents' minds.

There should also be some logical order to the questions. This means that sudden changes in topics and jumping around from topic to topic should be avoided. Transitional devices are sometimes necessary to smooth the flow when a change in subject matter occurs. Sometimes researchers will insert filter questions as a way to change the direction of the questioning. Most often, however, researchers will insert a brief explanation as a way of bridging a change in subject matter.

• Branching question

A technique used to direct respondents to different places in a questionnaire based on their response to the question at hand.

Design Branching Questions with Care A direction as to where to go next in the questionnaire based on the answer to a preceding question is called a **branching question.** For example, the initial question might be, "Have you bought a car within the last six months?" If the respondent answers yes, he or she is then instructed to go to another place in the questionnaire, where questions are asked about specific details of the purchase. Someone replying no to the same question would be directed to skip the question relating to the details of the purchase. The advantage to branching questions is that they reduce the number of alternatives that are needed in individual questions, while ensuring that those respondents capable of supplying the needed information still have an opportunity to do so. Those for whom a question is irrelevant are simply directed around it.

Branching questions and directions are much easier to develop for telephone or personal interviews than for mail surveys. With mail questionnaires the number of branching questions needs to be kept to an absolute minimum so that respondents do not become confused when responding, or refuse to cooperate because the task becomes too difficult. While they can be used more liberally with telephone and personal interview surveys, branching questions still need to be designed with care, since the evidence indicates that branching instructions increase the rate of item nonresponse for items immediately following the branch.[24] When using branching questions, it is generally good practice to (1) develop a flow chart of the logical possibilities and then prepare the branching questions and instructions to follow the flow chart, (2) place the question that follows the branch as close as possible to the original question so as to minimize the amount of page-flipping that is necessary,

[24]Donald J. Messmer and Daniel J. Seymour, "The Effects of Branching on Item Nonresponse," *Public Opinion Quarterly,* 46 (Summer 1982), pp. 270–277.

and (3) order the branching questions so that respondents cannot anticipate what additional information is required.[25]

The last point can be illustrated by a questionnaire seeking information about small appliance ownership. A skillfully designed questionnaire might begin by asking if a respondent owns any of a certain list of small appliances. If she answers yes to any, the researcher may then go on to ask the brand name, the store where purchased, and so on, of each. If instead the researcher had begun by asking, "Do you own a food processor?" and followed up with questions about brand, price, and so on, the respondent would soon recognize that "yes" answers to subsequent questions about appliance ownership would inevitably lead to many other questions and may decide it is less taxing to say no in the first place.

Ask for Classification Information Last   The typical questionnaire contains two types of information: basic information and classification information. Basic information refers to the subject of the study, for example, intentions or attitudes of respondents. Classification information refers to the other data we collect to classify respondents so as to extract more information about the phenomenon of interest.

---

[25]Sudman and Bradburn, *Asking Questions*, pp. 223–227.

Back to the Case

It had been a month since Karen Clark had begun working on the Wallach's questionnaire. She was surprised at how complicated such a seemingly simple project had been. After revising the survey's format, structure, and length, she had had to redraft each of the questions several times to eliminate ambiguous language, to avoid implicit assumptions, and to try not to tip off the respondent as to the answer she expected. It was hard work.

All that was left was to draft some questions asking for demographic characteristics. Karen was careful to write a question asking for income information using a scale. She followed that with a question about how much the family spent on groceries each week, and another asking about the use of food stamps.

These were important questions, and Karen was inclined to have interviewers ask them early in the study, but she thought she better run the idea by Susan first.

"Not a chance, Karen," said Susan upon hearing Karen's plan. "You'll be lucky to have these tired women talk to you at all, let alone tell you their intimate financial information right off the bat. First get the basic information we need for the study. Once the respondent is comfortable talking, then try to slip in a question about finances. And for goodness sake, save any sensitive questions for last!"

Susan has pointed out one of the primary principles governing questionnaire design. First present questions that relate to basic information, then ask those that seek classification information. The basic information is the meat of the study. Without it, there is no study.

Researchers should also avoid asking personal questions that may alienate the respondent until after the essential questions have been asked. Otherwise the respondent may refuse to answer further questions, and the interview will be lost. Research has found that respondents are also more likely to answer sensitive questions later in the interview after they have become comfortable with the interviewer and the interviewing process.

For instance, we might be interested in determining if a respondent's attitudes toward the need for seat belt legislation are in any way affected by the person's income. Income here would be a classification variable. Demographic/socioeconomic characteristics of respondents are often used as classification variables for understanding the results.

The proper questionnaire sequence is to present questions securing basic information first and those seeking classification information last. There is a logical reason for this. The basic information is most critical. Without it, there is no study. Thus, the researcher should not risk alienating the respondent by asking a number of personal questions before getting to the heart of the study, since it is not unusual for personal questions to alienate respondents most. Respondents who readily offer their opinions about television programming may balk when asked for their income. An early question aimed at determining their income may affect the whole tone of the interview or other communication. It is best to avoid this possibility by placing the classification information at the end.

Place Difficult or Sensitive Questions Late in the Questionnaire The basic information itself can also present some sequence problems. Some of the questions may be sensitive. Early questions should not be, for the reasons we mentioned earlier. If respondents feel threatened, they may refuse to participate in the study. Thus, sensitive questions should be placed in the body of the questionnaire and intertwined and hidden among some not-so-sensitive ones. Once respondents have become involved in the study, they are less likely to react negatively or refuse to answer when delicate questions are posed.

Step 7: Determine Physical Characteristics of Questionnaire

The physical characteristics of the questionnaire can affect the accuracy of the replies that are obtained. In one study, researchers asked consumers if they had purchased certain products. If they answered yes, they were then asked the specific brand of the product they had purchased. Two versions of the question seeking brand information were used, Form A and Form B. The only significant difference in the questions was that a set of parentheses was provided in Form B for the "other brand" category, whereas Form A had a line where respondents wrote in the name of those brands not on the original list. The difference in results regarding the percentage of households owning the two brands, F and G, among the 4,000 households surveyed was remarkable, as Table 10.3 indicates. Form B results were within a couple of percentage points of the results from the survey conducted one year earlier. It seems that respondents counted up from the bottom of the question when checking the brand category, and that the line on which the other brand was to be entered in Form A was too close to the ruled line separating this question from the next one.[26] In sum, the physical layout in Form A created confusion and produced inaccurate data.

The physical characteristics of a questionnaire can also affect how respondents react to it and the ease with which the replies can be processed. In determining the physical format of the questionnaire, a researcher wants to do those things that help get the respondent to accept the questionnaire, and facilitate handling and control by the researcher.

[26]Charles S. Mayer and Cindy Piper, "A Note on the Importance of Layout in Self-Administered Questionnaires," *Journal of Marketing Research,* 19 (August 1982), pp. 390–391.

Table 10.3   Brand Share among Owners

	Percentage Owning Brand		
	Form A	Form B	Net Difference
Product X			
Brand F	30	3	27
Brand G	47	71	24
Product Y			
Brand F	18	2	16
Brand G	27	41	14
Product Z			
Brand F	27	3	24
Brand G	35	58	23

Securing Acceptance of the Questionnaire The physical appearance of the questionnaire can influence respondents' cooperation. This is particularly true with mail questionnaires, but it applies as well to questionnaires used in personal interviews. If the questionnaire looks sloppy, respondents are likely to feel the study is unimportant and hence refuse to cooperate despite researchers' assurance that it is important. If the study is important, and there is no reason to conduct it if it is not, make the questionnaire reflect that importance. This means that good quality paper should be used for the questionnaires. It also means that the questionnaires should be printed, not mimeographed or otherwise photocopied.

It is also a good idea to include the name of the sponsoring organization and the name of the project on the first page or on the cover if the questionnaire is in book form. Both of these lend credibility to the study. However, since awareness of the sponsoring firm may bias respondents' answers, many firms use fictitious names for the sponsoring organization. This practice also helps eliminate phone calls or other inquiries from respondents asking for the results of the study.

Facilitate Handling and Control Several steps that facilitate handling and control by the researcher also contribute to acceptance of the questionnaire by respondents. These include questionnaire size and layout and question sequencing.

Questionnaire size is important.[27] Smaller questionnaires are better than larger ones if—and this is a big "if"—they do not appear crowded. Smaller questionnaires seem easier to complete; they appear to take less time and are less likely to cause respondents to refuse to participate. They are easier to carry in the field and are easier to sort, count, and file in the office than are larger questionnaires.

If, on the other hand, smaller size is gained at the expense of an uncluttered appearance, these advantages are lost. A crowded questionnaire has a bad appear-

[27]A. Regula Herzog and Jerald G. Bachman, "Effects of Questionnaire Length on Response Quality," *Public Opinion Quarterly,* 45 (Winter 1981), pp. 549–559.

ance, leads to errors in data collection, and results in shorter and less informative replies for both self-administered and interviewer-administered questionnaires. Researchers have found, for example, that the more lines or space left for recording the response to open-ended questions, the more extensive the reply will be. Similarly, the more information a respondent is given about the kind of information being sought, the better the reply is apt to be.[28] Both of these techniques, however, increase the physical size of the questionnaire needed for the study.

While post-card size probably represents the lower limit, letter size probably represents the upper limit to the size of an individual page in a questionnaire. When the questions will not all fit on the front and back of one sheet, multiple sheets need to be used. When this happens, one should make the questionnaire into a booklet rather than stapling or paper clipping the pages together. The method of binding not only facilitates handling but also reinforces an image of quality. So does numbering the questions, which also promotes respondent cooperation, particularly when branching questions are employed. Without numbered questions, instructions as to how to proceed, e.g., "If the answer to Question 2 is yes, please go to Question 5," cannot be used. Even with numbered questions, though, it is helpful if the respondent can be directed by arrows to the appropriate next question after a branching question. Another technique researchers have found useful with branch-type questions is the use of color coding on the questionnaire, where the next question to which the respondent is directed matches the color of the space in which the answer to the branching or filter question was recorded.

Numbering the questions also makes it easier to edit, code, and tabulate the responses.[29] It also helps if the questionnaires themselves are numbered. This makes it easier to keep track of the questionnaires and to determine which ones, if any, are lost. It also makes it easier to monitor interviewer performance and to detect interviewer biases, if any. The research director will be able to develop a log listing which questionnaires were assigned to which interviewers. Mail questionnaires are an exception to the principle that the questionnaires themselves be numbered. Respondents often interpret an assigned number on a mail questionnaire as a mechanism by which their responses can be identified. The accompanying loss in anonymity is threatening to many of them, and they may refuse to cooperate or even distort their answers.

Step 8: Reexamine and Revise Steps 1 through 7 If Necessary

A researcher should not expect that the first draft will result in a usable questionnaire. Rather, reexamination and revision are staples in questionnaire construction. Each question should be reviewed to ensure that the question is easy to answer and not confusing, ambiguous, or potentially offensive to the respondent. Neither should any question be leading or bias-inducing. How can one tell? An extremely critical attitude and good common sense should help. The researcher should examine each word in each question. The literature on question phrasing is replete with examples

---

[28]Charles F. Cannell, Lois Oksenberg, and Jean M. Converse, "Striving for Response Accuracy: Experiments in New Interviewing Techniques," *Journal of Marketing Research,* 14 (August 1977), pp. 306–315; Ed Blair, Seymour Sudman, Norman M. Bradburn, and Carol Stocking, "How to Ask Questions About Drinking and Sex: Response Effects in Measuring Consumer Behavior," *Journal of Marketing Research,* 14 (August 1977), pp. 316–321; and Andre Laurent, "Effects of Question Length on Reporting Behavior in the Survey Interview," *Journal of the American Statistical Association,* 67 (June 1972), pp. 298–305.

[29]These elementary steps, which are involved in the processing of all questionnaires, are discussed in Chapter 17.

of how some seemingly innocuous questions produced response problems.[30] When a potential problem is discovered, the question should be revised. After examining each question, and each word in each question, for its potential meanings and implications, the researcher might test the questionnaire in some role-playing situations, using others working on the project as subjects. This role playing should reveal some of the most serious shortcomings and should lead to further revision of the questionnaire.

Step 9: Pretest Questionnaire and Revise if Necessary

• Pretest

Use of a questionnaire (observation form) on a trial basis in a small pilot study to determine how well the questionnaire (observation form) works.

The real test of a questionnaire is how it performs under actual conditions of data collection. For this assessment, the questionnaire **pretest** is vital. The questionnaire pretest serves the same role in questionnaire design that test marketing serves in new product development. While the product concept, different advertising appeals, alternative packages, and so on, may all have been tested previously in the product development process, test marketing is the first place where they all come together. Thus, test marketing provides the real test of customer reactions to the product and the accompanying marketing program. Similarly, the pretest provides the real test of the questionnaire and the mode of administration.

Data collection should never begin without an adequate pretest of the questionnaire. The pretest can be used to assess both individual questions and their sequence.[31] It is best if there are two pretests. The first pretest should be done by personal interview, regardless of the actual mode of administration that will be used. An interviewer can watch to see if people actually remember data requested of them, or if some questions seem confusing or produce resistance or hesitancy among respondents for one reason or another. The pretest interviews should be conducted among respondents similar to those who will be used in the actual study, by the firm's most experienced interviewers.

The personal interview pretest should reveal some questions in which the wording could be improved or the sequence changed. If the changes are major, the revised questionnaire should again be pretested employing personal interviews. If the changes are minor, the questionnaire can be pretested a second time using mail, telephone, or personal interviews, whichever is going to be used for the full-scale study. This time though, less experienced interviewers should also be used in order to determine if typical interviewers will have any special problems with the questionnaire. The purpose of the second pretest is to uncover problems unique to the mode of administration.

Finally, the responses that result from the pretest should be coded and tabulated. We have previously discussed the need for the preparation of dummy tables prior to the development of the questionnaire. The tabulation of pretest responses can check on our conceptualization of the problem and the data and method of analysis necessary to answer it.

---

[30]Payne's book is particularly good in this regard. Chapter 13, for example, is devoted to the development of a passable question. When one considers that an entire chapter can be devoted to the development of one passable question (not a great question, mind you), one can appreciate the need for reexamining each question under a microscope for its potential implications. A condensed treatment of the things to be avoided in a question is to be found in Lyndon O. Brown and Leland L. Beik, *Marketing Research and Analysis,* 4th ed. (New York: Ronald, 1969), pp. 242–262. Sudman and Bradburn, *Asking Questions,* have recommendations specific to the type of question being asked (e.g., opinions versus demographic characteristics).

[31]An empirical examination of the usefulness of the pretest in uncovering various problems can be found in Shelby D. Hunt, Richard D. Sparkman, Jr., and James B. Wilcox, "The Pretest in Survey Research: Issues and Preliminary Findings," *Journal of Marketing Research,* 19 (May 1982), pp. 265–275.

[T]he tables will confirm the need for various sets of data. If we have no place to put the responses to a question, either the data are superfluous or we omitted some contemplated analysis. If some part of a table remains empty, we may have omitted a necessary question. Trial tabulations show us, as no previous method can, that all data collected will be put to use, and that we will obtain all necessary data.[32]

The researcher who avoids a questionnaire pretest and tabulation of replies is either naive or a fool. The pretest is the most inexpensive insurance the researcher can buy to ensure the success of the questionnaire and the research project. A careful pretest along with proper attention to the do's and don'ts presented in this chapter and summarized in Table 10.4 should make the questionnaire development process successful.

---

[32]Brown and Beik, *Marketing Research and Analysis,* pp. 265–266.

Table 10.4   Some Do's and Don'ts When Preparing Questionnaires

Step 1: Specify What Information Will Be Sought

1. Make sure that you have a clear understanding of the issue and what it is that you want to know (expect to learn). Frame your research questions, but refrain from writing questions for the questionnaire at this time.

2. Make a list of your research questions. Review them periodically as you are working on the questionnaire.

3. Use the "dummy tables" that were set up to guide the data analysis to suggest questions for the questionnaire.

4. Conduct a search for existing questions on the issue.

5. Revise existing questions on the issue, and prepare new questions that address the issues you plan to research.

Step 2: Determine Type of Questionnaire and Method of Administration

1. Use the type of data to be collected as a basis for deciding on the type of questionnaire.

2. Use degree of structure and disguise as well as cost factors to determine the method of administration.

3. Compare the special capabilities and limitations of each method of administration and the value of the data collected from each with the needs of the survey.

Step 3: Determine Content of Individual Questions

1. For each research question ask yourself, "Why do I want to know this?" Answer it in terms of how it will help your research. "It would be interesting to know" is not an acceptable answer.

2. Make sure each question is specific and addresses only one important issue.

3. Ask yourself whether the question applies to all respondents; it should, or provision should be made for skipping it.

4. Split questions that can be answered from different frames of reference into multiple questions, one corresponding to each frame of reference.

5. Ask yourself whether respondents will be informed about and can remember the issue that the question is dealing with.

6. Make sure the time period of the question is related to the importance of the topic. Consider using aided-recall techniques like diaries, records, or bounded recall.

7. Avoid questions that require excessive effort, that have hard-to-articulate answers, and that deal with embarrassing or threatening issues.

8. If threatening questions are necessary

   a. hide the questions among more innocuous ones.
   b. make use of a counterbiasing statement.
   c. phrase the question in terms of others and how they might feel or act.
   d. ask respondents if they have ever engaged in the undesirable activity, and then ask if they are presently engaging in such an activity.
   e. use categories or ranges rather than specific numbers.
   f. use the randomized-response model.

Step 4: Determine Form of Response to Each Question

1. Determine which type of question—open-ended, dichotomous, or multichotomous—provides data that fit the information needs of the project.

2. Use structured questions whenever possible.

3. Use open-ended questions that require short answers to begin a questionnaire.

4. Try to convert open-ended questions to closed (fixed) response questions to reduce respondent work load and coding effort for descriptive and causal studies.

continued

Table 10.4 *continued*

5. If open-ended questions are necessary, make the questions sufficiently directed to give respondents a frame of reference when answering.

6. When using dichotomous questions, state the negative or alternative side in detail.

7. Provide for "don't know," "no opinion," and "both" answers.

8. Be aware that there may be a middle ground.

9. Be sensitive to the mildness or harshness of the alternatives.

10. When using multichotomous questions, be sure the choices are exhaustive and mutually exclusive, and if combinations are possible, include them.

11. Be sure the range of alternatives is clear and that all reasonable alternative answers are included.

12. If the possible responses are very numerous, consider using more than one question to reduce the potential for information overload.

13. When using dichotomous or multichotomous questions, consider the use of a split ballot procedure to reduce order bias.

14. Clearly indicate if items are to be ranked or if only one item on the list is to be chosen.

Step 5: Determine Wording of Each Question
1. Use simple words.
2. Avoid ambiguous words and questions.
3. Avoid leading questions.
4. Avoid implicit alternatives.
5. Avoid implicit assumptions.
6. Avoid generalizations and estimates.
7. Use simple sentences and avoid compound sentences.
8. Change long, dependent clauses to words or short phrases.
9. Avoid double-barreled questions.
10. Make sure each question is as specific as possible.

Step 6: Determine Question Sequence
1. Use simple, interesting questions for openers.
2. Use the funnel approach, first asking broad questions and then narrowing them down.
3. Ask difficult or sensitive questions late in the questionnaire when rapport is better.
4. Follow chronological order when collecting historical information.
5. Complete questions about one topic before moving on to the next.

6. Prepare a flow chart whenever filter questions are being considered.
7. Ask filter questions before asking detailed questions.
8. Ask demographic questions last so that if respondent refuses, the other data are still usable.

Step 7: Determine Physical Characteristics of Questionnaire
1. Make sure the questionnaire looks professional and is relatively easy to answer.
2. Use quality paper and print; do not photocopy the questionnaire.
3. Attempt to make the questionnaire as short as possible while avoiding a crowded appearance.
4. Use a booklet format for ease of analysis and to prevent lost pages.
5. List the name of the organization conducting the survey on the first page.
6. Number the questions to ease data processing.
7. If the respondent must skip more than one question, use a "go to."
8. If the respondent must skip an entire section, consider color coding the sections.
9. State how the responses are to be reported, such as a check mark, number, circle, etc.

Step 8: Reexamine Steps 1–7 and Revise If Necessary
1. Examine each word of every question to ensure the question is not confusing, ambiguous, offensive, or leading.
2. Get peer evaluations of the draft questionnaire.

Step 9: Pretest Questionnaire and Revise If Necessary
1. Pretest the questionnaire first by personal interviews among respondents similar to those to be used in the actual study.
2. Obtain comments from the interviewers and respondents to discover any problems with the questionnaire, and revise it if necessary. When the revisions are substantial, repeat Steps 1 and 2 of the pretest.
3. Pretest the questionnaire by mail or telephone to uncover problems unique to the mode of administration.
4. Code and tabulate the pretest responses in dummy tables to determine if questions are providing adequate information.
5. Eliminate questions that do not provide adequate information, and revise questions that cause problems.

◆ Observational Forms

There are generally fewer problems in constructing observational forms than questionnaires, because the researcher is no longer concerned with the fact that the question and the way it is asked will affect the response. Through proper training of observers, the researcher can create the necessary expertise so that the data-collection instrument is handled consistently. Alternatively, the researcher may simply use a mechanical device to measure the behavior of interest and secure complete consistency in measurement. This is not to imply that observational forms offer no problems of construction. Rather, the researcher needs to make very explicit decisions about what is to be observed and the categories and units that will be used to record this behavior. Figure 10.3, which is the observation form used by a bank to evaluate the service provided by its employees having extensive customer contact, shows how detailed some of these decisions can be. In this case the observers acted as shoppers.

The statement that "one needs to determine what is to be observed before one can make a scientific observation" seems trite. Yet this is exactly the case. Almost any event can be described in a number of ways. When we watch someone making a cigarette purchase, we might report that (1) the person purchased one package of cigarettes, (2) the woman purchased one package of cigarettes, (3) the woman purchased a package of Tareyton cigarettes, (4) the woman purchased a package of Tareyton 100s, (5) the woman, after asking for and finding that the store was out of Virginia Slims, purchased a package of Tareyton 100s, and so on.

A great many additional variations are possible, such as adding the type, name, or location of the store where this behavior occurred. In order for this observation to be productive for scientific inquiry, we must predetermine which aspects of this behavior are relevant. In this particular example, the decision as to what to observe requires that the researcher specify the following:

- Who should be observed? Anyone entering the store? Anyone making a purchase? Anyone making a cigarette purchase?
- What aspects of the purchase should be reported? Which brand they purchased? Which brand they asked for first? Whether the purchase was of king size or regular cigarettes? What about the purchaser? Is the person's sex to be recorded? Is the individual's age to be estimated? Does it make any difference if the person was alone or in a group.
- When should the observation be made? On what day of the week? At what time of the day? Should day and time be reported? Should the observation be recorded only after a purchase occurs or should an approach by a customer to a salesclerk also be recorded even if it does not result in a sale?
- Where should the observation be made? In what kind of store? How should the store be selected? How should it be noted on the observational form—by type, by location, by name? Should vending-machine purchases also be noted?

The careful reader will note that these are the same kinds of who, what, when, and where decisions that need to be made in selecting the research design. The why and how are also implicit. The research problem should dictate the why of the observation, while the how involves choosing the observational device or form that will be used. A paper-and-pencil form should be very simple to use. It should parallel the logical sequence of the purchase act (for example, a male approaches the clerk, asks for a package of cigarettes, and so on, if these behaviors are relevant) and should permit the recording of observations by a simple check mark if possible. Again, careful attention to detail, exacting examination of the preliminary form, and an adequate pretest should return handsome dividends with respect to the quality of the observations made.

Figure 10.3

**Form Used by Observer
Acting as Shopper to
Evaluate Service
Provided by Bank
Employees**

Bank _____

Date _____ Time _____ Shopper's Name _____

Nature of Transaction: ☐ Personal   ☐ Telephone

    Details _____

    _____

    _____

    _____

A. For Personal Transactions:

   Bank Employee's Name _____

   1. How was name obtained?   ☐ Employee had name tag

                                      ☐ Name plate on counter or desk

                                      ☐ Employee gave name

                                      ☐ Shopper had to ask for name

                                      ☐ Name provided by other employee

                                      ☐ Other _____

                                      _____

B. For Telephone Transactions:

   Bank Employee's Name _____

   1. How was name obtained?   ☐ Employee gave name upon answering the telephone

                                      ☐ Name provided by other employee

                                      ☐ Shopper had to ask for name

                                      ☐ Employee gave name during conversation

                                      ☐ Other _____

                                      _____

C. Customer Relations Skills	**Yes**	**No**	**Does Not Apply**
1. Did the employee notice and greet you immediately?	☐	☐	☐
2. Did the employee speak pleasantly and smile?	☐	☐	☐
3. Did the employee answer the telephone promptly?	☐	☐	☐
4. Did the employee find out your name?	☐	☐	☐
5. Did the employee use your name during the transaction?	☐	☐	☐
6. Did the employee ask you to be seated?	☐	☐	☐
7. Was the employee helpful?	☐	☐	☐
8. Was the employee's desk or work area neat and uncluttered?	☐	☐	☐
9. Did the employee show a genuine interest in you as a customer?	☐	☐	☐

Figure 10.3

continued

C. Customer Relations Skills	Yes	No	Does Not Apply
10. *Did the employee thank you for coming in?*	☐	☐	☐
11. *Did the employee enthusiastically support the bank and its services?*	☐	☐	☐
12. *Did the employee handle any interruptions effectively? (phone calls, etc.)*	☐	☐	☐

Comment on any positive or negative details of the transaction that you found particularly noticeable.

_____

_____

_____

_____

_____

D. Sales Skills	Yes	No	Does Not Apply
1. *Did the employee determine if you had any accounts with this bank?*	☐	☐	☐
2. *Did the employee use "open-ended" questions in obtaining information about you?*	☐	☐	☐
3. *Did the employee listen to what you had to say?*	☐	☐	☐
4. *Did the employee sell you on the bank services by showing you what the service could do for you?*	☐	☐	☐
5. *Did the employee ask you to open the service which you inquired about?*	☐	☐	☐
6. *Did the employee ask you to bank with this particular bank?*	☐	☐	☐
7. *Did the employee ask you to contact him/her when visiting the bank?*	☐	☐	☐
8. *Did the employee ask you if you had any questions or if you understood the service at the end of the transaction?*	☐	☐	☐
9. *Did the employee give you brochures about other services?*	☐	☐	☐
10. *Did the employee give you his/her calling card?*	☐	☐	☐
11. *Did the employee indicate that you might be contacted by telephone, engraved card, or letter as a means of follow-up?*	☐	☐	☐
12. *Did the employee ask you to open or use other services? Check the following if they were mentioned.*	☐	☐	☐

☐ savings account

☐ checking account

☐ automatic savings

☐ Mastercharge

continued

Figure 10.3

continued

D. Sales Skills	Yes	No	Does Not Apply

☐ Master Checking

☐ safe deposit box

☐ loan services

☐ trust services

☐ automatic payroll deposit

☐ bank-by-mail

☐ automatic loan payment

☐ bank hours

☐ other _____

Comment on the overall effectiveness of the employee's sales skills.

_____

_____

_____

_____

_____

Source: Courtesy of Neil M. Ford.

◆ Summary

Learning Objective 1: Explain the role of research hypotheses in developing a questionnaire.
Research hypotheses guide the questionnaire by determining what information will be sought and from whom (since they specify what relationships will be investigated). Hence, they also affect the type of question and the form of response used to collect it.

Learning Objective 2: Define *telescoping error* and *recall loss* and explain how they affect a respondent's ability to answer questions accurately.
Telescoping error refers to people's tendency to remember an event as having occurred more recently than it did. Recall loss means they forget it happened at all. The degree to which the two types of error affect the accuracy of the reported information depends on the length of the period in question. For long periods, the telescoping effect is smaller while the recall loss is larger. For short periods, the reverse is true.

Learning Objective 3: Cite some of the techniques researchers use to secure respondents' cooperation in answering sensitive questions.
When asking sensitive questions, researchers may find it helpful to (1) hide the question in a group of other, more innocuous, questions; (2) state that the behavior or attitude is not unusual before asking the specific questions of the respondent; (3) phrase the question in terms of others and how they might feel or act; (4) state the response in terms of a number of categories that the respondent may simply check; (5) use the randomized-response model.

Learning Objective 4: Explain what is meant by an open-ended question.
An open-ended question is one in which respondents are free to reply in their own words rather than being limited to choosing from a set of alternatives.

Learning Objective 5: Name two kinds of fixed-alternative questions and tell the difference between them.

Two types of fixed-alternative questions are multichotomous and dichotomous questions. In a multichotomous question respondents are asked to choose the alternative that most closely reflects their position on the subject from a list of several alternatives. In a dichotomous question, only two alternatives are listed.

Learning Objective 6: List some of the primary rules researchers should keep in mind in trying to develop bias-free questions.

Among the rules of thumb that researchers should keep in mind in developing questions are (1) use simple words, (2) avoid ambiguous words and questions, (3) avoid leading questions, (4) avoid implicit alternatives, (5) avoid implicit assumptions, (6) avoid generalizations and estimates, and (7) avoid double-barreled questions.

Learning Objective 7: Explain what is meant by the funnel approach to question sequencing.

The funnel approach to question sequencing gets its name from its shape, starting with broad questions and progressively narrowing down the scope.

Learning Objective 8: Explain what is meant by a branching question and discuss when it is used.

A branching question is one which contains a direction as to where to go next on the questionnaire based on the answer given. Branching questions are used to reduce the number of alternatives that are needed in individual questions, while ensuring that those respondents capable of supplying the needed information still have an opportunity to do so.

Learning Objective 9: Explain the difference between basic information and classification information and tell which should be asked first in a questionnaire.

Basic information refers to the subject of the study; classification information refers to the other data we collect to classify respondents so as to extract more information about the phenomenon of interest. The proper questionnaire sequence is to present questions securing basic information first and those seeking classification information last.

Discussion Questions, Problems, and Projects

1. Evaluate the following questions.
   (a) ***Which of the following magazines do you read regularly?***

   _____ Time

   _____ Newsweek

   _____ Business Week

   (b) ***Are you a frequent purchaser of Birds Eye Frozen vegetables?***

   _____ Yes   _____ No

   (c) ***Do you agree that the government should impose import restrictions?***

   _____ Strongly agree

   _____ Agree

   _____ Neither agree nor disagree

   _____ Disagree

   _____ Strongly disagree

   (d) ***How often do you buy detergent?***

   _____ Once a week

   _____ Once in two weeks

   _____ Once in three weeks

   _____ Once a month

   (e) ***Rank the following in order of preference:***

   _____ Kellogg's Corn Flakes

   _____ Quaker's Life

   _____ Post Bran Flakes

     _____ Kellogg's Bran Flakes
     _____ Instant Quaker Oat Meal
     _____ Post Rice Krinkles

(f) *Where do you usually purchase your school supplies?*

(g) *When you are watching television, do you also watch most of the advertisements?*

(h) *Which of the following brands of tea are most similar?*
     _____ Liptons Orange Pekoe
     _____ Turnings Orange Pekoe
     _____ Bigelow Orange Pekoe
     _____ Salada Orange Pekoe

(i) *Do you think that the present policy of cutting taxes and reducing government spending should be continued?*
     _____ Yes   _____ No

(j) *In a seven-day week, how often do you eat breakfast?*
     _____ Every day of the week
     _____ 5–6 times a week
     _____ 2–4 times a week
     _____ Once a week
     _____ Never

2. Make the necessary corrections to the above questions.

3. Evaluate the following multichotomous questions. Would dichotomous or open-ended questions be more appropriate?

   (a) *Which one of the following reasons is most important in your choice of stereo equipment?*
        _____ Price
        _____ In-store service
        _____ Brand name
        _____ Level of distortion
        _____ Guarantee/warranty

   (b) *Please indicate your education level.*
        _____ Less than high school
        _____ Some high school
        _____ High school graduate
        _____ Technical or vocational school
        _____ Some college
        _____ College graduate
        _____ Some graduate or professional school

   (c) *Which of the following reflects your views toward the issues raised by ecologists?*
        _____ Have received attention
        _____ Have not received attention
        _____ Should receive more attention
        _____ Should receive less attention

   (d) *Which of the following statements do you most strongly agree with?*
        _____ Eastern Airlines has better service than Northwest Airlines
        _____ Northwest Airlines has better service than United Airlines
        _____ United Airlines has better service than Eastern Airlines
        _____ United Airlines has better service than Northwest Airlines
        _____ Northwest Airlines has better service than Eastern Airlines
        _____ Eastern Airlines has better service than United Airlines

4. Evaluate the following open-ended questions. Rephrase them as multichotomous or dichotomous questions if you think it would be appropriate.

   (a) *Do you go to the movies often?*

   (b) *Approximately how much do you spend per week on groceries?*

   (c) *What brands of cheese did you purchase during the last week?*

5. Assume you are doing exploratory research to find out people's opinions about television advertising.

    (a) Specify the necessary information that is to be sought.

    You have decided to design a structured-undisguised questionnaire and employ the personal interview method.

    (b) List the individual questions on a separate sheet of paper.
    (c) Specify the form of the response for each question (i.e., open-ended, multichotomous, dichotomous, scale). Provide justification for selecting a particular form of response.
    (d) Determine the number and sequence of each question. Reexamine and revise the questions.
    (e) Attach the final version of the questionnaire.
    (f) Pretest the questionnaire on a convenience sample of five students, and report the results of your pretest.

6. The objective of this study is to determine whether brand names are important for mothers purchasing children's clothing.

    (a) Specify the necessary information that is to be sought.

    You have decided to use a structured-undisguised questionnaire and to employ the telephone interview method.

    (b) List the individual questions on a separate sheet of paper.
    (c) Specify the form of the response for each question. Provide justification for selecting a particular form of response.
    (d) Determine the number and sequence of each question. Reexamine and revise the questions.
    (e) Attach the final version of the questionnaire.
    (f) Using the phone book as a sampling frame, pretest the questionnaire on a sample of five respondents, and report the results of your pretest.

7. A small brokerage firm was concerned with the declining number of customers and decided to do a quick survey. The major objective was to find out the reasons for patronizing a particular brokerage firm and to find out the importance of customer service. The following questionnaire was to be administered by telephone.

Good Afternoon Sir/Madam:

We are doing a survey on attitudes towards brokerage firms. Could you please answer the following questions? Thank you.

1. Have you invested any money in the stock market?

    _____ Yes   _____ No

If respondent replies *yes*, continue, otherwise terminate interview.

2. Do you manage your own investments or do you go to a brokerage firm?

    _____ Manage own investments   _____ Go to a brokerage firm

If respondent replies "go to a brokerage firm" continue, otherwise terminate interview.

3. How satisfied are you with your brokerage firm?

Very Satisfied	Satisfied	Neither Satisfied nor Dissatisfied	Dissatisfied	Very Dissatisfied
_____	_____	_____	_____	_____

continued

---

4. How important is personal service to you?

Very Important	Important	Not Particularly Important	Not at All Important
____	____	____	____

5. Which of the following reasons is the most important in patronizing a particular firm?

____ the commission charged by the firm

____ the personal service

____ the return on investment

____ the investment counseling

6. Approximately how long have you been investing through the brokerage firm you are currently using?

____ about 3 months   ____ about 9 months

____ about 6 months   ____ about 1 year or more

7. How much capital do you have invested?

____ $500–$750   ____ $1,000–$1,500

____ $750–$1,000   ____ $1,500 or more

Good-bye and thank you for your cooperation.

Evaluate the above questionnaire.

8. Assume that a medium-sized manufacturer of candy employs you to conduct an observational study in determining children's influence on adults in the purchase of candy.
   (a) List the variables that are relevant in determining this influence.
   (b) List the "observations" that might reflect each of these variables.
   (c) Develop an observational form that will be able to collect the needed information.
   (d) Observe three such purchases in a store/supermarket or the location that you specified above.
   (e) Report your findings.

9. This observational task can be conducted near the vending machines in the cafeteria, library, or business school. The objective is to observe the deliberation time taken at the various machines and determine the factors that influence the deliberation time.
   (a) List the variables that would be relevant in achieving the above objective.
   (b) List the "observations" that would reflect each of these variables.
   (c) Develop an observational form that will be able to collect the needed information.
   (d) Do five such observations and report your findings.

Suggested Additional Readings

For more elaborate treatments of how to go about constructing questionnaires, see

Stanley L. Payne, *The Art of Asking Questions* (Princeton, N.J.: Princeton University Press, 1979).

Seymour Sudman and Norman Bradburn, *Asking Questions: A Practical Guide to Questionnaire Design* (San Francisco: Jossey-Bass, 1982).

P. Labau, *Advanced Questionnaire Design* (Abt Books, 1981).

Herbert Schuman and Stanley Presser, *Questions and Answers in Attitude Surveys* (Orlando: Academic Press, 1981).

For a general bibliography in questionnaire construction, see

Wayne G. Daniel, *Questionnaire Design: A Selected Bibliography for the Survey Researcher* (Monticello, Ill.: Vance Bibliographies, 1979).

Chapter 11 Measurement Basics

+ + + +
+ + + +
+ + + +
+ + + +

Learning Objectives

Upon completing this chapter, you should be able to

1. Define the term *measurement* as it is used in marketing research.
2. List the four types of scales that can be used to measure an attribute.
3. Explain the primary difference between a ratio scale and an interval scale.
4. Cite some of the factors that may cause differences in two measures of the same attribute.
5. Name the two types of error that may affect measurement scores and define each.
6. Explain the concept of validity as it relates to measuring instruments.
7. Specify the two types of inferences a researcher makes in attempting to establish the validity of an instrument.
8. Cite the three types of direct assessment techniques used to infer the validity of a measure.
9. Outline the sequence of steps to follow in developing valid measures of marketing constructs.

Case in Marketing Research

Cases of Savvy, a shampoo specifically designed for oily hair, sat on the loading dock waiting to be shipped to Springfield for test marketing. At company headquarters, Steve Rollins, vice-president of marketing for Sunrise Brands, the shampoo's manufacturer, sat huddled with Jeremy Barton, research director, to plan the final test details.

"Well, Jeremy, advertising is ready, promotional coupons are set, and participating supermarkets and drugstores have agreed to set aside shelf space for us. I arranged for trial-size bottles to be sent to young women in our target market segment. I'm about ready to turn this project over to you."

"Fine," Jeremy responded, "I have a variety of instruments ready to measure consumer reaction. We plan to run qualitative studies to find out what purchasers liked and disliked about the product. We also are planning quantitative studies to measure how many and what kind of households got our samples, and who subsequently went on to purchase. We will also study awareness of our print and tele-

vision advertising. I figure we need to measure at 8, 14, and 20 weeks to get any valid reading on how we're doing. If it's September now, I think we should have some fairly comprehensive data for you to use in planning your national rollout by the beginning of next year."

"You know, Jeremy, I have a good feeling about this project," Steve said. "We've done our homework on this one. After listening to the tapes of all those focus groups with teenagers complaining about greasy hair, I think we're really on to something," Steve said. "Besides, R & D really outdid themselves in their low-oil product formulation, and the ad agency's 'Stop the Stringies with Savvy' is a brilliant campaign idea. Place an order for that sports car you've been lusting after, friend. We're about to hit the big time on this one."

"I hate to sound pessimistic, Steve, but if I were you, I wouldn't go spending my bonus check yet. You're new to this business. Maybe back in the soft drink industry consumers were loyal to their brands, but I've

seen too many shampoos come and go to count on anything in this market. Besides, I'm not so sure that our teen angels are as predictable as you might think. Let's wait for the test results before we pat ourselves on the back," Jeremy said.

"Don't be silly, Jeremy, my boy," Rollins said heartily. "Trust me. My daughter washes her hair as often as she brushes her teeth. If she and her pals like this shampoo as much as I think they will, we'll both be parking our Porsches in the executive parking lot."

Discussion Issues

1. What kinds of problems might a marketer encounter in trying to measure a consumer's attitude toward a new product?

2. What assumption is Steve Rollins making that could prove faulty? Why?

3. What kinds of questions should Jeremy Barton ask to determine consumers' attitudes toward the new shampoo?

Source: This fictitious case is based on the research conducted by S. C. Johnson & Son in launching Agree shampoo and creme rinse. Unlike our hapless researchers, S. C. Johnson researchers were thorough and successful. For more information see "Key Role of Research in Agree's Success Is Told," *Marketing News*, 12 (January 12, 1979), pp. 14–15.

Without realizing it, most of us spend the day engaging in various forms of measurement. We stagger out of bed, and hop onto the bathroom scale, hoping our midnight foray to the refrigerator will fail to register. We measure coffee into the coffeemaker, or stir a teaspoonful of instant coffee into a cup of water. We keep an eye on the clock so that we will not miss the bus or leave too little time to negotiate the rush-hour traffic on our way to class. We check the sports page for the score of the previous night's game—and perhaps the business section for the closing price on a favorite investment.

Most of the things we measure are fairly concrete: pounds on a scale, teaspoons of coffee, amount of gas in a tank. But how does one measure a person's attitude toward bubble gum? The likelihood of a teenager's using a certain brand of acne medication? A family's social class? Marketers are interested in measuring many attributes that laypeople rarely think of in terms of numerical values. In this chapter and the next, we will discuss how marketing researchers go about assigning numbers to various objects and phenomena.

◆ Scales of Measurement

◆ Measurement

Rules for assigning numbers to objects to represent quantities of attributes.

Measurement consists of "rules for assigning numbers to objects in such a way as to represent quantities of attributes."[1] Note two things about the definition. First, it indicates that we measure the attributes of objects and not the objects themselves. We do not measure a person, for example, but may choose to measure the individual's income, social class, education, height, weight, attitudes, or whatever, all of which are attributes of this person. Second, the definition is broad in that it does not specify how the numbers are to be assigned. In this sense, the rule is too simplistic and conveys a false sense of security, because there is a great temptation to read more meaning into the numbers than they actually contain. We often incorrectly attribute all the properties of the scale of numbers to the assigned numerals.

Consider the properties of the scale of numbers for a minute. Take the numbers 1, 2, 3, and 4. Now let the number 1 stand for one object, 2 for two objects, and so on. The scale of numbers possesses a number of properties. For example, we can say that 2 is larger than 1, and 3 is larger than 2, and so on. Also, we can say that the interval between 1 and 2 is the same size as the interval between 3 and 4, which is the same as that between 2 and 3, and so on. We can say still further that 3 is three times greater than 1, while 4 is four times greater than 1 and two times greater than 2, and so on.

When we assign numbers to attributes of objects, we must beware of the temptation to make these same arguments with the numbers in that it is unlikely that these relationships hold. We must determine what the properties of the attribute are and assign numbers in such a fashion that they accurately reflect the properties of the attribute. Errors at this point could mislead both the researchers and users of the research.

There are four types of scales on which an attribute can be measured, namely, nominal, ordinal, interval, and ratio.[2] Table 11.1 summarizes some of the more important features of these scales.

---

[1] Jum C. Nunnally, *Psychometric Theory,* 2nd ed. (New York: McGraw-Hill, 1978), p. 3.

[2] Our classification follows that of Stanley S. Stevens, "Mathematics, Measurement and Psychophysics," in Stanley S. Stevens, ed., *Handbook of Experimental Psychology* (New York: John Wiley, 1951), the most accepted classification in the social sciences.

Table 11.1   Scales of Measurement

Scale	Basic Comparisons[a]	Typical Examples	Measures of Average[b]
Nominal	Identity	Male/female	Mode
		User/nonuser	
		Occupations	
		Uniform numbers	
Ordinal	Order	Preference for brands	Median
		Social class	
		Hardness of minerals	
		Graded quality of lumber	
Interval	Comparison of intervals	Temperature scale	Mean
		Grade point average	
		Attitude toward brands	
Ratio	Comparison of absolute magnitudes	Units sold	Geometric mean
		Number of purchasers	Harmonic mean
		Probability of purchase	
		Weight	

[a]All the comparisons applicable to a given scale are permissible with all scales below it in the table. For example, the ratio scale allows the comparison of intervals and the investigation of order and identity, in addition to the comparison of absolute magnitudes.

[b]The measures of average applicable to a given scale are also appropriate for all scales below it in the table; i.e., the mode is also a meaningful measure of the average when measurement is on an ordinal, interval, or ratio scale.

Nominal Scale

One of the simplest properties of the scale of numbers is *identity*. A person's social security number is a **nominal scale** as are the numbers on football jerseys, lockers, and so on. These numbers simply identify the individual assigned the number. Similarly, if in a given study males are coded 1 and females 2, we have again made use of a nominal scale. The individuals are uniquely identified as male or female. All we need to determine an individual's sex is to know whether the person is coded as a 1 or as a 2. Note further that there is nothing implied by the numerals other than identification of the sex of the person. Females, although they bear a higher number, are not necessarily "superior" to males, or "more" than males, or twice as many as males as the numbers 2 and 1 indicate, or vice versa. We could just as easily reverse our coding procedure so that each female is a 1 and each male a 2.

The reason we could reverse our codes is that the only property conveyed by the numbers is identity. With a nominal scale, the only permissible operation is counting. Thus, the mode is the only legitimate measure of central tendency or average. It does not make sense in a sample consisting of sixty men and forty women to say that the average sex is 1.4, given males were coded 1 and females 2, even though the calculation 0.6 (1) + 0.4 (2) yields the number 1.4. All we can say is that there were more males in the sample than females, or that 60 percent of the sample was male.

• Nominal scale

Measurement in which numbers are assigned to objects or classes of objects solely for the purpose of identification.

Ordinal Scale

A second property of the scale of numbers is that of *order*. Thus, we could say that the number 2 is greater than the number 1, that 3 is greater than both 2 and 1, and that 4 is greater than all three of these numbers. The numbers 1, 2, 3, and 4 are ordered, and the larger the number the greater the property . Note that the **ordinal scale** implies identity, since the same number would be used for all objects that are the same. An example would be the assignment of the number 1 to denote freshmen, 2 to denote sophomores, 3 juniors, and 4 seniors. We could just as well use the numbers 10 for freshmen, 20 for sophomores, 25 for juniors, and 30 for seniors. This assignment would still indicate the class level of each person and the *relative standing* of two persons when compared in terms of who is further along in the academic program. Note that this is all that is conveyed by an ordinal scale. The difference in ranks says nothing about the difference in academic achievement between two ranks.

This is perhaps easier to see if we talk about the three top people in a graduating class. Assume that the top-ranked person's average grade is 3.85 on a four-point scale, the second-ranked person's average is 3.74, and the third-ranked person's is 3.56. While an ordinal scale will tell us that one person was ranked first and another was ranked second, it tells us nothing about the difference in academic achievement between the two. Nor does an ordinal scale imply that the difference in academic achievement between the first- and second-ranked people equals the difference between the second- and third-ranked people, even though the difference between 1 and 2 equals the difference between 2 and 3.

As suggested, we can transform an ordinal scale in any way we wish as long as we maintain the basic ordering of the objects. Again, whether we can use the ordinal scale to assign numerals to objects depends on the attribute in question. The attribute itself must possess the ordinal property to allow ordinal scaling that is meaningful. With ordinal scales, both the median and mode are permissible, or meaningful, measures of average. Thus, if twenty people ranked Product A first in comparison with Products B and C, while ten ranked it second and five ranked it third, we could say that (1) the average rank of Product A as judged by the median response was 1 (with thirty-five subjects, the median is given by the eighteenth response when ranked from lowest to highest) and that (2) the modal rank was also 1.

Interval Scale

A third property of the scale of numbers is that the *intervals* between the numbers are meaningful in the sense that the numbers tell us how far apart the objects are with respect to the attribute. This means that the differences can be compared. The difference between 1 and 2 is equal to the difference between 2 and 3. Further, the difference between 2 and 4 is twice the difference that exists between 1 and 2.

One classic example of an **interval scale** is the temperature scale, since it indicates what we can and cannot say when we have measured an attribute on an interval scale. Suppose the low temperature for the day was 40°F and the high was 80°F. Can we say that the high temperature was twice as hot (that is, represented twice the heat) as the low temperature? The answer is an unequivocal no. To see the folly in claiming 80°F is twice as warm as 40°F, one simply needs to convert these temperatures to their centigrade equivalents where $C = (5F - 160)/9$. Now we see that the low was 4.4°C and the high was 26.6°C, a much different ratio between low and high than was indicated by the Fahrenheit scale.

The example illustrates that we cannot compare the absolute magnitude of numbers when measurement is made on the basis of an interval scale. The reason is that in an interval scale, the zero point is established arbitrarily. For example, the same natural phenomenon, the freezing point of water, is represented by zero on the Celsius scale, but 32 on the Fahrenheit scale.[3] The zero position is therefore arbitrary.

What, then, can we say when measurement is made on an interval scale? First, we can say that 80°F is warmer than 40°F. Second, given a third temperature, we can compare the intervals; that is, we can say the difference in "heat" between 80°F and 120°F is the same as the difference between 40°F and 80°F, and that the difference between 40°F and 120°F is twice the difference between 40°F and 80°F. To see that this conclusion is legitimate, we can simply resort to the centigrade equivalents; 120°F represents 48.8°C, and the difference between 4.4°C (40°F) and 26.6°C (80°F) is the same as that between 26.6°C (80°F) and 48.8°C (120°F), namely, 22.2°. Further, the difference of 44.4°C between 4.4°C and 48.8°C is twice as great as that between 4.4°C and 26.6°C, as it was when the Fahrenheit scale was used. The comparison of intervals is legitimate with an interval scale because the relationships among the differences hold regardless of the particular constants chosen. With an interval scale, the mean, median, and mode are all meaningful measures of average.

Ratio Scales

+ Ratio scale

Measurement that has a natural, or absolute, zero and therefore allows the comparison of absolute magnitudes of the numbers.

The **ratio scale** differs from an interval scale in that it possesses a *natural,* or *absolute,* zero, one for which there is universal agreement as to its location. Height and weight are obvious examples. Because there is an absolute zero, comparison of the *absolute magnitude* of the numbers is legitimate. Thus, a person weighing 200 pounds is said to be twice as heavy as one weighing 100 pounds, and a person weighing 300 pounds is three times as heavy.

In a ratio scale, zero has an absolute empirical meaning—that is, that none of the property being measured exists. Further, we have already seen that the more powerful scales include the properties possessed by the less powerful ones. This means that with a ratio scale we can compare intervals, rank objects according to magnitude, or use the numbers to identify the objects (everything that interval, ordinal, and nominal scales do). And the geometric mean as well as the more usual arithmetic mean, median, and mode are meaningful measures of average when attributes are measured on a ratio scale.

+ Scaling of Psychological Attributes

Researchers decide which scale to use based on the attribute being measured in that the characteristic or qualities being measured may preclude use of a more powerful scale. For example, we may have to use a nominal rather than an ordinal scale because the qualities being measured may not lend themselves to a numerical ranking. That is, the properties implied by the numbers used for ranking may not correlate with the properties of the attribute being measured. Also, we cannot use an interval scale for an attribute that is only ordinal in nature. We introduce a serious error into our scale if we try to exceed the basic nature of the attribute with our

---

[3]The zero point on the Fahrenheit scale was originally established by mixing equal weights of snow and salt.

measure. Therefore it is critical to know something about the attribute itself before we assign numbers to it using some measurement procedure.

Further, the procedure used in constructing the scale determines the type of scale actually generated. The more powerful scales allow stronger comparisons and conclusions to be made. Thus, we can make certain types of comparisons that allow particular conclusions when measurement is on a ratio scale, say, that we cannot make when measurement is on an interval, ordinal, or nominal scale. There is a great temptation to assume that our measures have the properties of the ratio or at least the interval scale. Whether they do in fact is another question, and the simple condition that the attributes of the objects have been assigned numbers should not delude us. Rather, we should critically ask: What is the basic nature of the attribute? Have we captured this basic nature by our measurement procedure?

It is rare that a psychological construct can reasonably be assumed to have a natural, or absolute, zero.

> For example, what would an absolute zero of intelligence be? Or what is the absolute zero of attitude toward the Republican Party? There can be neutrality of feeling, and neutral position is often used as the zero point on the scale, but it does not represent an absolute lack of the attitude.[4]

The problem is no less real in marketing. Many of our constructs, borrowed from psychology and sociology, possess no more than interval measurement and some even less. We have to be very careful in conceptualizing the construct or characteristic so as not to delude ourselves or mislead others with our measures and, more importantly, *with our interpretation of those measures.*

The second problem we must face squarely is the ability of our measures to capture the construct as conceptualized. Even if an absolute zero logically exists, for example, do our measures determine it? The procedures used to generate the measure in large part determine the answer. If all we require is that the respondent rank five objects in terms of their overall desirability, we need to recognize that we have only generated an ordinal scale in the absence of further assumptions.

◆ Introduction to Psychological Measurement

As suggested earlier, part of the difficulty in measuring attitudes stems from the general difficulty in measuring any psychological construct or concept. Since we cannot physically see psychological constructs such as attitude, awareness, intentions, and so on, it is difficult to gauge whether our measures have measured them accurately. Even if we could see them, though, there would still be a question as to whether the measure we are using captures adequately the construct it is supposed to reflect. This problem is common to all scientific measurement.

The essence of the measurement problem is presented in Figure 11.1. The basic researcher or scientist uses theories in an attempt to explain phenomena. These theories or models consist of constructs (denoted by the circles with Cs in them), linkages among and between the constructs (single lines connecting the Cs), and data that connect the constructs with the empirical world (double lines). The single lines represent **conceptual** or **constitutive definitions,** in that a given construct is defined in terms of other constructs in the set. The definition may take the form of an equation that precisely expresses the interrelationship of the construct to the

◆ Constitutive (conceptual) definition

Definition in which a given construct is defined in terms of other constructs in the set, sometimes in the form of an equation that expresses the relationship among them.

---

[4]Wendell R. Garner and C. D. Creelman, "Problems and Methods of Psychological Scaling," in Harry Helson and William Bevan, eds., *Contemporary Approaches to Psychology* (New York: Van Nostrand, 1967), p. 4.

Figure 11.1

Schematic Diagram
Illustrating the Structure
of Science and the
Problem of Measurement

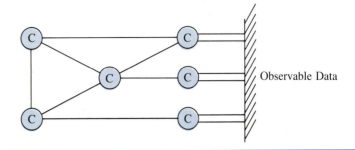

Observable Data

other constructs, such as the equation in mechanics that suggests that force equals mass times acceleration. Alternatively, the relationship may be only imprecisely stated, which is typically the case in the social sciences.

The double lines represent operational definitions. An **operational definition** describes how the construct is to be measured. It specifies the activities that the researcher must complete in order to assign a value to the construct (e.g., sum the scores on the ten individual statements to generate a total score.) In essence, the operational definition tells the investigator what to do and in what manner to measure the concept. Table 11.2, for example, shows how consumer sentiment toward marketing was assessed in one large study using Market Facts' mail panel by measuring respondents' reactions to product quality, product prices, advertising, and retailing and personal selling support. Conceptual definitions logically precede operational definitions and guide their development, for we must specify what a construct is before we can develop rules for assessing its magnitude.

The role of scientific inquiry is to establish the relationships that exist among the constructs of a model. It is necessary that some of the constructs be related to observable data if scientists are to accomplish their task. Otherwise, the model will be circular, with given unobservable constructs being defined in terms of other unobservable constructs. Since a circular model cannot be supported or refuted by empirical data, it is not legitimately considered a theory. Rather, a theory or system of explanation rests upon the condition that at least some of the constructs can be operationalized sufficiently so as to allow their measurement. Recall that measurement is defined as "rules for assigning numbers to objects to represent quantities of attributes." The rigor with which these rules are defined and the skill with which they are implemented determine whether the construct has been captured by the measure.

You would undoubtedly scoff at the following measurement procedure. John has blue eyes and Bill has brown eyes; therefore, John is taller than Bill. You might reply that the color of a person's eyes has nothing to do with the person's height, and, further, that if you wanted to see who was taller, the best procedure would be to measure them with a yardstick or to stand them side by side and compare their heights. You would be right on both counts. If I measured both John and Bill by asking them how tall they were, you would have probably voiced less objection to my procedure—unless John said he was taller while your observation of the two men showed that Bill was definitely the taller.

Now the interesting thing about most psychological constructs is that we cannot rely on visual comparisons to either confirm or refute a measure. We cannot see an attitude, a personality characteristic, a person's knowledge about or awareness of a particular product, or other psychological characteristics such as intelligence, mental anxiety, or whatever. These characteristics are all part of the consumer's black box.

• Operational definition

Definition of a construct that describes the operations to be carried out in order for the construct to be measured empirically.

Table 11.2   Illustration of Operational Definitions

Concept	Measurement[a]
	Sum of responses to following items, each measured on five-point disagree-agree scale.
Product Quality	The quality of most products I buy today is as good as can be expected.
	I am satisfied with most of the products I buy.
	Most products I buy wear out too quickly. (R)
	Products are not made as well as they used to be. (R)
	Too many of the products I buy are defective in some way. (R)
	The companies that make products I buy don't care enough about how well they perform. (R)
	The quality of products I buy has consistently improved over the years.
Price of Products	Most products I buy are overpriced. (R)
	Business could charge lower prices and still be profitable. (R)
	Most prices are reasonable considering the high cost of doing business.
	Competition between companies keeps prices reasonable.
	Companies are unjustified in charging the prices they charge.
	Most prices are fair.
	In general, I am satisfied with the prices I pay.
Advertising for Products	Most advertising provides consumers with essential information.
	Most advertising is very annoying. (R)
	Most advertising makes false claims. (R)
	If most advertising was eliminated, consumers would be better off. (R)
	I enjoy most ads.
	Advertising should be more closely regulated.
	Most advertising is intended to deceive rather than to inform consumers. (R)
Retailing or Selling	Most retail stores serve their customers well.
	Because of the way retailers treat me, most of my shopping is unpleasant. (R)
	I find most retail salespeople to be very helpful.
	Most retail stores provide an adequate selection of merchandise.
	In general, most middlemen make excessive profits. (R)
	When I need assistance in a store, I am usually *not* able to get it. (R)
	Most retailers provide adequate service.

[a]An (R) indicates scoring of the item needs to be reversed so that higher scores indicate more positive attitudes.

Source: Developed from the information in John F. Gaski and Michael J. Etzel, "The Index of Consumer Sentiment Toward Marketing," *Journal of Marketing*, 50 (July 1986), pp. 71–81.

Their magnitude must be inferred from our measurements. Since we cannot resort to a visual check on the accuracy of our measures, we must rely on evaluating the procedures we used to determine the measure. Eye color is certainly not height, but have we captured the sales representatives' satisfaction with their job if we ask them directly how satisfied they are? Probably not, for reasons that will become obvious as we continue our discussion.

Note that the problem of measuring the constructs is not unique to the researcher interested in scientific explanation. The practitioner shares this concern. The shampoo manufacturer in our opening case will need to know that the research is actually measuring consumer attitudes toward the new product and that the accuracy of the data is not being influenced by the interviewers asking the questions or by one of the many other factors with which research must contend. The ability to make these assessments relies heavily on an understanding of measurement, measurement error, and the concepts of reliability and validity. Understanding these concepts is the task to which we now turn.

◆ Variations in Measured Scores

You will recall that when we engage in measurement we are measuring the attributes of objects, not necessarily the objects themselves. Most measurement tasks present problems, but psychological measurement is particularly difficult at times since it usually involves a complex situation in which there are a great many factors that affect the attribute being measured. In addition, the measurement process itself may influence the results. For example, assume that certain tobacco companies are interested in measuring people's attitudes toward smoking in public places such as restaurants, office buildings, and medical waiting areas. An attitude scale to measure these feelings has been administered to a sample of respondents. A high score (maximum: 100) means that the respondent has a strong objection to smoking in public areas, while a low score (minimum: 25) indicates the opposite. If Mary scored 75, and Jane scored 40, we might conclude that Mary has a much more negative attitude toward smoking in public places than does Jane. But the validity of that conclusion would depend on the quality of the measurement. Let us consider some of the possible causes for the difference in the two scores.[5]

1. *A true difference in the characteristic we are measuring.* In an ideal situation, the difference in scores would reflect true differences in the attitudes of Mary and Jane and nothing else. This situation will rarely, if ever, occur. More likely, the different scores will also reflect some of the intruding factors that follow.

2. *True differences in other relatively stable characteristics of the individual that affect the score.* Not only does a person's position on an issue affect his or her score, but other characteristics can also be expected to have an effect. Perhaps the difference between Mary's and Jane's scores is simply due to the greater willingness of Mary to express negative feelings. Jane, by contrast, follows the adage, "If you can't say something nice, don't say anything at all." Her cooperation in the study has been requested, so she responds, but not truthfully.

3. *Differences due to transient personal factors.* A person's mood, state of health, fatigue, and so on, may all affect his or her responses. Yet these factors are temporary and can vary. Thus, if Mary, a nonsmoker, has just returned from a long wait in her dentist's smoke-filled waiting room, her responses may be decidedly different than if she had been interviewed several days earlier.

---

[5]These differences are adapted from Claire Selltiz, Lawrence S. Wrightsman, and Stuart W. Cook, *Research Methods in Social Relations,* 3rd ed. (New York: Holt, Rinehart and Winston, 1976), pp. 164–168. See also Duane F. Alwin and David J. Jackson, "Measurement Models for Response Errors in Surveys: Issues and Applications," in Karl F. Schuessler, ed., *Sociological Methodology 1980* (San Francisco: Jossey-Bass, 1979), pp. 69–119; and Frank E. Saal, Ronald G. Downey, and Mary Anne Lakey, "Rating the Ratings: Assessing the Psychometric Quality of Ratings Data," *Psychological Bulletin,* 88 (September 1980), pp. 413–428.

4. *Differences due to situational factors.* The situation surrounding the measurement also can affect the score. Mary's score might be different if her husband were there while the scale was being administered. Incidentally, this problem is the bane of researchers studying the decision-making process of married couples. When the husband is asked for the respective roles of husband and wife in purchasing a new automobile, for instance, one set of responses is secured; when the wife is asked, the responses are different; when the two are asked together, still a third set is obtained. Which is correct? It is hard to say, since the fact remains that the situation surrounding a measurement can affect the scores that are obtained.

5. *Differences due to variations in administration.* Much measurement in marketing involves the use of questionnaires administered by phone or in person. Since interviewers can vary in the way they ask questions, the responses also may vary as a function of the interviewer. The same interviewer may even handle two interviews differently enough to trigger a variance in recorded answers, although the respondents do not really differ on the characteristic.

6. *Differences due to the sampling of items.* As we attempt to measure any construct, we typically tap only a small number of the items relevant to the characteristic being measured. Thus, our attitude scale for the tobacco companies will contain only a sample of all the items or statements we could possibly have included. In fact, often we will not even know what all the relevant items are. If we added, deleted, or changed the wording of some items, we would undoubtedly change the outcome with respect to the scores of Mary and Jane. We must constantly be aware that our instrument reflects our interpretation of the construct and the

Back to the Case

"Steve, we've got trouble," Jeremy said tersely into the telephone from Springfield.

"What's the matter, Jeremy?" Steve asked.

"I can't understand what's going on here. Either our teenagers have stopped having greasy hair, or they're spending all their money on after-shave for their boyfriends for Christmas."

"What do you mean?" Steve asked.

"What I mean is that sales patterns have become very erratic in the past couple weeks. The week before Thanksgiving, sales started to drop off, and now this

week they're miserable. In some of our stores, a consumer is lucky to find our product at all, what with all the little baskets of shell-shaped soap, and kiddie shampoos in plastic reindeer bottles littering the aisles," Jeremy said.

"How are your telephone surveys going?" Steve asked.

"They're not so great either. For one thing, it's been really tough to reach people. Then when you do get them on the line, they seem rushed, distracted, and grouchy," Jeremy said.

"Sounds bad," Steve said. "Maybe we shouldn't have been in such a rush to get to test market. Our results might be very different in March than in December."

There are many factors that can influence scores on a measuring instrument. In addition to such things as a person's mood, willingness to express honest opinions, and ability to understand the questions being asked, situational factors beyond the researcher's control can wreak havoc with the reliability of the scores received.

items we use to measure it, and the resulting scores will vary according to the way in which items are chosen and the way those items are expressed.

Our final score is also influenced by the number of items presented. A man's height can serve as an indicator of his "size," but so can his weight, the size of his waistline, chest size, and so on. We certainly could expect to have a better measure of a man's size if we included all these items. So it is with psychological measurements. Other things being equal, a one-item scale is a less adequate sample of the universe of items relevant to a characteristic than is a twenty-five-item scale.

7. *Differences due to lack of clarity of the measuring instrument.* Sometimes a difference in response to a questionnaire or an item on a scale may represent differences in interpretation of an ambiguous or complex question rather than any fundamental differences in the characteristic one is attempting to measure. We saw in the last chapter how even simple words can be open to misinterpretation. In measuring complex concepts such as attitudes, the possibilities for misunderstanding increase greatly. One of the researcher's main tasks is to generate items or questions that mean the same thing to all respondents, so that the observed differences in scores are not caused by differences in interpretation.

8. *Differences due to mechanical factors.* "Circumstances such as broken pencils, check marks in the wrong box, poorly printed instructions, and lack of space to record responses fully, play their role in preventing the most effective functioning of a measuring instrument."[6]

Classification and Assessment of Error

The ideal in any scale is to generate a score that reflects true differences in the characteristic one is attempting to measure without interference from irrelevant factors. What we may in fact obtain is often something else. One type of error that may appear in our scores, **systematic error,** results from differences in stable characteristics that affect the person's score. Systematic errors are sometimes referred to as *constant errors,* since they affect the measurement in a constant way. An example would be the measurement of a man's height with a poorly calibrated wooden yardstick.

Another type of error, **random error,** is not constant but is instead due to transient aspects of the person or measurement situation. A random error is present when we repeat a measurement on an individual or group of individuals and do not get the same scores as the first time we did the measurement even though the characteristic being measured has not changed. For instance, if, unbeknownst to the researcher, a man who was measured once changed his shoes before being measured again, the two measures may not agree even though the man's actual height has not changed.

The distinction between systematic error and random error is critical because of the way the **validity,** or correctness, of a measure is assessed. Any scale or other measurement instrument that accurately measures what it was intended to measure is said to have validity. The validity of a measuring instrument is defined as "the extent to which differences in scores on it reflect true differences among individuals on the characteristic we seek to measure, rather than constant or random errors."[7] To accomplish this is a very difficult task. It is not accomplished by simply making

• Systematic error
Error in measurement that is also known as *constant error* since it affects the measurement in a systematic way.

• Random error
Error in measurement due to the transient aspects of the person or measurement situation.

• Validity
The extent to which differences in scores on a measuring instrument reflect true differences among individuals, groups, or situations in the characteristic that it seeks to measure, or true differences in the same individual, group, or situation from one occasion to another, rather than constant or random errors.

[6]Selltiz, Wrightsman, and Cook, *Research Methods,* p. 168.
[7]Ibid., p. 169.

up a set of questions or statements to measure a person's attitude toward smoking in public places, for example. The researcher must take the necessary steps to ensure the questionnaire does actually measure a person's attitude on this subject. This is never established unequivocally, but is always inferred. There are two types of inferences we make as we try to establish the validity of an instrument: (1) direct assessment of validity and (2) indirect assessment using reliability.[8]

[8]For detailed discussion of the conceptual relationships that should exist among the various indicants of reliability and validity and an empirical assessment of the evidence, see J. Paul Peter and Gilbert A. Churchill, Jr., "The Relationship Among Research Design Choices and Psychometric Properties of Rating Scales: A Meta-Analysis," *Journal of Marketing Research,* 23 (February 1986), pp. 1–10.

Research Window 11.1
Marketing Researchers Face the *Real* Pepsi Challenge: Interpreting Taste Tests

When Coca-Cola Co. uncorked its formula for the "New" Coke, executives boasted that it was the surest move they had ever made. They described as "overwhelming" the results of taste tests with 190,000 consumers, the majority of whom preferred the new recipe over old Coke.

History now records the introduction of the "New" Coke right up there with the debut of the Edsel as one of the greatest marketing debacles of all time. But what went wrong? If a marketer can't count on the results from 190,000 taste tests, then what is the role of research in the marketing mix?

Analysts now agree that what Coke failed to measure was the psychological impact of tampering with a ninety-nine-year-old soft drink. "When you have a product with a strong heritage that people could always count on being there, the mind becomes more important then physiological responses," said the research director for a rival cola.

Few products could stir as much emotion as all-American Coke, but other factors can also dilute the significance of taste tests. Certainly the image created by advertising affects people's perceptions of taste. That's why researchers often do both blind taste tests and tests in which brand names are revealed. "We did blind tests in the Pepsi Challenge commercials to eliminate brand influences," said an executive at one advertising firm. "But then we had to be very careful to say that people preferred the taste of Pepsi, not that they preferred Pepsi."

The color of a product also may make it seem tastier. When light-colored beer gets a shot of food coloring, consumers tend to describe it as heartier. Market researchers also say that 7-Up often beats colas in taste tests partly because people like its clear, light color. Yet, when the same people are asked what they take along on picnics or order at fast-food restaurants, they usually say a cola.

Measuring taste preferences is further confounded because the ability to discriminate between flavors varies greatly from one person to the next. Coca-Cola's marketing research director says that only about half the population has taste buds sensitive enough to distinguish between Coke and Pepsi. Indeed, "if you remove the caramel color from Coke, a lot of people won't be able to tell it from one of the clear drinks like Sprite," he said.

Testing conditions and procedures can also distort the results of taste studies. Researchers note that responses may be influenced by how hungry or thirsty a subject is, how questions are phrased, and even how the test samples of competing brands are numbered. Typically, companies choose numbers like 697 and 483 to label products because 1 and 2 and A and B carry definite connotations.

Other marketing consultants criticize taste tests as unrealistic because they often compare only two products, when in reality consumers have many more choices in supermarkets. In addition, taste tests are conducted in the unnatural setting

Direct Assessment of Validity

There are three types of direct assessment techniques we can use to infer the validity of a measure. We can look for evidence of its pragmatic validity, content validity, and construct validity.

Pragmatic Validity How well the measure actually predicts the criterion, whether it be a characteristic or specific behavior of the individual, is its **pragmatic validity.** An example would be the Graduate Management Admissions Test. The fact that this test is required by most of the major schools of business attests to its pragmatic validity; it has proved useful in predicting how well a student with a particular score on the exam will do in an accredited MBA program. The test score is used to predict

◆ **Pragmatic validity**

The usefulness of the measuring instrument as a predictor of some other characteristic or behavior of the individual; it is sometimes called *predictive validity* or *criterion-related validity.*

---

of a shopping mall, but research firms try to screen out as many other distorting influences as possible. They make sure test samples are kept at precisely the same temperature, and they serve only one sample from a can or bottle. To neu- tralize interviewees' palates, they usually feed people a cup of water and an unsalted cracker.

Source: Ronald Alsop, "Coke's Flip-Flop Underscores Risks of Consumer Taste Tests," *The Wall Street Journal,* 65 (July 18, 1985), p. 27.

Coca-Cola failed to consider the psychological impact of tampering with a 99-year-old soft drink and its strong all-American image when it followed the results of taste tests indicating a preference for the "New Coke."

the criterion of performance. An attitude scale example might be to use scores sales representatives achieve on a measuring instrument designed to assess their job satisfaction in predicting their likelihood of quitting. Both of these examples illustrate *predictive validity* or *criterion-related validity,* which are alternate terms for pragmatic validity, in that the attitude scores are used to predict a future behavior.

• **Concurrent validity**

The correlation between the predictor variable and the criterion variable when both are assessed at the same point in time.

However, there is another type of pragmatic validity known as **concurrent validity** that is concerned with the relationship between the predictor variable and the criterion variable when both are assessed at the same point in time. For example, the common tuberculin tine test, which is a routine part of many physical exams, is not meant to predict whether a person is apt to contract tuberculosis at some point in the future, but if the tuberculosis virus is present now.

Pragmatic validity is determined strictly by the correlation between the measuring instrument and the characteristic or behavior being measured. If the correlation is high, the measure is said to have pragmatic validity.

> Thus if it were found that accuracy in horseshoe pitching correlated highly with success in college, horseshoe pitching would be a valid measure for predicting success in college. This is not meant to imply that sound theory and common sense are not useful in selecting predictor instruments for investigation, but after the investigations are done, the entire proof of the pudding is in the correlations.[9]

Pragmatic validity is relatively easy to assess. It requires, to be sure, a reasonably valid way of measuring the criterion with which the scores on the measuring instrument are to be compared. Given that such scores are available, though (for example, the grades the student actually achieves in an MBA program or a tally of how many sales representatives actually quit), all that the researcher needs to do is to establish the degree of relationship, usually in the form of some kind of correlation coefficient, between the scores on the measuring instrument and the criterion variable. While easy to assess, pragmatic validity is rarely the most important kind of validity. We are often concerned with "what the measure in fact measures" rather than simply whether it predicts accurately or not.

• **Content validity**

The adequacy with which the domain of the characteristic is captured by the measure; it is sometimes called *face validity.*

Content Validity If the measurement instrument adequately covers the most important aspects of the construct that is being measured, it has **content validity.** Consider, for example, the characteristic of "spelling ability," and suppose that the following list of words was used to assess an individual's spelling ability: catcher, shortstop, rightfielder, foul, strike, walk, pitcher. Now, you would probably take issue with this spelling test. Further, the basis for your objection probably would be the fact that all the words relate to the sport of baseball. Therefore, you could argue that an individual who is basically a very poor speller could do well on this test simply because he or she is a baseball fan. You would be right, of course. A person with a good basic ability for spelling but little interest in baseball might, in fact, do worse on this spelling test than one with less native ability but a good deal more interest in baseball. The test could be said to lack content validity, since it does not properly sample the range of all possible words that could be used but is instead very selective in its emphasis.

Theoretically, to capture a person's spelling ability (in English) most accurately, we would have to administer a test that includes all the words in the English language. The person who spelled the greatest number of these words correctly would be said to have the most spelling ability. This is an unrealistic procedure. It would

---

[9]Nunnally, *Psychometric Theory,* p. 88.

take several lifetimes to complete. We therefore resort to sampling the range of the characteristic by constructing spelling tests that consist of samples of all the possible words that could be used. Different samplings of items can produce different comparative performances by individuals. We need to recognize that whether we have assessed the true characteristic depends on how well we have sampled the range of the characteristic. This is not only true for spelling ability, but also holds for psychological characteristics.

How can we ensure that our measure will possess content validity? We can never guarantee it, because it is partly a matter of judgment. We may feel quite comfortable with the items included in a measure, for example, while a critic may argue that we have failed to sample from some relevant aspect of the characteristic. While we can never guarantee the content validity of a measure, we can minimize the objections of the critics. The key to content validity lies in the *procedures* that are used to develop the instrument.

One way to define an appropriate domain, for example, is to search the literature and see how other researchers have defined the domain. The next step is to formulate a large number of items that broadly represent the range of attitudes that could be related to the topic in question. At this stage, the researcher may wish to

Back to the Case

"I can't believe all the things that have gone wrong with this test," Steve Rollins said. "First, the effect of the holidays all but invalidates our study. Now you're telling me that something is seriously wrong with the product?"

"Steve, I know you don't want to hear this, but I think we're going to have to dump all the Savvy we have on hand, mix a new batch, and start over. I thought we had nailed down all the aspects of the product and the promotion. We asked all the usual shampoo-related questions about smell, cleansing ability, and sudsing action, and lots about price, advertising approach, etc. But then in open-ended conversations with some of these girls, I discovered one aspect we hadn't considered as a variable," Jeremy said.

"What was that?" Steve asked.

"Color."

"Color? I thought we agreed that blue was a perfect color for teenagers. Other shampoos have colors. Prell's been dark green for years. If these kids are wacky enough to put blue mousse stripes in their hair, I thought they'd love it," Steve said.

"Another of your unfortunate stereotypes, Steve. Maybe your daughter likes her hair blue, or shocking pink, but these kids out here in the suburbs are a lot more conservative than your basic New York City teenager. Lots of them said they wouldn't buy our product because blue was an unnatural color and they didn't want any artificial ingredients in their shampoos," Jeremy said.

"Jeremy, we're not asking these kids to put the stuff on

their hamburgers. We want them to wash their hair with it," Steve said.

"Tell that to your teenager, Steve," said Jeremy. "As for me, I know when to go back to the drawing board. I'll be driving the old station wagon back to the city tonight. It's a good thing I didn't order that Porsche."

In addition to being careful not to let their own biases affect the instrument, researchers need to be careful to design attitude scales that measure the total potential domain of the construct being measured (e.g., the color of the shampoo in addition to its lathering action, control of oiliness, and so on). Only if the total domain is covered can the instrument be said to provide content validity.

include a wide variety of items with slightly different shades of meaning, since this original list will be narrowed down to produce the final instrument.

The collection of items must be large, so that after refinement the measure still contains enough items to adequately sample the entire range of the variable. In the example cited previously, a measure of a sales representative's job satisfaction would need to include items about each of the components of the job (duties, fellow workers, top management, sales supervisor, customers, pay, and promotion opportunities) if it is to be content-valid.

Construct Validity The measurement of constructs is a vital task, but **construct validity** is the most difficult type to establish. Not only must the instrument be internally consistent but it must also measure what it was intended to measure. That is, each item in the instrument must reflect the construct and must also show a correlation with other items in the instrument.[10]

Thus, a measuring instrument designed to measure attitude would be said to have construct validity if it indeed measured the attitude in question and not some other underlying characteristic of the individual that affects his or her score. Construct validity lies at the very heart of scientific progress. Scientists need constructs with which to communicate. So do you and I. In marketing we speak of people's socio-economic class, their personality, their attitudes, and so on, because these are all constructs for explaining marketing behavior. And while vital, they also are unobservable. We can observe behavior related to these constructs but not the constructs themselves. Rather, we try to operationally define a construct in terms of things we can observe. When we agree on the operational definition, precision in communication is advanced. Instead of saying that what is measured by these seventy-five items is the person's brand loyalty, we can speak of the notion of brand loyalty.

Once researchers have specified the domain of the construct, generated a set of items relevant to the breadth of the domain, refined the items, and ensured that the remaining items are internally consistent, the final step is to see how well the measure relates to measures of other constructs to which the construct in question is theoretically related. Does it behave as expected? Does it fit the theory or model relating this construct to other constructs?

For example, consider our earlier example relating job satisfaction to job turnover among sales representatives. Suppose we had developed a measure to assess a sales representative's job satisfaction. The construct validity of the measure could be assessed by determining if there is indeed a relationship between job-satisfaction scores and company turnover. Those companies in which the scores are low (indicating less job satisfaction) should experience more turnover than those with high scores. If they do not, one would question the construct validity of the job-satisfaction measure. In other words, the construct validity of a measure is assessed by whether the measure confirms or denies the hypotheses predicted from the theory based on the constructs.

The problem, of course, is that the failure of the hypothesized relationship to hold true for the phenomenon being observed may be due either to a lack of construct validity or to incorrect theory. We often try to establish the construct validity of a measure, therefore, by relating it to a number of other constructs rather than only

• **Construct validity**
Assessment of the construct, concept, or trait the instrument is supposed to be measuring.

[10]See Gilbert A. Churchill, Jr., "A Paradigm for Developing Better Measures of Marketing Constructs," *Journal of Marketing Research,* 16 (February 1979), pp. 64–73, for a procedure that can be used to construct scales having construct validity. See J. Paul Peter, "Construct Validity: A Review of Basic Issues and Marketing Practices," *Journal of Marketing Research,* 18 (May 1981), pp. 133–145, for an in-depth discussion of the notion of construct validity.

one. We also try to use those theories and hypotheses that have been tested by others and found to be sound.

If the trait or construct exists, it also should be measurable by more than one method. These methods should be independent insofar as possible. If they are all measuring the same construct, though, the measures should have a high level of correlation. This provides evidence of **convergent validity,** which is defined as "the confirmation of a relationship by independent measurement procedures." Another evidence of construct validity is **discriminant validity,** which requires that a measure not correlate too highly with measures from which it is supposed to differ.[11] Correlations that are too high suggest that the measure is not actually capturing an isolated trait or that it is simply reflecting **method variance,** which is the variation in scores attributable to the method of data collection. "The assumption is generally made . . . that what the test measures is determined by the content of the items. Yet the final score . . . is a composite of effects resulting from the content of the item and effects resulting *from the form of the items used*"[12] (emphasis added).

Indirect Assessment via Reliability

Reliability refers to the ability to obtain similar results by measuring an object, trait, or construct with independent but comparable measures. If we gave a group of people two different measures of intelligence, and the two sets of scores from the two measures correlated highly with each other, we would say that the measures are reliable in that each is able to replicate the scores of the other.

Evaluating the reliability of any measuring instrument consists of determining how much of the variation in scores is due to inconsistencies in measurement.[13] The reliability of the instrument should be established before it is used for a substantive study and not after.

Before discussing how evidence of reliability is obtained, we need to make a few points. If a measure is reliable, it is not influenced by transitory factors. However, a measure could be reliable but not necessarily valid. For example, let us assume we have devised a measure of upper body strength. The measure requires that subjects do a series of different exercises with some weights and suppose that the results from the various exercises agree. This would mean the measure was reliable. Suppose, though, that the weights used were mismarked. While reliable, then, the measure of body strength would be systematically off the mark, meaning it would be invalid.

Figure 11.2 illustrates the concept pictorially. The old rifle is unreliable. The new rifle is relatively reliable, but its sights are set incorrectly in the center diagram. The

---

• **Convergent validity**

Confirmation of the existence of a construct determined by the correlations exhibited by independent measures of the construct.

• **Discriminant validity**

Criterion imposed on a measure of a construct requiring that it not correlate too highly with measures from which it is supposed to differ.

• **Method variance**

The variation in scores attributable to the method of data collection.

• **Reliability**

Similarity of results provided by independent but comparable measures of the same object, trait, or construct.

---

[11]One convenient way of establishing the convergent and discriminant validity of a measure is through the multitrait-multimethod matrix of Campbell and Fiske. See Donald T. Campbell and Donald W. Fiske, "Convergent and Discriminant Validation by the Multitrait-Multimethod Matrix," *Psychological Bulletin,* 56 (1959), pp. 81–105. See also Neal Schmitt, Bryan W. Coyle, and Bruce B. Saari, "A Review and Critique of Analyses of Multitrait-Multimethod Matrices," *Multivariate Behavioral Research,* 12 (October 1977), pp. 447–478; and Donald P. Schwab, "Construct Validity in Organizational Behavior," in B. Staw and L. L. Cummings, eds., *Research in Organizational Behavior,* Vol. 2 (Greenwich, Conn.: JAI Press, 1980), pp. 3–43.

[12]L. J. Cronbach, "Response Sets and Test Validity," *Educational and Psychological Measurement,* 6 (1946), p. 475.

[13]See J. Paul Peter, "Reliability: A Review of Psychometric Basics and Recent Marketing Practices," *Journal of Marketing Research,* 16 (February 1979), pp. 6–17, for a detailed treatment of the issue of reliability in measurement. See Gilbert A. Churchill, Jr., and J. Paul Peter, "Research Design Effects on the Reliability of Rating Scales: A Meta-Analysis," *Journal of Marketing Research,* 21 (February 1984), pp. 360–375, for an empirical assessment of the factors that seem to affect the reliability of rating scales.

Figure 11.2

Illustration of Difference between Random and Systematic Error

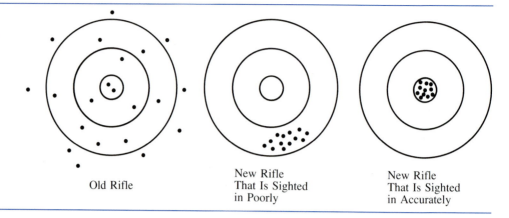

Old Rifle

New Rifle
That Is Sighted
in Poorly

New Rifle
That Is Sighted
in Accurately

right-hand diagram shows the new rifle with its sights set correctly. Only in the right-hand diagram could a user of any of the rifles be expected to hit the center of the target with regularity.

Although a measure that is reliable may or may not be valid, if it is not reliable, it is surely not valid. Conversely, if it is valid, it is surely reliable. A valid measure of height will be reliable, since it is actually measuring the trait in question. Reliability thus provides only negative evidence; it can prove the lack of validity but not the presence of it. Reliability is more easily determined than validity, however, so there has been a greater emphasis on it historically for inferring the quality of measures.

Stability One of the more popular ways of establishing the reliability of a measure is to measure the same objects or individuals at two different points in time and to correlate the obtained scores. Assuming that the objects or individuals have not changed in the interim, the two scores should correlate perfectly. To the extent that they do not, random disturbances were operating in either one or both of the test situations to produce random error in the measurement. The procedure is known as test-retest reliability assessment, and it establishes a measure's **stability.**

One of the critical decisions the researcher must face in determining the stability of a measure is how long to wait between successive administrations of the instrument. Suppose the researcher's instrument is an attitude scale. If the researcher waits too long, the person's attitude may change, thus producing a low correlation between the two scores. On the other hand, a short wait will likely produce test bias—people may remember how they responded the first time and be more consistent in their responses than is warranted by their attitudes.

To handle this problem, many researchers will use alternative forms for the two administrations. Instead of putting all the items in one form, the researcher generates two instruments that are as identical as possible in content. That is, each form should contain items from the same domains, and each domain of content should receive approximately the same emphasis in each form. Ideally, there would be a one-to-one correspondence between items on each of the two forms so that the means and standard deviations of the two forms would be identical and the inter-correlations among the items would be the same in both versions.[14] While it is next

+ Stability

Evidence of the reliability of a measure; determined by measuring the same objects or individuals at two different points in time and then correlating the scores; also known as test-retest reliability assessment.

[14]George W. Bohrnstedt, "Reliability and Validity Assessment in Attitude Measurement," in Gene F. Summers, ed., *Attitude Measurement* (Chicago: Rand McNally, 1970), p. 85.

to impossible to achieve the ideal, it is possible to construct forms that are roughly parallel, and parallel forms can be correlated across time to measure stability. The recommended time interval between administrations is two weeks.[15]

Equivalence In an attitude scale every item is theoretically acting as a measure of the attitude and a subject's score on one part of the scale should correlate with his or her score on another part of the scale. The **equivalence** measure of reliability focuses on the internal consistency of the set of items forming the scale.

The earliest measure of the internal consistency of a set of items was the *split-half reliability* of the scale. In assessing split-half reliability, the total set of items is divided into two equivalent halves; the total scores for the two halves are correlated; and this is taken as the measure of reliability of the instrument. Sometimes the division of items is made randomly, while at other times the even items are assumed to form one-half and the odd the other half of the instrument. The total score on the even items is then correlated with the total score obtained from the odd items.

Pointed criticism is increasingly being directed at split-half reliability as the measure of the internal consistency of a scale. The criticism focuses on the necessarily arbitrary division of the items into equivalent halves. Each of the many possible divisions can produce different correlations between the two forms or different reliabilities. Which division is correct or, alternatively, what is then the reliability of the instrument? For example, a ten-item scale has 126 possible splits or 126 possible reliability coefficients.[16]

An increasingly popular approach for assessing the internal consistency existing among the items on a scale looks at all the items simultaneously. Examining the rationale and calculation formulas would take us too far afield, but suffice it to say that the basic emphasis is on a search for the covariation that exists among the items. If the items are, in fact, reflecting the same trait, there should be substantial correlation among them. Lack of correlation of an item with other items in the scale is evidence that the item does not belong and should be deleted. Thus, measures of internal consistency are used when developing instruments and in establishing the internal consistency of the items in the final form. The two most popular measures are the KR20 coefficient for dichotomous items, and coefficient α for multichotomous items.[17]

The preceding discussion deals with the equivalence measure of reliability when applied to a single instrument. An alternate equivalence measure is used when different observers or different instruments measure the same individuals or objects at the same point in time. Do these methods produce consistent results? Are they equivalent as measured by the correlations among the total scores? An example would be a beauty contest. Do the judges, using the established criteria of beauty, talent, poise, and so on, rank the women in the same order in terms of winner, first runner-up, second runner-up, and so on? The reliability of the measure is greater to the extent that the judges agree. Figure 11.3, for example, depicts a situation in which the judgments of two different observers do not agree. This type of equivalence is the basis of convergent validation when the measures are independent.

[15]Nunnally, *Psychometric Theory,* p. 234, presents a rather scathing argument against test-retest reliability when alternative forms of the instrument are not available. See pages 232–236 in particular.

[16]In general, for a scale with $2n$ items, the total number of possible splits of the items into two halves is $(2n!)/2(n!)(n!)$. See Bohrnstedt, "Reliability and Validity," p. 86.

[17]See Nunnally, *Psychometric Theory,* Chaps. 6 and 7, pp. 190–255, for the rationale behind these coefficients and formulas for computing them.

Source: Reprinted with special permission of King Features Syndicate, Inc.

◆ Developing Measures

As a beginning researcher, it is easy to get confused over the issue of how one goes about developing measures of marketing constructs. How does one contend with the basic issues of reliability and validity, and how does one make the choices among the various coefficients that can be computed? Figure 11.4 diagrams a sequence of steps that can be followed to develop valid measures of marketing constructs.[18]

Step 1 in the process involves specifying the domain of the construct that is to be measured. Researchers need to be careful in specifying what is included in the domain of the construct and what is excluded. Consider measuring customer satisfaction with a new space heater the family recently purchased, for example. What attributes of the product and the purchase should be measured to assess accurately the family's satisfaction? Certainly one would want to be reasonably exhaustive in the list of product features to be included, incorporating such facets as cost, durability, quality, operating performance, and aesthetic features. But what about purchaser's reaction to the sales assistance received? What about the family members' reactions to subsequent advertising for a competitor's product offering the same features at lower cost? Or what about the family's reactions to news of some negative environmental effects of using the product? To detail which of these factors should be included or how customer satisfaction should be operationalized is beyond the scope of this book. But, obviously, researchers need to be very careful in specifying what is to be included in the domain of the construct being measured and what is to be excluded.

Step 2 in the process is to generate items that capture the domain as specified. Those techniques that are typically productive in exploratory research, including literature searches, experience surveys, and insight-stimulating examples, are generally productive here. The literature should indicate how the variable has been defined previously and how many dimensions or components it has. The search for ways to measure customer satisfaction would include product brochures, articles in trade magazines and newspapers, or results of product tests such as those published by *Consumer Reports.* The experience survey might include discussions with people in the product group responsible for the product, sales representatives, dealers, persons in marketing research, consumers, and outsiders who have a special expertise in heating equipment. The insight-stimulating examples could involve a comparison of competitors' products or a detailed examination of some particularly vehe-

---

[18]The procedure is adapted from Gilbert A. Churchill, Jr., "A Paradigm for Developing Better Measures of Marketing Constructs," *Journal of Marketing Research,* 16 (February 1979), pp. 64–73.

Figure 11.4

Suggested Procedure for Developing Measures

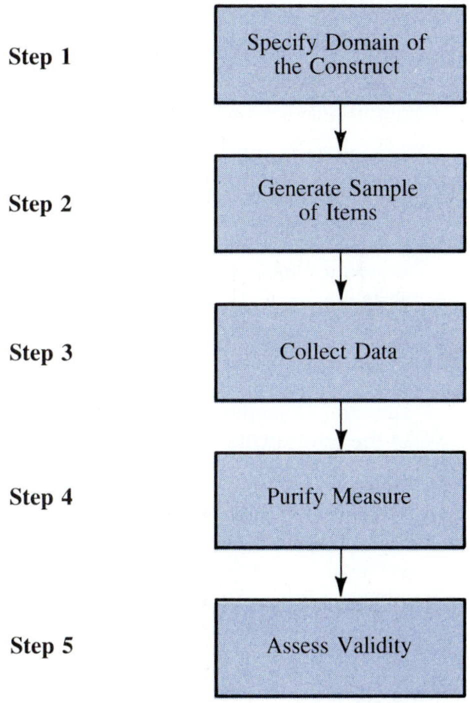

Step 1 → Specify Domain of the Construct

Step 2 → Generate Sample of Items

Step 3 → Collect Data

Step 4 → Purify Measure

Step 5 → Assess Validity

Source: Adapted from the procedure suggested by Gilbert A. Churchill, Jr., "A Paradigm for Developing Better Measures of Marketing Constructs," *Journal of Marketing Research,* 16 (February 1979), p. 66.

ment complaints in unsolicited letters about the performance of the product. Examples that reveal sharp contrasts or have striking features would be most productive. Focus groups also could be used to advantage at the item-generation stage.

Step 3 involves collecting data about the concept from a relevant sample of the target population—for example, all those who have purchased a space heater within the last six months.

Step 4 uses the data collected in Step 3 to purify the original set of items. The purification involves eliminating items that seemed to create confusion among respondents and items that do not discriminate between subjects with fundamentally different positions on the construct. The fundamental criterion that is used to eliminate items is how each item goes together with the other items. If all the items in a measure are drawn from the domain of a single construct, responses to those items should be highly correlated. If they are not, that is an indication that some of the items are not drawn from the appropriate domain and are producing error and unreliability, and those items should be eliminated. Several of the equivalence reliability coefficients mentioned earlier can be used to make this assessment, as can other statistical techniques.[19]

Step 5 in the process involves determining the validity of the purified measure. This involves assessing primarily its convergent, discriminant, and construct validity, since its content validity will have largely been addressed in Steps 1 through 4; and the assessment of its construct validity involves determining whether it behaves as expected, which in turn involves determining its pragmatic validity.

---

[19]See Churchill, "A Paradigm," for detailed discussion of which coefficients should be used and the rationale for their use.

◆ Summary

Learning Objective 1: Define the term *measurement* as it is used in marketing research.

Measurement consists of the rules for assigning numbers to objects in such a way as to represent quantities of attributes.

Learning Objective 2: List the four types of scales that can be used to measure an attribute.

The four types of scales on which an attribute can be measured are nominal, ordinal, interval, and ratio scales.

Learning Objective 3: Explain the primary difference between a ratio scale and an interval scale.

In an interval scale, the zero point is established arbitrarily. The ratio scale possesses a natural, or absolute, zero—one for which there is universal agreement as to its location.

Learning Objective 4: Cite some of the factors that may cause differences in two measures of the same attribute.

Some of the factors that may cause differences in two measures of the same attribute are (1) true differences in the characteristics being measured, (2) true differences in other relatively stable characteristics of the individual that affect the score, (3) differences due to transient personal factors, (4) differences due to situational factors, (5) differences due to variations in administration, (6) differences due to selective sampling, (7) differences due to lack of clarity of the measuring instrument, and (8) differences due to mechanical factors.

Learning Objective 5: Name the two types of error that may affect measurement scores and define each.

Two types of error may affect scores. The first type is *systematic error,* which results from differences in stable characteristics that affect the person's score. The second type is *random error,* which is due to transient aspects of the person or measurement situation.

Learning Objective 6: Explain the concept of validity as it relates to measuring instruments.

Any scale or other measurement instrument that actually measures what it was intended to measure is said to have validity. The validity of a measuring instrument is defined as "the extent to which differences in scores on it reflect true differences among individuals on the characteristic we seek to measure, rather than constant or random errors."

Learning Objective 7: Specify the two types of inferences a researcher makes in attempting to establish the validity of an instrument.

The two types of inferences we make as we try to establish the validity of an instrument are based on (1) direct assessment of validity and (2) indirect assessment of reliability.

Learning Objective 8: Cite the three types of direct assessment techniques used to infer the validity of a measure.

The three types of validity that can be directly assessed in a measure are pragmatic validity, content validity, and construct validity.

Learning Objective 9: Outline the sequence of steps to follow in developing valid measures of marketing constructs.

The following sequence of steps may be helpful in developing better measures of marketing constructs: (1) specify the domain of the construct, (2) generate a sample of items, (3) collect data, (4) purify the measure, and (5) assess validity.

Discussion Questions, Problems, and Projects

1. Identify the type of scale (nominal, ordinal, interval, ratio) being used in each of the following questions. Justify your answer.

◆

(a) ***During which season of the year were you born?***
    ____ winter   ____ spring   ____ summer   ____fall

(b) ***What is your total household income?*** _____

(c) ***Which are your three most preferred brands of cigarettes? Rank them from 1 to 3 according to your preference with 1 as most preferred.***

____ Marlboro	____ Salem
____ Kent	____ Kool
____ Benson and Hedges	____ Vantage

(d) ***How much time do you spend on traveling to school every day?***

____ under 5 minutes	____ 16–20 minutes
____ 5–10 minutes	____ 30 minutes and over
____ 11–15 minutes	

(e) ***How satisfied are you with Newsweek magazine?***

____ very satisfied	____ dissatisfied
____ satisfied	____ very dissatisfied
____ neither satisfied nor dissatisfied	

(f) ***On an average, how many cigarettes do you smoke in a day?***

____ over 1 pack	____ less than 1/2 pack
____ 1/2 to 1 pack	

(g) ***Which one of the following courses have you taken?***

____ marketing research	____ sales management
____ advertising management	____ consumer behavior

(h) ***What is the level of education for the head of the household?***

____ some high school	____ some college
____ high school graduate	____ college graduate and/or graduate work

2. The analysis for each of the above questions is given below. Is the analysis appropriate for the scale used?

   (a) About 50 percent of the sample was born in the fall, while 25 percent of the sample was born in the spring, and the remaining 25 percent was born in the winter. It can be concluded that the fall is twice as popular as the spring and the winter seasons.

   (b) The average income is $25,000. There are twice as many individuals with an income of less than $9,999 than individuals with an income of $40,000 and over.

   (c) Marlboro is the most preferred brand. The mean preference is 3.52

   (d) The median time spent on traveling to school is 8.5 minutes. There are three times as many respondents traveling less than 5 minutes as respondents traveling 16–20 minutes.

   (e) The average satisfaction score is 4.5 which seems to indicate a high level of satisfaction with *Newsweek* magazine.

   (f) Ten percent of the respondents smoke less than one-half pack of cigarettes a day, while three times as many respondents smoke over one pack of cigarettes a day.

   (g) Sales management is the most frequently taken course since the median is 3.2.

   (h) The responses indicate that 40 percent of the sample have some high school education, 25 percent of the sample are high school graduates, 20 percent have some college education, and 10 percent are college graduates. The mean education level is 2.6.

3. Discuss the notion that a particular measure could be reliable and still not be valid. In your discussion, distinguish between reliability and validity.

4. Find the following articles from the periodical section of your library. (i) G. A. Churchill, Jr., N. M. Ford, and O. C. Walker, Jr., "Measuring Job Satisfaction of Industrial Salesmen," *Journal of Marketing Research,* 11 (August 1974), pp. 254–260; and (ii) W. J. Lundstrom and L. M. Lamont, "The Development of a Scale for Measuring Consumer Discontent," *Journal of Marketing Research,* 13 (November 1976), pp. 373–381. For each of the articles, answer the following questions:

   (a) How was the reliability assessed? What techniques were specifically used?

   (b) What kinds of validity were assessed (predictive, content, and so forth)?

5. Feather-Tote Luggage is a producer of cloth-covered luggage, one of the primary advantages of which is its light weight. The company distributes its luggage through major department stores, mail order houses, clothing retailers, and other retail outlets such as stationery stores, leather good stores, and so on. The company advertises rather heavily, but it also supplements this promotional effort with a large field staff of sales representatives, numbering around 400. The numbers vary because one of the historical problems confronting Feather-Tote Luggage has been the large number of sales representatives' resignations. It is not unusual for 10 to 20 percent of the sales force to turn over every year. Since the cost of training a new sales representative is estimated at $5,000 to $10,000, not including the lost sales that might result because of a personnel switch, Mr. Harvey, the sales manager, is rightly concerned. He has been concerned for some time and therefore has been conducting exit interviews with each departing sales representative. On the basis of these interviews, he has formulated the opinion that the major reason for this high turnover is general sales representatives' dissatisfaction with company policies, promotional opportunities, and pay. But top management has not been sympathetic to Mr. Harvey's pleas regarding the changes needed in these areas of corporate policy. Rather, it has tended to counter Mr. Harvey's pleas with arguments that too much of what he is suggesting is based on his gut reactions and little hard data. Top management desires more systematic evidence that job satisfaction, in general, and these dimensions of job satisfaction, in particular, are the real reasons for the high turnover before it would be willing to change things.

Describe the procedures you would employ in developing a measure by which the job satisfaction of Feather-Tote Luggage sales representatives could be assessed. Indicate the type of scale you would use and why, and detail the specific steps you would undertake to assure the validity and reliability of this measure.

Suggested Additional Readings

For a procedure that can be used to construct scales having construct validity, see

Gilbert A. Churchill, Jr., "A Paradigm for Developing Better Measures of Marketing Constructs," *Journal of Marketing Research,* 16 (February 1979), pp. 64–73.

For a detailed treatment of the various types of reliability and the role of reliability in measurement, see

J. Paul Peter, "Reliability: A Review of Psychometric Basics and Recent Marketing Practices," *Journal of Marketing Research,* 16 (February 1979), pp. 6–17.

For an in-depth discussion of the notions of construct validity, see

J. Paul Peter, "Construct Validity: A Review of Basic Issues and Marketing Practices," *Journal of Marketing Research,* 18 (May 1981), pp. 133–145.

Chapter 12

Measuring Attitudes, Perceptions, and Preferences

Learning Objectives

Upon completing this chapter, you should be able to

1. List the various ways by which attitudes can be measured.
2. Name the most widely used attitude scaling techniques in marketing research and explain why researchers prefer them.
3. Explain how a Stapel scale differs from a semantic-differential scale.
4. Cite the one feature that is common to all ratings scales.
5. List three of the most common types of ratings scales.
6. Explain the difference between a graphic-ratings scale and an itemized-ratings scale.
7. Explain how the constant-sum scaling method works.
8. Identify the key decisions an analyst must make in order to complete a multidimensional scaling analysis.
9. Explain the basic principle behind conjoint analysis.

Case in Marketing Research

Executives at Marvell Toys knew that marketing to children was a highly volatile business. But their recent disastrous experience with their Fisticuffs Fighting Figures had left even the company's most seasoned marketers shell-shocked and confused.

Not only did children fail to respond to the toys, but the company had been deluged with angry letters from parents, educators, and consumer groups. The firm's higher-ups had vowed never to launch a product again without conducting extensive marketing research first.

Today Phil Stockton, a promising new employee in the company's marketing department, was meeting with Sally McGovern, a researcher from Dale & Barnett, a firm that specializes in conducting marketing research with children.

"Sally, nice to meet you," Phil said. "I've heard many good things about you and your firm from others here in the company. Unfortunately, we didn't call you in before we plunged ahead with the Fisticuffs fiasco. If we had, we might have saved a bundle of money and a lot of egg on our faces."

"Well, as you know, Phil, marketing to children is a lot more complicated in some ways than marketing to adults. Kids are a fickle bunch. What they love one week, they're bored with the next. And since they aren't the primary decision makers when it comes to purchasing an item, marketers often must find a way to get them to convince their parents that what they want is a good and useful item. All this is not to mention the tricks involved in measuring their attitudes toward a product in the development stages. I love this work, but others would tell you that it's a business only suited to the terminally vague," she laughed.

"Well, whether vaguely or precisely, we need to know how kids are likely to respond to our latest product, Love Bugs. After our experience with Fisticuffs, we thought we'd go for something soft and affectionate," Phil said.

"What are Love Bugs like, Phil?" Sally asked.

"They're basically stuffed animals in the shape of insects. There's a whole line of them in different colors. We're hoping to generate enough excitement about them that the kids will want to collect the whole set. There's Fuzzy the Fly, Grendel the Grasshopper, Polly the Praying Mantis, Topsy the Termite, and a bunch of others," Phil said, warming to his topic.

Sally looked a bit skeptical. "I'm glad you came to me, Phil. There's a lot of competition in this market, and it is wise to test carefully before plunging in. I have some ideas on how we might go about testing this line. Why don't you send me several complete sets of samples, and I'll go right to work," she said.

Discussion Issues

1. What problems might researchers expect to encounter in measuring children's attitudes?

2. How might children's attitudes and parents' attitudes differ on the same item?

3. What other information does Sally need about the new products before proceeding with her research?

One of the most pervasive notions in all of marketing is that attitudes play a pivotal role in consumer behavior. Consequently, an attempt to measure attitudes is incorporated in most of the major marketing models and in many, if not most, investigations of consumer behavior that do not rely on formal integrated models.[1] Marketers tend to emphasize the importance of attitudes. "Attitudes directly *affect* purchase decisions and these, in turn, *directly affect* attitudes through experience in using the product or service selected. In a broad sense, purchase decisions are based *almost solely* upon attitudes existing at the time of purchase, however these attitudes might have been formed"[2] (emphasis added).

Sometimes an entire industry will sponsor a study of attitudes. The advertising industry has always been especially interested in how advertising is perceived by the public. Table 12.1 reports the findings of a study sponsored by the American Association of Advertising Agencies to determine whether people's attitudes toward advertising were changing. The results of such a study would have important implications for the kinds of advertising the agencies produce, the frequency with which commercials are broadcast, or even the industry's efforts at self-regulation with regard to such concerns as truth in advertising and commercial clutter.

While industry studies such as this are not unusual, most often it is an individual firm that sponsors such a survey. Consider, for example, the following: (1) The appliance manufacturer's interest in present dealer and prospective dealer attitudes toward the company's warranty policy. If the dealers support the policy, the company feels they are more likely to give adequate, courteous service and, in the process, produce more satisfied customers. (2) The cosmetic manufacturer's interest in consumers' attitudes toward the company's new shampoo as it debuts in test market. Based on an early assessment of consumers' reactions, the company may decide to revise or fine tune its introductory marketing strategy before going national. (3) The industrial marketer's interest in the general job satisfaction of its highly trained, highly skilled field staff of sales representatives.

These examples indicate some of the many groups of people in whose attitudes the marketer typically is interested: the company's employees, its intermediaries, and its customers. Their attitude, stance, or predisposition to act can be important determinants of the company's success, and the marketer needs devices for measuring these attitudes. This chapter reviews some of those devices.

While the attitude concept is one of the most widely used in social psychology, it is used inconsistently. Both researchers and practitioners have trouble agreeing on interpretations of its various aspects. However, there does seem to be substantial agreement on the following points:[3]

1. Attitude represents a predisposition to act but does not guarantee that the actual behavior will occur. It merely indicates that there is a readiness to respond to an object. It is still necessary to do something to trigger the response.

---

[1]See, for example, James F. Engel, Roger D. Blackwell, and Paul Miniard, *Consumer Behavior,* 5th ed. (Hinsdale, Ill.: Dryden Press, 1985); J. Paul Peter and Jerry C. Olson, *Consumer Behavior: Marketing Strategy Perspectives* (Homewood, Ill.: Richard D. Irwin, Inc., 1987).

[2]James H. Myers and William H. Reynolds, *Consumer Behavior and Marketing Management* (Boston: Houghton Mifflin, © 1967), p. 146. For discussion of the role of attitudes and its impact on consumer behavior, see Robert B. Zajonc and Hazel Markus, "Affective and Cognitive Factors in Preferences," *Journal of Consumer Research,* 9 (September 1982), pp. 123–131.

[3]Adapted from the introduction by Gene F. Summers, ed., *Attitude Measurement* (Chicago: Rand McNally, 1970), p. 370. See also Engel, Blackwell, and Miniard, *Consumer Behavior.* One of the reasons for the many definitions of attitude is the age-old scientific problem of going from construct to operational definition, a problem that is reviewed in Chapter 11.

Table 12.1   Attitudes Toward Advertising: 1974–1985

	1974 % Agree	1985 % Agree		1974 % Agree	1985 % Agree
Consumer Benefits			**Entertainment Value**		
Advertising is a good way to learn about new products.	92%	92%	A lot of advertising is funny or clever.	72	81
Advertising is a good way to learn about what products and services are available.	88	87	A lot of advertising is enjoyable.	56	56
Advertising is a good way to find out how products and services work.	77	76	**Manipulation or Motivation**		
			Advertising makes people want things they don't really need.	78	84
Without advertising there would be fewer enjoyable programs on free TV.	74	75	Most ads try to work on people's emotions.	79	80
Advertising results in better products for the public.	57	60	It is really the manufacturers of products and not the advertising agencies who decide how truthful advertising is and what is said in ads.	60	63
Advertising gives you a good idea about products by showing the kinds of people who use them.	37	37	In general, advertisements present an honest picture of the products advertised.	41	30
Credibility			**Clutter or Intrusiveness**		
Most ads don't tell facts, but just create a mood.	72%	73%	There are too many commercials in a row on television.	87	92
Most advertising insults the intelligence of the average consumer.	60	72	The same ads are constantly shown again and again.	87	90
Products don't perform as well as the ads claim.	72	72			
People really "tune out" ads and don't remember what they've seen or heard soon after.	57	65			
Most advertising in in poor taste.	45	43			

Source: "Advertiser to Consumer: How 'm I Doin?" Ogilvy & Mather, *Listening Post,* 61 (April 1985), p. 2.

2. Attitudes are relatively persistent and consistent over time. They can be changed, to be sure, but alteration of an attitude that is strongly held requires substantial intervention.

3. There is a consistency between attitudes and behavior, and people act in such a fashion as to maintain this consistency.

4. Attitudes connote a preference and evaluation of an idea or object. They result in either positive or neutral or negative feelings for the idea or object.

The consistencies noted in this list led to our definition of attitude as representing a person's ideas, convictions, or liking with regard to a specific object or idea, presented in Chapter 7.

In addition to attitudes, marketers also have a keen interest in perceptions and preferences, and we will examine some of the techniques researchers use to measure attitudes, perceptions, and preferences in this chapter.

◆ Attitude-Scaling Procedures

There are a number of ways in which attitudes have been measured, including self-reports, observation of overt behavior, indirect techniques, performance of objective tasks, and physiological reactions.[4] By far the most common approach has been **self-reports,** in which people are asked directly for their beliefs or feelings toward an object or class of objects. A number of scales and scaling methods have been devised to measure these feelings. The main types will be reviewed here, but first let us briefly review the other approaches to attitude determination.

Observation of Behavior

The observation approach to attitude determination rests on the presumption that a subject's behavior is conditioned by his or her attitudes, and that we can therefore use the observed behavior to infer these attitudes. The behavior that the researcher wishes to observe is often elicited by creating an artificial situation. For example, to assess a person's attitude toward mandatory seat belt legislation, the subject might be asked to sign a strongly worded petition in favor of making seat belt usage a law. The individual's attitude toward seat belts would be inferred based on whether or not he or she signed. Alternatively, subjects might be asked to participate in a group discussion of the seat belt issue, and the researcher would note whether the individuals supported or opposed seat belt legislation in the discussion.

Indirect Techniques

The **indirect techniques** of attitude assessment use some unstructured or partially constructed stimuli as discussed in Chapter 8, such as word-association tests, sentence-completion tests, storytelling, and so on. Since the arguments concerning the use of these devices were detailed there, they will not be repeated here.

Performance of Objective Tasks

On the theory that people's **performance of objective tasks** will reflect their attitudes, one might ask a person to memorize a number of facts about an issue and then assess his or her attitude toward that issue from the facts that were successfully memorized. Thus, to assess a person's attitude toward seat belt legislation, one might ask him or her to memorize such facts as (1) the number of lives saved by seat belt usage, (2) the number of people who died in accidents because they could not remove their seat belts in time, and (3) the number of states that have adopted a mandatory seat belt law. The material should reflect both sides of the issue. The researcher then determines what facts the person remembered. The assumption is that subjects would be more apt to remember those arguments that are most consistent with their own position.

Physiological Reactions

Another approach to attitude measurement involves **physiological reaction,** which was discussed in Chapter 9. Here, through electrical or mechanical means, such as the psychogalvanic skin response technique, the researcher monitors the subject's

◆ Self-report Method of assessing attitudes in which individuals are asked directly for their beliefs about or feelings toward an object or class of objects.

◆ Indirect techniques Method of assessing attitudes that uses unstructured or partially structured stimuli such as word-association tests, sentence-completion tests, storytelling, and so on.

◆ Performance of objective tasks Method of assessing attitudes that rests on the presumption that a subject's performance of a specific assigned task (for example, memorizing a number of facts) will depend on the person's attitude.

◆ Physiological reaction Method of assessing attitudes in which the researcher monitors the subject's response, by electrical or mechanical means, to the controlled introduction of some stimuli.

[4]This classification of approaches is taken from Stuart W. Cook and Claire Selltiz, "A Multiple Indicator Approach to Attitude Measurement," *Psychological Bulletin,* 62 (1964), pp. 36–55.

response to the controlled introduction of some stimuli. One problem that arises in using these measures to assess attitude is that, with the exception of voice-pitch analysis, the individual's physiological response indicates only the intensity of the individual's feelings and not whether they are negative or positive.

Multiple Measures

Although self-report techniques for attitude assessment are the most widely used in marketing research studies because they are easy to administer, one should be aware of these other approaches, particularly when attempting to establish the validity of a self-report measure. They can provide useful insight into how the method of measurement, rather than differences in the basic attitudes of subjects, caused the scores to vary. This is consistent with the notion of using multiple indicators to establish the convergent and discriminant validity of a measure.

Self-Reports

Since attitude is one of the most pervasive concepts in all of sociopsychology, it is natural that researchers would devise a number of methods to measure it. Although many of the methods use self-reports, each method uses them in different ways. In this section, we shall review some of these self-report scales, particularly those that have novel features or have been used extensively in marketing studies. The discussion should give you an appreciation of the main types and their construction and use. Incidentally, in following the arguments, you will find it helpful to distinguish between how a scale is constructed and how it is used.

Summated-Ratings Scale   The *Likert scale,* also called a **summated-ratings scale,** is one of the most widely used attitude-scaling techniques in marketing research. It is particularly useful since it allows respondents to express the intensity of their feelings.[5]

Scale Construction   In developing a Likert, or summated-ratings scale, researchers devise a number of statements that relate to the product or attribute in question. Subjects are asked to indicate their degree of agreement or disagreement with each statement in the series. Table 12.2 is an example of a scale that might be used by a bank interested in comparing its image to those of its competitors.

In developing this type of scale, the researcher tries to generate statements about the characteristics of the object that could influence a person's attitude toward it. Each statement is then classified as either favorable or unfavorable.

Subjects are asked to indicate their degree of agreement or disagreement with each statement, and the various degrees of agreement are assigned scale values.[6] For our purposes, let's assume the values 1, 2, 3, 4, and 5 are assigned to the respective response categories. Now a subject could be considered to feel positively about the bank if he or she either agreed with a favorable statement or disagreed with an unfavorable statement. Consequently, it is necessary to reverse the scaling with neg-

Summated-ratings scale

Self-report technique for attitude measurement in which the subjects are asked to indicate their degree of agreement or disagreement with each of a number of statements; a subject's attitude score is the total obtained by summing over the items in the scale.

---

[5]The scale was first proposed by Rensis Likert, "A Technique for the Measurement of Attitudes," *Archives of Psychology,* No. 140 (1932).

[6]Paul E. Spector, "Choosing Response Categories for Summated Rating Scales," *Journal of Applied Psychology,* 61 (June 1976), pp. 374–375, contains a list of typical category descriptors and their numerical values.

Table 12.2   Example of Summated-Ratings Scale

	Strongly Disagree	Disagree	Neither Agree Nor Disagree	Agree	Strongly Agree
1. The bank offers courteous service.	_____	_____	_____	_____	_____
2. The bank has a convenient location.	_____	_____	_____	_____	_____
3. The bank has convenient hours.	_____	_____	_____	_____	_____
4. The bank offers low interest-rate loans.	_____	_____	_____	_____	_____

ative statements; a "strongly agree" response to a favorable statement and a "strongly disagree" response to an unfavorable statement would both receive scores of 5.

Using this scoring procedure, a total attitude score is then calculated for each subject. Researchers then evaluate the responses to determine which of the items discriminate most clearly between the high scorers and low scorers on the total scale. Those statements that generate mixed responses are weeded out, since they may tend to produce ambiguous results, or at the very least, may not be discriminating of attitude. In this way, the questionnaire is made internally consistent, so that every item relates to the same general attitude.[7]

Scale Use Once the list of statements has been refined, the remaining items are randomly ordered on the scale form so as to mix positive and negative statements. The scale is then ready to be administered to the desired sample of respondents. Once again, subjects are asked to indicate their degree of agreement with each statement. Subjects generally find it easy to respond, because the response categories allow the expression of the intensity of the feeling. The subject's total score is generated as the simple sum of the scores on each statement.

Unfortunately, interpretation of these summed scores is rarely simple. If, for example, the maximum favorable score on a particular twenty-item scale is 100, what do we say about a score of 78? Can we assume that the person's attitude toward the bank is favorable? We cannot, since the raw scores only assume meaning when we compare them to some standard. This problem is not unique to psychological scaling. It arises every day of our lives in a variety of ways. We are always making judgments on the basis of comparisons with some standard. Most typically the standard is established via our experiences and rarely is rigorously defined. Thus, when we say, "The man is very tall," we are in effect saying that on the basis of the experience we have, the man is taller than average.

In psychological scaling, this is formalized somewhat by clearly specifying the standard. Very often the standard is taken as the average score for all subjects, al-

---

[7]For an example, see William C. Lundstrom and Lawrence M. Lamont, "The Development of a Scale to Measure Consumer Discontent," *Journal of Marketing Research,* 13 (November 1976), pp. 373–381, which reports the procedures used and the results obtained in the development of a Likert scale to measure consumer discontent. For a generalizable procedure on how to go about constructing scales, see Gilbert A. Churchill, Jr., "A Paradigm for Developing Better Measures of Marketing Constructs," *Journal of Marketing Research,* 16 (February 1979), pp. 64–73.

though averages are also computed for certain predefined subgroups. The procedure is called *developing norms.* Comparisons can then be made against the norms to determine whether the person has a positive or negative attitude toward the object. Norms are not, of course, necessary for comparing subjects to determine which person has the more favorable attitude. Here one can simply compare the raw scores of the subjects. Nor are norms necessary when attempting to determine whether an individual's attitude has changed over time or whether a person likes one object better than another. One can simply compare the later and earlier scores or the difference in scores for the two objects.

Semantic-Differential Scale One of the most popular techniques for measuring attitudes in marketing research is the **semantic-differential scale.** It has been found to be particularly useful in corporate, brand, and product-image studies.

This scale grew out of some research by Osgood and his colleagues at the University of Illinois concerning the underlying structure of words.[8] The technique has been adapted, however, to make it suitable for measuring attitudes.

The original semantic-differential scale consisted of a great many bipolar adjectives, which were used to determine people's reactions to the objects of interest. Osgood found that most reactions could be categorized into one of three basic dimensions: (1) an *evaluation* dimension, represented by adjective pairs such as good-bad, sweet-sour, helpful-unhelpful; (2) a *potency* dimension, represented by adjective pairs such as powerful-powerless, strong-weak, deep-shallow; and (3) an *activity* dimension, represented by adjective pairs such as fast-slow, alive-dead, noisy-quiet. The same three dimensions tended to emerge regardless of the object being evaluated.[9] Thus, the general thrust in using the semantic-differential technique to form scales has been to select an appropriate sample of the accepted or basic adjective pairs so that a score could be generated for the object for each of the evaluation, potency, and activity dimensions. The object could then be compared to other objects using these scores.[10]

Marketers have taken Osgood's general idea and adapted it to fit their own needs. First, instead of applying the *basic* adjective pairs to the objects of interest, marketers have generated items of their own. These items have not always been antonyms, nor have they been single words. Rather, marketers have used phrases to anchor the ends of the scale, and some of these phrases have been attributes possessed by the product. For example, one end of the scale may be "good value for the money," and its opposite end, "poor value for the money." Second, instead of attempting to generate evaluation, potency, and activity scores, marketers have been more interested in developing profiles for the brands, stores, companies, or whatever is being compared, and total scores by which the objects could be compared. In this respect, the use of the semantic-differential approach in marketing studies has tended to

[8]Charles E. Osgood, George J. Suci, and Percy H. Tannenbaum, *The Measurement of Meaning* (Champaign, Ill.: University of Illinois Press, 1957).

[9]See David R. Heise, "The Semantic Differential and Attitude Research," in Summers, ed., *Attitude Measurement,* pp. 235–253, for an overview of the many studies in which the three dimensions were found. Factor analysis is the basic procedure employed to reduce a number of bipolar adjective pairs to basic dimensions.

[10]Several comparisons can be made: (1) The objects can be compared on the factor scores when the factors are considered one at a time; (2) the emotional value of the concept can be assessed by calculating the distance from the origin or neutral point to the object in three-space; and (3) the difference between objects or concepts in three-space can be assessed using Euclidean distance, since the three dimensions are independent of one another. For a discussion of these comparisons, see Heise, "The Semantic Differential and Attitude Research," pp. 241–244.

• Semantic-differential scale

Self-report technique for attitude measurement in which subjects are asked to check which cell between a set of bipolar adjectives or phrases best describes their feelings toward the object.

Figure 12.1

Example of Semantic Differential Scaling Form

Service is discourteous :____:____:____:____:____:____:____: Service is courteous

Location is convenient :____:____:____:____:____:____:____: Location is inconvenient

Hours are inconvenient :____:____:____:____:____:____:____: Hours are convenient

Loan interest rates are high :____:____:____:____:____:____:____: Loan interest rates are low

follow the summated-ratings approach to scale construction rather than the semantic differential tradition.

Let us again use the bank attitude-scaling problem to illustrate the semantic-differential method. First, a researcher would generate a large list of bipolar adjectives or phrases.[11] Figure 12.1 parallels Table 12.2 in terms of the attributes used to describe the bank, but it is arranged in a semantic-differential format. All we have done in Figure 12.1 is to try to express the things that could be used to describe a bank, and thus serve as a basis for attitude formation, in terms of positive and negative statements. Note that the negative phrase sometimes appears at the left side of the scale and other times at the right. This is to prevent a respondent with a positive attitude from simply checking either the right- or left-hand sides without even bothering to read the descriptions.

The scale would then be administered to a sample of subjects. Each respondent would be asked to read each set of bipolar phrases and to check the cell that best described his feelings toward the object. Respondents are usually instructed to consider the end positions in the scale as being very closely descriptive of the object, the center position as being neutral, and the intermediate positions as slightly descriptive and quite closely descriptive. Thus, for example, if the subject felt that Bank A's service was courteous, but only moderately so, he would check the sixth position reading from left to right.

The subject could be asked to evaluate two or more banks using the same scale.[12] When several banks are rated, the different profiles can be compared. Figure 12.2, for example (which is sometimes referred to as a **snake diagram** because of its shape), illustrates that Bank A is perceived as having more courteous service and a more convenient location and as offering lower interest rates on loans, but as having less convenient hours than Bank B. Notice that in constructing these profiles, all positive descriptors were placed on the right. This practice makes it much easier to interpret results. The plotted values represent the average score of all subjects on each descriptor. The profile that emerges gives a clear indication of how respondents perceive the differences between the two banks.

Rather than developing a profile, one can also total the scores on a semantic-differential scale in order to compare attitudes toward different objects (for example,

• Snake diagram

Diagram (so called because of its shape) that connects with straight lines the average responses to a series of semantic differential statements, thereby depicting the profile of the object or objects being evaluated.

[11]For a discussion of ways to go about this task, as well as other issues surrounding the construction of semantic differential scales, see John Dickson and Gerald Albaum, "A Method for Developing Tailor-made Semantic Differentials for Specific Marketing Content Areas," *Journal of Marketing Research,* 14 (February 1977), pp. 87–91.

[12]The most popular form of the semantic-differential scale places the objects being evaluated at the top and the descriptors used for the evaluation along the sides as the rows. One somewhat popular variation lists the descriptors at the top and the objects being evaluated along the side. For an empirical comparison of the two approaches, see Eugene D. Jaffe and Israel D. Nebenzahl, "Alternative Questionnaire Formats for Country Image Studies," *Journal of Marketing Research,* 21 (November 1984), pp. 463–471.

Figure 12.2
Contrasting Profiles of Bank A & B

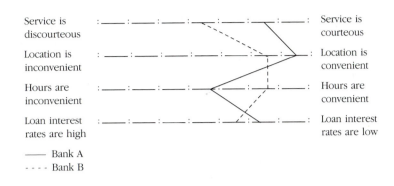

Service is discourteous ... Service is courteous

Location is inconvenient ... Location is convenient

Hours are inconvenient ... Hours are convenient

Loan interest rates are high ... Loan interest rates are low

——— Bank A
- - - - Bank B

alternative package designs). This score is arrived at by totaling the scores for the individual descriptors.

The popularity of semantic-differential scales in marketing research may be due to the ease with which they can be developed and the clarity with which they reveal results.[13] The technique also has the advantage of allowing subjects to express the intensity of their feelings toward company, product, package, advertisement, or whatever. When combined with proper item analysis techniques, the semantic-differential technique offers the marketing researcher a most valuable research tool.

Stapel Scale A modification of the semantic-differential scale that has received some attention in marketing literature is the **Stapel scale.** It differs from the semantic-differential scale in that (1) adjectives or descriptive phrases are tested separately instead of simultaneously as bipolar pairs, (2) points on the scale are identified by number, and (3) there are ten scale positions rather than seven. Respondents are told to rate how accurately each of a number of statements describes the object of interest, Bank A, for example. Instructions such as the following are given to respondents:

> You would select a *plus* number for words that you think describe (Bank A) accurately. The more accurately you think the word describes it, the larger the *plus* number you would choose. You would select a *minus* number for words you think do not describe it accurately. The less accurately you think a word describes it, the larger the *minus* number you would choose. Therefore, you can select any number from +5, for words that you think are very accurate, all the way to −5, for words that you think are very inaccurate.[14]

Proponents of the Stapel scale point out that this method not only frees the researcher from the formidable task of developing bipolar adjectives for each of the items on the test, but also permits finer discriminations in measuring attitudes. Despite these advantages, the Stapel scale has not been as warmly embraced as the semantic-differential scale, judging by the number of published marketing studies

• Stapel scale

Self-report technique for attitude measurement in which the respondents are asked to indicate how accurately each of a number of statements describes the object of interest.

[13]Barnett A. Greenberg, Jac L. Goldstucker, and Danny N. Bellenger, "What Techniques Are Used by Marketing Researchers in Business," *Journal of Marketing,* 41 (April 1977), pp. 62–68. For an example of the use of the semantic differential, see Sunil Mehrotra, Stuart Van Auken, and Subhash C. Lonial, "Adjective Profiles in Television Copy Testing," *Journal of Advertising Research,* 21 (August 1981), pp. 21–25.

[14]Irving Crespi, "Use of a Scaling Technique in Surveys," *Journal of Marketing,* 25 (July 1961), p. 71.

using each.[15] One problem with the Stapel scale is that many of the descriptors used to evaluate an object can be phrased one of three ways—positively, negatively, or neutrally—and the particular choice of phrasing seems to affect the results as well as subjects' ability to respond.[16] Nevertheless, it is a useful addition to the researcher's equipment arsenal, especially since it can be administered over the telephone.[17]

It should be pointed out that a total score on both the semantic-differential and Stapel scales is like a total score on a summated-ratings scale. The score 48, for example, is meaningless by itself but takes on meaning when compared to some norm or other score. There is a good deal of controversy as to whether semantic-differential, Stapel, or even summated-ratings total scores represent interval scaling, or, in actuality, ordinal scaling. While the controversy rages, marketers, like many psychological scaling specialists, have opted to assume that the scores represent interval scaling. While this assumption may not be entirely correct, it does allow researchers to use more powerful methods of analysis on the data generated.

Further, from a statistical point of view, the assumption of intervality often makes sense. Statistical tests of significance, for example, "do not care from where the numbers come" as long as the assumptions underlying the use of a particular statistical test are satisfied.[18] It is not necessary therefore to be overly concerned about the level of measurement from a *statistical* point of view. What we must be careful about, though, is the *interpretation* of the results (for example, arguing that a person with a score of 80 has twice as favorable an attitude toward an object as a person with a score of 40, unless, of course, the measurement scale is ratio).

◆ Other Ratings Scales

The previous discussion dealt with some of the main scaling methods that have been used to measure attitudes. The treatment was by no means exhaustive. Particularly conspicuous by its absence was a discussion of the importance of the various attributes to the individual. That is, in the bank example, even though the individual believes the bank has convenient hours, the person may not value this attribute, and, therefore, it may not affect his or her attitude toward the bank. On the other hand, if the individual places a strong emphasis on the convenience of a bank's location, and if he or she perceives the bank as being inconveniently located, this will have a negative, and perhaps a strongly negative, impact on his or her feeling toward the bank. There is a good deal of controversy as to how the importance of various attributes should be handled in determining a person's attitude toward an object. We shall not delve into this controversy, since it involves some very complex arguments as to how one determines which attributes are salient (that is, used in forming

---

[15]One study that compared the performance of the Stapel scale to the semantic differential found basically no difference between the results produced by, nor respondents ability to use, each. See Del I. Hawkins, Gerald Albaum, and Roger Best, "Stapel Scale or Semantic Differential in Marketing Research," *Journal of Marketing Research,* 11 (August 1974), pp. 318–322.

[16]Michael J. Etzel, Terrell G. Williams, John C. Rogers, and Douglas J. Lincoln, "The Comparability of Three Stapel Scale Forms in a Marketing Setting," in Ronald F. Bush and Shelby D. Hunt, eds., *Marketing Theory: Philosophy of Science Perspectives* (Chicago: American Marketing Association, 1982), pp. 303–306.

[17]Gregory D. Upah and Steven C. Cosmas, "The Use of Telephone Dials as Attitude Scales," *Journal of the Academy of Marketing Science,* (Fall 1980), pp. 416–426.

[18]There is evidence that demonstrates, for example, that there is little difference in results when ordinal data are analyzed by procedures appropriate to interval data. See Sanford Labovitz, "Some Observations on Measurement and Statistics," *Social Forces,* 46 (1967), pp. 151–160; Sanford Labovitz, "The Assignment of Numbers to Rank Order Categories," *American Sociological Review,* 35 (1970), pp. 515–524; and John Gaito, "Measurement Scales and Statistics: Resurgence of an Old Misconception," *Psychological Bulletin,* 87 (1980), pp. 564–567.

Table 12.3   Graphic-Ratings Scale

Please evaluate each attribute in terms of how important the attribute is to you personally by placing an "X" at the position on the horizontal line that most reflects your feelings.

Attribute	Not Important	Very Important
Courteous service	_____	
Convenient location	_____	
Convenient hours	_____	
Low interest-rate loans	_____	

an attitude) and how they should be measured.[19] Rather, we shall simply use importance values as a way of focusing on the differences among the general types of ratings scales.[20] Knowledge of the basic types should help in developing special scales for particular purposes.

There is one feature that is common to all ratings scales: "The rater places the person or object being rated at some point along a continuum or in one of an ordered series of categories; a numerical value is attached to the point or the category."[21] The scales differ, though, in the fineness of the distinctions they allow and in the procedures involved in assigning objects to positions. Three of the most common ratings scales are the graphic, the itemized, and the comparative.[22]

Graphic-Ratings Scale

• Graphic-ratings scale

Scale in which individuals indicate their ratings of an attribute by placing a check at the appropriate point on a line that runs from one extreme of the attribute to the other.

When using **graphic-ratings scales** individuals indicate their rating by placing a check at the appropriate point on a line that runs from one extreme of the attribute to the other. Many variations are possible. The line may be vertical or horizontal; it may be unmarked or marked; if marked, the divisions may be few or many as in the case of a *thermometer scale,* so called because it looks like a thermometer. Table 12.3 is an example of a horizontal, end-anchored only, graphic-ratings scale. Each individual would be instructed to indicate the importance of the attribute by check-

---

[19]This question is just one of the points of debate in attitude models. For an overview of the many points of controversy, as well as for an extensive bibliography of marketing studies, see William L. Wilkie and Edgar A. Pessemier, "Issues in Marketing's Use of Multiattribute Attitude Models," *Journal of Marketing Research,* 10 (November 1973), pp. 428–441. The empirical evidence suggests that incorporating importance weights seems to make very little difference in the predictive power of attitude models. See, for example, Neil E. Beckwith and Donald R. Lehmann, "The Importance of Differential Weights in Multiattribute Models of Consumer Attitude," *Journal of Marketing Research,* 10 (May 1973), pp. 141–145. Knowledge of the importance of various attributes can be important, though, in the design of marketing strategy. See, for instance, John A. Martella and John C. James, "Importance-Performance Analysis," *Journal of Marketing,* 41 (January 1977), pp. 77–79.

[20]Self-reports are just one of the ways attribute importance can be measured. Several other ways are using conjoint analysis, information display boards, or even deriving them statistically for groups of respondents. For examples of these approaches, see Roger M. Heeler, Chike Okechuku, and Stan Reid, "Attribute Importance: Contrasting Measurement," *Journal of Marketing Research,* 16 (February 1979), pp. 60–63; and Scott A. Neslin, "Linking Product Features to Perceptions: Self-Stated Versus Statistically Revealed Importance Weights," *Journal of Marketing Research,* 18 (February 1981), pp. 80–86.

[21]Claire Selltiz, Lawrence S. Wrightsman, and Stuart W. Cook, *Research Methods in Social Relations,* 3rd ed. (New York: Holt, Rinehart and Winston, 1976), pp. 403–404.

[22]*Ibid.,* pp. 404–406.

ing the appropriate position on the scale. The importance value would then be inferred by measuring the length of the line from the left origin to the marked position.

One of the great advantages of graphic-ratings scales is the ease with which they can be constructed and used. They provide an opportunity to make fine distinctions and are limited in this regard only by the discriminatory abilities of the rater.[23] Yet, for their most effective use, the researcher is advised to avoid making the ends of the continuum too extreme, since extremes tend to force respondents into the center of the scale, resulting in little useful information.

Itemized-Ratings Scale

* Itemized-ratings
scale

Scale distinguished by the fact that individuals must indicate their ratings of an attribute or object by selecting one from among a limited number of categories that best describes their position on the attribute or object.

The **itemized-ratings scale** is similar to the graphic-ratings scale except that the rater must select from a limited number of categories instead of placing a mark on a continuous scale. In general, five to nine categories work best in that they permit fine distinctions and yet seem to be readily understood by respondents. Of course, more can be used.[24]

There are a number of possible variations with itemized scales. Table 12.4, for example, depicts three different forms of itemized-ratings scales that have been used to measure customer satisfaction. Note that the categories are ordered in terms of their scale positions, and that while in some cases the categories have verbal descriptions attached, in other cases they do not. Category descriptions are not absolutely necessary in itemized-ratings scales, although their presence and nature does seem to affect the responses.[25] When they are used, it is important to ensure that the descriptors mean similar things to those responding.[26] When they are not used, it is tempting to conclude that a graphic-ratings scale is being used. That is an erroneous conclusion, however. The distinguishing feature of an itemized scale is that the possible response categories are limited in number. Thus, a set of faces varying systematically in terms of whether they are frowning or smiling used to capture a person's satisfaction or preference (appropriately called a *faces scale*) would be considered an itemized scale, even when no descriptions are attached to the face categories.[27]

---

[23]While easy to construct, there is some evidence that suggests graphic-ratings scales are not as reliable as itemized scales. See A. O. Gregg, "Some Problems Concerning the Use of Rating Scales for Visual Assessment," *Journal of the Market Research Society,* 8 (January 1980), pp. 29–43.

[24]Eli P. Cox III, "The Optimal Number of Response Alternatives for a Scale: A Review," *Journal of Marketing Research,* 17 (November 1980), pp. 407–422.

[25]Albert R. Wildt and Michael B. Mazis, "Determinants of Scale Response: Label Versus Position," *Journal of Marketing Research,* 15 (May 1978), pp. 261–267; and H. H. Friedman and J. R. Liefer, "Label Versus Position in Rating Scales," *Journal of the Academy of Marketing Science,* (Spring 1981), pp. 88–92.

[26]For lists of category descriptors and their numerical values, see James H. Myers and W. Gregory Warner, "Selected Properties of Selected Evaluation Adjectives," *Journal of Marketing Research,* 5 (November 1968), pp. 409–412. Spector, "Choosing Categories for Summated Rating Scales"; and Robert A. Mittelstaedt, "Semantic Properties of Selected Adjectives: Other Evidence," *Journal of Marketing Research,* 8 (May 1971), pp. 236–237.

[27]Faces scales are often used to measure the reactions of children. See, for example, M. E. Goldberg, G. J. Gorn, and W. Gibson, "TV Messages for Snack and Breakfast Foods: Do They Influence Children's Preferences?" *Journal of Consumer Research,* 5 (September 1978), pp. 73–81. Because of the ease with which they can be understood, they are also used to depict such things as corporate performance; see, for example, Bill Abrams, "With Computer Help, Marketing Professor Faces Up to Corporations Financial Data," *The Wall Street Journal,* 61 (July 22, 1981), p. 25.

Table 12.4   Three Different Forms of Itemized-Ratings Scales Used to Measure Satisfaction

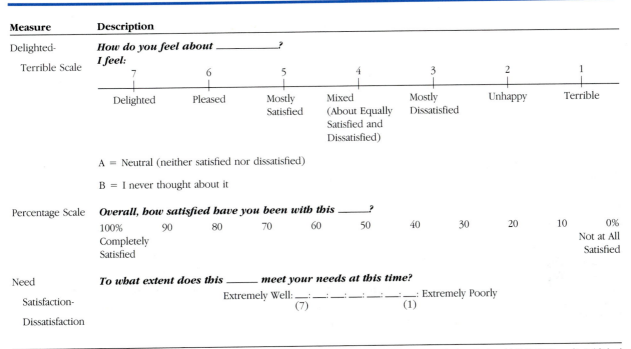

Measure	Description
Delighted-Terrible Scale	*How do you feel about* _____ *?*

I feel:

7	6	5	4	3	2	1
Delighted	Pleased	Mostly Satisfied	Mixed (About Equally Satisfied and Dissatisfied)	Mostly Dissatisfied	Unhappy	Terrible

A = Neutral (neither satisfied nor dissatisfied)

B = I never thought about it

Percentage Scale   *Overall, how satisfied have you been with this* _____ *?*

100% Completely Satisfied	90	80	70	60	50	40	30	20	10	0% Not at All Satisfied

Need Satisfaction-Dissatisfaction   *To what extent does this* _____ *meet your needs at this time?*

Extremely Well: __:__:__:__:__:__:__: Extremely Poorly
                (7)   (1)

Source: Adapted from Robert A. Westbrook, "A Rating Scale for Measuring Product/Service Satisfaction," *Journal of Marketing,* 44 (Fall 1980), p. 69. Published by the American Marketing Association.

Table 12.5   Itemized-Ratings Scale

Please evaluate each attribute in terms of how important the attribute is to you personally by placing "X" in the appropriate box.

Attribute	Not Important	Somewhat Important	Fairly Important	Very Important
Courteous service	☐	☐	☐	☐
Convenient location	☐	☐	☐	☐
Convenient hours	☐	☐	☐	☐
Low interest-rate loans	☐	☐	☐	☐

A summated-ratings statement is an example of a five-point itemized-ratings scale, while a semantic-differential adjective pair is an example of a seven-point scale. Table 12.5 is an itemized-ratings scale used to measure importance values; this four-point scale has the descriptor labels attached to the categories.

The itemized-ratings scale is also easy to construct and use, and although it does not permit the fine distinctions possible with the graphic-ratings scale, the clear definition of categories generally produces more reliable ratings.

Back to the Case

Sally McGovern sat with five-year-old Molly Levine on little chairs in Dale & Barnett's research center. Between them on the table was an acid-green stuffed animal with long antennae and bulging eyes.

Sally was explaining a measuring instrument to the little girl.

"Do you know what a happy face is, Molly?" she asked.

"Yes," she said. "I have a happy face sticker on my wall at home."

"See these three faces," she said, showing the child the following three-point funny-face scale:

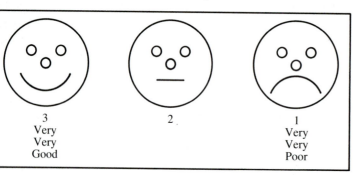

"One face is happy, one is sad, and the one in the middle is halfway between happy and sad," Sally said. "I'm going to show you some toys, and I want you to tell me which of these faces it makes you think of, okay?

"This is 'Polly the Praying Mantis,' " Sally continued. "Can you point to the face that best tells me how you feel about Polly?"

Without a moment's hesitation, Molly pointed to the sad face.

"Good work, Molly. Now here's a friend of Polly's, Fuzzy the Fly. How does he make you feel?" Sally asked.

Molly again pointed to the sad face.

"Okay, Molly. Here's another friend of Polly's and Fuzzy's. This is Grendel the Grasshopper. How does he make you feel?" Sally asked.

This time Molly pointed to the face in the middle, which had a straight line for a mouth.

"So Grendel doesn't make you happy or sad? He's just okay? Is that what you mean, Molly?" Sally probed.

"No," Molly said. "He makes me think of a mad face."

"A mad face? Why a mad face, Molly?" Sally asked.

"Cause I once caught a grasshopper outside and kept it in my room in a jar for a pet and it got out and went in my mom's room and she got mad," Molly explained.

"But we didn't say the middle face was a mad face, Molly," Sally said.

"It looks mad to me," Molly answered.

Measuring attitudes is one of the most difficult, and important, tasks a marketing researcher is likely to encounter. Measuring children's attitudes is even more complex since many of the measuring instruments commonly used for adults are inappropriate for children.

Researchers have tried several methods of adapting such techniques as the itemized-ratings scales to children's special needs. One version is the *faces scale,* which is a simplified adaptation of a ratings scale. The number of faces on the scale varies as to the age of the child involved. Three faces are generally used for the youngest group of children.

However, even such a simple technique as this has been found to be faulty. For a significant percentage of children, the middle, or neutral, face is perceived to be a "mad face." Hence for those children the scale does not really measure increasing or decreasing attitude across the scale and thus lacks validity.

Source: The information regarding measuring children's attitudes in this case is taken from Fred Cutler, "To Meet Criticisms of TV Ads, Researchers Find New Ways to Measure Children's Attitudes," *Marketing News,* 11 (January 27, 1978), p. 16.

Table 12.6   Comparative Ratings Scale

Please divide 100 points between the following two attributes in terms of the relative importance of each attribute to you.

Courteous service   _____

Convenient location   _____

Comparative-Ratings Scale

• Comparative-ratings scale

Scale requiring subjects to make their ratings as a series of relative judgments or comparisons rather than as independent assessments.

In graphic and itemized scales, respondents are not asked to compare two attributes with each other or with a standard given by researchers. For example, respondents may be asked to indicate how important convenient location is to them in choosing a bank, but not if convenient location is more or less important than convenient hours. In **comparative-ratings scales,** however, respondents are asked to judge each attribute with direct reference to the other attributes being evaluated.

The constant-sum scaling method is an example of a comparative-ratings scale that can be used to measure importance values. In the **constant-sum method,** the individual is instructed to divide some given sum among two or more attributes on the basis of their importance to him or her. Thus, in Table 12.6, if the subject assigned fifty points to courteous service and fifty points to convenient location, the attributes would be judged to be equally important; if the individual assigned eighty to courteous service and twenty to convenient location, courteous service would be considered to be four times as important.[28] Note the difference in emphasis with this method. All judgments are now made in comparison to some other alternative.

• Constant-sum method

A type of comparative-ratings scale in which an individual is instructed to divide some given sum among two or more attributes on the basis of their importance to him or her.

Respondents are generally asked to compare two attributes in this method, although it is possible to compare more. The individual could also be asked to divide 100 points among three or more attributes.[29]

Although comparative scales require more judgments from the individual than either graphic or itemized scales, they do tend to eliminate the **halo effects** that so often manifest themselves in scaling. Halo effects occur when there is carryover from one judgment to another.[30]

• Halo effect

Problem that arises in data collection when there is carryover from one judgment to another.

The problem researchers may encounter in using graphic or itemized scales to measure importance values is that respondents may be inclined to indicate that all, or nearly all, of the attributes are important. Yet empirical research indicates that when individuals are confronted by decisions that are complex because many alternatives or attributes are involved, they tend to simplify the decision by reducing the

---

[28]By considering all possible pairs of attributes in combination, one is able to construct scale values to reflect the importance ratings of each attribute to each individual. See Joy P. Guilford, *Psychometric Methods,* 2nd ed. (New York: McGraw-Hill, 1954), pp. 214–220, or Warren S. Torgerson, *Theory and Methods of Scaling* (New York: John Wiley, 1958), pp. 104–116, for a discussion of the procedure.

[29]See Valentine Appel and Babette Jackson, "Copy Testing in a Competitive Environment," *Journal of Marketing,* 39 (January 1975), pp. 84–86, and Clyde E. Harris, Jr., Richard R. Still, and Melvin R. Crask, "Stability or Change in Marketing Methods," *Business Horizons,* 21 (October 1978), pp. 32–40, for empirical examples based on the use of constant-sum scales.

[30]Comparative scales help to ensure that all respondents are approaching the rating task from the same perspective. See Richard R. Batsell and Yoram Wind, "Product Development: Current Methods and Needed Developments," *Journal of the Market Research Society,* 22 (1980), pp. 122–126.

number of alternatives or attributes they actually consider.[31] This is consistent with the notion that only certain attributes are salient when forming attitudes. The comparative scaling methods do allow more insight into the relative ranking, if not the absolute importance, of the attributes to each individual.

◆ Determining Which Scale to Use

When making the choice among scale types, number of scale points to use, whether or not to reverse some of the items, and so on, readers might find help in the findings of a very extensive study of the marketing measurement literature that examined these questions, and others, with respect to their impact on the reliability of measures.

The study, which reviewed the marketing literature over a twenty-year period, examined measures for which at least two indicators of quality were reported, and it quantitatively assessed the impact of a measure's features on its reliability.[32] As you may recall from Chapter 11, reliability gauges whether different measures of the same object, trait, or construct produce similar results. It is an important indicator of a measure's quality because it determines the impact of inconsistencies in measurement on the results. The general conclusion that emerged from the study is that many of the characteristics do not seem to affect the quality of the measure in any significant way. The exceptions are the number of items and the number of scale points. For both of these characteristics, the reliability of the measure increases as they increase. For the other characteristics, though, no choices are superior in all instances. Many of the choices are, and will probably remain, in the domain of researcher judgment, including the choice among semantic-differential, summated-ratings, or other ratings scales. All the scales have proven useful at one time or another. All rightly belong in the researcher's measurement tool kit. The nature of the problem, the characteristics of the respondents, and the planned mode of administration of the questionnaire will—and should—all affect the final choice. The respondent commitment to the task will also be a factor in the measure's reliability.[33]

◆ Multidimensional Scaling

Thus far in this chapter, we have emphasized the measurement of people's attitudes toward objects. Marketing managers are also interested in determining how people perceive various objects, be they products or brands. In its constant quest for a differential advantage, a firm needs to correctly position its products against competitive offerings. In order to do this, the product manager needs to identify the following:[34]

1. The number of dimensions consumers use to distinguish products.

2. The names of these dimensions.

---

[31]Jerome S. Bruner, Jacqueline J. Goodnaw, and George R. Austin, *A Study of Thinking* (New York: John Wiley, 1956); James G. Miller, "Sensory Overloading," in Bernard E. Flaherty, ed., *Psychophysiological Aspects of Space Flight* (New York: Columbia University Press, 1961), pp. 215–224; and Jacob Jacoby, "Perspectives on Information Overload," *Journal of Consumer Research,* 10 (March 1984), pp. 432–435.

[32]Gilbert A. Churchill, Jr., and J. Paul Peter, "Research Design Effects on the Reliability of Rating Scales: A Meta-Analysis," *Journal of Marketing Research,* 21 (November 1984), pp. 360–375.

[33]John R. Hauser and Steven M. Shugan, "Intensity Measures of Consumer Preference," *Operations Research,* 28 (March–April 1980), pp. 278–320.

[34]Glen L. Urban and John R. Hauser, *Design and Marketing of New Products* (Englewood Cliffs, N.J.: Prentice-Hall, 1980), p. 195.

3. The positioning of existing products along these dimensions.

4. Where consumers prefer a product to be on the dimensions.

One way in which managers can grasp the positioning of their brand versus competing brands is through the study of perceptual maps. Research Window 12.1, for example, depicts the situation in the automobile industry.

There are several ways by which perceptual maps can be created. The fundamental distinction is between nonattribute-based and attribute-based approaches. The attribute-based approaches rely on characteristic-by-characteristic assessments of the various objects using, for example, summated-ratings or semantic-differential

Back to the Case

"Phil, I have the results of our tests on the Love Bugs with me today, and I thought we should discuss them a bit before I leave them with you," Sally said.

"As I mentioned earlier, measuring children's attitudes is an art, not a science. Hence, I think you should weigh these results carefully before making any decisions," she continued.

"I sense some reservations here, Sally," Phil said. "Is this your way of leading up to telling me that the kids hated the Bugs?"

"Frankly, Phil, I wish I could be that clear-cut. Unfortunately, the results of our tests were very mixed. As you'll see in the report, some of the kids loved some of the Bugs. Some of the kids hated some of the Bugs. Some kids were indifferent. The only thing I can say with certainty is that Topsy the Termite made few friends," Sally said.

"We also ran a test to compare the responses of children to those of their parents on similar sets of questions. For example, we asked the kids, 'Who in your family decides what toys you get?

Would you say you? Or your mother and father?'

"We then asked the parents, 'Who decides what toys to buy the children?' and gave them the following choices: 'child decides, parent decides, or parent and child decide together.'

"The child's questionnaire is dichotomous; the parents' is multichotomous. Naturally, the child's question is not as statistically clean as the parent's, but with careful interpretation, some comparisons can be made," she said.

"Sally, this is all very interesting, but what is the bottom line? Do we market these Bugs or kill off the whole idea with a big can of Raid?" Phil asked.

"Phil, that's ultimately your decision, not mine. Read the report. Weigh all the information. Decide what level of risk you're willing to incur. My firm has made some recommendations at the end, but we make no guarantees of the product's success. I wish I could be more definitive," Sally said.

"I wish you could too," Phil said. "We need a big hit right

now. I was hoping you'd say these were going to be the Cabbage Patch Kids of the insect world, not a game of chance."

Several unique problems arise when researchers attempt to measure children's attitudes. Among them are:

1. Various scales are required for differing age groups.

2. Differing scales appear to be required for differing research objectives.

3. Scales differ drastically as to the classifications they allow.

While proper data-analysis techniques can overcome many of these concerns, the real problem arises when marketers attempt to take data from children's attitude studies and assume it is the "gospel truth."

It is especially important in such studies for researchers to point out clearly to marketing decision makers that children's attitudes are hard to measure and that children's attitude data must be used with caution.

scales. The ratings of the objects on each of the items are subsequently analyzed using various statistical techniques to identify the key dimensions or attributes consumers use to distinguish the objects.

In the nonattribute-based approaches, instead of asking a subject to rate objects on designated attributes (such as convenience, friendliness, or value for the money), one asks the individual to make some *summary* judgments about the objects. Then the researcher attempts to infer which characteristics were used to form those judgments. The reason for using this indirect approach is that in many cases the attributes may be unknown and the respondents unable or unwilling to represent their judgments accurately.

Typically, subjects are asked for their *perceptions of the similarity* between various objects and their *preferences* among these objects. An attempt is then made to locate the objects in a multidimensional space where the number of dimensions corresponds to the number of characteristics the individual used in forming the judg-

Research Window 12.1
Product Positioning in the Automotive Industry

Exasperated by the growing similarity of cars on the road, a former Detroit auto executive recently remarked that if all of today's models were lined up end to end, even the top officers of the Big Three car makers would have a hard time telling them apart at a respectable distance.

The comment addresses an increasing challenge for automotive stylists and marketers. As fuel-efficiency requirements have narrowed design and performance characteristics for cars, the auto companies have had to turn to more subtle ways of drawing distinctions between different models. An example of how that is done is the "brand image" map shown in the figure.

According to Mr. R. N. Harper, Jr., manager of product marketing plans and research, Chrysler draws up a series of such maps about three times a year, using responses to customer surveys. The surveys ask owners of different makes to rank their autos on a scale of 1 to 10 for such qualities as "youthfulness," "luxury," and "practicality." The answers are then worked into a mathematical score for each model and plotted on a graph that shows broad criteria for evaluating customer appeal.

The accompanying figure uses the technique to measure the images of the major divisions of

Perceptual Map of Automobiles

U.S. auto makers, plus a few import companies. Using it, Chrysler would conclude, for instance, that the position of its Plymouth division in the lower left-hand quadrant means that cars carrying the Plymouth name generally have a practical, though somewhat stodgy, image. The Chrysler nameplate, by contrast, is perceived as more lux-

• **Multidimensional scaling**

Approach to measurement in which people's perceptions of the similarity of objects and their preferences among the objects are measured, and these relationships are plotted in a multidimensional space.

ments. **Multidimensional scaling** analysis is the label that is used to describe the similarity- and preference-based approaches.[35]

The preference-based approaches for perceptual mapping are not used nearly as much as the similarity-based approaches. Our discussion, therefore, will concentrate on the similarity-based approaches, and in particular on the decisions that must be made in order to conduct multidimensional analysis.

---

[35]There are actually three basic types of techniques: fully metric, fully nonmetric, and nonmetric multidimensional scaling. They differ according to the kind of input data and output information used. *Fully metric* methods have metric input (interval or ratio-scaled data) and metric output, while *fully nonmetric* methods have ordinal input and generate ranked output. By far the most interesting from the marketing researcher's vantage point, at least as judged by the relative emphasis in the literature, are the *nonmetric methods,* which generate *metric output from ordinal input*. The nonmetric methods are emphasized here.

urious—though not nearly as luxurious as its principal competitors—Cadillac and Lincoln.

The map has other strategic significance, as well. By plotting on the map strong areas of customer demand, an auto maker can calculate whether its cars are on target. It can also tell from the concentration of dots representing competing models how much opposition it is likely to get in a specific territory on the map. Presumably, cars higher up on the graph should also fetch a higher price than models ranked toward the bottom, where the stress is on economy and practicality.

After viewing the results for its divisions, Chrysler concluded that Plymouth, Dodge and Chrysler all needed to present a more youthful image. It also decided that Plymouth and Dodge needed to move up sharply on the luxury scale.

Similarly, General Motors Corporation might find after looking at the map that its Chevrolet division, traditionally for entry-level buyers, ought to move down in practicality and more to the right in youthfulness. Another problem for GM on the map: the close proximity of its Buick and Oldsmobile divisions, almost on top of each other in the upper left-hand quadrant. That would suggest the two divisions are waging a

marketing war more against each other than the competition.

Chrysler also uses its marketing map to plot individual models—both those it sells currently and those it plans for the future. By trying to move a model into an unoccupied space on the map through changes in styling, price or advertising, the company believes it can better hope to carve out a distinctive niche in the market.

"The real advantage of the map," says Mr. Harper, "is that it looks at cars from a consumer perspective while also retaining some sort of tangible product orientation." He says, for example, that his bosses were delighted when, on a recent map, Chrysler's forthcoming Lancer and Commander models showed up on the map next to the Honda Accord. (The two new Chrysler compacts are due out this fall.) "That told us that consumers think of our two new cars exactly the way we hoped they would," says Mr. Harper. "It was tangible evidence of where the car would compete in the market. And frankly, that can be hard to get these days."

The attribute-based approaches are discussed only briefly later in this chapter because a full appreciation of them requires understanding of the essential purposes and operation of factor and discriminant analyses, topics that are not discussed in this book.[36]

Key Decisions in Multidimensional Scaling

In order to complete a multidimensional scaling analysis, an analyst must make a variety of decisions. Several of the key ones are pictured in Figure 12.3. The first of these is to specify the products or brands that will be used. While the purpose of the study will determine some of them, others will be left to the analyst to choose. In choosing, an analyst needs to recognize that the dimensions that appear in the perceptual map will be a direct result of the objects (known as a *stimulus set*) used to secure the judgments.

Suppose the study was being conducted to determine respondents' perceptions of various soft drinks. If no unsweetened or low-calorie soft drinks were included in the stimulus set, this very important dimension may not appear in the results. So as not to run such a risk, analysts may be tempted to include every conceivable product or brand in the stimulus set. This strategy, though, can place such a burden on respondents that their answers may be meaningless.

The burden on respondents is going to depend partly on the number of judgments each has to make and partly on the difficulty of each judgment. Both of these issues in turn depend upon how the similarity judgments are to be secured.[37] There are two main alternatives and a number of options under each alternative. The two major options are *direct* or *indirect similarity judgments,* two terms that are to some extent self-explanatory. The direct methods rely on data-collection mechanisms in which respondents compare stimuli using whatever criteria they desire and, on the basis of that comparison, state which of the stimuli are most similar, least similar, and so on.

In our soft drink example, for instance, respondents might choose to evaluate the pairs on the basis of "colaness" or "dietness." All possible pairs of the brands being evaluated could be formed, and respondents could be asked to rank-order the various pairs from most similar to least similar. (For example, which pair is more similar: Pepsi-Coke, 7-Up–Coke, or Pepsi–7-Up?) Alternatively, a brand could be singled out as a focal brand, and respondents could be asked to rank-order each of the other brands in terms of their similarity to the focal brand (if, for example, Coke were the focal brand, respondents might be asked to rank-order Pepsi, RC Cola, 7-Up, and Tab as to their similarities to Coke.) Each brand could serve, in turn, as the focal brand. While there are a number of alternative ways of collecting these judgments, they all have one thing in common: the respondents are asked to judge directly how similar the various alternatives are using criteria that they choose.

---

[36]See John R. Hauser and Frank S. Koppelman, "Alternative Perceptual Mapping Techniques: Relative Accuracy and Usefulness," *Journal of Marketing Research,* 16 (November 1979), pp. 495–506; and Joel Huber and Morris B. Holbrook, "Using Attribute Ratings for Product Positioning: Some Distinctions Among Compositional Approaches," *Journal of Marketing Research,* 16 (November 1979), pp. 507–516, for illustrations of the factor and discriminant analysis approaches to the generation of perceptual maps.

[37]For discussion of some of the main ways by which similarity judgments can be secured, see M. L. Davison, *Multidimensional Scaling* (New York: Wiley-Interscience, 1983); T. Deutcher, "Issues in Data Collection and Reliability in Multidimensional Scaling Studies—Implication for Large Stimulus Sets," in R. G. Golledge and J. N. Rayner, eds., *Proximity and Preference: Problems in the Multidimensional Scaling Analysis of Large Data Sets* (Minneapolis: University of Minnesota Press, 1982); or S. S. Schiffman, M. L. Reynolds, and F. W. Young, *Introduction to Multidimensional Scaling: Theory, Methods, and Applications* (New York: Academic Press, 1981).

Figure 12.3

Key Decisions When Conducting a Multidimensional Scaling Analysis

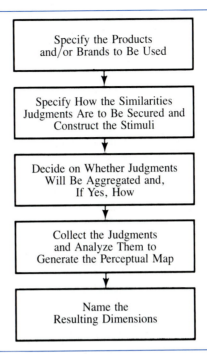

The indirect methods operate differently. Instead of respondents selecting the criteria on which to compare the alternatives, they are asked to evaluate each brand using prespecified criteria chosen by the analyst. Some kind of measure of similarity is then calculated for each pair of brands (for example, the correlation between the ratings of the brands).

The third decision analysts have to make is whether the judgments of individual respondents will be aggregated, or grouped together, so that group perceptual maps can be developed, or whether individual maps will be generated. The problem with individual maps is that they become very difficult for the marketing manager to use to develop marketing strategy. Managers typically look at marketing planning questions in terms of market segments, not individuals. Yet, as soon as the segment issue is raised, the question becomes one of deciding how the individual judgments will be aggregated. Is it likely that individuals used the same number of criteria (say, colaness, dietness, and sweetness) when evaluating the various brands? Even if they used the same number, are the criteria themselves likely to be the same? (What if some used colaness, dietness, and value for the money instead?) If they are not, what criteria should be used to group respondents? One of the most popular algorithms, INDSCAL, for example, assumes that all subjects use the same criteria to judge the similarity of objects but that they weight the dimensions differently when forming their judgments.[38]

Step 4 in Figure 12.3 involves the actual collection of the judgments and their processing. The processing involves two steps. First, an initial configuration must be determined for each of the dimensions. Different programs use different routines to generate an initial solution. Second, the points must be moved around until the fit

---

[38]For an overview of some marketing studies that have used various algorithms, see Lee G. Cooper, "A Review of Multidimensional Scaling in Marketing Research," *Applied Psychological Measurement,* 7 (Fall 1983), pp. 427–450.

is the best it can be in that dimensionality, using the criterion under which the program operates.

The last decision analysts have to make when conducting a nonmetric multidimensional scaling analysis involves what to call the dimensions. There are several procedures for naming the dimensions. The respondent can be asked to evaluate each of the objects (for instance, soft drinks) in terms of several attributes (colaness, dietness, price) determined by the researcher. The researcher then correlates the attribute scores each object receives with the coordinates for each object on the plotted diagram. In this method, the size of the respective correlation coefficients between attributes and dimensions is used to attach labels.

Another approach is to have the manager or researcher interpret the dimensions using his or her own experience and the visual configuration of points. Still a third approach is to attempt to relate the dimensions to the physical characteristics of the soft drinks as sweetness, color, or calories.

The practical fact is, however, that difficulty in naming the dimensions is one of management's major concerns with nonmetric multidimensional scaling analysis.

Attribute-Based Approaches

One of the advantages of the attribute-based approaches to the development of perceptual maps is that they do make the naming of dimensions easier. They also seem to be easier for respondents to use.[39] As mentioned earlier, the attribute-based approaches rely on having individuals rate various brands using (usually) either semantic-differential or summated-ratings scales. These judgments are usually then inputted to either discriminant analysis or factor analysis.

The emphasis in discriminant analysis is upon determining the combinations of attributes that best discriminate between the objects or brands. The dependent measures are the products rated (Coke, Pepsi, 7-Up), and the predictor variables are the attribute ratings. The analysis is typically run across groups of respondents to find a common structure. The dimensions are named by examining the weightings of the attributes that make up a discriminant dimension or by computing the correlations between the attributes and each of the discriminant scores. The use of discriminant analysis to develop perceptual maps seems to work particularly well when one is concerned with product design attributes that can be clearly and unequivocally perceived by consumers.[40]

Factor analysis relies on the assumption that there are only a few basic dimensions that underlie the attribute ratings. It examines the correlations among the attributes to identify these basic dimensions. The correlations are typically computed across brands and groups of consumers. The dimensions usually are named by examining the factor loadings that represent the correlations between each attribute and each factor. The use of factor analysis in the development of perceptual maps seems to be particularly useful when the marketing emphasis is on the formulation of communications strategy in which the linguistic relations between the attributes are key.[41]

[39]John R. Hauser and Frank S. Koppelman, "Alternative Perceptual Mapping Techniques: Relative Accuracy and Usefulness," *Journal of Marketing Research,* 16 (November 1979), pp. 495–506.

[40]Joel Huber and Morris B. Holbrook, "Using Attribute Ratings for Product Positioning: Some Distinctions Among Compositional Approaches," *Journal of Marketing Research,* 16 (November 1979), pp. 507–516.

[41]*Ibid.*

Comparison of Approaches in Multidimensional Scaling

The advantages of the attribute-based approach versus the nonattribute-based approach to multidimensional scaling are summarized in Table 12.7.[42] Most of the nonattribute-based applications in marketing use similarity judgments. Similarity measurement has the advantage of not depending on a predefined attribute set. But this feature is a two-edged sword. Although it allows respondents to use only those dimensions they normally use in making judgments among objects, it creates difficulties in naming the dimensions. Further, different consumers may use different dimensions, and then one must grapple with how best to combine consumers when forming maps. Constructing a separate map for each individual is prohibitively costly. Aggregating all the responses and then developing one map distorts reality in that it implies a homogeneity in perceptions that probably does not exist. The middle ground of grouping consumers into segments raises the whole issue of how the aggregation should be effected. Even individual consumers have been known to vary the criteria they use when making a series of judgments, indicating that the criteria depend on the products or brands in the stimulus set.

The fact that the criteria can change as the series of similarity judgments are made makes the already difficult problem of naming the dimensions even harder. One must be especially careful in using the similarity-based programs if the number of objects being judged is less than eight, as it is then very easy to develop an oversimplified picture of the competitive environment.

As previously mentioned, the attribute-based approaches make naming the dimensions easier and they also make the task of clustering respondents into groups with similar perceptions easier to deal with. They presume, however, that the list of attributes used to secure the ratings are relatively accurate and complete and that a person's perception or evaluation of a stimulus is some combination of the individual's reactions to the attributes making up the stimulus. Yet, people may not perceive or evaluate objects in terms of underlying attributes but may instead perceive them as some kind of whole that is not decomposable in terms of separate attributes. (For example, Corvette owners may not buy the car because of its handling, gas mileage, or even styling, but because of some undefinable attribute, or attributes—status, image, sexiness, playfulness, power?—that together make up a quality uniquely held by Corvette.)

Further, the measures used to group people imply some assumptions about how consumers' reactions to the various attribute scales should be combined. The attribute-based approaches are easier to use than the similarity method, since the programs employed are more readily available and less expensive to run.

Regardless of the approach taken, the appeal of multidimensional scaling lies in the maps produced by the technique. These maps can be used to provide insight into some very basic questions about markets, including, for product markets, the following:

1. The salient product attributes perceived by buyers in the market.

2. The combination of attributes buyers most prefer.

---

[42]For additional discussion of the advantages and the disadvantages of the nonattribute- and attribute-based approaches for the development of perceptual maps, see Hauser and Koppelman, "Alternative Perceptual Mapping . . ."; Huber and Holbrook, "Using Attribute Ratings . . ."; or Urban and Hauser, *Design and Marketing of New Products,* pp. 185–234.

Table 12.7   Comparison of the Nonattribute- and Attribute-based Approaches for Developing Perceptual Maps

Technique	Respondent Measures	Advantages	Disadvantages
Nonattribute-based similarity judgments	Judged similarity of various products and/or brands	Does not depend on a predefined attribute set. Allows respondents to use their normal criteria when judging objects. Allows for condition that perception of the "whole" may not be simply the sum of the perceptions of the parts.	Difficult to name dimensions. Difficult to determine if, and how, the judgments of individual respondents should be combined. Criteria respondents use depend on the stimuli being compared. Requires special programs. Provides oversimplified view of perceptions when few objects are used.
Attribute-based discriminant or factor analysis	Ratings on various products and/or brands on prespecified attributes	Facilitates naming the dimensions. Easier to cluster respondents into groups with similar perceptions. Easy and inexpensive to use. Computer programs are readily available.	Requires a relatively complete set of attributes. Rests on assumption that overall perception of a stimulus is made of the individual's reactions to the attributes making up the stimulus.

3. The products that are viewed as substitutes and those that are differentiated from one another.

4. The viable segments that exist in a market.

5. Those "holes" in a market that can support a new product venture.

Further, the technique also appears suited for product life-cycle analysis, market segmentation, vendor evaluation, the evaluation of advertisements, test marketing, sales representative–image and store-image research, brand-switching research, and attitude scaling.[43]

♦ Conjoint Measurement

♦ **Conjoint analysis**

Technique in which respondents' utilities or valuations of attributes are inferred from the preferences they express for various combinations of these attributes.

Like multidimensional-scaling analysis, **conjoint analysis** relies on the ability of respondents to make judgments about stimuli. In multidimensional-scaling analysis, the stimuli are products or brands, and respondents are asked to make judgments about their relative *similarity*. In conjoint analysis, the stimuli represent some *predetermined combinations of features, benefits, and attributes* offered by a product, and respondents are asked to make judgments about their *preference* for these various combinations. In essence, conjoint analysis seeks to determine which benefits or attributes buyers are willing to trade off to retain others. The basic aim is to determine which combinations of features respondents prefer most.

Respondents might use, for example, such attributes as miles per gallon, seating capacity, price, length of warranty, and so on in making judgments about which automobile they prefer. Yet, if asked to do so directly, many respondents might find it very difficult to state which attributes they were using and how they were combining them to form overall judgments. Conjoint analysis attempts to handle this prob-

---

[43]For a review of these applications, see Cooper, "A Review of Multidimensional Scaling in Marketing Research."

lem by estimating how much each of the attributes are valued on the basis of the choices respondents make among product concepts that are varied in systematic ways. In this type of analysis, researchers attempt to infer respondents' value systems based on their choices rather than on the respondents' own estimations.

Conjoint analysis presumes that the relative values of things considered jointly can be measured when they might not be measurable if taken one at a time. Quite often respondents are asked to express the relative value to them of various alternatives by ordering the alternatives from most desirable to least desirable. Researchers then attempt to assign values to the levels of each of the attributes in a way that is consistent with the respondents' rank-order judgments.

Example of Conjoint Analysis

Suppose we were considering introducing a new drip coffee maker and wished to assess how consumers evaluated the following levels of each of these product attributes.

- Capacity—4, 8, and 10 cups
- Price—$18, $22, and $28
- Brewing time—3, 6, 9, and 12 minutes

All three of these attributes are *motherhood* attributes, meaning that, other things being equal, most consumers would prefer either the most or least of each property—in this instance, the largest-capacity maker with the shortest brewing time and the lowest price. Unfortunately, life is not that simple. The larger coffee maker will cost more; faster brewing means a larger heating element for the same pot capacity, which also raises the cost. And a larger-capacity maker with no change in the heating element will require increased brewing time. In sum, a consumer is going to have to trade off one property to secure more of another. What the manufacturer is interested in determining is how consumers value these specific attributes. Is low price most valued, or are consumers willing to pay a higher price to secure some of the other properties? Which price? Which properties?

One way to answer these questions is to develop a set of index cards containing all possible combinations of these product attributes. If each card contains a combination of one possible aspect of each category (e.g., 4-cup capacity, $22 price, 6-minute brewing time) there would be thirty-six possible combinations.

Suppose we then asked a respondent to order these product descriptions or cards from least desirable (ranked 1) to most desirable (ranked 36). The respondent could be instructed, for example, to sort the cards first into four categories labeled very undesirable, somewhat undesirable, somewhat desirable, and very desirable, and then, after completing the sorting task, to order the cards in each category from least to most desirable. Suppose the ordering contained in Table 12.8 resulted from this process.

Note several things about these entries. First, the respondent least preferred the $28 maker with 4-cup capacity and 12-minute brewing time (ranked 1) and most preferred the 10-cup maker with 3-minute brewing time priced at $18 (ranked 36). Second, if the respondent cannot have her first choice, she is willing to trade off the short brewing time for a longer brewing time so that she could still get the 10-cup maker for $18 (ranked 35). She is not willing to trade off too much, however, as reflected by her third choice (ranked 34). Rather, she is willing to pay a little more to secure the faster 3-minute brewing time rather than having to endure an even slower 9-minute brewing time. In effect, she is willing to trade off price for brewing time.

Table 12.8   Respondent Ordering of Various Product Descriptions

| Capacity | 4 Cup | | | 8 Cup | | | 10 Cup | | |
Price	$18	$22	$28	$18	$22	$28	$18	$22	$28
Brewing Time:									
3 minutes	17	15	6	30	26	24	36	34	28
6 minutes	16	12	5	29	25	22	35	33	27
9 minutes	9	8	3	21	20	8	32	31	23
12 minutes	4	2	1	14	13	7	19	18	11

The type of question that conjoint analysis attempts to answer is, what are the individual's utilities for price, brewing time, and pot capacity in determining her choices? How much value does the individual place on each of these attributes in making her choice of products?

Procedure in Conjoint Analysis

The procedure for determining the individual's *utilities,* or values, for each of several product attributes followed in conjoint analysis is quite similar to that followed in multidimensional-scaling analysis. Again the technique is dependent on the availability of a high-speed computer. Just as in multidimensional scaling, the computer program emphasis is on generating an initial solution and subsequently on modifying that solution through a series of iterations to improve the goodness of fit.[44] More specifically, given a set of input judgments, the computer program will

1. Assign arbitrary utilities to each level of each attribute.
2. Calculate the utilities for each alternative by somehow combining, most typically adding, the individual utility values.
3. Calculate the goodness of fit between the ranking of the alternatives using these derived utility values and the original ordering of the input judgments.
4. Modify the utility values in a systematic way until the derived utilities produce evaluations that, when ordered, correspond as closely as possible to the order of the input judgments.

Based on the results determined by the computer, the researcher can determine the relative importance of each attribute. It is important to keep in mind that the importance values are dependent on the particular attributes chosen to structure the

[44]There are several programs available. One of the most popular is MONANOVA. See J. B. Kruskal, "Analysis of Factorial Experiments by Estimating Monotone Transformations of the Data," *Journal of the Royal Statistical Society,* Series B, 27 (1965), pp. 251–263; and J. B. Kruskal and F. Carmone, "Use and Theory of MONANOVA, a Program to Analyze Factorial Experiments by Estimating Monotone Transformations of the Data," unpublished paper, Bell Laboratories, 1968. For an empirical comparison involving MONANOVA versus other prediction schemes, see Dick R. Wittink and Philippe Cattin, "Alternative Estimation Methods for Conjoint Analysis: A Monte Carlo Study," *Journal of Marketing Research,* 18 (February 1981), pp. 101–106.

analysis. Thus, if higher prices had been used, the respondents' values may have been different, suggesting that price was relatively more important to the individual than if lower prices had been used.

An analysis such as this can be used to identify the optimal levels and importance of each attribute in structuring a new product offering. In addition, by grouping consumers who have similar preferences, products can be designed that come closer to satisfying particular market segments. Thus, conjoint analysis seems to have great promise at the concept-evaluation state of the product-development process.[45] In fact, conjoint analysis has been used successfully for products ranging from shampoos and panty hose to cameras and car rental agencies.[46]

General Comments on Conjoint Analysis

One can see that vital marketing questions in product design are being addressed by conjoint analysis. Further, the technique is not restricted to product evaluations. It can be used whenever one is making a choice among multi-attribute alternatives. With multi-attribute alternatives one typically does not have the option of having more of everything that is desirable and less of everything that is not desirable. Instead, most decisions involve trading off part of something in order to get more of something else. Conjoint analysis attempts to mirror the trade-offs one is willing to make. Consequently, while it has most often been used for product-design issues, including concept evaluation, it is also used quite regularly as an aid in pricing decisions, market-segmentation questions, or advertising decisions. It has been used less frequently for making distribution decisions, for evaluating vendors, for determining the rewards that salespeople value, and for determining consumer preferences for various attributes of health organizations (among other things).

◆ Summary

Learning Objective 1: List the various ways by which attitudes can be measured.

Attitudes can be measured by self-reports, observation of overt behavior, indirect techniques, performance of objective tasks, and physiological reactions.

Learning Objective 2: Name the most widely used attitude-scaling techniques in marketing research and explain why researchers prefer them.

The Likert scale, or summated-ratings scale, and the semantic-differential scale are the most widely used attitude-scaling techniques in marketing research. Both are particularly useful because they allow respondents to express the intensity of their feelings.

Learning Objective 3: Explain how a Stapel scale differs from a semantic-differential scale.

A Stapel scale differs from a semantic-differential scale in that (1) adjectives or descriptive phrases are tested separately instead of simultaneously as bipolar pairs, (2) points on the scale are identified by number, and (3) there are ten scale positions rather than seven. Respondents are told to rate how accurately each of a number of statements describes the object of interest.

---

[45]See Paul E. Green, J. Douglas Carroll, and Stephen M. Goldberg, "A General Approach to Product Design Optimization Via Conjoint Analysis," *Journal of Marketing,* 45 (Summer 1981), pp. 17–37, for a general procedure for optimizing product/service designs using input data based on conjoint-analysis methods.

[46]Paul E. Green and Donald S. Tull, *Research for Marketing Decisions,* 4th ed. (Englewood Cliffs, N.J.: Prentice-Hall, 1978), p. 491.

Learning Objective 4: Cite the one feature that is common to all ratings scales.

The one feature common to all ratings scales is that the rater places the person or object being rated at some point along a continuum or in one of an ordered series of categories; a numerical value is attached to the point or the category.

Learning Objective 5: List three of the most common types of ratings scales.

Three of the most common ratings scales are the graphic, the itemized, and the comparative scales.

Learning Objective 6: Explain the difference between a graphic-ratings scale and an itemized-ratings scale.

The itemized-ratings scale is similar to the graphic-ratings scale except that the rater must select from a limited number of categories instead of placing a mark on a continuous scale. In general, five to nine categories work well.

Learning Objective 7: Explain how the constant-sum scaling method works.

In the constant-sum method of comparative rating, the individual is instructed to divide some given sum among two or more attributes on the basis of their importance to him or her. Respondents are generally asked to compare two attributes in this method, although it is possible to compare more.

Learning Objective 8: Identify the key decisions an analyst must make in order to complete a multidimensional scaling analysis.

In order to complete a multidimensional scaling analysis, an analyst must (1) specify the products and/or brands to be used; (2) specify how the similarities judgments are to be secured and construct the stimuli; (3) decide on whether judgments will be aggregated and, if so, how; (4) collect the judgments and analyze them to generate the perceptual map; and (5) name the resulting dimensions.

Learning Objective 9: Explain the basic principle behind conjoint analysis.

In conjoint analysis, the stimuli represent some predetermined combinations of features, benefits, and attributes offered by a product, and respondents are asked to make judgments about their preference for these various combinations. In essence, conjoint analysis seeks to determine which benefits or attributes buyers are willing to trade off to obtain others. The basic aim is to determine which combinations of features respondents prefer most.

Discussion Questions, Problems, and Projects

1. (a) List at least eight attributes that students might use in evaluating bookstores.
   (b) Using these attributes, develop eight summated-ratings items and eight semantic-differential items by which attitudes towards (i) the university bookstore, and (ii) some other bookstore can be evaluated.
   (c) Administer each of the scales to ten students.
   (d) What are the average sample scores for the two bookstores using the scale of summated ratings? What can be said about students' attitudes towards the two bookstores?
   (e) Develop a profile analysis or snake diagram for the semantic-differential scale.
   (f) Based on the semantic-differential scale, what can be said about students' attitudes towards the two bookstores?

2. (a) Assume that a manufacturer of a line of cheese products wanted to evaluate customer attitudes towards the brand. A panel of 500 regular consumers of the brand responded to a questionnaire that was sent to them and that included several attitude scales that produced the following results:
   (i) the average score for the sample on a twenty-item summated-ratings scale was 105.
   (ii) the average score for the sample on a twenty-item semantic-differential scale was 106.

(iii) the average score for the sample on a fifteen-item Stapel scale was 52.

The vice-president has requested you to indicate whether his customers have a favorable or unfavorable attitude towards the brand. What would you tell him? Please be specific.

(b) Following your initial report, the vice-president has provided you with some more information. The following memo is given to you: "The company has been using the same attitude measures over the past eight years. The results of the previous studies are as follows:

Year	Summated Ratings	Semantic Differential	Stapel
1978	86	95	43
1979	93	95	48
1980	97	98	51
1981	104	101	55
1982	110	122	62
1983	106	112	57
1984	104	106	53
1985	105	106	52

We realize that there may not be any connection between attitude and behavior but it must be pointed out that sales peaked in 1982 and since then have been gradually declining." With this information, do your results change? Can anything more be said about customer attitudes?

3. Generate eight attributes that assess students' attitudes toward "take-home exams." Use the (i) graphic-, (ii) itemized-, and (iii) comparative-ratings scales to determine the importance of each of these attributes in students' evaluation of "take-home exams." (Note: In the case of the comparative-ratings scale use only five of the attributes.) Administer each of these scales to separate samples of five students.

(a) What are your findings with the graphic-ratings scale? Which attributes are important?

(b) What are your findings with the itemized-ratings scale? Which attributes are important?

(c) What are your findings with the comparative-ratings scale? Which attributes are important?

4. Find six print advertisements of different types of medium-sized automobiles (for example, Ford Fairmont Futura, Volkswagen Rabbit, Dodge 400, etc.). Append the six advertisements to this exercise.

(a) Form all possible pairs of these brands. Using the advertisements as input, rank the pairs in decreasing order of similarity (rank the most similar pair as 1) according to the way you perceive them.

(b) Complete the following table:

Perceived Similarity Judgments

Brand	1	2	3	4	5	6
1. ____						
2. ____						
3. ____						
4. ____						
5. ____						
6. ____						

(c) List the criteria that you used in determining the similarity of the brands.
(d) Now, rate the brands on the following two attributes, (i) style and (ii) features, using a seven-point semantic-differential scale. For example, if you think that a particular brand has a lot of style you would give it a rating of 6 or 7, and so on. Do this for all six brands on both the attributes.
(e) Complete the following distance matrix by computing the distances between each pair of objects. The distances can be computed with the following formula:

$$D_{ij} = \sqrt{(x_i - x_j)^2 + (y_i - y_j)^2}$$

where

x_i = rating of Brand i on Attribute 1 $i = 1 \ldots 6$
y_i = rating of Brand i on Attribute 2
x_j = rating of Brand j on Attribute 1
y_j = rating of Brand j on Attribute 2 $j = 1 \ldots 6$ $i \neq j$

For example, the distance between Brand 1 and Brand 2, is

$$D_{12} = \sqrt{(x_1 - x_2)^2 + (y_1 - y_2)^2}$$

Distance Matrix

Brand	1	2	3	4	5	6
1. ____						
2. ____						
3. ____						
4. ____						
5. ____						
6. ____						

Note: The pairs that are most similar on the two attributes have smaller distances. The pairs that are most dissimilar on the two attributes have larger distances.

(f) Convert the above distances to similarity values by assigning the rank of 1 to the two closest objects, the rank of 2 to the next closest objects, and so on. Assign the average of the ranks to those pairs in which the distances between the two objects are the same.

Calculated Similarity Judgments

Brand	1	2	3	4	5	6
1.						
2.						
3.						
4.						
5.						
6.						

(g) Compare the perceived similarity in part b of this question and the calculated similarity in part f.

5. Suppose you are interested in introducing a new toaster-oven and decide to use conjoint analysis to determine how people value different attributes.
   (a) List three product attributes that would be relevant to you.
   (b) List three levels of each of these product attributes you might use to assess respondents' utilities.
   (c) Assign utilities to each of these levels. For example, suppose size is one of the attributes. One might then assign higher utilities to each of the larger sizes.

	Attribute I		Attribute II		Attribute III	
Levels	**Utility**	**Levels**	**Utility**	**Levels**	**Utility**
1.					
2.					
3.					

   (d) Calculate the utilities for each alternative by assuming that the utilities for each attribute will combine additively. Complete the following table:

Utilities for the Feature Combinations Given the Assumed Values

Attribute I		**(1)**			**(2)**			**(3)**	
Attribute II	**(1)**	**(2)**	**(3)**	**(1)**	**(2)**	**(3)**	**(1)**	**(2)**	**(3)**
	___	___	___	___	___	___	___	___	___

Attribute III

(1)

(2)

(3)

   (e) Request a respondent to rank-order these product descriptions from least desirable (rank of 1) to most desirable (rank of 27).
       Note: 1. There are twenty-seven combinations.
                    2. Writing each combination on a separate index card would ease the task.
   (f) Now, complete the following table.

Respondents Ordering of Various Product Descriptions

Attribute I		**(1)**			**(2)**			**(3)**	
Attribute II	**(1)**	**(2)**	**(3)**	**(1)**	**(2)**	**(3)**	**(1)**	**(2)**	**(3)**
	___	___	___	___	___	___	___	___	___

Attribute III

(1)

(2)

(3)

(g) Plot the original order of the input judgments against the assigned utilities.

(h) Are the assigned utilities appropriate?

Suggested Additional Readings

For a general discussion of how to ask questions in attitude surveys, see

Howard Schuman and Stanley Presser, *Questions and Answers in Attitude Surveys* (Orlando: Academic Press, 1981).

For discussion of a general procedure that can be followed to develop attitude scales having desirable qualities, see

Gilbert A. Churchill, Jr., "A Paradigm for Developing Measures of Marketing Constructs," *Journal of Marketing Research,* 16 (February 1979), pp. 64–73.

For discussion of the various alternatives for conducting a multidimensional-scaling analysis, see

Glen L. Urban and John R. Hauser, *Design and Marketing of New Products* (Englewood Cliffs, N.J.: Prentice-Hall, 1980), especially pp. 185–234.

For discussion of the various issues surrounding conjoint analysis, see

Paul E. Green and V. Srinivasan, "Conjoint Analysis in Consumer Research: Issues and Outlook," *Journal of Consumer Research,* 5 (September 1978), pp. 103–123.

Part Four   Research Project

The fourth stage in the research process is to design the data-collection forms. As we learned from the chapters in this part, designing a questionnaire is still an art, not a science. Nonetheless, as we saw in Chapter 10, there is a pattern of steps that beginning researchers often find useful in developing questionnaires. The method outlined begins with specifying what information will be sought, and it ends with pretesting the questionnaire and revision. As was pointed out in the chapter, however, only rarely will actual questionnaire development be so orderly. More often, researchers will find themselves circling back to revise an earlier part of the questionnaire after subsequent development has proven it to be faulty in some respect.

We also learned in these chapters that the typical questionnaire contains two types of information: basic information and classification information. Basic information refers to the subject of the study, while classification information refers to the data collected about respondents, such as demographic and socioeconomic characteristics, that help in understanding the results. As we saw, the proper questionnaire sequence is to secure basic information first and classification information last, since without the basic information, there is no study.

Researchers for CARA decided to use a self-report attitude scale to measure local businesspeople's feelings toward various advertising media and their sales representatives. In the chosen format, respondents were asked to indicate the extent to which they agreed or disagreed with statements about sales representatives and advertising media by checking one of the blanks ranging from strong agreement to strong disagreement. This format allows researchers two advantages: they can measure a respondent's intensity of feeling, and responses can be easily scored.

In the CARA study, the various degrees of agreement were assigned the values of 5, 4, 3, 2, and 1, with "strongly agree" representing the value of 5 and "strongly disagree" representing the value of 1. A total attitude score for each respondent could thereby be calculated by summing the ratings of the individual items.

Respondents were asked to rate the importance of the attributes and characteristics used to describe sales representatives and advertising media by checking the three most important items in each category. Researchers thought this was important because an individual may strongly agree or disagree with an item but may not value that characteristic or attribute.

Each of the three categories of sales representatives contained twelve descriptive attributes. The attributes were ordered randomly, and the identical order was then used in each category. By using identical items in identical order, researchers could compare total attitude scores between the sales representative categories. If different items, or a different ordering of items within each category had been used, variation in the testing instrument might have been responsible for differences in resulting scores.

CARA Questionnaire

Section 1

Please indicate your opinion as to the extent to which you agree or disagree with the following statements for your television, radio, and newspaper sales representatives by placing an X in the appropriate blank. If you have more than one sales representative in any of these media, your opinions should include your general impressions of the sales representatives calling on you. If you have never been in contact with a sales representative in one or more of these media, please omit that section (or those sections) and proceed to the next. Don't worry over individual responses. It is your first impression to each item that is important.

Television Sales Representative

The TV sales representatives calling on me are:	Strongly Agree	Agree	Neither Agree Nor Disagree	Disagree	Strongly Disagree
1. Creative	_____	_____	_____	_____	_____
2. Reliable	_____	_____	_____	_____	_____
3. Sincere	_____	_____	_____	_____	_____
4. Results oriented	_____	_____	_____	_____	_____
5. Knowledgeable about my business	_____	_____	_____	_____	_____
6. Cooperative	_____	_____	_____	_____	_____
7. Available when needed	_____	_____	_____	_____	_____
8. Hard working	_____	_____	_____	_____	_____
9. Concerned about my particular advertising needs	_____	_____	_____	_____	_____
10. Able to get my ads placed quickly	_____	_____	_____	_____	_____
11. Aware of who my customers are	_____	_____	_____	_____	_____
12. Concerned about follow-through after the service	_____	_____	_____	_____	_____

Radio Sales Representative

The radio sales representatives calling on me are:	Strongly Agree	Agree	Neither Agree Nor Disagree	Disagree	Strongly Disagree
1. Creative	_____	_____	_____	_____	_____
2. Reliable	_____	_____	_____	_____	_____
3. Sincere	_____	_____	_____	_____	_____
4. Results oriented	_____	_____	_____	_____	_____
5. Knowledgeable about my business	_____	_____	_____	_____	_____
6. Cooperative	_____	_____	_____	_____	_____
7. Available when needed	_____	_____	_____	_____	_____
8. Hard working	_____	_____	_____	_____	_____
9. Concerned about my particular advertising needs	_____	_____	_____	_____	_____
10. Able to get my ads placed quickly	_____	_____	_____	_____	_____
11. Aware of who my customers are	_____	_____	_____	_____	_____
12. Concerned about follow-through after the service	_____	_____	_____	_____	_____

CARA Questionnaire   *continued*

Newspaper Sales Representative

The newspaper sales representatives calling on me are:	Strongly Agree	Agree	Neither Agree Nor Disagree	Disagree	Strongly Disagree
1. Creative	_____	_____	_____	_____	_____
2. Reliable	_____	_____	_____	_____	_____
3. Sincere	_____	_____	_____	_____	_____
4. Results oriented	_____	_____	_____	_____	_____
5. Knowledgeable about my business	_____	_____	_____	_____	_____
6. Cooperative	_____	_____	_____	_____	_____
7. Available when needed	_____	_____	_____	_____	_____
8. Hard working	_____	_____	_____	_____	_____
9. Concerned about my particular advertising needs	_____	_____	_____	_____	_____
10. Able to get my ads placed quickly	_____	_____	_____	_____	_____
11. Aware of who my customers are	_____	_____	_____	_____	_____
12. Concerned about follow-through after the service	_____	_____	_____	_____	_____

Please indicate what you believe are the three most important characteristics of a sales representative by placing an X in the appropriate blank. For example, if you feel Items 4, 8, and 10 are the most important characteristics, you would place an X in the blank next to each of these items.

The three most important characteristics of a media sales representative are:

1. Creativity _____
2. Reliability _____
3. Sincerity _____
4. An orientation towards results _____
5. A knowledge about my business _____
6. Cooperation _____
7. Availability when needed _____
8. Hard working _____
9. A concern about my particular advertising needs _____
10. The ability to quickly place my ads _____
11. Awareness of who my customers are _____
12. Concern about follow-through after the service _____

continued

CARA Questionnaire   *continued*

Section 2

Please indicate your opinion as to the extent to which you agree or disagree with the following statements about television, radio, and newspaper advertising regardless of whether you use that form of advertising or not. Place an X in the appropriate blank. Again, don't worry over individual responses since it is your first impression to each item that is important.

Television Advertising	Strongly Agree	Agree	Neither Agree Nor Disagree	Disagree	Strongly Disagree
1. People pay attention to the ads	_____	_____	_____	_____	_____
2. The ads reach my target market	_____	_____	_____	_____	_____
3. The ads do not cost too much	_____	_____	_____	_____	_____
4. The ads improve my sales volume	_____	_____	_____	_____	_____
5. The ads are creative	_____	_____	_____	_____	_____
6. The ads do not have to be repeated frequently to be effective	_____	_____	_____	_____	_____
7. The ads reach a large number of people	_____	_____	_____	_____	_____
8. The ads build up recognition of my business	_____	_____	_____	_____	_____
9. There is evidence the ads reach a known market	_____	_____	_____	_____	_____
10. Buying the ads is not a difficult process	_____	_____	_____	_____	_____
11. It is easy to monitor when the ads are being run	_____	_____	_____	_____	_____
12. The quality of the ads is high (good)	_____	_____	_____	_____	_____

Radio Advertising	Strongly Agree	Agree	Neither Agree Nor Disagree	Disagree	Strongly Disagree
1. People pay attention to the ads	_____	_____	_____	_____	_____
2. The ads reach my target market	_____	_____	_____	_____	_____
3. The ads do not cost too much	_____	_____	_____	_____	_____
4. The ads improve my sales volume	_____	_____	_____	_____	_____
5. The ads are creative	_____	_____	_____	_____	_____
6. The ads do not have to be repeated frequently to be effective	_____	_____	_____	_____	_____
7. The ads reach a large number of people	_____	_____	_____	_____	_____
8. The ads build up recognition of my business	_____	_____	_____	_____	_____
9. There is evidence the ads reach a known market	_____	_____	_____	_____	_____
10. Buying the ads is not a difficult process	_____	_____	_____	_____	_____
11. It is easy to monitor when the ads are being run	_____	_____	_____	_____	_____
12. The quality of the ads is high (good)	_____	_____	_____	_____	_____

CARA Questionnaire   *continued*

Newspaper Advertising	Strongly Agree	Agree	Neither Agree Nor Disagree	Disagree	Strongly Disagree
1. People pay attention to the ads	_____	_____	_____	_____	_____
2. The ads reach my target market	_____	_____	_____	_____	_____
3. The ads do not cost too much	_____	_____	_____	_____	_____
4. The ads improve my sales volume	_____	_____	_____	_____	_____
5. The ads are creative	_____	_____	_____	_____	_____
6. The ads do not have to be repeated frequently to be effective	_____	_____	_____	_____	_____
7. The ads reach a large number of people	_____	_____	_____	_____	_____
8. The ads build up recognition of my business	_____	_____	_____	_____	_____
9. There is evidence the ads reach a known market	_____	_____	_____	_____	_____
10. Buying the ads is not a difficult process	_____	_____	_____	_____	_____
11. It is easy to monitor when the ads are being run	_____	_____	_____	_____	_____
12. The quality of the ads is high (good)	_____	_____	_____	_____	_____

Please indicate what you believe are the three most important attributes of advertising by placing an X in the appropriate blank. For example, if you feel Items 4, 8, and 10 are the most important attributes, you would place an X in the blank next to each of those items.

The three most important attributes of advertising are that:

1. People pay attention to the ads _____
2. The ads reach my target market _____
3. The ads do not cost too much _____
4. The ads improve my sales volume _____
5. The ads are creative _____
6. The ads do not have to be repeated frequently to be effective _____
7. The ads reach a large number of people _____
8. The ads build up recognition of my business _____
9. There is evidence the ads reach a known market _____
10. Buying the ads is not a difficult process _____
11. It is easy to monitor when the ads are being run _____
12. The quality of the ads is high (good) _____

continued

Section 3: Classification Data

1. **What types of advertising have you used over the last 12 months?**

   Outdoor   _____

   Radio   _____

   Television   _____

   Newspaper   _____

   Magazine   _____

   Yellow Pages   _____

   Direct Mail   _____

   Shoppers   _____

   Other   _____

2. **Approximately what proportion of your total yearly advertising budget is spent on each of the following types of advertising?**

   Outdoor   _____

   Radio   _____

   Television   _____

   Newspaper   _____

   Magazine   _____

   Yellow Pages   _____

   Direct Mail   _____

   Shoppers   _____

   Other   _____

   Total =   100%

3. **How much do you spend annually on advertising?**

   0–$9,999   _____

   $10,000–$24,999   _____

   $25,000–$49,999   _____

   $50,000 and over   _____

4. **Which category best describes your position?**

   Manager   _____

   Owner/Manager   _____

   Secretary   _____

   Clerk   _____

   Other   _____

5. **Do you make decisions regarding advertising expenditures?**

   Yes   _____

   No   _____

6. **Do you use an advertising agency?**

   Yes   _____

   No   _____

Respondents were also asked to indicate which three of the twelve attributes they felt were the most important. These attributes were listed in the same order as the items in the sales representatives' scales.

The advertising media of television, radio, and newspaper were also described by twelve characteristics. These characteristics were randomly ordered, and each category used the identical order of items for the reason just cited. The twelve attributes were also listed in an importance scale in the same order as the items in the media categories, and respondents were asked to select the three attributes they believed to be most important.

Questions regarding the sales representatives were asked first so as to generate interest in the questionnaire. This section was followed by questions about attitudes toward the various media. Finally, researchers added a section requesting classification information. This section was last because, while important, it was the least critical to the study.

Researchers chose the twelve specific attributes used to describe the sales representatives and the advertising media based on their review of the literature, discussions with CARA members, and experience surveys with local retailers.

Cases to Part Four

Case 4.1   Rumstad Decorating Centers (B)

Rumstad Decorating Centers was an old-line Rockford, Illinois, business. The company was originally founded as a small paint and wallpaper supply store in 1929 by Mr. Joseph Rumstad, who managed the store until his retirement in 1970, at which time Jack Rumstad, his son, took over. In 1974 the original downtown store was closed and a new outlet was opened on the city's rapidly expanding west side. In 1983, a second store was opened on the east side of the city, and the name of the business was changed to Rumstad Decorating Centers.

Jack Rumstad's review of 1985 operations proved disconcerting. Both stores had suffered losses for the year (see Rumstad Decorating Centers, part A). The picture was far more dismal at the west side store. Losses at the east side store were 80 percent less than the previous year's, which was partially due to some major organizational changes. Further, the east side store had experienced a 25 percent increase in net sales and a 25 percent increase in gross profits over 1984. The west side store, in contrast, had shown a 21 percent decrease in net sales and a 31 percent decrease in gross profit.

Some preliminary research by Mr. Rumstad suggested the problem at the west side store might be traced to the store's location and/or its advertising. Was the location perceived as convenient? Were potential customers aware of Rumstad Decorating Centers, the products they carried, and where they were located? Did people have favorable impressions of Rumstad? How did attitudes toward Rumstad compare with those toward Rumstad's major competitors?

Mr. Rumstad realized he did not have the expertise to answer these questions. Consequently, he called in Mrs. Sandra Parrett, who owned and managed her own marketing research service in the Rockford area. Mrs. Parrett handled all liaison work with the client and assisted in the research design. In addition to Mrs. Parrett, Lisa Parrett, her daughter, supervised the field staff of four, analyzed data, and prepared research reports. Although the company was small, it had an excellent reputation within the business community.

Research Design

Rumstad agreed with Mrs. Parrett's suggestion that the best way to investigate Rumstad's concerns would be to use a structured, somewhat disguised questionnaire (see Figure 1). The sponsor of the research was to be hidden from the respondents so as to prevent them from answering "correctly" instead of honestly, and so that questions about two of Rumstad's main competitors, the Nina Emerson Decorating Center and the Wallpaper Shop, could be introduced. Both of these stores offered products and services similar to those carried by Rumstad, and they were located in the same area as Rumstad's west side store. The study was to be confined to the west side store because of cost; loss of profits for the last several years had severely constrained Rumstad's ability to engage in research of this sort. However, the west side store was so critical to the very survival of Rumstad Decorating Centers that Jack Rumstad was willing to commit funds to this investigation, although he repeatedly stressed to Mrs. Parrett the need to keep the cost as low as possible.

Even though the Emerson Decorating Center and the Wallpaper Shop were similar to Rumstad, there were differences in their marketing strategies. Both stores seemed to advertise more than did Rumstad, for example, although the exact amounts of their advertising budgets were not available. Emerson advertised in the *Shopper's World* (a weekly paper devoted exclusively to advertising that is distributed free), ran ads four times a year in the *Rockford Morning Star,* and did a small amount of radio and outdoor advertising. The Wallpaper Shop also advertised regularly in the *Shopper's World* but ran small ads daily in the *Morning Star* and daily radio commercials as well. Rumstad had formerly advertised in the *Morning Star* but now relied exclusively on the *Shopper's World.*

Figure 1   **Sample Questionnaire—Rumstad Decorating Centers**

Section I

For Questions 1–8, please indicate your opinion as to the importance of the following factors in choosing a decorating center. Place an X in the appropriate blank.

	Not Important	Slightly Important	Fairly Important	Very Important
1. Saw or heard an advertisement	___	___	___	___
2. Special sale	___	___	___	___
3. Convenient location	___	___	___	___
4. Convenient hours	___	___	___	___
5. Knowledgeable sales personnel	___	___	___	___
6. Good quality products	___	___	___	___
7. Additional services (e.g., matching paints, decorator services, etc.)	___	___	___	___
8. Reasonable prices in relation to quality	___	___	___	___

Below is a list of abbreviations for the three west side stores which will be referred to throughout the questionnaire:

Emerson Decorating Center — "Emerson"

Rumstad Decorating Center — "Rumstad"

Wallpaper Shop — "Wallpaper Shop"

Please indicate your response with an X in the appropriate blank.

9. Do you know where any of the following west side stores are located? (i.e., could you find any of these stores without referring to another source?)

	Yes	No
Emerson	___	___
Rumstad	___	___
Wallpaper Shop	___	___

10. When was the last time you heard or saw any advertisements for the following stores?

	Never	Within the Last Month	1–6 Months	More than 6 Months
Emerson	___	___	___	___
Rumstad	___	___	___	___
Wallpaper Shop	___	___	___	___

11. Please indicate the source(s) of any advertisements you have seen or heard.

	Have Not Seen/Heard	Shopper's World	Rockford Morning Star	Radio	TV	Other	Don't Recall
Emerson	___	___	___	___	___	___	___
Rumstad	___	___	___	___	___	___	___
Wallpaper Shop	___	___	___	___	___	___	___

12. Do you know which of the following items are available in these stores? If so, check the item(s) that apply.

	Don't Know	Paint	Paneling	Carpeting	Draperies	Other
Emerson	___	___	___	___	___	___
Rumstad	___	___	___	___	___	___
Wallpaper Shop	___	___	___	___	___	___

continued

Figure 1   *continued*

13. Which name brands of paint, if any, do you associate with the following stores?

	Benjamin Moore	Dutch Boy	Glidden	Pittsburgh	Do Not Associate Any Listed
Emerson	_____	_____	_____	_____	_____
Rumstad	_____	_____	_____	_____	_____
Wallpaper Shop	_____	_____	_____	_____	_____

14. Have you ever visited any of these west side stores?

	Never	Within Last Year	1–5 Yrs. Ago	More than 5 Yrs. Ago
Emerson	_____	_____	_____	_____
Rumstad	_____	_____	_____	_____
Wallpaper Shop	_____	_____	_____	_____

Section II

If you have visited or have knowledge of *one or more* of the stores listed below, please indicate your opinion as to the extent to which you agree or disagree with the following statements for each store(s). For instance, if you have knowledge of only one store, please answer each question for that particular store. If you have not visited or have no knowledge of any of these stores, omit this section and proceed to Section III.

	Strongly Agree	Agree	Neither Agree Nor Disagree	Disagree	Strongly Disagree
15. The location of the store is convenient.					
Emerson	_____	_____	_____	_____	_____
Rumstad	_____	_____	_____	_____	_____
Wallpaper Store	_____	_____	_____	_____	_____
16. The sales personnel are knowledgeable.					
Emerson	_____	_____	_____	_____	_____
Rumstad	_____	_____	_____	_____	_____
Wallpaper Store	_____	_____	_____	_____	_____
17. The store lacks additional services (e.g., matching paint, decorator services, etc.).					
Emerson	_____	_____	_____	_____	_____
Rumstad	_____	_____	_____	_____	_____
Wallpaper Store	_____	_____	_____	_____	_____
18. The store carries good quality products.					
Emerson	_____	_____	_____	_____	_____
Rumstad	_____	_____	_____	_____	_____
Wallpaper Store	_____	_____	_____	_____	_____
19. The prices are reasonable in relation to the quality of the products.					
Emerson	_____	_____	_____	_____	_____
Rumstad	_____	_____	_____	_____	_____
Wallpaper Store	_____	_____	_____	_____	_____

Figure 1 *continued*

	Strongly Agree	Agree	Neither Agree Nor Disagree	Disagree	Strongly Disagree
20. *The store hours are inconvenient.*					
Emerson	____	____	____	____	____
Rumstad	____	____	____	____	____
Wallpaper Store	____	____	____	____	____

Section III

1. Your sex: ____ Male   ____ Female

2. Your age: ____ Under 25   ____ 25–29   ____ 30–39   ____ 40–54 ____ 55 or over

3. How long have you lived in Rockford?
____ Less than 1 year   ____ 1–3 years   ____ 4 or more years

4. Do you: ____ Own a home or condominium   ____ Rent a house
____ Rent an apartment   ____ Other

5. When was the last time you painted or remodeled your residence?
____ Never   ____ Within past year   ____ 1–5 years ago   ____ More than 5 years ago

6. Approximately how many times have you received the weekly Shopper's World in the past 3 months?
____ Never   ____ 1–5 times   ____ 6–12 times

7. Do you read or page through the Shopper's World?
____ Do not receive it   ____ Never   ____ Less than ½ the time
____ About ½ the time   ____ More than ½ the time

Sample

Because of the financial constraints imposed on the study by Jack Rumstad, it was decided to limit the study to households within a two-mile radius of Rumstad, Emerson, and the Wallpaper Shop. Aldermanic districts within the two-mile radius were identified; there were four in all, and the wards within each district were listed. Two of the twelve wards were then excluded because they were outside of the specified area. Blocks within each of the remaining ten wards were enumerated, and five blocks were randomly selected from each ward. An initial starting point for each block was determined, and then the questionnaires were administered by the Parrett field staff at every sixth house on the block. All interviews were conducted on Saturday and Sunday. If there was no one at home or if the respondent refused to cooper-ate, the next house on the block was substituted; there was no one at home at thirty-nine households, and eighteen others refused to participate. The field work was completed within one weekend and produced a total sample of 123 responses.

Questions

1. Evaluate the questionnaire. Do you think the questionnaire adequately addresses the concerns raised by Rumstad?

2. How would you suggest the data collected be analyzed so as to best solve Rumstad's problem?

3. Do you think personal administration of the questionnaires was called for in this study, or would you suggest an alternative scheme? Why or why not?

Case 4.2   Calamity-Casualty Insurance Company[1]

Calamity-Casualty is an insurance company located in Dallas, Texas, that deals exclusively with automobile coverage. Its policy offerings include the standard features offered by most insurers, such as collision, comprehensive, emergency road service, medical, and uninsured motorist. The unique aspect of Calamity-Casualty Insurance is that all policies are sold through the mail. Agents do not make personal calls on clients, and the company does not operate district offices. As a result, Calamity-Casualty's capital-labor requirements are greatly reduced at a substantial cost savings to the company. A great portion of these savings are passed on to the consumer in the form of lower prices. The data indicate that Calamity-Casualty offers its policies at 20 to 25 percent below the average market rate.

The company's strategy of selling automobile insurance by mail at low prices has been very successful. Calamity-Casualty has traditionally been the third largest seller of automobile insurance in the Southwest. During the past five years, the company has consistently achieved an average market share of some 14 percent in the four states it serves—Arizona, New Mexico, Nevada, and Texas. This compares favorably to the 19 percent and 17 percent market shares realized by the two leading firms in the region. However, Calamity-Casualty has never been highly successful in Arizona. The largest market share gained by Calamity-Casualty in Arizona for any one year was 4 percent, which placed the company seventh among firms competing in that state.

The company's poor performance in Arizona greatly concerns Calamity-Casualty's board of executives. Demographic experts estimate that during the next six to ten years, the population in Arizona will increase some 10 to 15 percent, the largest projected growth rate of any state in the Southwest. Thus, for Calamity-Casualty to remain a major market force in the area, the company needs to improve its sales performance in Arizona.

In response to this matter, Calamity-Casualty sponsored a study that was conducted by the Automobile Insurance Association of America (AIAA), the national association of automobile insurance executives, to determine Arizona residents' attitudes toward and perception of the various insurance companies selling policies in that state. The results of the AIAA re-

search showed that Calamity-Casualty was favorably perceived across most categories measured. Calamity-Casualty received the highest ratings with respect to service, pricing, policy offering, and image. While these findings were well received by the company's board of executives, they provided little strategic insight into how Calamity-Casualty might increase sales in Arizona.

Since the company was committed to obtaining information useful for developing a more effective Arizona sales campaign, the executive board sought the services of Aminbane, Pedrone, and Associates, a marketing research firm specializing in insurance consulting, to help with the matter. After many discussions between members of the research team and executives at Calamity-Casualty, it was decided that the most beneficial approach toward designing a more appropriate sales campaign would be to ascertain the psychographic profiles of nonpurchasers and direct mail purchasers of Calamity-Casualty insurance. This would help the company better understand the personal factors influencing people's decision to respond or not to respond to direct mail solicitation.

Research Design

To gain insight as to which psychographic factors are important in describing purchasers of automobile insurance, some exploratory research was undertaken. Depth interviews were held with two insurance salespersons, who offered various insights on the subject. These experience interviews were followed by a focus-group meeting with Arizona residents who had received a direct mail offer from Calamity-Casualty. Finally, the research team consulted university professors in both psychology and mass communications to uncover other determinants of buyer behavior. Output from these procedures revealed three primary factors that could be used to describe purchasers of insurance by mail—namely, risk aversion, powerlessness, and convenience orientation. It was believed that people who were risk-averse, had a low

[1]The contributions of David M. Szymanski to the development of this case are gratefully acknowledged.

Table 1   Calamity-Casualty Marketing Research Questionnaire Items

Risk Aversion

1. It is always better to buy a used car from a dealer than from an individual.

2. Generally speaking, I avoid buying generic drugs at the drugstore.

3. It would be a disaster to be stranded on the road due to a breakdown.

4. It would be important to me to plan a long road trip very carefully and in great detail.

5. I would like to try parachute jumping sometime.

6. Before buying a new product, I would first discuss it with someone who had already used it.

7. Before deciding to see a new movie in a theater, it is important to read the critical reviews.

8. If my car needed even a minor repair, I would first get cost estimates from several garages.

Powerlessness

1. Persons like myself have little chance of protecting our personal interests when they conflict with those of strong pressure groups.

2. A lasting world peace can be achieved by those of us who work toward it.

3. I think each of us can do a great deal to improve world opinion of the United States.

4. This world is run by the few people in power, and there is not much the little guy can do about it.

5. People like me can change the course of world events if we make ourselves heard.

6. More and more, I feel helpless in the face of what's happening in the world today.

Convenience Orientation

1. I like to buy things by mail or catalog because it saves time.

2. I feel it is not worth the extra effort to clip coupons for groceries.

3. I would rather wash my own car than pay to have it washed at a car wash.

4. I would prefer to have an automatic transmission rather than a stick shift in my car.

5. When choosing a bank, I feel that location is the most important factor.

6. When shopping for groceries, I would be willing to drive a longer distance in order to buy at lower prices.

Note: Each item requires one of the following responses:

Responses	Code
S.A.—Strongly Agree	5
A.—Agree	4
N.—Neither Agree Nor Disagree	3
D.—Disagree	2
S.D.—Strongly Disagree	1

sense of powerlessness, and were convenience-oriented would be more favorably disposed toward direct mail marketing efforts and thus would be more likely to purchase Calamity-Casualty automobile insurance.

Method of Data Collection Given these factors of interest, the list of the items contained in Table 1 was generated to form the basis of a questionnaire to be administered to Arizona residents. Two samples of subjects were to be used—one of direct mail buyers and one of nonbuyers. The research team estimated that 175 subjects would be required from both samples to adequately assess the three constructs. Because a mail questionnaire dealing with psychographic subject matter might have a very low response rate, and because attitude toward direct mail was one of the attributes being measured, a telephone interview was believed to be best suited to the needs at hand.

Questions

1. Conceptually, what are the constructs risk aversion, convenience, and powerlessness?

2. Do you think the sample of items adequately assesses each construct? Can you think of any additional items that could or should be used?

Case 4.3   Consumer Medical Attitudes[1]

In planning and designing this research project, a number of practical concerns—such as implications and strategies for which the data might be used and methodological concerns for achieving the highest validity and reliability consistent with the resources available for the study—were considered.

Objectives of the Study

The purpose of this study is to assess attitudes and behavior of consumers concerning health care and physician services, with special attention to consumer support for possible solutions to the medical malpractice problem. More specifically, the objectives of this study are:

1. To describe criteria used by patients to select and evaluate health care by physicians.

2. To identify persons likely to bring a malpractice suit in specified situations.

3. To determine levels of support for alternative approaches for dealing with the malpractice study.

Research Methodology

Telephone Sample This study was conducted using a telephone questionnaire administered to a random sample of 1,500 adult residents in Ohio. The telephone format was selected after consideration of both mail and personal interviews, which it was felt would provide less reliable data in this particular study than would telephone interviews. The sample was drawn with the assistance of the Chicago-based Reuben Donnelly Company, which maintains telephone directories from all cities of the United States. It provided a computer-generated random sample of telephone numbers in Ohio cities and rural areas.

A sample of 1,500 is reliable and provides a reasonable base for making inferences about the Ohio adult population. However, all samples have some limitations. For example, persons who were not at home when calls were made or who do not have telephones could be underrepresented in this study. To minimize these problems, three callbacks were attempted at various time periods.

The interviewing for this study was completed by Dwight Spencer Associates from WATS line facilities in Columbus, Ohio, using skilled and continuously monitored interviewers.

Design and Pretest of Questionnaire The questionnaire used in this study was developed from prior studies on medical care and physician services as well as standardized forms used for securing demographic and attitudinal data. A preliminary form of the questionnaire was administered by telephone to twenty respondents in the Columbus area; it was further tested through a focus-group interview in which male and female consumers discussed each question and possible responses on the questionnaire.

After the telephone pretest, the focus-group interview, and consultation with the Ohio State Medical Association staff, numerous changes were made in order to clarify some questions unlikely to provide useful information in their original form. Very few difficulties were encountered in the administration of the final questionnaire. Even though it was lengthy—it took an average of nineteen minutes for completion—it was of sufficient interest and clarity that few terminations were encountered. Figure 1 contains the complete questionnaire.

[1]Source: W. Wayne Talarzyk, *Contemporary Cases in Marketing,* 3rd ed. (Chicago: The Dryden Press, 1983), pp. 116–128. This case has been adapted from Roger D. Blackwell and W. Wayne Talarzyk, *Consumer Attitudes toward Health Care and Medical Malpractice* (Columbus, Ohio: Grid, Inc., 1977). The adaptation was made with the permission of Grid, Inc. The research reported in the case was conducted under a grant from the Malpractice Research Fund of the Ohio State Medical Association.

Figure 1

**Medical Practices
Survey Form**

Hello. My name is _____
I am affiliated with _____
and we are working on a research project concerned with medical practices. I
have a number of questions that we are asking many people in Ohio, and we
will appreciate your opinion being included.

(CC)

(5)   1. *First, do you have a family doctor? That is, one you would go to most of
           the time when you are sick?* Yes 1 No 2

(6–7) 2. *Approximately how many times were you, your spouse, and children
           living at home treated during the past twelve months by a physician?* ☐ ☐
           (write in number.)

(8–9) 2a. *How many days were you or members of your family in a hospital
            during the past twelve months?* ☐ ☐

       3. *If you or members of your family were treated by more than one type of
          physician or specialist, how many times were you treated by each doctor
          during the past twelve months?*

                                                                   Number of Treatments

(10–11)   1. Family practice   _____

(12–13)   2. Surgeon   _____

(14–15)   3. OB-Gyn   _____

(16–17)   4. Ophthalmologist   _____

(18–19)   5. Pediatrician   _____

(20–21)   6. Internist   _____

(22–23)   7. Emergency room   _____

(24–25)   8. Other MD (specify _____)   _____

(26–27)   9. Other non-MD (specify _____)   _____

(28–29)   Total number of treatments   _____

(30)   4. *Thinking about your primary doctor or family doctor, can you think back
          and tell me how you happened to choose that doctor? (Record all reasons
          mentioned.) Were there any other reasons? (Check all reasons
          mentioned.)*

            1. Recommended by friend or relative   _____

            2. Recommended by another physician   _____

            3. Looked in yellow pages of directory   _____

            4. Recommended by hospital   _____

            5. Met the doctor socially or heard of him as a civic leader   _____

            6. Treated as member of hospital staff (emergency, etc.) _____

            7. Required physician (clinics, insurance, etc.)   _____

            8. Can't remember, always been our doctor, etc.   _____

            9. Other (specify) _____   _____

(31)   5. *Of those reasons, which one would be the most important for your choice?*
          _____ *(1–9)*

Note: Interviewer is to read orally all words except answer headings and instructions to interviewer.

continued

Figure 1

continued

6. *Here's an imaginary question. Suppose your present doctor were to move away suddenly and you had to choose a new one. I have a list of characteristics of doctors that people sometimes use to evaluate a doctor. I would like for you to rate each characteristic on a scale of 1 to 5 according to its importance to you personally. If something is very important to you, you should rate it as a 1; if it is somewhat important, you should rate it a 2; if it is neutral in importance, rate it 3; if it is somewhat unimportant, rate it a 4; and if it is very unimportant, rate it a 5.*

(32)   1. The doctor's office is near you.   1 2 3 4 5

(33)   2. The doctor has access to the hospital you want.   1 2 3 4 5

(34)   3. The doctor has a good personality and appearance.   1 2 3 4 5

(35)   4. How much the doctor charges   1 2 3 4 5

(36)   5. The doctor is willing to talk with you about your illness. 1 2 3 4 5

(37)   6. The doctor has many years of experience.   1 2 3 4 5

(38)   7. The doctor has never been sued for malpractice.   1 2 3 4 5

(39)   8. The doctor is recommended by other doctors.   1 2 3 4 5

(40)   9. The doctor has evening or weekend office hours.   1 2 3 4 5

(41)   10. The doctor is recommended by your friends.   1 2 3 4 5

(42)   11. How long it takes to get an appointment   1 2 3 4 5

(43)   7. *What is your feeling about the quality of health care given by your doctor? Would you describe it as:*

   1. Excellent _____ 2. Good _____

   3. Average _____ 4. Poor _____ or 5. Very poor _____

(44)   8. *What is your feeling about the quality of health care given by doctors in general?*

   1. Excellent _____ 2. Good _____

   3. Average _____ 4. Poor _____ or 5. Very poor _____

(45)   9. *What is your feeling about the charges you pay your doctor? Are they:*
   1. Entirely too high for the services provided you?   _____

   2. Too high for the services provided you?   _____

   3. Reasonable for the services provided you?   _____

   4. Low considering the services provided you?   _____

(46) 10. *In recent years, the amount that doctors pay for malpractice insurance has increased drastically. In a few words, what do you personally believe is the cause of increased costs of malpractice insurance?*

   _____

   _____

   _____

   1. Doctors are at fault.   _____

   2. Lawyers are at fault.   _____

   3. Insurance companies are at fault.   _____

   4. The government or laws are at fault.   _____

   5. Juries and/or judges are giving too much.   _____

Figure 1

continued

11. *Several ways of handling the malpractice problem have been proposed. We would like to describe some of these methods and ask you to rate your support for them on a 1 to 5 scale. If you would be strongly for this method, rate it 1. If you would be somewhat for the method, rate it a 2. If you are neutral, a 3; somewhat against it, a 4; and strongly against it, a 5.*

(47) 1. A law that lowerd the proportion of the settlement that lawyers could receive for malpractice suits.   1   2   3   4   5

(48) 2. A requirement that patients agree to arbitration of malpractice claims (the patient and the doctor would appoint skilled arbitrators to settle malpractice claims).   1   2   3   4   5

(49) 3. A state agency, something like the workmen's compensation bureau, which would collect malpractice insurance premiums from all physicians and decide what benefits would be given all patients with malpractice claims.   1   2   3   4   5

(50) 4. A state law which limited the amounts that could be collected by patients with malpractice claims.   1   2   3   4   5

(51) 5. A peer group review system in which a group of physicians reviewed malpractice claims and decided which ones should be taken to trial.   1   2   3   4   5

(52) 6. A release signed before a person is accepted as a patient agreeing not to sue for malpractice.   1   2   3   4   5

(53) 7. More time spent by your physician in explaining the risks or potential problems of your operation or medicine even though the charge for the doctor's services would be higher than now.   1   2   3   4   5

(54) 8. A state law which requires insurance companies to reduce malpractice rates to doctors in return for correspondingly higher rates on health insurance to the general public.   1   2   3   4   5

(55) 9. Countersuits by physicians against patients and their attorneys who sue for malpractice with no basis for the malpractice suit.   1   2   3   4   5

(56-58) **12.** *Of the malpractice suits that are brought against physicians, what percentage would you say are instances in which the doctor was negligent?* ☐☐☐%

(59-61) **13.** *Of the malpractice settlement, what percentage of the money do you believe goes to the lawyer?* ☐☐☐%

(62) **14.** *Let's assume that your doctor was unable to determine a cure for you, and you thought your doctor might be at fault. Would you be very likely to bring a malpractice suit, somewhat likely, undecided, somewhat unlikely, or very unlikely to bring a malpractice suit?*

1. Very likely _____   4. Somewhat unlikely _____

2. Somewhat likely _____   5. Very unlikely _____

3. Undecided _____

(63) **15.** *Let's assume that you developed a serious medical problem in which you thought your physician might be at fault. Would you be very likely to bring a malpractice suit, somewhat likely, undecided, somewhat unlikely, or very unlikely to bring a malpractice suit?*

1. Very likely _____   4. Somewhat unlikely _____

2. Somewhat likely _____   5. Very unlikely _____

3. Undecided _____

continued

Figure 1

continued

(64)   **16. Let's assume that your spouse or your parent died and you thought your physician might be at fault. Would you be very likely to bring a malpractice suit, somewhat likely, undecided, somewhat unlikely, or very unlikely to bring a malpractice suit?**

1. Very likely _____   4. Somewhat unlikely _____

2. Somewhat likely _____   5. Very unlikely _____

3. Undecided _____

(65)   **17. Have you ever personally brought a malpractice suit against a physician?**

1. Yes _____ (please continue) _____

2. No _____ (skip to Question 24) _____

(66)   **18. What happened to your suit? What is the current status?**

1. Dismissed with a settlement to you _____

2. Dismissed without a settlement to you _____

3. Brought to trial with a judgment to you _____

4. Brought to trial with no judgment to you _____

5. Case currently pending _____

(67)   **19. What was the specialty of the physician who was sued?**

1. Family practice _____

2. Surgeon _____

3. OB-Gyn _____

4. Ophthalmologist _____

5. Pediatrician _____

6. Other (specify _____) _____

(68)   **20. In a few words, can you tell me what caused you to decide to pursue a malpractice suit against the physician?**

_____

_____

_____

1. Self influences _____

2. Family influences _____

3. Physician influences _____

4. Other medical personnel (nurses, etc.) _____

5. Attorney influences _____

6. Other influences _____

7. Other reasons _____

(69-71)   **21. Of the amount that was paid to you, what percentage went to the attorney?**
□□□%

Figure 1

continued

(72)   **22. If you had to decide again to pursue the malpractice suit, would you be very likely to do it again, somewhat likely, undecided, somewhat unlikely, or very unlikely to bring the malpractice suit if you were able to do it over?**

1. Very likely   _____   4. Somewhat unlikely _____

2. Somewhat likely _____   5. Very unlikely   _____

3. Undecided   _____

(73)   **23. If you were to need medical treatment again, would you be very likely to go to the same physician, somewhat likely, undecided, somewhat unlikely, or very unlikely to go to the same physician again?**

1. Very likely   _____   4. Somewhat unlikely _____

2. Somewhat likely _____   5. Very unlikely   _____

3. Undecided   _____

24. Now, I would like to read some statements that some people agree with and some do not agree with. We would like to know if you strongly agree, somewhat agree, are neutral, somewhat disagree, or strongly disagree with each statement. There are no right or wrong answers. We are simply interested in your opinion about each statement.

(CC)(1–4)
Same as
Card 1

		SA	A	N	D	SD
(5)	1. I generally have a physical checkup at least once a year.	1	2	3	4	5
(6)	2. I generally approve of abortion if a woman wants one.	1	2	3	4	5
(7)	3. I have a great deal of confidence in my doctor.	1	2	3	4	5
(8)	4. About half of the physicians in Ohio are not really competent to practice medicine.	1	2	3	4	5
(9)	5. If I had a terminal illness, I would not want my physician to tell me.	1	2	3	4	5
(10)	6. Most doctors are overpaid.	1	2	3	4	5
(11)	7. I wish there were brochures which explained things to me when a doctor treats me.	1	2	3	4	5
(12)	8. I often watch TV programs that discuss health problems.	1	2	3	4	5
(13)	9. In most malpractice suits, the physician is actually negligent or in the wrong.	1	2	3	4	5
(14)	10. My physician adequately explains my medical problems to me.	1	2	3	4	5
(15)	11. Most physicians are ethical and responsible persons.	1	2	3	4	5
(16)	12. Most physicians are more concerned about making money than the welfare of their patients.	1	2	3	4	5
(17)	13. Most physicians in Ohio are not very competent.	1	2	3	4	5
(18)	14. It is wrong for a doctor to go on strike for any reason.	1	2	3	4	5
(19)	15. I usually read the nutrition information on food packages.	1	2	3	4	5
(20)	16. In most malpractice suits, the physician is not really to blame.	1	2	3	4	5

continued

Figure 1

continued

(21)   17. I believe that a very ill person should be allowed to die
            when there is no chance of recovering again.   1 2 3 4 5

(22)   18. I generally do exercises (like push-ups or sit-ups or
            jogging) at least twice a week.   1 2 3 4 5

(23)   19. I am careful about what I eat.   1 2 3 4 5

(24)   20. I usually have a good tan every year.   1 2 3 4 5

(25)   21. I frequently play tennis or other sports where I can get a
            lot of exercise.   1 2 3 4 5

(26)   22. I weigh about what my doctor says I should.   1 2 3 4 5

(27)   23. I usually go on a weight control diet at least twice a
            year.   1 2 3 4 5

(28)   24. It seems that I am sick a lot more than my friends are.   1 2 3 4 5

Finally, we have just a few questions to make sure we have all types of opinions represented in our survey.

(29)   *25. With what religion or denomination, if any, do you identify?*

   1. Catholic   _____   6. Other Protestant   _____
   2. Baptist   _____   (specify   )   _____
   3. Methodist   _____   7. Jewish   _____
   4. Lutheran   _____   8. Other (specify   ) _____
   5. Presbyterian   _____   9. None

(30)   *26. Would you consider your political views to be:*

   1. Very liberal   _____
   2. Somewhat liberal   _____
   3. Middle of the road   _____
   4. Somewhat conservative   _____
   5. Very conservative   _____

(31)   *27. Please stop me when I come to the category that describes your age.*

   1. Under 25   _____   4. 45 to 54   _____
   2. 25 to 34   _____   5. 55 to 64   _____
   3. 35 to 44   _____   6. 65 & older   _____

(32)   *28. What is the last year of school you have completed? (check appropriate category below)*

   1. Did not attend   _____
   2. Elementary or grammar school   _____
   3. Went to high school or trade school for less than 4 years   _____
   4. Graduated from high school or trade school   _____
   5. Some college, junior college, or technical school   _____
   6. Graduated from college   _____
   7. Some postgraduate work   _____
   8. Have postgraduate degree   _____

Figure 1

continued

(33)   **29. Is your residence in: (check appropriate category below)**

     1. A rural area   _____

     2. A small town   _____

     3. An urban area   _____

     4. A suburban area   _____

(34)   **30. Counting your spouse and children as well as yourself, how many persons in your family are living at home now?**

     _____ 1, _____ 2, _____ 3, _____ 4, _____ 5, _____ 6,

     _____ 7, _____ 8, _____ 9 or more

(35)   **31. Finally, as I read a number of income categories, please stop me when I come to the one that describes your household's total income last year (before taxes).**

     1. Less than $3,000   _____   6. $20,000 to $24,999 _____

     2. $3,000 to $7,999   _____   7. $25,000 to $34,999 _____

     3. $8,000 to $9,999   _____   8. $35,000 to $49,999 _____

     4. $10,000 to $14,999 _____   9. $50,000 or more   _____

     5. $15,000 to $19,999 _____

(36)   **32. Record sex of respondent:**

     1. Male _____   2. Female _____

Questions

1. In what ways do you believe the questionnaire in the research project could have been improved?

2. Evaluate the research methodology used in this study. What changes would you recommend in sample design, pretesting, and ways of gathering the data?

3. What methods of analysis would you recommend for evaluating the data acquired via this questionnaire?

Part Five   Sampling and Data Collection

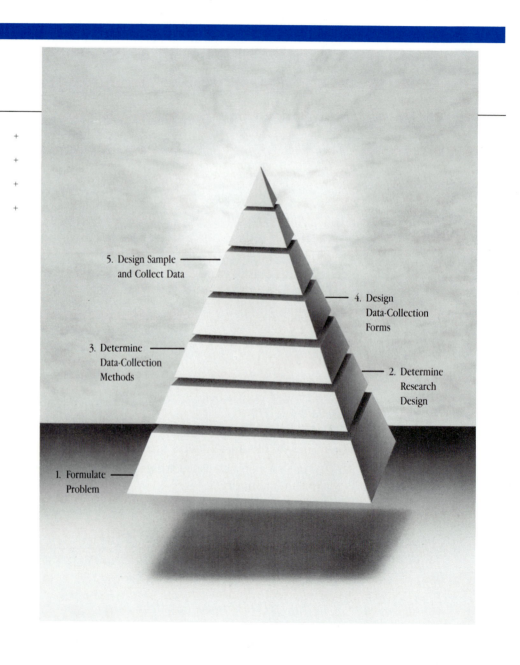

5. Design Sample and Collect Data

4. Design Data-Collection Forms

3. Determine Data-Collection Methods

2. Determine Research Design

1. Formulate Problem

Part Five focuses on the collection of data needed to answer a problem. Chapter 13 overviews the various types of sampling plans that can be used to determine the population elements from which data should be collected and also describes the nonprobability sampling and simple random sampling schemes from among the probability sampling plans. Chapter 14 then discusses two popular, but more complex, probability sampling schemes—stratified and cluster sampling. Chapter 15 treats the question of how many of these elements are needed to answer the problem with precision and confidence in the results. Chapter 16 discusses the many nonsampling errors that can arise in completing the data-collection task.

Chapter 13

Types of Samples and Simple Random Sampling

Learning Objectives

Upon completing this chapter, you should be able to

1. Distinguish between a census and a sample.
2. List the six steps researchers use to draw a sample of a population.
3. Define what is meant by a sampling frame.
4. Explain the difference between a probability sample and a nonprobability sample.
5. Distinguish between a fixed and sequential sample.
6. Explain what is meant by a judgment sample and describe its best use and its hazards.
7. Define what is meant by a quota sample.
8. Explain what is meant by a parameter in a sampling procedure.
9. Explain what is meant by derived population.
10. Explain why the concept of sampling distribution is the most important concept in statistics.

Case in Marketing Research

"Free tickets for a GBS show!" Danny Bigelow stood outside a Manhattan office building shivering in the damp, lingering chill of late March and trying hard to interest passing women in taking a few hours to preview the pilot of a new television show bucking for a slot on the network's fall schedule.

This was the second spring that Danny, an aspiring actor, had taken the job as recruiter for Global Broadcast Systems (GBS). Someday he hoped to be appearing on the screen, not hawking tickets to programs on the sidewalk. But for now, this was a good way to pay the rent until something better came along. Besides, during preview periods lots of producers from Los Angeles were in town trying hard to sell their shows, and one never knew when one of those guys with the expensive loafers and elegantly tailored jackets might notice him for an upcoming role, he thought, stamping his feet to keep warm.

Just then Danny spotted two women, obviously from out of town judging from their attire.

"Good afternoon, ladies. You must be chilly in those light jackets today. Why not warm up inside while previewing one of GBS's possible new fall television shows? I have free tickets right here. It will only take about an hour and a half of your time," Danny said, trying to be as charming as possible.

"What do you think, Martha?" a middle-aged woman in a bright cotton dress and linen jacket asked her companion.

"Sounds fine to me, Sylvia. My feet are killing me anyway, and we don't have to meet Delbert and Edwin back at the hotel until four. Then we can tell the folks back in Tulsa that we helped pick this fall's programs. Sounds like fun to me," Martha replied.

Danny smiled as he gave them their tickets and showed them where to stand inside. He only needed five more women for the afternoon show, and he could quit for the day.

Recruiting the right candidates was a problem in March, he remembered from last year. He was supposed to try to get as many out-of-towners as possible, but March was early for tourists in New York, and people in town for business were usually too busy to be interested.

Today he was assigned to recruit adult women to test a pilot for a daytime drama series, tentatively titled "Restless Spirits." On other days he might be asked to single out high school students to preview a show for the 8 P.M. time slot popular with teens, or a mixed group of adults for a Sunday night drama.

The network's busiest time was in the spring when most pilots for the fall season were being tested. During that period, all day, seven days a week, test audiences totaling over 30,000 people viewed episodes of proposed programs.

Danny worked hard then, and was usually exhausted by the end of May. But he knew the money he earned then would pay for his acting lessons and phone bills for the rest of the summer, so it was worth it.

Pulling his collar a little higher, he saw a potential recruit and her husband crossing the street and coming his way. Donning a smile, he approached them. "Free tickets for a GBS show!"

Discussion Issues

1. What problems might you foresee with the sample that Danny is recruiting?

2. What could television researchers do to overcome such problems?

3. If you were a researcher, what kinds of information would you want from Martha and Sylvia?

Source: This is a fictitious case based on the audience-testing process that occurs at CBS. See "Audience Testing: The Screening of America," which appeared in the company's employee newspaper, *Columbine,* edition 2, 1985, pp. 8–9.

• **Census**

A complete canvass of a population.

• **Sample**

Selection of a subset of elements from a larger group of objects.

• **Population**

Totality of cases that conforms to some designated specifications.

• **Sampling frame**

List of sampling units from which a sample will be drawn; the list could consist of geographic areas, institutions, individuals, or other units.

Once the researcher has clearly specified the problem and developed an appropriate research design and data-collection instruments, the next step in the research process is to select those elements from which the information will be collected. One way to do this is to collect information from each member of the population of interest by completely canvassing this population. A complete canvass of a population is called a **census.** Another way would be to collect information from a portion of the population by taking a **sample** of elements from the larger group and, on the basis of the information collected from the subset, to infer something about the larger group. One's ability to make this inference from subset to larger group depends on the method by which the sample of elements was chosen. A major part of this chapter is devoted to the "why" and "how" of taking a sample.

Incidentally, **population** here refers not only to people but also to manufacturing firms, retail or wholesale institutions, or even inanimate objects such as parts produced in a manufacturing plant; it is defined as the totality of cases that conform to some designated specifications. The specifications define the elements that belong to the target group and those that are to be excluded. A study aimed at establishing a demographic profile of frozen-pizza eaters requires specifying who is to be considered a frozen-pizza eater. Anyone who has ever eaten a frozen pizza? Those who eat at least one such pizza a month? A week? Those who eat a certain minimum number of frozen pizzas per month? Researchers need to be very explicit in defining the target group of interest. They also need to be very careful that they have actually sampled the target population and not some other population due to an inappropriate or incomplete **sampling frame,** which is the listing of the elements from which the actual sample will be drawn.

One might choose to sample rather than to canvass a whole population for several reasons. First, complete counts on populations of even moderate size are very costly and time-consuming. Often the information will be obsolete by the time the census is completed and the information processed. In some cases, a census is impossible. If, for example, researchers sought to test the life of a company's electric light bulbs by leaving all of its inventory of bulbs on until they burned out, they would have reliable data, but no product to sell.

Finally—and to novice researchers, surprisingly—one might choose a sample over a census for purposes of accuracy. Censuses involve larger field staffs, which in turn introduce greater potential for nonsampling error. This is one of the reasons the Bureau of the Census uses sample surveys to check the accuracy of various censuses. That is correct; samples are used to infer the accuracy of the census.[1]

---

[1]See "Census Bureau, Cities Skirmish Over Count; Money, Power at Stake," *The Wall Street Journal,* 60 (September 30, 1980), pp. 1 and 27, and "Census is Still Assailed, But Many Say Count Is Most Accurate Yet," *The Wall Street Journal,* 60 (December 9, 1980), pp. 1 and 24, for discussion of the controversy that surrounds the accuracy of the 1980 census.

◆ Required Steps in Sampling

Figure 13.1 outlines a useful six-step procedure that researchers can follow when drawing a sample of a population. Note that it is first necessary to define the population, or the collection of elements, about which the researcher wishes to make an inference. The researcher must decide if the relevant population consists of individuals, households, business firms, other institutions, credit-card transactions, or what? In making these decisions, the researcher also has to be careful to specify what units are to be excluded. Geographic boundaries and a time period for the study must always be specified, although additional restrictions are often placed on the elements. When the elements are individuals, for example, the relevant population may be defined as all those over eighteen years of age, or females only, or those with a high school education only.

In some cases, a combination of age, sex, education, race, and other restrictions could be used simultaneously. A study might specify, for example, high school–educated black women over eighteen years old who read *Vogue* magazine. In general though, the simpler the definition of the target population, the easier and less costly it is to find the sample.[2] Most important is that the researcher be precise in specifying exactly what elements are of interest and what elements are to be excluded. A clear statement of research purpose helps immeasurably in determining the appropriate elements of interest.

The second step in the sample-selection process is identifying the sampling frame, which, you will recall, is the listing of the elements from which the actual sample will be drawn. Say that the target population for a particular study is all the households in the metropolitan Dallas area. At first glance, the Dallas phone book would seem an easy and good example of a sampling frame. However, upon closer examination it becomes clear that the telephone directory provides an inaccurate listing of Dallas households, omitting those with unlisted numbers (and, of course, those without phones) and double-counting those with multiple listings. People who have recently moved and thus received new phones not yet listed are also omitted.

Experienced researchers have found that only rarely is there a perfect correspondence between the sampling frame and the target population in which they are interested. One of the researcher's more creative tasks in sampling is developing an appropriate sampling frame when the list of population elements is not readily available. Sometimes this means sampling geographic areas or institutions and then subsampling within these units when, say, the target population is individuals, but a current, accurate list of appropriate individuals is not available.

The third step in the procedure for drawing a sample is closely intertwined with the identification of the sampling frame. Choosing a sampling method or procedure depends largely on what the researcher can develop for a sampling frame. Different types of samples require different types of sampling frames. This chapter and the next review the main types of samples employed in marketing research. The connection between sampling frame and sampling method should become obvious from these discussions.

Step 4 in the sample selection process requires that sample size be determined. Chapter 15 discusses this question. Step 5 indicates that the researcher needs to actually pick the elements that will be included in the study. How this is done depends upon the type of sample being used, and consequently we will explore the

---

[2]Seymour Sudman, "Applied Sampling," in Peter H. Rossi, James D. Wright, and Andy B. Anderson, eds., *Handbook of Survey Research* (Orlando: Academic Press, 1983), pp. 145–194.

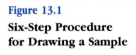

Figure 13.1

**Six-Step Procedure
for Drawing a Sample**

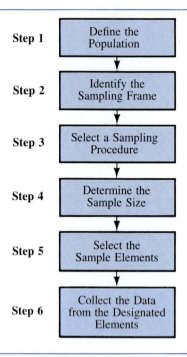

Step 1 — Define the Population

Step 2 — Identify the Sampling Frame

Step 3 — Select a Sampling Procedure

Step 4 — Determine the Sample Size

Step 5 — Select the Sample Elements

Step 6 — Collect the Data from the Designated Elements

topic of sample selection when we discuss sampling methods. Finally, the researcher needs to actually collect data from the designated respondents. A great many things can go wrong with this task. These problems are reviewed, and some methods for handling them are discussed in Chapter 16.

◆ Types of Sampling Plans

◆ **Probability sample**

Sample in which each population element has a known, nonzero chance of being included in the sample.

◆ **Nonprobability sample**

Sample that relies on personal judgment somewhere in the element selection process and therefore prohibits estimating the probability that any population element will be included in the sample.

Sampling techniques can be divided into the two broad categories of **probability** and **nonprobability samples.** In a probability sample each member of the population has a *known, nonzero* chance of being included in the sample. The chances of each member of the population being included in the sample may not be equal, but everyone has a known probability of inclusion. That probability is determined by the specific mechanical procedure that is used to select sample elements.

With nonprobability samples, on the other hand, there is no way of estimating the probability that any population element will be included in the sample. Thus, there is no way of ensuring that the sample is representative of the population. For example, all registered voters have a chance of being called for jury duty. If all the people who were called ultimately served on juries, and jurors were assigned to cases randomly, juries could be said to represent a probability sample. However, as any fan of courtroom dramas can tell you, an amazing amount of fancy footwork and folklore goes into the process of jury selection. One of the things a defendant pays an attorney for is his or her skill and judgment in picking a potentially sympathetic jury. Hence, a jury represents a nonprobability sample.

All nonprobability samples rely on personal judgment somewhere in the sample-selection process rather than a mechanical procedure to select sample members. While these judgments may sometimes yield good estimates of a population characteristic, there is no way of determining objectively if the sample is adequate. It is

Figure 13.2
Classification of Sampling Techniques

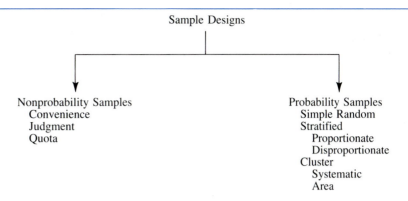

only when the elements have been selected with known probabilities that one is able to evaluate the precision of a sample result. For this reason, probability sampling is usually considered to be the superior method, in terms of being able to estimate the amount of sampling error present.

Samples can also be categorized by whether they are **fixed** or **sequential samples.** In fixed samples, the sample size is decided before the study begins, and all the needed information is collected before the results are analyzed. In our discussion we shall emphasize fixed samples since they are the type most commonly used in marketing research. Nevertheless, you should be aware that sequential samples can also be taken, and they can be used with each of the basic sampling plans we will discuss.

In a sequential sample, the number of elements to be sampled is not decided in advance but is determined by a series of decisions as the data are collected. For example, if after a small sample is taken, the evidence is not conclusive, more observations will be made. If the results are still inconclusive, the size of the sample will be expanded further. At each stage, a decision is made as to whether more information should be collected or whether the evidence is now sufficient to permit a conclusion. The sequential sample allows trends in the data to be evaluated as the data are being collected, and this affords an opportunity to reduce costs when additional observations show diminishing usefulness.[3]

Both probability and nonprobability sampling plans can be further divided by type. Nonprobability samples, for instance, can be classified as convenience, judgment, or quota, while probability samples can be simple random, stratified, or cluster, and some of these can be further divided. Figure 13.2 shows the types of samples we shall discuss in this chapter and the next. Except for convenience samples, Table 13.1 shows the relative frequency with which each type of sample is used by industry. These basic sample types can be combined into more complex sampling plans. If you understand the basic types, though, you should well understand the more complex designs.

• Fixed sample
Sample for which size is determined *a priori* and needed information is collected from the designated elements.

• Sequential sample
Sample formed on the basis of a series of successive decisions. If the evidence is not conclusive after a small sample is taken, more observations are taken; if it is still inconclusive after these additional observations, still more observations are taken. At each stage, then, a decision is made as to whether more information should be collected or whether the evidence is sufficient to draw a conclusion.

---

[3]For a good exposition of the principles and advantages of sequential sampling, see E. J. Anderton, R. Tudor, and K. Gorton, "Sequential Analysis: A Reappraisal for Market Research," *Journal of the Market Research Society,* 18 (October 1976), pp. 166–179; and E. J. Anderton, K. Gorton, and R. Tudor, "The Application of Sequential Analysis in Market Research," *Journal of Marketing Research,* 17 (February 1980), pp. 97–105.

Table 13.1   Relative Frequency with Which Various Sampling Techniques Are Used by Industry

	Type of Company		Consumer & Industrial	Retailer-Wholesaler	Utilities
	Consumer	Industrial			
Nonprobability Sampling Techniques					
Judgment sampling	52%	29%	40%	36%	39%
Quota sampling	60	18	33	36	56
Probability Sampling Techniques					
Simple random sampling	76	41	53	36	89
Stratified sampling	69	31	67	27	78
Cluster sampling	43	15	53	27	50
Total number of firms	(42)	(68)	(15)	(11)	(18)

Source: Adapted from Barnett A. Greenberg, Jac L. Goldstucker, and Danny N. Bellenger, "What Techniques Are Used by Marketing Researchers in Business?" *Journal of Marketing,* 41 (April 1977), pp. 64–65.

◆ Nonprobability Samples

As we stated earlier, nonprobability samples involve personal judgment somewhere in the selection process. Sometimes this judgment is imposed by the researcher, while in other cases the selection of population elements to be included is left to individual field workers. Since the elements are not selected by a mechanical procedure, it is impossible to assess the probability of any population member being included and thus, the degree of sampling error involved. Without knowing how much error results from a particular sampling procedure, researchers cannot gauge the accuracy of their estimates with any precision.

Convenience Samples

◆ **Convenience sample**

Nonprobability sample sometimes called an *accidental sample* because those included in the sample enter by accident, in that they just happen to be where the study is being conducted when it is being conducted.

Convenience samples are sometimes called *accidental samples* because those composing the sample enter by "accident"—they just happen to be where the information for the study is being collected. Examples of convenience samples abound in our everyday lives. We talk to a few friends, and on the basis of their reactions, we infer the political sentiment of the country; our local radio station asks people to call in and express their reactions to some controversial issue, and the opinions expressed are interpreted as prevailing sentiment; we ask for volunteers in a research study and use those who come forward.

The problem with convenience samples, of course, is that we have no way of knowing if those included are representative of the target population. And while we might hesitate to infer that the reactions of a few friends indicate prevailing political sentiment, we are often tempted to conclude that large samples, even though selected conveniently, are representative. The fallacy of this assumption is illustrated by a personal incident.

One of the local television stations in the city where the author resides conducted a daily public opinion poll several years ago on topics of interest to the local com-

Table 13.1   *continued*

Communications	Market Research & Consulting	Finance & Insurance	Other Services	Others	Total Sample Using Technique
23%	46%	27%	27%	27%	35%
32	39	43	53	20	37
59	73	87	67	53	63
32	61	73	60	53	53
23	49	53	27	13	34
(22)	(33)	(30)	(15)	(15)	(269)

munity. The polls were labeled the "Pulse of Madison" and were conducted in the following way. During the six o'clock news every evening, the station would ask a question about some controversial issue to which people could reply with a yes or no. Persons in favor would call one number; persons opposed would call another. The number of viewers calling each number was recorded electronically. Percentages of those in favor and opposed would then be reported on the ten o'clock news. With some 500 to 1,000 people calling in their opinions each night, the local television commentator seemed to interpret these results as reflecting the true state of opinion in the community.

On one six o'clock broadcast, the following question was posed: "Do you think the drinking age in Madison should be lowered to eighteen?" The existing legal limit was twenty-one. Would you believe that almost 4,000 people called in that night and that 78 percent were in favor of lowering the age requirement! Clearly, 4,000 responses in a community of 180,000 people "must be representative!" Wrong. As you may have suspected, certain segments of the population were more vitally interested in the issue than others. Thus, it was no surprise, when discussing the issue in class a few weeks later, to find that students had taken one-half-hour phone shifts on an arranged basis. Each person would call the yes number, hang up, call again, hang up, and so on, until it was the next person's turn. Thus, neither the size of the sample nor the proportion favoring the age change was surprising. The sample was simply not representative.

Further, increasing its size would not make it so. The representativeness of a sample must be ensured by the sampling procedure. When participation is voluntary or sample elements are selected because they are convenient, the sampling plan provides no assurance that the sample is representative. Empirical evidence, as a matter of fact, is much to the contrary. Rarely do samples selected on a convenience basis, regardless of size, prove representative. Convenience samples are not recommended, therefore, for descriptive or causal research. They may be used with exploratory designs in which the emphasis is on generating ideas and insights, but even here the judgment sample seems superior.

Judgment Samples

Judgment samples are often called *purposive samples;* the sample elements are handpicked because it is expected that they can serve the research purpose. Most typically, the sample elements are selected because it is believed that they are representative of the population of interest. One example of a judgment sample is seen every four years at presidential election time, when television viewers are treated to in-depth analyses of the swing communities. These communities are thought to be representative, since in previous elections the local winner has been the next president. Thus, by monitoring these pivotal communities, election analysts are able to offer an early prediction of the eventual winner. While election analysis and prediction have become much more sophisticated in recent years, the judgment sample of representative communities is still used.

As mentioned, the key feature of judgment sampling is that population elements are purposively selected. In some cases sample elements are chosen not because they are representative but rather because they can offer researchers the information they need. When the courts rely on expert testimony, they are in a sense using judgment samples. The same kind of philosophy may prevail in creating exploratory designs. When searching for ideas and insights, the researcher is not interested in sampling a cross section of opinion but rather in sampling those who can offer some perspective on the research question.

Back to the Case

Inside GBS Martha and Sylvia sat down at a table with about twenty-five other men and women. A hostess passed out forms to each person.

"Ladies and gentlemen, before we screen our program, 'Restless Spirits,' I'd appreciate it if you'd take a moment to fill out these questionnaires. We just need some information about your age, occupation, and where you're from," the hostess said.

Once the questionnaires were completed and handed back, the hostess spoke again. "Before you on the table are controls to our viewing system. As you watch the program, please push the green button if you like what you see on the screen, and the red button if you don't like it. Now, sit back and enjoy," she said.

As the program progressed, a microcomputer in the next room recorded the flow of viewer "yeas" and "nays," and combined those responses with those from other screenings of the same show.

The results were then translated into a videotaped graph of red and green lines that could be superimposed over the pilot tape, illustrating, moment by moment, audience likes and dislikes.

When the program ended, and the house lights came back up, the hostess began passing out another form. "Now, ladies and gentlemen, we'd appreciate it if you'd fill out one more questionnaire about the things you liked and didn't like about the program," she said.

Once the set of questionnaires was completed, the hostess led the group in an open-ended discussion about their reaction to the program.

Researchers at GBS are using a judgment sample, a type of nonprobability sample, to conduct their research. In this case, the population elements are chosen on the basis of the type of viewing audience to which the program is targeted.

The sample may not be representative of the target group, much less the general population, but it is probably the most practical and affordable way of securing audience reaction to a product—in this case, a television show—on which millions of dollars are being gambled.

• Snowball sample

Judgment sample that relies on the researcher's ability to locate an initial set of respondents with the desired characteristics; these individuals are then used as informants to identify still others with the desired characteristics.

The **snowball sample** is a judgment sample that is sometimes used to sample special populations.[4] This sample relies on the researcher's ability to locate an initial set of respondents with the desired characteristics. These individuals are then used as informants to identify others with the desired characteristics.

Imagine, for example, that a company wanted to determine the desirability of a certain product that would enable deaf people to communicate over telephone lines. Researchers might begin by identifying some key people in the deaf community and asking them for names of other deaf people who might be used in the study. Those asked to participate would also be asked for names of others who might cooperate.[5] In this way the sample "snowballs" by getting larger as participants identify still other possible respondents.

As long as the researcher is at the early stages of research when ideas or insights are being sought—and when the researcher realizes its limitations—the judgment sample can be used productively. It becomes dangerous, though, when it is employed in descriptive or causal studies and its weaknesses are conveniently forgotten.[6] The Consumer Price Index (CPI) provides a classic example of this. As Sudman points out, "the CPI is in only fifty-six cities and metropolitan areas selected judgmentally and to some extent on the basis of political pressure. In reality, these cities represent *only themselves* although the index is called the *Consumer Price Index for Urban Wage Earners and Clerical Workers,* and most people believe the index reflects prices everywhere in the United States. Within cities, the selection of retail outlets is done judgmentally, so that the *possible size of sample bias is unknown* (emphasis added).[7]

Quota Samples

• Quota sample

Nonprobability sample chosen in such a way that the proportion of sample elements possessing a certain characteristic is approximately the same as the proportion of the elements with the characteristic in the population; each field worker is assigned a quota that specifies the characteristics of the people he or she is to contact.

A third type of nonprobability sample, the **quota sample,** attempts to be representative of the population by including the same proportion of elements possessing a certain characteristic as is found in the population (see Research Window 13.1). Consider, for example, an attempt to select a representative sample of undergraduate students on a college campus. If the eventual sample of 500 contained no seniors, one would have serious reservations about the representativeness of the sample and the generalizability of the conclusions beyond the immediate sample group. With a quota sample, the researcher could ensure that seniors would be included and in the same proportion as they occur in the entire undergraduate student body.

Assume that a researcher was interested in sampling the undergraduate student body in such a way that the sample would reflect the composition of the student body by class and sex. Suppose further that there were 10,000 undergraduate stu-

---

[4]The technique was originally suggested by Leo A. Goodman, "Snowball Sampling," *Annals of Mathematical Statistics,* 32 (1961), pp. 148–170.

[5]AT & T used such a process for this communications problem, according to Robert Whitelaw, Division Manager for Market Research, in a speech "Research Solutions and New High Technology Service Concepts," which was delivered at the American Marketing Association's 1981 Annual Conference held in San Francisco, California, June 14–17, 1981.

[6]When certain very strict procedures are followed when listing members of the rare population, the snowball sample can be treated as a probability sample. For discussion of the requirements, see Martin R. Frankel and Lester R. Frankel, "Some Recent Developments in Sample Survey Design," *Journal of Marketing Research,* 14 (August 1977), pp. 280–293; or Patrick Biernacki and Dan Waldorf, "Snowball Sampling: Problems and Techniques of Chain Referred Sampling," *Sociological Methods and Research,* 10 (November 1981), pp. 141–163. For an example, see George S. Rothbart, Michelle Fine, and Seymour Sudman, "On Finding and Interviewing the Needles in the Haystack: The Use of Multiplicity Sampling," *Public Opinion Quarterly,* 46 (Fall 1982), pp. 408–421.

[7]Seymour Sudman, *Applied Sampling* (San Francisco: Academic Press, 1976), p. 10.

Research Window 13.1
The Ad Is Slick, Clever, Expensive—But Is Anybody Reading It?

Every year advertisers spend millions of dollars producing the ads that appear in publications ranging from *Advertising Age* to *Yankee* magazine. While a certain amount of copy and art testing can be done in-house at the agency before the ad is published, the real test of its success is when it appears in a publication alongside dozens of other ads designed equally carefully and fights for a reader's attention.

Starch INRA Hooper is a company that measures advertising readership in consumer, business, trade and professional magazines and newspapers, and reports its findings to advertisers and agencies—for a fee, of course. Since large sums are being gambled daily by advertisers seeking to get their message across to consumers, the Starch organization has been careful to design a sample for its research that can give subscribers fast—and accurate—information about the success of its advertising. Each year Starch interviews more than 100,000 people on their reading of over 75,000 advertisements. Approximately 1,000 individual issues are studied annually.

Starch uses a quota sample comprised of a minimum of 100 readers per sex. Starch has determined that at this sample size major fluctuations in readership levels stabilize. Adults, eighteen years and older, are personally interviewed face to face for all publications except those that are directed exclusively to special groups (e.g., for *Seventeen* magazine they would interview teenage girls).

Interviews are arranged to parallel the publication's geographic circulation. For *Los Angeles* magazine, for example, the study would focus on readers in southern California. A study of *Time* magazine would parallel its national circulation. Interviews are conducted in between twenty and thirty cities for each issue under study.

Each interviewer is assigned only a small quota of interviews in order to minimize interviewer bias. Interviews are distributed among people of varied ages, income levels, and occupations so

that collectively each study is broadly representative of the publication's audience. For certain business, trade, and professional publications, interviewing assignments are also designed to parallel the circulation by field of industry and job responsibility. For publications with small circulations, subscriber lists are used to help locate eligible respondents.

In each interview, interviewers ask respondents, who are permitted to look through the publication at the time of the interview, if they have seen or read any part of a particular advertisement. If the respondent answers yes, the interviewer follows up with more questions to determine the extent to which the respondent has read the ad.

Based on the respondent's answers, the interviewer classifies him or her as one of the following:

- *Noted reader:* a person who remembered having previously seen the advertisement in the issue being studied.
- *Associated reader:* a person who not only "noted" the advertisement, but also saw or read some part of it that clearly indicated the brand or advertiser.
- *Read-most reader:* a person who read half or more of the written material in the ad.

After all the ads are asked about, interviewers record basic classification data on sex, age, occupation, marital status, race, income, family size and composition so that sampling can be checked and cross tabulations of readership can be made.

Properly used, Starch data help advertisers and agencies to identify the types of advertisement layouts that attract and retain the highest readership and those that result in average or poor readership. For advertisers, this kind of information can be invaluable in designing an effective campaign for their products.

Source: "Starch Readership Report: Scope, Method, and Use," *Starch INRA Hooper,* Mamaroneck, NY 10543

To help ensure that a sample of undergraduate students is representative, quotas might be set for the number of freshmen, sophomores, juniors, and seniors to be included.

Source: Photo of Walgreen's pharmacist, Carmen Pineiro, teaching students at the University of Puerto Rico. Reprinted with permission from Walgreen Co.

dents in total and that 3,200 were freshmen, 2,600 sophomores, 2,200 juniors, and 2,000 seniors, and further that 7,000 were males and 3,000 females. In a sample of 1,000, the quota sampling plan would require that 320 sample elements be freshmen, 260 sophomores, 220 juniors, and 200 seniors, and further that 700 of the sample elements be male and 300 be female. The researcher would accomplish this by giving each field worker a quota—thus the name *quota sample*—specifying the types of undergraduates he or she is to contact. Thus, one field worker assigned 20 interviews might be instructed to find and collect data from

- Six freshmen—five male and one female
- Six sophomores—four male and two female
- Four juniors—three male and one female
- Four seniors—two male and two female

Note that the specific sample elements to be used would not be specified by the research plan, but would be left to the discretion of the individual field worker. The field worker's personal judgment would govern the choice of specific students to be interviewed. The only requirement would be that the interviewer diligently follow the established quota and interview five male freshmen, one female freshman, and so on.

Note further that the quota for this field worker accurately reflects the sex composition of the student population, but does not completely parallel the class composition; 70 percent (fourteen of twenty) of the field worker's interviews are with males but only 30 percent (six of twenty) are with freshmen, whereas freshmen represent 32 percent of the undergraduate student body. It is not necessary or even usual with a quota sample that the quotas per field worker accurately mirror the distribution of the control characteristics in the population; usually only the total sample has the same proportions as the population.

Note finally that quota samples still rely on personal, subjective judgment rather than objective procedures for the selection of sample elements. Here the personal judgment is that of the field worker rather than the designer of the research, as it might be in the case of a judgment sample. This raises the question of whether quota samples can indeed be considered representative even though they accurately reflect the population with respect to the proportion of the sample possessing each control characteristic. Three points need to be made in this regard.

First, the sample could be very far off with respect to some other important characteristic likely to influence the result. Thus, if the campus study is concerned with racial prejudice existing on campus, it may very well make a difference whether field workers interview students from urban or rural areas. Since a quota for the urban–rural characteristic was not specified, it is unlikely that those participating will accurately reflect this characteristic. The alternative, of course, is to specify quotas for all potentially important characteristics. The problem is that increasing the number of control characteristics makes specifications more complex. This in turn makes the location of sample elements more difficult—perhaps even impossible—and certainly more expensive. If, for example, geographic origin and socioeconomic status were also important characteristics in the study, the field worker might be assigned to find an upper-middle-class male freshman from an urban area. This is obviously a much more difficult task than simply locating a male freshman.

Also, it is difficult to verify whether a quota sample is representative. Certainly one can check the distribution of characteristics in the sample not used as controls to determine whether the distribution parallels that of the population. However, this type of comparison only provides negative evidence. It can indicate that the sample does not reflect the population if the distributions on some characteristics are different. If the sample and population distributions are similar for each of these characteristics, it is still possible for the sample to be vastly different from the population on some characteristic not explicitly compared.

Finally, interviewers left to their own devices are prone to follow certain practices.[8] They tend to interview their friends in excessive proportion. Since their friends are often similar to themselves, this can introduce bias. Interviewers who fill their quotas by stopping passers-by are likely to concentrate on areas where there are large numbers of potential respondents, such as business districts, railway and airline terminals, and the entrances to large department stores. This practice tends to over-represent the kinds of people who frequent these areas. When home visits are required, interviewers often succumb to the lures of convenience and appearance. They may conduct interviews only during the day, for example, resulting in an underrepresentation of working people. They often avoid dilapidated buildings or the upper stories of buildings without elevators.

Depending on the subject of the study, all of these tendencies have the potential for bias. They may or may not in fact actually bias the result, but it is difficult to correct them when analyzing the data. When the sample elements are selected objectively, on the other hand, researchers have certain tools they can rely on to make the question of whether a particular sample is representative less difficult. In these probability samples, one relies on the sampling procedure and not the composition of the specific sample to solve the problem of representation.

---

[8]Isidor Chein, "An Introduction to Sampling," in Claire Selltiz, Lawrence S. Wrightsman, and Stuart W. Cook, *Research Methods in Social Relations,* 3rd ed. (New York: Holt, Rinehart and Winston, 1976), pp. 520–521.

◆ Probability Samples

In a probability sample researchers can calculate the likelihood that any given population element will be included because the final sample elements are selected objectively by a specific process and not according to the whims of the researcher or field worker. Since the elements are selected objectively, researchers are then able to assess the reliability of the sample results, something not possible with nonprobability samples regardless of the careful judgment exercised in selecting individuals.

This is not to say that probability samples will always be more representative than nonprobability samples. Indeed, a nonprobability sample may be more representative. The advantage of probability samples is that they allow an assessment

Back to the Case

In the research department at GBS, two analysts sat down with a stack of about 400 questionnaires from viewers who had previewed "Restless Spirits." Each questionnaire had a number linking it with the graphs generated by responses from the red and green buttons.

"All right, Betty, first I want you to weed out all the men," Alice, the senior analyst, said to her young assistant. "Then eliminate anybody under eighteen or over sixty-five. After that go through the remaining stack and give me a geographic tally of the remaining viewers. From my preliminary look through the pile, it appears we still have too many New Yorkers for this group to be considered representative. We may have to eliminate some of them, too."

"What about the comments people made in the discussion?" Betty asked.

"They will have to be summarized and added to the final report," Alice said.

"So will all this information tell the network executives what programs to keep and which to can?" Betty asked.

"In some cases it will," Alice said. "Usually these tests produce three types of results. First there are programs that test as 'hit quality.' They almost always become series. The second group are those that test very poorly. They almost never make it to production. Then there is that vast, vague middle group that test average to below average. That's where art must supplement science," Alice said.

"What do you mean?" Betty asked.

"In marginal shows, we examine the data along with the executives, look at what people liked and didn't like, and decide if the show can be fixed," Alice said. "If it appears to be salvageable, the show's creators go into high gear and try to rework the show using viewer responses as guidelines. Ultimately, however, it is management, not the data,

that decides whether a show will fly or not," she said.

In audience testing, as in other forms of marketing research, the data are used for one thing: aiding in management decision making. When, as in television programming, millions of dollars ride on a decision, the data had better be accurate. Accurate data presume a sample that is accurate.

In a case such as this, where a nonprobability sample is used, there is no objective way for researchers to determine whether or not the sample used is actually representative. They must rely on past experience and "best guess" judgment—clearly a risky way to do business. Perhaps that is why so many shows launched with such fanfare in September fail to make it past the New Year!

of the amount of sampling error likely to occur, because a sample rather than a census was employed when gathering the data. Nonprobability samples, on the other hand, allow the investigator no objective method for evaluating the adequacy of the sample.

◆ Simple Random Sampling

Most people have had experience with simple random samples either in beginning statistics courses or in reading about the results of such samples in newspapers or magazines. In a simple random sample each unit included in the sample has a known and equal chance of being selected for study, and every combination of population elements is a sample possibility. For example, if we wanted a simple random sample of all students enrolled in a particular college, we might assign a number to each student on a comprehensive list of all those enrolled and then have a computer pick a sample randomly.

Parent Population

◆ Parent population

Totality of cases that conforms to some designated specifications; also called *target population.*

◆ Parameter

Fixed characteristic or measure of a parent or target population.

The **parent population,** or *target population,* is the population from which the simple random sample will be drawn. This population can be described by certain **parameters,** which are characteristics of the parent population, each representing a fixed quantity that distinguishes one population from another. For example, suppose the parent population for a study were all adults in Cincinnati. A number of parameters could be used to describe this population: the average age, the proportion with a college education, the range of incomes, and so on. Note that these quantities are fixed in value. Given a census of this population, we can readily calculate them. Rather than relying on a census, we usually select a sample and use the values calculated from the sample observations to estimate the required population values.

To see how this is done, consider the hypothetical population of twenty individuals shown in Table 13.2. There are several advantages in working with a small hypothetical population like this. First, the population's small size makes it easy to calculate the population parameters that might be used to describe it. Second, its size makes it relatively easy to see what might happen under a particular sampling plan. Both of these features make it easier to compare the sample results to the "true," but now known, population value than would be the case in the typical situation where the actual population value is unknown. The comparison of the estimate with the "true" value is thus more vivid than it otherwise would be.

Suppose we wanted to estimate the average income in this population from two elements selected randomly. Now the *population mean* income is a parameter. To estimate a population mean, denoted by μ, we would divide the sum of all the values by the number of values making up the sum. That is,

$$\text{population mean} = \mu = \frac{\text{sum of population elements}}{\text{number of population elements}}$$

In this case the calculation yields

$$\frac{5,600 + 6,000 + \ldots + 13,200}{20} = 9,400$$

Another parameter that might be used to describe the incomes in this population is the *population variance,* which is one measure of the spread of incomes. To

Table 13.2   Hypothetical Population

Element	Income (Dollars)	Education (Years)	Newspaper Subscription
1 A	5,600	8	X
2 B	6,000	9	Y
3 C	6,400	11	X
4 D	6,800	11	Y
5 E	7,200	11	X
6 F	7,600	12	Y
7 G	8,000	12	X
8 H	8,400	12	Y
9 I	8,800	12	X
10 J	9,200	12	Y
11 K	9,600	13	X
12 L	10,000	13	Y
13 M	10,400	14	X
14 N	10,800	14	Y
15 O	11,200	15	X
16 P	11,600	16	Y
17 Q	12,000	16	X
18 R	12,400	17	Y
19 S	12,800	18	X
20 T	13,200	18	Y

compute the population variance, we would calculate the deviation of each value from the mean, square these deviations, sum them, and divide by the number of values making up the sum. Letting σ^2 denote the population variance, the calculation yields

$$\text{population variance } \sigma^2 = \frac{\text{sum of squared differences of each population element from the population mean}}{\text{number of population elements}}$$

$$= \frac{(5{,}600{-}9{,}400)^2 + (6{,}000{-}9{,}400)^2 + \ldots + (13{,}200{-}9{,}400)^2}{20}$$

$$= 5{,}320{,}000$$

Derived Population

◆ Derived population

Population of all possible distinguishable samples that could be drawn from a parent population under a specific sampling plan.

◆ Statistic

Characteristic or measure of a sample.

The **derived population** consists of all the possible samples that can be drawn from the parent population under a given sampling plan. A **statistic** is a characteristic or measure of a sample. The value of a statistic used to estimate a particular parameter depends on the particular sample selected from the parent population under the sampling plan specified. Different samples yield different statistics and different estimates of the same population parameter.

Consider the derived population of *all* the possible samples that could be drawn from our hypothetical parent population of twenty individuals, under a sampling plan that specifies that a sample size of $n = 2$ be drawn by simple random sampling without replacement.

Let us assume, for the time being, that the information for each population element—in this case, the person's name and income—is written on a disk, placed in

Table 13.3　Derived Population of All Possible Samples of Size $n = 2$ with Simple Random Selection

k	Sample Identity	Mean	k	Sample Identity	Mean	k	Sample Identity	Mean	k	Sample Identity	Mean
1	AB	5,800	26	BI	7,400	51	CQ	9,200	76	EK	8,400
2	AC	6,000	27	BJ	7,600	52	CR	9,400	77	EL	8,600
3	AD	6,200	28	BK	7,800	53	CS	9,600	78	EM	8,800
4	AE	6,400	29	BL	8,000	54	CT	9,800	79	EN	9,000
5	AF	6,600	30	BM	8,200	55	DE	7,000	80	EO	9,200
6	AG	6,800	31	BN	8,400	56	DF	7,200	81	EP	9,400
7	AH	7,000	32	BO	8,600	57	DG	7,400	82	EQ	9,600
8	AI	7,200	33	BP	8,800	58	DH	7,600	83	ER	9,800
9	AJ	7,400	34	BQ	9,000	59	DI	7,800	84	ES	10,000
10	AK	7,600	35	BR	9,200	60	DJ	8,000	85	ET	10,200
11	AL	7,800	36	BS	9,400	61	DK	8,200	86	FG	7,800
12	AM	8,000	37	BT	9,600	62	DL	8,400	87	FH	8,000
13	AN	8,200	38	CD	6,600	63	DM	8,600	88	FI	8,200
14	AO	8,400	39	CE	6,800	64	DN	8,800	89	FJ	8,400
15	AP	8,600	40	CF	7,000	65	DO	9,000	90	FK	8,600
16	AQ	8,800	41	CG	7,200	66	DP	9,200	91	FL	8,800
17	AR	9,000	42	CH	7,400	67	DQ	9,400	92	FM	9,000
18	AS	9,200	43	CI	7,600	68	DR	9,600	93	FN	9,200
19	AT	9,400	44	CJ	7,800	69	DS	9,800	94	FO	9,400
20	BC	6,200	45	CK	8,000	70	DT	10,000	95	FP	9,600
21	BD	6,400	46	CL	8,200	71	EF	7,400	96	FQ	9,800
22	BE	6,600	47	CM	8,400	72	EG	7,600	97	FR	10,000
23	BF	6,800	48	CN	8,600	73	EH	7,800	98	FS	10,200
24	BG	7,000	49	CO	8,800	74	EI	8,000	99	FT	10,400
25	BH	7,200	50	CP	9,000	75	EJ	8,200	100	GH	8,200

a jar, and shaken thoroughly. The researcher then reaches into the jar, pulls out one disk, records the information on it, and puts it aside. She does the same with a second disk. Then she places both disks back in the jar and repeats the process. Table 13.3. shows the many possible results of following this procedure. There are 190 possible combinations of the twenty disks.

For each combination, one could calculate the sample mean income. Thus, for the sample AB,

$$k^{th} \text{ sample mean} = \frac{\text{sum of sample elements}}{\text{number of elements in sample}} = \frac{5,600 + 6,000}{2} = 5,800$$

Before discussing the relationship between the sample mean income (a statistic) and population mean income (the parameter to be estimated), a few words are in order regarding the notion of derived population. First, note that, in practice, we do not actually generate the derived population. This would be extremely wasteful of time and data. Rather, the practitioner merely generates one sample of the needed size. But the researcher will make use of the *concept* of a derived population and the associated notion of sampling distribution in making inferences. We shall see how in just a moment.

Second, note that the derived population is defined as the population of all possible distinguishable samples that can be drawn under a *given sampling plan.* Change any part of the sampling plan, and the derived population will also change. Thus, when selecting disks, if the researcher is to replace the first disk drawn, the

Table 13.3   *continued*

k	Sample Identity	Mean	k	Sample Identity	Mean	k	Sample Identity	Mean	k	Sample Identity	Mean
101	GI	8,400	126	IK	9,200	151	KQ	10,800	176	OP	11,400
102	GJ	8,600	127	IL	9,400	152	KR	11,000	177	OQ	11,600
103	GK	8,800	128	IM	9,600	153	KS	11,200	178	OR	11,800
104	GL	9,000	129	IN	9,800	154	KT	11,400	179	OS	12,000
105	GM	9,200	130	IO	10,000	155	LM	10,200	180	OT	12,200
106	GN	9,400	131	IP	10,200	156	LN	10,400	181	PQ	11,800
107	GO	9,600	132	IQ	10,400	157	LO	10,600	182	PR	12,000
108	GP	9,800	133	IR	10,600	158	LP	10,800	183	PS	12,200
109	GQ	10,000	134	IS	10,800	159	LQ	11,000	184	PT	12,400
110	GR	10,200	135	IT	11,000	160	LR	11,200	185	QR	12,200
111	GS	10,400	136	JK	9,400	161	LS	11,400	186	QS	12,400
112	GT	10,600	137	JL	9,600	162	LT	11,600	187	QT	12,600
113	HI	8,600	138	JM	9,800	163	MN	10,600	188	RS	12,600
114	HJ	8,800	139	JN	10,000	164	MO	10,800	189	RT	12,800
115	HK	9,000	140	JO	10,200	165	MP	11,000	190	ST	13,000
116	HL	9,200	141	JP	10,400	166	MQ	11,200			
117	HM	9,400	142	JQ	10,600	167	MR	11,400			
118	HN	9,600	143	JR	10,800	168	MS	11,600			
119	HO	9,800	144	JS	11,000	169	MT	11,800			
120	HP	10,000	145	JT	11,200	170	NO	11,000			
121	HQ	10,200	146	KL	9,800	171	NP	11,200			
122	HR	10,400	147	KM	10,000	172	NQ	11,400			
123	HS	10,600	148	KN	10,200	173	NR	11,600			
124	HT	10,800	149	KO	10,400	174	NS	11,800			
125	IJ	9,000	150	KP	10,600	175	NT	12,000			

derived population will include the sample possibilities *AA, BB,* and so on. With samples of Size 3 instead of 2, drawn without replacement, *ABC* is a sample possibility, and there are a number of additional possibilities as well—1,140 versus the 190 with samples of Size 2. Change the method of selecting elements by using something other than simple random sampling, and the derived population will also change.

Finally, note that picking a sample of a given size from a parent population is equivalent to picking a single element (one of the 190 disks) out of the derived population. This fact is basic in making statistical inferences.

Sample Mean versus Population Mean

If we were to evaluate the income of those in a simple random sample, could we assume that the sample mean will equal the parent population mean? To a large extent we generally assume there is a relationship; otherwise, it would be senseless to use the sample value to estimate the population value. But how much error is there likely to be?

Suppose we added up all the sample means in Table 13.3 and divided by the number of samples; that is, suppose we were to average the averages. By doing this, we would get the following:

$$\frac{5,800 + 6,000 \ldots + 13,000}{190} = 9,400$$

This is the mean of the parent population also. And this is what is meant by an *unbiased statistic;* its average value equals the population parameter that it is supposed to estimate. Note that the fact it is unbiased says nothing about any particular value of the statistic. Even though unbiased, a particular estimate may be very far from the true population value, for example, if either sample *AB* or sample *ST* were selected. In some cases, the true population value may even be impossible to achieve with any possible sample even though the statistic is unbiased; this is not true in the example, though, since a number of sample possibilities—for example, *AT*—yield a sample mean that equals the population average.

Next it is useful to take a look at the spread of these sample estimates, and particularly the relationship between this spread of estimates and the dispersion of incomes in the population. We saw previously that in order to compute the population variance, we needed to calculate the deviation of each value from the mean, square these deviations, sum them, and divide by the number of values making up the sum.

The variance of mean incomes could be calculated similarly. That is, we could calculate the variance of mean incomes by taking the deviation of each mean around its overall mean, squaring and summing these deviations, and then dividing by the number of cases.

Alternatively, we could determine the variance of mean incomes indirectly by using the variance of incomes in the parent population, since there is a direct relationship between the two quantities. More specifically, it turns out that when the sample is only a small part of the parent population, the variance of sample mean incomes is equal to the parent population variance divided by the sample size. In symbols, this means that

$$\sigma_{\bar{x}}^2 = \frac{\sigma^2}{n}$$

where $\sigma_{\bar{x}}^2$ is the variance of sample mean incomes, while σ^2 is the variance of incomes in the population, and n is the sample size.[9]

Third, consider the distribution of the estimates in contrast to the distribution of the variable in the parent population. Figure 13.3 indicates that the parent population distribution depicted by Panel A is spiked—each of the twenty values occurs once—and is symmetrical about the population mean value of 9,400. The distribution of estimates displayed in Panel B was constructed from Table 13.4 which in turn was generated by placing each of the estimates in Table 13.3 in categories according to size and then counting the number contained in each category. Panel B is the traditional histogram discussed in beginning statistics courses and represents the

---

[9]In the example at hand, the sample is 10 percent of the population since the procedure specifies samples of size $n = 2$ be drawn from a population of size $n = 20$. In a situation such as this in which the sample is a relatively large part of the population, the correct formula relating the two variances contains an additional term. Specifically it equals

$$\sigma_{\bar{x}}^2 = \frac{\sigma^2}{n} \frac{N-n}{N-1}$$

The additional term $\dfrac{N-n}{N-1}$ is called the finite population correction factor. It is, of course, close to 1 when the population is very large in comparison to the sample, and can then safely be ignored. The variance of mean incomes for the example using the formula turns out to be

$$\sigma_{\bar{x}}^2 = \frac{5,320,000}{2} \frac{20\text{-}2}{20\text{-}1} = 2,520,000$$

Figure 13.3

Distribution of Variable in Parent Population and Distribution of Estimates in Derived Population

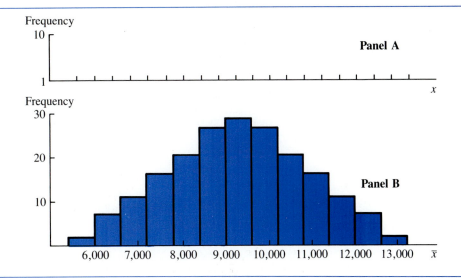

Table 13.4   Classification of Estimates by Size

Sample Mean	Number of Samples
$6,000 or less	2
$6,100 to 6,600	7
$6,700 to 7,200	11
$7,300 to 7,800	16
$7,900 to 8,400	20
$8,500 to 9,000	25
$9,100 to 9,600	28
$9,700 to 10,200	25
$10,300 to 10,800	20
$10,900 to 11,400	16
$11,500 to 12,000	11
$12,100 to 12,600	7
$12,700 or more	2

♦ Sampling distribution

Distribution of values of some statistic calculated for each possible distinguishable sample that could be drawn from a parent population under a specific sampling plan.

sampling distribution of the statistic. Note this: The notion of sampling distribution is the single most important notion in statistics; it is the cornerstone of statistical inference procedures. If one knows the sampling distribution for the statistic in question, one is in a position to make an inference about the corresponding population parameter. If on the other hand, one knows only that a particular sample estimate will vary with repeated sampling and has no information as to *how* it will vary, then it will be impossible to devise a measure of the sampling error associated with that estimate. Since the sampling distribution of an estimate describes how that estimate will vary with repeated sampling, it provides a basis for determining the reliability of the sample estimate. This is why probability sampling plans are so important to statistical inference. With known probabilities of inclusion of any population element in the sample, statisticians are able to derive the sampling distribution of various statistics. Researchers then rely on these distributions—be they for a sample mean, sample proportion, sample variance, or some other statistic—in making their inferences from single samples to population values. Note also that the distribution of sample means is mound-shaped and symmetrical about the population mean with samples of Size 2.

Recapitulating, we have shown that

1. The mean of all possible sample means is equal to the population mean.
2. The variance of sample means is related to the population variance.
3. The distribution of sample means is mound-shaped, whereas the population distribution is spiked.

• Central-limit theorem

Theorem that holds that if simple random samples of size n are drawn from a parent population with mean μ and variance σ^2, then when n is large, the sample mean $\bar{x}$ will be approximately normally distributed with mean equal to μ and variance equal to σ^2/n. The approximation will become more and more accurate as n becomes larger.

Central-Limit Theorem The third result of a mound-shaped distribution of estimates provides preliminary evidence of the operation of the **central-limit theorem,** which holds that if simple random samples of a given size, n, are drawn from a parent population with mean equal to μ, and variance equal to σ^2, then when the sample size n is large, the *distribution of sample means* will be approximately normally distributed with its mean equal to the population mean and its variance equal to the parent population variance divided by the sample size; that is,

$$\sigma_{\bar{x}}^2 = \sigma^2/n$$

The approximation will become more and more accurate as n becomes larger. Note the impact of this. It means that regardless of the shape of the parent population, the distribution of sample means *will be normal* if the sample is large enough. How large is large enough? If the distribution of the variable in the parent population is normal, then the distribution of means of samples of size $n = 1$ will be normal. If the distribution of the variable is symmetrical but not normal, then samples of very small size will produce a distribution in which the means are normally distributed. If the distribution of the variable is highly skewed in the parent population, then samples of a larger size will be needed.

The fact remains, though, that the distribution of the statistic, sample mean, can be assumed normal if only we work with a sample of sufficient size. We do not need to rely on the assumption that the variable is normally distributed in the parent population in order to make inferences using the normal curve. Rather, we rely on the central-limit theorem and adjust the sample size according to the population distribution so that the normal curve can be assumed to hold. Fortunately, the normal distribution of the statistic occurs with samples of relatively small size, as Figure 13.4 indicates.

Confidence Interval Estimates How does all of the preceding help us in making inferences about the parent population mean? After all, in practice we do not draw all possible samples of a given size, but only one, and we use the results obtained in it to infer something about the target group. It all ties together in the following way.

It is known that with any normal distribution, a specific percentage of all observations is within a certain number of standard deviations of the mean, for example, 95 percent of the values are within ± 1.96 standard deviations of the mean. The distribution of sample means is normal if the central-limit theorem holds and thus is no exception. Now, the mean of this sampling distribution is equal to the population mean μ, and its standard deviation is given by the square root of the variance of means, which is called the standard error of the mean, specifically $\sigma_{\bar{x}} = \sigma/\sqrt{n}$. Therefore, it is true that

Figure 13.4

Distribution of Sample Means for Samples of Various Sizes and Different Population Distributions

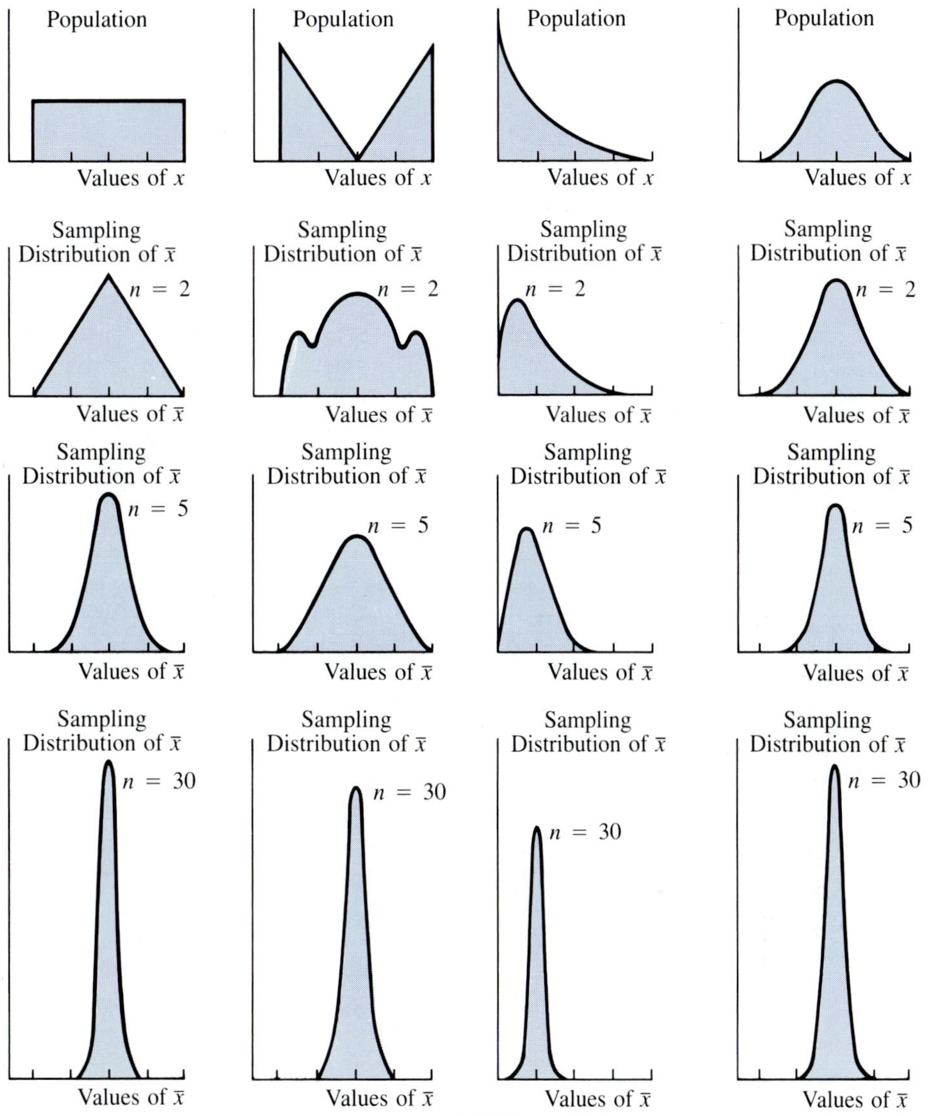

Source: Reproduced with permission from Ernest Kurnow, Gerald J. Glasser, and Frederick R. Ottman, *Statistics for Business Decisions* (Homewood, Ill.: Richard D. Irwin, Inc., © 1959), pp. 182–183.

- 68.26 percent of the sample means will be within $\pm\, 1\, \sigma_{\bar{x}}$ of the population mean
- 95.45 percent of the sample means will be within $\pm\, 2\, \sigma_{\bar{x}}$ of the population mean
- 99.73 percent of the sample means will be within $\pm\, 3\, \sigma_{\bar{x}}$ of the population mean

and in general that $\mu \,\pm\, z\sigma_{\bar{x}}$, will contain some certain proportion of all sample means depending on the selected value of z. This expression can be rewritten as an inequality relation that

$$\begin{pmatrix}\text{population} \\ \text{mean}\end{pmatrix} - z\begin{pmatrix}\text{standard error} \\ \text{of the mean}\end{pmatrix} \leq \begin{pmatrix}\text{sample} \\ \text{mean}\end{pmatrix} \leq \begin{pmatrix}\text{population} \\ \text{mean}\end{pmatrix} + z\begin{pmatrix}\text{standard error} \\ \text{of the mean}\end{pmatrix}$$

or

$$\mu \,-\, z\sigma_{\bar{x}} \leq \bar{x} \leq \mu \,+\, z\sigma_{\bar{x}} \tag{13.1}$$

which is held to be true a certain percentage of the time, and which implies that the sample mean will be in the interval formed by adding and subtracting a certain number of standard deviations to the mean value of the distribution. This inequality can be transferred to the equivalent inequality.

$$\genfrac{}{}{0pt}{}{\text{sample}}{\text{mean}} - (z)\left(\genfrac{}{}{0pt}{}{\text{standard error}}{\text{of the mean}}\right) \leq \genfrac{}{}{0pt}{}{\text{population}}{\text{mean}} \leq \genfrac{}{}{0pt}{}{\text{sample}}{\text{mean}} + (z)\left(\genfrac{}{}{0pt}{}{\text{standard error}}{\text{of the mean}}\right)$$

or

$$\bar{x} - z\sigma_{\bar{x}} \leq \mu \leq \bar{x} + z\sigma_{\bar{x}} \tag{13.2}$$

and if Equation 13.1 is true, say, 95 percent of the time ($z = 1.96$), then Equation 13.2 is also true 95 percent of the time. *When we make an inference on the basis of a single sample mean, we make use of Equation 13.2.*

It is important to note that Equation 13.2 says *nothing about the interval constructed from a particular sample as including the population mean.* Rather, the interval addresses the *sampling procedure.* The interval around a single mean may or may not contain the true population mean. Our confidence in our inference rests on the property that 95 percent of all the intervals we could construct under that sampling plan would contain the true value. We trust or hope that our sample is one of those 95 out of 100 that does (when we are 95 percent confident) include the true value.[10]

To illustrate this important point, suppose for the moment that the distribution of sample means of size $n = 2$ for our hypothetical example was normal. Table 13.5 illustrates the outcome pictorially for the first 10 out of the possible 190 samples that could be drawn under the specified sampling plan. Note that only 7 of the 10 intervals contain the true population mean. Confidence in the estimate arises because of the *procedure,* therefore, and not because of a particular estimate. The procedure suggests that with, say, a 95 percent confidence interval, if 100 samples were to be drawn and the sample mean and the confidence interval computed for each, 95 of the constructed intervals would include the true population value. The accuracy of a specific sample is evaluated only by reference to the procedure by which the sample was obtained. A sampling plan that is representative does not guarantee that a particular sample is representative. Statistical inference procedures rest on the representativeness of the sampling plan, and this is why probability samples are so critical to those procedures. Probability samples allow an estimate of the *precision* of the results in terms of how closely the estimates will tend to cluster

---

[10]The argument expressed here on the interpretation of a confidence interval is the traditional or classical statistics argument, which holds that the parameter being estimated is fixed in value. Thus, it is meaningless to interpret the statement probabilistically, since a given interval will or will not contain the population parameter. Bayesian analysts, though, adopt a different perspective. Bayesians hold that it is legitimate to assign personal probabilities to the states of nature, values of the unknown parameter in this case. One can then combine these judgments with sample information to produce posterior probabilities regarding the value of the unknown parameter. The confidence interval formed for a population mean is the same under the two approaches if one adopts the Bayesian assumption that the initial probabilities for each of the possible values of the unknown parameter are equal. The difference in perspectives, though, allows Bayesian analysts to interpret the resulting interval as a probability statement, that is, there is a 95 percent probability that the interval $\bar{x} \pm z\sigma_{\bar{x}}$ contains the true population mean. This interpretation tends to be much more satisfying to decision makers. For a discussion of the difference in the two perspectives, see Frankel, "Sampling Theory."

Table 13.5 Confidence Intervals for First Ten Samples Assuming the Distribution of Sample Means Was Normal

Sample Number	Sample Identity	Mean	Confidence Interval Lower Limit	Confidence Interval Upper Limit	Pictorial True $\mu = 9,400$
1	AB	5,800	2,689	8,911	
2	AC	6,000	2,889	9,111	
3	AD	6,200	3,089	9,311	
4	AE	6,400	3,289	9,511	
5	AF	6,600	3,489	9,711	
6	AG	6,800	3,689	9,911	
7	AH	7,000	3,889	10,111	
8	AI	7,200	4,089	10,311	
9	AJ	7,400	4,289	10,511	
10	AK	7,600	4,489	10,711	

about the true value. The greater the standard error of the statistic, the more variable the estimates and the less precise the procedure.

If it disturbs you that the confidence level applies to the procedure and not a particular sample result, you can take comfort in the fact that you can control the level of confidence with which the population value is estimated. Thus, if you do not wish to take the risk that you might have 1 of the 5 sample intervals in 100 that does not contain the population value, you might employ a 99 percent confidence interval, in which the risk is that only 1 in 100 sample intervals will not contain the population mean. Further, if you are willing to increase the size of the sample, you can increase your confidence and at the same time maintain the precision with which the population value is estimated. This will be explored more fully in Chapter 15.

There is one other perhaps disturbing ingredient in our procedure. The confidence interval estimate made use of three values: $\bar{x}$, z, and $\sigma_{\bar{x}}$. Now the sample mean $\bar{x}$ is computed from the selected sample, and z is specified to produce the desired level of confidence. But what about the standard error of the mean, $\sigma_{\bar{x}}$? It is equal to $\sigma_{\bar{x}} = \sigma/\sqrt{n}$, and thus in order to calculate it, we need to know the standard deviation of the variable in the population, that is, σ. What do we do if the population standard deviation, σ, is unknown? There is no problem, for two reasons. First, variation typically changes much more slowly than level for most variables of interest in marketing. Thus if the study is a repeat, we can use the previously discovered value for σ. Second, once the sample is selected and the information gathered, we can calculate the sample variance to estimate the population variance. The unbiased sample variance $\hat{s}^2$ is calculated as

$$\text{sample variance} = \hat{s}^2 = \frac{\text{sum of deviations around sample mean squared}}{\text{sample size minus 1}}$$

To compute the sample variance, then, we first calculate the sample mean. We then calculate the difference between each of our sample values and the sample mean, square these differences, sum them, and divide the sum by one less than the number of sample observations. The sample variance not only provides an estimate

Table 13.6   Symbols and Formulas Used for Means and Variances with Simple Random Samples

	Mean	Variance
Population	$\mu = \dfrac{\text{sum of population elements}}{\text{number of population elements}}$	$\sigma^2 = \dfrac{\text{sum of squared differences of each population element from the population mean}}{\text{number of population elements}}$
Sample	$\bar{x} = \dfrac{\text{sum of sample elements}}{\text{number of sample elements}}$	$\hat{s}^2 = \dfrac{\text{sum of squared differences of each sample element from the sample mean}}{\text{number of sample elements } - 1}$
		$\sigma_{\bar{x}}^2 = \dfrac{\sigma^2}{n}$ (when population variance is known)
Derived Population of Sample Means	$\dfrac{\text{average value} = \text{unknown}}{\text{population mean}}$	$s_{\bar{x}}^2 = \dfrac{\hat{s}^2}{n}$ (when population variance is unknown)

of the population variance, but it can also be used to secure an estimate of the standard error of the mean. When the population variance, σ^2, is known, the standard error of the mean, $\sigma_{\bar{x}}$, is also known since $\sigma_{\bar{x}} = \sigma/\sqrt{n}$. When the population variance, is unknown, the standard error of the mean can only be estimated. The estimate is given by $s_{\bar{x}}$, which equals the sample standard deviation divided by the square root of the sample size, that is $\hat{s}/\sqrt{n}$. The estimate calculation parallels that for the true value with the sample standard deviation substituted for the population standard deviation. Thus, if we draw sample *AB,* with a mean of 5,800,

$$\hat{s}^2 = \frac{(5,600 - 5,800)^2 + (6,000 - 5,800)^2}{1} = 80,000$$

and thus $\hat{s} = 283$ and $s_{\bar{x}} = \hat{s}/\sqrt{n} = 283/\sqrt{2} = 200$, and the 95 percent confidence interval is now

$$5,800 - 1.96(200) \le \mu \le 5,800 + 1.96(200) = 5,408 \le \mu \le 6,192,$$

which is somewhat smaller than before.[11]

Table 13.6 summarizes the computational formulas for the various means and variances used in this chapter.

Drawing the Simple Random Sample Although it was useful for illustrating the concepts of derived population and sampling distribution, the selection of sample elements from a jar containing all the population elements is not particularly rec-

---

[11]The *t* distribution would strictly be used when σ was unknown. We shall say more about this in Chapter 18.

ommended because of its great potential for bias. It is unlikely that the disks would be exactly uniform in size or feel, and slight differences here could affect the likelihood that any single element would be drawn. The national draft during the Vietnam war using a lottery serves as an example. Draft priorities were determined by drawing disks with birth dates stamped on them from a large container in full view of a television audience. Unfortunately, the dates of the year had initially been poured into the bowl systematically, January first and December last. Although the bowl was then stirred vigorously, December dates tended to be chosen first and January dates last. The procedure was later revised to produce a more random selection process.

The preferred way of drawing a simple random sample is through the use of a table of random numbers. Using a random number table involves the following sequence of steps. First, the elements of the parent population would be numbered serially from 1 to N; for the hypothetical population, the element A would be numbered 1, B as 2, and so on. Next, the numbers in the table would be treated so as to have the same number of digits as N. With $N = 20$, two-digit numbers would be used; if N is between 100 and 999, three-digit numbers would be required, and so on. Third, a starting point would be determined randomly. We might simply open the tables to some arbitrary place and point to a position on the page with our eyes closed. Since the numbers in a random number table are in fact random, that is, without order, it makes little difference where we begin.[12] Finally, we would proceed in some arbitrary direction, for example, up, down, or across, and would select those elements for the sample for which there is a match of serial number and random number.

To illustrate, consider the partial list of random numbers contained in Table 13.7. Since $N = 20$, we need work with only two digits, and therefore we can use the entries in Table 13.7 as is, instead of having to combine columns to produce numbers covering the range of serial numbers. Suppose we had previously decided to read down and that our arbitrary start indicated the eleventh row, fourth column, specifically the number 77. This number is too high and would be discarded. The next two numbers would also be discarded, but the fourth entry, 02, would be used, since 2 corresponds to one of the serial numbers in the list, Element B. The next five numbers would also be passed over as too large, whereas the number 05 would designate the inclusion of Element E. Elements B and E would thus represent the sample of two from whom we would seek information on income.

You should note that a simple random sample requires a serial numbered list of population elements. This means that the identity of each member of the population must be known. For some populations this is no problem, for example, if the study is to be conducted among *Fortune* magazine's list of the 500 largest corporations in the United States. The list is readily available, and a simple random sample of these firms could be easily selected. For many other populations of interest (for example, all families living in a particular city), the list of universe elements is much harder to come by, and applied researchers often resort to other sampling schemes.

---

[12]There are two major errors to avoid when using random number tables: (1) starting at a given place because one knows the distribution of numbers at that place and (2) discarding a sample because it does not "look right" in some sense and then continuing to use random numbers until a "likely looking" sample is selected. Sudman, "Applied Sampling," p. 165.

Table 13.7   Abridged List of Random Numbers

10 09 73 25 33	76 52 01 35 86	34 67 35 48 76	80 95 90 91 17	39 29 27 49 45
37 54 20 48 05	64 89 47 42 96	24 80 52 40 37	20 63 61 04 02	00 82 29 16 65
08 42 26 89 53	19 64 50 93 03	23 20 90 25 60	15 95 33 47 64	35 08 03 36 06
99 01 90 25 29	09 37 67 07 15	38 31 13 11 65	88 67 67 43 97	04 43 62 76 59
12 80 79 99 70	80 15 73 61 47	64 03 23 66 53	98 95 11 68 77	12 17 17 68 33
66 06 57 47 17	34 07 27 68 50	36 69 73 61 70	65 81 33 98 85	11 19 92 91 70
31 06 01 08 05	45 57 18 24 06	35 30 34 26 14	86 79 90 74 39	23 40 30 97 32
85 26 97 76 02	02 05 16 56 92	68 66 57 48 18	73 05 38 52 47	18 62 38 85 79
63 57 33 21 35	05 32 54 70 48	90 55 35 75 48	28 46 82 87 09	83 49 12 56 24
73 79 64 57 53	03 52 96 47 78	35 80 83 42 82	60 93 52 03 44	35 27 38 84 35
98 52 01 77 67	14 90 56 86 07	22 10 94 05 58	60 97 09 34 33	50 50 07 39 98
11 80 50 54 31	39 80 82 77 32	50 72 56 82 48	29 40 52 42 01	52 77 56 78 51
83 45 29 96 34	06 28 89 80 83	13 74 67 00 78	18 47 54 06 10	68 71 17 78 17
88 68 54 02 00	86 50 75 84 01	36 76 66 79 51	90 36 47 64 93	29 60 91 10 62
99 59 46 73 48	87 51 76 49 69	91 82 60 89 28	93 78 56 13 68	23 47 83 41 13
65 48 11 76 74	17 46 85 09 50	58 04 77 69 74	73 03 95 71 86	40 21 81 65 44
80 12 43 56 35	17 72 70 80 15	45 31 82 23 74	21 11 57 82 53	14 38 55 37 63
74 35 09 98 17	77 40 27 72 14	43 23 60 02 10	45 52 16 42 37	96 28 60 26 55
69 91 62 68 03	66 25 22 91 48	36 93 68 72 03	76 62 11 39 90	94 40 05 64 18
09 89 32 05 05	14 22 56 85 14	46 42 75 67 88	96 29 77 88 22	54 38 21 45 98
91 49 91 45 23	68 47 92 76 86	46 16 28 35 54	94 75 08 99 23	37 08 92 00 48
80 33 69 45 98	26 94 03 68 58	70 29 73 41 35	53 14 03 33 40	42 05 08 23 41
44 10 48 19 49	85 15 74 79 54	32 97 92 65 75	57 60 04 08 81	22 22 20 64 13
12 55 07 37 42	11 10 00 20 40	12 86 07 46 97	96 64 48 94 39	28 70 72 58 15

Source: This table is reproduced from page 1 of The Rand Corporation, *A Million Random Digits with 100,000 Normal Deviates* (New York: The Free Press, 1955). Copyright © 1955 and 1983 by The Rand Corporation. Used by permission.

♦ Summary

Learning Objective 1: Distinguish between a census and a sample.

A complete canvass of a population is called a census. A sample is a portion of the population taken from the larger group.

Learning Objective 2: List the six steps researchers use to draw a sample of a population.

The six steps researchers use in drawing a sample are (1) define the population, (2) identify the sampling frame, (3) select a sampling procedure, (4) determine the sample size, (5) select the sample elements, and (6) collect the data from the designated elements.

Learning Objective 3: Define what is meant by a sampling frame.

A sampling frame is the listing of the elements from which the actual sample will be drawn.

Learning Objective 4: Explain the difference between a probability sample and a nonprobability sample.

In a probability sample each member of the population has a known, nonzero chance of being included in the sample. The chances of each member of the population being included in the sample may not be equal, but everyone has a known probability of inclusion.

With nonprobability samples, on the other hand, there is no way of estimating the probability that any population element will be included in the sample. Thus, there is no way of ensuring that the sample is representative of the population. All nonprobability samples rely on personal judgment at some point in the sample-selection process. While these judgments may yield good estimates of a population characteristic, there is no way of determining objectively if the sample is adequate.

Learning Objective 5: Distinguish between a fixed and sequential sample.

In fixed samples, the sample size is decided before the study begins, and all the needed information is collected before the results are analyzed. In a sequential sample, the number

Table 13.7 *continued*

63 60 64 93 29	16 50 53 44 84	40 21 95 25 63	43 65 17 70 82	07 20 73 17 90
61 19 69 04 46	26 45 74 77 74	51 92 43 37 29	65 39 45 95 93	42 58 26 05 27
15 47 44 52 66	95 27 07 99 53	59 36 78 38 48	82 39 61 01 18	33 21 15 94 66
94 55 72 85 73	67 89 75 43 87	54 62 24 44 31	91 19 04 25 92	92 92 74 59 73
42 48 11 62 13	97 34 40 87 21	16 86 84 87 67	03 07 11 20 59	25 70 14 66 70
23 52 37 83 17	73 20 88 98 37	68 93 59 14 16	26 25 22 96 63	05 52 28 25 62
04 49 35 24 94	75 24 63 38 24	45 86 25 10 25	61 96 27 93 35	65 33 71 24 72
00 54 99 76 54	64 05 18 81 59	96 11 96 38 96	54 69 28 23 91	23 28 72 95 29
35 96 31 53 07	26 89 80 93 54	33 35 13 54 62	77 97 45 00 24	90 10 33 93 33
59 80 80 83 91	45 42 72 68 42	83 60 94 97 00	13 02 12 48 92	78 56 52 01 06
46 05 88 52 36	01 39 09 22 86	77 28 14 40 77	93 91 08 36 47	70 61 74 29 41
32 17 90 05 97	87 37 92 52 41	05 56 70 70 07	86 74 31 71 57	85 39 41 18 38
69 23 46 14 06	20 11 74 52 04	15 95 66 00 00	18 74 39 24 23	97 11 89 63 38
19 56 54 14 30	01 75 87 53 79	40 41 92 15 85	66 67 43 68 06	84 96 28 52 07
45 15 51 49 38	19 47 60 72 46	43 66 79 45 43	59 04 79 00 33	20 82 66 95 41
94 86 43 19 94	36 16 81 08 51	34 88 88 15 53	01 54 03 54 56	05 01 45 11 76
98 08 62 48 26	45 24 02 84 04	44 99 90 88 96	39 09 47 34 07	35 44 13 18 80
33 18 51 62 32	41 94 15 09 49	89 43 54 85 81	88 69 54 19 94	37 54 87 30 43
80 95 10 04 06	96 38 27 07 74	20 15 12 33 87	25 01 62 52 98	94 62 46 11 71
79 75 24 91 40	71 96 12 82 96	69 86 10 25 91	74 85 22 05 39	00 38 75 95 79
18 63 33 25 37	98 14 50 65 71	31 01 02 46 74	05 45 56 14 27	77 93 89 19 36
74 02 94 39 02	77 55 73 22 70	97 79 01 71 19	52 52 75 80 21	80 81 45 17 48
54 17 84 56 11	80 99 33 71 43	05 33 51 29 69	56 12 71 92 55	36 04 09 03 24
11 66 44 98 83	52 07 98 48 27	59 38 17 15 39	09 97 33 34 40	88 46 12 33 56
48 32 47 79 28	31 24 96 47 10	02 29 53 68 70	32 30 75 75 46	15 02 00 99 94
69 07 49 41 38	87 63 79 19 76	35 58 40 44 01	10 51 82 16 15	01 84 87 69 38

of elements to be sampled is not decided in advance but is determined by a series of decisions as the data are collected.

Learning Objective 6: Explain what is meant by a judgment sample and describe its best use and its hazards.

Judgment samples are those in which sample elements are handpicked because it is expected that they can serve the research purpose. Sometimes, the sample elements are selected because it is believed that they are representative of the population of interest.

As long as the researcher is at the early stages of research when ideas or insights are being sought—or when the researcher realizes its limitations—the judgment sample can be used productively. It becomes dangerous, though, when it is employed in descriptive or causal studies and its weaknesses are conveniently forgotten.

Learning Objective 7: Define what is meant by a quota sample.

The quota sampling technique attempts to ensure that the sample is representative of the population by selecting sample elements in such a way that the proportion of the sample elements possessing a certain characteristic is approximately the same as the proportion of the elements with the characteristic in the population. This is accomplished by assigning each field worker a quota that specifies the characteristics of the people the interviewer is to contact.

Learning Objective 8: Explain what is meant by a parameter in a sampling procedure.

A parameter is a characteristic of the parent population; it is a fixed quantity that distinguishes one population from another.

Learning Objective 9: Explain what is meant by derived population.

The derived population consists of all the possible samples that can be drawn from the parent population under a given sampling plan.

Learning Objective 10: Explain why the concept of sampling distribution is the most important concept in statistics.

The notion of the sampling distribution of the statistic is the cornerstone of statistical inference procedures. If one knows the sampling distribution for the statistic in question, one is in a position to make an inference about the corresponding population parameter. If, on the other hand, one knows only that a particular sample estimate will vary with repeated sampling and has no information as to *how* it will vary, then it will be impossible to devise a measure of the sampling error associated with that estimate. Since the sampling distribution of an estimate describes how that estimate will vary with repeated sampling, it provides a basis for determining the reliability of the sample estimate.

Discussion Questions, Problems, and Projects

1. For each of the following situations identify the appropriate target population and sampling frame.
   (a) A local chapter of the American Lung Association wants to test the effectiveness of a brochure titled "12 Reasons For Not Smoking" in the city of St. Paul, Minnesota.
   (b) A medium-sized manufacturer of cat food wants to conduct an in-home usage test of a new type of cat food in Sacramento, California.
   (c) A large wholesaler dealing in household appliances in the city of New York wants to evaluate dealer reaction to a new discount policy.
   (d) A local department store wants to assess the satisfaction with a new credit policy offered to charge account customers.
   (e) A national manufacturer wants to assess whether adequate inventories are being held by wholesalers in order to prevent shortages by retailers.
   (f) Your school cafeteria wants to test a new soft drink manufactured and sold by the staff of the cafeteria.
   (g) A manufacturer of cake mixes selling primarily in the Midwest wants to test market a new brand of cake mixes.

2. The management of a popular tourist resort on the west coast had noticed a decline in the number of tourists and length of stay over the past three years. An overview of industry trends indicated that the overall tourist trade was expanding and growing rapidly. Management decided to conduct a study to determine people's attitudes towards the particular activities that were available. They wanted to cause the minimum amount of inconvenience to their customers and hence adopted the following plan. A request was deposited in each hotel room of the two major hotels indicating the nature of the study and encouraging customers to participate. The customers were requested to report to a separate desk located in the lobby of the hotels. Personal interviews, lasting twenty minutes, were conducted at this desk.
   (a) What type of sampling method was used?
   (b) Critically evaluate the method used.

3. A national manufacturer of baby food was planning to enter the Canadian market. The initial thrust was to be in the provinces of Ontario and Quebec. Prior to the final decision of launching the product, management decided to test market the products in two cities. After reviewing the various cities in terms of external criteria such as demographics, shopping characteristics and so on, the research department settled on the cities of Hamilton, Ontario, and Sherbrooke, Quebec.
   (a) What type of sampling method was used?
   (b) Critically evaluate the method used.

4. The Juno Company, a manufacturer of clothing for large-sized consumers, was in the process of evaluating its product and advertising strategy. Initial efforts consisted of a number

of focus group interviews. The focus groups consisted of ten to twelve large men and women of different demographic characteristics who were selected by the company's research department using on-the-street observations of physical characteristics.

(a) What type of sampling method was used?

(b) Critically evaluate the method used.

5. The Hi-Style Company was a chain of beauty salons in San Diego, California. During the past five years the company had witnessed a sharp increase in the number of outlets it operated and the company's gross sales and net profit margin. The owner plans to offer a free service of hair analysis and consultation, a service for which other competing salons charge a substantial price. In order to offset the increase in operating expenses, the owner plans to raise the rates on other services by 5 percent. Prior to introducing this new service and increasing rates, the owner decides to do a survey using her customers as a sample and employing the method of quota sampling. Your assistance is required in planning the study.

(a) On what variables would you suggest the quotas be based? Why? List the variables with their respective levels.

(b) The owner has kept close track of the demographic characteristics of her customers over a five-year period and decides that these would be most relevant in identifying the sample elements to be used.

Variable	Level	Percent of Customers
Age	0–15 years	5%
	16–30 years	30%
	31–45 years	30%
	46–60 years	15%
	61–75 years	15%
	76 years and over	5%
Sex	Male	24%
	Female	76%
Income	$0–$9,999	10%
	$10,000–$19,999	20%
	$20,000–$29,999	30%
	$30,000–$39,999	20%
	$40,000 and over	20%

Based on these three quota variables, indicate the characteristics of a sample of 200 subjects.

(c) Discuss the possible sources of bias with the sampling method.

Suggested Additional Readings

For a good exposition of the principles and advantages of sequential sampling versus fixed samples, see

E. J. Anderton and R. Tudor, "The Application of Sequential Analysis in Market Research," *Journal of Marketing Research,* 17 (February 1980), pp. 97–105.

For a discussion of the use of snowball samples, see

Patrick Biernacki and Dan Waldorf, "Snowball Sampling: Problems and Techniques of Chain Referred Sampling," *Sociological Methods and Research,* 10 (November 1981), pp. 141–163.

For a more in-depth discussion of some of the more fundamental issues in sampling, see

Martin Frankel, "Sampling Theory," in Peter H. Rossi, James D. Wright, and Andy B. Anderson, eds., *Handbook of Survey Research* (Orlando: Academic Press, 1983), pp. 21–67.

Chapter 14

Stratified and Cluster Sampling

Learning Objectives

Upon completing this chapter, you should be able to

1. Specify the two procedures that distinguish a stratified sample.
2. Cite two reasons why researchers might opt to use a stratified sample rather than a simple random sample.
3. Note what points investigators should keep in mind when dividing a population into strata for a stratified sample.
4. Explain what is meant by a proportionate stratified sample.
5. Explain what is meant by a disproportionate stratified sample.
6. List the steps followed in drawing a cluster sample.
7. Explain the difference between a one-stage cluster sample and a two-stage cluster sample.
8. Explain why cluster sampling, though far less statistically efficient than comparable stratified samples, is the sampling procedure used most in large-scale field surveys employing personal interviews.
9. Distinguish between one-stage area sampling and simple, two-stage area sampling.
10. Note the quality that distinguishes probability-proportional-to-size sampling and explain when it is used.

Case in Marketing Research

Daniel Thackeray was facing his first big decision as the marketing director of Swanee Foods. The company was nearly ready to begin national distribution of its totally revamped line of frozen dinners, and it was Dan's job to pick the company that would monitor data from the new product's introduction.

As Dan shuffled through the stack of slick brochures touting various marketing research services available from a broad range of companies, he felt the burden of the decision weigh heavily on his shoulders. So much rested on a successful launch of the product. The company had already sunk millions into researching, reformulating, and repackaging its frozen dinners in an attempt to recapture its former preeminent position in the market. It was critical that whichever company won the Swanee account be able to use the most sophisticated data-analysis techniques possible to track the progress of the test.

As Dan sat mulling over the information before him, Doug Bradley, Swanee's director of advertising and promotion, stopped by the office.

"Do you have a minute to see some ads?" he asked. "We just got prints on our thirty-second spots for the frozen food line from the production lab."

"Sure, Doug, I'll be right down. I need a break from all these brochures. These companies all sound great on paper, so I'm having a tough time trying to figure out how to choose among them," Dan said.

"You know, Dan, we're going to need results practically overnight on this launch so we can fine-tune our marketing before Continental Foods gets wind of what we're doing. We need a company that can track the results of our sales promotions and advertising campaigns—and do it quickly. Sounds to me as if we need a pretty sophisticated organization," Doug said.

"You're right, Doug. I guess I can safely eliminate any company that doesn't do UPC scanner-based research. That's the only way we're going to get the results we need with the speed we want," Daniel said.

"There are two companies I've been particularly interested in that do research with scanners. But each employs a very different type of sample. One is a nationwide sample, and the other focuses in-depth on several strategically placed, representative markets around the country. Do you have any sense of which would be better for our needs?" Dan asked.

"I don't know," Doug said. "Why don't you have each group come in and make a presentation. Then you can ask them all the questions you want."

"Good idea. I'll call them both this afternoon. Now let's go see those commercials," Dan said.

Discussion Issues

1. If you were Dan Thackeray, what would you want to know about each company's sample?

2. What might be the advantage of testing in a limited number of carefully chosen locations?

3. What might be the advantage of using a national sample of all scanner-equipped supermarkets in the test?

In the preceding chapter we discussed the basic types of samples and how they are drawn. Simple random samples were used to illustrate the basis of statistical inference in which a parameter is estimated from a statistic. In this chapter we will take these concepts a bit further to explore two other types of probability samples: stratified samples and cluster samples.

◆ Stratified Sample

◆ **Stratified sample**

Probability sample that is distinguished by the two-step procedure where (1) the parent population is divided into mutually exclusive and exhaustive subsets, and (2) a simple random sample of elements is chosen independently from each group or subset.

A **stratified sample** is a probability sample that is distinguished by the following two-step procedure:

1. The parent population is divided into mutually exclusive and exhaustive subsets.

2. A simple random sample of elements is chosen independently from each group or subset.

Note that the definition says nothing about what criteria are used to separate the universe elements into subsets. That is because it is not the criteria that determine whether or not a stratified sample has been drawn. Admittedly, those criteria will make a difference as to the ultimate usefulness of the particular sample in question. But as long as the sample reflects the two-stage process, it is a stratified sample. Keep this distinction in mind. It will be useful later when distinguishing cluster samples from stratified samples.

The subsets into which the universe elements are divided are called *strata* or *subpopulations*. Note that our definition specified that this division be mutually exclusive and exhaustive. This means that every population element must be assigned to one, and only one, stratum and that no population elements are omitted in the assignment procedure.

To illustrate the process, suppose we again used the hypothetical population of twenty people used in the last chapter and shown again in Table 14.1. That population could be described by several parameters, such as the average income, the range in education, and the proportion subscribing to various newspapers. Now assume we divide the group into two strata on the basis of educational level. Table 14.2 shows the results of this stratification procedure. Elements A through J form the

Table 14.1   Hypothetical Population

Element	Income (Dollars)	Education (Years)	Newspaper Subscription	Element	Income (Dollars)	Education (Years)	Newspaper Subscription
1 A	5,600	8	X	11 K	9,600	13	X
2 B	6,000	9	Y	12 L	10,000	13	Y
3 C	6,400	11	X	13 M	10,400	14	X
4 D	6,800	11	Y	14 N	10,800	14	Y
5 E	7,200	11	X	15 O	11,200	15	X
6 F	7,600	12	Y	16 P	11,600	16	Y
7 G	8,000	12	X	17 Q	12,000	16	X
8 H	8,400	12	Y	18 R	12,400	17	Y
9 I	8,800	12	X	19 S	12,800	18	X
10 J	9,200	12	Y	20 T	13,200	18	Y

Table 14.2   Stratification of Hypothetical Population by Education

Stratum I Elements	Stratum I Elements	Stratum II Elements	Stratum II Elements
A	F	K	P
B	G	L	Q
C	H	M	R
D	I	N	S
E	J	O	T

first stratum (education of 12 years or less) and Elements K through T form the *second stratum* (education of more than 12 years). There is no particular reason to choose two strata. The parent population can be divided into any number of strata. We chose two as a convenient way of illustrating the technique.

The second step in the process requires that a simple random sample be drawn independently from *each* stratum. Let us again work with samples of Size 2, formed in this case by selecting one element from each stratum. (The number of elements from each stratum does not have to be equal, however.)

The procedure that would be used to select the two elements for the stratified sample is the same used in drawing a simple random sample. Within each stratum, the population elements would be serially numbered from 1 to 10. A table of random numbers would be consulted. The first number encountered between 1 and 10 would designate the element from the first stratum. The element from the second stratum could be selected after another independent start or by continuing from the first randomly determined start. In either case, it would again be designated by the first encounter with a number between 1 and 10.

Derived Population

Although only one sample of Size 2 will in fact be selected, let us look briefly at the derived population of all possible samples of Size 2 that could be selected under this sampling plan. This derived population along with the mean of each sample is displayed in Table 14.3.

Note that in this sampling plan there are only 100 possible sample combinations of elements, whereas with simple random sampling there were 190 possible combinations. That is because this type of sampling specified that one element be drawn from each stratum. In simple random sampling, you will recall that any two elements could be drawn from the population of items. In this sense, stratified sampling is always more restrictive than simple random sampling. Note further that every element has an equal chance of being included in the sample—1 in 10—since each can be the single element selected from the stratum in which it is in. This explains why we specified an additional requirement to define a simple random sample. Although simple random samples provide each element an equal chance of selection, other techniques can also. Thus, equal probability of selection is a necessary but not a sufficient condition for simple random sampling; in addition, each combination of n elements must be a sample possibility and as likely to occur as any other combination of n elements.

Table 14.3   Derived Population of All Possible Samples of Size 2 with Stratified Sampling

k	Sample Identity	Mean	k	Sample Identity	Mean	k	Sample Identity	Mean	k	Sample Identity	Mean
1	AK	7,600	26	CP	9,000	51	FK	8,600	76	HP	10,000
2	AL	7,800	27	CQ	9,200	52	FL	8,800	77	HQ	10,200
3	AM	8,000	28	CR	9,400	53	FM	9,000	78	HR	10,400
4	AN	8,200	29	CS	9,600	54	FN	9,200	79	HS	10,600
5	AO	8,400	30	CT	9,800	55	FO	9,400	80	HT	10,800
6	AP	8,600	31	DK	8,200	56	FP	9,600	81	IK	9,200
7	AQ	8,800	32	DL	8,400	57	FQ	9,800	82	IL	9,400
8	AR	9,000	33	DM	8,600	58	FR	10,000	83	IM	9,600
9	AS	9,200	34	DN	8,800	59	FS	10,200	84	IN	9,800
10	AT	9,400	35	DO	9,000	60	FT	10,400	85	IO	10,000
11	BK	7,800	36	DP	9,200	61	GK	8,800	86	IP	10,200
12	BL	8,000	37	DQ	9,400	62	GL	9,000	87	IQ	10,400
13	BM	8,200	38	DR	9,600	63	GM	9,200	88	IR	10,600
14	BN	8,400	39	DS	9,800	64	GN	9,400	89	IS	10,800
15	BO	8,600	40	DT	10,000	65	GO	9,600	90	IT	11,000
16	BP	8,800	41	EK	8,400	66	GP	9,800	91	JK	9,400
17	BQ	9,000	42	EL	8,600	67	GQ	10,000	92	JL	9,600
18	BR	9,200	43	EM	8,800	68	GR	10,200	93	JM	9,800
19	BS	9,400	44	EN	9,000	69	GS	10,400	94	JN	10,000
20	BT	9,600	45	EO	9,200	70	GT	10,600	95	JO	10,200
21	CK	8,000	46	EP	9,400	71	HK	9,000	96	JP	10,400
22	CL	8,200	47	EQ	9,600	72	HL	9,200	97	JQ	10,600
23	CM	8,400	48	ER	9,800	73	HM	9,400	98	JR	10,800
24	CN	8,600	49	ES	10,000	74	HN	9,600	99	JS	11,000
25	CO	8,800	50	ET	10,200	75	HO	9,800	100	JT	11,200

Sampling Distribution

Table 14.4 contains the classification of sample means by size, and Figure 14.1 displays the plot of this sample statistic. Note that in relation to Figure 13.3 for simple random sampling, stratified sampling can produce a more concentrated distribution of estimates. This suggests one reason why we might choose a stratified sample; stratified samples can produce sample statistics that are more precise, or that have smaller error due to sampling, than simple random samples. With education as a stratification variable, there is a marked reduction in the number of sample means that deviate widely from the population mean.

Table 14.4   Classification of Sample Means by Size with Stratified Sampling

Sample Mean	Number of Samples
7,300 to 7,800	3
7,900 to 8,400	12
8,500 to 9,000	21
9,100 to 9,600	28
9,700 to 10,200	21
10,300 to 10,800	12
10,900 to 11,400	3

Figure 14.1

Distribution of Sample Means with Stratified Sampling

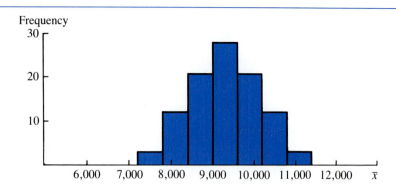

A second reason for drawing a stratified sample is that stratification allows the investigation of the characteristic of interest for particular subgroups. Thus, by stratifying, one is able to guarantee representation of those with a high school education or less, and those with more than a high school education. This can be extremely important when sampling from populations with rare segments. Suppose, for example, that a manufacturer of diamond rings wants to conduct a study of sales of the product by social class. Unless special precautions are taken, it is likely that the upper class—which represents only 3 percent of the total population—will not be represented at all, or will be represented by too few cases. Yet this may be an extremely important segment to the ring manufacturer. It is often true in marketing that a small subset of the population of interest will account for a large proportion of the behavior of interest—for example, consumption of the product. It then becomes critical that this subgroup be adequately represented in the sample. Stratified sampling is one way of ensuring adequate representation from each subgroup of interest.

Confidence Interval Estimate

In establishing a confidence interval with a simple random sample, we saw that we need three things to complete the confidence interval specifications given by

$$\bar{x} - zs_{\bar{x}} \leq \mu \leq \bar{x} + zs_{\bar{x}}.$$

1. The degree of confidence desired so that a z value can be selected.
2. A point estimate of the population mean given by the sample mean $\bar{x}$.
3. An estimate of the amount of sampling error associated with the sample mean, which was given by the standard error of the mean, $s_{\bar{x}} = \hat{s}/\sqrt{n}$, when the population variance was unknown.

The same three quantities are required for making inferences with a stratified sample. The only difference in the procedure occurs in the way Items 2 and 3 are generated. With stratified sampling, the sample estimate of the population mean and the standard error of estimate associated with this statistic are determined by weighting the individual strata results.

   More specifically, the analyst needs to compute the sample mean and the sample variance for each stratum. These would be calculated exactly as before, since a simple random sample is being taken from each stratum. The mean for the sample as a whole is then determined by weighting each of the respective strata means by the relative proportion of elements in the population that belong to the stratum. For example, if the population is divided into groups in such a way that one stratum contains one-fourth of all the population members, the sample mean for that stratum would receive a weight of .25 when one is determining the mean for the total sample. Similarly, the sample mean for a stratum that contains 10 percent of the population elements would be weighted .10 when one is estimating the overall sample mean.

The process to get the overall standard error of the mean is slightly more complex. The relative sizes of the respective strata are again used but the ratios are squared; for example, a stratum containing 10 percent of the population members would be weighted $(.10)^2 = .01$. Further, one needs to weight the variances of means by strata to get the overall variance of the mean. Then one takes the square root of the overall result to get the standard error of the mean for the overall sample. The variance of means for each stratum are obtained just as they were for a simple random sample, that is, by dividing the sample variance for the stratum by the sample size from that stratum.

Table 14.5 illustrates the procedure assuming Elements B and E were randomly selected from the first stratum and Elements N and S from the second stratum. Since each stratum contains ten of the twenty population elements, the sample mean for each stratum is weighted by one-half ($10 \div 20$) when one is determining the overall sample mean, while each variance of estimate is weighted .25. With the overall sample mean of 9,200 and standard error of estimate of 583, the 95 percent confidence interval ($z = 1.96$) is $9,200 \pm (1.96)583$ or $8,057 \leq \mu \leq 10,343$. This interval is interpreted as before. The true mean may or may not be in the interval, but since 95 of 100 intervals constructed by this process will contain the true mean, we are 95 percent confident that the true population mean income is between $8,057 and $10,343.[1]

Increased Precision of Stratified Samples We mentioned previously that one of the reasons one might choose a stratified sample is that such samples offer an opportunity for reducing sampling error or increasing precision. When estimating a mean, sampling error is given by the size of the standard error of the mean, $s_{\bar{x}}$; the smaller $s_{\bar{x}}$ is, the less the sampling error and the more precise the estimate will be as indicated by the narrower confidence interval associated with a specified degree of confidence.

Consider the example in Table 14.1 again. The total size of the population and the population within each stratum are fixed. The only way, therefore, for total sampling error to be reduced is for the variance of the estimate within each stratum to be made smaller. Now the variance of the estimate by strata in turn depends on the variability of the characteristic within the strata. Thus, the estimate of the mean can be made more precise to the extent that the population can be partitioned so that there is little variability within each stratum, that is, to the extent the strata can be made internally homogeneous.

A characteristic of interest will display a certain amount of variation in the population. The investigator can do nothing about this total variation because it is a fixed characteristic of the population. In the population in Table 14.1, for example, there

---

[1] Note that we are again assuming the normal distribution applies in making this inference. While this assumption is not strictly correct in this instance because of the size of the sample taken from each stratum, we are making it to allow more direct comparison with the interval constructed using simple random sampling. In most situations the normal distribution would hold because the central-limit theorem also applies to the individual strata means, and the linear combination of these means produces a normally distributed overall sample mean.

Table 14.5   Computation of Mean and Standard Error of Estimate for Stratified Sample

Stratum 1		Stratum 2	
Element	**Income**	**Element**	**Income**
B	6,000	N	10,800
E	7,200	S	12,800

Mean: $\bar{x}_1 = \dfrac{6{,}000 + 7{,}200}{2} = 6{,}600$ $\bar{x}_2 = \dfrac{10{,}800 + 12{,}800}{2} = 11{,}800$

Variance: $\hat{s}_1^2 = \dfrac{(6{,}000 - 6{,}600)^2 + (7{,}200 - 6{,}600)^2}{2 - 1}$ $\hat{s}_2^2 = \dfrac{(10{,}800 - 11{,}800)^2 + (12{,}800 - 11{,}800)^2}{2 - 1}$

$\qquad\qquad = 720{,}000$ $\qquad\qquad = 2{,}000{,}000$

Variance of estimate: $s_{\bar{x}_1}^2 = \dfrac{\hat{s}_1^2}{n_1} = \dfrac{720{,}000}{2} = 360{,}000$ $s_{\bar{x}_2}^2 = \dfrac{\hat{s}_2^2}{n_2} = \dfrac{2{,}000{,}000}{2} = 1{,}000{,}000$

Overall Sample

Mean: $\bar{x} = \dfrac{10}{20}(6{,}600) + \dfrac{10}{20}(11{,}800) = 9{,}200$

Variance of estimate: $s_{\bar{x}}^2 = \left(\dfrac{10}{20}\right)^2 (360{,}000) + \left(\dfrac{10}{20}\right)^2 (1{,}000{,}000) = 340{,}000$

Standard error of estimate: $s_{\bar{x}} = \sqrt{s_{\bar{x}}^2} = 583$

is a variation in incomes which the investigator can do nothing about. But the analyst can do something when dividing the elements of the population into strata so as to increase the precision with which the average value of the characteristic (i.e., average income) can be estimated. Specifically, the goal is to divide the population into strata so that the elements within any given stratum are as similar in value as possible and the values between any two strata are as disparate as possible. In this case, the division of the population between those who have more than a high school education and those who do not was a good way of separating the population into two strata since the elements within each stratum have similar incomes.

In the limit, if the investigator is successful in partitioning the population so that the elements in each stratum are exactly equal, there will be no error associated with the estimate of the population mean. That is right! The population mean could then be estimated without error because *the variability that exists between strata does not enter into the calculation of the standard error of estimate with stratified sampling.*

One can see this readily in a simple case with a limited number of values. Suppose that in a population of 1,000 elements, 200 had the value 5, 300 had the value 10, and 500 had the value 20. Now the mean of this population is $\mu = 14$, and the variance is $\sigma^2 = 39$. If a simple random sample of size $n = 3$ is employed to estimate this mean, then the standard error of estimate is

$$\sigma_{\bar{x}} = \dfrac{\sigma}{\sqrt{n}} = \dfrac{\sqrt{39}}{\sqrt{3}} = 3.61$$

and the width of confidence interval would be $\pm z$ times this value, 3.61. Suppose, on the other hand, a researcher employed a stratified sample and was successful in partitioning the total population so that all the elements with a value of 5 on the characteristic were in one stratum, those with the value 10 in the second stratum, and those with the value 20 in the third stratum. To generate a completely precise description of the mean of each stratum, the researcher would then need only to take a sample of one from each stratum. Further, when the investigator combined these individual results into a global estimate of the overall mean, the standard error of the estimate would be zero, since each stratum standard error of estimate is zero. The population mean value would be determined exactly.

Bases for Stratification The fact that variation among strata does not enter into the calculation of the standard error of estimate suggests the kinds of criteria that should be used to partition the population. The values assumed by the characteristic will be unknown, for if they were known, there would be no need to take a sample to estimate their mean level. What the investigator attempts to do, therefore, is to partition the population according to one or more criteria that are expected to be related to the characteristic of interest. It was no accident, therefore, that in our hypothetical example education was employed to divide the population elements into strata. As Table 14.1 indicates, there is a relationship between educational level and income level: the more years of school, the higher the income tends to be. Newspaper subscriptions, on the other hand, would have made a poor variable for partitioning the population into segments, since there is almost no relation between the paper to which a person subscribes and the individual's income. Whether one selects a "good" or a "bad" variable to partition the population does not affect whether a stratified sample is selected or not. It is significant in determining whether a good or poor sample is selected, but the two features defining a stratified sample are still (1) the partitioning of the population into subgroups and (2) the random selection of elements from each subgroup.

The calculation of the standard error of estimate provides some clue as to the number of strata that should be employed. Since the standard error of estimate depends only on variability within strata, the various strata should be made as homogeneous as possible. One way of doing this is to employ many, very small strata. In our education example, for instance, additional strata could be grade school education or less, some high school education, some college education, and graduate school education. Or even finer distinctions could be made. There are practical limits, though, to the number of strata that should be and are used in actual research studies. First, the creation of additional strata is often expensive in terms of sample design, data collection, and analysis. Second, there is an upper limit to the amount of variation that can be accounted for by any practical stratification. Regardless of the criteria by which the population is partitioned, a certain amount of variation is likely to remain unaccounted for, and thus the additional strata will serve no productive purpose.

Proportionate and Disproportionate Stratified Samples

♦ Proportionate stratified sample

Stratified sample in which the number of observations in the total sample is allocated among the strata in proportion to the relative number of elements in each stratum in the population.

Whether one chooses a stratified sample over a simple random sample depends in part on the trade-off between cost and precision. Although stratified samples typically produce more precise estimates, they also usually cost more than simple random samples. If the decision is made in favor of a stratified sample, the researcher must still decide whether to select a proportionate or disproportionate one.

With a **proportionate stratified sample,** the number of observations in the total sample is allocated among the strata in proportion to the *relative* number of ele-

Back to the Case

Dan Thackeray was just putting down the telephone when his secretary escorted a tall, dark-suited young woman into the office.

"Jill Bennett?" Dan asked, extending his hand. "I've been looking forward to meeting you. From our phone conversation, it sounds as though your company may be able to offer the services we're looking for."

"I hope so, Dan. As I mentioned to you earlier, Samson Scandata is one of the oldest firms in the business, so we have a lot of experience using our retail audit data to gauge new product introductions. But in our case, 'old' is by no means stodgy. We have state-of-the-art data-analysis tools and techniques that can tell you within days how well your product is doing," Jill said.

"I read your brochure," Dan said, "but I still had some questions about how your sample is chosen. Could you tell me a little more about it."

"Certainly. As you may know, there are over 235,000 retail food, drug, and mass-merchandise stores in the United States. Obviously, measuring consumer activity in every one is a physical as well as a practical and economic impossibility. The solution, therefore, lies in measuring a reliable and efficient sample of these outlets," Jill said.

"Our sample has been carefully designed so that it not only

reflects an accurate picture of that universe, but does so at a realistic cost by maintaining the most efficient cost/sample relationship possible," she continued.

"We make sure that our sample is not only the proper size, but also reflects the proper structure. It contains different sizes and types of stores in urban, suburban, and rural counties, from all geographic areas of the country. This structure is crucial for area-by-area and store-by-store type analyses to be possible. These analyses in turn allow clients to investigate sectional consumer preferences, the results of special marketing efforts in certain areas, and sales performance in each of their own sales territories," she said.

"In constructing this sample, we are always aware of our clients' budgets. We know that they need a sample that is not only accurate, but commercially efficient. The balance between these two requirements is maintained through the use of a technique known as disproportionate sampling. In the simplest terms, disproportionality of our sample is achieved by relating the sample selection to the store's volume, rather than the store count, which results in more large-volume stores and fewer small stores. As a result, the accuracy of our sample is

equivalent to a much larger—and, of course, much more expensive—sample," Jill said.

"Well, all this sounds impressive," Dan said, "but we're going to need results in a hurry. I understand you offer a scanning service?"

"Yes," Jill agreed. "We offer our Scanfast service as a supplement and enhancement to our basic index. We have found it provides clients a powerful analytical tool in the form of weekly sales data from a nationwide sample of scanner-equipped stores. In your case, such information could be used to determine how your new product is performing, whether or not it is hitting the sales targets you projected, if your sales are responding to your promotional campaigns, and whether competitors' activities are affecting your brand's performance."

"This has been very interesting, Jill," Dan said. "I'll get back to you within the week to let you know my decision."

A disproportionate sample can be a very useful and cost-efficient way of sampling, especially if there is a great variability among the strata. However, this technique presumes the researcher knows enough about the population of interest to be able to judge the degree of variability among the various strata.

Source: This fictitious case is based on ScanTrack and the Nielsen Food Index, two services offered by A. C. Nielsen Company.

ments in each stratum in the population. A stratum containing one-fifth of all the population elements would account for one-fifth of the total sample observations, and so on. Proportionate sampling was employed in our education example, since each stratum contains one-half of the population and they were sampled equally.

One advantage of proportionate allocation is that the investigator needs to know only the relative sizes of each stratum in order to determine the number of sample observations to select from each stratum with a given sample size. A **disproportionate stratified sample,** however, can produce still more efficient estimates. It involves balancing the two criteria of strata size and strata variability. With a fixed sample size, strata exhibiting more variability are sampled more than proportionately to their relative size. Conversely, those strata that are very homogeneous are sampled less than proportionately.

While a full discussion of how the sample size for each stratum should be determined would take us too far afield and would be much too technical for our purpose, some feel for the rationale behind disproportionate sampling is useful. Consider at the extreme a stratum with zero variability. Since all the elements are identical in value, a single observation tells all. On the other hand, a stratum that is characterized by great variability will require a large number of observations to produce a precise estimate of the stratum mean. One would expect, for example, great variability among the income levels of those people subscribing to *Newsweek* but much less among people subscribing to the glossy society magazine, *Town and Country*. One can expect greater precision when the various strata are sampled proportionate to the relative variability of the characteristic under study rather than proportionate to their relative size in the population.

A disproportionate stratified sample requires more knowledge about the population of interest than does a proportionate stratified sample. To sample the strata in relation to their variability, one needs knowledge of relative variability. Sampling theory is a peculiar phenomenon in that knowledge begets more knowledge. Disproportionate sampling can produce more efficient estimates than proportionate sampling, but the former method also requires that some estimate of the relative variation within strata be known. One can sometimes anticipate the relative homogeneity likely to exist within a stratum on the basis of past studies and experience. Sometimes the investigator may have to rely on logic and intuition in establishing sample sizes for each stratum. For example, one might expect that large retail stores would show greater variation than small stores in sales of some products. In a disproportionate sample, the large stores would be sampled more heavily as, for instance, they are in the Nielsen Retail Index.

• Disproportionate stratified sample

Stratified sample in which the individual strata or subsets are sampled in relation to both their size and their variability; strata exhibiting more variability are sampled more than proportionately to their relative size, while those that are very homogeneous are sampled less than proportionately.

• Stratified versus Quota Sample

Inexperienced researchers sometimes confuse stratified samples with quota samples. There are similarities. In each case, the population is divided into segments, and elements are selected from each segment. There is one key difference, though. In stratified samples, sample elements are selected by probability methods; in quota samples, elements are chosen based on a researcher's judgment. This difference has important implications. Since elements in a stratified sample are selected probabilistically, researchers can establish the sampling distribution of the statistic in question, and hence a confidence interval judgment. In a quota sample there is no objective way to assess the degree of sampling error. Therefore there is also no way to arrive at confidence interval estimates and statistical tests of significance.

◆ Cluster Sample

◆ Cluster sample

A probability sample
distinguished by a two-step
procedure in which (1) the
parent population is
divided into mutually
exclusive and exhaustive
subsets, and (2) a random
sample of subsets is
selected. If the investigator
then uses all of the
population elements in the
selected subsets for the
sample, the procedure is
one-stage cluster sampling;
if a sample of elements is
selected probabilistically
from the subsets, the
procedure is two-stage
cluster sampling.

Cluster samples are another probability sampling technique often used by researchers. Cluster sampling shares some similarities with stratified sampling, but also has some key differences. Cluster sampling involves the following steps:

1. The parent population is divided into mutually exclusive and exhaustive subsets.

2. A random sample of the subsets is selected.

If the investigator then uses all of the population elements in the selected subsets for the sample, the procedure is one-stage cluster sampling. If, on the other hand, a sample of elements is selected probabilistically from the selected subsets, the procedure is known as two-stage cluster sampling.

Note the similarities and differences between cluster sampling and stratified sampling. Although in each case the population is divided into mutually exclusive and exhaustive subgroups, in stratified sampling a sample of elements is selected *from each subgroup*. With cluster sampling, one chooses a *sample of subgroups*.

Remember that in stratified sampling, the goal is to separate the population into strata that are fairly homogeneous for a certain characteristic. In cluster sampling, the goal is to form subgroups that are similar to each other and are each small-scale models of the population. Each cluster should reflect the diversity of the whole population.

In our earlier example relating income to level of education, we noted that dividing the population into subgroups based on newspaper subscriptions was probably not a good idea for stratified sampling because that characteristic is not a good predictor of income. However, since the goal in cluster sampling is to form subgroups that are as heterogeneous as possible, newspaper subscriptions might be a good basis for dividing the population for this form of sample.

If all those subscribing to Paper X were considered to form one subgroup and all those subscribing to Paper Y a second subgroup, then one could be relatively safe in randomly selecting either subgroup to estimate the mean income in the population. While the distribution of incomes within each subgroup is not exactly the same as it is in the population, the range of incomes is such that there would be only a slight error if one were to estimate the mean income and variance of incomes of the population with the elements from either subset.

Admittedly, in practice clusters are not always formed to be as heterogeneous as possible. Because of the way cluster samples are often drawn, the defined clusters are homogeneous rather than heterogeneous in regard to the characteristic of interest. Beginning researchers often mistakenly then call the procedure *stratified sampling,* since it involves the construction of homogeneous subgroups of population elements. But as long as subgroups are subsequently selected for investigation randomly, the procedure is *cluster sampling* regardless of how the subgroups are formed. Admittedly, however, homogeneous subgroups produce less ideal cluster samples from a statistical efficiency viewpoint than do heterogeneous subgroups.

◆ Statistical efficiency

Measure used to compare
sampling plans; one
sampling plan is said to be
superior (more statistically
efficient) to another if, for
the same size sample, it
produces a smaller
standard error of estimate.

Statistical efficiency is a relative notion by which sampling plans can be compared. One sampling plan is said to be more statistically efficient than another if, for the same size sample, it produces a smaller standard error of estimate. When the characteristic of interest is the mean, for example, the sampling plan that produces the smallest value of the standard error of the mean, $s_{\bar{x}}$, for a given size sample is most statistically efficient. Cluster samples are typically much less statistically efficient than comparable stratified samples or even simple random samples because the probable margin of error with a fixed size sample is often greatest with cluster sampling.

Even with its typically lower statistical efficiency, cluster sampling is probably the sampling procedure used most in large-scale field surveys employing personal interviews. Why? Simply because cluster sampling is often more *economically efficient* in that the cost per observation is less. The economies permit the selection of a larger sample at a smaller cost. Since cluster sampling allows researchers to secure so many more observations for a given cost than they would be able to secure with stratified sampling, the margin of error associated with the estimate may actually be

Back to the Case

Dan had been impressed with Jill Bennett's presentation, but he was still curious about a new company, Fast/trac, that had been rumored to be an impressive performer in the scanner research area. Dan was skimming a story on the company that had appeared in a recent trade publication when his secretary announced that Roger Clemente, a Fast/trac account executive, was in the reception area.

Dan stood to shake hands as his secretary showed Roger into the office.

"Nice to meet you, Roger," Dan said. "I'm very interested in what Fast/trac has to offer. I've read a lot about your company, but I want to know more about your sample. Can you tell me what it is composed of?"

"With pleasure, Dan," Roger said. "Our sample is unique in that it is composed of 2,500 households in each of eight cities geographically dispersed across the United States. Included are such cities as Williamsport, Pennsylvania; Pittsfield, Massachusetts; Visalia, California; Midland, Texas; and Rome, Georgia. While no single test market is representative of the entire country, with markets

in eight of the nine census regions, representivity can certainly be achieved by judiciously combining areas."

"Why would this kind of sample be preferable to a national sample," Dan asked.

"The beauty of our system is that each of these markets represents a tightly controlled environment. The cities are chosen to be typical of the areas in which they are located, and thus results from tests can be generalized fairly accurately for the rest of the region," Roger said.

"In addition, the 2,500 households within each market represent a broad spectrum of the population. In essence, each market is a microcosm of the area," Roger said.

"I'm particularly interested in how your scanning service works," Dan said.

"That's really the heart of the system," Roger said. "Each participating household in our sample is given a card to present at the supermarket each time a purchase is made. The cashier types the identity code into a computerized register. When the bar codes on the items are scanned, the computer records

the purchases and funnels the information into a file on the shopper.

"Since each family in our sample is equipped with cable television, our clients are able to test product advertising, and quickly see how it affects consumer behavior," Roger continued. "I really think our company can offer you the kind of sophisticated, in-depth monitoring that is essential for getting quick information on how your new product is faring in the marketplace."

"I'm intrigued," Dan said. "Let me mull this over a bit, and get back to you within the week. Thanks for your time."

The sample that Fast/trac is offering is like a cluster sample in that each city is part of a subgroup of cities that are fairly homogeneous. Each city is also perceived to be a small-scale model of the population. However, the sample is unlike a cluster sample in that the cities are not selected probabilistically, but rather because they are believed to be representative. The selection of cities makes the sample a judgment sample.

Source: This fictitious case is based on BehaviorScan, a service offered by Chicago-based Information Resources, Inc.

smaller for cluster sampling. That is, cluster sampling is often more *efficient overall* than the other forms of sampling. Although it requires a larger sample for the same degree of precision, and is thus less statistically efficient, the smaller cost per observation allows samples so much larger that estimates with a smaller standard error can be produced for the same cost.

Systematic Sample

• Systematic sample

Form of cluster sampling in which every *k*th element in the population is designated for inclusion in the sample after a random start.

The **systematic sample** is a form of cluster sampling that offers one of the easiest ways of sampling many populations of interest. It involves selecting every *k*th element after a random start. Consider again the hypothetical population of twenty individuals, and suppose a sample of five is to be selected from this population. Number the elements from one to twenty. With twenty population elements and a sample size of five, the sampling fraction is $f = n/N = 5/20 = 1/4$, meaning that one element in four will be selected. The sampling interval $i = 1/f$ will be 4. This means that after a random start, every fourth element will be chosen. The random start, which must be some number between 1 and 4 — 1 and i in general — is determined from a random number table. Thus if the random start were 1, the first, fifth, ninth, thirteenth, and seventeenth items would be the sample. If it were 2, the second, sixth, tenth, fourteenth, and eighteenth items would be the sample, and so on.

Systematic sampling is one-stage cluster sampling since the subgroups are not subsampled, but rather all of the elements in the selected clusters are used. The subgroups or clusters in this case are

- Cluster I: A, E, I, M, Q
- Cluster II: B, F, J, N, R
- Cluster III: C, G, K, O, S
- Cluster IV: D, H, L, P, T

and one of these clusters is selected randomly for investigation. The random start, of course, determines the cluster that is to be used.

One can readily see the ease with which a systematic sample can be drawn. It is much easier to draw a systematic sample than it is to select a simple random sample of the same size, for example. With a systematic sample one needs to enter the random number table only once. The problem of checking for the duplication of elements, which is cumbersome with simple random samples, does not occur with systematic samples. All the elements are uniquely determined by the selection of the random start.[2]

A systematic sample can often be made more representative than a simple random sample. With our hypothetical population, for example, we are guaranteed representation from the low-income segment and the high-income segment with our systematic sampling plan. Regardless of which of the four clusters is chosen, one element must have an income of $6,800 or less; another must have an income of $12,000 or more; and the remaining three elements must have incomes between these two values. A simple random sample of Size 5 might or might not include low-income or high-income people.

The same is true when sampling from other populations. Thus, if we are sampling retail stores, we can guarantee representation of both small and large stores by

---

[2]For an example of the use of systematic sampling, see Mark E. Slama and Armen Tashchian, "Selected Socioeconomic and Demographic Characteristics Associated with Purchasing Involvement," *Journal of Marketing,* 49 (Winter 1985), pp. 72–82.

employing a systematic sample, if the stores can be arrayed from smallest to largest according to some criteria such as annual sales or square footage. The ability to guarantee representation from each size segment depends on the availability of knowledge about the size of each store so that they can be arrayed from smallest to largest and numbered serially. A simple random sample of stores would be apt to represent large stores inadequately since there are fewer large stores than small stores. Yet the fewer large stores account for a great proportion of all sales.

The degree to which the systematic sample will be more representative than a simple random sample thus depends on the clustering of objects within the list from which the sample will be drawn. The ideal list for a systematic sample will have elements similar in value on the characteristic (for example, similar levels of income, sales, education, and so on) close together and elements diverse in value spread apart.

At least one danger with systematic samples is that if there is a natural periodicity in the list of elements, the systematic sample can produce estimates seriously in error. For example, suppose we have the annual ticket sales of an airline by day and wish to analyze these sales in terms of length of trip. To analyze all 365 days may be prohibitively costly, but suppose the research budget does allow the investigation of 52 days of sales. A systematic sample of days using a sampling interval of 7 (365 ÷ 52) would obviously produce some misleading conclusions, since the day's sales would reflect all Monday trips, Friday trips, or Sunday trips, for example.[3] Of course, any other sampling interval would be acceptable, and in general, an enlightened choice of the sampling interval can do much to eliminate the problems associated with natural periodicities in the data. An appropriate choice of sampling interval, of course, depends on knowledge of the phenomenon and nature of the periodicity.

Area Sample

• Area sample

Form of cluster sampling in which areas (for example, census tracts, blocks) serve as the primary sampling units. The population is divided into mutually exclusive and exhaustive areas using maps, and a random sample of areas is selected. If all the households in the selected areas are used in the study, it is one-stage area sampling, while if the areas themselves are subsampled with respect to households, the procedure is two-stage area sampling.

In every probability sampling plan discussed so far, the investigator needs a list of population elements in order to draw the sample. A list identifying each population element is a necessary requirement for simple random samples, stratified samples, and systematic samples. The latter two procedures also require knowledge about some other characteristic of the population if they are to be designed optimally. For many populations of interest, however, such detailed lists are unavailable. Further, it will often prove prohibitively costly to construct them. When this condition arises, the cluster sample offers the researcher another distinct benefit—he or she only needs the list of population elements for the selected clusters.

Suppose, for example, that an investigator wishes to measure certain characteristics of industrial sales representatives such as their earnings, attitudes toward the job, hours worked, and so on. It would be extremely difficult, if not impossible, and certainly costly to develop an up-to-date roster listing each industrial sales representative. Yet such a list would be required for a simple random sample. A stratified sample would further require that the investigator possess knowledge about some

---

[3]Sudman suggests that when the "sampling interval i is not a whole number, the easiest solution is to use as the interval the whole number just below or above i. Usually, this will result in a selected sample that is only slightly larger or smaller than the initial sample required, and this new sample size will have no noticeable effect on either the accuracy of the results or the budget. For samples in which the interval i is small (generally for i less than 10), so that the rounding has too great an effect on the sample size, it is possible to add or delete the extra cases . . . it is usually easier to round down in computing i so that the sample is larger, and then to delete systematically." Sudman, *Applied Sampling,* p. 54.

Table 14.6   Possible Clusters to Use to Sample Various Types of Population Elements

Population Elements	Possible Clusters
College seniors	Colleges
Elementary school students	Schools
Manufacturing firms	Counties Localities Plants
Airline travelers	Airports Planes
Hospital patients	Hospitals

Source: Adapted from Seymour Sudman, *Applied Sampling* (New York: Academic Press, 1976), 70.

additional characteristics of each sales representative, for example, education or age, so that the population could be divided into mutually exclusive and exhaustive subsets. With a cluster sample, on the other hand, one could use the companies as sampling units. The investigator would generate a sample of business firms from the population of firms of interest. The business firms would be primary **sampling units** where a sampling unit is defined as "that element or set of elements considered for selection in some stage of sampling."[4] The investigator could then compile a list of sales representatives working for each of the selected firms, a much more realistic assignment. If the investigator then studied each of the sales representatives in each of the selected firms, it would be one-stage cluster sampling. If the researcher subsampled sales representatives from each company's list, it would be two-stage cluster sampling. Table 14.6 lists some possible clusters that could be used to sample various types of population elements.

> ◆ Sampling units
>
> Non-overlapping collections of elements from the population.

The same principle underlies area sampling. Current, accurate lists of population elements are rarely available. Directories of all those living in a city at a particular moment simply do not exist for many cities, and when they do exist, they are obsolete when published: people move, others die, new households are constantly being formed.[5] While lists of families are nonexistent, relatively accurate lists of primary sampling units are available in the form of city maps, if the area divisions of the city serve as the primary sampling units. While the complex details of area sampling are not relevant here, an appreciation for the rationale underlying the various approaches is.

One-Stage Area Sample   Suppose the investigator is interested in estimating the amount of wine consumed per household in the city of Chicago, and how consumption is related to family income. An accurate listing of all households is unavailable

---

[4]Earl R. Babbie, *The Practice of Social Research,* 2nd ed. (Belmont, Calif.: Wadsworth Publishing, 1979), p. 167.

[5]R. L. Polk and Company in Taylor, Michigan, publishes some 1,400 directories for most medium-sized cities in the range of 50,000 to 800,000 people. The directories contain both an alphabetical list of names and businesses and a street address directory of households. While the alphabetic list can contain a large percentage of inaccurate listings at any one time, the address directory is reasonably accurate since it only omits new construction after the directory is published and the directories are revised every two or three years.

for the Chicago area. A phone book when published is already somewhat obsolete, in addition to having the other inadequacies previously mentioned. One approach to this problem would be to

1. Choose a simple random sample of n city blocks from the population of N blocks.
2. Determine wine consumption and income for all households in the selected blocks and generalize the sample relationships to the larger population.

The probability of any household being included in the sample can be calculated. It is given simply as n/N since it equals the probability that the block on which it is located will be selected. Since the probabilities are known, the procedure is indeed probability sampling. Here, though, blocks have been substituted for households when selecting primary sampling units. The substitution is made because the list of blocks in the Chicago area can be developed from city maps. Each block can be identified, and the existence of this universe of blocks permits the calculation of the necessary probabilities.

Since each household on the selected blocks is included in the sample, the procedure is one-stage area sampling. Note that the blocks serve to divide the parent population into mutually exclusive and exhaustive subsets. Note further that the blocks do not serve very well as ideal subsets statistically for cluster samples; households on a given block can be expected to be somewhat similar with respect to their income and wine consumption rather than heterogeneous as desired.[6] On the other hand, the data-collection costs will be very low because of the concentration of households within each block.

Two-Stage Area Sample The distinguishing feature of the one-stage area sample is that all of the households in the selected blocks (or other areas) are enumerated and studied. It is not necessary to employ all items in a selected cluster; the selected areas themselves can be subsampled, and it is often quite advantageous to do so. Two types of two-stage sampling need to be distinguished:

1. Simple, two-stage area sample.
2. Probability-proportional-to-size area sample.

• Simple two-stage area sample

Form of cluster sampling in which a certain proportion of second-stage sampling units (e.g., households) is selected from each first-stage unit (e.g., blocks).

With **simple two-stage area sampling,** a certain proportion of second-stage sampling units (e.g., households) is selected from each first-stage unit (e.g., blocks). Consider a universe of 100 blocks; suppose there are 20 households per block; assume that a sample of 80 households is required from this total population of 2,000 households. The overall sampling fraction is thus $^{80}/_{2,000} = \frac{1}{25}$. There are a number of ways by which the sample can be completed, such as by (1) selecting 10 blocks and 8 households per block, (2) selecting 8 blocks and 10 households per block, (3) selecting 20 blocks and 4 households per block, or (4) selecting 4 blocks and 20 households per block. The last alternative would, of course, be one-stage area sampling, while the first three would all be two-stage area sampling.

The probability with which the blocks are selected is called the *block* or *first-stage sampling fraction* and is given as the ratio of n_B/N_B, where n_B and N_B are the number of blocks in the sample and in the population, respectively. For the first three

---

[6]When geographic clustering of rare populations occurs, it can be used to advantage in designing the sample. See, for example, Seymour Sudman, "Efficient Screening Methods for the Sampling of Geographically Clustered Special Populations," *Journal of Marketing Research,* 22 (February 1985), pp. 20–29.

schemes illustrated above, the first-stage sampling fractions would be, in order, 1 in 10, 1 in 12.5, and 1 in 5.

The probability with which the households are selected is the *household,* or *second-stage, sampling fraction.* Since there must be a total of 80 households in the sample, the second-stage sampling fraction differs for each alternative. The second-stage sampling fraction is given as $n_{H/B}/N_{H/B}$, where $n_{H/B}$ and $N_{H/B}$ are the number of households per block in the sample and in the population. For the first sampling scheme, the household sampling fraction is calculated to be $8/20 = 2/5$, while for the second scheme, it is $10/20 = 1/2$, and for the third scheme, $4/20 = 1/5$. Note that the product of the first-stage and second-stage sampling fractions in each case equals the overall sampling fraction of $1/25$.

Which scheme would be preferable? Although it is beyond the scope to present in this text the detailed calculation for determining this, we would like to illustrate the general principle. Economies of data collection would dictate that the second-stage sampling fraction be high. This means that a great many households would be selected from each designated block, as with the second scheme. Statistical efficiency would dictate a small second-stage sampling fraction, since it can be expected that the blocks would be relatively homogeneous and thus it would be desirable to have a very few households from any one block. The third scheme would be preferred on statistical grounds. Statistical sampling theory would suggest the balancing of these two criteria. There are formulas for this purpose that reflect essentially the cost of data collection and the variability of the characteristic within and between clusters, although a useful rule of thumb is that clusters of three to eight households per block or segment are near optimum for most social science variables.[7]

Simple two-stage area sampling is quite effective when there is approximately the same number of second-stage units (e.g., households) per first-stage unit (e.g., blocks). When the second-stage units are decidedly unequal, simple two-stage area sampling can cause bias in the estimate. To pursue our hypothetical example, some blocks in Chicago may contain multistoried low-income housing. Blocks in more affluent parts of the city may contain relatively few, single-family houses. In such a case, the number of second-stage units per first-stage unit would be vastly different. Sometimes this problem can be overcome by combining areas. When this option is not available or is cumbersome to implement, probability-proportional-to-size sampling can be employed.

• Probability-proportional-to-size sample

Form of cluster sampling in which a fixed number of second-stage units is selected from each first-stage cluster. The probabilities associated with the selection of each cluster are in turn variable because they are directly related to the relative sizes of each cluster.

Consider, for example, the data of Table 14.7 and suppose a sample of 20 elements is to be selected from this population of 2,000 households. With **probability-proportional-to-size sampling,** a *fixed* number of second-stage units is selected from each first-stage unit.[8] Suppose after balancing economic and statistical considerations that the number of second-stage units per first-stage unit is determined to be 10. Two first-stage units must be selected to produce a total sample of 20. The procedure gets its name from the way these first-stage units are selected. The probability of selection is variable in that it depends on the size of the first-stage unit. In particular, a table of four-digit random numbers would be consulted. The first two numbers encountered between 1 and 2,000 will be employed to indicate the blocks that

---

[7]Sudman, *Applied Sampling,* p. 81.

[8]For an empirical example that uses probability-proportionate-to-size cluster sampling, see Johnny Blair and Ronald Czaja, "Locating a Special Population Using Random Digit Dialing," *Public Opinion Quarterly,* 46 (Winter 1982), pp. 585–590.

Table 14.7   Illustration of Probability-Proportional-to-Size Sampling

Block	Households	Cumulative Number of Households
1	800	800
2	400	1,200
3	200	1,400
4	200	1,600
5	100	1,700
6	100	1,800
7	100	1,900
8	50	1,950
9	25	1,975
10	25	2,000

Research Window 14.1
Designing a Sample—Or, Who Are Those Nielsen Viewers Anyway?

How many times have your favorite television programs been cancelled because their ratings just weren't high enough? If you're like many people, you probably spent a moment thinking nasty thoughts about the folks whose viewing habits have such a powerful influence on what programs manage to stay on television—the Nielsen families. You've probably wondered who these people are and whether they really represent the opinions of the majority of television viewers.

The Nielsen people have gone to rather elaborate lengths to ensure that their households do represent a statistically reliable sample. After all, companies spend billions of dollars a year on television programming and advertising, and most of them base their judgments on information provided by the Nielsen Company.

The national Nielsen sample is, in reality, two separate samples of television households: the Nielsen Television Index (NTI) sample, which is used to obtain household tuning information, and the National Audience Composition (NAC) sample, which is used to obtain information regarding who is viewing a particular program. Some 1,200 households are used for NTI, and approximately 3,200 are used for NAC.

Although the end uses of the samples are slightly different, they are chosen via the same process: a multistage *area probability sample,* in which the sampling frame consists of small areas, and each area is selected with a probability equal to the proportion of the total housing units in the area. For example, if the Chicago area accounts for 5 percent of the total housing units in the United States, the Chicago area will have a 5 percent chance of being included in the Nielsen sample. To complete the definition, *multistage* means that the NTI/NAC sample consists of four stages: the selection of counties within the country, the selection of Census Enumeration Districts (EDs) or Block Groups (BGs) within the counties, the selection of blocks within the EDs/BGs, and the selection of housing units within the blocks.

Using computer tapes of the latest U.S. Census counts of all housing units in the country, Nielsen's Statistical Research Department predesignates the sample areas. Then trained surveyors visit these areas to identify and list housing units in the area. Sample housing units are selected from the lists, and the locations are given to the full-time Nielsen representatives whose job it is to secure cooperation from the selected house-

Geographic Hierarchy in
Metropolitan and
Nonmetropolitan Areas—
the Census Bureau's
definition of geographic
areas.

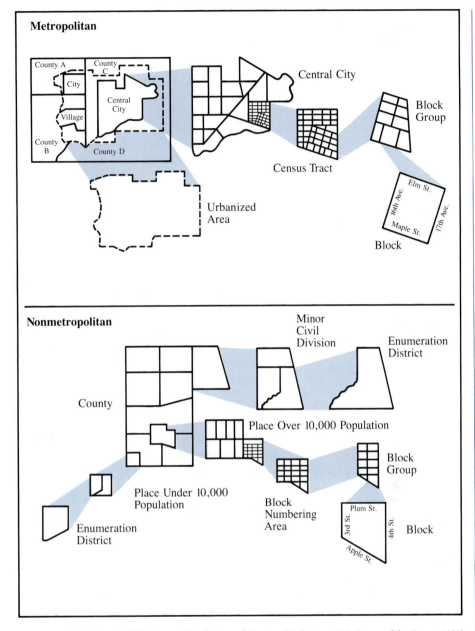

Source: Users' Guide Part A: 1980 Census of Population and Housing (Washington, D.C.: Bureau of the Census, 1982).

holds. Because of the skill and training of these field reps, most of the initially designated households agree to cooperate.

Work on the national sample does not end there. Every year the sample must be updated with new housing units to keep pace with population shifts and growth. In addition, the sample design provides for a systematic replacement of households over a period of five years for NTI

and three years for NAC—long enough to provide continuity of trend information. The end result of the Nielsen multistate area probability sampling technique is a geographically dispersed national sample of housing units.

Source: The Nielsen Ratings in Perspective (Northbrook, Ill.: Nielsen Media Research, 1980), p. 12.

will be used. All numbers between 1 and 800 will indicate the inclusion of Block 1; those from 801 to 1,200, Block 2; from 1,201 to 1,400, Block 3; and so on.

The probability that any particular household is included in the sample is equal, since the unequal first-stage selection probabilities are balanced by unequal second-stage selection probabilities. Consider, for example, Blocks 1 and 10, the two extremes. The first-stage selection probability for Block 1 is $800/2,000 = 1/2.5$, since 800 of the permissible 2,000 random numbers correspond to block 1. Only 25 of the permissible random numbers (1,976 to 2,000) correspond to Block 10, on the other hand, and thus the first-stage sampling fraction for Block 10 is $25/2,000 = 1/80$. Since 10 households are to be selected from each block, the second-stage sampling fraction for Block 1 is $10/800 = 1/80$, while for Block 10 it is $10/25 = 1/2.5$. The products of the first- and second-stage sampling thus compensate, since

$$\frac{800}{2,000} \times \frac{10}{800} = \frac{25}{2,000} \times \frac{10}{25}$$

which is also true for the remaining blocks.

Probability-proportional-to-size sampling is another illustration of how information begets information with applied sampling problems. One can avoid the bias of simple two-stage area sampling and can also produce estimates that are more precise when there is great variation in the number of second-stage units per first-stage unit. The price one pays, of course, is that probability-proportional-to-size sampling requires that one have detailed knowledge about the size of each first-stage unit. This is not quite as high a price as it might be since the Census Bureau has reported the number of households per block for all cities of over 50,000 in population as well as for a number of other urbanized areas.[9] Maps are included in each report. While somewhat obsolete when published, these map and block statistics can be updated. The local electrical utility will have records of connections current to the day, and so will the telephone company. In many cases, these statistics will be broken down by blocks.

Summary Comments on Probability Sampling

As you can probably begin to appreciate, sample design is a very detailed subject. Our discussion has concentrated on only a few of the fundamentals and, in particular, the basic types of probability samples. You should be aware, though, that the basic types can be, and are, combined in large-scale field studies to produce some very complex designs.

The Gallup Poll, for example, is probably one of the best known of all the polls. The sample for the Gallup poll for each survey "consists of 1,500 adults selected from 320 locations, using area sampling methods. At each location the interviewer is given a map with an indicated starting point and is required to follow a specified direction. At each occupied dwelling unit, the interview must attempt to meet sex quotas."[10] In sum, the Gallup poll uses a combination of area and quota sampling. Further, it is not uncommon to have several levels of stratification, such as by geo-

---

[9]*U.S. Census of Housing: 1980, Vol. III City Blocks,* HC(3)—No. (city number).

[10]Sudman, *Applied Sampling,* p. 71.

graphic area and density of population, precede several stages of cluster sampling. Thus, you cannot expect to be a sampling expert with the brief exposure to the subject contained here.[11] But you should be able to communicate effectively about sample design, and while you may not understand completely, say, why n_1 observations were taken from one stratum and n_2 from another, you should appreciate the basic considerations determining the choice.

♦ Summary

Learning Objective 1: Specify the two procedures that distinguish a stratified sample.

A stratified sample is a probability sample that is distinguished by the following two-step procedure: (1) the parent population is divided into mutually exclusive and exhaustive subsets, and (2) a simple random sample of elements is chosen independently from each group or subset.

Learning Objective 2: Cite two reasons why researchers might opt to use a stratified sample rather than a simple random sample.

Stratified samples can produce sample statistics that are more precise, meaning they have smaller error due to sampling, than simple random samples. Stratification also allows the investigation of the characteristic of interest for particular subgroups.

Learning Objective 3: Note what points investigators should keep in mind when dividing a population into strata for a stratified sample.

Investigators should divide the population into strata so that the elements within any given stratum are as similar in value as possible and so that the values between any two strata are as disparate as possible.

Learning Objective 4: Explain what is meant by a proportionate stratified sample.

With a proportionate stratified sample, the number of observations in the total sample is allocated among the strata in proportion to the *relative* number of elements in each stratum in the population.

Learning Objective 5: Explain what is meant by a disproportionate stratified sample.

Disproportionate stratified sampling involves balancing the two criteria of strata size and variability. With a fixed sample size, strata exhibiting more variability are sampled more than proportionately to their relative size. Conversely, those strata that are very homogeneous are sampled less than proportionately.

---

[11]Those interested in pursuing the subject further should see one of the excellent books on the subject, such as William G. Cochran, *Sampling Techniques,* 3rd ed. (New York: John Wiley, 1977); Morris H. Hansen, William N. Hurwitz, and William G. Madow, *Sample Survey Methods and Theory, Vol. 1, Methods and Applications* (New York: John Wiley, 1953); R. L. Jensen, *Statistical Survey Techniques* (New York: John Wiley, 1978); Graham Kalton, *Introduction to Survey Sampling* (Beverly Hills, Calif.: Sage Publications, 1982); Leslie Kish, *Survey Sampling* (New York: John Wiley, 1965); Richard L. Schaeffer, William Mendenhall, and Lyman Ott, *Elementary Survey Sampling,* 2nd ed. (North Scituate, Mass.: Duxbury Press, 1979); or Bill Williams, *A Sampler on Sampling* (New York: John Wiley, 1978). The little book by John Monroe and A. L. Finkner, *Handbook of Area Sampling* (Philadelphia: Chilton, 1959), provides an easy-to-read discussion of the design of an area sample. The books by Sudman, *Applied Sampling,* and A. C. Rosander, *Case Studies in Sample Design* (New York: Marcel Dekker, Inc., 1977), illustrate ways these sampling principles were applied to actual problems, while the articles by Seymour Sudman, "Improving the Quality of Shopping Center Sampling," *Journal of Marketing Research,* 17 (November 1980), pp. 423–431, and Edward Blair, "Sampling Issues in Trade Area Maps Drawn from Shopper Surveys," *Journal of Marketing,* 47 (Winter 1983), pp. 98–106, illustrate how the principles of sampling can be applied to improve sampling in shopping center studies.

Learning Objective 6: List the steps followed in drawing a cluster sample.

Cluster sampling involves the following steps: (1) the parent population is divided into mutually exclusive and exhaustive subsets, and (2) a random sample of the subsets is selected.

Learning Objectives 7: Explain the difference between a one-stage cluster sample and a two-stage cluster sample.

If an investigator uses all of the population elements in the selected subsets for the sample, the procedure is one-stage cluster sampling. If, on the other hand, a sample of elements is selected probabilistically from the selected subsets, the procedure is known as two-stage cluster sampling.

Learning Objective 8: Explain why cluster sampling, though far less statistically efficient than comparable stratifed samples, is the sampling procedure used most in large-scale field surveys employing personal interviews.

Cluster sampling is probably the sampling procedure used most in large-scale field surveys using personal interviews because it is often more economically efficient in that the cost per observation is less. The economies permit the selection of a larger sample at a smaller cost. Although cluster sampling requires a larger sample for the same degree of precision, and is thus less statistically efficient, the smaller cost per observation allows samples so much larger that estimates with a smaller standard error can be produced for the same cost.

Learning Objective 9: Distinguish between one-stage area sampling and simple, two-stage area sampling.

The distinguishing feature of the one-stage area sample is that all of the households in the selected blocks (or other areas) are enumerated and studied. With simple two-stage area sampling, a certain proportion of second-stage sampling units is selected from each first-stage unit.

Learning Objective 10: Note the quality that distinguishes probability-proportional-to-size sampling and explain when it is used.

With probability-proportional-to-size sampling, a fixed number of second-stage units is selected from each first-stage unit. This type of sampling is particularly useful when the number of second-stage units is unequal and so that simple two-stage area sampling could cause bias in the estimate.

Discussion Questions, Problems, and Projects

1. The Minnesota National Bank, headquartered in Minneapolis, Minnesota, has some 400,000 users of its credit card scattered throughout the state of Minnesota. The application forms for the credit card asked for the usual information on name, address, phone, income, education, and so on, that is so typical of such applications. The bank is now very much interested in determining if there is any relationship between the uses to which the card is put and the socioeconomic characteristics of the using party; for example, is there a difference in the characteristics of those people who use the credit card for major purchases only, such as appliances, and those who use it for minor as well as major purchases.
   (a) Identify the population and sampling frame that would be used by Minnesota National Bank.
   (b) Indicate how you would draw a simple random sample from the above sampling frame.
   (c) Indicate how you would draw a stratified sample from the above sampling frame.
   (d) Indicate how you would draw a cluster sample from the above sampling frame.
   (e) Which method would be preferred? Why?
2. Exclusive Supermarkets is considering entering the Boston market. Before doing so though, management wishes to estimate the average square feet of selling space among

potential competitors so as to plan better the size of the proposed new outlet. A stratified sample of supermarkets in Boston produced the following results.

Size	Total Number in City	Number of This Size in Sample	Mean Size of Stores in Sample	Standard Deviation of Stores in Sample
Small supermarkets	1,000	20	4,000 sq. ft.	2,000 sq. ft.
Medium supermarkets	600	12	10,000 sq. ft.	1,000 sq. ft.
Large supermarkets	400	8	60,000 sq. ft.	3,000 sq. ft

(a) Estimate the average-size supermarket in Boston. Show your calculations.
(b) Develop a 95 percent confidence interval around this estimate. Show your calculations.
(c) Was a proportionate or disproportionate stratified sample design used in determining the number of sample observations for each stratum? Explain.

3. The Store-More is a large department store located in Lansing, Michigan. The manager is worried about the constant overstocking of a number of items in the various departments. Approximately 3,000 items ranging from small multipurpose wrenches to lawnmowers are overstocked every month. The manager is uncertain whether the surpluses are primarily due to poor purchasing policies or poor store layout and shelving practices. The manager realizes the difficulty of scrutinizing the purchase orders, invoices, and inventory cards for all the items that are overstocked. He decides on choosing a sample of items but does not know how to proceed.
(a) Identify the population elements and sampling frame.
(b) What sampling method would you recommend? Why? Be specific.
(c) How would you draw the sample based on this sampling method?

4. The university housing office has decided to conduct a study to determine what influence living in dormitories versus off-campus housing has on the academic performance of the students. You are required to assist the housing office.
(a) What sampling method would you recommend? Why? Be specific.
(b) How would you draw the sample based on this sampling method?

5. Maxwell Federated operates a chain of department stores in the greater Chicago metropolitan area. The management of Maxwell Federated has been concerned of late with tight money conditions and the associated deterioration of the company's accounts receivable. It appears on the surface that more and more customers are becoming delinquent each month. Management wishes to assess the current state of delinquencies, to determine if they are concentrated in any stores, and to determine if they are concentrated among any particular types of purchases or purchasers.
(a) What type of sampling method would you recommend? Why? Be specific.
(b) How would you draw the sample based on this sampling method?

6. A retailer of household appliances is planning to introduce a new brand of dishwashers to the local market. He has decided to use two-stage area sampling and has secured an up-to-date map of your area but he does not know how to proceed and requires your assistance. Outline a step-by-step approach you would recommend for conducting the study.

Suggested Additional Readings

There are a number of excellent books that discuss in more detail than here the rationale for and various types of stratified and cluster samples. Three of the better and more extensive treatments can be found in

William Cochran, *Sampling Techniques,* 3rd ed. (New York: John Wiley, 1977).

Morris H. Hansen, William N. Hurwitz, and William G. Madow, *Sample Survey Methods and Theory, Vol. 1, Methods and Applications* (New York: John Wiley, 1953).

Leslie Kish, *Survey Sampling* (New York: John Wiley, 1965).

For more abbreviated but still useful treatments of the principles underlying survey sampling, see

Graham Kalton, *Introduction to Survey Sampling* (Beverly Hills: Sage Publications, 1982).

Richard L. Schaeffer, William Mendenhall, and Lyman Ott, *Elementary Survey Sampling,* 2nd ed. (North Scituate, Mass: Duxbury Press, 1979).

Bill Williams, *A Sampler on Sampling* (New York: John Wiley, 1978).

Seymour Sudman, *Applied Sampling* (San Francisco: Academic Press, 1976).

Chapter 15　Sample Size

Learning Objectives

Upon completing this chapter, you should be able to

1. Specify the key factor a researcher must consider in estimating sample size using statistical principles.

2. Cite two other factors researchers must also take into account when estimating a sample size and explain their relationship.

3. Explain in what way the size of the population influences the size of the sample.

4. Specify the circumstances under which the finite population correction factor should be used.

5. Explain the impact that cost has on sample size in stratified or cluster samples.

6. Cite the general rule of thumb for calculating sample size when cross-classification tables are used.

Case in Marketing Research

It was late on a Friday afternoon, and Leslie Jonas sat at her desk flipping through a recent issue of *Marketing News* when the phone rang.

"Leslie? This is Rebecca Hansen, from The Material World. Remember? We met at the 'Women in Communications' seminar on small businesses last month?"

"Oh, yes," Leslie said, remembering a small, energetic woman who spoke as quickly as she moved. "We discussed trends in the fabric business."

"Right," Rebecca said. "As I mentioned to you then, our industry is in a state of upheaval. As more women go to work, fewer have time to sew their own clothes. That's made the fashion fabric business something of a disaster area. But the good news is that these busy women also don't have time to sew draperies and slipcovers any more, so our home decorating business is booming.

"I'm calling you, Leslie, because we need to know how to reach these potential customers most economically. We have a sense that they would come from further away—and certainly spend more money—than our garment-sewing customers, but our figures are based more on gut instinct than on anything scientific. We'd like your company to do a small study for us to determine what our trading area really is, so we can maximize our advertising dollars," Rebecca said in a rush.

"Fine," Leslie responded. "We can do that. When would you like to get together?"

"Later this week would be best. Right now we're working on our budget and I'm all tied up," Rebecca said.

"I was wondering, though, if you could give me an idea now of what size sample we might need for a study of this type," she continued.

Leslie sighed. "Just once I'd like to get a new client whose first question isn't sample size," she thought.

Taking a deep breath, she delivered her usual response—an answer she knew was equivocal, unsatisfying, and even irritating to an anxious client—but the only one she could justify at this point.

"It depends, Rebecca, it depends. . . ."

Discussion Issues

1. On what factors might the sample size for Rebecca's study depend?

2. If you were Leslie Jonas, what information would you want about the population served by The Material World?

Thus far, our discussion of sampling has concentrated on sample type. Another important consideration is sample size. Unless the researcher is going to use a sequential sample, he needs some means of determining the necessary size of the sample before beginning data collection.

Beginning researchers might suppose that the sample should be as large as the client can afford, but the question of sample size is complex. It depends on, among other things, the type of sample, the statistic in question, the homogeneity of the population, and the time, money, and personnel available for the study. We cannot discuss all of these issues adequately in one chapter, but we will present the important statistical principles that determine sample size, using only simple random samples and a few of the more popular statistics. Readers interested in how sample size is determined for stratified or cluster samples should consult one of the standard references on sampling theory. Readers who would like to be able to use a simple random sample to estimate such things as population variance, which is beyond the scope of this chapter, will find help in a good intermediate-level statistics text. The principles are the same in each case, but the formulas differ since they depend on the sampling plan and the statistic in question.

♦ Basic Considerations in Determining Sample Size

Not surprisingly, the sampling distribution of the statistic is the key to determining sample size. You will recall that the sampling distribution of the statistic indicates how the sample estimates vary as a function of the particular sample selected. If a researcher knows the spread of the sampling distribution, he or she can then determine the amount of error that can be associated with any estimate. For instance, in Chapter 13, we saw that the error associated with the estimation of a population mean by a sample mean was given by the standard error of the mean $\sigma_{\bar{x}} = \sigma/\sqrt{n}$, or the population variance divided by the square root of the sample size when the population variance was known, and $s_{\bar{x}} = \hat{s}/\sqrt{n}$, or the sample variance divided by the square root of the sample size when the population variance was unknown. The first factor one must consider in estimating sample size, then, is the standard error of the estimate obtained from the known sampling distribution of the statistic.

A second consideration is how precise the estimate must be. For example, a researcher investigating mean income might want the sample estimate to be within $\pm\$100$ of the true population value. Or a less precise estimate might be required— say, one within $\pm\$500$ of the true value. When the problem involves estimating a population parameter, **precision** can be said to be measured by the magnitude of error, or the size of the estimating interval involved.

The degree of precision required will be greatly influenced by the importance of the decision involved in the study from a managerial perspective. If millions of dollars and hundreds of employees' jobs ride on the results of the study, the acceptable range of error is likely to be small. *Absolute precision* is expressed as within plus or minus so many units. *Relative precision* is expressed relative to the level of the estimate of the parameter.

Another factor that affects sample size is the degree of **confidence** the researcher requires in the estimate. With a sample of fixed size, there is a trade-off between degree of confidence and degree of precision. One can specify either the degree of precision, or the degree of confidence, but not both. It is only when sample size is allowed to vary that one can achieve both a specified precision and a specified degree of confidence in the result. Actually, the determination of

♦ Precision

Degree of error in a study or the size of the estimating interval. *Absolute precision* is expressed as within plus or minus so many units. *Relative precision* is expressed relative to the level of the estimate of the parameter.

♦ Confidence

The degree to which one can feel confident that an estimate approximates the true value.

sample size using statistical principles involves balancing the two considerations against each other.[1]

To understand the distinction between confidence and precision, suppose that we need to know the mean income of a certain population. The most precise measure of that particular parameter would be a point estimate of the mean, which is an estimate that involves a single value with no associated bounds of error. In the case of our study, calculations may show that the population mean income as estimated by the sample mean is $19,243. This point estimate is most assuredly wrong, and thus we can have no confidence in it despite its preciseness. On the other hand, we can have complete confidence in an estimate that the population mean income is between zero and $1 million, but that estimate is too imprecise to be of value.

The U.S. Census Bureau got even more caught up than usual with the issues surrounding precision and confidence after it published the results of the 1980 Census. Accurate census data are important because they are used to determine representation in the U.S. House of Representatives and are used as a basis for distribution of a variety of funds from federal and state governments.

---

[1]Bayesian analysts also consider the cost of wrong decisions when determining sample size. For a comparison of classical and Bayesian procedures for determining sample size, see Seymour Sudman, *Applied Sampling* (New York: Academic Press, 1976), pp. 85–105.

Back to the Case

Leslie Jonas sat in Rebecca Hansen's small office surrounded by colorful bolts of fabric, drapery rods, foam rubber cushions, and yards of pleater tape. Periodically Leslie lost sight of Rebecca as she darted behind a rack of drapery orders covered in plastic to retrieve a stack of fabric swatches or an order book.

"Sorry it's so crazy here, Leslie, but now that the kids are back in school, everybody seems to want to decorate," Rebecca said. "Now, what were you saying about precision and confidence?"

"I was asking how precise our estimates of the average number of miles these customers tend to travel to the store have to be. I'd also like to know how certain you need to be that that figure, once we determine it, is correct," Leslie said.

"Well, I want all these numbers to be very accurate, and I want to be able to have faith in them. We may only advertise in local newspapers, but even those costs add up. Our budget for marketing is tight, and we can't afford to spend a nickel on wasted space," Rebecca said.

"I understand," Leslie said. "My only problem with that request is that you have asked that we use a sample of no more than forty customers who have used your home decorating service over the last year. Using only that group, I can give you a fairly precise estimate of the average number of miles they traveled to the store—say within ±5 miles—but it might not be totally reliable. Or I can give you a broader estimate in which you can be relatively confident, but it won't be as precise."

"If we allow for the possibility of using a larger sample, our estimates could be more reliable, and precise," Leslie said.

As Leslie explained, with a fixed size sample, there is a trade-off between degree of confidence and degree of precision. This dilemma can be alleviated, however, if sample size is allowed to vary to produce an estimate with both the required precision and confidence.

Many people questioned the accuracy of the 1980 count, and some felt so certain that it was flawed that they filed suit against the Census Bureau. Research Window 15.1 describes some of the measures the bureau is taking to assure that the 1990 census will reflect the accuracy that user groups require.

◆ Sample Size Determination When Estimating Means

We can best see the interrelationship of the basic factors affecting the determination of sample size by looking at an example. Imagine that the Division of Tourism in a certain midwestern state wants to know the average amount that fishermen spend

Research Window 15.1
Seeking Consensus for the Census

Who said huge government agencies were immune to pressure from disgruntled consumers? Perhaps the IRS can still hang tough, but the U.S. Census Bureau is changing its ways in response to the fuss that followed the undercount in 1980. The numbers that were published following that census prompted at least fifty lawsuits from various people and groups who felt that the bureau's data were unrepresentative. Although none of the suits were successful, the bureau got the message.

In 1990 the bureau plans to verify its data by taking a sample survey after the census. Using computers, it will match the survey and the census results person by person. This will enable the bureau to adjust its undercount (and overcount) estimates for the country as a whole, as well as for small geographic areas. This technique was the source of the bureau's 1980 undercount estimates, including its estimates of illegal aliens, but in 1980 it was limited to the national level.

In planning for the 1990 census, the bureau has been investigating various adjustment methodologies. Once the data are in, the bureau will decide whether an adjustment is really necessary.

A major part of the planning for the census involves gaining a consensus about the acceptable standards for the quality of the adjusted and unadjusted figures. The bureau wants a consensus from the people and organizations it thinks of as "stakeholders"—groups that would doubtlessly include state and local officials who would be likely to sue the bureau again if they were dissatisfied with the 1990 figures.

To gain consensus, the bureau will announce the results of its research, and hold a number of public forums before the actual census to get an early sense of what stakeholders' reactions are likely to be. The proposed standards will then be submitted to Congress.

Not everyone agrees with this approach. Many people feel the bureau should be putting its time and money into making the census count complete. But most professional statisticians agree that the last three censuses have gone well beyond the point of diminishing returns in reducing the undercount to all but the impossibly hard-to-find. What needs to be done now is to support the Census Bureau's research, and to come to some kind of agreement on the "accuracy" an adjusted census should have.

As Harvard professor Michael A. Stoto told Congressman Robert Garcia's census oversight committee, "there are many dimensions of 'accuracy.'" These include absolute or proportional errors, errors in absolute population or in shares of the total, and overcounts as well as undercounts, not to mention random errors as well as the systematic ones the adjustment is intended to remedy. The stakeholders must examine their use of census data—political, economic, social, or whatever—and decide what accuracy means to them.

Source: Martha Farnsworth Riche, "The Consensus Census," *American Demographics,* 9 (January 1987), p. 8

Figure 15.1

**Sampling Distribution
of Sample Means**

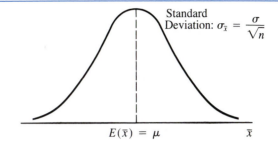

Standard
Deviation: $\sigma_{\bar{x}} = \dfrac{\sigma}{\sqrt{n}}$

$E(\bar{x}) = \mu$ $\bar{x}$

each year on food and lodging while on fishing trips within the state. Our job as researchers is to use a simple random sample to estimate the mean annual expenditure of those fishermen, using a list of all those who applied for fishing licenses within the year.[2] The central-limit theorem suggests that the distribution of sample means will be normal for samples of reasonable size regardless of the distribution of expenditures in the population of fishermen. Consider then the sampling distribution of sample means in Figure 15.1 and distinguish two cases: Case I, in which the population variance is known, and Case II, in which the population variance is unknown.

---

[2]The problem would be of interest to the tourist industry, and it also could be of interest to the division of state government concerned with economic development. The problem was chosen because the availability of a list of population elements allows a simple random sample to be selected.

Suppose that one wished to estimate the mean annual expenditure of fishermen in a certain state. The central-limit theorem suggests that the distribution of sample means will be normal for samples of reasonable size regardless of the distribution of expenditures in the population of fishermen.

Source: Courtesy of General Development Corporation.

Case I: Population Variance Known

The population variance might be known from past studies, even though the average expenditures for food and lodging might be unknown, since variation typically changes much more slowly than level.[3] This means that the spread of the distribution given by the standard error of estimate, $\sigma_{\bar{x}}$, as shown in Figure 15.1, is also known up to a proportionality constant, the square root of the sample size, since $\sigma_{\bar{x}} = \sigma/\sqrt{n}$. Thus we have some idea of the first ingredient in sample size determination, the standard error of estimate.

Suppose the director of tourism wanted the estimate to be within $\pm \$25$ of the true population value. Total precision would thus be $50, and half-precision, call it H, is $25. The reason we work with H instead of the full length of the interval is that the normal curve is symmetrical about the true population mean, and it simplifies the calculations to work with only one-half of the curve.

The remaining item that needs to be specified is the degree of confidence desired in the result. Suppose the director of tourism wants to be 95 percent confident that the interval the researcher constructs will contain the true population mean. This implies that z is approximately equal to 2.[4]

Now we have all we need for determining sample size, since it is known that a number of standard deviations on each side of the mean will include a certain proportion of all observations with a normal curve and, in particular, that two standard deviations will include 95 percent of all observations. In Figure 15.1, each observation is a sample mean; the distribution of these sample means is centered about the population mean; and two standard deviations are $2\sigma_{\bar{x}}$, or $z\sigma_{\bar{x}}$ in the general case. Since we want our estimate to be no more than $25 ($ = H$) removed from the true population value, we can simply equate the size of the specified half-interval with the number of standard deviations ($= z\sigma_{\bar{x}}$) to yield

$$H = z\sigma_{\bar{x}} \tag{15.1}$$

$$= z\frac{\sigma}{\sqrt{n}}$$

This equation can be solved for n, since H and z have been specified and σ is known from past studies. Specifically, n can be shown to be equal to

$$n = \frac{z^2}{H^2}\sigma^2 \tag{15.2}$$

or, in words,

$$\text{sample size} = \frac{\begin{array}{c} z, \text{ corresponding to desired} \\ \text{degree of confidence, squared} \times \text{population variance} \end{array}}{\text{desired level of precision squared}}$$

To illustrate, suppose the historic variation in expenditures on food and lodging as measured by the population standard deviation, σ, was $100. Then

$$n = \frac{(2)^2}{(25)^2}(100)^2$$

---

[3]See Morris H. Hansen, William N. Hurwitz, and William G. Madow, *Sample Survey Methods and Theory: Vol. 1: Methods and Applications* (New York: John Wiley, 1953) for one of the best treatments on securing variance estimates from past data, especially pages 450–455.

[4]The variable z more correctly equals 1.96 for a 95 percent confidence interval. The approximation $z = 2$ is used since it simplifies the calculations.

Figure 15.2   Nomograph to Determine Sample Size to Estimate a Mean with 95 Percent Confidence Level

Standard Deviation—σ	Sample Size—n	Half Precision—H
500	40000 / 35000	5
450	30000 / 25000	6
400	20000	
	15000	
350	10000 / 9000 / 8000 / 7000	7
	6000	8
300	5000	
	4000	9
250	3500 / 3000	
	2500	10
	2000	11
	1500	12
200	1000 / 900 / 800 / 700	13
175	600	14
	500	15
	400	16
150	350 / 300	
	250	18
	200	
125	150	20
100	100 / 90 / 80 / 70 / 60	25
90	50 / 40 / 35	
80	30	30
75	25	
70	20	35
65	15	
60	10	40
55		45
50	5 / 4	50

and $n = 64$. Thus only a relatively small sample needs to be taken to estimate the mean expenditure level when the population standard deviation is $100 and the allowed precision is $50.

Another way to solve estimation problems is to develop a *nomograph* for the equation and read off the sample size rather than calculate it. A nomograph, or *alignment chart,* is simply a graphical solution to an equation. When values of all but one of the variables in the equation are specified, the value of the remaining variable can be read from the graph. Figure 15.2 is a nomograph for Equation 15.2 when a 95 percent confidence level is desired. By placing a ruler, preferably a clear plastic ruler, on the values $H = 25$ and $\sigma = 100$, we can read the sample size from the column of sample sizes. For a 95 percent confidence level, the nomograph shows that $n = 64$.

Note what happens, however, if the estimate must be twice as precise: $25 is the total width of the desired interval and $H = 12.5$. Reading from Figure 15.2 or substituting in Equation 15.2,

$$n = \frac{(2)^2}{(12.5)^2}(100)^2$$

and $n = 256$; doubling the precision (halving the total width of the interval) increased the required sample size by a factor of 4. This is the basic trade-off between precision and sample size. Whenever precision is increased by a factor, c, sample size is increased by a factor of c^2. Thus, if the desired precision were $10 instead of $50—the estimate must be five times more precise ($c = 5$)—the sample size would be 1,600 instead of 64 ($c^2 = 25$).

One also pays dearly for increases in the degree of confidence. Suppose, for example, that 99 percent confidence is desired rather than 95 percent. We could use the nomograph for a 99 percent confidence interval as shown in Figure 15.3, or we could calculate the result directly, using Equation 15.2, but now letting $z = 3$ instead of 2 as before. Suppose $H = 25$ and $\sigma = 100$ as in the original situation. Then

$$n = \frac{(3)^2}{(25)^2}(100)^2$$

and $n = 144$, whereas $n = 64$ when $z = 2$. When z was increased by a factor of d ($d = \frac{3}{2}$ in the example), sample size increased by a factor of d^2 ($d^2 = \frac{9}{4}$ in the example).

The bottom line in all these calculations is that you should be well aware of the price that must be paid for increased precision and confidence. While we often desire very precise estimates in which we have a great deal of confidence, in the real world somebody must foot the bill incurred by each added degree of precision and confidence.

Case II: Population Variance Unknown

In our first case we used examples in which the population variance was known. What happens in the more typical case when the population variance is unknown? The procedure in estimating the sample size is the same except that an *estimated* value of the population standard deviation, σ, is used in place of the previously known value. Once the sample is selected, the variance calculated from the sample is *used in place of the originally estimated variance* when establishing confidence intervals.

Suppose, for example, that there were no past studies on which to base an estimate of σ. How does one then generate an estimate of the population standard

Figure 15.3   Nomograph to Determine Sample Size to Estimate a Mean with 99 Percent Confidence Level

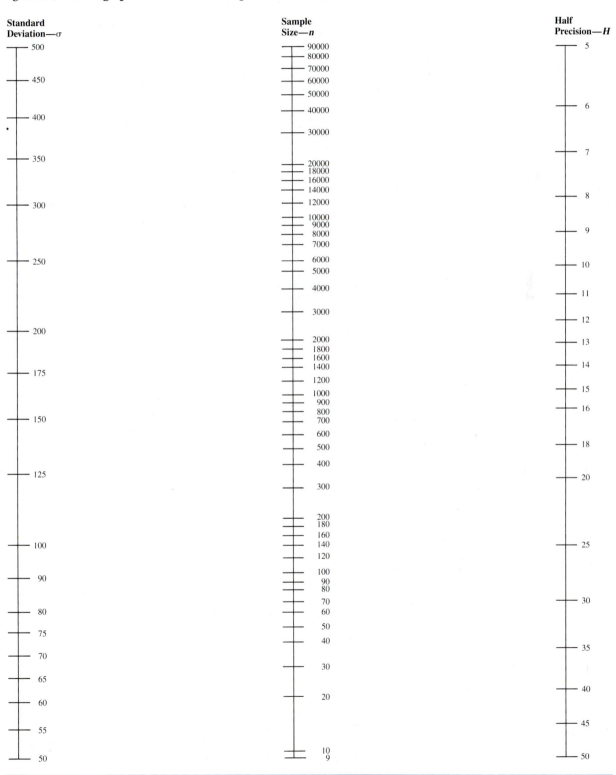

deviation? A pilot study is one way. An alternate is to take into account the fact that for a normally distributed variable, the range of the variable is approximately equal to plus or minus three standard deviations. Thus, if one can estimate the range of variation, one can estimate the standard deviation by dividing by 6. A little *a priori* knowledge of the phenomenon is often enough to estimate the range. If the estimate is in error, the consequence is a confidence interval more or less precise than desired. Let us illustrate.

Certainly there would be some licensed fisherman who would spend zero dollars on food and lodging while on fishing trips since they would only be making one-day trips. Some might also be expected to go on several one-week trips a year. Suppose that fifteen days a year were considered typical of the upper limit, and food and lodging expenses were calculated at $30 per day; the total dollar upper limit would be $450. The range would also be 450 (since they could not spend less than zero); and the estimated standard deviation would then be 450/6 = 75.

With desired precision of ±$25 and a 95 percent confidence interval, the calculation of sample size is now

$$n = \frac{z^2}{H^2}(\text{est. }\sigma)^2$$

$$= \frac{(2)^2}{(25)^2}(75)^2$$

and $n = 36$. The nomograph in Figure 15.2 could also be used to get the same result.

A sample of Size 36 would then be selected and the information collected. Suppose these observations generated a sample mean, $\bar{x} = 35$, and a sample standard deviation, $\hat{s} = 60$. The confidence interval is calculated as before[5] using the expression sample mean ±z (standard error of the mean), where now the standard error of the mean is estimated using the sample standard deviation, or in symbols $\bar{x} \pm zs_{\bar{x}}$, or

$$35 \pm 2\frac{\hat{s}}{\sqrt{n}} = 35 \pm 2\frac{60}{\sqrt{36}} = 35 \pm 20$$

or

$$15 \leq \mu \leq 55$$

Note what has happened. The desired precision was ±$25; the obtained precision is ±$20. The interval is narrower than planned (a bonus) because we overestimated the population standard deviation as judged by the sample standard deviation. If we had underestimated the standard deviation, the situation would have been reversed, and we would have ended up with a wider confidence interval than desired.

Case of Multiple Objectives

Researchers rarely conduct a study to determine only one parameter. It is much more typical for a study to involve multiple objectives. Let us assume more realisti-

[5]One would more strictly use the *t* distribution to establish the interval, since the population variance was unknown. The example was framed using the approximate $z = 2$ value for a 95 percent confidence interval so as to better illustrate the consequences of a poor initial estimate of σ.

Table 15.1   Sample Size Needed to Estimate Each of Three Means

	Variable		
	Expenditures on Food and Lodging	**Expenditures on Tackle and Equipment**	**Miles Traveled**
Confidence level	95 percent ($z = 2$)	95 percent ($z = 2$)	95 percent ($z = 2$)
Desired precision	±$25	±$10	±100 miles
Estimated standard deviation	±$75	±$20	±500 miles
Required sample size	36	16	100

cally, therefore, that in our study the researcher has been asked also to estimate the annual mean level of expenditures on tackle and equipment by licensed fishermen, and the number of miles traveled in a year on fishing trips. There are now three means to be estimated. Suppose each is to be estimated with 95 percent confidence and that the desired absolute precision and estimated standard deviation are as given in Table 15.1. Table 15.1 also contains the sample sizes needed to estimate each variable, which were calculated using Equation 15.2.

The three requirements produce conflicting sample sizes. Depending on the variable being estimated, n should equal 36, 16, or 100. The researcher must somehow reconcile these values to come up with a sample size suitable for the study as a whole. The most conservative approach would be to choose $n = 100$, the largest value. This would ensure that each variable is estimated with the required precision, assuming that the estimates of the standard deviations were accurate.

However, let us assume that of the three means to be determined, the estimate of miles traveled is the least critical. In such a case, it would be wasteful of resources to use a sample size of 100. A better approach would be to focus on those variables that are most critical and to select a sample sufficient in size to estimate them with the required precision and confidence. The variables for which a larger sample size is needed would then be estimated with either a lower degree of confidence or less precision than planned. Suppose in this case that the expenditure data are most critical and that the analyst, therefore, decides on a sample size of 36. Suppose also that the information from this sample of thirty-six fishermen produced a sample mean of $\bar{x} = 300$ and a sample standard deviation of $\hat{s} = 500$ miles traveled. The sample result is thus seen to agree with the original estimate of the population standard deviation, and so the confidence interval estimate will not be affected by inaccuracies here.

Using the standard expression, sample mean $\pm z$ (standard error of the mean), the confidence interval for miles traveled is calculated as

$$\bar{x} \pm z s_{\bar{x}} = \bar{x} \pm z \frac{\hat{s}}{\sqrt{n}} = 300 \pm 2 \frac{500}{\sqrt{36}}$$

or $133.3 \leq \mu \leq 466.7$. Whereas the desired precision was ±100 miles, the obtained precision is ±166.7 miles. In order to produce an estimate with the desired precision, the degree of confidence would have to be lowered from its present 95 percent level.

◆ Sample Size Determination When Estimating Proportions

The preceding examples all concern mean values. Marketers are also often interested in estimating other parameters such as the population proportion, π. In our example, the researcher might be interested in determining the proportion of licensed fishermen who are from out of state, or from rural areas, or who took at least one overnight trip.

At the beginning of this chapter we suggested three things were needed to determine sample size: a specified degree of confidence, specified precision, and knowledge of the sampling distribution of the statistic. As we noted earlier, the specific requirements of the research problem determine how the first two items will be specified. With percentages, though, precision means that the estimate will be within plus or minus so many percentage points of the true value, as, for example, within ± 5 percentage points of the true value.

The remaining consideration then is the sampling distribution of the sample proportion. If the sample elements are selected independently, as can reasonably be assumed if the sample size is small relative to the population size, then the theoretically correct distribution of the sample proportion is the binomial. But the binomial becomes indistinguishable from the normal with large samples or when the population proportion is close to one-half.[6] It is convenient to use the normal approximation when estimating sample size. After the sample is drawn and the sample proportion determined, the researcher can always fall back on the binomial distribution to determine the confidence interval if the normal approximation proves to be in error.

The distribution of sample proportions is centered about the population proportion (Figure 15.4). The sample proportion is an unbiased estimate of the population proportion. The standard deviation of the normal distribution of sample proportions, that is, the standard error of the proportion, denoted by σ_p, is equal to $\sqrt{\pi(1-\pi)/n}$. Since we are working again with the normal curve, the level of precision is again equated to the number of standard deviations the estimate can be removed from the mean value. But now the mean value is the population proportion, while the standard deviation is the standard error of the proportion, that is,

$$H = z\sigma_p \tag{15.3}$$

Substituting $\sqrt{\pi(1-\pi)/n}$ for σ_p and solving for n yields

$$n = \frac{z^2}{H^2}\pi(1-\pi) \tag{15.4}$$

or, in words,

$$\text{sample size} = \frac{z, \text{ corresponding to desired degree of confidence, squared} \times \text{population proportion} \times (1-\text{population proportion})}{\text{desired level of precision squared}}$$

Suppose the division of tourism is interested in knowing the proportion of all fishermen who took at least one overnight fishing trip in the past year. Suppose also

---

[6]The strict requirement is that $n\pi$ must be above a certain level if the normal curve is to provide a good approximation to the binomial, where π is the population proportion and n is the sample size. Some books hold that $n\pi$ must be greater than 5, while others suggest that the product must be greater than 10.

Figure 15.4

Approximate Sampling Distribution of the Sample Proportion

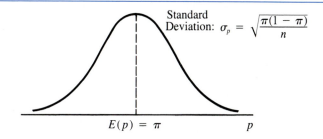

$$\text{Standard Deviation: } \sigma_p = \sqrt{\frac{\pi(1 - \pi)}{n}}$$

$$E(p) = \pi$$

that they wanted this estimate within ± 2 percentage points, and they wanted to be 95 percent confident ($z = 2$) in the result. Substituting these values in the formula (Equation 15.4) yields:

$$n = \frac{(2)^2}{(.02)^2}\, \pi(1 - \pi)$$

This equation contains two unknowns: the population proportion being estimated and the sample size. Thus, it is not solvable as it stands. In order to determine sample size, the researcher needs to estimate the population proportion. That is right! *The researcher must estimate the very quantity the study is being designed to discover in order to determine sample size.*

This fact is often bewildering and certainly disconcerting to decision makers and beginning researchers alike. Nevertheless, it is true that with proportions one is forced to make some judgment about the approximate value of the parameter in order to determine sample size. This is another example of how information begets information in sample design. To arrive at an initial estimate, researchers might consult past studies or other published data. Alternatively, they might conduct a pilot study. If neither of these options is available, they might simply use informed judgment—a best guess—as to the approximate likely value of the parameter.

A poor estimate will make the confidence interval more or less precise than desired. Suppose, for example, that the best considered judgment was that 20 percent of all licensed fishermen could be expected to take an overnight fishing trip during the year. Sample size is then calculated to be

$$n = \frac{(2)^2}{(.02)^2}\,(.20)(1 - .20)$$

and $n = 1,600$. After data are collected from the designated 1,600 fishermen, suppose that the sample proportion, p, actually turns out to be equal to 0.40. The confidence interval is then established, employing the sample standard error of the proportion, s_p, to estimate the unknown population standard error of the proportion, σ_p, where $s_p = \sqrt{\dfrac{pq}{n}}$ where p is the proportion engaging in the behavior in the particular sample selected, and $q = 1 - p$. In the example,

$$s_p = \sqrt{\frac{0.40\,(0.60)}{1,600}} = \sqrt{\frac{0.24}{1,600}} = 0.012$$

The confidence interval for the population proportion is given by the expression sample proportion $\pm$ *(z)* (standard error of the proportion) or

$$p \pm zs_p = 0.40 \pm 2(0.012)$$

or

$$0.376 \leq \pi \leq 0.424$$

Note the interval is wider than desired. This is because the sample proportion turned out to be larger than the *estimated* population proportion.

Suppose a wider interval than planned was unacceptable. One way of preventing it is to choose the sample size so as to reflect the "worst of worlds." Note from the formula that the largest sample size will be obtained when the product $\pi(1 - \pi)$ is greatest, since sample size is directly proportional to this quantity. This product is in turn greatest when the population proportion is $\pi = 0.5$, as might be intuitively expected, since if one-half of the population behaves one way and the other half the other way, then one would require more evidence for a valid inference than if a substantial proportion all behaved in the same way.

In the absence of any other information about the population proportion, then, one can always conservatively assume that π is equal to 0.5. The established confidence interval will simply be more precise to the extent that the sample estimate deviates from the assumed 0.5 value. Figures 15.5 and 15.6 are the nomographs for determining sample size to estimate a population proportion with 95 percent confidence level and 99 percent confidence level, respectively.

◆ Population Size and Sample Size

Although you may not have noticed it before, note it now: *The size of the population does not enter into the calculation of the size of the sample.* Except for one slight modification we will discuss shortly, the size of the population has *no direct effect* on the size of the sample.

Although this statement may initially seem strange, consider it carefully and you will see why it is true. When estimating a mean, if all population elements have exactly the same value of the characteristic (for example, if each of our fishermen spent exactly $74 per year on food and lodging), then a sample of one is all that is needed to determine the mean. This is true whether there are 1,000, 10,000, or 100,000 elements in the population. What directly affects the size of the sample is the variability of the characteristic in the population.

Suppose that our sample state offered some of the best fishing in the country and drew fishermen from across the nation as well as happy locals. If the parameter we sought to measure were mean number of miles traveled annually on fishing trips, there would be great variation in the characteristic. The more variable the characteristic, the larger the sample needed to estimate it with some specified level of precision. This idea not only makes intuitive sense, but we can see it directly expressed in the formulas for determining sample size to estimate a population mean. (See Equation 15.2.) Thus, population size affects sample size only indirectly through variability. In most cases, the larger the population, the greater the *potential* for variation of the characteristic.

It is also true that population size does not affect sample size when estimating a proportion. With a proportion, the determining factor, as we have seen, is the estimated proportion of the population possessing the characteristic; the closer the proportion is to 0.5, the larger the sample that will be needed, regardless of the size of

Figure 15.5   Nomograph to Determine Sample Size to Estimate a Proportion with 95 Percent Confidence Level

Estimated Proportion—π	Sample Size—n	Half Precision—H
.50	40000	.005
.45	35000	
.40	30000	
.35	25000	.006
	20000	
.30		.007
.28	15000	
	14000	
.25	12000	.008
	10000	
.22	9000	
	8000	.009
.20	7500	
	7000	
	6500	
.18	6000	.010
	5500	
	5000	
	4500	
.16	4000	.012
	3500	
.14	3000	
	2800	
	2600	.014
	2400	
	2200	
	2000	
	1800	
.12	1600	.016
	1500	
	1400	
	1200	.018
	1000	
.10	900	.020
	800	
	700	.022
.09	600	
	500	.025
	450	
.08	400	
	350	.028
	300	.030
.07	250	
	200	.035
	175	
.06	150	
		.040
	125	
	100	.045
.05	76	.050

Figure 15.6 Nomograph to Determine Sample Size to Estimate a Proportion with 99 Percent Confidence Level

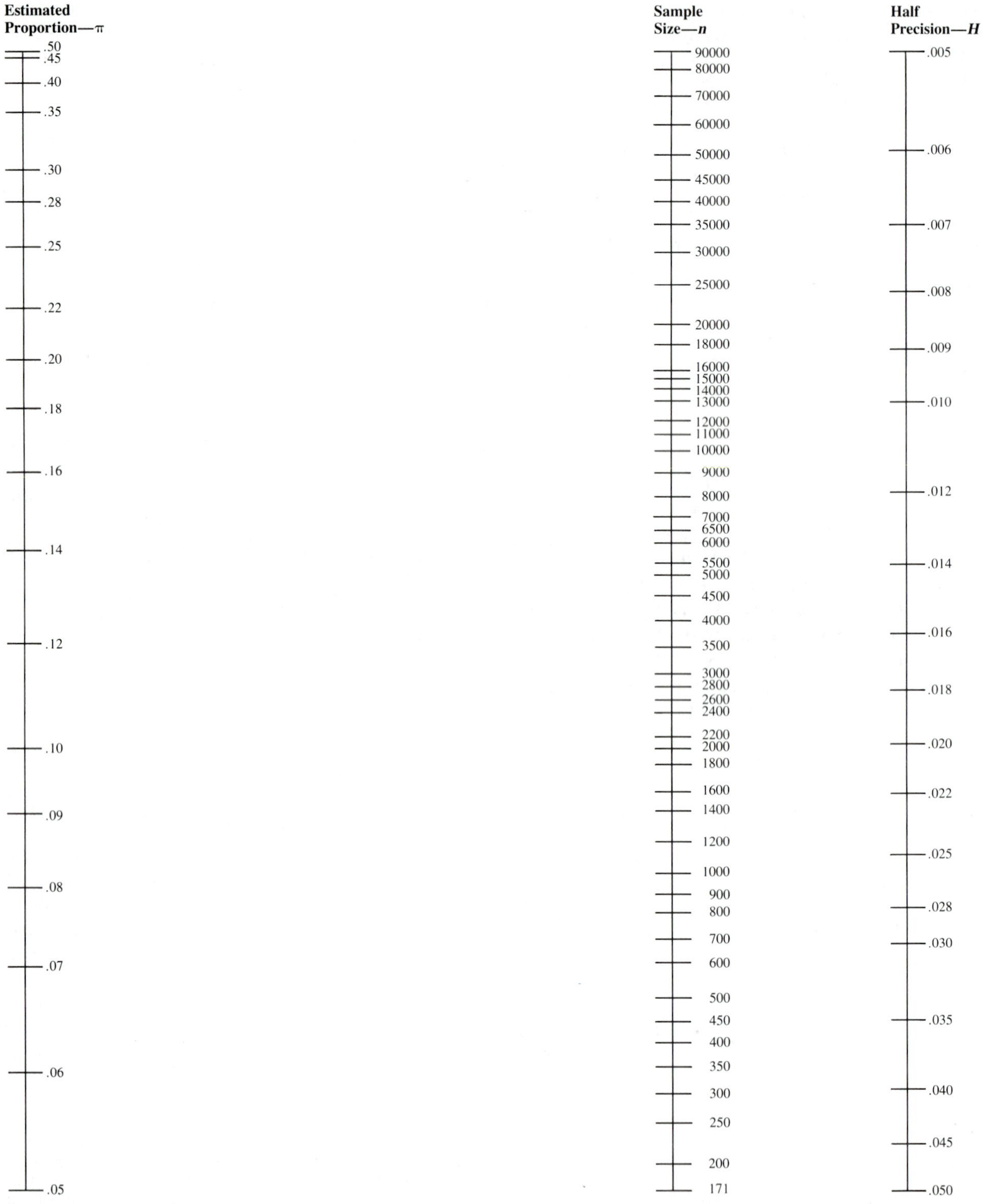

the population. A value of 0.5 signifies greatest variability because one-half of the population possesses the characteristic and one-half does not.

The procedures we have discussed so far apply to situations where the target population is essentially infinite. This is the case in most consumer-good studies. However, when we first began our discussion, we mentioned that there was one modification to the general rule that population size has no direct effect on sample size. In cases where the sample represents a large portion of the population, the formulas must be altered or they will overestimate the required sample. Since the larger the sample, the more expensive the study, the finite population correction factor should be employed.

As we have seen previously, the formula for the standard error of the mean is $\sigma_{\bar{x}} = \sigma/\sqrt{n}$ for most sampling problems. When the finite population correction factor is required, the formula becomes

$$\sigma_{\bar{x}} = \frac{\sigma}{\sqrt{n}}\sqrt{\frac{N-n}{N-1}}$$

where N denotes the size of the population and n denotes the size of the sample. The factor $(N - n)/(N - 1)$ is the finite population correction factor.

When the estimated sample represents more than 5 percent of the population, the calculated size should be reduced by the finite population correction factor.[7] If, for example, the population contained 100 elements and the calculation of sample size indicated that a sample of twenty was needed, fewer than twenty observations would, in fact, be taken if the finite population correction factor were employed.

The required sample would be given as $n' = nN/(N + n - 1)$, where n was the originally determined size and n' was the revised size. Thus, with $N = 100$ and $n = 20$, only seventeen sample elements would, in fact, be employed.

◆ Other Probability Sampling Plans

So far, the discussions of sample size have been based on simple random samples. You should be aware, though, that there are also formulas for determining sample size when other probability sampling plans are used. The formulas are more complex to be sure, but the same underlying principles apply. One still needs a knowledge of the sampling distribution of the statistic in addition to the research specifications regarding level of precision and degree of confidence.

The issue of sample size is compounded, though, by the fact that one now has a number of strata or a number of clusters with which to work. This means that one must deal with within-strata variability and within- and between-cluster variability in calculating sample size, whereas with simple random sampling only total population variability entered the picture. As before, the more variable the strata or cluster, the larger the sample that needs to be taken from it, other things being equal. This is precisely the basis for disproportionate stratified sampling discussed in Chapter 14.

Something else that must be equal, though, is cost. Cost did not enter directly into the calculation of sample size with simple random sampling, although it often

---

[7]The 5 percent correction factor is not a hard and fast rule. Some books contend that the finite population correction factor should be ignored if the sample includes no more than 10 percent of the population. Cochran suggests that the finite population correction can be ignored whenever the "sampling fraction does not exceed 5 percent and for many purposes even if it is as high as 10 percent," William G. Cochran, *Sampling Techniques,* 3rd ed. (New York: John Wiley, 1977), p. 25. Ignoring the finite population correction will result in overestimating the standard error of estimate.

does affect sample size. If the cost of data collection with a sample of the calculated size would exceed the research budget, the cost could be the factor keeping the sample size below what was indicated by the formulas. In fact, it is not unusual for the size of a simple random sample to be determined by dividing the data-collection budget by the cost per observation. From a strictly statistical viewpoint, however, cost per observation does not enter into the formulas for calculating sample size with simple random samples.

With stratified or cluster samples, cost exerts a direct impact. In calculating sample size, one has to allow for unequal costs per observation by strata or by cluster, and in implementing the sample size calculation, one has to have some initial estimate of these costs. The task then becomes one of balancing variability against costs and assessing the trade-off function relating the two. With a stratified sample, for example, if cost were the same by strata, one would want to sample most heavily the stratum that was most variable. On the other hand, if there was little variation within strata, one might choose to sample heavier those strata in which the cost per observation was less. Since it is unlikely that the cost per observation or variability will be the same for each stratum, the challenge becomes one of determining sample size by considering the precision likely to result from sampling each stratum at a given rate. Formulas are available for this purpose, as for cluster samples. We shall not go into these formulas here as they are readily available in the standard works on sampling theory and fall largely in the domain of the sampling specialist.[8] You should be aware, though, that, when dealing with stratified or cluster samples, cost per observation by subgroup enters directly into the calculation of sample size.

You should also be aware that there are formulas for determining sample size when the problem is one of hypothesis testing and not confidence interval estimation. Once again, the principles are the same, although there are some additional considerations such as the levels of Type I and Type II errors to be tolerated and the issue of whether it is necessary to detect subtle differences or only obvious differences. We shall not deal with these formulas, since they are also readily available in standard statistical works and their discussion would take us too far afield.

Sample Size Determination Using Anticipated Cross Classifications

Thus far, our discussion of how sample size is determined has been based primarily on the use of statistical principles, with a particular focus on the sampling error involved in the trade-off between degree of confidence and degree of precision. Until now we have limited ourselves to a discussion of these considerations since they are the most important ones theoretically. But in applied problems, the size of the sample is also going to be affected by certain practical considerations. In our discussion of stratified and cluster samples we already mentioned that the size of the budget for the study and the anticipated cost per observation would affect sample size. In addition to that, the size of the sample may also be affected by other, quite subjective factors. For example, researchers may find themselves increasing the size of the sample beyond what is required statistically in order to convince

[8]See, for example, Cochran, *Sampling Techniques;* Hansen, Hurwitz, and Madow, *Sample Survey Methods;* Leslie Kish, *Survey Sampling* (New York: John Wiley, 1965); R. L. Jensen, *Statistical Survey Techniques* (New York: John Wiley, 1978); Richard L. Schaeffer, William Mendenhall, and Lyman Ott, *Elementary Survey Sampling,* 2nd ed. (North Scituate, Mass.: Duxbury Press, 1979); Bill Williams, *A Sampler on Sampling* (New York: John Wiley, 1978); or Richard M. Jaeger, *Sampling in Education and the Social Sciences* (New York: Longman, 1984).

skeptical executives, who may have little understanding of sampling theory, that they can have confidence in the results of the study.

One of the more important practical bases for determining the size of sample that will be needed is the cross classifications to which researchers plan to subject the data. Suppose that in our task of estimating the proportion of all fishermen who took at least one overnight fishing trip in the past year, we also proposed to determine whether this pattern of behavior was somehow related to an individual's age and income. Assume that the age categories of interest were as follows: younger than 20, 20–29, 30–39, 40–49, and 50 and older. Assume the income categories of interest were as follows: less than $10,000, $10,000–$19,999, $20,000–$29,999, $30,000–$39,999, and $40,000 and over. There are thus five age categories and five income categories for which the proportion of fishermen taking an overnight trip would be estimated.

While we could estimate proportions for each of these variables separately, we should also recognize that the two variables are interrelated in that increases in incomes are typically related to increases in age. To allow for this interdependence, we need to consider the impact of the two variables simultaneously. The way to do

Back to the Case

A blast of a horn behind her startled Leslie Jonas out of her reverie. She had been so engrossed with rehearsing her pitch to Rebecca Hansen that she hadn't noticed that the light had turned green. Sheepishly, she pulled out of the intersection and headed east toward The Material World.

For a week now she had been mulling over the possibilities for Rebecca's study. She knew the shop had little to spend on a marketing research project, but she was convinced that Rebecca had a potentially winning business in hand if only she marketed it properly.

Three days ago she had seen an ad for a competing store's decorating services in the glossy city magazine that was so popular with the area's young, upscale working couples. If Rebecca could tap into that well-heeled,

image-conscious crowd, Leslie was sure she would do well.

The problem was to convince Rebecca that this market was worth the extra dollars she might spend cultivating it. To help make her case, Leslie had designed a marketing research study that went well beyond Rebecca's initial request. Instead of only finding the mean number of miles customers traveled to the store, Leslie was planning to propose a study that would also investigate shoppers' average age and income. If the results showed that an affluent, young local crowd was already attracted to the store, Leslie felt sure it would be relatively easy to convince Rebecca to spend the money to advertise to a similar crowd in a broader geographic area.

The idea was good, Leslie thought, but there was one basic

problem: money. If Rebecca balked at paying going rates for the study, should she drop her price to snare a potentially lucrative client, or should she just do the smaller-scale study Rebecca had requested?

Decisions, decisions. Real life was certainly more complicated than the elegant equations she had mastered in her marketing research texts!

Many factors other than statistical principles may influence the size of a sample. Among them are the potential cross classifications the data may be subjected to, as well as the very real consideration of cost. A researcher must determine what sample size would not only satisfy the requirements of the technique being used, but also the requirements of the client for whom the study is designed.

Table 15.2   Number and Proportion of Fishermen Staying Overnight as a Function of Age and Income

Income	Younger than 20	20–29	30–39	40–49	50 and older
Less than $10,000					
$10,000–$19,999					
$20,000–$29,999					
$30,000–$39,999					
$40,000 and over					

this is through a cross-classification table in which age and income jointly define the cells or categories in the table.[9]

Table 15.2, for instance, is a cross-classification table that could be used for the example at hand. Note that this dummy table is complete in all respects except for the numbers that actually go in each of the cells.[10] These would, of course, be determined by the data actually collected on the number and proportion of all those sampled who actually made at least one overnight trip. In the table there are twenty-five cells that need estimation. It is unlikely, however, that the decision maker for whom our study is designed is going to be comfortable with an estimate based on only a few cases of the phenomenon. Yet even with a sample of, say, 500 fishermen, there is only a potential of 20 cases per cell (i.e., 500 cases divided by 25 cells) if the sample is evenly divided with respect to the age and income levels considered. Further, it is very unlikely that the sample would split this way, which would put the researcher in the awkward position of estimating the proportion in a cell engaging in this behavior on the basis of fewer than 20 cases.

One can reverse this argument to estimate how large a sample should be taken. First, the researcher would calculate the number of cells in the intended cross classifications. That number can be found by multiplying the number of levels of the characteristics forming each of the cross classifications. In our study, researchers would multiply five (levels of income) by five (levels of age) to get twenty-five cells. If it was felt that the decision maker might need at least thirty observations per cell in order to feel comfortable with the cell's estimate, that would mean a sample of 750 subjects is needed. However, the sample of 750 is unlikely to be evenly distributed across the cells of the table, so the researchers would need to determine how the variables are likely to be distributed. Once the most important cells have been identified, the researcher can compute a sample size large enough to satisfy concerns about sufficient sampling. One general rule of thumb is that "the sample should be large enough so that there are 100 or more units in each category of the major breakdowns and a minimum of 20 to 50 in the minor breakdowns."[11] Major

---

[9]In Chapter 17 the procedures for setting up and analyzing cross-classification tables so that the proper inferences can be drawn are discussed.

[10]Refer again to Chapter 5 for a discussion of the notion of dummy tables and how they should be set up so that they are most productive.

[11]Sudman, *Applied Sampling*, p. 30.

Table 15.3   Typical Sample Sizes for Studies of Human and Institutional Populations

Number of Subgroup Analyses	People or Households		Institutions	
	National	**Regional or Special**	**National**	**Regional or Special**
None or few	1,000–1,500	200–500	200–500	50–200
Average	1,500–2,500	500–1,000	500–1,000	200–500
Many	2,500+	1,000+	1,000+	500+

Source: Seymour Sudman, *Applied Sampling* (New York: Academic Press, 1976), p. 87.

breakdowns refer to the cells in the most critical cross tabulations for the study, and minor breakdowns to the cells in the less important cross classifications.

Through all of this one has to make allowances for nonresponses, since some individuals designated for inclusion in the sample will be unavailable, and others will refuse to participate.[12] The researcher "builds up" the sample, so to speak, from the size of the cross-classification table with due allowance for these considerations.

Perhaps cross classification will not be the basic method used to analyze the data. Perhaps, instead, other statistical techniques will be used. If so, the same arguments for determining sample size apply. That is, one needs a sufficient number of cases to satisfy the requirements of the technique, so as to inspire confidence in the results. Different techniques have different sample size requirements, often expressed by the degrees of freedom required for the analysis. Readers interested in using a particular statistical technique for analysis should pay close attention to the sample size requirements for the techniques to be used safely. For now, we merely wish to reiterate the important point made earlier when introducing the research process— that the stages are very much related, and a decision with respect to one stage can affect all of the other stages. In this case a decision with respect to Stage 6 regarding the method of analysis can have an important impact on Stage 5, which precedes it, with respect to the size of the sample that should be selected. Therefore, the researcher needs to think through the entire research problem, including how the data will be analyzed, before beginning the data-collection process.

◆ Determining Sample Size Using Historic Evidence

A final method by which an analyst can determine the size of the sample to employ is to use the size that others have used for similar studies in the past. While this may be different from the ideal size in a given problem, the fact that the contemplated sample size is in line with that used for other similar studies is psychologically comforting, particularly to inexperienced researchers. Table 15.3, which summarizes the evidence, provides a crude yardstick in this respect. Note that national studies typically involve larger samples than regional or special studies. Note further that the number of subgroup analyses has a direct impact on sample size.

---

[12]Nonresponse and other nonsampling errors and what can be done about them are discussed in Chapter 16.

◆ Summary

Learning Objective 1: Specify the key factor a researcher must consider in estimating sample size using statistical principles.

The key factor a researcher must consider in estimating sample size is the standard error of the estimate obtained from the known sampling distribution of the statistic.

Learning Objective 2: Cite two other factors researchers must also take into account when estimating a sample size and explain their relationship.

When estimating a sample size, researchers must consider both how precise the estimate must be and the degree of confidence that is required in the estimate. With a sample of fixed size, there is a trade-off between degree of confidence and degree of precision. One can specify either the degree of precision or the degree of confidence, but not both. It is only when sample size is allowed to vary that one can achieve both a specified precision and a specified degree of confidence in the result. The determination of sample size involves balancing the two considerations against each other.

Learning Objective 3: Explain in what way the size of the population influences the size of the sample.

In most instances, the size of the population has no direct effect on the size of the sample but only affects it indirectly through the variability of the characteristic. In most cases the larger the population, the greater the *potential* is for variation of the characteristic; and sample size is directly proportional to variability.

Learning Objective 4: Specify the circumstances under which the finite population correction factor should be used.

In general, when the estimated sample represents more than 5 percent of the population, the calculated sample size should be reduced by the finite population correction factor.

Learning Objective 5: Explain the impact that cost has on sample size in stratified or cluster samples.

With stratified or cluster samples, cost exerts a direct impact. In calculating sample size, one has to allow for unequal costs per observation by strata or by cluster; and in implementing the sample size calculation, one has to have some initial estimate of these costs. The task, then, becomes one of balancing variability against costs and assessing the trade-off function relating the two.

Learning Objective 6: Cite the general rule of thumb for calculating sample size when cross-classification tables are used.

When calculating sample size by using cross-classification tables, the general rule of thumb is that the sample should be large enough so that there are 100 or more units in each category of the major breakdowns and a minimum of 20 to 50 in the minor breakdowns.

Discussion Questions, Problems, and Projects

1. A survey was being designed by the market research department of a medium-sized manufacturer of household appliances. The general aim was to assess customer satisfaction with the company's dishwashers. As part of this general objective, management wished to measure the average maintenance expenditure per year per household, the average number of malfunctions or breakdowns per year, and the number of times a dishwasher is cleaned within a year. Management wished to be 95 percent confident in the results. Further, the magnitude of the error was not to exceed ±$4 for maintenance expenditures, ±1 malfunction, and ±4 cleanings. The research department noted that while some households would spend nothing on maintenance expenditures per year, others might spend as much as $120. Also, while some dishwashers would experience no breakdowns within a year, the maximum expected would be no more than three. Finally, while some dishwashers might not be cleaned at all during the year, others might be cleaned as frequently as once a month.

(a) How large a sample would you recommend if each of the three variables are considered separately? Show all your calculations.

(b) What size sample would you recommend *overall* given that management felt that the expenditure on repairs was most important and the number of cleanings least important to know accurately?

(c) The survey indicated that the average maintenance expenditure is $30 and the standard deviation is $15. Estimate the confidence interval for the population parameter μ. What can you say about the degree of precision?

2. The management of a major dairy wanted to determine the average ounces of milk consumed per resident in the state of Montana. Past trends indicated that the variation in milk consumption (σ) was 4 ounces. A 95 percent confidence level is required and the error is not to exceed $\pm \frac{1}{2}$ an ounce.

(a) What sample size would you recommend? Show your calculations.

(b) Management wanted to double the level of precision and increase the level of confidence to 99 percent. What sample size would you recommend? Show your calculations. Comment on your results.

3. The manager of a local recreational center wanted to determine the average amount each customer spent on travelling to and from the center. On the basis of the findings, the manager was planning on raising the entrance fee. The manager noted that customers living near the center would spend nothing on travelling. On the other hand, customers living at the other side of town had to travel about 15 miles and spent about 20 cents per mile. The manager wanted to be 95 percent confident of the findings and did not want the error to exceed ± 10 cents.

(a) What sample size should the manager use to determine the average travel expenditure? Show your calculations.

(b) After the survey was conducted, the manager found the average expenditure to be $1.00, and the standard deviation was $0.60. Construct a 95 percent confidence interval. What can you say about the level of precision?

4. A large manufacturer of chemicals recently came under severe criticism from various environmentalists for its disposal of industrial effluent and waste. In response, management launched a campaign to counter the bad publicity it was receiving. A study of the effectiveness of the campaign indicated that about 20 percent of the residents of the city were aware of the campaign and the company's position. In conducting the study, a sample of 400 was used and a 95 percent confidence interval was specified. Three months later, it was believed that 30 percent of the residents were aware of the campaign. However, management decided to do another survey and specified a 99 percent confidence level and a margin of error of ± 2 percentage points.

(a) What sample size would you recommend for this study? Show all your calculations.

(b) After doing the survey it was found that 50 percent of the population was aware of the campaign. Construct a 99 percent confidence interval for the population parameter.

5. Score-It, Inc., is a large manufacturer of video games. The market research department is designing a survey in order to determine attitudes towards the products. Additionally, the percentage of households owning video games and the average usage rate per week is to be determined. The department wants to be 95 percent confident of the results and does not want the error to exceed ± 3 percentage points for video game ownership and ± 1 hour for average usage rate. Previous reports indicate that about 20 percent of the households own video games, and the average usage rate is 15 hours with a standard deviation of 5 hours.

(a) What sample size would you recommend assuming only the percentage of households owning video games is to be determined? Show all your calculations.

(b) What sample size would you recommend assuming only the average usage rate per week is to be determined? Show all your calculations.

(c) What sample size would you recommend assuming both the above variables are to be determined? Why?

After the survey was conducted, the results indicated that 30 percent of the households owned video games and the average usage rate was 13 hours with a standard deviation of 4.

(d) Compute the 95 percent confidence interval for the percentage of individuals owning video games. Comment on the degree of precision.

(e) Compute the 95 percent confidence interval for the average usage rate. Comment on the degree of precision.

6. The local gas and electric company in a city in the northeast United States recently started a campaign to encourage people to reduce unnecessary use of gas and electricity. To assess the effectiveness of the campaign, management wanted to do a survey to determine the proportion of people that had adopted the recommended energy saving measures.

(a) What sample size would you recommend if the error is not to exceed plus or minus .025 percentage points and the confidence level is to be 90 percent? Show your calculations.

(b) The survey indicated that the proportion adopting the measures was 40 percent. Estimate the 90 percent confidence interval. Comment on the level of precision. Show your calculations.

7. Assume you are a marketing research analyst for TV Institute, and you have just been given the assignment of estimating the percentage of all American households that watched the ABC movie last Sunday night. You have been told that your estimate should have a precision of ± 1 percentage point and that there should be a 95 percent "probability" of your being "correct" in your estimate. Your first task is to choose a sample of the appropriate size. Make any assumptions that are necessary.

(a) Recast the problem in a statistical format.

(b) Compute the sample size that will satisfy the required specifications.

(c) What is the required sample size if the precision is specified as ± 2 percentage points?

(d) What would be the sample size if the probability of being "correct" were decreased to 90 percent, keeping the precision at ± 1 percentage point?

(e) If you had only enough time to take a sample of size 100, what precision could you expect from your estimate? (Assume a 95 percent confidence interval.)

(f) Assume that instead of taking a sample from the entire country (60 million households), you would like to restrict yourself to one state with 1 million households. Would the sample size computed in Part b be too large? Too small? Explain.

8. Assume TV Institute has hired you to do another study estimating the average number of hours of television viewing per week per family in the United States. You are asked to generate an estimate within ± 5 hours. Further, there should be 95 percent confidence that the estimate is correct. Make any assumptions that are necessary.

(a) Compute the sample size that will satisfy the required specifications.

(b) What would be the required sample size if the precision were changed to ± 10 hours?

9. The manager of a local bakery wants to determine the average expenditure per household on bakery products. Past research indicates that the standard deviation is $10.

(a) Calculate the sample size for the various levels of precision and confidence. Show your calculations:

	Desired Precision ($\pm$)	Desired Confidence	Estimated Sample Size
1	0.50	0.95	
2	1.00	0.99	
3	0.50	0.90	
4	0.25	0.90	
5	0.50	0.99	
6	0.25	0.95	
7	1.00	0.90	
8	1.00	0.95	
9	0.25	0.99	

(b) Which alternative gives you the largest estimate for sample size? Explain.

10. A manufacturer of liquid soaps wishes to estimate the proportion of individuals using liquid soaps as opposed to bar soaps. Prior estimates of the proportions are listed below.
    (a) For the various levels of precision and confidence indicated, calculate the needed size of the sample.

	Desired Precision Percentage Points(±)	Desired Confidence	(%) Estimated Proportion	Estimated Sample Size
1	6	0.99	20	
2	2	0.90	10	
3	6	0.99	10	
4	4	0.95	30	
5	2	0.90	20	
6	2	0.99	30	
7	6	0.90	30	
8	4	0.95	10	
9	4	0.95	20	

(b) Which alternative gives the largest estimate of the sample size? Explain.

11. Your World, Inc., is a large travel agency located in Cincinnati, Ohio. Management is concerned about its declining leisure travel-tour business. It believes that the profile of those engaging in leisure travel has changed in the past few years. To determine if that is indeed the case, management decides to conduct a survey to determine the profile of the current leisure travel-tour customer. Three variables are identified that require particular attention. Prior to conducting the survey, the following three dummy tables are developed.

	Age			
Income	18–24	25–34	35–54	55+
0–$9,999				
$10,000–19,999				
$20,000–$29,999				
$30,000–$39,999				
$40,000 and over				

	Education			
Age	Some High School	High School Graduate	Some College	College Graduate
18–24				
25–34				
35–54				
55+				

	Education			
Income	Some High School	High School Graduate	Some College	College Graduate
0–$9,999				
$10,000–$19,999				
$20,000–$29,999				
$30,000–$39,999				
$40,000 and over				

(a) How large a sample would you recommend be taken? Justify your answer.
(b) The survey produced the following incomplete table for the variables of age and education. Complete the table on the basis of the assumption that the two characteristics are independent (even though that assumption is wrong). On the basis of the completed table, do you think an appropriate sample size was used? If yes, why? If not, why not?

Age	Education				
	Some High School	High School Graduate	Some College	College Graduate	Total
18–24					100
25–34					200
35–54					350
55+					350
Total	200	400	300	100	1,000

Suggested Additional Readings

For a more thorough discussion of the estimation of sample size for different types of samples and characteristics other than the mean and proportion, see

William Cochran, *Sampling Techniques,* 3rd ed. (New York: John Wiley, 1977).

Morris H. Hansen, William N. Hurwitz, and William G. Madow, *Sample Survey Methods and Theory, Vol. 1, Methods and Applications* (New York: John Wiley, 1953).

Leslie Kish, *Survey Sampling* (New York: John Wiley, 1965).

Richard L. Schaeffer, William Mendenhall, and Lyman Ott, *Elementary Survey Sampling,* 2nd ed. (North Scituate, Mass: Duxbury Press, 1979).

Chapter 16

Collecting the Data: Field Procedures and Nonsampling Errors

Learning Objectives

Upon completing this chapter, you should be able to

1. Explain what is meant by sampling error.
2. Cite the two basic types of nonsampling errors and describe each.
3. Outline several ways in which noncoverage bias can be reduced.
4. Explain what is meant by error due to nonresponse.
5. Cite the standard definition for response rate.
6. Identify the two main sources of nonresponse bias.
7. Define what is meant by contact rate.
8. Cite some of the factors that may contribute to a respondent's refusal to participate in a study.
9. Identify three factors that may be a source of bias in the interviewer-interviewee interaction.
10. Discuss the types of interviewer behavior that may lead to response bias.

Case in Marketing Research

Sarah Cho waved good-bye to her teenaged son, Donald, and headed out to her car just as a cold rain started to fall. Settling behind the wheel of her aging Toyota, Sarah checked her supplies one last time—a map of the Greater Greenfield area, a dozen No. 2 pencils, a stack of questionnaires, and a ponderous manual of instructions.

Nervously she headed out of the driveway toward her first destination. All those hours in class and additional hours spent poring over her books at the kitchen table were about to pay off as she began her job as an official field interviewer for the U.S. Census Bureau.

Until she took the job as an interviewer, Sarah thought, like most people, that all the Census Bureau did was count noses every ten years. She was surprised to find that the Bureau also collects information for any federal department or agency that needs facts from the field.

Sarah was also surprised to find that a sizable percentage of the people in her training group shared a background similar to hers. Many of the trainees were middle-aged housewives with children who were teenagers or older.

For her first assignment, Sarah was to begin work gathering data for the Current Population Survey, a continuing program on which national unemployment figures are based. She had until Saturday to track down a list of people and ask them about their work status during the previous week.

Today Sarah was scheduled to interview a list of people in an affluent section of the city, Greenacre Hills. She had dressed in her best new suit, and eagerly looked forward to getting a peak inside the door of the large homes set back from the streets on manicured lawns.

Greenacre Hills had been experiencing rapid growth recently as its woodsy terrain gave way to pricey subdivisions. Much of the development was so new that city maps did not yet reflect the current streets. Sarah had only a list of building permits to guide her.

The first site on her list was identified only by a building permit number and the description, "450 feet from the intersection of Matawan and Ivanhoe Roads."

When Sarah finally found the specified location, she was bewildered to find only pine trees on the lot.

After getting no response at the nearest house, she proceeded to the next number on her list: permit number 4579, issued to a family named McNally. Heading east on Matawan, she spotted a mailbox with the same name on a location that appeared to be that described on the permit.

Excitedly, she pulled into the driveway and rang the bell. A harried young woman with a French accent opened the door.

Sarah explained that she was seeking Beatrice McNally. The woman responded that both McNallys were out of town, and she had been hired to take care of the children until the following week. When a crash from the kitchen was followed by the yelp of a child, the babysitter hurriedly excused herself and shut the door.

After failing to locate three more addresses in the Greenacre Hills area, and finding no one at home at two more, a tired, frustrated Sarah decided she needed help. After locating the town hall, she roamed the halls until she found the office of the building inspector.

Explaining her dilemma, she asked the town official to help her match building permits with current addresses. This time Sarah was lucky. Within half an hour he had converted the elusive numbers into concrete addresses and had even given Sarah directions on how to find the streets in question.

Armed with the new information, Sarah headed out into the pouring rain to once again stalk her quarry.

Discussion Issues

1. Besides not-at-homes and problems in coverage of the specified sampling areas, what other problems might field interviewers expect to encounter when gathering data?

2. What measures might be helpful in alleviating such problems?

3. What problems might interviewers encounter in personal or telephone surveys that may not be a problem in mail surveys? What particular problems might mail surveys pose?

Source: This fictitious case is based on the experiences of a census interviewer as described in Flora Gee, "Adventures of a Census Interviewer," *Across the Board*, 17 (February 1980), pp. 2–4 and 73.

The data collection task is the one that most often comes to mind when people think of marketing research. At this stage in the research process, some kind of a field force is used, operating either in the field or from an office as in a phone or mail survey. In this chapter we will focus on the various things that can go wrong in conducting a field study, with a special emphasis on sources of error we have not discussed in earlier chapters. A person who understands the potential sources of error in data collection will have insights that will be useful in evaluating the research information upon which decisions must be based.

◆ Impact and Importance of Nonsampling Errors

◆ **Sampling error**

Difference between the observed values of a variable and the long-run average of the observed values in repetitions of the measurement.

◆ **Nonsampling errors**

Errors that arise in research that are not due to sampling; nonsampling errors can occur because of errors in conception, logic, misinterpretation of replies, statistics, arithmetic and errors in tabulating or coding, or in reporting the results.

Two basic types of errors arise in research studies: sampling errors and nonsampling errors. The concept of **sampling error** underlies much of the discussion in Chapters 13, 14, and 15. Basic to that discussion was the concept of the sampling distribution of some statistic, be it the sample mean, sample proportion, or whatever. The sampling distribution arises because of sampling error. The sampling distribution reflects the fact that the different possible samples that could be drawn under the sampling plan will produce different estimates of the parameter. The statistic varies from sample to sample simply because we are only sampling part of the population in each case. Sampling error then is "the difference between the observed values of a variable and the long-run average of the observed values in repetitions of the measurement."[1] As we saw, sampling errors can be reduced by increasing sample size. The distribution of the sample statistic becomes more and more concentrated about the long-run average value, as the sample statistic is more equal from sample to sample when it is based on a larger number of observations.

Nonsampling errors reflect the many other kinds of error that arise in research, even when the survey is not based on a sample. They can be random or nonrandom. Nonrandom, nonsampling errors are the more troublesome of the two. Random

---

[1]Frederick Mosteller, "Nonsampling Errors," *Encyclopedia of Social Sciences* (New York: Macmillan, 1968), p. 113. See also Charles F. Turner and Elizabeth Martin, eds., *Surveying Subjective Phenomena, Vol. 1* (New York: Russell Sage Foundations, 1985).

errors produce estimates that vary from the true value; sometimes these estimates are above and sometimes below the true value, but on a random basis. The result is that, if there are no sampling errors, the sample estimate will equal the population value. Nonrandom, nonsampling errors, on the other hand, tend to produce mistakes only in one direction. They tend to bias the sample value away from the population parameter. Nonsampling errors can occur because of errors in conception, logic, misinterpretation of replies, statistics, arithmetic, errors in tabulation or coding, or errors in reporting the results. They are so pervasive that they have caused one writer to lament

> The roster of possible troubles seems only to grow with increasing knowledge. By participating in the work of a specific field, one can, in a few years, work up considerable methodological expertise, much of which has not been and is not likely to be written down. *To attempt to discuss every way a study can go wrong would be a hopeless venture.*[2] (emphasis added)

Not only are nonsampling errors pervasive, but they are not as manageable as sampling errors. Sampling errors decrease with increases in sample size. Nonsampling errors do not necessarily decrease with increases in sample size. They may, in fact, increase. Also, sampling errors can be estimated if probability sampling procedures are used. With nonsampling errors, it is difficult even to predict the direction, much less the size, of the error.

True, nonsampling errors bias the sample value away from the population parameter, but in many studies it is hard to see whether they cause underestimation or overestimation of the parameter. Nonsampling errors also distort the reliability of sample estimates. The bias they cause may increase the standard error of estimates of particular statistics to such an extent that the confidence interval estimates turn out to be faulty.

One study, the Consumer Savings Project, conducted at the University of Illinois, demonstrated striking evidence of this phenomenon. In that study, researchers contrasted consumers' reports of financial assets and debts with known data.

> The empirical studies presented . . . indicate in striking fashion that nonsampling errors are not simply a matter of theory, but do in fact exist and are mainly responsible for the pronounced tendency of survey data to understate aggregates. . . . Not only was this bias present in the survey data, but in many instances the contribution of nonsampling errors to the total variance in the data was so large as to *render meaningless confidence intervals computed by the usual statistical formulas* . . . the magnitude of this type of error *tends, if anything, to increase with sample size.*[3] (emphasis added)

Further, more sophisticated samples are not the answer to eliminating nonsampling errors.

> If the findings of this project are any indication, increasing attention must be given to the detection and correction of nonsampling errors. Such attention will be needed particularly in the conduct of large-scale, well-designed probability samples, for as the efficiency of a sample design increases and the size of sampling variances decreases, the effect of nonsampling errors becomes progressively more important. Since nonsampling variances are virtually unaffected by sample size, we are faced with the paradoxi-

---

[2]Mosteller, "Nonsampling Errors," p. 113

[3]Robert Ferber, *The Reliability of Consumer Reports of Financial Assets and Debts* (Urbana, Ill.: Bureau of Economic and Business Research, University of Illinois, 1966), p. 261. There was a series of studies with respect to the single objective. Ferber's monograph provides an overview of the studies and results, although there are six monographs in all.

cal situation that the more efficient is the sample design, the more important are non-sampling errors likely to be and the more meaningless are confidence interval computations based on the usual error formulas.[4]

In the University of Illinois study, the amount of nonsampling error could be calculated since the reports consumers gave of their financial assets and debts could be contrasted with actual data regarding their financial condition. But suppose such data were not available. Researchers may suspect that the responses they are eliciting are not accurate, but how are they to predict the direction of the error? Should they assume consumers are overstating their assets, for example, to impress the interviewer, or understating them for fear the IRS may get wind of the information. And if they are misrepresenting their assets, how is a researcher to determine the magnitude of this amount? Is it $10,000 over the real figure or $2,000 under? Or vice versa?

As you can begin to see, nonsampling errors are frequently the most important errors that arise in research. In special Census Bureau investigations of their size, for example, nonsampling errors were found to be ten times the magnitude of sampling errors.[5] This is not an unusual finding. Rather, a consistent finding is that nonsampling error is the major contributor to total survey error, while random sampling error has minimal impact.[6] Nonsampling errors can be reduced, but their reduction depends on improving method rather than increasing sample size. By understanding the sources of nonsampling errors, the analyst is in a better position to reduce them.

• Nonobservation error

Nonsampling error that arises because of nonresponse from some elements designated for inclusion in the sample.

• Observation error

Nonsampling error that arises because inaccurate information is secured from the sample elements or because errors are introduced in the processing of the data or in reporting the findings.

• Types of Nonsampling Errors

Figure 16.1 offers a general overview of nonsampling errors.[7] They are of two basic types—errors due to nonobservation or to observation. **Nonobservation errors** result from a failure to obtain data from parts of the survey population. Nonobservation errors can happen because part of the population of interest was not included, or because some elements designated for inclusion in the sample did not respond. **Observation errors** occur because inaccurate information is secured from the sample elements, or because errors are introduced in the processing of the data or in reporting the findings. In many ways, they are more troublesome than nonobservation errors. With nonobservation errors, we at least know we have a problem because of noncoverage or nonresponse. With observation errors, we may not even be aware that a problem exists. The very notion of an observation error rests on the presumption that there is indeed some "true" value for the variable or variables. An observational error, then, is simply the difference between the re-

---

[4]*Ibid.,* p. 266. Wiseman and McDonald make a similar point with the comment, "The use of very sophisticated sampling schemes when other aspects of the data collection effort are much less sophisticated may result in higher costs than are justified for the resultant data quality." See Frederick Wiseman and Philip McDonald, "Noncontact and Refusal Rates in Consumer Telephone Surveys," *Journal of Marketing Research,* 16 (November 1979), p. 483.

[5]W. H. Williams, "How Bad Can 'Good' Data Really Be?," *The American Statistician,* 32 (May 1978), p. 61.

[6]See, for example, Ronald Andersen, Judith Kasper, Martin R. Frankel and Associates, *Total Survey Error* (San Francisco: Jossey-Bass, 1979), or Henry Assael and John Keon, "Nonsampling vs. Sampling Errors in Survey Research," *Journal of Marketing,* 46 (Spring 1982), pp. 114–123.

[7]Figure 16.1 is adapted from Leslie Kish, *Survey Sampling* (New York: John Wiley, © 1965), p. 519, and is reprinted by permission of John Wiley & Sons, Inc. Kish's Chap. 13, "Biases and Nonsampling Errors," is particularly recommended for discussion of the biases arising from nonobservation.

Figure 16.1

Overview of
Nonsampling Errors

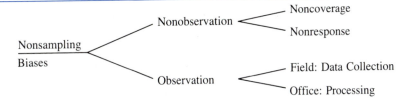

Source: Leslie Kish, *Survey Sampling* (New York: John Wiley & Sons, Inc., © 1965), p. 519. Reprinted by permission of John Wiley & Sons, Inc.

ported value and the "true" value. You can readily see that detection of an observation error places the researcher in the awkward position of knowing the very quantity the study is designed to estimate.

Nonobservation Errors

As is evident from Figure 16.1, there are two types of nonobservation errors: noncoverage errors and nonresponse errors. Each is capable of introducing significant bias in the results of a study, but analysts skilled enough to recognize the potential problem have several options for compensating for, or adjusting for, possible error.

⋆ Noncoverage error

Nonsampling error that arises because of a failure to include some units, or entire sections, of the defined survey population in the sampling frame.

Noncoverage Errors A source of significant error in a study can be noncoverage, but **noncoverage error** does not refer to sections of a population that are deliberately excluded from the survey, only those that were mistakenly excluded. Noncoverage, then, is essentially a sampling frame problem.

A good way to survey people is through the mail, but since the mailing list dictates the sampling frame, noncoverage errors can occur unless the mailing list is very specific.

For a general survey, for instance, noncoverage error might result from using a telephone directory for the sampling frame. Not every family has a phone, and some who have phones do not have them listed in the directory. Further, there are some important demographic differences between those having and not having phones.[8]

In a mail survey, where the mailing list dictates the sampling frame, noncoverage error can result from a mailing list that inadequately represents segments of the population. Experienced researchers know that rare is the mailing list that exactly captures the population that they wish to study, even though mailing lists are available for very specific population groups, as Table 16.1 indicates.

When the data are to be collected by personal interview, some form of area sample is typically used to pinpoint respondents. In this case, the sampling frame is one of areas, blocks, and dwelling units, rather than a list of respondents. However, this does not eliminate the incomplete frame problem. Maps of the city may not be totally current, and so the newest areas may not have a proper chance of being included in the sample. The instructions to the interviewer may not be sufficiently detailed. The direction, "Start at the northwest corner of the selected blocks, generate a random start, and take every fifth dwelling unit thereafter," may be inadequate to handle those blocks with a number of apartment units. The evidence indicates, for example, that lower-income households are avoided when the selection of households is made by the field staff rather than in the home office. Further, interviewers typically select the most accessible individuals within the household, contrary to instructions for random selection. This again means that a portion of the intended population is underrepresented in the study, while the accessible segment is overrepresented.

Nor is noncoverage bias eliminated in quota samples. Allowing interviewers flexibility in choosing respondents can open the door to substantial noncoverage bias. Interviewers typically underselect in both the high- and low-income classes. The research director may not discover this bias, since field staffers also have a tendency to falsify characteristics so that it appears that they interviewed the appropriate number of cases per cell. Further, the more elaborate and complex the quota sample, the more critical this "forcing" problem becomes. With three or four variables defining the individual cells, the interviewer may find it difficult to locate respondents who have all the prescribed characteristics, so they "cheat" a little bit on the characteristics defining difficult cells to fill.

• Overcoverage error

Nonsampling error that arises because of the duplication of elements in the list of sampling units.

Overcoverage error can arise because of duplication in the list of sampling units. Units with multiple entries in the sampling frame—for example, families with several phone listings—have a higher probability of being included in the sample than do sampling units with one listing. For most surveys, though, noncoverage is much more common and troublesome than overcoverage.

Noncoverage bias is not a problem in every survey. For some studies, clear, convenient, and complete sampling frames exist. For example, the department store wishing to conduct a study among its charge-account customers should have little trouble with frame bias. The sampling frame is simply those with charge accounts. There might be some difficulty in distinguishing active accounts from inactive accounts, but this problem can be addressed during the design stage of the study.

Similarly, the credit union in a firm should experience little noncoverage bias in conducting a study among its potential clientele. The population of interest here

---

[8]Randolph M. Grossman and Douglas K. Weiland, "The Use of Telephone Directories as a Sample Frame: Patterns of Bias Revisited," *Journal of Advertising,* 7 (Summer 1978), pp. 31–35; Patricia E. Moberg, "Biases in Unlisted Phone Numbers," *Journal of Advertising Research,* 22 (August–September 1982), pp. 51–55.

Table 16.1 Some Population Groups for Which Mailing Lists Are Available

Quantity		Price	Quantity		Price
550,000	**ATTORNEYS** (ALL)	$35/M	3,600	Auto Glass Replacement & Repair	$35/M
			9,600	Auto Muffler Shops	$35/M
355,000	Attorneys, Private Practice	$35/M	4,250	Auto Parking Lots & Garages	$35/M
300,000	Attorneys, American Bar Association Members		4,500	Auto Paint Shops	$35/M
	(Available by Specialty)	$45/M	45,350	Auto Parts & Supplies (Retail)	$35/M
203,200	Attorneys, Offices	$35/M	38,200	Auto Parts & Supplies (Wholesale)	$35/M
162,600	Attorneys, Individual Practice		154,000	Auto Repair Shops	$35/M
	(One Man Office)	$35/M	8,610	Auto Seat Cover, Top & Upholstery Shops	$35/M
240,400	Attorneys, Firms — Partners	$35/M	122,000	Auto Service Stations	$35/M
159,000	Attorneys, Senior Partners	$35/M	1,500	Auto Supply Chains	$75
40,600	Attorneys, Firms with 2 or more Attorneys	$35/M	36,350	Auto Towing & Wrecking	$35/M
24,100	Attorneys, Firms with 3 or more Attorneys	$35/M	35,600	Auto Telephone Licensees	$50/M
11,600	Attorneys, Firms with 5 or more Attorneys	$35/M	38,000	Auto Tire Dealers (Retail)	$35/M
7,650	Attorneys, Firms with 10 or more Attorneys	$40/M	5,500	Auto Tire Dealers (Wholesale)	$35/M
5,000	Attorneys, Firms with 15 or more Attorneys	$50/M	57,000	Auto Top & Body Repair	$35/M
3,700	Attorneys, Firms with 25 or more Attorneys	$60/M	12,500	Auto Transmission Shops	$35/M
135	Attorneys, Firms with 100 or more Attorneys	$75	21,800	Auto Truck Dealers	$35/M
42,000	Attorneys, Women	$35/M	37,000	Auto & Truck Renting & Leasing	$35/M
22,550	Attorneys, Administrative, Contract	$35/M	55,000,000	Automobile Owners, By Make, Year, Model	Inquire
23,800	Attorneys, Anti-Trust, Mergers & Acquisitions	$35/M	27,000	Aviation Executives	$35/M
27,000	Attorneys, Appeals	$35/M	3,000	Aviation Parts Mfrs.	$40/M
53,200	Attorneys, Banking, Securities	$35/M	9,100	Aviation Tower Operators	$35/M
21,500	Attorneys, Bankruptcy	$35/M	5,200	Awnings & Canopies Dealers	$35/M
3,600	Attorneys, Civil Rights	$50/M			
1,430	Attorneys, Communications, Federal	$75		**B**	
112,000	Attorneys, Corporate, Business	$35/M	12,500	Babies Wear Retail	$35/M
23,000	Attorneys, Corporation Staff (In-House)	$35/M	32,700	Bakeries, Retail	$35/M
22,000	Attorneys, Criminal	$35/M	6,500	Bakery Products Mfrs.	$35/M
2,950	Attorneys, Entertainment, Literary	$50/M	2,450	Balloon (Air) Owners	$40/M
20,500	Attorneys, Environmental, Energy	$35/M	10,500	Band Directors, High School	$35/M
81,000	Attorneys, Probate, Trust & Estate	$35/M			
22,000	Attorneys, Family Law, Divorce	$35/M		**BANKS**	
19,800	Attorneys, Government, All Levels	$35/M	13,940	Banks, Main Offices	$35/M
6,350	Attorneys, Health Care	$35/M	406	Banks with Assets $1 Billion or more	$75
1,200	Attorneys, Immigration	$75	653	Banks with Assets $500 Million or more	$75
70,500	Attorneys, Insurance, Negligence	$35/M	2,633	Banks with Assets $100 Million or more	$40/M
10,100	Attorneys, International Law, Foreign Trade	$35/M	3,529	Banks with Assets $75 Million or more	$40/M
23,750	Attorneys, Labor Relations, Arbitration	$35/M	5,259	Banks with Assets $50 Million or more	$35/M
28,000	Attorneys, Litigation	$35/M	8,772	Banks with Assets $25 Million or more	$35/M
12,100	Attorneys, Maritime, Admiralty	$35/M	12,517	Banks with Assets $10 Million or more	$35/M
10,200	Attorneys, Medical Malpractice	$50/M	13,620	Banks with Assets $5 Million or more	$35/M
12,000	Attorneys, Patent	$35/M	298	Banks with Assets less than $5 Million	$75
9,600	Attorneys, Public Utility, Communications	$35/M	23,250	Banks, Branches	$35/M
82,000	Attorneys, Real Estate, Property	$35/M	20,000	Banks, Cashiers	$35/M
52,000	Attorneys, Taxation	$35/M	200,000	Banks, Executives	$35/M
15,200	Attorneys, Tax Shelter	$50/M	64,500	Banks, Executives, Women	$35/M
10,500	Attorneys, Transportation	$35/M	3,654	Banks, Savings & Loan (HQ)	$35/M
81,000	Attorneys, Trial	$35/M	20,565	Banks, Savings & Loan (Branches)	$35/M
80,000	Attorneys, Young	$40/M	9,300	Banks, Trust Officers	$35/M
7,550	Auctioneers & Liquidators	$35/M	7,100	Barber & Beauty Supplies	$35/M
1,500	Audio Visual Dealers	$75	66,000	Barber Shops	$35/M
8,800	Audio Visual Education Directors	$40/M	91,100	Bars, Taverns, Cocktail Lounges	$35/M
3,000	Auditoriums, Arenas, Convention Halls	$35/M	2,200	Beauty Schools	$35/M
15,200	Auditors, Internal	$35/M	171,000	Beauty Shops	$35/M
10,750	Auditors, Internal (Foreign)	$95/M	130	Beer Brewers	$75
26,400	Auto Dealers, New Cars	$35/M	6,000	Beer Distributors	$35/M
56,500	Auto Dealers, Used Cars	$35/M	37,000	Behavioral Scientists	$35/M
36,000	Auto Dealers, Used, Independent	$40/M	150	Better Business Bureaus	$75
2,200	Auto Driving Schools	$35/M	1,800	Beverage Bottlers & Distributors	$75

Source: Alvin B. Zeller, Inc. 37 East 28th Street, New York, NY 10016. Reprinted with permission.

would be the firm's employees, and it could be expected that the list of employees would be current and accurate since it is needed to generate the payroll.

Noncoverage bias raises two questions for the researcher: (1) How pervasive is it likely to be? (2) What can be done to reduce it? One difficulty is that its magnitude can be estimated only by comparing the sample survey results with some outside criterion. The outside criterion can in turn be established through an auxiliary quality check of a portion of the results, or it may be available from another reliable and current study, such as the population census. Comparison with the census or another large sample, though, means that the basic sampling units must be similar in terms of operational definitions. If researchers plan to make such comparisons, they may want to plan the study in such a way that the bases used (e.g., dwellings or persons) lend themselves to effective comparisons.

Given that noncoverage bias is likely, what can the researcher do to lessen its effect? The most obvious step, of course, is to improve the quality of the sampling frame. This may mean taking the time to bring available city maps up to date, or it may mean taking a sample to check the quality and representativeness of a mailing list with respect to a target population. The unlisted-number problem common to telephone surveys can be handled by random-digit or plus-one dialing, although this will not provide adequate sample representation of those without phones.

There are usually limits to the degree to which an imperfect sampling frame can be improved. Once these limits are reached, the researcher can attempt to reduce noncoverage bias still further through the selection of sampling units or the adjustment of the results. When sampling from lists, for example, analysts often encounter the problem that both unwanted ineligibles and duplicates are included on the list, while some members of the target population are excluded. The first corrective step for this problem is to update the list, using supplementary sources if possible. While this would help reduce one aspect of the problem (excluded members), it might do little to eliminate ineligibles and duplicates. When the sample is drawn, however, all ineligibles can be ignored. Beware of the temptation to substitute the next name on the list since this would bias selection toward those elements that follow ineligible listings. The correct procedure is to draw another element randomly, if simple random selection procedures are being used. If systematic sampling procedures are being used, the sampling interval should be adjusted before the fact to allow for the percentage of ineligibles.

The problem of duplicates is handled by adjustment. Specifically, the results are weighted by the inverse of the probability of selection. In a study using a list of car registrations, for example, each contacted respondent would be asked, "How many cars do you own?" The response of someone who said two would be weighted by $\frac{1}{2}$, while that of someone who said three would be weighted by $\frac{1}{3}$.[9]

The appropriate sampling and adjustment procedures to account for inadequate sampling frames can become quite technical in complex sample designs and fall largely in the domain of the sampling specialist. We shall consequently not delve into these processes but shall simply note that noncoverage bias:

1. Is a nonsampling error and is therefore not dealt with in our standard error formulas.

2. Is not likely to be eliminated by increasing the sample size.

_____

[9]The general adjustment procedure for dealing with the problem of duplicates on a list is to weight sample elements discovered to have been listed k times by $1/k$. Sudman, *Applied Sampling,* p. 63. Most of the standard computer packages for statistically analyzing the data contain mechanisms by which the analyst can specify the weight to be applied to each sample observation.

Figure 16.2   Possible Outcomes When Attempting to Contact Respondents for Telephone Surveys

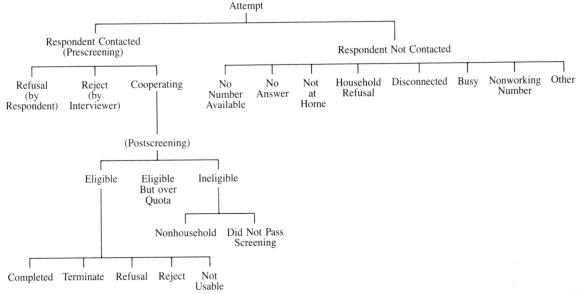

Source: Frederick Wiseman and Philip McDonald, *Toward the Development of Industry Standards for Response and Nonresponse Rates* (Cambridge, Mass.: Marketing Science Institute, 1980), p. 29

3. Can be of considerable magnitude.

4. Can be reduced, but not necessarily eliminated, by recognizing its existence, working to improve the sampling frame, and employing a sampling specialist to help reduce, through the sampling procedure, and adjust, through analysis, the remaining frame imperfections.[10]

• Nonresponse error

Nonsampling error that represents a failure to obtain information from some elements of the population that were selected and designated for the sample.

Nonresponse Errors Another source of nonobservation bias is **nonresponse error,** which represents a failure to obtain information from some elements of the population that were selected and designated for the sample. The first hurdle to overcome in dealing with nonresponse errors is simply anticipating all the things that can go wrong with an attempt to contact a designated respondent. Figure 16.2, for example, depicts the various outcomes of an attempted telephone contact. There is such a bewildering array of alternatives that even calculating a measure of the extent of the nonresponse problem becomes difficult.

In the late 1970s, several researchers became concerned that the marketing research industry had no uniform standard for measuring rates of response and nonresponse. Because the various research organizations used widely differing definitions and methods for calculating nonresponse, it was impossible to get an accurate assessment of the nonresponse problem. In an attempt to get a handle on the problem, the researchers conducted a study among a sample of members of the Council of American Survey Research Organizations (CASRO) and leading user companies. Each member was mailed a questionnaire that displayed actual contact and response data from three different telephone surveys, a telephone directory sample, a ran-

---

[10]Kish, *Survey Sampling,* pp. 530–531, offers a number of suggestions for decreasing the effect of noncoverage, as well as some general comments regarding the extent of noncoverage bias.

dom-digit sample, and a list sample. Respondents were asked to calculate the response, contact, completion, and refusal rates for each of the three surveys.[11] (Each of these rates is defined later in this text.) The difference in results was rather startling. The upper part of Table 16.2 displays the raw data from the telephone directory sample. Using the very same data, one responding organization reported the **response rate**—which is the number of interviews divided by the number of contacts—as 12 percent while another reported 90 percent. Nor was there agreement among the other firms. No more than three firms out of forty agreed on any single definition of the response rate, and those firms used three different definitions to arrive at their answers. The lower part of Table 16.2 displays the three most frequently used definitions and the definitions producing the minimum and maximum response rates.

Not only does the variation in definitions cause confusion when nonresponse rates are reported for a survey, but it also makes the treatment of the nonresponse error problem more difficult. It becomes hard to discern, for instance, whether a

* **Response rate**

The number of completed interviews with responding units divided by the number of eligible responding units in the sample.

---

[11]Frederick Wiseman and Philip McDonald, *Toward the Development of Industry Standards for Response and Nonresponse Rates* (Cambridge, Mass.: Marketing Science Institute, 1980).

Research Window 16.1
A Day in the Life of a Telephone Interviewer

Next time a caller interrupts your dinner to ask your opinion on brands of dishwashing detergent, be kind. It's not easy being a telephone interviewer, as Bernice Kanner, a journalist who frequently writes about advertising and marketing, found out when she volunteered to collect data for Burke Marketing Services, a large Cincinnati-based marketing research firm.

When Kanner sat down at the phone, Burke's director of national telephone research explained how the company's system works.

"We've had 2.5 million phone numbers randomly drawn," he said. "Our researchers work from page printouts, and by the time you sit down to dial, the randomization has already taken place." If the phone goes unanswered, Burke researchers try later, up to three times, he explained. "Otherwise you'd overly represent the homebound—the elderly, families with a baby or an invalid, or the unemployed," he said.

Kanner sat down with her list and began calling. Her impressions follow.

Dialing during the day is frustrating: in 62 percent of American households both men and women work. For those who don't, a Burke call is often the high point of the day. Monday night is peak dialing time, with all Burke's 117 stations busy; Tuesday night is second-best, followed by Sunday afternoon. Friday night is the worst: people tend to be tipsy or rushed. Calls are never made on Super Bowl Sunday, and if there's a flood in Mississippi, that area code is skipped.

Despite the intrusion—the average interview lasts seven to twelve minutes—few of those reached protest. Typically, 7 percent refuse to participate. One told me, "I'm not interested, babe." Some evade the issue by insisting that they never use the type of product in question. And wives often suspect the motives of women asking to speak to their husbands about TV-viewing habits. "Talk to me," they say. "I know all his habits."

And though the interviews sound robotized and repetitious, only 5 to 8 percent of those being interviewed get impatient. Fewer than 1 percent get furious enough to hang up. "It's remarkable how helpful people are," said the research director. "Some lug twenty-pound boxes of the product to the phone to read back number codes."

One helped from the next world. A Burke researcher had sent two cake mixes to a woman who subsequently died. Her husband said she had wanted Burke to know she liked the "A" particular method proved effective, or whether a different definition was responsible for a lower nonresponse error in a particular study. In an attempt to help to standardize findings so as to improve the practice of survey research, a special CASRO task force developed a definition of response rate that the industry is being encouraged to embrace as the standard definition. It follows:[12]

$$\text{response rate} = \frac{\text{number of completed interviews with responding units}}{\text{number of eligible responding units in the sample}}$$

The key requirement in accurately calculating the response rate is to properly handle eligibles. Table 16.3 shows how to calculate the response rate properly depending on whether there is or is not an eligibility requirement for inclusion in the sample.

Nonresponse is a problem in any survey in which it occurs because it raises the question of whether those who did respond are different in some important way

---

[12]"On the Definition of Response Rates," *CASRO Special Report* (Port Jefferson, N.Y.: The Council of American Survey Research Organizations, 1982).

---

mix better. Unfortunately, the results couldn't be used. She hadn't indicated why she'd picked that mix.

The Burke job manager gave Kanner a distilled version of the usual four-day training session on proper interviewing techniques.

"When you ask a question about shampoo, always add 'to wash your hair,'" she advised. A lot of people use shampoo for bubble bath. "Clarify by repeating the question. Or create a new question from the general-help card." She thrust one at Kanner, a list of directions and advice to keep in front of her while making calls.

"The main requisite is a conversational tone," the group manager said. What to do if the respondent gets peeved at seeming repetition? "Say you're just checking. Don't be shy about asking questions twice. That shows that you really want to know. Don't thank people for their time — they'll be less willing to volunteer it later. And for heaven's sake, don't lead the witness."

Kanner watched while the job manager demonstrated the process.

The first five calls were to out-of-service numbers, and the next two went unanswered. On the eighth try, a man was reached who didn't want to get involved. The ninth call hit pay dirt. The manager plunged into her spiel about dishwashing liquid, repeating the choices after each question: completely, somewhat, slightly, or not at all. She then asked about the respondent's age, education, job, and income. One person reached said she used whatever detergent she could buy with coupons. Unfortunately, the questionnaire didn't provide any way of recording that.

When Kanner took the phone, she hit five straight disconnecteds, several no-answers, and, finally, one woman who swore by Joy. Another said she was a senior citizen. "Do I still count?" she inquired.

The people at Burke believe their research benefits consumers as well as advertisers. "We want people to know that their opinion counts," said the research director. "The worst nightmare I have is that we connect with 1,000 people who are all D.K.'s [don't knows], who are all people with no opinion."

Source: This is a fictitious case based on Bernice Kanner, "What Makes an Ad Work," *New York,* 16 (May 23, 1983), pp. 16–20.

Table 16.2   Response Rate Calculations for Telephone Directory Sample

Panel A: Outcome of Telephone Call

Disconnected/nonworking telephone number	426
Household refusal	153
No answer, busy, not at home	1,757
Interviewer reject (language barrier, hard of hearing, . . .)	187
Respondent refusal	711
Ineligible respondent	366
Termination by respondent	74
Completed interview	501
Total	4,175

Panel B: Most Frequent, Minimum, and Maximum Response Rates

Most frequent

$$\frac{\text{Household refusals + Rejects + Refusals + Ineligibles + Terminations + Completed interviews}}{\text{All}} = \quad (1)$$

$$\frac{153 + 187 + 711 + 366 + 74 + 501}{\text{All}} = 48\%$$

$$\frac{\text{Rejects + Refusals + Ineligibles + Terminations + Completed interviews}}{\text{All}} = \quad (2)$$

$$\frac{187 + 711 + 366 + 74 + 501}{4,175} = 44\%$$

$$\frac{\text{Completed interviews}}{\text{All}} = \frac{501}{4,175} = 12\% \quad (3)$$

Minimum

$$\frac{\text{Completed interviews}}{\text{All}} = \frac{501}{4,175} = 12\%$$

Maximum

$$\frac{\text{Refusals + Ineligibles + Termination + Completed interviews}}{\text{Rejects + Refusals + Ineligibles + Termination + Completed interviews}} =$$

$$\frac{711 + 366 + 74 + 501}{187 + 711 + 366 + 74 + 501} = 90\%$$

Source: Frederick Wiseman and Philip McDonald, *Toward the Development of Industry Standards for Response and Nonresponse Rates* (Cambridge, Mass.: Marketing Science Institute, 1980), pp. 12 and 19. Reprinted with permission.

from those who did not respond. This is, of course, a question we cannot answer, although study after study has indicated that the assumption that those who did not respond were in fact equal to those who did is risky.

The two main sources of nonresponse bias are not-at-homes and refusals. Nonresponse bias can arise with studies using personal interviews, telephone, or mail surveys to secure the data. With mail surveys, though, the not-at-home problem becomes one of nonreceipt of the questionnaire. The questionnaire may simply have been lost in the mail, in which case the nonsampling error could be considered random and nonbiasing, or there may be more fundamental reasons for nonreceipt:

Table 16.3   The Impact of an Eligibility Requirement on the Calculation of the Response Rate

Example 1. Single-stage Sample, No Eligibility Requirement

Suppose a survey is conducted to obtain 1,000 interviews with subscribers of a particular magazine. A random sample of $n = 1,000$ is selected, and the initial data collection effort produces the following results.

Completed interviews   = 660
Refusals   = 115
Respondents not contacted = 225

For each of the 340 nonrespondents, substitute subscribers are selected until a completed interview is obtained. Assume that in this follow-up data collection effort 600 substitute names are required to secure the 340 interviews. The recommended response rate is:

$$660/1,000 = 66.0\%$$

and not

$$1,000/1,600 = 62.5\%$$

Example 2. Single-stage Sample, Eligibility Requirement

From a list of registered voters, a sample of $n = 900$ names is selected. Eligible respondents are defined as those planning to vote in an upcoming election. Assume the data collection effort produces the following results.

Completed interviews   = 300
Not contacted   = 250
Refused, eligibility not determined = 150
Ineligible   = 200

The recommended response rate is:

$$\frac{300}{300 + \left[\dfrac{300}{300 + 200}\right](250 + 150)} = \frac{300}{300 + 240} = 55.5\%.$$

As indicated, when using an eligibility requirement one first must estimate the number of eligibles among the nonrespondents. This is done by using the eligibility percentage, $(300/500) = 60\%$, obtained among persons successfully screened and applying this percentage to the nonrespondents. Thus, of the 400 nonrespondents, 60% (240) are estimated to have been eligible and the estimated response rate becomes (300/540) or 55.5%.

Source: Frederick Wiseman and Maryann Billington, "Comment on a Standard Definition of Response Rates," *Journal of Marketing Research*, 21 (August 1984), p. 337. Published by the American Marketing Association.

the addressee may have moved or died. These latter conditions would be a source of systematic, nonsampling error.

Not-at-Homes Replies will not be secured from some designated sampling units because the respondent will not be at home when the interviewer calls. The empirical evidence indicates that the percentage of **not-at-homes** has been increasing for a long time.[13] Obviously, much depends upon the nature of the designated respondent and the time of the call. Married women with young children are more apt to be at home during the day on weekdays than are men, married women without children, or single women. The probability of finding someone at home is also greater for low-income families and for rural families. Seasonal variations, particu-

• Not-at-homes

Nonsampling error that arises when replies are not secured from some designated sampling units because the respondents are not at home when the interviewer calls.

---

[13]Charlotte G. Steeh, "Trends in Nonresponse Rates," *Public Opinion Quarterly*, 45 (Spring 1981), pp. 40–57.

larly during the holidays, occur, as do weekday-to-weekend variations.[14] Further, it is much easier to find a "responsible adult" at home than a specific type of respondent, and thus the choice of the elementary sampling unit is key in the not-at-home problem.

Several things can be done to reduce the incidence of not-at-homes. For example, in some studies the interviewer might make an appointment in advance with the respondent. While this approach is particularly valuable in surveys of busy executives, it may not be justifiable in an ordinary consumer survey. A commonly used technique in the latter instance is the callback, which is particularly effective if the callback (preferably callbacks) is made at a different time than the original call. As a matter of fact, the nonresponse problem due to not-at-homes is so acute and so important to the accuracy of most surveys that one leading expert has suggested that small samples with four to six callbacks are more efficient than large samples without callbacks, unless the percentage of initial response can be increased considerably above normal levels.[15] Some data indicate, for example, that four to five calls are often needed to reach three-fourths of the sample of households (see Table 16.4).

An alternative to the *straight callback* is the *modified callback*. If the initial contact attempt and first few callbacks were made by an interviewer and a contact was not established, the interviewer might simply mail a self-administered questionnaire with a stamped, self-addressed envelope (or leave one at the door if an in-person survey is being made). If the not-at-home is simply a "designated-respondent-absent" rather than a "nobody-at-home," the interviewer can use the opportunity to inquire about the respondent's hours of availability.

One technique that is sometimes naively suggested for handling the not-at-homes is to substitute the neighboring dwelling unit, or, in a telephone survey, to call the next name on the list. This is a very poor way of handling the not-at-home condition. All it does is substitute more at-homes (who may be different from the not-at-homes in a number of important characteristics) for the population segment we are in fact trying to reach. This increases the proportion of at-homes in the sample and, in effect, aggravates the problem instead of solving it.

The proportion of reported not-at-homes is likely to depend on the interviewer's skill and the judgment used in scheduling initial contacts and callbacks. This suggests that one way of reducing not-at-home nonresponse bias is by better interviewer training, particularly with respect to how to schedule callbacks more efficiently.

The fact that interviewer effectiveness affects the number of not-at-homes also suggests one measure by which interviewers themselves can be compared and evaluated: by calculating the **contact rate** (K), which is the percentage of eligible as-

• Contact rate *(K)*

Measure used to evaluate and compare the effectiveness of interviewers in making contact with designated respondents; K = number of sample units contacted/total number of eligible sample units approached.

---

[14]The publication by the Bureau of the Census, *Who's Home When* (Washington: U.S. Government Printing Office, 1973), which contains data on the time of day when individuals with given socioeconomic characteristics may be expected to be home, is useful for planning personal or telephone interviews. See also M. F. Weeks, B. L. Jones, R. E. Folsum, Jr., and C. H. Benrud, "Optimal Times to Contact Sample Households," *Public Opinion Quarterly,* 44 (Spring 1980), pp. 101–114, while the report "Identifying Monthly Response Rates Aids in Mail Planning," *Specialty Advertising Report,* 15 (4th Quarter, 1979), contains a useful table for scheduling mail studies to coincide with the months in which people are most likely to respond.

[15]W. Edwards Deming, "On a Probability Mechanism to Attain an Economic Balance between the Resultant Error of Response and the Bias of Nonresponse," *Journal of the American Statistical Association,* 48 (December 1953), pp. 766–767. See also Benjamin Lipstein, "In Defense of Small Samples," *Journal of Advertising Research,* 15 (February 1975), pp. 33–40; and William C. Dunkelburg and George S. Day, "Nonresponse Bias and Callbacks in Sample Surveys," *Journal of Marketing Research,* 10 (May 1973), pp. 160–168, a study that provides "evidence on the rate at which sample values converge on their population distribution as the number of callbacks increases."

Table 16.4   Percentage of Sample Homes Reached with Each Call in Personal Interview and Telephone Surveys

Call	Personal Interview		Telephone	
	Percent	Cumulative Percent	Percent	Cumulative Percent
1	25	25	24	24
2	25	50	18	42
3	18	68	14	56
4	11	79	11	67
5	7	86	8	75
6	5	91	6	81
7	3	94	5	86
8	6	100	3	89[a]

[a]It took 17 calls to reach all the homes in the telephone survey.
Source: Robert M. Groves and Robert L. Kahn, *Surveys by Telephone* (Orlando, Fla.: Academic Press, 1979), pp. 56 and 58.

signments in which the interviewer makes contact with the designated respondent; that is,

$$K = \frac{\text{number of sample units contacted}}{\text{total number of eligible sample units approached}}$$

The contact rate measures the interviewer's persistence. Interviewers can be compared with respect to their contact rates and corrective measures can often be taken on that basis. The field supervisor may want to investigate the reasons for any individual interviewer's low contact rate. Perhaps this interviewer is operating in a traditionally high not-at-home area, such as a high-income section of an urban area. Alternatively, by examining the call reports for time of each call, the trouble may be traced to poor follow-up procedures. This condition would suggest additional training is necessary, which might then be provided by the field supervisor while the study is still in progress. The contact rate can also be used to evaluate an entire study with respect to the potential nonresponse caused by not-at-homes.

Refusals In almost every study, some respondents will refuse to participate. The rate of **refusals** will depend, among other things, on the nature of the respondent, the nature of the organization sponsoring the research, the circumstances surrounding the contact, the nature of the subject under investigation, and the skill of the interviewer.

The method used to collect the data also makes a difference. The empirical evidence indicates, for example, that personal interviews are most effective, and mail questionnaires least effective, in generating response. Telephone interviews are somewhat less successful on the average (about 10 percent) than personal interviews in getting target respondents to cooperate.[16]

◆ Refusals

Nonsampling error that arises because some designated respondents refuse to participate in the study.

---

[16]Julie Yu and Harris Cooper, "A Quantitative Review of Research Design Effects on Response Rates to Questionnaires," *Journal of Marketing Research,* 20 (February 1983), pp. 36–44.

Although different data-collection techniques will influence the types of people likely to cooperate in a survey, there does seem to be a tendency for females, non-whites, those who are less well-educated, who have lower incomes, and who are older, to be more likely to refuse to participate.[17]

The type of organization sponsoring the research can also make a difference in the number of refusals. People not only report differently to different sponsors, but

---

[17]T. De Maio, "Refusals: Who, Where, and Why," *Public Opinion Quarterly,* 44 (Summer 1980), pp. 223–233.

Back to the Case

After her frustrating day in Greenacre Hills, Sarah was almost looking forward to canvassing the Dixmont section of the city. Granted that it was a low-income neighborhood with a fairly high crime rate, but at least the houses were close together on streets that showed up on city maps, Sarah thought to herself.

Her first stop was a run-down brownstone with a malfunctioning doorbell. Since the lock on the entry-way door was also broken, she went inside and found the name she was looking for on the bank of mailboxes in the lobby.

Knocking on the door, Sarah was surprised to hear a frightened voice inside ask, "Who is it?"

"U.S. Census Bureau, miss," Sarah responded. "I need to ask a Josephine Chavez some questions."

"Let me see some identification," the woman demanded.

Sarah held her ID card up to the peephole in the door.

"Wait there," the woman said.

Sarah waited. And waited. After ten minutes, she knocked on the

door again. "Ms. Chavez? May I please talk to you?" she asked.

Just then Sarah heard footsteps on the stairway. Two uniformed policemen approached her and demanded to know what she was doing.

"I'm just a census interviewer," Sarah said, showing her ID.

"Sorry, lady," one of the officers said. "There have been a lot of robberies in this neighborhood, and people are understandably suspicious of people trying to get in their apartments.

"It's okay, Mrs. Chavez," the officer called through the door. "She's legitimate."

After conducting the interview with Mrs. Chavez, Sarah moved on to a section of dilapidated three-story buildings in search of Doris Simpson.

To her relief, Sarah easily found the address in question and was happy to see a light on in the front room.

In response to her knock, a gray-haired woman in a soiled housedress peeked out from behind a tattered curtain. "Go away. We don't want any," she

snarled.

"I'm not selling anything," Sarah said. "I'm from the Census Bureau. I just want to ask you some questions."

"We don't talk to no Asians," the woman said. "Git outta here, or I'll sic Sluggo on you."

Taking one glance at the vicious-looking mutt at the woman's feet. Sarah decided caution was more important than data and hurried down the steps.

There are a variety of reasons why respondents may refuse to participate in interviews. In urban areas, crime may make residents fearful of answering the door. Other people may fear that their answers will be used against them, or they may be reluctant to devote the amount of time necessary to completing the interview. In some cases, respondents may refuse to answer because they don't like the study's sponsor or the topic under investigation. In others, certain characteristics of the interviewer may bias the respondent against participation in the study.

they may also make their decision on whether or not to respond on the basis of who the sponsor is.

Sometimes the circumstances surrounding the contact can cause a refusal. A respondent may be busy, tired, or sick when contacted. And the subject of the research also affects the refusal rate. Those interested in the subject are most likely to respond. On the other hand, nonresponse tends to increase with the sensitivity of the information being sought.

Finally, interviewers themselves can have a significant impact on the number of refusals they obtain. Their approach, manner, and even their own demographic characteristics can affect a respondent's willingness to participate.

What can be done to correct the nonresponse bias introduced when designated respondents refuse their participation? There seem to be three available strategies:

1. The initial response rate can be increased.

2. The impact of refusals can be reduced through follow-up.

3. The obtained information can be extrapolated to allow for nonresponse.

Increasing Initial Response Rate   Improving the circumstances surrounding an interview or increasing the training of interviewers are logical ways to increase the response rate, but the nature of the respondent would seem to be one factor strictly beyond the researcher's control. After all, the problem dictates the target population, and this population is likely to contain households with different educational levels, income levels, cultural and occupational backgrounds, and so forth. However, the task is not as hopeless as it might seem. As will be shown later when we examine a model for interviewer-interviewee interaction, the interviewee's cooperation can be encouraged by an "appropriate choice" of interviewer. Cooperation can also be encouraged by convincing respondents of the value of the research and the importance of their participation. Advance notice may help, too.

Evidence suggests that the more information interviewers provide about the content and purpose of the survey, the higher the response rate will be in both personal and telephone interviews. A guarantee of confidentiality will secure further responses, since some individuals refuse to participate because they do not wish to be identified with their responses. Moreover, the research suggests that monetary incentives are effective in increasing response rates in mail surveys.[18] Interestingly, they are not effective when personal interviews are being used, except when the interviewing is being conducted at shopping malls.[19]

If the identification of the organization sponsoring the research is likely to increase nonresponse, researchers can overcome this bias by concealing that information or by hiring a professional research organization to conduct the field study. This is one reason why companies with established, sophisticated research departments of their own sometimes employ research firms to collect data.

It is difficult to generalize about the effectiveness of various inducements in increasing the response rate, because the effects of each technique are different from

[18]James R. Chromy and Daniel G. Horowitz, "The Use of Monetary Incentives in National Assessment Household Surveys," *Journal of the American Statistical Association,* 73 (September 1978), pp. 473–478; J. Duncan, "Mail Questionnaires in Survey Research: A Review of Response Inducement Techniques," *Journal of Management,* 5 (September 1979), pp. 39–55; and *The Use of Monetary and Other Gift Incentives in Mail Surveys: An Annotated Bibliography* (Monticello, Ill.: Vance Bibliographies, 1979).

[19]Frederick Wiseman, Marianne Schafer, and Richard Schafer, "An Experimental Test of the Effects of a Monetary Incentive on Cooperation Rates and Data Collection Costs in Central Location Interviewing," *Journal of Marketing Research,* 20 (November 1983), pp. 439–442.

Table 16.5   Impact of Selected Techniques on Response Rates

Techniques	Number of Response Rates Included in the Averages	Average Net Difference in Response Rates
Monetary Incentives		
Use/no use	49/30	15.3
Prepaid/not used	33/22	15.6
Promised/not used	13/7	5.8
Nonmonetary Incentives		
Premium/no premium	5/5	9.2
Offer of survey results/no offer	12/12	−2.6[a]
Response Facilitators		
Prior notification of survey/no prior notification	10/9	8.1
Foot-in-the-door/no prior request for respondent to do an initial task	34/12	18.3
Personalized cover letter/cover letter not personalized	35/32	6.6
Respondent promised anonymity/anonymity not promised	8/7	−0.4[a]
Deadline for responding specified/deadline not specified	7/7	−0.7[a]
Return postage provided/return postage not provided	6/5	1.3[a]
Follow-up letter sent/follow-up letter not sent	16/14	17.9

[a]Not a statistically significant difference.

Source: Developed from the data in Julie Yu and Harris Cooper, "A Quantitative Review of Research Design Effects on Response Rates to Questionnaires," *Journal of Marketing Research,* 20 (February 1983), pp. 36–44.

survey to survey. The data in Table 16.5 are interesting in this regard. In this quantitative analysis of the published literature on response rates from 1965 to 1981, some studies reported response rates for several different survey techniques.[20] Each response rate was treated as one observation when this occurred. The table looks at the average net difference in response rates when the technique was used, versus when it was absent. It suggests that on average, the three most effective ways to increase the response rate in a given study are (1) to get a "foot in the door" by having respondents comply with some small request before presenting them with the larger survey, (2) to follow up the initial request for cooperation with a letter to those who did not respond to the initial request, and (3) to offer a monetary incentive. Unfortunately, the study did not investigate whether the effectiveness of certain inducement techniques depended upon the method of data collection being used.

Increasing Response Rate by Follow-up   In some cases, the circumstances surrounding a contact are responsible for a respondent's refusal to participate. Since these circumstances may be temporary or changeable, follow-up actions may elicit a later response and thus increase the overall response rate. If a respondent declined

---

[20]Yu and Cooper, "A Quantitative Review of Research Design Effects."

participation because he or she was busy or sick, a callback at a different time or using a different approach may be enough to secure cooperation. In a mail survey, this may mean a follow-up mailing at a more convenient time. The key to the success of this follow-up may be appropriate training and control of the field staff.

Less can be done with the subject of the research itself if it is the source of nonresponse bias, since it is dictated by the problem to be solved. A sensitive research subject or one of little interest to the respondents is likely to elicit a high rate of refusals. However, the researcher should not overlook any opportunities of making the study more interesting—for example, by eliminating unnecessary questions.

If a respondent has refused to participate in a personal interview or a telephone survey for reasons other than circumstances, callbacks will be less successful. This is not so with mail surveys. Frequently responses are obtained with the second and third mailings from those who did not respond to the initial mailing. Of course, follow-up in a mail survey requires identification of those not responding earlier, which in turn requires identification of those who did respond, and we have already seen that reluctance to be identified may cause a refusal. Thus, identification of the respondents, which may serve to decrease one source of nonresponse, may increase another. The alternative, which is to send each new mailing to each designated sample member without screening those who have responded previously, can be expensive for the research organization and frustrating for the respondent.

Adjusting Results to Correct for Nonresponse A third strategy for correcting nonresponse bias involves estimating its effects and then adjusting the results.[21] Suppose that in estimating the mean income for some population, one secured responses from only a portion (p_r) of some designated sample. The proportion not responding could then be denoted p_{nr}. If $\bar{x}_r$ is the mean income of those responding, and $\bar{x}_{nr}$ the mean income of those not responding, then the overall mean would be

$$\bar{x} = p_r\bar{x}_r + p_{nr}\bar{x}_{nr}$$

This computation, of course, assumes that $\bar{x}_{nr}$ is known or at least can be estimated. An intensive follow-up of a sample of the nonrespondents is sometimes used to generate this estimate. The follow-up may be a modified callback (described earlier). While this rarely generates a response from each nonrespondent designated for the follow-up, it does allow a crude adjustment of the initial results. Ignoring the initial nonresponse is equivalent to assuming that $\bar{x}_{nr}$ is equal to $\bar{x}_r$, which is usually incorrect.

A second way to adjust the results is to keep track of those responding to the initial contact, the first follow-up, the second follow-up, and so on. The mean of the variable (or other appropriate statistic) is then calculated, and each subgroup is compared to determine whether any statistically significant differences emerge as a function of the difficulty experienced in making contact. If not, the variable mean for the nonrespondents is assumed equal to the mean for those responding. If a

[21]*Statistical Adjustment for Nonresponse in Sample Surveys: A Selected Bibliography with Annotations* (Monticello, Ill.: Vance Bibliographies, 1979); J. Scott Armstrong and Terry S. Overton, "Estimating Nonresponse Bias in Mail Surveys," *Journal of Marketing Research,* 14 (August 1977), pp. 396–402; Michael J. O'Neil, "Estimating the Nonresponse Bias Due to Refusals in Telephone Surveys," *Public Opinion Quarterly,* 40 (Summer 1976), pp. 218–232; and David Elliott and Roger Thomas, "Further Thoughts on Weighting Survey Results to Compensate for Nonresponse," *Survey Methodology Bulletin,* 15 (February 1983), pp. 2–11.

discernible trend is evident, the trend is extrapolated to allow for nonrespondents. This method is particularly valuable in mail surveys, where it is an easy task to identify those responding to the first mailing, the second mailing, and so on.

A third way by which the results from personal interviews can be adjusted is to use the scheme developed by Politz and Simmons that does not involve callbacks at all.[22] Rather, it relies on a single attempted contact with each sample member at a randomly determined time. During this contact, the respondent is asked if he or she was home at the time scheduled for the interview for the preceding five days. These five answers together with the time of contact provide information on the time the respondent was at home for six different days. The responses from each informant are then weighted by the reciprocal of their self-reported probability of being at home; for example, the answers of a respondent who was home one out of six times would receive a weight of 6. The basic rationale is that people who are usually not at home are more difficult to catch for an interview and therefore will tend to be underrepresented in the survey. Consequently, the less a subject reports being at home, the more that subject's responses should be weighted.

Evidence accumulated in past surveys also sometimes serves as the basis of the adjustment for nonresponse. Organizations that frequently conduct surveys using similar sampling procedures find this approach particularly useful. While no method of adjustment is perfect, any of them is better than assuming that nonrespondents are similar to respondents on the characteristic of interest. Yet this is the very assumption we make if no attempt is made to correct for nonresponse.

Item Nonresponse The preceding discussions all deal with *total nonresponse. Item nonresponse,* which can also be a problem, occurs when the respondent agrees to the total interview but refuses, or is unable, to answer some specific questions because of the content or form of the questions, or the amount of work required to produce the requested information. As we discussed earlier, researchers usually attempt to address these problems when developing the questionnaire and planning the methods for administering it. Sometimes, however, item nonresponses occur in spite of researchers' best efforts to avoid them.

Whether anything can then be done about item nonresponse depends on its magnitude. Here we must distinguish between flagrant item nonresponse, and isolated or sporadic nonresponse. If too many questions are left unanswered, the reply becomes unusable, and the treatment, or at least adjustment, is the same as that for a complete nonresponse. On the other hand, if only a few items are left unanswered on any questionnaire, the reply can often be made usable. At the very minimum, the "don't know" and "no answers" can be treated as separate categories when reporting the results. In many ways this is the best strategy because the little evidence that is available on item nonresponse suggests that the problem is extensive and nonrandom. Alternatively, the information from the missing item or items can sometimes be inferred from other information in the questionnaire.[23] This is especially true if

---

[22]While the technique also could possibly be used with telephone interviews, it was designed for personal interviews because of the tremendous expense of personal interview callbacks. Further, probing on the phone as to when a respondent was home during the last five days can cause mistrust. See Alfred Politz and Willard Simmons, "An Attempt to Get the Not-at-Homes into the Sample without Callbacks," *Journal of the American Statistical Association,* 49 (March 1949), pp. 9–32, for explanation of the technique. For an empirical investigation of the impact of weighting on bias, see James Ward, Bertram Russick, and William Rudelius, "A Test of Reducing Callbacks and Not-At-Home Bias in Personal Interviews by Weighting At-Home Respondents," *Journal of Marketing Research,* 22 (February 1985), pp. 66–73.

[23]Graham Kalton, *Compensating for Missing Survey Data* (Ann Arbor: Institute for Social Research, University of Michigan, 1983).

there are other questions on the questionnaire that relate to the same issue. The other questions are checked, and a consistent answer is formulated for the unanswered item. In the absence of such consistency checks, the statistical technique known as *regression analysis,* which measures the relationship between two or more variables, is sometimes used. The missing item is treated as the criterion variable, and the functional relationship is established between it and *a priori* related questions through regression analysis for those cases for which the item was answered. The equation is then used to estimate a response for the remaining questionnaires given the information they contain on the predictor variables.

Finally, a third way by which item nonresponse is handled is by substituting the average response for the item of those who did respond. This technique, of course, carries the assumption that those who did not respond to the item are similar to those who did. As we have suggested many times, this assumption may be risky, and therefore substituting the average should be done with caution.

♦ Completeness rate (C)

Measure used to evaluate and compare interviewers with respect to their ability to secure needed information from contacted respondents; the completeness rate measures the proportion of complete contacts by interviewer.

Response Rate versus Completeness Rate Just as the contact rate can be used to compare and evaluate interviewers with respect to not-at-homes, at least two ratios have been suggested for comparing interviewers with respect to refusals: the response rate, *R,* and the **completeness rate,** *C.* As explained earlier, the response rate equals the ratio of the number of completed interviews with responding units divided by the number of eligible responding units in the sample. The response rate reflects the interviewer's effectiveness at the door or on the phone.

The completeness rate applies to the individual items in the study. Most typically it will be used to evaluate interviewers with respect to the crucial questions involved in the study, for example, a respondent's income, debt, or asset position, although it can also be used to evaluate the whole contact. The completeness rate simply determines whether the response is complete or not, either with respect to the crucial questions or the whole questionnaire.

Observation Errors

Observation errors, defined earlier, may be more insidious than nonobservation errors, since the research analyst may not even be aware that they exist.

♦ Field error

Nonsampling error that arises during the actual collection of the data.

Field Errors By far the most prevalent type of observation error is the **field error,** which arises after the individual has agreed to participate in a study. Instead of cooperating fully, the individual refuses to answer specific questions, or provides an untruthful response. These errors have been referred to, respectively, as *errors of omission* and *errors of commission.*[24] In the last section we discussed errors of omission and item nonresponse. Now we wish to turn our attention to errors of commission, which are usually categorized as response errors.

When considering response errors, it is useful to keep in mind what occurs when respondents answer questions.[25] First, they need to understand what is being asked.

---

[24]Robert A. Peterson and Roger A. Kerin, "The Quality of Self-Report Data: Review and Synthesis," in Ben Enis and Kenneth Roering, eds., *Annual Review of Marketing 1981* (Chicago: American Marketing Association, 1981), pp. 5–20. See also, C. A. Muircheartaigh, "Response Errors," in C. A. Muircheartaigh and Clive Payne, eds., *The Analysis of Survey Data: Model Fitting* (London: John Wiley, 1977), pp. 193–239; and Duane F. Alvin and David J. Jackson, "Measurement Models for Response Errors in Surveys: Issues and Applications" in Karl F. Schuessler, *Sociological Methodology 1980* (San Francisco: Jossey-Bass, 1980), pp. 68–119.

[25]Charles F. Cannell, Peter U. Miller, and Louis Oksenberg, "Research on Interviewing Techniques," (Ann Arbor: Institute for Social Research, University of Michigan, 1981).

Second, they need to engage in a reasoning process to arrive at an answer. Typically, the respondent will try to assess the information needed for an accurate answer and then remember the attitudes, facts, or experiences that would be relevant to the question. He or she will then try to organize a response based on this information. Third, respondents need to evaluate the response in terms of its accuracy. Fourth, they need to evaluate the response in terms of other goals they might have, such as preserving their self-image or attempting to please the interviewer. Finally, they need to put into words the response that results from all of this mental processing. Reaching the final step is the object of the survey process. However, breakdowns can occur at any of the preceding steps, resulting in an inaccurate answer, a response error.

The factors that can cause response errors are so numerous that they almost defy categorization. One seemingly useful scheme for dealing with data-collection errors, though, is the interviewer-interviewee interaction model proposed by Kahn and Cannell (Figure 16.3).[26] The model suggests several things. First, each person brings certain background characteristics and psychological predispositions to the interview. While some of the background characteristics (such as age and sex) are readily observable, others are not, nor can the psychological state of the other person be seen. Yet both interviewer and interviewee will form some attitudes toward and expectations of the other person on the basis of their initial perceptions. Second, the interview is an interactive process and both interviewer and interviewee are important determinants of the process. Each party perceives and reacts to the specific behaviors of the other. Note, though, that there is no direct link between the boxes labeled behavior. Rather, the linkage is more complicated, "involving a behavior on the part of the interviewer or respondent, the perception of this behavior by the other principal in the interview, a cognitive or attitudinal development from that perception, and finally a resultant motivation to behave in a certain way. Only at this point is a behavioral act carried out, which in turn may be perceived by and reacted to by the other participant in the interview."[27]

The perceptions of this behavior may not be correct, just as the initial perceptions of each party may be in error. Nevertheless, such inferences will inevitably be made as both interviewer and respondent search for cues to help them understand each other and carry out the requirements imposed by the interview situation. In sum, not only do the specific behaviors of each party to the interaction affect the outcome, but so do the background characteristics and psychological predispositions of both interviewer and respondent.

The interviewer-interviewee interaction model is appealing for several reasons. One, it is consistent with the empirical evidence. Two, it offers some valuable insight on how response errors (as well as nonresponse errors due to refusals) can potentially be reduced. The model also applies to telephone and mail surveys, thereby further increasing its value. For example, the respondent's perceptions of the background characteristics and behavior of a telephone interviewer will likely affect the answers he or she provides. The respondent's background is certainly going to affect the person's reported responses. So will the person's suspicions regarding the true purpose of the study, or the individual's assumption of how confidential his or her responses will truly be. These factors can distort the respondent's answers regardless of the manner used to collect the data, and it is unlikely these distortions would be

---

[26]Robert L. Kahn and Charles F. Cannell, *The Dynamics of Interviewing* (New York: John Wiley, © 1957), p. 193. The figure is used by permission of John Wiley & Sons, Inc.

[27]*Ibid.,* p. 194.

Figure 16.3

A Model of Bias in the Interview

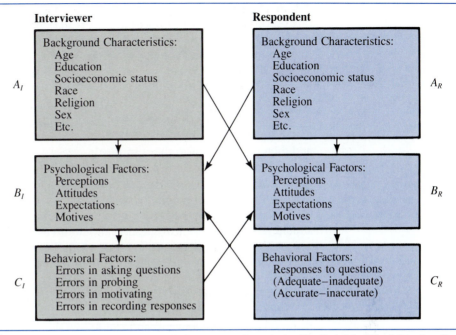

Source: Robert L. Kahn and Charles F. Cannell, *The Dynamics of Interviewing* (New York: John Wiley & Sons, Inc., © 1957), p. 193. Reprinted by permission of John Wiley & Sons, Inc.

random. At any rate, the model suggests certain actions that the researcher can take to generate accurate information.

Background Factors The empirical evidence supports the notion that background factors affect reported responses. More specifically, the evidence suggests that the interviewer is likely to get better cooperation and more information from the respondent when the two share similar backgrounds than if they are different. This is particularly true for readily observable characteristics, such as race, age, and sex, but applies as well to more unobservable characteristics, such as social class and income.[28] Consequently, it may be prudent to match the background characteristics of the interviewer and respondent as closely as possible, since the more characteristics the two have in common, the greater the probability of a successful interview.[29]

Unfortunately, researchers have found it difficult to implement this practice. Most interviewers are housewives who use interviewing as a way to supplement their family income. The job by no means attracts a balanced demographic cross section of people. So what can the researcher do to minimize such biases? He or she may be restricted to merely computing a measure of interviewer variability when analyzing the results. Possibly the field supervisor could revise interviewers' schedules in a specific project so as to improve background matches, but the most effective measure would be to recruit interviewers with diverse socioeconomic backgrounds.

---

[28]See, for example, the studies of Barbara Bailor, Leroy Bailey, and Joyce Stevens, "Measures of Interviewer Bias and Variance," *Journal of Marketing Research,* 14 (August 1977), pp. 337–343; Shirley Hatchett and Howard Schuman, "White Respondents and Race-of-Interviewer Effects," *Public Opinion Quarterly,* 39 (Winter 1975), pp. 523–528; and Patrick R. Cotter, Jeffrey Cohen, and Philip B. Coulter, "Race of Interviewer Effects on Telephone Interviews," *Public Opinion Quarterly,* 46 (Summer 1982), pp. 278–284.

[29]Kahn and Cannell, *The Dynamics of Interviewing,* pp. 197–199.

Psychological Factors The evidence regarding the impact of psychological factors on responses tends to support the notion that interviewers' opinions, perceptions, expectations, and attitudes affect the responses they receive.[30] Certainly these attitudes, opinions, expectations, and so on, are going to be conditioned by the interviewers' backgrounds, and since that is something we cannot control, how are we to control for these psychological factors? The primary way is through training. The fact that interviewers will have psychological predispositions is not critical, since these psychological factors are not observed by the respondent. What is critical is that these factors not be allowed to affect interviewers' behavior during the interview and thereby contaminate the response.

Most surveys, therefore, are conducted using a rather rigid set of procedures that interviewers must follow. The instructions should be clear and should be written. Further, they should state the purpose of the study clearly. They should describe the materials to be used, such as questionnaires, maps, time forms, and so on. They should describe how each question should be asked, the kinds of answers that are acceptable, and the kinds and timing of probes that are to be used, if any. The instructions should also specify the number and identity of respondents that interviewers need to contact, and the time constraints under which they will be operating. It is also important that the instructions be well organized and unambiguous.

The instructions must be clearly articulated; however, it is even more important that interviewers understand and can follow them. This suggests that practice training sessions will be necessary. It might also be necessary to actually examine the interviewers with respect to study purposes and procedures. Finally, interviewers might also be required to complete the questionnaire so that, if there is a pattern between the interviewers' answers and the answers they get when administering the questionnaire, it can be discerned.[31]

Behavioral Factors The respondents' background, attitudes, motives, expectations, and so on, are also potentially biasing. Whether they actually do introduce bias depends on how the interviewer and respondent interact. In other words, the predispositions to bias become operative only in behavior.

Unfortunately the evidence indicates that even when the rules are rigid and the questionnaires relatively simple and structured, interviewers do not follow the rules. They thereby introduce bias. In one classic study, fifteen college-educated interviewers interviewed the same respondent, who had previously been instructed to give identical answers to all fifteen.[32] All the interviews were recorded and were later analyzed for the incidence of errors by type and frequency. One of the most startling findings of the study was the sheer number of errors. For example, there were sixty-six failures to ask supplementary questions when inadequate responses were given, and the number of errors per interviewer varied from twelve to thirty-six. In another more recent study, it was found that ". . . one-third of the . . . interviewers deviated frequently and markedly from their instructions, sometimes failing to explain the

[30]Seymour Sudman, Norman Bradburn, Ed Blair, and Carol Stocking, "Modest Expectations: The Effects of Interviewers' Prior Expectations and Response," *Sociological Methods and Research,* 6 (November 1977), pp. 177–182; Eleanor Singer and Luanne Kohnke-Aguirre, "Interviewer Expectation Effects: A Replication and Extension," *Public Opinion Quarterly,* 43 (Summer 1979), pp. 245–260; and Eleanor Singer, Martin R. Frankel, and Marc B. Glassman, "The Effect of Interviewer Characteristics and Expectations on Response," *Public Opinion Quarterly,* 47 (Spring 1983), pp. 68–83.

[31]Donald S. Tull and Larry E. Richards, "What Can Be Done About Interviewer Bias," in Jagdish Sheth, ed., *Research in Marketing* (Greenwich, Conn.: JAI Press, 1980), pp. 143–162.

[32]L. L. Guest, "A Study of Interviewer Competence," *International Journal of Opinion and Attitude Research,* 1 (March 1947), pp. 17–30.

key terms or to repeat them as required, sometimes leaving them out altogether, shortening questions, or failing to follow up certain ambiguous answers in the manner required."[33]

At least three interviewer behaviors lead to response bias: (1) errors in asking questions and in probing when additional information is required, (2) errors in recording the answer, and (3) errors due to cheating.

While errors in asking questions can arise with any of the basic question types, the problem is particularly acute with open-ended questions where probing follows the initial response. No two interviewers are likely to employ the same probes. The content as well as the timing of the probes may differ. This raises the possibility that the differences in answers may be due to the probes that are used rather than any "true" differences in the position of the respondents.

The manner in which the initial question is phrased can also introduce error. Interviewers often reword the question to fit their perceptions of what the respondent is capable of understanding. They may also change the wording in a way that reflects their own opinion of what constitutes an appropriate answer.

Surprisingly, questions that include alternative answers possess great potential for interviewer bias. This bias occurs because the interviewer places undue emphasis on one of the alternatives in stating the question. Slight changes in tone can change the meaning of the entire question. In one of the most comprehensive studies to investigate interviewer error in asking questions, it was found, for example, that the average number of errors per question by type was:[34]

- Reading error   0.293
- Speech variations   0.116
- Probes   0.140
- Feedbacks to respondents   0.161

One of the interviewer's main tasks is keeping the respondent interested and motivated. At the same time, the interviewer must try to record what the respondent is saying by dutifully writing down the person's answers to open-ended questions or checking the appropriate box with closed questions. These dual, sometimes incompatible, responsibilities can also be a source of error. Interviewers may not correctly "hear" what the respondent is actually saying. This may be because the respondent is inarticulate and the response is garbled, or because an interviewer's own selective processes are operating. Interviewers may hear what they want to hear and retain what they want to retain. This is a common failing with all of us and, in spite of interviewer training, recording errors in the interview are all too common.[35]

Interviewer cheating can also be a source of response error. Cheating may range from the fabrication of a whole interview to the fabrication of one or two answers to make the response complete. The Advertising Research Foundation (ARF), for example, conducts validation studies for its members upon request by reinterviewing a sample of those who were reported to have been interviewed previously. Foundation researchers check to see if the interview actually took place and the

---

[33]W. A. Belson, "Increasing the Power of Research to Guide Advertising Decisions," *Journal of Marketing,* 29 (April 1965), p. 38. See also Martin Collins and Bob Butcher, "Interviewer and Clustering Effects in an Attitude Survey," *Journal of the Market Research Society,* 25 (January 1983), pp. 39–58.

[34]Norman M. Bradburn and Seymour Sudman, *Improving Interview Method and Questionnaire Design* (San Francisco: Jossey-Bass, 1979), p. 29.

[35]Martin Collins, "Interviewing Variability: A Review of the Problem," *Journal of the Market Research Society,* 22 (April 1980), pp. 77–95. For ways of investigating interviewer errors, see Jean Morton-Williams and Wendy Sykes, "The Use of Interaction Coding and Follow-up Interviews to Investigate Comprehension of Survey Questions," *Journal of the Market Research Society,* 26 (April 1984), pp. 109–127.

designated questions were asked. For the years 1972 and 1973, ARF found that 5.4 percent of the interviews across thirty-three separate studies could not be verified, and that an additional 7.9 percent contained at least two performance errors.[36] What was especially disturbing about these results is that it is generally believed that the surveys submitted for verification are among the best executed in the advertising area.

Most commercial research firms validate 10 to 20 percent of the completed interviews through follow-up telephone calls or by sending postcards to a sample of "respondents" to verify they have in fact been contacted. Generally, these follow-ups are most productive in detecting the flagrant cheating that occurs when a field worker fabricates the entire interview. They are much less effective in detecting more subtle forms of cheating in which (1) the interviewer asks only the key questions and fills in the remaining information later, (2) the interviewer interviews respondents in groups rather than separately as instructed, (3) the interviewer inter-

---

[36]Lipstein, "In Defense of Small Samples."

Back to the Case

It was late Friday night. A frazzled Sarah sat at her kitchen table going through her questionnaires. Out of fifty forms, she had only been able to complete thirty-two. Some of the others contained blanks where the respondent had refused to answer the question. Others were totally empty since the person in question had refused to participate in the interview at all.

Sarah knew that she had to have the questionnaires back by noon the following day. She was tired, frustrated, and upset that her first week on the job had been so unproductive. She was also embarrassed to face her supervisor with so many blanks.

Just then Sarah's son, Donald, wandered into the kitchen on the way to the refrigerator.

"What's the matter, Mom?" he asked, seeing her troubled expression.

"Oh, Donald. I made a mess of my first week," Sarah said. "I have all these blank forms, and questions with no responses, and I have to turn them in tomorrow."

"Look, Mom, why don't you just fill in the blanks yourself? Who's to know? You can guess some of the answers based on the kinds of houses the people lived in," Donald said. "Then next week things will be better."

"I'm tempted, Donald," Sarah said, "but it just wouldn't be right. Besides, they told us in the training program that someone would come by periodically and check up on the interviews that we were supposed to have completed. If it is found that I cheated, I could lose my job. Better I should face the music than be fired for something so dishonorable."

Frustrated interviewers are often tempted to cheat. There are many ways in which they can fabricate the data, ranging from making up an entire interview to more subtle methods such as interviewing respondents in groups, rather than separately as instructed. All these forms of cheating, however, tend to introduce response error into the data.

Research organizations must constantly be on the alert for such error and seek ways to alleviate it. Some firms conduct checks on a randomly selected number of interviews to see if they really occurred, and if the answers given are the same as those from the initial interview. Other firms focus on such preventive measures as thorough training of interviewers and careful monitoring of their performance.

views the wrong respondent because the designated respondent is inaccessible or difficult to contact, and (4) the interviewer employs one contact for information for two separate studies and thereby introduces contamination through respondent fatigue.

Another form of cheating, which is not exactly response error but which has a strong effect on all nonsampling errors, is padding bills. The interviewer may falsify the number of hours worked or the number of miles traveled. The problem is widespread because of the nature of the interviewing situation. The interviewer works without direct supervision in a basically low-paying job. Further, the supervisor's pay is normally geared to the interviewer's charges, so that the higher the interviewer's bills, the higher the supervisor's compensation. Bill padding drains resources from other parts of the study and thereby decreases the efficiency (value) of the information because it is obtained at higher cost.

As suggested previously, it is much more difficult to adjust for response errors than for nonresponse errors. Both their direction and their magnitude are unknown because, in order to estimate their effects, the true value must be known. The researcher's main hope lies in prevention rather than subsequent adjustment of the results. The various sources of errors themselves suggest preventives. For example, training can help reduce errors in asking questions and recording answers. Similarly, the way interviewers are selected, paid, and controlled could reduce cheating. Overall interviewer performance can be assessed by rating the quality of the work with respect to appropriate characteristics such as costs, types of errors, ability to follow instructions, and so on. We shall not elaborate on the recommended procedures for assessing these factors since that would be a book in its own right.[37] For our purposes, we need to recognize the existence of response errors, their sources, and their potentially devastating impact. The interviewer-interviewee interaction model is helpful in visualizing these sources and in indicating some methods of prevention.

Office Errors Our problems with nonsampling errors do not end with data collection. Errors can and do arise in the editing, coding, tabulating, and analyzing of the data.[38] For the most part, these errors can be reduced, if not eliminated, by exercising proper controls in data processing. These questions are discussed in the chapters dealing with analysis.

◆ Total Error Is Key

By this time the reader should understand the warning that total error, rather than any single type of error, is the key in designing a research investigation. The admonition particularly applies to sampling error. With a course in statistics behind them,

---

[37]Some useful general sources are: Ronald Anderson, Judith Kasper, Martin R. Frankel *et al., Total Survey Error* (San Francisco: Jossey-Bass, 1979); Bradburn and Sudman, *Improving Interview Method and Questionnaire Design;* Donald Dillman, *Mail and Telephone Surveys* (New York: John Wiley, 1978); Paul L. Erdos, *Professional Mail Surveys* (Malabar, Fla.: Robert E. Kreiger, 1983); Robert Ferber, ed., *Handbook of Marketing Research* (New York: McGraw-Hill, 1974), particularly Section II-B; Robert M. Groves and Robert L. Kahn, *Surveys by Telephone* (New York: Academic Press, 1979); and J. Rothman, "Acceptance Checks for Ensuring Quality in Research," *Journal of the Market Research Society,* 22 (July 1980), pp. 192–204.

[38]The reader who believes that analysis errors should be no problem should see Mosteller, "Nonsampling Errors," in which he devotes 9 of 19 pages to the discussion of potential errors in analysis. For an empirical example illustrating the potential extent of the problem, see David Elliot, "A Study of Variation in Occupation and Social Class Coding—Summary of Results," *Survey Methodology Bulletin,* 14 (May 1982), pp. 48–49.

students beginning their studies in research methods often argue for the "largest possible sample," reasoning that a large sample is much more likely to produce a statistic close to the population parameter being estimated than a small sample. What the student fails to appreciate, though, is that the argument applies only to sampling error. Increasing the sample size does, in fact, decrease sampling error. However, it may also increase nonsampling error because the larger sample requires more interviewers, for instance, and this creates additional burdens in selection, training, and control. Further, nonsampling error is a much more insidious and troublesome error than sampling error. Sampling error can be estimated. Many forms of nonsampling error cannot. Sampling error can be reduced through more sophisticated sample design or by using a larger sample. The path is clear and relatively well-traveled,

Table 16.6   Overview of Nonsampling Errors and Some Methods for Handling Them

Type	Definition	Methods for Handling
Noncoverage	Failure to include some units or entire sections of the defined survey population in the sampling frame	1. Improve basic sampling frame using other sources. 2. Select sample in such a way as to reduce incidence, e.g., by ignoring ineligibles on a list. 3. Adjust the results by appropriately weighting the subsample results.
Nonresponse	Failure to obtain information from some elements of the population that were selected for the sample	
Not-at-homes:	Designated respondent is not home when the interviewer calls.	1. Have interviewers make advance appointments. 2. Call back at another time, preferably at a different time of day. 3. Attempt to contact the designated respondent using another approach (e.g., use a modified callback).
Refusals:	Respondent refuses to cooperate in the survey.	1. Attempt to convince the respondent of the value of the research and the importance of his or her participation. 2. Provide advance notice that the survey is coming. 3. Guarantee anonymity. 4. Provide an incentive for participating. 5. Hide the identification of the sponsor by using an independent research organization. 6. Try to get a foot in the door by getting the respondent to comply with some small task before getting the survey. 7. Use personalized cover letters. 8. Use a follow-up contact at a more convenient time. 9. Avoid unnecessary questions. 10. Adjust the results to account for the nonresponse.

so the researcher should have little difficulty keeping sampling error within bounds. Not so with nonsampling errors. The path is not paved. New sources of nonsampling error are being discovered all the time, and even though known, many of these sources defy reduction by any automatic procedure. "Improved method" is critical, but what this ideal method should be is unknown. This chapter has attempted to highlight some of the better known sources of nonsampling error and ways of dealing with them.

Table 16.6 attempts to summarize what we have been saying about nonsampling errors and how they can be reduced or controlled. The table can be used as a sort of checklist for marketing managers and other users of research to evaluate the quality of the research prior to making substantive decisions on the basis of the

Table 16.6   *continued*

Type	Definition	Methods for Handling
Field	Although the individual participates in the study, he or she refuses to answer specific questions or provides incorrect answers to them.	1. Match the background characteristics of interviewer and respondent as closely as possible. 2. Make sure interviewer instructions are clear and written down. 3. Conduct practice training sessions with interviewers. 4. Examine the interviewers' understanding of the study's purposes and procedures. 5. Have interviewers complete the questionnaire and examine their replies to see if there is any relationship between the answers they secure and their own answers. 6. Verify a sample of each interviewer's interviews.
Office[a]	Errors that arise when coding, tabulating, or analyzing the data	1. Use field edit to detect the most glaring omissions and inaccuracies in the data. 2. Use second edit in the office to decide how data-collection instruments containing incomplete answers, obviously wrong answers, and answers that reflect a lack of interest are to be handled. 3. Use closed questions to simplify the coding, but when open-ended questions need to be used, specify the appropriate codes that will be allowed before collecting the data. 4. When open-ended questions are being coded and multiple coders are being used, divide the task by questions and not by data-collection forms. 5. Have each coder code a sample of the other's work to ensure a consistent set of coding criteria is being employed. 6. Follow established conventions; e.g., use numeric codes and not letters of the alphabet when coding the data for computer analysis. 7. Prepare a codebook that lists the codes for each variable and the categories included in each code. 8. Use appropriate methods to analyze the data.

[a]Steps to reduce the incidence of office errors are discussed in more detail in the analysis chapters.

research results. While not all of the methods for handling nonsampling errors will be applicable in every study, a systematic analysis of the research effort, using the table guidelines, should provide the proper appreciation for the quality of research information that is obtained.

◆ Summary

Learning Objective 1: Explain what is meant by sampling error.

Sampling error is the difference between the observed values of a variable and the long-run average of the observed values in repetitions of the measurement.

Learning Objective 2: Cite the two basic types of nonsampling errors and describe each.

There are two basic types of nonsampling errors: errors due to nonobservation and errors due to observation. Nonobservation errors result from a failure to obtain data from parts of the survey population. They occur because part of the population of interest was not included or because some elements designated for inclusion in the sample did not respond. Observation errors occur because inaccurate information was secured from the sample elements or because errors were introduced in the processing of the data or in reporting the findings.

Learning Objective 3: Outline several ways in which noncoverage bias can be reduced.

Noncoverage bias can be reduced, although not necessarily eliminated, by recognizing its existence, working to improve the sampling frame, and employing a sampling specialist to help reduce (through the sampling procedure) and adjust (through analysis) the remaining frame imperfections.

Learning Objective 4: Explain what is meant by error due to nonresponse.

Error due to nonresponse represents a failure to obtain information from some elements of the population that were selected and designated for the sample.

Learning Objective 5: Cite the standard definition for response rate.

Response rate may be defined as the number of completed interviews with responding units divided by the number of eligible responding units in the sample.

Learning Objective 6: Identify the two main sources of nonresponse bias.

The two main sources of nonresponse bias are not-at-homes and refusals.

Learning Objective 7: Define what is meant by contact rate.

The contact rate is defined as the percentage of eligible assignments in which the interviewer makes contact with the designated respondent; that is,

$$K = \frac{\text{number of sample units contacted}}{\text{total number of eligible sample units approached}}.$$

Learning Objective 8: Cite some of the factors that may contribute to a respondent's refusal to participate in a study.

The rate of refusals in a study will depend on, among other things, the nature of the respondent, the nature of the organization sponsoring the research, the circumstances surrounding the contact, the nature of the subject under investigation, and the skill of the interviewer. The method used to collect the data may also make a difference.

Learning Objective 9: Identify three factors that may be a source of bias in the interviewer-interviewee interaction.

The interviewer-interviewee interaction may be biased by background characteristics, psychological factors, and behavioral factors on the part of either the interviewer or the respondent, or both.

Learning Objective 10: Discuss the types of interviewer behavior that may lead to response bias.

At least three interviewer behaviors can lead to response bias: (1) errors in asking questions and in probing when additional information is required, (2) errors in recording the answer, and (3) errors due to cheating.

Discussion Questions, Problems, and Projects

1. Mrs. J. Hoffman was the owner of a medium-sized supermarket located in St. Cloud, Minnesota. She was considering altering the layout of the store so that, for example, the frozen food section would be near the section with fresh fruit and vegetables. These changes were designed to better accommodate customer shopping patterns and thereby increase customer patronage. Prior to making the alterations, she decided to administer a short questionnaire in the store to a random sample of customers. For a period of two weeks, three of the store cashiers were instructed to stand at the end of selected aisles and conduct personal interviews with every fifth customer. Mrs. Hoffman gave specific instructions that on no account were customers to be harassed or offended. Identify the major sources of noncoverage and nonresponse errors. Explain.

2. Tough-Grip Tires was a large manufacturer of radial tires located in New Orleans, Louisiana, that was experiencing a problem common to tire manufacturers. The poor performance of the auto industry was having a severe negative impact on the tire industry. To try and maintain sales and competitive positions, the various manufacturers were offering wholesalers additional credit and discount opportunities. Tough-Grip's management was particularly concerned about wholesaler reaction to a new discount policy they were considering. The first survey the company conducted to explore these reactions was unsatisfactory to top management. Management felt it was conducted in a haphazard manner and contained numerous nonsampling errors. Tough-Grip's management decided to conduct another study containing the following changes:

   - The sampling frame was defined as a list of 1,000 of the largest wholesalers that stocked Tough-Grip tires and the sample elements were to be randomly selected from this list.
   - A callback technique was to be employed with the callbacks being made at different times than the original attempted contact.
   - The sample size was to be doubled, from 200 to 400 respondents.
   - The sample elements that were ineligible or refused to cooperate were to be substituted for by the next element from the list.
   - An incentive of $1.00 was to be offered to respondents.

   Critically evaluate the steps that were being considered to prevent the occurrence of nonsampling errors. Do you think they are appropriate? Be specific.

3. A major publisher of a diverse set of magazines was interested in determining customer satisfaction with three of the company's leading publications: *Style Update, Business Profiles,* and *Hi-Tech Review.* The three magazines dealt, respectively, with women's fashions, business trends, and computer technology developments. Three sampling frames, consisting of lists of subscribers residing in Chicago, were formulated. Three random samples were to be chosen from these lists. Personal interviews using an unstructured-undisguised questionnaire were to be conducted. The publishing company had a regular pool of interviewers that it called upon whenever interviews were to be conducted. The interviewers had varying educational backgrounds, though 95 percent were high school graduates and the remaining 5 percent had some college education. In terms of age and sex, the range varied from eighteen years to forty-five years with 70 percent females and 30 percent males. The majority of interviewers were housewives and students. Prior to conducting a survey the company sent the necessary information in the mail and requested interviewers to indicate whether they were interested. The questionnaires, addresses and other detailed information were then sent to those interviewers replying affirmatively. After the interviewer completed his or her quota of interviews, the replies were sent back to the company. The company then mailed the interviewer's remuneration.

(a) Using the guidelines in Table 16.6, critically evaluate the selection, training and instructions given to the field interviewers.

(b) Using Kahn and Cannell's model in Figure 16.3, identify the major sources of bias that would affect the interviews.

4. The placement office at your university has asked you to assist it in the task of determining the size of starting salaries and the range of salary offers received by graduating seniors. The placement office has always gathered some information in this regard in that some seniors have historically come in to report the name of the company for which they are going to work and the size of their starting salaries. The office feels that these statistics may be biased, and thus it wishes to approach the whole task more systematically. This is why it has hired your expertise to determine what the situation was with respect to last year's graduating seniors.

(a) Describe how you would select a sample of respondents to answer the question of starting salaries. Why would you use this particular sample?

(b) What types of nonsampling errors might you expect to encounter with your approach, and how would you control for them?

5. Prepare a brief questionnaire regarding the television-viewing habits of adults in your city. Administer this instrument to a sample of subjects using at least ten telephone interviews and ten personal interviews. Discuss the extent of the nonresponse bias with each method.

6. For this exercise you will need to use the questionnaire on television-viewing habits developed in Exercise 5. In addition, develop questions designed to measure a respondent's attitude toward the television medium. Add these questions to the questionnaire on television-viewing habits. Administer this new questionnaire to one of your classmates. Then request the classmate you interviewed to administer his/her questionnaire so that you will be the interviewee. Refer to Figure 16.3, and discuss the background factors, psychological factors, and behavioral factors that might have led to bias in the interview. (Hint: After the interview it would be useful to discuss these aspects with your classmate, i.e., the interviewee. Explain what you meant by the various questions, and find out how your classmate interpreted these questions.)

Suggested Additional Readings

For general discussions of data quality, the differences between sampling and nonsampling error, and steps that can be taken to improve the quality of information gathered in marketing research studies, see

Ronald Anderson, Judith Kasper, Martin R. Frankel and Associates, *Total Survey Error* (San Francisco: Jossey-Bass, 1979).

Henry Assael and John Keon, "Nonsampling vs. Sampling Errors in Survey Research," *Journal of Marketing,* 46 (Spring 1982), pp. 114–123.

Robert A. Peterson and Roger A. Kerin, "The Quality of Self-Report Data: Review and Synthesis," in Ben Enis and Kenneth Roering, eds., *Annual Review of Marketing 1981* (Chicago: American Marketing Association, 1981), pp. 5–20.

Frederick Wiseman, ed., *Improving Data Quality in Sample Surveys* (Cambridge, Mass.: Marketing Science Institute, 1983).

Part Five   Research Project

The fifth stage in the research process is to design the sample and collect the data. As we learned from the chapters in this part, researchers generally prefer to use a sample of a population rather than a census of a population, not only because a sample is less costly to obtain, but because it is generally more accurate.

In these chapters we learned that researchers generally follow a six-step procedure for drawing a sample that includes defining the population, identifying the sampling frame, selecting a sampling procedure, determining the sample size, selecting the sample elements, and collecting the data from the designated elements. We investigated the different types of samples that researchers use and the advantages and disadvantages of each.

In the last chapter we investigated the second type of error that affects research studies: nonsampling error. As we discussed, there are two types of nonsampling error: those due to nonobservation and those due to observation. Nonobservation errors include coverage errors and nonresponse errors, while observation errors include field errors and office errors.

The problem with nonsampling error, we learned, is that unlike sampling error, it generally cannot be accurately estimated and corrected for. Like viruses for the common cold, new sources of nonsampling error are being discovered all the time—and, again like the common cold, are proving resistant to cure. A researcher's best tactic is to know as much as possible about the types of nonsampling errors that can occur and try to design a study that will prevent them.

Researchers for CARA were interested in assessing the attitudes of local businesspeople for their study. They decided to define the *local area* as the Fairview County area. *Businesspeople* were defined as individuals who make decisions regarding advertising expenditures for their firms. Researchers decided to exclude from the sample any firms that used an advertising agency or showed minimal interest in using any of the three major advertising media.

Researchers decided to use the latest Centerville Telephone Directory Yellow Pages as their sampling frame. Recall that a sampling frame is the list of elements from which the sample is drawn. They identified ten major categories of businesses from which to select the sample: building materials and hardware; automotive, sales and service; apparel; furniture and home furnishings; eating and drinking establishments; health and fitness; financial institutions; home entertainment; professional services; and a miscellaneous category including florists, jewelers, printers, book dealers, and retail photographic sales and services.

By further winnowing the list to eliminate those firms employing advertising agencies or expressing little interest in advertising, researchers compiled a final list of 3,086 businesses.

A systematic sampling plan was chosen for this study. Recall that in this type of sampling plan each element has a known *a priori* chance of inclusion in the sample. Each of the 3,086 businesses identified as a part of the sampling frame was classified as a member of one of the ten categories of business and was placed in alphabetical order within that category. The ten categories were then randomly ordered, and businesses were numbered from 1 to 3,086.

Researchers decided on a sample size of 600 and then determined two measures: the sampling interval and a random start. The sampling interval involved dividing the number of elements in the population (3,086) by the desired sample size (600). This number (5.14) was then rounded down to 5. A random number table was used to select the initial number between 1 and 5, and every fifth element was selected thereafter until the desired sample size was achieved.

Researchers then pretested the questionnaire by mailing twenty questionnaires to businesses selected by a systematic sampling plan. Half of the respondents were given a dollar for their cooperation; half were given nothing except thanks. Eighty percent of those receiving the incentive returned the questionnaire; only 10 percent of the others complied. Since CARA was interested in whether offering respondents an incentive would increase response similarly in the larger group, researchers decided to offer half the sample a dollar for responding and nothing to the other half.

A general rule for selecting sample size is that there should be 100 or more units for each category of the major breakdowns and 20 to 50 in the minor breakdowns. Researchers assumed that the section of the questionnaire requesting attitudes toward sales representatives would have the highest percentage of incomplete subsections. Based on the responses to that section in the pretest, they estimated that 150 questionnaires were necessary to fulfill the requirement for the major breakdowns. They also assumed that if the returned forms were evenly distributed among the four categories of annual advertising budgets, 25 units per minor breakdown should result, thus fulfilling the second general rule.

Since there was no assurance that an even distribution would occur, they decided to increase the number of returns to increase the probability that the desired number of units in the minor breakdowns would approach the desired level. Thus, they estimated the rates of return conservatively at 10 percent for those individuals not receiving a dollar and 50 percent for those receiving a dollar. Hence, a sample size of 300 for each group should have resulted in 30 and 150 returns for the no-dollar and dollar groups, respectively, which would be enough to satisfy the general rules mentioned.

CARA researchers recognized the sources of nonsampling error in their study. They knew, for example, that coverage errors in their sampling frame were inevitable because the Centerville Yellow Pages was not a complete list of all local businesses. Some of the businesses listed were no longer in existence, others were too new to have been listed, and others may have chosen not to be listed. Nevertheless, no alternative offered a better list of businesses at a reasonable cost.

By using only ten major categories of businesses, researchers also recognized that they had probably included some businesses that should not have been on the list and excluded others that should have been. Errors of inclusion and exclusion were also likely in their attempts to select only businesses not employing an advertising agency and businesses that would be interested in using the three major advertising media. Because of these biases, the researchers cautioned CARA representatives about generalizing the study's results to all businesses in Fairview County.

Nonresponse errors were evident in the response rates. Of the 600 questionnaires initially mailed, a total of 212 were returned. Of these, 165 were from the

300 which received a dollar, and 45 from the 300 which received no incentive. Thirty-four of the returned questionnaires were unusable, however, either because none of the pages were completed or because only classification data were given.

The study was interested in sampling from individuals who did not use an advertising agency, who were involved in making advertising decisions, and who held the positions of manager and/or owner. Within the three subsections (television, radio, and newspaper) of each of the two sections that assessed attitudes toward sales representatives and advertising media, a total of 168 questionnaires could be classified as being one of the desired categories or not. Of this total of 168, 141 did not use an advertising agency, 157 were decision makers, and 154 were owners and/or managers.

On the scale assessing the importance of the attributes of the sales representatives, 174 forms were classified by the desired categories. Four respondents did not fill out this section. Of the 174, 143 did not use an advertising agency, 162 were decision makers, and 160 were owners and/or managers.

The entire 178 questionnaires were classifiable by the desired categories on the scale assessing the importance of the characteristics of the advertising media. Of this total, 149 did not use an advertising agency, 166 were decision makers, and 160 were owners and/or managers.

Despite a predictable level of nonresponse, the results of the study seemed to indicate that the questionnaire generally secured responses from the population of interest on the variables mentioned.

Field errors occur when an individual who has agreed to participate in a study either refuses to answer specific questions or provides untruthful answers. CARA researchers noticed several instances of probable field error in the completed questionnaires. For example, on the scale measuring attitudes toward the advertising media of television, radio, and newspaper, 453 subsections were completed. Of this number, 133 were from the television category, 153 from the radio category, and 167 from the newspaper category. Since individuals were asked to fill out each subsection regardless of whether they used that type of advertising or not, there should not have been differences in these numbers. Researchers speculated that respondents may have been confused as to what their task was on this section, or they may merely have decided not to complete this section.

Respondents were also asked to approximate the proportion of their yearly advertising budget spent on nine different types of advertising. Researchers took the responses and determined the mean percentage scores for each category. The percentages did not add up to 100 percent, however, which indicated that some respondents had difficulty determining these proportions.

Cases to Part Five

Case 5.1   Rent Control Referendum

The arrival of spring, 1986, in Flint, Michigan, was accompanied by an upsurge of interest in the community's rent controversy. For several years, a small but highly vocal group of people, most of them living in the downtown area, had contended that apartment rents in the city were too high and that landlords were gouging the public. There had been a number of claims and counterclaims by both parties over the years, and while most of these had found their way into the local news, the issue remained at the level of an exchange of views until early 1986.

At this time, the downtown residents initiated a campaign for rent control. They petitioned the city council to pass legislation fixing rents at the previous year's level. The council refused to do so, but through a concerted campaign the residents succeeded in getting enough signatures to have the issue of rent control placed on the ballot as a public referendum in the fall elections.

This turn of events alarmed a group of realtors in the city, and they commissioned a study to investigate rents in the Flint area. The purpose of the study was to provide some hard data regarding the legitimacy of the claims of the two feuding parties—the residents who claimed they were being gouged and the landlords who claimed that although rents had risen, they had risen no faster than the price of many other things. The study was not intended to explore the perceived advantages and disadvantages of rent control. Its specific objective was to determine whether recent changes in apartment rents were greater or smaller than the changes in other consumer costs, as measured by the Consumer Price Index.

The original intention was to determine the percentage changes in rents for the last ten years. However, some initial exploratory research suggested that data for the last six years were sufficient. Also, since Census of Housing data were available for 1980, that year was picked as the base year for establishing rent changes.

The May Research Company, headed by Carol and Michelle May, was hired to conduct the investigation when it became apparent to the realty group that the information they were seeking was not available through any city agencies or as published data. Consequently, it was decided to generate a pseudo "rent index" by tracking the rents over the six-year period for apartment units selected at random. Insofar as possible, the study was to investigate whether the rates for different sized units had changed disproportionately.

Research Plan

The Flint area was arbitrarily divided into four sections of north, south, east, and west. The east side was chosen as an experimental district within which to test methodology, procedures, definitions, and data-collection methods, since it had a good mix of apartments in terms of age of buildings and number of rooms.

An apartment was defined as a unit with a refrigerator, stove, and bathroom, that was unfurnished but included utilities. A room was defined as any unit of space in an apartment that was surrounded by four walls and a doorway. Bathrooms and kitchenettes were to be counted as half-rooms, while porches, unfinished basements and attics, balconies, patios, hallways, and entryways were not to be counted when determining the size of the unit.

The sample was to be drawn using the Flint Block Statistics portion of the Census of Housing. A census block is sometimes more than one physical block. The census blocks within the east district were listed, and a simple random sample of sixty-four blocks was selected using a table of random numbers. A field worker was sent to each selected block and was instructed to use the random number assigned to select a building within the block. Specifically, the worker was told to start at the northwest corner of the block, to count buildings proceeding counterclockwise, and to use the building that corresponded to the assigned random number. If the designated building had no rental units, the next building was to be used. The apartments within the building were to be counted, and the table of random numbers was to be used to select the specific apartment that was to be included.

A very short, structured questionnaire was to be administered to an adult occupant of the apartment. Four basic items of information were requested: (1) whether the unit qualified as an apartment under the definition that was being used, (2) whether utilities were paid and whether the apartment was furnished, (3) current and previous rent, and (4) the name of the landlord. The name of the landlord was requested to afford a double check of the accuracy of the rent information provided. Both landlords and occupants could have reasons for inflating or under-

stating rents, and some tenants had not lived in their apartments continuously since 1980, the base year being used for the study.

While all occupant interviews were done in person, all landlord interviews were done by telephone. The landlord questionnaire was structured, and it was even shorter than the occupant questionnaire. All it asked for was the square footage of the unit and the monthly rent as of January 1 for 1980 through 1986.

Questions

1. What type of research design is being used? Is this design appropriate given the problem?

2. What type of sampling plan is being employed? Is this plan appropriate? Are there any changes in it you would recommend?

Case 5.2 Hart Machine Company[1]

Hart Machine Company of Newberry, South Carolina, is one of five major manufacturers of textile equipment in the country. It is also the only firm that specializes in the design and production of textile machinery rollers. Although its distribution is confined to the three-state area of Georgia, North Carolina, and South Carolina, company sales have been lucrative, averaging some $50 million annually. Part of Hart's success is due to the company being the only roller manufacturer headquartered in the Southeast, an area where 40 percent of the nation's textile mills are located. This location advantage allows Hart to offer customers both prompt shipment and service at low prices (due to lower transportation costs), factors that have helped catapult Hart Machine Company to the third highest position in the textile equipment industry during the relatively short seven-year period since Dean Hart founded it.

In an effort to determine how to best allocate sales personnel and to appraise the performance of current members of the selling team, Thomas Stein, the sales manager, decided to develop estimates of the sales potential for each state served by (1) measuring

the inventory of rollers currently used by textile mills and (2) obtaining estimates of manufacturers' future needs. He hoped to develop a feel for new product demand by first-time users and potential entrants into the textile mill industry as well as gain an indication of the replacement demand for Hart rollers by current users of the firm's product.

A search of the Standard Industrial Classification (SIC) codes identified nine three-digit textile mill industries that were candidates for Hart rollers. Fortunately, there was a good deal of published data available on these industries, and much of the data was broken down by geographic region, state, and county. Stein also had access to data on individual textile mills that employed twenty or more individuals. Stein thought this information was especially useful because only the larger mills possessed the scale of operations necessary to have textile machinery requiring Hart rollers. The published data (see Tables 1 and 2) also indicated that most of the mills (74 per-

---

[1]The contributions of David M. Szymanski to the development of this case are gratefully acknowledged.

Table 1   Total Number of Textile Mills by SIC Code Located in Georgia, North Carolina, and South Carolina

SIC Code	Type of Textile Mill	State			Total
		Georgia	North Carolina	South Carolina	
221	Weaving mills, cotton	45	48	44	137
222	Weaving mills, synthetics	34	76	108	218
223	Weaving and finishing	6	4	5	15
224	Narrow fabric mills	6	45	11	62
225	Knitting mills	45	597	47	689
226	Textile finishing	41	91	47	179
227	Floor covering mills	261	30	17	308
228	Yarn and thread mills	89	231	49	369
229	Miscellaneous textile goods	58	97	53	208
	Total	585	1,219	381	2,185

Source: U.S. Bureau of the Census, *County Business Patterns 1982,* for each of the states of Georgia, North Carolina, and South Carolina. U.S. Government Printing Office, Washington, D.C., 1984.

cent) in Georgia, North Carolina, and South Carolina qualified as likely prospects for Hart equipment in that they employed more than twenty people.

Because of limited research funds, the Hart Company decided to survey only a sample of textile plants in Georgia, North Carolina, and South Carolina. For each firm surveyed, Hart would attempt to ascertain the number of milling machines owned and oper-ated, their age, and the number and brand of rollers used in each piece of equipment. The researchers also hoped to gain information on each mill's perfor-mance—including plans for expansion or curtail-ment of different operations—and brand prefer-ences for roller supplies. From this information it would be possible to estimate the number of ma-chines per textile mill type as well as the new and

Table 2   Number of Textile Mills Employing 20 or More Persons by SIC Code for Georgia, North Carolina, and South Carolina between 1980 and 1982

Type of Textile Mill	Year = 1980			Total
	Georgia	North Carolina	South Carolina	
Weaving mills, cotton	45	47	51	143
Weaving mills, synthetics	26	68	98	192
Weaving and finishing mills, wool	5	4	4	13
Narrow fabric mills	3	34	12	49
Knitting mills	35	432	46	513
Textile finishing	36	69	34	139
Floor covering mills	153	10	14	177
Yarn and thread mills	89	223	50	362
Miscellaneous textile goods	32	56	34	122
Total	424	943	343	1,710

Table 3   Total Number of Textile Mills Employing More Than 20 Persons in Each of Hart Machine Company's Seven Sales Regions, 1982

Georgia

North sales region	324
South sales region	59
Total	383[a]

North Carolina

Northeast sales region	306
Southeast sales region	111
Western sales region	486
Total	903

South Carolina

East sales region	74
West sales region	225
Total	329[a]

[a]Due to differences in methods of reporting, totals differ slightly from those in Table 2.

replacement demand for Hart rollers in the three-state market area. This data would aid Stein in the allocation of sales personnel to different sectors and industries in relation to the demand for rollers. Currently, Hart's sales force is assigned to seven geo-graphic districts: the northern and southern sections of Georgia; the northeast, southeast, and western sections of North Carolina; and the eastern and western sections of South Carolina (see Table 3), according to the overall number of textile mills in each sector.

Industry figures indicate that the number of mills in each of the three states is declining across most industry types (see Table 2). Therefore, estimating the demand for rollers by each textile industry in each state could be crucial to optimal allocation of current sales personnel and to the determination of Hart's future sales force needs.

Having obtained a detailed listing of the addresses of the textile mills located in Georgia, North Carolina, and South Carolina by industry type, company officials tried to decide on the sampling plan that would best enable them to calculate the sales for Hart rollers quickly and inexpensively. Three plans were being considered for determining the mills at which production personnel were to be interviewed.

- Plan A, in which textile mills in each of the seven sales regions would be sampled in proportion to the district's size. For example, given that the northeast sales region in the North Carolina district accounts for approximately 19 percent (306/1,615 × 100) of the textile mills in the three-state area, 19 percent of the sample would come from the northeast sales region. Interviewers would be al-

Table 2   (continued)

	Year = 1981				Year = 1982		
Georgia	North Carolina	South Carolina	Total	Georgia	North Carolina	South Carolina	Total
43	44	48	135	37	40	43	120
25	70	97	192	29	67	106	202
4	4	4	12	4	2	4	10
4	34	10	48	4	35	11	50
34	427	39	500	33	414	37	484
32	71	35	138	30	64	37	131
144	9	13	166	136	12	12	160
85	211	52	348	79	204	46	329
39	56	33	128	33	65	34	132
410	926	331	1,667	385	903	330	1,618

lowed to pick the mills in which the interviews would be conducted.

- Plan B, in which after the total number of textile mills of each type in each sales region was determined, each of the sixty-three groups (9 SIC types × 7 regions) would be sampled in proportion to its size, and the plants at which the interviews would take place would be determined randomly.
- Plan C, in which two of the regions would be randomly selected, and production personnel at all of the plants in each of the two randomly selected regions would be interviewed.

Questions

1. What type of sampling plan is being proposed in each case?

2. What are the strengths and weaknesses of each plan? Which of the three plans would you recommend and why?

3. What other plans might the company consider?

Case 5.3   Holzem Business Systems

Holzem Business Systems serviced a number of small business accounts in the immediate area surrounding its Madison, Wisconsin, location. The company, which was headed by Mr. Claude Holzem, a certified public accountant, specialized in the preparation of financial statements, tax forms, and other reports required by various governmental units. Since its founding in 1962, the company had experienced steady, and sometimes spectacular, growth. Holzem, whose policy was high-quality service at competitive rates, was so successful in Dane County that it was far and away the dominant firm serving small businesses in the area. Further growth seemed to depend more on expansion into new areas than on further penetration of the Madison market.

Faced with such a prospect, Holzem conceived a plan that would capitalize on the substantial talent at the company's main office. What he envisioned was an operation in which area field representatives would secure raw data from clients. At the end of each day, they would transmit this information to headquarters using microcomputers with modems. There it would be coded and processed and the necessary forms prepared. These income statements, balance sheets, or tax forms would then be returned to the area representative. The field person would go over them with the client and would answer any questions that client might have.

In Holzem's mind, the system had a number of advantages. First, it allowed Holzem Business Systems to capitalize on the substantial expertise it had in its Madison office. The quality control for which the company had become noted could be maintained, as could the company's record of quick service. Second, the company would not need to hire CPAs as field representatives, because these area managers would not actually be preparing financial statements. This was believed to be particularly crucial because, as a result of recent heavy demand, there was a current shortage of available CPAs. They were commanding premium salaries. The prospect of using business college graduates who understood financial statements and could explain their significance to clients thus had significant cost advantages.

The big question confronting Holzem was whether there would be a demand for such a service. There was no question in his mind there was a need for accounting services among small businesses. His Madison experience had demonstrated this. But he was concerned that the physical distance between the client and the office might prove to be a psychological barrier for clients. If it proved necessary to establish full service branches in each area, then geographic expansion was less attractive to him.

In order to help him decide whether to go ahead, he commissioned a research study that had as its objectives identifying the perceived problems and the need for CPA services in general, and, in particular, potential client attitudes toward the type of service arrangement he envisioned.

Hathaway Research Associates, headed by James and Nancy Hathaway, was retained to do the study. It

Figure 1

**Regional Breakdown
of Counties**

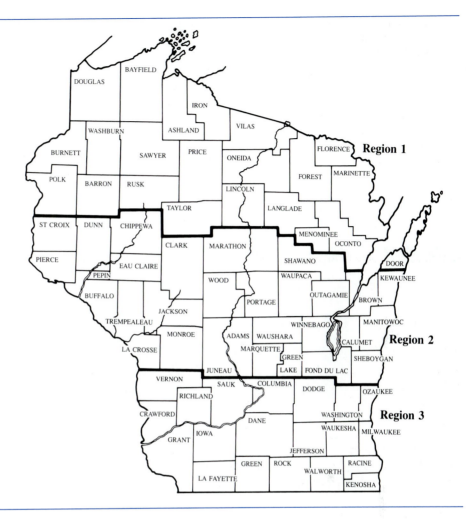

was to be conducted using personal interviews among a representative sample of small businesses within the state. For purposes of the study, a small business was defined as one employing fewer than fifty people. The study was to be confined to small businesses in the industries designated contract construction, manufacturing, wholesale trade, retail trade, and commercial services. These categories represented approximately 95 percent of all Holzem accounts, 85 percent of the total small businesses, and 81 percent of all businesses in the state.

Sampling Plan

The businesses serving as the sample were to be selected in the following way. First, the state was to be divided into the three regions depicted in Figure 1. Next, five counties were to be selected from each region by the following scheme.

1. The cumulative number of businesses was to be calculated from Table 1. The accumulation for the first ten counties in Region 1, for example, is as follows:

County	Number of Businesses	Cumulative Number of Businesses
Douglas	668	668
Burnett	147	815
Polk	488	1,303
Washburn	282	1,585
Barron	565	2,150
Bayfield	178	2,328
Sawyer	324	2,652
Rusk	229	2,881
Ashland	307	3,188
Iron	122	3,310

Table 1   Number of Small Businesses by Major Industry Category

County	Contract Construction	Manufacturing	Wholesale Trade	Retail Trade	Commercial Services	Total
Adams	14	10	3	49	27	103
Ashland	26	37	26	127	91	307
Barron	88	52	82	295	48	565
Bayfield	20	25	8	85	40	178
Brown	387	187	330	871	804	2,579
Buffalo	23	14	22	92	47	198
Burnett	22	12	7	82	24	147
Calumet	62	47	48	162	128	447
Chippewa	105	67	94	300	216	782
Clark	60	76	82	203	101	522
Columbia	98	55	84	360	208	805
Crawford	33	25	32	119	64	273
Dane	638	314	493	1,800	1,705	4,950
Dodge	143	98	119	370	258	988
Door	76	27	27	206	168	504
Douglas	49	30	43	339	207	668
Dunn	37	21	55	187	110	410
Eau Claire	122	39	113	415	331	1,020
Florence	4	6	1	29	6	46
Fond du Lac	178	94	131	546	374	1,323
Forrest	9	25	8	116	27	185
Grant	88	60	125	341	200	814
Green	71	49	82	234	122	558
Green Lake	60	28	28	150	84	350
Iowa	41	23	55	135	65	319
Iron	11	15	10	60	26	122
Jackson	27	14	29	120	49	239
Jefferson	120	88	111	400	283	1,002
Juneau	38	28	27	172	79	344
Kenosha	159	75	105	624	167	1,130
Kewaunee	44	35	32	112	76	299
La Crosse	167	91	159	573	450	1,440
Lafayette	31	29	50	106	58	274
Langlade	29	53	59	135	92	368
Lincoln	50	43	38	184	109	424
Manitowoc	161	102	119	464	338	1,184

Source: County Business Patterns

Table 1 *continued*

County	Contract Construction	Manufacturing	Wholesale Trade	Retail Trade	Commercial Services	Total
Marathon	244	148	196	520	432	1,540
Marinette	63	75	56	253	153	600
Marquette	27	11	9	68	34	149
Menominee	1	5	2	4	6	18
Milwaukee	1,200	1,238	1,711	4,914	5,708	14,771
Monroe	49	37	67	235	115	503
Oconto	49	43	50	143	97	382
Oneida	101	40	45	305	180	671
Outagamie	273	117	227	697	568	1,882
Ozaukee	151	109	95	313	245	915
Pepin	12	7	18	61	31	129
Pierce	50	27	29	206	104	416
Polk	59	44	51	234	100	488
Portage	83	42	71	280	171	647
Price	19	44	32	92	59	246
Racine	292	285	178	853	738	2,346
Richland	29	20	35	108	67	259
Rock	236	118	148	811	570	1,883
Rusk	24	34	34	95	42	229
St. Croix	80	44	61	225	144	554
Sauk	104	58	91	376	223	852
Sawyer	36	25	16	128	119	324
Shawano	65	58	61	232	110	526
Sheboygan	204	151	118	523	433	1,429
Taylor	29	28	36	93	57	243
Trempeleau	51	43	60	192	98	444
Vernon	37	39	52	154	85	367
Vilas	72	30	17	175	113	407
Walworth	144	106	90	522	345	1,207
Washburn	41	27	18	136	60	282
Washington	173	110	97	369	262	1,011
Waukesha	694	506	501	1,147	1,097	3,945
Waupaca	81	70	72	328	201	752
Waushara	26	22	30	114	71	263
Winnebago	244	157	151	759	632	1,943
Wood	141	83	104	427	303	1,058
Totals	8,475	5,995	7,466	26,655	20,957	69,548

2. A table of random numbers would be employed to determine which five counties would be selected. For example, if a number between 816 and 1,303 came up, Polk county would be used.

Hathaway Research Associates then planned to contact the state Department of Industry, Labor, and Human Relations (DILHR) for a list of individual firms within each county. DILHR used the unemployment computer tape to prepare such lists. This tape was compiled each year and reflected payments by firms into the state's unemployment compensation system. The records within the tape were maintained county by county, by SIC (Standard Industrial Classification) code within county, and in alphabetical order within the SIC code. Since the number of employees of each firm was indicated, DILHR could screen the master list and print out only those firms that satisfied the location, industry, and geographic criteria Hathaway Research Associates specified. DILHR would sell these lists of firms to interested clients, but it would provide only the name, address, and phone number of the selected businesses.

Hathaway Research Associates proposed to select forty businesses from each county by the following procedure:

1. The total number of businesses within the county was to be divided by 40 to get a sampling interval. The sampling interval would be different, of course, for each county.

2. A random start was to be generated for each county, using a table of random numbers. The random number was to be some number between 1 and the sampling interval, and this number was to be used to designate the first business to be included in the sample.

3. The sampling interval was to be added repeatedly to the random start, and every number generated in this manner was to designate a business to be included in the sample.

The preceding procedure was to be followed for all counties except Milwaukee and Dane. Holzem believed that if he were to expand into the Milwaukee market at all, he should do it with a completely self-sufficient branch and not with a satellite office tied to the Madison headquarters. He consequently instructed Hathaway Research Associates to exclude Milwaukee County from this part of the research investigation. Dane County was to be excluded because of the company's already successful penetration of this market.

Once the total sample of 600 businesses had been specified, Hathaway Research Associates planned to contact each firm by phone to set up an appointment for a personal interview with one of its highly trained field interviewers.

Questions

1. What kind of sample is being proposed by Hathaway Research Associates? Is this a good choice?

2. Is the sample a true probability sample (i.e., does every small business in Wisconsin have a known chance of selection)?

3. What is the probability that a small business in Menominee County (the county with the fewest small businesses) will be included in the sample? What is the probability that a small business in Waukesha County (of those counties eligible, the one with the most small businesses) will be included in the sample? Will this discrepancy cause any problems in analysis?

Case 5.4   Generic Drugs (B)

The State of Wisconsin passed a law in 1977 that permitted generic drugs to be substituted for brand name drugs when prescriptions were being filled. Consumers simply had to request the substitution

and the pharmacist was legally bound to make it. The legislation was designed to save customers money on their prescriptions. Thus, it proved disconcerting to the Department of Health and Social Services when, some eight years after its passage, few customers were taking advantage of the law by asking for the substitution.

Several hypotheses were advanced as to why this was happening, including the suggestions that the law had not been well publicized, consumers were not aware of its existence, consumers had unfavorable attitudes toward generic drugs, and there were a number of personal and situational factors, such as age, income, household size, and education that were affecting customers' use of the law (see Generic Drugs, Part A). It was decided that the best way to collect the needed information was through the use of self-administered questionnaires. Because of the difficulty of obtaining an accurate mailing list, the questionnaires were to be hand-delivered but returned by mail. Further, it was decided that the feasibility of the data-collection and sampling plans were to be determined by originally confining the study to Madison, the state capital and also the main campus location of the University of Wisconsin. Restricting the original investigation, it was recognized, would probably create some bias in the results because of a number of demographic differences between Madison and the remainder of the state.

Being the state capital and also home to the University of Wisconsin-Madison, the city of Madison was home to numerous professional people. Because of the number of doctors, lawyers, accountants, professors, and other professionals living there, the city had both a higher average education level and a higher average income than the state average or any other city within the state. Most of the professional people lived on the city's west side, typically in more spacious, more expensive housing.

Much of the industry in the city was government-related, although there were some very important exceptions, manufacturers such as Oscar Mayer and Ray-o-Vac and a number of insurance companies. Most of the manufacturing was concentrated on the city's east side, and consequently most of the city's blue-collar workers lived there. Homes on the east side were typically smaller and less expensive than those on the west side, so there were more of them in the same size area.

Sampling Plan

The 1,000 households to be surveyed were selected in the following manner. First, the city was divided into aldermanic districts using detailed maps. To ensure geographic representation of the city, samples were drawn from each aldermanic district. This was done by randomly choosing city blocks within each aldermanic district and then randomly selecting ten households in each of the selected blocks that would receive questionnaires.

Consider Aldermanic District 11, for example, which was located on the city's west side. The study was to be limited to residents of Madison over eighteen years of age. The total adult population in District 11 was 5,115, while the total adult population in the city was 122,016. The proportion of the total sample that was to come from Aldermanic District 11 was thus 5,115/122,016 = .0419. This meant that forty-two households [1,000 (.0419) = 42] were to be included in the sample.

The forty-two households were selected from five blocks within the district by first numbering all the blocks within the district, then randomly selecting five from this larger set of blocks. Ten households were interviewed on each of the first four blocks that were selected, and two households were interviewed in the fifth block. The households were selected by going around the block to count the number of dwelling units, then beginning at the southwest corner, following the detailed instructions for the count of dwelling units that were provided each field worker. Suppose, for example, there were fifty dwelling units in a selected block. The field worker was instructed to generate a random start between 1 and 5, using the table of random numbers each was provided. Suppose the number were 2; the field worker was then to drop off questionnaires at the second, seventh, twelfth, and so on, households in the initial numbering scheme.

Questions

1. What type of sample is being used to distribute questionnaires?

2. Is this a good choice?

Case 5.5   The Dryden Press

Until recently, the Dryden Press was a division of the publishing arm of CBS, Inc. The Dryden Press was established in the mid-1960s by Holt, Rinehart and Winston, which had traditionally been a strong social sciences publisher, as a response to the growth in enrollments that business schools were experiencing and the explosion in enrollments that was predicted. The venture represented one of the first forays by a traditional nonbusiness text publisher into the college business market. The experiment turned out to be very successful, and by the mid-1980s the Dryden Press was one of the top six publishers in the business area in sales. Company executives believed that one of the key reasons for Dryden's success was its ability to target books for specific market segments. The company was one of the first to recognize the potential growth in courses in consumer behavior and managerial economics, for example, and introduced the very successful texts by Engel, Kollat, and Blackwell in consumer behavior and by Brigham and Pappas in managerial economics in response. Through careful management of the revisions, these books still maintained strong market positions more than fifteen years after they had been introduced.

The Dryden Press editorial staff tried to maintain a posture of extreme sensitivity to changing market conditions brought about by the publication of new research findings or the changing demands placed on students due to changes in the environment and the needs of businesses. The editors made it a point to keep up with these changes so that the company would be prepared with new product when the situation demanded it. This was no small task, because the lead time on a book typically ran from three to four years from the time the author was first signed to a contract to when the book was actually published. It took most authors almost two years to develop a first draft of a book manuscript. The typical manuscript was then reviewed by a sample of experts in the field. Based on their reactions, most manuscripts would undergo some revision before being placed in production. The production process, which included such things as copy editing the manuscript, setting type, drawing figures, preparing promotional materials, proofreading, and so on, usually took about a year.

Research Questions and Objectives

In an attempt to anticipate any changes in the needs and desires of the market in consumer behavior texts, the editorial staff decided to find out the current level of use of the various texts in consumer behavior and the directions in which the market was moving. What were the market shares of the respective texts? What features of the various books were liked and disliked? Did the use of the various texts and the preference for certain features vary by class of school? Did four-year colleges have different requirements in consumer behavior texts than two-year schools? After a good deal of discussion among the members of the editorial staff, these general concerns were translated into specific research objectives. More specifically, the staff decided to conduct a research investigation that attempted to determine:

1. The importance of various topical areas in the teaching of consumer behavior within the next two to five years.

2. The importance and treatment of managerial applications in consumer behavior courses.

3. The level of satisfaction with the textbooks currently in use.

4. The relative market shares of the major consumer behavior textbooks.

5. The degree of switching of texts that goes on in consumer behavior courses from year to year.

6. The importance of various pedagogical aids such as glossaries, cases, learning objectives, and so on, in the textbook selection decision.

7. The importance of supplementary teaching tools such as student study guides, overhead transparency masters, and instructors' manuals in the consumer textbook selection decision.

The editorial staff thought it was important that the needed information be obtained from those who were actively involved in teaching consumer behavior courses. The staff also thought it imperative that only one respondent be used from any given school, even though the editors realized that some schools had multiple sections of the consumer behavior course and that different books might be used in different sections. For the most part, however, the editors believed that the same book would be used across sections, though not across courses, in the sense that the introductory courses at the undergraduate and graduate levels would use different books. The editors decided it would be better to target the questionnaires to one individual at each of the selected institutions and to simply have that person indicate on the questionnaire whether he or she normally taught a graduate or undergraduate course. Dryden could then analyze the responses to determine if there were any differences in them that could be attributed to the level at which the course was taught.

Method

There were several reasons why the editorial staff decided to use a mail questionnaire to collect the data. For one thing, the target population was geographically dispersed. Even though it was decided to limit the study only to those actively involved in teaching consumer behavior domestically, that still meant respondents could come from all over the United States, which in turn meant it could be prohibitive to collect this information by personal interview. At the same time, professors had no standard working schedule. Some might teach in the morning and some in the evening. When they were not teaching, some might work in their offices while others might work elsewhere. This variety of schedules and work conditions required that the questionnaires be available when the professors might be inclined to fill them out. Also, the objectives finally decided upon allowed the use of a relatively structured and undisguised questionnaire.

The big question facing the Dryden staff was how to draw a sample from the target population of those actively teaching the consumer behavior course, either at the undergraduate or graduate levels. For purposes of the study, "actively teaching" was operationally defined as having taught a consumer behavior course at least once in the last two years or being scheduled to teach one within the next year.

The company was considering drawing the sample from one of two lists it had at its disposal. One of the lists was an internal list consisting of all those professors whom the salespeople's reports indicated were interested in teaching specific courses such as financial planning, introductory accounting, marketing management, or consumer behavior. This meant that the salesperson had indicated on his or her reports that the professor was to receive sample copies of all those books in, say, consumer behavior that the Dryden Press publishes. Most of the entries on the list were developed from salespeople's calls, although some of them were obtained at the national association meetings where Dryden displayed its list of titles. Professors would often request sample copies of selected titles at the meetings so that they could review them before making an adoption decision. All requests for complimentary copies were sent for authorization to the salesperson serving the school. By approving the request, the salesperson was aware of the professor's interest and could follow it up in an attempt to get the adoption.

Because of how it was developed and used, the internal list paralleled the salespeople's territory structure. While most salespeople operated within one state and often within only part of a state, some operated across several states. Each salesperson was responsible for all the schools in his or her territory, including the universities with graduate programs, four-year colleges without graduate programs, and two-year institutions. The schools were listed alphabetically by salesperson, and each school had a computer code associated with it designating its type. Each professor on the list had a set of computer codes associated with the name that identified his or her interest areas.

The alternate list Dryden considered using was the printed membership directory of the Association for Consumer Research (ACR), an organization formed in the late 1960s for the pursuit of knowledge in the area of consumer behavior. Its membership is dominated by marketing professors (almost 80 percent of the total), although it also includes interested members from business and government as well as members representing other academic disciplines, such as sociology and psychology. The ACR directory was organized alphabetically by name of the member. Along with each member's name, the directory provided either the office or home address, depending on which the individual preferred to use, and both the office and home phone numbers. While about one-half of the addresses listed only the college at which the individual worked, the other 50 percent also listed the department. There were sixty-four pages in the directory, and all pages except the last one had sixteen names. A small percentage of the addresses were international.

Questions

1. Given the purposes of the study, how would you recommend a sample be drawn from:
   (a) Dryden's internal computer list?
   (b) The ACR printed membership directory?
2. Which approach would you recommend and why?

Case 5.6   First Federal Bank of Bakersfield

The Equal Credit Opportunity Act, which was passed in 1974, was partially designed to protect women from discriminatory banking practices. It forbade, for example, the use of credit evaluations based on sex or marital status. While adherence to the law has changed the way many bankers do business, women's perception that there is a bias against them by a particular financial institution often remains unless some specific steps are taken by the institution to counter that perception.

Close to a dozen "women's banks," that is, banks owned and operated by and for women, opened their doors during the 1970s with the specific purpose of targeting and promoting their services to this otherwise underdeveloped market. Today, while "women's banks" are evolving into full-service banks serving a wide range of clients, a number of traditional banks are moving in the other direction by attempting to develop services that are targeted specifically toward women. Many of these forward-looking institutions see such a strategy as a viable way to attract valuable customers and to increase their market share in the short term while gaining a competitive advantage by which they can compete in the long term as the roles of women in the labor force gain in importance. One can find, with even the most cursory examination of the trade press, examples of credit card advertising that depicts single, affluent, and head-of-the-family female card holders, financial seminar programs for affluent wives of professional men, informational literature that details how newly divorced and separated women can obtain credit, and entire packages of counseling, educational opportunities, and special services for women.

The First Federal Bank of Bakersfield was interested in developing its own program of this kind. The

executives were curious about a number of issues. Were women's financial needs being adequately met in the Bakersfield area? What additional financial services would women especially like to have? How do Bakersfield's women feel about banks and bankers? Was First Federal in a good position to take advantage of the needs of women? What channels of communication might be best to reach women who may be interested in the services that First Federal had to offer?

The executives believed that First Federal might have some special advantages if it did try to appeal to women. For one thing, the Bakersfield community gave evidence of being sensitive to the issues being raised by the feminist movement. For another, First Federal was a small, personal bank. The executives thought that women might be more comfortable in dealing with a smaller, more personalized institution and that the bank might not have the traditional "image problem" among women that many larger banks had.

Research Objectives

One program that bank executives believed might be particularly attractive to women was a series of financial seminars covering topics such as money management, wills, trusts, estate planning, taxes, insurance, investments, financial services, and establishing a credit rating. The executives wished to determine women's reactions to each of these potential topics and if there were a high level of interest, to further determine what the best format might be in terms of location, frequency, and length of each program. Consequently, they decided that the bank should conduct a research study that had the assessment of the financial seminar series as its main objective but that also would shed some light on the other, related issues. More specifically, the objectives of the research were as follows:

1. To determine what interest exists among women in the Bakersfield area for seminars on financial matters.

2. To identify the reasons why Bakersfield women would change, or have changed, their banking affiliations.

3. To examine the attitudes of Bakersfield women toward financial institutions and the people who run them.

4. To determine if there was any correlation between the demographic characteristics of women in the Bakersfield area and the services they might like to have.

5. To analyze the media usage habits of Bakersfield women.

Method

The assignment to develop a research strategy by which these objectives could be assessed was given to the bank's internal marketing research department. The department consisted of only five members— Beth Anchurch, the research director, and four project analysts. As Beth pondered the assignment, she was concerned about the best way to proceed. She was particularly concerned with the relatively short time horizon she was given for the project. Top executives thought there was promise in the seminar idea. If they were right, they wanted to begin designing and offering the seminars before any of their competitors came up with a similar idea. Thus, they specified that they would like the results of the research department's investigation to be available within forty-five to fifty days.

Beth was particularly concerned with whether the study should use mail questionnaires or telephone interviews. She had tentatively ruled out personal interviews because of the short deadline that had been imposed. After several days of contemplating the alternatives, she finally decided that it would be best to collect the information by telephone. Further, she decided that it would be better to hire out the telephone interviewing than to use her four project analysts to make the calls.

She believed that the multiple objectives of the project required a reasonably large sample of women

so that the various characteristics of interest would be sufficiently represented to enable some conclusions to be drawn about the population of Bakersfield as a whole. After pondering the various cross tabulations in which the bank executives would be interested, she finally decided that a sample of 500 to 600 adult women would be sufficient. The sample was to be drawn from the white pages of the Bakersfield telephone directory by the Bakersfield Interviewing Service, the firm that First Federal had hired to complete the interviews.

The sample was to be drawn using a scheme in which two names were selected from each page of the directory first by selecting two of the four columns on the page at random and then by selecting the fifteenth name in each of the selected columns. The decision to sample names from each page was made so that each interviewer could operate with certain designated pages of the directory, since each was operating independently out of her home.

The decision to sample every fifteenth name in the selected columns was determined in the following way. First, there were 328 pages in the directory with four columns of names per page. There were 80 entries per column on average, or approximately 26,240 listings. Using Bureau of the Census data on household composition, Beth estimated that 20 percent of all households would be ineligible for the study because they did not contain an adult female resident. This meant that only 20,992 (.80 × 26,240) of the listings would probably qualify. Since 500 to 600 names were needed, it seemed easiest to select two columns on each page at random and to take the same numbered entry from each column. The interviewer could then simply count or measure down from the top of the column. The number 15 was determined randomly; thus, the fifteenth listing in the randomly selected columns on each page was called. If the household did not answer or if the women of the house refused to participate, the interviewers were instructed to select another number from that column through the use of an abbreviated table of random numbers that each was supplied. They were to use a similar procedure if the household that was called did not have an adult woman living there.

First Federal decided to operate without callbacks because the interviewing service charged heavily for them. Beth thought it would be useful to follow up with a sample of those interviewed to make sure they indeed had been called, since the interviewers for Bakersfield Interviewing Service operated out of their own homes and it was impossible to supervise them

Table 1   Selected Demographic Comparison of Survey Respondents with Bureau of Census Data

Characteristic/Category	Percentage of Women	
	Survey	Census
Marital Status		
Married	53	42
Single	30	40
Separated	1	2
Widowed	9	9
Divorced	7	7
Age		
18–24	23	23
25–34	30	28
35–44	16	14
45–64	18	21
65+	13	14
Income		
Less than $10,000	9	29
$10,000–$19,999	19	29
$20,000–$50,000	58	36
More than $50,000	2	6
Refused	12	

more directly. She did this by selecting at random a handful of the surveys completed by each interviewer. She then had one of her project assistants call that respondent, verify the interview had taken place, and check the accuracy of the responses of a few of the most important questions. This audit revealed absolutely no instances of interviewer cheating.

The completed interview forms were turned over to First Federal for its own internal analysis. As part of this analysis, the project analyst compared the demographic characteristics of those contacted to the demographic characteristics of the population in the Bakersfield area as reported in the 1980 Census. The comparison is shown in Table 1. The analyst also prepared a summary of the nonresponses and refusals by interviewer. This comparison is shown in Table 2.

Questions

1. Compare the advantages and disadvantages of using telephone interviews versus personal interviews or mail questionnaires to collect the needed data.

2. Compare the advantages and disadvantages of using in-house staff versus a professional interviewing service to collect the data.

3. Do you think the telephone directory provided a good sampling frame given the purposes of the

Table 2   Results of Calls by Interviewer

	Number of Nonresponses			Number of Refusals		
Interviewer	Line Busy	No Answer	Ineligibles[a]	Initial	After Partial Completion	Number of Completions
1	7	101	36	15	0	30
2	2	45	13	16	0	30
3	11	71	23	17	7	30
4	14	56	47	35	6	39
5	9	93	10	23	13	30
6	5	102	28	63	14	35
7	6	36	17	16	0	18
8	7	107	23	13	0	30
9	11	106	36	47	0	30
10	10	55	6	35	9	30
11	38	83	48	92	0	30
12	5	22	3	8	0	9
13	23	453	102	65	7	99
14	12	102	27	31	0	19
15	7	173	29	66	0	34
16	2	65	9	33	0	22
Total	169	1,670	457	575	56	515
		1,839			631	

[a]No adult female resident.

study, or would you recommend an alternative sampling frame?

4. What type of sample is being used here? Still using the white pages of the telephone directory as the sampling frame, would you recommend some other sampling scheme? Why or why not?

5. If you were Ms. Anchurch, would you be happy with the performance of the Bakersfield Interviewing Service? Why or why not?

Case 5.7   WIAA Tournaments

The Wisconsin Interscholastic Athletic Association (WIAA) annually sponsors a number of state tournaments, all of which are held in the state capital of Madison. The tournaments include football, girls' tennis, girls' swimming, wrestling, boys' swimming, hockey, girls' basketball, boys' basketball, track, and boys' tennis, and the tournaments are held in the order listed. The first is usually held in late October and the last around the first week of June.

There were periodic discussions about the benefits and costs of these tournaments, in general and with respect to Madison in particular. In order to better assess the impact on Madison, the WIAA, in conjunction with the Greater Madison Chamber of Commerce, commissioned a study to determine the expenditures made in Madison that would not have been made if the tournaments had not been held there.

From the beginning, priorities were set concerning the importance of the various tournaments. The boys' basketball tournament was deemed most important because of the number of people it attracted. Further, it was decided to concentrate the study on the first three months of the calendar year, so football, girls' tennis, girls' swimming, track, and boys' tennis were not to be measured directly. Rather, total attendance at these events was known, and it was believed that if the attendance figures were multiplied by the per capita expenditure figures determined from the other events surveyed, a reasonable estimate could be obtained.

Data Collection

A self-administered questionnaire was used to collect the information (see Figure 1). The questionnaires were taped to predetermined seats at designated events. They were bright orange and had the words "PLEASE READ ME" stamped in green across the top so as to increase their visibility. The questionnaire instructed the respondent to complete it only after leaving the Madison area. It was hoped this would provide a more accurate picture of the person's total expenditures while in Madison. It was hoped that the individual would record expenditures as they were accruing and would complete the questionnaire soon after arriving home. Coding on the questionnaire denoted the tournament and the session in which it was distributed.

The target population was defined to include all ticket holders, contestants, and coaches attending the five individual WIAA tournaments surveyed. However, the most important segment with respect to economic impact were those people who were not from the Madison area but came to Madison expressly for the WIAA tournaments. Expenditure formulations did not include money spent by Madisonians except for the price of their tickets. It was believed that they would have spent approximately the same amount of money for other activities whether or not the tournaments were in Madison.

The seats to which the questionnaires were affixed were determined in the following way. First, the seats assigned various segments of the public were divided into groups by section number. Figure 2, for example, shows the seating arrangement for the basketball tournament. All those seats assigned to the general public made up one group, those assigned to competing team patrons another group, and so on. Second, sections within each group were determined randomly. Finally, seats within each section were determined so that the five major groups were sampled in the same proportion. This was done by dividing the total number of seats assigned each group by 20,

Figure 1   Questionnaire for WIAA Tournaments

Dear athletic fan:

Welcome to the WIAA tournaments! You are one of the selected few specially chosen to answer this questionnaire. Your past participation has made the WIAA tournaments a fun and exciting experience. Your cooperation in this survey will help us know you better. Due to the small size of the survey sample, please be sure to take this questionnaire home with you, and return it completed at your earliest convenience.

Thank you for giving us the help we need. Good luck in the competitions and have lots of fun!

Cordially,

Wisconsin Interscholastic Athletic Association

Greater Madison Chamber of Commerce

For official use only	□□□

Please check the most appropriate response for each of the questions:

1. *Are you from the Madison area (*including City & Town of Madison, Fitchburg, Middleton, Shorewood, Monona, Town of Burke, Maple Bluff)?*

   1 □ Yes   2 □ No

2. *If you answered "no" to Question 1, was the WIAA tournament your main reason for visiting Madison?*

   1 □ Yes   2 □ No

Residents of the Madison area* please omit Questions 3, 4 & 5.

3. *How many days and nights did you spend in the Madison area? Please round off parts of a day to a whole day.*

   A. DAYS — 1 □ One   2 □ Two   3 □ Three   4 □ Four   5 □ Five or more

   B. NIGHTS — □ None   2 □ One   3 □ Two   4 □ Three   5 □ Four   6 □ Five or more

Figure 2   Seat Assignments for Basketball Tournament

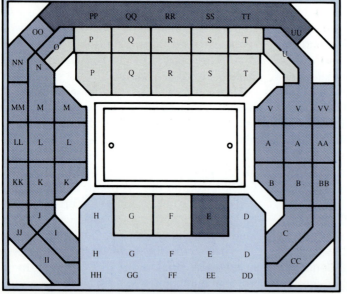

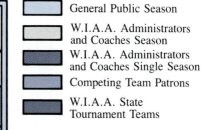

General Public Season

W.I.A.A. Administrators and Coaches Season

W.I.A.A. Administrators and Coaches Single Season

Competing Team Patrons

W.I.A.A. State Tournament Teams

Figure 1 *continued*

4. *How many days did you actually view the tournament games?*

   1 ☐ One   2 ☐ Two   3 ☐ Three

5. *How many people came to the Madison area with you but did not attend the games?*

   1 ☐ None   2 ☐ One   3 ☐ Two   4 ☐ Three   5 ☐ Four   6 ☐ Five or more

6. *Please give your best estimate of how much you spent in the following categories while you were in the Madison area:*

   A. Eating and drinking . . . . $_____

   B. Lodging (hotel, motel, tourist home, etc.) . . . . $_____

   C. Transportation companies (railroad, airline, bus—only if ticket was purchased locally,
       city or University bus, etc.) . . . . $_____

   D. Service stations (repair, parts, gasoline, etc.) . . . . $_____

   E. Auto dealers (car purchase only) . . . . $_____

   F. Apparel store (clothing, shoes, accessories, etc.) . . . . $_____

   G. Retail store (record, gift, drug, hardware, sporting goods, etc.) . . . . $_____

   H. Department, variety, discount or catalog stores . . . . $_____

   I.   Entertainment places (theatre, bowling alley, concert,
        amusement arcade, discotheque, etc.) . . . . $_____

   J.   Personal or business service (barber, beauty shop, dry cleaner,
        doctor, etc.) . . . . $_____

   K. Furniture and appliance store . . . . $_____

   L. City government (parking fee and traffic ticket) . . . . $_____

   M. Local households (babysitter, private parking, etc.) . . . . $_____

   TOTAL VISIT EXPENDITURE = $_____

since the overall sampling fraction was 1 in 20. A random start between 1 and the result of the division was determined from a random number table, and a questionnaire was affixed to that seat and every *k*th seat thereafter.

Both the sections sampled and the starting point were altered for each session of any tournament so as to lessen the likelihood of sampling people who held the same seat for more than one session. Further, the specific sampling pattern itself was altered for each tournament to reflect the forecast attendance and facility configuration.

The percentages of all questionnaires returned, by tournament, were: wrestling, 12 percent; swimming, 12 percent; hockey, 9 percent; girls' basketball, 15 percent; and boys' basketball, 20 percent. Per capita expenditures of those responding were then multiplied by the total number of people attending the event to determine total direct expenditures attributed to the event. These expenditures were then multiplied by an economic multiplier to reflect the fact that every dollar brought into the community has secondary effects because of the additional spending it triggers.

Questions

1. Evaluate the study design and method of data collection.

2. What kind of sample is being used? What is the rationale for sampling each group at the same rate?

Part Six   Data Analysis

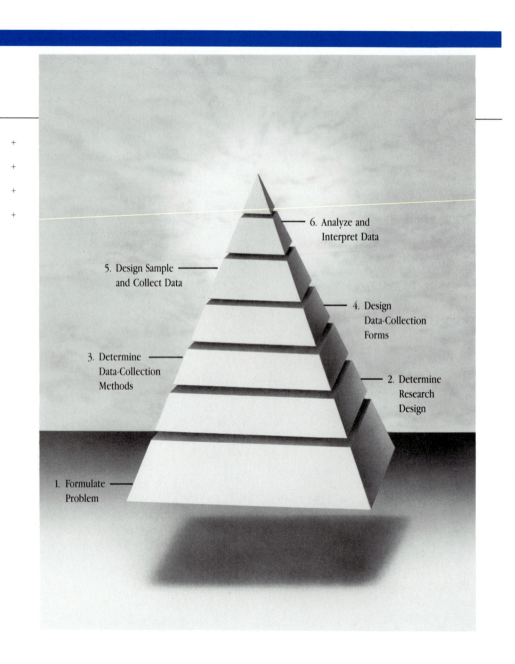

6. Analyze and
   Interpret Data

5. Design Sample
   and Collect Data

4. Design
   Data-Collection
   Forms

3. Determine
   Data-Collection
   Methods

2. Determine
   Research
   Design

1. Formulate
   Problem

After the data have been collected, the emphasis in the research process logically turns to analysis, which is the search for meaning in the collected information. This search involves many questions and several steps. Chapter 17 reviews the common steps of editing, coding, and tabulating the data. Some studies stop with these steps. Many involve additional analyses, however, particularly the testing for statistical significance, and Appendix 17A reviews some of the fundamentals regarding the testing for statistical significance. Chapter 18 and Appendix 18A then discuss the statistical procedures appropriate for determining whether some observed differences between and among groups are statistically significant. Finally, Chapter 19 and Appendix 19A discuss procedures for assessing the degree of association between variables.

Chapter 17

Data Analysis: Preliminary Steps

Learning Objectives

Upon completing this chapter, you should be able to

1. Explain the purpose of the field edit.
2. Define what is meant by coding in the research process.
3. List the three steps in the coding process.
4. Outline the conventions that are customarily followed when data are to be analyzed by a computer.
5. Describe the kinds of information contained in a codebook.
6. Define what is meant by tabulation and distinguish between the two types of tabulation.
7. Explain the various ways in which one-way tabulation can be used.
8. Assess the particular importance of cross tabulation.
9. Describe a method by which a researcher can determine what impact one variable has on another in a cross-tabulation table.

Case in Marketing Research

John Linsky, director of product development, got off the elevator at the fifteenth floor of the Capital Motors building and walked across the plush carpeting to the executive conference room. Under his arm he carried a report that he thought would not only be instrumental in changing the direction of the automobile manufacturer's product line, but would propel him into a position at the head of a division, at least, and perhaps even higher if everything worked according to his plan.

After shaking hands all around with the company's top executives, Linsky stood to make his presentation.

"Ladies and gentlemen," he said, "we all know that Capital Motors has built its reputation and greatness on producing top-quality cars at affordable prices. For our entire history, we've been known to make the car of choice for Middle America. We've grown and prospered under that strategy. But times are changing, and so must we.

Source: This fictitious case is based on an article by Bernie Whalen, "The 'Vanishing' Middle Class: A Passing Demographic Aberration," *Marketing News,* 18 (May 25, 1984), pp. 1 and 6–7.

"I have here a report, citing some of the best economic minds of our generation, that predicts that our primary market, the great middle class, is becoming an endangered species. Within years, this report shows, the country will be divided into two groups—those with a high income and those with a low. For all intents and purposes, the middle-income group will disappear.

"The threat this poses to our current marketing strategy is obvious. We cannot continue doing what we've been doing and hope to survive. We, too, must change with the times. That is why I propose that we start now to make plans to launch a 'new' Capital Motors. The luxury market is there for the taking. Look at the success of the BMW, the Audi, and the Mercedes. Even the Japanese are getting into the act with their luxury sports cars. If we start now, within a few years we, too, can develop products targeted to this market. Luxury touring cars. Sleek sports models. Even upscale station wagons. Of course, we may have to sacrifice our current market in the process, but I guarantee you that it will be worth it. Just look at these figures."

Linsky passed around a chart of census data showing the changes in annual household income between 1970 and 1982. Indeed, the argument seemed compelling. The figures did seem to show that during those twelve years, the lower and upper end of the spectrum increased while the middle class declined sharply from 48 percent of the population in 1970 to less than 41 percent by 1982.

Table 1 Annual Household Income (Constant Dollars)

Bracket	1970	1982
Under $15,000	33.5% 21,775,000	37.4% 31,416,000
$15,000– $35,000	48% 31,200,000	40.5% 34,020,000
Over $35,000	18.5% 12,025,000	22.1% 18,564,000
Household base	65 million	84 million

After studying the chart for a minute, the company's CEO spoke up. "Your argument has a certain appeal, John, but the implications to this company are just too vast to stake our future on an uncritical acceptance of these figures. I would like some time to examine these data more closely. If they hold up, we'll talk further. But something seems fishy here, and I don't plan to bet the ranch based on some economist's dire predictions. Economics isn't called the 'dismal science' for nothing."

Discussion Issues

1. If you were the CEO of Capital Motors, what further information would you want about the data Linsky presented?

2. What kind of questions would marketing researchers immediately ask about such data?

3. What social changes during this period might help to explain the data?

Imagine yourself as the director of a marketing research project. For weeks you have supervised a massive field study in numerous shopping malls. Now the foot soldiers in your data-collecting army have moved on to other projects, and you are left in your office surrounded by stacks of completed questionnaires. The battle to extract the information may be over, but you have not yet won the war until you can determine what all those data really mean.

In this chapter, we will begin to explore how analysts obtain meaning from raw data. All previous steps in the research process have been undertaken to support this search for meaning. The specific analytical procedures involved are closely related to the preceding steps, because the careful analyst looked ahead to this moment when he or she designed those other steps. The most astute researchers developed dummy tables as well, indicating how each item of information would be used. Thorough preparatory work probably revealed some undesirable data gaps and some "interesting" but not vital items that might have posed problems if they had not been dealt with at that time.

The search for meaning can take many forms. However, the preliminary analytical steps of editing, coding, and tabulating the data are common to most studies, so a review of what they are and how they are used is warranted.

♦ Editing

The basic purpose of editing is to impose some minimum quality standards on the raw data. Editing involves the inspection and, if necessary, correction of each questionnaire or observation form. Inspection and correction are often done in two stages: the field edit and the central-office edit.

Field Edit

• **Field edit**

Preliminary edit, typically conducted by a field supervisor, which is designed to detect the most glaring omissions and inaccuracies in a completed data-collection instrument.

The **field edit** is a preliminary edit designed to detect the most glaring omissions and inaccuracies in the data. It is also useful in helping to control the behavior of the field force personnel and to clear up any misunderstandings they may have about directions, procedures, specific questions, and so on.

Ideally, the field edit is done as soon as possible after the questionnaire or other data-collection form has been administered. In that way, problems can be corrected before the interviewing or observation staff is disbanded, and while the particular contacts that were the source of trouble are still fresh in the interviewer's or observer's mind. The preliminary edit is usually conducted by a field supervisor. Some of the items checked are described in Table 17.1.[1]

---

[1] The classification of items to be checked in the field edit is taken from Claire Selltiz, Lawrence S. Wrightsman, and Stuart W. Cook, *Research Methods in Social Relations,* 3rd ed. (New York: Holt, Rinehart and Winston, 1976), pp. 475–476. Reprinted by permission of Holt, Rinehart and Winston.

Table 17.1   Items Checked in the Field Edit

1. **Completeness:** This check for completeness involves scrutinizing the data form to ensure that no sections or pages were omitted, and it also involves checking individual items. A blank for a specific question could mean that the respondent refused to answer; alternatively, it may simply reflect an oversight on the respondent's part or that he did not know the answer. It may be very important for the purposes of the study to know which reason is correct. It is hoped that by contacting the field worker while the interview is fresh in his mind, the field editor can obtain the needed clarification.

2. **Legibility:** It is impossible to code a questionnaire that cannot be deciphered because of illegible handwriting or obscure abbreviations. It is a simple matter to correct this now, whereas it is often extremely time-consuming later.

3. **Comprehensibility:** Sometimes a recorded response is incomprehensible to all but the field interviewer. By detecting this now, the field editor can obtain the necessary clarification.

4. **Consistency:** Marked inconsistencies within an interview or observation schedule typically indicate errors in collecting or recording the data and may indicate ambiguity in the instrument or carelessness in its administration. For instance, if a respondent indicated that he saw a particular commercial on television last night on one part of the questionnaire, and later indicated that he did not watch television last night, the analyst would indeed be in a dilemma. Such inconsistencies can often be detected and corrected in the field edit.

5. **Uniformity:** It is very important that the responses be recorded in uniform units. For instance, if the study is aimed at determining the number of magazines read per week per individual, and the respondent indicates the number of magazines for which he or she has monthly subscriptions, the response base is not uniform, and the result could cause confusion in the later stages of analysis. If the problem is detected now, perhaps the interviewer can recontact the respondent and get the correct answer.

Central-Office Edit

• Central-office edit

Thorough and exacting scrutiny and correction of completed data-collection forms, including a decision about what to do with the data.

The field edit is typically followed by a **central-office edit,** which involves more complete and exacting scrutiny and correction of the completed returns. The work calls for the keen eye of a person well versed in the objectives and procedures of the study. To ensure consistency of treatment, it is best if one individual handles all completed instruments. If the work must be divided because of length and time considerations, the division should be by parts of the data-collection instruments rather than by respondents. That is, one editor would edit Part A of all questionnaires while the other would edit Part B.

Unlike the field edit, the central-office edit depends less on follow-up procedures and more on deciding just what to do with the data. Accurate follow-up is now more difficult because of the time that has elapsed. The editor must decide how data-collection instruments containing incomplete answers, obviously wrong answers, and answers that reflect a lack of interest will be handled. Since such problems are more prevalent with questionnaires than observational forms, we will discuss these difficulties from that perspective, although our discussion applies generally to all types of data-collection forms.

The study in which all the returned questionnaires are completely filled out is rare. Some will have complete sections omitted. Others will reflect sporadic item nonresponse. The editor's decision on how to handle these incomplete questionnaires depends on the severity of the omission. Questionnaires that omit complete sections are obviously suspect. Yet they should not automatically be thrown out. It might be, for example, that the omitted section refers to the influence of the spouse in some major durable purchase whereas the respondent is not married. This type of reply is certainly usable in spite of the incomplete section. If there is no logical justification for the large number of unanswered questions, the total reply would probably be thrown out, increasing the nonresponse rate for the study. Questionnaires containing only isolated instances of item nonresponse would be retained, although they might undergo some *data cleaning* after coding, a subject discussed later in this chapter.

Careful editing of the questionnaire will sometimes show that an answer to a question is obviously incorrect. For example, respondents might be asked for the type of store in which they purchased a camera in one part of the questionnaire and the name of the store in another. If the person responds "department store" to the first question and then gives the name of a catalog showroom to answer the second, one of the answers is incorrect. The editor may be able to determine which of the two answers is correct from other information in the questionnaire. Alternatively, the editor may need to establish policies as to which answer, if either, will be treated as correct when these inconsistencies or other types of inaccuracies arise. These policies will reflect the purposes of the study.

Editors must also be on the alert to spot completed questionnaires that have failed to engage the respondent's interest. Evidence of this lack of interest may be obvious or quite subtle. Consider, for example, a subject who checked the "5" position on a five-point scale for each of forty items in an attitude questionnaire, even though some items were expressed negatively and some positively. Obviously, that person did not take the study seriously, and the editor should probably throw out such a response. A discerning editor might also be able to pick up more subtle indications of disinterest, such as check marks that are not within the boxes provided, scribbles, spills on the questionnaire, and so on. An editor may not want to throw out these responses, but they should be coded so that it is later possible to run separate tabulations for the questionable instruments and obviously good questionnaires. Then the two groups could be compared to see whether lack of interest makes any difference in the results.

◆ Coding

◆ Coding

Technical procedure by which data are categorized; it involves specifying the alternative categories or classes into which the responses are to be placed and assigning code numbers to the classes.

Coding is "the technical procedure by which data are categorized. Through coding, the raw data are transformed into symbols—usually numerals—that may be tabulated and counted. The transformation is not automatic, however; it involves judgment on the part of the coder."[2]

The first step in coding is specifying the categories or classes into which the responses are to be placed.[3] There is no magic number of categories. Rather, the number will depend on the research problem being investigated and the specific items used to generate the information. Response choices should be mutually exclusive and exhaustive, so that every response logically falls into one and only one category. Multiple responses are legitimate for some questions—for example, if the question is "For what purposes do you use JELL-O?" and the responses include such things as "a dessert item," "an evening snack," "an afternoon snack," and so on. On the other hand, if the question focuses on the person's age, then only one age category is, of course, acceptable, and the code should indicate clearly which category.

Coding closed questions and most scaling devices is simple because the coding is established when the data-collection instrument is designed. Respondents then code

---

[2]Selltiz, Wrightsman, and Cook, *Research Methods,* p. 473.

[3]Some writers would make the specification of categories part of the editing rather than the coding function. Its placement in one or the other function is not nearly as important as the recognition that it is an extremely critical step with significant ramifications for the whole research effort.

themselves with their responses, or the interviewer codes them in recording the responses on the checklist provided.

Coding open-ended questions can be very difficult. The coder has to determine appropriate categories on the basis of answers that are not always anticipated.[4] Consider the following question, which was used in a study of the fast food franchise system of distribution:[5] "Please specify the product or service around which your franchise system is organized (for example, pancakes)." The expectation was that the respondents would reply with "hamburgers" or "chicken" or "pizza" and so on. Some did. Others responded with "hamburgers, hot dogs, and beverages." How should such a reply be treated? The decision, after much agonizing, was to establish the category of "multiple fast foods."[6]

If there are so many questionnaires that several coders are needed, inconsistency in coding may be an additional problem. To assure consistency of treatment, the work should be divided by task, not by dividing the questionnaires equally among the coders. By allowing coders to focus their energies on one, or a few questions, researchers can ensure that a consistent set of standards is being applied to each question. This approach is also more efficient, because coders can easily memorize just a few codes and thus do not have to consult the codebook for each instrument. When several persons do, in fact, code the same question on different batches of questionnaires, it is important that they also code a sample of the other's work to ensure that a consistent set of coding criteria is being employed.[7]

The second step in coding involves assigning code numbers to the classes. For example, sex might be assigned the letters M for male and F for female. Alternatively, the classes could be denoted by 1 for male and 2 for female. Generally, it is better to use numbers rather than letters to denote the classes. It is also better at this stage to use numerical data as it was reported on the data-collection form, rather than to collapse it into smaller categories. For example, it is not advisable to code age as 1 = under 20 years, 2 = 20–29, 3 = 30–39, and so on if actual ages of the people in years were provided. This would result in an unnecessary sacrifice of information in the original measurement and could just as easily be done at later stages in the analysis.

When a computer is being used to analyze the data, it is necessary to code the data so that they can be readily inputted to the machine. Regardless of how that input will be handled, whether by mark-sense forms or directly through a keyboard on a terminal, it is helpful to visualize the input in terms of an eighty-column card image. Further, it is advisable to follow certain conventions when coding the data.

1. Locate only one character in each column. When the question allows multiple responses, allow separate columns in the coding for each answer. Thus in our

---

[4]In one study that explicitly compared the responses to open and closed questions, marked differences were found in the response distributions to the two types of questions. The authors concluded that the responses to closed questions were the more valid, because the responses to open questions are often so vague that they are misclassified by coders. See H. Schuman and S. Presser, "The Open and Closed Question," *American Sociological Review*, 44 (1979), pp. 692–712. To improve the consistency with which similar answers are coded, some researchers have attempted to develop systems by which computers can code open-ended responses. For an illustration, see Colin McDonald, "Coding Open-Ended Answers With the Help of a Computer," *Journal of the Market Research Society*, 24 (January 1982), pp. 9–27.

[5]Urban B. Ozanne and Shelby D. Hunt, *The Economic Effects of Franchising* (Madison, Wis.: Graduate School of Business, The University of Wisconsin, 1971).

[6]*Ibid.*, p. 34.

[7]For discussion of a set of indices that can be used to investigate coder reliability as well as to determine which questions might be proving particularly troublesome, see Martin Collins and Graham Kalton, "Coding Verbatim Answers to Open Questions," *Journal of the Market Research Society*, 22 (October 1980), pp. 239–247.

One of the preliminary
steps in data analysis is
coding the data so that it
can be entered into a
computer.

Source: Courtesy of NCR Corporation.

JELL-O example, the coder should provide a separate column for those who use the product as a dessert item, an evening snack, and so on.

2. Use only numeric codes, not letters of the alphabet or special characters, like @, or blanks. Most computer statistical programs have trouble manipulating anything but numbers.

3. Use as many columns as are necessary to capture the variable for the field assigned to a variable. (Thus, if the variable is such that the ten codes from 0 to 9 are not sufficient to exhaust the categories, then one should use two columns, providing one hundred codes from 00 through 99. However, no more than one variable should be assigned to any field.)

4. Use standard codes for "no information." Thus, all "don't know" responses might be coded as 8, "no answers" as 9, and "does not apply" as 0. It is best if the same code is used throughout the study for each of these types of "no information."

5. Code in a respondent identification number on each record. This number need not, and typically will not, identify the respondent by name. Rather the number simply ties the questionnaire to the coded data. This is often useful information in data cleaning (discussed later). If the questionnaire requires more than eighty columns of code, it will not fit on one card image. Each card image then should be coded with the respondent identification number and a sequence number. Column 10 in Card Image 1 might then indicate how the respondent answered Question 2, while Column 10 in Card Image 2 might indicate whether the person is male or female.[8]

• Codebook

A book that describes each
variable, gives it a code
name, and identifies its
location in the record.

The final step in the coding process is to prepare a **codebook,** which contains the general instructions indicating how each item of data was coded. It lists the codes for each variable and the categories included in each code. It further indicates

[8]Philip S. Siedl, "Coding," in Robert Ferber, ed., *Handbook of Marketing Research* (New York: McGraw-Hill, 1974), pp. 2-178–2-199. This article provides an excellent overview of the issues that arise in coding data and how they can be handled.

where on the computer record the variable is located and how the variable should be read—for example, with a decimal point or as a whole number. The latter information is provided by the format specifications.

◆ Tabulation

Tabulation consists simply of counting the number of cases that fall into the various categories. The tabulation may take the form of a simple tabulation or a cross tabulation. **Simple tabulation** involves counting a single variable. It may be repeated for each of the variables in the study, but the tabulation for each variable is independent of the tabulation for the other variables. In **cross tabulation,** two or more of the variables are treated simultaneously. For instance, coding the number of people who bought Campbell's soup at a Kroger store is an example of a cross tabulation, since it measures two related characteristics. The tabulations may be done entirely by hand, entirely by machine, or partially by machine and partially by hand. Which is more efficient depends both on the number of tabulations necessary and on the number of cases in each tabulation. The number of tabulations is a direct function of the number of variables, while the number of cases is a direct function of the size of the sample. The fewer the number of tabulations required and the smaller the sample, the more attractive hand methods become. However, the attractiveness of either alternative also is highly dependent on the complexity of the tabulations. Complexity increases as the number of variables receiving simultaneous treatment in a cross tabulation increases. Complexity also increases as the number of categories per variable increases.

For hand tabulation a tally sheet is typically used. Consider the question, "How many trips did you make to the grocery store this past week?" The tally for a sample of Size 40 might look like this:

0	⊔⊔⊤	1		6
1	⊔⊔⊤	⊔⊔⊤	11	12
2	⊔⊔⊤	⊔⊔⊤		10
3	⊔⊔⊤	111		8
4 or more	1111			4

The hand tally also can be used to create cross-classification tables. Suppose one of the study questions was the relationship between shopping behavior and family size. Table 17.2 shows the cross tabulation that might then be constructed. The cross tabulation indicates, for instance, that of the six families that made zero trips to the grocery store, four were composed of only one member, one family had two members, and one family had four members. The cross tabulation thus provides information on the *joint occurrence* of shopping trips and family size.

Note that the right-hand totals (sometimes referred to as the *marginal totals*) are identical to the results for the straight tabulation. This shows that it is unnecessary to make straight tabulations for individual variables that will be included in two-way tables.

While the hand tabulation might be useful in very simple studies involving a few questions and a limited number of responses, most studies rely on computer tabulation using packaged programs. A great many such programs are available.[9] Some

---

[9]For a review of the features contained in the most popular statistical packages, see I. Francis, *Statistical Software: A Comparative Review* (Amsterdam: North Holland, 1981).

Table 17.2   Relationship between Family Size and Number of Shopping Trips

Number of Trips	Number of Members					
	1	2	3	4	5 or more	Total
0	1111	1		1		6
1	111	1111	111	11		12
2	1	111	1111	11		10
3		1	̶1̶1̶1̶1̶1̶	1	1	8
4 or more				1	111	4
Totals	8	9	12	7	4	40

will calculate summary statistics and will plot a histogram of the values in addition to reporting the number of cases in each category. The basic input to these statistical analyses will be the *data array,* which lists the value of each variable for each sample unit. Each variable occupies a specific place in the record for a sample unit, thereby making it easy to pick off the values for it from all of the cases. The location of each variable is given in the codebook.

Figure 17.1 shows an abbreviated version of a questionnaire that was sent to customers of a sporting goods retailer to determine their perceptions of buying sporting goods through the mail. Table 17.3 is an example of the data array that could result from such a study. Table 17.4 is the codebook to the study that describes what is contained in each column. Note that only one line had to be devoted to each sample unit or observation. If the amount of information sought from each sample unit were greater, so that it would not fit as an eighty-column card image record, additional lines would be devoted to each observation. The codebook would still indicate where the information for any particular variable was located.

There are a number of important questions concerning the analysis of data that can be illustrated using one-way tabulations and cross tabulations as vehicles. Consider, therefore, the data in Table 17.5. Suppose that the data were collected for a study focusing on car ownership. Suppose, in particular, that the following questions were of research interest:

- What characteristics distinguish families owning two or more cars from families owning one car?
- What are the distinguishing characteristics of those who buy station wagons? Foreign economy cars? Vans?
- Are there differences in the characteristics of families who financed their automobile purchase and those who did not?

Suppose that the data were collected from a probability sample of respondents using mailed questionnaires, and that the 100 people to whom the questionnaire was sent all replied. Thus, there are no problems of nonresponse with which to contend.

One-way Tabulation

The one-way tabulation, in addition to communicating the results of a study, can be used for several other purposes: (1) to determine the degree of item nonresponse, (2) to locate *blunders* (defined later), (3) to locate *outliers* (defined later), (4) to determine the empirical distribution of the variable in question, and (5) to calculate summary statistics. The first three of these are often referred to as *data cleaning*.

Figure 17.1   Part of the Questionnaire for Avery Sporting Goods

The following questionnaire was designed to give a well-known sporting goods company a better idea of people's perceptions of buying sporting goods and other general merchandise through catalogs. The first three columns of the data listed in Table 17.3 contain the customers' survey identification numbers.

1. *During the past year, what percentage of the sporting goods you purchased were ordered through a catalog?*

    _____   0 percent

    _____   1–10 percent

    _____   11–15 percent

    _____   16–20 percent

    _____   21+ percent

2. *How willing are you to purchase merchandise offered through the Avery Sporting Goods catalog?*

    _____ Not at all willing

    _____ Somewhat willing

    _____ Very willing

3. *Have you ever ordered any merchandise from the Avery Sporting Goods catalog?*

    _____ Never

    _____ Ordered before, but not within the last year

    _____ Ordered within the last year

	Not at All Confident	Slightly Confident	Somewhat Confident	Confident	Very Confident
4. *How confident are you that the following sporting goods purchased through a catalog would be of high quality?*					
a. Athletic clothing (shirts, warm-up suits, etc.)	_____	_____	_____	_____	_____
b. Athletic shoes	_____	_____	_____	_____	_____
c. Fishing equipment	_____	_____	_____	_____	_____
d. Balls (basketballs, footballs, etc.)	_____	_____	_____	_____	_____
e. Skiing equipment	_____	_____	_____	_____	_____
5. *How confident are you that the following sporting goods would be of high quality if purchased in a retail sporting goods store?*					
a. Athletic clothing (shirts, warm-up suits, etc.)	_____	_____	_____	_____	_____
b. Athletic shoes	_____	_____	_____	_____	_____
c. Fishing equipment	_____	_____	_____	_____	_____
d. Balls (basketballs, footballs, etc.)	_____	_____	_____	_____	_____
e. Skiing equipment	_____	_____	_____	_____	_____

Table 17.3   Listing of Raw Data

001111554344434
0021214455545453
0034135544245321
0043225543554324
0052115355453542

Item nonresponse is a significant problem in most surveys. Some percentage of the survey instruments invariably suffer from it. As a matter of fact, the degree of item nonresponse often serves as a useful indicator of the quality of the research. When it is excessive, it calls the whole research effort into question and suggests that the research objectives and procedures should be examined critically. When it is in bounds, it is still necessary for the research director to make a decision regarding what should be done about the missing items before analyzing the data. There are several possible strategies:

1. Leave the items blank, and report the number as a separate category. While this procedure works well for simple one-way and cross tabulations, it does not work well for a number of other statistical techniques.

2. Eliminate the case with the missing item in analyses using the variable. When using this approach, the analyst must continually report the number of cases on which the analysis is based, since the sample size is not constant across analyses. It also ignores the fact that a significant degree of nonresponse on a particular item might be informative in that it suggests respondents do not care very deeply about the issue being addressed by the question.

3. Substitute values for the missing items. Typically, the substitution will involve some measure of central tendency such as the mean, median, or mode. Alternatively, sometimes the analyst attempts to estimate the answer using other information contained in the questionnaire. The substitution of values makes maximum use of the data, since all the reasonably good cases are used. At the same time, it requires more work from the analyst, and it contains some potential for bias. It also raises the question of which statistical technique should be used to generate the estimate.[10]

---

[10]David W. Stewart, "Filling the Gap: A Review of the Missing Data Problem," unpublished manuscript, provides an excellent review of the literature on the missing data problem, including various methods for eliminating cases and estimating answers. On the basis of this review, he concludes several things: missing data points should be estimated regardless of whether the data are missing randomly or nonrandomly; for very small amounts of missing data, almost any of the estimation procedures work reasonably well; when larger amounts of data are missing and the average intercorrelation of variables is .20 or less, the substitution of the mean seems to work best; and when the average intercorrelation of the variables exceeds .20, a regression or principal components procedure is the preferred choice when linearity among the variables may be assumed. See also Jae-On Kim and James Curry, "The Treatment of Missing Data in Multivariate Analysis," *Sociological Methods and Research,* 6 (November 1977), pp. 215–240. For a study that empirically examines the question of whether or not missing items are random, see Richard M. Durand, Hugh J. Guffey, Jr., and John M. Planchon, "An Examination of the Random Versus Nonrandom Nature of Item Omissions," *Journal of Marketing Research,* 20 (August 1983), pp. 305–313.

Table 17.4   Portion of Codebook for Avery Sporting Goods Questionnaire

Column(s)	Question Number	Variable (Variable Number)	Coding Specification
1–3	—	Questionnaire identification number (VI)	—
4	1	Percentage of products purchased through a catalog (V2)	1 = 0 percent
			2 = 1–10 percent
			3 = 11–15 percent
			4 = 16–20 percent
			5 = 21 + percent
5	2	Willingness to purchase merchandise from the Avery Sporting Goods catalog (V3)	1 = Unwilling
			2 = Somewhat willing
			3 = Very willing
6	3	Ever ordered from the Avery Sporting Goods catalog (V4)	1 = Never ordered
			2 = Ordered before, but not within the last year
			3 = Ordered within the last year
			Coding Specifications 4a—5e
			1 = Not at all confident
			2 = Slightly confident
			3 = Somewhat confident
			4 = Confident
			5 = Very confident
7	4a	Confidence in buying athletic clothing through a catalog (V5)	
8	4b	Confidence in buying athletic shoes through a catalog (V6)	
9	4c	Confidence in buying fishing equipment through a catalog (V7)	
10	4d	Confidence in buying balls through a catalog (V8)	
11	4e	Confidence in buying skiing equipment through a catalog (V9)	
12	5a	Confidence in buying athletic clothing in a retail store (V10)	
13	5b	Confidence in buying athletic shoes in a retail store (V11)	
14	5c	Confidence in buying fishing equipment in a retail store (V12)	
15	5d	Confidence in buying balls in a retail store (V13)	
16	5e	Confidence in buying skiing equipment in a retail store (V14)	

◆ **Blunder**

Error that arises when editing, coding, key-punching, or tabulating the data.

There is no "right" or single answer as to how missing items should be handled. It all depends on the purposes of the study, the incidence of missing items, and the methods that will be used to analyze the data.

As mentioned earlier, another purpose of one-way tabulation is to locate **blunders,** which are simply errors that occur during editing, coding, or entering the data into the computer. Consider the one-way tabulation of the number of cars owned

Table 17.5 Raw Data for Car Ownership Study

Family Identifi- cation No.	(1) Income in Dollars	(2) Number of Members in Family	(3) Education of Household Head in Yrs.	(4) Region Where Live N = North S = South	(5) Life-Style Orientation L = Liberal C = Conservative	(6) Number of Cars Family Owns	(7) Did Family Finance the Car Purchase?	(8) Does Family Own Station Wagon?	(9) Does Family Own Foreign Economy Car?	(10) Does Family Own Van?
1001	16,800	3	12	N	L	1	N	N	N	Y
1002	17,400	4	12	N	L	1	N	N	N	N
1003	14,300	2	10	N	L	1	N	N	N	N
1004	15,400	4	9	N	L	1	N	N	N	N
1005	14,000	3	8	N	L	1	N	N	N	N
1006	17,200	2	12	N	L	1	N	N	Y	N
1007	17,000	4	12	N	L	1	N	N	N	N
1008	16,900	3	10	N	L	1	N	N	N	N
1009	16,700	2	12	N	L	1	N	N	N	N
1010	13,800	4	6	N	C	1	Y	N	N	N
1011	14,100	3	8	N	C	1	N	N	N	N
1012	16,300	3	11	N	C	1	N	N	N	N
1013	14,700	2	12	N	C	1	N	N	N	N
1014	15,400	4	12	N	C	1	N	N	N	N
1015	15,400	4	12	N	C	1	N	N	N	N
1016	15,900	3	11	N	C	1	Y	N	N	N
1017	16,300	3	12	N	C	1	N	N	N	N
1018	17,400	2	12	N	C	2	N	N	N	N
1019	17,300	2	12	N	C	1	N	N	N	N
1020	13,700	3	8	N	C	1	N	N	N	N
1021	16,100	2	12	N	C	1	N	N	Y	N
1022	16,300	4	12	N	C	1	Y	N	N	N
1023	13,800	3	6	N	C	1	N	N	N	N
1024	14,400	4	8	N	C	1	N	N	N	N
1025	15,300	2	9	N	C	1	Y	N	N	N
1026	15,900	3	12	N	C	1	N	N	N	N
1027	15,100	4	12	S	L	1	N	N	N	Y

ID										
1028	N	N	N	N	1	L	S	12	2	17,200
1029	N	Y	N	N	1	L	S	10	4	15,400
1030	N	N	N	N	1	L	S	12	3	15,600
1031	N	N	N	N	1	L	S	12	3	14,900
1032	Y	N	N	N	1	C	S	11	4	14,800
1033	N	N	N	N	1	C	S	12	4	14,600
1034	N	N	N	N	1	C	S	9	3	13,100
1035	Y	N	N	N	1	C	S	12	3	15,900
1036	N	N	N	N	1	C	S	12	4	16,700
1037	Y	N	N	N	1	C	S	12	4	17,300
1038	N	N	N	N	1	C	S	12	3	17,100
1039	Y	N	N	N	1	C	S	10	3	14,000
1040	N	N	N	N	1	C	S	10	3	13,600
1041	N	N	N	N	1	C	S	12	3	16,200
1042	Y	N	N	N	1	C	S	10	4	14,100
1043	N	N	N	N	1	C	S	8	2	12,700
1044	N	N	Y	N	1	L	N	13	4	16,000
1045	N	N	Y	N	2	L	N	16	3	15,400
1046	N	Y	N	Y	1	L	S	16	4	16,900
1047	N	N	Y	N	1	C	N	10	6	13,800
1048	N	N	N	Y	2	L	S	16	8	17,100
1049	N	Y	Y	N	2	C	N	15	5	16,800
1050	N	N	N	Y	1	L	N	8	5	12,900
1051	N	N	Y	N	1	L	S	8	6	13,700
1052	N	N	Y	N	2	C	N	12	8	16,800
1053	N	N	N	N	2	L	N	12	8	16,100
1054	N	N	Y	Y	1	C	N	12	6	15,700
1055	N	N	Y	N	1	L	N	12	2	18,200
1056	N	N	N	Y	1	L	N	12	3	19,800
1057	N	N	N	N	1	L	N	12	4	20,400
1058	N	N	N	N	1	L	N	12	2	19,000

Table 17.5 Raw Data for Car Ownership *continued*

Family Identifi-cation No.	(1) Income in Dollars	(2) Number of Members in Family	(3) Education of Household Head in Yrs.	(4) Region Where Live N = North S = South	(5) Life-Style Orientation L = Liberal C = Conservative	(6) Number of Cars Family Owns	(7) Did Family Finance the Car Purchase?	(8) Does Family Own Station Wagon?	(9) Does Family Own Foreign Economy Car?	(10) Does Family Own Van?
1059	17,600	4	12	N	L	1	Y	N	N	N
1060	32,000	3	12	N	L	1	N	N	N	N
1061	28,600	3	12	N	L	1	N	N	N	Y
1062	46,400	4	12	N	L	1	Y	N	Y	N
1063	21,200	2	12	N	L	1	Y	N	N	N
1064	19,300	4	10	N	C	1	Y	N	N	N
1065	17,700	4	10	N	C	1	Y	N	N	N
1066	32,400	3	12	N	C	2	N	N	Y	N
1067	38,700	3	12	N	C	1	N	N	N	Y
1068	24,200	2	12	S	L	1	Y	N	N	N
1069	25,100	3	12	S	L	2	N	N	N	Y
1070	23,300	4	12	S	L	1	N	N	N	Y
1071	20,200	2	12	S	L	1	Y	N	N	N
1072	19,300	3	10	S	C	2	N	N	N	Y
1073	18,200	4	12	S	C	1	N	N	N	N
1074	17,800	2	12	S	C	1	Y	N	N	N
1075	18,000	3	10	S	C	1	Y	N	N	Y
1076	31,300	4	16	N	L	1	N	Y	N	N
1077	26,900	4	16	N	L	2	N	N	N	N

ID										
1078	N	N	N	N	1	L	N	14	3	24,700
1079	N	N	N	N	1	L	N	17	3	27,300
1080	N	N	N	Y	2	L	N	13	2	18,100
1081	N	N	N	N	1	L	N	14	2	104,200
1082	Y	N	N	N	1	L	S	16	3	26,100
1083	N	N	N	N	1	L	S	13	4	19,300
1084	N	N	N	N	9	L	S	16	4	20,800
1085	Y	N	N	N	1	L	S	16	4	28,100
1086	Y	N	Y	Y	1	C	S	14	2	26,400
1087	N	N	Y	Y	2	L	N	10	6	18,300
1088	N	N	Y	Y	2	L	N	10	5	17,800
1089	N	N	N	Y	2	L	N	8	7	18,000
1090	N	Y	Y	N	2	L	N	12	9	19,600
1091	N	N	N	Y	2	L	N	12	11	24,200
1092	Y	Y	Y	Y	3	L	S	10	6	22,100
1093	N	N	N	N	2	L	S	12	5	49,000
1094	Y	N	Y	N	2	L	S	12	6	23,300
1095	Y	N	Y	Y	2	C	S	10	9	22,200
1096	N	Y	Y	Y	2	C	S	12	7	24,700
1097	N	Y	N	Y	3	L	N	16	6	27,300
1098	Y	N	N	Y	1	L	N	18	10	26,900
1099	N	Y	Y	N	2	L	S	15	7	21,200
1100	N	Y	Y	Y	2	C	S	16	5	23,800

Table 17.6   Cars per Family

Number of Cars Per Family	Number of Families
1	74
2	23
3	2
9	1

Table 17.7   Cars per Family

Number of Cars Per Family	Number of Families	Percent of Families
1	75	75
2	23	23
3	2	2
	100	100

per family in Table 17.6. A check of the original questionnaire indicates the family reporting ownership of nine cars had, in fact, one car. The "9" is a blunder. The simple one-way tabulation has revealed the error, and it can now be corrected at a very early stage in the analysis with a minimum of difficulty and expense.

The number of cases serving as a base for the one-way tabulation is 100, and thus the number entries are easily converted to percentages. In most cases, conversion will not be this simple. However, it is a good practice always to indicate percentages in the table since they aid communication. Hence, a more typical way of presenting our car study data, corrected for blunders, is shown in Table 17.7.

Note that the percentages are presented to zero decimal places. In this case the percentages were whole numbers because the sample size was 100, but in most cases they would have to be rounded off. Whole numbers should almost always be used, since they are easier to read and also because decimals may convey a greater accuracy than the figures can support, especially in a small sample. While in some cases the analyst might be justified in reporting percentages to one decimal place (rarely two decimal places, though), the general rule in reporting percentages is: *Unless decimals have a special purpose, they should be omitted.*[11]

Sometimes the percentages are presented in parentheses (see Table 17.8) immediately to the right or below the actual count entry in the table. Sometimes only the percentages are presented. In this case it is imperative that the total number of cases on which the percentages are based be provided.

[11]See the classic book by Hans Zeisel, *Say It with Figures,* 5th ed. (New York: Harper & Row, 1968), pp. 16–17, for conditions that would support reporting percentages with decimal-place accuracy.

Table 17.8   Income Distribution of Respondents in Car Ownership Study

Income	Number of Families		Cumulative Number of Families	
Less than $13,500	3	(3.0)	3	(3.0)
$13,500 to 15,400	23	(23.0)	26	(26.0)
$15,500 to 17,400	28	(28.0)	54	(54.0)
$17,500 to 19,400	14	(14.0)	68	(68.0)
$19,500 to 21,400	7	(7.0)	75	(75.0)
$21,500 to 23,400	4	(4.0)	79	(79.0)
$23,500 to 25,400	6	(6.0)	85	(85.0)
$25,500 to 27,400	6	(6.0)	91	(91.0)
$27,500 to 29,400	2	(2.0)	93	(93.0)
$29,500 to 55,400	6	(6.0)	99	(99.0)
More than $55,400	1	(1.0)	100	(100.0)
Total number of families	100	(100.0)		

• **Outlier**

Observation so different in magnitude from the rest of the observations that the analyst chooses to treat it as a special case.

Still another use of the one-way tabulation is to locate **outliers,** which are not errors but rather observations so different in magnitude from the rest of the observations that the analyst chooses to treat them as special cases. This may mean eliminating the observation from the analysis or determining the specific factors that generate this unique observation. For instance, if the family in our earlier example had really owned nine cars, this figure would be considered an outlier, since it is highly unusual for a family to own that many cars.

For another case, consider the tabulation of incomes contained in Table 17.8 but ignore the right-hand column for the moment. The tabulation indicates there is only one family with an income greater than $55,400. Table 17.5 indicates that this family (Number 1081) had an annual income of $104,200. This is clearly out of line with the rest of the sample and is properly considered an outlier. What the analyst chooses to do with this observation depends on the objectives of the study. In this case, it is not unreasonable for a family to have such an income, and so the observation will be retained in the analysis.

• **Histogram**

Form of bar chart on which the values of the variable are placed along the abscissa, or X axis, and the absolute frequency or relative frequency of occurrence of the values is indicated along the ordinate, or Y axis.

A fourth use of the one-way frequency tabulation is to determine the *empirical distribution* of the characteristic in question. The distribution often is best visualized through a **histogram,** a form of bar chart in which the values of the variable are placed along the abscissa, or X axis, and the absolute frequency or relative frequency of occurrence of the values is indicated along the ordinate, or Y axis. The histogram for the income data in Table 17.8 appears as Figure 17.2, with the incomes over $29,500 omitted because their inclusion would have required an undue extension of the income axis. It is readily apparent that the distribution of incomes is skewed to the right. The actual distribution can be compared to some theoretical distribution to determine whether the data are consistent with some *a priori* model. Further insight into the empirical distribution of income can be obtained by constructing the **frequency polygon,** which is obtained from the histogram by connecting the midpoints of the bars with straight lines. The frequency polygon for incomes is superimposed on the histogram in Figure 17.2.

• **Frequency polygon**

Figure obtained from a histogram by connecting the midpoints of the bars of the histogram with straight lines.

◆ **Cumulative distribution function**

Function that shows the number of cases having a value less than or equal to a specified quantity; the function is generated by connecting points representing the given combinations of *X*s (values) and *Y*s (cumulative frequencies) with straight lines.

An alternative way of gaining insight into empirical distribution is through the empirical **cumulative distribution function.** Once again, the one-way tabulation is the source of the data. In this case, though, the number of observations with a value less than or equal to a specified quantity is determined; that is, the cumulative frequencies are generated. Thus, in the right-hand column of Table 17.8, we see that there are three families with incomes less than $13,500, whereas there are twenty-six families (3 + 23) with incomes of $15,400 or less and fifty-four families (3 + 23 + 28) with incomes of $17,400 or less. These cumulative frequencies are denoted along the ordinate in Figure 17.3, while the abscissa again contains incomes. The empirical cumulative distribution function is generated by connecting the points representing the given combinations of *X*s (values) and *Y*s (cumulative frequencies) with straight lines.

The cumulative distribution function can also be used to determine whether the distribution of observed incomes is consistent with some theoretical or assumed distribution. In addition, it can be used to calculate some of the commonly used

Research Window 17.1
Are the Rich Really Getting Richer?

Headlines all over the country proclaimed the news: "Major Study Proves Rich Getting Richer." The results of a University of Michigan study released by Democrats on the Joint Economic Committee showed beyond a shadow of a doubt that the nation's wealthy were getting richer faster than ever, and faster than anyone else. The startling conclusion was that the richest 0.5 percent of Americans had 25 percent of the nation's wealth in 1963, but a full 35 percent by 1986.

The rich smiled and patted their Gold Cards, while the social reformers mounted plans to take up their cudgels and redistribute the wealth.

But there was something funny about the figures. Wealth is rarely measured, because it is such a loose concept, but census data have been showing a gradual *decline* in the concentration of income. How can wealth be getting more concentrated if income is getting less concentrated?

Noting this oddity, the Federal Reserve, which had commissioned the report, warned when it released the data that they seemed irregular. People in the Treasury looked at the numbers more closely and were amazed to learn that the study, if accurate, meant that the wealthy had huge new

holdings in unincorporated business assets. The magnitude of those investments just didn't jibe with the Fed's own estimates.

Sensing that something had gone awry, the Fed took a closer look at the Michigan report and found a seemingly small error that shot the validity of all the data to smithereens. One wealthy family was reported as having $200 million in unincorporated business assets, when the family actually had $2 million in such assets. A keypuncher in Ann Arbor was probably to blame. This one error got compounded every time the figure was used because the sample was so small. A correction subsequently issued by the Joint Economic Committee showed that once this error was fixed, the study showed a statistically insignificant increase in the concentration of wealth.

The Michigan researchers and the Fed should have been more careful, but such mistakes do happen. Static analysis, deficit forecasts, and GNP predictions are showing that economic data are prone to error.

In this case, it was hard to say who was more disappointed with the corrected results: the rich, who found that their assets were growing at only the same rate as everyone else's, or the politicians, who had been delighted to use the report to make political hay.

Source: "Soak the Politicians," *The Wall Street Journal,* 66 (August 22, 1986), p. 16.

Figure 17.2

Histogram and Frequency Polygon of Incomes of Families in Car Ownership Study

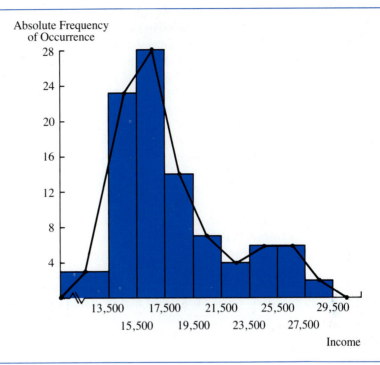

Figure 17.3

Cumulative Distribution of Incomes of Families in Car Ownership Study

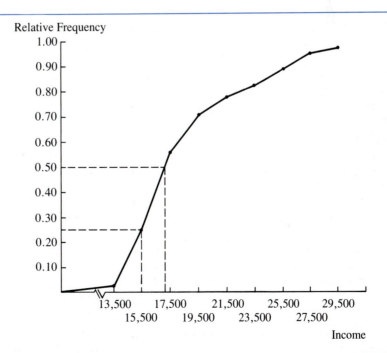

measures of location such as the median, quartiles, and percentiles. These can simply be read from the plot once the cumulative relative frequencies are entered. In our case, the cumulative relative frequencies are equal to the cumulative absolute frequencies divided by 100, since there are 100 cases.

By definition, the sample median is that value for which 50 percent of the values lie below it and 50 percent are above it. To read the sample median from the plot of the cumulative distribution, simply extend a horizontal line from 0.50 on the relative frequency ordinate until it intersects the graph, and then drop a vertical line from the point of intersection to the X axis. The point of intersection with the X axis is the approximate sample median. In the case at hand, the sample median equals $17,300. The quality of the approximation could be checked by actually determining the median using the detailed data.

Sample quartiles could be determined in similar fashion. The first sample quartile (also known as the twenty-fifth percentile) is that value for which 25 percent of the observations are below it. The first sample quartile is determined by drawing a horizontal line from 0.25 on the relative frequency ordinate until it intersects the graph, dropping a vertical line from the point of intersection to the horizontal axis, and reading off the value of the first quartile at the point of intersection with the X axis. The first quartile is thus found to be $15,300. The procedure for the third quartile (seventy-fifth percentile) or any other percentile would be the same as that for the median or first quartile. The only change would be where the horizontal line commenced.

The one-way tabulation is also useful in calculating other summary measures, like the mode, mean, and standard deviation. The mode or the most frequently occurring item can be read directly from the one-way tabulation. Thus, Table 17.7 suggests that most families own one car. The mean, or "average" response, can be calculated from a one-way tabulation by weighting each value by its frequency of occurrence, summing these products, and dividing by the number of cases. The average number of cars per family given the data in Table 17.7 would thus be estimated as follows:

Value	Frequency	Value × Frequency
1	75	75
2	23	46
3	2	6
	100	127

The result is 127/100 = 1.27 cars per family.

The standard deviation provides a measure of spread in the data. It is calculated from the one-way tabulation by taking the deviation of each value from the mean and squaring these deviations. The squared deviations are then multiplied by the frequency with which each occurs, these products are summed, and the sum is divided by one less than the number of cases to yield the sample variance. The square root of the sample variance then yields the sample standard deviation. The calculation of the standard deviation is thus very similar to that for ungrouped data, except for the fact that each value is weighted by the frequency with which it occurs. The standard deviation for the data in Table 17.7 is thus calculated as follows:

Value	Value-Mean	(Value-Mean)^2	Frequency	Frequency Times Difference Squared
1	-.27	.0729	75	5.4675
2	.73	.5329	23	12.2567
3	1.73	2.9929	2	5.9858
				23.7100

Table 17.9   Family Income and Number of Cars Family Owns

Income	Number of Cars		
	1 or Less	2 or More	Total
Less than $17,500	48	6	54
More than $17,500	27	19	46
Total	75	25	100

This yields a variance of $23.7100/99 = .2395$ and a standard deviation of $\sqrt{.2395} = .4894$.

The one-way tabulation as a communication vehicle for the results has not been discussed. The reader needs only to look at Table 17.5 to see how much insight can be gathered about the variable income and then compare that with the insight generated in the one-way tabulation contained in Table 17.8. Considering that one-way tabulations also serve as a basic input to the histogram, frequency polygon, empirical cumulative distribution function, and in calculating summary statistics, it is an unwise analyst indeed who does not take the time to develop them.

Cross Tabulation

While the one-way tabulation is useful for examining the variables of the study separately, cross tabulation is a most important mechanism for studying the relationships among and between variables. In cross tabulation the sample is divided into subgroups so as to learn how the dependent variable varies from subgroup to subgroup. It is clearly the most used data-analysis technique in marketing research. Some would call it the bread-and-butter of applied research. Most marketing research studies go no further than cross tabulation, while many of the studies that do use more sophisticated analytical methods still contain cross tabulation as a significant component. Thus, the analyst and decision maker both need to understand how cross tabulations are developed and interpreted.

Consider the question of the relationship, if any, between the number of cars that the family owns and family income. To keep the example simple, suppose the analyst is simply interested in determining if a family above average in income is more likely to own two or more cars than a family below average in income. Suppose further that $17,500 is the median income in the population and that this figure is to be used to split the families in the sample into two groups, those with below-average and those with above-average incomes.

Table 17.9 presents the two-way classification of the sample families by income and number of cars. Looking at the marginal totals, we see that seventy-five families have one car or less, while twenty-five families have two cars or more. We also see that the sample is fairly representative of the population, at least as far as income is concerned; fifty-four families fall into the below-average income group using the $17,500 cutoff.

Does the number of cars depend on income? It certainly seems so on the basis of Table 17.9 since nineteen of the families owning two or more cars are in the upper income group. Is there anything that can be done to shed additional light on the relationship? The answer is yes. Compute percentages. Tables 17.10 and 17.11 are mathematically equivalent to Table 17.9, but are based on percentages calculated

Table 17.10   Number of Cars by Family Income

	Number of Cars			
Income	1 or Less	2 or More	Total	Number of Cases
Less than $17,500	89%	11%	100%	54
More than $17,500	59%	41%	100%	46

Table 17.11   Family Income by Number of Cars

Income	1 or Less	2 or More
Less than $17,500	64%	24%
More than $17,500	36%	76%
Total	100%	100%
(Number of cases)	(75)	(25)

in different directions: horizontally in Table 17.10 and vertically in Table 17.11. The tables contain quite different messages. Table 17.10 suggests that multiple-car ownership is affected by family income; 41 percent of the families with above-average incomes had two or more automobiles, while only 11 percent of the below-average-income families did so. This is an unambiguous finding. Table 17.11, on the other hand, conveys a different story. It suggests that 64 percent of those who owned one car had below-average incomes, while only 24 percent of those who owned two or more cars were below average in income. Does this mean that multiple-car ownership paves the way to higher incomes? Definitely not. Rather, it simply illustrates a fundamental rule of percentage calculations: Always calculate percentages in the direction of the causal factor, or across the effect factor.[12] In this case, income is logically considered the cause, or independent variable, and multiple-car ownership the effect, or dependent variable. The percentages are correctly calculated, therefore, in the direction of income as in Table 17.10.[13]

One very useful way to determine the direction in which to calculate percentages is to think about the problem in terms of **conditional probabilities,** or the probability of one event occurring given that another event has occurred or will occur. Thus, the notion that a family is likely to have two or more cars *given* that it is a high-income family makes sense, while the notion that a family is likely to have a high income *given* that it has two or more cars does not.

The two-way cross tabulation, although it provides some insight into a dependency relationship, is not the final answer. Rather, it represents a start. Consider the relationship between multiple-car ownership and size of family. Table 17.12 indicates the number of small and large (five or more members) families that possess

* Conditional probability

Probability that is assigned to an Event A when it is known that another Event B has occurred or that would be assigned to A if it were known that B would occur.

---

[12]See Zeisel, *Say It with Figures,* p. 28, for a slightly modified statement of the percentage-direction-calculation rule that takes into account the representativeness of the sample.

[13]At times the direction of causation will not be straightforward, and the calculation of percentages can logically proceed in either direction. *Ibid.,* pp. 30–32.

Table 17.12   Number of Cars and Size of Family

	Number of Cars		
Size of Family	4 or Less	5 or More	Total
4 or less	70	8	78
5 or more	5	17	22
Total	75	25	100

two or more cars. Now, analysts would logically consider family size a cause of multiple-car ownership, and not vice versa. Thus, the percentages would be properly computed *in the direction of size of family, or across number of cars.* Table 17.13 presents these percentages and suggests that the number of cars a family owns is affected by the size of the family—77 percent of the large families have two or more cars, while only 10 percent of the small families do.

This result raises the question: Does multiple-car ownership depend on family size or, as previously suggested, on family income? The proper way to answer this question is through the *simultaneous* treatment of income and family size. In effect, the two-way cross-classification table needs to be partitioned and a three-way table of income, family size, and multiple-car ownership formed. One way of doing this is illustrated in Table 17.14. This table is, in one sense, two cross-classification tables of multiple-car ownership versus income—one for small families of four or fewer members, and one for large families of five or more members.

Table 17.13   Number of Cars by Size of Family

	Number of Cars			
Size of Family	1 or Less	2 or More	Total	Number of Cases
4 or less	90%	10%	100%	(78)
5 or more	23%	77%	100%	(22)

Table 17.14   Number of Cars by Income and Size of Family

	Four Members or Less: Number of Cars			Five Members or More: Number of Cars			Total Number of Cars		
Income	1 or Less	2 or More	Total	1 or Less	2 or More	Total	1 or Less	2 or More	Total
Less than $17,500	44	2	46	4	4	8	48	6	54
More than $17,500	26	6	32	1	13	14	27	19	46
Total	70	8	78	5	17	22	75	25	100

Table 17.15   Number of Cars by Income and Size of Family

Income	Four Members or Less: Number of Cars			Five Members or More: Number of Cars			Total Number of Cars		
	1 or Less	2 or More	Total	1 or Less	2 or More	Total	1 or Less	2 or More	Total
Less than $17,500	96%	4%	100% (46)	50%	50%	100% (8)	89%	11%	100% (54)
More than $17,500	81%	19%	100% (32)	7%	93%	100% (14)	59%	41%	100% (46)

Once again we would want to compute percentages in the direction of income within each table. Table 17.15 contains these percentages, which indicate that multiple-car ownership depends both on income and on family size. For small families of four or less, 19 percent of those with above-average incomes have two or more cars, while only 4 percent of those with below-average incomes have more than one automobile. For large families, 93 percent of those with above-average incomes and 50 percent of those with below-average incomes have more than one vehicle.

The preceding comparisons highlight the effect of income on multiple-car ownership, holding family size constant. We could also compare the effect of family size on multiple-car ownership, holding income constant. We would still find that each provides a partial explanation for multiple-car ownership. Now, you may have felt a bit uncomfortable with the presentation of the data in Tables 17.14 and 17.15. The information is there to be mined, but perhaps you may have wondered whether it could not be presented in a more revealing manner. It can, if you are willing to accept a couple of refinements in the manner of presentation. Look specifically at the first row of the first section of Table 17.15 as it is reproduced as Table 17.16. All of the information contained in this table can be condensed into one figure, 4 percent. This is the percentage of small, below-average-income families that have two or more cars. It follows that the complementary percentage, 96 percent, represents those that have one automobile or none.

Table 17.17 shows the rest of the data in Table 17.15 treated in the same way. The entry in each case is the percentage of families in that category that own two or more automobiles. Table 17.17 conveys the same information as Table 17.15, but it delivers the message with much greater clarity. The separate effect of income on multiple-car ownership, holding family size constant, can be determined by reading down the columns, while the effect of family size, holding income constant, can be determined by reading across the rows. Omitting the complementary percentages has helped reveal the structure of the data. Consequently, we will use this form of

Table 17.16   Ownership for Small, Below-Average-Income Families

Income	Number of Cars		
	1 or Less	2 or More	Total
Less than $17,500	96%	4%	100% (46)

Table 17.17   Percentage of Families Owning Two or More Cars by Income and Size of Family

	Size of Family		
Income	1 or Less	2 or More	Total
Less than $17,500	4%	50%	11%
More than $17,500	19%	93%	41%

• Total association

Association existing between the variables without regard to the levels of any other variables; also called the *zero-order association* between the variables.

• Conditional association

Association existing between two variables when the levels of one or more other variables are considered in the analysis; the other variables are called *control variables.*

presentation whenever we attempt to determine the effect of several explanatory variables, considered simultaneously, in the pages that follow.

The original association between number of cars and family income reflected in Table 17.10 is called the **total** (or *zero-order*) **association** between the variables. Table 17.17, which depicts the association between the two variables within categories of family size, is called a *conditional table* that reveals the **conditional association** between the variables. Family size here is a *control variable.* Conditional tables that are developed on the basis of one control variable are called *first-order* conditional tables, while those developed using two control variables are called *second-order* conditional tables, and so on.

Which variable has the greater effect on multiple-car ownership, income or family size? A useful method for addressing this question is to calculate the difference in proportions as a function of the level of the variable.[14] This can be done for the zero-order tables as well as the conditional tables of higher order. Consider again Table 17.10, concentrating on the impact of income on the probability of the family having multiple cars. The proportion of low-income families that have two or more cars is 0.11, while the proportion of high-income families is 0.41. The probability of having multiple cars is clearly different depending on the family's income; specifically, high income increases the probability of having two or more cars by 0.30 (0.41 − 0.11) over low income. A similar analysis applied to Table 17.13 suggests the probability of multiple-car ownership is clearly different depending on family size. While 0.10 of the small families have multiple cars, 0.77 of the large families do. Thus, large family size increases the probability of having two or more cars by 0.67 (0.77 − 0.10) over small family size.

To determine whether income or family size has the greater impact, it is necessary to consider them simultaneously using a similar analysis. Table 17.17 contains the data that are necessary for this analysis. Let us first consider the impact of income. The proper way to determine the effect of income is to hold family size constant, which means, in essence, that we must investigate the relationship between income and multiple-car ownership for small families and then again for large families. Among small families, having high income increases the probability of having multiple cars by 0.15 (0.19 − 0.04). Among large families, having high income increases the probability of having multiple cars by 0.43 (0.93 − 0.50). The size of the associations between income and multiple-car ownership are different for different family sizes. This means there is a statistical interaction between the independent vari-

---

[14]See Ottar Hellevik, *Introduction to Causal Analysis: Exploring Survey Data by Crosstabulation* (London: George Allen & Unwin, 1984).

Table 17.18   Conditions That Can Arise with the Introduction of an Additional Variable into a Cross Tabulation

Initial Conclusion	With the Additional Variable	
	Change Conclusion	**Retain Conclusion**
Some relationship	I A. Refine explanation B. Reveal spurious explanation C. Provide limiting conditions	II
No relationship	III	IV

ables, and in order to generate a single estimate of the effect of income on car ownership, some kind of *average* of the separate effects needs to be computed. The appropriate average is a weighted average that takes account of the sizes of the groups on which the individual effects were calculated. There were 78 small families in the sample of 100 cases and 22 large families; the weight for small families is thus 0.78 and for large families 0.22. The weighted average is thus

$$0.15(0.78) + 0.43(0.22) = .21$$

which suggests that on average, high versus low income increases the probability of owning multiple cars by .21.

To investigate the impact of family size, it is necessary to hold income constant, or alternatively, to investigate the impact of family size on multiple-car ownership for low-income families, then for high-income families, and then to generate a weighted average of the two results if they are not the same. Among low-income families, being large in size increases the probability of having multiple cars by 0.46 (0.50 − 0.04) compared to small families. Among high-income families, large size increases the probability by 0.74 (0.93 − 0.19) versus small size. Since there were 54 low-income families and 46 high-income families, the appropriate weights for weighting the two effects are 0.54 and 0.46, respectively. The calculation yields

$$0.46(0.54) + 0.74(0.46) = .59$$

as the estimate for the impact of family size on multiple-car ownership. Family size has a more pronounced effect on multiple-car ownership than does income. It increases the probability of having two or more cars by 0.59, whereas income increases it by 0.21.

The preceding example highlights an important application of cross tabulation—the use of an additional variable to refine an initial cross tabulation. In this case, family size was used to refine the relationship between multiple-car ownership and income. This is only one of the many applications of successive cross tabulation of variables, and, in fact, a number of conditions can occur when additional variables are introduced into a cross tabulation, as shown in the various panels of Table 17.18. The two-way tabulation may initially indicate the existence or nonexistence of a relationship between the variables. The introduction of a third variable may occasion no change in the initial conclusion, or it may indicate that a substantial change is in order.

Panel I: Initial Relationship Is Modified by Introduction of a Third Variable

Now that we have considered Panel I-A ("Refine explanation") in the preceding discussion, let us turn to an analysis of the alternative conditions. Consider Panel I-B ("Reveal spurious explanation"). One of the purposes of the automobile-owner-ship study was to determine the kinds of families that purchase specific kinds of automobiles. Consider vans. It was expected that van ownership would be related to life-style and, in particular, that those with a liberal orientation ("swingers") would be more likely to own vans than would those who are conservative by nature. Table 17.19 was constructed, employing the raw data on car ownership in Table 17.5, to test this hypothesis. Contrary to expectation, conservatives are more apt than liberals to own vans; 24 percent of the conservatives and only 16 percent of the liberals in the sample owned vans.

Is there some logical explanation for this unexpected finding? Consider the addition of a third variable, the region of the country in which the family resides, to the analysis. A clear picture of the relationship among the three variables considered simultaneously can be developed employing our previously agreed upon convention; that is, simply report the percentage in each category. The complement, 100 minus the percentage, then indicates the proportion not owning vans.

As Table 17.20 indicates, van ownership is not related to life-style. Rather, it depends on the region of the country in which the family resides. When region is held constant, there is no difference in van ownership between liberals and conservatives. Families living in the South are much more likely to own a van than are families who live in the northern states. It just so happens that people in the South are more conservative with regard to their life-style than people in the North. The original relationship is therefore said to be spurious.

While it seems counterproductive to calculate the difference in proportions to determine the impact of each variable for each of the potential conditions in

---

Table 17.19   Van Ownership by Life-style

	Own Van?		
Life-style	**Yes**	**No**	**Total**
Liberal	9(16%)	46(84%)	55(100%)
Conservative	11(24%)	34(76%)	45(100%)

Table 17.20   Van Ownership by Life-style and Region of Country

	Region of Country		
Life-style	**North**	**South**	**Total**
Liberal	5%	41%	16%
Conservative	5%	43%	24%

Table 17.18, it does seem useful to do it for this case to demonstrate what is meant by a *main effect* without a statistical interaction. The example is also useful in reinforcing how the difference-in-proportions calculation can be used to isolate the causal relationships that exist in cross-tabulation data. Consider first the zero-order association between van ownership and life-style contained in Table 17.19. Being a conservative increases the probability of van ownership by 0.08 (0.24 − 0.16) compared to being liberal. Yet Table 17.20 shows that this is a spurious effect that is due to region of the country, since it disappears when region is held constant. Among those living in the North, the partial association between van ownership and life-style is 0.00 (0.05 − 0.05). Among those living in the South, there is a slightly higher probability of van ownership among conservatives, namely 0.02 (0.43 − 0.41). This effect is so small that it can be attributed to rounding error, particularly since the proportions were carried to only two decimal places and the number of cases is so small. Regardless of the region of the country in which the family resides, their liberal or conservative orientation has no effect on whether or not they own a van.

Note, conversely, that the effect of region is pronounced and consistent. Among liberal families, living in the South increases the probability of van ownership 0.36

Back to the Case

"Come in, Stephanie," J. B. Wainwright, chairman of Capital Motors, called from inside his office to Stephanie Davison, the company's head of marketing research, when he saw her pause at his secretary's desk. "I've been looking forward to seeing you. I hope you can shed some light on those figures Linsky was tossing around at last week's meeting. Are we headed for disaster, or can I put away the life vests?"

Stephanie laughed. "Don't worry, J. B. I don't think the 'great middle class' is sinking yet. The figures were interesting, but they only tell part of the story."

"Well, come in and enlighten me," J. B. said, "before I'm tempted to run out and invest all my pension funds in caviar futures."

Stephanie perched on the edge of a stylish but uncomfortable armchair beside J. B.'s desk

and pulled some papers from a file on her lap.

"I've analyzed the data John presented, J. B., and concluded that while his information may be technically accurate, it tells only part of the story. Take a look at the time period the data track. Remember the post–World War II Baby Boom took place between 1946 and 1965. During that time, 70 million people were born. Millions of those Baby Boomers started flooding the labor market in the early 1970s.

"At about that time, these young people, generally with modest incomes, were also starting households. In fact, households headed by people under age thirty-five increased 50 percent during that time, and that group accounts for a large percentage of the under-$15,000 bracket," Stephanie said.

"At the same time, the over-sixty-five age group was also expanding, contributing to a further increase in the lower-income brackets. Not only were these two groups causing the under-$15,000 bracket to swell, but social and life-style changes also caused the numbers in that category to grow.

"The number of households headed by one individual—divorced, separated, or unmarried people with children as well as singles—increased dramatically during that decade," Stephanie said. "These household types also have relatively lower incomes."

"While these numbers may account for the growth of the lower-income brackets, to what factor do you attribute the upper-end growth?" J. B. asked.

Stephanie smiled. "You're looking at it," she said.

(0.41 − 0.05) compared to living in the North. Among conservative families, living in the South increases the probability by 0.38 (0.43 − 0.05). Within rounding error, the effect is the same for families with both philosophical orientations, which means there is no interaction among the two predictor variables. Rather, there is only a main effect of region on van ownership, and the best estimate of its size is given by either of these estimates or their average.

Consider now the question of ownership of foreign economy cars. (Panel I-C, "Provide limiting conditions"). Does it depend on the size of the family? Table 17.21 suggests it does. Smaller families are *less* likely to own a foreign economy car than are larger families! Only 8 percent of the small families, but 27 percent of the large families, have such automobiles. This relationship is interesting because it runs counter to what we might intuitively expect to find. Can it be accounted for?

Let us expand this cross classification by adding a variable for the number of cars the family owns. Table 17.22 presents the percentage data, which indicate that it is only when large families have two or more cars that they own a foreign economy car. No large families with one car owned such an automobile. The introduction of

"During the 1970s there was a tremendous influx of women into the labor force. In households where the wife does not work, the median income is $21,000; when the wife works part-time, it's $28,000. In the 50 million households in which both husband and wife work full-time, the median income is $32,000—meaning in 25 million households it's *more than* $32,000," she said.

"Women's incomes largely explain why poverty and affluence can be rising at the same time. Indeed, between 1970 and 1982, census data show that the $25,000 to $35,000 income bracket recorded the largest percentage increase—from 16.9 percent of households to 23.4 percent. The $35,000 households increased nearly 4 percent," Stephanie continued.

"So what you're saying, if I

read you correctly, is that the growth in the low-income brackets caused by the Baby Boomers' starting households was a passing demographic aberration?" J. B. asked. "As these people age, and start making more money, they should swell the ranks of the middle class, right?"

"Absolutely," Stephanie said. "It's also important to look at the absolute numbers of households by income level. While there is no doubt that the upper- and lower-income brackets have increased, so has the middle class. There are about 10 percent more middle-income households today than there were in 1970."

"Well, that's a relief," said J. B. "I guess I won't scrap plans for our new mid-size wagon and economy coupe yet. But I'm still intrigued by the growth in the upper end. Should we consider a luxury line?"

As marketing researchers well know, numbers can lie. Raw data are often misleading. They must be analyzed, explained, and put into context and perspective before they can be acted upon.

In the case in question, while the census data may have been accurate, examining them out of context caused them to be misinterpreted. Census data must be looked at over a continuum. Rarely would you get two extremes occurring simultaneously with the middle falling apart. The income shifts in the 1970s were caused by a passing demographic aberration. In this case, had age of respondents been added as another variable to the analysis, the bulge caused by the Baby Boom would have become apparent.

Table 17.21   Foreign Economy Car Ownership by Family Size

	Own Foreign Economy Car?		
Size of Family	Yes	No	Total
4 or less	6 (8%)	72(92%)	78(100%)
More than 4	6(27%)	16(73%)	22(100%)

Table 17.22   Foreign Economy Car Ownership by Family Size and Number of Cars

	Number of Cars		
Size of Family	1 or Less	2 or More	Total
4 or less	6%	25%	8%
More than 4	0%	35%	27%

the third variable has revealed a condition that limits foreign economy-car owner-ship—multiple-car ownership where large families are concerned.

The recent study investigating the effectiveness of aspirin in treating blood clotting after surgery provides an interesting, important application of how the addition of a third variable to an analysis can reveal a limiting condition. The two-way tabulation of those treated with aspirin or a placebo versus the presence or absence of blood clots revealed aspirin was effective in reducing the incidence of clots. When the sample was broken down by sex of the patient, though, it was found that aspirin was very useful in preventing blood clotting in men but not at all useful in treating women.[15]

Panel II: Initial Conclusion of a Relationship Is Retained Consider now the analysis of station wagon ownership based on the data in Table 17.5. At first, it would seem to be related to family size. A case could be made that larger families have a greater need for station wagons than smaller families.

The cross tabulation of these two variables in Table 17.23 suggests that larger families are indeed more likely to own stations wagons; 68 percent of the large families and only 4 percent of the small families own them.

Consider, however, whether income might also affect station wagon ownership. As Table 17.24 indicates, income has an effect over and above family size. As one goes from a small to a large family, there is a substantial increase in the likelihood of owning a station wagon. With high-income families, however, the increase is larger. Alternatively, if one focuses solely on large families, there is an increase in station wagon ownership from below-average to above-average income groups. The initial conclusion, though, is retained: large families do display a greater tendency to purchase station wagons. Further, the effect of family size on station wagon own-ership is much larger than the effect of income.

---

[15]See Joann S. Lublin, "Aspirin Found to Cut Blood Clotting Risks in Men, Not Women," *The Wall Street Journal,* 57 (December 8, 1977), p. 26.

Table 17.23   Station Wagon Ownership by Family Size

| | Own Station Wagon? | | |
Size of Family	Yes	No	Total
Less than 4	3 (4%)	75(96%)	78(100%)
More than 4	15(68%)	7(32%)	22(100%)

Table 17.24   Station Wagon Ownership by Family Size and Income

| | Income | | |
Size of Family	Less Than $17,500	More Than $17,500	Total
Less than 4	4%	3%	4%
More than 4	63%	71%	68%

Panel III: Relationship Is Established with Introduction of a Third Variable
Suppose one of the purposes of the study is to determine the characteristics of
families who financed the purchase of their automobile. Consider the cross tabulation of installment debt versus education of the household head. Table 17.25 results
when the families included in Table 17.5 are classified into one of two educational
categories—those with a high school education or less and those with some college
training. As is evident, there is no relationship between education and installment
debt; the percentage of families with outstanding car debt is 30 percent in each case.

Table 17.26 illustrates the situation when income is also considered in the analysis. For below-average incomes, the presence of installment debt increases with education. For above-average incomes, installment debt decreases with education. The
effect of education was obscured in the original analysis because the effects canceled
each other. When income is also considered, the relationship of installment debt to
education is quite pronounced.

**Panel IV: Conclusion of No Relationship Is Retained with Addition of a
Third Variable** Consider once again the question of station wagon ownership. We
have seen previously that it is related to family size. Let us forget this result for a
minute and begin the analysis with the question: Is station wagon ownership affected

Table 17.25   Financed Car Purchase by Education of Household Head

Education of Household Head	Financed Car Purchase?		
	Yes	No	Total
High school or less	24(30%)	56(70%)	80(100%)
Some college	6(30%)	14(70%)	20(100%)

by region of the country in which the family lives? Table 17.27 provides an initial answer. Station wagon ownership does not depend on region; 18 percent of the sample families living in both the North and in the South own wagons.

Let us now consider the relationship when family size is again taken into account. Table 17.28 presents the data. Once again the percentages are constant across regions. There is minor variation, but this is due to round-off accuracy. Small families display a low propensity to purchase station wagons, regardless of whether they live

Back to the Case

Stephanie thought a moment before answering J. B.'s question. "I hate to hedge, J. B., but the most accurate answer I can give you about the wisdom of entering the luxury market is, it depends," she said.

"Let me explain a bit about census data. The brackets used by the Census Bureau are largely determined by the format and reporting practices of their surveys. While they can tell us who makes what, they leave a lot to be desired when it comes to information about how that money is spent," Stephanie added.

"For example, a child-free couple with a $25,000 annual income may have a very nice middle-class life. A couple with the same income, five children, and a big mortgage, may have trouble making ends meet. The first couple may have a fair amount of discretionary income; the second may have trouble stretching the grocery budget to the end of the month," she said.

"Now, the Census Bureau uses the $35,000 figure as the starting point to figure discretionary income for a family of four. Families with significant discretionary income are typically considered high-income households. How-

ever, in the marketing community, $35,000 usually doesn't qualify as high-income. Most research firms offering data on the 'affluent' consumer market usually start at $40,000 or $50,000," Stephanie said.

"The bureau also considers a 'poverty' income level for a family of four at under $10,000," she said.

"So, if we use the Bureau's poverty cutoff and the marketing community's definition of upper-income as $50,000 plus, we would see that there has been very little change from 1970 to 1982. I broke these figures out in my office. Here's a table that shows the percentage of change during those years in three categories," Stephanie said.

Household Income:
Poverty, Middle, Affluent

Bracket	1970	1982
$10,000−	21.8%	23.9%
$10,000–$50,000	70.4	67.2
$50,000+	7.8	8.9

"As the table shows, the middle-income group has shown a very small change. The upper-in-

come group has grown slightly, but I don't know if it's enough to base a whole new product line on. I guess I'd want to see more information before making such a costly decision," she said.

"I agree," said J.B. "I'm not averse to changing with the times, but I want to be sure that the times really are changing before I commit the company to a radical departure from our current strategy. After all, I'll be the one on the firing line before the board of directors and the stockholders. And that can be a pretty uncomfortable position unless you're convinced that what you're doing is right."

As this case shows, a researcher must also be aware of possible semantic differences that could dramatically affect the interpretation of the data. One research organization's "high-income" family may be a member of the debt-ridden middle class by another firm's standards.

In this scenario, researchers may want to add another variable to the analysis—how many households have x amount of discretionary income available to spend on cars—before making a decision of such magnitude.

Table 17.26   Financed Car Purchase by Education of Household Head and Income

Education of Household Head	Income		Total
	Less Than $17,500	More Than $17,500	
High school or less	12%	58%	30%
Some college	40%	27%	30%

Table 17.27   Station Wagon Ownership by Region

Region	Own Station Wagon?		Total
	Yes	No	
North	11(18%)	49(82%)	60(100%)
South	7(18%)	33(82%)	40(100%)

Table 17.28   Station Wagon Ownership by Region and Family Size

Region	Size of Family		Total
	4 or Less	More Than 4	
North	4%	69%	18%
South	3%	67%	18%

in the North or the South. Large families have a high propensity, and this, too, is independent of where they live. The original lack of relationship between station wagon ownership and region of residence is confirmed with the addition of the third variable, family size.

Summary Comments on Cross Tabulation   The previous examples should confirm the tremendous usefulness of cross tabulation as a tool in analysis. We have seen applications in which a third variable (1) helped to uncover a relationship not immediately discernible and (2) triggered the modification of conclusions drawn on the basis of a two-variable classification. You may have paused to ask yourself, why stop with three variables? Would the conclusion change with the addition of a fourth variable? A fifth? Indeed it might. The problem is that one never knows for sure when to stop introducing variables. The conclusion is always susceptible to change with the introduction of the "right" variable or variables. The analyst is always in the position of "inferring" that a relationship exists. Later research may demonstrate that the inference was incorrect. This is why the accumulation of studies, rather than a single study, supporting a particular relationship is so vital to the advancement of knowledge.

Table 17.29   The Researcher's Dilemma

Researcher's Conclusion	True Situation	
	No Relationship	Some Relationship
No relationship	Correct decision	Spurious noncorrelation
Some relationship	Spurious correlation	Correct decision if concluded relationship is of proper form

Table 17.29 is an overview of the dilemma the researcher faces. The true situation is always unknown. If it were known, there would be no need to research it. Instead, the researcher is always in the position of making statements about an unknown true situation. The analyst may conclude that there is no relationship, or that there is some relationship between two or more variables when in fact there is none or there is some. Only one of the four possibilities in Table 17.29 *necessarily* corresponds to a correct conclusion—when the analyst concludes there is no relationship and in fact there is no relationship. Two of the other possibilities are necessarily incorrect, while one contains the possibility for error. That is, suppose the true situation is one of some relationship between or among the variables. The analyst has reached a correct conclusion only if he or she concludes that there is some relationship and, further, discovers its correct form.

Spurious noncorrelation means that the analyst concludes there is no relationship when, in fact, there is one. *Spurious correlation* occurs when there is no relationship among the variables, but the analyst concludes that a relationship exists.

The opportunities for error are great. Consequently, one may be tempted to continue adding variables to the analysis *ad infinitum.* Fortunately, both theory and data will prevent the anxious—or overly ambitious—analyst from pursuing this course. Theory will constrain him or her because certain tabulations simply will not make any sense. The data will also act as a barrier to endless cross tabulations for several reasons. First, note that the analyst will want to add variables successively to the analysis in the form of higher-dimensional cross-classification tables. This can be accomplished only if the analyst has correctly anticipated the tabulations that would be desirable. This is most important. It is too late to say, "If only we had collected information on variable *X*!" once the analysis has begun. The relationships to be investigated, and thus the cross tabulations that should be appropriate, must be specified before the data are collected. Ideally, the analyst would construct dummy tables before beginning to collect the data. The dummy tables would be complete in all respects except for the number of observations falling in each cell. As a practical matter, it is usually impossible to anticipate all the cross tabulations one will want to develop. Nevertheless, careful specification of these tables at problem-definition time can return substantial benefits.

The analyst also is going to be limited by the size of the sample. In our example, since we started with 100 observations, the two-way tables were not particularly troublesome. Yet as soon as we introduced the third variable, cell sizes became extremely small. This occurred even though we treated all variables as dichotomies. Families were either below average or above average in income; they were either small or large; they lived either in the North or in the South, and so on. This was done purposely so as to simplify the presentation. Yet even here the three-way tabulation offers eight cells ($2 \times 2 \times 2$) into which the observations may be placed. Assuming an even allocation of the cases to the cells, this only allows 12.5 cases per cell. This is clearly a small number upon which to base any kind of conclusion.

The problem, of course, would have been compounded if a greater number of levels had been used for any of the variables. Consider what would happen if the families had been divided into four income groups rather than two, given that the number of cells is the product of the number of levels for the variables being considered. For example, four income levels, three educational levels, and four family size levels would generate a cross-tabulation table with forty-eight separate cells (4 × 3 × 4). One would need a much larger sample than 100 to have any confidence in the suggested relationships.

◆ Summary

Learning Objective 1: Explain the purpose of the field edit.

The field edit is a preliminary edit designed to detect the most glaring omissions and inaccuracies in the data. It is also useful in helping to control the actions of the field force personnel and to clear up any misunderstandings they may have about directions, procedures, specific questions, and so on.

Learning Objective 2: Define what is meant by coding in the research process.

Coding is the technical procedure by which data are categorized. Through coding, the raw data are transformed into symbols—usually numerals—that may be tabulated and counted. The transformation is not automatic, however; it involves judgment on the part of the coder.

Learning Objective 3: List the three steps in the coding process.

The coding process involves the three steps of (1) specifying the categories or classes into which the responses are to be placed, (2) assigning code numbers to the classes, and (3) preparing the codebook.

Learning Objective 4: Outline the conventions that are customarily followed when data are to be analyzed by a computer.

When data are to be analyzed by computer, a number of conventions should be followed in assigning the code numbers, including the following:

1. Locate only one character in each column.
2. Use only numeric codes.
3. Assign as many columns as are necessary to capture the variable.
4. Use the same standard codes throughout for "no information."
5. Code in a respondent identification number on each record.

Learning Objective 5: Describe the kinds of information contained in a codebook.

The codebook contains the general instructions indicating how each item of data was coded. It lists the codes for each variable and the categories included in each code. It further indicates where on the computer record the variable is located and how the variable should be read.

Learning Objective 6: Define what is meant by tabulation and distinguish between the two types of tabulation.

Tabulation consists simply of counting the number of cases that fall into the various categories. The tabulation may take the form of a simple tabulation or a cross tabulation. Simple tabulation involves counting a single variable. In cross tabulation, two or more of the variables are treated simultaneously.

Learning Objective 7: Explain the various ways in which one-way tabulation can be used.

In addition to communicating the results of a study, one-way tabulation can be used: (1) to determine the degree of item nonresponse, (2) to locate blunders, (3) to locate outliers, (4) to determine the empirical distribution of the variable in question, and (5) to calculate summary statistics.

Learning Objective 8: Assess the particular importance of cross tabulation.

Cross tabulation is one of the more useful devices for studying the relationships among and between variables since the results are easily communicated; further, cross tabulation can provide insight into the nature of a relationship since the addition of one or more variables to a two-way cross-classification analysis is equivalent to holding each of the variables constant.

Learning Objective 9: Describe a method by which a researcher can determine what impact one variable has on another in a cross-tabulation table.

A useful method for determining the impact one variable has on another variable in a cross-tabulation table is to compute the difference in proportions with which the dependent variable occurs as a function of the levels of the independent variable. This can be done for the zero-order tables as well as the conditional tables of higher order. The higher-order tables are used to remove the effects of other variables that might be affecting the dependent variable.

Discussion Questions, Problems, and Projects

1. The WIST television station was conducting research in order to help develop programs that would be well received by the viewing audience and would be considered a dependable source of information. A two-part questionnaire was administered by personal interviews to a panel of 3,000 respondents residing in the city of Houston. The field and office edits were simultaneously done, so that the deadline of May 1st could be met. A senior supervisor, Marlene Howe, was placed in charge of the editing tasks and was assisted by two junior supervisors and two field workers. The two field workers were instructed to discard instruments that were illegible or incomplete. Each junior supervisor was instructed to scrutinize 1,500 of the instruments for incomplete answers, wrong answers, and responses that indicated a lack of interest. They were instructed to discard instruments that had more than five incomplete or wrong answers (the questionnaire contained thirty questions). In addition, they were asked to use their judgment in assessing whether the respondent showed a lack of interest and, if so, to discard the questionnaire.
   (a) Critically evaluate the above editing tasks. Please be specific.
   (b) Make specific recommendations to George Wist, the owner of the WIST television station, as to how the editing should be done.

2. (a) Establish response categories and codes for the question, "What do you like about this new brand of cereal?"
   (b) Code the following responses using your categories and codes.
      1. "$1.50 is a reasonable price to pay for the cereal."
      2. "The raisins and nuts add a nice flavor."
      3. "The sizes of the packages are convenient."
      4. "I like the sugar coating on the cereal."
      5. "The container does not tear and fall apart easily."
      6. "My kids like the cartoons on the back of the packet."
      7. "It is reasonably priced compared to other brands."
      8. "The packet is attractive and easy to spot in the store."
      9. "I like the price, it is not so low that I doubt the quality and at the same time it is not so high to be unaffordable."
      10. "The crispness and lightness of the cereal improve the taste."

3. (a) Establish response categories and codes for the following question that was asked of a sample of business executives. "In your opinion, which types of companies have not been affected by the present economic climate?"
   (b) Code the following responses using your categories and codes.
      1. Washington Post
      2. Colgate Palmolive
      3. Gillette
      4. Hilton Hotels
      5. Chase Manhattan
      6. Prentice-Hall
      7. Hoover
      8. Fabergé

9. Marine Midlands Banks   13. Singer
10. Zenith Radio   14. Saga
11. Holiday Inns   15. Bank America
12. Dryden Press

4. A large manufacturer of electronic components for automobiles recently conducted a study to determine the average value of electronic components per automobile. Personal interviews were conducted with a random sample of 400 respondents. The following information was secured with respect to each subject's "main" vehicle when he or she had more than one.

Average Dollar Value of Electronic Equipment Per Automobile

Dollar Value of Electronic Equipment	Number of Automobiles
Less than $50	35
$51 to $100	40
$101 to $150	55
$151 to $200	65
$201 to $250	65
$251 to $300	75
$301 to $350	40
$351 to $400	20
More than $400	5
Total number of automobiles	400

(a) Convert the above information into percentages.
(b) Compute the cumulative absolute frequencies.
(c) Compute the cumulative relative frequencies.
(d) Prepare a histogram and frequency polygon with the average value of electronic equipment on the X axis and the absolute frequency on the Y axis.
(e) Graph the empirical cumulative distribution function with the average value on the X axis and the relative frequency on the Y axis.
(f) Locate the median, first sample quartile, and third sample quartile on the cumulative distribution function graphed in Part e of this project.
(g) Calculate the mean and standard deviation and variance for the frequency distribution. (Hint: Use the midpoint of each class interval and multiply that by the appropriate frequency. For the interval starting at $401, assume the midpoint is 425.5.)

5. Select a convenience sample of fifty students on your campus and ask them the following two questions: Are you a part-time or full-time student? How many hours did you spend studying last week?
(a) Compute the average number of hours spent studying. Show your calculations.
(b) Complete the following cross-classification table.

	Hours Spent Studying		
Status	Less Than Average	More Than Average	Total
Full-time			
Part-time			
Total			

(c) Do your findings confirm the hypothesis that the hours spent studying depend on the status of the student? Compute the necessary percentages.

6. A social organization was interested in determining if there were various demographic characteristics that might be related to people's propensity to contribute to charities. The organization was particularly interested in determining if individuals above forty years of age were more likely to contribute larger amounts than individuals below forty. The average contribution in the population was $1,500 and this figure was used to divide the individuals in the sample into two groups, those that contributed large amounts or more than average versus those that contributed less than average. The following table presents a two-way classification of the sample of individuals by contributions and age.

Table 1   Personal Contributions and Age

Personal Contribution	Age 39 or less	Age 40 or more	Total
Less than or equal to $1,500	79	50	129
More than $1,500	11	60	71
Total	90	110	200

In addition, the social organization wanted to determine if contributions depended on income and/or age. The following table presents the simultaneous treatment of age and income. The median income in the population was $18,200 and this figure was used to split the sample into two groups.

Table 2   Personal Contributions by Age and Income

Personal Contributions	Income Less than or equal to $18,200 — Age 39 or Less	Income Less than or equal to $18,200 — Age 40 or More	Income More than $18,200 — Age 39 or Less	Income More than $18,200 — Age 40 or More	Total — Age 39 or Less	Total — Age 40 or More
Less than or equal to $1,500	63	22	16	28	79	50
More than $1,500	7	18	4	42	11	60
Total	70	40	20	70	90	110

(a) Does the amount of personal contributions depend on age? Generate the necessary tables to justify your answer.

(b) Does the amount of personal contributions depend on age alone? Generate the necessary tables to justify your answer.

(c) Present the percentage of contributions of more than $1,500 by age and income in tabular form. Interpret the table.

7. A large toy manufacturer wanted to determine the characteristics of families who had purchased a new electronic game that was designed and marketed for all age groups. Management needs your assistance in interpreting the following two cross-classification tables.

Table 1   Purchased Electronic Games versus Number of Children

	Purchased Electronic Games		
Number of Children	Yes	No	Total
Less than or equal to 1	63	87	150
More than 1	21	29	50

Table 2   Purchased Electronic Games versus Number of Children and Age of Head of Household

	Age of Head of Household		
Number of Children	Less than 45	More than 45	Total
Less than or equal to 1	14%	46%	42%
More than 1	38%	19%	42%

(a) What does Table 1 indicate? Explain and show calculations where necessary.
(b) What does Table 2 indicate? Have your conclusions changed or remained the same? Explain.

8. A local telephone company wanted to determine the demographic characteristics of users of answering services. Management needs your help in interpreting the following two tables.

Table 1   Use of Answering Services versus Education

Education of Household Head	Use of Answering Service		
	Yes	No	Total
High school or less	48	72	120
Some college or more	20	60	80

Table 2   Use of Answering Services versus Education and Income

Education of Household Head	Income		
	Less Than $18,200	More Than $18,200	Total
High school or less	15%	45%	40%
Some college or more	15%	42%	25%

(a) What does Table 1 indicate? Explain and provide calculations where necessary.

(b) What does Table 2 indicate? Have your conclusions changed or remained the same? Explain.

Suggested Additional Readings

For useful discussion of the purposes and procedures to follow when editing and coding data, see

John A. Sonquist and William C. Dunkelberg, *Survey and Opinion Research: Procedures for Processing and Analysis* (Englewood Cliffs, N.J.: Prentice-Hall, 1977), especially pages 41–196.

Philip S. Siedl, "Coding," in Robert Ferber, ed., *Handbook of Marketing Research* (New York: McGraw-Hill, 1974), pp. 2-178 to 2-199.

For especially insightful discussions of the use of cross-tabulation analysis to reveal the underlying patterns in data, see the classic work

Hans Zeisel, *Say It with Figures,* 5th ed. (New York: Harper and Row, 1968), or

Ottar Hellevik, *Introduction to Causal Analysis: Exploring Survey Data by Cross-tabulation* (London: George Allen & Unwin, 1984).

Appendix 17A   Hypothesis Testing

In Chapter 17 we discussed the preliminary data-analysis steps of editing, coding, and tabulation. That chapter demonstrated the importance and potential value of these preliminary procedures, which are common to almost all research studies. Some studies stop with tabulation and cross tabulation. However, many others involve additional analyses, particularly the formal test of a statistical hypothesis or the establishment of a confidence interval. This appendix reviews these procedures.

When marketers prepare to launch a research study, they generally begin with a speculation, or guess, about a phenomenon in their environment. "I'll bet," the advertising manager might say to the marketing director, "that if we hired a sultry celebrity to promote our shampoo, sales would increase." Or the sales manager might say to the company's financial officer, "If my department only had more money to spend on training, our people would be more productive."

In marketing, as in other scientific fields, such unproven propositions are called hypotheses. Through the use of statistical techniques, we are often able to determine whether there is empirical evidence to confirm such hypotheses. Many of the procedures discussed in the next few chapters are used to test specific hypotheses. It is therefore useful to review some basic concepts that underlie hypothesis testing in classical statistical theory, such as framing the null hypothesis, setting the risk of error in making a wrong decision, and the general steps involved in testing the hypothesis.[1]

Null Hypothesis

Marketing research studies are unable to prove results. At best, they can indicate which of two mutually exclusive hypotheses are more likely to be true on the basis of observed results. The general forms of these two hypotheses and the symbols attached to them are as follows:[2]

---

[1]Bayesian statistical theory assumes a different posture with respect to hypothesis testing than does classical statistics. Because classical statistical significance-testing procedures are much more commonly used in marketing research though, only the basic elements underlying classical statistical theory are presented here.

[2]E. J. Davis, "Appendix 2: Statistical Tests," in Margaret Crimp, *The Marketing Research Process* (Englewood Cliffs, N.J.: Prentice-Hall, 1981), p. 236.

- H_0, the hypothesis that our results do not show any significant differences between population groups over whatever factors have been measured; and
- H_a, the alternate hypothesis that differences shown in our results reflect real differences between population groups.

The first of these hypotheses, H_0, is known as the *null hypothesis*. One simple fact underlies the statistical test of an hypothesis: A researcher may reject a null hypothesis, but he or she can never accept it—except conditionally—since further evidence may subsequently prove it wrong. In other words, one "rejects" the null hypothesis (and accepts the alternate hypothesis) or "does not reject" the null hypothesis on the basis of the evidence at hand. It is wrong to conclude, however, that since the null hypothesis was not rejected, it can be accepted as valid.

A naive qualitative example should illustrate the issue.[3] Suppose we are testing the hypothesis that "John Doe is a poor man." We observe that Doe dines in cheap restaurants, lives in the slum area of the city in a run-down building, wears worn and tattered clothes, and so on. Although his behavior is certainly consistent with that of a poor man, we cannot "accept" the null hypothesis that he is poor. It is possible that Doe may in fact be rich, but extremely frugal. We can continue gathering information about him, but for the moment we must decide "not to reject the null hypothesis." One single observation, for example, that indicates he has a six-figure bank account or that he owns 100,000 shares of AT & T stock, would allow the immediate rejection of the null hypothesis and "acceptance" of the alternate hypothesis that "John Doe is rich."

The upshot of this discussion is that the researcher needs to frame the null hypothesis in such a way that its rejection leads to the acceptance of the desired conclusion, that is, the statement or condition he or she wishes to verify. For example, suppose a firm was considering introducing a new product if it could be expected to secure more than 10 percent of the market. The proper way to frame the hypotheses then would be

$$H_0: \pi \leq 0.10$$
$$H_a: \pi > 0.10$$

If the evidence leads to the rejection of H_0, the researcher would then be able to accept the alternative that the product could be expected to secure more than 10 percent of the market, and the product would be introduced. If H_0 cannot be rejected, though, the product should not be introduced unless more evidence to the contrary becomes available. The example as framed involves the use of a *one-tailed* statistical test in that the alternate hypothesis is expressed directionally, that is, as being greater than 0.10. The one-tailed test is most commonly used in marketing research, although there are research problems that warrant a *two-tailed* test; for example, the market share achieved by the new formulation of Product X is no different from that achieved by the old formulation, which was 10 percent. A two-tailed test would be expressed as

$$H_0: \pi = 0.10$$
$$H_a: \pi \neq 0.10$$

There is no direction implied with the alternate hypothesis; the proportion is simply expressed as not being equal to 0.10.

The one-tailed test is more commonly used than the two-tailed test in marketing research for two reasons. First, there is typically some preferred direction to the outcome, for example, the greater the market share, the higher the product quality, the lower the expenses, the better. The two-tailed alternative is used when there is no preferred direction in the outcome or when the research is meant to demonstrate the existence of a difference but not its direction. Second, the one-tailed test, when it is appropriate, is more powerful statistically than the two-tailed alternative.

---

[3]The author expresses his appreciation to Dr. B. Venkatesh of Burke Marketing Services, Inc., for suggesting this example to illustrate the rationale behind the framing of null hypotheses.

Table 17A.1   Judicial Analogy Illustrating Decision Error

Verdict	True Situation: Defendant Is	
	Innocent	Guilty
Innocent	Correct decision: probability $= 1 - \alpha$	Error: probability $= \beta$
Guilty	Error: probability $= \alpha$	Correct decision: probability $= 1 - \beta$

Most students seem to experience some difficulty in framing one-tailed statistical tests and commonly reverse the inequalities in the null and alternate hypotheses. Suppose the two hypotheses are incorrectly framed as

$$H_0: \pi \geq 0.10$$
$$H_a: \pi < 0.10$$

and the sample results are $p = 0.15$. Even though the evidence is consistent with the results desired, the researcher cannot reasonably suggest that avenue because the null hypothesis can never be accepted, only rejected. The researcher could recommend the product introduction, though, if the two hypotheses were reversed in sign and the null hypothesis was rejected.

Types of Errors

Since the result of statistically testing a null hypothesis would be to reject it or not reject it, two types of errors may occur. First, the null hypothesis may be rejected when it is true. Second, it may not be rejected when it is false and, therefore, should have been rejected. These two errors are, respectively, termed *Type I error* and *Type II error* or α *error* and β *error,* which are the probabilities associated with their occurrence. The two types of errors are not complementary in that $\alpha + \beta \neq 1$.

To illustrate each type of error and to demonstrate that they are not complementary, consider a judicial analogy.[4] Since under U.S. criminal law, a person is innocent until proven guilty, the judge and jury are always testing the hypothesis of innocence. The defendant may, in fact, be either innocent or guilty, but based on the evidence the court may reach either verdict regardless of the true situation. Table 17A.1 displays the possibilities. If the defendant is innocent and the jury finds him innocent, or if the defendant is guilty and the jury finds him guilty, the jury has made a correct decision. If, however, the defendant truly is innocent and the jury finds the person guilty, they have made an error, and similarly if the defendant is guilty and they find him innocent. The jury must find one way or the other, and thus the probabilities of the jury's decision must sum vertically to 1. Thus if we let α represent the probability of incorrectly finding the person guilty when he is innocent, then $1 - \alpha$ must be the probability of correctly finding him innocent. Similarly, β and $1 - \beta$ represent the probabilities of findings of innocence and guilt when he is guilty. It is intuitively obvious that $\alpha + \beta$ is not equal to 1, although later discussion will indicate that β must increase when α is reduced if other things remain the same. Since our society generally holds that finding an innocent person guilty is more serious than finding a guilty person innocent, α error is reduced as much as possible in our legal system by requiring proof of guilt "beyond any reasonable doubt."

Table 17A.2 contains the corresponding research situation. Just as the defendant's true status is unknown to the jury, the true situation regarding the null hypothesis is unknown to the researcher. The researcher's dilemma parallels that of the jury in that he has limited information with which to work. Suppose the null hypothesis is true. If the researcher concludes

[4]R. W. Jastram, *Elements of Statistical Inference* (Berkeley, Calif.: Book Company, 1947), p. 44.

Table 17A.2   Types of Errors in Hypothesis Testing

	True Situation: Null Hypothesis is	
Research Conclusion	**True**	**False**
Do not reject H_0	Correct decision Confidence level Probability $= 1 - \alpha$	Error: Type II Probability $= \beta$
Reject H_0	Error: Type I Significance level Probability $= \alpha$	Correct decision Power of test Probability $= 1 - \beta$

it is false, he has made a Type I (α) error. The significance level associated with a statistical test indicates the probability with which this error may be made. Since sample information will always be somewhat incomplete, there will always be some α error. The only way it can be avoided is by never rejecting the null hypothesis (never finding anyone guilty, in the judicial analogy). The *confidence level* of a statistical test is $1 - \alpha$, and the more confident we want to be in a statistical result, the lower we must set α error. The *power* associated with a statistical test is the probability of correctly rejecting a false null hypothesis. One-tailed tests are more powerful than two-tailed tests because, for the same α error, they are simply more likely to lead to a rejection of a false null hypothesis. β error represents the probability of not rejecting a false null hypothesis. There is no unique value associated with β error.

Procedure

The relationship between the two types of errors is best illustrated through example, and the example would be most productive if developed following the general format of hypothesis testing. Figure 17A.1 shows the typical sequence of steps that researchers follow in testing hypotheses. Suppose the problem was indeed one of investigating the potential for a new product and that the research centered around testing consumer preferences. Suppose that, in the judgment of management, the product should not be introduced unless at least 20 percent of the population could be expected to prefer it, and that the research calls for 625 respondents to be interviewed for their preferences.

Step 1 The null and alternate hypotheses would be

$$H_0: \pi \le 0.20$$
$$H_a: \pi > 0.20$$

The hypotheses are framed so that if the null hypothesis is rejected, the product should be introduced.

Step 2 The appropriate sample statistic is the sample proportion. Although the sample proportion is theoretically binomially distributed, the large sample size permits the use of the normal approximation.[5] The z test therefore applies. The z statistic in this case equals

---

[5]The binomial distribution tends toward the normal distribution for a fixed π as sample size increases. The tendency is most rapid when $\pi = 0.5$. With sufficiently large samples, normal probabilities may be used to approximate binomial probabilities with πs in this range. As π departs from 0.5 in either direction, the normal approximation becomes less adequate, although it is generally held that the normal approximation may be used safely if the smaller of $n\pi$ or $n(1 - \pi)$ is 10 or more. If this condition is not satisfied, binomial probabilities can either be calculated directly or found in tables that are readily available. In the example, $n\pi = 625(0.2) = 125$, and $n(1 - \pi) = 500$, and thus there is little question as to the adequacy of the normal approximation to binomial probabilities.

Figure 17A.1

**Typical Hypothesis-
Testing Procedure**

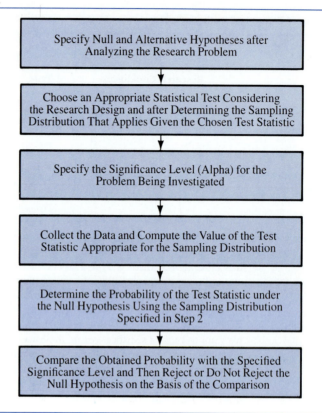

$$z = \frac{p - \pi}{\sigma_p}$$

where p is the sample proportion preferring the product, σ_p is the standard error of the proportion, or the standard deviation of the distribution of sample ps. And σ_p in turn equals

$$\sqrt{\frac{\pi(1 - \pi)}{n}} = \sqrt{\frac{0.20(0.80)}{625}} = 0.0160$$

where n is the sample size. Note this peculiarity of proportions. As soon as we have hypothesized a population value, we have said something about the standard error of the estimate. The proportion is the most clear-cut case of "known variance," since the variance is specified automatically with an assumed π. The researcher thus knows all of the values for calculating z except p before ever taking the sample and further knows *a priori* the distribution to which the calculated statistic will be related. This is true in general, and the researcher should have these conditions clearly in mind before taking the sample.

Step 3 The researcher selects a significance level (α) using the following reasoning: In this situation α error is the probability of rejecting H_0 and concluding that $\pi > 0.2$, when in reality $\pi \leq 0.2$. This conclusion will lead the company to market the new product. However, since the venture will be profitable only if $\pi > 0.2$, a wrong decision to market would be financially unprofitable, possibly disastrous. The probability of Type I error should, therefore, be minimized as much as possible. The researcher recognizes, though, that the probability of a Type II error increases as α is decreased, other things being equal. Type II error in this case implies concluding $\pi \leq 0.2$ when in fact $\pi > 0.2$, which in turn suggests that the company would table the decision to introduce the product when it could be profitable. The

Figure 17A.2

Probability of
$z = 1.500$ **with a One-Tailed Test**

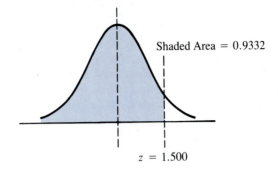

Shaded Area = 0.9332

$z = 1.500$

opportunity lost from making such an error could be quite serious. Although, as explained later, the researcher does not know what β would be, he or she knows that α and β are interrelated and that an extremely low value of α, say, 0.01 or 0.001, would produce intolerable β errors. The researcher decides, therefore, on an α level of 0.05 as an acceptable compromise.[6]

Step 4 Since Step 4 involves the computation of the test statistic, it can only be completed after the sample is drawn and the information collected. Suppose 140 of the 625 sample respondents preferred the product. The sample proportion is thus $p = 140/625 = 0.224$. The basic question that needs to be answered is conceptually simple. "Is this value of p too large to have occurred by chance from a population with $\pi = 0.2$?" Or, in other words, "What is the probability of getting $p = 0.224$ when $\pi = 0.2$?"

$$z = \frac{p - \pi}{\sigma_p} = \frac{0.224 - 0.20}{0.0160} = 1.500$$

Step 5 The probability of occurrence of a z value of 1.500 can be found from standard tabled values of areas under the normal curve. (See Table 1 at the end of the book.) Figure 17A.2 shows the procedure. The shaded area between $-\infty$ and 1.500 equals 0.9332; this means the area to the right of $z = 1.500$ is $1.000 - 0.9332$ or 0.0668. This is the probability of securing a z value of 1.500 under a true situation of $\pi = 0.2$.

Step 6 Since the calculated probability of occurrence is higher than the specified significance level of $\alpha = 0.05$, the null hypothesis is not rejected. The product would not be introduced because, while the evidence is in the right direction, it is not sufficient to conclude beyond "any reasonable doubt" that $\pi > 0.2$. If the decision maker had been able to tolerate a 10 percent chance of committing a Type I error, the null hypothesis would have been rejected and the product marketed, since the probability of getting a sample $p = 0.224$ when the true $\pi = 0.20$, is, as we have seen, 0.0668.

Power

The example illustrates the importance of correctly specifying the risk of error. If a 10 percent chance of an α error were tolerable and the researcher specified $\alpha = 0.05$, a potentially profitable opportunity would have been bypassed. The choice of the proper significance level involves weighing the costs associated with the two types of error, which is unfortunately a

---

[6]We shall have more to say about the choice of $\alpha = 0.05$ and its interpretation after we have introduced the notion of power.

procedure that most researchers ignore, choosing out of habit, $\alpha = 0.10$ or 0.05. Perhaps this lapse is due to the difficulty encountered in specifying β error, or Type II error.

The difficulty arises because β error is not a constant. Recall that it is the probability of not rejecting a false null hypothesis. Other things being equal, we would prefer a test that minimized such errors. Alternatively, since the power of a test equals $1 - \beta$, we would prefer the test with the greatest power so that we would have the best chance of rejecting a false null hypothesis.[7] Now clearly our ability to do this depends on "how false H_0 truly is." It could be "just a little bit false" or "way off the mark," and the probability of an incorrect conclusion would certainly be higher in the first case.

Consider again the hypotheses

$$H_0: \pi \leq 0.2$$
$$H_a: \pi > 0.2$$

where $\sigma_p = 0.0160$ and $\alpha = 0.05$ as before. Any calculated z value greater than 1.645 will cause us to reject this hypothesis, since this is the z value that cuts off 5 percent of the normal curve. The z value can be equated to the *critical* sample proportion through the formula

$$z = \frac{p - \pi}{\sigma_p}$$

$$1.645 = \frac{p - 0.20}{0.0160}$$

or $p = 0.2263$. Thus, any sample proportion greater than $p = 0.2263$ will lead to the rejection of the null hypothesis that $\pi \leq 0.2$. This means that if 142 or more $[0.2263(625) = 141.4]$ of the sample respondents prefer the new product, the null hypothesis will be rejected and the product introduced, while if 141 or less of the sample respondents prefer it, the null hypothesis will not be rejected and the new product will not be introduced.

The likelihood of a sample proportion of $p = 0.2263$ is much greater for certain values of π than for others. Suppose, for instance, that the true but unknown value of π is 0.22. The sampling distribution of the sample proportion is again normal, but now it is centered about 0.22. The probability of obtaining the critical sample proportion $p = 0.2263$ under this condition is found again from the normal curve table, where now[8]

$$z = \frac{p - \pi}{\sigma_p} = \frac{0.2263 - 0.22}{0.0166} = 0.380$$

The shaded area between $-\infty$ and $z = 0.380$ is given in Table 1 at the end of the book as 0.6480, and thus the area to the right of $z = 0.380$ is equal to $1.000 - 0.6480 = 0.3520$ (see Panel B in Figure 17A.3). This is the probability that a value as large or larger than $p = 0.2263$ would be obtained if the true population proportion was $\pi = 0.22$. It is also the power of the test in that if π is truly equal to 0.22, the null hypothesis is false and 0.3520 is the probability that the null will be rejected. Conversely, the probability that $p < 0.2263$ equals $1 - 0.3520 = 0.6480$, which is β error. The null hypothesis is false, and yet the false null hypothesis is not rejected for any sample for which the proportion $p < 0.2263$.

Suppose that the true population condition was $\pi = 0.21$ instead of $\pi = 0.22$, and the null hypothesis was again $H_0: \pi \leq 0.20$. Since the null hypothesis is less false in this second case, we would expect power to be lower and the risk of β error to be higher because the null hypothesis is less likely to be rejected. Let us see if that is indeed the case. The z value corresponding to the critical $p = 0.2263$ is 1.000. Power given by the area to the right of

---

[7]See Alan G. Sawyer and A. Dwayne Ball, "Statistical Power and Effect Size in Marketing Research," *Journal of Marketing Research,* 18 (August 1981), pp. 275–290, for a persuasive argument as to why marketing researchers need to pay more attention to power in their research designs. The article also offers a number of suggestions on how to improve statistical power.

[8]Note that σ_p is now $\sqrt{0.22(0.78)/625} = 0.0166$, since a different specification of π implies a different standard error of estimate.

Figure 17A.3

Computation of β Error and Power for Several Assumed True Population Proportions for the Hypothesis π ≤ 0.2

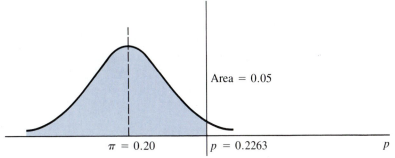

Area = 0.05

$\pi = 0.20$ $p = 0.2263$ p

Panel A: Critical Proportion under Null Hypothesis

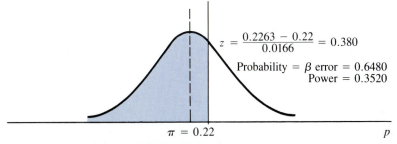

$$z = \frac{0.2263 - 0.22}{0.0166} = 0.380$$

Probability = β error = 0.6480
Power = 0.3520

$\pi = 0.22$ p

Panel B: Probability of Realizing Critical Proportion When $\pi = 0.22$, Which Means Null Hypothesis Is False

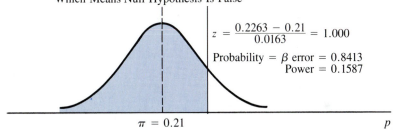

$$z = \frac{0.2263 - 0.21}{0.0163} = 1.000$$

Probability = β error = 0.8413
Power = 0.1587

$\pi = 0.21$ p

Panel C: Probability of Realizing Critical Proportion When $\pi = 0.21$, Which Means Null Hypothesis Is False

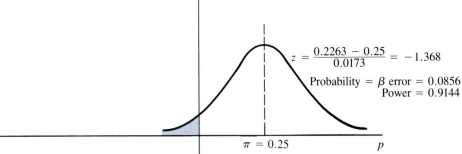

$$z = \frac{0.2263 - 0.25}{0.0173} = -1.368$$

Probability = β error = 0.0856
Power = 0.9144

$\pi = 0.25$ p

Panel D: Probability of Realizing Critical Proportion When $\pi = 0.25$, Which Means Null Hypothesis Is False

$z = 1.000$ is 0.1587 (the β error is 0.8413), and the expected result is obtained (see Figure 17A.3, Panel C).

Consider one final value, true $\pi = 0.25$. The null hypothesis of $\pi = 0.20$ would be "way off the mark" in this case, and we would expect there would only be a small chance that it would not be rejected and a Type II error would be committed. The calculations are displayed

Table 17A.3　**β Error and Power for Different Assumed True Values of π and the Hypotheses, $H_0 : \pi \leq 0.20$ and $H_a : \pi > 0.20$**

Value of π	Probability of Type II, or β, Error	Power of the Test: $1 - \beta$
0.20	$(0.950) = 1 - \alpha$	$(0.05) = \alpha$
0.21	0.8413	0.1587
0.22	0.6480	0.3520
0.23	0.4133	0.5867
0.24	0.2133	0.7867
0.25	0.0856	0.9144
0.26	0.0273	0.9727
0.27	0.0069	0.9931
0.28	0.0014	0.9986
0.29	0.0005	0.9995
0.30	0.0000	1.0000

in Figure 17A.3, Panel D; $z = -1.368$, and the area to the right of $z = -1.368$ is 0.9144. The probability of β error is 0.0856, and the *a priori* expectation is confirmed.

Table 17A.3 contains the power of the test for other selected population states, and Figure 17A.4 shows these values graphically. Figure 17A.4 is essentially the power curve for the hypothesis,

$$H_0: \pi \leq 0.20$$
$$H_a: \pi > 0.20$$

and it confirms that the farther away the true π is from the hypothesized value in the direction indicated by the alternate hypothesis, the higher the power. Note that power is not defined for the hypothesized value, because if the true value in fact equals the hypothesized value, a β error cannot be committed.

Note that since power is a function rather than a single value, the researcher attempting to balance Type I and Type II errors logically needs to ask how false the null hypothesis is likely to be and to establish his or her decision rule accordingly. This requirement possibly explains why so many researchers content themselves with the specification of Type I, or α, error and allow β error to fall where it may. The example provides an excellent opportunity to illustrate the dangers in this approach.

The failure to even worry about, much less explicitly take into account, the power of the statistical test represents one of the fundamental problems with the classical statistics hypothesis-testing approach as it is commonly practiced in marketing research. Another common problem is the widespread tendency to misinterpret a "statistically significant result." There are several common misinterpretations.[9] One of the most frequent is to view a *p* value as representing the probability that the results occurred because of sampling error. Thus, the commonly used *p* = 0.05 is taken to mean that there is a probability of only 0.05 that the results were caused by chance, and thus there must be something fundamental causing them.

---

[9]For an excellent discussion of some of the most common misinterpretations of classical significance tests and some recommendations on how to surmount the problems, see Alan G. Sawyer and J. Paul Peter, "The Significance of Statistical Significance Tests in Marketing Research," *Journal of Marketing Research,* 20 (May 1983), pp. 122–133.

Figure 17A.4

**Power Function for
Data of Table 17A.3**

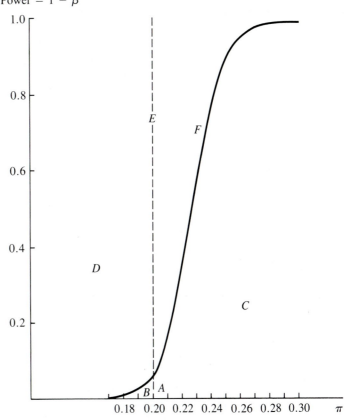

Probability of Rejecting H_0: $\pi \leq 0.20$
Power = $1 - \beta$

A—Type I error; true null hypothesis is rejected; significance level.
B—Type I error; true null hypothesis is rejected.
C—No error; false null hypothesis is rejected.
D—No error; true null hypothesis is not rejected.
E—No error; true null hypothesis is not rejected; confidence level.
F—Type II error; false null hypothesis is not rejected.

In actuality, a p value of 0.05 means that if, and this is a big if, the null hypothesis is true, the odds are only 1 in 20 of getting a sample result of the magnitude that was observed. Unfortunately, there is no way in classical statistical significance testing to determine whether the null hypothesis is true.

A p value reached by classical methods is not a summary of the data. Nor does the p value attached to a result tell how strong or dependable the particular result is. . . . Writers and readers are all too likely to read .05 as $p(H/E)$, "the probability that the *H*ypothesis is true, given the *E*vidence." As textbooks on statistics reiterate almost in vain, p is $p(E/H)$, the probability that this *E*vidence would arise if the (null) *H*ypothesis is true.[10]

[10]Lee J. Cronbach and R. E. Snow, *Aptitudes and Instructional Methods: A Handbook for Research on Interactions* (New York: Irvington, 1977), p. 52.

A second very frequent misinterpretation is to hold that the α or p level chosen is in some way related to the probability that the research hypothesis, typically captured in the alternative hypothesis, is true. Most typically, this probability is taken as the complement of the α level. Thus, a p value of 0.05 is interpreted to mean that its complement, $1 - 0.05 = 0.95$, is the probability that the research hypothesis is true. "Related to this misinterpretation is the practice of interpreting p values as a measure or the degree of validity of research results, i.e., a p value such as p < .0001 is "highly statistically significant" or "highly significant" and therefore much more valid than a p value of, say, 0.05."[11] Both of these related interpretations are wrong.

The only logical conclusion that can be drawn when a null hypothesis is rejected at some predetermined p level is that sampling error is an unlikely explanation of the results, given that the null hypothesis is true. In many ways that is not saying very much, because, as was just argued, the null hypothesis is a weak straw man; it is set up to be false. The null, as typically stated, holds that there is no relationship between a certain two variables, say, or that the groups are equal with respect to some particular variable. Yet, we do not really believe that. Rather, we investigate the relationship between variables because we believe there is some association between them, and we contrast the groups because we believe they are different with respect to the variable. Further, we can control our ability to reject the null hypothesis simply by the power we built into the statistical test, primarily through the size of the sample used to test it. "Given sufficiently high statistical power, one would expect virtually *always* to conclude the exact null hypothesis is false.[12]

Marketing researchers, then, need to be wary when interpreting the results of their hypothesis-testing procedures so that they do not mislead themselves and others. They need constantly to keep in mind both types of errors that it is possible to make. Further, they need to make sure they do not misinterpret what a test of significance reveals. It represents no more than a test against the null hypothesis. One useful way of avoiding misinterpretation is to calculate confidence intervals when possible, as this gives decision makers a much better feel for how much faith they can have in the results.

A test of significance is very much a yes-no affair: either the sample result is statistically significant, or it is not. On the other hand, "the confidence interval not only gives a yes or no answer, but also, by its width, gives an indication of whether the answer should be whispered or shouted."[13] While not every test of significance can be put in the form of a confidence interval estimate, many of them can, and it is advisable to put them in that form when the opportunity arises.[14]

---

[11]Sawyer and Peter, "The Significance," p. 123. For other useful discussions of what statistical tests of significance mean, see Mick Alt and Malcolm Brighton, "Analyzing Data or Telling Stories?" *Journal of the Market Research Society,* 23 (October 1981), pp. 209–219; and Norval D. Glenn, "Replications, Significance Tests and Confidence in Findings in Survey Research," *Public Opinion Quarterly,* 47 (Summer 1983), pp. 261–269.

[12]*Ibid.,* p. 125.

[13]Mary G. Natrella, "The Relation between Confidence Intervals and Tests of Significance," *American Statistician,* 14 (1960), p. 22.

[14]For an excellent discussion of the relationship between tests of significance and confidence interval estimates, see *Ibid.,* pp. 20–22, 33.

Chapter 18

Data Analysis: Examining Differences

+ + + +

+ + + +

+ + + +

+ + + +

Learning Objectives

Upon completing this chapter, you should be able to

1. Explain the basic use of a chi-square goodness-of-fit test.

2. Discuss the similarities and differences between the chi-square goodness-of-fit test and the Kolmogorov-Smirnov test.

3. Specify which test would be appropriate if one were testing an hypothesis about a single mean, given that the variance is known. Which would be appropriate if the variance were unknown?

4. Identify the tests that would be appropriate if the analysis involves two means from independent samples.

5. Specify the appropriate test if the analysis involves the difference between two parent-population proportions.

Case in Marketing Research

Mike Mihalic, director of catalog sales for Avery Sporting Goods, led Patrick Hayes from Samson Marketing Services through Avery's newest store toward his office in the back.

"This is fantastic, Mike," Pat said, as he wound his way past rows of tennis rackets and running shoes, Nautilus equipment, and golf clubs. "Owning this place is like having a license to print money," he said, noting the line at the register of customers laden with merchandise.

"It's been great, Pat," Mike said. "So good, in fact, that we're planning to open another three stores in the next eight months. I only wish I could say that our catalog division was doing as well."

"What's happening there, Mike?" Pat asked, settling into a chair across from Mike's cluttered desk. "Your catalog sales have always been the bedrock of your business."

"That's true," Mike said. "They've been good enough to allow us to expand into a retail operation, but they're just not growing the way they used to."

"So what are you planning to do? Bail out of direct mail?" Pat asked.

"Oh no," Mike said, looking alarmed. "Far from it. The catalog allows us to reach a national market at a fairly low cost. What we'd like to do is to revitalize that segment of the market. In fact, the reason I called you in was to ask if Samson would be interested in conducting a survey of our past customers for us as a way of beginning to get a handle on how we can improve our sales in that area."

"You know we'd be delighted to help," Pat said. "What exactly did you have in mind?"

"Well, to begin with, we'd like to know what our mail-order customers think about our products and services. I'd also like to get a better feel for who our customers really are. How old they are, how much they make . . . you know, things like that," Mike said.

"I think those are good ideas, Mike, but my experience with this business makes me want to take the study one step further. I think we really ought to investigate how customers feel about buying merchandise, especially sporting goods, through the mail versus in a retail outlet. I think that perception may be important in how we subsequently formulate our marketing strategy."

"Sounds logical to me, Pat," Mike said. "Why don't you go ahead and draft a proposal for a study. I'll tell Sid Green at the mailing house to run a list of names of our catalog customers for you."

"Fine," Pat said. "One last question: How much have you budgeted for this study?"

"Well, it's like this, Pat. We've been spending a lot on advertising for the retail stores, and postage rates have just gone up . . . Look, why don't we talk about it over lunch?" Mike finished feebly.

"Sure thing, buddy," Pat said, smiling, and readying himself to hear once more the "we don't have much money, but we want a large sample and lots of variables" speech.

Discussion Issues

1. If you were the marketing research director on this survey, what variables would you want to investigate in the study?

2. How might some of those variables be interrelated?

3. Assuming a mail survey is to be used, what might you do to increase the response rate?

A question that arises regularly in the analysis of research data is, are the research results statistically significant? Could the result have occurred by chance due to the fact that only a sample of the population was contacted, or does it actually indicate an underlying condition in the population? To answer, we use one of several tests of statistical significance. This chapter reviews some of the more important tests for examining the statistical significance of differences. The difference at issue might be the difference between some sample result and some expected population value, or the difference between two or more sample results. Different types of tests are applicable for different types of problems. The first part of the chapter reviews the χ^2 (chi-square) goodness-of-fit test, which is especially useful with nominal data. The second part reviews the Kolmogorov-Smirnov test, which is useful with ordinal data. The latter sections focus on the tests that are applicable when examining differences in means or proportions.

◆ Goodness of Fit

It is often the case in marketing studies that an analyst must determine whether a certain pattern of behavior shown by the data corresponds to the pattern that was expected when the study was devised. As an illustration, consider a breakfast food manufacturer who has recently developed a new cereal called *Score*. The cereal will be packaged in the three standard sizes: small, large, and family size. In the past, the manufacturer has found that for every small package, three of the large and two of the family size are also sold. The manufacturer wishes to see if this same tendency would hold with this new cereal, since a change in consumption patterns could have significant production implications. The manufacturer therefore decides to conduct a market test to determine the relative frequencies with which consumers would purchase the various sizes.

Suppose that, in an appropriate test market, over a one-week period, 1,200 boxes of the new cereal were sold and that the distribution of sales by size was as follows:

Number Buying			
Small	**Large**	**Family**	**Total**
240	575	385	1,200

As some quick multiplication would show, these figures do not match the pattern established earlier with other cereal brands. Does this preliminary evidence indicate that the firm should expect a change in the purchase patterns of the various sized packages with Score?

◆ **Chi-square goodness-of-fit test**

Statistical test to determine whether some observed pattern of frequencies corresponds to an expected pattern.

This is the type of problem for which the **chi-square goodness-of-fit test** is ideally suited. (Note the *chi* is a Greek letter that rhymes with sky.) The variable of interest has been broken into k mutually exclusive categories ($k = 3$ in the example), and each observation logically falls into one of the k classes or cells. The trials (purchases) are independent, and the sample size is large.

All that is necessary to employ the test is to calculate the *expected* number of cases that would fall in each category and to compare that with the *observed* number actually falling in the category, using the statistic

$$\chi^2 = \sum_{i=1}^{k} \frac{[O_i - E_i]^2}{E_i}$$

where

- O_i is the observed number of cases falling in the ith category.
- E_i is the expected number of cases falling in the ith category.
- k is the number of categories.

The expected number falling into a category is generated from the null hypothesis, which in this case is that the composition of sales of Score by package size would follow the manufacturer's normal sales. As we noted earlier, that is that for every small package, three large and two family sizes would be sold. In terms of the proportion of all sales, that means:

$$\text{small size: } \frac{1}{1 + 3 + 2} = 1/6,$$

$$\text{large size: } \frac{3}{1 + 3 + 2} = 3/6, \text{ and}$$

$$\text{family size: } \frac{2}{1 + 3 + 2} = 2/6$$

or that one-sixth of the sales could be expected to be in the small package size, one-half in the large size, and one-third in the family size if sales of the new cereal follow traditional patterns. If the 1,200 boxes sold in test market followed the normal or expected pattern, then 200 ($1/6 \times 1,200$) would have been the small size, 600 ($1/2 \times 1,200$) would have been the large size, and 400 ($1/3 \times 1,200$) would have been the family size. How does the observed pattern compare to the expected pattern? The approximate χ^2 statistic is computed as

$$\chi^2 = \frac{(240 - 200)^2}{200} + \frac{(575 - 600)^2}{600} + \frac{(385 - 400)^2}{400} = 9.60$$

The chi-square distribution is one of the statistical distributions that is completely determined by its degrees of freedom, ν. The term *degrees of freedom* refers to the number of things that can vary independently. For example, suppose you had five numbers for which you calculated an average. Then, by knowing any four of the numbers and the average, you would be able to determine the fifth number. In effect, you have used up one degree of freedom in the numbers by calculating the average. The degrees of freedom in the chi-square test are determined by how many cells in a table are free to vary.[1] For example, if we had the following table,

	B_1	B_2	
A_1	x	x	5
A_2	x	x	7
	4	8	

and we are given one of the cell values, say, the upper left value,

[1]Paul R. Winn, Ross H. Johnson, *Business Statistics* (New York: Macmillan Publishing Co., Inc., 1978), pp. 274–275.

	B_1	B_2	
A_1	1	④	5
A_2	③	④	7
	4	8	

then the circled values are all fixed, given that we know the marginal totals. If we know $A_1B_1 = 1$, then every other value is automatically determined. Because of this, we say that only one cell is free to vary.

In the example, the number of degrees of freedom is one less than the number of categories k, that is, $v = k - 1 = 2$, because the sum of the differences between the observed and expected frequencies is zero; both the expected and observed frequencies must sum to the total number of cases; given any $k - 1$ differences, the remaining difference is thus fixed, and this results in the loss of one degree of freedom.

Back to the Case

Pat Hayes stashed an unwieldy package containing a new basketball for his son and a squash racket for himself behind the door in Mike Mihalic's office, sat down at a table in the corner, and opened his briefcase.

"You'll be pleased to know that we've finished analyzing much of the data, and I have some results for you to mull over, Mike," Pat said.

"Great," Mike said. "What did you find out?"

"As you know, after pretesting our questionnaire with 25 customers, we mailed it to 225 randomly chosen individuals from the mailing list you supplied me. We offered each of these people a $3 coupon toward their next catalog purchase to encourage them to respond. As a result, we got 124 usable surveys, for a 55 percent response rate," Pat said.

"One of the primary things we wanted to investigate in this study was whether people who have bought from Avery in the past are willing to do so again. That would give us a sense of their general level of satisfaction with the mail-order buying experience," Pat said.

"In order to conduct this analysis we ran the data through a program called *SPSS*, which is short for *Statistical Package for the Social Sciences*. It's a widely used program for statistical analysis. This table is a result of the two-way tabulation that SPSS produced for the variables I mentioned," Pat said, handing Mike the following table.

Mike looked confused.

"Let me explain," Pat said. "This is a table of two variables: the willingness of individuals on Avery's mailing list to purchase from a catalog, and whether or not those same individuals ever purchased from the catalog in the past. Willingness to buy through the Avery Sporting Goods catalog is the dependent variable we are interested in explaining."

"Look now at the column percentages," Pat instructed Mike. "These percentages suggest that the 'most willing' group of purchasers among the catalog recipients are those who ordered from Avery within the past year. Over three-fourths of these people who did order within the past year (40.5 + 35.7 percent) are somewhat willing to order from Avery again. At the same time, almost one-fourth (23.8 percent) of those who bought within the last year are not willing to place another order. It might be worth your while, Mike, to investigate that group further to find out why they're so unhappy," Pat said.

"I know this is getting a bit statistical for you, Mike," Pat said, "but bear with me for one more minute. Look down at that figure that's given where it says 'raw chi

Suppose the researcher has chosen a significance level of $\alpha = 0.05$ for this test. The tabled value of χ^2 for two degrees of freedom and $\alpha = 0.05$ is 5.99 (see Table 2 in the appendix at the end of the book). Since the calculated value ($\chi^2 = 9.60$) is larger, the conclusion is that the sample result would be unlikely to occur by chance alone. Rather, the preliminary market-test results suggest that sales of Score will follow a different pattern than is typical. The null hypothesis of sales in the ratio of 1:3:2 is rejected.

The chi-square test outlined here is an approximate test.[2] The approximation is relatively good if, as a rule of thumb, the expected number of cases in each category is five or more, although this value can be as low as 1 for some situations.[3]

---

[2]The correct distribution to test the hypothesis is the hypergeometric. The hypergeometric distribution, however, is unwieldy for anything but very small samples. The chi-square distribution approximates the hypergeometric for large sample sizes. For a discussion of this point, as well as the other conditions surrounding a goodness-of-fit test, see Leonard A. Marascuilo and Maryellen McSweeney, *Nonparametric and Distribution Free Methods for the Social Sciences* (Belmont, Calif.: Brooks/Cole, 1977), pp. 243–248.

[3]W. G. Cochran, "The χ^2 Test of Goodness of Fit," *Annuals of Mathematical Statistics,* 23 (1952), pp. 315–345.

Cross Tabulation of Willingness to Purchase from Avery's Catalog (V3) with Whether Respondent Has Purchased from It Before (V4)

Count Row Percent Column Percent Total Percent		V4 Never Ordered 1	Ordered before But Not within Past Year 2	Ordered within Past Year 3	Row Total
V3					
Unwilling	1	20 40.0 46.5 16.1	20 40.0 51.3 16.1	10 20.0 23.8 8.1	50 40.3
Somewhat Willing	2	7 20.0 16.3 5.6	11 31.4 28.2 8.9	17 48.6 40.5 13.7	35 28.2
Very Willing	3	16 41.0 37.2 12.9	8 20.5 20.5 6.5	15 38.5 35.7 12.1	39 31.5
Column Total		43 34.7	39 31.5	42 33.9	124 100.0

Raw chi square = 10.997 with four degrees of freedom
Significance = .027

square.' Basically, that figure measures whether the results of our analysis are statistically significant, or whether they were just a matter of chance. In this case, the value is such that we can say with some certainty that the two variables we measured are indeed related. That is, a customer's willingness to purchase through the Avery catalog seems to be influenced by whether or not he or she has purchased from it before."

In this analysis, the chi-square value of $\chi^2 = 10.997$ with four degrees of freedom is significant at the .027 level. This indicates that the null hypothesis of independence between the two variables would typically be rejected in favor of the alternative that willingness to purchase from Avery's catalog is a function of having purchased from it before.

The previous example illustrated the use of the chi-square distribution to test a null hypothesis regarding k population proportions, $\pi_1, \pi_2, \ldots, \pi_k$. The proportions were needed to generate the expected number of cases in each of the k categories. Viewed in this light, the test of a single proportion discussed when reviewing the logic of hypothesis testing in the appendix to Chapter 17 is a special case; in the goodness-of-fit test, the single parameter π is replaced by the k parameters $\pi_1, \pi_2, \ldots, \pi_k$.

Another use of the chi-square goodness-of-fit test is in determining whether a population distribution has a particular form. For instance, we might be interested in finding out whether a sample distribution of scores might have arisen from a normal distribution of scores.[4] To investigate, we could construct the sample frequency histogram. The intervals would correspond to the k cells of the goodness-of-fit test. The observed cell frequencies would be the number of observations falling in each interval. The expected cell frequencies would be the number falling in each interval, if indeed the sample came from a normal distribution with mean μ and variance σ^2. If the population mean and variance were unknown, the sample mean and variance could be used as estimates. This would result in the loss of two additional degrees of freedom, but the basic test procedure would remain unchanged.

♦ Kolmogorov-Smirnov Test

The **Kolmogorov-Smirnov test** is similar to the chi-square goodness-of-fit test in that it uses a comparison between observed and expected frequencies to determine whether observed results are in accord with a stated null hypothesis. But the Kolmogorov-Smirnov test takes advantage of the ordinal nature of the data.

Consider, for example, a manufacturer of cosmetics who is testing four different shades of a foundation compound, very light, light, medium, and dark. The company has hired a marketing research firm to determine whether any distinct preference exists toward either extreme. If so, the company will manufacture only the preferred shades. Otherwise, it will market all shades. Suppose that in a sample of 100, 50 persons preferred the very light shade, 30 the light shade, 15 the medium shade, and 5 the dark shade. Do these results indicate some kind of preference?

Since shade represents a natural ordering, the Kolmogorov-Smirnov test can be used to test the preference hypothesis. The test involves specifying the cumulative distribution function that would occur under the null hypothesis, and comparing that with the observed cumulative distribution function. The point at which the two functions show the maximum deviation is determined, and the value of this deviation is the test statistic.

The null hypothesis for the cosmetic manufacturer would be that there is no preference for the various shades. Thus it would be expected that 25 percent of the sample would prefer each shade. The cumulative distribution function resulting from this assumption is presented as the last column of Table 18.1.

Kolmogorov-Smirnov D, which is equal to the *absolute value of the maximum deviation* between the observed cumulative proportion and the theoretical cumulative proportion, is $0.80 - 0.50 = 0.30$. If the researcher chooses an $\alpha = 0.05$, the critical value of D for large samples is given by $1.36/\sqrt{n}$, where n is the sample size. In our case of a sample size of 100, the critical value is 0.136. Calculated D exceeds

---

[4]The reader interested in the details of such a test should see Samuel Richmond, *Statistical Analysis*, 2nd ed. (New York: Ronald, 1964), pp. 291–295.

When the data are ordinal, the Kolmogorov-Smirnov test is useful for determining if some observed pattern of results corresponds to some expected pattern.

Source: Courtesy of J.P. Morgan & Co. Incorporated.

the critical value, and thus the null hypothesis of no preference among shades is rejected. The data indicate a statistically significant preference for the lighter shades.

The careful reader will have noticed that the hypothesis of no preference could also have been tested with the chi-square goodness-of-fit test. When the data are ordinal though, the Kolmogorov-Smirnov test is the preferred procedure. It is more powerful than chi-square in almost all cases, is easier to compute, and does not require a certain minimum expected frequency in each cell as does the chi-square test.

Table 18.1   Observed and Theoretical Cumulative Distributions of Foundation Compound Preference

Shade	Observed Number	Observed Proportion	Observed Cumulative Proportion	Theoretical Proportion	Theoretical Cumulative Proportion
Very light	50	0.50	0.50	0.25	0.25
Light	30	0.30	0.80	0.25	0.50
Medium	15	0.15	0.95	0.25	0.75
Dark	5	0.05	1.00	0.25	1.00

The Kolmogorov-Smirnov test can also be used to determine whether two independent samples have been drawn from the same population or from populations with the same distribution. An example would be a manufacturer interested in determining whether consumer preference among sizes for a new brand of laundry detergent was the same as for the old brand. To apply the test, we would simply need to create a cumulative frequency distribution for each sample of observations using the same intervals. The test statistic would be the value of the maximum deviation between the two observed cumulative frequencies.[5]

◆ Hypotheses about One Mean

A recurring problem in marketing research studies is the need to make some statement about the parent-population mean. Recall that when sampling from a parent population with known variance that the distribution of sample means is normal, the mean of the sample means is equal to the population mean, and the variance of the sample means, $\sigma_{\bar{x}}^2$, is equal to the population variance divided by the sample size; that is, $\sigma_{\bar{x}}^2 = \sigma^2/n$. Thus, it should not prove surprising to find that the appropriate statistic for testing a hypothesis about a mean when the population variance is *known* is

$$z = \frac{\bar{x} - \mu}{\sigma_{\bar{x}}}$$

where

- $\bar{x}$ is the sample mean
- μ is the population mean
- $\sigma_{\bar{x}}$ is the standard error of the mean, which is equal to $\sigma/\sqrt{n}$, where n is the sample size and σ is the population standard deviation.

The z statistic is appropriate if the sample comes from a normal population, or if the variable is not normally distributed in the population, but the sample is large enough for the central-limit theorem to be operative. What happens, though, in the more realistic case in which the population variance is unknown?

When the parent-population variance is unknown, then, of course, the standard error of the mean, $\sigma_{\bar{x}}$, is unknown, since it is equal to $\sigma/\sqrt{n}$. The standard error of the mean must then be estimated from the sample data. The estimate is $s_{\bar{x}} = \hat{s}/\sqrt{n}$, where $\hat{s}$ is the unbiased sample standard deviation; that is,

$$\hat{s} = \sqrt{\frac{\sum_{i=1}^{n} (X_i - \bar{x})^2}{n - 1}}$$

Or, in words,

$$\hat{s} = \sqrt{\frac{\text{the sum of the deviations of the sample observations around the sample mean squared}}{\text{sample size minus 1}}}$$

---

[5]See Marascuilo and McSweeny, *Nonparametric and Distribution Free Methods,* pp. 250–251. See also Jean Dickinson Gibbons, *Nonparametric Statistical Inference,* 2nd ed. (New York: Marell Dekker, Inc., 1985).

The test statistic now becomes

$$\frac{\text{(sample mean minus hypothesized value of population mean)}}{\text{estimated standard error of the mean}}$$

or $(\bar{x} - \mu)/s_{\bar{x}}$, which is t distributed with $n - 1$ degrees of freedom if the conditions for the t test are satisfied.

To use the t statistic appropriately for making inferences about the mean, two basic questions need to be answered:

- Is the distribution of the variable in the parent population normal, or is it asymmetrical?
- Is the sample size large or small?

If the variable of interest is normally distributed in the parent population, then the test statistic $(\bar{x} - \mu)/s_{\bar{x}}$ is t distributed with $n - 1$ degrees of freedom. This is true whether the sample size is large or small. For small samples, we actually use t with $n - 1$ degrees of freedom when making an inference. Although t with $n - 1$ degrees of freedom is also the theoretically correct distribution for large n, the distribution approaches and becomes indistinguishable from the normal distribution for samples of thirty or more observations. The test statistic $(\bar{x} - \mu)/s_{\bar{x}}$ is therefore referred to a table of normal deviates when one is making inferences with large samples. Note, though, that this is because the theoretically correct t distribution (since σ is unknown) has become indistinguishable from the normal curve.

What happens if the variable is not normally distributed in the parent population when σ is unknown? If the distribution of the variable is symmetrical or displays only moderate skew, or asymmetry, there is no problem. The t test is quite robust to departures from normality. However, if the variable is highly skewed in the parent population, the appropriate procedure depends upon the sample size. If the sample is small, the t test is inappropriate. Either the variable has to be transformed so that it is normally distributed, or one of the distribution-free statistical tests must be used. If the sample is large, the normal curve could be used for making the inference, provided the following two assumptions are satisfied.

1. The sample size is large enough so that the sample mean $\bar{x}$ is normally distributed because of the operation of the central-limit theorem. The greater the degree of asymmetry in the distribution of the variable, the larger the size of the sample that is needed to satisfy this assumption.
2. The sample standard deviation $\hat{s}$ is a close estimate of the parent-population standard deviation σ. The higher the degree of variability is in the parent population, the larger the size of the sample needed to justify this assumption.

The possible hazards involved in ignoring the nature of the distribution of data were cited by Robert L. Lavidge, president of Elrick and Lavidge, Inc., a marketing research firm:

> Consider the test of a new product. On the average, consumers wanted it neither really hot nor really mild. The mean rating of the test participants was quite close to the middle of the scale which had "very mild" and "very hot" as its bipolar adjectives. This happened to fit the client's preconceived notion. However, examination of the distribution of the ratings revealed the existence of a large proportion of consumers who wanted the sauce to be mild and an equally large proportion who wanted it to be hot.

Table 18.2   Summary Table of Inferences about a Single Mean

	σ Known	σ Unknown
Distribution of variable in parent population is normal or symmetrical.	Small n: Use $z = \dfrac{\bar{x} - \mu}{\sigma_{\bar{x}}}$ Large n: Use $z = \dfrac{\bar{x} - \mu}{\sigma_{\bar{x}}}$	Small n: Use $t = \dfrac{\bar{x} - \mu}{s_{\bar{x}}}$ where $s_{\bar{x}} = \hat{s}/\sqrt{n}$ and $\hat{s} = \sqrt{\dfrac{\sum_{i=1}^{n}(X_i - \bar{x})^2}{n - 1}}$ and refer to t table for $n - 1$ degrees of freedom. Large n: Since the t distribution approaches the normal as n increases, use $z = \dfrac{\bar{x} - \mu}{s_{\bar{x}}}$ for $n > 30$.
Distribution of variable in parent population is asymmetrical.	Small n: There is no theory to support the parametric test. One must either transform the variate so that it is normally distributed and then use the z test, or one must use a distribution-free statistical test. Large n: If the sample is large enough so that the central-limit theorem is operative, use $z = \dfrac{\bar{x} - \mu}{\sigma_{\bar{x}}}$	Small n: There is no theory to support the parametric test. One must either transform the variate so that it is normally distributed and then use the t test, or one must use a distribution-free statistical test. Large n: If sample is large enough so that (1) the central-limit theorem is operative and (2) $\hat{s}$ is a close estimate of σ, use $z = \dfrac{\bar{x} - \mu}{s_{\bar{x}}}$

Relatively few wanted the in-between product, which would have been suggested by looking at the mean rating alone.[6]

Table 18.2 summarizes the situation for making inferences about a mean for known and unknown parent-population standard deviation, σ, and normally distributed and asymmetrical parent-population distributions.

To illustrate the application of the t test, consider a supermarket chain that is investigating the desirability of adding a new product to the shelves of its associated stores. Since many products must compete for limited shelf space, the store has determined that it must sell 100 units per week in each store in order for the item to be sufficiently profitable to warrant handling it. Suppose that the research department decides to investigate the item's turnover by putting it in a random sample of

[6]"How to Keep Well-Intentioned Research from Misleading New-Product Planners," *Marketing News,* 18 (January 6, 1984), Section 2, p. 8.

Table 18.3   Store Sales of Trial Product per Week

Store i	Sales X_i	Store i	Sales X_i
1	86	6	93
2	97	7	132
3	114	8	116
4	108	9	105
5	123	10	120

ten stores for a limited period of time. Suppose further that the average sales per store per week were as shown in Table 18.3.

Since the variance of sales per store is unknown and has to be estimated, the t test is the correct parametric test if the distribution of sales is normal. The normality assumption seems reasonable and could be checked using one of the goodness-of-fit tests. The little sales evidence available does not indicate any real asymmetry, so let us assume that the normality assumption is satisfied.

A one-tailed test is appropriate, since it is only when the sales per store per week reach at least 100 units that the product will be introduced on a national scale. The null and alternate hypotheses are

$$H_0: \mu \leq 100$$
$$H_a: \mu > 100$$

and suppose the significance level is to be $\alpha = 0.05$. From the data in Table 18.3,

$$\text{sample mean} = \frac{\text{sum of observations}}{\text{sample size}}$$

or

$$\bar{x} = \frac{\sum\limits_{i=1}^{n} X_i}{n} = 109.4$$

and

$$\text{sample standard deviation} = \frac{\text{square root of sum of deviations around sample mean squared}}{\text{sample size minus 1}}$$

or

$$\hat{s} = \sqrt{\frac{\sum\limits_{i=1}^{n} (X_i - \bar{x})^2}{(n - 1)}} = 14.40$$

and therefore the estimated standard error of the mean is $s_x = \hat{s}/\sqrt{n} = 4.55$. Calculations yield

$$t = \frac{\overline{x} - \mu}{s_{\overline{x}}} = \frac{109.4 - 100}{4.55} = 2.07$$

Critical t as read from the t table with $\nu = n - 1 = 9$ degrees of freedom is 1.833 ($p = .95$). (See Table 3 in the appendix at the end of the book.) It is unlikely that the calculated value would have occurred by chance if the sales per store in the population were indeed less than or equal to 100 units per week.

Some insight into the sales per store per week that might be expected if the product were introduced on a national scale can be obtained by calculating the confidence interval. The appropriate formula is

sample mean $\pm\, t$ (estimated standard error of the mean)

or

$$\overline{x} \pm ts_{\overline{x}}.$$

For a 95 percent confidence interval and 9 degrees of freedom, $t = 1.833$, as we have already seen. The 95 percent confidence interval is thus $109.4 \pm (1.833)(4.55)$, or 109.4 ± 8.3, or, alternatively, $101.1 \le \mu \le 117.7$.

Suppose the product is placed in fifty stores and that the sample mean and sample standard deviation are the same, that is, $\overline{x} = 109.4$, $\hat{s} = 14.40$. The test statistic would now be $z = 4.62$, which would be referred to a normal table since the t is indistinguishable from the normal for samples of this size. Calculated z is greater than critical $z = 1.645$ for $\alpha = 0.05$, and, as expected, the same conclusion is warranted. The evidence is stronger now because of the larger sample of stores; the product could be expected to sell at a rate greater than 100 units per store per week.

The impact of the larger sample and the opportunity it provides to use the normal curve can also be seen in the smaller confidence interval the larger sample produces. When the normal curve rather than t distribution applies, the formula $\overline{x} \pm ts_{\overline{x}}$ for calculating the confidence interval changes to $\overline{x} \pm zs_{\overline{x}}$, where the appropriate z value is read from the normal curve table. Since for a 95 percent confidence interval, $z = 1.645$, the interval is $109.4 \pm (1.645)(4.55)$ or 109.4 ± 7.5, which yields the estimate $101.9 \le \mu \le 108.6$, a slightly narrower interval than that produced when ten stores rather than fifty were in the sample.

♦ Hypotheses about Two Means

Consider testing a hypothesis about the difference between two population means. Assuming the samples are independent, there are three cases to consider:

- The two parent-population variances are known.
- The parent-population variances are unknown but can be assumed to be equal.
- The parent-population variances are unknown and cannot be assumed to be equal.

Variances Are Known

Experience has shown that the population variance usually changes much more slowly than does the population mean. This means that the "old" variance can often be used as the "known" population variance for studies that are being repeated. For example, we may have annually checked the per capita soft drink consumption of people living in different regions of the United States. If we were now to test a hypothesis about the differences in per capita consumption of a new soft drink, we could use the previously determined variances as "known" variances for our new soft drink. Consider that our problem is indeed one of determining whether there are any differences between Northerners and Southerners in their consumption of a new soft drink our company has recently introduced, called Spark. Further, past data indicate that per capita variation in the consumption of soft drinks is 10 ounces per day for Northerners and 14 ounces per day for Southerners as measured by the standard deviation, that is, $\sigma_N = 10$ and $\sigma_S = 14$.

The null hypothesis is that there is no difference between Northerners and Southerners in their consumption of Spark, or that their mean consumption is equal (H_0: $\mu_N = \mu_S$), while the alternate hypothesis is that there is a difference (H_a: $\mu_N \neq \mu_S$). It so happens that if $\bar{x}_N$ and $\bar{x}_S$, the sample means, are normally distributed random variables, then their sum or difference is also normally distributed. The two sample means could be normally distributed because per capita consumption is normally distributed in each region or because the two samples are large enough that the central-limit theorem is operative. In either case, the test statistic is $z =$ the sample mean of the first sample minus the sample mean of the second sample minus the hypothesized population mean in the first sample minus the hypothesized population mean in the second sample, all divided by the standard error of the difference in the two means; or

$$ z = \frac{(\bar{x}_1 - \bar{x}_2) - (\mu_1 - \mu_2)}{\sigma_{\bar{x}_1 - \bar{x}_2}} $$

where

- $\bar{x}_1$ is the sample mean for the first (northern) sample
- $\bar{x}_2$ is the sample mean for the second (southern) sample
- μ_1 and μ_2 are the unknown population means for the northern and southern samples
- $\sigma_{\bar{x}_1 - \bar{x}_2}$ is the standard error of estimate for the difference in means and is equal to the square root of the sum of the two variances in means, specifically,

$$ \sqrt{\sigma_{\bar{x}_1}^2 + \sigma_{\bar{x}_2}^2}, $$

where, in turn, $\sigma_{\bar{x}_1}^2 = \sigma_1^2/n_1$ and $\sigma_{\bar{x}_2}^2 = \sigma_2^2/n_2$. Now σ_1^2 and σ_2^2 are the "known" population variances of $\sigma_1^2 = (10)^2 = 100$ and $\sigma_2^2 = (14)^2 = 196$.

Suppose that a random sample of 100 people from the North and South, respectively, is taken and that $\bar{x}_1 = 20$ ounces per day and $\bar{x}_2 = 25$ ounces per day. Does this result indicate a real difference in consumption rates? The standard error of estimate is

$$ \sigma_{\bar{x}_1 - \bar{x}_2} = \sqrt{\frac{100}{100} + \frac{196}{100}} = \sqrt{2.96} = 1.720 $$

and the calculated z is

$$ z = \frac{(20 - 25) - (\mu_N - \mu_S)}{1.720} = \frac{-5 - 0}{1.720} = -2.906 $$

Calculated z exceeds the critical tabled value of -1.96 for $\alpha = 0.05$, and the null hypothesis is rejected. There is a statistically significant difference in the per capita consumption of Spark by Northerners and Southerners.

The confidence interval for the difference in the two means is given by the formula

$$(\overline{x}_1 - \overline{x}_2) \pm z\sigma_{\overline{x}_1 - \overline{x}_2}$$

For a 95 percent confidence interval, $z = 1.96$, and the interval estimate of the difference in consumption of Spark by the two groups is $-5 \pm (1.96)(1.720) = -5 \pm 3.4$. Northerners, on average, are estimated to drink 1.6 to 8.4 ounces of Spark less per day than Southerners.

Variances Are Unknown

When the two parent-population variances are unknown, the standard error of the test statistic $\sigma_{\overline{x}_1 - \overline{x}_2}$ is also unknown, since $\sigma_{\overline{x}_1}$ and $\sigma_{\overline{x}_2}$ are unknown and have to be estimated. As was true with one sample, the sample standard deviations are used to estimate the population standard deviations;

$$\hat{s}_1^2 = \frac{\sum_{i=1}^{n_1}(X_{i1} - \overline{x}_1)^2}{(n_1 - 1)}$$

is used to estimate σ_1^2 and

$$\hat{s}_2^2 = \frac{\sum_{i=1}^{n_2}(X_{i2} - \overline{x}_2)^2}{(n_2 - 1)}$$

is used to estimate σ_2^2, and the estimates of the standard error of the means become

$$s_{\overline{x}_1} = \hat{s}_1/\sqrt{n_1} \text{ and } s_{\overline{x}_2} = \hat{s}_2/\sqrt{n_2}$$

The general estimate of the standard error of the difference in two means, $\sigma_{\overline{x}_1 - \overline{x}_2}$, is then

$$s_{\overline{x}_1 - \overline{x}_2} = \sqrt{s_{\overline{x}_1}^2 + s_{\overline{x}_2}^2} = \sqrt{\frac{\hat{s}_1^2}{n_1} + \frac{\hat{s}_2^2}{n_2}}$$

Although unknown, if the two parent-population variances *can be assumed equal,* a better estimate of the common population variance can be generated by pooling the samples to calculate

$$\hat{s}^2 = \frac{\sum_{i=1}^{n_1}(X_{i1} - \overline{x}_1)^2 + \sum_{i=1}^{n_2}(X_{i2} - \overline{x}_2)^2}{n_1 + n_2 - 2}$$

where $\hat{s}^2$ is the pooled sample variance used to estimate the common population variance. Note that the calculation of the pooled sample variance involves summing the squares of the deviations of the first sample around their mean and adding that total to the sum of the squares of the deviations of the second sample around their mean. In this case the estimated standard error of the test statistic $s_{\overline{x}_1 - \overline{x}_2}$ reduces to

$$S_{\bar{x}_1 - \bar{x}_2} = \sqrt{\frac{\hat{s}_1^2}{n_1} + \frac{\hat{s}_2^2}{n_2}} = \sqrt{\frac{\hat{s}^2}{n_1} + \frac{\hat{s}^2}{n_2}} = \sqrt{\hat{s}^2\left(\frac{1}{n_1} + \frac{1}{n_2}\right)}$$

If the distribution of the variable in each population can further be assumed to be normal, the appropriate test statistic is

$$t = \frac{(\bar{x}_1 - \bar{x}_2) - (\mu_1 - \mu_2)}{S_{\bar{x}_1 - \bar{x}_2}}$$

which is t distributed with $\nu = n_1 + n_2 - 2$ degrees of freedom.

Suppose, for example, that a manufacturer of floor waxes has recently developed a new wax. The company is considering two different containers for the wax, one plastic and one metal. The company decides to make the final determination on the basis of a limited sales test in which the plastic containers are introduced in a random sample of ten stores and the metal containers are introduced in an *independent* random sample of ten stores. The test results are contained in Table 18.4.

$$\text{Calculated } t = \frac{(\bar{x}_1 - \bar{x}_2) - (\mu_1 - \mu_2)}{S_{\bar{x}_1 - \bar{x}_2}} = \frac{(403.0 - 390.3) - (0)}{8.15} = 1.56.$$

This value is referred to a t table for $\nu = n_1 + n_2 - 2 = 18$ degrees of freedom. The test is two-tailed because the null hypothesis is that they were unequal; there was no *a priori* statement that one was expected to sell better than the other. For $\alpha = 0.05$, say, and 18 degrees of freedom, critical $t = 2.101$. (One needs to look in the column headed $1 - \alpha = .975$ rather than at .95 in Table 3 in the appendix, since this is a two-tailed test.) Since calculated t is less than critical t, the null hypothesis of no difference would not be rejected. The sample data do not indicate that the plastic container could be expected to outsell the metal container in the total population, even though it did so in this limited experiment.

The example again demonstrates the importance of explicitly determining the statistical significance level by appropriately balancing Type I and Type II errors. Here α error was set arbitrarily equal to 0.05. This led to nonrejection of the null hypothesis and the conclusion that the plastic container would not be expected to outsell the metal container in the total population. Yet if the decision maker had been able to tolerate an α error of 0.20, say, just the opposite conclusion would have been warranted, since interpolating in Table 3 in the appendix for 18 degrees

Table 18.4   Store Sales of Floor Wax in Units

Store	Plastic Container	Metal Container	Store	Plastic Container	Metal Container
1	432	365	6	380	372
2	360	405	7	422	378
3	397	396	8	406	410
4	408	390	9	400	383
5	417	404	10	408	400

Back to the Case

Pat Hayes and Mike Mihalic came back from lunch and settled once again at the table in Mike's office, which was littered with old coffee cups, computer print-outs, and back issues of the Avery Sporting Goods catalog.

"I noticed your eyes were glazing over when I started talking about statistical significance before lunch, Mike, so I wanted to wait until we had a break before launching into my other findings," Pat said.

"There's more?" Mike asked.

"Sure thing. We felt there was a lot of valuable information hidden in these questionnaires that would be useful to you in developing a strategy for the renaissance of the direct mail business. Stick with me, buddy, and there's a promotion in your future," Pat said, laughing.

Mike smiled wanly, anticipating more tables and numbers.

"Now, look at this," Pat said, directing Mike's attention to a long question that had appeared in the survey. "We asked people how confident they felt about purchasing these various sporting goods items by mail. Now the beauty of this question is that there is an index, called CATCON, short for 'catalog confidence' that is designed to measure the amount of confidence people have when purchasing products from a catalog. The CATCON index in this case is what you would get if you added up the score of the responses for items 'a' through 'e' on question 4." (See Figure 17.1).

"So what does this all mean?" Mike asked.

"Well, the really interesting thing we found is that the score differs based on the customer's sex. Look at this table," Pat said, thrusting a small chart in front of Mike.

"The table shows that the mean score for men is higher than it is for women. Since our sample was fairly small, you may well ask whether that difference is really statistically significant," Pat said.

"Right," Mike said. "I was just about to ask that very question."

"You bet it is," Pat said. "Just check out the value of *t*."

This is an example of a hypothesis about two means, since its goal was to assess whether there was a difference in the degree of confidence between males and females when buying from catalogs. It was a two-tailed test, since the alternate hypothesis was that they were unequal — there was no belief beforehand that one sex would be more confident than the other. In this case, the null hypothesis is rejected, since there indeed is a statistically significant difference between men's and women's confidence when catalog shopping.

Difference in Means for CATCON Index between Males and Females

Variable/Group	Number of Cases	Mean	Standard Deviation	Standard Error	Pooled Variance Estimate			Separate Variance Estimate		
					t Value	Degrees of Freedom	Two-Tail Probability	*t* Value	Degrees of Freedom	Two-Tail Probability
CATCON										
1. Males	65	21.462	2.001	.248	33.87	121	.000	33.87	119.42	.000
2. Females	58	9.224	2.000	.263						

of freedom indicates that the probability of getting calculated $t = 1.56$ under an assumption of no difference in the population means is approximately 15 percent. Assuming the production and other costs associated with each container were the same, it would clearly seem that the final packaging decision should favor the plastic container. If the production and other costs were not the same, then these costs should be reflected in the statistical decision rule.[7]

The preceding discussion assumes that the samples are independent and that the variable of interest is normally distributed in each of the parent populations. The normality assumption was again necessary to justify the use of the t distribution. What happens, though, if the variable is not normally distributed or the samples are not independent? The lower half of Table 18.5 summarizes the approach for non-normal parent distributions for known and unknown σ, while the next section treats the case of **related samples.**

Samples Are Related

A manufacturer of camping equipment wished to study consumer color preferences for a sleeping bag it had recently developed. The bag was of medium quality and price. Traditionally, the high-quality, high-priced sleeping bags used by serious campers and backpackers came in the earth colors, such as green and brown. Previous research indicated that the low-quality, low-priced sleeping bags were frequently purchased for children, to be used at slumber parties. Vivid colors were preferred by this market segment, with bright reds and oranges leading the way. Production capacity restrictions would not allow the company to produce sets in both colors. To make the comparison, it selected a random sample of five stores into which it introduced bags of both types. The sales per store are indicated in Table 18.6. Do the data present sufficient evidence to indicate a difference in the average sales for the different colored bags?

An analysis of the data indicates a difference in the two means of $(\overline{x}_1 - \overline{x}_2) = (50.2 - 45.2) = 5.0$. This is a rather small difference, considering the variability in sales that exists across the five stores. Further, application of the procedures of the last section suggests that the difference is not statistically significant. The pooled estimate of the common variance is

$$\hat{s}^2 = \frac{\sum_{i=1}^{n_1}(X_{i1} - \overline{x}_1)^2 + \sum_{i=1}^{n_2}(X_{i2} - \overline{x}_2)^2}{n_1 + n_2 - 2} = \frac{1512.8 + 1222.8}{8} = 341.95$$

and

$$s_{\overline{x}_1 - \overline{x}_2} = \sqrt{\hat{s}^2\left(\frac{1}{n_1} + \frac{1}{n_2}\right)} = \sqrt{341.95\left(\frac{1}{5} + \frac{1}{5}\right)} = 11.70.$$

Calculated t is thus

$$t = \frac{(\overline{x}_1 - \overline{x}_2) - (\mu_1 - \mu_2)}{s_{\overline{x}_1 - \overline{x}_2}} = \frac{(50.2 - 45.2) - 0}{11.70} = 0.427$$

---

[7]The Bayesian posture would be to introduce the plastic container even with the obtained sample results if the opportunity costs associated with each alternative were the same. If they were not the same, then the Bayesian approach would incorporate these costs directly into the decision rule regarding which container should be produced.

Table 18.5   Summary Table of Inferences about the Difference in Two Means

	σ Known	σ Unknown
Distribution of variables in parent populations is normal or symmetrical.	Small n: Use $z = \dfrac{(\bar{x}_1 - \bar{x}_2) - (\mu_1 - \mu_2)}{\sigma_{\bar{x}_1 - \bar{x}_2}}$ where $\sigma_{\bar{x}_1 - \bar{x}_2} = \sqrt{\dfrac{\sigma_1^2}{n_1} + \dfrac{\sigma_2^2}{n_2}}$ Large n: Use $z = \dfrac{(\bar{x}_1 - \bar{x}_2) - (\mu_1 - \mu_2)}{\sigma_{\bar{x}_1 - \bar{x}_2}}$	Small n: Can you assume $\sigma_1 = \sigma_2$? 1. Yes: Use pooled variance t test where $t = \dfrac{(\bar{x}_1 - \bar{x}_2) - (\mu_1 - \mu_2)}{s_{\bar{x}_1 - \bar{x}_2}}$ and $s_{\bar{x}_1 - \bar{x}_2} =$ $\sqrt{\dfrac{\sum\limits_{i=1}^{n_1}(X_{i1} - \bar{x}_1)^2 + \sum\limits_{i=1}^{n_2}(X_{i2} - \bar{x}_2)^2}{n_1 + n_2 - 2}\left(\dfrac{1}{n_1} + \dfrac{1}{n_2}\right)}$ with $(n_1 + n_2 - 2)$ degrees of freedom. 2. No: Approach is shrouded in controversy. Might use Aspin-Welch test. Large n: Use $z = \dfrac{(\bar{x}_1 - \bar{x}_2) - (\mu_1 - \mu_2)}{s_{\bar{x}_1 - \bar{x}_2}}$ and use pooled variance if variances can be assumed equal, and unpooled variance if equality assumption is not warranted.
Distribution of variables in parent populations is asymmetrical.	Small n: There is no theory to support the parametric test. One must either transform the variates so that they are normally distributed and then use the z test, or one must use a distribution-free statistical test. Large n: If the individual samples are large enough so that the central-limit theorem is operative for them separately, it will also apply to their sum or difference. Use $z = \dfrac{(\bar{x}_1 - \bar{x}_2) - (\mu_1 - \mu_2)}{\sigma_{\bar{x}_1 - \bar{x}_2}}$	Small n: There is no theory to support the parametric test. One must either transform the variates so that they are normally distributed and then use the t test, or one must use a distribution-free statistical test. Large n: One must assume that n_1 and n_2 are large enough so that the central-limit theorem applies to the individual sample means. Then it can also be assumed to apply to their sum or difference. Use $z = \dfrac{(\bar{x}_1 - \bar{x}_2) - (\mu_1 - \mu_2)}{s_{\bar{x}_1 - \bar{x}_2}}$ employing a pooled variance if the unknown parent-population variances can be assumed equal, and use unpooled variance if the equality assumption is not warranted.

which is less than the critical value $t = 2.306$ found in the table for $\alpha = 0.05$ and $v = n_1 + n_2 - 2 = 8$ degrees of freedom. The null hypothesis of there being no difference in sales of the two types of colors cannot be rejected on the basis of the sample data.

But wait a minute! A closer look at the data indicates a marked inconsistency with this conclusion. The bright-colored sleeping bags outsold the earth-colored ones in each store, and indeed an analysis of the per-store differences (the procedure is detailed further on) indicates that there is a statistically significant difference in the sales of the two bags. The reason for the seeming difference in conclusions—the

Table 18.6   Per-store Sales of Sleeping Bags

Store	Bright Colors	Earth Colors
1	64	56
2	72	66
3	43	39
4	22	20
5	50	45

difference is not significant versus it is significant—arises because the t test for the difference in two means is *not appropriate* for the problem. The difference in means test assumes that the samples are independent. These samples are not. Sales of bright-colored and earth-colored bags are definitely related, since they are both found in the same stores. Note how this example differs from the floor wax example, in which the metal containers were placed in one sample of stores and the plastic containers were located in an independent sample of stores. We need a procedure that takes into account the fact that the observations are related.

The appropriate procedure is the t test for related samples. The procedure is as follows. Define a new variable d_i, where d_i is the difference between sales of the bright-colored bags and the earth-colored bags for the ith store. Thus

$$d_1 = 64 - 56 = 8$$
$$d_2 = 72 - 66 = 6$$
$$d_3 = 43 - 39 = 4$$
$$d_4 = 22 - 20 = 2$$
$$d_5 = 50 - 45 = 5$$

Now calculate the mean difference by averaging the individual store-to-store differences

$$\bar{d} = \frac{\sum_{i=1}^{n} d_i}{n} = \frac{8 + 6 + 4 + 2 + 5}{5} = 5.0$$

and the standard error of the difference by determining the sum of the deviations around the mean squared, specifically

$$s_d = \sqrt{\frac{\sum_{i=1}^{n}(d_i - \bar{d})^2}{n - 1}} = \sqrt{\frac{20}{4}} = 2.24$$

The test statistic is the sample mean difference minus the hypothesized population mean difference, divided by the standard error of the difference, divided by the square root of the sample size, or symbolically,

$$t = \frac{\bar{d} - D}{s_d/\sqrt{n}}$$

where D is the difference that is expected under the null hypothesis. Since there is no *a priori* reason why one color would be expected to sell better than the other, the appropriate null hypothesis is that there is no difference, while the alternate hypothesis is that there is; thus,

$$H_0: D = 0$$
$$H_a: D \neq 0$$

Calculated t is therefore

$$t = \frac{5.0 - 0}{2.24/\sqrt{5}} = 5.0$$

This value is referred to a t table for $\nu =$ (number of differences minus 1) degrees of freedom; in this case, there are five paired differences, and thus $\nu = 4$. Critical t for $\nu = 4$ and $\alpha = 0.05$ is 2.776, and thus the hypothesis of no difference is rejected. The sample evidence indicates that the bright-colored sleeping bags are likely to outsell the earth-colored ones.

An estimate of how greatly the sales per store of the bright-colored sleeping bags would exceed those of the earth-colored bags can be calculated from the confidence interval formula, sample mean difference $\pm t$ (standard error of the mean difference), or

$$\bar{d} \pm t(s_d/\sqrt{n}).$$

Research Window 18.1

Caveat Emptor . . . or, Beware the Butchers!

Calvin Hoddock told this story about the possible pitfalls of marketing research:

"There are two types of research professionals playing with exotic techniques—the butchers and the surgeons (sometimes referred to as the technicians and the magicians). There are a lot more butchers around than surgeons.

"A butcher is statistically oriented—mesmerized with his exotic techniques but divorced from marketing reality. The surgeon is a sound statistician who is marketing-oriented. Surgeons are very hard to find in this business.

"Let me show you what a butcher can do to a research study. A large segmentation study was conducted in a health-oriented category. After substantial number crunching, there was an agonized meeting among the client, the advertising agency, and the supplier. Despite tons of numbers, the study did not discriminate. There were very few useful data in the study, a valid but unpalatable finding, after spending $75,000.

"It was decided to reanalyze the study with another supplier. Fortunately, the new supplier was a surgeon and discovered something that the butcher had overlooked. The homemaker purchased the product and tried to get other family members to use it. She was particularly unsuccessful in getting her husband to use the product. He resisted it for a number of 'macho reasons.'

"Because the butcher did not understand this basic marketing dynamic, he merged the data of males and females together. The net result was to average everything out, leading to a lack of discrimination.

"Beware of the butchers in the business. We have too many of them. They have a high propensity to produce bad numbers. On the surface, however, their techniques are presumably statistically pristine and powerful."

Source: "Hoddock Cites 'Pitfalls' of Marketing Research," *Marketing News,* 12 (June 1, 1979), p. 1.

The 95 percent confidence interval is

$$5.0 \pm (2.776)(2.24/\sqrt{5}) = 5.0 \pm 2.8$$

suggesting that sales of the bright-colored bags would be in the range of 2.2 to 7.8 bags greater per store on average.

Hypotheses about Two Proportions

The appendix to Chapter 17 reviewed the essential nature of hypothesis testing, employing as an example the testing of an hypothesis about a single population proportion. In this section, we want to illustrate the procedure for testing for the difference between two population proportions.[8]

The test for the difference between two population proportions is basically a large sample problem. The samples from each population must be large enough so that the normal approximation to the exact binomial distribution of sample proportions can be used. As a practical matter, this means that np and nq should be greater than 10 for each sample, where p is the proportion of "successes" and q is the proportion of "failures" in the sample and n is the sample size.

To illustrate, suppose a cosmetics manufacturer is interested in comparing male college students and male nonstudents in terms of their use of hair spray. Suppose random samples of 100 students and 100 nonstudents in Austin, Texas, are selected and their use of hair spray in the last three months is determined. Suppose further that 30 students and 20 nonstudents had used hair spray within this period. Does this evidence indicate that a significantly higher percentage of college students than nonstudents use hair spray?

Since we are interested in determining whether the two parent-population proportions are different, the null hypothesis is that they are the same, that is,

$$H_0: \pi_1 = \pi_2$$
$$H_a: \pi_1 \neq \pi_2$$

where Population 1 is the population of college students, and Population 2 is the population of nonstudents. The sample proportions are $p_1 = 0.30$ and $p_2 = 0.20$ and therefore $n_1 p_1 = 30$, $n_1 q_1 = 70$, $n_2 p_2 = 20$, $n_2 q_2 = 80$, and the normal approximation to the binomial distribution can be used. The test statistic is z = first sample proportion minus second sample proportion minus hypothesized proportion for the first population minus hypothesized proportion for the second population divided by the standard error of the difference in the two sample proportions; or

$$z = \frac{(p_1 - p_2) - (\pi_1 - \pi_2)}{\sigma_{p_1 - p_2}}$$

---

[8]The tests for population proportions are logically considered with nominal data because they apply in situations where the variable being studied can be divided into those cases *possessing* the characteristic and those cases *lacking* it, and the emphasis is on the number or proportion of cases falling into each category. Marketing examples abound: "prefer A" versus "do not prefer A," "buy" versus "do not buy," "brand loyal" versus "not brand loyal," "sales representatives meeting quota" versus "sales representatives not meeting quota." The test for the significance of the difference between two proportions is treated here because the hypothesis is examined using the z test, and the procedure relies on an "automatic pooled sample variance" estimate. It was thought that these notions would be better appreciated after the discussion of the test of means rather than before.

where $\sigma_{p_1-p_2}$ is the standard error of the difference in the two sample proportions. The one question that still remains in the calculation of z is what does $\sigma_{p_1-p_2}$ equal?

A general statistical result that is useful for understanding the calculation of $\sigma_{p_1-p_2}$ is that *the variance of the sum or difference of two independent random variables is equal to the sum of the individual variances.* For a single proportion, the variance is $\pi(1 - \pi)/n$, and thus the variance of the difference is

$$\sigma^2_{p_1-p_2} = \sigma^2_{p_1} + \sigma^2_{p_2} = \frac{\pi_1(1 - \pi_1)}{n_1} + \frac{\pi_2(1 - \pi_2)}{n_2}$$

Note that the variance of the difference is given in terms of the two unknown population proportions, π_1 and π_2. Although unknown, the two population proportions have been assumed equal, and thus we have a "natural" case of a *pooled variance estimate*; $s^2_{p_1-p_2}$ is logically used to estimate $\sigma^2_{p_1-p_2}$, where

$$s^2_{p_1-p_2} = pq\left(\frac{1}{n_1} + \frac{1}{n_2}\right)$$

and

$$p = \frac{\text{total number of successes in the two samples}}{\text{total number of observations in the two samples}}$$
$$q = 1 - p.$$

For the example,

$$p = \frac{30 + 20}{100 + 100} = \frac{50}{200} = 0.25,$$

$$s^2_{p_1-p_2} = (0.25)(0.75)\left(\frac{1}{100} + \frac{1}{100}\right) = 0.00375,$$

and

$$s_{p_1-p_2} = 0.061.$$

Calculated z is found as follows:

$$z = \frac{(0.30 - 0.20) - (0)}{0.061} = \frac{0.10}{0.061} = 1.64,$$

while critical $z = 1.96$ for $\alpha = 0.05$. The sample evidence does not indicate that there is a difference in the proportion of college students and nonstudents using hair spray.

The 95 percent confidence interval is calculated by the formula, (first sample proportion − second sample proportion) ± z (estimated standard error of the difference in the two proportions), or $(p_1 - p_2) \pm zs_{p_1-p_2}$, which is $(.30 - .20) \pm 1.96(0.061) = .10 \pm .12$, and which yields a similar conclusion. The interval includes zero, suggesting there is no difference in the proportions using hair spray in the two groups.

◆ Summary

Learning Objective 1: Explain the basic use of a chi-square goodness-of-fit test.

The chi-square goodness-of-fit test is appropriate when a nominally scaled variable falls naturally into two or more categories and the analyst wishes to determine whether the observed number of cases in each cell corresponds to the expected number.

Learning Objective 2: Discuss the similarities and differences between the chi-square good-ness-of-fit test and the Kolmogorov-Smirnov test.

The Kolmogorov-Smirnov test is similar to the chi-square goodness-of-fit test in that it uses a comparison between observed and expected frequencies to determine whether observed results are in accord with a stated null hypothesis. But the Kolmogorov-Smirnov test takes advantage of the ordinal nature of the data.

Learning Objective 3: Specify which test would be appropriate if one were testing an hypothesis about a single mean, given that the variance is known. Which would be appropriate if the variance were unknown?

In testing an hypothesis about a single mean, the z test is appropriate if the variance is known, while the t test applies if the variance is unknown.

Learning Objective 4: Identify the tests that would be appropriate if the analysis involves two means from independent samples.

In an analysis that involves two means from independent samples, the z test is used if the variances are known. If the variances are unknown but assumed equal, a t test using a pooled sample variance applies.

Learning Objective 5: Specify the appropriate test if the analysis involves the difference between two parent-population proportions.

The test of the equality of proportions from two independent samples involves a "natural" pooling of the sample variances. The z test applies.

Discussion Questions, Problems, and Projects

1. A large publishing house recently conducted a survey to assess the reading habits of senior citizens. The company published four magazines specifically tailored to suit the needs of senior citizens. Management hypothesized that there were no differences in the preferences for the magazines. A sample of 1,600 senior citizens interviewed in the city of Albuquerque, New Mexico, indicated the following preferences for the four magazines.

Publication	Frequency of Preference
1. Golden Years	350
2. Maturation	500
3. High Serenity	450
4. Time for Living	300
Total	1,600

Management needs your expertise to determine whether there are differences in senior citizens' preferences for the magazines.

(a) State the null and alternate hypotheses.
(b) How many degrees of freedom are there?
(c) What is the chi-square critical table value at the 5 percent significance level?
(d) What is the calculated χ^2 value? Show all your calculations.
(e) Should the null hypothesis be rejected or not? Explain.

2. Silken-Shine Company is a medium-sized manufacturer of shampoo. During the past years the company has increased the number of product variations of Silken-Shine shampoo that are available from three to five to increase its market share. Management conducted a survey to compare sales of Silken-Shine shampoo with sales of Rapunzel and So-Soft, their two major competitors. A sample of 1,800 housewives indicated the following frequencies with respect to most recent shampoo purchased.

Shampoo	Number Buying
1. Silken-Shine	425
2. Rapunzel	1,175
3. So-Soft	200
Total	1,800

Past experience had indicated that three times as many households preferred Rapunzel to Silken-Shine and that in turn twice as many households preferred Silken-Shine to So-Soft. Management wants to determine if the historic tendency still holds, given Silken-Shine Company has increased the range of shampoos available.

(a) State the null and alternate hypotheses.
(b) How many degrees of freedom are there?
(c) What is the chi-square critical table value at the 5 percent significance level?
(d) What is the calculated χ^2 value? Show all your calculations.
(e) Should the null hypothesis be rejected or not? Explain.

3. A manufacturer of music cassettes wants to test four different cassettes varying in tape length: 30 minutes, 60 minutes, 90 minutes, and 120 minutes. The company has hired you to determine whether customers show any distinct preference toward either extreme. If there is a preference toward any extreme, the company would manufacture only cassettes of the preferred length; otherwise, the company is planning to market cassettes of all four lengths. A sample of 1,000 customers indicated the following preferences.

Tape Length	Frequency of Preference
30 minutes	150
60 minutes	250
90 minutes	425
120 minutes	175
Total	1,000

(a) State the null and alternate hypotheses.
(b) Compute Kolmogorov-Smirnov D by completing the following table.

Tape Length	Observed Number	Observed Proportion	Observed Cumulative Proportion	Theoretical Proportion	Theoretical Cumulative Proportion
30 min.					
60 min.					
90 min.					
120 min.					

(c) Compute the critical value of D at $\alpha = 0.05$. Show your calculations.
(d) Would you reject the null hypothesis? Explain.
(e) What are the implications for management?
(f) Explain why the Kolmogorov-Smirnov test would be used in this situation.

4. Liberty Foods markets vegetables in six different sized cans: A, B, C, D, E, and F. Through the years the company has observed that sales of all its vegetables in the six can sizes are in the proportion 6:4:2:1.5:1.5:1, respectively. In other words, for every one case of F that is sold, six cases of size A, four of size B, 2 of size C, 1.5 of size D, and 1.5 of size E are also sold.

The marketing manager would like the sales data for a new canned vegetable—pureed carrots—compared with the pattern for the rest of Liberty's product line to see if there is any difference. Based on a representative sample of 600 cases of pureed carrots, he observes that 30 percent were Size A, 20 percent B, 10 percent C, 10 percent D, 15 percent E, and 15 percent F.

(a) The marketing manager has asked you to determine whether the pureed carrots' sales pattern is similar to the pattern for other vegetables by using the chi-square goodness-of-fit test. Show all your calculations clearly.

(b) You are now asked to determine the above with the use of the Kolmogorov-Smirnov test. Show all your calculations clearly.

(c) What can you conclude from the use of the two test statistics? Are your results from the two tests conflicting or similar?

(d) Which test statistic would you prefer? Why?

5. A medium-sized manufacturer of paper products was planning to introduce a new line of tissues, hand towels, and toilet paper. However, management had stipulated that the new products should be introduced only if average monthly purchases per household were $2.50 or more. The product was market tested, and the diaries of the 100 panel households living in the test-market area were checked. They indicated that average monthly purchases were $3.10 per household with a standard deviation of $0.50. Management is wondering what decision it should make and has asked for your recommendation.

(a) State the null and alternate hypotheses.

(b) Is the sample size considered large or small?

(c) Which test should be used? Why?

(d) At the 5 percent level of significance, would you reject the null hypothesis? Support your answer with the necessary calculations.

6. The president of a chain of department stores had promised the managers of the various stores a bonus of 8 percent if the average monthly sales per store increased $300,000 or more. A random sample of twelve stores yielded the following sales increases:

Store	Sales	Store	Sales
1	$320,000	7	$380,000
2	$230,000	8	$280,000
3	$400,000	9	$420,000
4	$450,000	10	$360,000
5	$280,000	11	$440,000
6	$320,000	12	$320,000

The president is wondering whether this random sample of stores indicates that the population of stores has reached the goal. (Assume the distribution of the variable in the parent population is normal.)

(a) State the null and alternate hypotheses.

(b) Is the sample size considered small or large?

(c) Which test should be used? Why?

(d) Would you reject the null hypotheses at the 5 percent level of significance? Support your conclusion with the necessary calculations.

7. Joy Forever is the owner of two jewelry stores located in Corpus Christi and San Antonio. During the past year the San Antonio store had spent a considerable amount on in-store displays as compared to the Corpus Christi store. Joy Forever wants to determine if the in-store displays resulted in increased sales. The average sales for a sample of 100 days for the San Antonio and Corpus Christi stores were $21.8 million and $15.3 million. (Past experience has shown that $\sigma_{SA} = 8$ and $\sigma_{CC} = 9$ where σ_{SA} is the standard deviation in sales for the San Antonio store and σ_{CC} is the standard deviation for the Corpus Christi store.)

(a) State the null and alternate hypotheses.
(b) What test would you use? Why?
(c) What is the calculated value of the test statistic? Show your calculations.
(d) What is the critical tabled value at 5 percent significance level?
(e) Would you reject the null hypothesis? Explain.
(f) What can Joy Forever conclude?

8. Come-and-Go Company, a large travel agency located in Portland, Oregon, wanted to study consumer preferences for its package tours to the East. For the past five years Come-and-Go had offered two similarly priced packaged tours to the East that only differed in the places included in the tour. A random sample of five months' purchases from the past five years was selected. The number of consumers that purchased the tours during these five months is listed below.

Month	Packaged Tour I	Packaged Tour II
1	90	100
2	70	60
3	120	80
4	110	90
5	60	80

The management of Come-and-Go needs your assistance to determine whether there is a difference in preferences for the two tours.
(a) State the null and alternate hypotheses.
(b) What test would you use? Why?
(c) What is the calculated value of the test statistic? Show your calculations.
(d) What is the critical tabled value at the 5 percent significance level?
(e) Would you reject the null hypothesis? Explain
(f) What can the management of Come-and-Go Company conclude about preferences for the two tours?

9. The manager of the Budget Department Store recently increased the store's use of in-store promotions in an attempt to increase the proportion of entering customers who made a purchase. The effort was prompted by a study made a year ago that showed 65 percent of a sample of 1,000 parties entering the store made no purchase. A recent sample of 900 parties contained 635 who made no purchases. Management is wondering whether there has been a change in the proportion of entering parties who make a purchase.
(a) State the null and alternate hypotheses.
(b) What is the calculated value? Show your calculations clearly.
(c) Based on your results, would you reject the null hypothesis? Explain.

Suggested Additional Readings

Most of the statistical tests discussed in this chapter can be found in any introductory statistics texts, and readers are encouraged to refer to the text they used in their introductory statistics course for more details on any of the methods that are discussed.

Appendix 18A   Analysis of Variance

In Chapter 18 we used the example of packaging floor wax in plastic and metal containers to examine that statistical test of the difference in two population means. Let us now reconsider the data of Table 18.4 to demonstrate an alternate approach to the problem. Known as the

• Analysis of variance
(ANOVA)

Statistical test employed
with interval data to
determine if $k(k \geq 2)$
samples came from
populations with equal
means.

analysis of variance (ANOVA), it has the distinct advantage of being applicable when there
are more than two means being compared. The basic idea underlying the analysis of variance
is that the parent-population variance can be estimated from the sample in several ways, and
comparisons among these estimates can tell us a great deal about the population. Recall that
the null hypothesis involving the two types of containers was that the two parent-population
means were equal; that is, $\mu_1 = \mu_2$. If the null hypothesis is true, then, except for sampling
error, the following three estimates of the population variance should be equal:

1. The *total variation,* computed by comparing each of the twenty sales figures with the
   grand mean.
2. The *between-group variation,* computed by comparing each of the two treatment means
   with the grand mean.
3. The *within-group variation,* computed by comparing each of the individual sales figures
   with the mean of its own group.

If, however, the hypothesis is not true, and there is a difference in the means, then the
between-group variation should produce a higher estimate than the within-group variation,
which considers only the variation within groups and is independent of differences between
groups.

These three separate estimates of the population variation are computed in the following
way when there are k treatments or groups.

1. Total variation: sum of squares total SS_T, given by the sum of the squared deviations of
   each observation from the grand mean. Now the grand mean of all n observations turns
   out to be equal to

$$\frac{432 + \cdots + 408 + 365 + \cdots + 400}{20} = 396.7$$

and the sum of squares total equals

$$SS_T = (432 - 396.7)^2 + \cdots + (408 - 396.7)^2$$
$$+ (365 - 396.7)^2 + \cdots + (400 - 396.7)^2$$

The difference between *each observation* and the *grand mean* is determined; the differences are squared and then summed.

2. Between-group variation: sum of squares between groups SS_B. To calculate between-group
   variation, it is first necessary to calculate the means for each group. The mean sales of the
   plastic container turn out to be equal to 403.0, and those for the metal container to be
   equal to 396.7. The sum of squares between groups is thus

$$SS_B = 10(403.0 - 396.7)^2 + 10(390.3 - 396.7)^2$$

The difference between each *group mean* and the *overall mean* is determined; the difference is squared; each squared difference is weighted by the number of observations making up the group, and the results are summed.

3. Within-group variation: sum of squares within groups SS_W. The calculation of the sum of
   squares within groups involves calculating the difference between each observation and
   the mean of the group to which it belongs, specifically,

$$SS_W = (432 - 403.0)^2 + \cdots + (408 - 403.0)^2$$
$$+ (365 - 390.3)^2 + \cdots + (400 - 390.3)^2$$

The difference between *each observation* and its *group mean* is determined; the differences are squared and then summed.

Let us take a closer look at the behavior of these three sources of variation. First, SS_T
measures the overall variation of the n observations. The more variable the n observations,

the larger SS_T becomes. Second, SS_B reflects the total variability of the means. The more nearly alike the k means are, the smaller SS_B becomes. If they differ greatly, SS_B will be large. Third, SS_W measures the amount of variation within each column or treatment. If there is little variation among the observations making up a group, SS_W is small. When there is great variability, SS_W is large.

It can be shown that $SS_T = SS_B + SS_W$ and that each of these sums of squares, when divided by the *appropriate number of degrees of freedom*, generates a mean square that is essentially an unbiased estimate of the population variance.[1] Further, if the null hypothesis of no difference among population means is true, they are all estimates of the same variance and should not differ more than would be expected because of chance. If the variance between groups is significantly greater than the variance within groups, the hypothesis of equality of population means will be rejected.

In other words, we can view the variance within groups as a measure of the amount of variation in sales of containers that may be expected on the basis of chance. It is the *error variance* or *chance variance*. The between-group variance reflects error variance plus any group-to-group differences occasioned by differences in popularity of the two containers. Therefore, if it is found to be significantly larger than the within-group variance, this difference may be attributed to group-to-group variation, and the hypothesis of equality of means is discredited.

But what are these degrees of freedom? The total number of degrees of freedom is equal to $n - 1$, since there is only a single constraint, the grand mean, in the computation of SS_T. For the within-group sum of squares, there are n observations and k constraints, one constraint for each treatment mean. Hence, the degrees of freedom for the within group sum of squares equals $n - k$. There are k values, one corresponding to each treatment mean, in the calculation of SS_B, and there is one constraint imposed by the grand mean; hence, the degrees of freedom for the between-group sum of squares is $k - 1$.

The separate estimates of the population variance or the associated mean squares are

$$MS_T = \frac{SS_T}{df_T} = \frac{SS_T}{n - 1}$$

$$MS_B = \frac{SS_B}{df_B} = \frac{SS_B}{k - 1}$$

$$MS_W = \frac{SS_W}{df_W} = \frac{SS_W}{n - k}$$

The mean squares computed from the sample data are merely estimates of the true mean squares. The true mean squares are in turn given by the expected values of the corresponding sample mean squares. Given that the samples are independent, that the population variances are equal, and that the variable is normally distributed in the parent population, it can be shown that these expected values are

$$E(MS_W) = \sigma^2 = \text{error variance or chance variance}$$

and

$$E(MS_B) = \sigma^2 + \text{treatment effect.}$$

The ratio $E(MS_B)/E(MS_W)$ will equal 1 if there is no treatment effect. It will be greater than 1 if there is a difference in the sample means. Since the two expected values are not known, the sample mean squares are used instead to yield the ratio

$$\frac{MS_B}{MS_W} = F$$

---

[1] See Geoffrey Keppel, *Design and Analysis: A Researcher's Handbook,* 2nd ed. (Englewood Cliffs, N.J.: Prentice-Hall, 1982), pp. 24–64, for the derivation.

Table 18A.1   Analysis of Variance of Sales of Plastic versus Metal Containers

Source of Variation	Sum of Squares	Degrees of Freedom	Mean Square	F Ratio
Between group	806.5	1	806.5	2.43
Within group	5,978.1	18	332.1	
Total	6,784.6	19		

which follows the F distribution. The F distribution depends on two degrees of freedom, one corresponding to the mean square in the numerator and one corresponding to the mean square in the denominator. Since MS_B and MS_W are only sample estimates of the true variances, one should not expect the ratio MS_B/MS_W to be exactly 1 when the treatment effect is zero, nor should one immediately conclude that there is a difference among the group means when the ratio is greater than 1. Rather, given a significance level and the respective degrees of freedom for the numerator and denominator, a critical value of F may be read from standard tables. The critical value indicates the magnitude of the ratio that can occur because of random sampling fluctuations, even when there is no difference in the group means, that is, $E(MS_B)/E(MS_W) = 1$. The entire analysis is conveniently handled in an analysis of variance table.

Table 18A.1 is the analysis of variance table for the plastic and metal container sales data. The calculated F value is referred to an F table for 1 and 18 degrees of freedom (see Table 4 in the appendix at the back of this textbook). Using the same α as before, $\alpha = 0.05$, critical F is found to be 4.41, and again the sample evidence is not sufficient to reject the hypothesis of the equality of the two means. This should not be surprising since it can be shown that when the comparison is between two means (the degrees of freedom in the numerator of the F ratio are then $\nu_1 = k - 1 = 1$), $F = t^2 = (1.56)^2 = 2.43$.[2] Both tests are identical in this special case, and if one test does not indicate a significant difference between the two means, neither will the other.[3]

Randomized-Block Design

• Randomized-block design

Experimental design in which: (1) the test units are divided into blocks or homogeneous groups using some external criterion, and (2) the objects in each block are randomly assigned to treatment conditions. The randomized-block design is typically employed when there is one extraneous influence to be explicitly controlled.

Imagine what might have happened if, by chance, the stores selected to handle the plastic containers were all substantially larger than those handling the metal containers. Any difference in sales between the two groups could have been because the larger stores routinely have more traffic and hence greater sales.

If a closer analysis of the situation shows that such outside influences may distort the results of an experiment, a **randomized-block design** can be employed. This design involves the grouping of "similar" test units into blocks and the random assignment of treatments to test units in each block. Similarity is determined by matching the test units on the expected extraneous source of variation, for example, store size in the container example. The hope is that the units within each block will be more alike then will units selected completely at random. Since the differences between blocks can be taken into account in the variance analysis, for the same number of observations the error mean square should be smaller than it would be if a completely randomized design had been used. The test should therefore be more efficient.

---

[2]It can be shown mathematically that if a random variable is t distributed with ν degrees of freedom, then t^2 is F distributed with $\nu_1 = 1$, $\nu_2 = \nu$ degrees of freedom; that is, if $t \sim t_\nu$, then $t^2 \sim F_{1,\nu}$.

[3]For an insightful discussion of how one should set up hypotheses for analysis of variance, see Richard K. Burdick, "Statement of Hypothesis in the Analysis of Variance," *Journal of Marketing Research,* 20 (August 1983), pp. 320–324.

Latin-Square Design

• Latin-square design

Experimental design in which (1) the number of categories for each extraneous variable we wish to control is equal to the number of treatments, and (2) each treatment is randomly assigned to categories according to a specific pattern. The Latin-square design is appropriate where there are two extraneous factors to be explicitly controlled.

The **Latin-square design** is appropriate when there are two extraneous factors that can cause serious distortion in the results. Suppose a company wanted to test the effectiveness of three different plans for frequency of sales calls by their sales representatives on potential customers. The plans varied with regard to how often the sales rep would be required to call on various-sized accounts. The manufacturer wanted to know which of the three would produce the most sales.

In order to test the plan, the firm chose a sample of thirty salespeople from among its sales staff of five hundred. The company was concerned that differences in sales ability might affect the results of the test. Consequently, it decided to match the sales representatives in terms of their ability, employing their past sales as the matching criterion. The company thus formed ten blocks of three relatively equal sales representatives each. The call-frequency plans were then assigned randomly to each of the sales representatives within a block, resulting in a randomized-block design.

Now suppose further that the firm decided to conduct the investigation not only with sales reps of different ability but also among sales representatives having different sized territories. Suppose, in fact, we had divided the sales representatives into three classes on the basis of ability—outstanding, good, and average—and the territories into the three classes—large, average, and small. There are thus nine different conditions with which to cope. One way of proceeding would be to use randomized blocks and test each of the three call plans under each of the nine conditions. This would require a sample of twenty-seven sales representatives. An alternative approach would be to try each call plan only once with each size territory and each level of ability. This would require a sample of only nine test units or sales representatives. The primary gain in this case would be administrative control. In other cases, there may be cost advantages associated with the use of fewer test units. The interesting point is that if differences in territory size do indeed have an effect, the Latin-square design with nine test units could be as efficient as the randomized-block design with many more test units.

The Latin-square design requires that the number of categories for each of the extraneous variables we wish to control be equal to the number of treatments. With three call plans to investigate, it was no accident that we divided the sales representatives into three ability levels and the territories into three size categories. The Latin-square design also requires that the treatments be randomly assigned to the resulting categories. This is typically accomplished by selecting one of the published squares at random and then randomizing the rows, columns, and treatments using this square.[4]

Factorial Designs

• Factorial design

Experimental design that is used when the effects of two or more variables are being simultaneously studied; each level of each factor is used with each level of each other factor.

So far we have considered designs that involve only one experimental variable, although it may have had multiple levels, for example, three different call plans. It is often desirable to investigate the effects of two or more factors in the same experiment. For instance, it might be desirable to investigate the sales impact of the shape as well as the construction material of containers for floor wax. Suppose that in addition to packaging a new floor wax in metal or plastic containers, two shapes, A and B, were being considered for the containers. Package shape and package type would both be called *factors*. There would be two different levels of each factor, four different treatments in all since they can be used in combination, and a **factorial design** would be used. A factorial design is one in which the effects of two or more independent treatment variables are considered simultaneously.

There are three very good reasons why one might want to use a factorial design.[5] First, it allows the interaction of the factors to be studied. The plastic container might sell better in Shape A, while the metal container sells better in Shape B. This type of effect can be investi-

---

[4]See R. A. Fisher and F. Yates, *Statistical Tables* (Edinburgh: Oliver and Boyd, 1948) for Latin squares from 4 × 4 to 12 × 12.

[5]The following argument is basically that of William C. Guenther, *Analysis of Variance* (Englewood Cliffs, N.J.: Prentice-Hall, 1964), pp. 99–100.

gated only if the factors are considered simultaneously. Second, a factorial design allows a saving of time and effort since all the observations are employed to study the effects of each of the factors. Suppose separate experiments were conducted, one to study the effect of container type and another to study the effect of container shape. Then some of the observations would yield information about type and some about shape. By combining the two factors in one experiment, all the observations bear on both factors. "Hence one two-factor experiment is more economical than two one-factor experiments."[6] Third, the conclusions reached have broader application since each factor is studied with varying combinations of the other factors.[7] This result is much more useful than it would be if everything else had been held constant.

The factorial design may be used with any of the single-factor designs previously discussed — completely randomized, randomized block, and Latin square. The underlying model changes, as does the analysis of variance table, but the principle remains the same.

----

[6]Guenther, *Analysis of Variance,* p. 100. For an example of the insight that can be gained from a factorial experiment, see J. B. Wilkinson, J. Barry Mason, and Christie H. Paksoy, "Assessing the Impact of Short-Term Supermarket Strategy Variables," *Journal of Marketing Research,* 19 (February 1982), pp. 72–86.

[7]One can often use select combinations of factor levels rather than every possible combination, which greatly simplifies the experiment. See Charles W. Holland and David W. Cravens, "Fractional Factorial Experimental Designs in Marketing Research," *Journal of Marketing Research,* 10 (August 1973), pp. 270–276.

Chapter 19

Data Analysis: Investigating Associations

Learning Objectives

Upon completing this chapter, you should be able to

1. Explain the difference between regression and correlation analysis.

2. List the three assumptions that are made about the error term in the least-squares solution to a regression problem.

3. Discuss what the Gauss-Markov theorem says about the least-squares estimators of a population parameter.

4. Define what is meant by the standard error of estimate.

5. Specify the relationship that a correlation coefficient is designed to measure.

6. Discuss the difference between simple regression analysis and multiple-regression analysis.

7. Explain what is meant by multicollinearity in a multiple-regression problem.

8. Describe when a partial-regression coefficient is used and what it measures.

9. Explain the difference between the coefficient of multiple determination and the coefficient of partial determination.

10. Describe how the use of dummy variables and variable transformations expands the scope of the regression model.

Case in Marketing Research

Two salesmen from a prominent running-shoe manufacturer had just launched into a fervent description of their newest model when the phone rang in Mike Mihalic's office at Avery Sporting Goods.

"Mike, it's Pat Hayes from Samson Marketing Services," Cindy Allen, Mike's secretary, called in from the outer office.

"Can you guys wait just a minute?" Mike asked the two salesmen.

"Pat," he said, picking up the phone, "what have you got for me?"

"Mike, remember when we planned the catalog study, you said you wanted to know more about the demographics of your customers? Well, I've just completed a rather thorough analysis of the data we collected, and I think I've come up with some interesting findings. They're a little complex to go into on the phone. When might we get together to discuss them?" Pat asked.

"Well, I'm tied up right now, but I'm eager to see what you've come up with since we're about to begin planning our big spring mailing," Mike said. "How about first thing tomorrow morning?"

"I'll be there," Pat said.

"Now, gentlemen," Mike said turning back to the salesmen, "what were you saying about the new ankle-support feature on your shoes?"

Discussion Issues

1. If you were Mike Mihalic, what information might you still want from the catalog buying study?

2. How might that information be correlated with the data Pat Hayes has already uncovered?

3. How might you use such data in developing subsequent mailings?

In the discussion of data analysis so far, we have been primarily concerned with testing for the significance of *differences* obtained under various research conditions, whether between a sample result and an assumed population condition, or between two or more sample results. Quite often, however, the researcher must determine whether there is any *association* between two or more variables and, if so, the strength and functional form of the relationship.

Typically, we try to predict the value of one variable (for example, consumption of a specific product by a family) on the basis of one or more other variables (for example, income and number of family members). The variable being predicted is called the *dependent* or, more aptly, the *criterion variable.* The variables that form the basis of the prediction are called the *independent,* or *predictor, variables.*

◆ Simple Regression and Correlation Analysis

◆ Regression analysis

Statistical technique used to derive an equation that relates a single criterion variable to one or more predictor variables; when there is one predictor variable, it is simple regression analysis while it is multiple-regression analysis when there are two or more predictor variables.

◆ Correlation analysis

Statistical technique used to measure the closeness of the linear relationship between two or more intervally scaled variables.

Regression analysis and **correlation analysis** are widely used among marketing researchers for studying the relationship between two or more variables. Although the two terms are often used interchangeably, there is a difference in purpose. Correlation analysis measures the *closeness* of the relationship between two or more variables. The technique considers the joint variation of two measures, neither of which is restricted by the experimenter. Regression analysis, on the other hand, is used to derive an *equation* that relates the criterion variable to one or more predictor variables. It considers the frequency distribution of the criterion variable when one or more predictor variables are held fixed at various levels.[1]

It is perfectly legitimate to measure the closeness of the relationship between variables without deriving an estimating equation. Similarly, one can perform a regression analysis without investigating the closeness of the relationship between the variables. But, since it is common to do both, the body of techniques, rather than one or the other, is usually referred to as either regression or correlation analysis.

To save you endless frustration in trying to determine how the term *regression analysis* fits with the technique about to be discussed, we should pause to mention that, like many terms in our language, the name bears no useful relationship to the technique, although we will not delve into its semantic history here.[2]

As regards correlation analysis, we should also comment on the distinction between correlation and causation. The use of the terms *dependent* (criterion) and *independent* (predictor) *variables* to describe the measures in correlation analysis stems from the mathematical functional relationship between the variates and is in no way related to dependence of one variable on another in a causal sense. For example, while the techniques may show some correlation between high income and a tendency to take winter vacations to the Caribbean, it would be a mistake to assume that having a high income *causes* a person to head south when the thermometer plummets.

There is nothing in correlation analysis, or any other mathematical procedure, that can be used to establish causality. All these procedures can do is measure the nature and degree of *association* or *covariation* between variables. Statements of

---

[1]Although the regression model theoretically applies to fixed levels of the predictor variables (Xs), it can also be shown to apply when the Xs themselves are random variables, assuming certain conditions are satisfied. See John Neter, William Wasserman, and Michael H. Kutner, *Applied Linear Regression Models* (Homewood, Ill.: Richard D. Irwin, 1983), pp. 83–84; or Thomas H. Wonnacott and Ronald J. Wonnacott, *Regression: A Second Course in Statistics* (New York: John Wiley, 1981), pp. 49–50.

[2]Donald R. Lehmann, *Market Research and Analysis,* 2nd ed. (Homewood, Ill.: Richard D. Irwin, 1985), p. 482.

causality must spring from underlying knowledge and theories about the phenomena under investigation. They in no way spring from the mathematics.[3] In Research Window 19.1, the former director of marketing research at General Mills urges researchers to look beyond the welter of data they devote their energies to collecting

---

[3]See Darrell Huff, *How to Lie with Statistics* (New York: Norton, 1954), pp. 87–99, for a discussion of this point using some rather humorous anecdotes.

Research Window 19.1
The Importance of Theory in Marketing Research

If marketing researchers want to acquire true marketing "knowledge" they should devote more time and effort to developing and validating marketing theories, according to Lawrence D. Gibson, former director of marketing research, General Mills Inc., Minneapolis.

"There's a funny notion around that theories are vague, ephemeral, and useless, and data are nice, hard, real things. And that somehow knowledge is associated with facts and data. This is nonsense. Knowledge is an interrelated set of validated theories and established facts, not just facts. In marketing, we are profoundly ignorant of what we're doing because we're woefully short on theory while we're drowning in data."

Deploring the lack of validated marketing theories and the overabundance of marketing "facts," Gibson quoted the scientist, R. B. Braithwaite: "The world is not made up of empirical facts with the addition of the laws of nature. What we call the laws of nature are simply theories, the conceptual devices by which we organize our empirical knowledge and predict the future."

And he quoted Albert Einstein: "The grand aim of all science is to cover the maximum number of empirical facts, by logical deduction, into the smallest number of axioms, axioms which represent that remainder which is not comprehended."

In other words, Gibson said, "the axioms and theories are not our knowledge, they are our ignorance. They're part of the problem we assume away." A theory, he said, is how "scientists choose to organize their knowledge and perceptions of the world. Theories are pretty well laid out, simplistic, general, have predicted usefulness, and fit the facts.

"Theory is basic to what data you choose to collect," he said. "You can't observe all the veins of all the leaves of all the branches of all the trees of all the forests in the world. You've got to choose what facts you choose to observe, and you're going to be guided in some sense by some kind of theory. And when you turn around to use the data, you're also going to be guided by theory. It will have a profound effect on what you do."

This shows up in the way researchers go about analyzing different kinds of data. For example, when working with observational data, people simply don't realize the weak theoretical ground on which they stand. They wander around the data, merrily trying to find out what makes sense.

"Perhaps you've seen some fairly typical versions of this. The creative analyst looks at the data and the survey and they don't make sense. 'Make sense' means the findings are congenial to his prior judgment. But the world isn't working the way he thought it was supposed to be working.

"So he cross-tabs by big cities versus little cities. Still doesn't make sense. But he is very creative, and observes there are more outer-directed people in big cities than in little cities, so he now cross-tabs by inner-directed versus outer-directed by city size, and—lo and behold—he finds out he was right all along!

"Now, obviously, as long as you keep analyzing and don't like what you see, and stop analyzing when you do like what you see, the world always will look to you the way it's supposed to look. You'll never learn anything."

Source: "Marketing Research Needs Validated Theories," *Marketing News,* 17 (January 21, 1983), p. 14. Published by the American Marketing Association. Reprinted with permission.

and consider the theory that directs marketing inquiry. Without the theory, the mathematics are useless.

The subject of regression and correlation analysis is best discussed through example. Consider, therefore, the national manufacturer of a ballpoint pen, Click, which is interested in investigating the effectiveness of the firm's marketing efforts. The company uses regional wholesalers to distribute Click and supplements their efforts with company sales representatives and spot television advertising. The company plans to use annual territory sales as its measure of effectiveness. These data and information on the number of sales representatives serving a territory are readily available in company records. The other characteristics to which they seek to relate sales—television spot advertising and wholesaler efficiency—are more difficult to determine. To obtain information on television spot advertising in a territory, researchers must analyze advertising schedules and study area coverage by channel to determine what areas each broadcast might reach. Wholesaler efficiency requires rating the wholesalers on a number of criteria and aggregating the ratings into an overall measure of wholesaler efficiency, where 4 is outstanding, 3 is good, 2 is average, and 1 is poor. Because of the time and expense required to generate these advertising and distribution characteristics, the company has decided to analyze only a sample of sales territories. The data for a simple random sample of forty territories are contained in Table 19.1.

The effect of each of the marketing-mix variables on sales can be investigated in several ways. One very obvious way is to simply plot sales as a function of each of the variables. Figure 19.1 contains these plots, which are called *scatter diagrams*. Panel A suggests that sales increase as the number of television spots per month increases. Panel B suggests that sales increase as the number of sales representatives serving the territory increases. Finally, Panel C suggests that there is little relationship between sales in a territory and the efficiency of the wholesaler serving the territory.

A close look at Panels A and B also suggests that it would be possible to summarize the relationship between sales and each of the predictor variables by drawing a straight line through the data points. One way to generate the relationship between sales and either television spots or number of sales representatives would be to "eyeball" it; that is, one could usually draw a straight line through the points in the graphs. Such a line would represent the line of "average" relationship. It would indicate the average value of the criterion variable, sales, for given values of either of the predictor variables, television spots or number of sales representatives. One could then enter the graph with, say, the number of television spots in a territory, and could read off the average level of sales expected in the territory. The difficulty with the graphic approach is that two analysts might generate different lines to describe the relationship. This simply raises the question of which line is more correct or fits the data better.

An alternative approach is to mathematically fit a line to the data. The general equation of a straight line is $Y = \alpha + \beta X$, where α is the Y intercept and β is the slope coefficient. In the case of sales Y and television spots X_1, the equation could be written as $Y = \alpha_1 + \beta_1 X_1$, while for the relationship between sales Y and number of sales representatives X_2, it could be written as $Y = \alpha_2 + \beta_2 X_2$, where the subscripts indicate the predictor variable being considered. As written, each of these models is a *deterministic model*. When a value of the predictor variable is substituted in the equation with specified α and β, a unique value for Y is determined, and no allowance is made for error.

When investigating social phenomena, there is rarely, if ever, zero error. Thus in place of the deterministic model, we might substitute a *probabilistic model* and

Table 19.1   Territory Data for Click Ball Point Pens

Territory	Sales (in Thousands) Y	Advertising (TV Spots per Month) X_1	Number of Sales Representatives X_2	Wholesaler Efficiency Index X_3
005	260.3	5	3	4
019	286.1	7	5	2
033	279.4	6	3	3
039	410.8	9	4	4
061	438.2	12	6	1
082	315.3	8	3	4
091	565.1	11	7	3
101	570.0	16	8	2
115	426.1	13	4	3
118	315.0	7	3	4
133	403.6	10	6	1
149	220.5	4	4	1
162	343.6	9	4	3
164	644.6	17	8	4
178	520.4	19	7	2
187	329.5	9	3	2
189	426.0	11	6	4
205	343.2	8	3	3
222	450.4	13	5	4
237	421.8	14	5	2
242	245.6	7	4	4
251	503.3	16	6	3
260	375.7	9	5	3
266	265.5	5	3	3
279	620.6	18	6	4
298	450.5	18	5	3
306	270.1	5	3	2
332	368.0	7	6	2
347	556.1	12	7	1
358	570.0	13	6	4
362	318.5	8	4	3
370	260.2	6	3	2
391	667.0	16	8	2
408	618.3	19	8	2
412	525.3	17	7	4
430	332.2	10	4	3
442	393.2	12	5	3
467	283.5	8	3	3
471	376.2	10	5	4
488	481.8	12	5	2

make some assumptions about the error. For example, let us work with the relationship between sales and the number of television spots and consider the model

$$Y_i = \alpha_1 + \beta_1 X_{i1} + \epsilon_i$$

where Y_i is the level of sales in the ith territory, X_{i1} is the level of advertising in the ith territory, and ϵ_i is the error associated with the ith observation. This is the form of the model that is used for regression analysis. The error term is part and parcel of the model. It represents a failure to include all factors in the model, the fact that there is an unpredictable element in human behavior, and the condition that there

Figure 19.1

Scatter Diagrams of Sales versus Marketing-Mix Variables

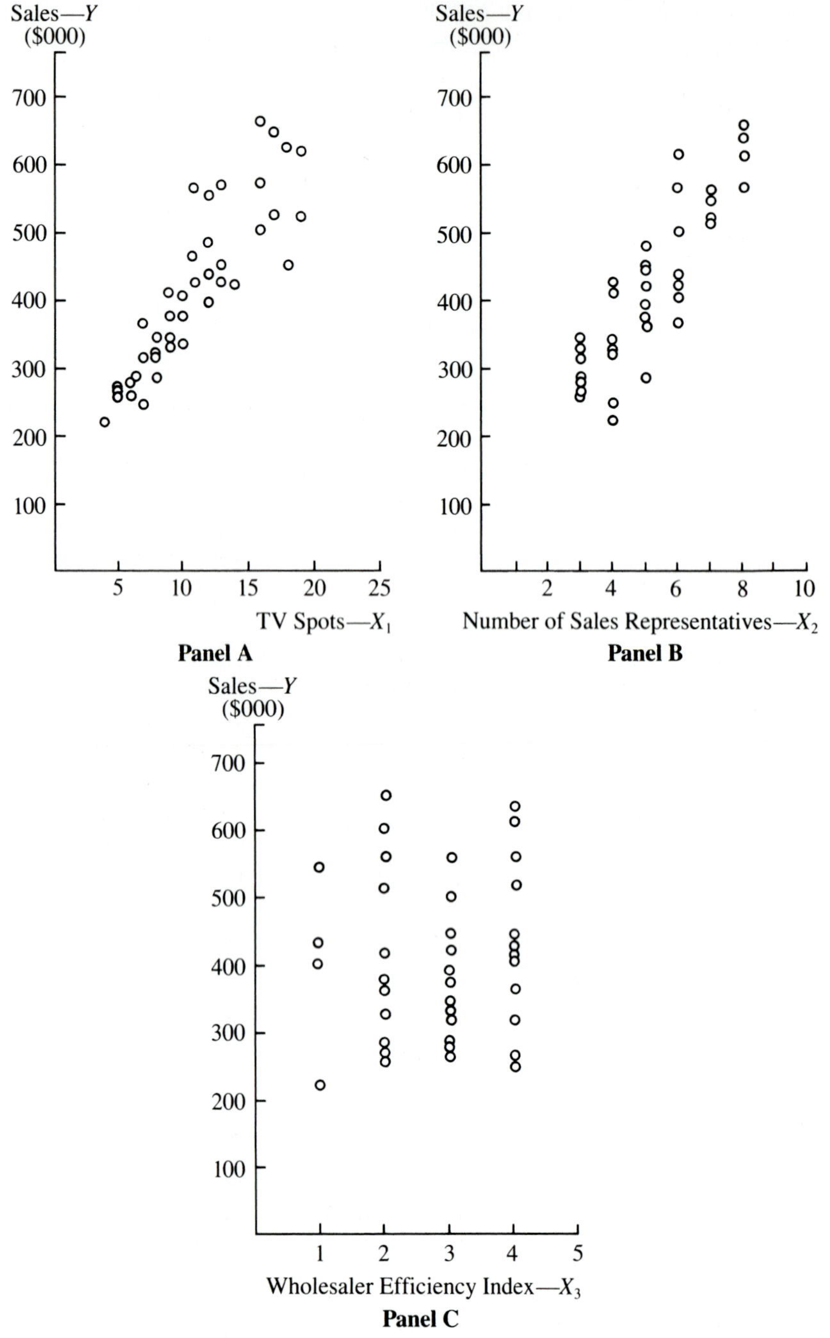

Panel A — Sales—Y ($000) versus TV Spots—$X_1$

Panel B — Sales—Y ($000) versus Number of Sales Representatives—X_2

Panel C — Sales—Y ($000) versus Wholesaler Efficiency Index—X_3

are errors of measurement.[4] The probabilistic model allows for the fact that the Y value is not uniquely determined for a given X_i value. Rather, all that is determined for a given X_i value is the "average value" of Y. Individual values can be expected to fluctuate above and below this average.

---

[4]Strictly speaking, the regression model requires that errors of measurement be associated only with the criterion variable and that the predictor variables be measured without error. See Wonnacott and Wonnacott, *Regression*, pp. 293–299, for a discussion of the problems and solutions when the predictor variables also have an error component.

Figure 19.2

Relationship between Y and X_1 in the Probabilistic Model

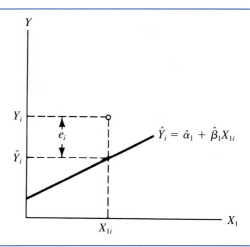

The mathematical solution for finding the *line of best fit* for the probabilistic model requires that some assumptions be made about the distribution of the error term. The line of best fit could be defined in a number of ways. The typical way is in terms of the line that minimizes the sum of the deviations squared about the line (the *least-squares solution*). Consider Figure 19.2 and suppose that the line drawn in the figure is the estimated equation. Employing a caret (^) to indicate an estimated value, the error for the ith observation is the difference between the actual Y value, Y_i, and the estimated Y value, $\hat{Y}_i$; that is, $e_i = Y_i - \hat{Y}_i$. The least-squares solution is based on the principle that the sum of these squared errors should be made as small as possible; that is, $\sum_{i\,=\,1}^{n} e_i^2$ should be minimized. The sample estimates $\hat{\alpha}_1$ and $\hat{\beta}_1$ of the true population parameters α_1 and β_1 are determined so that this condition is satisfied.

There are three simplifying assumptions made about the error term in the least-squares solution:

1. The mean or average value of the error term is zero.

2. The variance of the error term is constant and is independent of the values of the predictor variable.

3. The values of the error term are independent of one another.

Given these assumptions, it is possible to solve formulas to secure estimates for the population parameters, $\hat{\alpha}$, the intercept, and $\hat{\beta}$, the slope, by hand, although it is much more common to use a computer to estimate them.[5]

---

[5]For those who would like to try solving for each of these values, the formulas are

$$\hat{\alpha} = \bar{y} - \hat{\beta}\bar{x},$$

$$\hat{\beta} = \frac{n \sum\limits_{i=1}^{n} X_i Y_i - \left(\sum\limits_{i=1}^{n} X_i\right)\left(\sum\limits_{i=1}^{n} Y_i\right)}{n \sum\limits_{i=1}^{n} X_i^2 - \left(\sum\limits_{i=1}^{n} X_i\right)^2}$$

where

$$\bar{y} = \sum\limits_{i=1}^{n} \frac{Y_i}{n} \text{ and } \bar{x} = \sum\limits_{i=1}^{n} \frac{X_i}{n}$$

If we used the data in Table 19.1 for sales *(Y)* and television spots per month *(X₁)*, it would turn out that the estimate for $\hat{\alpha}$ would be 135.4, and $\hat{\beta}_1$ would be 25.3.[6]

------

[6]Many of the results contained in the discussion were determined by computer and thus may differ slightly from those generated using hand calculations because of the rounding errors associated with the latter method.

Back to the Case

Pat Hayes and Mike Mihalic each snared a doughnut from a box on the secretary's desk as they headed into Mike's office in the back of the sporting goods store.

After wiping powdered sugar off his fingers, Pat delved into his briefcase for a thick file.

"Mike, I know you find some of this statistical information rather heavy going," he said, pulling a sheaf of papers from the file, "but the results are so interesting that I think it's worthwhile to show you how I came up with the figures."

"I'm all ears, Pat," Mike said. "J. B. Stuart, vice-president of marketing for the whole chain, is due in the office tomorrow. I'd

like to be able to dazzle him with some statistics. Besides, it's very important that this spring mailing we're planning do well. My credibility rests on it."

"Fine," Pat said. "Let's get started. Remember the last time I was here we discussed the CAT-CON index? That index measured how confident people felt about buying merchandise through the mail. We got that data from responses to Question #4 in our survey.

"Now, in addition to that general measure, we wanted to know how people felt about buying from Avery specifically. To determine that factor, we came up with an 'attitude toward Av-

ery' index, called ATTAVRY, using responses to Questions 7 through 11.

"Here those are," Pat said, handing Mike the corresponding part of the questionnaire.

"ATTAVRY was formed in such a way that higher scores implied more favorable attitudes about buying from Avery. The responses to the five questions were summed to produce the ATTAVRY score for each subject," Pat said.

"We also wanted to know if that attitude was related in any way to the respondent's demographic characteristics. This table that we compiled shows whether the ATTAVRY index varies as a

Questions 7–11 from Avery Sporting Goods Questionnaire

	Strongly Disagree	Disagree	Neither Agree nor Disagree	Agree	Strongly Agree
7. In general, Avery Sporting Goods sells a high-quality line of merchandise.	_____	_____	_____	_____	_____
8. Avery Sporting Goods carries all of the most popular name-brand sporting equipment.	_____	_____	_____	_____	_____
9. Avery Sporting Goods has a very high-quality catalog.	_____	_____	_____	_____	_____
10. The descriptions of the products shown in the Avery catalog are very accurate.	_____	_____	_____	_____	_____
11. The selection of sporting goods available through the Avery catalog is very broad.	_____	_____	_____	_____	_____

The equation is plotted in Figure 19.3. The slope of the line is given by $\hat{\beta}_1$. The value 25.3 for β_1 suggests that sales increase by $25,300 for every unit increase in television spots. As mentioned previously, this is an estimate of the true population condition based on our particular sample of forty observations. A different sample would most assuredly generate a different estimate. Further, we have not yet asked whether this is a statistically significant result or whether it could have occurred by

function of the person's occupation," he said, handing Mike the following table.

"You may remember that we coded blue-collar workers as 0 and white-collar workers as 1. Using simple regression analysis, we determined that the results are both statistically and practically significant. You see where it says the 'adjusted R-square' value is .752," Pat said, pointing to the third line in the table.

Mike nodded.

"That means that approximately 75 percent of the variation in the ATTAVRY index—the measure of people's

attitude toward buying from Avery—can be accounted for or explained by the variation in occupation. There is a positive relationship between the two variables ($B = 11.534$)," Pat said.

"I hate to sound dumb, but what, exactly, does that mean?" Mike asked.

"In a nutshell, that white-collar workers have more favorable attitudes toward Avery than blue-collar workers," Pat said.

This scenario illustrates how simple regression analysis can be used to study the relationship

between two variables. In this case, the two variables were respondents' attitudes toward Avery and their type of occupation. The dependent, or criterion, variable was their attitude; occupation was the independent, or predictor, variable.

Remember, that while this technique can be used to determine whether there is a relationship between the two variables, it does not imply that one *causes* the other. The fact that a respondent has a white-collar job does not *cause* him to buy from a sporting goods catalog.

Simple Regression Analysis of ATTAVRY versus Occupation

Dependent variable. . .ATTAVRY
Variable(s) entered on step number 1. *V*41

		Analysis of Variance	DF	Sum of Squares	Mean Square	F
Multiple *R*	.869	Regression	1	4071.174	4071.174	374.512
R-squared	.754	Residual	122	1326.213	10.871	
Adjusted *R*-squared	.752					
Standard error	3.297					

Variables in the Equation

Variable	B	Beta	Standard Error β	F
*V*41	11.534	.869	.596	374.512
(Constant)	9.727			

Figure 19.3

Plot of Equation Relating Sales to Television Spots

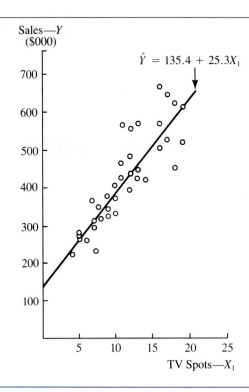

chance. Nevertheless, it is a most vital item of information that helps in determining whether advertising expense is worth the estimated return. The estimate of the intercept parameter is $\hat{\alpha}_1 = 135.4$; this indicates where the line crosses the Y axis, since it represents the estimated value of Y when the predictor variable equals zero.

Standard Error of Estimate

An examination of Figure 19.3 shows that while the line seems to fit the points fairly well, there is still some deviation in the points about the line. The size of these deviations measures the goodness of the fit. We can compute a numerical measure of the variation of the points about the line in much the same way as we compute the standard deviation of a frequency distribution.

Just as the sample mean is an estimate of the true parent-population mean, the line given by $\hat{Y}_i = \hat{\alpha}_1 + \hat{\beta}_1 X_{i1} + e_i$ is an estimate of the true regression line $Y_i = \alpha_1 + \beta_1 X_{i1} + \epsilon_i$. Consider the variance of the random error ϵ around the true line of regression, that is, σ_ϵ^2 or $\sigma_{Y/X}^2$. When the population variance σ^2 is unknown, an unbiased estimate is given by the square of the sample standard deviation, $\hat{s}$,

$$\hat{s} = \frac{\sum\limits_{i=1}^{n}(X_i - \bar{x})^2}{(n-1)}$$

Similarly, let $s_{Y/X}^2$ be an unbiased estimate of the population variance about the regression line, $\sigma_{Y/X}^2$. Now it can be shown that the sample estimate of the variance about the regression line is related to the sum of the squared errors, specifically, it equals

Figure 19.4

Rectangular Distribution of Error Term

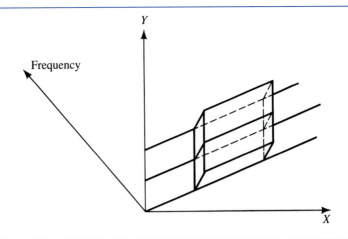

$$s_{Y/X}^2 = \frac{\sum\limits_{i=1}^{n} e_i^2}{(n-2)} = \frac{\sum\limits_{i=1}^{n}(Y_i - \hat{Y}_i)^2}{(n-2)}$$

where n is again the sample size, and $s_{Y/X}^2$ is an unbiased estimator of $\sigma_{Y/X}^2$, where Y_i and $\hat{Y}_i$ are, respectively, the observed and estimated values of Y for the ith observation. The square root of the above quantity $s_{Y/X}$ is often called the **standard error of estimate,** although the term *standard deviation from regression* is more meaningful.

• **Standard error of estimate**

Term used in regression analysis to refer to the absolute amount of variation in the criterion variable that is left "unexplained," or unaccounted for by the fitted regression equation.

The interpretation of the standard error of estimate parallels that for the standard deviation. Consider any X_{i1} value. The standard error of estimate means that for any such value of television spots X_{i1}, Y_i (sales) tends to be distributed about the corresponding $\hat{Y}_i$ value—the point on the line—with a standard deviation equal to the standard error of estimate. Further, the variation about the line is the same throughout the entire length of the line. The point on the line, the arithmetic mean, changes as X_{i1} changes, but the distribution of Y_i values around the line does not change with changes in the number of television spots. Figure 19.4 depicts the situation under the assumption that the error term is rectangularly distributed, for example.[7] Note that the assumption of constant $s_{Y/X}$, irrespective of the value of X_{i1}, produces parallel bands around the regression line.

The smaller the standard error of estimate, the better the line fits the data. For the line relating sales to television spots it is $s_{Y/X} = 59.6$.

Inferences about the Slope Coefficient

Earlier we calculated the value of the slope coefficient, $\hat{\beta}_1$, to be 25.3. At that time we did not yet raise the question of whether that result was statistically significant or could have been due to chance. To deal with that question requires an additional assumption, namely, that the errors are normally distributed rather than rectangularly distributed as previously assumed. Before proceeding, though, let us emphasize that the least-squares estimators of the parent population parameters are BLUE, that

---

[7]This assumption will be modified shortly to that of normally distributed errors. It is made this way now in order to make more vivid the fact that the assumption of normally distributed errors is necessary only if statistical inferences are to be made about the coefficients.

is, they are the *best*, *linear*, *unbiased* *estimators* of the true population parameters regardless of the shape of the distribution of the error term. All that is necessary is that the previous assumptions be satisfied. This is the remarkable result of the Gauss-Markov theorem. It is only if we wish to make statistical inferences about the regression coefficients that the assumption of normally distributed errors is required.

It can be shown that if the ϵ_i are normally distributed random variables, then $\hat{\beta}_1$ is also normally distributed. That is, if we were to take repeated samples from our population of sales territories and calculate a $\hat{\beta}_1$ for each sample, the distribution of these estimates would be normal and *centered* around the *true population* parameter β_1. Further, the variance of the distribution of $\hat{\beta}_1$'s, $\sigma_{\hat{\beta}_1}^2$, can be shown to be equal to

$$\sigma_{\hat{\beta}_1}^2 = \frac{\sigma_{Y/X_1}^2}{\sum_{i=1}^{n}(X_{i1} - \bar{x}_1)^2}$$

Since the population $\sigma_{Y/X}^2$ is unknown, $\sigma_{\hat{\beta}_1}^2$ is also unknown and has to be estimated. The estimate is generated by substituting the standard error of estimate $s_{Y/X}$ for $\sigma_{Y/X}$

$$s_{\hat{\beta}_1}^2 = \frac{s_{Y/X_1}^2}{\sum_{i=1}^{n}(X_{i1} - \bar{x}_1)^2}$$

The situation so far is as follows: Given the assumption of normally distributed errors, $\hat{\beta}_1$ is also normally distributed with a mean of β_1 and unknown variance $\sigma_{\hat{\beta}_1}^2$. Since the variance of the distribution of the sample is unknown, we need to use a similar procedure to that used when making an inference about the mean when the population variance is unknown. That set of conditions requires a t test to examine statistical significance. The test for the significance of β_1 has a similar requirement. The null hypothesis is that there is no linear relationship between the variables, while the alternate hypothesis is that a linear relationship does exist, that is,

$$H_0: \beta_1 = 0$$
$$H_a: \beta_1 \neq 0$$

The test statistic is $t = (\hat{\beta}_1 - \beta_1)/s_{\hat{\beta}_1}$; that is, the slope estimated from the sample minus the hypothesized slope, divided by the standard error of estimate, which is t distributed with $n - 2$ degrees of freedom. In the example,

$$s_{\hat{\beta}_1}^2 = \frac{s_{Y/X_1}^2}{\sum_{i=1}^{n}(X_{i1} - \bar{x}_1)^2} = \frac{(59.6)^2}{723.6} = 4.91$$

$$s_{\hat{\beta}_1} = \sqrt{4.91} = 2.22$$

$$t = \frac{\hat{\beta}_1 - \beta_1}{s_{\hat{\beta}_1}} = \frac{25.3 - 0}{2.22} = 11.4$$

For a 0.05 level of significance, the tabled t value for $\nu = n - 2 = 38$ degrees of freedom is 2.02. Since calculated t exceeds critical t, the null hypothesis is rejected; $\hat{\beta}_1$ is sufficiently different from zero to warrant the assumption of a linear relationship between sales and television spots. Now this does not mean that the true relationship between sales and television spots is *necessarily* linear, only that the evidence indicates that Y (sales) changes as X_1 (television spots) changes, and that we may obtain a better prediction of Y using X_1 and the linear equation than if we simply ignored X_1.

What if the null hypothesis is not rejected? As we have noted, β_1 is the slope of the assumed line over the region of observation and indicates the linear change in Y for a one-unit change in X_1. If we do not reject the null hypothesis that β_1 equals zero, it does not mean that Y and X_1 are unrelated. There are two possibilities. First, we may simply be committing a Type II error by not rejecting a false null hypothesis. Second, it is possible that Y and X_1 might be perfectly related in some curvilinear manner, and we have simply chosen the wrong model to describe the physical situation.

Correlation Coefficient

So far we have been concerned with the functional relationship of Y to X. Suppose we were also concerned with the *strength of the linear relationship* between Y and X. This leads to the notion of the **coefficient of correlation.** Two additional assumptions are made when discussing the correlation model. First, X_i is also assumed to be a random variable. A sample observation yields both an X_i and Y_i value. Second, it is assumed that the observations come from a bivariate normal distribution, that is, one in which the X variable is normally distributed and the Y variable is also normally distributed.

Now consider the drawing of a sample of n observations from a bivariate normal distribution. Let ρ represent the strength of the linear association between the two variables in the parent population. Let r represent the sample estimate of ρ. Suppose the sample of n observations yielded the scatter of points down in Figure 19.5 and consider the division of the figure into the four quadrants formed by erecting perpendiculars to the two axes at $\bar{x}$ and $\bar{y}$.

Consider the deviations from these bisectors. Take any point P with coordinates (X_i, Y_i) and define the deviations

$$x_i = X_i - \bar{x}$$
$$y_i = Y_i - \bar{y}$$

where the small letters indicate deviations around a mean. It is clear from an inspection of Figure 19.5 that the product $x_i y_i$ is

- Positive for all points in Quadrant I.
- Negative for all points in Quadrant II.
- Positive for all points in Quadrant III.
- Negative for all points in Quadrant IV.

Hence, it would seem that the quantity $\sum_{i=1}^{n} x_i y_i$ could be used as a measure of the linear association between X and Y,

- For if the association is positive so that most points lie in the Quadrants I and III, $\sum_{i=1}^{n} x_i y_i$ tends to be positive.
- While if the association is negative so that most points lie in the Quadrants II and IV, $\sum_{i=1}^{n} x_i y_i$ tends to be negative.
- While if no relation exists between X and Y, the points will be scattered over all four quadrants and $\sum_{i=1}^{n} x_i y_i$ will tend to be very small.

The quantity $\sum_{i=1}^{n} x_i y_i$ has two defects, though, as a measure of linear association between X and Y. First, it can be increased arbitrarily by adding further observations, that is, by increasing the sample size. Second, it can also be arbitrarily influenced by

• Coefficient of correlation

Term used in regression analysis to refer to the strength of the linear association between the criterion variable and a predictor variable.

Figure 19.5

Scatter of Points for Sample of n Observations

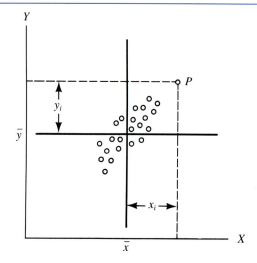

changing the units of measurement for either X or Y or both, for example, by changing feet to inches. These defects can be removed by making the measure of the strength of linear association a dimensionless quantity and dividing by n. The result is the *Pearsonian*, or *product-moment, coefficient of correlation*, that is,

$$r = \frac{\sum_{i=1}^{n} x_i y_i}{n s_X s_Y}$$

where s_X is the standard deviation of the X variable and s_Y is the standard deviation of the Y variable.

The correlation coefficient computed from the sample data is an estimate of the parent-population parameter ρ, and part of the job of the researcher is to use r to test hypotheses about ρ. It is unnecessary to do so for the example at hand because the test of the null hypothesis H_0: $\rho = 0$ is equivalent to the test of the null hypothesis H_0: $\beta_1 = 0$. Since we have already performed the latter test, we know that the sample evidence leads to the rejection of the hypothesis that there is no linear relationship between sales and television spots; that is, it leads to the rejection of H_0: $\rho = 0$.

The product-moment coefficient of correlation may vary from -1 to $+1$. Perfect positive correlation, where an increase in X determines exactly an increase in Y, yields a coefficient of $+1$. Perfect negative correlation, where an increase in X determines exactly a decrease in Y, yields a coefficient of -1. Figure 19.6 depicts these situations and several other scatter diagrams and their resulting correlation coefficients. An examination of these diagrams will provide some appreciation of the size of the correlation coefficient associated with a particular degree of scatter. The square of the correlation coefficient is the **coefficient of determination.** By some algebraic manipulation, it can be shown to be equal to

$$r^2 = 1 - \frac{s_{Y/X}^{\,2}}{s_Y^{\,2}}$$

that is, $r^2 = 1$ minus the standard error of estimate squared, divided by the sample variance of the criterion variable. In the absence of the predictor variable, our best

◆ **Coefficient of determination**

Term used in regression analysis to refer to the relative proportion of the total variation in the criterion variable that can be "explained," or accounted for, by the fitted regression equation.

Figure 19.6

Sample Scatter Diagrams and Associated Correlation Coefficients

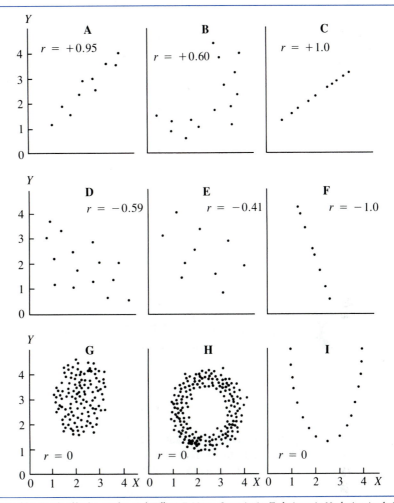

Source: Ronald E. Frank, Alfred A. Kuehn, and William F. Massy, *Quantitative Techniques in Marketing Analysis* (Homewood, Ill.: Richard D. Irwin, Inc., 1962), p. 71. Used with permission.

estimate of the criterion variable would be the sample mean. If there were low variability in sales from territory to territory, the sample mean would be a good estimate of the expected sales in any territory. However, high variability would render it a poor estimate. Thus, the variance in sales s_Y^2 is a measure of the "badness" of such an estimating procedure. The introduction of the covariate X might produce an improvement in the territory sales estimates. It depends on how well the equation fits the data. Since $s_{Y/X}^2$ measures the scatter of the points about the regression line, $s_{Y/X}^2$ can be considered a measure of the "badness" of an estimating procedure that takes account of the covariate. Now if $s_{Y/X}^2$ is small in relation to s_Y^2, the introduction of the covariate via the regression equation can be said to have substantially improved the predictions of the criterion variable, sales. Conversely, if $s_{Y/X}^2$ is approximately equal to s_Y^2, the introduction of the covariate X can be considered not to have helped in improving the predictions of Y. Thus, the ratio $s_{Y/X}^2/s_Y^2$ can be considered to be the ratio of variation left unexplained by the regression line divided by the total variation; that is,

$$r^2 = 1 - \frac{\text{unexplained variation}}{\text{total variation}}$$

The right side of the equation can be combined in a single fraction to yield

$$r^2 = \frac{\text{total variation} - \text{unexplained variation}}{\text{total variation}}$$

Total variation minus unexplained variation leaves "explained variation," that is, the variation in Y that is accounted for or explained by the introduction of X. Thus, the coefficient of determination can be considered to be equal to

$$r^2 = \frac{\text{explained variation}}{\text{total variation}}$$

where it is understood that total variation is measured by the variance in Y. For the sales and television spot example, $r^2 = 0.77$. This means that 77 percent of the variation in sales from territory to territory is accounted for, or can be explained, by the variation in television spot advertising across territories. Consequently, we can do a better job of estimating sales in a territory if we take account of television spots than if we neglect this advertising effort.

◆ Multiple-Regression Analysis

The basic idea behind multiple-regression analysis is the same as that behind simple regression: to determine the relationship between independent and dependent, that is, predictor and criterion, variables. Multiple-regression analysis allows the introduction of additional variables, so the equation constructed reflects the values of several rather than one predictor variable. The objective in introducing additional variables is to improve our predictions of the criterion variable.

A wry observer of many a research project once offered some astute insights on the behavior of variables and the way in which they may be correlated (see Research Window 19.2). You may want to keep them in mind while you read this section on multiple-regression analysis.

Research Window 19.2
Walkup's Laws of Statistics

Law No. 1
Everything correlates with everything, especially when the same individual defines the variables to be correlated.

Law No. 2
It won't help very much to find a good correlation between the variable you are interested in and some other variable that you don't understand any better.

Law No. 3
Unless you can think of a logical reason why two variables should be connected as cause and ef-

fect, it doesn't help much to find a correlation between them. In Columbus, Ohio, the mean monthly rainfall correlates very nicely with the number of letters in the names of the months!

Source: Lewis E. Walkup, "Walkup's First Five Laws of Statistics," *The Bent,* (Summer 1974) publication of Tau Beta Pi, National Engineering Honor Society, University of Missouri Alumni Magazine; as quoted in Robert W. Joselyn, *Designing the Marketing Research Project* (New York: Petrocelli/Charter, 1977), p. 175.

Revised Nomenclature

A more formal, revised notational framework is valuable for discussing multiple-regression analysis. Consider the general regression model with three predictor variables. The regression equation is

$$Y = \alpha + \beta_1 X_1 + \beta_2 X_2 + \beta_3 X_3 + \epsilon$$

which is a simplified statement of the more elaborate and precise equation,

$$Y_{(123)} = \alpha_{(123)} + \beta_{Y1.23} X_1 + \beta_{Y2.13} X_2 + \beta_{Y3.12} X_3 + \epsilon_{(123)}$$

In this more precise system, the following holds true:

- $Y_{(123)}$ is the value of Y that is estimated from the regression equation, in which Y is the criterion variable and X_1, X_2, and X_3 are the predictor variables.
- $\alpha_{(123)}$ is the intercept parameter in the multiple-regression equation, in which Y is the criterion variable and X_1, X_2, and X_3 are the predictor variables.
- $\beta_{Y1.23}$ is the coefficient of X_1 in the regression equation, in which Y is the criterion variable and X_1, X_2, and X_3 are the predictor variables. It is called the **coefficient of partial (or net) regression.** Note the subscripts. The two subscripts to the left of the decimal point are called *primary subscripts*. The first identifies the criterion variable, and the second identifies the predictor variable of which this β value is the coefficient. There are always two primary subscripts. The two subscripts to the right of the decimal point are called *secondary subscripts*. They indicate which other predictor variables are in the regression equation. The number of secondary subscripts varies from zero for simple regression to any number, $k - 1$, where there are k predictor variables in the problem. In this case, the model contains three predictor variables, $k = 3$, and there are two secondary subscripts throughout.
- $\epsilon_{(123)}$ is the error associated with the prediction of Y when X_1, X_2, and X_3 are the predictor variables.

When the identity of the variables is clear, it is common practice to use the simplified statement of the model. The more elaborate statement is helpful, though, in interpreting the solution to the regression problem.

• **Coefficient of partial (or net) regression**

Quantity resulting from a multiple-regression analysis, which indicates the average change in the criterion variable per unit change in a predictor variable, holding all other predictor variables constant; the interpretation applies only when the predictor variables are independent, as required for a valid application of the multiple-regression model.

Multicollinearity Assumption

The assumptions that we made about the error term for the simple regression model also apply to the multiple-regression equation. And the multiple-regression model requires the additional assumption that the predictor variables are not correlated among themselves. When the levels of the predictor variables can be set by the researcher, the assumption is easily satisfied. When the observations result from a survey rather than an experiment, the assumption is often violated, because many variables of interest in marketing vary together. For instance, higher incomes are typically associated with higher education levels. Thus, the prediction of purchase behavior employing both income and education would violate the assumption that the predictor variables are independent of one another. **Multicollinearity** is said to be present in a multiple-regression problem when the predictor variables are correlated among themselves.

• **Multicollinearity**

Condition said to be present in a multiple-regression analysis when the predictor variables are not independent as required but are correlated among themselves.

Coefficients of Partial Regression

Consider what would happen if we introduced a number of sales representatives into our problem of predicting territory sales. We could investigate the two-variable relationship between sales and the number of sales representatives. This would involve, of course, the calculation of the simple regression equation relating sales to number of sales representatives. The calculations would parallel those for the sales and television spot relationship. Alternatively, we could consider the simultaneous influence of television spots and number of sales representatives on sales using multiple-regression analysis. Assuming that is indeed the research problem, the regression model would be written

$$Y_{(12)} = \alpha_{(12)} + \beta_{Y1.2}X_1 + \beta_{Y2.1}X_2 + \epsilon_{(12)}$$

indicating that the criterion variable, sales in a territory, is to be predicted employing two predictor variables, X_1 (television spots per month) and X_2 (number of sales representatives).

Once again, the parameters of the model could be estimated from sample data employing least-squares procedures. Let us again distinguish the sample estimates from the true, but unknown, population values by using a caret to denote an estimated value. Let us not worry about the formulas for calculating the regression coefficients. They typically will be calculated on a computer anyway and can be found in almost any introductory statistics book. The marketing analyst's need is how to interpret the results provided by the computer.

For this problem, the equation turns out to be

$$\hat{Y} = \hat{\alpha}_{(12)} + \hat{\beta}_{Y1.2}X_1 + \hat{\beta}_{Y2.1}X_2 = 69.3 + 14.2X_1 + 37.5X_2$$

This regression equation may be used to estimate the level of sales to be expected in a territory, given the number of television spots and the number of sales representatives serving the territory. Like any other least-squares equation, the line (a plane in this case, since three dimensions are involved) fits the points in such a way that the sum of the deviations about the line is zero. That is, if sales for each of the forty sales territories were to be estimated from this equation, the positive and negative deviations about the line would exactly balance.

The level at which the plane intercepts the Y axis is given by $\hat{\alpha}_{(12)} = 69.3$. Consider now the coefficients of partial regression, $\hat{\beta}_{Y1.2}$ and $\hat{\beta}_{Y2.1}$. *Assuming the multicollinearity assumption is satisfied,* these coefficients of partial regression can be interpreted as the average change in the criterion variable associated with a unit change in the appropriate predictor variable while holding the other predictor variable constant. Thus, assuming there is no multicollinearity, $\hat{\beta}_{Y1.2} = 14.2$ indicates that on the average, an increase of $14,200 in sales can be expected with each additional television spot in the territory if the number of sales representatives is not changed. Similarly, $\hat{\beta}_{Y2.1} = 37.5$ suggests that each additional sales representative in a territory can be expected to produce $37,500 in sales, on the average, if the number of television spots is held constant.

In simple regression analysis, we tested the significance of the regression equation by examining the significance of the slope coefficient employing the t test. Calculated t was 11.4 for the sales and television spot relationship. The significance of the regression could also have been checked with an F test. In the case of a two-variable regression, calculated F is equal to calculated t squared; that is, $F = t^2 = (11.4)^2 = 130.6$, while in general calculated F is equal to the ratio of the mean square due to regression to the mean square due to residuals. In simple regression, the calculated F value would be referred to an F table for $v_1 = n - 2$ degrees of freedom. The conclusion would be exactly equivalent to that derived by testing the significance of the slope coefficient employing the t test.

In the multiple-regression case, *it is mandatory that the significance of the overall regression be examined using an F test.* The appropriate degrees of freedom are

$v_1 = k$ and $v_2 = n - k - 1$, where there are k predictor variables. Critical F for $v_1 = 2$ and $v_2 = 40 - 2 - 1 = 37$ degrees of freedom, and a 0.05 level of significance is 3.25. Calculated F for the regression relating sales to television spots and the number of sales representatives is 128.1. Since calculated F exceeds critical F, the null hypothesis of no relationship is rejected. There is a statistically significant linear relationship between sales and the predictor variables, number of television spots and number of sales representatives.

The slope coefficients can also be tested individually for their statistical significance in a multiple-regression problem, given the overall function is significant. The t test is again used, although the validity of the procedure is highly dependent on multicollinearity that exists within the data. If the data are highly multicollinear, there will be a tendency to commit Type II errors; that is, many of the predictor variables will be judged as not being related to the criterion variable when in fact they are. It is even possible to have a high R^2 value and to conclude that the overall regression is statistically significant but that none of the coefficients are significant. The difficulty with the t tests for the significance of the individual slope coefficients arises because the standard error of estimate of the least-squares coefficients, $s_{\hat{\beta}i}$, increases as the dependence among the predictor variables increases. And, of course, as the denominator of calculated t gets larger, t itself decreases, occasioning the conclusion of no relationship between the criterion variable and the predictor variable in question.

Is multicollinearity a problem in our example? Consider again the simple regression of sales on television spots; $\hat{\beta}_1$ ($\hat{\beta}_{Y1}$ in our more formal notational system) was equal to 25.3. Thus, when the number of sales representatives in a territory was not considered, the average change in sales associated with an additional television spot was \$25,300. Yet when the number of sales representatives was considered, the average change in sales associated with an additional television spot was \$14,200, $\hat{\beta}_{Y1.2} = 14.2$. Part of the sales effect that we were attributing to television spots was in fact due to the number of sales representatives in the territory. We were thus overstating the impact of the television spot advertising because of the way decisions have historically been made in the company. Specifically, those territories with the greater number of sales representatives have received more television advertising support (or vice versa). Perhaps this was logical since they contained a larger proportion of the consuming public. Nevertheless, the fact that the two predictor variables are not independent (the coefficient of simple correlation between television spots and number of sales representatives is 0.78) has caused a violation of the assumption of independent predictors. Multicollinearity is present within this data set.

A multicollinear condition within a data set reduces the efficiency of the estimates for the regression parameters. This is because the amount of information about the effect of each predictor variable on the criterion variable declines as the correlation among the predictor variables increases. The reduction in efficiency can be easily seen in the limiting case as the correlation between the predictor variables approaches 1 for a two-predictor model. Such a situation is depicted in Figure 19.7, where it is assumed that there is a perfect linear relationship between the two predictor variables, television spots and number of sales representatives, and also that there is a strong linear relationship between the criterion variable sales and television spots. Consider the change in sales from \$75,000 to \$100,000. This change is associated with a change in the number of television spots, from three to four. This change in television spots is also associated with a change in the number of sales representatives, from four to five. What is the effect of a television spot on sales? Can we say it is $100 - 75 = 25$, or \$25,000? Most assuredly not, for historically a sales

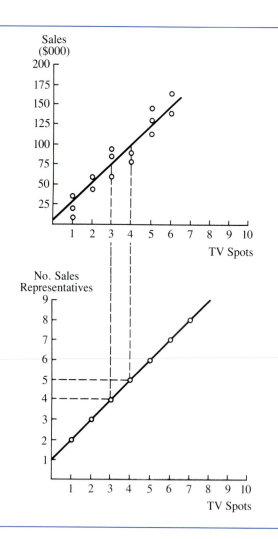

Figure 19.7

Hypothetical Relationship between Sales and TV Spots and between TV Spots and Number of Sales Representatives

representative has been added to a territory whenever the number of television spots has been increased by one (or vice versa). The number of television spots and of sales representatives varies in perfect proportion, and it is impossible to distinguish their separate influences on sales, that is, their influence when the other predictor variable is held constant.

Very little meaning can be attached to the coefficients of partial regression when multicollinearity is present, as it is in our example. The "normal" interpretation of the coefficients of partial regression as "the average change in the criterion variable associated with a unit change in the appropriate predictor variable while holding the other predictor variables constant" simply does not hold.[8] The equation may still be quite useful for prediction, assuming conditions are stable. That is, it may be used to predict sales in the various territories for given levels of television spots and number of sales representatives *if* the historical relationship between sales and each of the predictor variables, and between or among the predictor variables themselves,

---

[8]M. G. Kendall, *A Course in Multivariate Analysis* (London: Charles Griffin, 1957), p. 74.

can be expected to continue.[9] The partial-regression coefficients should not be used, though, as the basis for making marketing strategy decisions when significant multicollinearity is present.[10]

Coefficients of Multiple Correlation and Determination

• Coefficient of multiple determination

In multiple-regression analysis, the proportion of variation in the criterion variable that is accounted for by the covariation in the predictor variables.

• Coefficient of multiple correlation

In multiple-regression analysis, the square root of the coefficient of multiple determination.

One item of considerable importance in simple regression analysis is the measure of the closeness of the relationship between the criterion and predictor variables. The coefficient of correlation and its square, the **coefficient of multiple determination,** are used for this purpose. In multiple regression, there are similar coefficients for the identical purpose.

The **coefficient of multiple correlation** is formally denoted by $R_{Y.123}$, where the primary subscript identifies the criterion variable and the secondary subscripts identify the predictor variables. When the variables entering into the relationship are obvious, the abbreviated form, R, is used. The coefficient of multiple determination is denoted formally by $R_{Y.123}^2$ and informally by R^2. It represents the proportion of variation in the criterion variable that is accounted for by the covariation in the predictor variables. In the investigation of the relationship between sales and television spots and number of sales representatives, $R_{Y.12}^2 = 0.874$. This means that 87.4 percent of the variation in sales is associated with variation in television spots and number of sales representatives. The introduction of the number of sales representatives has improved the fit of the regression line; 87.4 percent of the variation in sales is accounted for by the two-predictor variable model, whereas only 77.5 percent was accounted for by the one-predictor model. The square root of this quantity, $R_{Y.12} = 0.935$, is the coefficient of multiple correlation. It is always expressed as a positive number.

Coefficients of Partial Correlation

There are two additional quantities to consider when interpreting the results of a multiple-regression analysis that were not present in simple regression analysis: the coefficient of partial correlation and its square, the coefficient of partial determination.

Recall that in the simple regression analysis relating sales Y to television spots X_1 the coefficient of simple determination could be written

$$r_{Y.1}^2 = 1 - \frac{\text{unexplained variation}}{\text{total variation}}$$

[9]There are some things that the analyst faced with multicollinear data can do. See R. R. Hocking, "Developments in Linear Regression Methodology: 1959–1982," *Technometrics,* 25 (August 1983), pp. 219–230, and Ronald D. Snee, "Discussion," *Technometrics,* 25 (August 1983), pp. 230–237, for a discussion of the problem and some alternative ways for handling it.

[10]There is another interpretation danger in the example that was not discussed. It is not unreasonable to assume that both the number of sales representatives serving a territory and the number of television spots per month were both determined on the basis of territorial potential. If this is the case, the implied causality is reversed, or at least confused; instead of the number of sales representatives and number of television spots determining sales, sales in a sense (potential sales anyway) determine the former quantities, and they in turn could be expected to affect realized sales. If this is actually the case, the coefficient estimating procedure needs to take into account the two-way "causation" among the variables. See Wonnacott and Wonnacott, *Regression,* pp. 284–292, for a discussion of the problems and the logic underlying the estimation of simultaneous-equation systems.

and recall also that the unexplained variation was given by the square of standard error of estimate, $s_{Y.1}^2$, since the standard error of estimate measures the variation in the criterion variable that was unaccounted for by the predictor variable X_1. Total variation, of course, was given by the variance in the criterion variable s_Y^2. Thus,

$$r_{Y.1}^2 = 1 - \frac{s_{Y.1}^2}{s_Y^2}$$

The last term in this formula is the ratio of the variation remaining in the criterion variable, after taking account of the predictor variable X_1, to the total variation in the criterion variable. It measures the relative degree to which the association between the two variables can be used to provide information about the criterion variable.

Now consider the multiple-regression case with two predictor variables, X_1 and X_2. Denote the standard error of estimate by $s_{Y.12}$ and its square by $s_{Y.12}^2$. The standard error of estimate measures the variation still remaining in the criterion variable Y after the two predictor variables X_1 and X_2 have been taken into account. Since $s_{Y.1}^2$ measures the variation in the criterion variable that remains after the first predictor variable has been taken into account, the ratio $s_{Y.12}^2/s_{Y.1}^2$ can be interpreted as measuring the relative degree to which the association among the three variables Y, X_1, and X_2 provides information about Y over and above that provided by the association between the criterion variable and the first predictor variable alone. In other words, the ratio $s_{Y.12}^2/s_{Y.1}^2$ measures the *relative degree* to which X_2 adds to the knowledge about Y after X_1 has already been fully utilized. The ratio is the basis for the **coefficient of partial determination,** which in the sales (Y) versus television spots (X_1) and number of sales representatives (X_2) example is

$$r_{Y2.1}^2 = 1 - \frac{s_{Y.12}^2}{s_{Y.1}^2} = 1 - \frac{(45.2)^2}{(59.6)^2} = 1 - 0.576 = 0.424$$

• **Coefficient of partial determination**

Quantity resulting from a multiple-regression analysis that indicates the proportion of variation in the criterion variable that is not accounted for by an earlier variable or variables and that is accounted for by the addition of a new variable into the regression equation.

• **Coefficient of partial correlation**

In multiple-regression analysis, the square root of the coefficient of partial determination.

This means that 42.4 percent of the variation in sales that is not associated with television spots is incrementally associated with the number of sales representatives. Alternatively, the errors made in estimating sales from television spots are, as measured by the variance, reduced by 42.4 percent when the number of sales representatives X_2 is added to X_1 as an additional predictor variable. The square root of the coefficient of partial determination is the **coefficient of partial correlation.**

In our example there were two predictors. Thus, we defined the coefficient of partial determination for the number of sales representatives X_2 as $r_{Y2.1}^2$. We could have similarly defined a coefficient of partial determination for television spots. It would be denoted as $r_{Y2.1}^2$, and it would represent the percentage of the variation in sales not associated with X_2 that is incrementally associated with X_1; this latter coefficient would show the incremental contribution of X_1 after the association between Y and X_2 had already been considered.

When there are more than two predictors, we could define many more coefficients of partial determination. Each would have two primary subscripts indicating the criterion variable and the newly added predictor variable. There could be a great many secondary subscripts, as they always indicate which predictor variables have already been considered. Hence, if we had three predictor variables, we could calculate $r_{Y2.1}$, $r_{Y3.1}$, $r_{Y1.2}$, $r_{Y3.2}$, $r_{Y1.3}$, and $r_{Y2.3}$. These would all be *first-order* partial correlation coefficients since they have one secondary subscript indicating that one other predictor variable is taken into account. We could also calculate $r_{Y1.23}$, $r_{Y2.13}$, and $r_{Y3.12}$. These are all *second-order* partial correlation coefficients. Each has two secondary subscripts indicating that the incremental contribution of the variable is being considered after two other predictor variables have already been taken into account. Simple correlation coefficients, of course, have no secondary coefficients; they are, therefore, often referred to as *zero-order* partial correlation coefficients.

Dummy Variables

The analysis of the sales data of Table 19.1 is still not complete. No attention has yet been given to the effect of distribution on sales, particularly as measured by the wholesaler efficiency index. One way of considering the effect of wholesaler efficiency on sales would be to introduce the index directly; that is, the X_3 value for each observation would simply be the value recorded in the last column of Table 19.1. Letting X_3 represent the wholesaler efficiency index, the multiple-regression equation, using the informal notational scheme, would be

$$Y = \alpha + \beta_1 X_1 + \beta_2 X_2 + \beta_3 X_3 + \epsilon$$

The least-squares estimate of β_3 in this equation turns out to be $\hat{\beta}_3 = 11.5$. Note what this number implies if the predictor variables are independent. It means that the estimated average change in sales is $11,500 for each unit change in the wholesaler efficiency index. This means that a fair distributor could be expected to sell $11,500 more on the average than a poor one; a good one could be expected to average $11,500 more than a fair one; and an excellent one could be expected to sell $11,500 more on the average than a good one. The sales increments are assumed constant for each change in wholesaler rating. The implication is that the wholesaler efficiency index is an intervally scaled variable and that the difference between a poor and a fair wholesaler is the same as the difference between a fair one and a good one. This is a questionable assumption with an index that reflects ratings.

An alternative way of proceeding would be to convert the index into a set of **dummy variables** or, more appropriately, **binary variables.** A binary variable is one that takes on one of two values, 0 (zero) or 1. Thus, it can be represented by a single binary digit. Binary variables are used mainly because of the flexibility one has in defining them. They can provide a numerical representation for attributes or characteristics that are not essentially quantitative. For example, one could introduce sex into a regression equation using the dummy variable X_i, where

$$X_i = 0 \quad \text{if the person is a female}$$
$$X_i = 1 \quad \text{if the person is a male}$$

• Dummy (or binary) variable

Variable that is given one of two values, 0 or 1, and that is used to provide a numerical representation for attributes or characteristics that are not essentially quantitative.

The technique is readily extended to handle multichotomous as well as dichotomous classifications. For instance, suppose one wanted to introduce the variable social class into a regression equation, and suppose there were three distinct class levels: upper class, middle class, and lower class. This could be handled using two dummy variables, say X_1 and X_2, as follows:

	X_1	X_2
■ If a person belongs to the upper class	1	0
■ If a person belongs to the middle class	0	1
■ If a person belongs to the lower class	0	0

There are several other logically equivalent coding schemes, for example, the following:

	X_1	X_2
■ If a person belongs to the upper class	0	0
■ If a person belongs to the middle class	1	0
■ If a person belongs to the lower class	0	1

Back to the Case

"What you've discovered about the relationship between attitude toward Avery and occupation may be helpful in designing our next mail campaign, Pat," said Mike, "but there were other things I was interested in, too. How about whether these customers are married or not? How about how long they've worked?"

"Slow down," Pat said, laughing. "I was just getting to that. Ready for a few more tables?"

"Why not," Mike said. "If we keep up at this pace, J. B. Stuart will be so impressed with my profound knowledge of my market, he may even go for my idea of offering autographed baseballs with every $50 purchase."

"Well, then, let me tell you about the multiple-regression analysis we did," Pat said. "That's sure to impress him."

"What's that?" Mike asked.

"You asked about years worked and marital status. Well, we used a multiple-regression

analysis to determine if the AT-TAVRY index was related to those other demographic characteristics," Pat said.

"Since marital status can be broken into a variety of categories, we had to convert the categories into four dummy variables with the following equivalences using SPSS's recode ability," Pat said, handing Mike the following chart.

"Now here's a table showing the output," he continued, passing the table on page 638 across the desk.

"Once again, we determined that the overall regression equation was statistically significant. Further, we discovered that the variables, taken together, account for 93 percent of the variation in the ATTAVRY index, as you can see from the adjusted R squared value of .931," Pat said.

"These results are particularly interesting since they give us a chance to see the values for each

of the categories of marital status, as they are keyed to the dummy variables. Look at this list," Pat said, handing a small table to Mike.

$$D2 = 2.851$$
$$D3 = 4.387$$
$$D4 = 7.006$$
$$D5 = 7.577$$

"If we consider single people as the null state, we can see that marriage—even if it ends in divorce or death—seems to help to predispose people toward buying from Avery. Look at the $D2$ value, for example. It shows that there is an increase in the ATTAVRY index of 2.85 on average if the person is married rather than single," Pat said.

"What if I want to know the difference between, say, married people and divorced people," Mike asked.

"Easy," Pat said. "Just subtract the two. In that particular case, divorced people have an ATTAVRY index approximately 5.16 higher on average than married people, since $D4 - D2 = 5.155$."

"This is fascinating stuff, Pat," Mike said. "Now all I need for assured success is a large list of divorced white-collar men, and I'll be all set! Maybe these guys are all workaholics with no time to shop, but who want to lavish

V43 =	Implying	D2	D3	D4	D5
1	Single	0	0	0	0
2	Married	1	0	0	0
3	Separated	0	1	0	0
4	Divorced	0	0	1	0
5	Widowed	0	0	0	1

Multiple-Regression Analysis of ATTAVRY Index versus Several Demographic Characteristics

Dependent variable . . . ATTAVRY
Variable(s) entered on step number   1   D2
                                         V41
                                         V42
                                         D5
                                         D4
                                         D3

		Analysis of Variance	DF	Sum of Squares	Mean Square	F
Multiple R	.967	Regression	6	5042.459	840.410	277.036
R squared	.934	Residual	117	354.928	3.034	
Adjusted R squared	.931					
Standard error	1.742					

Variables in the Equation

Variable	B	Beta	Standard Error B	F
D2	2.851	.165	.627	20.668
V41	3.753	.283	.600	39.081
V42	.213	.368	.029	55.626
D5	7.577	.550	.935	65.625
D4	7.006	.391	.948	54.618
D3	4.387	.267	.646	46.076
(Constant)	4.491			

their kids with fancy sporting goods on weekends . . . ."

Pat laughed. "Listen, Mike. My job is to analyze the numbers. I'll leave the direct mail strategy to you. I'll be interested in hearing how your mailing turns out. Meanwhile, what kind of price can you give me on one of those autographed baseballs? I know a

certain seven-year-old who would be thrilled to have one."

Multiple-regression analysis allows researchers to analyze the relationship between several predictor variables at the same time. By measuring the strength of their relationship, researchers can improve their predictions of the criterion variable.

The other question researchers must ask in a multiple-regression analysis is whether the predictor variables are correlated among themselves, that is, whether they are multicollinear. Would you suspect, in this case, that the variables of years worked, occupation, and marital status are related?

It is therefore most important that the analyst interpreting the output from a regression run employing dummy variables pay close attention to the coding of the variables. It should be clear that an m category classification is capable of unambiguous representation by a set of $m - 1$ binary variables and that an mth binary would be entirely superfluous. As a matter of fact, the use of m variables to code an m-way classification variable would render most regression programs inoperative.

Suppose that we were to employ three dummy variables to represent the four-category wholesaler efficiency index in the Click ballpoint pen example as follows:

	X_3	X_4	X_5
■ If a wholesaler is poor	0	0	0
■ If a wholesaler is fair	1	0	0
■ If a wholesaler is good	0	1	0
■ If a wholesaler is excellent	0	0	1

The regression model is

$$Y = \alpha + \beta_1 X_1 + \beta_2 X_2 + \beta_3 X_3 + \beta_4 X_4 + \beta_5 X_5 + \epsilon.$$

The least-squares estimates of the wholesaler efficiency parameters are as follows:[11]

$$\hat{\beta}_3 = 9.2$$
$$\hat{\beta}_4 = 20.3$$
$$\hat{\beta}_5 = 33.3$$

These coefficients indicate that on the average a fair wholesaler could be expected to sell $9,200 more than a poor one; a good wholesaler could be expected to sell $20,300 more than a poor one, and an excellent wholesaler, $33,300 more than a poor one. Note that all of these coefficients are interpreted with respect to the "null" state, that is, with respect to the classification for which all of the dummy variables are defined to be zero—the classification "poor" in this case.[12]

The analyst wishing to determine the difference in sales effectiveness between other classifications must look at coefficient differences. Thus, if the researcher wanted to calculate the estimated difference in expected sales from a good wholesaler and a fair wholesaler, the appropriate difference would be $\hat{\beta}_4 - \hat{\beta}_3 = 20.3 - 9.2 = 11.1$ thousand dollars ($11,100). Similarly, an excellent wholesaler could be expected on the average to sell $\hat{\beta}_5 - \hat{\beta}_4 = 33.3 - 20.3 = 13.0$ thousand dollars ($13,000) more than a good one.

The use of dummy variables indicates that the relationship between sales and the wholesaler efficiency index is not linear as was assumed when the index was introduced as an intervally scaled variable. Instead of an across-the-board increase of $11,500 with each rating change, the respective increases are 9.2 ($9,200) from poor to fair, 11.1 ($11,100) from fair to good, and 13.0 ($13,000) from good to excellent.

---

[11] The data were artificially created employing specified parameter values and a random error term in a linear equation. The parameters were actually $\beta_3 = 2.0$, $\beta_4 = 22.0$; and $\beta_5 = 32.0$.

[12] For a useful discussion of some alternative ways to code dummy variables and the different insights that can be provided by the various alternatives, see Jacob Cohen and Patricia Cohen, *Applied Multiple Regression/Correlation Analysis for the Behavioral Sciences,* 2nd ed. (Hillsdale, N.J.: Lawrence Erlbaum Associates, 1983), pp. 181–222.

Variable Transformations

The use of dummy variables greatly expands the scope of the regression model. They allow the introduction of classificatory and rank-order variables in regression problems. As we have seen, they also allow nonlinear criterion variable/predictor variable relationships to be dealt with. Another technique that expands the obvious scope of the regression model is that of variable transformations.

A **variable transformation** is simply a change in the scale in which the given variable is expressed. Consider the model

$$Y = \alpha X_1^{\beta_1} X_2^{\beta_2} X_3^{\beta_3} \epsilon$$

in which the relationship among the predictors and between the predictors and the error is assumed to be multiplicative. At first glance, it would seem that it would be impossible to estimate the parameters α, β_1, β_2, and β_3 using our normal least-squares procedures. Now consider the model

$$W = \alpha' + \beta_1 Z_1 + \beta_2 Z_2 + \beta_3 Z_3 + \epsilon'$$

This is a linear model, and so it can be fitted by the standard least-squares procedures. But consider the fact that it is exactly equivalent to our multiplicative model if we simply let

$$
\begin{aligned}
W &= \ln Y & Z_2 &= \ln X_2 \\
\alpha' &= \ln \alpha & Z_3 &= \ln X_3 \\
Z_1 &= \ln X_1 & \epsilon' &= \ln \epsilon
\end{aligned}
$$

We have converted a nonlinear model to a linear model using variable transformations. To solve for the parameters of our multiplicative model, we simply (1) take the natural log of Y and each of the Xs, (2) solve the resulting equation by the normal least-squares procedures, (3) take the antilog of α' to derive an estimate of α, and (4) read the values of the β_i since they are the same in both models.

The transformation to natural logarithms involves the transformation of both the criterion and predictor variables. It is also possible to change the scale of either the criterion or predictor variables. Transformations to the exponential and logarithmic are some of the most useful since they serve to relax the constraints imposed by the following assumptions.[13]

- The relationship between the criterion variable and the predictor variables is additive.
- The relationship between the criterion variable and the predictor variables is linear.
- The errors are *homoscedastic* (i.e., are equal to a constant for all values of the predictors).

Dummy variables are one form of transformation, and we have already seen how they allow the treatment of nonlinear relationships.

---

[13]See Ronald E. Frank, "Use of Transformations," *Journal of Marketing Research,* 3 (August 1966), pp. 247–253, for a discussion of these conditions and how the proper transformation can serve to fulfill them. See Leonard Jon Parsons and Piet Vanden Abeele, "Analysis of Sales Call Effectiveness," *Journal of Marketing Research,* 18 (February 1981), pp. 107–113, for an example that uses the log transformation.

Variable transformation

Change in scale in which a variable is expressed.

◆ Summary Comments on Data Analysis

We have now come to the end of our section on data analysis. As we have seen, there are many sophisticated techniques analysts use to determine the meaning of collected data. While the computer has made data analysis much easier, and has provided researchers with many more opportunities for examining various facets of the data, we would be remiss if we did not close this chapter on a note of caution.

In Research Window 19.3 a well-known writer of the pre–computer era points out the hazards inherent in forecasting the future based on data collected in the past. For those of you who will be researchers, or even, simply, users of data, equations and statistical techniques will be important, but no more important than a heavy dose of common sense.

Research Window 19.3

Life on the Mississippi—742 Years from Now

Mark Twain may not have been a statistician, but he knew enough about the tricks numbers can play to write this little spoof for those who would predict "logical" outcomes based on past data.

"In the space of one hundred and seventy-six years the Lower Mississippi has shortened itself two hundred and forty-two miles. This is an average of a trifle over one mile and a third per year. Therefore, any calm person, who is not blind or idiotic, can see that in the Old Oölitic Silurian Period, just a million years ago next November, the Lower Mississippi River was upward of one million three hundred thousand miles long, and stuck out over the Gulf of Mexico like a fishing-rod. And by the same token any person can see that seven hundred and forty-two years from now the Lower Mississippi will be only a mile and three-quarters long, and Cairo and New Orleans will have joined their streets together, and be plodding comfortably along under a single mayor and a mutual board of aldermen. There is something fascinating about science. One gets such wholesale returns of conjecture out of such a trifling investment of fact."

Mark Twain knew about the tricks numbers can play.

Source: UPI/Bettmann Newsphotos.

Source: From *Life on the Mississippi,* p. 156, by Mark Twain.

◆ Summary

Learning Objective 1: Explain the difference between regression and correlation analysis.

Analysts use correlation analysis to measure the *closeness* of the relationship between two or more variables. The technique considers the joint variation of two measures, neither of which is restricted by the experimenter.

Regression analysis refers to the techniques used to derive an *equation* that relates the criterion variable to one or more predictor variables. It considers the frequency distribution of the criterion variable when one or more predictor variables are held fixed at various levels.

Learning Objective 2: List the three assumptions that are made about the error term in the least-squares solution to a regression problem.

There are three simplifying assumptions made about the error term in the least-squares solution:

1. The mean or average value of the disturbance term is zero.
2. The variance of the disturbance term is constant and is independent of the values of the predictor variable.
3. The values of the error term are independent of one another.

Learning Objective 3: Discuss what the Gauss-Markov theorem says about the least-squares estimators of a population parameter.

According to the Gauss-Markov theorem, the least-squares estimators are BLUE, that is, they are the *b*est, *l*inear, *u*nbiased *e*stimators of the true population parameters regardless of the shape of the distribution of the error term.

Learning Objective 4: Define what is meant by the standard error of estimate.

The standard error of estimate is an absolute measure of the lack of fit of the equation to the data.

Learning Objective 5: Specify the relationship that a correlation coefficient is designed to measure.

The correlation coefficient measures the strength of the linear relationship between Y and X.

Learning Objective 6: Discuss the difference between simple regression analysis and multiple-regression analysis.

The basic idea behind multiple-regression analysis is the same as that behind simple regression: to determine the relationship between independent and dependent, that is predictor and criterion, variables. In multiple-regression analysis, however, several predictor variables are used to estimate a single criterion variable.

Learning Objective 7: Explain what is meant by multicollinearity in a multiple-regression problem.

Multicollinearity is said to be present in a multiple-regression problem when the predictor variables are correlated among themselves.

Learning Objective 8: Describe when a partial-regression coefficient is used and what it measures.

If the predictor variables are not correlated among themselves, each partial-regression coefficient indicates the average change in the criterion variable per unit change in the predictor variable in question, holding the other predictor variables constant.

Learning Objective 9: Explain the difference between the coefficient of multiple determination and the coefficient of partial determination.

The coefficient of multiple determination measures the proportion of the variation in the criterion variable accounted for, or "explained," by all the predictor variables, while the coefficient of partial determination measures the relative degree to which a given variable adds to our knowledge of the criterion variable over and above that provided by other predictor variables.

Learning Objective 10: Describe how the use of dummy variables and variable transformations expands the scope of the regression model.

Dummy or binary variables allow the introduction of classificatory or nominally scaled variables in the regression equation, while variable transformations considerably increase the scope of the regression model since they allow certain nonlinear relationships to be considered.

Discussion Questions, Problems, and Projects

1. The Crystallo Bottling Company, which provides glass bottles to various soft drink manufacturers, has the following information pertaining to the number of cases per shipment and the corresponding transportation cost:

Number of Cases per Shipment	Transportation Costs in Dollars
1,500	200
2,200	260
3,500	310
4,300	360
5,800	420
6,500	480
7,300	540
8,200	630
8,500	710
9,800	730

The marketing manager is interested in studying the relationship between the number of cases per shipment and the transportation costs. Your assistance is required in performing a simple regression analysis.

(a) Plot the transportation costs as a function of the number of cases per shipment.
(b) Interpret the scatter diagram.
(c) Calculate the coefficients $\hat{\alpha}$ and $\hat{\beta}$ and develop the regression equation.
(d) What is the interpretation of the coefficient $\hat{\alpha}$ and $\hat{\beta}$?
(e) Calculate the standard error of estimate.
(f) What is the interpretation of the standard error of estimate you calculated?
(g) Compute the t value with $n - 2$ degrees of freedom with the use of the following formula for the square root of the variance of the distribution of β's

$$s_{\hat{\beta}} = \sqrt{\frac{s_{Y/X}^2}{\sum_{i=1}^{10} (X_i - \bar{x})^2}}$$

$$t = \frac{\hat{\beta}_1 - \beta_1}{s_{\hat{\beta}_1}}$$

where β is assumed to be zero under the null hypothesis of no relationship; that is,

$$H_0 : \beta_1 = 0$$
$$H_a : \beta_1 \neq 0$$

(h) What is the tabled t value at a 0.05 significance level?
(i) What can you conclude about the relationship between transportation costs and number of cases shipped?

(j) The marketing manager wants to estimate the transportation costs for 18 cases.
    (i) Use the regression model to derive the average value of Y_0.
    (ii) Provide a confidence interval for the estimate using the following:

$$s_{\hat{Y}/X_{01}}^2 = s_{Y/X_1}^2 \left[\frac{1}{n} + \frac{(X_{01} - \bar{x})^2}{\sum_{i=1}^{10} (X_{i1} - \bar{x})^2} \right]$$

$$\hat{Y}_0 \pm t\, s_{\hat{Y}/X_{01}} =$$

2. The marketing manager of Crystallo Company wanted to determine if there was an association between the size of carton and the transportation cost per shipment. (The company followed a policy of including the same size cartons for any particular shipment.) The information pertaining to size of carton is given below. Refer to the previous question for information on the transportation costs per shipment.
  (a) Calculate the correlation coefficient.
  (b) Interpret the correlation coefficient.
  (c) Calculate the coefficient of determination.
  (d) Interpret the coefficient of determination.

3. The marketing manager of Crystallo Company is considering multiple-regression analysis with the number of cartons per shipment and the size of cartons as predictor variables and transportation costs as the criterion variable (refer to the previous problem). He has devised the following regression equation.

$$\hat{Y} = \hat{\alpha}_{(12)} + \hat{\beta}_{Y1.2}X_1 + \hat{\beta}_{Y2.1}X_2 = -41.44 - 3.95\,X_1 + 24.44\,X_2$$

where X_1 is the number of cartons per shipment and X_2 is the size of the carton.
  (a) Interpret $\hat{\alpha}_{(12)}$, $\hat{\beta}_{Y1.2}$, and $\hat{\beta}_{Y2.1}$.
  (b) Is multiple regression appropriate in this situation? If yes, why? If no, why not?

4. An analyst for a large shoe manufacturer had developed a formal linear regression model to predict sales of its 122 retail stores located in different SMSAs in the United States. The model is as follows:

$$Y_{(123)} = \alpha_{(123)} + \beta_{1.23}X_1 + \beta_{2.13}X_2 + \beta_{3.12}X_3$$

where

    X_1 = population in surrounding area in thousands
    X_2 = marginal propensity to consume
    X_3 = median personal income in surrounding area in thousands of dollars
    Y = sales in thousands of dollars.

Some empirical results were as follows:

Variable	Regression Coefficient	Coefficient Standard Errors ($s_{\beta i}$)
X_1	$\hat{\beta}_{1.23} = 0.49$	0.24
X_2	$\hat{\beta}_{2.13} = -0.40$	95
X_3	$\hat{\beta}_{3.12} = 225$	105
$R^2 = 0.47$	$\hat{\alpha} = -40$	225

  (a) Interpret each of the regression coefficients.
  (b) Are X_1, X_2, and X_3 significant at the 0.05 level? Show your calculations.
  (c) Which independent variable seems to be the most significant predictor?
  (d) Provide an interpretation of the R^2 value.

(e) The marketing research department of the shoe manufacturer wants to include an index that indicates whether the service in each store is poor, fair, or good. The coding scheme is as follows:

$$1 = \text{poor service}$$
$$2 = \text{fair service}$$
$$3 = \text{good service}$$

(i) Indicate how you would transform this index so that it could be included in the model. Be specific.

(ii) Write out the regression model including the preceding transformation.

(iii) Suppose two of the parameters for the index are 4.6 and 10.3. Interpret these values in light of the scheme you adopted.

5. a. List the assumptions underlying regression analysis.
   b. List the possible limitations of regression analysis.
   c. Identify one important practical application of regression analysis for a marketing manager.

6. Refer to the following article: William Qualls, Richard W. Olshavsky and Ronald E. Michaels, "Shortening of the PLC—An Empirical Test," *Journal of Marketing,* 45 (Fall 1981), pp. 76–80.
   a. What regression model have the authors used to derive Figure I of the study? What was the purpose of this model?
   b. Was the regression coefficient found to be significant? What was the level of significance?

7. Refer to the following article: Lawrence A. Crosby and James R. Taylor, "Consumer Satisfaction with Michigan's Container Deposit Law: An Ecological Perspective," *Journal of Marketing,* 46 (Winter 1982), pp. 47–60.
   a. Refer to Table 3 of the study. What does this table indicate?
   b. What does the following footnote indicate: "Unless indicated otherwise, all *rs* are significant at the 95 percent confidence level?" What hypothesis is this a test of?
   c. Which two variables have the highest correlation coefficient?

Suggested Additional Readings

For detailed discussion of regression and correlation analysis, see

John Neter, William Wasserman, and Michael H. Kutner, *Applied Linear Regression Models* (Homewood, Ill.: Richard D. Irwin, 1983).

Thomas H. Wonnacott and Ronald J. Wonnacott, *Regression: A Second Course in Statistics* (New York: John Wiley, 1981).

Jacob Cohen and Patricia Cohen, *Applied Multiple Regression/Correlation Analysis for the Behavioral Sciences,* 2nd ed. (Hillsdale, N.J.: Lawrence Erlbaum Associates, 1983).

Appendix 19A   Nonparametric Measures of Association

Chapter 19 focuses on the product-moment correlation as the measure of association. While the product-moment correlation coefficient was originally developed to deal with continuous variables, it has proven quite robust to scale type and can sometimes handle variables that are ordinal or dichotomous as well as those that are interval.[1] Though widely applicable, it is not universally applicable. This appendix therefore treats some alternate measures of association, namely, the contingency table and coefficient that are appropriate for nominal data and

---

[1]Jum C. Nunnally, *Psychometric Theory,* 2nd ed. (New York: McGraw-Hill, 1978), especially pp. 117–150.

also the Spearman's rank-order correlation coefficient and the coefficient of concordance, which are suited to the analysis of rank-order data.

Contingency Table

One problem researchers often encounter in analyzing nominal data is the independence of variables of classification. In Chapter 17, for example, we examined a number of questions involving the relationship between automobile purchases and family characteristics. At that time, we conducted no statistical tests of significance, thus avoiding the question of whether the results reflected sample aberrations or represented true population conditions. If statistical tests had been run at that time, they would have been primarily of the chi-square contingency-table type, which is ideally suited for investigating the independence of variables in cross classifications.

Consider, for example, a consumer study involving the preferences of families for different sizes of washing machines. *A priori,* it would seem that larger families would be more prone to buy the larger units and smaller families the smaller units. To investigate this question, suppose the manufacturer checked a random sample of those purchasers who returned their warranty cards. Included on the warranty cards was a question on the size of the family. Although not a perfect population for analysis, the manufacturer felt it was good enough for this purpose since some 85 percent of all warranty cards are returned. Furthermore, it was a relatively economical way to proceed, since the data were internal. The study could be carried out by checking a random sample of warranty cards for family size and machine purchased.

A random sample of 300 of these cards provided the data in Table 19A.1. The assignment is to determine if family size affects the size of the machine that is purchased. The null hypothesis is that the variables are independent; the alternate is that they are not. Suppose a significance level of $\alpha = 0.10$ was chosen for the test. To calculate a χ^2 statistic, one needs to generate the expected number of cases likely to fall into each category. *The expected number is generated by assuming that the null hypothesis is indeed true;* that is, that there is no relationship between size of machine purchased and family size. Suppose size of machine purchased is denoted by the variable A and size of family by the variable B and that

$$A_1 = \text{purchase of an 8-lb. load washing machine}$$
$$A_2 = \text{purchase of a 10-lb. load washing machine}$$
$$A_3 = \text{purchase of a 12-lb. load washing machine}$$
$$B_1 = \text{family of one to two members}$$
$$B_2 = \text{family of three to four members}$$
$$B_3 = \text{family of five or more members}$$

If variables A and B are indeed independent, then the probability of occurrence of the event A_1B_1 (a family of one to two members purchased an 8-lb. load machine) is given as the product of the separate probabilities for A_1 and B_1; that is,

$$P(A_1B_1) = P(A_1)P(B_1)$$

by the multiplication law of probabilities for independent events. Now $P(A_1)$ is given by the number of cases possessing the characteristic A_1, n_{A_1}, over the total number of cases n. $P(A_1)$ is thus

$$\frac{n_{A_1}}{n} = \frac{70}{300} = \frac{7}{30}$$

Similarly, $P(B_1)$ is given by the number of cases having the characteristic B_1, n_{B_1}, over the total number of cases, or $P(B_1) = n_{B_1}/n = 40/300 = 2/15$. The joint probability $P(A_1B_1)$ is

$$P(A_1B_1) = P(A_1)P(B_1) = \left(\frac{7}{30}\right)\left(\frac{2}{15}\right) = \frac{7}{225}$$

Table 19A.1   Size of Washing Machine versus Size of Family

Size of Washing Machine Purchased	Size of Family in Members			Total
	1 to 2	3 to 4	5 or more	
8-lb. load	25	37	8	70
10-lb. load	10	62	53	125
12-lb. load	5	41	59	105
Total	40	140	120	300

Given a total of 300 cases, the number expected to fall in the cell A_1B_1, E_{11} is given as the product of the total number of cases and the probability of any one of these cases falling into the A_1B_1 cell, that is,

$$E_{11} = nP(A_1B_1) = 300(7/225) = 9.33$$

Although this is the underlying rationale for generating the expected frequencies, there is an easier computational form. Recall that $P(A_1) = n_{A_1}/n$ and that $P(B_1) = n_{B_1}/n$ and that $P(A_1B_1) = P(A_1)P(B_1)$. The formula for E_{11} upon substitution then reduces to

$$E_{11} = nP(A_1B_1) = nP(A_1)P(B_1)$$
$$= n \frac{n_{A_1}}{n} \frac{n_{B_1}}{n} = \frac{n_{A_1}n_{B_1}}{n}$$
$$= \frac{70 \times 40}{300} = 9.33$$

Thus to generate the expected frequencies for each cell, one needs merely to multiply the marginal frequencies and divide by the total. The remaining expected frequencies, which are calculated in like manner, are entered below the cell diagonals in Table 19A.2. The calculated χ^2 value is thus

$$\chi^2 = \sum_{i=1}^{3} \sum_{j=1}^{3} \frac{[O_{ij} - E_{ij}]^2}{E_{ij}}$$

$$= \frac{(25 - 9.33)^2}{9.33} + \frac{(37 - 32.67)^2}{32.67} + \frac{(8 - 28.00)^2}{28.00}$$

$$+ \frac{(10 - 16.67)^2}{16.67} + \frac{(62 - 58.33)^2}{58.33} + \frac{(53 - 50.00)^2}{50.00}$$

$$+ \frac{(5 - 14.00)^2}{14.00} + \frac{(41 - 49.00)^2}{49.00} + \frac{(59 - 42.00)^2}{42.00}$$

$$= 26.318 + 0.574 + 14.286 + 2.669 + 0.231 + 0.180 + 5.786 + 1.306 + 6.881$$

$$= 58.231$$

where O_{ij} and E_{ij}, respectively, denote the actual number and expected number of observations that fall in the ij cell. Now the expected frequencies in any row add to the marginal total. This must be true because of the way the expected frequencies were calculated. Thus, as soon as we know any two expected frequencies in a row, say, 9.33 and 32.67 in Row A_1, for example, the third expected frequency is fixed, because the three must add to the marginal total. This means that there are only $(c - 1)$ degrees of freedom in a row, where c is the number of columns. A similar argument applies to the columns; that is, there are $r - 1$ degrees of

Table 19A.2   Size of Washing Machine versus Size of Family: Observed and Expected Frequencies

Size of Washing Machine Purchased	Size of Family in Members			Total
	B_1 1 to 2	B_2 3 to 4	B_3 5 or more	
A_1—8-lb. load	25 9.33	37 32.67	8 28.00	70
A_2—10-lb. load	10 16.67	62 58.33	53 50.00	125
A_3—12-lb. load	5 14.00	41 49.00	59 42.00	105
Total	40	140	120	300

freedom per column, where r is the number of rows. The degrees of freedom in total in a two-way contingency table are thus given by

$$v = (r - 1)(c - 1)$$

In our problem $v = (3 - 1)(3 - 1) = 4$. Using our assumed $\alpha = 0.10$, the tabled critical value of χ^2 for four degrees of freedom is 7.78 (see Table 2 in the appendix). Computed $\chi^2 = 58.231$ thus falls in the critical region. The null hypothesis of independence is rejected. Family size is shown to be a factor in determining size of washing machine purchased.

In one form or another, the chi-square test is probably the most widely used test in marketing research, and the serious student is well advised to become familiar with its requirements. Table 19A.3 summarizes them.

Contingency Coefficient

While the χ^2 contingency-table test indicates whether two variables are independent, it does not measure the strength of association when they are dependent. The contingency coefficient can be used for this latter purpose. Since the contingency coefficient is directly related to the χ^2 test, it can be generated by the researcher with relatively little additional computational effort. The formula for the contingency coefficient, call it C, is

$$C = \sqrt{\frac{\chi^2}{n + \chi^2}}$$

where n is the sample size and χ^2 is calculated in the normal way.

Recall that calculated χ^2 for the data in Table 19A.1 was 58.23, and that since the calculated value was larger than the critical tabled value, the null hypothesis of independence was rejected. While the conclusion that naturally follows—that family size affects the size of washing machine purchased—is an interesting finding, it is only part of the story. Although the variables are dependent, what is the strength of the association between them? The contingency coefficient helps answer this question. The contingency coefficient is

$$C = \sqrt{\frac{58.23}{300 + 58.23}} = 0.403$$

Table 19A.3   Requirements for the Chi-Square Test

1. The test deals with frequencies. Percentage values need to be converted to counts of the number of cases in each cell.[a]

2. The chi-square distribution, although continuous, is being used to approximate the distribution of a discrete variable. This results in the computed value being proportionately inflated if too many of the expected frequencies are small. It is generally agreed that only a few cells (less than 20 percent) should be permitted to have expected frequencies less than 5, and none should have expected frequencies less than 1.[b] Categories may be meaningfully combined to conform to this rule.

3. Multiple answers per respondent should not be analyzed with chi-square contingency-table analysis in that the normal tabled critical values of the chi-square statistic for a specified alpha error no longer apply when more than one cross-tabulation analysis is conducted with the same data. If multiple answers per respondent are to be analyzed, special tables should be used for testing the statistical significance of the results.[c]

4. Each observation should be independent of the others. The chi-square test would not be appropriate, for example, for analyzing observations on the same individuals in a pretest–post-test experiment.[d]

[a]The test can also be used with proportions, but this type of application is much rarer. For an example, see George W. Snedecor and William G. Cochran, *Statistical Methods,* 6th ed. (Ames, Iowa: Iowa State University Press, 1967), pp. 240–242.

[b]Snedecor and Cochran, *Statistical Methods,* p. 235, suggest the χ^2 test is accurate enough if only the latter condition is satisfied, and they recommend combining classes only to ensure cell sizes of at least 1. When there is only one degree of freedom, Yates' correction for continuity can be applied, which improves the test and removes cell size requirements. See F. Yates, "Contingency Tables Involving Small Numbers and the χ^2 Test," *Journal of the Royal Statistical Society,* 1, pp. 217–235.

[c]See C. Mitchell Dayton and William D. Schafer, "Extended Tables of t and Chi Square for Bonferroni Tests with Unequal Error Allocation," *Journal of the American Statistical Association,* 68 (March 1973), pp. 78–83.

[d]When the observations are related, rather than being independent, the McNemar or Cochran Q tests can be employed when the data are nominal. These tests are discussed in a number of nonparametric statistics books. See, for example, Leonard A. Marascuilo and Maryellen McSweeney, *Nonparametric and Distribution-Free Methods for the Social Sciences* (Belmont, Calif.: Brooks/Cole, 1977); or Wayne W. Daniel, *Applied Nonparametric Statistics* (Boston: Houghton Mifflin, 1978).

Does this value indicate strong or weak association between the variables? We cannot say without comparing the calculated value against its limits. When there is no association between the variables, the contingency coefficient will be zero. Unfortunately though, the contingency coefficient does not possess the other attractive property of the Pearsonian product-moment correlation coefficient of being equal to 1 when the variables are completely dependent or perfectly correlated. Rather, its upper limit is a function of the number of categories. When the number of categories is the same for each variable, that is, when the number of rows r equals the number of columns c, the upper limit on the contingency coefficient for two perfectly correlated variables is

$$\sqrt{(r-1)/r}$$

In the example at hand, $r = c = 3$, and thus the upper limit for the contingency coefficient is

$$\sqrt{\frac{2}{3}} = 0.816$$

The calculated value is approximately halfway between the limits of zero for no association and 0.816 for perfect association, suggesting there is moderate association between size of family and size of washing machine purchased.

Spearman's Rank-Order Correlation Coefficient

The Spearman correlation coefficient, denoted r_s, is one of the best known coefficients of association for rank-order data. The coefficient is appropriate when there are two variables

Table 19A.4 Distributor Performance

Distributor	Service Ranking X_i	Overall Performance Ranking Y_i	Ranking Difference $d_i = X_i - Y_i$	Difference Squared d_i^2
1	6	8	−2	4
2	2	4	+2	4
3	13	12	+1	1
4	1	2	−1	1
5	7	10	−3	9
6	4	5	−1	1
7	11	9	+2	4
8	15	13	+2	4
9	3	1	+2	4
10	9	6	+3	9
11	12	14	−2	4
12	5	3	+2	4
13	14	15	−1	1
14	8	7	+1	1
15	10	11	−1	1

$$\sum_{i=1}^{15} d_i^2 = 52$$

per object, both of which are measured on an ordinal scale so that the objects may be ranked in two ordered series.[2]

Suppose, for instance, that a company wishes to determine whether there was any association between the overall performance of a distributor and the distributor's level of service. Again, there are many measures of overall performance: sales, market share, sales growth, profit, and so on. The company in our example feels that no single measure adequately defines distributor performance, but that overall performance is a composite of all of these measures. Thus, the marketing research department is assigned the task of developing an index of performance that effectively incorporates all of these characteristics. The department is also assigned the responsibility of evaluating each distributor in terms of the service he or she provides. This evaluation is to be based on customer complaints, customer compliments, service turnaround records, and so on. The research department feels that the indices it develops to measure these characteristics could be employed to rank-order the distributors with respect to overall performance and service.

Table 19A.4 contains the ranks of the company's fifteen distributors with respect to each of the performance criteria. One way to determine whether there is any association between service and overall performance would be to look at the differences in ranks based on each of the two variables. Let X_i be the rank of the ith distributor with respect to service and Y_i be the rank of the ith distributor with regard to overall performance, and let $d_i = X_i - Y_i$ be

---

[2]The Spearman rank correlation coefficient is a shortcut version of the product-moment correlation coefficient, in that both coefficients produce the same estimates of the strength of association between two sets of ranks. The rank correlation coefficient is easy to conceptualize and calculate, so it is often used when the data are ranked. See Nunnally, *Psychometric Theory,* pp. 134–135.

the difference in rankings for the ith distributor. Now if the rankings on the two variables are exactly the same, each d_i will be zero. If there is some discrepancy in ranks, some of the d_is will not be zero. Further, the greater the discrepancy, the larger will be some of the d_is. Therefore, one way of looking at the association between the variables would be to examine the sum of the d_is. The difficulty with this measure is that some of the negative d_is would cancel some of the positive ones. To circumvent this difficulty, the differences are squared in calculating the Spearman rank-order correlation coefficient. The calculation formula is as follows:[3]

$$r_s = 1 - \frac{6 \sum_{i=1}^{n} d_i^2}{n(n^2 - 1)}$$

in the example at hand,

$$\sum_{i=1}^{15} d_i^2 = 52$$

and

$$r_s = 1 - \frac{6(52)}{15(15^2 - 1)} = 1 - \frac{312}{3,360} = 0.907$$

Now the null hypothesis for the example would be that there is no association between service level and overall distributor performance, while the alternate hypothesis would suggest there is a relationship. The null hypothesis that $r_s = 0$ can be tested by referring directly to tables of critical values of r_s or, when the number of sample objects is greater than 10, by calculating the t statistic

$$t = r_s \sqrt{\frac{n - 2}{1 - r_s^2}}$$

which is referred to a t table for $v = n - 2$ degrees of freedom. Calculated t is

$$t = 0.907 \sqrt{\frac{15 - 2}{1 - (0.907)^2}} = 7.77$$

while critical t for $\alpha = 0.05$ and $v = 13$ degrees of freedom is 2.16. Calculated t exceeds critical t, and the null hypothesis of no relationship is rejected. Overall distributor performance is related to service level. The upper limit for the Spearman rank-order correlation coefficient is 1, since if there were perfect agreement in the ranks, $\sum_{i=1}^{n} d_i^2$ would be zero. Thus, the relationship is significant and relatively strong.

Coefficient of Concordance

So far we have been concerned with the correlation between *two* sets of rankings of n objects. There has been an X and Y measure in the form of ranks for each object. There will be cases in which we wish to analyze the association among three or more rankings of n objects or individuals. When there are k sets of rankings, Kendall's *coefficient of concordance, W,* can be employed to examine the association among the k variables.

---

[3]See Leonard A. Marascuilo and Maryellen McSweeney, *Nonparametric and Distribution-Free Methods for the Social Sciences* (Belmont, Calif.: Brooks/Cole, 1977), pp. 429–439, for the development of the logic underlying the computational formula. An alternate measure of rank correlation is provided by Kendall's tau coefficient. See M. G. Kendall, *Rank Correlation Methods* (London: Griffin, 1948), pp. 47–48, for a discussion of the rationale behind the tau coefficient; and Edgar Pessemier and Moshe Handelsman, "Temporal Variety in Consumer Behavior," *Journal of Marketing Research,* 21 (November 1984), pp. 435–444, for a marketing example that uses it.

Table 19A.5   Branch Manager Rankings

| | Rank Advocated by | | | |
Branch Manager	Vice-President Marketing	General Sales Manager	Marketing Research Department	Sum of Ranks R_i
A	4	4	5	13
B	3	2	2	7
C	9	10	10	29
D	10	9	9	28
E	2	3	3	8
F	1	1	1	3
G	6	5	4	15
H	8	7	7	22
I	5	6	6	17
J	7	8	8	23

One particularly important use of the coefficient of concordance is in examining interjudge reliability. Consider a computer equipment manufacturer interested in evaluating its domestic sales branch managers. Many criteria could be used: sales of the branch office, sales in relation to the branch's potential, sales growth, and sales representative turnover are just a few. Assume that the company feels that different executives in the company would place different emphasis on the various criteria and that a consensus with respect to how the criteria should be weighted would be hard to achieve. The company therefore decides that the vice-president in charge of marketing, the general sales manager, and the marketing research department should all attempt to rank the ten branch managers from best to worst and that these rankings will be examined to determine whether there is agreement among them (see Table 19A.5).

The right-hand column of Table 19A.5 contains the sum of ranks assigned to each branch manager. Now if there were perfect agreement among the three rankings, the sum of ranks, R_i, for the top-rated branch manager would be $1 + 1 + 1 = k$, where $k = 3$. The second-rated branch manager would have sum of ranks $2 + 2 + 2 = 2k$, and the nth-rated branch manager would have the sum of ranks $n + n + n = nk$. Accordingly, when there is perfect agreement among the k sets of rankings, the R_i would be $k, 2k, 3k, \ldots, nk$. If there is little agreement among the k ratings, the R_i would be approximately equal. Thus, the degree of agreement among the k rankings could be measured by the variance of the n sums of ranks; the greater the agreement, the larger would be the variance in the n sums.

The coefficient of concordance, W, is a function of the variance in the sums of ranks. It is calculated in the following way. First, the sum of the R_i for each of the n rows is determined. Second, the average R_i, $\bar{R}$, is calculated by dividing the sum of the R_i by the number of objects. Third, the sum of the squared deviations is determined; call this quantity s, where

$$s = \sum_{i=1}^{n} (R_i - \bar{R})^2$$

The coefficient of concordance is then computed as

$$W = \frac{s}{\frac{1}{12}k^2(n^3 - n)}$$

The denominator of the coefficient represents the maximum possible variation in sums of ranks if there were perfect agreement in the rankings. The numerator, of course, reflects the actual variation in ranks. The larger the ratio, the greater is the agreement among the evaluations.

$$\bar{R} = \frac{\sum\limits_{i=1}^{n} R_i}{n} = \frac{13 + 7 + \ldots + 23}{10} = \frac{165}{10} = 16.5$$

$$s = (13 - 16.5)^2 + (7 - 16.5)^2 + \ldots + (23 - 16.5)^2 = 720.5$$

and

$$\frac{1}{12} k^2 (n^3 - n) = \frac{1}{12} (3)^2 (10^3 - 10) = 742.5$$

Thus

$$W = \frac{720.5}{742.5} = 0.970$$

The significance of W can be examined by using special tables when the number of objects being ranked is small, in particular, when $n \leq 7$. When there are more than seven objects, the coefficient of concordance is approximately chi-square distributed where $\chi^2 = k(n - 1)$ W with $v = n - 1$ degrees of freedom. The null hypothesis is that there is no agreement among the rankings, while the alternate hypothesis is that there is some agreement. For an assumed $\alpha = 0.05$, critical χ^2 for $v = n - 1 = 9$ degrees of freedom is 16.92, while calculated χ^2 is

$$\chi^2 = k(n - 1) W = 3 (9)(0.970) = 26.2$$

Calculated χ^2 exceeds critical χ^2, and the null hypothesis of no agreement is rejected, because there indeed is agreement. Further, the agreement is good, as is evidenced by the calculated coefficient of concordance. The limits of W are zero with no agreement and 1 with perfect agreement among the ranks. The calculated value of W of 0.970 suggests that while the agreement in the ranks is not perfect, it is certainly good. The marketing vice-president, the general sales manager, and the marketing research department are applying essentially the same standards in ranking the branch managers.

Kendall has suggested that the best estimate of the true ranking of n objects is provided by the order of the various sums of ranks, R_i, when W is significant.[4] Thus, the best estimate of the true ranking of the sales managers is that F is doing the best job, B the next best job, and that C is doing the poorest job.

---

[4]Kendall, *Rank Correlation Methods,* p. 87.

Part Six   Research Project

The sixth stage in the research process is to analyze and interpret the data. All the earlier steps in the research process were undertaken to support this search for meaning. Most data analysis begins with the preliminary steps of editing, coding, and tabulating the data. The results are often analyzed further to determine if the differences are statistically significant, or if there is any correlation between the variables.

CARA researchers had begun their study with two objectives:

1. Identify business decision-makers' attitudes toward the advertising media of newspaper, radio, and television.
2. Identify business decision-makers' attitudes toward the advertising sales representatives of those media.

In analyzing the data collected from the questionnaires, researchers calculated the percentage of respondents who agreed that their sales representatives possessed the attributes listed on the questionnaire and who agreed that the categories of advertising media were characterized by the listed items. They calculated this by determining what proportion of the total number of respondents checked the "strongly agree" or "agree" category for each item.

Business Decision-Makers' Attitudes toward Advertising Media

CARA researchers found that the characteristics of television advertising that garnered the highest percentage of agreement were (1) that the ads reach many people (86 percent), (2) that they build up recognition (80 percent), and (3) that people pay attention (67 percent). The highest categories for radio advertising were that (1) the ads reach many people (73 percent), (2) that they build up recognition (67 percent), and (3) that they are easy to buy (54 percent). Respondents agreed that (1) newspaper ads were easy to monitor (77 percent), (2) built up recognition (70 percent), (3) reached many people (70 percent), and (4) were easy to buy (70 percent). The items on which respondents expressed the lowest percentage of agreement for television advertising were that (1) few repeats were necessary (20 percent) and (2) the items were not costly (10 percent). For radio advertising, the items of lowest agreement were that (1) the ads were not costly (34 percent) and that (2) few repeats were necessary (17 percent). For newspaper advertising, the lowest categories were that (1) the ads are creative (27 percent) and (2) few repeats are necessary (27 percent).

Business Decision-Makers' Attitudes toward Advertising Sales Representatives

When analyzing the data, CARA researchers found that 68, 62, and 62 percent of respondents felt their television sales representatives were cooperative, knowledgeable, and available, respectively, and these represented the items with the highest percentage of agreement in this category. For radio representatives, the highest percentage of agreement was found concerning their cooperation (72 percent), ability to quickly place ads (68 percent), and availability (64 percent). The highest rated items for newspaper representatives were cooperation (73 percent), the ability to place ads quickly (64 percent), and reliability (62 percent). The items with the lowest percent of agreement for television sales representatives were creativity (42 percent), awareness of client's customers (40 percent), and follow-through (37 percent). For radio representatives, the lowest items were follow-through (35 percent), awareness of client's customers (43 percent), and knowledgeability (28 percent). Follow-through, awareness, and knowledgeability were also the lowest items for newspaper representatives, with, respectively, 33 percent, 30 percent, and 29 percent of respondents agreeing.

Importance Scales

A chi-square test of independence was used to test whether respondents differed on the number of times they checked a given attribute or characteristic and to see whether these frequencies differed from the theoretical (expected) frequencies. Comparisons of the observed and expected frequencies for each individual attribute of sales representatives and characteristic of advertising media indicated that no significant differences existed between respondents who were decision makers and respondents who were not. The same type of comparison also revealed no significant differences between respondents who were owners and/or managers and those who were not.

A chi-square goodness-of-fit test was used to assess whether respondents ascribed different values to the attributes and characteristics listed in the sales-representatives and advertising-media sections of the study. Significant differences were found in the observed and expected frequencies of the attributes of sales representatives (see Table 1). Not all attributes were rated equally important. Figure 1 portrays graphically the number of times each attribute was chosen as one of the three most important attributes. The most important attributes were creativity, knowledge about the client's business, concern about particular

Table 1   Chi-Square Test: Characteristics of Advertising

Item No.	1	2	3	4	5	6	7	8	9	10	11	12
Observed Frequencies	91	54	23	73	80	11	17	18	75	13	48	23

Expected Frequencies   All cells = 43.83 $df = 11$ $\chi^2 = 222.67$[a]

[a]Statistically significant, $p < .001$

Figure 1   Number of Times an Attribute Was Chosen as One of the Three Most Important

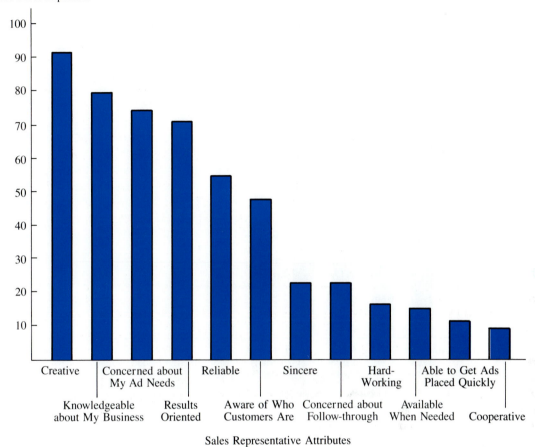

Number of Times As One of
the Three Most Important

Sales Representative Attributes

Table 2   Chi-Square Test: Attributes of Sales Representatives

Item No.	1	2	3	4	5	6	7	8	9	10	11	12
Observed Frequencies	75	98	28	122	15	8	47	99	17	1	5	23

Expected Frequencies   All cells = 43.83 $df = 1$ $\chi^2 = 444.35$[a]

[a]Statistically significant, $p < .001$

advertising needs, and an orientation toward results. The least important attributes were sincerity, concern about follow-through, hardworking, availability, ability to place ads quickly, and cooperation.

Significant differences were also noted when the observed and expected frequencies of the characteristics of advertising media were tested (see Table 2).

Figure 2   Number of Times a Characteristic Was Chosen as One of the Three Most Important

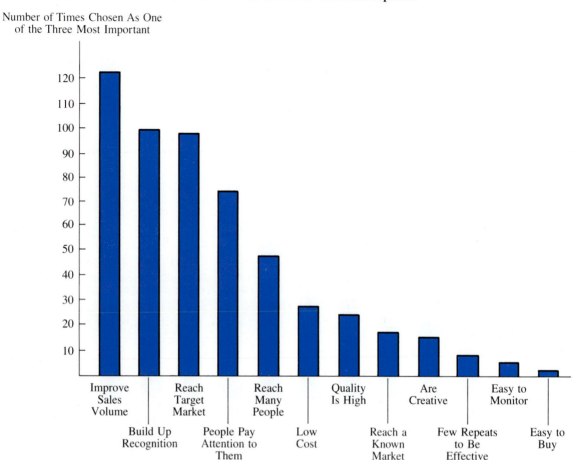

Number of Times Chosen As One
of the Three Most Important

The hypothesis that each of the characteristics was of equal importance was rejected. Figure 2 displays the observed frequencies associated with each characteristic. The most important characteristics were whether the ads improved sales volume, whether they built recognition of the business, whether they were costly, and whether people paid attention to them. The least important characteristics were whether the ads were of high quality, whether there was evidence that the ads reached a known market, whether they were creative, whether repetition was necessary for effectiveness, whether they were easy to monitor, and whether the ad-buying process was difficult.

Cases to Part Six

Case 6.1   University of Wisconsin-Extension: Engineering Management Program[1]

Introduction

The University of Wisconsin-Extension is the outreach campus of the University of Wisconsin System. It is responsible for offering high-quality continuing education to adults in a variety of professions from around the country.

The Management Institute is one of the many specialized departments within the UW-Extension. It conducts programs aimed at providing education and training in at least a dozen areas of business management and not-for-profit management. Extension Engineering is another of the specialized departments. Since 1901, it has grown from its summer school origins into one of the finest organizations of its kind. Extension Engineering has offered institutes and short courses annually since 1949. It has a dedicated full-time faculty of engineering and science professors, most of whom have extensive business and industrial experience.

Opportunity for an Engineering Management Program

In the spring of 1984, William Nitzke, the director of Extension Engineering client services, set out to explore the possibility of establishing a certificate program in engineering management. He recognized this opportunity after speaking with attendees of Extension Engineering seminars and reading several articles that made reference to the need for management training for engineers. Mr. Nitzke believed it would be feasible to develop a coordinated curriculum in engineering management by combining the strengths of the Management Institute and Extension Engineering. This new program would include a comprehensive series of management courses specifically created to provide engineers with skills to better meet the challenges of management positions.

Background   More than half of the chief executives in major U.S. companies are engineers, and most of the middle management positions are filled by engineers.[2] Moreover, the American Association of Engineering Societies reports that about two-thirds of all engineers spend two-thirds of their careers in supervisory or management positions.[3] Yet, the crowded engineering curricula at major colleges and universities allow little room for courses that prepare engineers for the types of problems they will have to face as managers. Thus, many engineers, as they evolve in their careers, find themselves promoted into management positions without formal training and unprepared to deal with a quite different set of challenges. One estimate suggests that nearly a million engineering supervisors and managers are currently not well prepared for their positions.[4]

Major corporations throughout the United States are becoming aware that their technically capable engineers are inadequately trained to handle the management-related problems they confront. As a result, the efficiencies of the corporations are affected, and the full potential of the engineers as managers is not realized.

The Management Institute of the UW-Extension does provide programs for the nonmanagement manager. However, neither Extension Engineering nor the Management Institute offers a coordinated or comprehensive series of programs specifically designed for engineers or similar professions. Further,

---

[1]The contributions of Maria Papas Heide to the development of this case are gratefully acknowledged.

[2]*Management for Engineers,* University of Kentucky and University of Missouri Rolle joint sponsorship, October 5, 1983.

[3]Merrit A. Williamson, "Engineering Schools Should Teach Management Skills," *Professional Engineer,* 53 (Summer 1983), pp. 11–14.

[4]*Ibid.*

according to secondary data and direct client inquiry, few continuing education opportunities presently exist on a national level for engineers to gain specialized management training. The Extension Engineering department consequently decided it would attempt to establish itself and the Management Institute as a leading-edge provider of professional development programs in engineering management by being one of the first continuing education institutes to offer a certificate program in Engineering Management.

The original conceptualization of the certificate program held that engineers would be granted a certificate only after successful completion of ten to twelve seminars from the total set available. Each seminar was to run three to five days. About five to six of these seminars would be required and the other five to six would be electives.

A study was undertaken to discover the degree of interest in this type of specialized management training among engineers who had previously attended Extension Engineering seminars. The thought was that the original conceptualization could be modified easily enough depending on the findings from the study.

More specifically, the research was to address the following specific issues:

1. The overall general interest in an engineering management program offered by the UW-Extension.

2. The appeal of earning a certificate in contrast to taking selected seminars on an "as needed" basis.

3. The preferred design of a certificate engineering management program with respect to schedules of attendance, availability of correspondence seminars, and years to complete the certificate requirements.

4. The type of seminar topics that should comprise the certificate engineering management curriculum.

Research Method and Results The study had several stages. In the first preliminary stage, letters were sent to 212 recent attendees of UW-Extension engineering seminars, requesting them to participate in a telephone interview regarding the proposed engineering management program. Reply postcards were received from 100 of the attendees, providing a response rate of 47 percent. The respondents fit into the following categories:

Percentage

38	Agreed to participate in telephone interview.
49	Did not wish to participate in the telephone interview but were willing to complete a written questionnaire and/or were interested in receiving information on the program when it was developed.
13	Were not interested in an Engineering Management program.
100	

The respondents contacted for the telephone interviews were very helpful in designing the written questionnaire, which was subsequently pretested on attendees of a current Extension Engineering seminar. After incorporating the changes suggested from the pretest, a final version of the written questionnaire was mailed to 2,000 randomly selected participants of Extension Engineering seminars within the past two years. A second mailing of the questionnaire to the same 2,000 respondents followed two weeks after the first mailing. The questionnaires for 123 of the names on the mailing list were returned as undeliverable. A total of 502 usable surveys, providing a response rate of 27 percent, were returned from the first and second mailings.

In the second mailing, a reply postcard was included along with the questionnaire. The postcard was provided as an inducement for those contacted who were unwilling to complete an entire questionnaire to at least return a postcard answering the critical question regarding their interest in an Engineering Management program. One hundred ninety-one (191) usable postcards were returned. Including both the surveys and the postcards in which the single critical question regarding interest was answered, the response rate was 35 percent. It was found that 69 percent of all the respondents were interested in a program offering management seminars specifically designed for engineers.

One of the open-ended questions was, "What are the three most important management-related problems you (or the engineers you supervise) face at work?" The question was designed to gather some insights into the most common areas of management-related difficulties faced by all types of engineers. The question also specifically addresses the fourth research objective listed earlier: to determine the type of seminar topics that should comprise the certificate engineering management curriculum. A representative sample of the responses provided by the engineers to this question is listed in Table 1.

Table 1   Sample of Verbatim Responses Regarding the Most Important Management-Related Problems Engineers Face

1. Increasing productivity
2. Management/union relationships
3. Management does not relate to employees
4. Quality of job performed
5. Dealing with changing priorities
6. Human relations
7. Client/public interactions and manipulation
8. Quality control of projects
9. Getting bogged down on minor items and losing sight of the big picture
10. Keeping employees happy
11. Communicating technical items to nontechnical persons
12. Utilization of time
13. The lack of ability of some to see the big picture
14. Motivation of subordinates to achieve consistent level of performance
15. Quality of workmanship
16. Obtaining appropriate information on a timely basis
17. Contract administration
18. Communications between scattered segments of company
19. Contractor performance
20. Designing job to be motivating
21. Effective sharing of information
22. Managing employees for maximum productivity
23. More efficient use of time
24. Management of information related to many projects in progress simultaneously
25. Personnel management
26. Communicating with other divisions of the company
27. Peer communications
28. Motivating those I supervise
29. Lack of defined career plan
30. Ability to communicate in nonengineering terms
31. Handling below-standard employees with union ties
32. Long-term motivation
33. Data exchange
34. Time constraints
35. Motivation of subordinates
36. Getting the most productivity out of subordinates
37. Information exchange with other departments
38. Cope with upcoming computers
39. Salary management
40. Understanding of contract management
41. Sometimes lack of enthusiasm
42. Correspondence
43. Determining accurate fee estimates
44. Evaluation/selection of "best" applicant for position
45. Satisfying the client

46. Problem identification and solving
47. Bureaucracy
48. Building confidence
49. Market entry/penetration
50. Timely responses from other departments
51. Bolstering morale
52. Lack of salary increases
53. Learning computer management tools
54. Holding effective meetings
55. Results tracking
56. Contract compliance
57. Interface with other project groups
58. Understanding and setting goals
59. Making sales contacts
60. Gaining recognition and promotion for qualified people
61. Conveying engineering problems to nontechnical management
62. Effective technical writing
63. Cost reduction
64. Follow-through on projects
65. Personal development with respect to career
66. Priority rank of assignments
67. Keeping good relationship with employees
68. Improving work habits
69. Figuring of project costs
70. Researching and compiling information to generate realistic cost proposal
71. Interdepartmental coordination of work efforts
72. Low productivity
73. Seeing the forest through the trees
74. Getting time to do my own work while supervising other workers
75. Dealing with hostile public
76. Lack of devotion of employees
77. Accomplish the volume of work in the given time
78. Skill in making sound management decisions
79. Politics with the company (how they affect decisions)
80. Estimating time to perform work
81. Budget control and forecasting
82. In-house cost estimating/tracking
83. Purchasing policies
84. Interpersonal relations
85. Scheduling
86. Motivating others to contribute as a team toward a project goal
87. Database optimization and report use
88. Lack of supervisory training
89. Estimating engineering man hours required
90. Knowing what the boss really wants

continued

Table 1   *continued*

91. Meeting mandated deadlines
92. Motivating the people who work under you to try to achieve goals set
93. Upward communication
94. Business planning (growth projections, marketing plans, etc.)
95. Lack of initiative and curiosity
96. Understanding other people's work-related problems
97. Communications with upper management
98. Discipline (self and principles of application)
99. Financial management of firm
100. Time management
101. Work load distribution
102. Unions
103. System bureaucracy
104. Sales and marketing of services
105. Work appropriation
106. Performance evaluation
107. Keeping employees interested, enthusiastic, and committed to job
108. Salary adjustments
109. Scheduling individual items in a project so project is completed on time
110. Information collection and dissemination
111. Project management—getting a project to run smoothly
112. Developing people
113. Task prioritization
114. Performance/salary structure relationship
115. Engineer performance review
116. Selling ideas
117. Politics
118. Effective presentation of the results
119. Cost analysis/control
120. Monitoring jobs in progress
121. Effective communications with associates
122. Providing opportunities for advancement
123. The inability to rate people properly
124. Achieving desired end results
125. Making effective use of computer-based systems
126. Training
127. Lack of coordination of effort
128. Keeping projects within budget
129. Reducing duplication of effort
130. Cost awareness
131. Conveying concise direct ideas to engineers in written form
132. Inefficient budgeting and financial expertise
133. Not getting continual feedback on my performance— feel like a machine expected to do a task
134. Public speaking
135. Distribution of assignments

136. Transfer of knowledge
137. Meeting budgets
138. Correcting those I supervise
139. Written communication
140. Establishing priorities
141. Management at meetings
142. Decision making
143. Application of appropriate disciplinary actions
144. Long-range planning
145. Conducting effective presentations
146. Creating and controlling project budgets
147. Employee handling
148. Making the right decision based on facts
149. Cross training in other departments
150. Manpower projection
151. Financial control
152. Work flow between departments
153. Getting ideas across
154. Distribution and best use of manpower
155. Communications
156. Management perception of engineers as people vs. tools
157. Commitment and performance
158. Rating of subordinates
159. Convincing top management of your ideas
160. Preparation and management of budgets
161. Managing people
162. Manpower allotment
163. Meeting schedules that change rapidly
164. Evaluation of employees
165. Failure of those in management positions to take control
166. To communicate more effectively
167. Clear division of responsibility between groups
168. Negotiating
169. Documenting
170. Conducting effective meetings
171. Keeping projects on schedule
172. Project administration
173. Understanding financial management
174. Understanding leadership roles
175. Keeping a project within the cost restrictions
176. Delegation of authority as well as responsibility
177. Lack of honest constructive performance appraisal
178. Hiring/interviewing
179. Project work staffing
180. Counseling employees
181. Controlling employees
182. Supervisor does not aid me as he might in helping to pursue and achieve goals set down in annual performance review

Questions

1. Establish what you believe would be a relatively exhaustive and useful set of codes that could be used to code the responses to the question and to answer the fourth objective for the study.

2. Use your *a priori* codes to code the verbatim responses listed in Table 1. Establish additional codes if needed to account for unanticipated categories of responses.

3. Summarize what the sample of data suggests about the problems faced by the engineers who responded to this survey. Recommend the types of seminars that should be included in the engineering management curriculum.

Case 6.2 WCOL-TV[1]

WCOL-TV is the local affiliate of the CBS network in Columbus, Ohio. The station is managed by Maurice Edward, who in 1986 commissioned an audience viewership study among the staff and students at Ohio State University. The study was done in November 1986 so as to coincide with the Nielsen and Arbitron ratings. The study was undertaken since these services, because of the transient nature of this community, did not include the university community in their viewership ratings of local news programs.

Edward believed that WCOL-TV had a much higher market share with its local news than either the ABC or NBC affiliates, particularly among university staff and students, and he commissioned the study to either support or refute this conjecture. If it was true, it would provide one more weapon in the station's arsenal when it came to selling advertising time. At the same time he wished to determine the features of each network's local news broadcast that were liked and disliked, the channel switching that occurred between the programs broadcast immediately prior to the 6:00 P.M. local news and during the local news, and the channel switching that occurred between the 6:00 P.M. news and the 11:00 P.M. news.

Research Method and Results

The self-administered questionnaire was developed by the owner and founder of MEC Research Agency, Mary Elizabeth Crosby, to address Edward's concerns. It was pretested on a judgment sample of staff and students. Other than rewording of some of the Likert-type statements regarding features, the questionnaire developed by the agency proved satisfactory. The final questionnaire was subsequently mailed to a sample of faculty, staff, and students selected from the staff-student directory. The study team believed that this directory provided a reasonably good sampling frame, as it was published soon after fall registration.

The directory is organized into two parts, one listing faculty and staff and the other students; 79 percent of the listings are students and 21 percent faculty and staff. In order to select the desired sample of 800, a random start was generated and that name and every eightieth name thereafter was used. This produced a sample of 170 staff and 630 students. Of the 800 questionnaires sent with self-addressed stamped return envelopes, 385 were returned.

The Likert-type statements on the questionnaire were coded 1 through 5, with 5 assigned to the "strongly agree" response category. The means and standard deviations of the ratings for each of the

---

[1]The location and channels for this case are disguised for proprietary reasons at the request of the sponsor.

Table 1   Mean Scores and Standard Deviations of Likert Statements Regarding Features

Statement	WCOL-TV Channel 12	WRXY-TV Channel 4	WKLM-TV Channel 2
1. Newscasts cover topics of viewer concern.	3.698(.7825)	3.886(.6402)	3.727(.7887)
2. Pace of newscast is slow.	3.294(1.0203)	3.365(1.0054)	3.273(.9684)
3. Weather reports are timely.	3.560(.9788)	3.515(.9483)	3.870(.9914)
4. News team members take their work seriously and achieve credibility.	3.520(.9988)	3.788(.8323)	3.896(.7360)
5. Sports stories are up to date.	3.535(.7432)	3.743(.7075)	3.787(.7221)
6. Personalities frequently insert opinionated statements.	3.040(.9661)	3.154(.9929)	3.250(1.0344)
7. Friendliness of the personalities is evident.	3.770(.8501)	3.738(.8962)	3.724(.7933)
8. Weather report is not clear and understandable.	3.872(.8228)	3.721(.9395)	3.895(1.1025)
9. Newscasters and individuals interviewed are identified.	3.952(.6261)	3.976(.6982)	3.842(.6938)
10. Fastbreaking stories are given major importance in the newscast.	3.654(.8006)	3.721(.7563)	3.645(.8900)
11. Personalities are neatly dressed and have a well-groomed appearance.	3.866(.6565)	4.029(.6496)	4.000(.7297)
12. Field reports from the location of the news event are rare.	3.632(.9117)	3.743(.9202)	3.627(.7671)
13. Newscast mixes human interest stories with hard news (crimes, disasters).	3.748(.7450)	3.848(.5848)	3.649(.7908)
14. Newscast contains enough local news without undue emphasis on national news.	3.611(.9293)	3.713(.7528)	3.605(.8178)
15. There is too much emphasis on college sports.	3.177(1.1337)	3.419(.9485)	3.493(1.0827)
16. News is presented in an easily understood language.	4.016(.5511)	3.981(.6502)	4.093(.5244)
17. Visual aids used in the weather report are readable.	3.635(.9087)	3.740(.8243)	4.000(.8736)
18. Newscasts report happenings at the university.	3.419(.8397)	3.667(.8397)	3.632(.9379)
19. Transitions between segments of the news program seem abrupt.	3.389(.8576)	3.467(.8443)	3.307(.8216)
20. Weather report is accurate.	3.220(1.0229)	3.375(.7782)	3.636(.8722)
21. On-the-scene film reports are frequent.	3.581(.8751)	3.600(.8390)	3.613(.7692)
22. Quality of operational and technical production is low.	3.240(1.0806)	3.333(.9268)	3.526(.9306)
23. There are too many commercials.	2.157(.9954)	2.667(1.0712)	2.421(1.1805)
Total number	97	95	58

three local news broadcasts are shown in Table 1. The ratings were generated by asking respondents, "Which TV channel do you most often watch for the news?" and asking them to complete the scales with this channel in mind. The responses to the first three questions on the questionnaire and the questions that elicited these responses are contained in Table 2. Finally, Tables 3 and 4 contain, respectively, the cross tabulations of Questions 1 and 2 and of Questions 1 and 3.

Question

1. What would you tell Edward about how the local news on Channel 12 is perceived as opposed to perceptions of that on the NBC (Channel 4) and ABC (Channel 2) affiliates?

Table 2   Response by Question

1. On which of the following originating stations do you watch the 6:00 p.m. news?
- 97   12(CBS) WCOL-TV
- 95   4(NBC) WRXY-TV
- 58   2(ABC) WKLM-TV
- 135   I do not watch the 6:00 p.m. news on television.

2. Prior to the 6:00 news, do you watch?
- 129   12(CBS)—National news
- 63   4(NBC)—National news
- 44   2(ABC)—National news
- 149   I do not watch the 6:00 p.m. news on television.

3. On which of the following stations do you watch the 11:00 p.m. news?
- 69   12(CBS) WCOL-TV
- 75   4(NBC) WRXY-TV
- 57   2(ABC) WKLM-TV
- 184   I do not watch the 11:00 p.m. news on television.

Table 3   Cross Tabulation of Question 1 versus Question 2

Station Watched Prior to 6:00 p.m. News	Station Watched for 6:00 p.m. News			Do Not Watch	Total
	12(WCOL-TV)	4(WRXY-TV)	2(WKLM-TV)		
12(WCOL-TV)	72	24	12	21	129
4(WRXY-TV)	4	48	8	3	63
2(WKLM-TV)	5	8	27	4	44
Do not watch	16	15	11	107	149
Total	97	95	58	135	385

Table 4   Cross Tabulation of Question 1 versus Question 3

Station Watched for 6:00 p.m. News	Station Watched for 11:00 p.m. news			Do Not Watch	Total
	12(WCOL-TV)	4(WRXY-TV)	2(WKLM-TV)		
12(WCOL-TV)	53	9	5	30	97
4(WRXY-TV)	6	48	11	30	95
2(WKLM-TV)	3	4	33	18	58
Do not watch	7	14	8	106	135
Total	69	75	57	184	

Case 6.3   Fabhus, Inc.

Fabhus, Inc., a manufacturer of prefabricated homes located in Atlanta, Georgia, had experienced steady, sometimes spectacular, growth since its founding in the early 1950s. In the late 1970s and into the early 1980s, however, inflation coupled with extremely high interest rates on mortgage loans caused a severe decline in the entire home-building industry.

In an attempt to offset the dramatic decline in sales, company managers decided to use marketing research to get a better perspective on their customers, so that they could better target their marketing efforts. After much discussion among the members of the executive committee, it was finally determined the following questions should be addressed in this research effort.

1. What is the demographic profile of the typical Fabhus customer?

2. What initially attracts these customers to a Fabhus home?

3. Do Fabhus home customers consider other factory-built homes when making their purchase decision?

4. Are Fabhus customers satisfied with their homes? If they are not, what particular features are unsatisfactory?

Research Method and Results

The research firm that was called in on the project suggested a mail survey to past owners. Preliminary discussions with management suggested that Fabhus had its greatest market penetration near its factory. As one moved further from the factory, the share of the total new housing business that went to Fabhus declined. The company suspected this might result from the higher prices of the units due to shipping charges. Fabhus relied on a zone-price system in which prices were based on the product delivered at the construction site.

Local dealers actually supervised construction. Each dealer had pricing latitude and could charge more or less than Fabhus's suggested list price. Individual dealers were responsible for seeing that customers were satisfied with their Fabhus home, although Fabhus also had a toll-free number customers could call if they were not satisfied with the way their dealer handled the construction or if they had problems moving in.

Based on the potential impact distance and dealers might have, the research team believed it was important to sample purchasers in the various zones as well as customers of the various dealers. Since Fabhus's records of houses sold were kept by zone, and by date sold within zone, sample respondents were selected in the following way:

First, the number of registration cards per zone were counted. Second, the sample size per zone was determined so that the number of respondents per zone was proportionate to the number of homes sold in the zones. Third, a sample interval, k, was chosen for each zone, a random start between 1 and k was generated, and every kth record was selected. The mail questionnaire shown in Figure 1 was sent to the 423 households selected.

A cover letter informing Fabhus's customers of the general purpose of the survey accompanied the questionnaire, and a new one-dollar bill was included with each survey as an incentive to respond. Further, the anonymity of the respondents was guaranteed by enclosing a self-addressed postage-paid postcard in the survey. Respondents were asked to mail the postcard when they mailed their survey. All of those who had not returned their postcards in two weeks were sent a notice reminding them that their survey had not been returned. The combination of incentives, guaranteed anonymity, and follow-up prompted the return of 342 questionnaires for an overall response rate of 81 percent.

A complete list of the data is available from your instructor.

Questions

1. Using the data provided by your instructor and analytic techniques of your own choosing, address as best you can the objectives that prompted the research effort in the first place.

2. Do you think the research design was adequate for the problems posed? Why or why not?

Figure 1   Factory-built Home Owners Survey

1. *How did you first learn of the factory-built home that you bought? (check one, please)*

☐ Friend or relative   ☐ Direct mail

☐ Another customer   ☐ Newspaper

☐ Realtor   ☐ Radio

☐ Model home   ☐ TV

☐ Yellow pages   ☐ Don't remember

☐ National magazine   ☐ Other _____
                                    (please specify)

2. *Did you own the land your home is on before you first visited your home builder?*

☐ Yes   ☐ No

3. *How long have you lived in your home?* _____ *years*

4. *Where did you live before purchasing your factory-built home? (please check one)*

☐ Rented a house, apartment, or mobile home

☐ Owned a mobile home

☐ Owned a conventionally built home

☐ Owned another factory-built home

☐ Other _____
          (please specify)

5. *Please rate your overall level of satisfaction with your home. (please check one)*

☐ Very satisfied

☐ Somewhat satisfied

☐ Somewhat dissatisfied

☐ Very dissatisfied

6. *How important to you were each of the following considerations in purchasing your factory-built home? (please check a box for each item)*

Considerations	Extremely Important	Important	Slightly Important	Not Important
Investment value	☐	☐	☐	☐
Quality	☐	☐	☐	☐
Price	☐	☐	☐	☐
Energy features	☐	☐	☐	☐
Dealer	☐	☐	☐	☐
Exterior style	☐	☐	☐	☐
Floor plan	☐	☐	☐	☐
Interior features	☐	☐	☐	☐
Delivery schedule	☐	☐	☐	☐

continued

Figure 1   *continued*

7. *Below, please list any other homes you looked at before purchasing the home you chose. Please state the reason you did not purchase the other home.*

Name of Home	Factory-built?	Reason for Not Purchasing
_____	☐ Yes ☐ No	_____
_____	☐ Yes ☐ No	_____
_____	☐ Yes ☐ No	_____
_____	☐ Yes ☐ No	_____

Now would you please tell us about you and your family.

8. *How many children do you have living at home?* _____ *children*

9. *What is the age of the head of your household? (check one please)*

☐ Under 20   ☐ 45–54

☐ 20–24   ☐ 55–64

☐ 25–34   ☐ 65 or over

☐ 35–44

10. *What is the occupation of the head of the household? (check one please)*

☐ Professional or official   ☐ Labor or machine operator

☐ Technical or manager   ☐ Foreman

☐ Proprietor   ☐ Service worker

☐ Farmer   ☐ Retired

☐ Craftsman   ☐ Other _____
                                         (please specify)
☐ Clerical or sales

11. *Which of the following categories includes your family's total annual income? (check one please)*

☐ Under $6,000   ☐ $24,000–29,999

☐ $6,000–11,999   ☐ $30,000–35,999

☐ $12,000–17,999   ☐ $36,000–41,999

☐ $18,000–23,999   ☐ $42,000 or over

12. *Is the spouse of the head of the household employed? (check one please)*

☐ Spouse employed full-time

☐ Spouse employed part-time

☐ Spouse not employed

☐ Not married

One final question:

13. *Would you recommend your particular factory-built home to someone interested in building a new home?*

☐ Yes   ☐ No

**Thank you very much for completing this survey.
Your help in this study is greatly appreciated.**

Case 6.4   Local Government Pooled Investment Fund

The Local Government Pooled Investment Fund (LGPIF) enables governments in the state of Wisconsin to invest any idle local funds, including state aid payments, in the State Investment Pool. The local funds are pooled with the state funds and invested by the State Investment Board to earn the same return as those in the State Investment Pool.

The operation of the LGPIF is quite simple. The local governing body designates the State Investment Fund as a public depository. An officer is designated as the local official authorized to transfer funds to the state treasurer for deposit in the fund. The official then communicates to the state treasurer's office in writing the local government's desire to participate.

Local governments participating in the fund earn interest at the same rate as the state board on short-term investments. All participants in the State Investment Fund share equally in interest earnings, computed on the average yield for a quarter-term investment and based on the average daily balance of each participant's share of the fund. Each participant in the fund therefore earns interest computed at the average rate for the quarter, regardless of the amount of money deposited in the fund or the term of deposit. Funds may be deposited by check or wire transfer and are returned in the same manner when they are withdrawn. Requests for withdrawals, if received before 10:00 A.M., are honored the same day.

Unless specifically requested, a receipt for amounts deposited is not sent. Instead, each local government receives a monthly statement of deposits and withdrawals that indicates the daily balances on which earnings were based.

The officers of the State Investment Fund have a great deal of investment expertise since that is their full-time job. They are in daily communication with banks, securities' dealers, and other investors to achieve the highest competitive rate. With millions of dollars pooled in the fund, the board is able to purchase securities in large blocks, at high yields, and for long periods of time. All of these advantages result in much higher average returns for members of the pool than a local government would be able to earn on its own.

In light of the high rates of interest earned by the fund's investments and the fact that local governments can participate in the program, it proved disconcerting when only 5 percent of all eligible local units of government had decided to participate by the first anniversary of the enabling legislation. Consequently, the state budget office, under the direction of the director of budget operations, commissioned a study to determine why additional support had not materialized and to make recommendations of how participation in the pool could be increased.

Study Design

Some exploratory study of participants and nonparticipants suggested that nonparticipation might be traced to (1) lack of awareness of the fund and its potential value, (2) concern about involvement in the investment of local funds, (3) pressure to keep the funds locally, and (4) mistrust of the operation of the fund and secondary purposes for which it might be used, for example, to revise state aid formulas.

It was determined that the best way to explore these possibilities was through a survey of local treasurers using mail questionnaires. Since many of the treasurers worked only part-time and did not maintain regular office hours, it would have been very difficult and expensive to conduct a telephone interview with them. Personal interviews were ruled out because of the wide geographic distribution of the units in addition to the difficulty of making sure the treasurer would be in when the interviewer called.

The questionnaire shown in Figure 1 was sent to both participants and nonparticipants in the fund. Participants were defined to include those local units of government that had passed resolutions to invest in the fund even if they were not currently doing so. There were 100 such local units, including 37 cities, 17 counties, and 46 towns and villages, and it was decided to send all 100 questionnaires.

The nonparticipants were sampled by first dividing the total set of eligible local government units into three subgroups of cities, counties, and towns and villages, of which there were respectively 172, 55, and 1,508 units. Second, a simple random sample was chosen from each subgroup. Specifically, 49 cities, 46 counties, and 100 towns and villages were sent questionnaires addressed to the treasurer. All treasurers

Figure 1   Local Government Pooled Investment Fund Questionnaire

---

Instructions: Please complete the following questionnaire by checking *only one* response unless otherwise indicated. The last two questions call for your own specific comments.

1. *Are you aware of the Local Government Pooled Investment Fund?*

   _____ Yes _____ No If not, please answer only questions 7 through 15.

2. *Have you received information on the Local Government Pooled Investment Fund?*

   _____ Yes _____ No If not, please answer only questions 7 through 15.

3. *If so, how well did the brochures explain the program?*

   _____ The information was vague

   _____ The information was vague and failed to answer my questions

   _____ The information was clear but failed to answer my questions

   _____ The information was adequate

4. *Where has the majority of your information regarding the pool come from?*

   _____ Newspapers

   _____ Brochures

   _____ Meetings/workshops

   _____ Officials from other units of government

   _____ Other, specify: _____

5. *With whom have you discussed the program? What was his or her reaction? (Check as many as are appropriate.)*

   _____ Mayor, manager, or other chief executive   _____ Favorable   _____ Neutral   _____ Unfavorable

   _____ Your board or council   _____ Favorable   _____ Neutral   _____ Unfavorable

   _____ Financial officers from other local units of government   _____ Favorable   _____ Neutral   _____ Unfavorable

   _____ Local banks   _____ Favorable   _____ Neutral   _____ Unfavorable

   _____ Other, specify:_____   _____ Favorable   _____ Neutral   _____ Unfavorable

   _____ Discussed it with no one

6. *Which of the following applies to your situation? (Check as many as are appropriate.)*

   _____ By governing board or council resolution, funds *must be* invested in local financial institutions.

   _____ By governing board or council resolution, funds *cannot be* invested through the Local Government Investment Fund.

   _____ No resolutions have been passed restricting investment activity.

7. *In which of the following do you currently hold your funds? (Check as many as are appropriate.)*

   _____ Checking account

   _____ Passbook savings account

   _____ Certificates of deposit

   _____ Bonds or Treasury bills

   _____ Local Government Pooled Investment Fund

   _____ Other, specify: _____

Figure 1   *continued*

8. *Of those options listed in Question 7, which do you feel would provide the highest rate of return on your funds?* _____

9. *In your opinion is it the treasurer's responsibility to invest idle funds?*
   _____ Yes_____ No

10. *Under existing state law do you think it is legal to invest your funds?*
    _____ Yes_____ No

11. *In which months of the year do your greatest cash payouts occur?* _____
    _____
    In which months of the year does your revenue significantly exceed your expenditures? _____

12. *How many hours a week do you work as treasurer?_____ hours*

13. *As treasurer, I would like to know more about: (Check as many as are appropriate.)*
    _____ Local government investment opportunities
    _____ Cash-flow management
    _____ Long-range financial planning
    _____ Other, specify: _____
    _____ Feel no need for additional information on these subjects

14. *Do you feel an obligation to keep your funds invested in local bank(s)?*
    _____ Yes_____ No

15. *In order for us to invest our funds outside the local community, the interest rate we would receive would need to be higher than offered locally by at least*
    _____ 1/2%   _____ 2 1/2%
    _____ 1%   _____ 3%
    _____ 1 1/2%   _____ Higher than 3%
    _____ 2%   _____ Higher interest rates would not affect our decision

16. *Do you feel your funds would be more secure in*
    _____ Local Government Pooled Investment Fund
    _____ Local banks
    _____ Both are equally secure

17. *Do you feel that the channels of communication concerning the Local Government Pooled Investment Fund could be improved?*
    _____ No
    _____ Yes, how? _____

18. *Have the interest rates earned on the Local Government Pooled Investment Fund over the past year changed your feeling toward the pool?*
    _____ No_____ Yes
    _____ Not aware of level of interest rates earned on Pooled Investment Fund

continued

Figure 1   *continued*

19. What are your feelings toward the following existing features of the Local Government Pooled Investment Fund?

	Excellent Feature	Good Feature	Neutral	Bad Feature	Very Bad Feature
A. No minimum deposit required	_____	_____	_____	_____	_____
B. Rate of interest earned not known until end of quarter	_____	_____	_____	_____	_____
C. Money can be withdrawn at any time without penalty	_____	_____	_____	_____	_____
D. Money will be received within one day after it is requested	_____	_____	_____	_____	_____
E. Rate of interest earned not dependent on amount invested or terms invested	_____	_____	_____	_____	_____
F. No receipt received for amount deposited	_____	_____	_____	_____	_____
G. Money can be withdrawn by telephone call to state treasurer's office	_____	_____	_____	_____	_____
H. Local Government Pooled Investment Fund is administered by the state	_____	_____	_____	_____	_____
I. Money invested in Pooled Investment Fund cannot be recycled in local economy	_____	_____	_____	_____	_____
J. Rate of interest earned on Pooled Investment Fund has been consistently above that earned on certificates of deposit	_____	_____	_____	_____	_____

20. Of those features listed in Question 19, which ones, if changed, would prompt your local government to join the Pooled Investment Fund? (Circle as many as are appropriate.)

A   B   C   D   E   F   G   H   I   J

List any other changes which would prompt you to join _____

_____

_____

21. What other kinds of information would you like to receive concerning the Local Government Pooled Investment Fund Program? _____

_____

_____

who did not return the questionnaire within a three-week cutoff period were contacted by phone to encourage their participation.

Results

The overall response to the questionnaire was good; 205 of the 295 treasurers that were sent questionnaires returned them. As might be expected, proportionately more participants than nonparticipants in the fund completed and returned their questionnaires.

The form used to code the data and the data itself are available from your instructor.

Question

1. Using the data supplied by your instructor, examine the major hypotheses that have been advanced regarding nonparticipation.

Case 6.5   Como Western Bank[1]

Como Western Bank is one of several commercial lending institutions located in the Colorado community of Brentwood Hills. The bank maintains four branch offices with one branch located in each of the east-west, north-south districts of town. Its main office is located in downtown Brentwood Hills.

During the past decade, changes in the banking industry in Brentwood Hills have paralleled those taking place nationally in that the environment has become increasingly complex and competitive. Deregulation, technological innovation, and changing interest rates have all made it difficult for banks to attract and keep customers. Local banks must now compete with insurance companies, multi-service investment firms, and even the government for clients. As a result, lending institutions like Como Western are focusing increased attention on meeting consumer needs and developing strategies to increase their client base.

A 1972 study of commercial banking in Brentwood Hills showed Como Western to have an above-average proportion of older households, long-time residents of the community, and middle-income persons as customers. The bank appeared to be less successful in attracting younger households, college graduates, and new residents of Brentwood Hills. In addition, the study found non-customers of Como Western to have a weak image of the bank, while customers held a very positive image.

Bank officials sensed that these results also typified the situation in 1987. However, because the officials were in the process of developing a comprehensive marketing plan, they desired more up-to-date and detailed information to aid in formulating an appropriate marketing strategy. Therefore, bank officials contracted with the Mestousis Research Agency to study current bank customers. The agency was a small local one. It was led by its founder, Mike Mestousis, and Kathy Rendina, who served as the principal investigator on most projects. In addition, it employed six clerical people. The objectives of the study given to the Mestousis agency were: (1) determine the demographic profiles of present bank customers; (2) determine customer awareness, use, and overall perception of current bank services; and (3) identify new bank services desired by customers.

Research Method

The Mestousis agency proposed and the bank's directors agreed that the study should be conducted in two phases. The first phase was designed to increase the research team's familiarity with Como Western's current clientele and service offerings. Several methods of inquiry were used. They included personal interviews with customers, bank employees, and members of the bank's board of directors, as well as a literature search of studies relating to the banking industry. Based upon information gathered through

[1]The contributions of David M. Szymanski to the development of this case are gratefully acknowledged.

these procedures, a questionnaire to be used in the second portion of the project was developed.

Because the information being sought was general but yet personal in nature, the mail survey was deemed appropriate for data-collection purposes. To encourage a high response rate, a cover letter describing the research objectives and importance of responding was written by the bank president and mailed with each questionnaire, along with a stamped, self-addressed envelope. Furthermore, those who returned the questionnaire became eligible to participate in a drawing to win one of five fifty-dollar bills. To ensure anonymity, the name and address of the respondent was to be sealed in a separate envelope and returned with the questionnaire.

The questionnaire itself was also designed to encourage high response. The instructions made it clear that the information would be held in strict confidence, and the more sensitive questions were asked last. In addition, the questionnaire was extensively pretested using bank customers of various ages and backgrounds.

Several weeks before the questionnaire was mailed, customers were notified via the bank's newsletter of the possibility that they would be receiving the questionnaire.

Sampling Plan and Results

The relevant population for the study was defined as all noncommercial customers of Como Western Bank who lived in Brentwood Hills and who were not employees of the bank. The total number of customers meeting these requirements was 10,300. A printout of bank customers revealed that bank records list customers in block according to zip codes.

The researchers were of the opinion that 500 survey responses were required to adequately perform the analysis. Anticipating a 30–35 percent response rate, 1,500 to 1,600 surveys needed to be mailed. Given 10,300 population elements and the estimated sample size of 1,600, the researchers decided to send a questionnaire to one of every six names on the list. They generated the first name randomly using a table of random numbers. It was the fourth name on the list. They consequently sent questionnaires to the fourth, tenth, sixteenth, and so on, names on the list. In all, 1,547 questionnaires were sent and 673 were returned for a response rate of approximately 44 percent.

A copy of the questionnaire, coding form, and a listing of the data are available from your instructor.

Questions

1. Evaluate the general research design.
2. Evaluate the sampling plan.
3. Using the data supplied by your instructor, evaluate what the results suggest with respect to
   (a) The demographic characteristics of Como Western's customers?
   (b) Customer awareness, use, and perceptions of the various services provided by Como Western?
   (c) The relationship, if any, between age and income of the respondents and their overall evaluation of the services provided by Como Western?
4. What new services, if any, should Como Western offer?

Case 6.6   Joseph Machine Company

The Joseph Machine Company, which was named after its founder and longtime owner/manager Gerald Joseph, produced pumps and air compressors. Joseph Machine had for some time been concerned with improving the procedures by which its sales force was selected. The company had always hired engineering graduates for this work because an equipment sale demanded some technical sophistication on the part of the sales representative. A sales representative simply had to be able to respond to a customer's technical questions about the equipment, and also to explain how the customer's processing system might be better designed. Assuming that a prospective sales candidate had an engineering degree (mechanical or electrical degrees were preferred, but others were accepted as well), the hiring decision was made primarily on the basis of a personal interview with several executives in the company. Those doing the interviewing often disagreed as to what kinds of credentials and candidates were acceptable.

The company was interested in determining whether there were some more objective criteria that could be employed in the hiring decision. An examination of sales performance literature suggested that a sales representative's personality and intellectual abilities are often primary determinants of success. The company therefore decided to administer personality and IQ tests to each of its sales representatives to determine whether there was any association between these characteristics and the representative's performance. Total sales for the past year in relation to territory quota, expressed as an index, were to be employed as the performance criterion, and Joseph Machine wished to control for any differences in performance that might be attributable to time on the job.

The following data resulted from the investigation:

Sales Representative	Performance Index	IQ Test	Personality Score	Time on Job (in Months)	Sales Representative	Performance Index	IQ Test	Personality Score	Time on Job (in Months)
1	122	130	86	78	21	99	116	69	53
2	105	100	62	48	22	102	113	82	89
3	103	93	85	81	23	98	109	81	75
4	95	81	72	62	24	100	86	68	71
5	97	98	78	98	25	99	92	61	74
6	106	114	68	63	26	99	92	75	79
7	100	87	79	72	27	113	81	71	87
8	115	82	67	85	28	114	103	79	84
9	78	115	70	59	29	110	114	76	106
10	101	114	64	55	30	98	92	83	109
11	115	92	84	117	31	92	105	81	80
12	120	81	84	103	32	106	81	79	85
13	88	89	56	49	33	103	81	84	95
14	110	82	87	110	34	111	85	55	67
15	96	92	82	77	35	102	98	54	61
16	93	85	65	60	36	102	84	74	83
17	92	85	70	74	37	88	109	65	45
18	103	114	64	82	38	105	85	66	93
19	121	85	83	115	39	94	91	62	64
20	95	99	84	102	40	108	81	79	63
					41	84	101	59	41

Questions

1. Is there any relationship between a sales representative's performance and IQ? Performance and personality score?

2. Do the relationships change when time on the job is held constant?

3. What amount of performance can be attributed to all three factors considered simultaneously?

4. Evaluate your method of analysis and also evaluate the procedure being employed by Joseph Machine Company to improve its sales representative selection procedures.

Part Seven   Research Reports and Marketing Intelligence

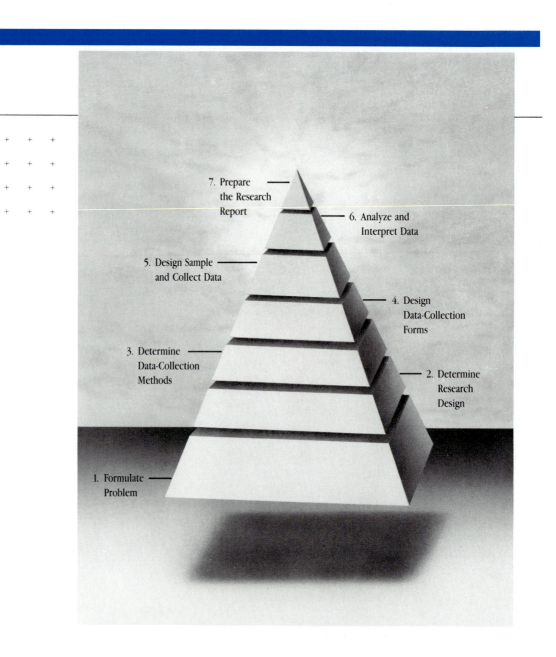

7. Prepare the Research Report

6. Analyze and Interpret Data

5. Design Sample and Collect Data

4. Design Data-Collection Forms

3. Determine Data-Collection Methods

2. Determine Research Design

1. Formulate Problem

Part Seven consists of three chapters. Chapter 20 discusses one of the most important parts of the whole research process, the research report. The research report often becomes the standard by which the entire research effort is assessed, and it is important that the report contributes positively to the evaluation of the effort. Chapter 20 deals with the criteria a research report should satisfy, and the form a research report can follow so that it does contribute positively to the research effort. Chapter 21 then discusses how to deliver effective oral reports and also reviews some of the graphic devices that can be employed to communicate important findings more forcefully. In Chapter 22 the relationship between the project emphasis to research stressed in the book, and decision support systems is discussed. Chapter 22 also discusses some of the more important issues that must be addressed when designing decision support systems.

Chapter 20

The Written Research Report

Learning Objectives

Upon completing this chapter, you should be able to

1. Specify the fundamental criterion by which all research reports are evaluated.
2. Identify and discuss the four criteria that a report should meet if it is to communicate effectively with readers.
3. Outline the main elements that make up a standard report form.
4. Explain the kind of information that is contained in the summary.
5. Distinguish between a conclusion and a recommendation.
6. Describe the kind of information that should be contained in the introduction.
7. Describe the kind of information that should be contained in the body.
8. Describe the kind of information that should be contained in the appendix.

Case in Marketing Research

It was Monday morning, a day Jessica Ellis had looked forward to with both exhilaration and trepidation. The previous Friday afternoon, her boss, Kathy Moran, had told her that she had been chosen to write the company's final research report for Oakhurst Valley Hospital.

Jessica knew that if she did well on this important assignment, her future at Pierce Research Associates would be assured. But as she flipped the light on in her office and saw the piles of computer printouts, rows of manila file folders, and stacks of questionnaires that seemed to cover every available surface, her heart sank. How would she ever manage to organize all this information into a concise, well-written, convincing document?

Just then Kathy Moran stopped by. "Hi, Jessica. I'm glad to see you're here early. We have lots to do if this report is to be ready by next Monday morning."

"Next Monday morning? I thought we had two weeks," Jessica said in alarm.

"Well, we did as of last Friday. However, I just got a call from Glen Roper, the director of marketing at Oakhurst, and he said that the hospital's CEO, Benson Stockbridge, has to be out of town that day. The only other time he has available is Monday the 14th. We'll have to be ready," Kathy said.

"Also, I wanted to give you this additional data. We just finished running the final cross tabs, and I thought you'd want this table we've generated as part of the report," she said.

"Now, we went over all the data and our recommendations last Friday, so I think you should be all set to write. Just remember, we have a lot riding on this account. The hospital market is just becoming aware of the need for research such as ours. I think we've come up with some pretty interesting findings on this ac-count, findings that should revitalize Oakhurst if the people in charge follow through on our suggestions. If we do well here, we are sitting on a potential gold mine. But it all depends on our report. All this work will have been for naught if the report isn't good. Do you have any other questions?" Kathy asked.

Overwhelmed by the job before her, Jessica shook her head. "Not at the moment," she said.

"Well, if you need me, I'll be right down the hall," Kathy said. "Good luck."

1. If you were Jessica Ellis, what questions would you have asked?

2. What factors do you think might distinguish a good report from a bad one?

3. If the research itself has been good, why is the report still so important?

A frustrated executive of a large corporation once remarked that "he is convinced reports are devices by which the informed ensure that the uninformed remain that way."[1] To avoid creating the kind of report that executive was thinking of requires considerable amounts of knowledge, skill, and attention to detail. If length were the criterion of importance of a chapter, there would be an inverse relationship between this chapter and the criterion. This chapter is short, but its subject is vital to the success of the research effort. Regardless of the sophistication displayed in other portions of the research process, the project is a failure if the research report fails.

The empirical evidence indicates that the research report is one of the five most important variables affecting the use of research information.[2] The research steps discussed in the preceding chapters of this text determine the content of the research report, but since the report is all that many executives will see of the project, it becomes the yardstick for evaluation. The writer must ensure that the report informs without misinforming.

The report must tell readers what they need and wish to know. Typically, executives must be convinced of the usefulness of the findings. They are more interested in results than methods. However, to act on the report effectively, they must know enough about the methods that were used to recognize their weaknesses and bounds of error. It is the researcher's responsibility to convey this information to the decision maker in sufficient detail and in understandable form.

In this chapter and the next, we will offer some guidelines for developing successful research reports. In this chapter we will focus on the criteria by which research reports are evaluated and the parts and forms of the written research report.

♦ Research Report Criteria

Research reports are evaluated by one fundamental criterion—how well they communicate with the reader. The "iron law" of marketing research holds, for example, that "people would rather live with a problem they cannot solve than accept a solution they cannot understand."[3] The reader is not only the reason that the report is prepared, but also the standard by which its success is measured. This means that the report must be tailor-made for its reader or readers, with due regard for their technical sophistication, interest in the subject area, the circumstances under which they will read the report, and the use they will make of it.

The technical sophistication of the readers determines their capacity for understanding methodological decisions, such as experimental design, measurement device, sampling plan, analysis technique, and so on. Readers with little technical sophistication will more than likely take offense at the use of unexplained technical jargon. "The readers of your reports are busy people, and very few of them can balance a research report, a cup of coffee, and a dictionary at one time."[4] Unex-

[1] Reprinted by special permission from William J. Gallagher, *Report Writing for Management,* p. 1. Addison-Wesley Publishing Company, Inc., Reading, Massachusetts, Copyright © 1969. All rights reserved. Much of this introductory section is also taken from this excellent book. See also Richard Hatch, *Business Communication,* 2nd ed. (Chicago: Science Research Associates, 1983).

[2] The other variables are the extent of interaction researchers have with managers, the research objectives, the degree of surprise in the results, and the stage of the product or service in its life cycle. See Rohit Deshpande and Gerald Zaltman, "A Comparison of Factors Affecting Researcher and Manager Perceptions of Market Research Use," *Journal of Marketing Research,* 21 (February 1984), pp. 32–38.

[3] Walter B. Wentz, *Marketing Research: Management, Method, and Cases,* 2nd ed. (New York: Harper & Row, 1979), p. 61.

[4] Stewart Henderson Britt, "The Communication of Your Research Findings," in Robert Ferber, ed., *Handbook of Marketing Research* (New York: McGraw-Hill, 1974), p. 1-90.

plained jargon may even make such persons suspicious of the report writer. Researchers should try to be particularly sensitive to this hazard, because, being technical people, they may fail to realize that they are using technical language unless they remind themselves to watch for it.

While the readers' backgrounds and need for methodological detail will determine the upper limit for the technical content of the report, it is the readers' individual preferences that must guide the report writer.

Some executives demand a minimum report; they want only the results—not a discussion of how the results were obtained. Others want considerable information on the

Back to the Case

After working late on the report for Oakhurst Valley Hospital for two nights in a row, a tired Jessica Ellis finally had a rough draft to show Kathy Moran. Jessica sat quietly on a chair in the corner of Kathy's office and tried hard to read the older woman's reaction from the expression on her face.

Finally, after what seemed like hours, Kathy looked up. "Well, I think it's a beginning, Jessica," she said, "but we're not home free. For one thing, the tone is all wrong. Now, think. Who is going to read this report?"

"Glen Roper," Jessica responded quickly.

"Right," Kathy said. "And who else?"

"Well, Mr. Stockbridge, I assume," Jessica said slowly.

"You better believe it," Kathy said. "Also, the hospital's financial officer, and possibly members of the board of directors, and surely some of the department heads, and, for all we know, the members of the Ladies Auxiliary.

"Now, what do all those people, with the exception of Roper, have in common?" Kathy asked.

"I don't know," Jessica said in confusion.

"They all think a cross tab is something that holds your tie in place, and a conjoint analysis is what the doctor does when he reads the X ray of some football player's knee. We know that Glen Roper will understand our more sophisticated techniques, since he has an MBA in marketing, and we do have to convince him that we've done our job. But the rest of these people know very little about statistical techniques. In fact, if they're typical of the general population, they are absolutely mystified by fancy equations and suspicious of anybody who talks in mathematical jargon. However, these same people are going to be very instrumental in deciding if the hospital ultimately acts on our recommendations," Kathy said.

"I suggest you take this report back to your office and write it with those people in mind," she continued. "Save the truly technical stuff for the appendix, where Glen can pore over it to his heart's content. But write the rest with the head of pediatrics in mind . . . that is, a guy who is

obviously bright, but knows a whole lot more about the causes of strep throat in toddlers than about multicollinearity. Got it?"

"Right," Jessica said, with a small sigh. "So much for dazzling them with my expertise."

"Trust me, Jessica. You'll dazzle them more with a well thought out report in language they can understand, than in trying to strut your numbers," Kathy said.

A research report—and, indeed, the whole research project—is only as successful as its ability to communicate with its intended audience. The report's readers must be able to understand the study's results before they can act on them. If the report is too technically sophisticated for its readers, then the chances are excellent that it will find its home on a shelf rather than be put to good use.

If the report will be read by many audiences with varying levels of technical capacity, the writer must structure the report so that different sections address the needs and abilities of each audience.

research methods used in the study. Many executives place a premium on brevity, while others demand complete discussion. Some are interested only in the statistical results and not in the researcher's conclusions and recommendations.

Thus, *the audience determines the type of report*. Researchers must make every effort to acquaint themselves with the *specific preferences of their audience*. They should not consider these preferences as unalterable, but *any deviations from them should be made with reason and not from ignorance!*[5] (emphasis added)

The report writer's difficulties in tailoring the report are often compounded by the existence of several audiences. The marketing vice-president might have a different technical capacity and level of interest than the product manager responsible for the product discussed in the report. There is no easy solution to this problem of "many masters." The researcher must recognize the potential differences that may arise and may have to exercise a great deal of ingenuity to reconcile them. Occasionally, a researcher may find it necessary to prepare several reports, each designed for a specific audience, although more often the conflicting demands can be satisfied by one report that contains both technical and nontechnical sections for different readers.

◆ Writing Criteria

A report that achieves the goal of communicating effectively with readers is generally one that meets the specific criteria of completeness, accuracy, clarity, and concise-ness.[6] These criteria are intimately related. An accurate report, for example, is also a complete report. For discussion purposes, however, it is helpful to discuss the criteria as if they were distinct.

Completeness

◆ Completeness

Criterion used to evaluate a research report; specifically, whether the report provides all the information readers need in a language they understand.

A report is **complete** when it provides all the information readers need in language they understand. This means that the writer must continually ask whether every question in the original assignment has been addressed. What alternatives were ex-amined? What was found? An incomplete report implies that supplementary reports, which are annoying and delay action, will be forthcoming.

The report may be incomplete because it is too brief or too long. The writer may omit necessary definitions and short explanations. On the other hand, the report may be lengthy but not profound, due to a reluctance to waste any collected infor-mation. In a report full of non-vital information, the main issues are often lost in the clutter. Also, if the report is big, it may discourage readers from even attempting to digest its contents.

Readers are thus the key to determining completeness. Their interest and abilities determine what clarification should be added and what findings should be omitted. In general, the amount of detail should be proportionate to the amount of direct control users can exercise over the areas under discussion. For example, if the in-tended reader is a product's advertising manager, it would generally be wise to omit a lengthy discussion of possible improvements to production techniques.

---

[5]Harper W. Boyd, Jr., Ralph Westfall, and Stanley F. Stasch, *Marketing Research: Text and Cases,* 6th ed. (Homewood, Ill.: Richard D. Irwin, 1985), p. 665.

[6]Gallagher, *Report Writing,* p. 78.

Table 20.1   Some Examples of Sources of Inaccuracy in Report Writing

A. *Simple Errors in Addition or Subtraction*

"In the United States, 14 percent of the population has an elementary school education or less, 51 percent has attended or graduated from high school, and 16 percent has attended college."

An oversight such as this (14 + 51 + 16 do not equal 100 percent) can be easily corrected by the author, but not so easily by the reader because he or she may not know if one or more of the percentage values is incorrect or if a category might have been left out of the tally.

B. *Confusion between Percentages and Percentage Points*

"The company's profits as a percentage of sales were 6.0 percent in 1982 and 8.0 percent in 1987. Therefore, they increased only 2.0 percent in five years."

In this example, the increase is, of course, 2.0 percentage points, or 33 percent.

C. *Inaccuracy Caused by Grammatical Errors*

"The reduction in the government's price supports for dairy products has reduced farm income $600 million to $800 million per year."

To express a range of reduction, the author should have written: "The reduction in the government's price supports for dairy products has reduced farm income $600-800 million per year."

D. *Confused Terminology Resulting in Fallacious Conclusion*

"The Jones' household annual income increased from $10,000 in 1964 to $30,000 in 1984, thereby tripling the family's purchasing power."

While the Jones' household annual income may have tripled in the 20 years, the family's purchasing power certainly did not as the cost of living, as measured by the consumer price index, more than tripled in the same period.

Accuracy

• Accuracy

Criterion used to evaluate a research report according to whether the reasoning in the report is logical and the information correct.

The previously discussed steps in the research process are obviously vital to accuracy, but, given accurate input, the research report may generate inaccuracies because of carelessness in handling the data, illogical reasoning, or inept phrasing.[7] Thus, **accuracy** is another writing criterion. Table 20.1 illustrates some examples of sources of inaccuracy in report writing.

The possession of advanced degrees is no safeguard against the hazards detailed in Table 20.1. In fact, the more educated a person is, the more apt he may be to sink into the morass of excess verbiage. Consider the president of a major university who, in the late 1960s, wrote a letter to soothe anxious alumni after a spell of campus unrest. "You are probably aware," he began, "that we have been experiencing very considerable potentially explosive expressions of dissatisfaction on issues only partially related." He meant that the students had been hassling them about different things.[8] In Research Window 20.1, Jock Elliott, chairman emeritus of the advertising agency Ogilvy & Mather, shows how one corporate vice-president also sank into the quicksand of his own words.

[7]See Gallagher, *Report Writing,* pp. 80–83, for a number of examples that display some of the inaccuracies that may arise. The examples are particularly interesting in that they have been extracted from actual company reports.

[8]Taken from William Zinsser, *On Writing Well,* 3rd ed. (New York: Harper and Row, 1985), pp. 7–8, a modern classic for writers that is as helpful as it is fun to read.

Inaccuracies also arise because of grammatical errors in punctuation, spelling, tense, subject and verb agreement, and so on.[9] Careful attention to detail in these areas is essential for any report writer.

Clarity

◆ **Clarity**

Criterion used to evaluate a research report; specifically, whether the phrasing in the report is precise.

The writing criterion of **clarity** is probably failed more than any other. Clarity is produced by clear and logical thinking and precision of expression. When the underlying logic is fuzzy or the presentation imprecise, readers experience difficulty in understanding what they read. They may be forced to guess, in which case the corollary to Murphy's law applies, "If the reader is offered the slightest opportunity to misunderstand, he probably will."[10] Achieving clarity, however, requires effort.

---

[9]Gallagher, *Report Writing*, Chap. 10, "Reviewing for Accuracy: Grammar," pp. 156–177, has examples of how these inaccuracies can confuse and misinform. See also Charles T. Brusaw, Gerald J. Alred, and E. Watter Oliv, *The Business Writers Handbook*, 2nd ed. (New York: St. Martins Press, 1982).

[10]Gallagher, *Report Writing*, p. 83.

Research Window 20.1
How to Write Your Way Out of a Job

Jock Elliott, the chairman emeritus of the Ogilvy & Mather advertising agency, is a man who appreciates good writing. After all, his business is built on his employees' ability to communicate with clients and consumers.

Elliott makes no bones about the importance of being able to write well in order to advance in a career. "As you sail along on your career," he writes, "bad writing acts as a sea anchor, pulling you back, good writing as a spinnaker, pulling you ahead."

In the following excerpt from an article he wrote, he tells about one prospective employee who sank beneath the waves, weighed down by the anchor of his own words:

"Last month I got a letter from a vice-president of a major management consulting firm. Let me read you two paragraphs. The first:

Recently, the companies of our Marketing Services Group were purchased by one of the largest consumer research firms in the U.S. While this move well fits the basic business purpose and focus of the acquired MSG units, it is personally restrictive. I will rather choose to expand my management opportunities with a career move into industry.

"What he meant was: The deal works fine for my company, but not so fine for me. I'm looking for another job.

"Second paragraph:

The base of managerial and technical accomplishment reflected in my enclosed resumé may suggest an opportunity to meet a management need for one of your clients. Certainly my experience promises a most productive pace to understand the demands and details of any new situation I would choose.

"What he meant was: As you can see in my resume, I've had a lot of good experience. I am a quick study. Do you think any of your clients might be interested in me?

"At least, that's what I think he meant.

"This fellow's letter reveals him as pompous. He may not *be* pompous. He may only be a terrible writer. But I haven't the interest or time to find out which. There are so many people looking for jobs who don't sound like pompous asses.

"Bad writing done him in—with me, at any rate."

Jock Elliott, "How Hard It Is to Write Easily," *Viewpoint: By, For, and About Ogilvy & Mather,* 2 (1980), p. 18.

The first, and most important, rule is that the report be well organized.[11] In order for this to happen, you must first clarify for yourself the purpose of your report and how you intend to accomplish it. Make an outline of your major points. Put the points in logical order and place the supporting details in their proper position. Tell the reader what you are going to cover in the report and then do what you said you were going to do. Use short paragraphs and short sentences. Do not be evasive or ambiguous; once you have decided what you want to say, come right out and say it. Choose your words carefully, making them as precise and understandable as possible. See Table 20.2 for some specific suggestions when choosing words.

Do not expect your first draft to be satisfactory. Expect to rewrite it several times. When rewriting, attempt to reduce the length by half. That forces you to simplify and remove the clutter. It also forces you to think about every word and its purpose, to evaluate whether each word is helping you say what you wish to say. Jock Elliott has some very pointed comments on writing clearly.

> Our written and spoken words reflect what we are. If our words are brilliant, precise, well ordered and human, then that is how we are seen.
>
> When you write, you must constantly ask yourself: What am I trying to say? If you do this religiously, you will be surprised at how often you don't know what you are trying to say.
>
> You have to *think* before you start every sentence, and you have to *think* about every word.
>
> Then you must look at what you have written and ask: Have I said it? Is it clear to someone encountering the subject for the first time? If it's not, it is because some fuzz has worked its way into the machinery. The clear writer is a person clearheaded enough to see this stuff for what it is: fuzz.
>
> It is not easy to write a simple declarative sentence. Here is one way to do it. Think what you want to say. Write your sentence. Then strip it of all adverbs and adjectives. Reduce the sentence to its skeleton. Let the verbs and nouns do the work.
>
> If your skeleton sentence does not express your thought precisely, you've got the wrong verb or noun. Dig for the right one. Nouns and verbs carry the guns in good writing; adjectives and adverbs are decorative camp followers.[12]

Conciseness

• Conciseness

Criterion used to evaluate a research report; specifically, whether the writing in the report is crisp and direct.

Although the report must be complete, it must also be **concise.** This means that the writer must be selective in what is included. The researcher must avoid trying to impress the reader with all that has been found. If something does not pertain directly to the subject, it should be omitted. The writer must also avoid lengthy discussions of commonly known methods. Given that the material is appropriate, conciseness can still be violated by writing style. This commonly occurs when the writer is groping for the phrases and words that capture an idea. Instead of finally coming to terms with the idea, the writer writes around it, restating it several times, in different ways, hoping that repetition will overcome poor expression. Concise writing, on the other hand, is effective because "it makes maximum use of every

---

[11]Kenneth Roman and Joel Raphaelson, *Writing That Works* (New York: Harper and Row, 1981). This book gives some excellent advice on how to write more effective reports as well as memos, letters, and speeches. See also Kenneth Roman and Joel Raphaelson, "Don't Mumble and Other Principles of Effective Writing," *Viewpoint: By, For, and About Ogilvy & Mather,* 2 (1980), pp. 19–36. The little book by William Strunk, Jr., and E. B. White, *The Elements of Style* (New York: Macmillan, 1959), is a classic on how to write clearly.

[12]Jock Elliott, "How Hard It Is to Write Easily," *Viewpoint: By, For, and About Ogilvy & Mather,* 2 (1980), p. 18.

Table 20.2   Some Suggestions When Choosing Words for Marketing Research Reports

1. *Use short words.* Always use short words in preference to long words that mean the same thing.

Use this	Not this
Now	Currently
Start	Initiate
Show	Indicate
Finish	Finalize
Use	Utilize
Place	Position

2. *Avoid vague modifiers.* Avoid lazy adjectives and adverbs and use vigorous ones. Lazy modifiers are so overused in some contexts that they have become clichés. Select only those adjectives and adverbs that make your meaning precise.

Lazy modifiers	Vigorous modifiers
Very good	Short meeting
Awfully nice	Crisp presentation
Basically accurate	Baffling instructions
Great success	Tiny raise
Richly deserved	Moist handshake
Vitally important	Lucid recommendation

3. *Use specific, concrete language.* Avoid technical jargon. There is always a simple, down-to-earth word that says the same thing as the show-off fad word or the vague abstraction.

Jargon	Down-to-earth English
Implement	Carry out
Viable	Practical, workable
Net net	Conclusion

Source: Table adapted from Chapter 2 of *Writing That Works* by Kenneth Roman and Joel Raphaelson. Copyright © 1981 by Kenneth Roman and Joel Raphaelson. Reprinted by permission of Harper & Row, Publishers, Inc.

word . . . no word in a concise discussion can be removed without impairing or destroying the function of the whole composition. . . . To be concise is to express a thought completely and clearly in the fewest words possible."[13]

One helpful technique for ensuring that the report is concise is reading the draft aloud. This often reveals sections that should be pruned or rewritten.[14]

> Silent reading allows him [the writer] to skim over the familiar material and thus impose an artificial rapidity and structural simplicity on something that is in reality dense and tangled. The eye can grow accustomed to the appearance of a sentence, but it is much more difficult for the tongue, lips, and jaw to deal with what the eye might accept readily.

[13]Gallagher, *Report Writing*, p. 87.

[14]*Ibid.*, p. 84.

Table 20.2   *continued*

Jargon	Down-to-earth English
Suboptimal	Less than ideal
Proactive	Active
Bottom line	Outcome

4. *Write simply and naturally — the way you talk.* Use only those words, phrases, and sentences that you might actually say to your reader if you were face to face. If you wouldn't say it, if it doesn't sound like you, don't write it.

Stiff	Natural
The reasons are fourfold	There are four reasons
Importantly	The important point is
Visitation	Visit

5. *Strike out words you don't need.* Certain commonly used expressions contain redundant phrasing. Cut out the extra words.

Don't write	Write
Advance plan	Plan
Take action	Act
Study in depth	Study
Consensus of opinion	Consensus
Until such time as	Until
The overall plan	The plan

◆ Forms of Report

The organization of the report influences all the criteria of report writing. While good organization cannot guarantee clarity, conciseness, accuracy, and completeness, poor organization can preclude them. There is no single, acceptable organization for a report. Once again, the writer should be guided by the nature and needs of the reader in choosing the most appropriate format for the report. The following format is sufficiently flexible to allow the inclusion or exclusion of elements to satisfy particular needs.

1. Title page
2. Table of contents

   3. Summary
      a. Introduction

      b. Results

      c. Conclusions

      d. Recommendations

   4. Introduction

   5. Body
      a. Methodology

      b. Results

      c. Limitations

   6. Conclusions and recommendations

   7. Appendix
      a. Copies of data-collection forms

      b. Detailed calculations supporting sample size, test statistics, and so on

      c. Tables not included in the body

      d. Bibliography

Title Page

The title page indicates the subject of the report, the name of the organization for whom the report is made, the name of the organization submitting it, and the date. If the report is done by one department within a company for another, the names of organizations or companies are replaced by those of individuals. Those for whom the report is intended are listed on the title page, as are the departments or people preparing the report. If a report is confidential, it is especially important to list the names of the individuals authorized to see it on the title page.

Table of Contents

The table of contents lists, in order of appearance, the divisions and subdivisions of the report with page references. In short reports, the table of contents may simply contain the main headings. The table of contents will also typically include tables and figures and the pages on which they may be found. For most reports, exhibits will be labeled as either tables or figures, with maps, diagrams, and graphs falling into the latter category.

Summary

The summary is the most important part of the report. It is the heart and core. Many executives will read only the summary. Others will read more, but even they will use the summary as a guide to those questions about which they would like more information.

The true summary is not an abstract of the whole report in which everything is restated in condensed form, nor is it a simple restatement of the subject, nor is it a brief statement of the significant results and conclusions. A true summary gives the high points of the entire body of the report. A properly written summary saves the time of busy executives without sacrificing their understanding. A good test of a summary is self-sufficiency. Can it stand on its own, or does it collapse without the full report?

A good summary contains the necessary background information, as well as the important results and conclusions. Whether it contains recommendations is determined to an extent by the reader. Some managers prefer that the writer suggest appropriate action, while others prefer to draw their own conclusions on the basis of the evidence contained in the study. Although the good summary contains the necessary information, it will rarely be broken down through the use of headings and subheadings. The summary that requires such subdivisions is, in all likelihood, too long.

The summary begins with an introduction that should provide the reader with enough background to appreciate the results, conclusions, and recommendations of the study. The introduction should state who authorized the research and for what purpose. It should state explicitly the problem(s) or hypotheses that guided the research.

Following the introduction should be a section in which the study's significant findings or results are presented. The results presented in the summary must agree, of course, with those in the body of the report, but only the key findings are presented here. A useful approach is to include one or several statements reporting what was found with regard to each problem or objective mentioned in the introduction.

The final two sections of the summary are conclusions and recommendations, which follow a discussion of the results. Conclusions and recommendations are not the same. A conclusion is an opinion based on the results. A recommendation is a suggestion as to appropriate future action.

Conclusions should be included in the summary section. The writer is in a much better position to base conclusions on the evidence than is the reader, as the writer has greater familiarity with the methods used to generate and analyze the data. The writer is at fault if conclusions are omitted and readers are allowed to draw their own. Recommendations, though, are another matter. Some managers simply prefer to determine the appropriate courses of action themselves and do not want the writer to offer recommendations. Others hold that the writer, being closest to the research, is in the best position to suggest a course of action. For example, the Lipton Company has the philosophy that it is the responsibility of the marketing research people to interpret the findings. As Dolph von Arx, the executive vice-president, comments: "We feel strongly that our market research people must go beyond reporting the facts. We want them to tell us what *they* think the facts mean—both in terms of conclusions, and, if possible, indicated actions. Those who are responsible for making the decisions may or may not accept those conclusions or recommendations, but we want this input from our Market Research people."[15]

Introduction

Whereas in the summary the readers' interests are taken into account, in the report's formal introduction their education and experience are considered. The introduction provides the background information readers need to appreciate the discussion in the body of the report. Some form of introduction is almost always necessary. Its length and detail, though, depend upon the readers' familiarity with the subject, the report's approach to it, and the treatment of it.[16] As a general rule, a report with wide distribution will require a more extensive introduction than a report for a narrow audience.

The introduction often serves to define unfamiliar terms or terms that are used in

---

[15]Dolph von Arx, "The Many Faces of Market Research," paper delivered at meeting of the Association of National Advertisers, Inc., New York, April 3, 1985.

[16]Gallagher, *Report Writing,* p. 54.

a specific way in the report. For instance, in a study of market penetration of a new product, the introduction might be used to define the market and name the products and companies considered "competitors" in calculating the new product's market share.

The introduction may provide some pertinent history, answering such questions as the following: What similar studies have been conducted? What findings did they produce? What circumstances led to the present study? How was its scope and emphasis determined? Clearly, if readers are familiar with the history of this project and related research or the circumstances that inspired the current research, these items can be omitted. A report going to executives with little background in the particular product or service dealt with would probably have to include them.

The introduction should state the specific objectives of the research. If the project was part of a larger, overall project, this should be mentioned. Each of the subproblems or hypotheses should be explicitly stated. After reading the introduction, readers should know just what the report covers and what it omits. They should appreciate the overall problem and how the subproblems relate to it. They should be aware of the relationship between this study and other related work. And they should appreciate the need for the study and its importance. Through all of this, the introduction should serve to win the readers' confidence and dispel any prejudices they may have.

Body

The details of the research — its method, results, and limitations — are contained in the body of the report. One of the hardest portions of the report to write is that giving the details of the method. The writer has a real dilemma here. Sufficient information must be presented so that readers can appreciate the research design, data-collection methods, sample procedures, and analysis techniques that were used without being bored or overwhelmed. Technical jargon, which is often a succinct way of communicating a complex idea, should be omitted since many in the audience will not understand it.

Readers must be told whether the design was exploratory, descriptive, or causal. They should also be told why the particular design was chosen and what its merits are in terms of the problem at hand. Readers should also be told whether the results are based on secondary or primary data. If primary, were they based on observation or questionnaire? And if the latter, were the questionnaires administered in person, or by mail or telephone? Once again it is important to mention why the particular method was chosen. What were its perceived advantages over alternative schemes? This may mean discussing briefly the perceived weaknesses of the other data-collection schemes that were considered.

Sampling is a technical subject, and the writer cannot usually hope to convey all the nuances of the sampling plan in the body of the report, but must be somewhat selective in this regard. At the very minimum, the researcher should answer the following questions:

1. How was the population defined? What were the geographical, age, sex, or other bounds?

2. What sampling units were employed? Were they business organizations or business executives? Were they dwelling units, households, or individuals within a household? Why were these particular sampling units chosen?

3. How was the list of sampling units generated? Did this produce any weaknesses? Why was this method used?

4. Were any difficulties experienced in contacting designated sample elements? How were these difficulties overcome and was bias introduced in the process?

5. Was a probability or nonprobability sampling plan employed? Why? How was the sample actually selected? How large a sample was selected? Why was this size sample chosen?

In essence, the readers need to understand at least three things with respect to the sample: What was done? How was it done? Why was it done?

There is very little that can be said about the method of analysis when discussing research methods, since the results tend to show what has been done in this regard. It often proves quite useful, though, to discuss the method in general before detailing the results. Thus, if statistical significance is established through chi-square analysis, the writer might provide the general rationale and calculation procedure for the chi-square statistic, as well as the assumptions surrounding this test and how well the data supported the assumptions. This enables readers to separate what was found from how it was determined. The distinction may not only help the readers' understanding, but also prevent repetition in the report. The procedure is outlined with its key components once, and the results are then simply reported in terms of these components.

The results section of the body of the report presents the findings of the study in some detail, often including supporting tables and figures, and accounts for the bulk of the report. The results need to address the specific problems posed, and must be presented with some logical structure.[17] The first of these requirements directs that information that is interesting but irrelevant in terms of the specific problems that guided the research be omitted. The second requirement directs that the tables and figures not be a random collection, but reflect some psychological ordering.[18] This may mean by subproblem, geographic region, time, or other criterion that served to structure the investigation.

Tables and figures should be used liberally when presenting the results. While the tables in the appendix are complex, detailed, and apply to a number of problems, the tables in the body of the report should be simple summaries of this information. Each table should address only a single problem and it should be especially constructed to shed maximum light on this problem. Guidelines for constructing tables follow:[19]

1. Order the columns or rows of the table by the marginal averages or some other measure of size. If there are many similar tables, keep the same order in each one.

2. Put the figures to be compared into columns rather than rows, and, if possible, put the larger numbers at the top of the columns.

3. Round the numbers to two effective digits.

4. Give brief verbal summaries of each table that guide the reader to the main patterns and exceptions.

---

[17]Some of the many structures and the conditions under which they can be used are contained in Jessamon Dawe, *Writing Business and Economic Papers: Theses and Dissertations* (Totowa, N.J.: Littlefield, Adams, 1975), pp. 75–86.

[18]See Gallagher, *Report Writing,* pp. 50–68, for a discussion of the psychological order of things in research reports.

[19]See A. S. C. Ehrenberg, "Rudiments of Numeracy," *Journal of the Royal Statistical Society,* Series A, 140 (1977), pp. 277–297; and A. S. C. Ehrenberg, "The Problem of Numeracy," *American Statistician,* 35 (May 1981), pp. 67–71, for a particularly informative discussion using examples of how adherence to these principles can dramatically improve readers' abilities to comprehend the information being presented in tables.

Figure 20.1 **Guidelines for** **Producing Better** **Tables**	The following table (Table 1) presents some sales figures for a product being sold in eight cities in the United Kingdom. At first glance, it may seem to be fairly well laid out. But look again. How would you summarize the information in the table to someone over the phone?

Table 1   Quarterly Sales of Product X in Eight Cities

£'000	Quarter 1	Quarter 2	Quarter 3	Quarter 4
Bolton	31.3	29.1	25.2	29.3
Edinburgh	135.1	126.9	132.1	208.3
Hull	70.3	81.3	70.9	84.0
Leeds	276.8	258.6	223.0	336.2
Luton	23.5	27.5	22.7	27.1
Plymouth	41.4	44.0	33.2	50.2
Sheffield	233.4	220.1	193.6	220.9
Swansea	62.3	66.4	61.8	76.7

Looked at more carefully, the table seems a jumble. It appears that no thought was given to communicating what the numbers really say. The main difficulty is that the cities are listed alphabetically. There is no apparent pattern in each column.

Now look at the same information as presented in Table 2.

Table 2   The Cities Ordered by Population Size (Rounded and with Averages)

Sales in £'000	QI	QII	QIII	QIV	Av.
Sheffield	230	220	190	220	220
Leeds	280	260	220	340	270
Edinburgh	140	130	130	210	150
Hull	70	81	71	84	76
Swansea	62	66	62	77	67
Plymouth	41	44	33	50	42
Luton	23	27	23	27	25
Bolton	31	29	25	29	29
Average	110	107	94	130	110

See how ordering the information by following the steps outlined below improves the table's readability:

■ Order the columns or rows of the table by the marginal averages. In this case, the cities are ordered by the size of their adult populations.
■ Round off the numbers to two effective digits..
■ Order the columns of the table by marginal averages or some other measures of size. In this case, the average sales per city appear in the right-hand margin; the average sales per quarter appear at the bottom of the columns.
■ Give brief verbal summaries that guide the reader to the main patterns and exceptions.

Figure 20.1

continued

The heading of Table 2 informs the reader that the cities are ordered by population size, and that sales are recorded in pounds sterling, a form of British currency. Knowing this information, and examining the table as it's now laid out, we can begin to see major patterns emerge: the bigger the cities, the higher the sales! Exceptions are also clear, such as sales in Leeds being relatively high and sales in Luton relatively low (averages of 270 and 25).

Trends over time are also easier to take in. Although not typical, the column averages help us see that sales in each city were mostly steady quarter by quarter, but lower in QIII and higher in QIV. We can also see that the QIV increases were largest in Leeds and Edinburgh.

The difference between Tables 1 and 2 is the difference between a good table and a poor one. In a good table, the patterns and exceptions should be obvious at a glance, at least once one knows what they are.

Next time you have trouble reading a table, ask yourself if the information could be better ordered. The fault may not be in your ability to comprehend the information, but in the table itself.

Source: A.S.C. Ehrenberg, "The Problem of Numeracy," *The American Statistician,* 35 (May 1981), pp. 67–71.

Figure 20.1 gives an example of how these guidelines can yield better tables.

Figures, like tables, should address only one subproblem. Further, they should be chosen carefully for the type of message they can most effectively convey, but this subject will be discussed in the next chapter.

It is impossible to conduct the "perfect" study, because every study has its limitations. The researcher knows what the limitations of his or her efforts are, and these limitations should not be hidden from the reader. Researchers sometimes fear that a frank admission of the study's limitations may diminish the reader's opinion of the quality of the research. Often the contrary is true. If some limitations are not stated and readers discover them, they may begin to question the whole report and assume a much more skeptical, critical posture than they would have had the limitations been stated explicitly. Stating them also allows the writer to discuss whether, and by how much, the limitations might bias the results. Their exclusion, and later discovery, encourages readers to draw their own conclusions in this regard.

When discussing the limitations, the writer should provide some idea of the accuracy with which the work was done. The writer should specifically discuss the sources of nonsampling error and the suspected direction of their biases. This often means that the researcher provides some limits by which the results are distorted due to these inaccuracies. Readers should be informed specifically as to how far the results can be generalized. To what populations can they be expected to apply? If the study was done in Miami, readers should be warned not to generalize the results to the southern states or all the states. The writer should provide the proper caveats for readers and not make readers discover the weaknesses themselves. However, the writer should not overstate the limitations either, but should assume a balanced perspective.

Conclusions and Recommendations

The results lead to the conclusions and recommendations. In this section, the writer shows the step-by-step development of the conclusions and states them in greater detail than in the summary. There should be a conclusion for each study objective or problem. As one book puts it, "readers should be able to read the objectives, turn to the conclusions section, and find specific conclusions relative to each objective."[20] If the study does not provide evidence sufficient to draw a conclusion about a problem, this should be explicitly stated.

---

[20]Boyd, Westfall, and Stasch, *Marketing Research,* p. 672.

Appendix

The appendix contains material that is too complex, too detailed, too specialized, or not absolutely necessary for the text. The appendix will typically contain as an exhibit a copy of the questionnaire or observation form used to collect the data. It will also contain any maps used to draw the sample as well as any detailed calculations used to support the determination of the sample size and sample design. The appendix may include detailed calculations of test statistics and will often include detailed tables from which the summary tables in the body of the report are generated.

Back to the Case

It was late Thursday afternoon, and the rest of the company's employees were putting on their coats and preparing to go home when Jessica gathered together the last tables for the report's appendix and headed down the hall to Kathy Moran's office.

"Kathy, do you have time to look at this before you go home?" Jessica asked.

"Sure thing. I'm planning on staying late with the people in the graphics department to work on some charts for our presentation Monday anyway. Let's see what you have," Kathy said.

Kathy read quickly but intently, occasionally circling a word or deleting a phrase as she went through the report. Toward the end, Jessica noticed that her reading slowed. Finally, she looked up.

"I'm reading the 'results' section of the report, Jessica, and I see no mention of the problems we had with data collection," Kathy said.

"Of course not, Kathy," Jessica said. "I would never mention those! I wouldn't want Oakhurst to think we didn't do a good job."

"On the contrary," Kathy said, "if you didn't mention them, we wouldn't be doing a good job."

"What do you mean?" Jessica asked.

"If you remember correctly, our field interviewers had a lot of trouble reaching families where both spouses worked. They also got turned down a good deal when they attempted to interview the elderly. And, from the looks of the completed questionnaires, it is clear that the southeastern end of town is substantially underrepresented," Kathy said.

"Is that where the low-income housing project is?" Jessica asked.

Kathy nodded. "I would grant you that most of the people who read this report wouldn't notice these omissions. However, Glen Roper is one sharp guy, and you can bet that he'll be going over the data with a fine-tooth comb. If he discovers that we failed to note our sources of nonsampling bias, the whole report will be suspect. It's better to be clear about the report's limitations than to gloss them over and be called on it later," Kathy said.

"This makes me edgy," Jessica said, "but I trust your judgment. I'll add a section that outlines our problems. Anything else?"

"Other than that, I think it's great," Kathy said. "Want to come to Monday's meeting so I can show you off?"

Jessica smiled. "Only if I can first spend the weekend sleeping to get rid of the circles under my eyes," she laughed.

Researchers often fear that by stating the report's limitations they are discrediting their work. More often, the reverse is true. There is no such thing as a "perfect" research study. By acknowledging the study's limitations and biases, researchers can guide readers in gauging just how far the results can be generalized, and what factors may still be unaccounted for. On the other hand, if the study's limitations are hidden by the researcher and subsequently discovered by the reader, the validity of the whole project, as well as the credentials of the researcher, may be called into question.

The writer should recognize that the appendix will be read by only the most technically competent and interested reader. Therefore, the writer should not put material in the appendix if its omission from the body of the report would create gaps in the presentation.

◆ Summary

Learning Objective 1: Specify the fundamental criterion by which all research reports are evaluated.

Research reports are evaluated by one fundamental criterion—communication with the reader. The reader is not only the reason that the report is prepared, but also the standard by which its success is measured.

Learning Objective 2: Identify and discuss the four criteria that a report should meet if it is to communicate effectively with readers.

A report that achieves the goal of communicating effectively with readers is generally one that meets the specific criteria of completeness, accuracy, clarity, and conciseness.

Learning Objective 3: Outline the main elements that make up a standard report form.

A standard report generally contains the following elements: title page, table of contents, summary, introduction, body, conclusions and recommendations, and appendix.

Learning Objective 4: Explain the kind of information that is contained in the summary.

A true summary gives the high points of the entire body of the report, including necessary background information, as well as important results and conclusions.

Learning Objective 5: Distinguish between a conclusion and a recommendation.

A conclusion is an opinion based on the results. A recommendation is a suggestion as to appropriate future action.

Learning Objective 6: Describe the kind of information that should be contained in the introduction.

An introduction provides background information, defines unfamiliar terms, outlines pertinent history, and states the specific objectives of the research. Through all this, the introduction should serve to win the readers' confidence and dispel any prejudices they may have.

Learning Objective 7: Describe the kind of information that should be contained in the body.

The details of the research are contained in the body of the report. This includes details of method, results, and limitations.

Learning Objective 8: Describe the kind of information that should be contained in the appendix.

The appendix contains materials that are too complex, too detailed, too specialized, or not absolutely necessary for the text. The appendix will typically contain as an exhibit a copy of the questionnaire or observation form used to collect the data.

Discussion Questions, Problems, and Projects

1. The owner of a medium-sized home-building center specializing in custom-designed and do-it-yourself bathroom supplies requested the Liska and Leigh Consulting Firm to prepare a report on the customer profile of the bathroom design segment of the home-improvement market. Evaluate the following sections of the report.

   The customer market for the company can be defined as the do-it-yourself and bathroom design segments. A brief profile of each follows.

The do-it-yourself (DIY) market consists of individuals in the 25–45 age group living in a single dwelling. DIY customers are predominantly male, although an increasing number of females are becoming active DIY customers. The typical DIY customer has an income in excess of $20,000 and the median income is $22,100 with a standard deviation of 86. The DIY customer has an increasing amount of leisure time, is strongly value- and convenience-conscious, and displays an increasing desire for self-gratification.

The mean age of the custom bathroom design segment is 41.26 and the annual income is in the range of $25,000 to $35,000. The median income is $29,000 with a standard deviation of 73. The custom bathroom design customers usually live in a single dwelling. The wife is more influential and is the prime decision maker about bathroom designs.

2. Discuss the difference between conclusions and recommendations in research reports.

3. Assume that Wendy's International, Inc., wants to diversify into another fast food area. You are required to prepare a brief report for the company executives outlining an attractive opportunity. In preparing the report, go through the following steps:
   (a) Decide on the particular fast food area you think most appropriate.
   (b) Collect secondary data relating to the area and analyze consumption trends over the past five years (or ten years).
   (c) Decide on the outline of the report and its various sections.
   (d) Develop the appropriate tables and charts to support your analysis.
   (e) Write the report.

4. Describe the information that should be contained in the summary, and discuss why this is the most important part of the research report.

5. In presenting a report to a group of grocery store managers, a researcher stated the following: "The data from the judgment sample of 10 grocery stores was analyzed and the results show that the 95 percent confidence interval for average annual sales in the population of grocery stores is $1,000,000 ± $150,000."
   (a) As far as the audience is concerned, what is wrong with this statement?
   (b) Rewrite the statement. Be sure to include all of the relevant information while correcting the problem.

Suggested Additional Readings

For excellent, succinct treatments of how to write better, see

Kenneth Roman and Joel Raphaelson, *Writing That Works* (New York: Harper and Row, 1981).

William Strunk, Jr., and E. B. White, *The Elements of Style* (New York: Macmillan Company, 1959).

William Zinsser, *On Writing Well,* 3rd ed. (New York: Harper and Row, 1985).

Chapter 21

The Oral Research Report

+ + + +

+ + + +

+ + + +

+ + + +

Learning Objectives

Upon completing this chapter, you should be able to

1. Specify the first rule to keep in mind when preparing an oral report.
2. Describe the two most common forms of organization for oral reports.
3. Discuss the key points a presenter should keep in mind regarding the use of visual aids.
4. Explain how the time allotted for an oral presentation should be organized.
5. Describe the circumstances in which a pie chart is most effective.
6. Explain the best use of a line chart.
7. Describe the circumstances in which a stratum chart is most effective.
8. Cite the reason why bar charts are so widely used.
9. Describe the circumstances in which a grouped-bar chart is most effective.

Case in Marketing Research

It was 8:30 Monday morning when Kathy Moran and Jessica Ellis pulled into the parking lot at Oakhurst Valley Hospital. While Jessica was unloading a portfolio of flip charts and overhead transparencies from the trunk, Kathy spotted Glen Roper, the hospital's director of marketing, locking his car nearby.

"Hi, Glen," she called across the lot.

"Kathy! You're here early. I thought our meeting wasn't until ten o'clock," Glen said.

"It isn't, but I'm a former Girl Scout, and I still believe in being prepared," Kathy said with a laugh. "I wanted time to check out the room, test the sound system, and find the coffee machine before we're 'on' at ten."

"Sounds wise to me," Glen said. "I'll show you where we'll be meeting."

"By the way, Glen," Kathy said, "This is Jessica Ellis. She was a research associate on the Oakhurst project and was responsible for writing the report. Jessica is one of the rapidly rising stars in our organization."

"Pleased to meet you, Jessica," Glen said. "What can I tell you about Oakhurst before the meeting begins?"

"I guess at this point I'm mostly interested in how many people will be at the meeting and who they are," Jessica said.

"Frankly, this meeting is likely to be much larger than I had originally intended," Glen said. "Initially I thought we'd hold it in the board room with some of the directors; Mr. Stockbridge, the CEO; the medical director; a few people from my staff; the public relations head; and our financial officer. However, there's been so much interest in the idea of alternative-care centers that there are now going to be several department heads, some of the nursing staff, the social service people, and even the president of the Ladies Auxiliary, who happens, by the way, to be Stockbridge's wife. It's really a mixed group. To accommodate everybody I've had to move the meeting to the amphitheatre in the west wing. I tried to reach you yesterday to let you know about the changes, but I guess we missed each other."

Kathy and Jessica exchanged glances.

"It's a good thing we got here early," Kathy said. "We've got our work cut out for us."

Discussion Issues

1. If you were in charge of delivering the final oral report on your company's research project, what kind of information would you want in advance?

2. How would you use that information in preparing your report?

3. How might your oral report differ from your written report?

In addition to the written report, most marketing research investigations require one or more oral reports. Often clients, or those in the company for whom the study is being undertaken, want progress reports during the course of the project. Almost always they require a formal oral report at the conclusion of the study. The principles surrounding the preparation and delivery of the oral report parallel those for the written report.

◆ Preparing the Oral Report

As we emphasized in the preceding chapter, the first requirement is to know the audience. What is their technical level of sophistication? What is their involvement in the project? Their interest? Once again, researchers may want to present more detailed reports to those who are deeply involved in the project or who have a high level of technical sophistication than to those who are only slightly involved or interested.

In general, it is better to err on the side of too little technical detail rather than too much. Executives want to hear and see what the information means to them as managers of marketing activities. What do the data suggest with respect to marketing actions? They can ask for the necessary clarification with respect to the technical details if they want it.

Another important consideration is how the presentation is organized. There are two popular forms of organization. Both begin by stating the general purpose of the study and the specific objectives that were addressed. They differ, however, with respect to when the conclusions are introduced. In the most popular structure, the conclusions are introduced after all of the evidence supporting a particular course of action is presented. This allows the presenter to build a logical case in sequential fashion. By progressively disclosing the facts, the presenter has the opportunity to deal with audience concerns and biases as they arise, and thus lead them to the conclusion that the case builds.

In the alternative structure, conclusions are presented immediately after the purpose and main objectives. This structure tends to involve managers immediately in the findings. It not only gets them to think about what actions the results suggest, but also alerts them to pay close attention to the evidence supporting the conclusions. This format allows managers to evaluate the strength of the evidence supporting an action, since they know beforehand the conclusions that were drawn from it.

The structure a presenter decides to use should depend on the particular company's style and preferences and on the presenter's own level of comfort with each form of organization. In either case, the evidence supporting the conclusions must be presented systematically, and the conclusions drawn must be consistent with the evidence.

A third important element in an effective oral presentation is the use of appropriate visual aids. Depending on the size of the group and the physical facilities in which the meeting is held, flip charts, transparencies, slides, and even chalkboards can all be used to advantage. Regardless of which type of visual is used, make sure it can be read easily by those in the back of the room. Keep the visuals simple so they can be understood at a glance. Whenever possible, use figures rather than tables to make the points, as figures are more easily understood.

◆ Delivering the Oral Report

Honor the time limit set for the meeting. Use no more than a third to a half of the time set aside for the formal presentation. But be careful not to rush the presentation of the information contained in the charts. Remember, the audience is seeing

Back to the Case

It has been a frenzied hour and a half at Oakhurst for Kathy and Jessica, making additional copies of a handout, finding chalk for the blackboard, testing the microphone on the podium, and making some last-minute revisions in the amount of detail Kathy would present in her report.

Now Jessica sat with the other members of Pierce Research Associates while Kathy presented the group's conclusions to the assembled audience.

"We at Pierce know that the idea of alternative-care centers is a popular one here at Oakhurst," Kathy said. "We understand the necessity of finding a new competitive niche in this highly competitive environment. But after extensive study, we must recommend against that particular route of expansion. As you will see when I present our data, it is clear that while 67 percent of the population said they were in favor of establishing such centers, 85 percent of those answering our survey also said they had family doctors. When we probed further, it became obvious that most of the people polled thought the centers were a great alternative 'for other people.'

"While we are unanimous in our belief that building alternative-care centers would not be

wise, we have isolated a market that we feel is currently being underserved in this community, and may present a profitable route for Oakhurst to pursue. That is the field of urgent-care centers. I will discuss that concept more thoroughly later in my presentation," Kathy continued.

Jessica looked around her. There wasn't a happy face in the audience. The members of the Pierce staff knew that their report was going to bring unwelcome news to the Oakhurst community. Jessica only hoped that Kathy's skill and diplomacy would help them over the rough spots until the hospital could be convinced of the real message in their findings.

As Kathy finished her presentation, there was an expectant rustle in the audience.

"I've left the last half-hour of my talk for questions and answers," Kathy said. "Please feel free to ask any of us to clear up any points that may be confusing, or about anything we may have touched on too briefly."

The hall was quiet, expectant. Then a booming voice from the upper level of the amphitheatre asked, "What makes you so sure that those people who so heartily endorsed our alternative-care idea won't use it?" All eyes turned to Benson Stockbridge, the hospital's CEO.

"A good question, Mr. Stockbridge, and one of the trickiest marketing researchers must deal with. What we have here is the difference between attitudes and intentions. While most people had the attitude that the centers would be good, on average they also had had their own family doctors for eleven or more years. In spite of what they said about the concept, when we asked additional questions about expected use, it was clear they had no intention of using the facility themselves. We designed our research very carefully to go beyond what people say, to see what they plan to do, and how those two relate."

One popular way of structuring an oral presentation is to present the study's findings early in the report, immediately following the purpose and main objectives of the research. This format allows the audience to see how the evidence subsequently presented supports the conclusions that were presented.

It is also important to leave ample time for a question-and-answer period following the formal presentation. In this way the audience can ask for clarification of any confusing material, and the presenter can use the questions asked as a way of emphasizing the points made earlier in the talk.

them for the first time. Order your presentation in such a way that there is enough time both to present and discuss the most critical findings. Reserve the remaining time for questions and further discussion.

One of the unique benefits of the oral presentation is that it allows interaction. A question-and-answer period may be the most important part of your presentation. It allows you to clear up any confusion that may have arisen during the course of your talk, to emphasize points that deserve special attention, and to get a feeling for the issues that are of particular concern or interest to your audience. The nature of the questions raised during a progress report may help you structure your final report to best advantage.

Research Window 21.1
How to Use a Microphone Well

Bungling at the microphone can create a "sound barrier" between you and your audience. But using a sound system effectively can connect you and bring your ideas to the audience in a powerful, intimate way. Here's some useful advice.

- **The mike must be aimed at your mouth, about six to eight inches away from you.** Adjust the microphone height to mouth level quickly, before you say a word. Then point the mike toward your mouth. Don't hunch over to reach the mouthpiece; instead, as recording engineer David Satz says, "let the microphone address you."

- **Check out the sound system before you speak.** "You have a right to have someone there who knows the system," says Satz, "and you have a right to a few moments of practice." If possible, meet with the sound operator.

- **When you test a microphone, just talk into it normally and ask someone to listen.** Never blow into it.

- **Let the sound system work for you.** Let *it* do the broadcasting. Keep your volume, inflections, and pacing in your normal range. Listen to how well the system is working for those ahead of you and, when it's your turn, adjust your voice as necessary.

- **When using a hand-held microphone,** hold it in front of you, aimed at your mouth (not under your chin). Be careful that your handling of the microphone does not make noises—watch out for clunking finger rings.

- **In a question-and-answer session,** don't aim your microphone at the questioner. Instead, repeat the question over the sound sys-

Correct use of a microphone is very important to a successful presentation of ideas.

Source: Used with permission of The Coca-Cola Company.

tem (following this procedure also gives you an extra moment to frame an answer).

- **Know when not to use a sound system.** If you can be heard comfortably by all the people in the room without amplification, by all means, talk without a microphone. Relying on a sound system for a few dozen people, or in a room with excellent acoustics, distances you from your audience. Check your audibility by stepping away from the mike and asking listeners in the back if they can hear you. Unless you see puzzled stares, proceed on your own steam.

Source: John Stoltenberg, "How to Use a Microphone Well," *Working Woman* (February 1986), p. 79.

Use the time-honored principles of public speaking when delivering the message: Keep the presentation simple and uncluttered so that the audience does not have to backtrack mentally to think about what was said, and choose words and sentences that are appropriate for the tongue. That means spoken speech, your usual vocabulary, and simple phrases.[1] Finally, if the situation demands that you use a microphone, use it well. Research Window 21.1 offers some specific suggestions in this regard.

◆ Graphic Presentation of the Results

The old adage that a picture is worth a thousand words is equally true for business reports. A picture, called a *graphic illustration* in the case of the research report, can indeed be worth a thousand words when it is appropriate to the presentation and well-designed. When inappropriate or poorly designed, such an illustration may actually detract from the value of the written or oral research report. In this section, we will review briefly some of the most popular forms of graphics and when each is best used.[2]

In a research report, graphic illustration generally involves the presentation of quantities in graph form. To be effective, it must be more than simply converting a set of numbers into a drawing; the picture must give the readers an accurate understanding of the comparisons or relationships that they would otherwise have to search for in the numbers in the report and perhaps fail to see. If well done, the graphic illustration will give the readers this understanding more quickly, more forcefully, more completely, and more accurately than could be done in any other way.[3]

Graphic presentation is not the only way to present quantitative information, nor is it always the best. Sometimes text and tables are better used. Graphics should be used only when they serve the purpose better than do these other modes. Written textual material is generally the most useful in explaining, interpreting, and evaluating results, while tables are particularly good for providing emphasis and for vivid demonstrations of important findings. Particularly since some readers tend to shy away from graphic presentation as "too technical," it should be used with discretion and designed with care.

At one time graphic presentation was expensive and often delayed the presentation of reports because the visuals had to be drawn by graphic artists. Computer graphics are changing that. The development of computer software for graphically portraying the results of the study now makes the preparation of visuals fast and inexpensive. There is no longer any excuse for not using graphics when appropriate.[4]

---

[1]There are a number of excellent books available on making effective oral presentations. See, for example, Dorothy Sarnoff, *Make the Most of Your Best: A Complete Program for Presenting Yourself and Your Ideas with Confidence and Authority* (Garden City, N.Y.: Doubleday, 1983).

[2]The presentation by no means includes all the graph forms that could be used, just some of the more common ones. Those interested in more detail should see Mary E. Spear, *Practical Charting Techniques* (New York: McGraw-Hill, 1969); Calvin F. Schmid, *Handbook of Graphic Presentation* (New York: Ronald, 1954); Paul Douglas, *Communication through Reports* (Englewood Cliffs, N.J.: Prentice-Hall, 1957); Robert L. Shurter, *Written Communications in Business* (New York: McGraw-Hill, 1957); and Edward R. Tufte, *The Visual Display of Quantitative Information* (Cheshire, Conn.: Graphics Press, 1983).

[3]American Management Association, *Making the Most of Charts: An ABC of Graphic Presentation, Management Bulletin* 28 (New York: American Telephone and Telegraph Company, 1960).

[4]See Hirotaka Takeuchi and Allan H. Schmidt, "New Promise of Computer Graphics," *Harvard Business Review,* 58 (January–February 1980), pp. 122–131, for discussion of the elements necessary for generating report graphics by computer and the development trends with respect to these elements.

Advances in computer graphics allow marketing researchers to communicate complex information more effectively than ever before.

Source: Courtesy of Wang Laboratories, Inc.

There are three basic kinds of graphics: charts that show how much, maps that show where, and diagrams that show how. Since charts are generally the most useful of the three types, the following discussion focuses on some of the more common chart types.

• Pie chart

Circle representing a total quantity and divided into sectors, with each sector showing the size of the segment in relation to that total.

Pie Chart

Probably one of the more familiar charts, the **pie chart** is simply a circle divided into sections, with each of the sections representing a portion of the total. Since the sections are presented as part of a whole, or total, the pie chart is particularly effective for depicting relative size or emphasizing static comparisons. Figure 21.1 (re-

Figure 21.1

Personal Consumption Expenditures by Major Category for 1986

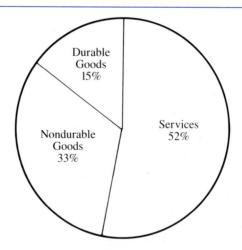

sulting from the data of Table 21.1), for instance, shows the breakdown of personal consumption expenditures by major category for 1986. The conclusion is obvious. Expenditures for services account for the largest proportion of total consumption expenditures. Further, expenditures for services and nondurable goods completely dwarf expenditures for durable goods.

Research Window 21.2
Computer Graphics Take the Worry out of Charts and Graphs

Advances in personal computer hardware and software in the past few years have put the use of charts and graphs for reports within easy reach of most marketing researchers. These advances create opportunities to attack the thorniest problem marketing researchers face: communicating complex information to research users.

The effective use of report graphics attacks this problem directly. Graphics actually can improve the communication of information and add impact to the message delivered. The reason for this is simple: typically, research deals with quantitative information; yet people are more comfortable dealing with verbal, and especially visual, information. Charts and graphs can help.

The new technology has many advantages over the laborious, time-consuming, and expensive methods previously used. When using computer software to generate a chart, it is easier to detect errors; and correcting them is as easy as correcting a misspelled word with a word processor. In addition, the software will always draw bars in bar charts to the right height.

When creating charts and graphs becomes easy and inexpensive, researchers are more likely to explore many different ways of presenting the information. This is the kind of experimentation that refines the communication power of a chart. It may involve just changing the scale, exploding a wedge in a pie chart, or doing something more dramatic, like rearranging bars or changing the format from a bar chart to a line chart. Using good business graphics software, many of these changes can be made simply by pushing one button instead of another. All of them can be done in a matter of minutes.

As an example, the accompanying two charts use exactly the same data presented in different ways to communicate different messages. Chart

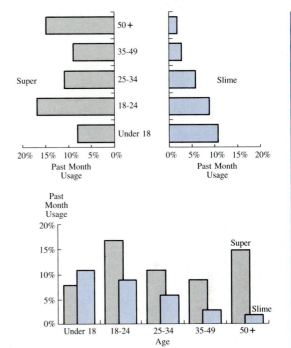

Chart 1A (top) Profile of Sauce Usage by Age
Chart 1B (bottom) Differences in Sauce Usage by Age

1A emphasizes the pattern of brand use across age groups for two products; Chart 1B emphasizes different use of the two brands within each age group.

The microcomputer technology that makes all this possible is changing rapidly. However, the three key elements that are needed to begin remain the same: the right personal computer hardware, the right software or programs to generate the graphics, and the time and willingness to use the first two.

Source: George Parker, "Graphic Advances for Software," *Marketing News*, 20 (January 3, 1986), pp. 64 and 69.

Table 21.1   Personal Consumption Expenditures for 1970–1986 (Billions of Dollars)

		Durable Goods			Nondurable Goods				Services
Year	Total Personal Consumption Expenditures	Total Durable Goods	Motor Vehicles & Parts	Furniture & Household Equipment	Total Nondurable Goods	Food	Clothing and Shoes	Gasoline and Oil	
1970	621.70	85.20	36.20	35.20	265.70	138.90	46.80	22.40	270.80
1971	672.20	97.20	45.40	37.20	278.80	144.20	50.60	23.90	296.20
1972	737.10	111.10	52.40	41.70	300.60	154.90	55.40	25.40	325.30
1973	812.00	123.30	57.10	47.10	333.40	172.10	61.40	28.60	355.20
1974	888.10	121.50	50.40	50.60	373.40	193.70	64.80	36.60	393.20
1975	976.40	132.20	55.80	53.50	407.30	213.60	69.60	40.40	437.00
1976	1,084.30	156.80	72.60	59.10	441.70	230.60	75.30	44.00	485.70
1977	1,204.40	178.20	84.80	65.70	478.80	249.80	82.60	48.10	547.40
1978	1,346.50	200.20	95.70	72.80	528.20	275.90	92.40	51.20	618.00
1979	1,507.20	213.40	96.60	81.80	600.00	311.60	99.10	66.60	693.70
1980	1,668.10	214.70	90.70	86.30	668.80	345.10	104.60	84.80	784.50
1981	1,915.10	239.90	100.50	92.70	740.60	376.50	119.90	92.70	934.70
1982	2,050.70	252.70	108.90	95.70	771.00	398.80	124.40	89.10	1,027.00
1983	2,234.50	289.10	130.40	107.10	816.70	421.90	135.10	90.20	1,128.70
1984	2,428.20	331.20	154.50	118.90	870.10	449.90	147.20	90.70	1,227.00
1985	2,600.50	359.30	169.20	126.80	905.10	469.30	155.20	91.90	1,336.10
1986	2,799.80	414.50	204.70	140.00	932.80	494.00	166.60	74.20	1,452.40

Source: Economic indicators.

Figure 21.1 has three slices, and it is easy to interpret. Had the information been broken into finer categories (for example, if the separate components of durable and nondurable goods had been depicted), a greater number of sections would have been required. Although more information would have been conveyed, emphasis would have been lost. As a rule of thumb, no more than six slices should be generated; the division of the pie should start at the twelve o'clock position; the sections should be arrayed clockwise in decreasing order of magnitude; and the exact percentages should be provided on the graph.[5]

♦ Line chart

Two-dimensional chart constructed on graph paper in which the *X* axis represents one variable (typically time) and the *Y* axis another variable.

Line Chart

The pie chart is a one-scale chart, which is why its best use is for static comparisons of the phenomena at a point in time. The **line chart** is a two-dimensional chart that is particularly useful in depicting dynamic relationships such as time-series fluctua-

---

[5]Jessamon Dawe and William Jackson Lord, Jr., *Functional Business Communication,* 3rd ed. (Englewood Cliffs, N.J.: Prentice-Hall, 1983).

Back to the Case

Jessica was impressed with Kathy's ability to use the question-and-answer period skillfully to reinforce the company's findings. As more and more people asked questions, Jessica could sense a gradual softening in the hostility to Pierce's initial recommendation, and an increased open-mindedness to the alternative that they had suggested.

Kathy recognized a hand in the middle of the audience. It was Tyler McGillis, the hospital's chief financial officer.

"Ms. Moran," he said, "would you please explain again why you think this urgent-care idea would work here at Oakhurst?"

"Certainly, Mr. McGillis," Kathy said. "Let's look at this pie chart. It shows that your four competitors have completely saturated the market for emergency services. There is clearly no room for Oakhurst to gain a foothold in this area.

"However, if we look at this bar chart on emergency room services, an appealing opportunity becomes clear. In our survey, we found that while the need for true emergency services—those dealing with accidents, heart attack victims, etc.—is being met, there is a fairly substantial segment of that population whose needs are not being adequately served. Those are the people with what we might call 'minor emergencies.' They are the 'other' segment on the chart. Those 'others' include such things as the kid who needs a couple of stitches in a knee; the elderly person who has

fallen in the bathroom and has no broken bones but is bruised and shaken up; the out-of-towner with a sudden fever and no family doctor nearby. Those people typically sit in a hospital emergency room, sometimes for hours, while the more serious cases are being attended to. If Oakhurst had what we might call an 'urgent-care facility,' it would meet a need that no other hospital in the area is presently serving."

Jessica looked over at Glen Roper. He was smiling. Even crusty old Stockbridge looked interested. "The battle is won," she thought to herself and breathed a small sigh of relief.

Graphic illustration is often an important part of an oral presentation. If well-designed and appropriate to the report, charts and graphs can often make a point more clearly than is possible with words or numbers.

With the development of computer graphics, it is now possible for a researcher to generate such graphics easily and inexpensively.

Note: For more information about marketing research in the health-care industry, see Paul H. Keckley, "Using and Misusing Marketing Research in the Healthcare Industry," *Healthcare Financial Management,* (December 1985), pp. 31–35. Also please note that the art in this case is included only to illustrate a point and is in no way meant to reflect actual data from the health-care industry.

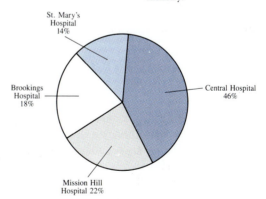

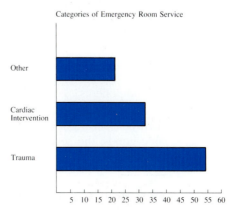

Categories of Emergency Room Service

Figure 21.2   **Retail Sales of New Passenger Cars**

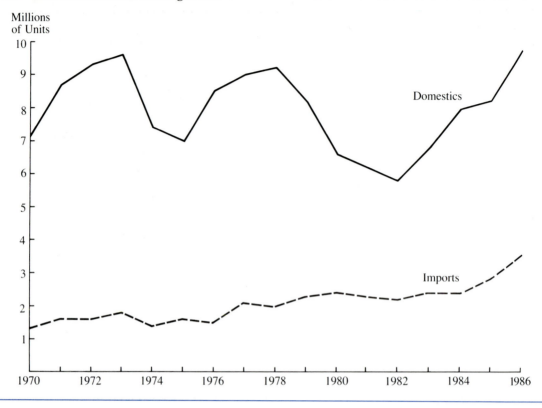

tions of one or more series. For example, Figure 21.2 (produced from the data of Table 21.2) shows that, for 1970–1986, new car sales of imports were subject to much less fluctuation than were domestic sales.

The line chart is probably used even more often than the pie chart. It is typically constructed on graph paper with the X axis representing time and the Y axis values of the variable or variables. When more than one variable is presented, it is recommended that the lines for different items be distinctive in color or form (dots and dashes in suitable combinations) with identification of the different forms given in a legend.[6]

Stratum Chart

• Stratum chart

Set of line charts in which quantities are aggregated or a total is disaggregated so that the distance between two lines represents the amount of some variable.

The **stratum chart** serves in some ways as a dynamic pie chart in that it can be used to show relative emphasis by sector (for example, quantity consumed by user class) and change in relative emphasis over time. The stratum chart consists of a set of line charts whose quantities are grouped together (or a total that is broken into its components). For example, Figure 21.3 (again resulting from the data of Table 21.1) shows personal consumption expenditures by major category for the seventeen-year period of 1970–1986. The lowest line shows the expenditures just for durable goods, the second lowest line shows the total expenditures for durable plus nondurable goods. Personal consumption expenditures for nondurable goods are

[6]Dawe and Lord, *Functional Business Communication.*

Table 21.2   Retail Sales of New Passenger Cars (Millions of Units)

Year	Domestics	Imports	Total
1970	7.10	1.30	8.40
1971	8.70	1.60	10.30
1972	9.30	1.60	10.90
1973	9.60	1.80	11.40
1974	7.40	1.40	8.80
1975	7.00	1.60	8.60
1976	8.50	1.50	10.00
1977	9.00	2.10	11.10
1978	9.20	2.00	11.20
1979	8.20	2.30	10.50
1980	6.60	2.40	9.00
1981	6.20	2.30	8.50
1982	5.80	2.20	8.00
1983	6.80	2.40	9.20
1984	8.00	2.40	10.40
1985	8.20	2.80	11.00
1986	9.70	3.50	13.20

Source: Economic indicators.

thus shown by the area between the two lines. So it is with the remaining areas. We would need seventeen pie charts (one for each year) to capture the same information, and the message would not be as obvious.

The X axis typically represents time in the stratum chart, and the Y axis again captures the value of the variables. The use of color or distinctive crosshatching is strongly recommended to distinguish the various components in the stratum chart. As was true for the pie chart, no more than six components should be depicted in a stratum chart.

Bar Chart

• Bar chart

Chart in which the relative lengths of the bars show relative amounts of variables or objects.

The **bar chart** can be either a one-scale or two-scale chart. This feature, plus the many other variations it permits, probably accounts for its wide use. Figure 21.4, for example, is a one-scale chart. It also shows personal consumption expenditures by major category at a single point in time. Figure 21.4 presents the same information as Figure 21.1 but is, in at least one respect, more revealing; it not only offers some appreciation of the relative expenditures by major category, but also indicates the magnitude of the expenditures by category. Given the total amount of personal consumption expenditures for 1986, readers could, of course, also generate this information from the pie chart. However, it would involve additional calculations on their part.

Figure 21.5, on the other hand, is a two-scale bar chart. It uses the data contained in Table 21.2 and shows total automobile sales for the period 1970–1986. The Y axis represents quantity, and the X axis, time.

Figure 21.3   Personal Consumption Expenditures by Major Category, 1970–1986

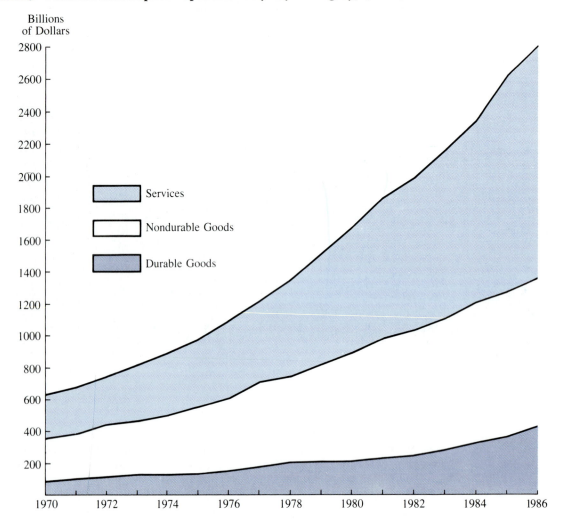

Figure 21.4   Personal Consumption Expenditures by Major Category for 1986

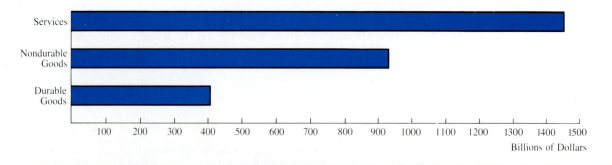

Figure 21.5   Total Automobile Sales, 1970–1986

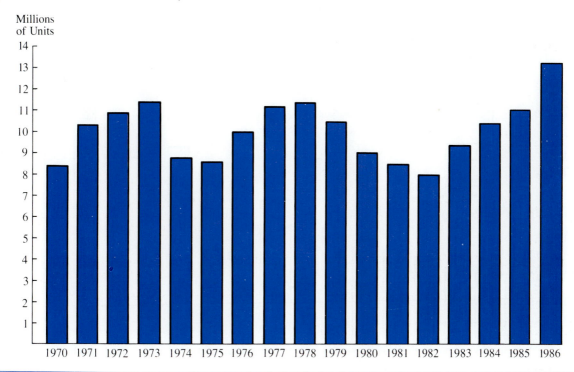

Figures 21.4 and 21.5 show that the bar chart can be drawn either vertically or horizontally. When emphasis is on the change in the variable through time, the vertical form is preferred, with the X axis as the time axis. When time is not a variable, either the vertical or horizontal form is used.

Bar Chart Variations

> • Pictogram
>
> Bar chart in which pictures represent amounts—for example, piles of dollars for income, pictures of cars for automobile production, people in a row for population.

As previously suggested, bar charts are capable of great variation. One variation is to convert them to **pictograms.** Instead of using the length of the bar to capture quantity, amounts are shown by piles of dollars for income, pictures of cars for automobile production, people in a row for population, and so on. This can be a welcome change of pace for the reader if there are a number of graphs in the report.[7]

A variation of the basic bar chart—the grouped-bar chart—can be used to capture the change in two or more series through time. Figure 21.6, for example, shows the change in consumption expenditures by the three major categories for the period 1970–1986. Just as distinctive symbols are effective in distinguishing the separate series in a line chart, distinctive coloring and/or crosshatching is equally helpful in a grouped-bar chart.

---

[7]Pictograms are especially susceptible to perceptual distortions. Report users have to be especially careful when reading them so that they are not misled with respect to the correct conclusions. See Patricia Ramsey and Louis Kaufman, "Presenting Research Data: How to Make Weak Numbers Look Good," *Industrial Marketing,* 67 (March 1982), pp. 66, 68, 70, and 74.

Figure 21.6   **Personal Consumption Expenditures by Major Category, 1970–1986**

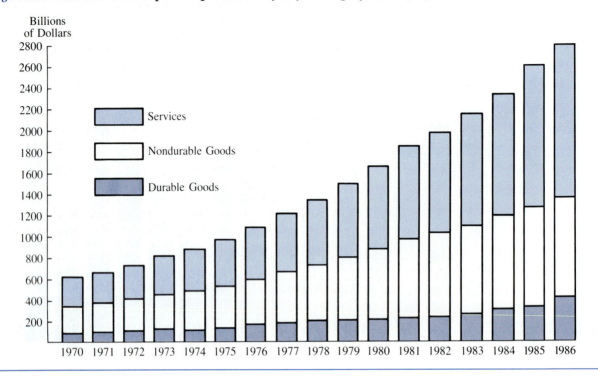

Figure 21.7   **Personal Consumption Expenditures by Major Category, 1975–1986**

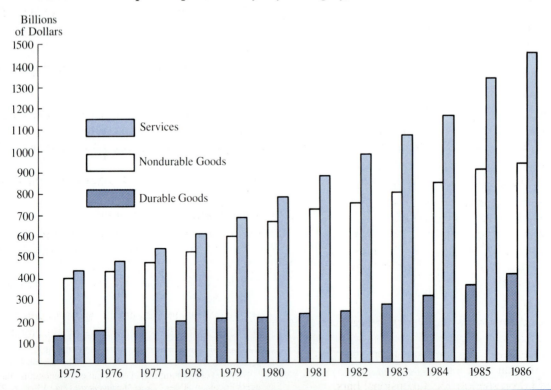

There is also a bar chart equivalent to the stratum chart—the divided-bar chart. Its construction and interpretation are similar to those for the stratum chart. Figure 21.7, for example, is a divided-bar chart of personal consumption expenditures by major category. It shows both total and relative expenditures through time. It, too, makes use of distinctive crosshatching for each component. Research Window 21.3 offers some suggestions on using graphics in slide presentations.

◆ Summary

Learning Objective 1: Specify the first rule to keep in mind when preparing an oral report.
As with written reports, the first rule when preparing an oral report is to know your audience.

Learning Objective 2: Describe the two most common forms of organization for oral reports.
There are two popular forms of organization for oral reports. Both begin by stating the general purpose of the study and the specific objectives that were addressed. In the most popular structure, the conclusions are introduced after all of the evidence supporting a particular course of action is presented. This allows the presenter to build a logical case in sequential fashion. In the alternative structure, conclusions are presented immediately after the purpose and main objectives. This format allows managers to evaluate the strength of the evidence supporting an action, since they know beforehand the conclusions that were drawn from it.

Research Window 21.3
Putting Slide Graphics to Use

Word slides
- Keep them brief: Use key words only.
- Use bullets and color to highlight key points.
- Break up the information to make a series of slides (a progressive or "build" series). Use color to show the new line added to each slide.

Tabular slides
- Use to show lists.
- Keep items brief as possible; arrange them to fill the slide area so the type can be as large as possible.

Box Charts
- Use for organization charts, flow charts.
- Simplify to keep them legible.
- Break up complex charts into a series. (Show flow chart divided by time periods; show organization chart with the overall chart and departmental "close up.")

Bar charts
- Use them for data arranged in segments (by month, year, etc.).
- Choose vertical or horizontal bars (both within horizontal slide format).
- Add drop shadow for dimensional bars.
- Show complex facts clearly by using multiple or segmented bars.
- Divide extensive data into a progressive disclosure series.

Pie charts
- Use them to emphasize the relationship of the parts to the whole.
- Select single pie or double pie.
- Consider options such as drop shadow for dimensional effect, pulled-out slices, etc.
- Arrange the slices to make your point most effectively.
- Divide the slice into a series if that improves effectiveness.

Line graphs and area graphs
- Use these to display trends or continuous data.
- Decide whether line graph or area graph shows your point better.
- Select baseline and scale for maximum effectiveness.
- Use callouts to identify key points in graph.
- Divide extensive data into a series of graphs.

Source: Leslie Blumberg, "For Graphic Presentations, Managers Focus on Slides," *Data Management* (May 1983), p. 22.

Learning Objective 3: Discuss the key points a presenter should keep in mind regarding the use of visual aids.

The visual aids used in an oral report should be easily understood and should be easily seen by those in the back of the room.

Learning Objective 4: Explain how the time allotted for an oral presentation should be organized.

Honor the time limit set for the meeting. Use no more than a third to a half of the time set aside for the formal presentation. Reserve the remaining time for questions and discussion.

Learning Objective 5: Describe the circumstances in which a pie chart is most effective.

A pie chart is a one-scale chart, which is particularly effective in communicating a static comparison.

Learning Objective 6: Explain the best use of a line chart.

The line chart is a two-dimensional chart that is particularly useful in depicting dynamic relationships such as time-series fluctuations of one or more series.

Learning Objective 7: Describe the circumstances in which a stratum chart is most effective.

The stratum chart is in some ways a dynamic pie chart in that it can be used to show relative emphasis by sector and change in relative emphasis over time.

Learning Objective 8: Cite the reason why bar charts are so widely used.

The bar chart can be either a one-scale or two-scale chart. This feature, plus the many other variations it permits, probably accounts for its wide use.

Learning Objective 9: Describe the circumstances in which a grouped-bar chart is most effective.

A variation of the basic bar chart, the grouped-bar can be used to capture the change in two or more series through time.

Discussion Questions, Problems, and Projects

The management of the Seal-Tight Company, manufacturers of metal cans, presents you with the following information.

The Seal-Tight Company
A Comparative Statement of Profit and Loss for the Fiscal Years 1982–1986

	1982	1983	1984	1985	1986
Net sales	$40,000,000	$45,000,000	$48,000,000	$53,000,000	$55,000,000
Cost and expenses					
Cost of goods sold	$28,000,000	$32,850,000	$33,600,000	$39,750,000	$40,150,000
Selling and admin. expenses	4,000,000	4,500,000	4,800,000	5,300,000	5,500,000
Depreciation	1,200,000	1,350,000	1,440,000	1,590,000	1,650,000
Interest	800,000	900,000	960,000	1,060,000	1,100,000
	$34,000,000	$39,600,000	$40,800,000	$47,700,000	$48,400,000
Profits from operations	6,000,000	5,400,000	7,200,000	5,300,000	6,600,000
Estimated taxes	$ 2,400,000	$ 2,160,000	$ 2,880,000	$ 2,120,000	$ 2,640,000
Net profits	$ 3,600,000	$ 3,240,000	$ 4,320,000	$ 3,180,000	$ 3,960,000

1. Develop a visual aid to present the company's distribution of sales revenues in 1986.

2. Develop a visual aid that would compare the change in the net profit level to the change in the net sales level.

3. Develop a visual aid that will present the following expenses (excluding COGS) over the five-year period: selling and administration expenses and depreciation and interest expenses.

4. The management of Seal-Tight has the following sales data relating to its two major competitors.

	1982	1983	1984	1985	1986
Metalmax Co.	$35,000,000	$40,000,000	$42,000,000	$45,000,000	$48,000,000
Superior Can Co.	$41,000,000	$43,000,000	$45,000,000	$46,000,000	$48,000,000

You are required to prepare a visual aid to facilitate the comparison of the sales performance of Seal-Tight Company with its major competitors.

Suggested Additional Readings

For an excellent discussion of how to make effective oral presentations, see

Dorothy Sarnoff, *Make the Most of Your Best: A Complete Program for Presenting Yourself and Your Ideas with Confidence and Authority* (Garden City, N.Y.: Doubleday, 1983).

For discussion of how to develop effective graphics, see

Mary E. Spear, *Practical Charting Techniques* (New York: McGraw-Hill, 1969).

Edward R. Tufte, *The Visual Display of Quantitative Information* (Cheshire, Conn.: Graphics Press, 1983).

Chapter 22

The Research Project and the Firm's Marketing Intelligence System

+ + + +
+ + + +
+ + + +
+ + + +

Learning Objectives

Upon completing this chapter, you should be able to

1. Explain the difference between a project emphasis in research and a marketing information system (MIS) or decision support system (DSS) emphasis.
2. Define what is meant by a marketing information system.
3. Cite some of the problems inherent in a marketing information system.
4. Define what is meant by a decision support system.
5. What feature most clearly differentiates DSS from MIS?

Case in Marketing Research

Driving in a light rain through the lush midwestern farmland, Jerry Mendelsohn had plenty of time to think about what he had seen that day at the giant corporate offices of Beecham Foods. As a data-processing manager for a consulting firm, Mendelsohn had visited Beecham in the early 1970s and had come away very impressed with its sophisticated financial systems. Now, more than fifteen years later, as the information officer of yet another company, he had again visited Beecham and been shocked at what he had seen.

Over the past decade, the company had been transforming itself from a producer of cake mixes and other baking products into a diversified food and restaurant giant. While the company focused on managing its radical growth, its information systems had been neglected and had fallen into disrepair. Attempting to keep a hold on their personal areas of operations, the company's managers had begun using a variety of personal computers as a way of bypassing the company's over-stressed central information systems.

As the person charged with bringing order out of chaos, Mendelsohn knew he had a big job ahead of him. The problems were many. As the company focused its attention, resources, and creativity on its new areas of business, management information systems had suffered. They had been perceived by the company as a largely unwarranted expense and thus funded inconsistently. New acquisitions of companies had brought other problems. Whenever a company was added, so was another set of computers and another data-processing department. The operations of smaller companies could sometimes be integrated into the existing organization, but major acquisitions entailed major headaches. Often they were linked with the parent company by what Mendelsohn could only characterize as "wooden technical bridges."

By the early 1980s, top management had begun to recognize the problems. The biggest impact of the failure of systems came in the area of market information, where Beecham found itself losing out to competitors whose analysis of market intelligence allowed them to respond better to conditions.

That was when they had turned to Jerry Mendelsohn. As one of the top information strategists in the business, he was charged with the responsibility of designing a system that would keep up with the strategic direction of the corporation, as well as provide individual product managers with the information they needed to make decisions.

It was going to be a big job, Jerry knew, but an exciting one too. It wasn't often that he got to design an entire system, practically from scratch.

Discussion Issues

1. If you were Jerry Mendelsohn, what questions would you want answered before beginning to design an information system?

2. What kinds of marketing information might be included in such a system?

3. How might each department's different needs for the same data—sales information, for example—be reconciled most efficiently?

Source: This fictitious case is based on Pillsbury's actual experience in designing a corporate information system. For more details on Pillsbury's information strategy, see Daniel Ruby, "Microcomputers Form the Cornerstone of Firm's New Information Strategy," *PC Week,* (February 11, 1986), pp. 39–42.

The subject of marketing research can be approached in a number of ways. In this book we have used a *project emphasis* as the basis for our discussion. Using this perspective, we focused on how to define a problem and then develop the research needed to answer it. Because we have broken the research process down into components small enough to be discussed in the space of a chapter, it may seem to be a series of disconnected bits and pieces. However, as pointed out in Chapter 2, the research process is anything but a set of disconnected parts. All the steps are highly interrelated, and a decision made at one stage has implications for the others as well. Now that we have closely examined each of the individual components of the research process, in this chapter we will look once again at how they work together. We will also review some of the key decisions that must be made as the process unfolds.

A research project should not be viewed as an end in itself. Projects arise because managerial problems need solving. The problems themselves may concern the identification of market opportunities, the evaluation of alternative courses of action, or control of marketing operations. Since these activities, in turn, are the essence of the managerial function, research activity can also be viewed from the broader perspective of the firm's marketing intelligence system. The second part of this chapter, therefore, focuses on the nature and present status of marketing intelligence.

♦ The Research Process Revisited

Earlier in this text, we suggested marketing research involved the systematic gathering, recording, and analyzing of data about problems relating to the marketing of goods and services. We pointed out that these activities are logically viewed as a sequence of steps called the research process. The stages of the process were identified as follows:

1. Formulate the problem.
2. Determine the research design.
3. Determine data-collection method.
4. Design data-collection forms.
5. Design sample and collect data.
6. Analyze and interpret the data.
7. Prepare the research report.

The decision problem logically comes first. It dictates the research problem and the design of the project. However, the transition from problem to project is not an automatic one. It is not unusual for a researcher to go from problem specification to tentative research design and then back to problem respecification and modified research design. This back-and-forth process is perfectly natural, and, in fact, reflects one of the researcher's more important roles: to help to define and redefine the problem so that it can be researched, and, more important, answer the decision maker's problem.

While this task might appear to be simple in principle, in practice it can be formidable, as it requires a clear specification of objectives, alternatives, and environmental constraints and influences. The decision maker may not readily provide these to the researcher, who then must dig them out in order to design effective research.

In some cases research may not even be necessary. If the decision maker's views are so strongly held that no amount of information might change them, the research will be wasted. It is up to the researcher to determine this before, rather than after, conducting the research. Often this can be accomplished by asking "what if" questions. What if consumer reaction to the product concept is overwhelmingly favorable? What if it is unfavorable? What if it is only slightly favorable? If the decision maker indicates that he or she will make the same decision in each case, there may be important objectives that have never been explicitly stated. This is a critical finding. Every research project should have one or more objectives, and one should not proceed to the other steps in the process until these can be explicitly stated.

It is also important to ask at this point whether the anticipated benefits of the research are likely to exceed the expected costs. It is a mistake to assume that simply because something might change as a result of the research, the research is warranted. It may be that the likelihood of finding something that might warrant a change in the decision is so remote that the research still will be wasted. Researchers constantly need to ask: Why should this research be conducted? What could we possibly find out that we do not already know? Will the expected benefits from the research exceed its costs? If the answers indicate research, then the question logically turns to, what kind?

If the problem cannot be formulated as some specific "if-then" conjectural relationships exploratory research is in order. The primary purpose of exploratory research is gathering some ideas and insights into the phenomenon. The output of an exploratory study will *not* be answers but more specific questions or statements of tentative relationships. The search for such insights demands a flexible research design. Structured questionnaires or probability sampling plans are not used in exploratory research, since the emphasis is not on gathering summary statistics but on gaining insight into the problem. The personal interview is much more appropriate than the telephone interview, and that in turn is more appropriate than a mail survey, since the unstructured question is most useful in the experience survey. Interviewees should be handpicked because they can provide the wanted information. In such cases, a convenience or judgment sample is very much in order, whereas it would be completely out of place in descriptive or causal research. Focus groups can also be productive.

The researcher may also want to conduct a survey of the literature or an analysis of selected cases. These steps can be advantageous in exploratory research, particularly if the researcher remembers that the goal of exploratory research is to discover ideas and tentative explanations of the phenomenon, and not to fix on one idea as being the sole definitive explanation. The analysis of published data may be particularly productive if it reveals sharp contrasts or other striking features that may help to illuminate the reasons behind the phenomenon under investigation.

If exploratory research has succeeded in generating one or more specific hypotheses to be investigated, the next research step would logically be descriptive or causal research. The design the researcher actually selects depends largely on how convinced he or she is that the tentative explanation is indeed the correct explanation for the phenomenon. Of course, the feasibility and cost of conducting the experiment are also important factors in determining research design. While experiments typically provide more convincing proof of causal relationships, they also usually cost more than descriptive designs. This is one of the reasons why descriptive designs are the most commonly employed type in marketing research.

Whereas exploratory designs are flexible, descriptive designs are rigid. Descriptive designs demand a clear specification of the who, what, when, where, how, and why of the research before data collection begins. They generally employ structured questionnaires or scales because these forms provide advantages in coding and tabulating. In descriptive designs, the emphasis is on generating an accurate picture of the relationships between and among variables. Probability sampling plans are desirable, but if the sample is to be drawn using nonprobabilistic methods, it is important that a quota sample be used. Descriptive studies typically rely heavily on cross-tabulation analysis or other means of investigating the association among variables, such as regression analysis, although the emphasis can also be on the search for differences. The great majority of descriptive studies are cross-sectional, although some do use longitudinal information.

Experiments are the best means we have for making inferences about cause and effect relationships, since, if designed properly, they provide the most compelling evidence regarding concomitant variation, time order of occurrence of variables, and elimination of other factors. A key feature of the experiment is that the researcher

Research Window 22.1
The Research Results May Be Enlightening—But Will They Be Used?

Every year private firms spend millions of dollars on marketing research, yet little is known about the factors affecting the use of this research. Two studies attempted to find answers to that question. One addressed the issue from the research consumer's perspective; the other studied researchers' perceptions of factors likely to affect managerial use of marketing research information.

The research consumers studied were marketing managers in consumer products/service businesses. The researchers included in the sample were originally culled from the *Membership Roster* of the American Marketing Association, and then narrowed to a list of only those who worked for agencies specializing in research on consumer products or services.

The research showed that there were some important differences between managers and researchers in terms of what they perceive to be the most important factors influencing research use.

Both communities agreed that the degree of interaction between researchers and managers had an important affect on the potential use of marketing information. However, researchers consider this to be the most important factor, whereas marketing managers do not rate it as highly as the organizational structure of the firm to which the manager belongs, or the technical quality of the final research report. Researchers

tend to place the technical quality aspects of a report well below not only the extent of researcher-manager interaction, but also below the political acceptability of their recommendations and the degree to which they have been able to uncover new avenues and directions for the client firm.

Researchers generally felt that the degree to which a research recommendation was politically acceptable to key managers in the client firm was a very important factor in determining whether the research was used. Research is not conducted in a political vacuum. As one senior research executive in an in-house research department at a leading U.S. corporation said,

> Most major products in our corporation have champions, i.e., people who are committed to the concept. There are also champions on the other side, i.e., those who are opposed to the product. We find it desirable to meet with both sets of champions separately . . . to extract an understanding of what market research can accomplish. We try to negotiate with them what they will accept as supporting or negative evidence so that, when it comes, either way we won't have any arguments.

If this is the position taken by a researcher within the company, imagine the difficulty an external research supplier might have in determining what marketing research can be expected to accomplish in a firm. If the research shows that

is able to control who will be exposed to the experimental stimulus (the presumed cause). Depending on the nature of the experiment, subjects may be individual consumers, members of panels, or other elements from the population of interest. Sampling plays little role in experiments other than in determining which objects are going to be assigned to which treatment conditions.

Because the goal is to test a specific relationship, causal designs also demand a clear specification of what is to be measured and how it is to be measured. Structured data-collection instruments such as questionnaires and scales are often used. Researchers also rely heavily on the observation method for collecting data, because this method tends to produce more objective and accurate information.

The major objective in analyzing experimental results is to determine if there are differences between those exposed to the experimental stimulus and those not ex-

the pet product of a senior marketing manager (its "champion") is not faring well in the marketplace, the manager may be as likely (or more likely) to criticize the research study than to find fault with the product. Hence, it is understandable that researchers place a high value on the political acceptability of research findings in judging their chances of being used.

Another variable that differs substantially between researchers and managers is whether surprising new findings are likely to be used. The researchers think that the more surprising the results, the more likely they are to be acted upon. Managers disagree. While researchers value findings that provide new, hitherto unknown directions, managers say they are more likely to use research that reduces uncertainty and verifies existing information.

In keeping with this finding, the study's authors also found that managers dislike findings that do not coincide with their expectations. As they noted, "researchers saw the variable surprise as being of minor importance in influencing research use, in sharp contrast to managers who saw surprise as a kind of filter or reality test which helped them evaluate market research results. It is conceivable that researchers underrate the degree to which their clients dislike being taken by surprise. Both in the mail survey of managers and in our personal interviews we repeatedly found marketing managers using re-

search as an uncertainty-reducer. Market research was required to fill an information gap. If in the process of doing so it also led to unforeseen, unanticipated, and perhaps counter-intuitive findings, managers were likely to be upset. Managers do not like being told they may be wrong, or even out of touch."

Finally, while researchers consider the quality of a report's presentation and technical quality to be equally important in influencing research use, managers single out the technical quality as being the most important attribute of the report, but downplay the importance of the form of presentation. The study's authors explained this finding by noting that because managers cannot comfortably tell researchers that they do not like findings that do not coincide with expectations, they may select one or several of the research report attributes to censure. The technical quality of the report is frequently the attribute selected.

Future marketing researchers may want to keep the words of one research supplier in mind: "It is more important to recognize the comfort zones of the [client firm] and then let the technicality of the presentation reflect what is comfortable to the manager."

Source: Rohit Deshpande and Gerald Zaltman, "A Comparison of Factors Affecting Researcher and Manager Perceptions of Market Research Use," *Journal of Marketing Research,* 21 (February 1984), pp. 32–38.

posed. Although researchers generally use analysis of variance to investigate and measure these differences, other techniques (for example, the *t* test for the difference in means of independent or correlated samples) are used as well.

The previous paragraphs should indicate how significantly the steps are interrelated and, in particular, how the basic nature of the research design implies a number of things with respect to the structure of the data-collection form, design of the sample, collection, and analysis of the data. A decision about appropriate research design does not completely determine the latter considerations, of course, but simply suggests their basic nature. The analyst still has to determine their specific format. For example, is the structured questionnaire to be disguised or undisguised? Is the probability sample to be simple, stratified, or cluster? How large a sample is needed? Does the data-collection instrument dictate a data analysis procedure for nominal, ordinal, interval, or ratio data? These questions, too, will be determined in large part by the way the research question is framed, although the ingenuity displayed by the designer of the research will determine their final form. The researcher will have to balance the various sources of error that can arise in the process when determining this final form. In effecting this balance, the researcher must be concerned with assessing and minimizing total error; this often means assuming additional error in one of the parts of the process so that total error can be decreased.

Once the research has been completed, several factors influence whether or not the results will actually be used. Research Window 22.1 reports the findings of two studies that were done to determine those factors.

◆ The Research Project and the Marketing Intelligence System

Very early in this book we suggested that the fundamental purpose of marketing research is to assist marketing managers with the decisions they must make within any of the domains of their responsibilities. As directors of the firms' marketing activities, marketing managers have an urgent need for information, or *marketing intelligence*. They might need to know about the changes that should be expected in customer purchasing patterns, the types of marketing institutions that might evolve, which of several alternative product designs might be the most successful, the shape of the firm's demand curve, or any of a number of other issues that could affect the way they plan, solve problems, or evaluate and control the marketing effort.

Marketing research has traditionally been responsible for this intelligence function. As the formal link with the environment, marketing research generates, transmits, and interprets feedback originating in the environment regarding the success of the firm's marketing plans, and the strategies and tactics employed in implementing those plans.

The project emphasis in research, which has been used in this book, is just one of the ways by which marketing intelligence is provided. Two other ways are through *marketing information systems (MIS)* and *decision support systems (DSS)*.[1] In the final section of this chapter, we will explore some of the differences between

---

[1]Information systems can be discussed at both the functional and corporate levels. When discussing corporate information systems, MIS stands for *management* information system, and it is understood that DSS refers to the structure of the decision support system for the whole company. Since our interest is marketing intelligence, we will use the term MIS to refer to the *marketing* information system and DSS to refer to the structure of the information system to support marketing decision making.

the project emphasis and these alternative schemes for providing marketing intelligence. One interesting way to visualize the difference between these two perspectives is to think of one as a flash bulb and the other as a candle.

The difference between marketing research and marketing intelligence is like the difference between a flash bulb and a candle. Let's say you are dancing in the dark. Every

Back to the Case

Jerry Mendelsohn was back at Beecham headquarters for his first meeting with top management since he had begun designing the company's information systems. While he knew the company's executives were basically in favor of the proposed system, he still anticipated some problems since the capital investment required was substantial.

Standing at a small lectern in the company's plush conference room, Jerry began his presentation to the assembled group of officers.

"Ladies and gentlemen," he said, "as you know, Beecham has some serious problems with regard to its information systems. However, we also have a unique opportunity. Because we are, in essence, beginning anew, we can take advantage of new technology. By contrast, our competitors, who may have temporarily been ahead of us with systems put together over the past decade, will find themselves at a disadvantage as their systems become progressively more outdated.

"By using personal computers," Jerry continued, "we can distribute computer power throughout the company, giving user management unlimited access to strategically critical information. If we can get users to apply PCs creatively within the overall architecture of the system, we can leapfrog the competition.

"Of course, PCs are just one aspect of the overall plan. Most important is a complete overhaul of the company's data base and the communications networks that support the baseline systems."

A hand went up at the back of the room. It was Sarah Margolin, senior vice-president of marketing. "How do you envision information sharing on this system, Mr. Mendelsohn?" she asked.

"In any MIS, basic company information — sales data, distribution information, financial reports, etc. — is shared. However, beyond the generalized company information requirements, I see a need for a more specific information system. In the case of your area, I would propose a highly sophisticated and flexible decision support system," Jerry said.

"How might that work?" Sarah asked.

"Imagine that the product manager in charge of cake mixes commissioned a marketing research study of a new, easy-to-use mix," Jerry said. "The data from that study — information on how added convenience affects users' perceptions of the product, pricing information, effectiveness of promotional strategies — might be highly useful to the product manager in charge of your new line of instant rice mixes. With this system, the manager of the side dish line would have available the information from the cake mix study."

"It sounds interesting," Sarah Margolin said, "but I would like to know more specifically if this system can help us manage similar functions over a variety of brands. Could you investigate how we currently handle our advertising expenditures, for example, and let me know how this system might improve our current methods?"

A management information system is one way by which a constant flow of information is provided to a company's managers. At the functional level the abbreviation of MIS can also refer to the *marketing information system*. These systems can be used to extract and report various data from the company's central data base in a form that meets the needs of a number of different managers.

90 seconds you are allowed to set off a flash bulb. You can use those brief intervals of intense light to chart a course, but remember everybody is moving, too. Hopefully, they'll accommodate themselves roughly to your predictions. You might get bumped and you may stumble every so often, but you can dance along.

On the other hand, you can light a candle. It doesn't yield as much light but it's a steady light. You are continually aware of the movements of other bodies. You can adjust your own course to the courses of others. The intelligence system is a kind of candle. It's no great flash on the immediate state of things, but it provides continuous light as situations shift and change.[2]

Historically, one of the problems of the research project emphasis has been its sporadic nature. A project is often devised in times of crisis and carried out with urgency. This has led to an emphasis on data collection and analysis instead of the development of pertinent information on a regular basis. One suggestion for closing the gap is to think of management in terms of an ongoing process of decision making that requires a constant flow of information rather than as a repeated exercise in crisis intervention, or "putting out fires," as managers often refer to it.

Marketing Information Systems

• Marketing information system (MIS)

Set of procedures and methods for the regular, planned collection, analysis, and presentation of information for use in making marketing decisions.

The earliest attempts at providing a regular flow of information to decision makers focused on **marketing information systems (MIS).** These systems were defined as "a set of procedures and methods for the regular, planned collection, analysis, and presentation of information for use in making marketing decisions."[3] The emphasis in MIS is in the establishment of systems that produce information needed for decision making on a recurring basis rather than on the basis of one-time research studies.

In designing a marketing information system, analysts typically begin by conducting a detailed analysis of each decision maker who might use the system, in order to secure an accurate, objective assessment of each manager's decision-making responsibilities, capabilities, and decision-making style. The analysis typically focuses on securing answers to such questions as the following:[4]

1. What types of decisions is each decision maker regularly called upon to make?
2. What type of information is needed to make these decisions?
3. What types of information does the decision maker regularly receive?
4. What types of special studies are periodically requested?
5. What types of information would the decision maker like to receive but is not presently receiving?
6. What information should be received daily, weekly, monthly, yearly?
7. What magazines and trade journals should be received regularly?
8. What types of data analysis programs would the decision maker like to receive?
9. What improvements would the decision maker like to see made in the current information system?

[2]Statement by Robert J. Williams, who was the creator of the first recognized marketing information system at the Mead Johnson division of the Edward Dalton Company. "Marketing Intelligence Systems: A DEW Line for Marketing Men," *Business Management,* 29 (January 1966), p. 32.

[3]Donald F. Cox and Robert E. Good, "How to Build a Marketing Information System," *Harvard Business Review,* 45 (May–June 1967), pp. 145–154.

[4]Philip Kotler, "A Design for the Firm's Marketing Nerve Center," *Business Horizons,* 9 (Fall 1966), pp. 63–74. See also William R. King, "Developing Useful Decision Support Systems," *Management Decision,* 15 (Fall 1978), pp. 263–273.

When Pillsbury transformed itself from a producer of baking products into a diversified food and restaurant giant, it had to make dramatic changes in its information systems.

Source: Courtesy of The Pillsbury Company.

Given these information specifications, designers would then attempt to specify, get approval for, and subsequently generate a series of reports that would go to the various decision makers.[5] Table 22.1, for example, shows the types of sales analysis reports and sales expense and margin reports developed for a sales information system for a consumer food products company for which the author served as consultant. As might be obvious from Table 22.1, each report was designed so that its form and purpose met the needs of a number of managers with similar job titles. System support people spent a lot of time working with individual decision makers to develop good report formats and efficient systems for extracting and combining information from the various data banks, a typical occurrence when designing MISs. It is common to have separate data banks for general sales data, market data, product data, sales representative data, and consumer data in an MIS.[6]

To understand how an MIS might work, imagine that three executives, a marketing manager, a director of marketing research, and a sales manager in a consumer prod-

[5]See Raymond McLeod, Jr., and John Rogers, "Marketing Information Systems: Uses in the Fortune 500," *California Management Review,* 25 (Fall 1982), pp. 106–118, for the results of a survey conducted among the executives of the Fortune 500 that highlights the relative emphasis on marketing information systems and their use by management in the reporting firms.

[6]See Van Mayros and D. Michael Werner, *Marketing Information Systems* (Radnor, Pa.: Chilton, 1982), for detailed list of the data elements that might go into each one of these data banks.

Table 22.1   Sales Analysis and Sales Expense and Margin Reports in a Consumer Food Products Company

Report Name	Purpose	Frequency	Distribution[a]
A. Sales Analysis Reports			
Region	To provide sales information in units and dollars for each sales office or center in the region as well as a regional total	Monthly	One copy of applicable portions to each regional manager
Sales Office or Center	To provide sales information in units and dollars for each district manager assigned to a sales office	Monthly	One copy of applicable portions to each sales office or center manager
District	To provide sales information in units and dollars for each account supervisor and retail salesperson reporting to the district manager	Monthly	One copy of applicable portions to each district manager
Salesperson Summary	To provide sales information in units and dollars for each customer whom the salesperson calls upon	Monthly	One copy of applicable portions to each salesperson
Salesperson Customer/Product	To provide sales information in units and dollars for each customer whom the salesperson calls upon	Monthly	One copy of applicable portions to each salesperson
Salesperson/Product	To provide sales information in units and dollars for each product that the salesperson sells	Quarterly	One copy of applicable portions to each salesperson
Region/Product	To provide sales information in units and dollars for each product sold within the region. Similar reports would be available by sales office and by district.	Monthly	No general distribution; used for special sales analysis when needed
Region/Customer Class	To provide sales information in units and dollars for each class of customer located in the region. Similar reports would be available by sales office and by district.	Monthly	No general distribution; used for special sales analysis when needed
B. Sales Expense and Margin Reports			
Salesperson Compensation and Expense Report	To provide a listing of salesperson compensation and expenses by district	Monthly	District managers
Salesperson Sales Expense Report	To provide comparative information regarding the ability of the salespeople to manage their expenses	Monthly	District managers
Salesperson Margin Report	To highlight the contribution of profit being made by the various salespeople	Monthly	District managers
Sales Office and Center Margin Report	To highlight the profitability of the various districts within a sales office or center	Monthly	Center managers
Region Margin Report	To highlight the profitability of the various centers within a region	Monthly	Region managers

[a]To understand the report distribution, it is useful to know that salespeople were assigned accounts in sales districts. Salespeople were assigned one or, at most, a couple of large accounts and were responsible for all the grocery stores, regardless of geography, affiliated with these large accounts, or they were assigned a geographic territory and were responsible for all of the stores within that territory. All sales districts were assigned to sales offices or sales centers. The centers were, in turn, organized into regions.

ucts company must make a decision about a new line of frozen yogurt bars. The designer who planned the MIS would have had to anticipate the various information that each executive might want in making the decision about the yogurt bars, and the form that information should take to be most useful to them. The designer would then have to specify the data that would need to be in the system, how that data could be secured, how the data should be stored, how the data in separate data banks should be accessed and combined, and what the report formats should be like.

Once these analysis and design steps were completed, the system would be constructed, which is essentially a programming task. Programmers would write and document the programs that would make data retrieval as efficient as possible with respect to the use of computer time and memory. When all the procedures were debugged so that the system was operating correctly, it would be put on-line. Once implemented, the company's decision makers could ask for any of the previously defined reports. In the early days of MIS, these requests would go through the computer or information systems departments, which would issue a hard copy or printed report. (See Research Window 22.2 for a glossary of terms useful in communicating with people in a firm's computer department.) More recently, it has become common for managers to access such reports directly through computer terminals sitting on their desks.

Research Window 22.2
A Glossary of Computer Terms for the Slightly Bewildered

Today's savvy marketing researchers need to know more than the fact that a dummy table is not where the slow readers sit. If they want state-of-the-art data analysis, they need to be able to carry on deep and meaningful discussions with the company's computer experts as well. These people can be enormously helpful—but only if you can communicate with them in their own language. To aid in that process, we offer a few terms that will help in understanding those technological wizards who ride herd over the company's information systems.

Bug—an elusive creature living in a program that makes it incorrect. The activity of "debugging," or removing bugs from a program, ends when people get tired of doing it, not when the bugs are removed.

Design—what you regret not doing later on.

Documentation—instructions translated from Swedish by a Japanese person for English-speaking persons.

Hardware—the parts of a computer system that can be kicked.

Information center—a room staffed by professional computer people whose job it is to tell you why you cannot have the information you require.

On-line—the idea that a human being should always be accessible to a computer.

Regression analysis—mathematical techniques for trying to understand why things are getting worse.

Strategy—a long-range plan whose merit cannot be evaluated until sometime after those creating it have left the organization.

Systems programmer—a person in sandals who has been in the elevator with a senior vice-president and is ultimately responsible for a phone call you are to receive from your boss.

Source: Charles Bassine, "The Computer Expert's Glossary," *Datamation*, 31 (January 15, 1985), p. 104.

Decision Support Systems

When they were first proposed, MISs were held up as a cureall for management's information needs. The reality, however, often fell short of the promise. The primary reasons were as much behavioral as technical. People tend to resist change, and with MIS, the changes are often substantial. Furthermore, many decision makers are reluctant to disclose to others what factors they use and how they combine those factors when making a decision about a particular issue. But without such disclosure it is next to impossible to design reports that will give them the information they need in the form they need it. Even when managers are willing to disclose their decision-making calculus and information needs, there are problems.

Different managers typically emphasize different things and, consequently, have different data needs. There are very few report formats that are optimal for different users. The developers either have to design "compromise" reports that are satisfactory for a number of users, but not ideal for any single user, or they have to engage in the laborious task of programming to meet each user's needs one at a time. Sometimes top management provides inadequate support for the changes that necessarily accompany MIS, and this failure of support is a common finding in unsuccessful attempts to develop such systems.

Many firms underestimate the costs and time required to establish such systems, usually because they underestimate the size of the task, and/or the changes in organizational structure, key personnel, and electronic data-processing systems that will be required. By the time the system can be developed, the personnel for which it is designed often have different responsibilities, or the economic and competitive environments around which it is designed have changed. Thus, they are often obsolete soon after being put on-line, necessitating that the whole process of analysis, design, development, and implementation begin anew.

Another fundamental problem with MIS is that the systems do not lend themselves to the solution of ill-structured problems, which are the most common kind of problems managers face. The notion of ill-structured problems is addressed in Simon's[7] description of decision making as "a process involving the three stages of intelligence, design, and choice," and in the following explanation by another expert in the field.

> Intelligence refers to the gathering of information from the decision-making system's environment and exploring that information in an effort to recognize the existence of problems. Design refers to the clarification of a problem, to the creation of potential solutions to the problem, and to the assessment of a potential solution's feasibility. Finally, the choice stage involves the act of choosing one of the feasible solutions and investigating the implementation of that solution. . . . If a problem encountered in decision making cannot be fully clarified and if the exploration of potential solutions cannot be completed before a choice must be made, then the problem is said to be ill-structured. Otherwise, the problem is well-structured and can (in principle, at least) be programmed.[8]

Many of the activities performed by managers cannot be programmed, nor can they be performed routinely or delegated, because they involve personal choices.[9]

[7]Herbert A. Simon, *The New Science of Management Decisions* (New York: Harper and Row, 1960).

[8]Robert H. Bonczek, Clyde W. Holsapple, and Andrew B. Whinston, "Developments in Decision Support Systems," undated manuscript, Management Information Research Center, Krannert Graduate School of Management, Purdue University, pp. 3–4.

[9]P. G. Keen and G. R. Wagner, "DSS: An Executive Mind-Support System," *Datamation,* 25 (November 1979), pp. 117–122.

Since a manager's decisions are often tailored to specific situations or formed by unexpected choices, standardized reporting systems lack the necessary scope and flexibility to be useful. Nor can managers, even if they are willing to, specify in advance what they want from programmers and model builders, because decision making and planning are often exploratory. As decision makers and their staffs learn more about a problem, their information needs and methods of analysis evolve. Further, decision making often involves exceptions and qualitative issues that are not easily programmed.

As these problems with MIS became more apparent, the emphasis in supplying marketing intelligence on a regular basis changed from the production of preformatted, batch reports to a **decision support system (DSS)** mode, where a DSS has been defined as "a coordinated collection of data, systems, tools, and techniques with supporting software and hardware by which an organization gathers and interprets relevant information from business and environment and turns it into a basis for marketing action."[10]

A DSS concentrates on the design of data systems, model systems, and dialog systems that can be used interactively by managers. See Figure 22.1.[11] The **data system** includes the processes used to capture and the methods used to store data coming from marketing, finance, and manufacturing, as well as information coming from any number of external or internal sources. Marketing research as discussed in this book would typically supply some of the information input to the data system. Other inputs might come from purchase of syndicated commercial marketing information services like National Purchase Diary Panel or Nielsen Retail Index. Still other information input to the data bank would come from the sales function via invoices or perhaps from salesperson call reports that detail which accounts salespeople are calling upon and how frequently.

In sum, the data system would hold data from a variety of sources and in a variety of forms. The fundamental criterion as to whether a particular piece of data might find itself in the data bank is whether it is useful for marketing decision making. The basic task of a DSS is to capture relevant marketing data in reasonable detail and to put that data in a truly accessible form. It is crucial that the data-base management capabilities built into the system can organize the data the same way a manager does, regardless of the form that organization assumes.

At Ocean Spray, for example, a DSS was developed that allows managers to plan and track the progress of the more than 4,000 sales promotions the company initiates each year. Sales promotion was an early automation target at Ocean Spray because of the many details involved in planning strategy for the sixty-three different sizes and flavors of sauces, juices, and drinks the company markets through sixty-eight retail brokers.

Before the DSS was developed, managers had planned their promotions manually using a time-oriented matrix. Each promotion was positioned on a grid according to its start date, case projections, and promotion terms. In addition, managers allocated case projections by month and calculated trade expenses by promotion type.

Decision support system (DSS)

A coordinated collection of data, system tools, and techniques with supporting software and hardware, by which an organization gathers and interprets relevant information from business and environment and turns it into a basis for marketing action.

Data system

The part of a decision support system that includes the processes used to capture and the methods used to store data coming from a number of external and internal sources.

---

[10]John D. C. Little, "Decision Support Systems for Marketing Managers," *Journal of Marketing,* 43 (Summer 1979), p. 11. See also John D. C. Little, Lakshmi Mohna, and Antoine Hatorin, "Yanking Knowledge from the Numbers: How Marketing Decision Support Systems Can Work for You," *Industrial Marketing,* 67 (March 1982), pp. 46, 50–56.

[11]Figure 22.1 and this surrounding discussion are adapted from the excellent treatment of the subject by Ralph H. Sprague, Jr., and Eric D. Carlson, *Effective Decision Support Systems* (Englewood Cliffs, N.J.: Prentice-Hall, 1982), Chaps. 1 and 2.

Figure 22.1

**Components of a
Decision Support
System**

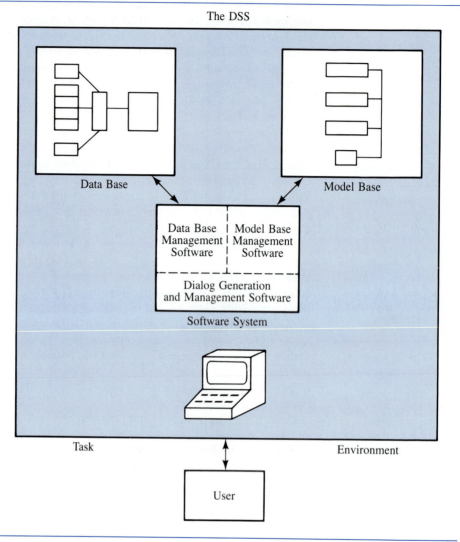

The DSS

Data Base

Model Base

Data Base
Management
Software

Model Base
Management
Software

Dialog Generation
and Management Software

Software System

Task   Environment

User

Source: Ralph H. Sprague, Jr./Eric D. Carlson, *Building Effective Decision Support Systems,* © 1982, p. 29. Adapted by
permission of Prentice-Hall, Inc., Englewood Cliffs, NJ.

The DSS automated the production of promotion plan details and calculated trade
expenses for each manager. The system also enables the managers to access the data
base to perform "what if" analyses.

"A manager can change any variable, such as length of deal or amount of off-
invoice allowed, to see what the potential impact would be," according to one
Ocean Spray executive. "He may ask, 'What will the impact be on my trade expenses
for a particular month if I move a promotion up two weeks?'"

Officials at Ocean Spray stress that the system does not determine what the case
objective should be in a promotion. That is still up to the manager, who works with
the field salespeople to arrive at a decision.

However, the data base helps the managers make their determinations with
greater confidence. "Built into the data base is a history of what each promotion
distribution has been, by product and by market," a company manager noted. "Pro-

motions tend to be consistent from year to year. Thus, a manager has a good idea of how a promotion will distribute over the weeks it runs."

The data base was recently enhanced when the company began getting computer tapes from Selling Areas-Marketing, Inc. (SAMI), the research company that reports on warehouse withdrawals. "Our invoice history provides information on how the trade is buying a promotion," an Ocean Spray executive explained, "and SAMI data gives us the consumer sell-through. The managers now have a more complete picture of what is going on during a promotion period."[12]

Whenever managers look at data, they have a preconceived idea of how something works and, therefore, what is interesting and worthwhile in the data. These ideas are called *models*.[13] Most managers also want to manipulate data to gain a better

[12]Thayer C. Taylor, "Software Juices up Ocean Spray Promotions," *Sales & Marketing Management,* 136 (May 1986), pp. 74–75.

[13]John D. C. Little and Michael N. Cassettari, *Decision Support Systems for Marketing Managers* (New York: American Management Association, 1984), p. 14.

Back to the Case

As Sarah Margolin had suggested, Jerry Mendelsohn had been spending time investigating Beecham's advertising services department. Once again, he was surprised by what he saw.

Beecham's products ranged from ice cream to fish dinners, baking products to frozen vegetables. The company spent $80 million annually advertising these twenty-five to thirty brands. But the truly surprising finding was that the advertising department tracked and analyzed the weekly spending for radio, television, billboards, newspapers, and magazines for each of the brands by hand.

Jerry was eager to tell Sarah Margolin how the system he had proposed would improve the management and control of the complex advertising function.

Over lunch, he told her what he had in mind.

"While I admire the sheer volume of work that your advertising services department has been able to handle," he said, "it nonetheless falls short of the ideal way of managing such massive amounts of information. In doing this all by hand, you have been in the position of reacting to the information instead of leading it or managing it."

"I agree," Sarah said, "but how do you propose to remedy the situation?"

"I would suggest a system designed around personal computers," Jerry said. "Not only should managers in the advertising department have PCs, but they should also be linked with each of your major advertising agencies. In that way, media buyers at the agency, as well as product managers, can easily see where the advertising dollars have been spent, how each medium is producing, what remains in the budget at any given point,

and even deadlines for various publications. By automating, you'll not only get a better handle on the information, but your managers will be able to make better decisions based on that information."

Decision support systems such as the one discussed here allow managers the flexibility and individuality they need to make decisions specific to their functions. Standardized reporting systems are not often equipped to handle such specific requests for information.

Decision support systems typically are designed to be used interactively by managers. Such dialog systems allow managers to explore information in the system and generate reports in a form that best suits their needs rather than in a format most convenient for generalized company purposes.

♦ Model system

Model system
The part of a decision support system that includes all the routines that allow the user to manipulate the data so as to conduct the kind of analysis the individual desires.

Dialog system
The part of a decision support system that permits users to explore the data bases by employing the system models to produce reports that satisfy their particular information needs. Also called *language systems.*

understanding of a marketing issue. These manipulations are called *procedures.* The **model system** includes all the procedures that allow the user to manipulate the data so as to conduct the kind of analysis he or she desires.

The routines for manipulating the data may run the gamut: from summing a set of numbers to conducting a complex statistical analysis or to finding an optimization strategy using some kind of nonlinear programming routine. While many sophisticated techniques are available and can be useful for some purposes, "the most frequent operations are basic ones: segregating numbers into relevant groups, aggregating them, taking ratios, ranking them, picking out exceptional cases, plotting and making tables."[14]

The **dialog systems,** which are also called *language systems,* are the most important and clearly differentiate DSS from MIS. The dialog systems permit managers who are not programmers themselves to explore the data bases using the system models to produce reports that satisfy their own particular information needs. The reports can be tabular or graphical, and the report formats can be specified by individual managers. The dialog systems can be passive, which means that the analysis possibilities are presented to the decision makers for selection via menu, a few simple key strokes, light pen, or a mouse device; or they can be active, requiring the users to state their requests in a command mode. A key feature is that, instead of funneling their data requests through a team of programmers, managers can conduct their analyses by themselves (or through one of their assistants) using the dialog system. This allows them to target the information they want without being overwhelmed with irrelevant data. Managers can ask a question and, on the basis of the answer, can ask a subsequent question, and then another, and another, and so on.

> With the right DSS, for example, a marketing VP evaluating the sales of a recently introduced test instrument could "call up" sales by month, then by the year, breaking them out *at his* (or her) *option* by, say, customer segments. As he works at his CRT terminal, his inquiries could go in several directions depending on the decision at hand. If his train of thought raises questions about monthly sales last year compared to forecasts, he wants his information system to follow along and give him answers immediately.
>
> He might see that his new product's sales were significantly below forecast. Forecasts too optimistic? He compares other products' sales to his forecasts and finds that the targets were accurate. Something wrong with the product? Maybe his sales department is getting insufficient leads, or isn't putting leads to good use? Thinking about how to examine that question, he checks ratios of leads converted to sales—product by product. The results disturb him. Only 5 percent of the new product's leads generate orders compared to the company's 12 percent all-product average. Why? He guesses that the sales force isn't supporting the new product enough. Quantitative information from the DSS perhaps could provide more evidence to back that suspicion. But already having enough quantitative knowledge to satisfy himself, the VP acts on his intuition and experience and decides to have a chat with his sales manager.[15]

From the previous discussion, it should be obvious that DSS and MIS are both concerned with improving information processing so that better marketing decisions can be made. DSS differs from MIS, though, in a number of ways.[16] First, DSS tends

---

[14]*Ibid.,* p. 15.

[15]Michael Dressler, Ronald Beall, and Joquin Ives Brant, "What the Hot Marketing Tool of the '80s Offers You," *Industrial Marketing,* 68 (March 1983), pp. 51 and 54.

[16]For discussion of the features that differentiate DSS from MIS, see Sprague and Carlson, *Effective Decision Support Systems;* and Bonczek, Holsapple, and Whinston, "Developments in Decision Support Systems."

A dialog system in a DSS permits managers to explore on their own the data bases which use system models to produce reports that satisfy their own particular information needs.

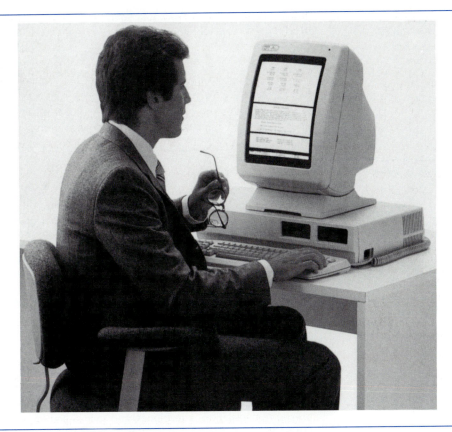

Source: Courtesy of CPT Corporation.

to be aimed at the poorly structured, underspecified problems that managers face rather than at those problems that can be investigated using a relatively standard set of procedures and comparisons. Second, DSS attempts to combine the use of models and analytical techniques and procedures with the more traditional data access and retrieval functions. Third, such systems specifically incorporate features that make them easy to use in an interactive mode by noncomputer people. These features might include such things as menu-driven procedures for doing an analysis and graphic display of the results. Regardless of how the interaction is structured, these systems have the ability to respond to users' specific informational requests in "real time," meaning the time available for making the decision. Fourth, they emphasize flexibility and adaptability. They can accommodate different decision makers with diverse styles as well as changing environmental conditions.

An analysis of the current status of DSS suggests that there are probably three types of systems currently in place—data-retrieval, market analysis, and modeling systems.[17] Data-retrieval systems represent the most elementary DSS. They allow decision makers to extract, sort, summarize, and list data from any of a number of existing data files. Data-retrieval systems are quite useful in helping managers answer the question, "What has happened?" However, managers usually want to know more than simple history. Good managers like to find out "why did so-and-so happen?" This is a question that is typically answered by analyzing expected relation-

---

[17]See Richard D. Canning, "What's Happening with DSS?" *EDP Analyzer,* 22 (July 1984), pp. 1–12, for further discussion of the three types of systems.

ships between the phenomena of interest and other marketing variables. Systems capable of addressing the "why" question are called *market analysis systems.* The most sophisticated systems currently in place are able to go beyond analysis and address questions like, "What would happen if?" Many of these systems, called *modeling systems,* currently rely on electronic spreadsheet programs such as Visicalc or Lotus 1-2-3, or upon one of the financial planning programs especially designed for handling modeling issues. More powerful computer packages are being developed every day; many managers are likely to gravitate to these powerful modeling programs as they become more comfortable in interacting directly with computers and as these packages are made easier to use.

◆ Summary

Learning Objective 1: Explain the difference between a project emphasis in research and a marketing information system (MIS) or decision support system (DSS) emphasis.

The difference between the project emphasis in research that has been assumed in this book and marketing information system (MIS) or decision support system (DSS) emphases is that both of the latter rely on the continual monitoring of the firm's activities, competitors, and environment, while the former emphasizes the in-depth, but nonrecurring, study of some specific problem or environmental condition.

Learning Objective 2: Define what is meant by a marketing information system.

A marketing information system is a set of procedures and methods for the regular, planned collection, analysis, and presentation of information for use in making marketing decisions. The thrust in designing MIS is the detailed analysis of each decision maker who might use the system, in order to secure an accurate, objective assessment of each manager's decision-making responsibilities, capabilities, and style — and, most important, each manager's information needs. Given the specification of information needs, system support people develop report formats and efficient systems for extracting and combining information from various data banks.

Learning Objective 3: Cite some of the problems inherent in a marketing information system.

Marketing information systems require managers to disclose their decision making processes, which many managers are reluctant to do. Further, the report formats are typically compromises that try to satisfy the different styles of the different users. Also, the development time required for these systems often means that they quickly become obsolete.

Learning Objective 4: Define what is meant by a decision support system.

A decision support system is a coordinated collection of data, systems, tools, and techniques with supporting software and hardware, by which an organization gathers and interprets relevant information from business and the environment and turns it into a basis for marketing action. A DSS concentrates on the design of data systems, model systems, and dialog systems.

Learning Objective 5: What feature most clearly differentiates DSS from MIS?

The dialog systems are most important and most clearly differentiate DSS from MIS. They allow managers to conduct their own analyses while they, or one of their assistants, sit at a computer terminal. This allows managers to analyze problems using their own personal views of what might be happening in a given situation, relying on their intuition and experience, rather than on a series of prespecified reports.

Discussion Questions, Problems, and Projects

1. Twenty years ago the marketing information system was emphasized as being the solution to a host of problems arising from irregular research efforts. The promise was never realized and current emphasis is on the design of decision support systems rather than mar-

keting information systems. How do you account for the gap between the promise and delivery of MIS? Do you think DSSs will suffer the same fate as MISs? Why or why not?

2. You are requested to design a decision support system for a hypothetical manufacturer of automotive parts.
   (a) What data should be included in the system (e.g., sales by sales area or by product line, age, and type of automobile driven)?
   (b) What data sources might be used to create the information system?
   (c) Describe how you would structure the system conceptually, including what elements you would build into each of the subsystems.

3. Arrange an interview with a manager of one of the local businesses for the expressed purpose of discussing a decision support system.
   (a) Complete the following:
      Name of the company: _____
      _____
      Name and title of the manager you interviewed: _____
      _____
   (b) Briefly describe the DSS that the company is currently using, emphasizing especially the functions that are served by it (e.g., production, sales management, etc.).
   (c) Briefly write your assessment of the person's familiarity with the concept. Is the person more concerned with the technical questions (e.g., how information is stored) or with the overall concept and its impact on the organization's decision-making capabilities?
   (d) Briefly describe the company's use of the DSS, including how they determine which managers get what access to what data and how, their experience with the system, and so on.

Suggested Additional Readings

For useful discussions of the structure and use of decision support systems, see

John D. C. Little, "Decision Support Systems for Marketing Managers," *Journal of Marketing,* 43 (Summer 1979), pp. 9–27.

Ralph H. Sprague, Jr., and Eric D. Carlson, *Effective Decision Support Systems* (Englewood Cliffs, N.J.: Prentice-Hall, 1982).

Part Seven   Research Project

The seventh and final stage in the research process is to prepare the research report. As we noted in the chapters in this section, despite the sophistication that may have been displayed in the earlier stages in the research process, the project will be a failure if the research report fails. Since the research report is all that most executives will see of the project, it is the yardstick by which that research will be evaluated.

A standard research report generally contains the following elements: title page, table of contents, summary, introduction, body, conclusions and recommendations, and appendix. Most marketing research projects also conclude with an oral report. Most effective oral presentations keep their technical detail to a minimum and make use of appropriate visual aids.

Both written and oral reports are judged by one fundamental criterion: how well they communicate with the audience, be it a reader or listener. The report must be tailor-made for the reader or readers, with due regard for their technical sophistication, interest in the subject area, the circumstances under which they will read the report, and the use they will make of it.

In the continuing case we have featured at the end of each section, we have discussed much of the material that would appear in a research report on such a project. For example, much of the information that would normally appear in an introduction, appears at the end of Part Two, where the first stage in the research process, problem formulation, is discussed. Information about the design of the study that would be included in the body of the report appears in subsequent sections that discuss the research design, the method of data collection, the design of the data-collection form, the design of the sample, and the data-collection process. Information that would generally appear in the section of the report devoted to conclusions was discussed at the end of Part Six. Certain items such as test statistics and calculations, tables, and a bibliography have been omitted because of length restrictions.

It is important, however, for students to see what the executive summary to such a research report would look like, since in many ways it encapsulates the rest of the document. A good executive summary contains necessary background information as well as the important results and conclusions, and it is thus the one part of the study that can truly stand alone.

This marketing research project was sponsored by the Centerville Area Radio Association (CARA). Its purpose was to identify specific problems that area businesses have with regard to advertising so that CARA advertising sales representatives can work to solve these through their marketing actions. The research objectives were as follows:

1. Identify business decision makers' attitudes toward the advertising media of newspaper, radio, and television.
2. Identify business decision makers' attitudes toward the advertising sales representatives of newspaper, radio, and television.

A five-page questionnaire was developed to measure these attitudes. The questionnaire was designed to test several hypotheses, the first being that different types of advertising media were perceived differently. CARA members were interested in investigating the different perceptions of newspaper, radio, and television as advertising media, since these three were the primary competitors for advertising budgets among Centerville-area businesses.

Another hypothesis was that the advertising sales representatives for the three types of media were also perceived differently from one another. Perceptions were measured through use of scaled ratings of itemized individual attributes of (1) the medium and (2) the sales representatives for each medium. It was hypothesized that attitudes would be further differentiated by the level of annual advertising expenditures made by the respondent's company. Moreover, the particular attributes of sales representatives and advertising media were tested to determine their importance to the respondents.

Also, it was hypothesized that the percentages of businesspeople who felt the sales representatives from each of the three media that possessed each of a number of desirable attributes would differ, as would the percentages of businesspeople who felt the advertising media themselves had the listed characteristics. Additionally, it was deemed important to determine the estimated proportion of advertising expenditures for each of nine advertising categories.

The position title of the respondent, whether or not the respondent made advertising decisions, and whether or not the business used an advertising agency, were used to categorize and, if necessary, exclude individuals from the final data analysis.

The research method consisted of mailing a questionnaire to 600 area businesses. A systematic probability sample of 600 was drawn from Yellow Pages listings of businesses identified by CARA as representative of those with which they do business or would like to do business. These businesses fell into ten broad categories:

1. Building material and hardware.
2. Automotive, sales and service.
3. Apparel.
4. Furniture and home furnishings.
5. Eating and drinking establishments.
6. Health and fitness.
7. Financial institutions.
8. Home entertainment.
9. Professional services.
10. A miscellaneous category consisting of florists, printers, bookstores, jewelers, and photographic sales and services.

In an effort to ensure an adequate response rate, a one-dollar bill was enclosed in 300 of the mailed questionnaires. The remaining 300 did not receive a dollar. The questionnaires were color-coded (cream-colored for the ones that received the dollar bill and white for the others), so that response rates for the two groups could be calculated. Systematic probability sampling was also used to determine which businesses would receive a questionnaire with a one-dollar bill inside.

The questionnaires were mailed April 8th. The cutoff date for accepting returned questionnaires was April 24th. One hundred sixty-five (165) cream-colored questionnaires were returned while 47 of the white ones were returned, for a total of 212. The results indicate that the inclusion of the dollar bill made a difference. Thirty-four (25 cream, 9 white) of the questionnaires returned were unusable due to incompleteness.

The hypothesis that there were differences in attitudes toward the three advertising media was not supported by the data. There were no significant differences in respondents' attitudes toward newspaper, radio, and television as advertising media.

With regard to the hypothesis that there were differences in attitudes toward newspaper, radio, and television sales representatives, there were no significant differences except when individuals whose business used an advertising agency were included with those who did not.

The classification of attitude scores by advertising expenditures revealed an inverse linear relationship: as advertising expenditures increased, attitudes toward advertising sales representatives became increasingly negative.

There were significant differences in the ratings of the *importance* of the different characteristics of the media and the various attributes of sales representatives. More particularly, the analysis of the item-importance scores indicated that it would be worthwhile for radio sales representatives to become more knowledgeable about their clients' areas of business and more aware and concerned about their clients' particular advertising needs. Radio representatives should make it clear to business clients that radio advertising can build up recognition of a business as well as or better than television advertising. Further, if radio advertising can improve a business's sales volume and can reach its target market better than television advertising, and as well as or better than newspaper advertising, this should be clearly indicated to business clients.

Appendix

Table 1 Cumulative Standard Unit Normal Distribution

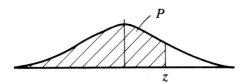

Values of P corresponding to Z for the normal curve. Z is the standard normal variable. The value of P for $-Z$ equals one minus the value of P for $+Z$, (e.g., the P for -1.62 equals $1 - .9474 = .0526$).

Z	.00	.01	.02	.03	.04	.05	.06	.07	.08	.09
.0	.5000	.5040	.5080	.5120	.5160	.5199	.5239	.5279	.5319	.5359
.1	.5398	.5438	.5478	.5517	.5557	.5596	.5636	.5675	.5714	.5753
.2	.5793	.5832	.5871	.5910	.5948	.5987	.6026	.6064	.6103	.6141
.3	.6179	.6217	.6255	.6293	.6331	.6368	.6406	.6443	.6480	.6517
.4	.6554	.6591	.6628	.6664	.6700	.6736	.6772	.6808	.6844	.6879
.5	.6915	.6950	.6985	.7019	.7054	.7088	.7123	.7157	.7190	.7224
.6	.7257	.7291	.7324	.7357	.7389	.7422	.7454	.7486	.7517	.7549
.7	.7580	.7611	.7642	.7673	.7704	.7734	.7764	.7794	.7823	.7852
.8	.7881	.7910	.7939	.7967	.7995	.8023	.8051	.8078	.8106	.8133
.9	.8159	.8186	.8212	.8238	.8264	.8289	.8315	.8340	.8365	.8389
1.0	.8413	.8438	.8461	.8485	.8508	.8531	.8554	.8577	.8599	.8621
1.1	.8643	.8665	.8686	.8708	.8729	.8749	.8770	.8790	.8810	.8830
1.2	.8849	.8869	.8888	.8907	.8925	.8944	.8962	.8980	.8997	.9015
1.3	.9032	.9049	.9066	.9082	.9099	.9115	.9131	.9147	.9162	.9177
1.4	.9192	.9207	.9222	.9236	.9251	.9265	.9279	.9292	.9306	.9319
1.5	.9332	.9345	.9357	.9370	.9382	.9394	.9406	.9418	.9429	.9441
1.6	.9452	.9463	.9474	.9484	.9495	.9505	.9515	.9525	.9535	.9545
1.7	.9554	.9564	.9573	.9582	.9591	.9599	.9608	.9616	.9625	.9633
1.8	.9641	.9649	.9656	.9664	.9671	.9678	.9686	.9693	.9699	.9706
1.9	.9713	.9719	.9726	.9732	.9738	.9744	.9750	.9756	.9761	.9767
2.0	.9772	.9778	.9783	.9788	.9793	.9798	.9803	.9808	.9812	.9817
2.1	.9821	.9826	.9830	.9834	.9838	.9842	.9846	.9850	.9854	.9857
2.2	.9861	.9864	.9868	.9871	.9875	.9878	.9881	.9884	.9887	.9890
2.3	.9893	.9896	.9898	.9901	.9904	.9906	.9909	.9911	.9913	.9916
2.4	.9918	.9920	.9922	.9925	.9927	.9929	.9931	.9932	.9934	.9936
2.5	.9938	.9940	.9941	.9943	.9945	.9946	.9948	.9949	.9951	.9952
2.6	.9953	.9955	.9956	.9957	.9959	.9960	.9961	.9962	.9963	.9964
2.7	.9965	.9966	.9967	.9968	.9969	.9970	.9971	.9972	.9973	.9974
2.8	.9974	.9975	.9976	.9977	.9977	.9978	.9979	.9979	.9980	.9981
2.9	.9981	.9982	.9982	.9983	.9984	.9984	.9985	.9985	.9986	.9986
3.0	.9987	.9987	.9987	.9988	.9988	.9989	.9989	.9989	.9990	.9990
3.1	.9990	.9991	.9991	.9991	.9992	.9992	.9992	.9992	.9993	.9993
3.2	.9993	.9993	.9994	.9994	.9994	.9994	.9994	.9995	.9995	.9995
3.3	.9995	.9995	.9995	.9996	.9996	.9996	.9996	.9996	.9996	.9997
3.4	.9997	.9997	.9997	.9997	.9997	.9997	.9997	.9997	.9997	.9998

Source: Paul E. Green, *Analyzing Multivariate Data* (Chicago: Dryden Press, 1978).

Table 2   Selected Percentiles of the χ^2 Distribution

Values of χ^2 corresponding to P

ν	$\chi^2_{.005}$	$\chi^2_{.01}$	$\chi^2_{.025}$	$\chi^2_{.05}$	$\chi^2_{.10}$	$\chi^2_{.90}$	$\chi^2_{.95}$	$\chi^2_{.975}$	$\chi^2_{.99}$	$\chi^2_{.995}$
1	.000039	.00016	.00098	.0039	.0158	2.71	3.84	5.02	6.63	7.88
2	.0100	.0201	.0506	.1026	.2107	4.61	5.99	7.38	9.21	10.60
3	.0717	.115	.216	.352	.584	6.25	7.81	9.35	11.34	12.84
4	.207	.297	.484	.711	1.064	7.78	9.49	11.14	13.28	14.86
5	.412	.554	.831	1.15	1.61	9.24	11.07	12.83	15.09	16.75
6	.676	.872	1.24	1.64	2.20	10.64	12.59	14.45	16.81	18.55
7	.989	1.24	1.69	2.17	2.83	12.02	14.07	16.01	18.48	20.28
8	1.34	1.65	2.18	2.73	3.49	13.36	15.51	17.53	20.09	21.96
9	1.73	2.09	2.70	3.33	4.17	14.68	16.92	19.02	21.67	23.59
10	2.16	2.56	3.25	3.94	4.87	15.99	18.31	20.48	23.21	25.19
11	2.60	3.05	3.82	4.57	5.58	17.28	19.68	21.92	24.73	26.76
12	3.07	3.57	4.40	5.23	6.30	18.55	21.03	23.34	26.22	28.30
13	3.57	4.11	5.01	5.89	7.04	19.81	22.36	24.74	27.69	29.82
14	4.07	4.66	5.63	6.57	7.79	21.06	23.68	26.12	29.14	31.32
15	4.60	5.23	6.26	7.26	8.55	22.31	25.00	27.49	30.58	32.80
16	5.14	5.81	6.91	7.96	9.31	23.54	26.30	28.85	32.00	34.27
18	6.26	7.01	8.23	9.39	10.86	25.99	28.87	31.53	34.81	37.16
20	7.43	8.26	9.59	10.85	12.44	28.41	31.41	34.17	37.57	40.00
24	9.89	10.86	12.40	13.85	15.66	33.20	36.42	39.36	42.98	45.56
30	13.79	14.95	16.79	18.49	20.60	40.26	43.77	46.98	50.89	53.67
40	20.71	22.16	24.43	26.51	29.05	51.81	55.76	59.34	63.69	66.77
60	35.53	37.48	40.48	43.19	46.46	74.40	79.08	83.30	88.38	91.95
120	83.85	86.92	91.58	95.70	100.62	140.23	146.57	152.21	158.95	163.64

Source: Adapted with permission from *Introduction to Statistical Analysis* (2d ed.) by W. J. Dixon and F. J. Massey, Jr., McGraw-Hill Book Company, Inc., 1957.

Table 3   Upper Percentiles of the *t* Distribution

v \ $1-\alpha$	.75	.90	.95	.975	.99	.995	.9995
1	1.000	3.078	6.314	12.706	31.821	63.657	636.619
2	.816	1.886	2.920	4.303	6.965	9.925	31.598
3	.765	1.638	2.353	3.182	4.541	5.841	12.941
4	.741	1.533	2.132	2.776	3.747	4.604	8.610
5	.727	1.476	2.015	2.571	3.365	4.032	6.859
6	.718	1.440	1.943	2.447	3.143	3.707	5.959
7	.711	1.415	1.895	2.365	2.998	3.499	5.405
8	.706	1.397	1.860	2.306	2.896	3.355	5.041
9	.703	1.383	1.833	2.262	2.821	3.250	4.781
10	.700	1.372	1.812	2.228	2.764	3.169	4.587
11	.697	1.363	1.796	2.201	2.718	3.106	4.437
12	.695	1.356	1.782	2.179	2.681	3.055	4.318
13	.694	1.350	1.771	2.160	2.650	3.012	4.221
14	.692	1.345	1.761	2.145	2.624	2.977	4.140
15	.691	1.341	1.753	2.131	2.602	2.947	4.073
16	.690	1.337	1.746	2.120	2.583	2.921	4.015
17	.689	1.333	1.740	2.110	2.567	2.898	3.965
18	.688	1.330	1.734	2.101	2.552	2.878	3.922
19	.688	1.328	1.729	2.093	2.339	2.861	3.883
20	.687	1.325	1.725	2.086	2.528	2.845	3.850
21	.686	1.323	1.721	2.080	2.518	2.831	3.819
22	.686	1.321	1.717	2.074	2.508	2.819	3.792
23	.685	1.319	1.714	2.069	2.500	2.807	3.767
24	.685	1.318	1.711	2.064	2.492	2.797	3.745
25	.684	1.316	1.708	2.060	2.485	2.787	3.725
26	.684	1.315	1.706	2.056	2.479	2.779	3.707
27	.684	1.314	1.703	2.052	2.473	2.771	3.690
28	.683	1.313	1.701	2.048	2.467	2.763	3.674
29	.683	1.311	1.699	2.045	2.462	2.756	3.659
30	.683	1.310	1.697	2.042	2.457	2.750	3.646
40	.681	1.303	1.684	2.021	2.423	2.704	3.551
60	.679	1.296	1.671	2.000	2.390	2.660	3.460
120	.677	1.289	1.658	1.980	2.358	2.617	3.373
∞	.674	1.282	1.645	1.960	2.326	2.576	3.291

v = degrees of freedom

Source: Taken from Table III of R. A. Fisher and F. Yates: *Statistical Tables for Biological, Agricultural, and Medical Research,* published by Longman Group UK Ltd., London (previously published by Oliver & Boyd Ltd., Edinburgh, 1963). Used by permission of the authors and publishers.

Table 4   Selected Percentiles of the F Distribution

$F_{.90(\nu_1, \nu_2)}$ $\alpha = 0.1$

ν_1 = degrees of freedom for numerator

ν_2	1	2	3	4	5	6	7	8	9	10	12	15	20	24	30	40	60	120	∞
1	39.86	49.50	53.59	55.83	57.24	58.20	58.91	59.44	59.86	60.19	60.71	61.22	61.74	62.00	62.26	62.53	62.79	63.06	63.33
2	8.53	9.00	9.16	9.24	9.29	9.33	9.35	9.37	9.38	9.39	9.41	9.42	9.44	9.45	9.46	9.47	9.47	9.48	9.49
3	5.54	5.46	5.39	5.34	5.31	5.28	5.27	5.25	5.24	5.23	5.22	5.20	5.18	5.18	5.17	5.16	5.15	5.14	5.13
4	4.54	4.32	4.19	4.11	4.05	4.01	3.98	3.95	3.94	3.92	3.90	3.87	3.84	3.83	3.82	3.80	3.79	3.78	3.76
5	4.06	3.78	3.62	3.52	3.45	3.40	3.37	3.34	3.32	3.30	3.27	3.24	3.21	3.19	3.17	3.16	3.14	3.12	3.10
6	3.78	3.46	3.29	3.18	3.11	3.05	3.01	2.98	2.96	2.94	2.90	2.87	2.84	2.82	2.80	2.78	2.76	2.74	2.72
7	3.59	3.26	3.07	2.96	2.88	2.83	2.78	2.75	2.72	2.70	2.67	2.63	2.59	2.58	2.56	2.54	2.51	2.49	2.47
8	3.46	3.11	2.92	2.81	2.73	2.67	2.62	2.59	2.56	2.54	2.50	2.46	2.42	2.40	2.38	2.36	2.34	2.32	2.29
9	3.36	3.01	2.81	2.69	2.61	2.55	2.51	2.47	2.44	2.42	2.38	2.34	2.30	2.28	2.25	2.23	2.21	2.18	2.16
10	3.29	2.92	2.73	2.61	2.52	2.46	2.41	2.38	2.35	2.32	2.28	2.24	2.20	2.18	2.16	2.13	2.11	2.08	2.06
11	3.23	2.86	2.66	2.54	2.45	2.39	2.34	2.30	2.27	2.25	2.21	2.17	2.12	2.10	2.08	2.05	2.03	2.00	1.97
12	3.18	2.81	2.61	2.48	2.39	2.33	2.28	2.24	2.21	2.19	2.15	2.10	2.06	2.04	2.01	1.99	1.96	1.93	1.90
13	3.14	2.76	2.56	2.43	2.35	2.28	2.23	2.20	2.16	2.14	2.10	2.05	2.01	1.98	1.96	1.93	1.90	1.88	1.85
14	3.10	2.73	2.52	2.39	2.31	2.24	2.19	2.15	2.12	2.10	2.05	2.01	1.96	1.94	1.91	1.89	1.86	1.83	1.80
15	3.07	2.70	2.49	2.36	2.27	2.21	2.16	2.12	2.09	2.06	2.02	1.97	1.92	1.90	1.87	1.85	1.82	1.79	1.76
16	3.05	2.67	2.46	2.33	2.24	2.18	2.13	2.09	2.06	2.03	1.99	1.94	1.89	1.87	1.84	1.81	1.78	1.75	1.72
17	3.03	2.64	2.44	2.31	2.22	2.15	2.10	2.06	2.03	2.00	1.96	1.91	1.86	1.84	1.81	1.78	1.75	1.72	1.69
18	3.01	2.62	2.42	2.29	2.20	2.13	2.08	2.04	2.00	1.98	1.93	1.89	1.84	1.81	1.78	1.75	1.72	1.69	1.66
19	2.99	2.61	2.40	2.27	2.18	2.11	2.06	2.02	1.98	1.96	1.91	1.86	1.81	1.79	1.76	1.73	1.70	1.67	1.63
20	2.97	2.59	2.38	2.25	2.16	2.09	2.04	2.00	1.96	1.94	1.89	1.84	1.79	1.77	1.74	1.71	1.68	1.64	1.61
21	2.96	2.57	2.36	2.23	2.14	2.08	2.02	1.98	1.95	1.92	1.87	1.83	1.78	1.75	1.72	1.69	1.66	1.62	1.59
22	2.95	2.56	2.35	2.22	2.13	2.06	2.01	1.97	1.93	1.90	1.86	1.81	1.76	1.73	1.70	1.67	1.64	1.60	1.57
23	2.94	2.55	2.34	2.21	2.11	2.05	1.99	1.95	1.92	1.89	1.84	1.80	1.74	1.72	1.69	1.66	1.62	1.59	1.55
24	2.93	2.54	2.33	2.19	2.10	2.04	1.98	1.94	1.91	1.88	1.83	1.78	1.73	1.70	1.67	1.64	1.61	1.57	1.53
25	2.92	2.53	2.32	2.18	2.09	2.02	1.97	1.93	1.89	1.87	1.82	1.77	1.72	1.69	1.66	1.63	1.59	1.56	1.52
26	2.91	2.52	2.31	2.17	2.08	2.01	1.96	1.92	1.88	1.86	1.81	1.76	1.71	1.68	1.65	1.61	1.58	1.54	1.50
27	2.90	2.51	2.30	2.17	2.07	2.00	1.95	1.91	1.87	1.85	1.80	1.75	1.70	1.67	1.64	1.60	1.57	1.53	1.49
28	2.89	2.50	2.29	2.16	2.06	2.00	1.94	1.90	1.87	1.84	1.79	1.74	1.69	1.66	1.63	1.59	1.56	1.52	1.48
29	2.89	2.50	2.28	2.15	2.06	1.99	1.93	1.89	1.86	1.83	1.78	1.73	1.68	1.65	1.62	1.58	1.55	1.51	1.47
30	2.88	2.49	2.28	2.14	2.05	1.98	1.93	1.88	1.85	1.82	1.77	1.72	1.67	1.64	1.61	1.57	1.54	1.50	1.46
40	2.84	2.44	2.23	2.09	2.00	1.93	1.87	1.83	1.79	1.76	1.71	1.66	1.61	1.57	1.54	1.51	1.47	1.42	1.38
60	2.79	2.39	2.18	2.04	1.95	1.87	1.82	1.77	1.74	1.71	1.66	1.60	1.54	1.51	1.48	1.44	1.40	1.35	1.29
120	2.75	2.35	2.13	1.99	1.90	1.82	1.77	1.72	1.68	1.65	1.60	1.55	1.48	1.45	1.41	1.37	1.32	1.26	1.19
∞	2.71	2.30	2.08	1.94	1.85	1.77	1.72	1.67	1.63	1.60	1.55	1.49	1.42	1.38	1.34	1.30	1.24	1.17	1.00

ν_2 = degrees of freedom for denominator

Source: Adapted with permission from *Biometrika Tables for Statisticians*, Vol. 1 (2nd ed.), edited by E. S. Pearson and H. O. Hartley, Cambridge University Press, 1958.

Table 4 Selected Percentiles of the F Distribution *continued*

$$F_{.95}(v_1, v_2) \qquad \alpha = 0.05$$

v_1 = degrees of freedom for numerator

v_2 \ v_1	1	2	3	4	5	6	7	8	9	10	12	15	20	24	30	40	60	120	∞
1	161.4	199.5	215.7	224.6	230.2	234.0	236.8	238.9	240.5	241.9	243.9	245.9	248.0	249.1	250.1	251.1	252.2	253.3	254.3
2	18.51	19.00	19.16	19.25	19.30	19.33	19.35	19.37	19.38	19.40	19.41	19.43	19.45	19.45	19.46	19.47	19.48	19.49	19.50
3	10.13	9.55	9.28	9.12	9.01	8.94	8.89	8.85	8.81	8.79	8.74	8.70	8.66	8.64	8.62	8.59	8.57	8.55	8.53
4	7.71	6.94	6.59	6.39	6.26	6.16	6.09	6.04	6.00	5.96	5.91	5.86	5.80	5.77	5.75	5.72	5.69	5.66	5.63
5	6.61	5.79	5.41	5.19	5.05	4.95	4.88	4.82	4.77	4.74	4.68	4.62	4.56	4.53	4.50	4.46	4.43	4.40	4.36
6	5.99	5.14	4.76	4.53	4.39	4.28	4.21	4.15	4.10	4.06	4.00	3.94	3.87	3.84	3.81	3.77	3.74	3.70	3.67
7	5.59	4.74	4.35	4.12	3.97	3.87	3.79	3.73	3.68	3.64	3.57	3.51	3.44	3.41	3.38	3.34	3.30	3.27	3.23
8	5.32	4.46	4.07	3.84	3.69	3.58	3.50	3.44	3.39	3.35	3.28	3.22	3.15	3.12	3.08	3.04	3.01	2.97	2.93
9	5.12	4.26	3.86	3.63	3.48	3.37	3.29	3.23	3.18	3.14	3.07	3.01	2.94	2.90	2.86	2.83	2.79	2.75	2.71
10	4.96	4.10	3.71	3.48	3.33	3.22	3.14	3.07	3.02	2.98	2.91	2.85	2.77	2.74	2.70	2.66	2.62	2.58	2.54
11	4.84	3.98	3.59	3.36	3.20	3.09	3.01	2.95	2.90	2.85	2.79	2.72	2.65	2.61	2.57	2.53	2.49	2.45	2.40
12	4.75	3.89	3.49	3.26	3.11	3.00	2.91	2.85	2.80	2.75	2.69	2.62	2.54	2.51	2.47	2.43	2.38	2.34	2.30
13	4.67	3.81	3.41	3.18	3.03	2.92	2.83	2.77	2.71	2.67	2.60	2.53	2.46	2.42	2.38	2.34	2.30	2.25	2.21
14	4.60	3.74	3.34	3.11	2.96	2.85	2.76	2.70	2.65	2.60	2.53	2.46	2.39	2.35	2.31	2.27	2.22	2.18	2.13
15	4.54	3.68	3.29	3.06	2.90	2.79	2.71	2.64	2.59	2.54	2.48	2.40	2.33	2.29	2.25	2.20	2.16	2.11	2.07
16	4.49	3.63	3.24	3.01	2.85	2.74	2.66	2.59	2.54	2.49	2.42	2.35	2.28	2.24	2.19	2.15	2.11	2.06	2.01
17	4.45	3.59	3.20	2.96	2.81	2.70	2.61	2.55	2.49	2.45	2.38	2.31	2.23	2.19	2.15	2.10	2.06	2.01	1.96
18	4.41	3.55	3.16	2.93	2.77	2.66	2.58	2.51	2.46	2.41	2.34	2.27	2.19	2.15	2.11	2.06	2.02	1.97	1.92
19	4.38	3.52	3.13	2.90	2.74	2.63	2.54	2.48	2.42	2.38	2.31	2.23	2.16	2.11	2.07	2.03	1.98	1.93	1.88
20	4.35	3.49	3.10	2.87	2.71	2.60	2.51	2.45	2.39	2.35	2.28	2.20	2.12	2.08	2.04	1.99	1.95	1.90	1.84
21	4.32	3.47	3.07	2.84	2.68	2.57	2.49	2.42	2.37	2.32	2.25	2.18	2.10	2.05	2.01	1.96	1.92	1.87	1.81
22	4.30	3.44	3.05	2.82	2.66	2.55	2.46	2.40	2.34	2.30	2.23	2.15	2.07	2.03	1.98	1.94	1.89	1.84	1.78
23	4.28	3.42	3.03	2.80	2.64	2.53	2.44	2.37	2.32	2.27	2.20	2.13	2.05	2.01	1.96	1.91	1.86	1.81	1.76
24	4.26	3.40	3.01	2.78	2.62	2.51	2.42	2.36	2.30	2.25	2.18	2.11	2.03	1.98	1.94	1.89	1.84	1.79	1.73
25	4.24	3.39	2.99	2.76	2.60	2.49	2.40	2.34	2.28	2.24	2.16	2.09	2.01	1.96	1.92	1.87	1.82	1.77	1.71
26	4.23	3.37	2.98	2.74	2.59	2.47	2.39	2.32	2.27	2.22	2.15	2.07	1.99	1.95	1.90	1.85	1.80	1.75	1.69
27	4.21	3.35	2.96	2.73	2.57	2.46	2.37	2.31	2.25	2.20	2.13	2.06	1.97	1.93	1.88	1.84	1.79	1.73	1.67
28	4.20	3.34	2.95	2.71	2.56	2.45	2.36	2.29	2.24	2.19	2.12	2.04	1.96	1.91	1.87	1.82	1.77	1.71	1.65
29	4.18	3.33	2.93	2.70	2.55	2.43	2.35	2.28	2.22	2.18	2.10	2.03	1.94	1.90	1.85	1.81	1.75	1.70	1.64
30	4.17	3.32	2.92	2.69	2.53	2.42	2.33	2.27	2.21	2.16	2.09	2.01	1.93	1.89	1.84	1.79	1.74	1.68	1.62
40	4.08	3.23	2.84	2.61	2.45	2.34	2.25	2.18	2.12	2.08	2.00	1.92	1.84	1.79	1.74	1.69	1.64	1.58	1.51
60	4.00	3.15	2.76	2.53	2.37	2.25	2.17	2.10	2.04	1.99	1.92	1.84	1.75	1.70	1.65	1.59	1.53	1.47	1.39
120	3.92	3.07	2.68	2.45	2.29	2.17	2.09	2.02	1.96	1.91	1.83	1.75	1.66	1.61	1.55	1.50	1.43	1.35	1.25
∞	3.84	3.00	2.60	2.37	2.21	2.10	2.01	1.94	1.88	1.83	1.75	1.67	1.57	1.52	1.46	1.39	1.32	1.22	1.00

v_2 = degrees of freedom for denominator

Table 4　Selected Percentiles of the F Distribution *continued*

$$F_{.975}(\nu_1, \nu_2) \qquad \alpha = 0.025$$

ν_1 = degrees of freedom for numerator

ν_2 \ ν_1	1	2	3	4	5	6	7	8	9	10	12	15	20	24	30	40	60	120	∞
1	647.8	799.5	864.2	899.6	921.8	937.1	948.2	956.7	963.3	968.6	976.7	984.9	993.1	997.2	1001	1006	1010	1014	1018
2	38.51	39.00	39.17	39.25	39.30	39.33	39.36	39.37	39.39	39.40	39.41	39.43	39.45	39.46	39.46	39.47	39.48	39.49	39.50
3	17.44	16.04	15.44	15.10	14.88	14.73	14.62	14.54	14.47	14.42	14.34	14.25	14.17	14.12	14.08	14.04	13.99	13.95	13.90
4	12.22	10.65	9.98	9.60	9.36	9.20	9.07	8.98	8.90	8.84	8.75	8.66	8.56	8.51	8.46	8.41	8.36	8.31	8.26
5	10.01	8.43	7.76	7.39	7.15	6.98	6.85	6.76	6.68	6.62	6.52	6.43	6.33	6.28	6.23	6.18	6.12	6.07	6.02
6	8.81	7.26	6.60	6.23	5.99	5.82	5.70	5.60	5.52	5.46	5.37	5.27	5.17	5.12	5.07	5.01	4.96	4.90	4.85
7	8.07	6.54	5.89	5.52	5.29	5.12	4.99	4.90	4.82	4.76	4.67	4.57	4.47	4.42	4.36	4.31	4.25	4.20	4.14
8	7.57	6.06	5.42	5.05	4.82	4.65	4.53	4.43	4.36	4.30	4.20	4.10	4.00	3.95	3.89	3.84	3.78	3.73	3.67
9	7.21	5.71	5.08	4.72	4.48	4.32	4.20	4.10	4.03	3.96	3.87	3.77	3.67	3.61	3.56	3.51	3.45	3.39	3.33
10	6.94	5.46	4.83	4.47	4.24	4.07	3.95	3.85	3.78	3.72	3.62	3.52	3.42	3.37	3.31	3.26	3.20	3.14	3.08
11	6.72	5.26	4.63	4.28	4.04	3.88	3.76	3.66	3.59	3.53	3.43	3.33	3.23	3.17	3.12	3.06	3.00	2.94	2.88
12	6.55	5.10	4.47	4.12	3.89	3.73	3.61	3.51	3.44	3.37	3.28	3.18	3.07	3.02	2.96	2.91	2.85	2.79	2.72
13	6.41	4.97	4.35	4.00	3.77	3.60	3.48	3.39	3.31	3.25	3.15	3.05	2.95	2.89	2.84	2.78	2.72	2.66	2.60
14	6.30	4.86	4.24	3.89	3.66	3.50	3.38	3.29	3.21	3.15	3.05	2.95	2.84	2.79	2.73	2.67	2.61	2.55	2.49
15	6.20	4.77	4.15	3.80	3.58	3.41	3.29	3.20	3.12	3.06	2.96	2.86	2.76	2.70	2.64	2.59	2.52	2.46	2.40
16	6.12	4.69	4.08	3.73	3.50	3.34	3.22	3.12	3.05	2.99	2.89	2.79	2.68	2.63	2.57	2.51	2.45	2.38	2.32
17	6.04	4.62	4.01	3.66	3.44	3.28	3.16	3.06	2.98	2.92	2.82	2.72	2.62	2.56	2.50	2.44	2.38	2.32	2.25
18	5.98	4.56	3.95	3.61	3.38	3.22	3.10	3.01	2.93	2.87	2.77	2.67	2.56	2.50	2.44	2.38	2.32	2.26	2.19
19	5.92	4.51	3.90	3.56	3.33	3.17	3.05	2.96	2.88	2.82	2.72	2.62	2.51	2.45	2.39	2.33	2.27	2.20	2.13
20	5.87	4.46	3.86	3.51	3.29	3.13	3.01	2.91	2.84	2.77	2.68	2.57	2.46	2.41	2.35	2.29	2.22	2.16	2.09
21	5.83	4.42	3.82	3.48	3.25	3.09	2.97	2.87	2.80	2.73	2.64	2.53	2.42	2.37	2.31	2.25	2.18	2.11	2.04
22	5.79	4.38	3.78	3.44	3.22	3.05	2.93	2.84	2.76	2.70	2.60	2.50	2.39	2.33	2.27	2.21	2.14	2.08	2.00
23	5.75	4.35	3.75	3.41	3.18	3.02	2.90	2.81	2.73	2.67	2.57	2.47	2.36	2.30	2.24	2.18	2.11	2.04	1.97
24	5.72	4.32	3.72	3.38	3.15	2.99	2.87	2.78	2.70	2.64	2.54	2.44	2.33	2.27	2.21	2.15	2.08	2.01	1.94
25	5.69	4.29	3.69	3.35	3.13	2.97	2.85	2.75	2.68	2.61	2.51	2.41	2.30	2.24	2.18	2.12	2.05	1.98	1.91
26	5.66	4.27	3.67	3.33	3.10	2.94	2.82	2.73	2.65	2.59	2.49	2.39	2.28	2.22	2.16	2.09	2.03	1.95	1.88
27	5.63	4.24	3.65	3.31	3.08	2.92	2.80	2.71	2.63	2.57	2.47	2.36	2.25	2.19	2.13	2.07	2.00	1.93	1.85
28	5.61	4.22	3.63	3.29	3.06	2.90	2.78	2.69	2.61	2.55	2.45	2.34	2.23	2.17	2.11	2.05	1.98	1.91	1.83
29	5.59	4.20	3.61	3.27	3.04	2.88	2.76	2.67	2.59	2.53	2.43	2.32	2.21	2.15	2.09	2.03	1.96	1.89	1.81
30	5.57	4.18	3.59	3.25	3.03	2.87	2.75	2.65	2.57	2.51	2.41	2.31	2.20	2.14	2.07	2.01	1.94	1.87	1.79
40	5.42	4.05	3.46	3.13	2.90	2.74	2.62	2.53	2.45	2.39	2.29	2.18	2.07	2.01	1.94	1.88	1.80	1.72	1.64
60	5.29	3.93	3.34	3.01	2.79	2.63	2.51	2.41	2.33	2.27	2.17	2.06	1.94	1.88	1.82	1.74	1.67	1.58	1.48
120	5.15	3.80	3.23	2.89	2.67	2.52	2.39	2.30	2.22	2.16	2.05	1.94	1.82	1.76	1.69	1.61	1.53	1.43	1.31
∞	5.02	3.69	3.12	2.79	2.57	2.41	2.29	2.19	2.11	2.05	1.94	1.83	1.71	1.64	1.57	1.48	1.39	1.27	1.00

ν_2 = degrees of freedom for denominator

Table 4 Selected Percentiles of the *F* Distribution *continued*

$F_{.99}(\nu_1, \nu_2)$ $\alpha = 0.01$

ν_1 = degrees of freedom for numerator

ν_2 = degrees of freedom for denominator

ν_2 \ ν_1	1	2	3	4	5	6	7	8	9	10	12	15	20	24	30	40	60	120	∞
1	4052	4999.5	5403	5625	5764	5859	5928	5982	6022	6056	6106	6157	6209	6235	6261	6287	6313	6339	6366
2	98.50	99.00	99.17	99.25	99.30	99.33	99.36	99.37	99.39	99.40	99.42	99.43	99.45	99.46	99.47	99.47	99.48	99.49	99.50
3	34.12	30.82	29.46	28.71	28.24	27.91	27.67	27.49	27.35	27.23	27.05	26.87	26.69	26.60	26.50	26.41	26.32	26.22	26.13
4	21.20	18.00	16.69	15.98	15.52	15.21	14.98	14.80	14.66	14.55	14.37	14.20	14.02	13.93	13.84	13.75	13.65	13.56	13.46
5	16.26	13.27	12.06	11.39	10.97	10.67	10.46	10.29	10.16	10.05	9.89	9.72	9.55	9.47	9.38	9.29	9.20	9.11	9.02
6	13.75	10.92	9.78	9.15	8.75	8.47	8.26	8.10	7.98	7.87	7.72	7.56	7.40	7.31	7.23	7.14	7.06	6.97	6.88
7	12.25	9.55	8.45	7.85	7.46	7.19	6.99	6.84	6.72	6.62	6.47	6.31	6.16	6.07	5.99	5.91	5.82	5.74	5.65
8	11.26	8.65	7.59	7.01	6.63	6.37	6.18	6.03	5.91	5.81	5.67	5.52	5.36	5.28	5.20	5.12	5.03	4.95	4.86
9	10.56	8.02	6.99	6.42	6.06	5.80	5.61	5.47	5.35	5.26	5.11	4.96	4.81	4.73	4.65	4.57	4.48	4.40	4.31
10	10.04	7.56	6.55	5.99	5.64	5.39	5.20	5.06	4.94	4.85	4.71	4.56	4.41	4.33	4.25	4.17	4.08	4.00	3.91
11	9.65	7.21	6.22	5.67	5.32	5.07	4.89	4.74	4.63	4.54	4.40	4.25	4.10	4.02	3.94	3.86	3.78	3.69	3.60
12	9.33	6.93	5.95	5.41	5.06	4.82	4.64	4.50	4.39	4.30	4.16	4.01	3.86	3.78	3.70	3.62	3.54	3.45	3.36
13	9.07	6.70	5.74	5.21	4.86	4.62	4.44	4.30	4.19	4.10	3.96	3.82	3.66	3.59	3.51	3.43	3.34	3.25	3.17
14	8.86	6.51	5.56	5.04	4.69	4.46	4.28	4.14	4.03	3.94	3.80	3.66	3.51	3.43	3.35	3.27	3.18	3.09	3.00
15	8.68	6.36	5.42	4.89	4.56	4.32	4.14	4.00	3.89	3.80	3.67	3.52	3.37	3.29	3.21	3.13	3.05	2.96	2.87
16	8.53	6.23	5.29	4.77	4.44	4.20	4.03	3.89	3.78	3.69	3.55	3.41	3.26	3.18	3.10	3.02	2.93	2.84	2.75
17	8.40	6.11	5.18	4.67	4.34	4.10	3.93	3.79	3.68	3.59	3.46	3.31	3.16	3.08	3.00	2.92	2.83	2.75	2.65
18	8.29	6.01	5.09	4.58	4.25	4.01	3.84	3.71	3.60	3.51	3.37	3.23	3.08	3.00	2.92	2.84	2.75	2.66	2.57
19	8.18	5.93	5.01	4.50	4.17	3.94	3.77	3.63	3.52	3.43	3.30	3.15	3.00	2.92	2.84	2.76	2.67	2.58	2.49
20	8.10	5.85	4.94	4.43	4.10	3.87	3.70	3.56	3.46	3.37	3.23	3.09	2.94	2.86	2.78	2.69	2.61	2.52	2.42
21	8.02	5.78	4.87	4.37	4.04	3.81	3.64	3.51	3.40	3.31	3.17	3.03	2.88	2.80	2.72	2.64	2.55	2.46	2.36
22	7.95	5.72	4.82	4.31	3.99	3.76	3.59	3.45	3.35	3.26	3.12	2.98	2.83	2.75	2.67	2.58	2.50	2.40	2.31
23	7.88	5.66	4.76	4.26	3.94	3.71	3.54	3.41	3.30	3.21	3.07	2.93	2.78	2.70	2.62	2.54	2.45	2.35	2.26
24	7.82	5.61	4.72	4.22	3.90	3.67	3.50	3.36	3.26	3.17	3.03	2.89	2.74	2.66	2.58	2.49	2.40	2.31	2.21
25	7.77	5.57	4.68	4.18	3.85	3.63	3.46	3.32	3.22	3.13	2.99	2.85	2.70	2.62	2.54	2.45	2.36	2.27	2.17
26	7.72	5.53	4.64	4.14	3.82	3.59	3.42	3.29	3.18	3.09	2.96	2.81	2.66	2.58	2.50	2.42	2.33	2.23	2.13
27	7.68	5.49	4.60	4.11	3.78	3.56	3.39	3.26	3.15	3.06	2.93	2.78	2.63	2.55	2.47	2.38	2.29	2.20	2.10
28	7.64	5.45	4.57	4.07	3.75	3.53	3.36	3.23	3.12	3.03	2.90	2.75	2.60	2.52	2.44	2.35	2.26	2.17	2.06
29	7.60	5.42	4.54	4.04	3.73	3.50	3.33	3.20	3.09	3.00	2.87	2.73	2.57	2.49	2.41	2.33	2.23	2.14	2.03
30	7.56	5.39	4.51	4.02	3.70	3.47	3.30	3.17	3.07	2.98	2.84	2.70	2.55	2.47	2.39	2.30	2.21	2.11	2.01
40	7.31	5.18	4.31	3.83	3.51	3.29	3.12	2.99	2.89	2.80	2.66	2.52	2.37	2.29	2.20	2.11	2.02	1.92	1.80
60	7.08	4.98	4.13	3.65	3.34	3.12	2.95	2.82	2.72	2.63	2.50	2.35	2.20	2.12	2.03	1.94	1.84	1.73	1.60
120	6.85	4.79	3.95	3.48	3.17	2.96	2.79	2.66	2.56	2.47	2.34	2.19	2.03	1.95	1.86	1.76	1.66	1.53	1.38
∞	6.63	4.61	3.78	3.32	3.02	2.80	2.64	2.51	2.41	2.32	2.18	2.04	1.88	1.79	1.70	1.59	1.47	1.32	1.00

Index*

Aaker, David A., 250n
ABC "Telefirst," 58
Abeele, Piet Vanden, 641n
Abernathy, J. R., 280n
Abrams, Bill, 46n, 58n, 346n
Absolute magnitude, 313
Absolute (natural) zero, 313, 314
Accidental sample, 396
Accuracy (in research report), **683**–684
Achenbaum, Alvin R., 110n
Ackoff, Russell I., 46n, 49n
Adam home computers, 45
Adler, Lee, 14n, 58n, 59n
Administrative control (for interviews and questionnaires), **229**–231, 232
Advertising Research Foundation, 46, 207n, 499–500
AIO analysis, 186
Airwick Industries, 58
Albaum, Gerald, 342n, 344n
Algorithms, 355
Alignment chart, 454
Alred, Gerald J., 684n
Alsop, Ronald, 59n, 205n, 249n, 321n
Alt, Mick, 580n
Alvin, Duane F., 317n, 495n
American Airlines, 4
American Express, 184
American Marketing Association, 6–8, 720
code of ethics, 37
American Telephone and Telegraph (AT & T), 399n
Analysis of selected cases, 81, **84**–87, 719
Analysis of variance (ANOVA), 609–613, 722
Andersen, Ronald, 478n, 501n
Anderson, John F., 274n
Anderton, E. J., 395n
ANOVA, 609–613, 722
Appel, Valentine, 349n
Area sample, 220, **434**–440
noncoverage error in, 480
probability-proportional-to-size sample, 436, 437–441
Arens, William F., 112n
Armstrong, J. Scott, 493n
Association (between variables), 616, 646. See also Regression analysis
Atkin, Charles, K., 241n
Attitude, 187–189
and communication methods, 196, 203, 214, 215
interviewers', and response errors, 498
measurement of, 314, 317–319, 336–344. See also Attitude scale

Attitude scale, 338–344, 361. See also Self-report
data-collection method for, 270
equivalence in, 327, 329
fictional example of, 323
internal consistency of, 327, 340
and multidimensional scaling, 358
and norms, 341
split-half reliability in, 327
stability in, 326–327
Attributes, measurement (scaling) of, 313–330. See also Scales (ratings)
Audimeter, 163, 245–246
Audit
pantry, 243
product, 158–159
store, 155–156, 158
Audits & Surveys' Burgoyne, Inc., 117
Audits & Surveys' National Total-Market Index, 158–159
Austin, George R., 350n
Awareness/knowledge, 189–192
data-collection method for, 196, 203
measurement of, 314
Ayer, N. W., & Son, 9

Babbie, Earl R., 435n
Bachman, Jerald G., 294n
Bagozzi, Richard P., 250n
Bailey, Leroy, 497n
Bailor, Barbara, 497n
Ball, A. Dwayne, 576n
Banks, Sharon K., 218n
Bar chart, 547, 705, **709**–710
fictional example of, 707
pictogram, 711
variations of, 710–713, 714
Barban, Arnold M., 248n
Barnes, James G., 238n
Barrett, Jane, 278n
Bartels, Robert, 9n
Bassine, Charles, 727n
Batsell, Richard R., 349n
Bayer, Alan E., 288n
Bayesian analysts (or theory), 412n, 449n, 570n, 599n
Beall, Ronald, 732n
Becherer, Richard C., 186n
Beckwith, Neil E., 345n
Behavior, 185–194
and attitudes/opinions, 187–189, 196, 336–337
and communication vs. observation methods, 195–197

---

*Note: The lowercase *n* after a page number indicates the information can be found in a footnote or source note on that page; the lowercase *t,* in a table; and the lowercase *f* in a figure. Running glossary terms, and the page on which the terms are defined, appear in boldface type.

Behavior *(continued)*
  defined, **193**–194
  and fixed-alternative questions, 203
  interviewers', and response errors, 498–501
    profile of average consumer, 92
Behaviorscan, 160
Beik, Leland L., 296n, 297n
Belch, George E., 108n
Belk, Russell W., 111n
Bellenger, Danny N., 205n, 207n, 343n
Belson, W. A., 499n
Bennett, Peter, 5n
Bennett, S. E., 275n
Benrud, C. H., 488n
Benton, William, 238
Benton and Bowles, 238
Berchman, Tracy R., 229n
Berdie, Douglas R., 274n
Berger, James O., 47n
Bermont, Hubert, 181
Bernhardt, Kenneth I., 205n, 207n
Berni Corporation, 59, 217
Berry, Elizabeth, 164n, 246n
Best, Roger, 344n
Bias. *See various types and* Nonsampling error
Biernacki, Patrick, 399n
Big Brothers of Fairfax County, Case 1.1,
    66–67
Billington, Maryann, 487n
Binary variable, 637–640
Birnbaum, Jeffrey H., 219n
Bishop, George F., 275n, 276n
Blackwell, Roger D., 336n
Blair, Ed, 202n, 295n, 441n, 498n
Blair, John R., 20n, 218n, 221n, 437n
Blankenship, A. B., 221n, 274n
Blankertz, Donald F., 92n, 94n
Block (first-stage) sampling fraction, 436, 440
Bloom, Derek, 247n
BLUE estimators, 625–626
Blumberg, Leslie, 713n
Blunch, Niels J., 283n
Blunder, 538, 541–546
Bohrnstedt, George W., 326n, 327n
Bonczek, Robert H., 728n, 732n
Bonita Baking Company (A), Case 1.3, 67–68
Bonita Baking Company (B), Case 2.2,
    127–129
Bonoma, Thomas V., 85n
Bouchard, Thomas J., Jr., 243n, 244n
Boudreaux, Michael, 20n
Boughton, Paul D., 51n
Bovée, Courtland L., 112n
Boyd, Harper W., 81n, 202n, 216n, 278n, 682n,
    693n
Bradburn, Norman M., 202n, 274n, 285n, 292n,
    295n, 296n, 498n, 499n, 501n
Brain-wave research, 251
Braithwaite, R. B., 617
Branching question, 291–292, 295, 303
Brand awareness, 275n
Brand loyalty, 97–98, 324
Brand-switching matrix, 97–98, 118
Brand-tracking studies, 27
Brand-transition matrix, 98n
Brandt, Michael T., 8n
Brant, Joquin Ives, 732n
Brighton, Malcolm, 580n

Britt, Stewart Henderson, 680n
Brown, Lyndon O., 296n, 297n
Bruner, Jerome S., 350n
Brusaw, Charles T., 684n
Buchanan, L., 214n
Buckman, Glen A., 251n
Burdick, Richard K., 611n
Burger King, 4
Burke, Marketing Services, 484–485, 571n
Burns, Alvin C., 186n
Burns, Kevin, 107n
Burton, John P., 278n
Bush, Alan J., 228n
Butcher, Bob, 499n

Cabbage-Patch Kids, 45–46
Calamity-Casualty Insurance Company, Case
    4.2, 378–380
Calder, Bobby J., 208n
Callbacks, 486, 493, 494
Calvin Klein, 190
Campbell, Cathy, 280n
Campbell, Donald T., 109n, 202n, 216n, 325n
Campbell Soup Company, 47, 210
Campos, George, 146
Cannell, Charles F., 229n, 295n, 495n, 496,
    496n, 497n
Canning, Richard D., 733n
Cantril, Hadley, 283n
Cappo, Joe, 51n
CARA. *See* Centerville Area Radio Association
Carlson, Eric D., 729n, 730n, 732n
Carlson, Eugene, 183n
Carman, James M., 250n
Carmone, F., 360n
Carroll, J. Douglas, 361n
CASRO (Council of American Survey Research
    Organizations), 228, 483, 485
Cassettari, Michael N., 731n, 732n
Categories (in coding), 32, 534. *See also*
    Tabulation
Cattin, Philippe, 360n
Causal research, 29, 75, 87, 104–117, 719.
    See also Causality
  and convenience sample, 397
  experiments in, 79, 87. *See also* Experiment
  vs. exploratory and descriptive research, 104
  fictional example, 115
  and hypotheses, 77, 104
  and judgment sample, 417
  and snowball sample, 399
  and structured observation, 240
  and test marketing, 78, 79
Causality (causal relationships), 104–118, 616–
    617
  and concomitant variation, 105, 118
  vs. correlation (or association), 616–617
  and cross tabulation, 552, 558
  fictional example of, 623
  and percentages, calculation of, 552
  and time order of variables, 105–106, 118
Cause-and-effect relationships. *See* Causality
Census, 144, 172, 392. *See also* Censuses,
    economic
  Bureau of U.S.
    accuracy of, 449–450
    definition of geographic areas, 439f
    data available, example of, 145t

Census *(continued)*
 interviewers (fictional example), 475–476, 490
 and Nielsen television area probability sample, 438–439
 and nonsampling error, 478, 482
 and probability-proportional-to-size area sampling, 440
 vs. sample, 392, 404, 416
Censuses, economic, 172–176
Centerville Area Radio Association (CARA), Research Project, 64–65, 123–124, 254–255, 367–373, 507–509, 655–658, 736–738
Central-limit theorem, 410, 426*n*
 in hypothesis testing, 590, 591
 and sample size, 451
Central-office edit, 532, **533**–534
Chance fork, 53
Charts, 547, 704–713. *See also various types of charts*
Chase, Donald A., 207*n*
Chein, Isidor, 402*n*
Chestnut Ridge Country Club, Case 2.5, 135–138
Chevrolet pickup truck (vs. Ford), 185, 189
Chi-square goodness-of-fit test, 584–587, 604
 fictional example, 587
 vs. Kolmogorov-Smirnov test, 589, 605
 requirements for, 650*t*
Chicago Daily News, 50–51, 58
Childers, Terry L., 221*n*
Children, testing, 346*n*
 fictional example, 348, 351
Chonko, Lawrence B., 35*n*
Chromy, James R., 491*n*
Chrysler Corporation, 352–353
Churchill, Gilbert A., Jr., 186*n*, 320*n*, 324*n*, 325*n*, 329*n*, 340*n*, 350*n*
Clarity (in research report), **684**–685
Classification information (vs. basic information), 303
Cluster sample, 422, **431**–440, 441. *See also* Area sample; Systematic sample
 and cost, 464
 fictional example, 432
 and sample size, 448, 463, 464, 468
Coca-Cola Corporation, 320–321
Cochran, William G., 441*n*, 464*n*, 587*n*, 650*n*
Code of ethics, 37
Codebook, 536–537, 538, 565
Coders, 534, 535
Coding, 32, 532, **534**–537, 565
 consistency in, 240, 535
 dichotomous questions, 284
 and nonsampling errors, 477
 from pretest, 296
 and questionnaire design, 295
Coefficient α, 327
Coefficient of concordance, 647, 652–654
Coefficient of correlation, 627–630, 643
Coefficient of determination, 628–630
Coefficient of multiple correlation, 635
Coefficient of multiple determination, 635, 643
Coefficient of partial correlation, 635, **636**–637

Coefficient of partial determination, 635, **636**–637, 643
Coefficient of partial (or net) regression, 631–635, 643
Coefficients, 327, 328, 329
 contingency, 646, 649–650
 Pearsonian, 628
 product-moment, 628
 slope, inferences about, 625–627
 Spearman's rank-order correlation, 647, 650–652
 tau, 652*n*
Cohen, Jacob, 640*n*
Cohen, Jeffrey, 497*n*
Cohen, Patricia, 640*n*
Coleco Industries, 45
ColecoVision, 45
Collins, Martin, 499*n*, 535*n*
Communication, 195–197, 202–216. *See also* Questionnaires
 and dichotomous questions, 284
 vs. observation, 196, 197, 299
Como Western Bank, Case 6.5, 673–674
Comparative-ratings scale, 349–350, 362
Completeness (in research report), **682**
Completeness rate *(C),* 484, 495
Computer
 coding for, 535–537, 565
 and conjoint analysis, 360
 and data analysis, 642. *See also* Marketing information system and decision support system
 and data search, 152–153
 and mail questionnaires, 222, 228
 and multidimensional scaling, 360
 programs for marketing information systems, 727
 programs for simulated test markets, 117
 programs for tabulation, 537–538
 and telephone and personal interviews, 222, 228
 terms for (glossary), 727
Computer graphics, 703, 705
Conceptual definition, 314–316
Conciseness (in research report), **685**–686
Concomitant variation, 105, 118, 720
Concurrent validity, 322
Conditional association, 555
Conditional probability, 552–556
Coney, Kenneth A., 275*n*
Confidence (level), **448**–449. *See also* Confidence interval estimate
 (trade-off with) sample size, 413, 454, 468
 of statistical tests, 573
Confidence interval estimate
 when estimating proportions, 459, 460
 with known/unknown population variance, 452, 454, 456
 with multiple objectives, 457
 and nonsampling errors, 477, 478
 and quota sample, 430
 and significance-testing procedures, 570, 580
 in simple random sample, 410–413
 in stratified sample, 425–428
Conjoint analysis, 358–361, 362
Conner, Paul W., 51*n*
Constant error, 319
Constant-sum method, 349, 362

Constitutive (conceptual) definition, 314–316
Construct validity, 321, 324–325, 329
Consumer
    behavior, 92, 185–194. *See also* Behavior
    and brand loyalty, 97–98
    diary. *See* Panels
    groups (regarding ethics in marketing
        research), 35
Consumer Mail Panel, 77, 160, 166, 168
Consumer market services, 95, 160, 162–163
Consumer Medical Attitudes, Case 4.3, 380–
    387
Consumer Price Index (CPI), 399
Consumer Price Index for Urban Wage Earners
    and Clerical Workers, 399
Consumer Reports, 328
Consumer Savings Project (University of
    Illinois), 477, 478
Contact rate *(K),* 484, 488, 495, 504
Content validity, 321, 322–324, 329
Contingency coefficient, 646, 647–650
Contrived setting, 244–245
Controlled test market, 117
Control variables, 555
Convenience sample, 395, 396–397, 719
Convergent validity, 325, 329, 339
Converse, Jean M., 295*n*
Cook, Stuart W., 75*n*, 80*n*, 18*n*, 82*n*, 83*n*, 85*n*,
    202*n*, 203*n*, 317*n*, 319*n*, 345*n*, 532*n*,
    534*n*
Cook, Thomas D., 109*n*
Cooper, Harris, 489*n*, 492*n*
Cooper, Lee G., 355*n*, 358*n*
Cornish, Edward, 238*n*
Corporate culture, 46, 62
Correlation analysis, 616, 618, 643. *See also*
    Regression analysis
Cosmas, Steven C., 344*n*
Cotter, Patrick R., 497*n*
Coulter, Philip B., 497*n*
Council of American Survey Research
    Organizations (CASRO), 228, 483, 485
Counterbiasing statement, 280
Covariation. *See* Association
Cox, Donald F., 724*n*
Cox, Eli P., 346*n*
Cox, Keith K., 205*n*
Cox, William E., Jr., 84*n*
Coyle, Bryan W., 325*n*
Crask, Melvin R., 349*n*
Cravens, David W., 613*n*
Creelman, C. D., 314*n*
Crespi, Irving, 343*n*
Criterion (or dependent) variable, 616, 620*n*
    fictional example, 639
    improving the predictions of the, 630, 643–
        644
    when predictor variable is absent, 628–629
    and variable transformation, 641
Criterion-related validity, 321–322
Cronbach, L. J., 325*n*, 579*n*
Cross-classification analysis, 103. *See also*
    Cross tabulation
Cross classifications, anticipated, 464–467. *See*
    also Cross tabulation
Cross-sectional study (analysis), **95,** 96, 98,
    102–104, 118
    and chi-square contingency table, 647

types of, 102. *See also* Field study; Sample
    survey
Cross tabulation, 537, 551–565, 566
    and descriptive research, 720
    fictional example, 587
    and item nonresponse, 540
Cumulative distribution function, 548–551
    in example of Kolmogorov-Smirnov test, 588,
        590
Curry, James, 540*n*
Curtis Publishing Company, 9*n*
Cutler, Fred, 348*n*
Czaja, Ronald, 218*n*, 221*n*, 437*n*
Czepiel, John, 250*n*

Dancer, Fitzgerald, sample, 117
Daniel, Wayne G., 274*n*, 650*n*
Darden, Damon, 113*n*, 114*n*
Data
    accuracy of, 282, 293, 497, 534
    on behavior, 185–194, 196. *See also*
        Behavior
    commercially supplied, 4, 30. *See also*
        Marketing research, firms for
    demographic/socioeconomic, 184–185, 196,
        197
        fictional example, 183, 185, 189
        and questionnaire design, 203, 293
    as feedback, 5, 6
    ineligible, 482
    new vs. existing, 4
    objectivity of, 197
    primary, 30. *See also* Primary data
    secondary, 29–30. *See also* Secondary data
Data analysis, 32, 529. *See also* Regression
    analysis
    and adjustment of data for, 482, 483, 493–
        494, 501
    and associations, 616–644
    and the computer era, 642
    and data-collection errors, 476
    and data on knowledge vs. opinions, 215
    dialog system for, 732
    and DSS vs. MIS, 733
    errors (or hazards) in, 501*n*, 591–592, 602,
        642
        fictional example, 531–532, 558–559, 562
    and item nonresponse, 285
    model system for, 732
    and no-opinion answers, 494
    preliminary steps in, 532–566
    and the research process, 532
    and the research report, 691
    and (marketing) research theory, 617–618
    and sample size, 467
    and statistical tests, 584–605. *See also*
        Statistical tests
    summary comments on, 642
    and television diaries, 246
Data array, 538
Data cleaning, 534, 538
Data collection, 29–32
    and callbacks, 488
    by communication, 195–197. *See also*
        Communication
    control in, 222, 229–231, 293
    costs of, 196–197, 245, 251
        and area sample, 437

Data collection *(continued)*
    and sample size, 463–464
    and sequential sample, 395
  errors (hazards) in, 144, 295, 476
  field methods of, 31. *See also* Field studies
  forms for, 29, 30, 202, 721, 722. *See also*
      Observation, forms for; Questionnaires
  methods for, 29–30, 195–197, 231. *See also*
      Interviews; Panels; Samples
  and multidimensional scaling, 354
  by observation, 195–197. *See also*
      Observation
  and pretest, 296
  of primary data. *See* Primary data
  by questionnaire, 202–216. *See also*
      Questionnaire
  and research design, 74, 721, 722
  of secondary data. *See* Secondary data
  staff for, 31–32. *See also* Interviewers
Data interpretation, 32
Data processing, 501, 728
Data-retrieval system, 733
Data sources, 151–168. *See also* Publications
Data system, 729–731
Davis, Linden A., Jr., 18*n*
Davison, M. L., 354*n*
Dawe, Jessamon, 691*n*, 706*n*, 708*n*
Day, George S., 488*n*
Dayton, C. Mitchell, 650*n*
Decimals (in research reports), 546
Decision fork, 53
Decision maker
  and environment, 45, 62
  (impact of) personality of, 46–47. *See also*
      Marketing research, wasted
  relationship with researcher, 44, 50, 51–52,
      62
  risk, attitudes toward, 47–49
Decision making, 44–53, 62–63. *See also*
      Decision Maker
  and central-office edit, 580
  and computer programming, 727–729
  and confidence intervals, 580
  and "ill-structured problems," 728
  and MIS, 724
  and nonsampling error, 503–504
  and (research) project emphasis, 724
  and (research) proposal, 56
  and risk, attitudes toward, 47–49
Decision problem, 50–53, 63
Decision support system (DSS), 15–16, **728**–
    734
Decision tree, 52–53, 63
Degrees of freedom (in statistical distribution),
    585–587
DeMaio, T., 490*n*
Demby, Emanuel H., 20*n*
Deming, W. Edwards, 488*n*
Depth interview, 204–205. *See also* Focus-
    group interview
Derived population, 405–407
  in stratified sample, 423
Descriptive research, 29, 75–79, 87, 92–104,
    719–720
  and convenience sample, 397, 417
  cross-sectional vs. longitudinal studies for, 95
  errors in, 93–94
  vs. exploratory, 92

fictional example, 86, 103, 115
  purposes of, 92–93, 117
  and questionnaire design, 268, 719
  and snowball sample, 399
  and structured observation, 240
  types of, 95–104
Deshpande, Rohit, 32*n*, 680*n*, 721*n*
Deterministic model, 618
Deutcher, T., 354*n*
Dialog system, 729, 732
Diary. *See* Panels
Dichotomous question, 284–285, 303
  and dummy variables, 637
  and internal consistency, 327
Dickson, John, 342*n*
Dillman, Donald, 501*n*
Dimensions in semantic-differential scales, 341
Direct Mail Marketing Association, 220
Directories, 172–181, 435*n*
Directory of Directories, 152, 180
Discriminant analysis, 354, 356
Discriminant validity, 325, 329, 339
Disguise, 202
Disguised observation, 241–244
Disproportionate stratified sample, 430, 441
  fictional example, 429
  and sample size, 463
Distribution (concept of). *See* Sampling
    distribution
Distribution services
  Audits & Surveys' National Total-Market
      Index, 158–159
  Nielsen Retail Index, 156–157
  Nielsen Scantrack, 157–158
  Selling Areas—Marketing, Inc. (SAMI), 159
  and standard test markets, 116
DMI (Dun and Bradstreet "Market Identifiers"),
    155, 156*f*
Donnelly, James H., Jr., 54*n*
Double-barreled question, 290, 303
Douglas, Paul, 703*n*
Downey, Ronald G., 317*n*
Dressler, Michael, 732*n*
Drives (vs. motives), 193
Dryden Press, The, Case 5.5, 520–522
DSS. *See* Decision support system
Dummy table, 93–95, 118
  cross-classification, for determining sample
      size, 466
  and cross tabulation, 564
  and data analysis, 532
  and questionnaire design, 268–269, 296–297
Dummy (or binary) variable, 637–640, 641,
    643, 644
Dun and Bradstreet, 155, 156*f*
Duncan, J., 491*n*
Dunkelburg, William C., 488*n*
Dunn, S. Watson, 248*n*
Duplicated data, 480, 481
DuPont, 245, 250
Durand, Richard, 540*n*
Duzy, Kenneth, 152*n*
Dyer, Robert F., 8*n*

Eastman Kodak, 4
Economy
  and consumer intentions, 192
  impact on decision making, 45, 62

Edel, Richard, 77*n*
Editing, 32, 532–534, 565
  and questionnaire design, 295
Edwards, Linda, 251*n*
Ehrenberg, A. S. C., 691*n*, 693*n*
Einstein, Albert, 617
Electrical observation, 338–339
Elliott, David, 493*n*, 501*n*
Elliott, Jock, 683, 684, 684*n*, 685*n*
Elrick and Lavidge, Inc., 591
Empirical distribution, 538, 547. *See also*
    Cumulative distribution function
Emulators (in VALS terminology), 198
Encyclopedia of Associations, 152, 180
Encyclopedia of Business Information Sources,
    153–154, 180
Engel, James F., 336*n*
Environment
  impact on decision making, 45–46, 62
  impact on marketing research, 5, 7
Equivalence, 327, 329
Erdos, Paul L., 221*n*, 274*n*, 501*n*
Errors of commission/omission, 495–501. *See*
    also various types of errors
Ethics in marketing research, 33–39
  regarding observation methods, 241–242
Etzel, Michael J., 316*n*, 344*n*
Experience survey, 81, **82**–84, 88, 328, 719
Experiment, 79, 87, **107**–117, 118, 719–722.
    See also Observation; Test marketing
  field, 108–109, 118
  laboratory, 107–108, 118, 244, 245, 252
  problems in, 111–115
  validity of, 109–110, 244
Experimental research. *See* Causal research;
    Experiment
Exploratory research, 28–29, **75**–77, 79–86,
    87–88. *See also* Hypothesis
  and convenience sample, 397
  vs. descriptive research, 92
  fictional example, 115
  and focus-group interview, 210
  and individual depth interview, 205
  and judgment sample, 397, 398
  and marketing constructs, 328
  projective methods for, 215
  purpose of, 92
External data, 4, **149**–151
  key sources, 151–155, 168. *See also* Data
    sources; Publications
  steps in using, 150*t*–151*t*
External validity, 109, 244
Eye camera, 248–249
Eye-tracking, 248–249

Fabhus, Inc., Case 6.3, 666–668
Faces scale, 346, 348
Factor analysis, 341*n*, 354, 356
Factorial design, 612–613
Faria, Anthony J., 152*n*, 153*n*
Federal Reserve Board, 192, 548
Ferber, Robert, 92*n*, 94*n*, 98*n*, 100*n*, 101*n*,
    144*n*, 477*n*, 478*n*, 501*n*
Fern, Edward F., 210*n*
Fero, Marcia Newlands, 125*n*
Field edit, 532, 533, 565
Field error (bias), **495**–501
Field experiment, 108–109, 118
Field staff, 230, 231, 532. *See also* Interviewer

Field study, 102–103. *See also* Field error
  fictional example, 475–476
  and probability sampling, 440
  and sample design, 440
  vs. sample survey, 102, 118
Figures (in research reports), 691, 693, 700
Fine, Michelle, 399*n*
Finite population correction factor, 463, 468
Finkner, A. L., 441*n*
First Federal Bank of Bakersfield, Case 5.6,
    522–525
First-stage sampling fraction, 436–437, 440
Fisher, R. A., 612*n*
Fiske, Donald W., 325*n*
Fiske, Susan T., 187*n*
Fixed-alternative question, 202–203, 232, 303
  and interviewer bias, 499
  types of, 280–285
Fixed sample, 395, 416
Flegal, David W., 60*n*, 61*n*
Focus-group interview, 205–210, 232
  in experience survey, 84
  fictional example, 201, 209
  vs. individual depth interview, 205, 208–209
  and marketing constructs, 329
  moderator of, qualifications for, 206*t*–207*t*
  and research design, 719
Follow-up
  callbacks, 486, 493, 494
  and contact rate, 489. *See also* Response
    rate
  and field vs. central-office edit, 533
  and interviewer cheating, 500–501
  on mail questionnaire, 230, 493
  and nonresponse error, 491, 492–493
  and refusals, 491
  for simulated test market, 117
  on telephone vs. personal interview, 220–221
Folsom, R. E., Jr., 488*n*
Forced-distribution test market, 117
Ford, Neil M., 186*n*
Ford Motor Company, 77
Ford pickup truck (vs. Chevrolet), 185, 189
Fox, James Alan, 280*n*
Foy, Larry, 125*n*
Francis, I., 537*n*
Frank, Ronald E., 641*n*
Frankel, K., 399*n*, 412*n*
Frankel, Lester R., 399*n*
Frankel, Martin R., 399*n*, 478*n*, 498*n*, 501*n*
Frazer, Cara S., 186*n*
Freeman, Laurie, 79*n*
Frequency polygon, 547, 551
Frey, James H., 221*n*
Fried, Edreta, 283*n*
Friedman, H. H., 346*n*
Funnel approach, 291, 303

Gaito, John, 344*n*
Gallagher, William J., 680*n*, 682*n*, 684*n*, 686*n*,
    689*n*, 691*n*
Gallup Poll, 440
Galvanic skin response test. *See*
    Psychogalvanometer
Gardner, David M., 111*n*
Gardner, Fred, 164*n*, 246*n*
Garner, Wendell, R., 314*n*
Gaski, John F., 316*n*
Gatchel, Robert J., 248*n*

Gatty, Bob, 158*n*
Gauss-Markov theorem, 626, 643
Gee, Flora, 476*n*
General Mills, 46, 57, 187–189, 617
General Motors, 278
Generalized questions, 290
Generic Drugs (A), Case 3.1, 256
Generic Drugs (B), Case 5.4, 518–519
Geurts, Michael D., 280*n*
Gibbons College Library, Case 2.4, 131–135
Gibson, Lawrence D., 6*n*, 20*n*, 57*n*, 111, 617
Gibson, W., 346*n*
Giges, Nancy, 79*n*
Gill, Sam, 275*n*
Gillette Company, 27
Glasser, G. J., 218*n*
Glassman, Mark B., 498*n*
Glenn, Norval D., 580*n*
Goldberg, M. E., 346*n*
Goldberg, Stephen M., 361*n*
Goldstucker, Jac L., 205*n*, 207*n*, 343*n*
Good, Robert E., 724*n*
Goodman, Leo A., 399*n*
Goodnaw, Jacqueline J., 350*n*
Goodness of fit, 584–587
Gorn, G. J., 346*n*
Gorton, K., 395*n*
Government publications, 149, 172–178
Graphic presentations, 703–713. *See also*
    various types
Graphic-ratings scale, 345–346
    vs. comparative-ratings scale, 349
    vs. itemized-ratings scale, 347, 362
Grass, Robert C., 250*n*
Green, Paul E., 361*n*
Greenberg, Barnett A., 343*n*
Greenberg, B. G., 280*n*
Gregg, A. O., 346*n*
Gregg, J. P., 249*n*
Grossman, Randolph M., 480*n*
Groves, Robert, 218*n*, 222*n*, 231*n*, 489*n*, 501*n*
GTE (Sylvania Division), 153
Guengel, Pamela G., 229*n*
Guenther, William C., 612*n*, 613*n*
Guest, I. L., 498*n*
Guffey, Hugh J., Jr., 540*n*
Guilford, Joy P., 349*n*
Gulledge, Larry, 241*n*

Hair, Joseph F., Jr., 228*n*
Haire, Mason, 213*n*
Haley, Russell I., 114*n*, 115*n*
Halo effect, 349
Handelsman, Moshe, 569*n*
Hansen, F., 251*n*
Hansen, Morris H., 441*n*, 451*n*, 464*n*
Hardin, Michael, 62*n*
Harris, Clyde E., Jr., 349*n*
Harrison, Mary Carolyn, 186*n*
Hartley, Steven W., 186*n*
Hart Machine Company, Case 5.2, 511–514
Hatch, Richard, 680*n*
Hatchett, Shirley, 497*n*
Hauser, John R., 350*n*, 354*n*, 356*n*, 357*n*
Hawkins, Del I., 275*n*, 344*n*
Heeler, Roger M., 345*n*
Heide, Maria Papas, 659*n*
Heise, David R., 341*n*
Hellevik, Ottar, 555*n*

Henkin, Joel, 206*n*
Herzog, A. Regula, 294*n*
Hess, John M., 208*n*
Higgenbotham, James B., 205*n*
Higgins, Kevin, 85*n*
Hill, Richard W., 231*n*
Hingson, Ralph, 278*n*
Histogram, 538, **547,** 551
    in chi-square test, 588
Hochstim, Joseph R., 30*n*
Hocking, R. R., 635*n*
Holbrook, Morris B., 354*n*, 356*n*, 357*n*
Holland, Charles W., 613*n*
Hollander, Sidney, Jr., 92*n*, 94*n*
Hollis, Pamela G., 189*n*
Holm, Cynthia K., 35*n*
Holsapple, Clyde W., 728*n*, 732*n*
Holzem Business Systems, Case 5.3, 514–518
Homoscedastic values, 641
Honomichl, Jack J., 9*n*, 13*n*, 167*n*, 247*n*
Horowitz, Daniel G., 491*n*
Horvitz, D. G., 280*n*
Household sampling fraction, 437, 440
Houston, Michael J., 84*n*
Huber, Joel, 354*n*, 356*n*, 357*n*
Huff, Darrell, 617*n*
Hughes, G. David, 114*n*, 115*n*
Human observation, 245
Hunt, Shelby D., 35*n*, 36*n*, 296*n*, 535*n*
Hurwitz, William N., 441*n*, 452*n*, 464*n*
Huxley, Stephen J., 231*n*
Hypergeometric distribution, 587*n*
Hypothesis(es) 77–79. *See also* Causality;
        Hypothesis testing
    best data for development of, 87
    and descriptive research, 92, 93
    example of in causality, 105
    in experience survey, 83
    and field studies, 103
    and focus groups, 232
    in observation methods, 240
    and questionnaire design, 268, 269, 275
Hypothesis testing, 570–580
    fictional example, 598
    and null hypothesis, 570–580. *See also* Null
        hypothesis
    about one mean, 590–594, 605
    and power (concept of), 575–580
    and related samples, 599–603
    and sample size, 464
    and setting the risk of error, 570, 573, 575–
        576
    steps in, 573–575
    about two means, 594–603, 605. *See also*
        Analysis of variance (ANOVA)
    about two proportions, 603–604, 605
    and Type I and Type II errors, 572–575
Hypothetical outcomes, 49, 50, 56

Implicit alternative, 289–290, 303
Implicit assumption, 290
Indirect techniques (for attitude scaling), **338**
INDSCAL, 355
Industrial market services, 155
Information control, 222–229, 232
Information manager, 152
Information Resources, Inc., 162
    Behaviorscan, 162–163
Ingrassia, Lawrence, 205*n*

Illiterate America, 221
Inner-directed people, 187, 197–198
Insight-stimulating examples, 84, 88, 328–329.
    See also Analysis of selected cases
Intention, 192–193
    data collection on, 196, 203
    measurement of, 314
Internal data, 4, 82, **149–151**
Internal validity, 109, 110
International Reading Association, 221
Interval scale, 310, **312**–313, 314
    vs. ordinal scale, 344
    and product-moment correlation, 646
    vs. ratio scale, 313, 330
    and self-reports, 344
Interview
    depth, 204–205
    in experience survey, 82–84
    focus-group. *See* Focus-group interview
    informal (in experience survey), 83
    mall intercept, 228n
    and noncoverage error, 480
    personal. *See* Personal interview
    for simulated test market, 117
    structured (in experience survey), 83
    telephone. *See* Telephone interview
    unstructured (in analysis of selected cases),
        84
Interviewer. *See also* Field staff
    cheating by, 230, 499–501
    instructions to, 498, 223f–224f, 225f–227f
    and training to increase response rate, 491,
        492, 498
Interviewer errors (causing bias), 295, 402,
        498–501
    and background (of interviewer), 491, 497
    and noncoverage error, 480
    and psychological/behavioral factors, 498–
        501, 504
    and response error (bias), 496, 497–501
Interviewer-interviewee interaction
    model for, 491, 496
    as source of error, 501, 504
Interviewer performance
    and callbacks, 488
    and completeness rate, 495
    and contact rate, 488–489
    and field edit, 532
    and measurement, 318
    and questionnaire design, 295
    and refusals, 489, 491
Item nonresponse, 285, 291, 494–495
    and central-office edit, 533–534
    as indicator of quality of research, 540
    and one-way tabulation, 538, 540–541
    and substitution of values, 540
Item omission. *See* Item nonresponse
Itemized-ratings scale, 346–347
    vs. comparative-ratings scale, 349
    fictional example, 348
    vs. graphic-ratings scale, 362
Izod brand shirts, 187–189

Jackson, Babette, 349n
Jackson, David J., 317n, 495n
Jacob, Herbert, 148n
Jacoby, Jacob, 283n
Jaffe, Eugene D., 342n
James, John C., 345n

Jastram, R. W., 572n
Jensen, R. L., 441n, 464n
John, George, 84n
Johnson, H. Webster, 152n, 153n
Johnson, Ross H., 585n
Joiner, Brian L, 280n
Jones, B. L., 488n
Joselyn, Robert W., 44n, 630n
Joseph Machine Company, Case 6.6, 674–675
Journey into China, 111, 112
Judgment sample, 395, 397, **398**–399, 417
    and research design, 719

Kahn, Robert L., 218n, 231n, 489n, 496, 496n,
        497n, 501n
Kalton, Graham, 277n, 282n, 441n, 494n, 535n
Kalwani, Manohar U., 193n
Kanner, Bernice, 33n, 50n, 59n, 184n, 190n,
        209n, 246n, 484–485, 485n
Kaplan, Charles P., 145n
Karson, Marvin J., 193n
Kasper, Judith, 478n, 501n
Kassarjian, Harold H., 186n, 212n
Katz, Martin, 61n
Kaufman, Louis, 711n
Kearns, Walter, 144
Keckley, Paul H. 707n
Keen, P. G., 728n
Kelleher, Joanne, 144n
Kendall, K. W., 186n
Kendall, M. G., 634n, 652n, 654, 654n
Kendall's coefficient of concordance, 647,
        652–654
Kenner, 59
Kenny, David A., 104n, 105n
Keppel, Geoffrey, 107n, 610n
Kerin, Roger A., 220n, 221n, 285n, 495n
Kerlinger, Fred N., 79n, 102n, 107n, 211n, 241n
Key informant search, 82, 88
Keypunching, blunders in, 541, 548
Khost, Henry P., 117n
Kiechel, W., III, 152n
Kilpatrick, F. P., 210n
Kim, Jac-On, 540n
Kimberly-Clark, 78
King, William R., 724n
Kish, Leslie, 441n, 478n, 483n
Klein, Frederick C., 244n
Klompmaker, Jay E., 114n, 115n
Klopfer, W. G., 211n
Knowledge. *See also* Awareness
    consumers', 232
    vs. opinions, 215
Kohnke-Aguirre, Luanne, 498n
Kolmogorov-Smirnov test, 584, **588**–590
    vs. chi-square test, 589, 605
Koppelman, Frank S., 354n, 356n, 357n
Kornhauser, Arthur, 268n, 274n
Koten, John, 4n, 8n
KR20 coefficient, 327
Kreisman, Richard, 163n
Kruskal, J. B., 360n
Kutner, Michael H., 616n

LaBarbera, Priscilla, 250n
Laboratory experiment, 107–108, 244, 245,
        252
    vs. field experiment, 108, 109, 118
Laczniak, Gene R., 82n

Lakey, Mary Anne, 317*n*
Lamont, Lawrence M., 340*n*
Landon, E. Laird, Jr., 218*n*
Language system, 732
Latin-square design, 612, 613
Laurent, Andre, 295*n*
Lavidge, Robert L., 591
Lawrence, Raymond J., 92*n*, 202*n*
Leading question, 289, 295, 303
Lean Cuisine, 85
Least-squares solution, 621, 625, 632, 643
   and variable transformation, 641
Lehmann, Donald R., 345*n*, 616*n*
Levine, Joel, 46*n*
Liefer, J. R., 346*n*
Life cycle of consumer, 274–275
Life cycle of product, 358
Life-style (AIO) analysis, 186, 196, 197
Like (soft drink), 112
Likert, Rensis, 339*n*
Likert scale. *See* Semantic-differential scale
Lincoln, Douglas J., 344*n*
Line chart, 705, **706**–708, 713, 714. *See also*
   Stratum chart
Lipstein, Benjamin, 488*n*, 500*n*
Lipton Company, 689
Literature search, 81–82, 328, 719
Little, John D. C., 729*n*, 731*n*, 732*n*
Local Government Pooled Investment Fund,
   Case 6.4, 669–673
Locander, William B. 278*n*
Lockley, Lawrence C., 9*n*
Loeb, Margaret, 96*n*
Longitudinal study (analysis), **95**–101, 118,
   720. *See also* Panels
Lonial, Subhash C., 343*n*
Lord, William Jackson, Jr., 706*n*, 708*n*
Lotus 1-2-3, 734
Lublin, Joann S., 560*n*
Lundstrom, William J., 67*n*, 127*n*, 340*n*
Lynch, John G., Jr., 109*n*

McCarthy, E. Jerome, 5*n*, 6*n*
McDaniel, Stephen W., 18*n*
McDonald, Colin, 535*n*
McDonald, Philip, 478*n*, 484*n*, 486*n*
MacLachlan, James, 250*n*
McLeod, Raymond, Jr., 725*n*
McNemar test, 650*n*
McSweeney, Maryellen, 587*n*, 650*n*, 652*n*
Machalaba, Daniel, 221*n*
Madden, Charles S., 18*n*
Madow, William G., 441*n*, 452*n*, 464*n*
Mahajan, Vijay, 113*n*
Maier, Ernest L., 152*n*, 153*n*
Mail questionnaire, 216, 218–221, 232. *See*
   also Questionnaire design;
   Questionnaires; Questions
   and adjustment of data for nonresponse, 494
   appearance of, 295
   bias in, 228, 229
   branching questions in, 291
   and computer assistance, 222, 228
   example of, 368–372, 539*f*
   example of with cover letter, 271*f*–274*f*
   follow-up on, 493
   format of, 294

   and information control, 222, 228–229, 230
   and interviewer-interviewee interaction model,
      496
   monetary incentives for, 491
   and not-at-homes, 486
   and numbering, 295
   and refusals, 489
   and research design, 719
   and sampling control, 216
   and sampling frame, 216–217
Mailing lists, 31
   for consumer studies, 220
   example of, 481*t*
   and noncoverage error, 480
   as sampling frame, 218–219
Main effect (in statistics terminology), 558
Manager. *See* Decision maker; Marketing
   manager
Mangione, Thomas W., 278*n*
Maps (for area sampling), 220
Maps, perceptual, 351–356, 357
Marascuilo, Leonard A., 587*n*, 650*n*, 652*n*
Market analysis system, 734
Market Facts (research firm), 76–77, 166, 315
Market Research Corporation of America,
   160–162
Market segmentation, 184
   and conjoint analysis, 361
   and multidimensional scaling, 358
   and perceptual maps, 355
Market test, 110. *See also* Test marketing
Marketing concept, 4–5, 9–10
Marketing costs, 111, 112
Marketing information services, 155–168. *See*
   also under specific names
Marketing information system (MIS), 15–16,
   724–727
   and decision maker, 724–725, 728
   and decision making, 724, 732
   vs. DSS, 732–733, 734
   emphasis on vs. project emphasis, 718, 722–
      724, 734
   fictional example, 717, 723
   problems with, 728–729, 734
Marketing intelligence system. *See* Marketing
   information system
Marketing manager, 4–5
Marketing mix, 5, 21, 49–50
   evaluated by marketing research, 4, 8
   and longitudinal analysis, 98
   and test marketing, 110–111
Marketing process, 5, 6
Marketing research, 5, 21. *See also* Research
   design; Research process
   activities, 5–9, 17–20
     survey of firms, 7*t*
   and advertising agencies, 11
   and broadcasters, 10
   budget for, 15, 46
     survey of firms, 17*f*
   in consumer goods industries, 46
   and corporate culture, 46
   costs of, 56, 61, 112, 719. *See also*
     Marketing Research, budget for and
     decision making, 46, 718–719, 722. *See*
     also Decision making and decision
     support system (DSS), 15–16, 722
   departments of, 9–10, 13–14
     survey of firms, 10*f*

Marketing research *(continued)*
and environment of firm/decision maker, 5, 6, 8, 45, 46
errors in, 33, 39. *See also various types*
ethics in, 33–39, 241–242
and financial institutions, 10, 46, 58
firms for, 13, 155–168, 491. *See also*
    Research supplier
    and controlled test markets, 117
    Market Facts, 76–77, 166, 315
and government agencies, 13
and industrial manufacturing companies, 10, 19
jobs in, 4, 17–20, 21
    list of, 19t
    salaries of, 20f
and legal suits, 8n
and management of firm, 4–5, 46. *See also*
    Decision Making; Marketing research, wasted
manager of, 4–5, 6
and marketing information system (MIS), 15–16, 722
organization of, 14–15, 21
origins/growth of, 9–10
philosophy of, 26–27, 39
problems in, 47, 58, 718
    ethical, 35–36, 39
process of. *See* Research process
project emphasis in, 677, 718, 722
and public utilities, 13
and publishers, 10
purpose of, 8t, 52, 54
role in the firm, survey results, 7t
and schools, 13
strategy, 26–27, 39
successful, 59, 85, 682, 695
and trade associations, 13
and transportation companies, 13
types of, 9, 10
    unusual, 26
uses of, 4–9
variables affecting use of, 680
wasted, 46, 51, 58–59, 718–719, 720–721
Marketing survey, 4, 9
Markus, Gregory B., 97n
Markus, Hazel, 336n
Marquis, Kent H., 178n
Martell, Chris, 221n
Martella, John A., 345n
Martin, Elizabeth, 476n
Maryles, Daisy, 59n
Mason, J. Barry, 613n
Mathiowetz, Nancy, 222n
Maxwell House, 214
Mayer, Charles S., 14n, 293n
Mayros, Van, 725n
Mazis, Michael B., 346n
Mean(s). *See also* Hypothesis testing, about one mean/two means
differences in, 584, 594–603.
    analysis of variance (ANOVA), 608–613, 722
geometric, and ratio scale, 313
and interval scale, 313
and median and mode, 313
and one-way tabulation, 540, 550
population, vs. sample mean, 407–415
and ratio scale, 313

sample, vs. population mean, 407–415
sample size when estimating, 450–457. *See also* Standard error of estimate
in stratified sample, 425–428
symbols for, 414t
Measurement, 310–330, 336–362, 721
of attitudes, 317–319, 336–344. *See also* Attitude scale
of attributes, 313–330
developing constructs for, 328–329, 330
errors in, 319–321, 330. *See also* Validity
fictional example, 309, 318, 335
problems in, 317–319, 330
reliability of, 317, 325–326, 328
scales of, 310–314, 330. *See also* Scales
statistical tests of, 344
validity of, 319–325, 328, 329, 330
Mechanical observation, 195, 245–251, 338–339
and brain-wave research, 251
by camera, eye, 248–249, 252
by camera, on-site, 241
by eye-tracking, 248–249
by psychogalvanometer, 247–248, 252, 338–339
    vs. voice-pitch analysis, 250–251, 252
by response latency, 249–250, 252
by scanner, 195, 246–247
by tachistoscope, 248, 252
by voice-pitch analysis, 249, 250–251, 252, 339
Median
and interval scale, 313
and one-way tabulation, 550
and ordinal scale, 312
and ratio scale, 313
Mehrotra, Sunil, 343n
Mendenhall, William, 441n, 646n
Menu Census, 162
Messmer, Donald J., 291n
Method variance, 325
Metzger, G. D., 218n
Miles, Milton C., 85
Miller, James G., 350n
Miller, Peter U., 229n, 495n
Miniard, Paul, 336n
MIS. *See* Marketing information system
Mitchell, Arnold, 187n, 188n
Mittelstaedt, Robert A., 346n
Moberg, Patricia E., 218n, 480n
Mode
and interval scale, 313
and one-way tabulation, 550
and ordinal scale, 312
and ratio scale, 313
Model
and decision support system, 733
defined, 731
for interviewer-interviewee interaction, 491, 496
for repeat purchasing tendencies, 113n, 117
for simulated test market, 117
Model system, 729, 732
Modeling system, 733, 734
MONANOVA, 360n
Monroe, John, 441n
Morris, Betty, 114n, 210n
Morton-Williams, Jean, 499n
Mosinee Paper Company, 82

Mosteller, Frederick, 476n, 477n, 501n
Motes, William H., 100n
"Motherhood" attributes, 359
Motivation, 193, 196
  and questionnaire design, 210
Motive, 193
Muircheartaigh, C. A., 495n
Muller, Eitan, 113n
Mullett, Gary M., 193n
Multichotomous question, 281–285
  and dummy variables, 637
  and internal consistency, 327
Multicollinearity, 631, 643
  and coefficients of partial regression, 632,
    633, 634–635
  fictional example, 639
Multidimensional scaling, 350–358, 362
  compared to conjoint analysis, 360
  defined, **353**
Multiple-regression analysis, 630–642, 643. *See
    also various coefficients of*
Multitrait-multimethod matrix, 325n
Murray, Alan, 80n
Myers, James H., 185n, 190n, 191n, 193n,
    336n, 346n
Myers, John H., 148n

Narasimhan, Chakravarthi, 113n
National Family Opinion (NFO) Panel, 160, 166,
    270
National Geographic Society, 111, 112
National Opinion Research Council, 231n
National Purchase Diary (NPD) Panel, 4, 13,
    160
  vs. Nielsen Retail Store Audit, 95–96
  sample page from, 161f
Natural setting, 244–245
Nebenzahl, Israel D., 342n
Need-driven people, 187, 197–198
Needham, Harper, and Steers, 186
Nelson, Ronald G., 251n
Nemmers, Erqin Esser, 148n
Nescafe, 213–214
Neslin, Scott A., 345n
Nestle Enterprises, 85
Neter, John, 616n
Neu, Morgan, 249
Nevin, John R., 108n
NFO (National Family Opinion) Panel, 160, 166,
    270
Nielsen, A. C. (biography), 167
Nielsen, A. C., Company, 9n, 13
  data on test marketing, 113, 117
Nielsen Retail Index, 155, 156–157
  vs. Audits & Surveys' National Total-Market
    Index, 158–159
  and decision support system, 729
Nielsen Retail Store Audit, 95, 96
Nielsen Scantrack, 157–158
Nielsen Television Index, 160, 163–164
  and area probability sample, 438–439
  and example of causality, 107
Noelle-Neumann, E., 289n
Nominal scale (or data), 310, **311,** 313–314
  and chi-square test, 584
  and nonparametric measures of association,
    646
  and population proportions, 603n
Nomograph, 454, 456, 460

Noncoverage error, 479–483, 504
Nonobservation error, 478–495, 504
  noncoverage error, 479–483, 504
  nonresponse error, 483–495, 504
  overcoverage error, 480, 481
Nonparametric measures of association, 646–
    654
Nonprobability sample, 31, 394–395, 396–
    402, 416
  fictional example, 403, 421
  vs. probability sample, 403–404
  types of, 395
Nonresponse, 228n, 231n
  and nonobservation errors, 478, 483–495
  and sample size, 467
Nonresponse error, 483–495, 504. *See also*
    Item nonresponse
  adjusting for, 493–494, 501
  vs. response error, 501
  and substituting values, 540
Nonsampling error (or bias), 285, **476**–504
  checklist for, 503
  nonobservation error, 478–495, 504
    noncoverage, 479–483, 504
    nonresponse error, 483–495, 504
    overcoverage error, 480, 481
  observation error, 478, 495–501, 504
    field error, 495–501
    office error, 501
  random vs. nonrandom, 476–477
  in research report, 693
  and sample size, 467
  and sampling error, 476–478, 501–504
  and total error, 478
  types of, 479f
Noonan, A. C., 238n
Nostalgia, Inc., Case 2.1, 125–127
Not-at-homes, 486, **487**–489
NPD. *See* National Purchase Diary Panel
Null hypothesis, 570–580
  in example of chi-square test, 587, 588
  fictional example, 587
  in Kolmogorov-Smirnov test, 588–589
Nunnally, Jum C., 310n, 322n, 327n, 646n,
    651n

O'Brien, John, 288n
Observation, 195, 238–252, 721
  vs. communication, 196, 197, 299
  and construct validity, 324
  contrived vs. natural setting for, 244–245
  disguised vs. undisguised, 241–244
  electrical devices for, 245–251
  and ethics, 241–242
  fictional example, 243
  flexibility in, 239
  forms for, 296, 299, 300f–302f. *See also*
    Questionnaires
  human, 245–246, 251
  mechanical devices for, 195, 245–251, 252.
    See also Mechanical observation
  natural vs. contrived setting for, 244–245
  structured vs. unstructured, 239–241
  vs. surveys, 244
Observation error, 478, 495–501, 504
  field error, 495–501
  office error, 501
Ocean Spray, 729–731
O'Dell, William F., 76–77

Office errors, 501. *See also* Central-office edit
Ogilvy & Mather, 683
Okechuku, Chike, 345*n*
Oksenberg, Lois, 229*n*, 295*n*, 495*n*
Oldendick, Robert W., 275*n*, 276*n*
Oliv, E. Walton, 684*n*
Olson, Jerry C., 336*n*
O'Neil, Michael J., 493*n*
Open-ended question, 202, 203, **204**–205, **280**–281
    and bias, 499
    coding of, 204–205, 534–535
    example of, 229
    and information control, 222
    and questionnaire design, 270
    and response error, 499
    tabulation of, 222
Operational definition, 315, 324
Opinion, 187–189, 196
    vs. knowledge, 215
Oppenheim, A. N., 274*n*
Order bias, 283
Ordinal scale (for data), 310, **312,** 313–314
    and Kolmogorov-Smirnov test, 584, 588, 589
    and product-moment correlation, 646
    and self-reports, 344
O'Rourke, Diane, 221*n*
Osgood, Charles, 341, 341*n*
Ott, Lyman, 441*n*, 464*n*
Outer-directed people, 187, 197–198
Outlier, 538, **547**
Output planning, 95
Overcoverage error, 480, 481
Overton, Terry S., 493*n*
Ozanne, Urban B., 535*n*

Paksoy, Christie H., 613*n*
Pampers, 78, 81, 113
Panel (omnibus), 96–99, 118
Panel (true), 95–100, 118
Panels, 95–101, 118, 219
    and brand-switching matrix, 97
    Consumer Mail Panel, 77, 160, 166, 168
    for experiments, 721
    fictional example, 86
    Menu Census, 162
    National Family Opinion (NFO) Panel, 166, 270
    National Purchase Diary (NPD) Panel. *See* National Purchase Diary (NPD) Panel
    product purchase diary, 99
    product request diary, 99, 99*t*–100*t*
    television viewing log, 99
    and turnover table, 96, 97
Parameter, 404
    vs. statistic, 406
Parasuraman, A., 15*n*
Parent population, 404. *See also* Population
    vs. derived population, 407
    and increasing initial response rate, 491
Parker, George, 705*n*
Parker Pen Company, 96
Parlin, Charles, 9*n*
Parsons, Leonard Jon, 641*n*
Payne, Stanley L., 231*n*, 274*n*, 283*n*, 284*n*, 286*n*, 296*n*
Pearsonian coefficient of correlation. *See* Product-moment coefficient

People meter, 245–246
Pepsi Corporation, 320–321
Pepsodent toothpaste, 238
Percentages (in research report), 546, 552
    and conditional probabilities, 552–556
Perception Research Services, Inc., 249
Perceptual maps, 351–356, 357
Performance of objective tasks, 338, 361
Periodicity, 434
Perreault, William D., Jr., 5*n*, 6*n*
Persinos, John F., 49*n*
Personal interview, 216
    and attitude scale, 270
    bias in, 228, 229, 486, 494
    and branching questions, 291
    and computer assistance, 222, 228
    and field force, 230
    and information control, 222, 229, 230, 232
    and measurement, 318
    and monetary incentives, 491
    and nonresponse, 486, 494
    for pretest, 296
    and questionnaire format, 294
    and refusals, 489
    and research design, 719
    and sampling control, 220
    at shopping malls, 491
Personality (data on), **185**–187
Pessemier, Edgar A., 345*n*, 656*n*
Peter, J. Paul, 54*n*, 320*n*, 324*n*, 325*n*, 336*n*, 350*n*, 578*n*, 580*n*
Peterson, Robert A., 220*n*, 221*n*, 285*n*, 495*n*
Philip Morris, 112
Phillips, Lynn W., 84*n*
Physiological reaction, 338–339, 361. *See also* Mechanical observation
Pictogram, 711
Pie chart, 704–706, 713, 714
    fictional example, 707
Pillsbury, 46*n*, 47, 205, 717*n*, 725*n*
Piper, Cindy, 293*n*
Planchon, John M., 540*n*
Plummer, Joseph T., 187*n*
Plus-one dialing, 218, 482
Pocketpiece (Nielsen report), 163
Politz, Algred, 494, 494*n*
Polk, R. L., & Company, 238, 435*n*
Pooled variance estimate, 604
Population, 392
    derived, 405–407
    and parameters, 404
    parent, 404, 407, 491
Population mean, 404. *See also* Mean(s)
Population parameters, 404
Population size and sample size, 460–463
Population variance, 404–405. *See also* Variance(s)
Position bias, 283
Posten, Carol, 247*n*
Potency Dimension, 341
Powell, Terry E., 218*n*
Power (of statistical tests), 575–580
Pragmatic validity, 321–322, 329
Precision, 448–449
    and cost, 464
    when estimating proportions, 458–459
    when population variance is known/unknown, 452–456
    (trade-off with) sample size, 413, 454, 468

Precision *(continued)*
  in stratified samples, 426–428
  when there are multiple objectives, 457
Predetermined question, 202
Predictive validity, 321–322
Predictor (or independent) variable, 616, 620*n*
  binary, 637–640, 643
  dummy, 637–640, 641
  and variable transformation, 641
Presser, Stanley, 275*n*, 276*n*, 284*n*, 535*n*
Prestbo, John A., 26*n*
Preston, Ivan L., 8*n*
Pretest (for questionnaire), **296**–297
Primary data, 30, 144, 184–197
  collection of, 195–197
  fictional example, 183, 185
  and questionnaire design, 270, 281
  vs. secondary data, 155, 168, 184
  types of, 184–194
Primary source, 148, 149
Pringle's potato chips, 113
Probabilistic model, 618–621
Probability-proportional-to-size area sample, 436, 437–441
Probability sample, 31, 394–395, 403–404, 416. *See also* Cluster sample; Simple random sample; Stratified sample
  and field studies, 103
  when not used, 81, 82
  and research design, 719, 720
  and sampling errors, 477
  and snowball sample, 399*n*
  and statistical inference, 409–410
  summary comments on, 440
  of telephone numbers, 218
  types of, 395*f*
Problem formulation, 28, 33, 44–63, 718
  and cross tabulation, 564
  and exploratory research, 79–80
  fictional example, 43
  and research design, 75
Problem solving. *See* Exploratory research
Proctor & Gamble, 26, 78–79, 81, 113
Product concept, 296, 361
Product-moment coefficient, 628, 646, 650
Product purchase diary, 99
Product request diary, 99, 99*t*–100*t*
Program strategy, 26, 27, 39
  vs. project strategy, 26–27
Project strategy, 26, 39
  vs. program strategy, 26–27
Projective method, 210–215, 232
Proportionate stratified sample, 428–430, 441
Proportions
  hypothesis testing about, 603–604, 605
  sample size when estimating, 458–460
Psychogalvanic skin response, 338. *See also* Psychogalvanometer
Psychogalvanometer, 247–248
  vs. voice-pitch analysis, 250–251, 252
Psychographic analysis, 186
Psychological measurement, 313–317. *See also* Attributes, measurement of Publications
  government, 149, 172–178
  guides to, 179–181
  privately produced, 178–179
Purchase behavior. *See* Behavior

Purchase-intention scale, 282
Pym, G. A., 238*n*

Quaker Oats, 16
Quartiles (on histograms), 550
Questionnaires, 202–232. *See also* Mail questionnaire; Questionnaire design; Questions
  administration of, 216–231, 232
  and causal research, 721
  for interview, example of, 223*f*–227*f*
  length of, 229
  stimulus, in projective methods, 215, 232
  structured, and exploratory research, 719
  structured-disguised, 215–216
  structured-undisguised, 202–203
  unstructured-disguised, 210–215, 216
  unstructured-undisguised, 204–209
  wording in, 295–296. *See also* Attitude scale
Questionnaire design, 268–297, 302–303
  and pretest, 296–297
  and project strategy, 26
  summary of steps in, 269*f*, 297*t*–298*t*
Questions, 270–280
  ambiguous, 288–289, 295, 303
  answering, process of, 495–496
  bias in, 283, 303
  branching, 291–292, 295, 303
  color-coded, 295
  and computer assistance, 228
  dichotomous. *See* Dichotomous question
  double-barreled, 290, 303
  filter, 276, 295–296
  fixed-alternative. *See* Fixed-alternative question
  generalized, 290, 303
  leading, 289, 295, 303
  multichotomous (multiple-choice). *See* Multichotomous question
  open-ended. *See* Open-ended question
  order of. *See* Questions, sequence of.
  personalized, 228
  sensitive (or offensive), 278–280, 293, 295, 302
    examples of, 279*t*
    and refusals, 491
  sequence of (order or position of), 290–293, 294, 303
    automatic, 222
    bias caused by, 283, 284
    and pretest, 296
  wording of, 285–290, 302
Quota sample, 100, 395, **399**–402, 417
  and Gallup Poll, 440
  noncoverage error in, 480
  and research design, 720
  vs. stratified sample, 430

Raddock, Steve, 238*n*
Raiffa, Howard, 47*n*
Ramsey, Patricia, 711*n*
Random-digit dialing, 218, 482, 485–486
Random error, 319, 330, 486
Randomized-block design, 611, 612, 613
Randomized-response model, 280, 302
Raphaelson, Joel, 685*n*
Ratings scales. *See* Scales
Ratio scale, 310, **313,** 314
  vs. interval scale, 313, 330

Raymond, Charles, 47*n*
Recall (and retention rates), 191
Recall loss, 276–277, 302
Recklefs, Roger, 114*n*
Recognition method, 164, 191
Refusal rate, 484
Refusals, 486, 489–491, 504
  fictional example, 490
  and interviewer-interviewee interaction model, 496
Regression analysis, 495, 540*n*, 616. *See also*
    Correlation analysis
  vs. correlation analysis, 616, 643
  multiple-, 630–642, 643
  and research design, 720
  simple, 616–630, 632, 643
    fictional example, 623
Reid, L. N., 214*n*
Reid, Stan, 345*n*
Reiling, Lynn G., 114*n*
Reinmuth, James E., 280*n*
Related samples, 599–603
Reliability, 317, **325**–326, 328, 403
  and equivalence, 327, 329
  interjudge, and the coefficient of concordance, 653
  and nonsampling error, 477
  and (choice of) ratings scale, 350
  and sampling distribution, 418
  split-half, 327
Rent Control Referendum, Case 5.1, 510–511
Report, research. *See* Research report
Research analyst (investigator), 49, 718–719, 722
  and analysis of selected cases, 85–86
  at Quaker Oats, 16, 19
Research design, 74–84, 87, 719. *See also*
    Causal research; Descriptive research;
    Exploratory research
  choice of, 28–29
  and observation form, 299
  principle of, 75, 87
  process of, 32–33
Research problem, 50, 63
Research process, 27, 28–33, 722
  and data analysis, 467
  and research request step in, 51–52
  and sample size, 467
  summary of steps in, 34*t*, 39
Research project, 718, 722–724, 734
Research proposal, 51, **54**–57, 63
  example of, 55*t*, 57*t*
  justification of marketing research in, 54, 58–60
Research report, 32, 677, 680
  first rule of, 680, 700, 713
  oral, 700–715
    fictional example, 699, 701–702, 707
    figures vs. tables for, 700. *See also* Charts
    length of, 700–702, 714
    microphone, use of in, 702, 703
    tables for, 703, 713
    visual aids for, 700, 714. *See also*
      Computer graphics; Graphic
      presentations
  and progress reports, 700
  written, 680–695, 700
    (discussion of) bias or nonsampling error in, 693

fictional example, 679, 681, 694
figures for, 691, 693. *See also* Charts
length of, 682
tables for, 691–693
words to avoid/use, 686*t*, 687*t*
Research request step (statement), **51**–52
Research supplier, 60–62. *See also* Marketing
    research, firms for
Response bias. *See* Response error
Response error, 282, 495–501
  and effect of interviewer, 491, 496, 497–501
  vs. nonresponse, 501
Response latency, 249–**250,** 252
Response rate, 483, 484–**485,** 504. *See also*
    Nonresponse error
  vs. completeness rate, 495
  and quantitative analysis of, 492
  ways of increasing, 491–493
Retention rates, 191
Reve, Torger, 84*n*
Reynolds, M. L., 354*n*
Reynolds, R. J., 96
Reynolds, William H., 185*n*, 190*n*, 191*n*, 193*n*,
    336*n*
Rich, Clyde I., 218*n*
Richard, Lawrence M., 186*n*
Richards, Larry E., 498*n*
Riche, Martha Farnsworth, 450*n*
Richmond, Samuel, 588*n*
Roberts, Johnnie L., 153*n*
Rogers, John C., 344*n*, 725*n*
Rogosa, David, 97*n*
Roman, Kenneth, 685*n*
Rosander, A. C., 441*n*
Rothbart, George S., 399*n*
Rothman, J., 501*n*
Ruby, Daniel, 717*n*
Rudelius, William, 494*n*
Rumstad Decorating Centers (A), Case 2.3,
    129–131
Rumstad Decorating Centers (B), Case 4.1,
    374–377
Russick, Bertram, 494*n*
Russo, J. E., 249*n*

Saal, Frank E., 317*n*
Saari, Bruce B., 325*n*
Sackmary, Benjamin D., 94*n*
Salespeople
  and conjoint analysis, 361
  factors in success of, 186
SAMI (Selling Areas—Marketing, Inc.), 159, 731
Sample, 30, **392**
  accidental, 396
  area, 220, 434–440
    noncoverage error in, 480
  vs. census, 392, 404, 416
  cluster. *See* Cluster sample
  convenience, 395, 396–397, 719
  disproportionate stratified sample. *See*
      Disproportionate stratified sample
  fixed, 395, 416
  judgment, 395, 397, 398–399, 417
    and research design, 719
  nonprobability. *See* Nonprobability sample
  probability. *See* Probability sample
  proportionate stratified sample, 428–430, 441
  purposive, 398

Sample *(continued)*
quota. *See* Quota sample
random. *See* Simple random sample
selected, 482
selection of, 393–394, 416
sequential, 395, 416–417
simple random. *See* Simple random sample
snowball, 399
stratified. *See* Stratified sample
systematic, 433–434, 482
types of, 395*f*
Sample design, 30–32, **392,** 440–441
accuracy and cost of various types, 428, 434, 437
in causal research, 29
cost and accuracy of various types, 428, 434, 437
in descriptive research, 29
fictional example, 237, 391
and measurement, 318–319
and nonsampling errors, 477–478
and sample size, 31, 459
and sampling frame, 30–31
Sample mean, 406, 407–415. *See also* Mean(s)
in stratified sample, 424, 425, 426
Sample proportion, 458–460. *See also* Proportions
Sample size, 31, 448–468
basic considerations in determining, 448–450
and Bayesian analysts, 449*n*
and central-limit theorem, 451
(trade-off with) confidence level, 413, 454, 468
and convenience sample, 396–397
and cost, 463–464, 468
and (anticipated) cross classifications, 464–467, 468
and data analysis, 467
examples of typical, 467*t*
fictional example of determining, 447, 449, 465
when estimating means, 450–457
when estimating proportions, 458–460
and fixed vs. sequential sample, 395
and historic evidence, 467
and hypothesis testing, 464, 591
key factor in determining, 448, 468
and nonsampling error, 477, 482, 502
and population size, 460–463, 468
and population variance, known/unknown, 452–456
(trade-off with) precision, 413, 454, 468
rule of thumb for determining, 466, 468
and sampling distribution, 448, 451, 458, 463
and sampling error, 476, 477
and sampling theory, 448, 464
for simple random samples, 448–463
and subgroup analysis, 467
and total error, 33, 502
Sample survey, 102, 103, 500
vs. field study, 102, 118
Sample variance, 413–414
in stratified sample, 425–428
Sampling control, 216, 219–220, 221, 232
and quota sample, 402
Sampling distribution, 406, **409,** 410, 418
and chi-square test, 588
hazards of ignoring, 591–592
and sample size, 448, 451, 458, 463

and sampling error, 476
and stratified sample, 424, 426
Sampling error, 218–219, 418, **476.** *See also* Total error
and field study, 103
and hypothesis-testing, 580
vs. nonsampling error, 476–478, 501–504
and probability sample, 395, 404
and quota sample, 430
and sample size, 476, 477
and sampling distribution, 476
and simple random sample, 407
and snowball sample, 399
and stratified sample, 424, 426
and systematic sample, 434
Sampling frame, 30–31, **216**–217, **392,** 393, 416
improving the, 482
and noncoverage error, 479–480, 482
Sampling interval, 434, 448, 482
Sampling specialist, 482, 483
Sampling theory, 430, 437
and sample size, 448, 464
Sampling unit, 220, **435**
and data array, 538
and not-at-homes, 487, 488, 489
Sarnoff, Dorothy, 703*n*
Sawyer, Alan G., 108*n*, 576*n*, 578*n*, 580*n*
Scales (ratings), 310–330, 338–344, 721. *See also* Measurement
attitude. *See* Attitude scale
choice of, 350
coding of, 534–535
common feature of, 345, 362
comparative-ratings, 349–350
constant-sum method, 349
errors in, 319–321, 330. *See also* Validity
and fixed-alternative questions, 284–285
graphic-ratings. *See* Graphic-ratings scale
interval. *See* Interval scale
itemized-ratings. *See* Itemized-ratings scale
Likert. *See* Summated-ratings scale
and multichotomous questions, 285
multidimensional. *See* Multidimensional scaling
nominal. *See* Nominal scale
ordinal. *See* Ordinal scale
Osgood's dimensions in, 341
of psychological attributes, 313–330. *See also* Attitude scale
purchase-intention, 282
ratio. *See* Ratio scale
and research design, 719–720
semantic-differential. *See* Semantic-differential scale
snake diagram, 342–343
Stapel, 343–344, 361
summated-ratings. *See* Summated-ratings scale
self-report, 338, 339–344, 361
steps in developing, 328–329, 330
thermometer, 345
validity of, 321–325, 328, 329, 330
and variable transformation, 641
Scanners in supermarkets, 162–163, 195, 246–247
fictional example, 421
Scatter diagrams, 618, 624, 628
Schaeffer, Richard L., 441*n*, 464*n*

Schafer, Marianne, 491n
Schafer, Richard, 491n
Schafer, William D., 650n
Schanenger, Charles M., 185n
Schellinck, D. A., 186n
Schiffman, S. S., 354n
Schmid, Calvin, F., 703n
Schmitt, Allan H., 703n
Schmitt, Neal, 325n
Schneider, Kenneth C., 35n
Schrier, Fred I., 187n, 192n, 193n
Schuman, Herbert, 275n, 276n
Schuman, Howard, 276n, 284n, 497n, 535n
Schumer, Fern, 247n
Schwab, Donald P., 325n
Schwartz, David A., 241n, 251n
Sciglimpaglia, Donald, 67n, 127n
Search and deliberation, 239, 240, 241, 244
Searle, G. D., 59
Sebestik, Jutta P., 221n
Second-stage (household) sampling fraction, 437, 440
Secondary data, 29–30, **144**–168, 184
　disadvantages of, 155, 168, 185
　errors in, 147–149
　external vs. internal, 160
　fictional example, 152, 183
　from government (U. S.), 149, 172–179
　internal vs. external, 160
　key sources of, 151–155, 168
Secondary source, 148
Selective perception, 215
Self-report, 338, 339–344, 361
　comparative-ratings scale, 349–350
　constant-sum method, 349
　graphic-ratings scale. See Graphic-ratings scale
　itemized-ratings scale. See Itemized-ratings scale
　Likert scale. See Summated-ratings scale
　semantic-differential scale. See Semantic-differential scale
　snake diagram, 342–343
　Stapel scale, 343–344, 361
　summated-ratings scale. See Summated-ratings scale
Selling Areas—Marketing, Inc., (SAMI), 159, 731
Sellitz, Claire, 75n, 80n, 81n, 82n, 83n, 85n, 104n, 105n, 106n, 202n, 203n, 317n, 319n, 345n, 532n, 534n
Semantic-differential scale, 341, 343, 361
　vs. itemized-ratings scale, 347
　and multidimensional scaling, 351–352, 356
　Osgood's dimensions in, 341
　vs. Stapel scale, 344, 361
Sen, Subrata K., 113n
Sendak, Paul E., 108n
Sentence completion, 212–213, 215, 338
Sequence bias, 228
Sequential sample, 395, 416–417
Sevin, Charles H., 150n
Sewall, Murphy A., 193n
Seymour, Daniel J., 291n
Sharma, Subhash, 113n
Shawkey, Bruce, 220n
Sheatsley, Paul B., 268n, 274n
Shimp, Terence A., 8n
Shugan, Steven M., 350n

Shurter, Robert L., 703n
Siedl, Philip S., 536n
Siedler, John, 84n
Silk, Alvin J., 193n
Similarity judgments, 354, 355, 357
Simmons, Willard, 494, 494n
Simmons Media/Marketing Services, 160, 165–166
Simon, Herbert A., 728, 728n
Simon, Julian L., 74n
Simple random sample, 404–415
　and area sample, 434
　bias in, 415
　and cluster sample, 433–434
　and ineligibles, 482
　and sample size, 448, 463, 464
　and stratified sample, 422, 423, 424
Simple tabulation, 537, 540, 565
Simulated test market (STM), **117,** 119
Singer, Eleanor, 498n
Skinner, Steven J., 221n
Slama, Mark E., 433n
Slides (for graphic presentation), 713
Sloan, Pat, 50n
Slope coefficients, inferences about, 625–627
　in multiple-regression analysis, 633
　in simple regression analysis, 632
Smith, Charlie, 245
Smith, Kent, 79
Snake diagram, 342–343
Snedecor, George W., 650n
Snee, Ronald D., 635n
Snow, R. E., 579n
Snowball sample, 399
Sobczynski, Anna, 85n
Solomon, Julie B., 113n
Spagna, Gregory J., 282n
Sparkman, Richard D., Jr., 296n
Spear, Mary E., 703n
Spearman's rank-order correlation coefficient, 647, 650–652
Spector, Paul E., 339n, 346n
Split ballot, 284
Split-half reliability, 327
Spradley, Jimmy, 48–49
Sprague, Ralph H., Jr., 729n, 730n, 732n
Spurious correlation/noncorrelation, 564
Stability, 326–327
Standard Candy of Nashville, 48–49
Standard error of estimate, 624–**625,** 643
　in cluster sample, 431
　mean, 410
　and nonsampling error, 477, 482
　and population proportion, 458–460
　and population size, 463
　in regression analysis, 624–625
　and sample size, 448, 468
　and statistical efficiency, 431
　in stratified sample, 425–428
Standard test market, 116
Standardized Marketing Information Services, 155–168, 169
Standardization (in questionnaires), 202–203, 210, 230
Stapel scale, 343–344, 361
Starch Advertisement Readership Service (Starch INRA Hooper, Inc.), 160, 164–165, 249, 400
　example of report by, 191

Stasch, Stanley F., 81*n*, 202*n*, 278*n*, 682*n*, 693*n*
Statistic, 405, 406, 408
Statistical efficiency, 431–433, 437
Statistical tests, 32, 570, 584–605
    analysis of variance (ANOVA), 608, 609–613, 722
    chi-square. *See* Chi-square goodness-of-fit test
    factorial design, 612–613
    goodness-of-fit. *See* Chi-square goodness-of-fit test
    Kolmogorov-Smirnov. *See* Kolmogorov-Smirnov test
    Latin-square design, 612, 613
    and measurement, 430
    one-tailed and two-tailed, 571–572, 573
    power of, 573, 575–580
    and quota sample, 430
    randomized-block design, 611, 612, 613
    in research report, 691, 694
Statistical theory
    Bayesian, 412*n*, 449*n*, 570*n*, 599*n*
    classical, 412*n*, 570
Statistics
    and one-way tabulation, 538, 551
    and probability sampling, 409
    and sampling distribution, 409, 418
    summary, 102, 538, 550–551
Stech, Charlotte G., 487*n*
Steinhorst, R. Kirk, 280*n*
Stem, Donald E., Jr., 280*n*
Sterling Drug, 58
Stevens, Joyce, 497*n*
Stevens, Stanley S., 310*n*
Stewart, David W., 147*n*, 148*n*, 151*n*, 540*n*
Still, Richard R., 349*n*
STM (simulated test market), 117, 119
Stocking, Carol, 202*n*, 295*n*, 498*n*
Storytelling, 213–214, 215, 338
Stouffer, 84, 85
Strata, dividing, 422
    in cluster sample, 431, 441
    in stratified sample, 428–430
    variability and sample size, 463, 464
Stratified sample, 422–430, 440, 441
    and area sample, 434–435
    vs. cluster sample, 422
    and cost, 464
    proportionate vs. disproportionate, 428–430
    vs. quota sample, 430
    and sample size, 448, 464, 468
    vs. simple random sample, 441
Stratum chart, 708–709, 714
Structure (in questionnaires), **202**
Structured observation, 239–241
Strunk, William, Jr., 685*n*
Subpopulations, 422
Substituting values for missing data, 540
Suchomel Chemical Company, Case 3.2, 257–258
Suci, George J., 341*n*
Sudman, Seymour, 98*n*, 100*n*, 101*n*, 202*n*, 228*n*, 231*n*, 274*n*, 285*n*, 292*n*, 295*n*, 296*n*, 393*n*, 399*n*, 415*n*, 434*n*, 436*n*, 437*n*, 440*n*, 441*n*, 449*n*, 466*n*, 498*n*, 499*n*
Summary statistics, 102, 538, 550–551

Summated-ratings scale, 339–340, 361
    vs. itemized-ratings scale, 347
    and multidimensional scaling, 351–352, 356
    vs. semantic-differential scale, 342, 344
    vs. Stapel scale, 344
Summers, Gene F., 336*n*
Suncoast National Bank, Case 3.3, 258–263
Sunset Books (children's book publisher), 59, 83
Supervisory Training at the Management Institute, Case 1.2, 67
Supplier, research, 60–62
Survey Research Center at University of Michigan, 192
Swint, Albert G., 218*n*
Swinyard, William R., 108*n*
Sykes, Wendy, 499*n*
Symbols for means and variances, 414*t*
Systematic error, 319, 330, 487
Systematic sample, 433–434, 482
Szymanski, David M., 131*n*, 135*n*, 511*n*, 673*n*

Tables (for research reports), 691–693, 700, 703
Tabulation, 32, 537–565
    by computer, 537–538
    cross. *See* Cross tabulation
    of dichotomous questions, 284
    by hand tally, 537
    and nonsampling error, 477
    one-way, 538–551
    from pretest, 296, 297
    and questionnaire design, 294, 295
    simple, 537, 540, 565
Tachistoscope, 248, 252
Takeuchi, Hirotaka, 703*n*
Tally sheet, 537
Tannenbaum, Percy H., 341*n*
Target population. *See* Parent population
Tashchian, Armen, 433*n*
TAT (thematic apperception test), 213
Tauber, Edward, 247*n*
Taulkie, E. S., 211*n*
Tax code (example of exploratory research), 79–80
Taylor, Shelley E., 187*n*
Taylor, Thayer C., 731*n*
Telecom Research, 58–59
Telephone interview, 27, 216, 221*n*. *See also* Telephone sampling
    and adjusting for nonresponse, 494*n*
    and administrative control, 229–231, 232
    and attitude scale, 270, 274*n*
    bias in, 228, 229, 486
    and branching questions, 291
    and computer assistance, 222, 228
    and information control, 222, 229, 230, 232
    and measurement, 318
    and refusals, 489
    and research design, 719
    and sampling control, 220
Telephone sampling, 218–221, 216–221, 393. *See also* Telephone interview
    interviewer effect on, 484–485
    and interviewer-interviewee interaction model, 496
    and noncoverage error, 480
    and nonresponse error, 483–484, 486
    problems in, 31

Telescoping error, **276**–277, 302
Television viewing
  Nielsen data. *See* Nielsen Television Index
  and nonprobability sample, 403
  and observation methods, 245–246, 251
    fictional example, 239
  and panel data, 99
  Simmons data, 160, 165–166
Test market, 116–117, 119
Test marketing, 26, 58, **110**–115, 119
  fictional example, 86, 115
  and hypotheses, 78, 79
  models for 113*n*, 117
  and multidimensional scaling, 358
  (compared to) pretest, 296
  types of, 116–117
Test-retest reliability assessment, 326, 327*n*
Thematic apperception test (TAT), 213
Thermometer scale, 345
Thomas, Roger, 493*n*
Tigert, Douglas, 186*n*
Time order of variables, 105–106, 118, 720
Time series analysis. *See* Longitudinal analysis
Torgerson, Warren S., 349*n*
Total association, 555
Total error, 39, 426, 501–504, 722
  and nonsampling error, 478
  vs. part (or stage) error, 33
  and sampling error vs. nonsampling error,
    501–504
Toy Manufacturers of America, 4
Toys "Я" Us, 4
Tracy, Eleanor Johnson, 112*n,* 114*n*
Tracy, Paul E., 280*n*
Treistman, J., 249*n*
Tuchfarber, Alfred J., 275*n*, 276*n*
Tudor, R., 395*n*
Tufte, Edward R., 703*n*
Tull, Donald S., 361*n*, 498*n*
Turner, Charles F., 476*n*
Turnover table, 96, 97–98, 118
Twain, Mark, 642, 642*n*
Twedt, Dik Warren, 6*n*, 7*n*, 10*n*, 19*n*
Tyebjee, Tyzoon T., 218*n*, 228*n*, 250*n,*
Type I and Type II errors
  in determining sample size, 464
  in multiple-regression analysis, 633
  in testing null hypothesis, 572–575, 576, 577,
    578

Udell, Jon G., 82*n*
Undisguised observation, 241–244
Universal Product Code, 157–158
University of Wisconsin–Extension: Engineering
    Management Program, Case 6.1,
    659–663
Unstructured observation, 239–241
Upah, Gregory D., 344*n*
Urban, Glen L., 350*n*
Utilities, 358, 360

Validity, 319–325, 328, 329, 330. *See also
    various types.*
VanValey, Thomas L., 145*n*
Variable transformation, 641, 644
Variables
  criterion (or dependent). *See* Criterion
    variable

functional relationships of, 616–627
  linear relationships of, 627–630
  predictor. *See* Predictor variable
Variance(s), 404–405, 610
  known/unknown, in determining sample size,
    452–456
  known/unknown, in hypothesis testing, 590–
    591, 594–599
  population, and sample variance, 413–414
  in stratified sample, 425–428
  symbols for, 414*t*
Variation, total, 629–630, 635–636
Venkatesh, B., 571*n*
Verdoorn, P. J., 144*n*
Verille, Perry, 18*n*
Visicalc, 734
Voice-pitch analysis, 249, **250**–251, 252
  and attitude scaling, 339
Von Arx, Dolph, 689, 689*n*
Von Peckmann, Frederick, 214*n*

Wagner, G. R., 728*n*
Waksberg, Joseph, 218*n*
Waldorf, Dan, 399*n*
Walker, Orville, C., Jr., 186*n*
Walkup, Lewis E., 630*n*
Wallace, Wallace H., 250*n*
Warner, W. Gregory, 346*n*
Wasserman, William, 616*n*
Watson, Paul J., 248*n*
WCOL–TV, Case 6.2, 663–665
Webb, Eugene J., 243*n*
Webster, Frederick E., Jr., 214*n*
Weeks, M. F., 488*n*
Weiland, Douglas K., 480*n*
Weinstein, A., 251*n*
Wells, William D., 207*n*
Wentz, Walter B., 26*n*, 680*n*
Werner, D. Michael, 725*n*
Westbrook, Robert A., 347*n*
Westfall, Ralph, 81*n*, 202*n*, 216*n*, 278*n*, 682*n*,
    693*n*
Whalen, Bernie, 46*n*, 58*n*, 531*n*
Whinston, Andrew B., 728*n*, 732*n*
White, E. B., 685*n*
Whitelaw, Robert, 399*n*
WIAA Tournaments, Case 5.7, 525–527
Wiggins, Kevin, 114*n*
Wilcox, James B., 35*n*, 296*n*
Wildt, Albert R., 346*n*
Wilkie, William L., 345*n*
Wilkinson, J. B., 613*n*
Williams, Bill, 441*n*, 464*n*
Williams, Robert J., 724*n*
Williams, Terrell G., 344*n*
Williams, W. H., 478*n*
Williamson, Merrit A., 659*n*
Wind, Yoram, 349*n*
Winer, Russell S., 101*n*
Winn, Paul R., 585*n,*
Wiseman, Frederick, 478*n*, 484*n*, 486*n*, 487*n*,
    491*n*
Wittink, Dick R., 360*n*
Wonnacott, Ronald J., 616*n*, 635*n*
Wonnacott, Thomas H., 616*n*, 635*n*
Woodside, A. G., 214*n*
Word association, 212, 338
Worthing, Parker M., 108*n*

Wrangler, 50
Wrightsman, Lawrence S., 75*n*, 80*n*, 81*n*, 82*n*,
    83*n*, 85*n*, 202*n*, 203*n*, 317*n*, 319*n*, 345*n*,
    532*n*, 534*n*

Yarnell, Laurie N., 217*n*
Yates, F., 612*n*, 650*n*
Young, F. W., 354*n*
Yu, Julie, 489*n*, 492*n*

Zajone, Robert B., 336*n*
Zaltman, Gerald, 32*n*, 680*n*, 721*n*
Zeisel, Hans, 97*n*, 546*n*, 552*n*
Zeller, Alvin B., 481*n*
Zero-order association, 555, 566
Zikmund, William G., 67*n*, 127*n*
Zinsser, William, 683*n*
Zuckerkandel, Samuel, 250*n*